W9-COB-467

Computer Service and Repair

A Guide to Upgrading, Configuring, Troubleshooting, and Networking Personal Computers

by

Richard M. Roberts

Publisher
The Goodheart-Willcox Company, Inc.
Tinley Park, Illinois
www.g-w.com

Manufactured in the United States of America.

Library of Congress Catalog Card Number 2003067505

International Standard Book Number 1-59070-335-9

1 2 3 4 5 6 7 8 9 – 05 – 08 07 06 05 04

The Goodheart-Willcox Company, Inc. Brand Disclaimer: Brand names, company names, and illustrations for products and services included in this text are provided for educational purposes only and do not represent or imply endorsement or recommendation by the author or the publisher.

The Goodheart-Willcox Company, Inc. Safety Notice: The reader is expressly advised to carefully read, understand, and apply all safety precautions and warnings described in this book or that might also be indicated in undertaking the activities and exercises described herein to minimize risk of personal injury or injury to others. Common sense and good judgment should also be exercised and applied to help avoid all potential hazards. The reader should always refer to the appropriate manufacturer's technical information, directions, and recommendations; then proceed with care to follow specific equipment operating instructions. The reader should understand these notices and cautions are not exhaustive.

The publisher makes no warranty or representation whatsoever, either expressed or implied, including but not limited to equipment, procedures, and applications described or referred to herein, their quality, performance, merchantability, or fitness for a particular purpose. The publisher assumes no responsibility for any changes, errors, or omissions in this book. The publisher specifically disclaims any liability whatsoever, including any direct, indirect, incidental, consequential, special, or exemplary damages resulting, in whole or in part, from the reader's use or reliance upon the information, instructions, procedures, warnings, cautions, applications, or other matter contained in this book. The publisher assumes no responsibility for the activities of the reader.

Library of Congress Cataloging-in-Publication Data

Roberts, Richard M.
Computer service and repair: a guide to upgrading, configuring, troubleshooting, and networking personal computers/ Richard M. Roberts. — [New ed.].
p. cm.
Includes index.
ISBN 1-59070-335-9
1. Microcomputers—Maintenance and repair. I. Title.

TK7887.R62 2005
004. 16—dc2 2003067505

Introduction

Personal computer (PC) support has evolved into one of the largest service industries in the world. The demand for skilled technicians to maintain, support, and upgrade PCs is ever growing. It is a rewarding and challenging career that can take you anywhere in the world. If you enjoy tinkering with PCs or have ever wondered how they work and what it takes to repair them, this course is for you. If you wish to learn computer networking, programming, administration, or any of the computer sciences, then this is the perfect place to start. A good foundation in PC technology will provide you with a base of knowledge that will make learning the other technical areas much easier.

Most computer troubleshooting is performed at the keyboard using knowledge about the PC system. You need to have a good understanding of how the components work hand-in-hand with the operating system software rather than knowing how the electronic parts (transistors, resistors, and capacitors) function. PC repair started out as a domain dominated by electronic technicians with thousands of hours of training. It has evolved into a specialized field of PC technicians requiring little to no electronics background at all.

Computer systems are built better than ever before. The constant problems caused by failing components encountered 30 years ago are seldom found today. Computers still do fail because of bad components, but now the majority of failures are due to software problems or they are caused by the computer users themselves. Only a small percentage of computer failures actually require component replacement. What is needed is someone who can diagnose the problem and determine if it is hardware related, software related, or user generated. This is the job of the PC technician. Remember that with PC repair, it is important to complete all lab activities. They are designed to give you valuable computer experiences and enhance the skills you are being taught. This will better prepare you for the CompTIA examination if you choose to take it, and better prepare you for a career as a PC technician.

I wish you much success in your future.

Sincerely,

Richard Roberts

The Author

For the past 35 years, Richard Roberts has been designing curriculum, teaching Electricity and Electronics as well as Computer Technology, and supervising technical teachers. Mr. Roberts is an accomplished programmer and computer technician. He has experience as the system administrator for Novell NetWare, Microsoft NT, and IBM token ring networking systems. He possesses a Bachelor's degree in Technical Education and a Master's degree in Administration/ Supervision. He also has current CompTIA A+, Network+, and iNet+ certifications.

His computer experiences started as early as 1974, when he began programming and teaching the Motorola 6800, which eventually evolved into the Motorola 68000—the core processor of the Apple Macintosh computer system. Since then, Mr. Roberts has maintained his teaching status to both instructors and students as the technology has evolved, and he has remained at a state-of-the-art technical level through research, teaching, and applications. He is currently an adjunct instructor at South Florida Community College. He also coauthored the textbook ***Electricity and Electronics*** as well as designed and programmed the accompanying interactive CD-ROM.

In addition to his current position, Mr. Roberts has taught at Erwin Technical Center and Tampa Bay Technical High School, and he has taught adults in the military service. His time is now divided between computer consulting and applications, teaching students and instructors, and writing textbooks and other ancillary instructional materials. Occasionally, he goes fishing, but not too often.

Using This Text

Each chapter begins with a number of learning objectives. These are the goals you should set to accomplish while working through the chapter. In addition to your objectives, each chapter begins with a list of these new terms, which are important for you to learn as you move through the chapter. When these words are introduced in the text, they are printed in a ***bold italic*** typeface. At that point in the text, you will find these terms defined in the margin.

As you read this text, you will also notice some other words or phrases that stand out. File names that you encounter will appear like notepad.exe, student.txt, or io.sys. Any data you must enter, be it by typing at the DOS and Run prompts or button/tabs/menus that you will click on with your mouse are set out like **dir C:** or **Start | Programs | Accessories | System Tools**. Any Internet addresses within the text are in the traditional Web style and in blue, such as www.g-w.com. Internet address listed under Interesting Web Sites for More Information at the end of each chapter are in the traditional Web style, underlined, and in blue, such as www.g-w.com.

Be sure to read any A+ Notes, Tech Tips, or Warnings that you encounter. A+ Notes contain tips that will help you study for the CompTIA A+ Certification exams. Tech Tips are useful tidbits that might come in handy in the field. Take heed when you see a Warning. Warnings alert you when an act may damage your computer or yourself. Losing all of your data is the most common danger you will encounter with computers. You may also encounter some dangerous voltages, especially when dealing with monitors. Most of those repairs should be left to special technicians.

Each chapter concludes with a summary of some of the key information you should take from the chapter, a large number of questions, a list of useful Web sites, and laboratory activities for you to try. Each chapter has two sets of questions. The first set of questions tests your general comprehension of the material in the chapter. The second set of questions mimics the style of the CompTIA A+ Certification exams. The questions asked here are on topics that the exams commonly probe.

Hands-on experience is the only way to become proficient in PC repair, so be sure to attempt the activities at the end of each chapter. If you can complete the activities in this text and in the accompanying laboratory manual, you should have no problem passing the A+ Certification exams. Each chapter concludes with a complete Laboratory Activity. Be sure to work through each of these activities. Suggested Laboratory Activities are also included. These activities are loosely structured proceedings that you can attempt on your own or if you have free time in class.

Never forget, the world of PCs changes rapidly. Consequently, PC repair and the CompTIA A+ Certification exams must change with it. Each chapter includes a list of Web sites where you can find the latest information on the topics covered. Be sure to check the CompTIA Web site (www.comptia.org) frequently for the latest information on what subjects are being added to the exams and what subjects are being dropped. Also, check the author's Web site (www.RMRoberts.com) for text updates, interesting links, and bonus laboratory material.

Acknowledgments

I would like to thank the following people who helped make this textbook possible by supplying information, details, photographs, artwork, and software.

Adam Forbes, Crucial Technology
Al Platt, US Postal Service
Beverly A. Summers, Fluke Corporation
David Goss, American Microsystems LTD
Erkki Lepre, F-Secure Corporation
Gabriel Rouchon, Swiftech Inc.
George Alfs, Intel Corporation
Heather Jardim, Kingston Technology Company, Inc.
Howard Burnside, Electronics Instructor, Retired
Jason Cambria, NeoWorx, Inc.
Jeremy VanWagnen, TechSmith Corporation
Jim Spare, Canesta, Inc.
John Stott, Citicorp

Kevin Franks, Winternals Software LP
Melody Chalaban, Belkin Corporation
Michelle Flippen, Tiny Software, Inc.
Stu Sjouwerman, Sunbelt Software
Tom Way and Joanna Moore, IBM Corporation
Walter Ernie, Computer and Electronics Instructor
and special thanks to Carl Marchand

Trademarks

CompTIA Authorized Quality Curriculum

The logo of the CompTIA Authorized Curriculum Program and the status of this or other training material as "Authorized" under the CompTIA Authorized Curriculum Program signifies that, in CompTIA's opinion, such training material covers the content of CompTIA's related certification exams. CompTIA has not reviewed or approved the accuracy of the contents of this training material and specifically disclaims any warranties of merchantability or fitness for a particular purpose. CompTIA makes no guarantee concerning the success of persons using any such "Authorized" or other training material in order to prepare for any CompTIA certification exam. The contents of this training material were created for the CompTIA A+ Core Hardware and A+ Operating System Technologies exams covering CompTIA certification exam objectives that were current as of 08/01/2003.

How to Become CompTIA Certified

This training material can help you prepare for and pass a related CompTIA certification exam or exams. In order to achieve CompTIA certification, you must do the following:

1. Select a certification exam provider. For more information please visit http://www.comptia.org/certification/test_locations.htm.
2. Register for and schedule a time to take the CompTIA certification exam(s) at a convenient location.
3. Read and sign the Candidate Agreement, which will be presented at the time of the exam(s). The text of the Candidate Agreement can be found at www.comptia.org/certification.
4. Take and pass the CompTIA certification exam(s).

For more information about CompTIA's certifications, such as their industry acceptance, benefits, or program news, please visit www.comptia.org/certification.

CompTIA is a non-profit information technology (IT) trade association. CompTIA's certifications are designed by subject matter experts from across the IT industry. Each CompTIA certification is vendor-neutral, covers multiple technologies, and requires demonstration of skills and knowledge widely sought after by the IT industry.

To contact CompTIA with any questions or comments:

Please call + 1 630 268 1818 or e-mail CompTIA at questions@comptia.org.

Chapter Listing

Table of Contents

Chapter 6

Chapter 7

Chapter 8

Chapter 9

Magnetic Storage Devices .329

Chapter 10

CD Technology .381

Chapter 11

Printers .407

Chapter 12

Chapter 13

Chapter 22

Introduction to a Typical PC

After studying this chapter, you will be able to:

- Explain the role of computers.
- Explain what a computer is.
- Describe computer data.
- Identify the major components of a typical PC.
- Describe the power-on sequence of a typical PC.
- Explain how the major components interact with each other.
- Interpret the common prefixes associated with the computer's size and speed.
- Define electrostatic discharge.
- Identify common tools used to service a PC.

A+ Exam—Key Points

Some of the very basic questions on the A+ Certification exams deal with cable and connector identification. Cable and connector identification can be difficult for students new to PC technology, but anyone who has worked with a PC for some time will be able to answer them.

Be sure you can identify various connectors and cables including:

- DB-9
- DB-25
- RJ-11
- PS/2 or mini-DIN
- IEEE-1394
- USB

Be able to differentiate between serial and parallel data transmission. Examine and memorize all typical computer cable end connectors. For example, look at the end of the monitor cable. Does it use pins or a socket? The same goes for the PC unit. Always check the CompTIA Web page for the latest test objectives. A complete listing of hardware identification and installation requirements is listed there.

Key Words and Terms

The following words and terms will become important pieces of your computer vocabulary. Be sure you can define them.

A+ Certification
American Standard Code for Information Interchange (ASCII)
analog
anti-static wrist strap
basic input/output system (BIOS)
battery
binary number system
bit
byte
central processing unit (CPU)
chip
complementary metal oxide semiconductor (CMOS)
CompTIA
computer
cooling fan
data
device bay
digital
electrostatic discharge (ESD)
expansion card
expansion card slot
hard drive
hexadecimal number system
hot swap
integrated circuit (IC)
motherboard
parallel
peripheral
random access memory (RAM)
serial
word

This unit introduces you to the basic concepts you need to know to understand computer hardware and software. The unit briefly covers many topics. These topics are expanded into complete chapters later in the textbook. This text presents the personal computer based on the IBM-compatible computer architecture, better known as the PC, and prepares you for CompTIA's A+ Certification exams.

The ***CompTIA*** organization is a not-for-profit, vendor-neutral organization that certifies the competency level of technicians through examinations written to test specific areas. The CompTIA organization has prepared the examinations to test individuals with 500 hours of PC repair, installation, and support experiences. The certification awarded on successful completion of the exams is called ***A+ Certification.*** It is recognized throughout the industry as a certification of basic PC repair and support skills. The combination of this textbook and its accompanying Laboratory Manual prepares you for the certification exams. There is more information in Chapter 20—A+ Certification Exam Preparation–Core Hardware and Chapter 21—A+ Certification Exam Preparation–Operating Systems Technologies. You can also visit the CompTIA Web site at www.comptia.org for the latest information.

CompTIA
a not-for-profit, vendor-neutral organization that certifies the competency level of computer service technicians.

A+ Certification
certification awarded on successful completion of the A+ Core Hardware and A+ Operating Systems Technologies exams.

The Role of Computers

Computers are found in every aspect of our lives. There is not an industry that operates without a computer. Computers can be found in banks, Wall Street businesses, military aircraft, automobiles, televisions, communication systems, home appliances, satellites, submarines, and police stations. Computers can vary in size from the small, simple microprocessor that you might find in a coffeepot or a clock radio to huge mainframe systems that are used in research and government systems. **Figure 1-1** shows the microchip along with a large computer system and a typical home or business PC.

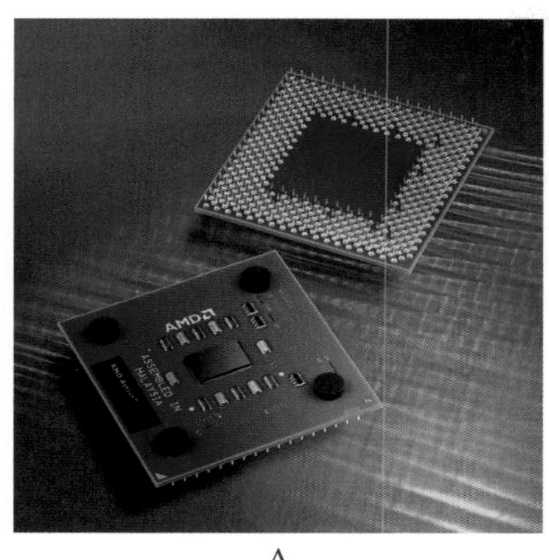

A

B

C

Figure 1-1. A microchip (AMD Athlon™ XP processor) alongside a large computer system for a research center, and, of course, a typical home PC. (Advanced Microprocessor Devices, Inc. and International Business Systems Corporation)

At first, the makeup of a computer can seem intimidating. However, as you progress through this text, you will see that the mechanics of a computer are quite simple. The difficulty is overcome by understanding the interaction of hardware and software, grasping different operating systems, and recognizing upgrade and compatibility issues.

If you know which part is defective, it is a relatively easy task to replace the part. The challenge is determining which part is defective or determining if the problem is hardware related or software related.

The aim of this textbook is to systematically teach you the necessary skills to be successful in the world of computer technology. In this chapter, we will take a quick look at the major components of a typical PC and introduce basic computer concepts such as computer data and software. As your studies progress through the text, each part and concept will be covered in great depth, but for now it is best to have an overall view of the PC system. No component can be fully understood without realizing how it interacts with the other components in the system.

This chapter covers introductory level knowledge of the computer system before going into depth at a technician level.

Digital Electronics

digital
a system that uses discrete values.

analog
a system using a continuous, infinite range of values.

All electronic components fall into one of two categories, analog or digital. Digital electronics is a system that is best represented by a simple switch. There can only be two conditions in the switch circuit. The switch is either on or off. No other state exists. Look at **Figure 1-2,** which shows a typical switch wired to a lamp. The switch controls all the power to the lamp. The lamp can be turned on or off. No other electrical condition can exist for this simple circuit. ***Digital*** electronics in computers use on and off conditions. There is either full voltage or no voltage applied to the circuit.

Analog electronics use and produce varying voltage levels. Analog electrical circuits can be represented with a dimmer switch. **Figure 1-3** shows a dimmer switch connected to a lamp. In this circuit, the intensity of the lamp varies as the dimmer switch is turned. The light from the lamp can have different intensities because the dimmer switch varies the amount of electrical energy that reaches the lamp.

A computer is constructed of some very complex digital circuits. These digital circuits are combined into modules such as circuit board cards. As a PC technician, you will usually only be responsible for replacing the module, not repairing the digital circuits. You do not need an extensive electronics background to repair the PC.

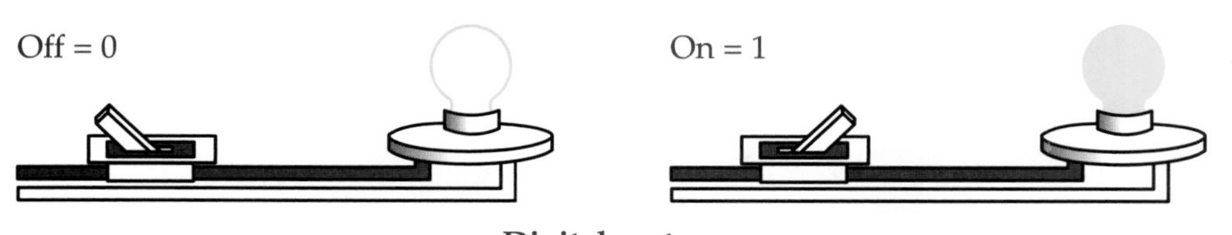

Figure 1-2. Typical on/off switch wired to lamp.

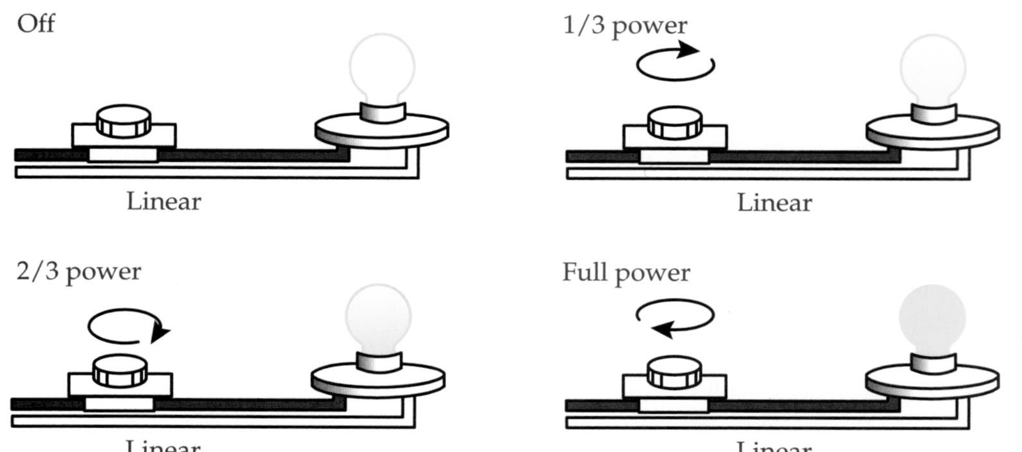

Figure 1-3. A typical dimmer switch.

What Is a Computer?

The PC is a fantastic piece of engineering technology. A ***computer*** is an assembly of electronic modules that interact with computer programs known as software to create, modify, transmit, store, and display data. The computer has rapidly evolved from a simple electronic device into a highly sophisticated piece of electronic technology.

computer
an assemblage of electronic modules that interact with software to create, modify, transmit, store, and display data.

Science fiction writers have attributed human qualities to computers such as Father in *Alien: Resurrection.* The computer can appear to be intelligent, but in reality it only processes and stores data. Processing data is limited to such things as sorting items, comparing, and locating previously stored data. In addition, computers perform mathematical calculations at amazing speeds. However, the computer cannot think. The computer can only be programmed.

This leads to another basic question: What is data? ***Data*** is information. This information comes in many forms. Data can be text (such as *ABC* or *123*), graphics (pictures), and sounds (like music or voices). **Figure 1-4** is an illustration presenting text, sound, and a picture, followed by digital electrical voltage symbols.

data
information, which can be presented in alpha/numeric form (such as ABC or 123), visual form (pictures), and audible form (like music or voices).

Data inside the computer is represented electronically as high and low voltages. The voltages are pulsed through the system. These pulses of high and low voltages create what is called a *digital signal.* Many things can be done with these pulses of electrical energy. Data can be displayed on a computer monitor or can be stored in memory chips, on a hard drive, a floppy disk, or a compact

Picture

ectronic componen
ne of two categories, digi
analog type devices. Digit
electronics has two states
conditions, on oand off. An
e expressed at many diff
vels between on and o

Text

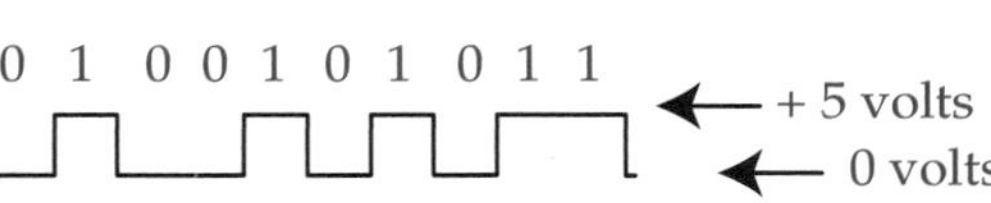

Figure 1-4.
Sound, pictures, and text are all forms of data. Each can be represented by a code comprised of ones and zeros, the binary number system. (Union Tools, Inc.)

disc (CD). When written to a hard drive or to floppy disks, the electrical pulses are converted to magnetic patterns on the surface of the disk.

Data in a computer system is represented as ones and zeros. The pattern of ones and zeros is known as the *binary system.* You will be introduced to the binary system later in this chapter. Some of the digital patterns represent words, pictures, and sounds. Other digital patterns represent commands such as load file, find file, save file, or activate the diskette drive. Remember, the computer does not contain any intelligence. It simply manipulates, stores, and displays data.

Computer Data Codes

Data can be almost anything. It can be numbers, text, pictures, and sounds. Computer data and functions are expressed in a variety of ways. They can be expressed as voltage levels, numeric systems such as binary and hexadecimal, and symbolic codes such as ASCII. Although computer data and commands can be expressed in many different forms and still have the same meaning, the form selected should be the one that is easiest to grasp for the given material. For example, it is much easier to express memory locations as hexadecimal values rather than binary values although the memory location could be expressed in either value. The computer technician must be very familiar with each of these forms of data expression.

binary number system a system in which all numbers are expressed as combinations of 0 and 1. Also known as the base 2 number system.

Binary Number Code

The ***binary number system*** consists of entirely ones and zeros. It is the perfect numbering system to represent digital electronic systems. Just as a digital device has only two states (on and off), the binary system utilizes only two numbers, 0 and 1. Look at **Figure 1-5** to see how the binary number system is used to express different values from zero to fifteen.

Figure 1-5.
The binary number system can be used to represent any integer in the decimal system. This chart shows binary numbers counting up to 15.

Binary	Decimal
0000	0
0001	1
0010	2
0011	3
0100	4
0101	5
0110	6
0111	7
1000	8
1001	9
1010	10
1011	11
1100	12
1101	13
1110	14
1111	15

Binary can be compared to a switch. If the switch is closed, the lamp will be on. This state is represented by a 1. When the switch is in the off position, the lamp is dark. This state is represented by a 0.

This may seem like a system too simple to represent data in a computer, but let's compare it to the Morse code system. The Morse code system consists of only two tones, a short beep and a long beep. These sounds are referred to as a dot and a dash respectively. See **Figure 1-6.** This code resembles a binary system. It has two conditions. The dots and dashes can be combined in sequences that represent the alphabet and the numerals 0–9. The Morse code system has been used to transmit information all over the world.

Graphics are transmitted in a similar fashion using a facsimile (fax) machine. The light and dark areas are represented by the presence or absence of a transmitted voltage. Again, this is a form similar to digital electronics. See **Figure 1-7,** which depicts two rotating drums. One drum is a transmitter and the other is a receiver. As you can see, the two-state condition of digital electronics can be much more powerful than it first appears.

The ones and zeros of the binary system are used to represent the high and low voltage signals that travel throughout the computer system. They also represent data stored on disks or in memory chips.

Hexadecimal Number Code

The hexadecimal code is based on the number base 16, similar to how the binary code is based on the number base 2. The ***hexadecimal number system*** uses 16 characters. See **Figure 1-8.**

hexadecimal number system
a system in which all numbers are expressed in combinations of 16 alphanumeric characters (0–F). Also known as the base 16 number system.

The hexadecimal system uses numerals 0–9 from the decimal number system and six additional characters from the alphabet, A–F. This combination of number and letter characters forms the hexadecimal number system. Binary numbers are too long and awkward to be used to express computer values such as memory locations. Thus, hexadecimal numbers are used instead. The hexadecimal code uses less space.

The hexadecimal system best matches the hardware system of most computers. As you will learn, data lines in a computer are eight, sixteen, thirty-two, or sixty-four lines wide. They use increments of eight and sixteen, which work beautifully with a hexadecimal system.

In addition, the number values you will encounter that are used to express memory sizes (such as 256, 512, and 1024) are increments of 16. As you can see,

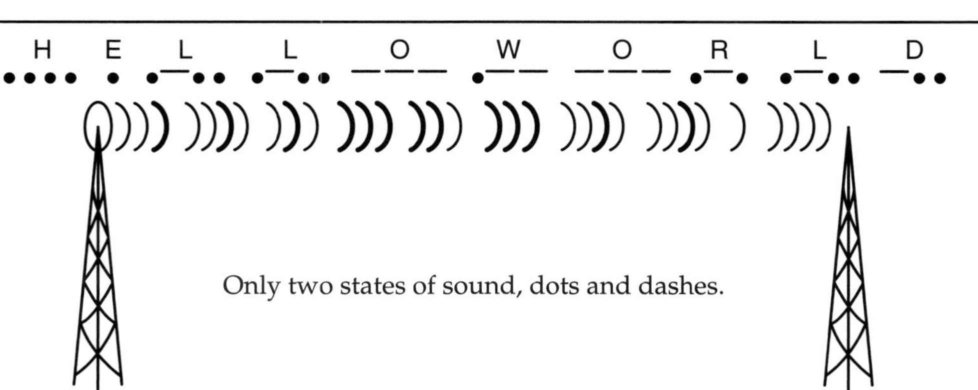
H E L L O W O R L D
Only two states of sound, dots and dashes.

Figure 1-6. Morse code transfers letters between two antennas using combinations of two states, dots and dashes.

Figure 1-7.
Voltage highs and lows can be used to send pictures across phone lines.

Original News Photograph.

The original photo is mounted on the rotating drum. A light transmitter and receiver convert the light and dark areas of the image into matching voltage levels.

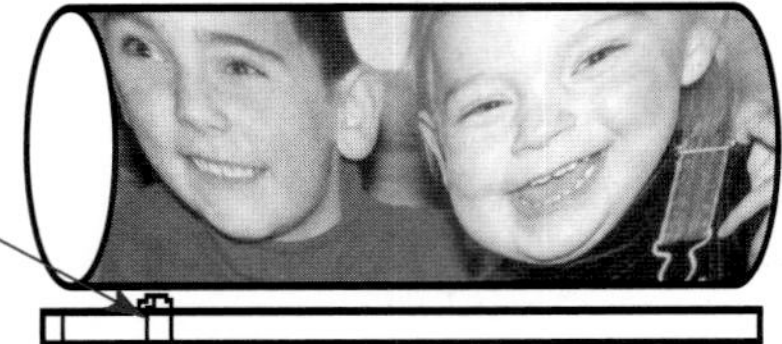
A transducer moves along the drum while it spins, converting the image into electrical signals.
Rotating drum.

Copy converted from electrical signal back to photograph.

Data is converted into electrical signals. The signals are carried across telephone lines to the destination telephoto machine where the image is recreated.

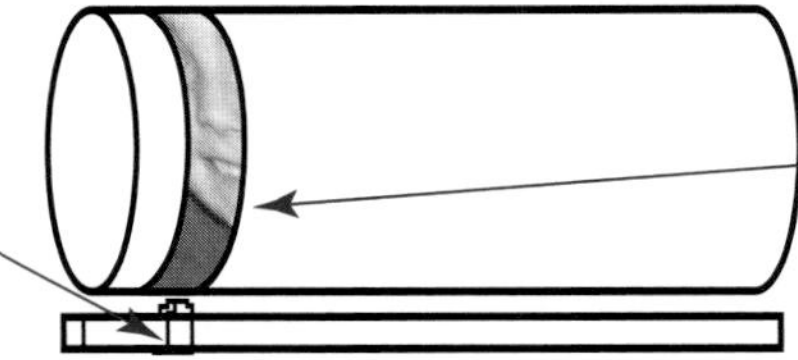
A writing stylus converts the electrical signals into an image.
Electronic voltage levels converted to drawing.

The first facsimile or "telephography" machine was put into commercial use in 1924. A transparency of a photograph was placed on a spinning drum. The image was converted into electrical signals representing the light and dark areas in the photograph. The electrical signals were converted back into a photographic image at the destination.

a number system based on 16 is used to best match the digital electronic system of computers.

Both binary and the hexadecimal numbering system will be used to express values and illustrate computer operation many times throughout the study of computer systems.

Hexadecimal	Decimal
0	0
1	1
2	2
3	3
4	4
5	5
6	6
7	7
8	8
9	9
A	10
B	11
C	12
D	13
E	14
F	15

Figure 1-8. Hexadecimal numbers include the digits 0–9 and the letters A–F.

ASCII Code

ASCII (pronounced *as-key*) stands for ***American Standard Code for Information Interchange.*** It was the first attempt to standardize computer character codes among the varieties of hardware and software. When a key on a computer keyboard is pressed, say the letter *M*, all computer systems display the letter *M* on the monitor screen. When the letter *M* is sent to the printer, the letter *M* is printed as expected. **Figure 1-9** is a listing of character codes and their ASCII code representatives.

The ASCII system was a great attempt to standardize the computer coding system, but it had limitations. The extended character set is unique to certain systems, such as IBM or equivalent machines. The extended character set must be used with a compatible software system or unexpected characters are generated. In addition, the standard form of ASCII does not allow for such common requirements of word-processing packages such as **bold,** *italic,* underline, or variations in fonts. ASCII was meant for symbol compatibility used for basic data files. ASCII is still used today, especially when data needs to be transferred between two different software programs.

ASCII (American Standard Code for Information Interchange)
the first attempt to standardize computer character codes among the varieties of hardware and software.

Bits, Bytes, and Words

Bit, byte, and word are basic computer units of data based on the binary number system. The term ***bit*** is short for *b*inary dig*it*. A bit is a single binary unit of one or zero. A ***byte*** is equal to eight bits. Early computers processed data in patterns of these eight-bit bytes.

A ***word*** is the total amount of bytes a computer can process at one time. Consequently, the length of a word can vary from computer to computer. For

bit
short for binary digit. A bit is a single binary unit of one or zero.

byte
equal to eight bits.

word
the total amount of bytes a computer can process at one time.

Figure 1-9.
ASCII code.

Table of Standard ASCII Characters		
0	NUL	Null
1	SOH	Start of header
2	STX	Start of text
3	ETX	End of text
4	EOT	End of transmission
5	ENQ	Enquiry
6	ACK	Acknowledgment
7	BEL	Bell
8	BS	Backspace
9	HT	Horizontal tab
10	LF	Line feed
11	VT	Vertical tab
12	FF	Form feed
13	CR	Carriage return
14	SO	Shift out
15	SI	Shift in
16	DLE	Data link escape
17	DC1	Device control 1
18	DC2	Device control 2
19	DC3	Device control 3
20	DC4	Device control 4
21	NAK	Negative acknowledgment
22	SYN	Synchronous idle
23	ETB	End of transmit block
24	CAN	Cancel
25	EM	End of medium
26	SUB	Substitute
27	ESC	Escape
28	FS	File separator
29	GS	Group separator
30	RS	Record separator
31	US	Unit separator
32	SP	Space
33	!	
34	"	
35	#	
36	$	
37	%	
38	&	
39	'	
40	(	
41	)	
42	*	
43	+	
44	,	
45	-	
46	.	
47	/	
48	0	
49	1	
50	2	
51	3	
52	4	
53	5	
54	6	
55	7	
56	8	
57	9	
58	:	
59	;	
60	<	
61	=	
62	>	
63	?	
64	@	

(Continued)	
65	A
66	B
67	C
68	D
69	E
70	F
71	G
72	H
73	I
74	J
75	K
76	L
77	M
78	N
79	O
80	P
81	Q
82	R
83	S
84	T
85	U
86	V
87	W
88	X
89	Y
90	Z
91	[
92	\
93	]
94	^
95	_
96	`
97	a
98	b
99	c
100	d
101	e
102	f
103	g
104	h
105	i
106	j
107	k
108	l
109	m
110	n
111	o
112	p
113	q
114	r
115	s
116	t
117	u
118	v
119	w
120	x
121	y
122	z
123	{
124	|
125	}
126	~
127	DEL

example, many computer systems process either 32 or 64 bits at one time. Hence, a word in those machines would consist of 32 bits (4 bytes) or 64 bits (8 bytes) respectively. Computers are often compared by the size of the word they can process.

Bit	=	0 or 1	1
Byte	=	eight bits	01011110
Word	=	1 to 8 bytes	10010010 11110000 00110011 10101010

Serial and Parallel Data Transfer

Data is transferred in one of two modes in a computer system: series or parallel. Ports on a computer are similarly classified as serial or parallel ports. In a ***serial*** transfer, data is sent through a port one bit at a time in successive order. Modems are used to communicate with other computers over telephone lines. Because of the limited capacity in a telephone line, data is transferred through modems in a serial fashion. Other examples of serial data transfer are the keyboard and mouse.

serial occurring one at a time. In serial transfer, data is transmitted one bit at a time.

In ***parallel*** transfer, more than one bit is sent side by side. In parallel port transfer, data is sent eight bits at a time. An example is a port for the transmission of data to a printer. Most printers have data transferred to them through parallel ports. In general, data is transferred at a much higher rate through a parallel port than a serial port. Data is transferred in parallel on the computer bus system between devices such as the hard drive, RAM, and the CPU. **Figure 1-10** shows a comparison between serial and parallel data transfer.

parallel side-by-side. In parallel transfer, more than one bit of data is transferred at a time.

Figure 1-10.
Serial and parallel data transfer. Serial transfers one bit at a time. Parallel transfers multiple bits, usually multiples of 8 (1 byte), at a time.

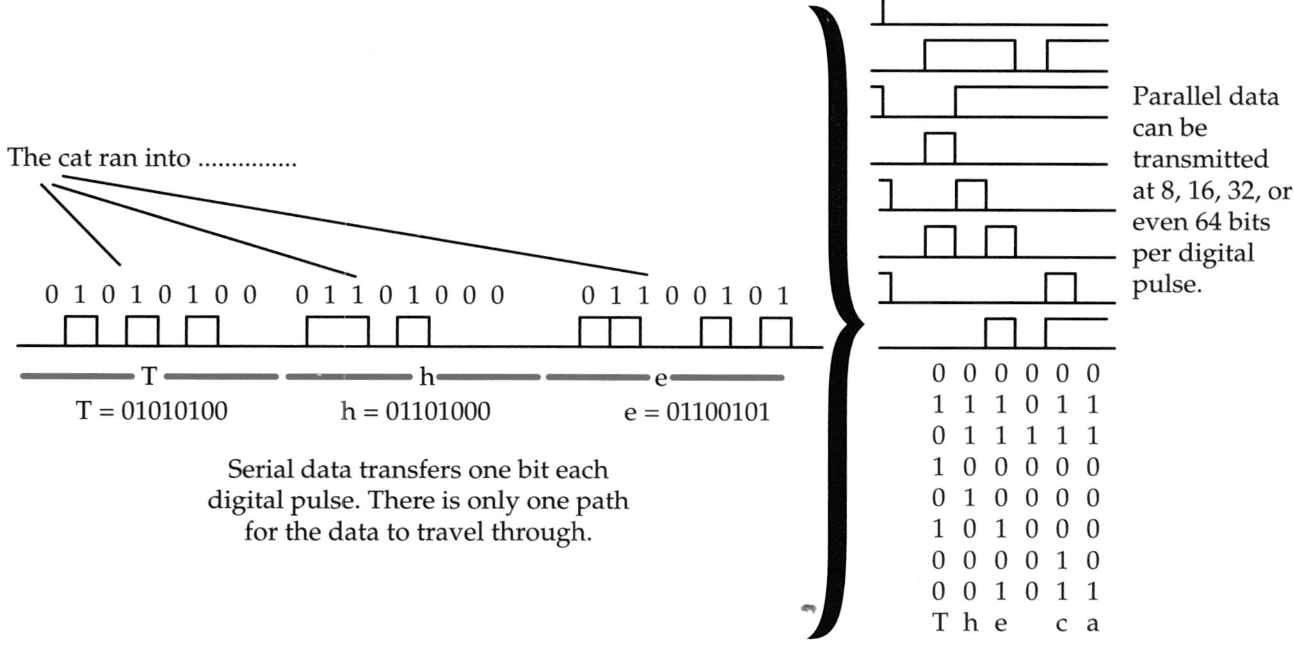

Computer Numerical Values

Metric prefixes are commonly used to express the speed and size of computer systems and hardware. Prefixes are usually used in combination with the word bit (b) or byte (B). For example, *speed* is usually expressed in *bits. Storage space* is usually expressed as *bytes*. See **Figure 1-11** for a listing of commonly used metric prefixes.

There is some confusion when using metric prefixes for expressing computer sizes. There can be two possible values for a large expression such as a megabyte. The nominal value for megabyte using the base 10 number system is equal to 1,000,000. In computer systems, a 1-megabyte item such as memory is 1,048,576 (2^{20}) bytes (the power of 2 raised to the 20th). The large values expressed for computer systems are based on the binary number system. **Figure 1-12** compares the values of the base 10 number system and the base 2 number system.

Figure 1-11.
Metric prefix chart.

Metric name	Symbol	Number base 10	Number base 2	Common name	Numeric equivalent for the base 10 number system
Pico	P	10^{-12}	2^{-40}	trillionth	0.000 000 000 001
Nano	N	10^{-9}	2^{-30}	billionth	0.000 000 001
Micro	μ	10^{-6}	2^{-20}	millionth	0.000 001
Milli	m	10^{-3}	2^{-10}	thousandth	0.001
Base unit		1			1
Kilo	K	10^{3}	2^{10}	thousand	1,000
Mega	M	10^{6}	2^{20}	million	1,000,000
Giga	G	10^{9}	2^{30}	billion	1,000,000,000
Terra	T	10^{12}	2^{40}	trillion	1,000,000,000,000
Peta	P	10^{15}	2^{50}	quadrillion	1,000,000,000,000,000
Exa	E	10^{18}	2^{60}	quintillion	1,000,000,000,000,000,000

Figure 1-12.
Base 10 and base 2 comparisons. You get more for your meg when you are using base 2 terminology.

Prefix	Base 2 number system	Base 10 number system
Kilobyte	1,024	1,000
Megabyte	1,048,576	1,000,000
Gigabyte	1,073,741,824	1,000,000,000
Terabyte	1,099,511,627,776	1,000,000,000,000
Petabyte	1,125,899,906,842,624	1,000,000,000,000,000
Exabyte	1,152,921,504,606,846,976	1,000,000,000,000,000,000

Take a Tour outside the Computer Case

Look at **Figure 1-13.** A minimal workstation consists of a computer and input and output devices. The computer itself is a case that houses the motherboard, CPU, memory, hard disk drive, and other associated electronics parts and modules that make up the computer system. The typical input devices found at a workstation are a keyboard and mouse, but there are many other different devices that can be used as input devices. These input devices will be covered later in the textbook. The typical output devices found at the workstation are the computer monitor, printer, and speakers. The monitor, printer, and speakers are classified as peripherals. ***Peripherals*** are optional equipment used to display data or to input data. The monitor displays data in the form of words and pictures. The printer displays data in a printed form on paper. The speakers convert data into sound such as music and spoken language.

peripherals
optional equipment used to input or output data.

There are many different case styles that are used to contain and protect the electronic parts of the computer system. Some of the most common case styles are referred to as desktop, tower, mini tower, micro tower, laptop, and notebook.

Figure 1-13.
Front view of a typical PC.

Case selection is usually based on individual taste. The outside of the computer system allows access to the electronic parts inside. Data can be entered into the computer system through the disk drive, CD drive, keyboard, mouse, or one of the ports in the back. See **Figure 1-14.**

Exterior Connections

The exterior connections to a computer are well worth a closer look. The following connectors are some of the more common connectors that you will find on a PC. More information is given on these connectors in the sections detailing the components with which they work.

There are a variety of exterior connectors used with computer equipment. Many times the type of connector can help reveal the identity of the card it is attached to or what type of equipment most likely connects to it. For example, the mouse and the keyboard may use the exact same style of connector, such as the mini-DIN type. However, they may not be interchangeable. The mouse must connect to the mini-DIN connector identified for the mouse cable, and the keyboard must connect to the mini-DIN connector identified for the keyboard cable. **Figure 1-15** shows the design of the DIN and mini-DIN connectors.

The DB connector looks similar in shape to the letter *D*, see **Figure 1-16.** The DB connector typically is classified as a 9-, 15-, or 25-pin connector. The DB connector is commonly used to connect items such as a joystick, monitor, or printer. The DB connector at the back of a sound card is sometimes referred to as a game port. When a 15-pin D shell connector is arranged with three rows of five connections, it can be referred to as a HD-15. The HD represents high density and is usually used for monitor connections.

There are two types of RJ connectors commonly used with a PC: RJ-11 and RJ-45. The RJ-11 is used for modem telephone connections. The RJ-45 is used for network connections. The RJ-11 uses four conductors and four pins, while the RJ-45 uses eight conductors and eight pins, see **Figure 1-17.**

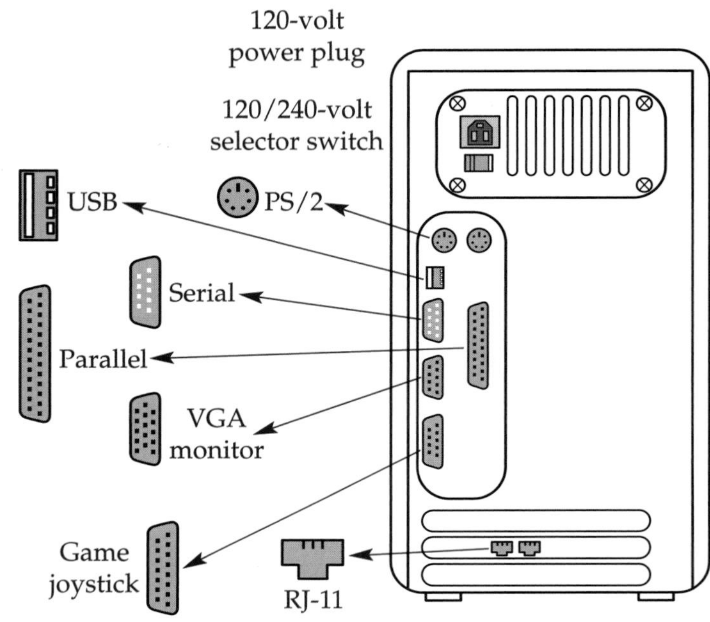

Figure 1-14. Ports accessible at the back of a typical PC unit. There are a variety of ports on the back of a computer to handle the various peripherals that may be attached.

Figure 1-18 shows a picture of a network card. Network cards can come with different kinds of connectors. They may use an RJ-45, a DB-15, or a BNC connector. Some network cards come with multiple connectors to allow them to be used with any standard type of network wiring. Each type of wiring requires a different type of connector.

The FireWire connector, also known as the IEEE 1394 connector, can connect up to 63 devices that can be hot swapped. The term ***hot swap*** means the devices

hot swap
to plug in or unplug a device while the PC is running.

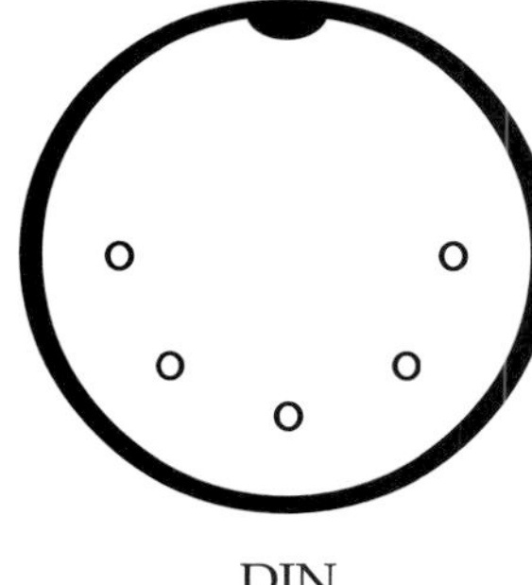

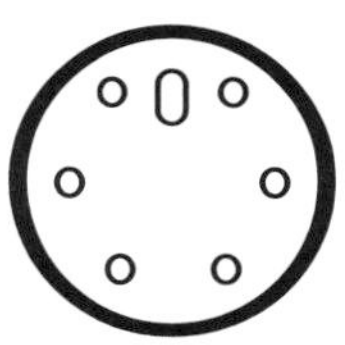

Figure 1-15.
DIN and mini-DIN connectors.

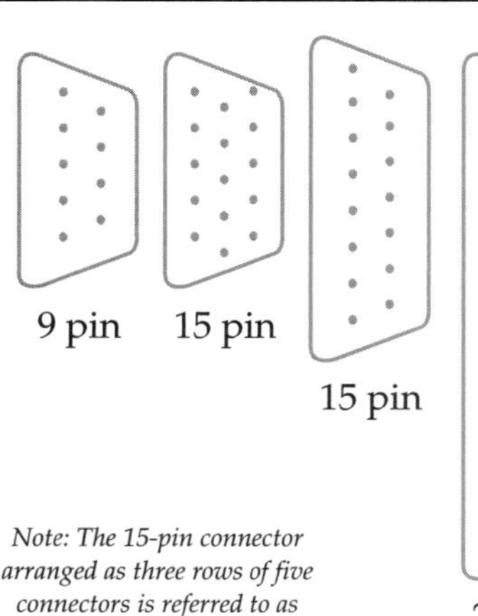

Various DB connectors

Figure 1-16.
Selection of sizes of DB connectors and a typical DB connector. DB connectors are used for both serial and parallel ports.

can be plugged in or unplugged while the PC is running. FireWire was designed for Apple computers by Lucent Technologies and is proprietary. FireWire is seen more often on Apple equipment than on PC equipment. It is designed for very high-speed data transfers such as those required for video equipment. The high-speed data transfer rates make it an excellent choice to upload video images from a camera to a PC. FireWire is also used for other equipment connections such as hard disk drives, CD-ROM drives, DVD drives, and printers. **Figure 1-19** shows a pair of FireWire connectors.

The Universal Serial Bus (USB) is another type of connection used on PCs, **Figure 1-20.** The USB is a multipurpose connector that allows many different devices to connect to the PC in a daisy chain fashion or by the use of a hub. The USB design allows for connections to peripheral devices that formerly may have required opening the PC case and inserting an adapter card. With the USB port, the need to open the case to connect many of the different devices has been eliminated.

Figure 1-17. RJ-45 and RJ-11 connectors.

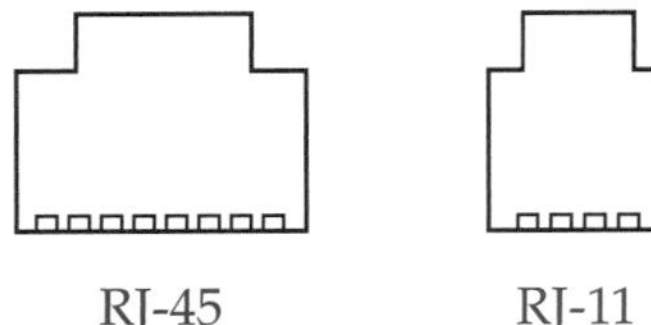

Figure 1-18. Typical PCMCIA network adapter for a laptop. This network adapter comes with a USB connector. Devices that convert the USB connection to other types of connections are readily available.

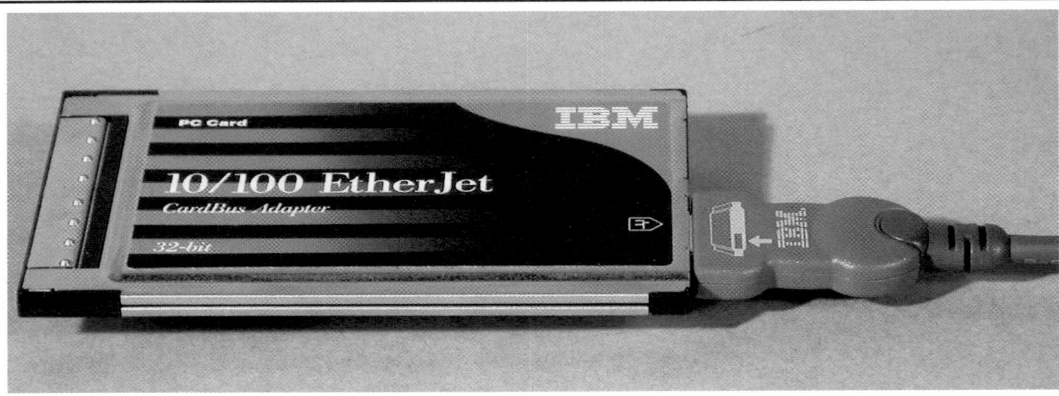

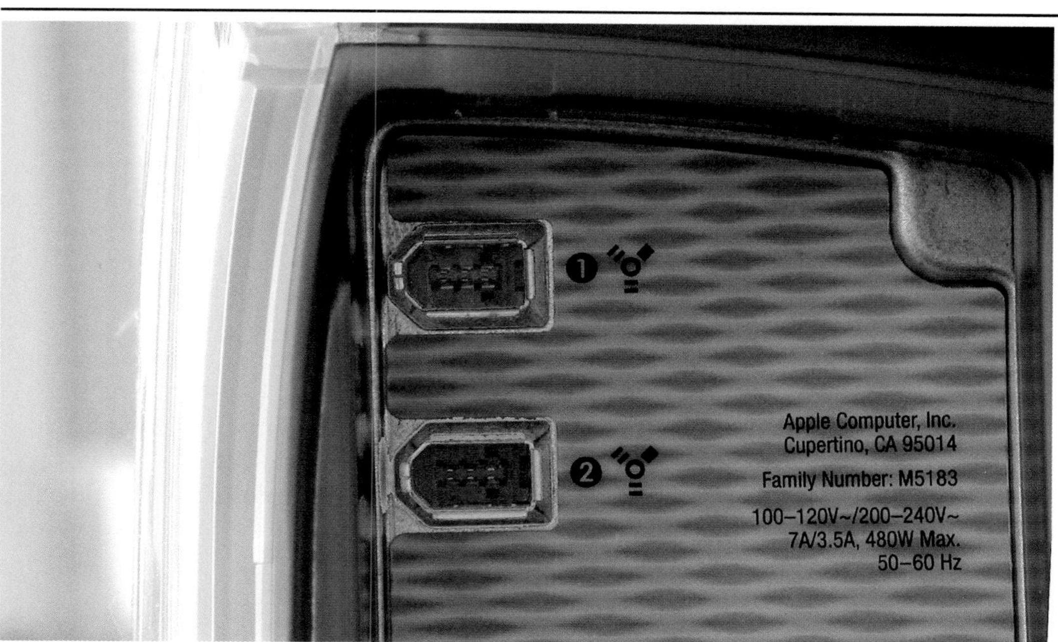

Figure 1-19. FireWire ports are high-speed connections.

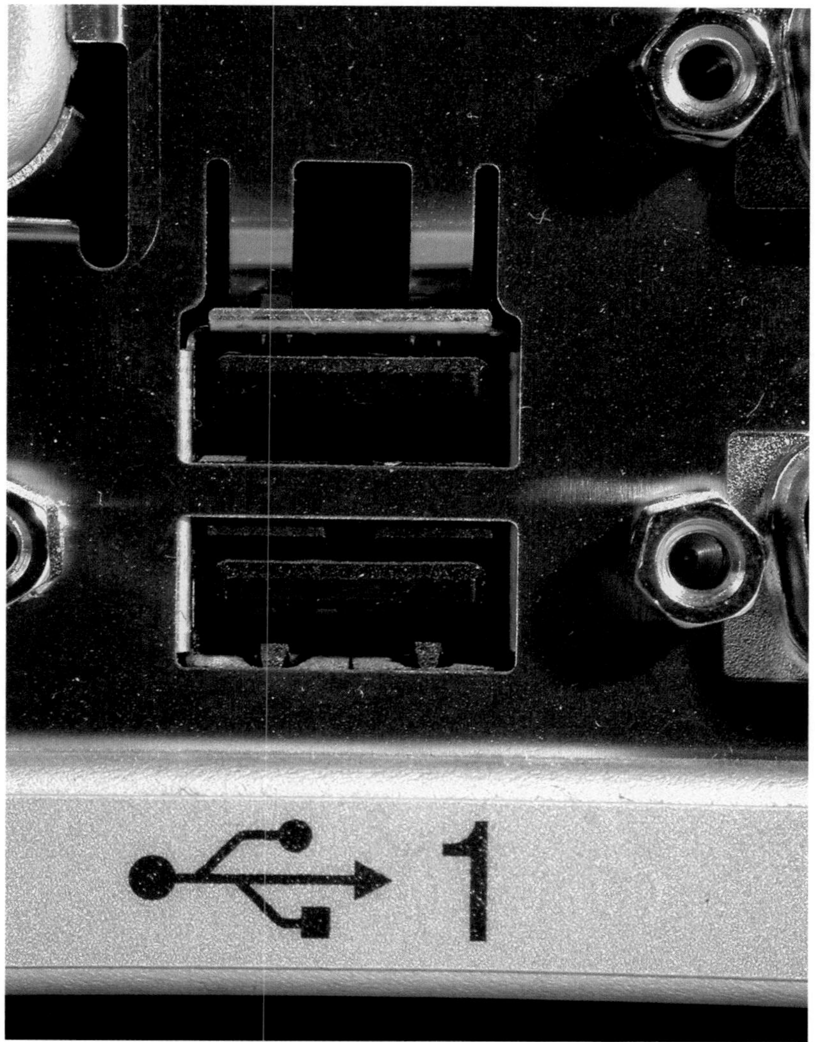

Figure 1-20. Photo of USB port.

Another very desirable advantage of USB is that you can connect up to 127 devices through the USB port in a daisy chain fashion, **Figure 1-21.** Before USB, it was quite possible to run out of a sufficient number of ports to support the numerous types of equipment that might be needed for a special workstation. For example, a workstation used by a graphics designer might require connections to a scanner, digital camera, microphone, laser printer, color inkjet printer, poster-size plotter printer, and a digital graphics tablet for freehand drawings. The USB and FireWire ports are capable of supporting numerous devices required by a single workstation. Legacy workstations could only be used to support a limited number of devices.

device bay
a drive bay designed to accommodate the easy hot swap of devices such as hard disk drives, tape drives, CD-RW drives, and DVD drives.

The ***device bay*** is relatively new for PCs. It is designed to accommodate the easy hot swap of devices such as hard drives, tape drives, CD-RW drives, and DVD drives. The device bay is prewired for either USB or FireWire and allows devices to easily slide into or out of the PC case. A device installed into the device bay looks as though it was installed internally. By installing the device into the device bay, the problem of long cords running across and around valuable desk space can been eliminated.

central processing unit (CPU)
the brain of the computer. Most of the computer's calculating takes place in the central processing unit. In PCs, the central processing functions are carried out by a single chip, which is called a microprocessor.

Take a Tour inside the Computer Case

The inside of a PC is filled with a number of standard components and expansion slots that allow each machine to be customized with a tremendous variety of interesting tools, **Figure 1-22.** The equipment that follows details only the common computer components. These are devices you will find in almost every system.

CPU

In the simplest of terms, the ***central processing unit (CPU)*** is the brain of the computer, **Figure 1-23.** The terms *Pentium® 4, Celeron, K6,* and others are the names given to identify various models of CPUs. The CPU consists of millions

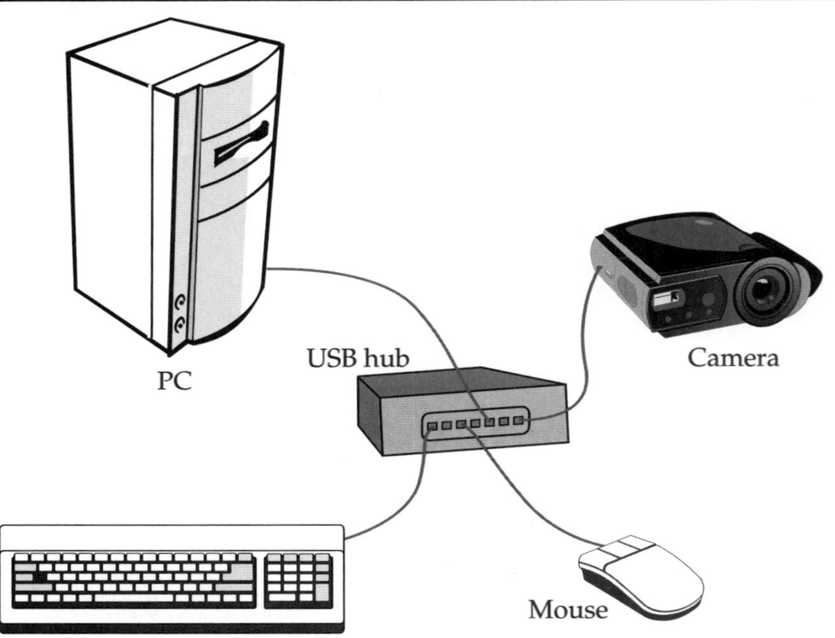

Figure 1-21.
A USB hub can be used to connect multiple USB devices to a PC.

of microscopic electronic components called *transistors*. The transistors are electrically connected together in such a way they are able to interact with computer programs and process data.

All the other computer components depend on the actions of the CPU. The CPU controls the data in the computer. Commands are issued to the CPU via software. The CPU translates the commands into actions, such as save the data on the screen to memory, open a new file, and locate a file called MyHomeWork.

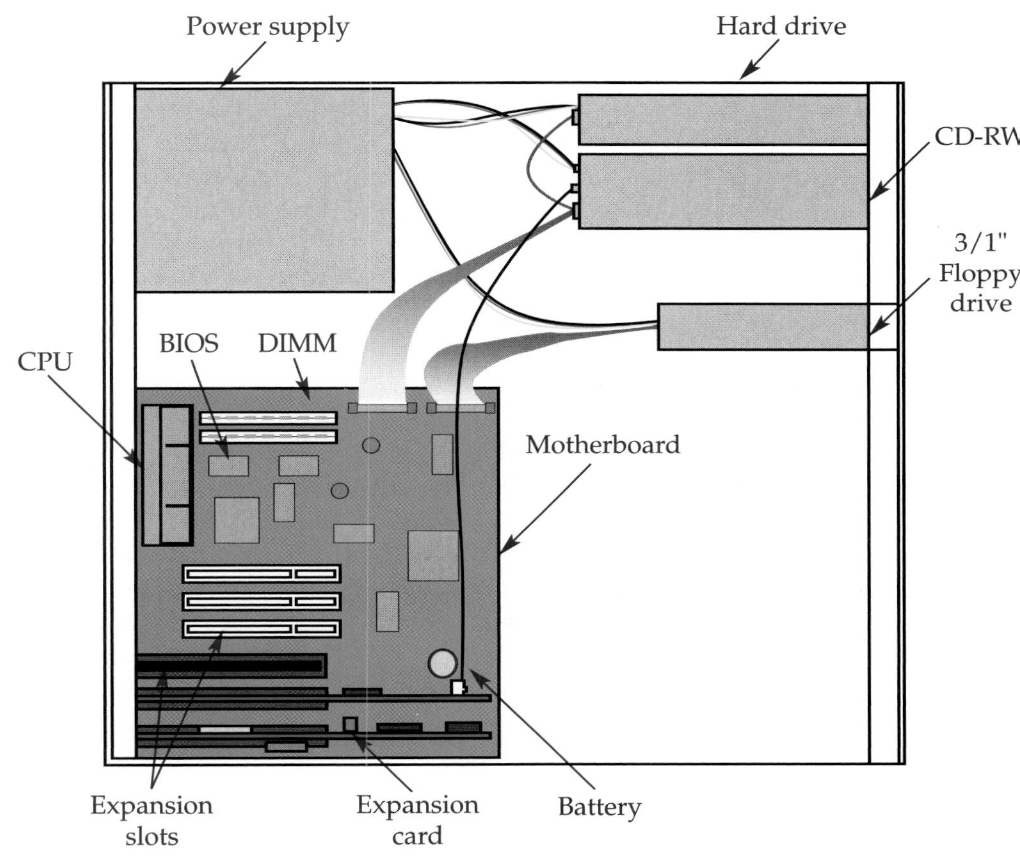

Figure 1-22. These components are common to the PC. Depending on the style of the unit (tower, desktop, or laptop), the arrangement of the parts will vary. This sketch shows a tower PC.

Figure 1-23. The CPU is the brain of the computer. Shown is the Pentium® 4 processor. (Intel Corp.)

As discussed earlier, the CPU does not think or possess any human intelligence as some movies may depict. A CPU simply carries out the program codes written in the software program.

Power Supply

The power supply converts the typical 120-volt ac power from the wall outlet to dc voltage levels used by the various computer components, **Figure 1-24.** Once the 120 volts of ac power is converted to a lower dc voltage, usually 3.3, 5, or 12 volts, cables carry the electrical energy to the motherboard, disk drives, and other major components.

hard drive
a magnetic storage media consisting of a set of magnetic disks and read/write heads housed inside a hard case.

motherboard
a circuit board covered by a maze of conductors, which provide electrical current to the computer components and expansion slots. Also used to refer to the main circuit board and all of its electronic components (chipset).

Hard Drive

The ***hard drive*** (also called the internal drive or hard disk) is where computer programs and data are stored, **Figure 1-25.** A hard drive is made up of several disks in a stack inside a sealed box. Computer programs and data are stored on the hard drive as magnetic impulses. Data is transmitted to and from the hard drive through a flat ribbon cable attached to the hard drive on one end and to the motherboard on the opposite end. The hard drive is connected to the power supply by several brightly colored wires that supply the electrical energy needed to run the hard drive system.

Motherboard

The motherboard is usually a rectangular piece of circuit board covered with many conductors that provide electrical energy paths to the computer components and expansion slots, **Figure 1-26.** The ***motherboard*** provides a way to distribute the digital signals carrying data, control instructions, and distribute small amounts of electrical power to the many different components mounted on the board. The electrical system of pathways is referred to as the *computer bus.*

Figure 1-24.
The power supply converts 120 volts to a level usable to a PC.

RAM

Random access memory (RAM) is the location where computer programs are loaded to from the hard drive, **Figure 1-27.** RAM is classified as a *volatile* memory system. Volatile simply means that the data and programs loaded in RAM are lost when power is turned off. Increasing a computer's RAM is one of the most common computer upgrades performed. RAM is usually mounted into several parallel slots on the motherboard. The amount of RAM in a typical home PC

random access memory (RAM) a volatile memory system into which programs are loaded. When the computer's power is shut off, all data stored in RAM is lost.

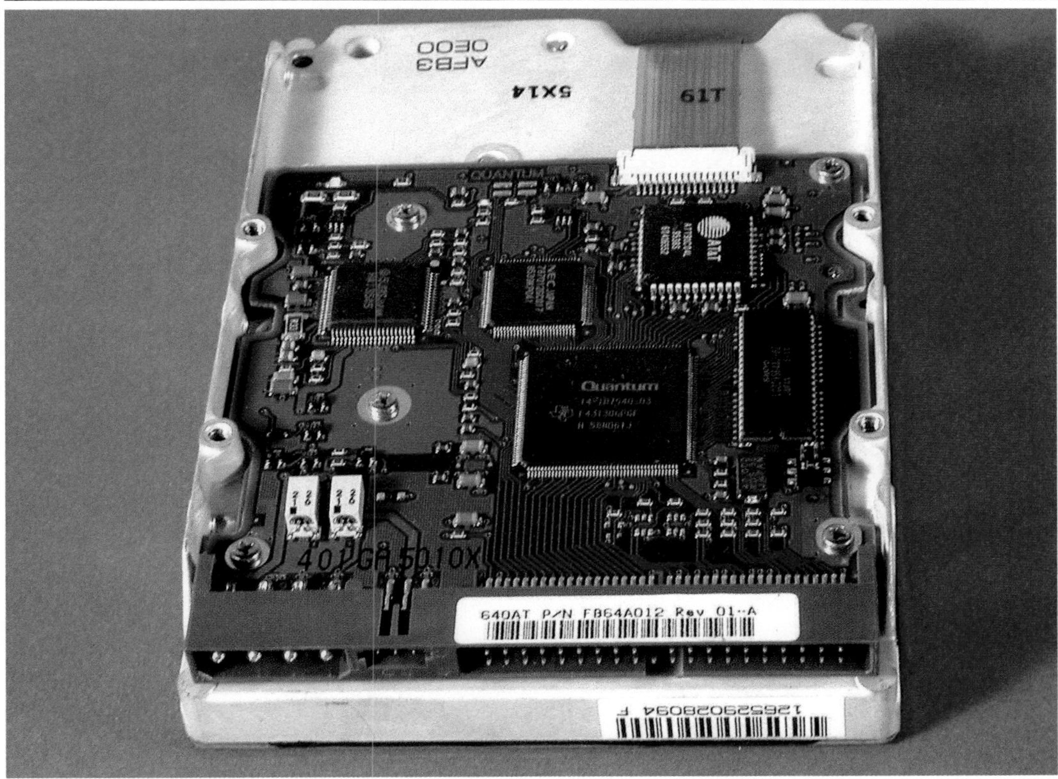

Figure 1-25.
Hard drives are the most common storage device used with a PC.

Figure 1-26.
Almost all computer data runs through the motherboard.

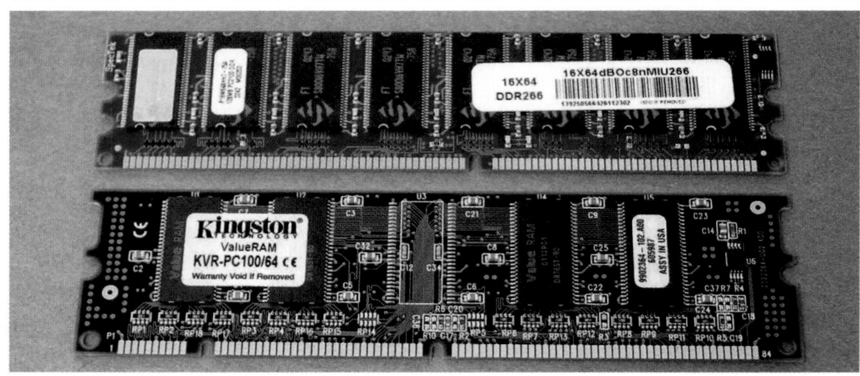

Figure 1-27. RAM modules are easy additions to the PC.

could be 128MB, 256MB, 512MB, or more. Depending on the type of applications to be run, the amount of RAM required will vary.

RAM is a place where data is temporarily stored. When a computer is turned off, the RAM is emptied. When a computer is started, new information is loaded into RAM. When you draw a picture, the data that represents the picture is in RAM and is transferred to the screen. Look at **Figure 1-28.** The text on the screen is really a reflection of the data in RAM.

basic input/output system (BIOS) special firmware that permits the compatibility between the CPU and devices such as the hard drive, CD-ROM drive, and monitor.

BIOS and CMOS Chips

The term ***BIOS*** is an acronym for ***basic input/output system.*** The terms BIOS and CMOS are often interchanged, but they are really two distinct

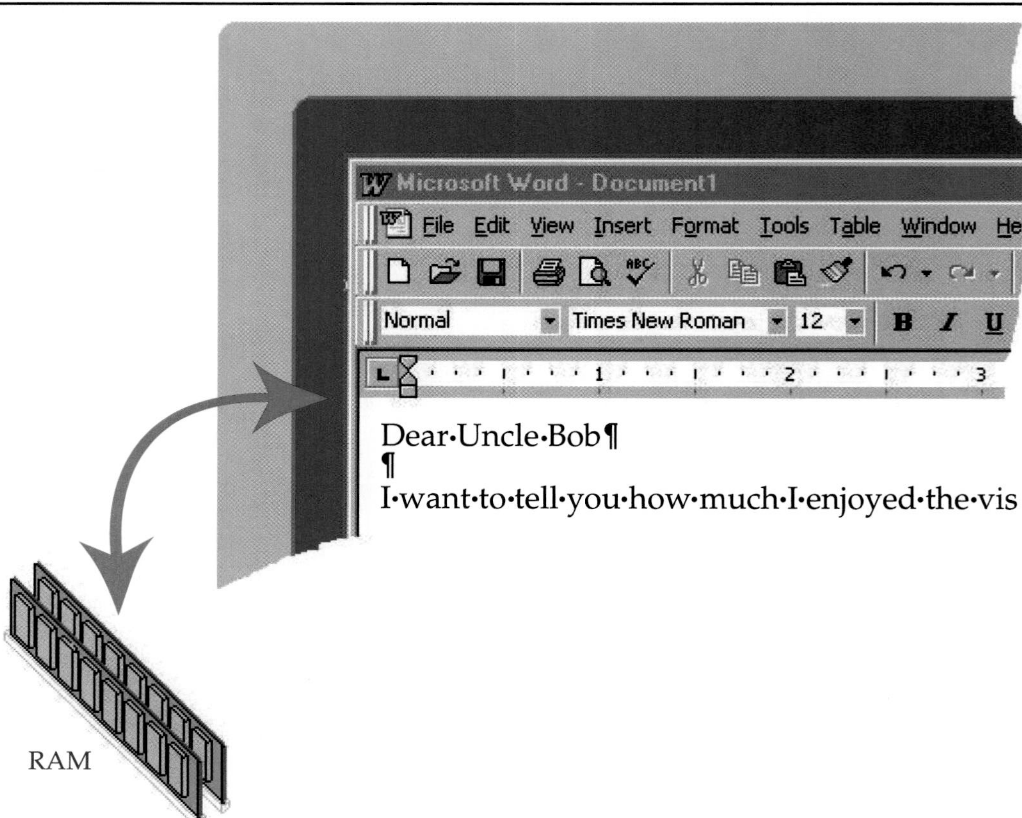

Figure 1-28. As you type data into a word-processing program, the information is stored in RAM.

concepts. The BIOS is stored in a special type of memory chip and consists of software programs that support the compatibility between the CPU and devices such as the hard drive, CD-ROM drive, and monitor. The BIOS includes the BIOS Setup program, which is responsible for setting and storing the date and time and information about the computer hardware. CMOS is a type of integrated circuit chip that stores the data required by the BIOS Setup program.

Originally, the BIOS was permanently etched into a ROM (read only memory) chip. ROM BIOS was permanent and could only be changed by replacing the ROM chip. Today, BIOS software is stored on an EEPROM (electrically erasable programmable read only memory) chip. An EEPROM is reprogrammable and is often referred to as *flash ROM*. Flash ROM can be erased electrically and reprogrammed with an updated version of a software program. Flash ROM retains its data when the power supply to the computer is disconnected or turned off.

complementary metal oxide semiconductor (CMOS) the chip that stores the BIOS Setup program data.

The CMOS chip is a hardware component. ***CMOS*** stands for ***complementary metal oxide semiconductor,*** which describes the electronic technology used to construct the chip. The CMOS chip is where the BIOS Setup program stores information about the computer's hardware.

battery the component that supplies voltage to the CMOS chip. Without the battery, the information stored in the CMOS chip would be lost every time the computer was shut off.

Battery

The ***battery*** supplies voltage to the CMOS chip, which contains the BIOS Setup data, **Figure 1-29.** Without the battery, the computer would lose the date, time, and all the important information about the hardware components stored in the CMOS chip when the computer power switch is turned off.

expansion cards a board that can be easily installed in a computer to enhance or expand its capabilities.

Expansion Cards

Expansion cards are sometimes called *interface cards* or *host adapters.* ***Expansion cards*** allow the computer to be custom-designed to meet the needs of different consumers, **Figure 1-30.** A certain computer may have video circuitry

Figure 1-29.
Batteries allow information such as the date and time to be saved while a PC is powered down.

A

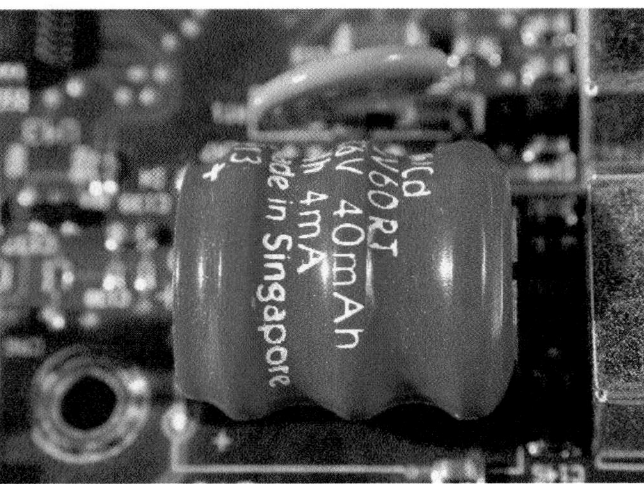

B

integrated into the motherboard that only allows for minimal video performance, or it may have a separate video card. The performance of this video system would be adequate for accounting or word-processing functions. However, it would be substandard for computer-aided drafting or game applications. To remedy this, a new expansion video card can be added to the computer system.

Other typical expansion cards are network interface cards, modems, and digital cameras. There are many more computer items that can be added with expansion cards.

Expansion Card Slots

expansion card slots receptacles for expansion cards which allow them to connect to the motherboard's circuitry.

Expansion cards fit snugly into ***expansion card slots,*** **Figure 1-31.** The expansion card slots allow the expansion card to connect directly to the electronic circuitry in the motherboard. This allows the expansion card to communicate directly or indirectly with other components on the motherboard or with the CPU. There are a number of types of expansion slots. They come with

Figure 1-30. Expansion cards allow computers to do many different things. This is an ISA-type sound card.

Figure 1-31. Expansion card slots.

names such as ISA, EISA, and PCI. These types of expansion slots will be discussed in detail in Chapter 3—Motherboards.

Cooling Fans

The ***cooling fan*** supplies a constant stream of air across the computer components. The typical CPU comes equipped with a fan mounted directly to the CPU to assist in the cooling process. Electronic components are damaged by excessive heat.

cooling fan
a fan that supplies a constant stream of air across the computer components.

Cables

There are several different types of cables commonly used inside the PC case. These cables connect the motherboard to devices such as the hard drive, floppy drive, and CD-RW drive.

Figure 1-32 shows a typical flat ribbon cable used to connect a hard drive to the motherboard. The cable consists of many parallel conductors. Some of the conductors are used to transfer data and others are used to transmit control signals between the motherboard and the device.

Electrical power for the devices can also be transmitted through the flat ribbon cable, but many devices consume more electrical power than the flat ribbon cable and motherboard are designed to safely carry. When a large volume of electrical power is required for a device, a separate power cable that runs directly from the power supply is used.

Figure 1-33 shows the flat ribbon cable for a 31/2″ floppy drive. Note the twist in the cable used for the floppy drive. The twist is required when more than one floppy drive is connected to the motherboard. The PC control system uses the twist to separately identify the two drives.

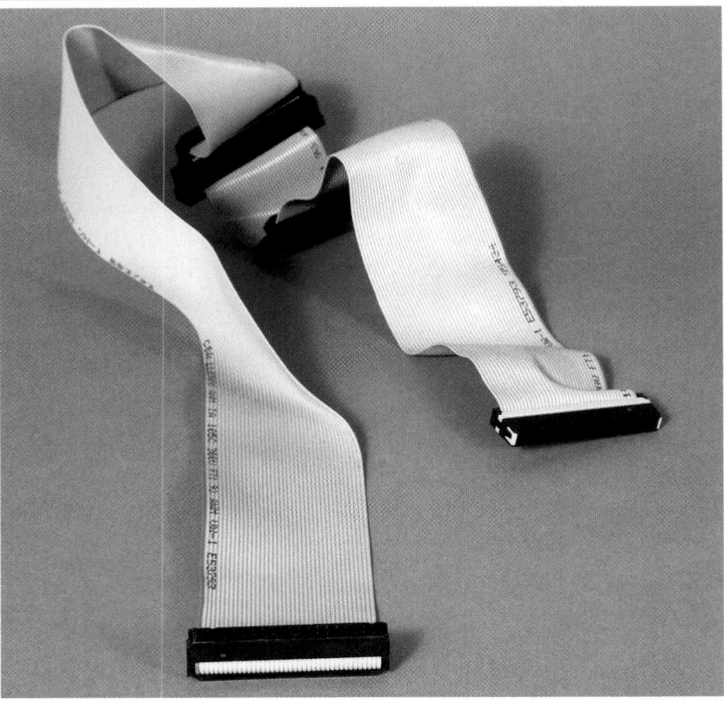

Figure 1-32.
Flat ribbon cable used to connect devices such as a hard drive or CD drive to the motherboard.

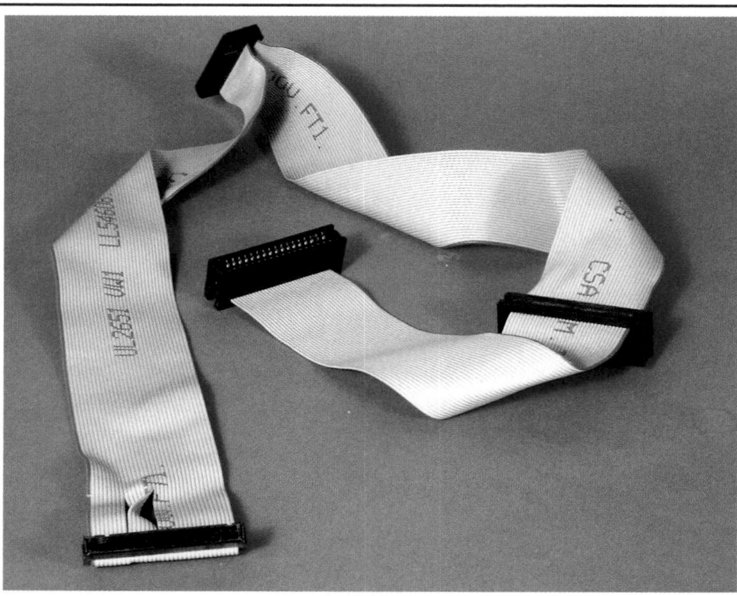

Figure 1-33.
Flat ribbon cable for connecting a floppy drive to the motherboard. Take special note of the twist in the section of cable near the connector on the left. The end with the twist connects to the floppy drive.

How the Major Parts Work Together

The following scenario traces how a sequence of events occurs in a typical PC system. In this example, a user moves from turning on the computer through saving text data. Please note that there are many different PCs. They all have unique start-up features and program interactions.

1. When the power switch is turned to the *on* position, electrical power from the wall outlet moves through the power supply where it is converted to a much lower dc voltage (or voltages). This stepped-down power is used to run the major components of the computer system including the motherboard, disk drives, and expansion cards. The fan starts up, providing a rush of cool air across the components.
2. Next, the BIOS system is activated and performs a POST. The POST (power-on self-test) checks the components in the computer system such as RAM, ROM, hard drive, and keyboard to ensure they are in proper working order. Information will flash across the computer's monitor, providing information such as the type and model number of the BIOS system and the amount of memory.
3. After the BIOS program checks the system, the operating system takes control. There are many different types of operating systems, but for our example, Windows software will be used.
4. The CPU now waits for activity to be generated by the mouse, keyboard, modem, or some other input device. The CPU constantly checks if a key is pressed or the mouse is moved or clicked. The CPU checks these items thousands of times per second.
5. The mouse pointer is moved to an icon and the mouse is clicked to activate a desired program—a word-processing program in this example. The software represented by the icon is activated. It now shares control of the computer with the CPU.

6. Some typing is done, and then the save command is issued by clicking a save-the-data icon in the word-processing program. The program now attempts to save to a disk. When the word-processing program saves, the operating system takes over in conjunction with the BIOS program. The operating system interprets the command issued from the word-processing program and translates it to a set of instructions that the BIOS can interpret.
7. The BIOS system, in turn, translates the instructions to the disk system. It activates the disk motor and actuator arm, moving it to the next available sector on the disk. Information about available disk space is kept in the file allocation table (FAT). The operating system and BIOS system work together until all data is transferred and recorded on disk.
8. Control is then returned to the word-processing program, so long as an error has not occurred. Possible errors are disk full or unable to read disk.

The cooperation between the word-processing program, operating system, and BIOS system goes unnoticed by the user.

Integrated Circuits

The term "chip" is often used in the computer industry. A ***chip*** is actually the final product of the manufacturing of an integrated circuit. An ***integrated circuit (IC)*** is a collection of transistors, resistors, and other electronic components reduced to an unbelievable small size. In fact, over six million transistors manufactured as an integrated circuit can fit into an area the size of a dime. Chips are commonly found on circuit boards. They are the black, square and rectangular devices.

chip
a semiconductor containing an integrated circuit.

integrated circuit
a collection of transistors, resistors, and other electronic components reduced to an unbelievable small size.

Manufacturing an Integrated Circuit

The manufacturing process that creates an IC consists of many hundreds of steps in a process covering a period of several months. The first step in the manufacture of a chip is the design of the circuit. The circuit is drawn on a very large scale. When the design is completed and all drawings are finished, the manufacturing process is ready to begin. First, the drawings are photographed. The negative of the drawing's photograph is used as a template in the manufacturing process. See **Figure 1-34.**

An ingot of pure silicon is made and then sliced into thin wafers to serve as the base of the IC. Silicon is the same as most common beach sand, but it is extremely pure. The material cannot contain any impurities that might cause adverse effects in the manufacturing of the IC. A series of layers are produced over the surface of the silicon wafer using a process called *photolithography.*

Photolithography is described in the following sequence of events. First, a heat process vaporizes silicon dioxide. Then various other chemicals are used to form many extremely thin layers over the surface of the wafer. After each layer is formed, a coating of a chemical called *photoresist* is laid over the entire surface of the wafer. The photoresist reacts when exposed to ultraviolet light.

The negative from the photograph made of the circuit is used as a stencil. The negative is called the *photomask.* When ultraviolet light shines through the mask, it causes the photoresist to leave a pattern of soft and hard surfaces in the exact pattern of the designed circuit. The soft photoresist is then washed away leaving an etched pattern of valleys and ridges on the surface of the wafer.

Figure 1-34.
A—A circuit drawing uses a template to form circuits on silicon wafers. B—Fine layers are created in the silicon. The layers are controlled in such a way to create the millions of transistors and other electronic components used in the integrated circuit. (International Business Systems Corporation)

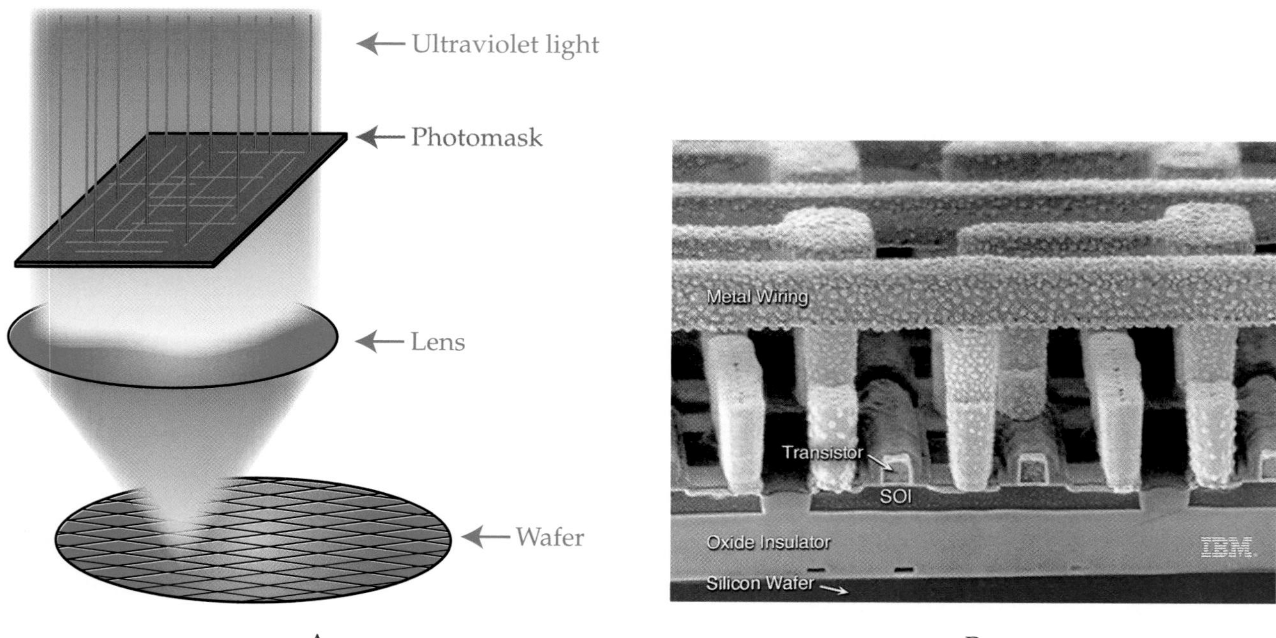

These valleys are filled with conductive materials. The process of filling in these valleys is called doping or implantation. This process is repeated many more times until twenty or more layers are developed over the surface of the entire wafer. A single wafer consists of many integrated circuits. The wafer is cut into individual integrated circuits and then packaged.

One of the most difficult parts of packaging the integrated circuit is connecting the very fine wires between the actual wafer circuits and the much larger pins on the outside of the package. The entire wafer and thin connection wires are encapsulated in a hard insulating material resembling black plastic.

Modern computer technology would not be possible without the techniques used in building integrated circuits. The ICs used in computers have many specialized purposes. For example, the CPU is a very large and complex IC that controls all the PC activities. The computer modem, used to communicate across telephone lines, has a specialized chip that changes computer data into a stream of various voltage levels that represent the data. It also converts the stream back into digital data at the receiving end. There are various other chips scattered across the motherboard that have special purposes. Some assist the CPU with data flow across the motherboard. Others control devices such as the hard drive and floppy drive. The RAM used in computers is nothing more than a group of ICs mounted on an insulated circuit board.

Electrostatic Discharge

Electrostatic discharge, or ***ESD,*** is best defined in the world of computer maintenance as the transfer of static electrical energy from one object to another, such as a computer chip. ESD can destroy the miniature circuits inside a computer chip. Static charges are usually created by friction. When two dissimilar materials are rubbed together, an electric charge is produced.

A common example of static electricity buildup and discharge is when you walk across a surface such as a rug and then reach out and touch a doorknob. You feel a sharp snap as the electrical charge of your body discharges to the doorknob. This is ESD.

You have learned about how ICs are manufactured and can appreciate the small scale of the circuit. An electrostatic discharge will damage the tiny circuits inside the chip. To avoid ESD, technicians wear a ground strap when handling static sensitive devices, **Figure 1-35.** The ***anti-static wrist strap*** bleeds off any static charge buildup on a technician's body and allows safe handling of an integrated circuit device.

electrostatic discharge (ESD) a release of energy (electrical current), created when an object with an electrostatic charge makes contact with a conductor.

anti-static wrist strap a strap, typically worn around the wrist, that connects the technician to ground and bleeds off any electrostatic charge.

Tech Tip:
Static buildup is always greatest when the air is dry and cool.

Tool Kit

Computer repair requires a minimum number of tools, **Figure 1-36**. A standard tool kit can vary from a small pouch to a more elaborate tool case.

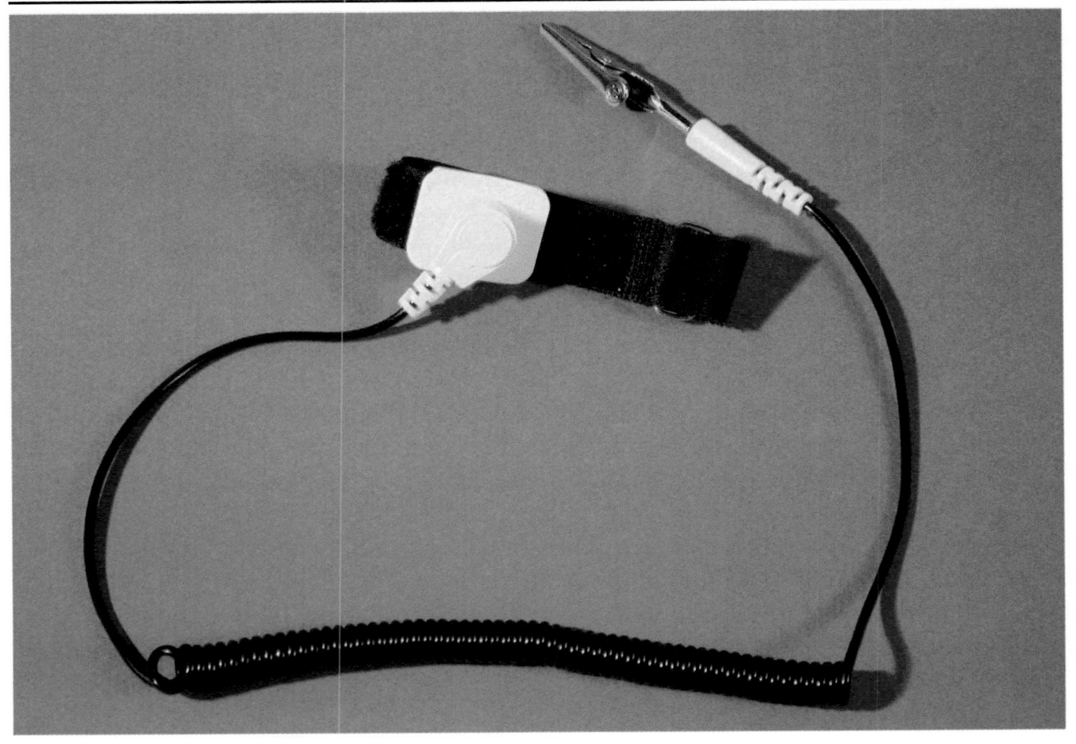

Figure 1-35. Ground strap.

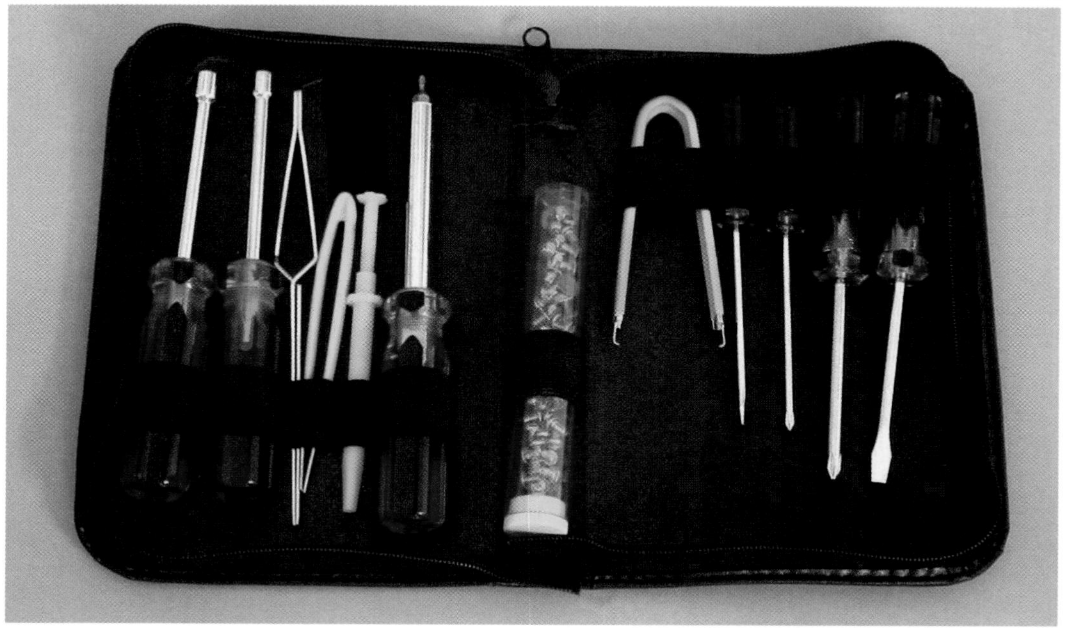

Figure 1-36. Standard small tool kit. This kit contains the basics. More elaborate kits are available.

A variety of flat tip, Phillips, and star drivers are needed. Canned compressed air, a chip puller, anti-static wrist strap, multimeter, extra screws, and a Torx driver set are also helpful tools. Additionally, some type of extraction tool for retrieving dropped screws and other parts is definitely needed.

Warning:
Do not use magnetic extraction devices when working on computers. In fact, you should *not* keep any magnetic devices in your tool kit including magnetic screwdrivers. As you will learn in Chapter 9—Magnetic Storage Devices, data is often stored on magnetic computer disks and tapes. Magnetic devices such as magnetic screwdrivers or extraction tools can destroy the data. Accidents can and will happen, but many can be prevented by not having any materials around your work location that can cause such destruction.

Software Tool Kit

You will find that a software tool kit is just as important as a hardware tool kit. You will probably depend more on your skills using software than hardware to troubleshoot, diagnose, and repair PCs. As you progress through the textbook, there will be many suggestions about software to add to your tool kit. There will also be many references to third party suppliers and shareware available for your use.

Many software tools can be found as shareware. Shareware is software programming that is freely distributed, usually by downloading from the Internet. Shareware is not always free for your unlimited use. It is usually intended for use on a trial basis only. The distributor expects the subscriber to purchase the software at a later date.

Summary

- There are two major classifications of electronic components, analog and digital. An analog system consists of many various voltage levels. A digital system usually contains only two voltage levels.
- The three common codes associated with PCs are binary, hexadecimal, and ASCII.
- The binary system consists of only two numbers: zero and one. The binary number system is used to represent the digital circuits of a computer.
- The hexadecimal numbering system has sixteen characters. It uses the digits *0–9* and the letters *A–F*.
- ASCII code is a standardized system of codes used to represent computer characters and symbols.
- A bit consists of a single 0 or 1 and is represented by the lowercase *b*.
- A byte consists of eight bits and is represented by the uppercase *B*.
- A peripheral is an optional piece of equipment used for input or output.
- A central processing unit (CPU) controls all the actions and processes data through the computer system.
- An integrated circuit (IC) is a collection of transistors, resistors, and other electronic components reduced to an extremely small size.
- Electrostatic discharge (ESD) is a static charge of electricity that can damage integrated circuits.
- *Never* use any type of magnetic tool around a PC.

Review Questions

Answer the following questions on a separate sheet of paper. Please do not write in this book.

1. Explain or compare the typical PC vs. human characteristics.
2. What components are found in a typical computer workstation?
3. Describe the difference between a digital and an analog electronic device.
4. Which of the following items acts like an analog system, and which is most like a digital system?
   a. Automobile gas pedal
   b. Streetlight
   c. Drawbridge
   d. Car horn
   e. Wind speed
   f. Slide trombone
   g. Drum
   h. Flashlight
5. Complete the following statement. There are eight _____ in one _____.

6. Data can be _____.
   a. text
   b. sound
   c. picture
   d. All the answers are correct.
7. The binary number system consists of the decimal numbers _____ and _____.
8. List the characters for the hexadecimal number system from zero to fifteen.
   0 = ___ 1 = ___ 2 = ___ 3 = ___ 4 = ___ 5 = ___ 6 = ___ 7 = ___ 8 = ___
   9 = ___ 10 = ___ 11 = ___ 12 = ___ 13 = ___ 14 = ___ 15 = ___
9. RAM provides (temporary, permanent) _____ storage of data.
10. What is the purpose of the battery mounted on the motherboard?
11. Explain the difference between the CMOS chip and BIOS.
12. What happens during the POST?
13. Define a *bit.*
14. Define a *byte.*
15. Define a *word.*
16. What letter symbol represents bit?
17. What letter symbol represents byte?
18. How many bytes are in a 32-bit word?
19. What are the two numeric values for 1 megabit?
    a. Base 10 _____ = 1M
    b. Base 2 or binary _____ = 1M
20. Why are expansion slots provided on a computer motherboard?
21. What is the function of BIOS?
22. What is another name commonly used for an integrated circuit?
23. Why should you not have a magnetic screwdriver in your tool kit?
24. What is the purpose of an anti-static wrist strap?
25. Give an example of a serial input device.

26. Convert the following acronyms to complete words and capitalize the letter of the word used to construct the acronym. Example: CPU = Central Processing Unit.
    a. BIOS =
    b. RAM =
    c. ROM =
    d. ASCII =
    e. POST =
    f. ESD =
    g. CMOS =
    h. IC =

Sample A+ Exam Questions

Answer the following questions on a separate sheet of paper. Please do not write in this book.

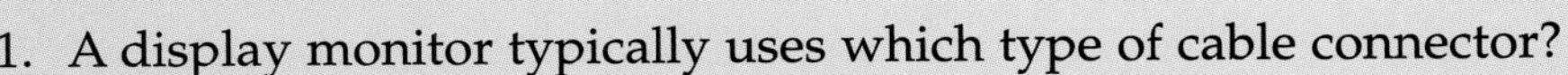

1. A display monitor typically uses which type of cable connector?
    a. DB-9
    b. DB-15
    c. 9-pin serial
    d. 25-pin parallel
2. A typical hard drive uses which type of cable connector?
    a. flat ribbon cable
    b. DB-15
    c. RJ-45
    d. PS/2
3. A modem typically uses which type of connector to connect to the telephone line?
    a. RJ-45
    b. DB-9
    c. RJ-11
    d. PS/2
4. The maximum number of devices that can be connected to an IEEE 1394 connector is ______.
    a. 7
    b. 24
    c. 63
    d. 127

5. The maximum number of devices that can be connected using a USB connector is _____.
   a. 7
   b. 24
   c. 63
   d. 127
6. Firmware is associated with which of the following items?
   a. RAM
   b. BIOS
   c. DVD
   d. Speaker amplifier system
7. Which of the following is *not* a standard expansion card architecture?
   a. ISA
   b. PCI
   c. EISA
   d. ICP
8. The acronym CMOS represents which of the following answers?
   a. Complementary mechanical operating system
   b. Complementary metal oxide semiconductor
   c. Complementary media operating system
   d. Complementary metallic opposition semiconductor
9. Which is the accepted method for a technician to deal with ESD?
   a. Always use insulated hand tools.
   b. Place the PC on a rubber mat before disassembly.
   c. Disconnect the ground before servicing a PC.
   d. Always wear an anti-static wrist strap before touching PC components.
10. Which type of tool should *never* be used for PC repair?
    a. Stainless steel
    b. Plastic handled
    c. Magnetic tipped
    d. Wooden handled

Suggested Laboratory Activities

Do not attempt any suggested laboratory activities without your instructor's permission. Certain activities can render the PC operating system inoperable.

1. Remove the case from three different PCs and compare the hardware. The PCs may differ by age or manufacture. Take note of similarities as well as differences. Identify all the major components.
2. Select a major brand of PC and use the Internet to access the Web site of the manufacturer. Look for technical reference material to help you identify the component locations on the motherboard and on the outside of the case.

Interesting Web Sites for More Information

www.cbi.umn.edu
www.computerhistory.org
www.karbosguide.com
www.intel.com
www.pcguide.com

Close-up view of the end of a cable for a floppy drive. Examine the twist near the connector. The twist identifies this connector as the one you will plug into the floppy drive.

Chapter 1
Laboratory Activity
Part Identification

After completing this laboratory activity, you will be able to:

- ❑ Identify the major components outside of a PC case.
- ❑ Identify the major parts inside a PC case.

Introduction

In this lab, you will learn to identify the major components inside a typical PC. You will be asked questions throughout the lab activity that will later be reviewed in your classroom as an instructor-lead activity. Answer all questions to the best of your ability. Short answers are acceptable. *Do not* remove any of the major components or disconnect any of the wiring or connections during this activity. This is strictly a visual identification exercise. You may use your textbook to help you identify the components.

Equipment and Materials

- Anti-static wrist strap.
- Pen or pencil and notebook paper.

Procedure

1. ______ Report to your assigned PC for this activity.
2. ______ Is the assigned PC a desktop model or a tower?
3. ______ On a separate sheet of paper, note if each of the following components is in your unit.

   ______ Floppy drive

   ______ CD drive

   ______ DVD drive
4. ______ Look at the back of the case and identify the types of port access the unit has. You may use the following illustration to assist you in identification.
5. ______ On a separate sheet of paper, sketch and identify each of the following ports.

   ______ 15-pin D-shell connector used to connect to the monitor

   ______ RJ-11 used to connect to a phone line

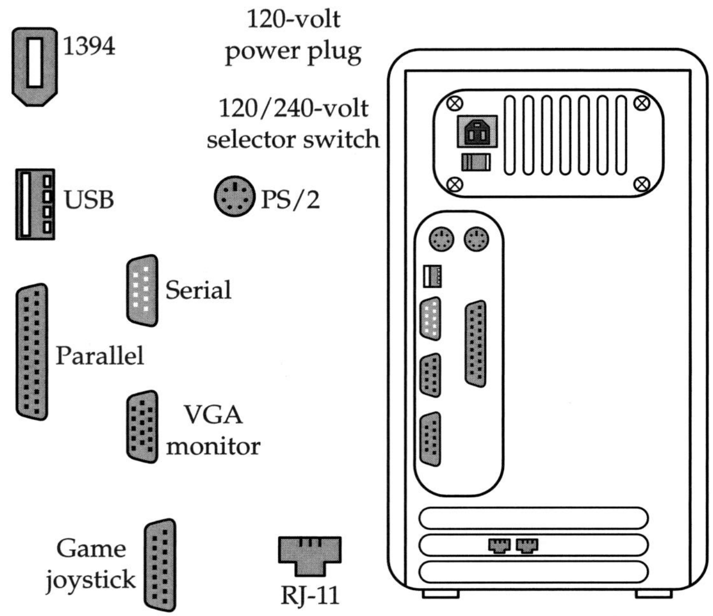

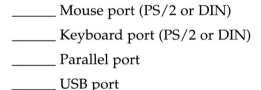

______ Mouse port (PS/2 or DIN)

______ Keyboard port (PS/2 or DIN)

______ Parallel port

______ USB port

6. ______ Watch the instructor as the removal of the case is demonstrated. There are many different case styles used to house the internal components of a PC. The variations can be quite confusing, and damage to the case can result if it is improperly disassembled. Watch closely and do not disassemble the case until given approval by the instructor.

7. ______ After removing the outside case cover, inspect the contents inside. Try to locate and identify the power supply unit. It is usually a large metallic box with many different colored wires running to other devices inside the PC. Another way to identify the power supply is to find where the 120-volt power cord enters the PC. The 120-volt power cord usually connects directly to the power supply. Does the power supply have a cooling fan as part of its total assembly? If so, where is the fan located? Approximately how many sets of power conductors are leaving the power supply unit and going to other components?

8. ______ Look on the power supply unit for markings related to the wattage of the power supply. Once you have located the markings, write the wattage rating of the unit below.

9. ______ Identify the CPU. It should be mounted on the motherboard and have some sort of heat sink attached to it. It may also have a fan unit. Does the CPU in your unit have a heat sink? Does the CPU in your unit have a fan mounted to it?

10. ______ Look for the random access memory modules (RAM). They will be either SIMMs or DIMMs. The following illustration depicts the general appearance of a memory module. How many memory units are installed? Do the memory modules have chips on both sides or one side?

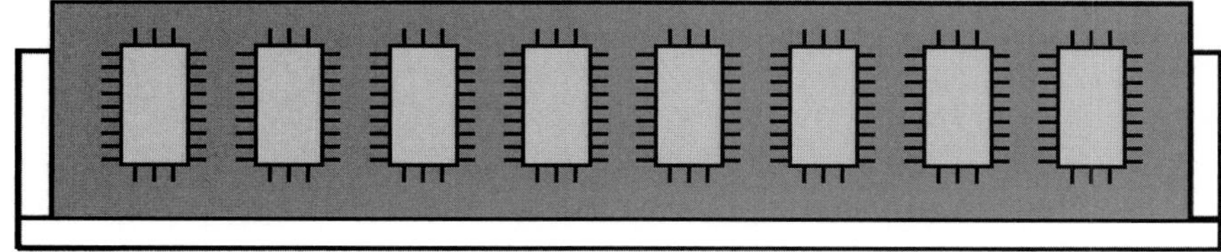

11. ______ Identify the main system board, or motherboard. It is a very large electronic circuit board that covers much of the area inside the case. How many expansion slots are located on the motherboard?

How many of the slots are PCI and how many are ISA? PCI slots are usually shorter than ISA slots and white in color. ISA slots are longer than PCI and usually dark brown or black in color.

How many of the expansion slots have adapter cards installed in them?

Look closely at how the motherboard is mounted to the case. How much space is between the motherboard and the metal case?

Why do you think there is a space between the motherboard and the case?

12. ______ Look at the back of the floppy drive.

Does it have any conductors from the power supply connected to it? Does the floppy drive have a flat ribbon cable connected to it?

If it does have a flat ribbon cable connected to it, where does the other end of the flat cable connect?

Does the flat ribbon cable have a red or blue stripe on one edge?

Does the flat ribbon cable going to the floppy drive have any conductors twisted in the cable?

13. ______ Identify the hard drive. It is a box mounted entirely inside the computer case. It will have wires from the power supply plugged into it as well as a flat ribbon cable.

Does the hard drive have a flat ribbon cable going to it? If so, where is the other end attached?

Does the flat ribbon cable have a red or blue stripe on one edge?

Are there power cables from the power supply going to the hard drive?

Does the flat ribbon cable going to the hard drive have a twist in part of the conductors?

14. ______ Look at the various chips mounted on the motherboard. Do they appear to be soldered in place or plugged into sockets?

15. ______ Can you locate the CMOS battery? Look for either a circular silver disk approximately 1″ in diameter, a blue barrel shaped device approximately 3/4″ in diameter, or a rectangular box approximately 2″× 3/4″ × 3/4″. The battery normally has the voltage printed on it.

16. ______ If you are unable to identify any items, call your instructor for assistance.

17. ______ Lastly, it is often necessary to make a sketch of the PC components' layout. The sketch is used as a guide for reassembly after certain PC components have been disassembled. For example, if you must replace a motherboard, every wire connection point should be identified. Make a sketch of the PC layout. It should look similar to the example that follows. The one shown here is very small, and the labeling is limited. Make yours larger on a separate sheet of paper. Be sure to identify fan, LED, and switch connections. Draw the sketch with as much detail as possible, as it will help during

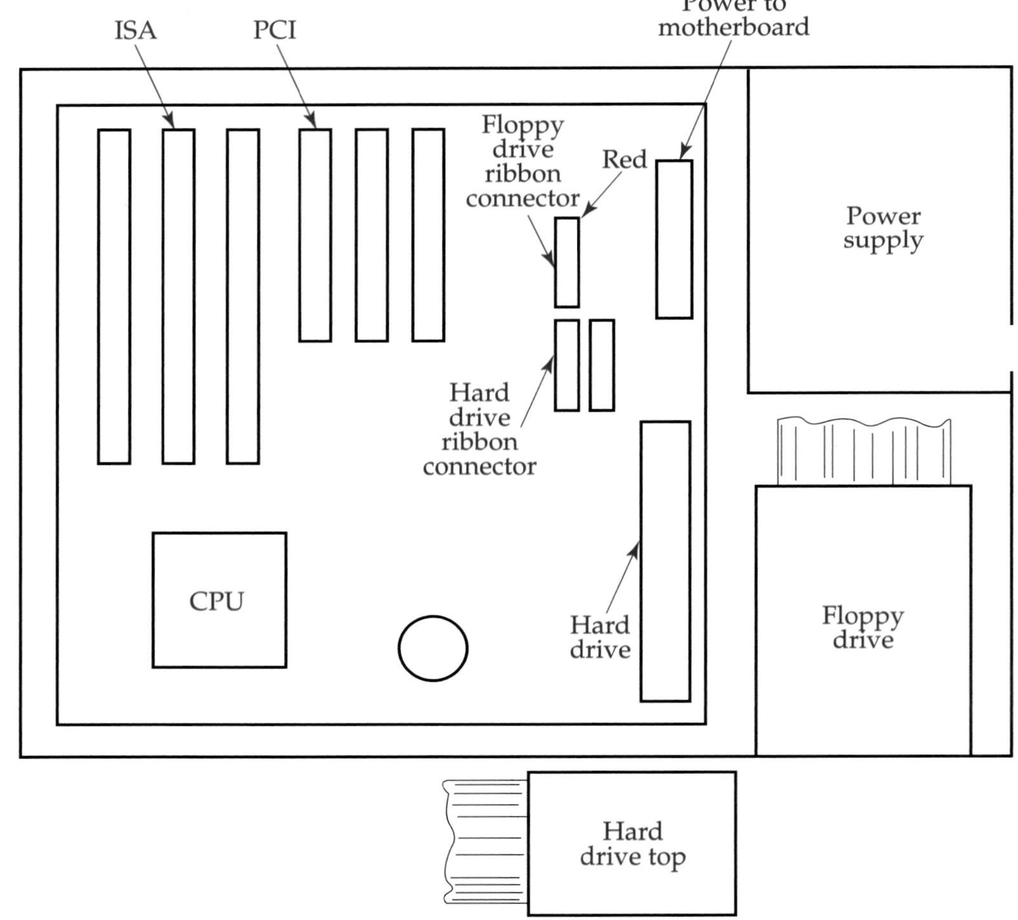

reassembly. Notice how the red mark on the flat ribbon data cable going to the hard drive and floppy drive has been identified on each end. Do the best you can, and then turn it in to your instructor for review. Before you begin, see if your instructor wants you to draw it in the workbook or on a separate sheet of paper.

Internet Assignment

1. Find the motherboard layout for the PC you are working on. Go to the manufacturer's Web site and see if you can locate the motherboard's schematic diagram. You will need the PC's model number.

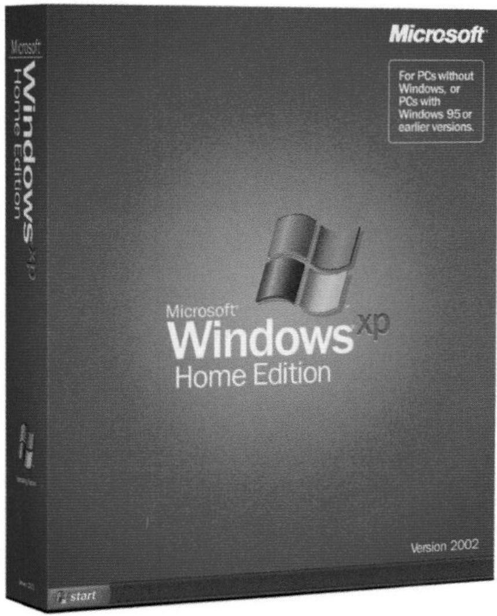

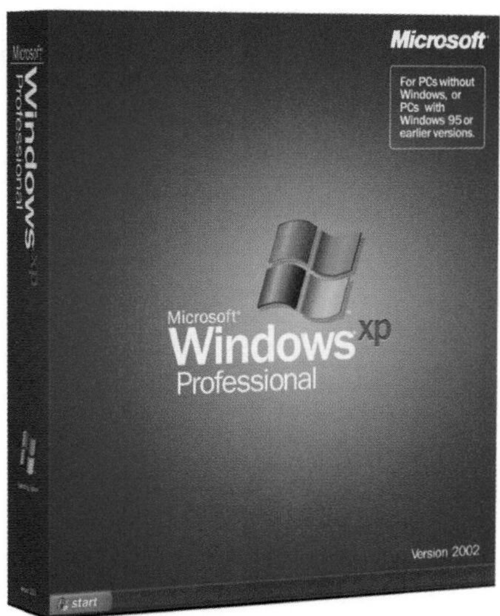

Microsoft's operating system, Windows XP, comes in two versions. One is designed for the home user and the other is designed for business. (Microsoft Corporation)

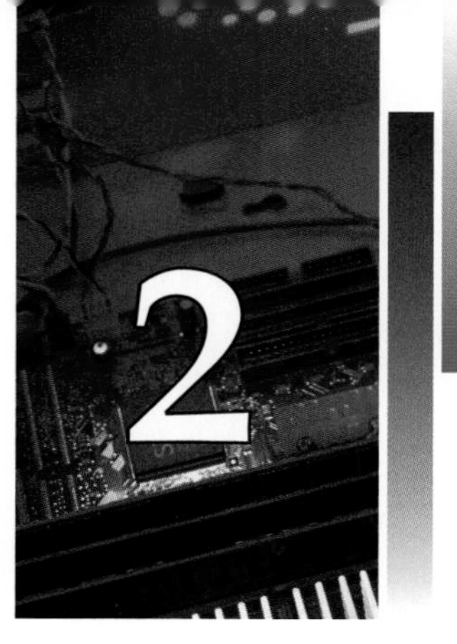

2 Operating Systems

After studying this chapter, you will be able to:

- ❑ Identify various computer operating systems.
- ❑ Explain minimum requirements of an operating system.
- ❑ Describe the three core DOS files.
- ❑ Identify DOS limitations.
- ❑ Explain the differences between the various versions of the Windows operating system.
- ❑ Describe how to create a DOS boot disk.
- ❑ Describe the boot process.
- ❑ Describe the relationship of application software, operating systems, BIOS, and system hardware components.
- ❑ Describe the common characteristics of different operating systems.

A+ Exam—Key Points

There will most likely be at least one question about allowable file names involving either 8.3 or long file name structure. Be familiar with the allowed or disallowed symbols. You must also know the basic text line commands such as **ver**, **dir**, **attrib**, **mem**, **scandisk**, **defrag**, **edit**, **copy**, **xcopy**, **format**, and **fdisk**. *Note that many of these commands will be covered in more detail in later chapters of the textbook.* Even with an excellent knowledge of the Windows operating system, the lack of sufficient knowledge of text line commands can result in failure on the CompTIA A+ Certification exams.

In addition, be sure you can define multitasking, both preemptive and cooperative.

A+

Key Words and Terms

The following words and terms will become important pieces of your computer vocabulary. Be sure you can define them.

application software
booting
bootstrap program
bugs
cabinet (cab) files
cold boot
configure
cooperative multitasking
directory
disk operating system (DOS)
DOS system boot disk
drivers
extensions
external commands
file
file allocation table (FAT)
graphical user interface (GUI)
internal commands
kernel
legacy
multitasking
operating system (OS)
pathname
Plug and Play (PnP)
POST (power-on self-test)
preemptive multitasking
registry
root directory
source code
subdirectory
text line command
warm boot
Windows system disk

This unit introduces you to various common operating systems. Understanding the operating system is essential for troubleshooting a PC system. The operating systems introduced in this unit include MS-DOS, PC-DOS, Linux, and the Windows families (including Windows 3.x, Windows 95, Windows 98, Windows Me, Windows NT Workstation, Windows 2000, and Windows XP).

To gain in-depth knowledge of an operating system, the operating system and its various options must be put to use. It is imperative that you supplement textbook studies with actual hands-on practice with these common operating systems. The Laboratory Manual for this text is designed to give you the necessary skills and first-hand knowledge required to pass the A+ Certification exams and to become a proficient PC technician.

Major Operating Systems

There are many operating systems on the market. Some are commonly known while others are obscure. For the purpose of this text, we will cover only the operating systems that are covered on the A+ Certification exams. The tests currently cover some text line commands, Windows 98, Me, XP, NT workstation, and 2000. Linux is also discussed in this text because it is likely that you will encounter it in the field. However, Linux is not covered in the A+ Certification exams. Linux has its own separate certification offered by CompTIA.

What Is an Operating System?

Before operating systems were commonplace, users had to write code for all of the common tasks. If you wanted to save data, you had to write the code that told your computer to do so.

An ***operating system (OS)*** provides a computer user with a file system structure and with a means of communicating with the computer system hardware. The operating system communicates with disk storage units, screen displays, printers, memory, and other computer components. It is also the job of the operating system to make sure programs running on the computer do not interfere with each other.

operating system (OS)
software that provides the user with a file system structure and allows the user to communicate with the computer system's hardware.

Operating system software has evolved over the years. Think of the evolution of computer software and hardware as a group of inventors constantly building a better mousetrap. What is a leading edge operating system one day may not be the next day. In fact, it will likely become obsolete only a few years later. It is the constant evolution of the computer that makes it so confusing. Each operating system has its individual strengths and weaknesses.

The core of any operating system is referred to as the ***kernel.*** Just as plants bud and grow from a single seed or kernel, so does the operating system software. The core program is enhanced by other software applications that refine the computer system. Associated with the core can be programs that provide for user interface style, security, and specialized file systems.

kernel
the core of the operating system.

Operating systems allow application software to communicate with the BIOS, which in turn translates the request of the application software into instructions that the hardware can understand. Examine **Figure 2-1.**

An operating system provides a user with the ability to interact with the computer hardware and peripherals. As you can see, users give instructions to the computer system via application software such as word-processing, graphics, and gaming software. The operating system provides a communication system between the software application and the BIOS. In some cases, the operating system can communicate directly with the hardware components.

Operating System Characteristics

The way an operating system handles activities such as storing data, interfaces with the user, and presents information on the screen can be referred to as operating system characteristics. Most operating systems appear similar when judged by their screen display. However, there are many differences in the way they handle activities, especially data storage.

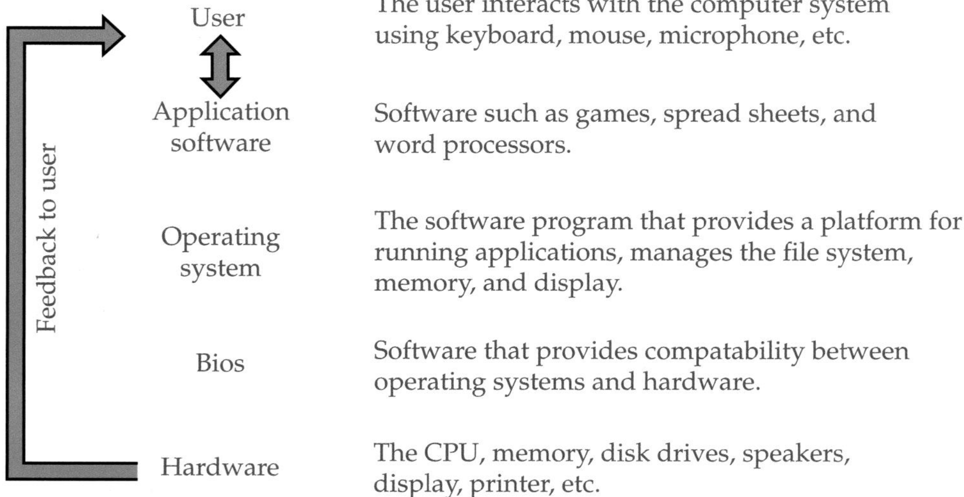

Figure 2-1. Typical relationship of computer hardware and software components.

Multitasking

multitasking running two or more programs at the same time.

Multitasking is the ability of an operating system to support two or more programs running at the same time. With multitasking, it seems to the user that both programs are running simultaneously. However, in reality, they are not. The computer simply switches control between the programs giving the illusion they are running at the same time.

An example of multitasking is using the printer while, at the same time, using e-mail, surfing the Internet, or running another computer application such as a game. The computer runs the software in between sending packets of data to the printer.

Note that you may also hear the term *thread* or *threads* used. These terms refer to a form of multitasking when more than one CPU is installed on a motherboard. Data and parts of a program can be shared between two or more CPUs. This is called *threading* instead of multitasking.

Not all operating systems support multitasking. In addition, those that support multitasking do not all support it in the same way. DOS, for example, does not support multitasking. Only one program can be run at a time. If a second program is loaded, the first is unloaded from RAM. If the printer is printing, another program cannot run until the printer has finished. The two major classifications of multitasking are preemptive and cooperative.

Preemptive multitasking

preemptive multitasking multiple programs sharing control of the operating system.

Preemptive multitasking, sometimes referred to as *time slicing,* allows multiple programs to share control of the operating system. No single program can totally take charge of the computer system. All programs running in the preemptive mode of multitasking are sharing RAM. If two programs attempt to use the same area of RAM at the same time, the computer will lock up. Windows 95, Me, XP, NT, 2000, and OS/2 use preemptive multitasking.

Cooperative multitasking

cooperative multitasking one program dominating the operating system but allowing another program to run while the primary program is idle.

With ***cooperative multitasking,*** one program dominates the operating system but will allow another program to run while the primary program is idle. This type of multitasking is common to the Macintosh operating system and Windows 3.x.

User Interface

There are two dominant user interfaces used to issue commands on a computer system, *text line command* and *graphical user interface*. Graphical user interface is usually referred to as GUI (pronounced *gooey*).

Text line command

text line command commands issued by entering text at a command prompt.

A ***text line command*** interface means that commands for the computer are issued by typing in text at a command prompt. DOS, PC-DOS, and UNIX are typical text line command systems. See **Figure 2-2.**

Some common DOS commands are **dir**, **copy**, and **mem**. These commands call up a directory, copy a file or disk, and list your memory resources, respectively. See **Figure 2-3** for a chart of some common DOS commands.

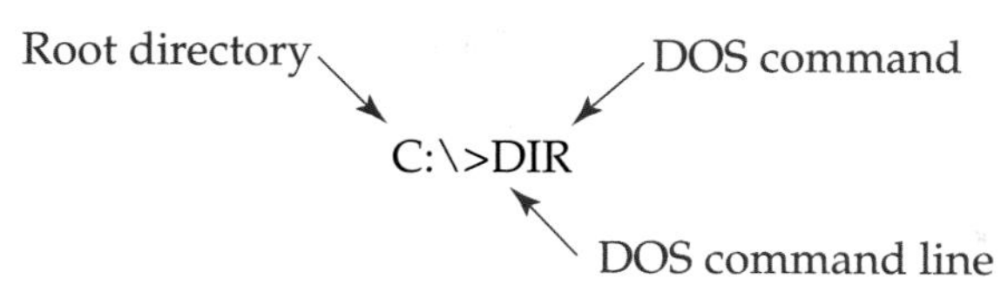

Figure 2-2.
This is a typical DOS command line.

Figure 2-3.
Chart of commonly used DOS commands.

Command	Example	Definition
mem	**C: mem**	Displays information about the type and amount of system memory.
cd	**C:\>cd\games**	Changes the command line from the current directory to another directory. In the example, a command is issued to the computer changing the current command line from the root directory of drive C to a directory on drive C called games.
copy	**C:\>copy a:memo1 c:**	The **copy** command copies data from one location to another. In the example, a file named memo1 is being copied from drive A to drive C.
dir	**C:\>dir**	The command **dir** will display the current directory. All the files and directories directly connected to the root directory will be displayed.
exit	**C:\>exit**	When DOS is accessed from Windows, and the command **exit** is issued at the DOS command line, DOS is closed and control returns to the Windows desktop.
md	**C:\>md c:\games**	The command **md** is used to create or make a directory. In the example, a directory called games is created.
rd	**C:\>rd c:\games**	The command **rd** is used to delete or remove a directory. In the example, the directory called games is being removed from the root directory of drive C.
chkdsk	**C:\>chkdsk a:**	The **chkdsk** command is used to check a disk for errors and displays the findings on the monitor screen.
format	**C:\>format a:**	The command **format** prepares a disk for first time usage. Today most disks are already formatted or prepared to store data and programs. You must be careful issuing the command format because it can erase all data on the disk being formatted. In the example, the command **format** is being issued at the DOS prompt to prepare a disk in drive A before storing data on it.

There are many more commands than the few listed, but these are some of the most commonly used. DOS was the major operating system used by PCs in the 1980s. However, DOS was difficult to use. Users had to memorize many different commands to become proficient with the DOS operating system.

Today, text line commands are still used, especially when troubleshooting. Text line commands are particularly important when a PC fails to complete its startup process and take the user to the graphical user screen. Troubleshooting tools such as Recovery Console, used in Windows 2000 and Windows XP, can only be run using text line commands. It is important that the technician be able to use the text line command prompt.

Windows 2000, Me, and XP do not use DOS but rather a DOS emulator. The DOS emulator has the look and feel of a real DOS prompt and functions similarly. Many of the restrictions or limitations of DOS are not found in the emulator program. For example, many of the restricted characters not allowed in DOS file names can be used in the Windows DOS emulator.

Windows XP uses DOS-like commands in the Command Console utility. The Command Console utility allows a computer technician to communicate with the Windows XP operating system after a system GUI failure. When a computer system fails during the startup process, there is no graphical user interface. The only means of communicating with the computer system is by using a non-graphical user interface such as the Command Console. Many of the text line commands used in Command Console look and work exactly like the old DOS commands. See **Figure 2-4.** The commands are designed to look and feel like the older DOS commands so that technicians can easily understand them.

Figure 2-4. Windows XP text line commands.

```
C:\WINDOWS\System32\command.com

C:\>help
For more information on a specific command, type HELP command-name
ASSOC    Displays or modifies file extension associations.
AT       Schedules commands and programs to run on a computer.
ATTRIB   Displays or changes file attributes.
BREAK    Sets or clears extended CTRL+C checking.
CACLS    Displays or modifies access control lists (ACLs) of files.
CALL     Calls one batch program from another.
CD       Displays the name of or changes the current directory.
CHCP     Displays or sets the active code page number.
CHDIR    Displays the name of or changes the current directory.
CHKDSK   Checks a disk and displays a status report.
CHKNTFS  Displays or modifies the checking of disk at boot time.
CLS      Clears the screen.
CMD      Starts a new instance of the Windows command interpreter.
COLOR    Sets the default console foreground and background colors.
COMP     Compares the contents of two files or sets of files.
COMPACT  Displays or alters the compression of files on NTFS partitions.
CONVERT  Converts FAT volumes to NTFS.  You cannot convert the
         current drive.
COPY     Copies one or more files to another location.
DATE     Displays or sets the date.
DEL      Deletes one or more files.
DIR      Displays a list of files and subdirectories in a directory.
DISKCOMP Compares the contents of two floppy disks.
DISKCOPY Copies the contents of one floppy disk to another.
DOSKEY   Edits command lines, recalls Windows commands, and creates macros.
ECHO     Displays messages, or turns command echoing on or off.
ENDLOCAL Ends localization of environment changes in a batch file.
ERASE    Deletes one or more files.
EXIT     Quits the CMD.EXE program (command interpreter).
FC       Compares two files or sets of files, and displays the differences
         between them.
FIND     Searches for a text string in a file or files.
FINDSTR  Searches for strings in files.
FOR      Runs a specified command for each file in a set of files.
FORMAT   Formats a disk for use with Windows.
FTYPE    Displays or modifies file types used in file extension associations.
GOTO     Directs the Windows command interpreter to a labeled line in a
         batch program.
GRAFTABL Enables Windows to display an extended character set in graphics
         mode.
HELP     Provides Help information for Windows commands.
IF       Performs conditional processing in batch programs.
LABEL    Creates, changes, or deletes the volume label of a disk.
MD       Creates a directory.
MKDIR    Creates a directory.
```

There are also newer text line commands that complement today's more sophisticated operating systems. So when you hear someone say "*DOS is dead*" or "*DOS is no longer used,*" you can reply, "*Yes, you are correct, but text-based commands are an essential part of troubleshooting.*" There will be much more about command line support in Chapter 15—PC Troubleshooting and in the Laboratory Manual.

Graphical user interface

graphical user interface (GUI) an operating system interface that allows the user to perform functions by selecting on-screen icons rather than by issuing text line commands.

Although DOS and DOS-like systems controlled over 80 percent of the market during the 1980s, the user-friendly ***graphical user interface (GUI)*** system of Macintosh gained popularity. Creating GUIs for the PC in the form of Windows 3.1 and Windows NT helped Microsoft retain control of the operating system market. In most operating systems that are used today, the GUI displays the file system consisting of folders, icons, and names. One great advantage of using the GUI is that the entire file structure is easily displayed and interpreted. Examine **Figure 2-5** and **Figure 2-6.** Shown is a typical GUI display of a file system organization.

The relative relationship between files and folders is simple to interpret. Two window styles appear. One is based on the program Windows Explorer, and the other uses a more traditional folder display. Each window style displays the same file structures. The two styles differ only in their presentation. Figure 2-5 uses a series of cascading windows to display information about the software's organization of files and their location in the file system on the hard drive. Figure 2-6 uses Windows Explorer to display the same information, only it resembles a more advanced DOS file structure.

A typical GUI is seen in **Figure 2-7.** This is a typical Windows 98 desktop. The desktop view for Windows 95, 98, 2000, Me, NT, 2000, and XP are very similar. On the desktop are a number of program icons.

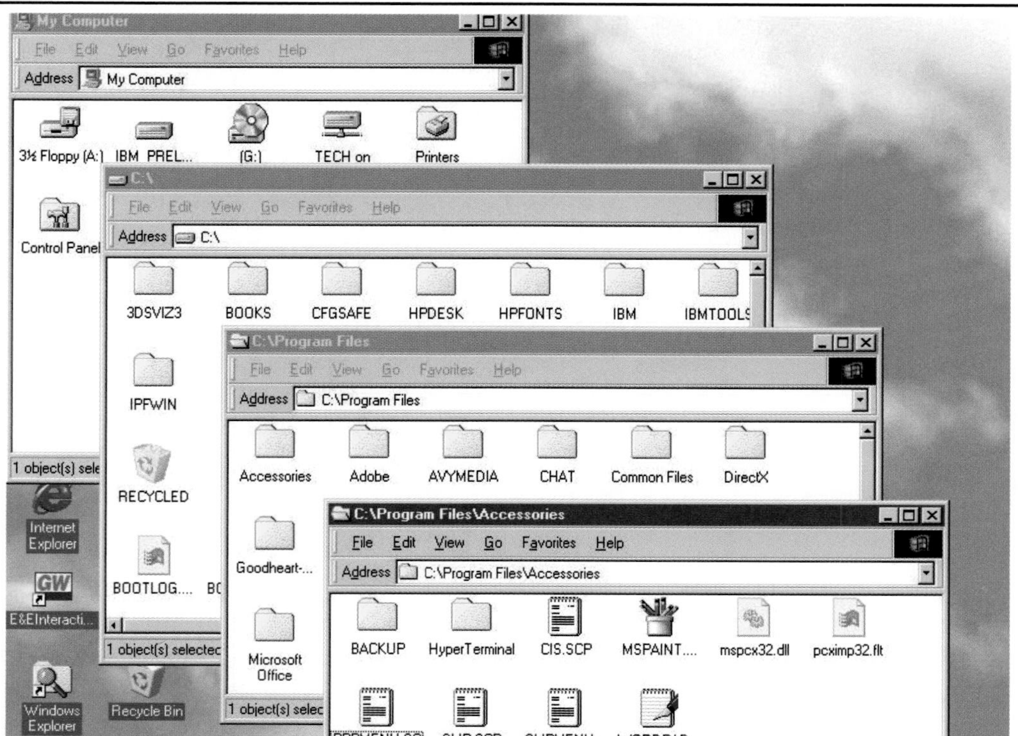

Figure 2-5.
File structure is shown here through cascading windows.

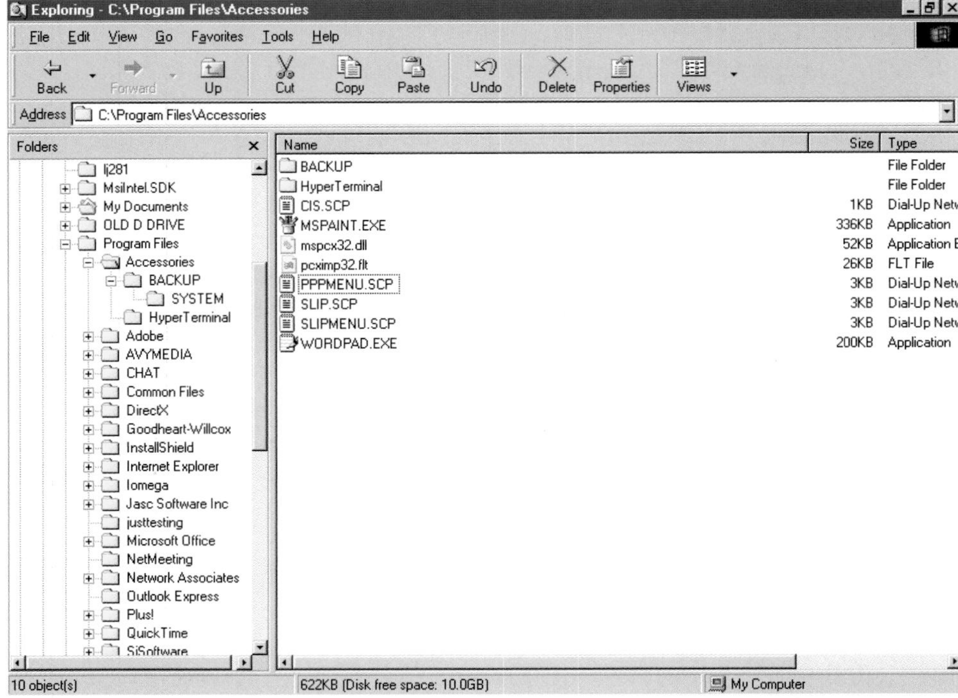

Figure 2-6.
File structure can also be seen using Windows file managing software Windows Explorer.

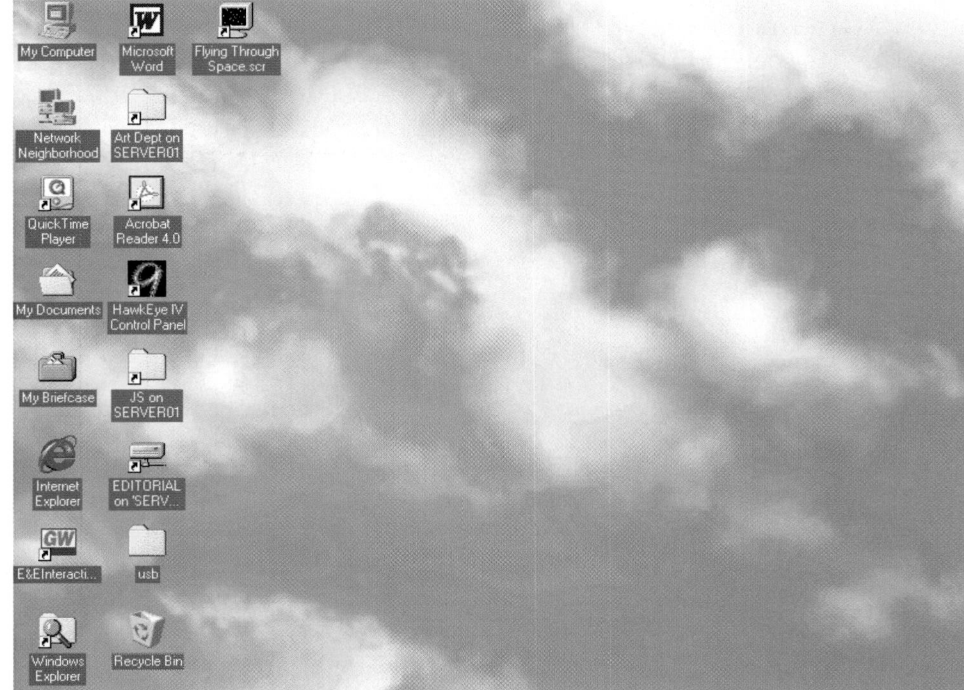

Figure 2-7.
Typical opening GUI for Windows. While the mechanics behind the interface can be very different between the various versions of Windows, the appearance of the GUI has remained fairly constant.

File System Structure

There are many different file systems, but they do have common characteristics. Programs and files are stored on computers in much the same way regardless of the operating system used.

The basic structure is made of directories, subdirectories, and files. A ***file*** is a collection of data or a program. ***Directories*** and ***subdirectories*** are groupings of files. The distinction between directories and subdirectories is in how they relate to each other. This will become apparent shortly. Examine **Figure 2-8.** This is a typical directory and file structure. It shows the relationship of the root directory, directories, subdirectories, and files.

The ***root directory*** is at the top of the directory structure. In this case, C:\ appears at the top. Thus, the root directory is C: (your hard drive). Next, there are two directories stemming from the root directory, Games and School. Directory and subdirectory are relative terms. Looking at the example again, you will see that English is a subdirectory to School. Both English and School are directories, but the placement in the structure determines which is a subdirectory in relation to the other. Directories can contain files. Under the directory Games, you can see several game files such as Hearts and Solitaire.

file
a collection of data that forms a single unit.

directory
a file used to group other files together in a hierarchical file structure. A directory is analogous to a file folder in a conventional, paper filing system. Directories are referred to as folders in many operating systems.

subdirectory
a file that subdivides the contents of a directory. A subdirectory is analogous to a folder within a folder in a conventional, paper filing system. Subdirectories are referred to as subfolders in many operating systems.

Pathname

A file ***pathname*** is used to identify the location of a specific file. Look again at Figure 2-6. The pathname for the file is displayed near the top of the window's dialog box. The display is C:\Program Files\Accessories. C: is the root of the file, \Program Files is the first directory folder, and \Accessories is the subdirectory of \Program Files. The entire string of characters is referred to as the file pathname.

pathname
a string of characters used to identify a file's location in the directory structure.

A Closer Look at DOS

The ***disk operating system (DOS)*** is the operating system that was first widely accepted and used throughout the world. It is still used today but to a limited degree. It has been overshadowed by many more powerful operating systems. It is important to have a basic understanding of DOS because it set the standards for the other operating systems used today. In fact, DOS 7 is actually integrated into the Windows 98 operating system to ensure downward compatibility with some older programs that were designed to run under DOS. Text line commands are still very much a part of the A+ Certification exams. To pass the exams, you must acquire a basic understanding of text line commands.

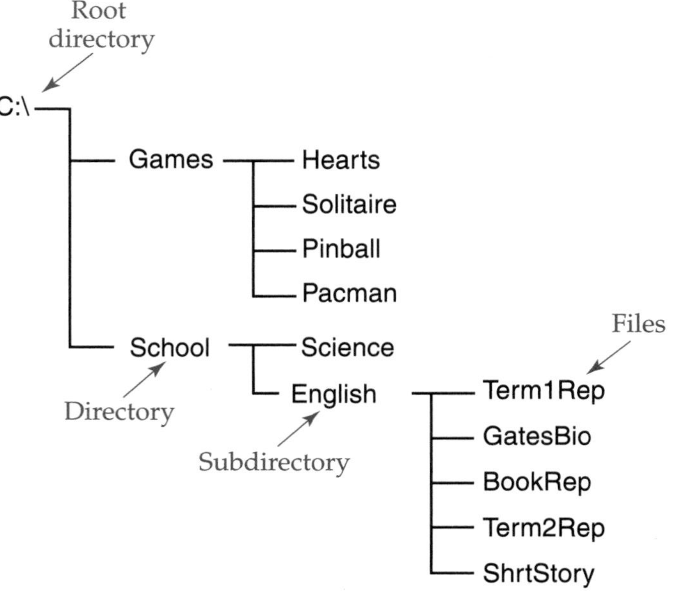

Figure 2-8.
Typical directory and file structure.

root directory
the directory at the top of the file structure hierarchy. A root directory is analogous to a file cabinet drawer in a conventional, paper filing system. A root directory is also referred to as the root.

DOS Core Files

The core files associated with DOS are io.sys, msdos.sys, and command.com. These three files are the minimum set of files required to operate a DOS-compatible computer system. The IBM system has its own version of DOS called PC-DOS. In the IBM system, the io.sys and msdos.sys files are called ibmio.com and ibmdos.sys. Command.com is still referred to as command.com.

These are important files. If erased, the computer would fail to complete its starting routine. Command.com is a program that interprets commands, such as copy and erase, which are issued at the DOS prompt.

Tech Tip:
Note that io.sys and msdos.sys are *hidden files*. To prevent users from accidentally erasing them, the operating system "hides" them. You still have access to these files, but in the default operating system settings, they will not show up in your file structure. When using Windows Explorer, the option for viewing hidden files must be activated.

disk operating system (DOS)
an operating system typically requiring the user to issue text line commands to perform operations.

DOS system boot disk
a floppy disk that contains the files necessary to run a computer with DOS.

DOS System Boot Disk

A ***DOS system boot disk*** is a floppy disk that contains the files necessary to run a computer with DOS. The three files necessary are the DOS core files: io.sys, msdos.sys, and command.com. A DOS boot disk is a very handy troubleshooting tool because a computer can have one of several different problems related to the boot sequence and hard drive.

To create a DOS boot disk, you simply place a floppy disk into the drive and enter the command **format a: /s** at the DOS command prompt. DOS will then copy the necessary files to the floppy disk in **drive A:**. To test the disk, insert it into the standard 3 1/2" floppy drive while the computer is off. Then turn the power to the computer on. The computer will automatically start using the system files of the operating system located on the boot disk. A DOS prompt will appear on the screen similar to that in **Figure 2-9.**

```
MS-DOS Prompt
AUTOEXEC NAI            225  10-26-01  1:54p autoexec.nai
PZ5          <DIR>           05-31-01  2:00p PZ5
SETUPXLG TXT            440  08-27-01 11:28a SETUPXLG.TXT
LJ281        <DIR>           08-27-01 11:50a lj281
RESCUE~1 TXT         47,749  09-05-01 10:39a Rescued document
RESCUE~2 TXT          1,727  09-05-01  1:32p Rescued document
RESCUE~3 TXT          1,727  09-05-01  1:32p Rescued document
RESCUE~4 TXT          1,724  09-05-01  1:32p Rescued document
RESCUE~5 TXT         49,026  09-05-01  1:32p Rescued document
        22 file(s)        359,360 bytes
        16 dir(s)      10,298.86 MB free

C:\>
```

Figure 2-9.
A typical DOS prompt.

Command.com

Command.com is a compact software program that allows the user to interact with the computer using standard DOS commands. Another name for the command.com software program is the *command interpreter.* The command interpreter contains a set of software programs that are activated by text entered at the command prompt. These commands are known as ***internal commands*** because the required software to run these commands resides inside the command.com program file.

internal commands a set of programs that are wholly contained within the command processor program (command.com).

Following are examples of several common internal commands.

Command	System Response
ver	Displays the software version running on the computer.
dir	Displays a list of files, directories, and subdirectories.
time	Displays the time.
date	Displays the date.
copy	Copies a file or group of files from one location to another location.
del	Deletes a file.
rename	Changes the name of a file.

The DOS operating system also uses several ***external commands.*** They are individual, executable files found in addition to the internal commands of the command.com file. The external commands can be viewed in the DOS directory structure. The external commands typically have an .exe file extension.

external commands individual, executable files that extend DOS's functionality beyond the limits of its internal commands.

Following are several examples of common external DOS commands.

Command	System Response
edit	Starts a text editor program similar to a word processor.
format	Prepares a disk for storing data.
chkdsk	Checks the condition of a disk and displays a report.
print	Prints a text file to a printer.

Msdos.sys

Msdos.sys is the kernel of the operating system. This program contains many smaller programs that process all the common commands needed to communicate between the user and the hardware, such as the processor. For IBM systems with PC-DOS, the program is called ibmdos.sys.

Io.sys

The io.sys file contains generic drivers necessary for communicating with hardware devices such as the monitor, floppy drive, hard drive, and keyboard. The io.sys file works in conjunction with the msdos.sys file to boot the computer. For IBM systems with PC-DOS, it is called ibmbio.com.

Naming DOS Files

DOS has a definitive system for naming files usually referred to as the *eight point three* (or 8.3) naming convention. A DOS file name is divided into two

extension
the second part of a filename. An extension is typically three characters long and indicates the function of the file.

parts by a period. The first part of the name consists of one to eight characters, and the second part, called the ***extension,*** consists of three characters.

In most cases when you are naming a file, the second part is optional and is completed automatically by a software application. For example, a word processing application may automatically save the file with the .txt extension. **Figure 2-10** lists some common name extensions.

Not all characters are available for use in a DOS name. Acceptable characters consist of the following:

A through Z
0 through 9
Underscore _
Caret ^
Dollar sign $
Tilde ~
Exclamation point !
Number sign #
Percent sign %
Ampersand &
Hyphen -
Braces { }
Parentheses ( )
At sign @
Apostrophe '
backtick `

Figure 2-10. Common file extensions.

.bmp	A bitmap graphics file.
.com	An executable command file.
.dll	A dynamic link library—collection of data or functions that can be used by Windows applications.
.doc	A document file.
.exe	An executable file—one that is a program and will run if the name is typed at the DOS prompt.
.ini	A file containing configuration information for Windows.
.log	A file that lists actions that have occurred.
.pif	A program information file—holds information about how Windows should run non-Windows applications.
.txt	A text file.

Certain characters are *not* used as part of the file name because they have special meanings in DOS. Common characters that are not allowed include back slashes, commas, and spaces. Periods can only be used for the separation of the name and extension. Other characters that cannot be used consist of the following:

| + = * > < ? : [ ]

Many different operating systems as well as application programs restrict the use of special characters in a file name.

A Closer Look at Microsoft Windows

The most widely used operating system today is Microsoft Windows. Windows 98 and later versions are found on most machines. The A+ Certification requires knowledge of Windows 98, Me, NT Workstation, 2000, and XP. References to all systems are discussed when appropriate.

Desktop

Windows 95 and later versions, including NT and 2000, are very similar. In fact, you might say they set the standard for today. Even the newest Linux desktop looks remarkably like a Windows desktop. The desktop allows the user easy access to many of the most common software programs used. Look at **Figure 2-11.**

At the bottom left of the screen is the **Start** button. This button is used to launch and access existing programs. When the mouse arrow is clicked on the **Start** button, a menu similar to **Figure 2-12** will pop up. Many options are made

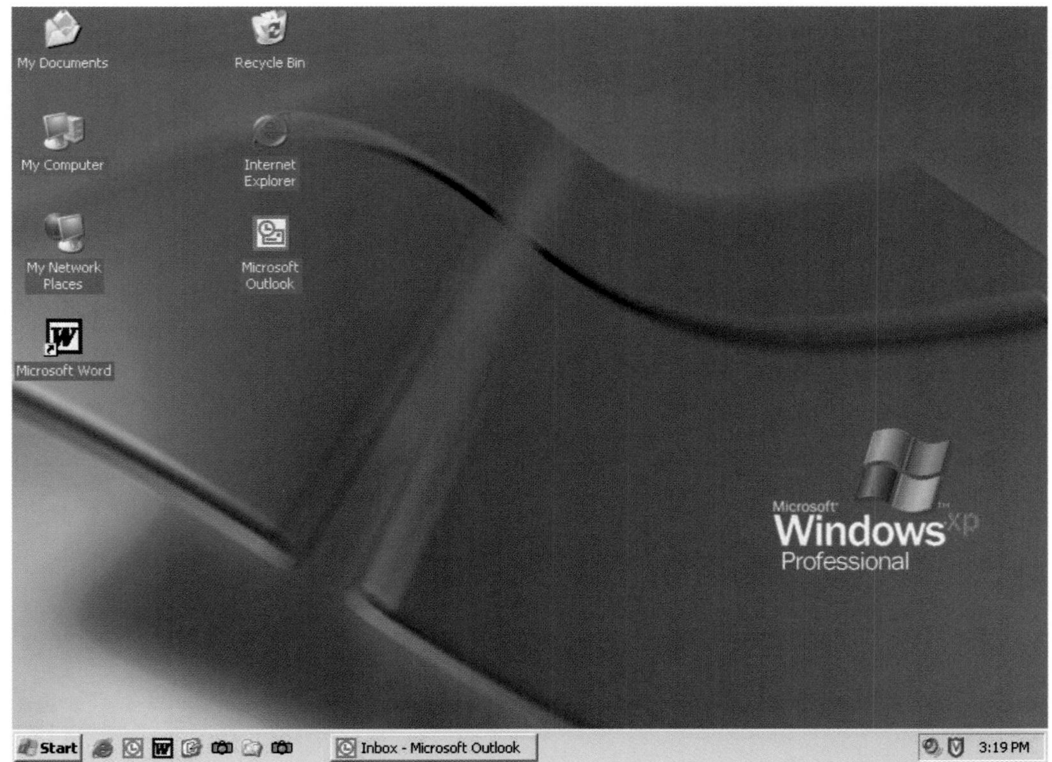

Figure 2-11. Typical Windows desktop.

available through this menu. These options include **Help**, **Find**, **Settings**, **Documents**, **Programs**, and **Shut Down**.

Long File Names

Beginning with Windows 95 and Windows NT, Windows operating systems were designed to overcome the DOS file name restriction of a maximum of eight characters (the 8.3 naming convention). The long file name structure allows file names of up to 255 characters to be used.

This long file name feature allows for the content of the file to be described in some detail. This provides relief from brief, cryptic, eight-character file names. For example, using the long file standard, a file could be saved as Term1 Science Paper The Factors Affecting Ocean Tides. There are still certain characters or symbols that cannot be used in the file name. The characters that are still not allowed in the long file name system consist of the following:

| * > < ? : \ / "

These characters have a special meaning to the operating system and will produce errors or unwanted results when used.

Windows System Disk

Windows system disk
a disk containing all the files necessary to start the PC and load the operating system.

A Windows system disk, also called a boot disk, is easily created from Windows Explorer. The ***Windows system disk*** contains the following files: command.com, io.sys, and msdos.sys. This is very similar to the DOS boot disk. However, a Windows system disk also contains additional files, drivers, and compression utilities that are not associated with the DOS boot disk such as drvspace.bin.

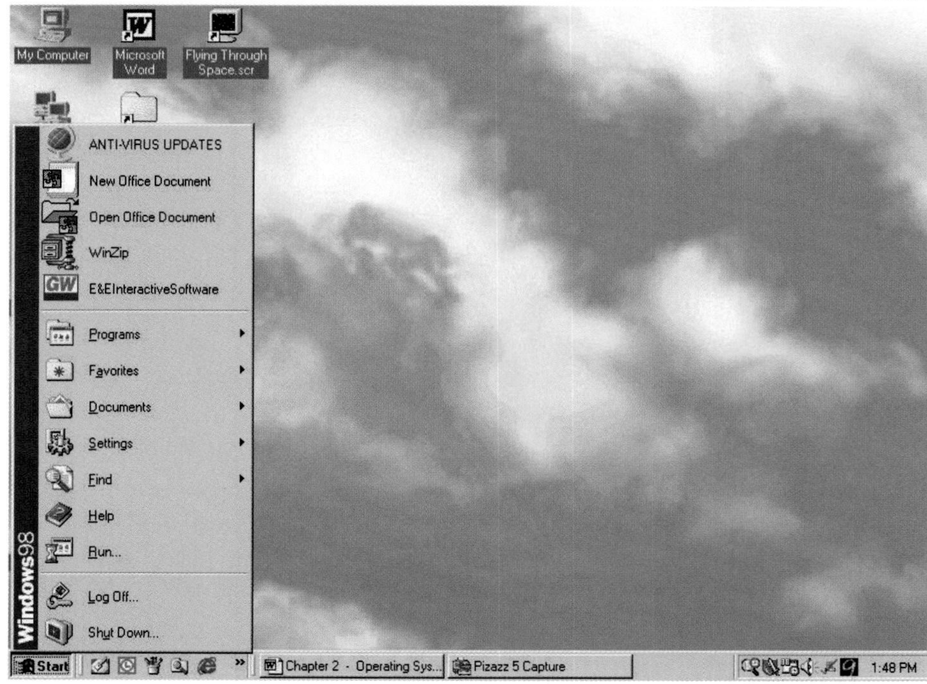

Figure 2-12. Windows desktop showing the **Start** menu.

A+ Note:
The A+ Certification exams generally refer to only command.com, io.sys, and msdos.sys.

Boot Sequence

Following are the major steps for a typical MS-DOS or Windows startup sequence (or ***booting*** process). It is important to remember that config.sys and autoexec.bat are not required by Windows 95 and later. They are included to allow downward compatibility with legacy programs. The term legacy is used often when discussing computer hardware and software. ***Legacy*** refers to older technology kept intact for use by newer technology systems. Today, the config.sys files are mostly located in the io.sys.

booting
the process of starting the computer and loading the operating system.

legacy
older technology kept intact for use by newer technology systems.

POST

The ***POST (power-on self-test)*** is a short routine that is part of the BIOS program. It does a simple check of the major computer components to see if they are installed and working. The POST routine is located on the BIOS chip.

power-on self-test (POST)
a routine check of the computer's hardware that executes every time the computer is turned on.

Bootstrap Program

The bootstrap program is usually located in the BIOS but transferred to the hard drive. The ***bootstrap program*** is a short program that loads into memory some basic files and then turns the startup operation over to the operating system. The name comes from the expression "to pull oneself up by one's bootstraps." For DOS and Windows 95, 98, and Me operating systems, the bootstrap program generally loads in this order:

bootstrap program
a short program that loads some basic files into memory, and then turns the startup operation over to the operating system.

1. io.sys
2. msdos.sys
3. config.sys
4. command.com
5. autoexec.bat

Windows NT, 2000, and XP operating systems require four files to successfully boot. The required files are NTLDR, ntdetect.com, boot.ini, and ntoskrnl.exe. If any of these files are missing, Windows NT-based systems will not complete the boot process.

1. NTLDR loads the operating system and all necessary information after the POST is completed. NTDLR remains resident in memory and frequently regains control after relinquishing control to other programs such as ntdetect.com.
2. Ntdetect.com detects basic hardware and sends the information to the NTLDR.
3. Boot.ini identifies the location of the operating system.

4. The ntoskrnl.exe file loads the operating system kernel. You can think of ntoskrnl.exe as the operating system. Each version of operating system has a unique kernel that cannot be exchanged. For example, Windows 2000, Windows XP, and Windows XP Home Edition use similar but distinctly different kernels.

A+ Note:
The A+ Certification exams usually stress knowledge of the boot sequence. Exercises in the accompanying Laboratory Manual will assist you in better understanding the boot process.

Warm and Cold Booting

cold boot turning on the computer at the power switch.

warm boot using the reset button or key combination to restart a computer that is already running.

There are two styles of booting a computer, a cold (or hard boot) and a warm (or soft boot). A ***cold boot*** means that the electrical power switch is used to turn on the computer. A ***warm boot*** is used to restart a computer that is already running. A warm boot can be initiated by a software program as part of a typical installation such as installing a game. Another common style of initiating a warm boot is by pressing the [Ctrl], [Alt], and [Delete] keys simultaneously.

Config.sys

The config.sys file is activated when the computer is booted. In early versions of Windows, it was used to customize, disable, or enable certain operating system features such as the maximum number of files that can be opened at the same time. The config.sys file also was responsible for loading device drivers that control hardware devices such as advanced video adapter boards. The config.sys file is still found in the boot process of newer operating systems, but it is included only to support legacy software applications. The *registry* now does the tasks formerly performed by config.sys. The registry is discussed later in this chapter.

The config.sys file is a simple ASCII text file that can be easily altered by any text editor such as Notepad. You should *never* attempt to alter or edit the config.sys file with an *advanced* form of text editor. Advanced features such as bold, italics, and special fonts can be saved into the config.sys file. This can cause the computer to crash or produce unpredictable results. Before attempting to make changes to or experimenting with your config.sys file, you should always make a backup copy. Making backup copies of files and using specific commands is covered in the Laboratory Manual for this text.

Figure 2-13 shows some common commands used in a config.sys file. These are only a few of the config.sys commands that can be found in a typical config.sys file.

Autoexec.bat

Autoexec.bat is a file used to load and run programs at startup. The autoexec.bat is an optional file for Windows 95 version OSR2 (Operating System Revision 2) and later. It is not required for modern operating systems. The

Commands	Functions
files	Used to specify how many files can be opened at one time.
devicehigh	Loads a device drive into upper memory.
buffers	Specifies how much memory is allocated for transferring files to and from disks.
lastdrive	Sets the maximum number of available drives that can be set up on a computer.
rem	Used to place text in a file as notes. Anything following the command **rem** will not be executed.
set	Sets the value for the environment such as the DOS prompt appearance.
stacks	Used to specify how much memory is reserved for hardware interrupts.

Figure 2-13. Commands that can be found in a config.sys file.

autoexec.bat is required to run older, legacy programs usually associated with DOS. **Figure 2-14** shows some typical commands used in the autoexec.bat file. **Figure 2-15** shows an example of an autoexec.bat file taken from a Windows 95 system.

The Windows Family

In 1983, Windows was introduced as the first Microsoft graphic user interface for the PC operating system. It was built on top of the DOS system. It was not a new operating system. It simply displayed the file structure on the screen differently than the text-only screen. With the introduction of the Windows 95 came a new operating system that was not completely dependent on DOS. Many other iterations have followed. The current A+ Certification exams no longer cover Windows 3.x or Windows 95 but it is worth taking a quick look at all versions of Windows.

Commands	Functions
echo	Hides or displays messages on the display, using the switches on and off.
path	Sets up a search path to locate executable files.
prompt	Determines the appearance of the DOS prompt.
rem	Used to place remarks in the file that will not be executed.
set	Sets up, displays, or removes DOS variables.
shell	Used to specify the location of the command interpreter to be used.
pause	Suspends the program until any key is pressed.

Figure 2-14. Commands that can be found in an autoexec.bat file.

Figure 2-15. Typical autoexec.bat file.

```
@ECHO OFF
SET BLASTER=A220 I5 D1 H5 P330 T6
SET CTCM=C:\WINDOWS
rem - By Windows Setup - C:\WINDOWS\COMMAND\MSCDEX.EXE
rem - /D:MSCD001
PATH C:\BITWARE\
```

Windows 3.x

The Windows 3.x programs consist of Windows 3.0, 3.1, and 3.11. These programs are known as graphical user interface (GUI) systems. These GUI systems were not truly new operating systems, but rather they were an additional layer placed above MS-DOS. Windows 3.x gave you a graphic display to issue commands as opposed to entering commands from the DOS prompt. However, below the GUI, a Windows 3.x computer is running DOS.

Windows version 3.0 was not well received by all computer users. Because of the additional layer on top of the MS-DOS operating system, the computer ran slower, especially when operating gaming programs. However, the Windows system was well received by new users or people who were not adept in DOS commands and utilities.

A+ Note:
Windows 3.0, 3.1, 3.11, and Windows 95 operating systems are no longer on the A+ Certification exams. You should be familiar with them simply as a reference when compared to current systems.

Windows 95

The release of Windows 95 produced many changes in the Microsoft operating system. Some of the significant changes to Windows 95 consisted of the following:

- Plug and Play (PnP).
- Right mouse click.
- 32-bit operating system.
- Enhanced CD player.

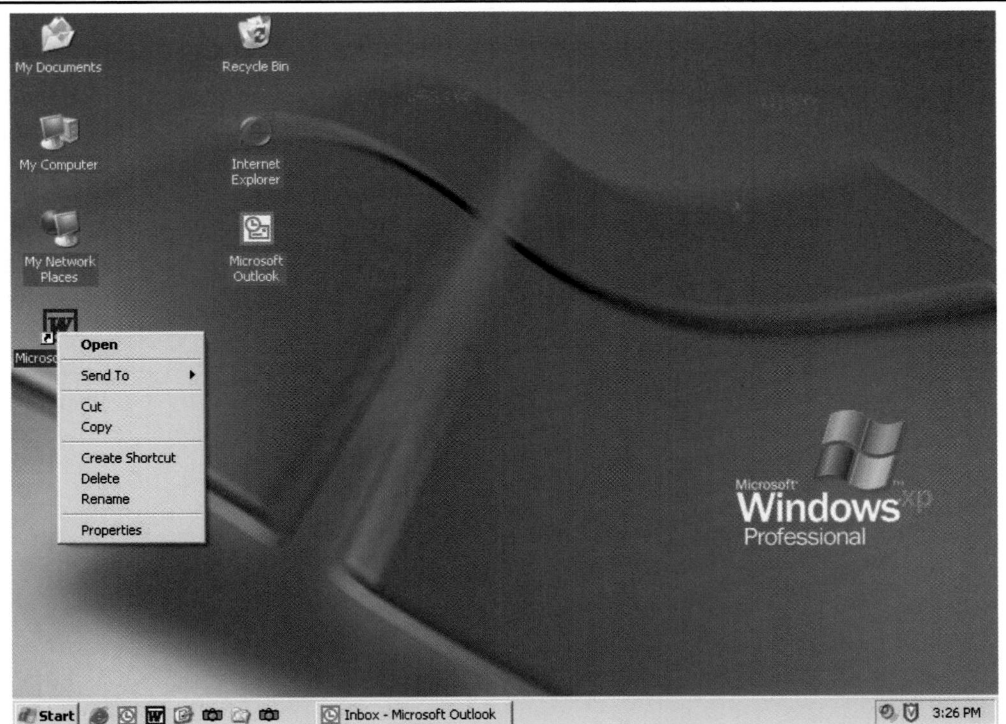

Figure 2-16. Shortcut menu.

Plug and Play (PnP) allows hardware devices to be configured (installed) automatically. For example, when an adapter card is installed into a slot and the computer is turned on, the new card is automatically detected by the computer system as a new piece of hardware. The computer then configures all the resources that previously required manual entry—settings such as the interrupts and memory allocation. To utilize PnP capability, the device to be installed must be a PnP device. Otherwise, the computer cannot set it up automatically.

Plug and Play (PnP) a BIOS function that enables the automatic detection and configuration of new hardware components. Also the automatic assignment of system resources such as DMA channels, interrupts, memory, and port assignments.

The right mouse click was new with Windows 95. The right mouse click displays a shortcut menu with access to features such as **Open**, **Explore**, **Find**, **Create Shortcut**, **Rename**, and **Properties**. See **Figure 2-16.** These features are examined in-depth in your Laboratory Manual.

Windows could now handle 32 bits of data as well as 16 bits. This meant that programs written for 32-bit systems would run much faster than on the Windows 3.x predecessor. Windows 95 maintained its downward compatibility by still including DOS as part of the operating system.

Windows 98

The release of the Windows 98 operating system was delayed several times. It was originally a project code named Memphis and later called Windows 97. It offered support for new technologies such as DVD, MMX, AGP, and FAT32. Windows 98 also introduced integration of a Web browser as part of the operating system. The integration of the Web browser caused a lot of controversy and helped involve Microsoft in an antitrust suit that made its way to the United States Supreme Court. Windows 98 is downward compatible with earlier versions of Windows and DOS.

Windows NT

Windows NT was actually developed by Microsoft to replace the MS-DOS system but became too large and powerful for the typical PC at that time. That is why Windows NT (New Technology) is similar in appearance to any other windows operating system. NT is designed in two versions. One version is to be used as a stand-alone PC platform and the other as a file server operating system.

A file server is a powerful PC connected to many PCs via a network. File servers are covered in more depth in Chapter 16—Introduction to Networking. Windows NT is a 32-bit system. It supports preemptive multitasking.

Security is enhanced in Windows NT. It provides a means of limiting access to users. In fact, even if only one person is using an NT system, that single user must set up their own individual security system in order to be able to access the computer files and operating system.

Windows Me

Windows Me (Millennium Edition) follows the graphical user interface style that is so common with the Windows operating system. Windows Me is more stable than its Windows 98 and 95 predecessors. While the basic operating system remains the same, there are several changes in the Windows Me operating system that were needed because of the evolution of home computing and equipment. The following are some of the changes.

Today it is common to have more than one PC in a household. With more than one PC in the home, there needed to be a means of sharing items such as Internet connections, printers, files, and software. The home user needed to start setting up a small network system. The Windows Me system introduced an advanced network wizard designed especially for the home or small office user. It makes it much easier for a novice to properly set up a network for sharing equipment, software, and Internet connections.

As the digital media world expands and improves, the operating system needs to provide more support and more drivers for digital music and video cameras. Windows Me also included more sophisticated data compression techniques for video files.

A system restore tool was added to the system. The tool is designed to automatically capture changes in the entire PC system every ten hours or once a day. The data is saved and can be used to restore the PC back to the way it was when it last worked correctly. A system file protection tool was also added to the design. It prevents a poorly written program from overwriting or replacing critical system files while installing software.

An important note about Windows Me is its technologies are written over the original Windows 95 kernel. This was the last in the series of operating systems that were written over the Windows 95 kernel. Newer systems have been written over the Windows NT kernel.

Windows 2000

Windows 2000 continues to improve the many features of the Windows operating system. One of the major changes in the operating system is the new hard drive file system known as *dynamic file system* (also called NFTS5.0). In Windows 2000, the standard file allocation table (FAT) file system as well as

NTFS4.0 are referred to as *basic file system.* The dynamic file system is a major improvement to the NTFS file system for storing and retrieving files from the hard drive. File allocation tables are discussed later in this chapter and in detail in Chapter 9—Magnetic Storage Devices. The new system improves security and allows multiple hard drives to be handled as one large volume. To the user, the multiple drives appear as one.

Tech Tip:
Microsoft named the new file system technology "dynamic disk." Technicians and writers immediately began referring to the new file system as NTFS5.0 to differentiate it from the existing NTFS 4.0 file system.

Windows XP

In October of 2001, the first versions of Windows XP (eXPerience) were released. Windows XP was the first major change in the Microsoft operating system for the home user since Windows 95 came on the market. Windows Me is the last operating system technology written on the Windows 95 and Windows 98 kernel.

Windows XP is written using a modified NT kernel. The NT kernel is a much more stable operating system when compared to the typical Windows 95, 98, and Me series.

Two Windows XP operating systems were created: one for home use, called Windows XP Home Edition, and the other for business use, called Windows XP Professional Edition. Windows XP is the dominant replacement for all Windows systems. PC systems running Windows NT, 2000, 98, or Me should easily upgrade to Windows XP. There may be some difficulty with earlier software versions and some older hardware. Check the hardware compatibility listing at the Microsoft Web site to be sure.

Additional Non-Windows Operating Systems

The following operating systems are not covered on the A+ Certification exams. However, it can prove useful to know something of these systems as you may encounter them in the field.

Linux

Linux is a derivative of UNIX. UNIX is a mainframe computer operating system originally developed in the 1970s. Linux can run on Intel as well as Motorola processors. In other words, Linux can be installed on a Macintosh and on IBM-PC clones as well. Since it can be downloaded very inexpensively (or free), it is becoming very popular. There are several common varieties of Linux on the market such as Red Hat, SuSE, Caldera, and Debian.

Linux is a powerful operating system that can be installed on a single PC, or like Windows NT, it can be used as a file server operating system. The source code can be readily downloaded. ***Source code*** is the actual programming code used to make the operating system. No other major operating system does this. Most source codes are closely guarded company secrets. Having the source code for an operating system allows you to modify it for your own needs.

source code
the programming code used to make the operating system.

OS/2

OS/2 was developed by Microsoft for IBM computer systems. It is very similar to the Windows operating systems. At the time it was released, it was very impressive, with features that had only been found in the Macintosh operating system, such as the ability to use long file names. OS/2 is compatible with Windows and DOS as well. However, programs written specifically for OS/2 will not run on Windows or DOS.

OS 9

OS 9 was developed jointly by Microware Systems and Motorola. Motorola manufactures the CPU found in the Macintosh computer system. OS 9 was developed in the early 1980s but is still in use today. It is the operating system behind many industrial technologies as well as WebTV boxes.

Common Operating System Terminology

There are several technical terms that must be introduced early for your studies to be successful. The following terminology is presented at an introductory level. Throughout the following chapters the following concepts will be introduced in more detail.

File Allocation Tables

file allocation table (FAT)
a table used by the operating system to record and recall the locations of files on the disk.

No introduction to operating systems would be complete without mentioning file allocation tables. A ***file allocation table (FAT)*** is used by the operating system to keep track of all files on the disk. It maintains a table of all areas on the disk, and it tracks which areas are used and which are not. File allocation tables are covered in much greater depth in Chapter 9—Magnetic Storage Devices.

There are several different file allocation tables with which you must be familiar. These tables are FAT12, FAT16, FAT32, VFAT, HPFS, and NTFS. In a typical operating system installation, you will be asked to choose between several FAT options. When in doubt, choose FAT16. It is compatible with most operating systems. As you study operating systems more in-depth, you will see the need for other types of file allocation systems.

Configuration

configuration
setup for use with specific hardware and software.

When a computer system is ***configured,*** the type of hardware and software the system planned for use is recorded. Configuration files contain information such as the amount of memory and the type of floppy drive, modem, and video adapter present in the system. Configuration information is stored in the config.sys file of DOS systems. Early Windows systems stored configuration information in the win.ini and system.ini files. Starting with Windows 95, configuration information is stored in the registry. The config.sys file is still found in the boot process of the newer operating systems, but it is included only to support legacy software applications.

Registry

The registry is found in Windows 95, 98, Me, NT, 2000, and XP. The ***registry*** is essentially a database that stores configuration information. The major sections of the registry are listed below.

registry
a database that stores configuration information.

- HKEY_CLASSES_ROOT: Object linking and embedding (OLE) information and how files are associated with each other.
- HKEY_CURRENT_USERS: Information for the current user of this workstation.
- HKEY_LOCAL_MACHINE: Information specific to the local computer.
- HKEY_USERS: Information for each user of this workstation.
- HKEY_CURRENT_CONFIG: Display and printer settings.

The registry is accessed by entering **regedit** in the **Run** window found in the **Start** menu. **Figure 2-17** shows the Windows XP Registry Editor.

Warning:
Changes in the registry can completely disable your computer operating system. Do not experiment with your registry settings unless under supervision of your instructor.

There are two main registry files which you will work with in the future: system.dat and user.dat. The system.dat files contain information about the machine settings. The user.dat file contains information about individuals who use this particular computer station. Registry files can be copied to disk, installed on another machine, backed up, and modified.

Another set of configuration files are files ending with an .ini extension. These configuration files are replaced by the Windows registry settings for the Windows 95 and later operating systems. Many computer systems still contain .ini files to maintain a downward compatibility with some software programs.

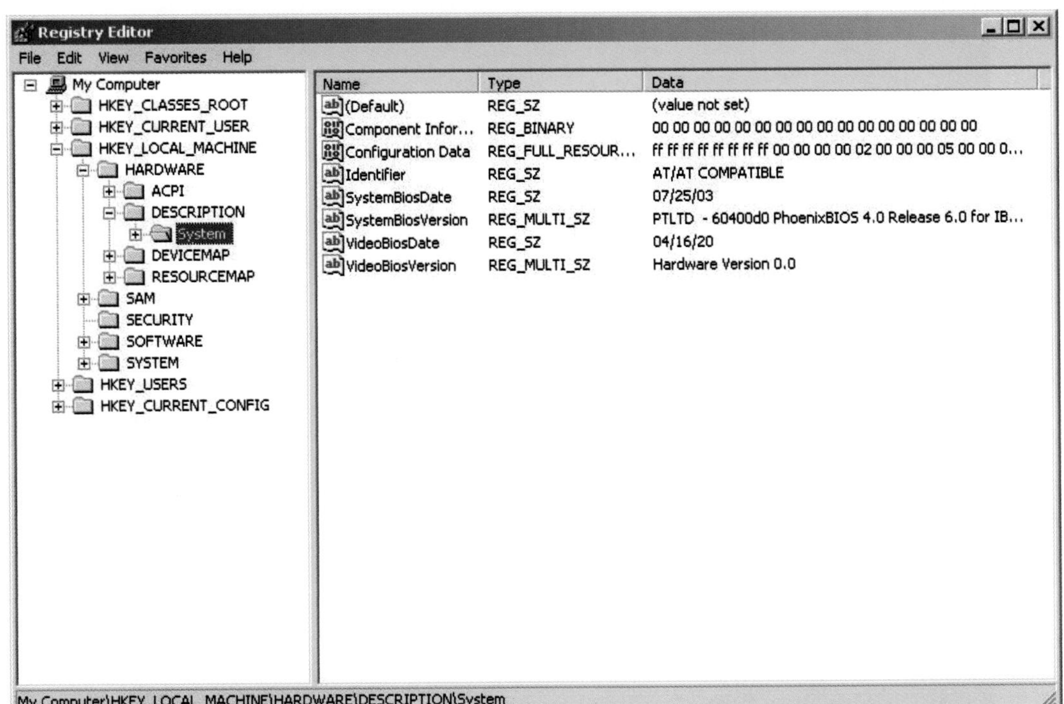

Figure 2-17.
Windows XP Registry Editor.

Application Software

application software software designed for a specific purpose such as creating databases or spreadsheets, word processing, producing graphics, or just for entertainment.

Application software, also referred to as end-user software, is designed for a specific purpose such as creating databases or spreadsheets, word processing, producing graphics, or just for entertainment. It is not an operating system.

The typical application software relies on the operating system to communicate with PC hardware such as the hard drive or CD-ROM drive. When a word-processing program issues a save command, the command is interpreted by the OS, which in turn passes it through the CPU and on to the hardware.

Software Drivers

drivers software that enables proper communication between the PC and peripheral devices.

Software ***drivers*** are small packages of programs that need to be installed on a computer system to allow proper communication between the PC and the peripheral device. Common devices that require drivers are printers, modems, monitors, and storage devices. Drivers act as translators, converting common commands issued from the CPU to the device in use.

PC and software systems are constantly evolving, but not necessarily in the same time frame. For example, you may install a printer that is much newer than the technology of the software installed on a computer. The computer may not have the software programs necessary to communicate correctly with the printer. A typical scenario is when a new printer is installed on a PC and the self-test runs perfectly. However, when a file you have created on the PC is sent to the printer, it prints out a garbled set of meaningless symbols or an endless stream of blank pages. This is a classic case of incorrect driver software.

cabinet (cab) files compressed files that contain the operating system software.

Drivers for an MS-DOS system usually have a .sys file extension, while Windows systems usually use a .drv extension. Many driver files are stored in the Windows directory and are known as ***cabinet*** (or ***cab***) ***files.*** Cab files are compressed files that contain the software necessary to communicate with the operating system. When hardware, such as a printer, is upgraded or changed, the driver file necessary to communicate with the operating system is usually found in the .cab files.

Software Patches

bugs errors in programming.

Software patches are fixes for operating systems and application software that have already been released. They also contain system updates when the system has been compromised. Although software systems go through countless hours of testing, many have errors in programming. These errors are referred to as ***bugs.*** Patches for software programs can assist in correcting bugs and are readily available for download off the Internet.

Summary

- Operating systems provide two main services: file management and user interface with the hardware system.
- The core program of an operating system is referred to as the kernel.
- Multitasking is the appearance to the user that two or more applications are running at the same time.
- Two types of multitasking are cooperative and preemptive. Preemptive multitasking rapidly switches between programs in a continuous cycle. With cooperative multitasking, one program is active while others are paused waiting to be called.

- Computer commands can be issued through a graphical user interface or through text line commands.
- A computer system file structure is a hierarchical organization of directories, subdirectories, and files.
- The three DOS core files are io.sys, msdos.sys, and command.com.
- Command.com is the interpreter for DOS internal commands.
- Msdos.sys is the kernel of the operating system.
- Io.sys contains the generic driver programs that are necessary to communicate with the BIOS and the hardware system.
- DOS uses the 8.3 naming convention.
- Windows 95 and later use long file naming convention allowing up to 255 characters in a file name.
- Files ending in .ini are configuration files.
- The power-on self-test (POST) is a BIOS program that does a simple check of major components when power is applied to the PC.
- The config.sys file is a text file that enables, disables, and customizes system features. It has been replaced by the registry in newer operating systems.
- Plug and Play is a technology that allows many different devices to be installed automatically in a PC with minimal user intervention.
- The file allocation table (FAT) is used to keep track of file locations on storage media such as disks.
- The registry is a database that contains information about the PC hardware and software system.
- The registry can be accessed by the regedit program but should not be altered by inexperienced users.
- Software drivers are programs required to allow the CPU to communicate with hardware devices properly.
- Cabinet files are compressed files containing drivers.
- Software patches are fixes for operating systems after the original release of the program.

Review Questions

Answer the following questions on a separate sheet of paper. Please do not write in this book.

1. What are the two main services provided by an OS?
2. Convert the following acronyms to complete words and capitalize the letter of the word used to construct the acronym. Example: CPU = Central Processing Unit.
    a. OS =
    b. NT =
    c. DOS =
    d. PnP =

3. Why are text-based commands used in Windows XP?
4. List five symbols that are not allowed in DOS naming convention.
5. List five symbols that are *not* allowed in Windows 98 naming convention.
6. List five special symbols that are allowed in Windows 98 naming convention.
7. Check the following file names. List the file names that are not valid using the DOS naming convention and give the character or reason why that name is not valid.

   big/boy

   big*top

   myfile$

   BLUEHOLLIDAY

   jimsfile

   report(feb)

   rep feb

   $CHOOL1

   rep#105
8. Which file names are invalid using Windows 95 long name format? (Indicate why each is not acceptable.)

   myreport

   MYREPORT#12

   mymemo*for*jim

   MYMEMO/TO/JIM

   my+memo+to+jim

   mymemo:jim

   MEMO1999~CA$H

   memo1999?

   MEMOJune2001=
9. What four files are required to boot a Windows NT operating system?
10. What is the name of the Windows XP file that loads the kernel?
    a. ntdetect.com
    b. NTLDR
    c. boot.ini
    d. ntoskrnl.exe
11. What is the name of the Windows XP operating system file that detects system hardware components?
12. The purpose of FAT is to ______.
    a. keep track of the number of times the PC starts
    b. record the amount of memory used
    c. record file locations on disk
    d. supply power to the screen display

13. What is a kernel?
14. What three files are found on a MS-DOS boot disk?
15. Arrange the following components into the correct boot sequence.
    IO.SYS
    COMMAND.COM
    AUTOEXEC.BAT
    POST
    Bootstrap Program
    CONFIG.SYS
    MSDOS.SYS
16. The _____ is the operating system itself.
    a. kernel
    b. io.sys
    c. basic
    d. file allocation table
17. An operating system does what? Select all that apply.
    a. Manages file storage.
    b. Provides communication between the user and the computer system.
    c. Provides software to communicate with the BIOS.
    d. Provides communication between the user and the hard drive.
18. A warm boot may be initiated by pressing which three keys simultaneously?
19. A spreadsheet program is an example of a(n) _____.
    a. patch
    b. operating system
    c. application
    d. driver
20. A software program designed to support communication between a specific printer and a PC is commonly referred to as a(n) _____.
    a. patch
    b. operating system
    c. application
    d. driver
21. Errors in software are commonly referred to as _____ and are corrected by installing a software _____.
22. Which command is used to create a DOS boot disk?
    a. **format**
    b. **format /s**
    c. **format /boot**
    d. **system format**

23. A database that stores system configuration information is called the _____.
    a. autoexec
    b. sysconfig
    c. registry
    d. sysreg

Sample A+ Exam Questions

Answer the following questions on a separate sheet of paper. Please do not write in this book.

1. Which file name is acceptable when using the DOS 8.3 naming convention?
    a. memo\23
    b. memo*23
    c. memo_23
    d. memo>23
2. The operating feature that allows two programs to appear to be running simultaneously is called _____.
    a. multiprocessing
    b. multitasking
    c. program coordination
    d. kernel sharing
3. Which operating system does *not* support multitasking?
    a. DOS
    b. Windows 98
    c. Windows 2000
    d. Windows XP
4. Which file is *not* required to boot a Windows XP operating system?
    a. command.com
    b. NTLDR
    c. Ntdetect.com
    d. boot.ini
5. Which command will create a DOS boot disk?
    a. **boot.dos**
    b. **format /s**
    c. **fdisk**
    d. **makeboot**
6. Which command removes a file called memo.txt from a directory structure?
    a. **remove memo.txt**
    b. **del memo.txt**
    c. **memo.txt del**
    d. **delete memo.txt**

7. DOS commands are carried out by which program below?
   a. io.sys
   b. msdos.sys
   c. command.com
   d. doscom.com
8. Which of the following commands can be used to check the condition of a floppy disk?
   a. **chkdsk**
   b. **checkdisk**
   c. **chkdisk**
   d. **diskchk**
9. In Windows 98, the config.sys file has been replaced by which of the following?
   a. io.sys
   b. sysmon.sys
   c. registry
   d. configsub.com
10. Which is the correct order of the typical boot process in Windows 98?
    a. command.com, autoexec.bat, io.sys, config.sys, msdos.sys
    b. command.com, io.sys, config.sys, autoexec.bat, msdos.sys
    c. io.sys, msdos.sys, config.sys, command.com, autoexec.bat
    d. autoexec.bat, io.sys, command.com, msdos.sys, config.sys

Suggested Laboratory Activities

Do not attempt any suggested lab activities without your instructor's permission. Certain lab activities could render the PC operating system inoperable.

1. Access the DOS prompt from the **Start** menu of the PC desktop. When the DOS prompt appears on the screen, type the various DOS commands followed by a forward slash symbol and question mark. For example, typing **ver/?** reveals information on the screen about the **ver** command. Some operating systems use **/help** in place of the **/?**. Take notes from the screen and then try using the command. Explore the following commands: **ver**, **mem**, **dir**, **cls**, **xcopy**, **copy**, **time**, **prompt**, and **date**. Only explore the function of the DOS commands with your instructor's permission. There are many commands that can cause PC operation problems if used incorrectly.

Warning:
Do not attempt to use the **fdisk** or **format** command until you have been given instruction by your teacher. These commands can permanently erase data and files and leave the PC inoperative.

2. Experiment with the long file naming convention. Try the special symbols and see what effect they have when attempting to save a file.

3. Do an Internet search to find more information about DOS commands.
4. Make a system startup disk and inspect the content of the disk. You can learn how to make a system startup disk by choosing **Help** from the **Start** menu. Use the search words "Startup disk" after accessing help.

Interesting Web Sites for More Information

www.ibm.com
www.global.acer.com
www.dell.com
www.ami.com

Chapter 2
Laboratory Activity
Windows XP Upgrade Installation

After completing this laboratory activity, you will be able to:

- ❑ Upgrade a PC with an existing Windows 98, or later, operating system to a Windows XP operating system.
- ❑ Determine the minimum requirements for a Windows XP installation.
- ❑ Identify information required for a typical installation.
- ❑ Explain the Windows XP installation process in general terms.

Introduction

In this laboratory activity, you will install Windows XP as an upgrade for an existing Windows operating system previously installed on a computer system. Windows XP (eXPerience) operating system was released in October of 2001. Windows XP comes in two flavors: Windows XP Professional and Windows XP Home Edition. The Windows XP professional is designed to replace the Windows NT and Windows 2000 family of network operating systems, while the Windows Home Edition is designed to replace the Windows 9x and Windows Me editions. The Windows XP operating system is built on the Windows NT technology, which is more stable than the Windows 9x series.

The minimum requirements for installing the Windows XP operating system are as follows:

233 MHz Pentium or higher microprocessor
128MB of RAM recommended (64MB minimum)
4GB of RAM Maximum
1.5GB of unused hard drive space
VGA monitor
Keyboard and mouse
CD-ROM or DVD drive

Note:
When networking the PC, a network adapter card is required.

Before you begin upgrading to Windows XP, you should check the hardware compatibility list located at Microsoft Tech support (www.microsoft.com/hcl/). Don't assume that because a previous version of Windows is already installed on the PC that the hardware used in the PC is compatible with the Windows XP operating system. Check the listing of hardware for potential problems. Note that Windows XP does perform a hardware check as part of the upgrade procedure. However, the automatic hardware detection program is not completely reliable. Always check the Microsoft Web site for the very latest information.

Near the beginning of the installation process, the Windows XP installation wizard will present a screen giving you an option to connect to the Microsoft Web site to check the hardware compatibility list and to look for updates to the operating system.

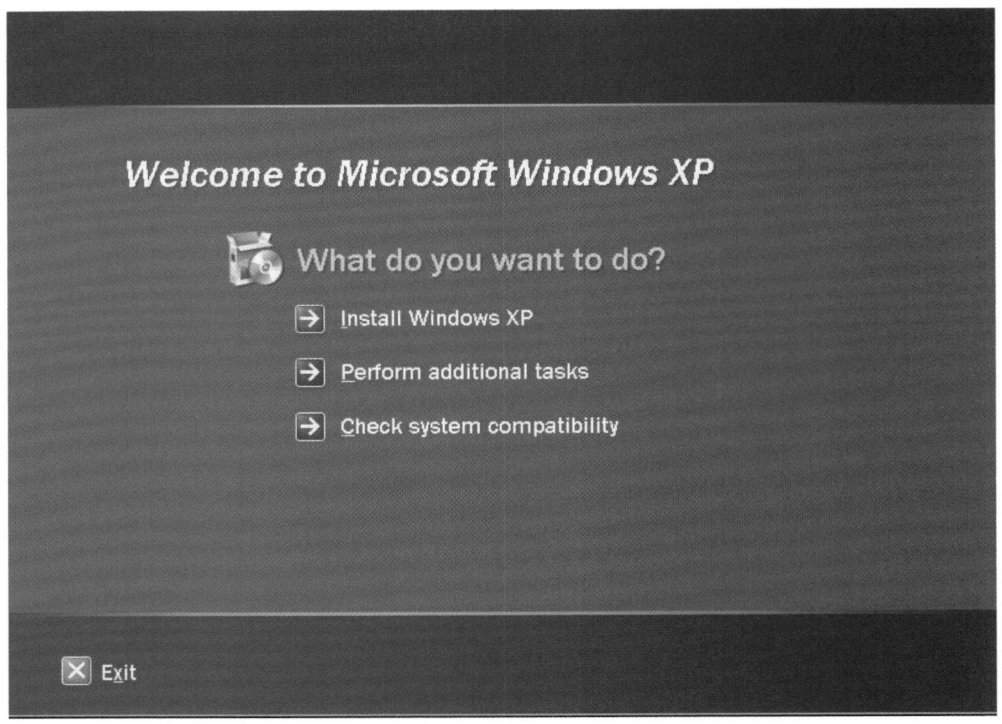
Welcome to Microsoft Windows XP
What do you want to do?
Install Windows XP
Perform additional tasks
Check system compatibility
Exit

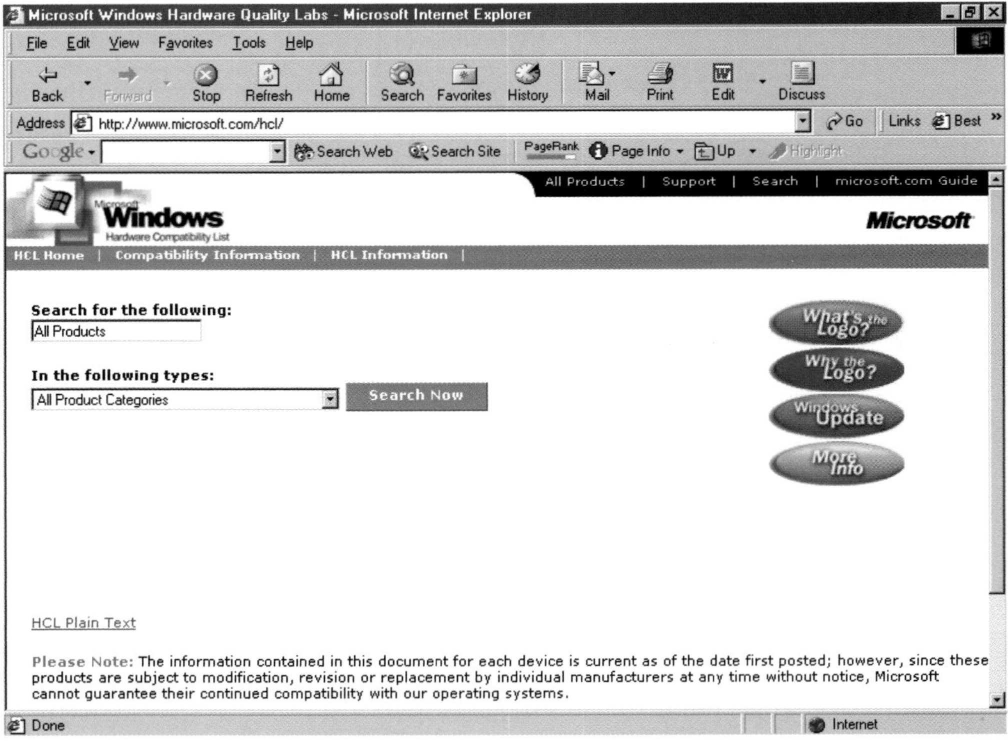
Microsoft Windows Hardware Quality Labs - Microsoft Internet Explorer
File Edit View Favorites Tools Help
Back Forward Stop Refresh Home Search Favorites History Mail Print Edit Discuss
Address http://www.microsoft.com/hcl/
Go Links Best
Search Web Search Site PageRank Page Info Up Highlight
All Products | Support | Search | microsoft.com Guide
Windows
Hardware Compatibility List
Microsoft
HCL Home | Compatibility Information | HCL Information |
Search for the following:
All Products
In the following types:
All Product Categories
Search Now
What's the Logo?
Why the Logo?
Windows Update
More Info
HCL Plain Text
Please Note: The information contained in this document for each device is current as of the date first posted; however, since these products are subject to modification, revision or replacement by individual manufacturers at any time without notice, Microsoft cannot guarantee their continued compatibility with our operating systems.
Done
Internet

If you select the option to **Visit the compatibility Web site**, a screen image similar to the one that follows will appear.

The hardware compatibility Web site allows you to search for compatible equipment by operating system and by type of product such as chipset, RAM, displays, and more. The following image is a screen capture of the hardware compatibility list taken from the Microsoft Web site. This is a partial list of displays that are compatible with various Windows operating systems. The circle with "Compatible" inside is used to identify the compatible displays by operating system.

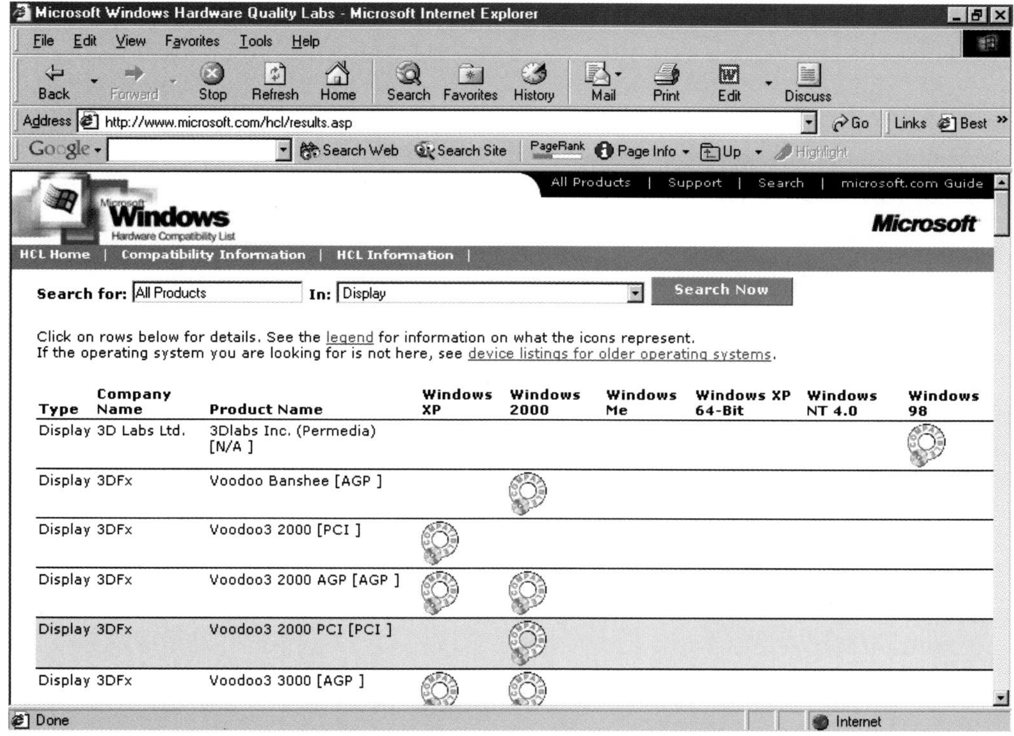

If your specific equipment is not on the compatibility list, you will need to go to the manufacture's Web site and download an updated version of the hardware driver that is compatible with Windows XP.

Certain information may be required for your upgrade to Windows XP. The exact order and specific information can vary depending if the PC is part of a network and on what type of network system it is a part of. Below is a list of typical information you will need before you begin the installation wizard. The following information will be supplied by your instructor:

Computer name
Domain name
Workgroup
Organization
User name
Password
IP address
Name of DHCP server

Write the information down on a separate sheet of paper so you can refer to it during the upgrade process. During a typical system upgrade, much of the information will be transferred to the new operating system from the old, but not necessarily all of the information listed.

When you start the actual system upgrade process, you will insert the CD into the CD-ROM or DVD drive after the PC has been booted. The installation wizard will direct you through the entire upgrade process. When in doubt about a screen prompt, check with your instructor. Usually choosing the default option will be fine. Because you may be installing the new operating system on a computer in a network arrangement, your instructor will brief you on any particular changes that may be required for the installation.

When the upgrade is complete, you will be prompted to create a user account. The user account uniquely identifies each user of the PC and allows each user to load their specific settings and files when they log on to the PC.

When performing a Windows XP operating system upgrade, you must perform the upgrade over an existing compatible operating system. The only compatible operating systems for upgrades are Windows 98 (any edition), Windows Me, Windows NT 4.0 (with service pack 6 installed), or Windows 2000. Other operating systems are not compatible for a successful upgrade. Some systems that are not compatible are Windows 95, DOS, and various Linux versions.

Equipment and Materials

- A typical PC containing a processor that operates at 233 MHz or better, contains 128MB RAM (preferred, 64MB minimum), has a hard disk drive with at least 1.5GB of unused disk space, and is loaded with one of the following operating systems: Windows 98, Windows 2000, Windows Me, Windows NT 4.0 Service pack 6, Windows XP (either Home Edition or Professional).

Procedure

1. ______ Before you begin the installation process, gather all required materials, and then report to your assigned PC station.
2. ______ Boot the PC and check that the machine has the minimum installation requirements. If the PC has the minimum requirements, you may proceed to step 3. If it does not have the minimum hardware requirements, notify your instructor.
3. ______ Access the Readlst.txt file on the installation CD-ROM. Read the information carefully.
4. ______ With the PC booted to its operating system, insert the installation CD-ROM containing the Windows XP operating system. The CD-ROM may automatically start the installation process. The automatic startup of the installation depends on the PC system equipment and BIOS. Wait approximately 2 minutes. If the installation has not automatically begun, start the installation process

manually. You can manually start the program by typing and running **D:setup.exe** from the **Run** option in the **Start** menu. See the figures that follow. *(Note: It is assumed D: is the CD-ROM or DVD device. If this is not the case, substitute the correct drive letter in the command. If you are having difficulty, you can also Browse… until you locate the program.)*

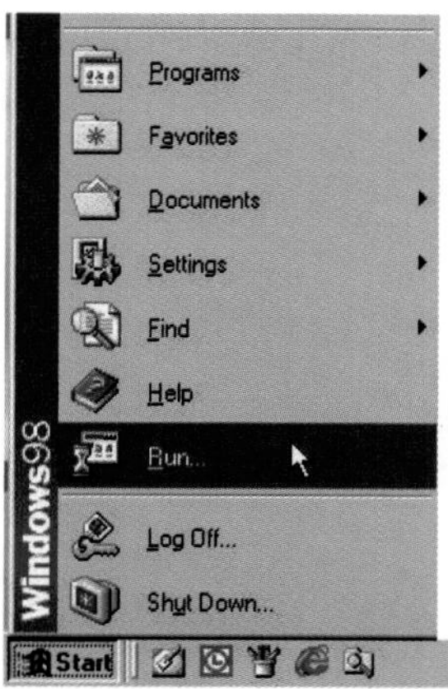

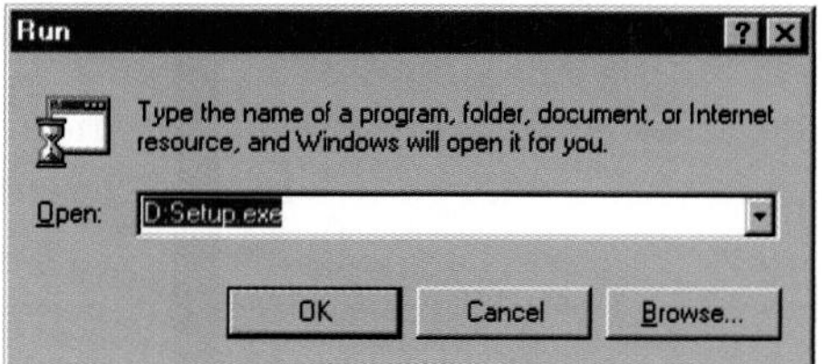

5. ______ Select the **Install Windows XP** from the menu selections by clicking the item.

6. ______ Select the default **Upgrade (Recommended)** from the dialog screen.

7. ______ Take note of the list on the left side of the screen display. This is a list of the installation activities as they occur during the system upgrade process. The amount of time for the total installation process is also listed. Observe the listing on the left as the installation wizard takes you through the installation upgrade process. You will be prompted for information throughout the installation process. This information includes asking you to accept the licensing agreement and to choose a file system, as well as inquiring about other details such as your regional settings, location, choice of language, name, organization, computer name, and administrator password.

8. ______ After the Windows XP operating system is installed, the computer should reboot and you will be prompted to log on for the first time. It is during this time you will have the option to activate your installed copy of Windows XP. You will also be prompted to set up user accounts for the PC. Check with your instructor about the specific requirements of these two prompts. The instructor may not want you to activate the Windows XP operating system. Activation requires using a modem to contact the Microsoft Web site and activate the software operating system. This is Microsoft's solution to prevent the pirating of their operating systems. When the system is activated, Microsoft creates a database describing the hardware of the PC system on which the original copy of the Windows XP operating system has been installed. If the specific hardware does not match when activating a second installation on another PC, the installation is disabled.

9. ______ Before ending this lab activity, check with the instructor to see if you will be leaving the upgraded operating system on the PC or uninstalling it.

10. ______ Complete the review questions at the end of this laboratory activity.

Review Questions

Answer the following questions on a separate sheet of paper. Please do not write in this book.

You may need to use the Read1st.txt file located on the Windows XP installation CD-ROM to answer some of the following questions.

1. What is the minimum CPU speed for Windows XP?
2. What is the recommended amount of RAM and the minimum amount of RAM required for a typical Windows XP installation?
3. What is the maximum amount of RAM that Windows XP can support?
4. What is the recommended amount of free hard drive space required for a Windows XP installation?
5. What is the minimum monitor resolution required for Windows XP?
6. What does the acronym HCL represent?
7. From the list that follows, select the items that are recommended for completion before performing a Windows XP upgrade.
   a. Be sure that an anti-virus program is installed and running during the installation process.
   b. Perform a virus scan.
   c. Back up important files.
   d. Contact your ISP and notify them that you are installing a new operating system.
   e. Format the hard drive.
   f. Access and read the Read1st.txt file located on the CD-ROM.
8. Which of the following operating systems can Windows XP satisfactorily upgrade? Choose all that apply.
   a. Windows 95
   b. Windows 98
   c. Windows 2000
   d. Windows NT 4.0 with Service pack 6
   e. DOS 6.0
   f. Linux

There are many unique and proprietary designs for motherboards. The motherboard shown here was cleverly engineered so that all the PC's components could be packaged into a case that fits into the PC keyboard. (Cybernet Manufacturing, Inc.)

3 Motherboards

After studying this chapter, you will be able to:

- Identify major parts of a motherboard.
- Identify common motherboard form factors.
- Explain motherboard bus architecture.
- Identify expansion slot architectures.
- Identify the important system resources and explain what they are used for.
- Identify and explain IRQs.
- Explain the role of a chipset.
- Explain the purpose of the CMOS Setup program.
- Explain the procedure for upgrading a flash BIOS.

A+ Exam—Key Points

The test will ask many questions about system resources, especially IRQ settings. Memorize IRQ and I/O settings for COM1, COM2, COM3, COM4, LPT1, and LPT2.

There will be several questions concerning CMOS and BIOS. Typical questions will address the process of upgrading BIOS, changing CMOS settings, and changing and setting the CMOS Setup password.

Knowledge of expansion slot architecture will be required. There may also be a question to test basic knowledge of form factors.

Key Words and Terms

The following words and terms will become important pieces of your computer vocabulary. Be sure you can define them.

- Accelerated Graphics Port (AGP)
- address bus
- backplane
- BIOS
- bus
- bus mastering
- chipset
- CMOS setup
- control bus
- data bus
- direct memory access (DMA)
- Enhanced Parallel Port (EPP)
- I/O bus
- expansion card slot
- Extended Capabilities Port (ECP)
- Extended Industry Standard Architecture (EISA)
- field replacement unit (FRU)
- flash BIOS
- form factor
- I/O port address
- IEEE 1394 (FireWire)
- Industry Standard Architecture (ISA)
- internal bus
- IRQ
- local bus
- memory address range
- memory bus
- Micro Channel Architecture (MCA)
- north bridge
- Peripheral Component Interconnect (PCI)
- Plug and Play (PNP)
- POST (power-on self-test)
- power bus
- south bridge
- Universal Serial Bus (USB)
- Video Electronics Standards Association (VESA) local bus

The *motherboard* is considered the most important element of a computer's design. All major components connect to and transmit data across the motherboard. The motherboard is the communications center for input and output devices such as the memory, CPU, keyboard, mouse, parallel port, serial port, monitor, and network connection. The motherboard also provides the connection points required by the fans, speakers, on/off switches, LED indicator lights, and CMOS battery.

The motherboard provides a means for expanding and customizing the system by inserting expansion boards into slots provided as direct connections to the bus architecture. There are various special purpose chips that control communications between the different buses and devices mounted on the motherboard. The motherboard is also referred to as the *system board, main board,* and *planar board.*

Motherboard Construction

The motherboard provides a physical surface on which to mount electronic components such as resistors, capacitors, chips, slots, and sockets. The motherboard is a combination of insulating material and electronic circuit paths constructed of small thin conductors. See **Figure 3-1.** The motherboard is constructed mainly from electrical insulation material. Insulation material does not conduct electrical energy. The small electrical circuits that run across the surface of the motherboard are called *traces*. Traces provide the paths between all the different components mounted on the motherboard. This confines the flow of electrical energy to the path created by the traces. The electrical circuit paths provide a means of sending and receiving data between the components mounted on and connected to the motherboard.

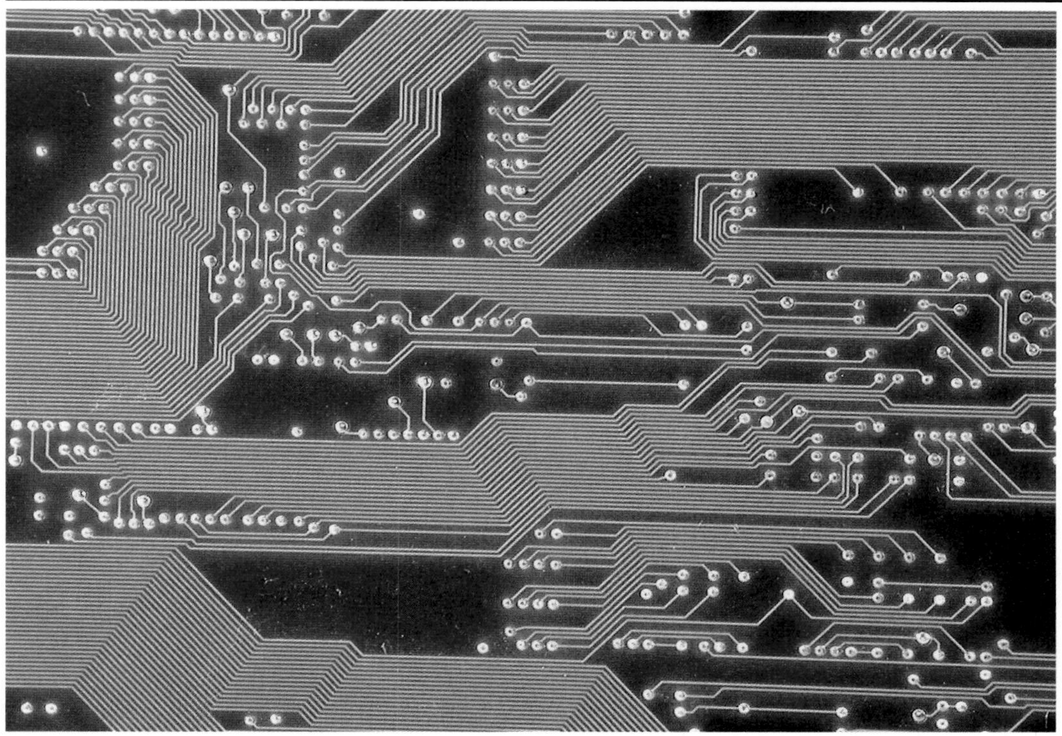

Figure 3-1. Close-up view of motherboard circuit paths.

The insulated motherboard does not allow the electrical energy to come in contact with the case. An electrical short circuit would be created if electrical energy were allowed to flow to the metal PC case. A short circuit would also be created if electrical energy could flow directly between the traces on the motherboard.

The thin conductors also provide power to low-power devices. Large-power consumption devices, such as the disk drives, are provided power directly from the power supply through much larger conductors. Many of the thin conductors on the motherboard are grouped together to make up what is referred to as a bus. A ***bus*** is a collection of conductors that works together for a specific purpose.

There are many bus type classifications such as data bus, control bus, memory bus, internal bus, I/O bus, address bus, and power bus. The ***data bus*** is used to move data between components. The data is moved between components grouped as 8, 16, 32, or 64 bits. The amount of data that can be moved at one time is referred to as the bus width.

Signals are transmitted across the ***control bus*** to activate devices such as disk drives and modems. The ***memory bus*** connects directly to the memory, and the ***I/O bus*** (or ***expansion bus***) runs along the expansion slots. The ***internal bus*** is part of the integrated circuit inside the CPU unit. The ***local bus*** (or ***system bus***) connects directly to the CPU and provides communications to high-speed devices mounted closely to the CPU. The ***address bus*** connects the CPU with the main memory module. It identifies memory locations where data is to be stored or retrieved. Lastly, the ***power bus*** is used to send electrical power to small consumption devices such as speakers, lights, and switches. Larger consumption devices such as disk drives connect directly to the power supply using larger conductors. As you can see, there are many different bus types and classifications. The name usually implies the purpose of the bus.

bus
a collection of conductors that connect multiple components, allowing them to work together for a specific purpose.

data bus
a bus used to move data between components.

control bus
a bus which delivers command signals from the processor to devices.

memory bus
a bus that connects the processor to the memory.

I/O bus
a bus that connects the processor to the expansion slots.

internal bus
part of the integrated circuit inside the CPU.

local bus
a bus system that connects directly to the CPU and provides communications to high-speed devices mounted closely to the CPU.

A bus may also be a collection of bus types. For example, the local bus consists of power, data, control, and memory bus lines. It therefore consists of the power bus, data bus, control bus, and memory bus. For this reason, the local bus may be referred to by other names such as the system bus or memory bus. Intel has coined the local bus as the *front side bus (FSB)*. This term is used quite often when specifying motherboard bus speeds.

Tech Tip:
The motherboard is considered a field replacement unit. A *field replacement unit (FRU)* is any major part of a computer system that could be completely replaced on site rather than attempting a repair in the field. Most of the components mounted on a motherboard are chips soldered into place. Only a highly skilled electronics technician should attempt repair and replacement of motherboard chips.

address bus
a bus system that connects the CPU with the main memory module. It identifies memory locations where data is to be stored or retrieved.

power bus
a bus system that sends electrical power for small consumption devices such as speakers, lights, and switches.

field replacement unit (FRU)
any major part of a computer system that could be completely replaced on site rather than repaired.

form factor
the physical shape or outline of a motherboard and the location of the mounting holes. Also called a footprint.

Form Factors

The ***form factor*** describes the physical shape or outline of a motherboard and the location of the mounting holes. Sometimes the form factor is called the *footprint*. A motherboard form factor must be considered when upgrading a PC system. The form factor determines if the motherboard will fit the PC case style you intend to use. Another device that conforms to a form factor is the power supply. The power supply must match the form factor of the case and motherboard. The most common form factors are the XT, AT, Baby AT, LPX, ATX, NLX, and backplane.

XT, AT, and Baby AT Form Factors

The original PC by IBM used an XT form factor for its motherboard. This was in 1983 and was the truly first standardized form factor for motherboards. The XT used an 8-bit data bus system. The next standard size was the AT (Advanced Technology) form factor. It was slightly larger than the XT and provided a 16-bit data bus.

As chip technology advanced, it became possible to reduce the size of the motherboard back to the original size and shape of the XT. This next board was called the Baby AT. Even though it was the same size as the XT board, there would have been a lot of confusion caused by naming it an XT. Then there would have been two different boards, one 8 bit and the other 16 bit, that were the same size. This is the reason for calling the 16-bit board the Baby AT. See **Figure 3-2.**

ATX Form Factor

The Baby AT remained popular until 1996 when the ATX, a new style of motherboard, gained popularity. The ATX is incompatible with most other motherboard form factors. See **Figure 3-3.**

The ATX looks similar to a Baby AT board that has been turned 90° inside the computer case. The ATX requires a new shape of power supply so that both the motherboard and power supply will fit inside the same case. The most welcomed feature of the ATX motherboard is the new style of power supply connector mounted on the motherboard. The new power supply connector is

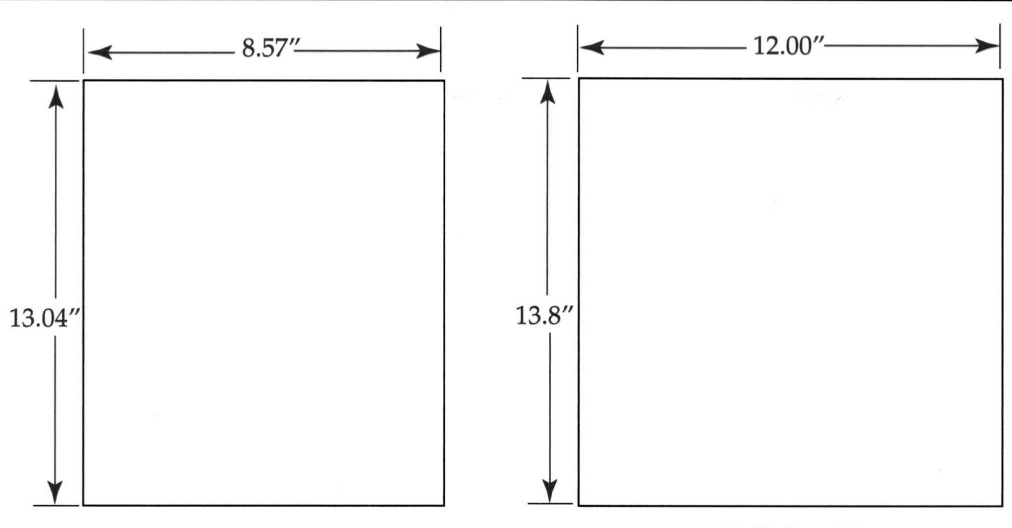

Figure 3-2.
Comparison of the Baby AT and the full-size AT form factor.

designed to prevent the power supply from being plugged into the motherboard with the polarity reversed. This would result in a blown motherboard.

We will take a closer look at power supply connectors in Chapter 5—Power Supplies. For quick identification, an ATX form factor motherboard uses a 20-pin power supply connector, and an AT form factor motherboard uses a 12-pin connector.

LPX Form Factor

The LPX was designed to allow for a low profile desktop computer or slim tower. The motherboard has no expansion slots as the typical motherboard does. It has a slot usually mounted in the middle of the motherboard used to host a *bus riser card.* See **Figure 3-4.**

The adapter cards are plugged into the bus riser card at right angles. This style of installing expansion cards allows the cards to be inserted in parallel

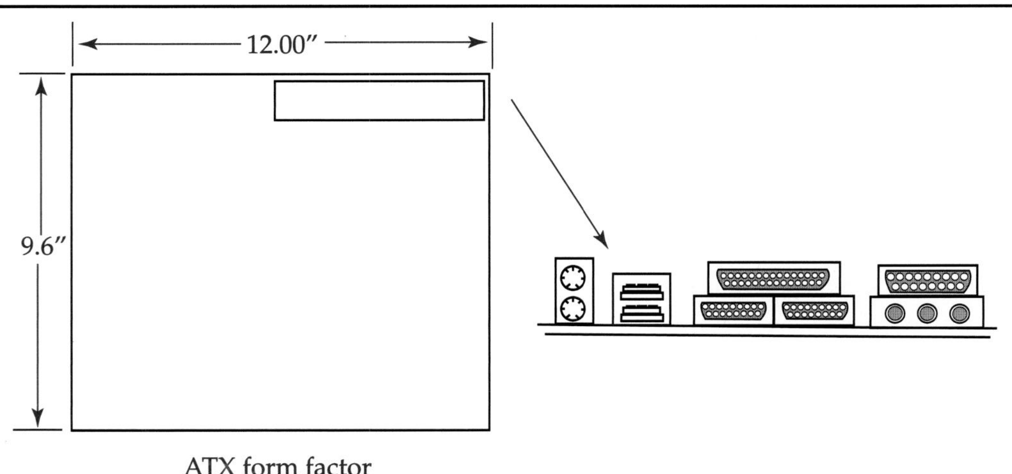

Figure 3-3.
ATX form factor and back view.

Figure 3-4.
LPX form factor and back view.

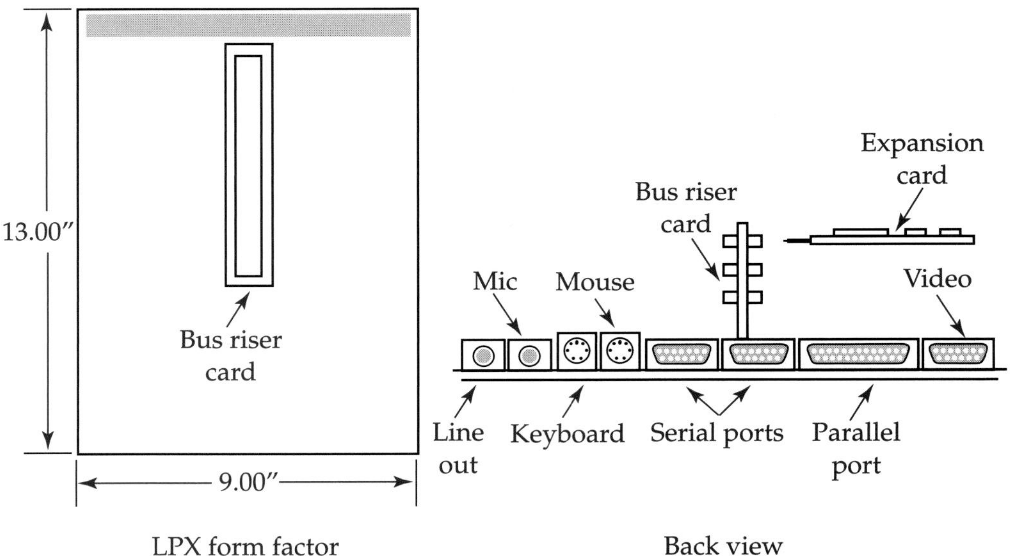

with the surface of the motherboard. The expansion boards installed parallel with the motherboard is what allows for the low profiles of the computer case.

The LPX is not considered a true standard that allows for upgrading but rather a proprietary style. The bus riser card is not always located in the same spot. This variation can cause a problem when changing or upgrading the motherboard. Obtaining a motherboard from the same manufacturer is usually required to get the correct layout. This style of motherboard is popular in lower priced computer systems.

NLX Form Factor

Another motherboard style, the NLX, uses the same principle as the bus riser card design. However, rather than placing the bus riser card in the middle of the motherboard, it is located at the end of the board. In fact, the edge of the motherboard actually plugs into the riser card.

The major advantage of the NLX board over the LPX is that the NLX is standardized in the industry. This means you can replace or upgrade any NLX board with any other NLX board in the industry. The NLX is very popular among the leading PC manufacturers such as Gateway, Hewlett-Packard, IBM, NEC, and Micron. The board width is a standard 9.00″ while the length can vary from 10.00″ to 13.6″. Even though the length may vary, it is still considered a standard. See **Figure 3-5** and **Figure 3-6.**

The ATX and NLX continue to be the most popular design used by computer manufacturers and should stay standard for some time.

backplane
a circuit board with an abundance of slots along the length of the board.

Backplane

A backplane system is not a true motherboard design, but it must be considered with motherboards. A ***backplane*** is a circuit board with an abundance of slots along the length of the board, **Figure 3-7.** Expansion cards slide into the

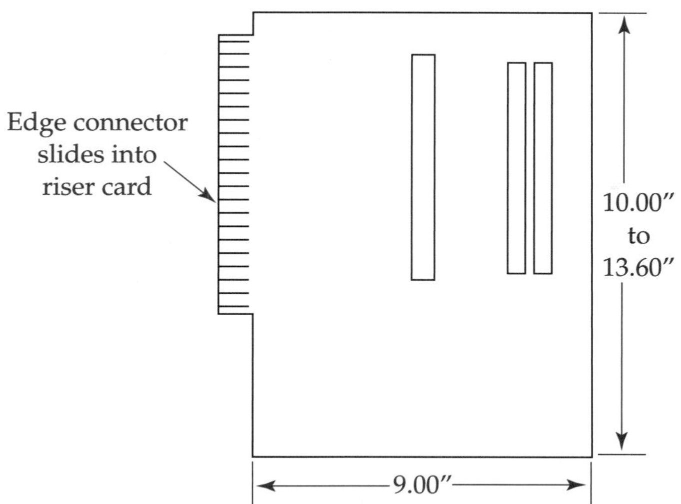

Figure 3-5.
NLX form factor. Take special note of the edge connector on the left side of the motherboard. The motherboard fits into the riser expansion card.

Figure 3-6.
NLX motherboard. (Intel Corp.)

expansion slots. Even the CPU can insert into an expansion slot on the backplane. The main idea of the design is to ensure easy upgrades of any and all components. This style is very popular in heavy industry. The backplane is considered proprietary.

There are two main classifications of backplane boards, active and passive. In a *passive* design, all the typical circuits and chips found on the motherboard are found on the adapter cards and not on the backplane. An *active* backplane design contains the usual circuitry found on any typical motherboard with the exception of the main processor itself. The processor is usually installed into an expansion slot to allow for an easy upgrade as more advanced processors come on the market.

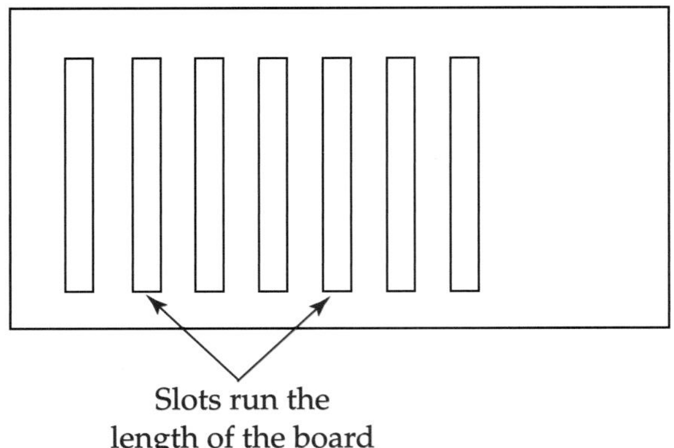

Figure 3-7. Typical backplane design is simply a series of slots spanning across the motherboard.

Motherboard Bus System Architecture

The original PC had a simple bus architecture. There was one bus that connected all major components to the RAM and CPU. The CPU transmitted data to and from components on the motherboard at the same speed. See **Figure 3-8.** The original bus architecture consisted of one bus. The speed of the bus matched the processor speed.

As the PC evolved, the CPU processing speed increased and soon surpassed the speed capabilities of the bus structure. At high frequencies, a bus system can transmit electromagnetic energy just like a radio transmitter. The bus inside the CPU is very short. In fact, it is microscopic. This allows data to move at high speeds without generating electromagnetic interference. The bus outside the CPU is a great deal longer, and interference is a significant problem. This is the main reason for limited speed of data transmission on a bus system.

The electrical occurrence of *inductive reactance* limits the speed of electrical energy flow through a conductor. Inductive reactance has a choking effect on the flow of electrical energy. The amount of choking effect is directly related to the speed of data transmission (frequency) and the length of the conductor (bus wire

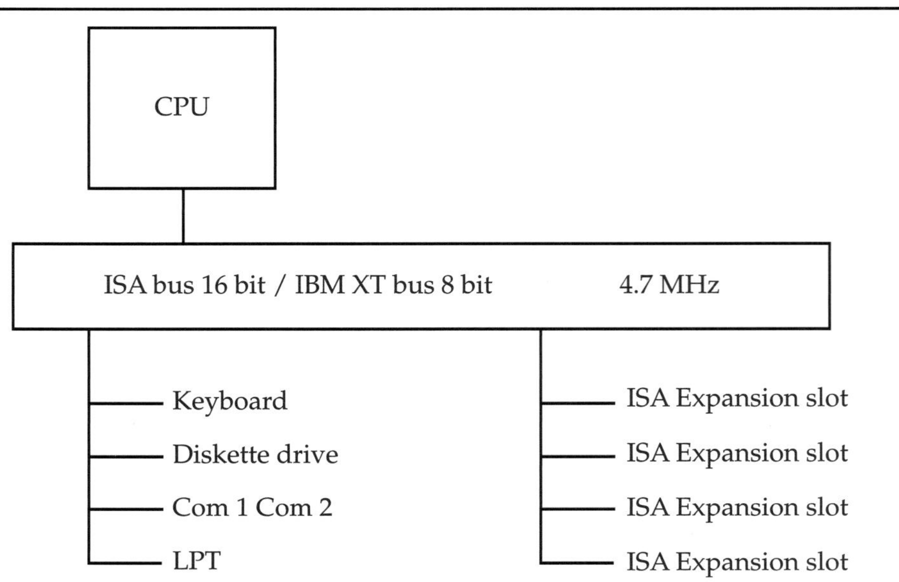

Figure 3-8. PC using a single bus to communicate and transfer data to all components inside and outside the computer. All components run at the same speed as the CPU.

length). The choking effect increases in direct proportion with the speed of data transmission and the length of the data path. Consequently, CPU transfer speeds in excess of 600 MHz are too fast for any expansion card currently on the market.

A PC is designed with several different bus speeds and chipsets that control data flow through the bus system. A current local bus is designed as a 64-bit bus. Common speeds for the local bus are 100, 133, 200, 400, 533, and 800 MHz. These speeds are too high to communicate to input/output (I/O) devices through the expansion card slots. Thus, the I/O bus, or expansion bus, became the second type of bus designed as part of the motherboard. The two bus systems, local and I/O, are separated by computer chips that act as buffers for passing data at two or more different speeds. The chips allow the bus from the CPU and RAM to communicate with the slower I/O bus. Also, the data transmitted across the 64-bit width of the local bus is converted to the 16-bit width of a much smaller I/O bus used for an ISA adapter card. See **Figure 3-9** and **Figure 3-10** for two views of the bus system in a PC.

In Figure 3-9, note the relationship of the CPU, RAM, chip bridges, typical ports and/or external devices, and the ISA, PCI, and USB bus architecture. Also, note that the CPU does not communicate directly with I/O devices. The CPU communicates with RAM, which in turn transmits the communication through the bridge chip(s) to the I/O devices. Because of the speed differences between the CPU and the devices such as COM1, the CPU must go into a state of rest called the wait state. The CPU must wait while the data is converted from 16 bit to 64 bit and vice versa.

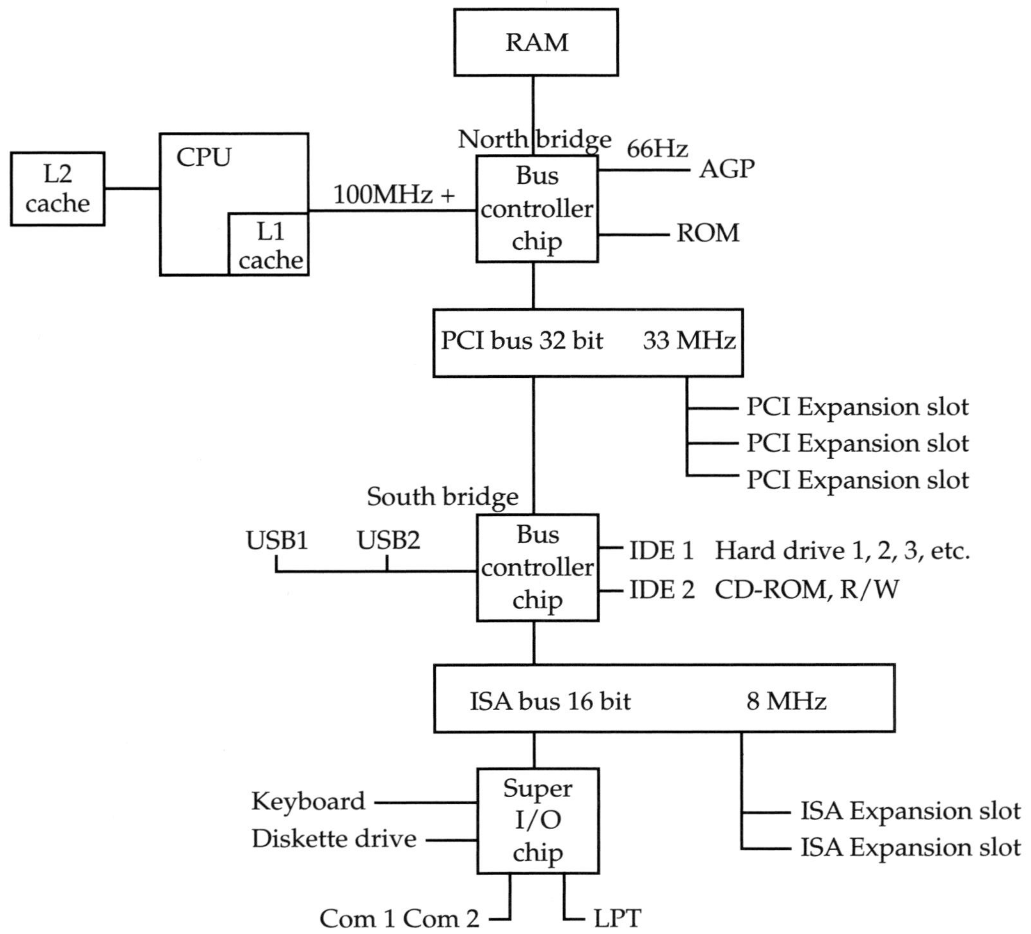

Figure 3-9. Modern bus architecture with incorporation of chipsets to provide communication between buses of different speeds.

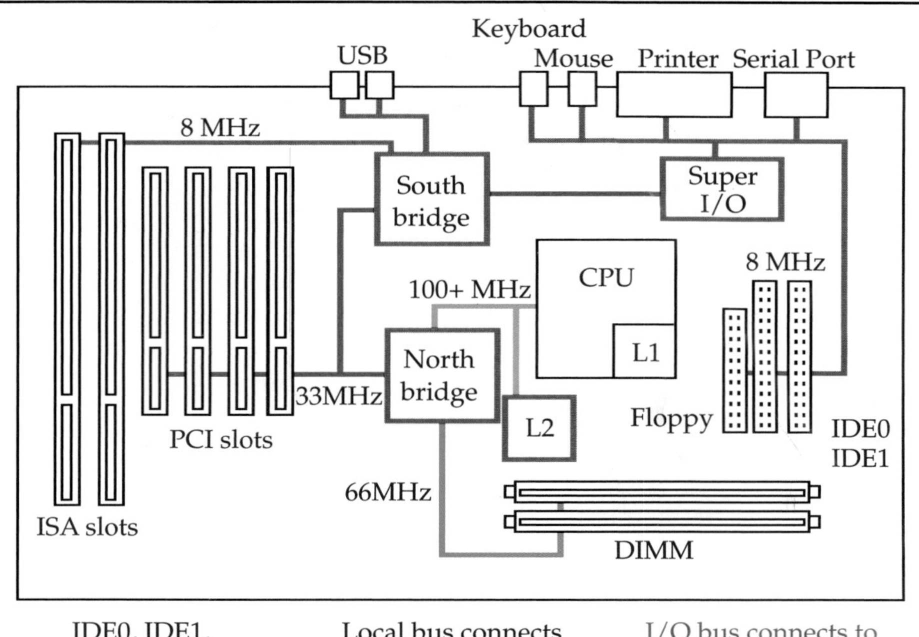

Figure 3-10. The motherboard bus structure can be classified into two general types: local bus and I/O bus. The local bus is also referred to as the system bus or the front side bus and is the fastest bus on the motherboard. The I/O bus is slower than the local bus and is used to serve the ports and slots located on the motherboard. Notice how the chipset controls the speed of data from the CPU.

expansion card slots connectors that allow devices to be quickly and easily plugged into the bus system.

Expansion Card Slots

Expansion card slots provide a quick and easy method of connecting devices directly into the motherboard bus system. This allows you to modify or customize the computer system. There are several styles of expansion slots that have evolved with the computer motherboards. These slots include ISA, EISA, MCA, VESA, PCI, AGP, AMR, CNR, USB, and IEEE 1394. *(USB and IEEE 1394 are not physically designed as a traditional slot. However, they are a type of hardware expansion architecture.)*

Expansion slots are designed to hold inserted cards called adapters, expansion cards, interface cards, and daughter boards. This allows the technician to modify the existing computer system for such features as network cards, which allow communications with a network. Television and radio adapter cards are available to allow tuning a favorite radio station or watching television programs on the PC.

Industry Standard Architecture (ISA) an I/O (expansion) bus system featuring a 16-bit data bus.

ISA

The ***Industry Standard Architecture (ISA)*** is the oldest bus system found on PC motherboards, **Figure 3-11**. Some new motherboards still come with ISA slots to allow the interfacing of legacy hardware components. The ISA data bus is 16 bits wide, which means it communicates 16 bits of data simultaneously at a bus speed of 8.33 MHz. The original ISA bus structure of the IBM in 1981 was only 8 bits with a bus speed of 4.77 MHz.

In addition to the 16 data lines, there are address lines on the bus that designate the location for sending the data. There are clock lines, which control the timing on the bus and voltage lines, which distribute positive, negative, and ground level voltages for cards on the bus.

Figure 3-11.
Illustrations of typical 8-bit and 16-bit ISA adapter card edge.

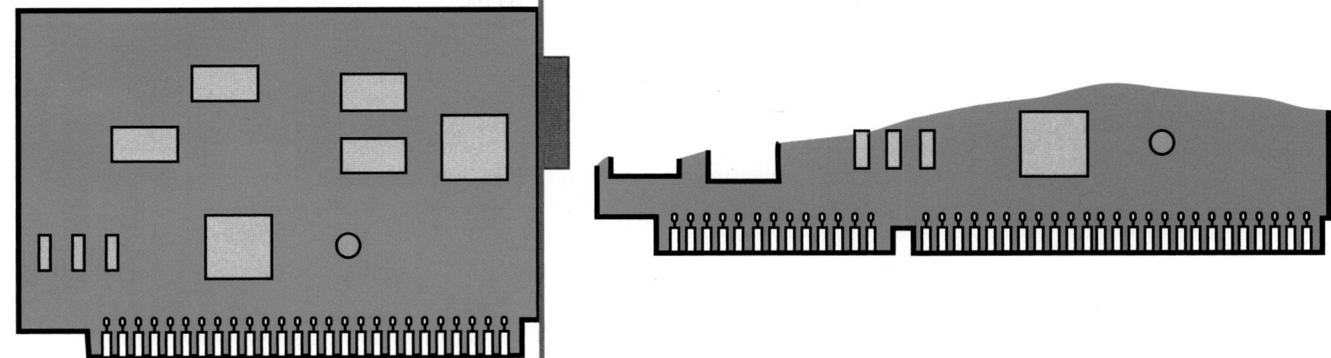

Typical 8-bit ISA Expansion Card

This card uses only 8 parallel lines used for transmitting data. Note that 8-bit ISA boards can fit into slots designed for 16 bit ISA cards

Typical 16-bit ISA Expansion Card

It has 18 more connectors than the ISA card. It transmits data over 16 data lines providing twice the data lines as 8-bit ISA.

Tech Tip:
ISA is used for internal ports such as keyboard, mouse, diskette drive, and parallel ports. The ISA is the only bus system left on PC motherboards to assure backward compatibility. Today, the newest motherboards are equipped with only PCI slots. The components listed here will work just as well on a more advanced bus system. See Figure 3-11.

MCA

The first major revolution in bus design came with the development of ***Micro Channel Architecture (MCA)*** by IBM. MCA has a 32-bit data width and a higher data transfer speed than ISA. See **Figure 3-12.**

The MCA bus was also considered an intelligent bus system because it could automatically assign interrupt requests (IRQs) without human intervention. This was a remarkable feat at the time because most adapter devices required the setting of switches or jumpers to identify the IRQ. One of the most significant features of the MCA bus was that it was patented by IBM and could be used by other PC manufacturers only if they paid royalties. In response to the proprietary MCA bus system came the EISA.

Micro Channel Architecture (MCA)
an I/O (expansion) bus system featuring a 32-bit data bus. MCA and ISA cards and slots are not physically compatible.

EISA
an I/O (expansion) bus with a 32-bit data bus. Designed in response to IBM's MCA bus system. EISA buses are backward compatible with ISA cards. This means that an ISA card would fit and function in an EISA expansion slot.

EISA

Extended Industry Standard Architecture (EISA) was developed jointly by Compaq, AST Research, Epson, Hewlett-Packard, NEC, Olivetti, Tandy, Wyse, and Zenith Data Systems in response to the development of IBM's MCA bus system. These companies are often referred to as the "gang of nine" in the history of PC development. In contrast to the MCA, the EISA was developed to be royalty-free. The EISA bus is 32-bits wide with a bus speed of 20 MHz, **Figure 3-13.**

ISA and MCA are not physically compatible. However, ISA and EISA are considered physically compatible. An ISA adapter card can fit into an EISA bus slot. MCA bus slots require an adapter card physically designed according to the MCA standard.

Figure 3-12.
The MCA expansion card features Plug and Play capabilities.

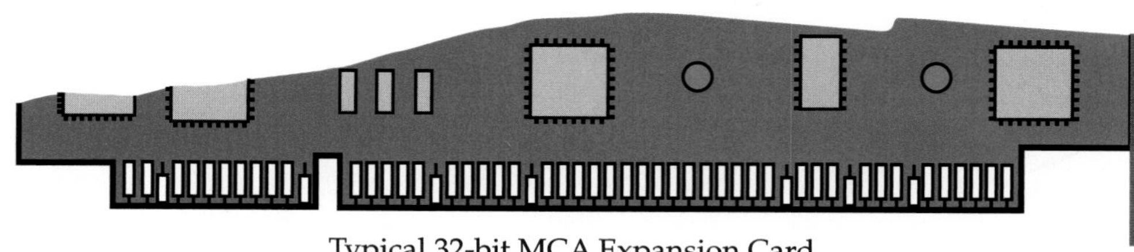

Typical 32-bit MCA Expansion Card

Figure 3-13.
The EISA uses 97 connectors designed in two levels. It can transmit 32 bits of data and supports Plug and Play like the MCA card.

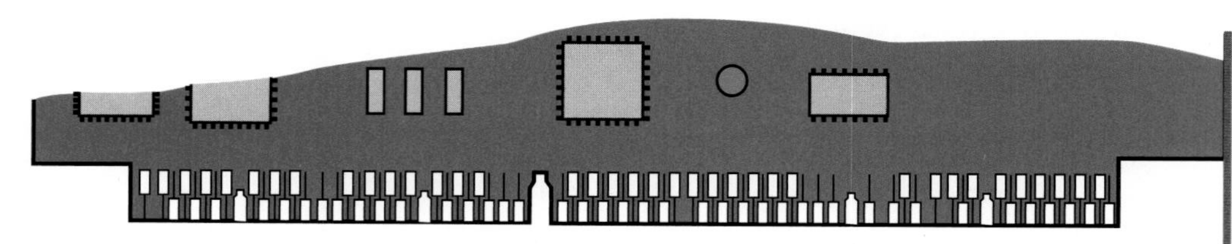

Typical 32-bit EISA Expansion Card

Video Electronics Standards Association (VESA) local bus
a bus system that could handle a higher data transfer rate than MCA or EISA. The VL-Bus was developed by a consortium of video adapter and monitor manufacturers.

Peripheral Component Interconnect (PCI)
a bus system featuring a 32-bit data bus that provides a high-speed bus structure needed for faster CPUs.

VESA Local Bus

The ***Video Electronics Standards Association (VESA) local bus*** (often called the VL-Bus) was developed by a consortium of video adapter and monitor manufacturers. A consortium is an association of competitors that combine their efforts to organize something they could not do individually. In this case, the group developed a standard video system for PCs.

The VESA bus could handle a higher data transfer rate than MCA or EISA. It was placed close to the processor on the motherboard, and it transferred data at the same rate as the CPU. As CPU speeds soon increased, the VESA bus soon became obsolete. The VESA design could not keep pace with the higher CPU speeds and was soon replaced by PCI. See **Figure 3-14.**

PCI

The ***Peripheral Component Interconnect (PCI),*** **Figure 3-15,** provides a high-speed bus structure needed for faster CPUs. The PCI standard has undergone changes needed to meet the needs of high-speed data transfers. High-speed data transfers are required for devices such as video graphic displays, TV tuners, high-end audio systems, high-speed gigabit network interfaces, and other devices that can be incorporated into the PC system through a PCI slot.

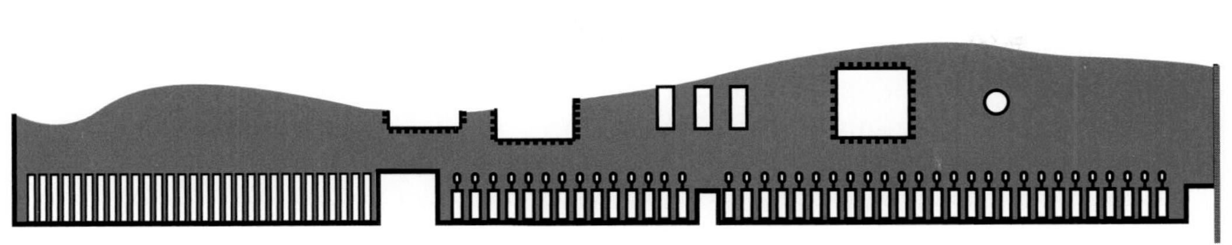

Figure 3-14. The VESA expansion card was designed for video adapters. It was based on the ISA standard, and the slot is compatible to ISA cards. The additional portion of the card consists of 36 more pairs of contacts to carry local bus data.

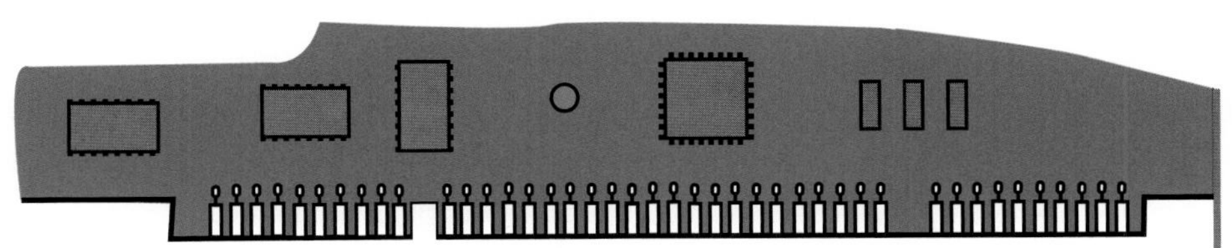

Figure 3-15. The edge connector of a 32-bit PCI expansion card. PCI cards are not compatible with other types of cards.

The original PCI evolved into the PCI 2.0 and PCI-X specifications. PCI-X is the latest version of the PCI standard. The original PCI bus speed of 33 MHz increased to 66 MHz (PCI 2.0) and then to 133 MHz (PCI-X). PCI-X is capable of obtaining a maximum data transfer rate of 1 GBps compared to the original PCI data transfer rate of 132 MBps.

Tech Tip:
The maximum data transfer rate is calculated by multiplying the bus speed by the bus width.

The newly proposed PCI-X 2.0 standard raises the bus frequency to 266 MHz and 533 MHz. This raises the maximum data transfer rate to over 2 GBps and 4 GBps respectively. To find more about the PCI-X standard, check the www.pcisig.com Web site.

The PCI bus can communicate to the ISA bus as well as to the local bus, using chips called bridges or chipsets. These chips provide buffering and make the different bus speeds compatible.

PCI is also designed with a buffer system. A buffer system holds data while the CPU is busy with other chores. When the CPU is available, the data is transferred from the buffer to the CPU to be acted on. The PCI slot is the most common slot found on current motherboards.

Parallel Ports

Parallel port technology has changed quite a bit since it was first introduced as a high-speed data transfer port. It was considered high speed as compared to the existing serial port of that time. The parallel port was capable of transferring data through several lines at the same time, resulting in data being transferred in bytes. Transferring data in bytes was eight times faster than serial data transfers.

The original parallel port standard was for a unidirectional port. The port was designed to send data to the printer. The port was used for output only. Later, the bi-directional port was designed, which allowed the parallel port not only to be used for output but also to be used for input into the computer system.

Enhanced Parallel Port (EPP) a parallel port standard that allows a throughput as high as 2 Mbps. The EPP is also referred to as the IEEE-1284 standard.

The original parallel port data transfer rate was 50 kbps, which was sufficient for dot matrix printers. The dot matrix was designed for alphanumeric character printing and low-resolution graphics. When laser printers came on the market, a standard with a higher data throughput was required. The laser printer introduced a higher quality printed image for both alphanumeric characters and graphic images. The ***Enhanced Parallel Port (EPP)*** standard met the requirements. The EPP could produce a throughput as high as 2 Mbps. The EPP was also referred to as the IEEE-1284 standard.

Extended Capabilities Port (ECP) a parallel port standard that provides for bi-directional communication and has extended capabilities to support multiple devices.

The next parallel printer port was the ***Extended Capabilities Port (ECP)***. The throughput was still limited to 2 Mbps, but the port's capabilities were extended, as the name implies. The capabilities were extended to support multiple devices. Common parallel port devices are printers, scanners, and faxes. The throughput of each parallel port device ranges from approximately 500 kbps to 2 Mbps. The transfer of data is bi-directional and automatically adjusts throughput to match the slowest device while exchanging data.

USB

Universal Serial Bus (USB) a bus system designed to replace the function of expansion slots with a data transfer rate as high as 480 Mbps. The USB is accessed by plugging a USB device into the bus at a port opening in the case. Additional devices (up to 127) can be connected to the bus in a daisy chain configuration.

Universal Serial Bus (USB) is designed to replace the existing variety of ports and expansion slots. The USB 2.0 can achieve a data transfer rate as high as 480 Mbps. USB technology conserves the use of IRQ assignments because it only requires the use of one IRQ. For example, when two or more devices are connected to a USB port, they automatically share the same IRQ address without creating a conflict. Each device takes turns communicating through the USB port. For USB to work properly, an operating system and a recently developed chipset such as Intel's 440LX must be used.

The USB is designed as a port rather than a traditional slot. It is accessed by plugging a USB device into the bus at a port opening in the case. See **Figure 3-16.** Devices are simply daisy chained when using USB cables and connectors. There is no need to open the computer case. Look at **Figure 3-17.** In the picture, you see two variations of the USB connector. The one on the left is a USB type A connector, and the one on the right is a USB type B connector.

The original USB (USB 1.1) supports 1.5 Mbps and 12 Mbps, and USB 2.0 supports 480 Mbps. The USB port connects to many different types of input and output peripherals and is capable of supporting up to 127 devices. The cable consists of four wires or conductors—two data lines (D+ and D–), a voltage bus (Vbus), and a ground (GND). See **Figure 3-18.**

The combination of the Vbus and GND carry power to each device connected to the USB port. Since the actual amount of electrical power carried on the electrical power lines is low, devices requiring additional power use their own electrical power supply.

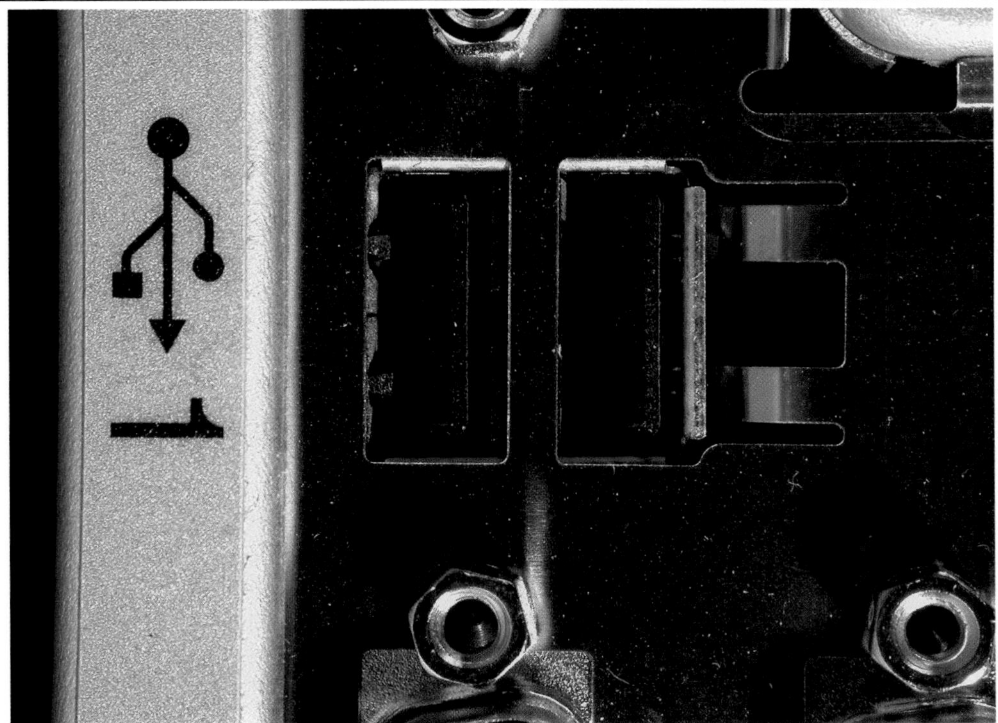

Figure 3-16.
USB devices can be plugged into ports in a PC's case.

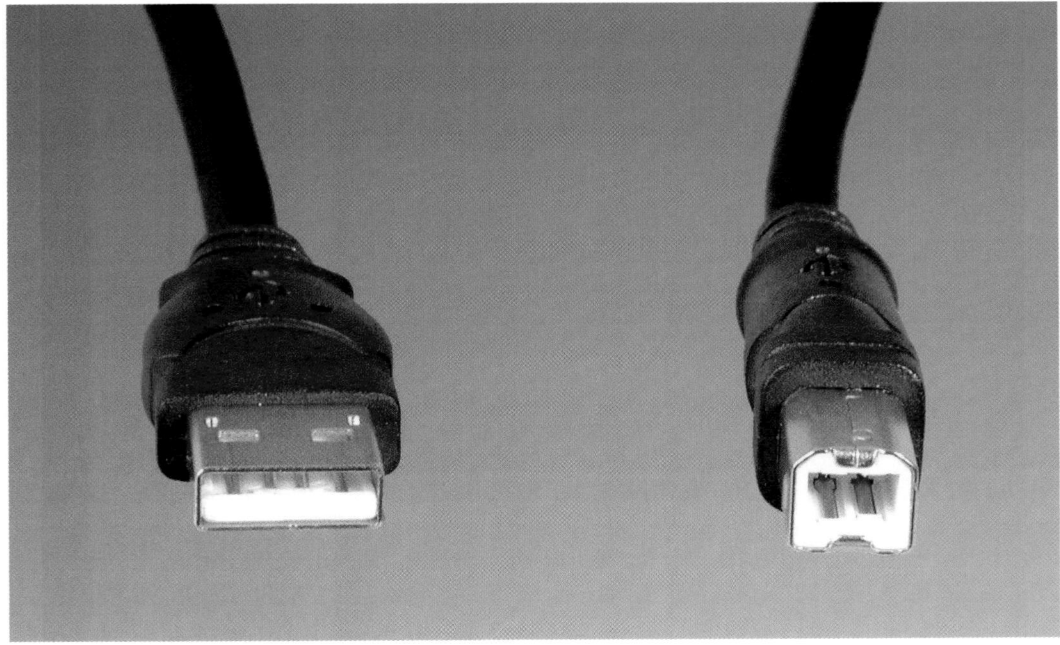

Figure 3-17.
Two variations of the USB connector, type A and type B.

The USB carries commands and data on the two twisted data lines. The twist in the data pair is designed to support high-speed data transfers. The twist is engineered for maximum throughput. Placing a twist in cable pairs reduces the amount of inductive reactance and helps achieve the high data rates. This technique is also incorporated in some other computer high data-rate cables like newer hard disk drive cables.

Figure 3-18.
USB cable design.

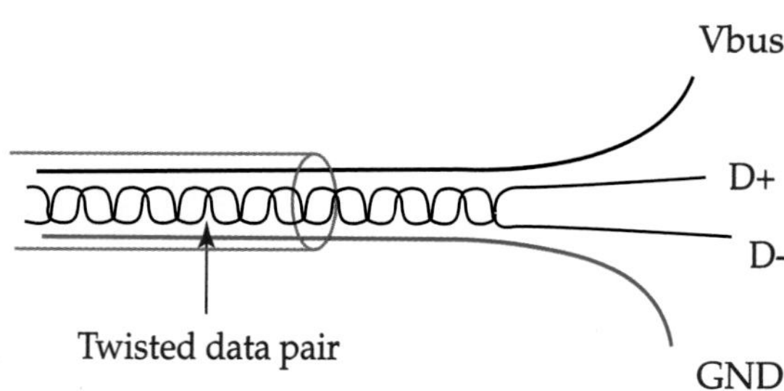

The USB is designed for Plug and Play support. Devices connected to the port are automatically detected, and communication between the computer system and the device begins. The various equipment that connect to the USB port are assigned an address for identification purposes. Data is moved along the data lines as packets of information. This is similar to the way networks communicate. The topic of data packets is covered in detail in Chapter 16—Introduction to Networking.

IEEE 1394 (FireWire)

FireWire (IEEE 1394) a bus system that provides a high rate of data transfer (speeds of 400 Mbps). A single IEEE 1394 port can serve up to 63 external devices in daisy chain fashion.

Specification ***IEEE 1394*** was first introduced by Apple computer systems and called by the trade name **FireWire, Figure 3-19.** Other manufacturers call the similar systems names such as I-link and Lynx. FireWire technology provides a high rate of data transfer (400 Mbps) needed for devices such as video cameras. A single IEEE 1394 port can serve up to 63 external devices in daisy chain fashion.

With the introduction of USB and 1394, manufacturers have been reducing the number of slots available on the motherboard. The use of USB and FireWire can eliminate the need for expansion slots as well as parallel and serial ports. USB and FireWire can be used to connect any device that presently uses motherboard adapter slot technology.

AGP

Accelerated Graphics Port (AGP) a bus designed exclusively for the video card. It supports data transfer of 32 bits at 254.3 MBps, 508.6 MBps, 1.017 GBps, and 2.034 GBps.

The ***Accelerated Graphics Port (AGP),*** **Figure 3-20,** was designed exclusively for the video card, especially 3-D graphic support. There is usually only one slot of this type on any motherboard. The slot is designed to fit as close as possible to the CPU and RAM to allow for high data transfer rates. The bandwidth for transferring data to and from the AGP can be significantly faster than PCI. AGP supports 32-bit data transfers at speeds of 254.3 MBps, 508.6 MBps, 1.017 GBps, and 2.034 GBps, while PCI 2.1 supports 64-bit transfers with a maximum throughput of 508.6 MBps. The actual rates vary according to PC hardware and chipsets. Chipsets are covered later in this chapter.

AGP offers the best support for graphics programs. The most powerful feature of AGP is DIME (direct memory execution). DIME is the direct access to main memory used strictly to support the video. This means the video card can use large portions of RAM rather than only the memory modules located on the video card.

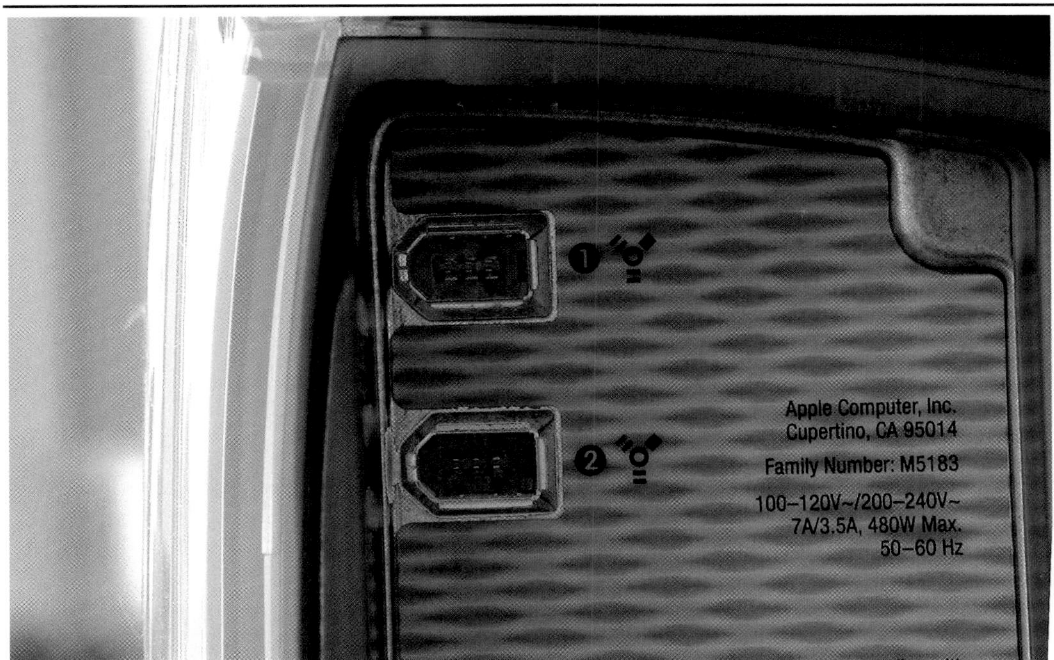

Figure 3-19.
IEEE 1394 (FireWire) ports.

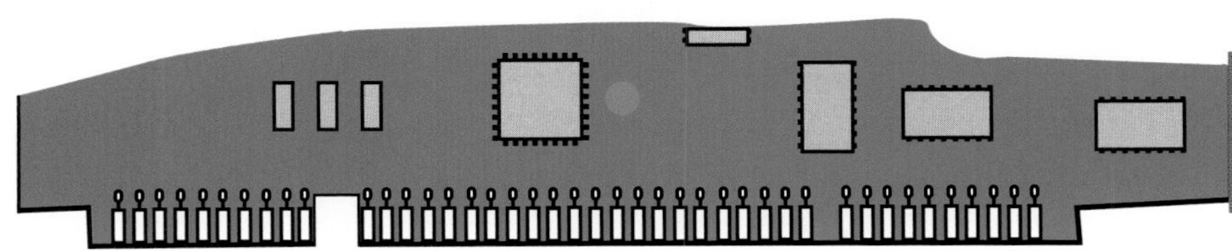

Figure 3-20.
The edge connector of a 32-bit AGP expansion card.

AMR, ACR, and CNR

There are many devices that are commonly used in a standard desktop computer system. By combining the functions of several separate technologies into a single unit, a more economical device can be produced. Manufacturers can combine the functions of Audio, USB, modem, DSL, Network connection (Ethernet), wireless access technologies, and more. Three special motherboard slot specifications that meet this need are Audio Modem Riser (AMR), Advanced Communications Riser (ACR), and Communications Network Riser (CNR). The combined technologies are incorporated into one riser board, which is inserted into a slot on the motherboard. See **Figure 3-21.**

CNR is a royalty free standard developed by Intel Corporation. ACR is an organization that developed the ACR standard and is supported by 3COM, AMD, Lucent Technologies, VIA Technologies, Motorola, Texas Instruments, ACER, PCTEL, and others.

Figure 3-21.
The ACR riser is designed with a 120-pin PCI connector. The connector is reversed and slightly offset from the other PCI connectors found on the motherboard.

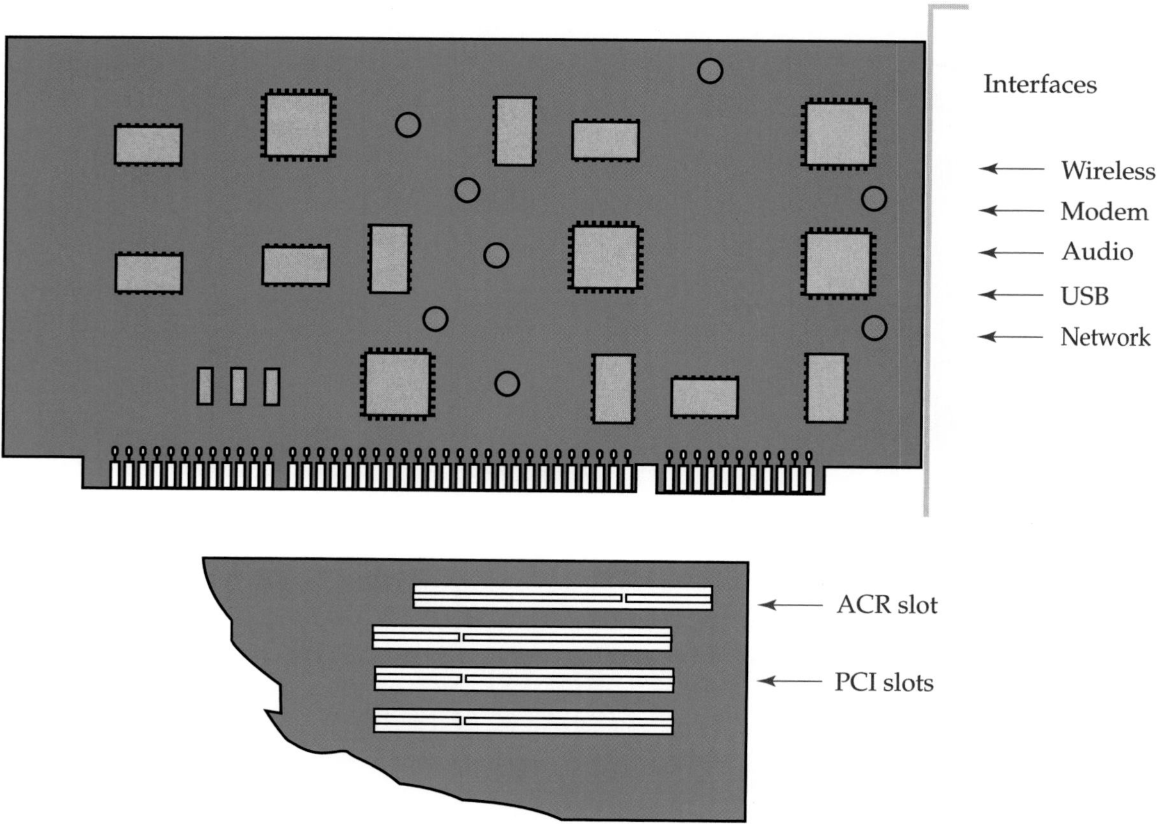

The AMR technology was released first and was closely followed by CNR. CNR is the more popular choice by computer hardware manufactures because it is royalty free and uses the same space as the PCI slot. With CNR sharing a PCI slot on the motherboard, the manufacturer does not need to make a major design change in the motherboard structure and circuitry the way they would for an AMR slot. AMR was later replaced by ACR. ACR is backward compatible with AMR.

The Intel CNR board can support on a single card up to four different devices out of a possible seven types of devices. The slot location is typically located at the edge of the motherboard, far away from components that could produce interference. The riser cards incorporate audio devices whose data can be corrupted by stray electromagnetic interference generated by other high-speed components.

Riser board technology is favorable for development of low cost motherboard manufacturing, but there are two problems. First, if one or more of the devices incorporated into the riser board goes bad, the entire board will need to be replaced at a higher cost than if replacing a single item such as a modem card. Second, the cost of a replacement board is higher because you need to go through the original manufacturer.

System Resources

System resources are resources that must be assigned and made available for devices such as printers, modems, disk drives, a mouse, or a sound card. The major system resources to consider are the I/O port address, memory addresses, IRQ, and DMA settings. System resource assignments can be viewed under Device Manager in Windows.

To see the system resources assigned on your computer, right-click the **My Computer** icon on the desktop. A right-click brings up a shortcut menu. Select the **Properties** option. The **System Properties** dialog box will display, **Figure 3-22.** Choose the Device Manager tab. You should see a screen similar to the one in **Figure 3-23.**

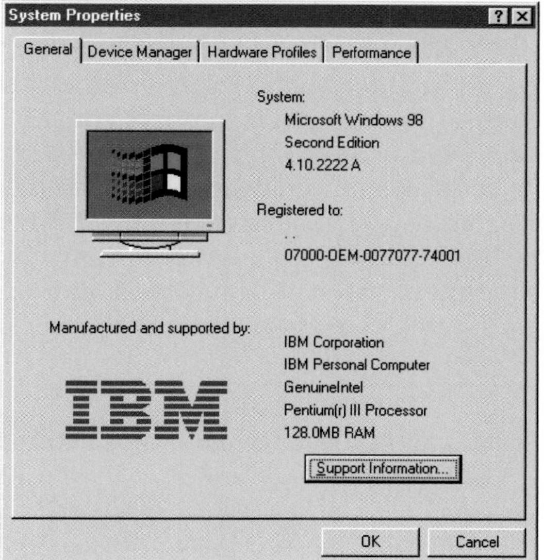

Figure 3-22. System Properties dialog box.

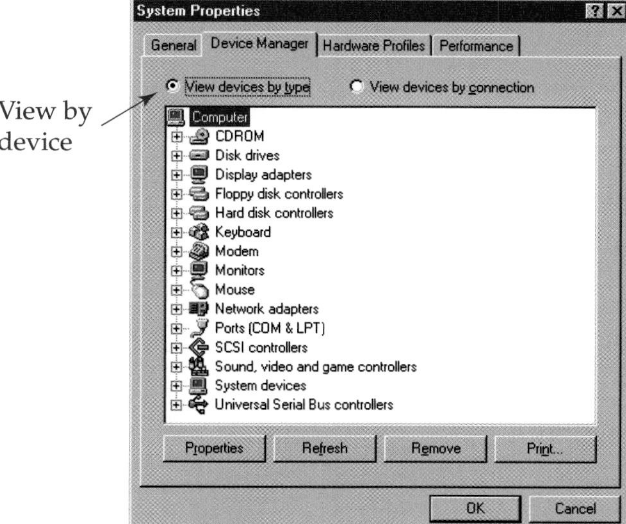

Figure 3-23. Device Manager shows a list of the devices connected to the PC.

The **System Properties** dialog box allows you to view properties of all hardware devices connected to the motherboard. In addition, the **System Properties** dialog box allows you to change the system resource assignments.

I/O Port and Memory Address Range

Each device has a unique memory address range. Components such as DVD drives, hard drives, and monitors require part of the computer system's memory to be used for temporary data storage.

I/O port address a memory address expressed in hexadecimal notation, which is used to identify a computer device such as a video card.

Memory address range an assigned section of memory used as a temporary storage area for data before it is transferred.

A ***memory address range*** is an assigned section of memory used as a temporary storage area for data before it is transferred. An ***I/O port address*** is assigned to a device for identification. A device must be identified for communication purposes. Both the I/O port and the memory address are expressed as a range and in hexadecimal notation such as 02E8h–02EFh. (Remember the small letter "h" is included in the number expression to identify it as a hexadecimal unit rather than a conventional numeric expression.) Some devices have an I/O port address and a name as well, such as COM3 or LPT1. See **Figure 3-24.**

A memory address is often mistaken for an I/O port address because a memory address also uses hexadecimal numbers for their assignments. Look at the resources assigned to a video graphics card in **Figure 3-25.** The memory address range is the area used to store large amounts of video information, and the I/O port is used to control communications between the video card and the CPU. For example, if a command is issued on the bus for I/O port address number 03B0, then the device that is assigned port number 03B0 accepts the command. If a large amount of video information is sent to the video card, the information is temporarily stored in the memory location range of 000B0000–000BFFFF.

Tech Tip:
Not all hardware devices have an assigned memory range but most do have an assigned I/O port address range.

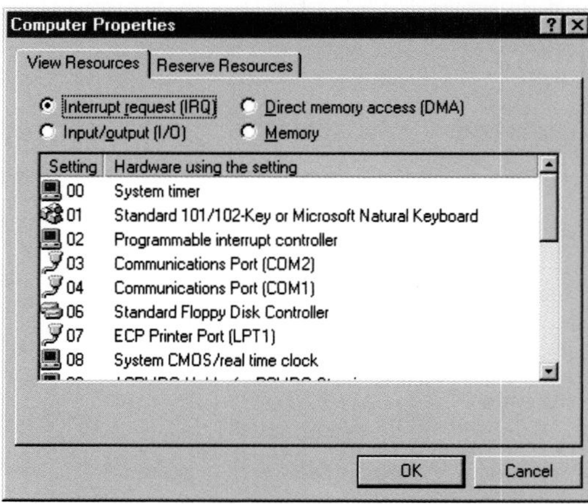

Figure 3-24. Computer Properties dialog box.

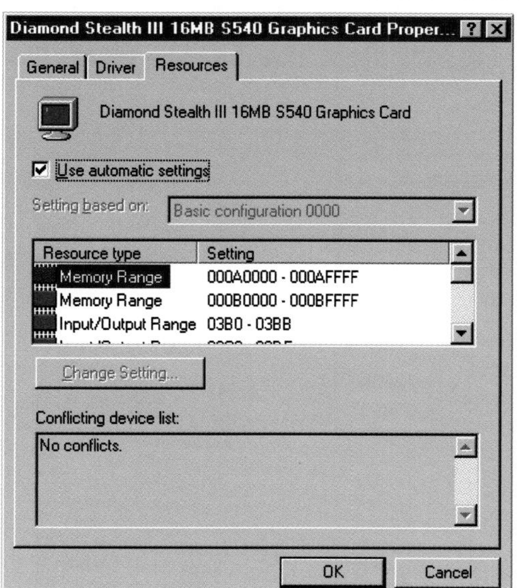

Figure 3-25. Resources assigned to a video graphics card.

IRQ Settings

Devices connected to a computer motherboard need the attention of the CPU. The only way to share the attention of the CPU with the individual devices is through an orderly system of IRQ settings. ***IRQ*** is an acronym for interrupt request. An IRQ literally interrupts the processes taking place in the CPU to give attention to some device such as a keyboard. There are also software interrupts in addition to hardware interrupts. Software interrupts are programmed into the software and call for the CPU's attention. Hardware interrupts are physically wired to the computer bus.

IRQ
IRQ is an acronym for interrupt request. An IRQ is a signal that interrupts the processes taking place in the CPU and requests that the processor pay attention to a specific device.

The table listed in **Figure 3-26** shows a listing of typical hardware IRQ assignments. Early PC designs used only eight IRQs numbered 0 through 7. Today 16 IRQ settings are the standard, numbered 0 through 15. A number of IRQ settings, such as the system timer, keyboard, COM1, LPT, primary IDE, and secondary IDE, are standard.

Tech Tip:
When the IRQ design evolved from 8 to 16 IRQs, it was created by cascading IRQ 2 to IRQ 9. This means that IRQ 2 should never be assigned to any device. The assignment for IRQ 2 is communicating with IRQ 9.

IRQs are also assigned priorities. A lower number for an IRQ means a higher priority. Look at the system timer on the chart. It is assigned to IRQ 0. This gives it the highest priority, as it should be. The system timer is responsible for the timing of all devices including the CPU.

Another important aspect of IRQ assignments are *IRQ conflicts* that arise when two or more devices assigned the same IRQ setting try to access the CPU at the same time. When this happens, the conflicting request for attention can cause some strange occurrences. Usually only one of the two devices will have

Figure 3-26.
Table of IRQ settings cascading from IRQ 2 to IRQ 9. Note that this is a typical set of IRQ assignments. They will not match all machines. Many IRQs will have more than one device assigned to them, especially controller chips.

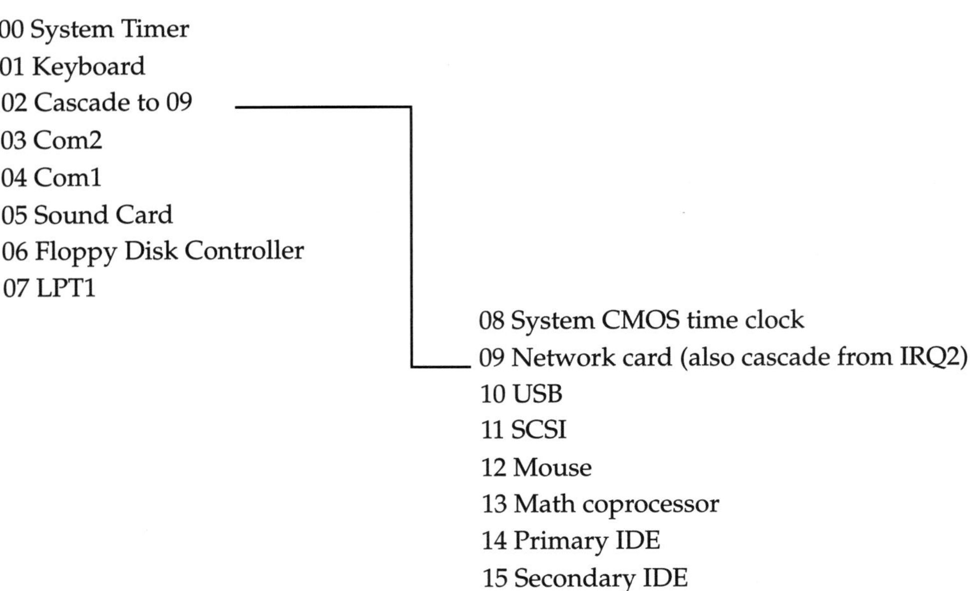

access to the CPU, leaving the other the appearance of being dead. Two IRQ assignments *can* be shared if the devices are not going to be used at the same time. An example of two such devices would be a scanner and a camera. A digital camera can share an IRQ assignment with a scanner because it is highly unlikely both would be used at the same time. However, if the mouse and a floppy drive were assigned the same IRQ setting, a problem would arise. If the mouse was identified first by the CPU, then the floppy drive would appear disabled. If the floppy drive was identified first by the CPU, the mouse would appear to be disabled. Today many chipsets are identified by IRQs and are shared with other chipsets and devices.

Plug and Play (PnP) remedies most of the assignment problems. Plug and Play technology automatically assigns IRQ settings as well as other system resources. For Plug and Play to work, the BIOS, operating system software, and hardware must all be Plug and Play compliant. Before Plug and Play technology, system resources had to be assigned manually. This was very difficult at times. With Plug and Play, the user is usually unaware of the process of system resources being assigned when devices are added. The hardware device is usually automatically detected when the system starts up. The needed resources are assigned without user intervention. There are some occasions when Plug and Play technology does not work, and system resources have to be assigned manually. This happens most often when very new hardware and legacy hardware coexist in the same system.

A+ Note:
I/O addresses and IRQs can vary from machine to machine, but there are some common settings for the COM and LPT ports that you should memorize for the A+ Certification exams.

COM1 IRQ 4 and I/O address 3F8–3FF
COM2 IRQ 3 and I/O address 2F8–2FFh
COM3 IRQ 4 and I/O address 3E8–3EFh
COM4 IRQ 3 and I/O address 2E8–2EFh
LPT1 IRQ 7 and I/O address 378–37Fh

Examine **Figure 3-27.** Here you see an interrupt request assignment viewed through the **System Properties** dialog box. This window is often used to verify or change IRQ settings. To view these settings, double-click the device you are interested in. You can also right-click the device and choose **Properties.**

DMA Channels

In the early days of computers, the CPU was designed to control all devices and their functions. For example, when data was moved from the floppy disk to the RAM memory, each bit would have to be transferred to the CPU, and then the CPU would transfer the bit to the memory location. DMA allows the floppy disk drive to transfer all the data directly to memory without the involvement of the CPU.

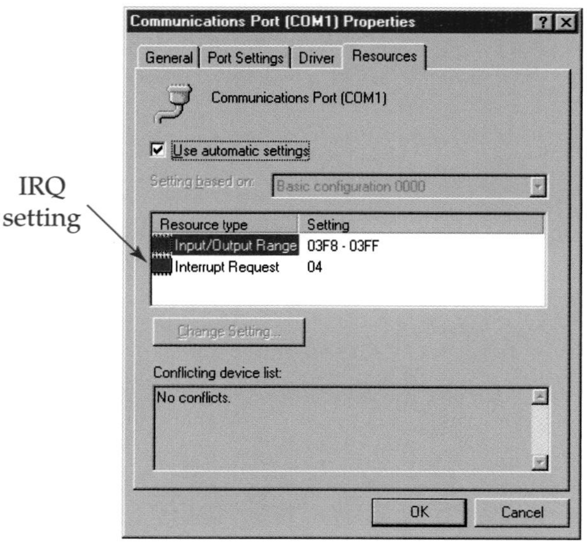

Figure 3-27. Through the **System Properties** dialog box, you can view specific device properties. This can show you the IRQ being used by any device.

direct memory access (DMA) a combination of software and hardware that allows certain system devices direct access to the RAM.

Direct memory access (DMA) is a combination of software and hardware that allows certain system devices direct access to the memory. Without DMA, all data must be transferred to memory under the control of the CPU. Waiting for the CPU to take action can cause a bottleneck for the transfer of data in the computer system. If the data does not need the CPU's special attention, a device that has DMA can transfer the data directly into memory via the DMA controller.

The DMA controller is a chip that connects certain devices directly to memory, bypassing the CPU. Each DMA controller has four channels. There is one device connected per channel. The typical motherboard has a total of eight channels available for devices. **Figure 3-28** shows the DMA assignment for LPT1 on a PC. DMA settings, like IRQs and I/O settings, can be viewed through the **Systems Properties** dialog box.

Bus Mastering

bus mastering a feature of some buses that allows data to be transferred directly between two devices without the intervention of the CPU.

Bus mastering is another method of control that allows data to be transferred directly between two devices without the intervention of the CPU. Control of the bus is usually taken while the CPU is busy with a task that does not require the use of the bus system.

Even though bus mastering and DMA sound similar, they are different. The main difference between bus mastering and DMA is the intent of the device. Bus mastering takes control of the bus system to which it is attached, while DMA is used to access the memory system. DMA is designed to allow devices to communicate directly to and from the memory (RAM) without the intervention of the CPU. Bus mastering technology allows devices to carry out specific tasks such as communicating with each other without direct intervention of the CPU. It allows devices to carry out their individual tasks without using the CPU for each and every bit transfer. While the CPU is busy with other tasks such as

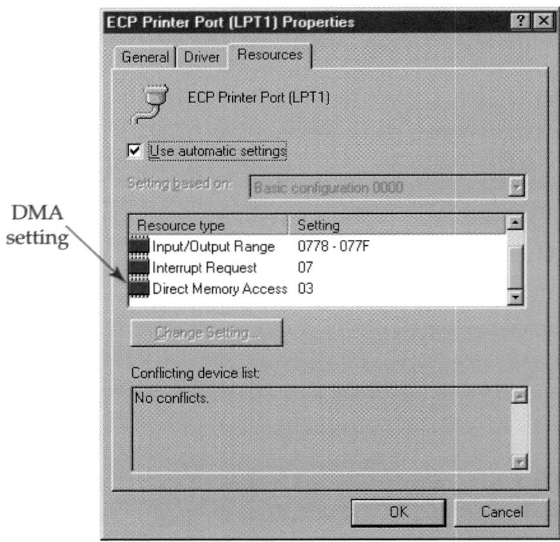

Figure 3-28. The System Properties dialog box will also show you DMA assignments for devices.

calculations, the bus master controller controls the communication between two devices on the bus system.

Both DMA and bus mastering are designed to speed up the common operations involving data flow. To use either technology, the device as well as the BIOS, the operating system software, and the motherboard chipset must be designed to support the technology.

Chipsets

The very early PC systems had many more individual components mounted on the motherboard than do today's PCs. These numerous components were eventually redesigned into units referred to as chipsets. ***Chipsets*** contain all the electronic circuitry required to carry out certain common motherboard functions, such as communication between the PCI and ISA bus, controlling direct memory access, directing interrupt requests, and serving as temporary memory.

The chipset is commonly divided into the north bridge and the south bridge. The ***north bridge*** is used to transfer and control higher data speed systems such as graphics and DVD hardware. The ***south bridge*** controls the slower devices associated with the PCI and ISA buses.

chipset
a name for the collection of electronic circuitry required to carry out certain common motherboard functions.

north bridge
the portion of the chipset that controls higher data speed systems such as graphics and DVD hardware.

south bridge
the portion of the chipset that controls the slower devices associated with the PCI and ISA buses.

Plug and Play

Plug and Play (PnP) is the automatic assignment of system resources such as DMA channels, interrupts, memory, and port assignments. As the name implies, with Plug and Play you simply plug in a device (such as a network card) and the system software automatically assigns the system resources. There is no need to manually configure the system resources. For Plug and Play to work, the BIOS, the hardware being installed, and the operating system must all support Plug and Play technology.

Before Plug and Play, expansion cards required the installer to set jumpers or dip switches into specific configurations to identify such things as the card's IRQ setting and port address.

Plug and Play works well most of the time, but not for every case. There are times when you must intervene. Not all operating systems support Plug and Play. Windows 95 and later as well as the Windows NT series support Plug and Play to different degrees depending on the version and device drivers available.

Examine **Figure 3-29.** Jumpers are used to select certain options associated with the device they are mounted near. For example, jumper settings can determine the data transmission speed or operating voltage. Jumpers are similar in appearance to motherboard low power connection points such as for indicator lights (LEDs), switches, and low-power speakers.

Plug and Play (PnP)
the automatic assignment of system resources such as DMA channels, interrupts, memory, and port assignments.

BIOS and CMOS

Many technicians use the terms BIOS and CMOS interchangeably, but in reality they are two different distinct terms. The ***BIOS*** is a read only memory (ROM) chip that contains a group of software programs written in machine language. *Machine language* is a language that uses hexadecimal codes to write a program. It is the language that your computer understands. It is many times faster than other programming languages, but it is much more difficult to write.

BIOS
a read only memory module designed to initiate three different activities: the power-on self-test (POST), the CMOS Setup program, and communications between the system hardware and operating system.

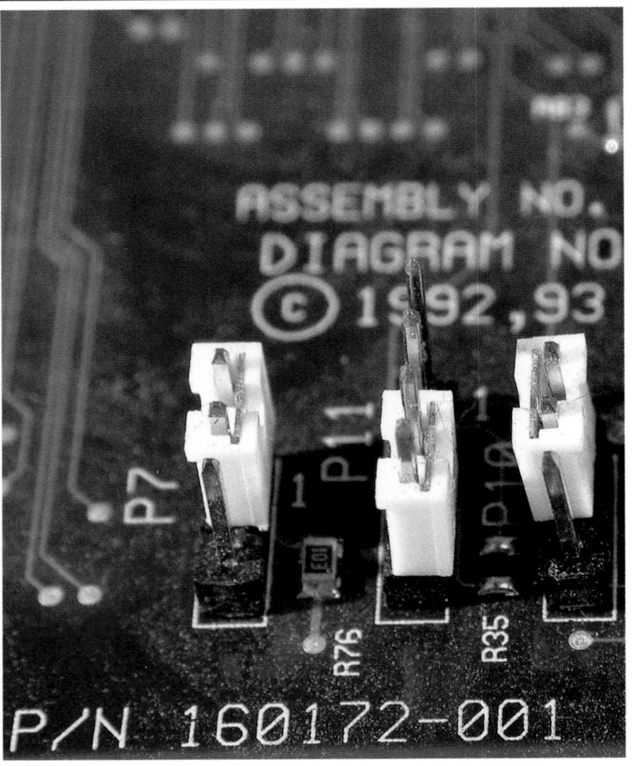

Figure 3-29.
Set of jumpers found on a motherboard. Moving or removing jumper connections can change a variety of PC settings.

The BIOS program is designed to initiate three different activities, the power-on self-test (POST), the CMOS Setup program (also called the *BIOS Setup program)*, and communications between the system hardware and operating system. The BIOS also controls the sequence of boot devices. This feature allows you to determine which device is looked at first when locating the bootstrap program.

When the bootstrap program is located, it is loaded and started. The sequence of looking at the boot devices ceases. The usual setting of boot device sequence is the floppy drive, the hard drive, and last (if bootable) the CD-ROM drive. Sometimes computers are set to boot from the hard drive first as a time saving measure or for security reasons.

Another interesting feature of the BIOS is the setting of password protection for the CMOS Setup program. By password protecting the CMOS Setup program, unauthorized personnel cannot change the settings either intentionally or accidentally. Curious PC users often inadvertently change BIOS setting.

Sometimes people forget their password. If this happens, the CMOS will have to be erased. This will allow a new password to be programmed into CMOS. Some motherboards are equipped with a jumper simply for erasing the data in CMOS. Moving the jumper to the "clear CMOS" position will erase all CMOS data, even the password. Moving the jumper back to its original location will allow the settings to be reentered.

Tech Tip:
The exact process and terminology of clearing the CMOS data can vary between motherboard manufacturers.

Upgrading BIOS

Upgrading BIOS is fairly common when upgrading hardware systems on older machines. In addition, upgrading the BIOS is not just for hardware concerns. Certain software programs can require an upgraded version of the BIOS. For example, when Plug and Play was introduced to consumers, problems arose when trying to use the new Plug and Play technology. The appropriate software operating system may have been available and a Plug and Play device installed, however, the system could not detect or support the device until the BIOS was upgraded.

To upgrade the BIOS program on early computer motherboards, the BIOS chip had to be replaced or an ultraviolet light had to be used to erase the program stored on the BIOS chip in order to reprogram it. The first programs were electrically etched into the microscopic circuitry inside the BIOS chip. The style of chip was referred to as programmable read-only memory (PROM). These were programmed once by the manufacturer and could not be reprogrammed. They simply had to be replaced.

Another variation of the BIOS chip called the erasable programmable read-only memory (EPROM) was developed. This chip had a transparent window usually covered by a foil patch. The foil patch was a sticker with the BIOS manufacturer name and part identification on it. When the label was removed, a window exposing the circuitry inside the chip was revealed. If an ultraviolet light was shined through the exposed window, the program in the chip would be erased. This process allowed the chip to be reprogrammed. These past techniques are no longer used.

Modern PCs use flash BIOS. ***Flash BIOS*** is an electrically erasable programmable read only memory (EEPROM) module, which can be erased electrically and then reprogrammed. Flash BIOS is easily reprogrammed using software available through the motherboard manufacturer's Web site and an updated BIOS program file.

flash BIOS
BIOS that is stored on a reprogrammable chip, allowing for easy upgrades.

Warning:
Upgrading the BIOS can render the PC inoperable. Visit the manufacturer's Web site first and read all information pertaining to upgrading the BIOS. Follow the manufacturer's instructions for upgrading your particular BIOS.

The following are general instructions for upgrading a flash BIOS. *Always* follow the manufacturer's instructions for upgrading a specific BIOS.

1. Download the BIOS upgrade program and the updated BIOS program file from the motherboard manufacturer's Web site.
2. Copy the BIOS upgrade program and the updated BIOS program file onto a bootable floppy disk.
3. Boot the PC with bootable floppy disk.
4. Run the BIOS upgrade program.
5. When the BIOS upgrade program asks for the name of the BIOS program file, enter the exact name of the BIOS program file.

6. If the BIOS upgrade program asks you if you want to back up the contents of the BIOS, answer "yes." Having a backup of the BIOS is vital if you need to return the BIOS to its original state. The BIOS upgrade program will then back up the original contents of the BIOS, erase the contents from the BIOS, and write the new BIOS program file to the BIOS.
7. When the procedure has successfully completed, reboot your PC and enter the CMOS Setup program. Do not be alarmed if you do not see the new BIOS date and information in the CMOS Setup screen.
8. Enter the CMOS Setup program and set it to its default settings.
9. Save the changes and reboot the computer.
10. When the computer is rebooting, enter the CMOS Setup program again. You will now see the date of the new BIOS program.
11. Enter the correct settings for your system.
12. Save the changes and reboot the computer.

Tech Tip:
Details vary somewhat for different motherboards and BIOS upgrade procedures. For detailed steps on upgrading a particular BIOS, consult the manufacturer's Web site.

CMOS Setup

The term CMOS (pronounced *c-moss*) stands for complementary metal oxide semiconductor. CMOS is a type of low-power consuming semiconductor chip technology. In the electronics field, there are many different types of devices designed from CMOS technology. In the computer field, it is understood to refer to the location where the BIOS settings or data are stored.

CMOS Setup (or BIOS Setup) a program that allows you to identify the type of hard drive and other storage systems in the PC, set up a password for accessing the PC and the CMOS Setup program, select certain power management features, and select the boot order of bootable devices.

To store the BIOS setting in the CMOS, the ***CMOS Setup (or BIOS Setup)*** program is used. The BIOS runs a setup routine that identifies the major components and certain features for the computer. The CMOS Setup allows you to identify the type of hard drive and other storage systems. The CMOS Setup program also allows you to set up a password for accessing the machine and the BIOS settings. It also allows you to select certain power management features. The BIOS allows you to select the boot options for selecting in what order the hard drive, floppy drive, and CD-ROM drive are sequenced. It also allows you to identify the type of chipset installed.

The CMOS Setup program is activated by a special set of keyboard strokes during the boot up period. The instructions for accessing the CMOS Setup program are often displayed on the screen. When they are not displayed, accessing a computer's CMOS Setup can be difficult. There are many different ways to access the CMOS Setup. Examine **Figure 3-30.** These key combinations could prove helpful for the troublesome machine. Keep in mind that what works for a particular brand one day may not work in the future. Another way to find the right key combination is to check the company's Web site. You may have to open the computer's case and look at the brand and model number on the BIOS chip.

Figure 3-31 shows a typical CMOS Setup routine screen. Not all CMOS Setup screens look the same, but they are similar in appearance and in function.

BIOS Manufacturer	Key(s) to Press
AMI	[Del] or [Esc] key during POST
Award, Phoenix	[Ctrl] + [Alt] + [Esc] or [Ctrl] + [Alt] + [S] or [F2] during POST
Computer Manufacturer	
Dell	[Ctrl] + [Alt] + [Enter]
Compact	[F2] or [F10] or [Ctrl] + [Alt] + [F2]
DTK	[Esc]
IBM PS/2	[Ctrl] + [Alt] + [Del] followed by [Ctrl] + [Alt] + [Ins]
Gateway 2000	[F1]
Sony PC	[F3] while booting followed by [F1] at Sony logo
NEC	[F1] when cursor flashes on screen

Figure 3-30.
Possible key combinations for accessing the CMOS Setup program.

Figure 3-31.
Screen displays for CMOS Setup program and exit.

System Time:	[14:45:47]
System Date	[06/09/2000]
Language	English
Diskette A:	[1.44 MB, 31/2]
Diskette B:	[Not Installed]
>IDE Adapter 0 Master	[C:2.2 GB]
>IDE Adapter 0 Slave	[None]
>IDE Adapter 1 Master	[None]
>IDE Adapter 1 Slave	[None]
Video Systems:	[EGA/VGA]
>Memory and Cache	
>Boot Options	
>Keyboard Features	

Above is a typical first screen display of CMOS setup program.

Save Changes & Exit
Discard Changes & Exit
Get Default Values
Load Previous Values
Save Changes

Typical exit screen leaving the CMOS setup routine.

POST

The *POST (power-on self-test)* is a simple diagnostic program that is initiated when electrical power is applied to the computer system. The POST verifies that the major computer components are installed and in working order.

The devices checked may vary slightly from computer to computer depending on the BIOS. The POST checks hardware such as the CPU, ROM, RAM, keyboard, monitor, mouse, and hard drive. The test it performs is not as sophisticated as diagnostic software, but it will check for major problems. When the POST is finished, it usually makes one "beep" sound to let you know that the POST is complete and everything is in working order. If an error is detected during the POST, an error code is usually displayed on the screen and a series of beeps are heard that match the code. The codes and beep pattern vary according to the different BIOS chip manufacturers. A list of error codes and beep codes can be obtained from the Web site of the manufacturer.

Motherboard Component Identification

There are many different motherboard manufacturers. The process of identifying many of the jumper and connection locations as well as chips and other major components can be very confusing. **Figure 3-32** shows a typical component layout drawing for a motherboard.

Figure 3-32.
ATX motherboard layout.

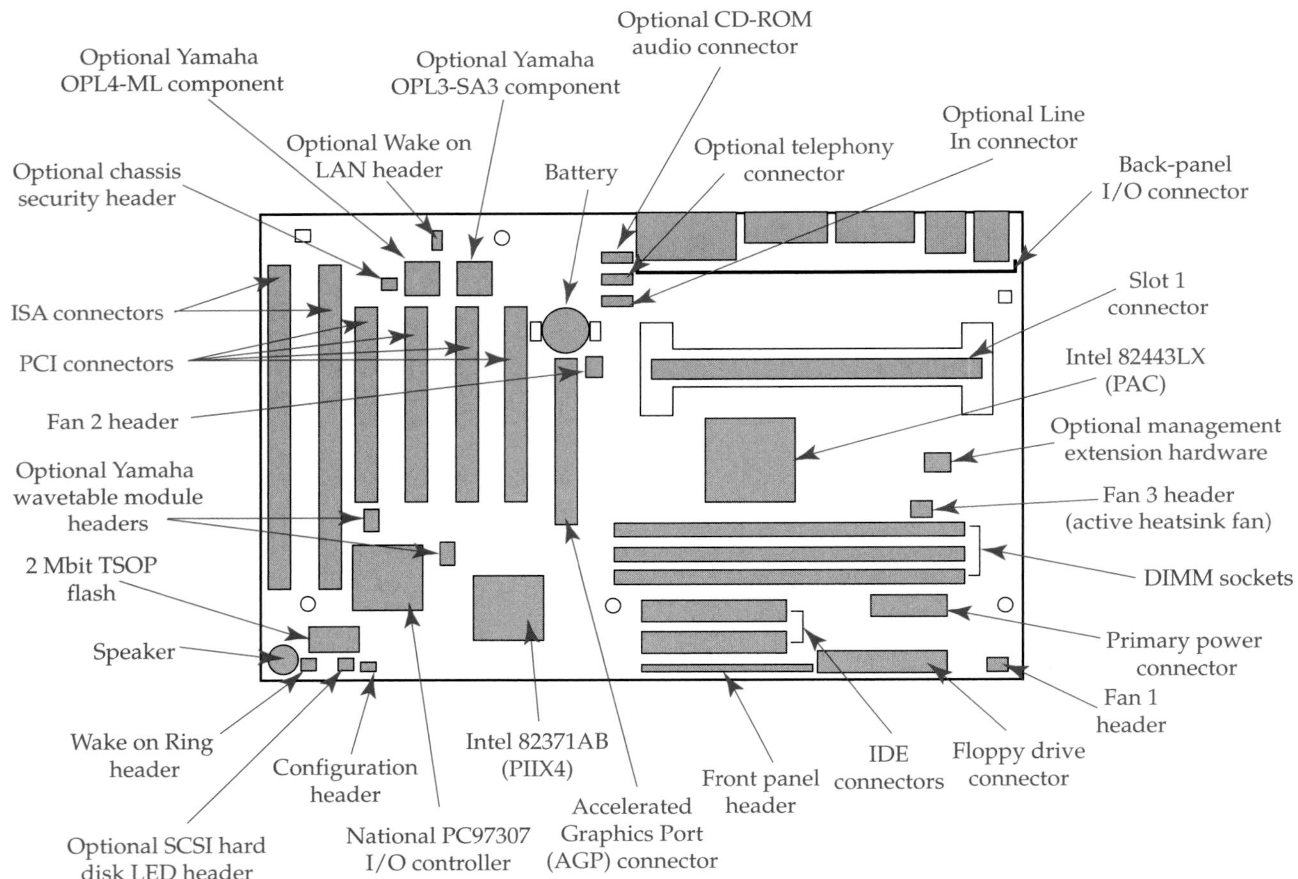

Components are identified by their relative position and outline on each motherboard. All major components can be easily identified. Component layouts are usually readily available at the manufacturer's Web site. Once the Web page for the manufacturer is located, the technician should proceed to one of the following links: site map, specifications, publications, manuals, or support. Most manufacturers have information available through downloads.

Troubleshooting Motherboards

The motherboard is one of the most expensive parts to replace, and problems with it are some of the most difficult to diagnose. Understanding all the peripheral devices that are associated with the PC is required to effectively diagnose a defective motherboard. Many times, the process of diagnosing a problem requires third-party diagnostic software or hardware.

The difficulty in diagnosing a motherboard fault is that all major components use the motherboard circuitry. For example, a technician is troubleshooting a modem problem. The technician first examines the modem itself and all of its connections. After all methods of diagnosing the modem have been exhausted, the motherboard chipset or circuitry could be at fault. The motherboard must be changed in order to be absolutely sure.

Substitution can be expensive when trying to determine if the CPU or motherboard is at fault. Both are expensive parts. Before replacing the motherboard, always start with a simple inspection of some common failure points. Many times electronic equipment failures are nothing more than loose connections. All the jumpers and connections on and to the motherboard should be checked. A detailed drawing of the component layout (from the manufacturer's Web site) will help locate all possible connections and jumpers. Many times, the simple act of reconnecting jumpers and connections will remedy the problem.

Sometimes a computer can be repaired simply by removing and reinstalling the CPU. The connection pins can become oxidized and stop the flow of electrical energy. Removing and reinserting often clears a sufficient amount of the thin coating of oxidation to clear the fault.

Obvious signs of lightning or high voltage surge damage should be sought. A small burnt area on the motherboard bus at the connection to a component is a sure sign. The backside of the motherboard should also be inspected for damage.

At times, a fault disappears when the cover is removed from the PC. This is often a sign of a pinched cable or a loose connection. Wires and cables can become trapped between the case and metal framework during assembly. The cable may not be completely damaged at the time it becomes caught, but, over time, the framework pinches through the cable.

As you progress through your studies, your knowledge base will grow and so will your troubleshooting skills.

Summary

- Motherboard form factor describes the shape and size of the motherboard.
- There are several types of motherboard slots available such as ISA, EISA, MCA, AGP, and PCI.
- The latest motherboard designs no longer include ISA slots. In addition, the development of USB and FireWire has reduced the number of remaining PCI slots required for system expansion.
- USB 1.1 supports data transfer rates of 1.5 Mbps and 12 Mbps, and USB 2.0 supports transfer rates as high as 480 Mbps.
- System resources are I/O port address, memory address range, interrupt request (IRQ), and direct memory access (DMA).
- Direct memory access (DMA) allows devices to communicate directly with the memory system without constant intervention by the CPU.
- Bus mastering allows devices to communicate directly with each other without constant intervention by the CPU.
- Chipsets combine many individual electronic systems into one or two chips.
- The north bridge controls communication between high-speed modules while the south bridge controls slower communications.
- Plug and Play (PnP) automatically detects new hardware and assigns system resources.
- The BIOS performs three major tasks, POST, CMOS Setup, and communication between the operating system and hardware.
- The CMOS chip stores information such as time, date, and type of hard drive installed.
- The power-on self-test (POST) tests the major components (video, keyboard, mouse, memory, etc.) to see if they are working.

Review Questions

Answer the following questions on a separate sheet of paper. Please do not write in this book.

1. What are three alternate names used for motherboard?
2. What is a field replacement unit?
3. Define the following bus types.
   Memory
   Address
   Data
   Power
   Local
   Expansion
   Internal
   Control

4. A bus can consist of two or more other types of bus. True or False?
5. Form factor describes the _____ of the motherboard.
   a. bus type
   b. shape
   c. voltage level
   d. chipset
6. What is the major difference between an NLX and an LPX form factor?
7. Which is the fastest bus system?
   a. ISA
   b. EISA
   c. MCA
   d. PCI
8. An ISA adapter card will fit into a(n) _____ slot.
   a. EISA
   b. MCA
   c. PCI
   d. any standard
9. Will a Baby AT fit into the same case as an XT?
10. What are the advantages to incorporating the CNR or ACR riser system into a motherboard design?
11. What are the four major system resources used by computer devices?
12. List how to access a view of IRQ assignments for a PC. Start with *Right-click* **My Computer**.
13. What IRQ setting is used for COM2?
14. What IRQ setting is used for COM1?
15. What three things are necessary for Plug and Play to work?
16. Which IRQ has the highest priority?
   a. 3
   b. 5
   c. 2
   d. 15
17. What do the acronyms EPP and ECP represent?
18. What is the maximum throughput of USB 2.0?
19. What is the maximum throughput of USB 1.1?
20. Which has the highest data transfer rate, USB or IEEE 1394?
21. What is the maximum number of devices that can be attached to an IEEE 1394 port?

22. What is the total number of hardware IRQs?
23. Explain how IRQ assignments can be shared.
24. Early PC systems used _____ IRQs while today _____ IRQ settings are available.
25. What can be done to protect the CMOS Setup program from accidental changes?
26. How many channels does a DMA controller have?
27. How many devices can be connected to each channel of a DMA controller?

Sample A+ Exam Questions

Answer the following questions on a separate sheet of paper. Please do not write in this book.

1. Which form factor uses a bus riser card?
   a. AT
   b. ATX
   c. NLX
   d. XT
2. Which architecture supports the fastest transfer speeds?
   a. ISA
   b. PCI
   c. USB 1.1
   d. IEEE 1394
3. Which slot design is exclusively used for video cards?
   a. PCI
   b. AGP
   c. USB
   d. IEEE 1394
4. IRQ settings can be accessed in Windows 98 through the _____.
   a. Device Manager
   b. System Resource icon in Control Panel
   c. IRQ icon in Control Panel
   d. System Resources dialog box.
5. Which IRQ setting is associated with COM1?
   a. 3
   b. 4
   c. 5
   d. 6

6. Which I/O port address is usually assigned to COM1?
   a. 03F8
   b. 02F8
   c. 03A0
   d. 02A0
7. Where does the computer store information about the type of hard drive installed?
   a. At sector 2 of the hard drive.
   b. In the CMOS.
   c. In the system ROM chip.
   d. In the system RAM chip.
8. What is required for Plug and Play technology to work correctly? Select all that apply.
   a. Plug and Play BIOS
   b. An operating system that supports Plug and Play
   c. Device Manager must support Plug and Play
   d. The hardware device being installed must be equipped to support Plug and Play
9. Which of the following technologies is used to control data flow on the system bus?
   a. Bus mastering
   b. Bus routing
   c. Bus directory
   d. Active bus
10. Which of the following items controls the speed of data flow across different bus architectures on a motherboard?
    a. BIOS
    b. Motherboard chipsets
    c. DMA channels
    d. IEEE 1394

Suggested Laboratory Activities

Do not attempt any suggested laboratory activities without your instructor's permission. Certain activities can render the PC operating system inoperable.

1. Completely remove a motherboard. Make a drawing and label all connections to the motherboard to assist you during reinstallation.
2. Access the Web site of the motherboard's manufacturer. Look for a drawing on the site that identifies all of the major parts of the motherboard. Identify the type of chipset and BIOS that it uses. List the various features associated with the motherboard chipset.

3. Access the CMOS Setup program on your assigned PC station. Write down all the settings you find in the CMOS Setup program, such as the hard drive, floppy disk drive, and CD-ROM drive configurations. Look for a Help option. It will usually be displayed on the screen as you move the cursor into each setting's input field. Locate the security password system in the BIOS.
4. Access **Device Manager** and study the way the system resources are displayed and assigned. Identify the IRQ, memory, and DMA assignments for various devices. Record your findings and use them as a study guide.
5. Execute **msinfo32.exe** from the **Run** program in the **Start** menu. Examine the information displayed, such as memory, DMA, and I/O assignments. Look at the various information that can be displayed and explore the options available in the **Tools** menu.
6. Access the Web site of the BIOS manufacturer American Mega Trends (www.ami.com). Locate and read the procedure for upgrading a system BIOS. Download the utility for identifying motherboards that are equipped with AMI BIOS chips. Download and print a copy of the common AMI beep and POST codes. Download and print a copy of the AMI glossary of terms.
7. Access the Phoenix Web site (www.phoenix.com) and locate the beep codes associated with the BIOS. Look for downloads and manuals.

Interesting Web Sites for More Information

www.asus.com

www.micron.com

www.giga-byte.com

www.j-mark.com

www.tekram.com

www.soyo.com

www.motherboards.org

Chapter 3
Laboratory Activity

Identifying PC BIOS and Operating Systems

After completing this laboratory activity, you will be able to:

- ❑ Identify the BIOS manufacturer and version.
- ❑ Identify the Windows operating system.
- ❑ Access and modify the BIOS CMOS settings.
- ❑ Check the browser setup and version.

Introduction

In this activity, you will learn to identify the manufacturer and version of the BIOS, Windows operating system, and browser information.

The BIOS (Basic Input/Output Operating System) translates commands given by the operating system program into actions carried out by the PC system hardware. The type of hardware that makes up the PC system must be identified before the BIOS program can carry out commands that affect the system hardware. When the hardware is identified, the BIOS program stores the data in a CMOS (Complimentary Metal-Oxide Semiconductor). The CMOS must use a small battery to retain the settings after power to the computer is turned off.

The PC's hardware is usually identified automatically though Plug and Play technology. The Plug and Play technology automatically detects the hardware and assigns settings to the CMOS data collection. For the Plug and Play technology to work, three things are required: the hardware being installed, the BIOS, and the operating system must be Plug and Play compliant. All three requirements must be met for Plug and Play technology to work properly. For example, you may attach a Plug and Play device to a PC that is using a Plug and Play operating system, such as Windows 98. However, if the BIOS is not Plug and Play, the device will need to be installed manually. You may also upgrade the BIOS to a Plug and Play BIOS.

Typically, when the PC first boots, BIOS information is flashed across the screen. For example, a message similar to the one below may appear in the upper-left quadrant of the screen.

AMIBIOS 1992 C American Megatrends, Inc.
BIOS Version 1.00.07
0032 KB memory
Press Fl to enter setup

The above information displays the BIOS manufacture and version. The amount of RAM is displayed, and then instructions are given for accessing the CMOS Setup program. The exact method of accessing the CMOS Setup program is not standard and is not always displayed on the screen. You may need to consult the PC or BIOS manufacturer through its Web site to identify the exact steps necessary to access the CMOS Setup program.

Equipment and Materials

- Typical PC with Windows 95, or later, operating system.

Procedure

1. ______ Turn on the PC and closely watch for instructions for accessing the CMOS Setup program. If the information is not displayed, you may need to ask the instructor. On a separate sheet of paper, write down the instructions for accessing the CMOS Setup program.
2. ______ After accessing the CMOS Setup program, find and record on a separate sheet of paper the answers to the questions in the following list. You will not be familiar with much of the information recorded. This is normal. The information displayed in the BIOS settings will become clear to you as you progress through the course. What is important for you to understand is the type of information contained in the BIOS settings and what can be changed. There are many different BIOS-settings programs available and not all will exactly match the information being requested below. Answer all questions to the best of your ability.

   ______ Is the system date and time displayed?

   ______ Can the system time and date be changed?

   ______ Is the BIOS version displayed?

   ______ Is the amount of extended memory displayed and if so, how much memory does the PC have?

   ______ What information can be viewed about the floppy drives?

   ______ What information about the hard drive is present?

   ______ Are there any security features present and if so, describe them.

   ______ What information about the monitor is displayed?

   ______ What are the "Boot Options"?

   ______ What information is provided about the serial ports?

   ______ Is there any information about the CPU?
3. ______ Now that you have found the listed information, make special note of how the BIOS settings program is exited. You usually must exit by choosing an option such as: **Use default settings, Save changes,** or **Do not retain changes to settings.** It is important to realize that changes are not automatically retained by the CMOS.
4. ______ If time permits, and you have instructor approval, change the system time indicated in the CMOS Setup program as well as the date. Again, make sure you have instructor approval first.

5. ______ Return the system time and date settings to the correct settings and then shut down the PC system.

Review Questions

Answer the following questions on a separate sheet of paper. Please do not write in this book.

1. How did you access the CMOS Setup program?
2. Why aren't the CMOS settings lost after the power is turned off to the PC?
3. Where is the manufacturer of the BIOS and the version displayed?
4. If instructions for accessing the CMOS Setup program are not displayed on the screen, how could you find the information needed to determine the proper keystroke sequence for accessing the CMOS Setup program?

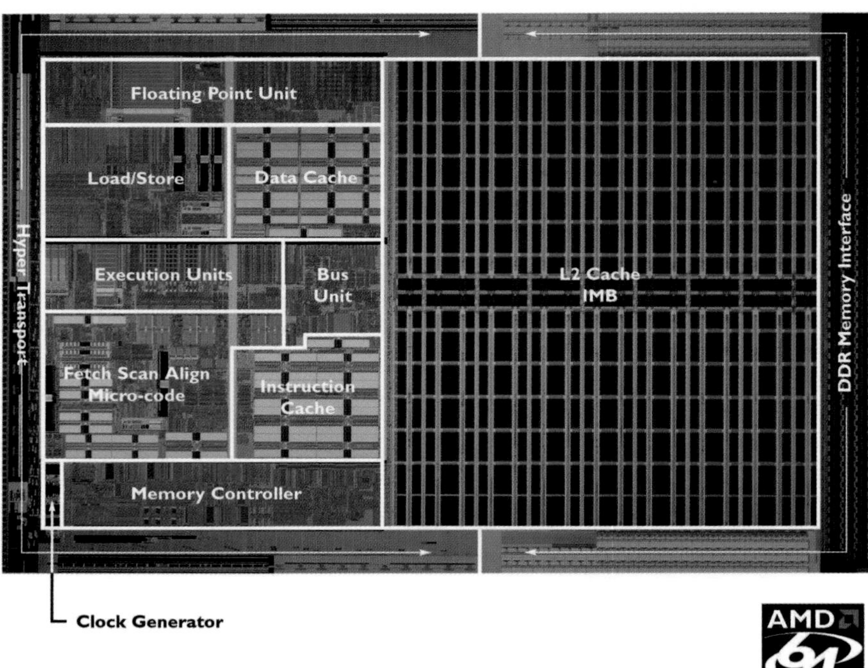

AMD Opteron™ Processor die. Note the major parts of this CPU. (Advanced Microprocessor Devices, Inc.)

4 CPU

After studying this chapter, you will be able to:

- Identify the operation, function, and purpose of the CPU.
- Differentiate between the internal and external bus system.
- Identify and explain the major portions of a CPU.
- Briefly review the evolution of the CPU.
- Identify sockets and SEC connections associated with the CPU.
- Identify and explain the purpose of a voltage regulator.
- Explain real and protected modes of operation.
- Define the terms multiple branch prediction, superscalar technology, and MMX technology as it applies to the CPU.

A+ Exam—Key Points

The CompTIA exam may ask questions concerning key developmental stages of the CPU and what socket is associated with which processor. Some examples of questions might include the following:

- When was the first L3 cache introduced?
- What socket is used for a Pentium 4 processor?
- Which processor can utilize a 400 MHz FSB?

Key Words and Terms

The following words and terms will become important pieces of your computer vocabulary. Be sure you can define them.

arithmetic logic unit (ALU)
assembly language
bus unit
cache
clock doubling
compiler
complex instruction set computer (CISC)
control unit
decode unit
Dual Independent Bus (DIB)
dynamic execution
front side bus (FSB)
instruction set
instructions
L1 cache
L2 cache
L3 cache
math coprocessor
MMX processor
multiple branch prediction
overclocking
pin grid array (PGA)
protected mode
real mode
reduced instruction set computer (RISC)
registers
register unit
Single Edge Contact (SEC)
superscalar
System Management Mode (SMM)
virtual mode
zero insertion force (ZIF) socket

CPU stands for *c*entral *p*rocessing *u*nit, and it does exactly what its name implies. It is *central* in that all other components are dependent on the CPU. See **Figure 4-1.** It is a *processor* in that it processes data. It is a *unit* in that it is very much a self-contained device that is modular in design. The CPU is replaced as an entire unit.

Instructions and Data

The CPU has been given the status of the computer's brain. It has evolved over the years from a simple chip composed of only 27,000 transistors in early

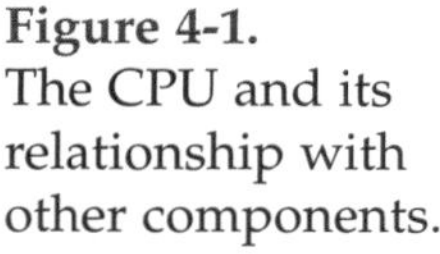

Figure 4-1.
The CPU and its relationship with other components.

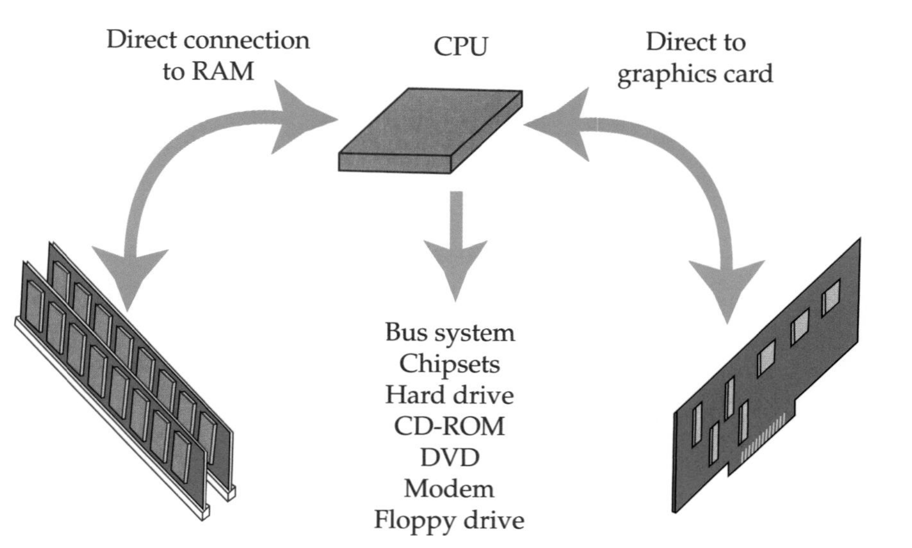

1978 to a highly sophisticated integrated chip composed of over 9 million transistors. The CPU follows commands called ***instructions*** and then processes data. The data is normally stored in RAM or introduced into the system by some device such as a keyboard, mouse, microphone, hard disk drive, or CD-ROM drive.

Every processor runs from a set of commands called the ***instruction set.*** The instruction set is the lowest language level used to program a computer. The instruction set is written in a language called ***assembly language.*** Assembly is one step above actual machine language. When code is written in a high-level language such as BASIC or C++, it must be compiled before it can run the computer as a stand-alone program or executive program. A ***compiler*** is a special program that translates the higher-level language into machine language based on the CPU's instruction set. The instruction set contains commands such as add, subtract, compare, add one to, subtract one from, get the next one, two, or four bytes from, and put the next one, two, or four bytes at.

The CPU has several registers. ***Registers*** are small pockets of memory used to temporarily store data that is being processed by the CPU. For example, when adding two numbers together, one number is stored in register A and the other number is stored in register B. The add command adds the contents of register A to the contents of register B and places the result in register C. Next, the contents can be moved from register C to a RAM address.

Assembly language programs are translated into machine language code. The program is written as a series of commands and bytes of data to be acted on byte by byte. Writing code in assembly language is painstakingly difficult. It takes an extremely long time to write even a simple program. However, it produces the fastest execution possible. Assembly translated into machine language is used when speed or compact size is a necessity. The kernel code of operating systems and BIOS programs are usually written to some degree in assembly code. Most other common programs are written for computers using a higher-level language that is then translated from the higher-level language to machine-like code. However, using a higher-level language and then compiling the code results in a larger, slower program.

The machine level programs are lengthy but appear transparent to the user because of the sheer speed at which the instructions are carried out by the computer. Programming in machine language is an entire science and only needs to be briefly explained to give you the necessary insight on how a CPU functions with data.

instructions
commands given to the processor.

instructional set
a set of basic commands that control the processor.

assembly language
a low-level language in which a CPU's instruction set is written.

compiler
a special program that translates the higher-level language into machine language based on the CPU's instruction set.

registers
small pockets of memory, within the processor, that are used to temporarily store data that is being processed by the CPU.

CPU Operation

A CPU is in a state of constant operation. When not processing commands to process data, the CPU is:

- Refreshing memory.
- Checking for communication from other devices through the system of hardwired IRQs and software IRQs.
- Monitoring system power.
- Performing any other programmed duties.

Look at **Figure 4-2** to see how a CPU performs the simple operation of addition. This series demonstrates how the registers are used to manipulate data. To add the numerical value of two numbers together, three registers are used. The

Figure 4-2.
Illustrated in this series are the steps that a CPU takes to add two numbers together.

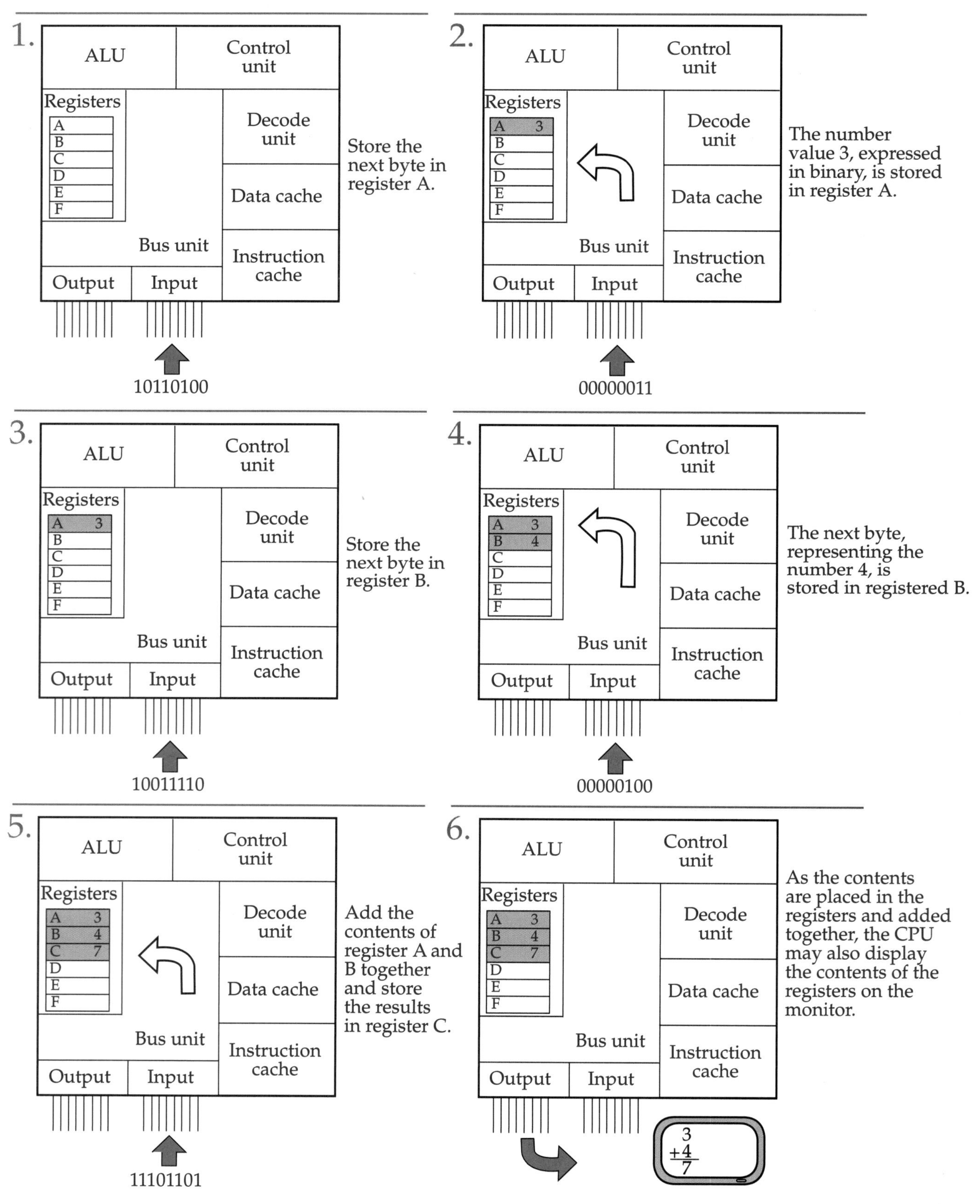

value 3 is placed in register A. The value 4 is placed in register B. Then the contents of the two registers are added together and stored in register C. While this action seems simple, there are many other activities going on at the same time that are controlled by the CPU. For example, the CPU is refreshing the RAM, checking IRQ status (checking for keyboard input, mouse input, and other such input), and displaying the contents of the registers on the monitor screen.

CPU Parts

The following is a simplified discussion of CPU operation, but it should give you some idea of how the major parts work together to perform operations on data. The ***bus unit*** connects all the other major components together, accepts data, and sends data through the input and output bus sections. There is an *instruction cache* and a *data cache.* The term ***cache*** (pronounced cash) means a small temporary memory storage area. Cache is used to separate and store incoming data and instructions.

A ***decode unit*** does what the name implies. It decodes instructions sent to the CPU. Under the direction of a control unit, it not only decodes the series of instructions and data but also sends the data on to other areas in an understandable format.

The ***control unit*** controls the overall operation of the CPU. It takes instructions from the decode unit and directs command instructions to the arithmetic logic unit and data to be manipulated to the register area. The ***arithmetic logic unit (ALU)*** performs mathematical functions on data stored in the register area. It also performs data manipulations such as comparing two pieces of data stored in the registry unit. It can do comparisons such as "equal to," "greater than," and "less than."

The ***register unit*** is composed of many separate, smaller storage units. Each register has a unique identity. In our model, each is labeled with a letter of the alphabet. The main difference between register storage and cache is that registers contain a single data element. A single data element is a number (25684) or a letter (A, a, B, b, C, etc.). The data and instruction cache can hold multiple pieces of data and commands. The ALU performs manipulations on the data stored in registers, such as adding or subtracting the contents of register A to or from the contents of register B. The ALU can also do comparisons on the contents of A or B, such as determining which is larger.

Manipulating a list of words in alphabetical order is an example of a comparison of the contents of two or more registers. Each letter is given a numeric value, processed through the CPU in pairs, and then stored in either cache or RAM in the appropriate order. The series of comparisons can consist of over a thousand repetitions. The CPU operates at such a high speed that the process appears very brief. This is the great value of the computer. A computer can perform repetitive tasks such as sorting the addresses of 2,000,000 names for a phone book in a few minutes. Performed manually, the same operation would take weeks or even months to perform. Animation on the screen of the display unit has also been made possible because of the great speed of the control unit, the ALU, and the registers. See **Figure 4-3.**

bus unit
the network of circuitry that connects all the other major components together, accepts data, and sends data through the input and output bus sections.

cache
a small temporary memory area that is used to separate and store incoming data and instructions.

decode unit
a CPU component that decodes instructions and data and transmits the data to other areas in an understandable format.

control unit
a CPU component that controls the overall operation of the CPU.

arithmetic logic unit (ALU)
a CPU component that performs mathematical functions on data stored in the register area.

register unit
a CPU component containing many separate, smaller storage units known as registers.

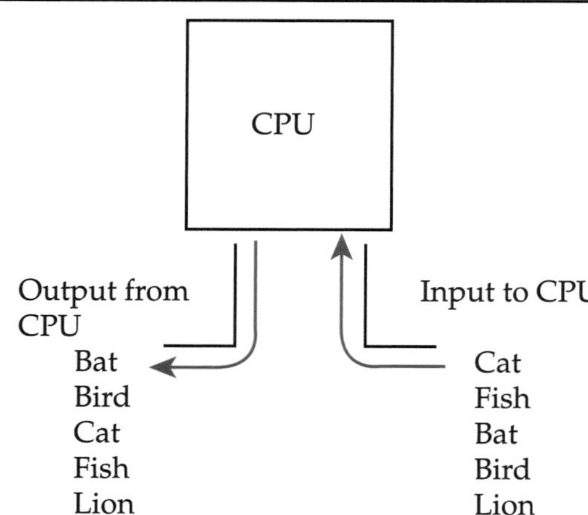

Figure 4-3. A list of words are entered into the CPU and stored in cache. The control unit sends pairs of words to the registry broken down by letter and then compares each pair until all possible combinations are exhausted.

CPU Power

Not all business conducted with a PC requires the use of a powerful CPU. A simple word processing package will work with most any CPU. However, extreme software gaming, CAD/CAM (computer-aided drafting/computer-aided manufacturing), scientific simulations and research, and large corporate financial record calculations require powerful CPUs. CPU power can be taken even further. Many of the very sophisticated operations, such as weather predictions and medical research, have requirements well beyond a PC and must turn to the use of a mainframe or a super computer.

Imagine a CAD drawing of a shopping center or mall that can be manipulated on the display unit. A person can walk through the *virtual mall* and look at the simulation as though they were actually in the mall itself. They can see the entire layout through a shopper's perspective. Or, imagine many popular game scenarios as you navigate through a maze of hallways. Animation, especially those involving three-dimensional images, is CPU intensive.

One form of animation technology requires the redrawing of every line in the image for each display change. See **Figure 4-4.** Before redrawing each line, a calculation has to be made based on the X, Y, and Z coordinates of each end of the line. The distance and angle of the new location is used as part of the algorithm. An algorithm is similar to a recipe. You simply insert the X, Y, and Z coordinates of the existing position of each line end and then input the new X, Y, and Z coordinates.

Rather than inputting the exact coordinates manually, they can be *implied* by the use of a mouse, keyboard, or game control device. To give a realistic feeling, an illustration containing hundreds or even thousands of lines must be computed in a fraction of a second and then displayed on the screen. This type of operation requires a high-speed CPU with many advanced data processing techniques.

Remember that the CPU receives a constant stream of alternating commands and data. Early CPUs required all data to be transferred through the CPU. For example, if a memo were being typed, the CPU would act on each letter in the memo. Now, modern systems allow for bus mastering and direct memory access. These additions allow repetitive actions that do not require manipulation of data to simply be passed on to memory, the screen, the printer, or data storage areas such as the hard drive.

Figure 4-4. These three illustrations show the concept behind animation technology using X, Y, and Z coordinates.

1.

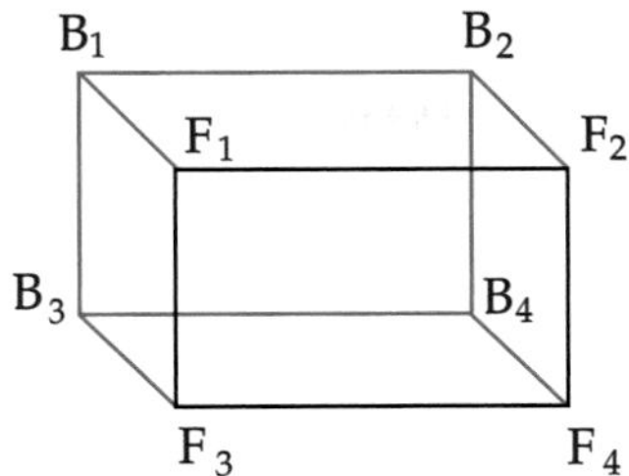

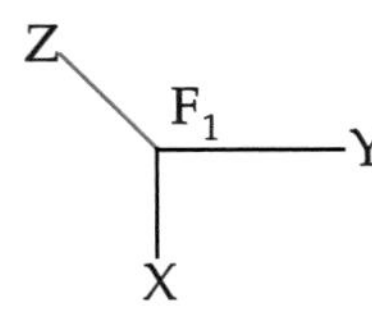

Using point F_1 as a reference, each corner of the object is calculated using trigonometric functions using the distances from F_1 based on the length of the X, Y, and Z axis.

2.

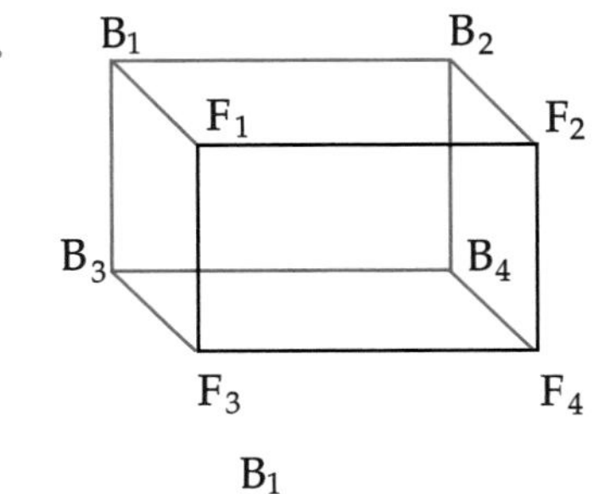

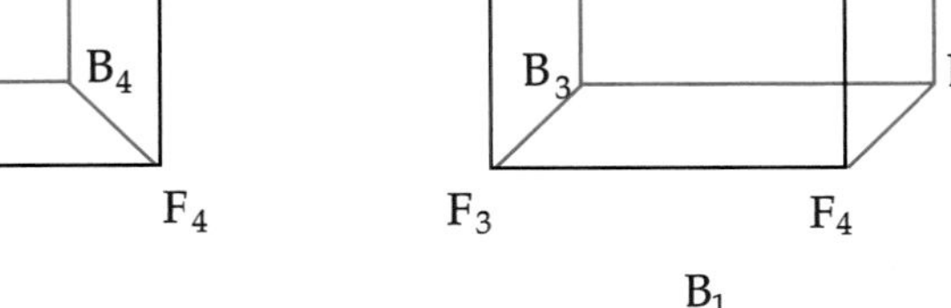

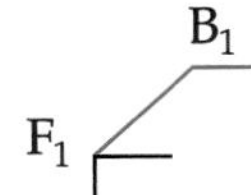

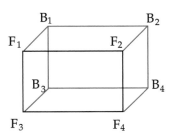

Original point B_1

New location of point B_1

Each individual point location must be calculated and then plotted.

3.

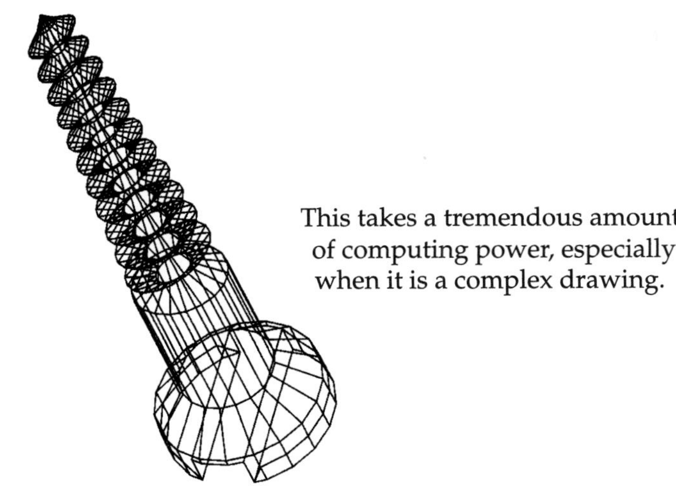

This takes a tremendous amount of computing power, especially when it is a complex drawing.

Each step of the processor requires a clock beat. The clock sends a repetitive signal to all parts of the computer system to keep all data transmissions in step with the other parts. The transmission of data throughout the PC is a combination of series and parallel transmissions and many different devices operating at different speeds. For example, the keyboard is a serial device. Keyboard data must be converted to parallel data and then be transmitted in step with the other parts of the computer.

Processor Speed

The CPU has been progressively made to operate faster and more efficiently. The modifications to data processing methods are given special names to describe their actions. Modifications to the CPU include RISC, superscalar technology, dynamic execution, and additional cache. In this next section, we will take a closer look at processor speed and these special modifications to the CPU.

Comparison of CPUs is usually based on speed and bus width. The speed is how fast the CPU can process data and commands. The bus width is how many bits can be passed simultaneously on parallel circuits, for example 8, 16, 32, and 64 bits simultaneously.

The CPU moves data and carries out commands as a series of binary numbers. The CPU or processor speed is measured in hertz (Hz), or cycles per second. With CPUs, this means the number of digital pulses in one second. A digital signal is a fluctuation of electrical energy. In digital electronics, a complete cycle is one complete sequence of the digital signal shape. Look at **Figure 4-5** to see a complete cycle of the digital signal illustrated.

The term *frequency* is used to express the number of cycles in one second. Thus, if there are 25 complete digital cycles in one second, the frequency is 25 hertz (25 Hz). A CPU that runs at 1 MHz carries out instructions and data movement at one million digital pulses per second. Bus width and speed combine to express amount of data transfer. See **Figure 4-6** for a drawing explaining the speed of a CPU.

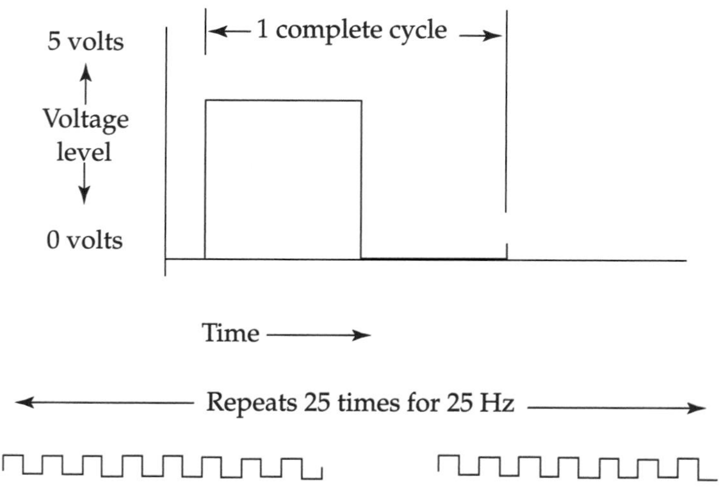

Figure 4-5. Complete cycle of a digital signal. A 5-volt digital signal rises and falls to a 5-volt level. The number of times it repeats the pattern in one second is the frequency of the signal. A 25 Hz signal repeats 25 times in one second.

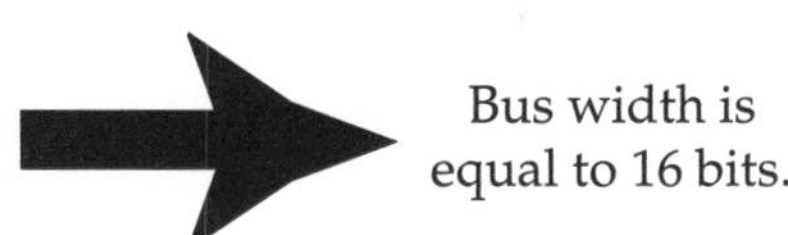
10110100101101001011010010110100
11011011110110111101101111011011
00001110000011100000111000001110
00101000001010000010100000101000
11101101111011011110110111101101
00010001000100010001000100010001
11101010111010101110101011101010
10101010101010101010101010101010
11100010111000101110001011100010
11000101110001011100010111000101
10101001101010011010100110101001
11111010111110101111101011111010
00001010000010100000101000001010
11100010111000101110001011100010
01010010010100100101001001010010
11011001110110011101100111011001
Frequency of data flow is 5 MHz.
Bus width is equal to 16 bits.
Total data is equal to the bus width multiplied by the speed of the data.
16 bits x 5 MHz = 80 Mbps
Mbps (Megabits per second)

Figure 4-6. The rate of data transfer is based on the width and speed of the bus system.

As computer systems shifted from text-based command operating systems to Graphical User Interface (GUI), speed became an extremely important factor. The intense graphics of OS/2 or Windows requires a faster computer system. Graphics functions demand a lot of processor attention.

Keep in mind that the speed of processing data is not entirely dependent on the speed of the electronics. The instruction set used to process data as well as special methods such as pipeline burst, RISC, and cache technique also influence the speed of processing data.

Enhancing CPU Operation

Processors are continually getting faster and more powerful. Each new generation of CPU can operate on shorter clock cycles. However, a CPU's abilities can be enhanced in a number of ways in addition to simply producing chips that operate at a faster MHz rate. These improvements include changes to the local bus, the addition of cache, and the addition of a math coprocessor.

Local Bus

The *local bus* is connected directly to the CPU chip. It is always the highest speed bus in the entire computer system. The local bus is the bus system connecting certain components directly to the CPU. RAM and video card slots are examples of components connected directly to the CPU to better enhance performance. The local bus is also referred to as the *system bus* or the *front side bus*. A lot of the terminology used is dependent on the manufacture of the product or even the generation of the technology. The latest series of Pentium processors use the term ***front side bus (FSB)*** when referencing what has been known as the local bus.

front side bus (FSB) another term for local bus.

The shorter the distance between the two devices, the higher the data transfer rate can be. It is not the length the data has to travel, but rather the effect of inductive reactance that causes a choking effect on the electrical impulses. As the length of the data path increases, so does the choking effect.

The only practical way to decrease this choking effect as the length of the path increases is to lower the data flow rate. Thus, the inductive reactance slows down the speed that a processor can run.

L1, L2, and L3 Cache

The processor bus speed is the highest data transfer speed in the entire computer system. To enhance the speed of data processing, a special block of RAM memory was developed and manufactured as an integral part of the processor. This feature began with the 486 processor. This special memory unit is called cache.

L1 cache
a cache contained within the processor that is designed to run at the processor's speed.

The cache in the CPU is called the ***L1 cache.*** L1 cache is designed to run at the same speed as the CPU. It is the most costly memory to produce when compared on a per byte basis. As design engineers must create a CPU and computer system that will work at a high speed while staying within a reasonable cost that the customer can afford, L1 cache is smaller on less expensive processors.

L1 cache produces faster CPU processing of data. Data can be stored temporarily in the L1 cache rather than in a RAM module. The bus speed to L1 cache is many times faster than the bus speed from the CPU to the RAM. By storing data in L1 cache, the movement of data being manipulated by the CPU is greatly increased.

L2 cache
a cache mounted outside of the processor. (Note: the Pentium III incorporates the L2 cache in the processor chip.)

L3 cache
the cache mounted on the motherboard when L1 and L2 caches are incorporated into the CPU chip.

L2 cache is separate from the processor but mounted as close as possible to the processor to keep the transfer rates high. The ***L2 cache*** is used to increase the speed of transmitting data to and from the processor to other parts of the motherboard.

L1 and L2 cache also differ in one other significant way. L1 cache is made from static RAM technology. L2 cache uses dynamic RAM technology, which is slower than the L1 cache. The terms static and dynamic memory type will become clearer when you complete Chapter 6—Memory. **Figure 4-7** shows the layout of a modern cache system.

The Pentium III incorporates both L1 and L2 cache into the CPU die. The L1 cache is divided into a data cache and an instruction cache. The L2 cache performs at a much higher rate of data transfer than previous L2 caches since it is built in to the processing unit. Earlier models simply installed the L2 cache in close proximity to the CPU. When L1 and L2 caches are incorporated into the CPU chip, the cache on the motherboard becomes ***L3 cache.***

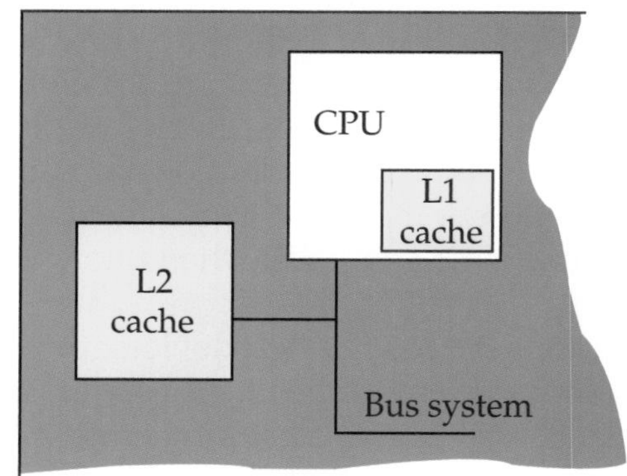

Figure 4-7.
Starting with the 486 processor, the L1 cache was incorporated into the CPU and the L2 cache was mounted on the motherboard in close proximity to the CPU.

Math Coprocessor

Early processors were limited to whole number mathematical calculations. For more advanced calculations, a second chip called the ***math coprocessor*** had to be installed on the motherboard. Math coprocessors are also called *floating-point units (FPU).*

math coprocessor
a component of the CPU that improves the processor's ability to perform advanced mathematical calculations.

Beginning with the 486 CPU, the math coprocessor was integrated into the processor chip, thus eliminating the need for a separate math coprocessor chip. Math coprocessor ability was a requirement for sophisticated graphics programs such as AutoCAD. *AutoCAD* is a computer-aided drafting software program that depends on complicated math routines such as sizing drawings, changing scales, and even changing views of the object being drawn.

Math coprocessor identification numbers are always one higher than the processor series they are designed to match. For example, a 386 processor would use a 387-math coprocessor.

Processor Descriptive Features

Processor descriptive features are a collection of terms used to explain, identify, and compare processing units.

System Management Mode

System Management Mode (SMM) was first developed for laptop computers to save electrical energy when using a battery. SMM was introduced in the 486SL processor and became a standard for all Pentium processors and later.

System Management Mode (SMM)
a standby mode developed for laptop computers in order to save electrical energy when using a battery.

The power management is controlled by software usually set up by the BIOS setup routine. Power management will put the CPU and the computer system into a state of rest or sleep and can actually shut down the complete PC system.

Clock Doubling

The processor must remain *in step* or *in synchronization* with the other electronic components mounted on the motherboard. To accomplish higher processing speeds for the CPU while maintaining a common synchronization with other components on the board, CPU clock-doubling technology was developed.

The internal speed of the processor is referred to as the clock rate. Clock rate as well as bus speed is measured in Hz. As the speed of the processor has increased, the bus on the motherboard has failed to keep up with the processor speed. ***Clock doubling*** is simply the multiplying of the speed of the motherboard bus to run the CPU. Originally, the speed was multiplied by 2, but multiples of 3, 4, and more quickly followed.

clock doubling
running the CPU at a multiple of the bus frequency.

A crystal oscillator circuit produces the digital beat of the computer system. Simply put, a crystal is sliced very thin and electrical energy is connected to it. With the proper additional circuitry, a steady repetitive digital pulse is produced. This beat is the external bus speed of the motherboard.

Using microscopic digital circuitry at the clock input of the CPU, the steady beat can be doubled, tripled, quadrupled, or more. The technique is referred to as clock "doubling" even though now it more than doubles the frequency of the internal CPU digital pulse. Look at the chart in **Figure 4-8** to see how clock doubling affects the speed of the CPU while maintaining a lower motherboard bus speed that is in sync with the CPU.

Figure 4-8.
A chart comparing the CPU internal clock rate to the motherboard bus speed and some common clock doubling speeds.

CPU	CPU speed	Clock doubling multiplier	Motherboard system bus speed
386	25 MHz	None	25 MHz
486DX	66 MHz	2	33 MHz
586	133 MHz	4	33 MHz
Pentium	100 MHz	1.5	66 MHz
Pentium	133 MHz	2	66 MHz
Pentium	200 MHz	3	66 MHz

Overclocking

Certain styles of CPU can operate at various frequencies. Sometimes CPU manufacturers substitute higher-speed processors than the computer system manufacturers order. While higher-speed processors are more expensive than lower-speed processors, the CPU manufacturers feel it is more important to be able to supply a CPU to the manufacturer when needed rather than wait until more of the requested lower-speed processors can be produced.

overclocking
forcing a processor to operate faster than its approved speed.

When computer-savvy people discovered the practice of substituting higher-speed processors in place of lower-speed processors, ***overclocking*** (sometimes called *speed margining*) was born.

Overclocking is *not* the same as clock doubling, but it is derived from the same techniques. Some motherboards are equipped with jumper settings that allow you to change the input frequency to the CPU. Consumers began to raise the input speed to the CPU to see if it would run at the higher speed. Many CPUs did, in fact, perform well.

The practice of overclocking is not supported by the manufacturing industry and voids the warranty status of the processor. When a processor runs at a higher speed than it is designed for, excessive heat develops that may damage the chip. The CPU may freeze up and come to a complete stop with or without a fatal error message. Remember that fatal error messages are issued by normally working processors that have a software or hardware problem.

RISC

reduced instruction set computer (RISC)
a type of CPU architecture that is designed with a fewer number of transistors and commands.

Reduced instruction set computer (RISC) is a type of CPU architecture that is designed with a fewer number of transistors and commands. This architecture produces a CPU that is both cheaper and faster. The trade-off is that the system software has to carry modifications to allow for fewer CPU instructions. This puts greater responsibility on the software written for them.

CISC

complex instruction set computer (CISC)
a CPU with a more complex instruction set.

Complex instruction set computer (CISC) is, as the name implies, a CPU with a more complex instruction set. The CPU die is designed to accept many machine language commands that manipulate or process complex mathematical formulas.

There is an increase in the number of transistors required to produce a CISC-based CPU. The added complexity causes an increase in clock cycles to produce the desired results. This type of system is best utilized by complex programming techniques. CISC is designed as the opposite of RISC systems.

MMX

In 1997, the ***MMX processor*** was introduced. The MMX processor was based on a standard processor with the addition of 57 commands that enhanced its abilities to support graphics technology. Many of the commands replaced functions normally carried out by the sound and video card. This allowed for faster processing of video and sound data. The L1 cache was made larger to assist in speeding the animation of frames.

MMX processor
a processor with an additional 57 commands that enhance its abilities to support multimedia technology.

The meaning behind letters *MMX* is debatable. Some claim it stands for Multi-Media eXtensions. Others claim it stands for Matrix Math eXtensions. Intel, the company that developed MMX technology, claims that MMX was not meant to be an acronym at all.

Multiple Branch Prediction

Multiple branch prediction is a technique that guesses what data element will be needed next rather than waiting for the next command to be issued. It is especially accurate in repetitive tasks and can significantly speed up CPU operations. Multiple branch prediction has proven to be over ninety percent accurate.

multiple branch prediction
a technique that predicts what data element will be needed next, rather than waiting for the next command to be issued.

Superscalar Technology

The 486 and all processors before it could only process one instruction at a time. Beginning with the Pentium, processing multiple instructions at the same time was possible. The act of processing more than one instruction at the same time is called ***superscalar*** execution.

superscalar
processing multiple instructions simultaneously.

CPUs are designed with two pipelines. Pipelines are parallel paths on which data travels to the CPU sections. This parallel path concept is what makes the CPU capable of performing two data manipulation functions at the same time. Two data words can be processed during the same clock tick. Again, the speed of the processor is now improved far beyond the limits of the clock. Superscalar technology is dependent not only on a new physical design of the processor, but also on an additional set of instructional commands to operate the twin pipelines while still maintaining backward compatibility with previous processors. All modern processors use superscalar technology.

dynamic execution
a term coined by Intel to describe the enhanced, the superscalar, and the multiple branch prediction features associated with the Pentium II processor.

Dynamic Execution

The term ***dynamic execution*** was coined by Intel to describe the enhanced superscalar and multiple branches predict features associated with the Pentium II processor. Dynamic execution is a combination of new physical features and additional instruction set commands manufactured into the processor chip. It is a technique that looks ahead at instructions coming to the processor. If an instruction can be carried out faster than the instruction preceding it, it is moved ahead of its current position and then executed.

dual independent bus (DIB)
a bus system architecture in which one bus connects to the main memory and the other connects with the L2 cache.

Dual Independent Bus

Dual Independent Bus (DIB) is a bus architecture introduced with the Pentium Pro and Pentium II. As the name implies, there are two separate or independent bus systems incorporated into the processor chip. One bus connects to the main memory and the other connects with the L2 cache. Both buses can be used simultaneously rather than singly to increase program execution speed.

Real, Protected, and Virtual Modes

real mode
an operating mode in which only the first 1MB of a system's RAM can be accessed. Also an operating mode in which the 286 or later processor emulates an 8088 or 8086 processor.

protected mode
an operating mode which supports multitasking and allows access to memory beyond the first 1MB.

virtual mode
an operational mode in which the processor can operate several real mode programs at once and access memory higher than the first 1MB.

Real mode is supported by the 286 processor and later. It is used to operate within the first 1MB of memory. In real mode, multitasking is not supported. The 286 processor acts like an 8088 or 8086 processor with the legacy limitations. In ***protected mode,*** the processor supports multitasking and accesses more than 1MB of memory. In ***virtual mode,*** the processor can operate several real mode programs at once and access memory higher than the first 1MB.

The various stages or modes are used in the Windows operating systems as a diagnostic tool. The operating system runs the processor as a simple device such as the early 8088 and 8086 processor. While in protected mode, each program is given its own section of memory and cannot access the other memory locations. This prevents one program from using another program's section of memory, causing a conflict that results in CPU crash.

Moore's Law

In 1965 Gordon Moore, cofounder of Intel, predicted that computers would double in calculating power approximately every 12 months. So far, he has been pretty close to correct. The amount of time has lengthened slightly to about 18 months.

Computers have evolved technically at a rate unsurpassed by any other technology in history. Other technologies have evolved at a snail's pace when compared to the computer. The continuing rapid development of the computer is difficult to predict, but most experts agree that this present rate will continue for some time.

CPU Voltages

CPU operation voltage has decreased over the years. The reason for decreasing the operating voltage levels is to reduce the amount of heat generated by the CPU when processing data.

Motherboards are designed in different ways to achieve different CPU voltage levels. Some boards are equipped with a set of jumpers located beside the CPU. Various voltage levels can be achieved by moving the jumper position. This is a very common method on third-party motherboards. Another method is the use of a voltage regulator. A voltage regulator is installed on the motherboard beside the CPU. The voltage regulator is easy to spot. It is usually equipped with its own small heat sink for cooling purposes. Starting with the Pentium, applied voltage from the motherboard was reduced from 5 volts to 3.5 volts.

Tech Tip:
Always read the motherboard documentation to ensure the correct jumper setting corresponds to the correct voltage level of the CPU. An incorrect jumper setting can easily damage the CPU.

Cooling the CPU

As the CPU evolved to higher data speeds, the heat generated by the processor circuits also increased. Electrical circuits generate heat in proportion to the speed of data flow. Electronic integrated circuits start to break down at approximately 160° F (71°C). To counteract the effect of heat generated by the processor, heat sinks and internal fan units became standard equipment for the CPU. See **Figure 4-9.**

A heat sink is designed to remove and dissipate heat from the CPU. Heat sinks are attached to the CPU by heat conductive paste. The paste ensures a good fit between the surface of the processor and heat sink. Without the paste, the heat sink could warp slightly, resulting in poor physical contact between the surfaces, and the CPU could heat up to a dangerous level.

Heat sinks come in various shapes and sizes. The heat sink is designed with a series of fin structures for increased surface area. The larger the surface area is, the better its ability to cool. Top end, high performance computers may incorporate a cooling system similar to the one in **Figure 4-10.** This is a liquid cooling system complete with a pump, lines, a radiator heat exchange unit, and a CPU heat exchange unit. Liquid cooling provides a superior cooling effect compared to the air exchange systems. Liquid cooling is often installed on overclocked systems. When overclocked, the CPU generates higher than normal heat levels. Fan and heat sink combination units will not normally remove the additional heat generated by an overclocked CPU.

An internal fan may be attached directly to the CPU or used in conjunction with a heat sink. Never operate a CPU without a fan if it is required. Certain motherboards are designed with a heat detection device located near or under the CPU unit. The detection device reports high temperatures experienced by the CPU due to fan or heat sink failure. The motherboard's circuitry is designed

Figure 4-9.
CPUs and some chips require cooling fans to assist in removing excessive damaging heat. High heat will damage a CPU as well as other chips. The large fan in the photograph is mounted on a Pentium 4 processor. Directly behind the large fan is a smaller fan mounted on the north bridge.

Figure 4-10.
Liquid cooling system. (Swiftech Inc.)

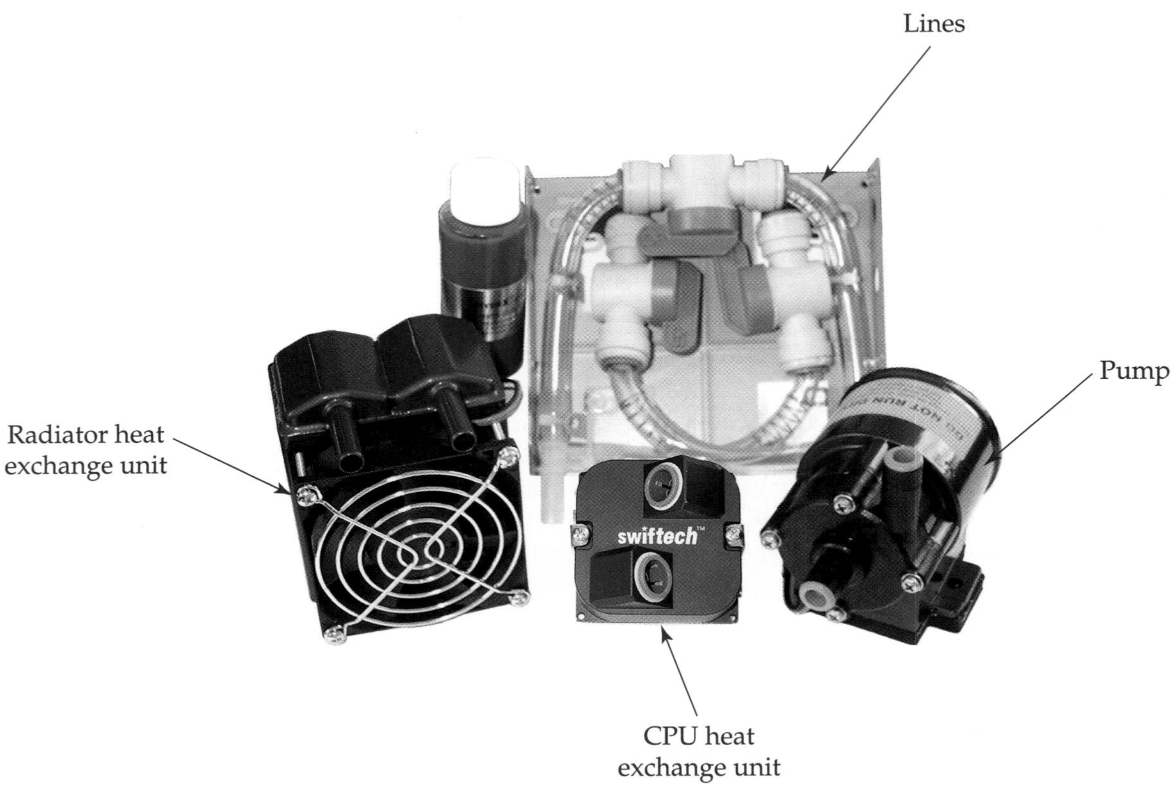

to shut down the unit if excessive heat is detected. The speed and temperature monitoring features are not supported by all motherboards or BIOS systems.

Processor Manufacturers

While there are a large number of past and present CPUs to choose from, three companies have produced most of these chips. These three competitors are Intel, AMD, and Cyrix.

Intel

Intel is the dominant force in the manufacturing of CPUs for PCs. Intel has been at the top in sales since introducing the 8086 processor to the market in the 1970s. Sales of Intel's 8088 chip were great enough to propel Intel into the Fortune 500.

Intel has continued to dominate the computer processor manufacturing market through the years. Today, Intel controls the vast majority of computer chip manufacturing. Intel not only manufactures CPUs but also chipsets, motherboards, and wireless and networking devices.

AMD

Advanced Micro Devices (AMD) has long been Intel's biggest competitor. Originally AMD manufactured math coprocessors, but when the math coprocessor began to be integrated into the CPU chip, AMD began manufacturing its own CPU.

AMD began its series with the 486 and designed its processor to be compatible with the Intel series. Both Intel and AMD manufacture excellent CPUs.

Tech Tip:
You must be careful when upgrading a PC. For example, the AMD Slot A is physically compatible with the Intel Slot 1 design. However, the two processors are not compatible by electrical connection. The data lines, as well as the control lines are not in the same position. You must also check if the BIOS and the motherboard chipset support the processor. Most of the information needed to determine the processor upgrade can be obtained from the motherboard manufacturer's Web site. Always check before attempting to perform an upgrade.

VIA Cyrix

Cyrix is a CPU manufacturer that was acquired by VIA Technologies. While the Cyrix CPU does not command a large portion of the desktop industry, it is a quality product at a reasonable price, especially for lower cost models.

Processor Evolution

Familiarity with the CPU evolution will assist you on the A+ Certification exams as well as give you some insight into the future development of the processor. There may be several questions on an exam asking you to identify which processor first implemented a specific feature. The following brief outline should help prepare you for such questions.

In the past, numbers such as 286, 386, 486 always identified CPUs. It was easy to identify the latest technology (and to predict the name of the next processor). Intel tried to protect their processor by trying to trademark the processor number. The courts ruled against them saying that a company cannot trademark a number. Consequently, Intel changed their practice by naming their processor line with a non-numerical nomenclature. Thus started the Pentium, Pentium Pro, Celeron, and so on. This change in practice has made it much more difficult to identify where any particular processor belongs in the evolution of processors.

8086

The first PC introduced by IBM contained an Intel 8086 processor chip. The processor ran at 4.77 MHz and contained a 16-bit internal bus and was capable of a 16-bit external bus. Standard small computer systems used an 8-bit bus structure for the motherboards. At the time, making a 16-bit motherboard for the 8086 seemed like an expensive waste. This is an important point to note about the development of the PC. Simply making a more advanced processor doesn't necessarily mean the rest of the computer industry will follow suit. Developing a more sophisticated computer chip also requires more sophisticated software and support hardware. A CPU that can transmit data using a 16-, 32-, or 64-bit bus width cannot be effective without other hardware and software capable of handling that same improved bus width. The 8086 was re-engineered to accommodate the 8-bit external bus and was re-released in 1979.

8088

Next in the line of development was the 8088, which was released in 1979. It was a 16-bit internal CPU that had an 8-bit external bus. The speed of the CPU was 5 and 8 MHz. The 8088 is famous because it was the chip used in the original IBM PC.

80286

The 80286 (or 286) was released in 1982. It also had a 16-bit internal bus width, but the speed of the processor was significantly increased to 12 MHz. The 80286 introduced a significant advancement in computer industry known as protected mode. *Protected mode,* as mentioned earlier in this chapter, is the capability to assign specific areas of the computer memory to specific software programs. Each program is provided protection from interference from the other program. Look at **Figure 4-11.**

In real mode, only one computer software program could be loaded into memory at one time. To load a second program, the first had to be unloaded from memory. An interesting point to note with the 80286 is that it could change from real mode to protected mode but not return to real mode. To return to real mode from protected mode, the computer had to be re-booted. The 80286 could address up to 16MB of memory.

80386DX

The 80386DX processor was given the DX suffix to separate it from other 386 models such as the SX and SL. The 80386 was released in 1985. It made vast improvements over the 80286. The 80386 could address up to 4GB of memory, had a 32-bit bus width, and could boast a processor speed up to 33 MHz. The processor could also support multitasking.

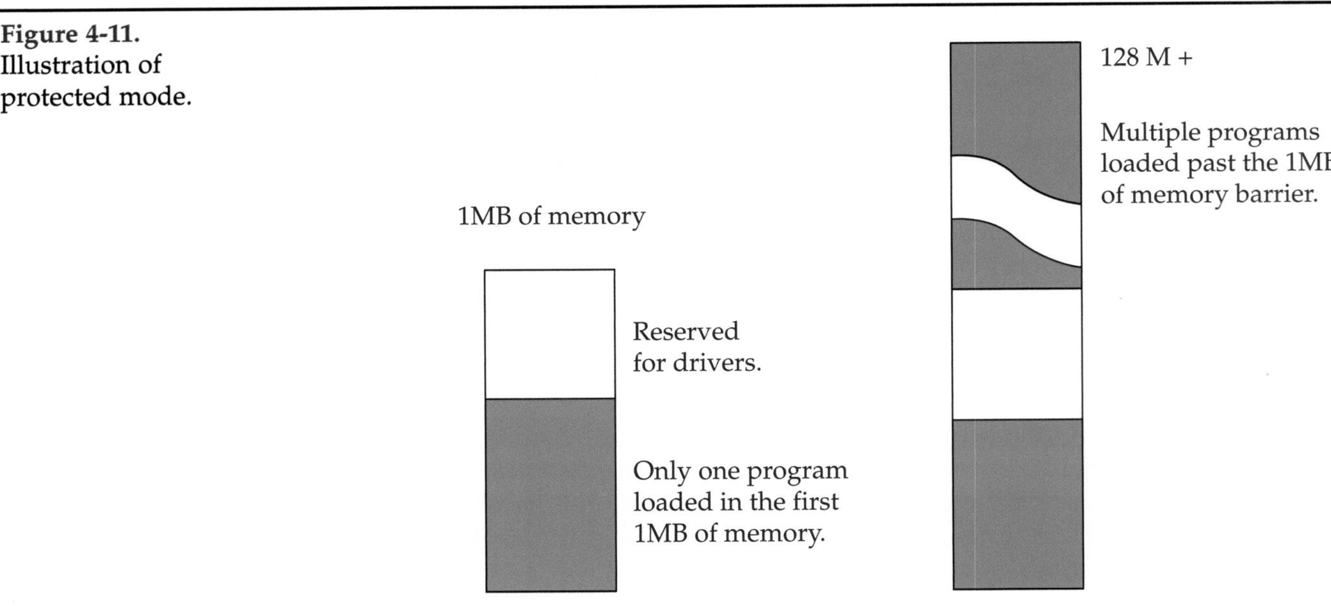
128 M +
Multiple programs loaded past the 1MB of memory barrier.
1MB of memory
Reserved for drivers.
Only one program loaded in the first 1MB of memory.
Real Mode
Protected Mode

Figure 4-11. Illustration of protected mode.

Tech Tip:
Names of processors are often reduced to their last three digits. For example, an 80386 is usually referred to as simply a 386 processor.

80386SX

The 386SX model was introduced in 1988 with features similar to the 80386DX. The SX model of the 386 was designed as a cheaper version of CPU for lower end users. It could only address a 16-bit external bus, a step back from the DX model, which could address a 32-bit external bus.

80386SL

The 386SL was introduced in 1990. It was developed with power management in mind to be used for the laptop industry. It is important to remember that portable (laptop and notebook) computers have such a restricted space to mount components in that they usually have problems performing adequate cooling. For this reason, they are usually less optimized than their full desktop or tower counterparts.

80486DX

The 486DX was introduced in 1989 and runs at speeds of 25, 33, and 50 MHz. It utilizes a built-in L1 memory cache and incorporates the math coprocessor into the CPU. This model also uses pipeline techniques.

80486SX

The 486SX model was introduced in 1991 as an inexpensive 486 model. It lacks the built-in math coprocessor and has a maximum speed of 33 MHz.

80486SL

The 486SL was introduced in 1992 with power management features.

80486DX2

The 486DX2 was also introduced in 1992. Its major feature was a clock doubler to speed up the internal speed of the CPU.

80486DX4

The 486DX4 was introduced in 1994. Its major feature was the internal clock rate tripled in the CPU. The typical processor clock rates are 75 and 100 MHz.

Pentium

Introduced in 1993, the Pentium ran with a maximum clock rate of 200 MHz. The bus width was raised to 64-bit. It was classified as CISC architecture, and it is designed with many RISC features such as pipelining and superscaling.

Pentium Overdrive

The Pentium Overdrive was introduced in 1995 with a maximum clock rate of 100 MHz. It was designed as an upgrade for the 486-based computer and was equipped with an overdrive socket mounted on the motherboard.

Pentium Pro

The Pentium Pro was introduced in 1995 with a maximum clock rate of 200 MHz.

Pentium with MMX

Introduced in 1997, the Pentium with MMX operates with a maximum clock rate of 233 MHz. The chip was designed for multimedia applications.

MMX OverDrive

The MMX OverDrive was introduced in 1997 and operates at a maximum clock rate of 200 MHz. It was designed as an upgrade for the Pentium processor.

Pentium II

Introduced in 1997, the Pentium II operates with a maximum clock rate of 450 MHz. It was the first design with the Single Edge Contact (SEC) processor package.

Pentium III

The Pentium III was introduced in 1999 and continued to be reintroduced in variations through 2000. There are 70 new instructions added to its machine language command set to increase its ability to manipulate graphics, video, audio, and speech recognition abilities. Its maximum processing speed is approximately 1 GHz. It has over 28 million transistors and can address 64GB of memory. The CPU core voltage is 1.5 volts.

AMD Duron

The AMD Duron is available in speeds of 800, 850, and 900 MHz. It supports a 200 MHz front side bus. It parallels the Pentium III classes of processors.

VIA Cyrix III

The VIA Cyrix III is built from a 0.18 micron manufacturing technology and is installed in a typical Socket 370 motherboard interface. The CPU is designed for 500 MHz to 700 MHz speeds. It has a 128KB L1 cache and a 100/133 MHz front side bus. It is completely compatible with any X86 technology. (X86 technology refers to general PC technology based on the sequence of development such as the 8086, 80286, and 80386.)

AMD Athlon

The AMD Athlon processor is available in a wide range of speeds from 900 MHz to 1.4 GHz and has front side bus speeds of 200 and 266 MHz. The Athlon is designed for advanced multimedia applications. It parallels the Pentium 4 class of processors.

Pentium 4

The Pentium 4 processor was introduced in November of 2000. Versions of this processor have surpassed 2 GHz. The Pentium 4 is commonly found in speeds of 1.3 GHz, 1.4 GHz, 1.5 GHz, and 1.7 GHz.

The Pentium 4 is a 32-bit processor that can interface with the motherboard using a 400 MHz front side bus. There are 144 new programming instructions added to the processor to improve video, audio, and three-dimensional (3D) applications.

The typical design of the Pentium 4 is to be used with a motherboard that can handle the 400 MHz front side bus to access RDRAM, an extremely fast type of RAM. The motherboard must also be equipped with the 850 chipset or better to perform at 3.2GB data transfer speeds.

Celeron

The Intel Celeron processor was developed as a low cost desktop processor. There are four models of Celeron. Each carries the name of one of the four Pentium models. For example, there is Pentium Celeron, Pentium II Celeron, Pentium III Celeron, and Pentium IV Celeron. The main difference in the Celeron models is they do not carry a large cache. Smaller cache is cheaper to produce, which results in a low cost CPU with the Pentium name. Without the larger cache, the processor has a lower data processing throughput speed, or overall lower performance. Advertisements for low cost desktop computers often boast of having a Pentium or a Pentium 4 processor inside but fail to fully identify the processor as a Celeron. The Celeron is only mentioned in the fine print or in the model specifications. The average consumer purchases the desktop unaware of the lower performance.

Pentium Xeon

The Pentium Xeon processor was designed for high-end applications such as network servers and for communication between multiple CPUs installed on the same server. The processor has a front side bus that operates at 533 MHz and a speed that ranges from 1.8 GHz to 3 GHz. The Pentium Xeon uses a socket 603 and has L3 cache (an L1 cache range of 8KB to 12KB and an L2 cache range of 512KB to 2MB).

Xeon MP

The Xeon MP is designed for server applications. It has a core frequency range from 1.4 GHz to 2.8 GHz and supports a front side bus of 400 MHz. The Xeon MP mounts into a socket 603. The processor contains an L1 cache of 20KB, an L3 cache of 256KB, and an additional L3 1MB cache located on the motherboard. The three-cache system produces a very high data throughput, out performing any processor with similar core frequency.

Itanium

Intel designed two Itanium processors, Itanium1 and Itanium2. The Intel Itanium 2 processor is a high-end CPU designed for large enterprise servers and technical applications requiring a high degree of processing power.

The Itanium incorporates three levels of cache, L1, L2, and L3. The L3 motherboard cache size ranges from 3MB to 6MB. The L2 is 256KB, and the on-chip L1 cache is 32KB. It uses a 400 MHz bus.

Intel designed a plastic rail to help support the Itanium processor when mounted on the 478 socket. The 478 socket was first introduced with the Pentium 4. The plastic mounting rail surrounds the socket and is designed to ensure that the cooling mechanism makes perfect contact with the processor surface. The processor surface must be in proper alignment with and fit snugly to the heat dissipation mechanism. Without proper alignment with the processor surface, the processor would fail to transfer excessive heat to the cooling assembly. The CPU would heat in a short period of time, causing a system failure.

Athlon MP

The Athlon MP processor is designed primarily for server applications and mounts to the motherboard via a socket A. Its CPU internal clock speed range is 1.8 GHz to 2.2 GHz. The L1 cache is 128KB and L2 cache 512KB. It supports a 266 MHz front side bus. Do not confuse the AMD Athlon MP with the Intel Xeon MP.

AMD Duron

The AMD Duron was designed as a low-end desktop processor to compete with the low cost Intel Celeron. The L2 cache is only a modest 64KB. The reduced size of the L2 cache lowers the overall throughput and reduces the costs of the processor. The front side bus is available in the 100 MHz and 200 MHz range, which also reduces the overall cost of the CPU. The Duron installs into a Socket 462, or a Socket A.

Athlon XP

The Athlon XP can be found in servers, high-end workstations, and normal desktop computer systems. Athlon XP has 128KB L1 and 512KB L2 cache integrated into the CPU. An additional cache on the motherboard is referred to as L3 and ranges in size according to the motherboard manufacturer. The CPU operates at 1700 GHz to 3200 GHz with a front side bus speed of 333 MHz to 400 MHz. The XP installs into a Socket 462, or a Socket A.

AMD Opteron

The AMD Opteron is a high-end processor designed and developed for network servers. The Opteron eliminated the 4GB memory address barrier associated with earlier processors. The 4GB memory access limitation is a trait of the 32-bit design, but the Opteron uses a 64-bit memory address design, allowing for greater memory capacity. Total possible accessible memory is 256 TB, but that number is impractical for now. The typical core processor speeds range from 800 GHz to 2600 GHz, but the processor can produce a throughput of 19GB or more by using multiple paths to process data. The 64 KB L1 cache and the 1024 KB (1 MB) L2 cache are both integrated into the CPU chip. The Opteron mounts into a Socket 940 micro PGA.

AMD Athlon 64

The AMD Athlon 64 is an extremely powerful desktop CPU. As the name implies, it uses 32 and 64-bit processing technology. L1 and L2 cache are integrated into the CPU chip, and an L3 cache is mounted on the motherboard. The Athlon 64 is designed to mount in a 940-pin socket. Normally the increased number of pins would increase the overall dimensions of the CPU socket. The

Athlon 64 CPU, however, uses the Socket 940 m (micro) PGA. The micro PGA reduces the socket pin grid array area, reducing the overall size of the CPU socket even with an increase in the number of pins.

Tech Tip:
Servers and high-end workstations generally use the Athlon XP, the Athlon MP, and the Athlon Opteron. Desktop systems generally use the Athlon Duron, the Athlon XP, and the Athlon 64. High performance processors typically require large heat sinks, and cooling fans. For this reason, portable PCs (Laptop, PDA, and notebooks) must use slower performing processors.

The charts in **Figure 4-12** show a selection of characteristics for some common Intel and AMD processors. To see more information about various CPUs, visit www.geek.com/procspec/procspec.htm. This Web site has an in-depth amount of information on Intel, AMD, Sun, Alpha, VIA, and HP CPUs.

Socket and Slot Styles

The CPU is physically packaged in two main styles, a socket design and a Single Edged Contact (SEC) cartridge. **Figure 4-13** and **Figure 4-14** show various socket designs and the SEC cartridge. The type and size of CPU sockets have evolved over the years. The pattern of pins is referred to as the ***pin grid array (PGA).***

pin grid array (PGA) the pattern of pins on a CPU.

Intel Processor Chart
Desktop Models

Name	Bits	Clock speed	Bus speed	Socket/Slot	L1 cache	L2 cache
Pentium	32	166–233 MHz	66 MHz	Socket 7	32KB	512KB on motherboard
Pentium II	32	233–300 MHz	66–100 MHz	Slot 1	32KB	512KB on cartridge
Pentium III	32	450 MHz–1 GHz	100–133 MHz	Slot 1 or Socket 370	32–64KB	256–512KB on chip
Pentium 4	32	1.7 GHz–3.0 GHz	400–533 MHz	Socket 478	20KB	256KB on chip
Itanium 1	64	800 MHz	266 MHz	Socket 478	32KB	96KB–4MB on chip
Itanium 2	128	1.3–1.56 GHz	400 MHz	Socket 478	32KB	256–6MB on chip
Xeon	32	1.8–3 GHz	400–533 MHz	Socket 603	8–12KB	512–2MB on chip
Xeon MP	32	1.4–2.8 GHz	400 MHz	Socket 603	20KB	256KB on chip

A

(continued)

Figure 4-12. Charts showing the alignment of different processors and the generation to which they belong. These charts show the Intel and AMD lines of processors.

Figure 4-12
(continued).

AMD Processor Chart
Desktop Models

Name	Bits	Clock speed	Bus speed	Socket/Slot	L1 cache	L2 cache
K6	32	166–300 MHz	60–66MHz	Super 7	64KB	512KB on motherboard
K6-2	32	266–550 MHz	66 and 100MHz	Super 7	64KB	512KB on motherboard
K6-III	32	400–450MHz	100MHz	Super 7	64KB	256KB on chip
K7 Athlon	32	500MHz–1.2GHz	200MHz	Slot A	128KB	512KB on cartridge
Duron	32	600–1.3GHz	100–200MHz	Socket 462/ socket A	64–128KB	64KB
Athlon XP	32–64	1.7–3.2GHz	333–400MHz	Socket 462/ socket A	128KB	512KB on chip
Athlon 64	32–64	800–1.6GHz	333MHz	Socket 754	128KB	245–1MB on chip
Operton	32–64	800–2.6GHz	333–666MHz	Socket 940	128KB on chip	1MB on chip
Athlon MP	32	2.13–2.8GHz	133–266MHz	Socket A	128KB	512KB on chip

Note: On some models, when L1 and L2 cache are manufactured on the chip, an L3 cache exists on the motherboard.
Note: Socket A is designed for AMD Athlon and Duron processors. Socket A is synonymous with socket 462.

B

zero insertion force (ZIF) socket
a processor socket equipped with a lever to assist in the installation of the processor chip.

Single Edge Contact (SEC)
a processor configuration in which the CPU is mounted on a circuit board and the edge of the circuit board inserts into the motherboard socket.

A ***zero insertion force (ZIF) socket*** is designed with a lever to assist in the installation of the CPU chip. The original socket design required many pounds of force to insert the CPU pins into the CPU socket. Many times this resulted in damage to the pins and even damage to the motherboard. To alleviate the use of severe force, the ZIF socket was designed. It requires practically no force at all to insert the CPU chip into the socket while the lever arm is raised. Once the CPU is inserted into the socket, the lever is lowered, which in turn causes each pin to fit tightly into the socket. The ZIF socket literally clamps each pin into place.

As the system bus is expanded and more instructional code features are added, more connections to the CPU are required. The socket system has also evolved, increasing the number of pins. One design, which started with the Pentium II, was the ***Single Edge Contact (SEC).*** It is similar in design to an adapter card. The CPU is mounted on a circuit board, and the edge of the circuit board inserts into the motherboard socket. The SEC cartridge-type processor also incorporates a heat sink and fan as part of the complete assembly. Examine Figure 4-14.

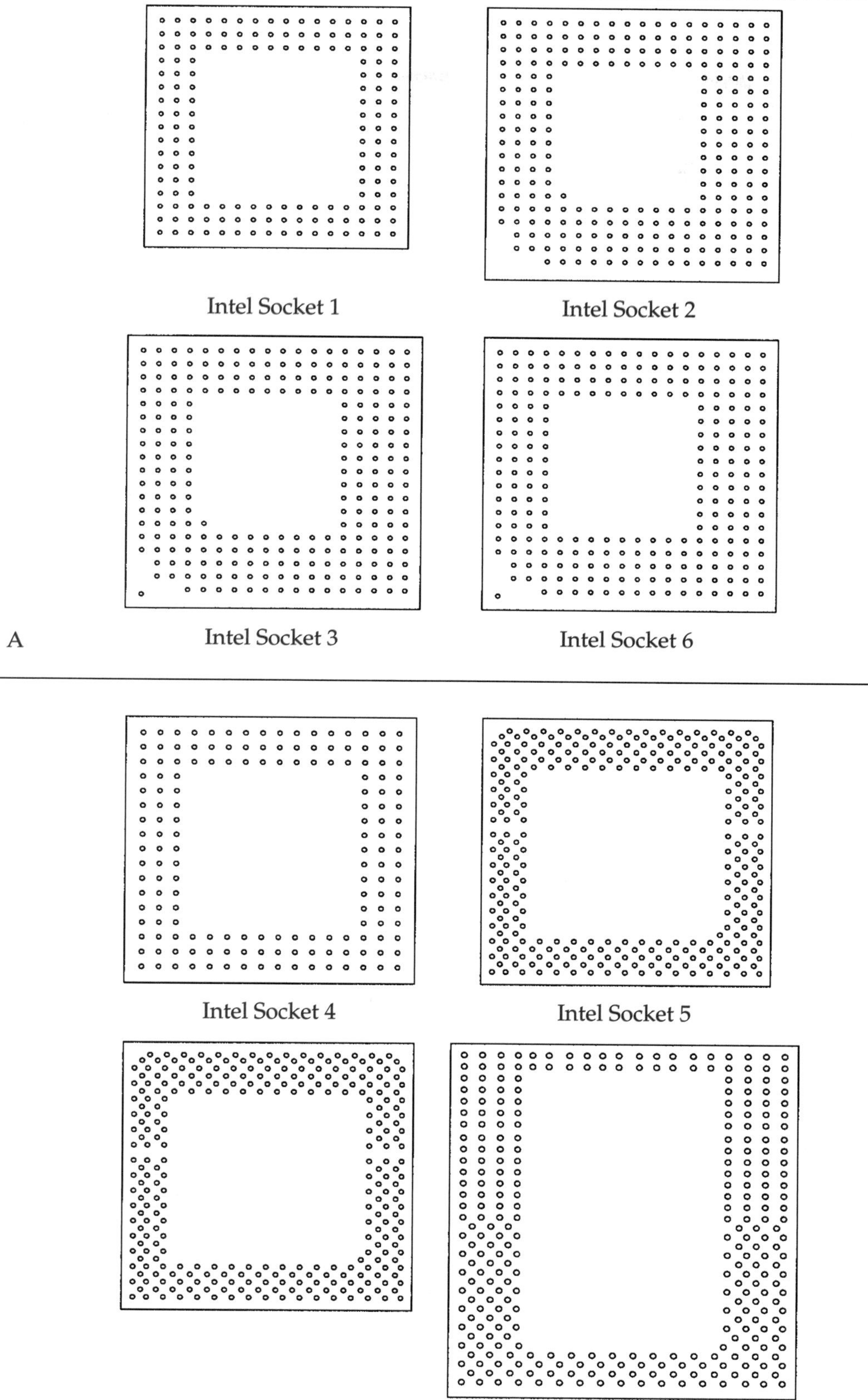

Figure 4-13. Illustration of various socket designs. A—Socket designs used for 486 processors. B—Socket designs used for the Pentium and Pentium Pro processors. C—Socket designs used for the PIII, P4, Xeon, and Itanium processors. D—Socket designs used for the Athlon, Duron, and Opteron processors.

(continued)

Figure 4-13
(continued).

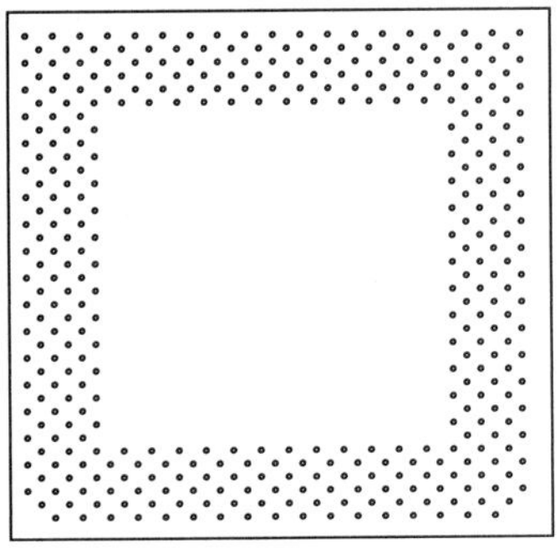

Intel Socket 370

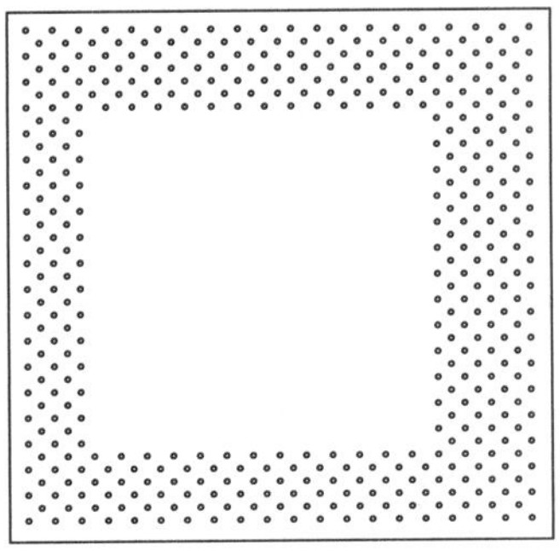

Intel Socket 423

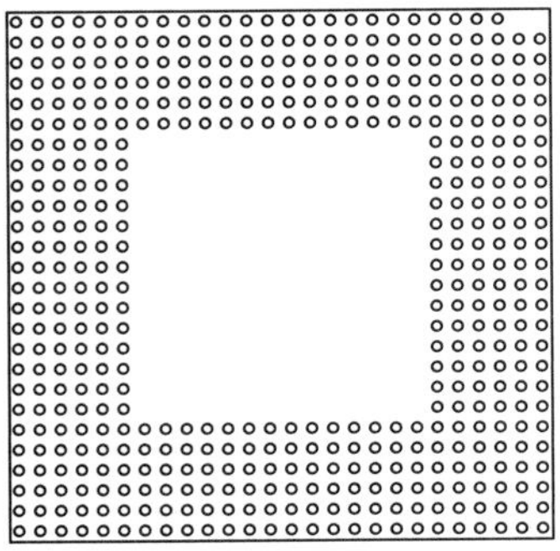

C

Intel Socket 478B

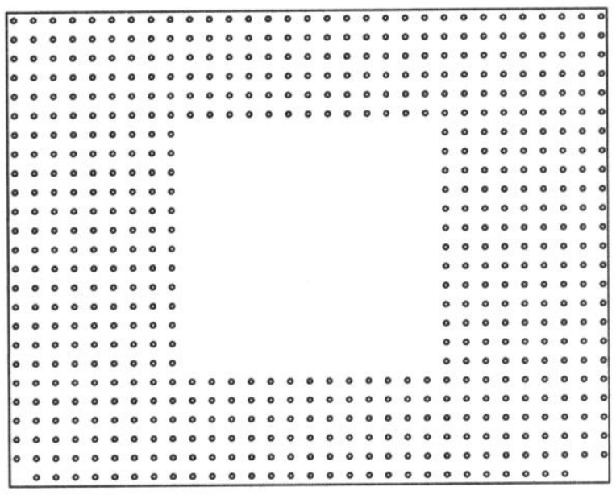

Intel Socket 603

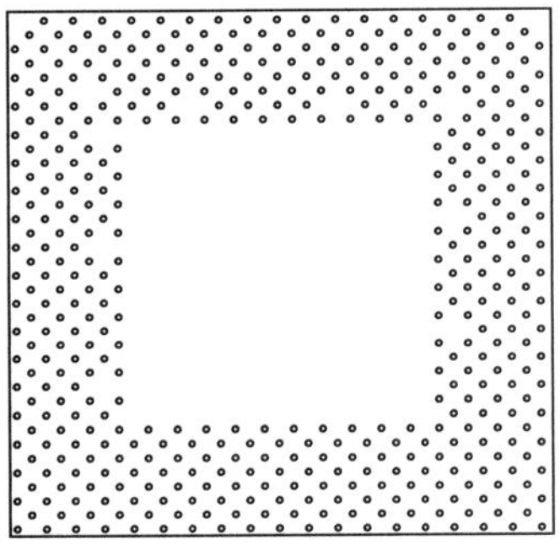

AMD Socket 462

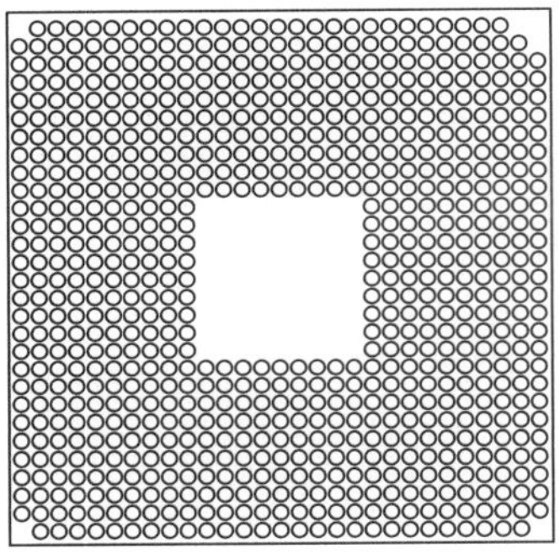

AMD Socket 754

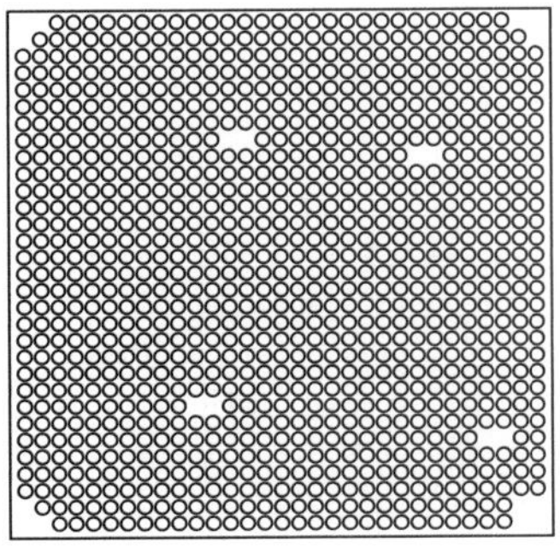

D

AMD Socket 940

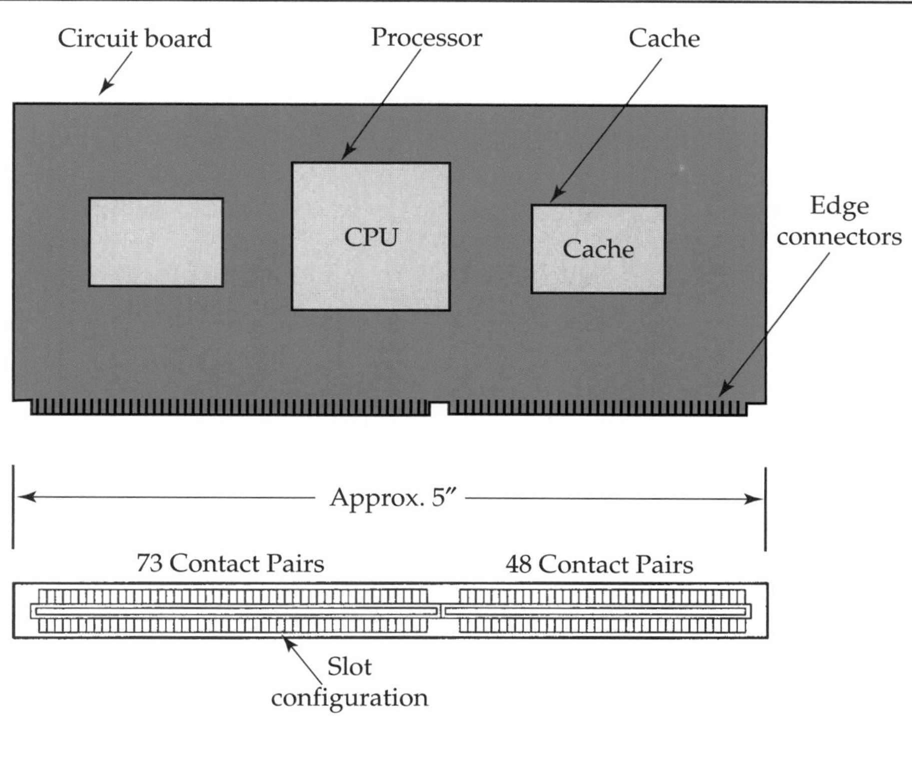

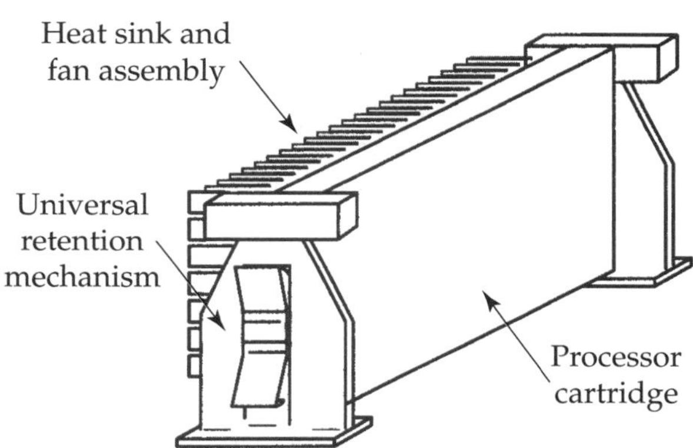

Figure 4-14. Detailed assembly of Pentium II or III SEC cartridge-type processors. The processor is mounted on a circuit board and then enclosed in a cartridge package. A fan and heat sink assembly is added for cooling. The cartridge and heat sink assembly is attached to a universal retention mechanism for weight support.

Both Intel and AMD have SEC cartridge-type possessors. Intel's SEC cartridge-type processors are inserted into a Slot 1 socket, and AMD's SEC cartridge-type processors are inserted into a Slot A socket. Both sockets look similar; however, they are electrically different. *Never* insert a processor designed for a Slot A socket into a Slot 1 socket or a processor designed for a Slot 1 socket into a Slot A socket.

Tech Tip:
Remember that Slot A is used for AMD processors and Slot 1 is used for Intel processors. A good memory aid is to associate the uppercase "A" in Slot A with the "A" in AMD. Since the "1" in Slot 1 looks similar to an uppercase "I", you can associate the number "1" with the letter "I" in Intel.

Questions to Ask before Upgrading a CPU

The process of upgrading the CPU can range from easy to nearly impossible. An important point is to be aware of the physical arrangement of the processor case before upgrading the CPU. The motherboard must be compatible with the physical style of the CPU package. The degree of likelihood for a logical upgrade is based on several computer system conditions. Questions you should first answer include:

- What are you trying to achieve by upgrading the CPU?
- Is the upgrade processor compatible physically with the motherboard socket or slot?
- Will the chipset and BIOS support the upgraded processor?
- Does the motherboard bus speed, rather than the CPU speed, limit the increase in speed you desire?

Transferring data to and from the hard drive or a scanner is mostly an issue involving the motherboard bus speed and port speeds and not the speed of the CPU. If an increase in the speed of downloading information from the Internet is the challenge, a new processor is not likely to increase the download speed. Download speed is more dependent on the cabling system between the downloading site and the computer and the modem speed. If typing is the main function performed at the computer, upgrading the CPU will have little to no effect on the user's typing speed.

As you can see, upgrading a processor may not meet your desires. If you crunch a lot of data or play games that contain intensive graphics and sound, you may very well improve the performance of the computer system by upgrading the CPU. Often, it is more practical to replace the CPU and the motherboard to achieve the desired results.

Summary

- The CPU is constantly evolving with manufacturers' attempts to improve processing power.
- Both L1 and L2 cache are small areas of memory close to the processor. L1 is usually incorporated into the integrated circuit of the processor.
- When L1 and L2 cache are incorporated into the CPU, the cache off the CPU chip is referred to as L3 cache.
- Math coprocessors became integrated into the CPU chip beginning with the 486.
- Clock doubling is how the internal parts of the CPU keep in step with the motherboard bus system while allowing the CPU to operate at a higher speed.
- Overclocking is running a CPU faster than the speed it is rated for.
- RISC is used to produce a less costly CPU.
- MMX technology was developed mainly for multimedia applications.
- The speed of the processor is increased not only by clock speed but also by data processing techniques such as superscalar technology, multiple branch prediction, and MMX.
- Superscalar technology is the ability of the CPU to carry out more than one instruction during a single clock beat.

- Real mode is when a CPU is running under the standard DOS restrictions such as only 1MB of memory and no multitasking.
- Protected mode is running the CPU with multitasking capabilities.
- Moore's law states that the calculating power of the CPU doubles every 12 months. In reality, it is actually approximately every 18 months.
- To combat the heating problem associated with the higher CPU speeds, heat sinks and internal fans became part of the CPU assembly. The voltage required to operate the CPU has also been reduced from 5 volts to 3.5 volts or lower.

Review Questions

Answer the following questions on a separate sheet of paper. Please do not write in this book.

1. What three methods or devices are used to cool the CPU?
2. What is cache?
3. Which processor first introduced L1 cache?
4. Which processor was specifically designed for improved video animation?
5. What three methods are used to combat the CPU heat problem?
6. What does the term *superscalar* mean?
7. When did superscalar begin?
8. What is System Management Mode?
9. What does the arithmetic logic unit do?
10. What is a math coprocessor?
11. What is a ZIF socket?
12. Where is L3 cache located?
13. What does the term *clock doubling* mean?
14. What does overclocking mean?
15. What is a dual independent bus, and when was it introduced?
16. Which processor first integrated the math coprocessor into the CPU chip?
17. State Moore's law.
18. What is protected mode?
19. What is real mode?
20. How many more instructional commands were added to the instruction set of a CPU with MMX technology?
21. What socket is used for an AMD Athlon 64 processor?
22. Which socket is used for an Athlon processor, a Slot A or a Slot 1?
23. Which AMD processor is most similar to the Intel Celeron?
24. Which Athlon processor contains the largest L2 cache?
25. What type of socket is used for the Pentium 4?

Sample A+ Exam Questions

Answer the following questions on a separate sheet of paper. Please do not write in this book.

1. Which of the following are true statements concerning the L1 cache? Choose all that apply.
   a. It is generally incorporated into the CPU.
   b. It generally transfers data faster than external cache.
   c. It is usually much larger in storage size than motherboard RAM.
   d. It is a form of temporary memory storage.
2. A CPU register is best described as what?
   a. A cache memory used to store hardware information
   b. A temporary memory storage unit
   c. The CPU clock signal generator
   d. The trademark associated with the brand of CPU
3. Which statement best describes the location of the front side bus?
   a. The FSB connects directly to the USB port.
   b. The FSB connects directly to the CPU.
   c. The FSB connects directly to the backside bus.
   d. The FSB connects directly to the HDD interface connector.
4. Which is the best definition of the term *superscalar*?
   a. A CPU die that is unusually physically large in cross-sectional area
   b. A CPU specially designed with a set of instructions to scale AutoCAD drawings
   c. A CPU design that supports the processing of more than one instruction at the same time
   d. A CPU design that automatically overclocks the processor speed
5. Which mode allows the CPU to access more than 1MB of RAM?
   a. Real mode
   b. Protected mode
   c. RISC mode
   d. Safe mode
6. When upgrading a CPU, which three items below should be given consideration?
   a. BIOS version
   b. CPU socket/slot type
   c. Size of the RAM
   d. Motherboard chipset

7. The acronym SEC represents what?
   a. System energy control
   b. Secret encryption code
   c. Single edge contact
   d. Solid edge connector
8. Which technology was developed for multimedia applications?
   a. RISC
   b. PGA
   c. MMX
   d. SMM
9. Which factors directly affect the speed of data manipulation by the CPU? Choose two.
   a. Clock frequency
   b. Bus width
   c. Voltage level
   d. System temperature
10. When replacing or upgrading the CPU, you should always do what?
   a. Leave the fan assembly off and run the system for a while to be sure the new CPU is operating correctly.
   b. Move the jumpers on the motherboard to test for the highest overclocking speed that the CPU can safely handle.
   c. Check the manufacturer's Web site for the latest upgrade or replacement information.
   d. Replace the BIOS as a matter of routine practice.

Suggested Laboratory Activities

Do not attempt any suggested laboratory activities without your instructor's permission. Certain activities can render the PC operating system inoperable.

1. Go to the AMD Web site and access the instructions for installing/replacing an AMD processor, such as the K6.
2. Get to the Intel Web site and access the instructions for installing/replacing Pentium III and Pentium 4 processors.
3. Select a PC in the lab, visit the manufacturer's Web site, and locate step-by-step procedures for replacing the CPU.
4. Go on the Internet and download a shareware utility to measure CPU performance.
5. Visit the Intel Web site and AMD Web site and research the latest CPU technologies.

Interesting Web Sites for More Information

www.amd.com
www.ibm.com
www.idt.com
www.intel.com
www.intel.com/design/quality/celeron/parts.htm
www.intel.com/design/quality/celeron/ppga/integration.htm
www.mips.com
www.motorola.com
www.nec.com
www.sun.com
www.ti.com

Chapter 4
Laboratory Activity
Installing a Pentium 4 Processor

After completing this laboratory activity, you will be able to:

- ❑ Identify the required socket used for an Intel Pentium 4 processor.
- ❑ Explain the key steps to installing an Intel Pentium 4 processor.
- ❑ Explain the importance of properly applying the thermo compound.

Introduction

In this lab activity you will install a Pentium 4 processor and fan and heat sink assembly. The Pentium 4 is designed by Intel, and installs into a 478-pin micro pin grid array (μPGA). The symbol for micro (μ) is often used in the acronym. The micro PGA uses less space on the motherboard for the socket because the pins are placed closer together than in any other previous socket design.

The installation of the Pentium 4 processor can be quite complex when compared to earlier processor installations. One of the most critical aspects of installing the processor is the installation of the fan and heat sink assembly. The fan and heat sink assembly requires electrical power to operate properly. Electrical power is provided by a three-pin connection located on the motherboard in close proximity to the processor.

Note:
You may need additional instructional sheets if the fan and heat sink assembly does not match the one in this lab activity.

Heat exchange between the cooling unit and the processor is also critical. Simply mounting the fan and heat sink assembly on the processor is not sufficient. A thermo compound must be installed between the processor and fan and heat sink assembly to ensure heat will dissipate in the most efficient manner. Without the thermo compound, the heat conduction between the processor and the fan and heat sink assembly is significantly reduced and can cause the processor to overheat. Excessive heat can damage the processor.

The thermo compound looks like a cream-colored, grease-type material. The thermo compound may come in a separate container or be already spread on the processor and protected by a clear plastic cover. If it is already spread on the processor, the protective plastic cover must be removed before installing the fan and heat sink assembly.

Sometimes thermo compound is supplied in a tube. When in a tube, simply open the tube and squeeze the compound onto the base of the heat sink or onto the surface of the processor. Rather than using your finger, you may use a small piece of plastic that comes with the packaging to smear the thermo compound evenly across the surface area.

Note:
When replacing a defective processor, some of the thermo compound may be removed and should be replaced.

Some key points to remember while installing a processor include the following:

- Always wear a ground strap when handling static-sensitive devices such as a processor.
- Always place the static-sensitive materials (processor and motherboard) on an anti-static mat or inside the original plastic package. Never lay them on a workbench unless the workbench has been designed to handle static-sensitive devices.
- The fan and heat sink assembly must be designed specifically for the Pentium 4 processor model you are installing.
- Thermo compound must be installed between the processor and the fan and heat sink assembly.
- If the thermo compound is already spread on the fan and heat sink assembly and protected by a clear plastic cover, the protective plastic cover must be removed before installation.
- A Pentium 4 processor requires a special motherboard with a 478-pin micro pin grid array (μPGA) and a power supply with a rating sufficient to support the processor. The power supply should indicate that it is designed for a Pentium 4 processor.

For more information on Pentium 4 installation procedures, visit Intel's support Web site at www.support.intel.com/support.

Equipment and Materials

- Pentium 4 processor (model determined by instructor) and fan and heat sink assembly.
- Motherboard with a 478-pin mPGA socket and retention frame.
- Anti-static mat or packaging for processor and motherboard.
- Additional instruction sheets may be required for this lab activity, especially if the fan and heat sink assembly do not match the one in this activity.

Procedure

1. ______ Gather all materials required for this lab activity and report to your assigned lab location.

Note:
When handling the motherboard or the Pentium 4 processor, be sure to take the proper electrostatic discharge (ESD) precautions.

2. ______ If available, read the motherboard manual prior to installing the processor. Read the section specific to processor installation.

3. ______ If the retention frame is not already installed on the motherboard, remove the four white pushpins from the black fasteners in each corner of the frame. The four black fasteners should remain fully seated in the retention frame.

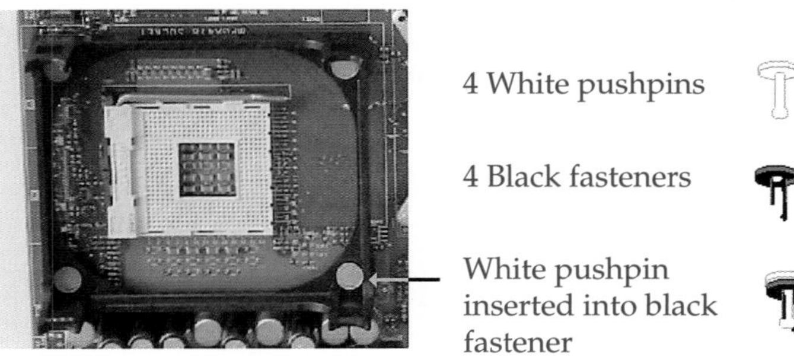

4. ______ If the retention frame is already installed, skip to step 8.
5. ______ Place the retention frame on the motherboard, aligning it with the four corner holes that surround the processor socket.
6. ______ Secure the retention frame to the motherboard by gently pressing on the black fasteners until they snap into place.
7. ______ Insert the four white pushpins into the black fasteners, one at each corner of the retention frame.
8. ______ Carefully remove the processor from its box. Do *not* handle or touch the processor pin area.
9. ______ Place the socket ZIF lever in the fully released position. The fully released position is when the lever is in the upright position.

10. ______ Look closely at the processor pin grid pattern to ensure the pin pattern on the processor matches the pin pattern of the socket. The socket has one corner pin hole missing near the hinge area of the ZIF socket lever. This is where pin 1 is located. Align pin 1 on the processor with pin 1 on the socket and insert the processor. There is a dot on the back of the processor, which indicates pin 1. No force is required to insert the processor pins into the socket.

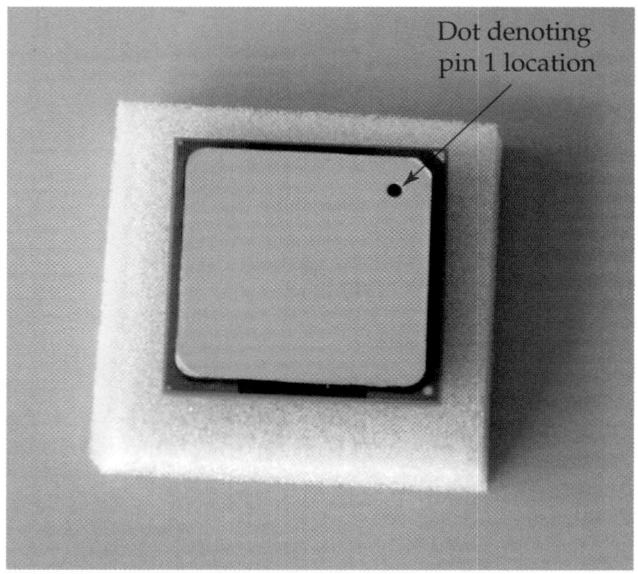

11. ______ After the processor has been inserted into the socket, close the ZIF socket lever by pushing the lever down to its lowest position.

12. ______ If the processor fan and heat sink assembly already have thermo compound applied, remove the plastic cover. Do *not* touch the white patch containing the thermo compound.

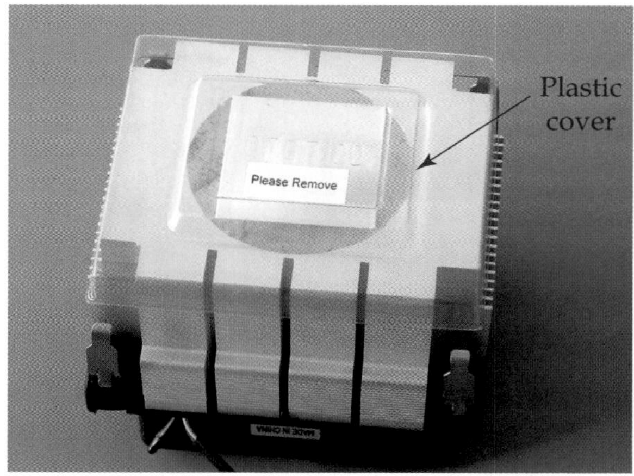

13. ______ If the thermo compound is included in an applicator with the processor, apply the entire thermal compound material to the center of the processor's surface.

14. ______ Make sure the lever of the fan and heat sink assembly is in the unlocked position. (See the following illustration.)

15. ______ Align the fan and heat sink assembly with the retention frame (the fan and heat sink assembly is symmetrical with the retention frame) and place it on the processor. The retaining clips on the fan and heat sink assembly should align with the holes in the retention frame. Make sure the fan and heat sink assembly cable is not trapped between the assembly and retention frame. Allow the heat sink base to compress (without rotating or twisting) the thermal compound material.

16. ______ Move the lever of the fan and heat sink assembly to the locked position. The lever action will insert all four retaining clips into the holes of the retention frame. It is important to *not* allow the heat sink assembly to rotate or twist on the processor's surface. Securing the fan and heat sink assembly while closing the lever ensures the thermal interface material is not damaged and the processor will operate correctly.

17. ______ Once the lever is locked, verify that the fan and heat sink assembly is securely retained and that the retaining clips are properly engaged with the retention frame.
18. ______ Connect the fan and heat sink assembly fan cable to the motherboard fan power header. Consult the motherboard manual to determine the correct fan header to use.
19. ______ Call your instructor to have your project inspected. Do *not* energize your project until the instructor has inspected and approved it.

Review Questions

Answer the following questions on a separate sheet of paper. Please do not write in this book.

1. Why should a ground strap be worn during installation or removal of a processor?
2. How do you properly install the Pentium 4 processor?
3. What does the acronym μPGA represent?
4. How many socket pins are used with a Pentium 4 processor?
5. What is the purpose of the thermo compound?
6. Where would you look to find more specific information about the Pentium 4 processor?
7. Any power supply can be used with a Pentium 4 processor. True or False?

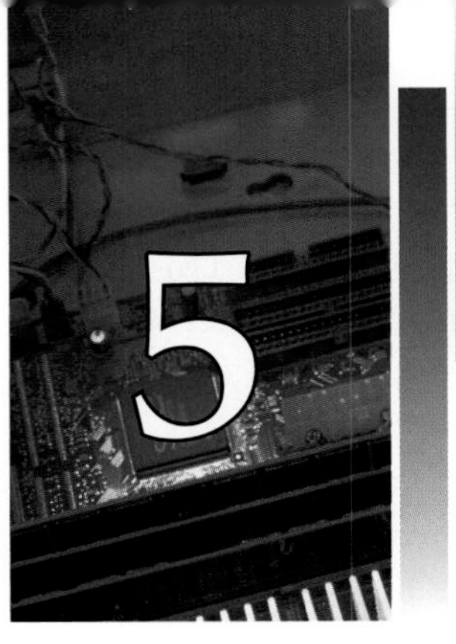

5 Power Supplies

After studying this chapter, you will be able to:

- Define electrical energy.
- Describe the terms ampere, volt, and ohm in relation to electrical energy.
- Explain the wattage rating of a power supply unit.
- Determine power supply requirements for a PC.
- Identify possible commercial power problems.
- Use a digital multimeter to troubleshoot a power supply.
- Apply wattage values when selecting the proper power supply and computer devices.
- Identify various power supply form factors.
- Explain the use of UPS and power protection devices.

A+ Exam—Key Points

There will be some basic questions about meters and reading resistance of wires and fuses. There will also likely be a basic question about wattage.

Key Words and Terms

The following words and terms will become important pieces of your computer vocabulary. Be sure you can define them.

Advanced Power Management (APM)
alternating current (ac)
ampere (A)
backfeed
continuity
current
cycle
dedicated circuit
direct current (dc)
fuse
metal oxide varistor (MOV)
mini connector
Molex connector
power
power good signal
resistance
soft power
standby power connection
uninterruptible power supply (UPS)
volt (V)
voltage
volt-amperes (VA)
watts (W)

This unit introduces you to the basic concepts of electrical energy. This chapter is not intended to turn you into an electronics technician. Rather, this chapter will familiarize you with the terminology and basic electrical concepts needed to ensure success as a computer technician and success on the A+ Certification exams.

You will learn how to use a multimeter to test voltage and resistance and to test the standard features of computer power supplies. The basis of this chapter is the discussion and illustration of the PC power supply unit. The power supply is easy to understand and simple to replace, but making a mistake connecting a power supply can damage the motherboard. This would be a very expensive mistake.

What Is Electrical Energy?

Electrical energy is best defined as the flow of electrons. Most people only know that electricity can be supplied from a wall outlet or from a battery. This is fine for what you need to achieve in this unit. In fact, these will likely be the only two areas of concern you will have when working with PCs.

The flow of electrons is described by terms that express electrical values such as voltage, current, resistance, and power. Each term will be explained on an individual basis and in relation to each other. The terminology may seem confusing at first, but it is fairly simple. Familiarity with these terms is essential for A+ certification.

AC and DC

direct current (dc)
electrical current that flows in one direction.

alternating current (ac)
electrical current that reverses direction cyclically.

cycle
the completed sequence of flow, first in one direction and then in the other.

Direct current (dc) electrical energy flows from negative to positive. A dc power source has two terminals, one positive and the other negative. The positive terminal is indicated by the color red and a plus "+" sign. The negative terminal is indicated by the color black and a minus "–" sign. DC electrical energy flows in a steady motion from negative to positive. Look at the left side of **Figure 5-1.**

Alternating current (ac) has no negative or positive markings because an alternating current system is in a state of constant change or alternating polarities. The current in an ac circuit flows in one direction and then in the opposite direction. Examine the right side of Figure 5-1. The completed sequence of flow, first in one direction and then in the other is called a ***cycle.*** Current flows in one direction during the first half cycle and then in the opposite direction the next half cycle. See **Figure 5-2** for an illustration of one ac cycle.

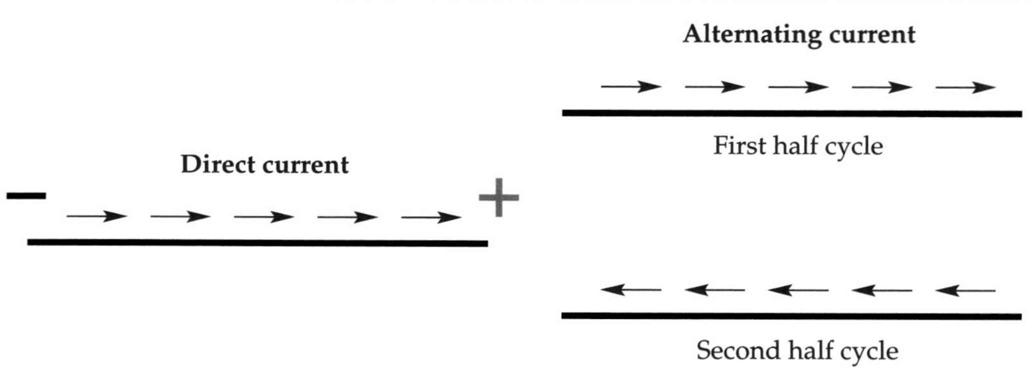

Figure 5-1. Illustrations of ac and dc flow.

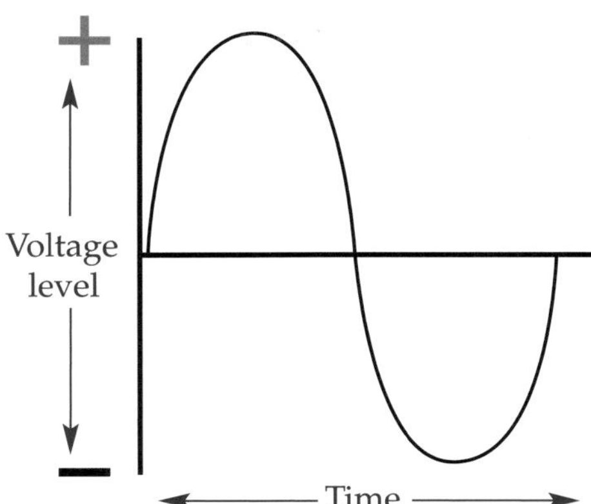

Figure 5-2.
An ac voltage is commonly plotted as a graph with the voltage level plotted along the vertical axis and the time plotted along the horizontal axis.

This pattern is repeated as long as power is applied to the circuit. The frequency of how often the cycle is repeated is expressed in hertz (Hz) and is based on a time period of one second. Standard household electrical energy is 60 Hz. This means that the direction of the current changes at a rate of 60 times per second or 60 Hz. See **Figure 5-3.**

Voltage and Current

Voltage and current are two measures of electrical power that are tested by technicians in the diagnosis of problems related to the PC. Measurements are usually taken with a universal multimeter. The multimeter and its operation are covered later in this chapter.

Voltage and current are directly related to each other when measuring electrical quantities. ***Voltage,*** measured in ***volts (V),*** is the amount of electrical pressure present in a circuit or power source. ***Current,*** measured in ***amperes (A),*** is the amount of electron flow. Do not mistake the ampere measurement of electrical energy as speed. It is the measure of volume of electrical energy flowing through the system.

Electrical energy can be compared to water in a pipe. Water flow is measured in gallons per minute (GPM) as well as pounds per square inch (PSI). GPM is the rate of flow or volume of water while PSI is the amount of pressure used to produce the flow. Electrical energy is similar. The voltage of the electrical source produces the force for moving the amount of electrical energy, or current, flowing through the wires and devices. The letter *V* represents voltage and the letter *A* or the abbreviation *amp* usually represents amperes.

voltage
the amount of electrical pressure present in a circuit or power source.

volts
a scale used in measuring electrical pressure (electromotive force).

current
the electron flow in a circuit.

amperes
a scale used in measuring the volume of electron flow in a circuit.

Resistance

Resistance is the opposition to the flow of electrical energy. The unit of resistance is the ohm and is expressed with the letter symbol *R* or the symbol omega (Ω).

Electrical components that manipulate the voltage and current levels in a circuit have measurable resistance values that can be expressed in ohms. Computer technicians very seldom, if ever, are required to take accurate resistance readings. The resistance readings taken by PC technicians are usually to

resistance
the opposition to the flow of electrical energy.

Figure 5-3.
A complete ac cycle is illustrated with a series of ac cycles. The cycle pattern represents the rise and fall of a voltage level. This pattern repeats 60 times in one second (60 Hz) for standard household electrical energy.

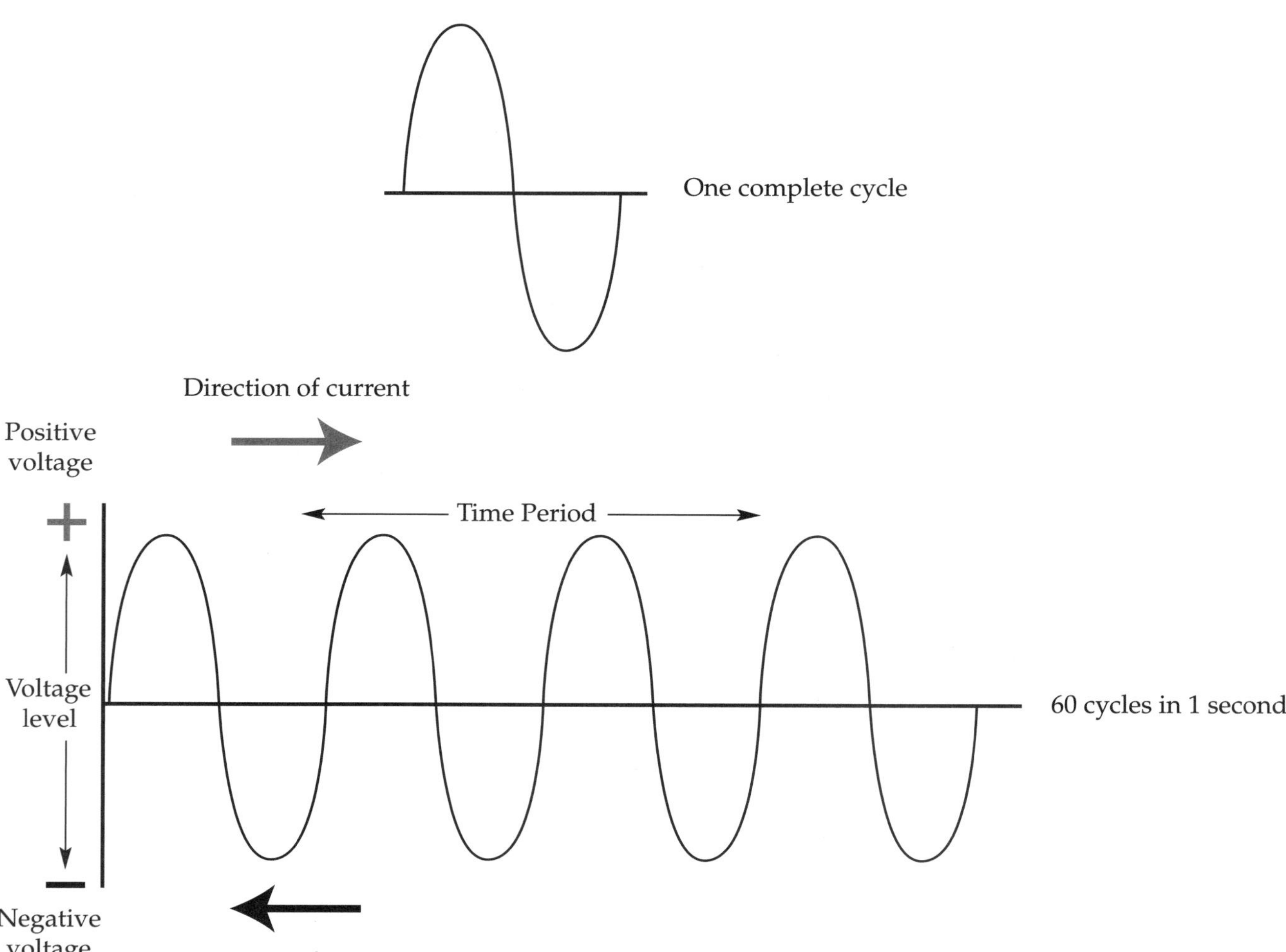

check for electrical continuity. ***Continuity*** is the ability of a device or component to allow an unobstructed flow of electrical energy. Examine **Figure 5-4.**

continuity
a state of connectedness. In electronics, an unbroken circuit is said to have continuity.

fuse
an inexpensive, passive component that is engineered to burn open at a predetermined amperage, protecting the rest of the circuit from overload.

In the illustration, there are two electrical wires. These wires are referred to as *conductors* when using electrical terminology. A complete conductor, one that has no breaks, will have a resistance reading of zero. There is no significant resistance to be measured. When a conductor has a break in its path, referred to as an *open,* there is an immeasurable amount of resistance. This extreme condition of high resistance is referred to as *infinity.* As the term infinity implies, the reading is so high it is beyond the capability of the multimeter to read it. It is imperative that you learn these two readings, what they mean, and the conditions that cause them. This is the key to using the ohmmeter function to troubleshoot certain PC items.

Now let's look at a switch and a fuse. A ***fuse*** is constructed of two metallic end pieces with a thin strand of wire stretched between them. The wire is engineered to burn open at a predetermined ampere value. The fuse is covered in either a tube of clear glass or opaque ceramic material.

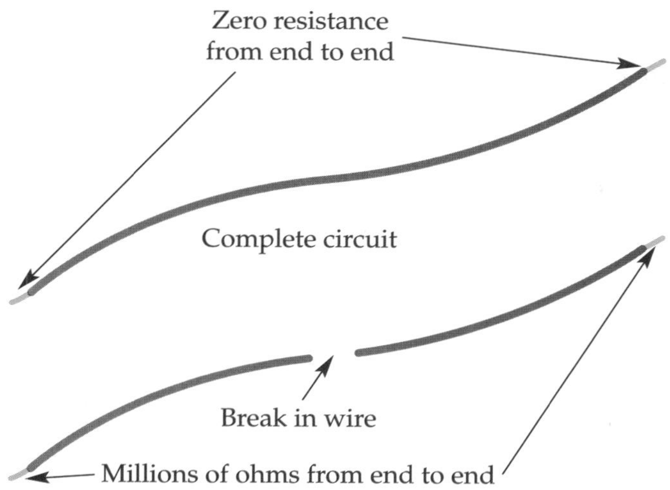

Figure 5-4.
Drawing of two wires, one complete and the other open. A complete circuit has (almost) no resistance. An open circuit (like a broken wire) has a very high or infinite resistance.

To check a fuse with a multimeter, the meter function should be set to measure resistance. Place the meter probes across the fuse, one probe on each end of the fuse. The reading should be zero for a good fuse and infinity for a bad fuse. A bad fuse is when the small wire inside the fuse is burnt to an open condition. The path for the electricity no longer exists, **Figure 5-5.**

Warning:
Be sure the electrical power supplying the fuse is turned off.

Testing switches is very similar to testing fuses. An open switch will show an infinite resistance. A closed switch should show zero ohms of resistance, **Figure 5-6.** As with testing a fuse, *make sure the electrical power to the switch is disconnected.*

Backfeed

Resistance values can fool an untrained electronics technician. There is a situation when a resistance reading taken on a circuit component such as a switch will give false information. An open switch can, in fact, have what appears as a resistance value other than infinity. The meter may be reading through the electronic components mounted in the system and indicate a value anywhere between zero and infinity.

Look at the drawing in **Figure 5-7.** In the illustration, the ohmmeter is reading through the circuit components even after the switch is opened. This is referred to as ***backfeed*** and is a very common condition. To avoid backfeed situations, the component to be read should be removed from the circuit whenever possible. This is not always practical. At times, it is more appropriate to take voltage readings to indicate the condition of fuses, breakers, and switches.

backfeed
a type of ohmmeter reading in which the resistance is measured through the circuit components even though the circuit is open.

Checking Power Outlets

Checking a power outlet is a very common task. See **Figure 5-8.** The meter probes are simply inserted into a wall outlet to check for electrical power. There is no polarity when reading ac voltage sources, so the polarity markings on the meter need not be observed.

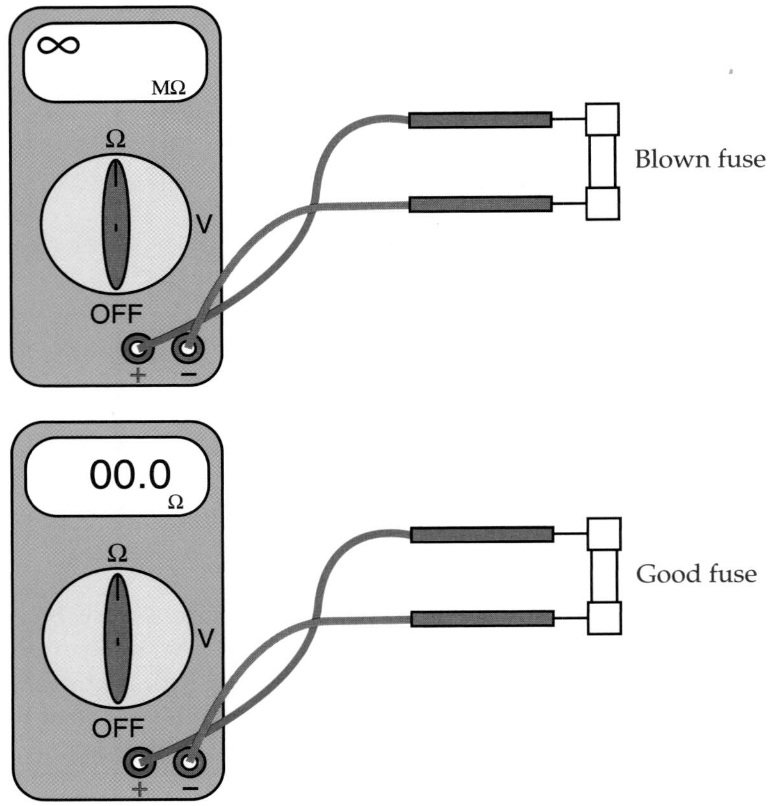

Figure 5-5.
A blown fuse will have a resistance reading too high to be displayed, even in the megaohm range. A good fuse will display zero resistance.

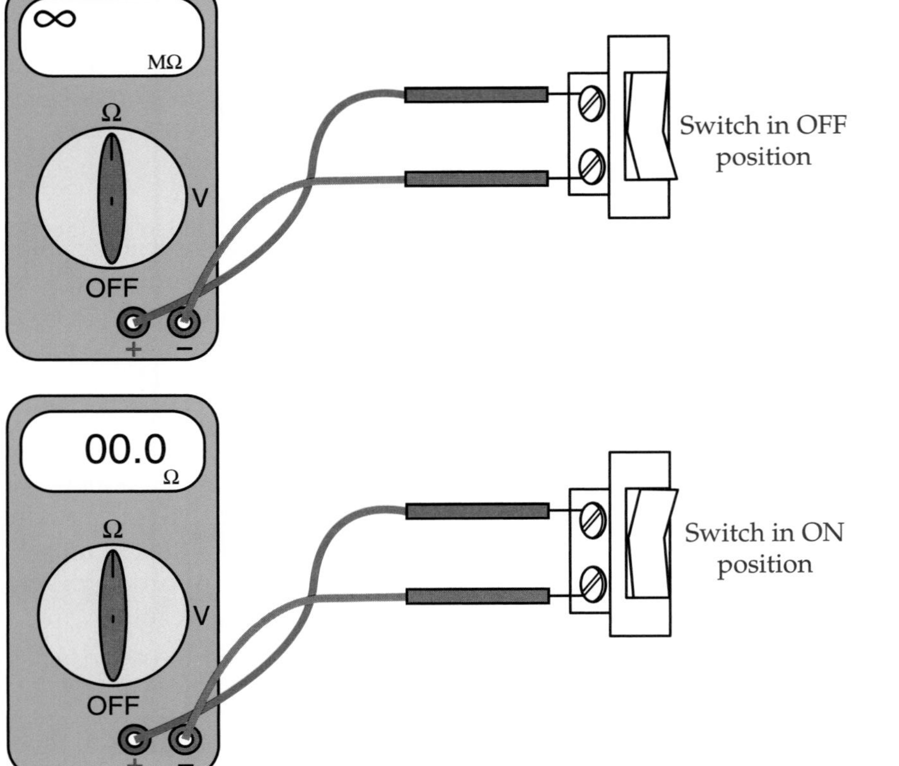

Figure 5-6.
A closed switch has zero resistance while an open switch shows infinite resistance.

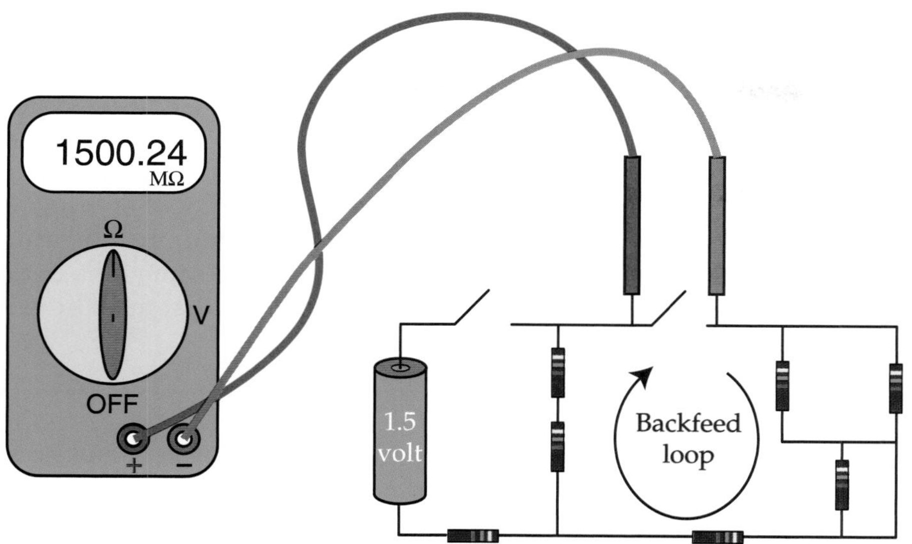

Figure 5-7. Reading resistance across an open switch can give you a false resistance reading. The ohmmeter reads the resistance through the rest of the circuit instead of the resistance across the open switch.

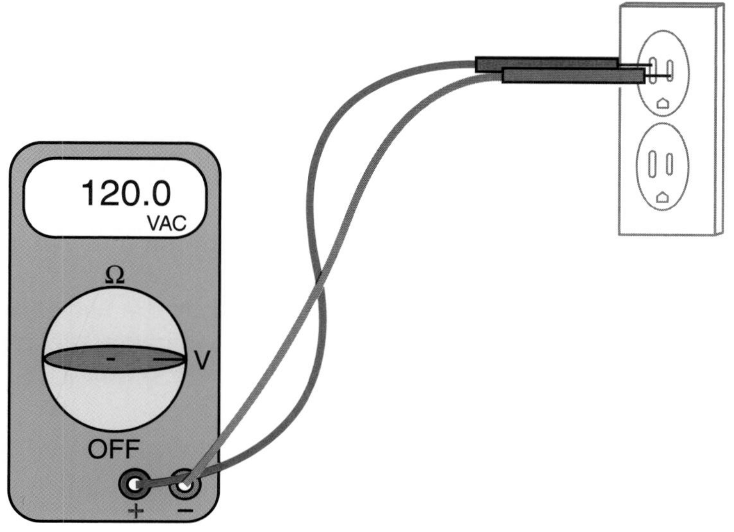

Figure 5-8. Meter connected to a wall outlet. Polarity need not be observed. Be careful when making this test. Keep your fingers away from the exposed probe tips.

Warning:
Never touch the tips of the meter leads when taking readings. Once you start this practice, it may soon develop into a very bad habit. Low voltages (below 50 volts) will not normally harm you, and you normally do not feel any electrical sensation. Touching a 120-volt ac line is an entirely different story. You will definitely feel the sensation of electrical energy. It is possible to incur a permanent injury or even death. Safety is a habit. Develop safe habits when reading low voltages and you will automatically use the same habits when reading a much higher voltage.

A good voltage reading is considered to be plus or minus 10% of the 120-volt rating. In actuality, the voltage can drop or rise considerably more before affecting a PC.

Two other important considerations when taking voltage readings are the weather and the time of day. Low voltage is common on extremely hot or cold days when electrical heat or air conditioning control building temperature. Heating and air conditioning call for a large demand on the electrical system inside a building. The highest demand for electrical power is usually between the hours of 4:00 PM and 6:00 PM. During this time period, most households are actively using power because of those coming home from school or work. The demand for heat or cooling increases and often combines with the power needed for the preparation of the evening meal. During the same time period, many businesses are still operating. This is the time period that most brownouts occur.

Tech Tip:
When checking for low voltage, it is best to have the air conditioning or heating system operating at maximum so that you can see the system under maximum strain. This is especially important when checking an intermittent problem and a low voltage condition is suspect.

Clean Electrical Power

Clean power is a term that means the commercial electrical supply is steady, at the correct voltage level, and does not contain voltage spikes. Clean power can be difficult to obtain without additional equipment being added to the supply system. High voltage power line switching, lightning, cars hitting electric poles, or routine line maintenance can cause voltage spikes. When a spike occurs, an abnormally high level of voltage is sent through the electrical system. See **Figure 5-9** for an illustration of line spike in relation to normal ac voltage pattern.

Line voltage spikes can be reduced or eliminated by the use of line conditioning equipment. A common method of ensuring a constant clean power supply is the use of uninterruptible power supplies (UPS). The UPS system will be discussed later in this chapter.

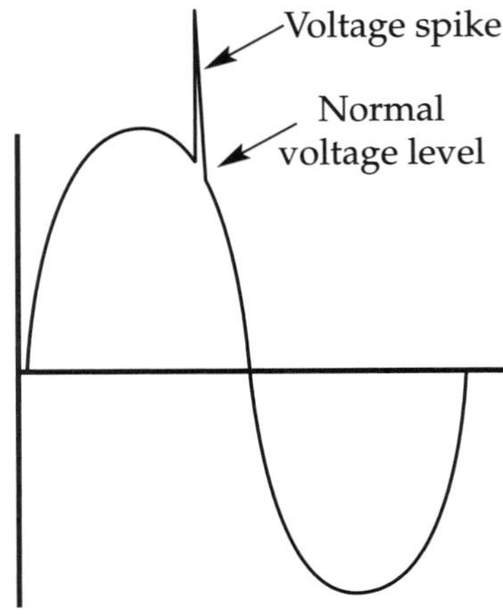

Figure 5-9.
A voltage line spike can be caused by many things (motors, switches, lightning). The increased voltage in the spike damages electronic components by exceeding the voltage limitation of the component.

Power

The amount of electrical energy provided or used by equipment is ***power*** and it is measured in ***watts (W).*** Wattage is the product of voltage and current. In other words, to determine the amount of power expressed in watts that a dc circuit is using, the electrical pressure measured in volts is multiplied by the electrical current measured in amps.

power
the amount of electrical energy provided or used by equipment.

Watts = Volts × Amps

A computer drawing 3 amps when connected to a 120-volt source would consume *approximately* 360 watts of electrical energy. Notice that the term "approximately" is used here. When calculating wattage values associated with ac power, there are other electrical factors, such as induction, to be taken into account. The power value of an ac circuit is expressed as ***volt-amperes (VA).***

watts (W)
a scale used in measuring electrical power.

volt-amperes (VA)
an alternative scale for measuring electrical power.

A power supply's output capacity is rated in watts and in VA. Watts and VA are not the same expression. Wattage is considered the "true" power rating of a device. It is measured with a very expensive wattmeter or calculated with a more exact formula. VA is considered the "apparent" power. It is called the apparent power because the voltage and amperes values derived from a multimeter are not true values. These values are distorted from electrical factors in the circuit, such as induction. Look at **Figure 5-10.** Total load is calculated from a group of computers and a printer, which are rated by current, amperes, and wattage. Notice that the calculated power rating derived from the formula V × A is higher than the total power rating derived from adding the individual watt values. The power rating derived from adding the individual watt values is the true power rating. This is a very brief explanation of a very complicated topic. The electronic theory involved for a complete understanding of electronic system loads is beyond the scope of this text. If you have a real desire to know more about electronics, an introductory level course in basic dc and ac circuits is recommended.

When sizing the load capacity of a computer configuration, there are two choices. All the watt values can be added together to arrive at the total load in watts, or all the ampere loads can be added together and then compared to the amperage rating of the power supply.

Wattage measurements are used in two primary ways: power consumption and power supplied. The amount of power consumed by devices such as monitors or hard drives is expressed in watts. When wattage is written on a device

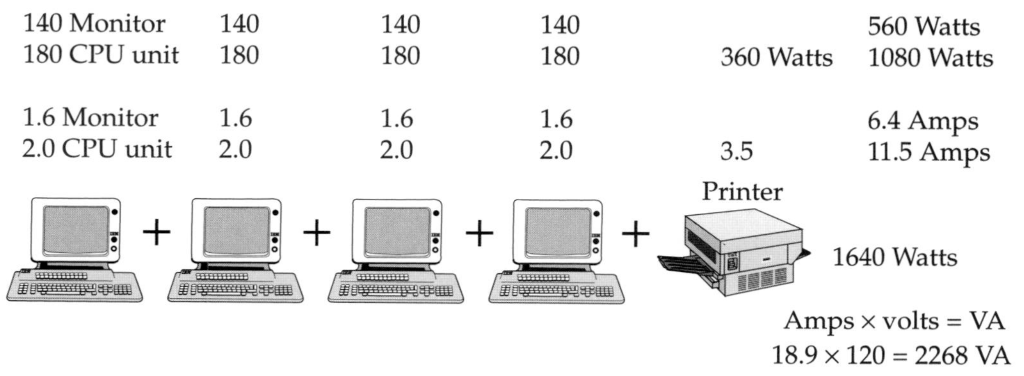

Figure 5-10.
The total wattage rating can be quite a bit different than the calculated wattage rating based on the formula of volts × amps. It is not unusual for the calculated wattage using volts and amps to be larger than the wattage totals.

that uses or consumes electrical power, the watts label is used to express the amount of power used or consumed by that device. When watts is used as a label on a device that supplies electrical energy such as a generator or power supply, it represents the amount of power that can be provided safely from that unit. Power supplies and generators can actually supply more power than they are rated for. However, when excess amounts of power are taken from a power supply, excessive heating occurs. This can permanently damage the power supply.

When changing power supplies, a power supply with equal or greater wattage marked on the label must be used. A power supply with less wattage capability may work for a while, but it will surely burn up after a period of time.

To determine how much equipment can be connected to a power strip, the wattage ratings of each piece of equipment should be added together. A typical power strip should not connect to a total of over 1600 watts of equipment. Also, *never* daisy chain (string in series) power strips, **Figure 5-11.** When daisy chained together, the first strip carries the total load of both strips.

Another consideration when using extension cords is wire size. A cord with less than number 16-gauge wire should not be used. Wire smaller than 16 gauge can pose a fire hazard. Wire gauge is used to indicate the size of wire and also how much current it can safely handle without excessive heat. Remember, the larger the number, the smaller the wire. **Figure 5-12** shows a wire size chart with current ratings.

Parts of a Digital Multimeter

A digital multimeter is used to measure current, resistance, and voltage values. As the name implies, the meter is constructed from digital circuits, and it is used in place of multiple meters. The multimeter replaces the use of individual

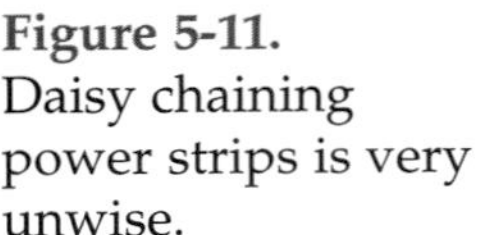

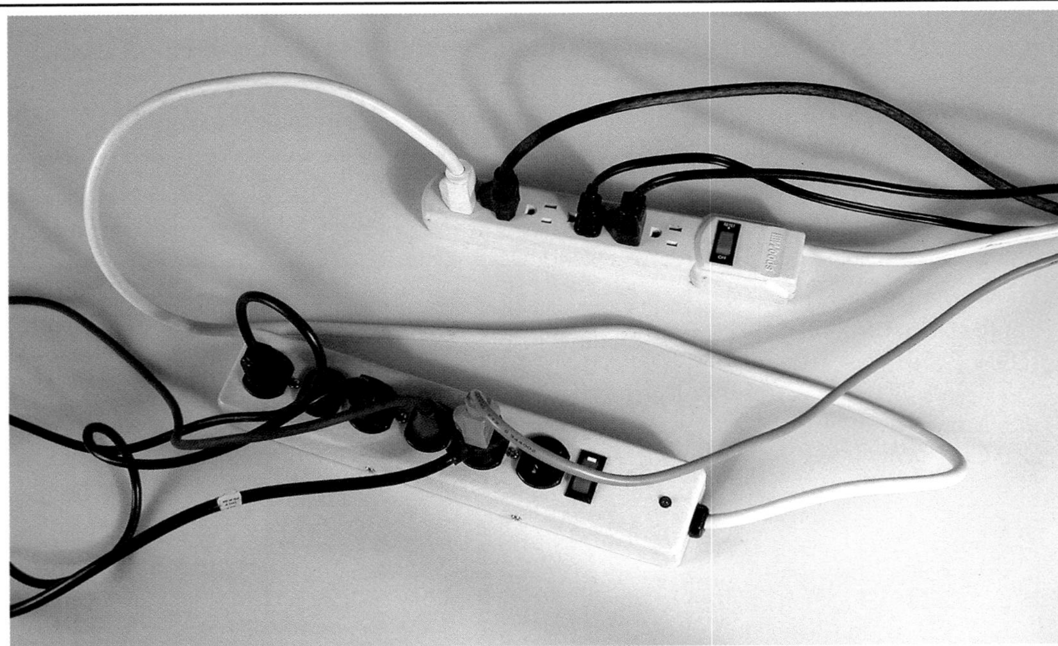

Figure 5-11. Daisy chaining power strips is very unwise.

Wire Size	Ampere Rating
12	20
14	15
16	7
18	5

Figure 5-12.
Wire size chart with current ratings. Note that this chart reflects current carrying capacities of typical conductors. It does not take into consideration the type of insulation or the application, which can change the current rating for the listed conductors.

volt, ohm, and amp meters. It is an all-in-one type of meter. Look at **Figure 5-13.** Shown is a typical digital multimeter with major parts labeled.

The display area displays a numeric value of the electrical quality being measured such as voltage, current, or resistance. The numeric display expresses the value with a decimal point when appropriate. The numeric value displayed in the meter window is coordinated with the range dial setting and with the location of where the meter leads are plugged.

The range should be set to a level higher than the expected value to be read. In other words, a meter with voltage ranges of 5, 50, and 500 should be set to 50 to take an expected 12-volt reading. Some meters come with automatic range selection. The selector switch dial is set to voltage, and the meter automatically sets the correct range when it is connected to the circuit being measured.

There are several locations where the test leads can be plugged. Examine **Figure 5-14.** Notice the plug-in points (or jacks) on the meter. One is black with a negative "–" symbol beside it and the other is red with a plus "+" sign beside it. These identify the appropriate polarity position of the electrical input. The test leads correspond in the colors red and black, which represent positive and negative power respectively. Also, take special note of the ac marking on some of the meter jacks. Be sure the test leads are plugged into the appropriate jacks when taking current readings.

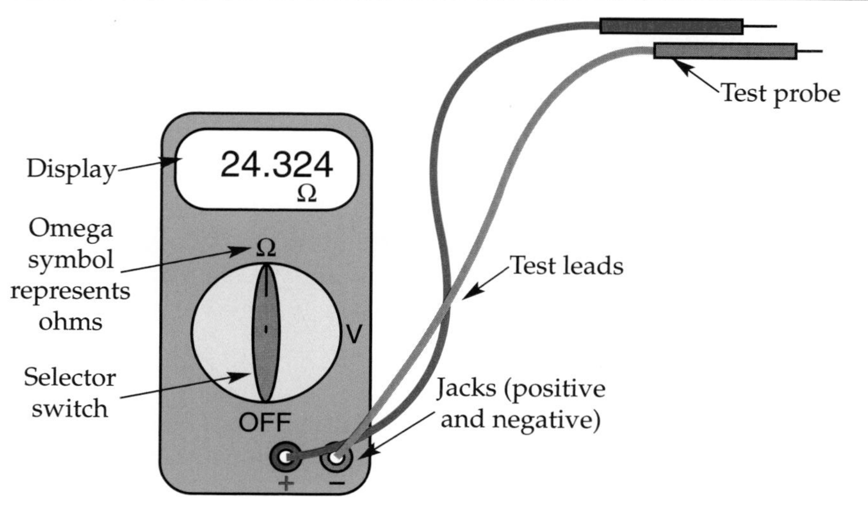

Figure 5-13.
A typical auto-range meter is very simple in design. You simply select the function you wish (volts or resistance here), and then touch the parts with the probe tips.

Figure 5-14. Meters come with multiple jacks for the test probes. Be sure to place the test probes in the proper jacks. (Fluke Corp. Reproduced with permission.)

Probes

The meter is equipped with two test leads with probes at the end of each. The probes are for touching test points. One test lead is black and the other is red. This color combination is universal. The black lead is for the negative side of a reading. It plugs into the meter at the jack that is marked in black, has a negative sign, or both. The red lead plugs into the jack with the red marking or the plus sign for voltage and resistance readings. For current readings, there is usually a different position in which to be plugged. As a PC technician, you typically never need to take a current reading. Current readings are much more complicated and require knowledge of electronic components to correctly connect the meter. Voltage readings and occasionally resistance readings are required.

Never touch the probes with your fingertips when taking readings even when the voltage is low. Make electrical safety a habit. Forming safe habits is essential. If you touch the bare tip of the probe during routine checks of low voltage where there is not sufficient voltage to harm you, you may create a bad habit. This can lead to touching the tips when reading dangerously high voltages.

Display Area

The display area is where the measured value is displayed. For example, when reading voltage, the display will give a numeric value of the voltage and possibly indicate if it is an ac or dc voltage value. It may also indicate if you are out of the correct range selection value.

Range Selection

The range selector is used to choose the appropriate value to be read: voltage, current, or resistance. The dial indicator should be placed in the lowest range that is greater than the value to be read. If it is placed higher than the next highest value, an accurate reading will not be obtained. The reading will be a rounded-off value, rather than an accurate reading. If you go below the desired level, you will probably not get a reading at all. In fact, a warning will appear in the display area of most good meters.

Some meters are equipped with an auto-range feature. It will automatically select the correct range for the reading you are taking. I highly recommend this type of meter for anyone not familiar with basic electronics.

Procedures for Reading Voltage

Before taking any readings, you should have some idea of the level of voltage you expect to read. For example, a common wall outlet is 120 volts ac. A power supply unit might be 12, 5, or 3.5 volts dc depending on the exact power supply connection.

Warning:
Never wear an anti-static or ground strap while taking meter readings. The ground strap makes you an excellent conductor of electricity, which is a dangerous situation when taking meter readings.

To read ac or dc voltages:

1. Insert the meter leads into the appropriate jacks on the face of the meter. The red lead is inserted into the jack marked with the letter "V" or a "+" symbol. (Generally, you will never use the jacks marked with an "A" or a "mA" as they are used for current readings.)
2. Insert the black lead into the jack marked "COM" or with the "–" symbol. The common is usually black and the input voltage jack is usually red.
3. Turn the selector switch to voltage AC. On some meters this can require the use of two separate switches. One switch selects ac or dc voltage and the other switch selects the voltage range. If you do not have an auto-range meter, set the range selector to the next highest voltage level over what you expect to read. (This is where an auto-range meter is handy.)
4. Touch the test locations with the probes. Keep your fingers away from the tips of the probes.
5. Read the display and record the voltage. It should be within 10% of the expected voltage level.

Procedures for Reading Resistance

To read resistance:

1. Insert the meter leads into the appropriate jacks on the face of the meter. The red lead is inserted into the jack marked with the letter "V" or a "+" symbol.

2. Insert the black lead into the jack marked with "COM" or with a "–" symbol. The common is usually black.
3. Be absolutely sure the power is OFF before attempting to read resistance.

Warning:
Electrical voltage can damage a meter if the meter is set up to read resistance.

4. Set the selector switch to the *highest* value of resistance.
5. Touch the test probes together to see if the meter is working properly. The reading should be zero. If not, the battery inside the unit could be weak. The ohmmeter portion of a multimeter depends on battery power to take a resistance reading.
6. Touch the probes to the part (fuse or cable) to be tested.
7. When doing a resistance check on a fuse or a cable, you should read either zero resistance or infinity. A good fuse will cause a reading of zero resistance as will a good cable. A bad fuse will cause a reading of infinity as will a cable that is not complete from end to end.

Checking Fuses, Cables, and Switches

When checking fuses, cables, and switches there are only two resistance values that are typically displayed on a digital meter display: zero ohms and infinity. A typical low ampere value fuse found in electronic equipment is simple in construction. The fuse is a cylinder shape of glass or ceramic with a metal cap on each end. Inside the cylinder is the fuse link. The fuse link is a thin metal wire that burns and splits into two parts at a predetermined ampere value.

The easiest way to tell if the fuse is good (or not) is to remove it from the fuse holder and take a resistance reading across the fuse. Since the fuse is made of a small metal wire, it will have very low resistance. When tested with the ohmmeter, the meter will indicate zero resistance. If the fuse is burned open, it will have a resistance value too high to read. You would be trying to read through the air or space inside the tube. This reading is known as infinity. This means the resistance reading is beyond the capabilities of the meter range.

The same principle applies to a cable and switches. Before reading a switch or cable with an ohmmeter, they must be removed from the PC. A cable should read zero resistance from one end to the other. A cable with a broken wire will read infinity. See **Figure 5-15** for an illustration of a cable with a meter attached, illustrating both a good reading and a bad cable reading.

A switch can be difficult to remove from the circuit and the type of switch present must be identified. Some switches used today are capacitor-type switches. These switches cannot be adequately diagnosed with an ohmmeter. Capacitor switches are usually very small in comparison to the physical size of mechanical switches. If a switch is suspected as the problem, it may be best to simply replace the switch with a known good switch rather than attempting to diagnose it with a meter.

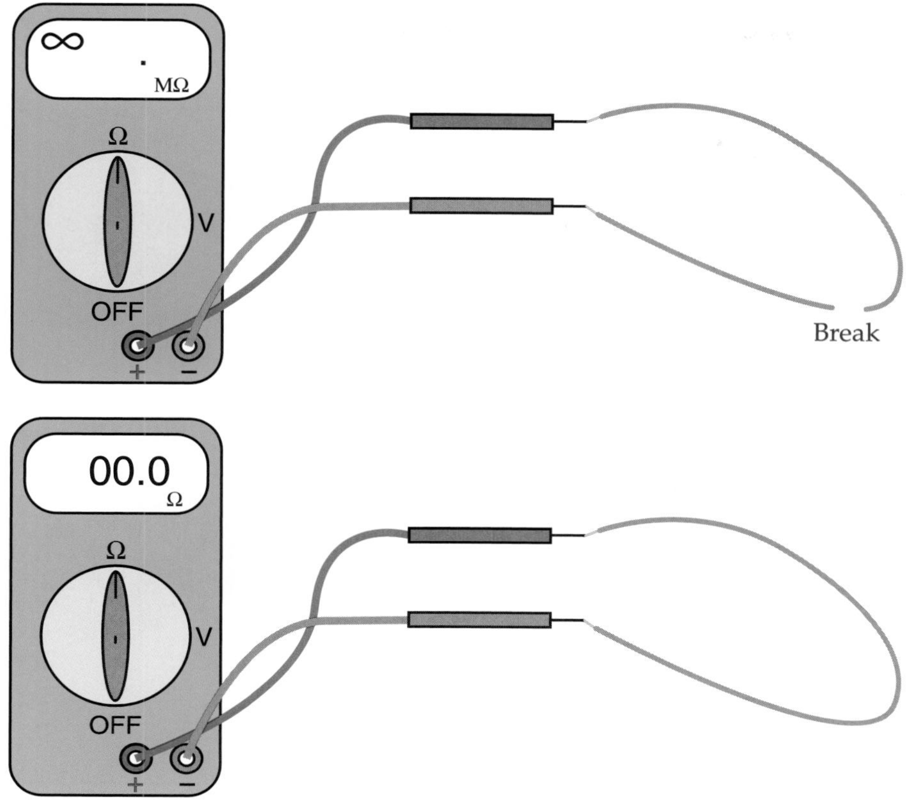

Figure 5-15.
A good conductor will read zero resistance. A conductor with a break (or open) will read infinity, the highest possible resistance reading.

Branch Circuits

Many computer problems can be generated by the electrical system inside the residential home or small business. A typical electrical panel distributes electricity to electrical circuits throughout a home. The electrical power in home settings and some businesses all tie back to the same electrical panel. Electrical equipment running anywhere in that environment can cause a power problem for the computer system.

For example, the operation of a vacuum cleaner or a power tool can generate voltage spikes that can disrupt the computer process. The computer can be damaged, develop a glitch, or simply lock up. It is imperative that a surge protector of some sort be installed at the computer location. See **Figure 5-16** for a drawing of a typical home distribution center.

A branch circuit is the technical name for the wiring from an electrical panel to the final outlet on that circuit. A typical commercial installation uses two electrical distribution panels: one panel for lighting and the other panel for distributing power to equipment. **Figure 5-17** is an illustration showing side-by-side panels. One panel is for lighting and the other is for power.

Computers are located in every type of business location from small travel agency offices to heavy manufacturing operations. It is important to know the type of equipment that a company operates from the same electrical distribution panel that serves the computer station.

The type of electrical distribution and the equipment connected to that electrical system is of major concern to reliable computer operation. An office

Figure 5-16.
Typical home distribution.

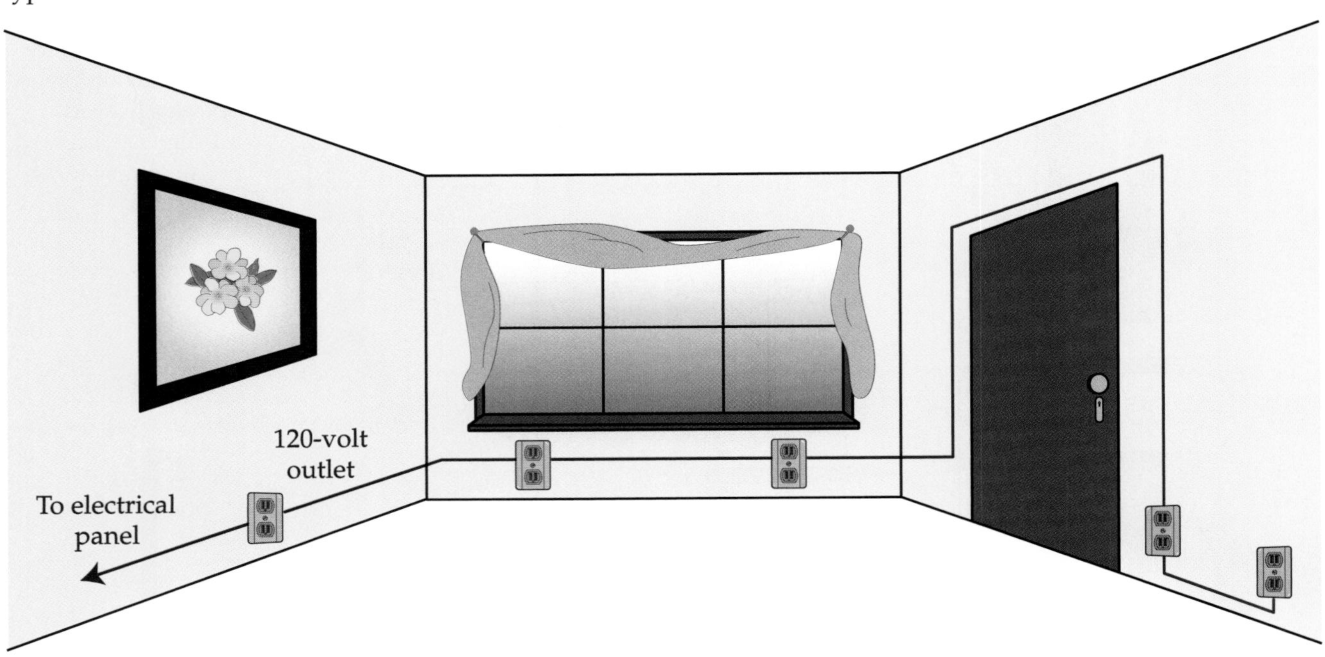

Figure 5-17.
Heavy machinery should have its own electrical panel. It should not be on the same panel as computer equipment.

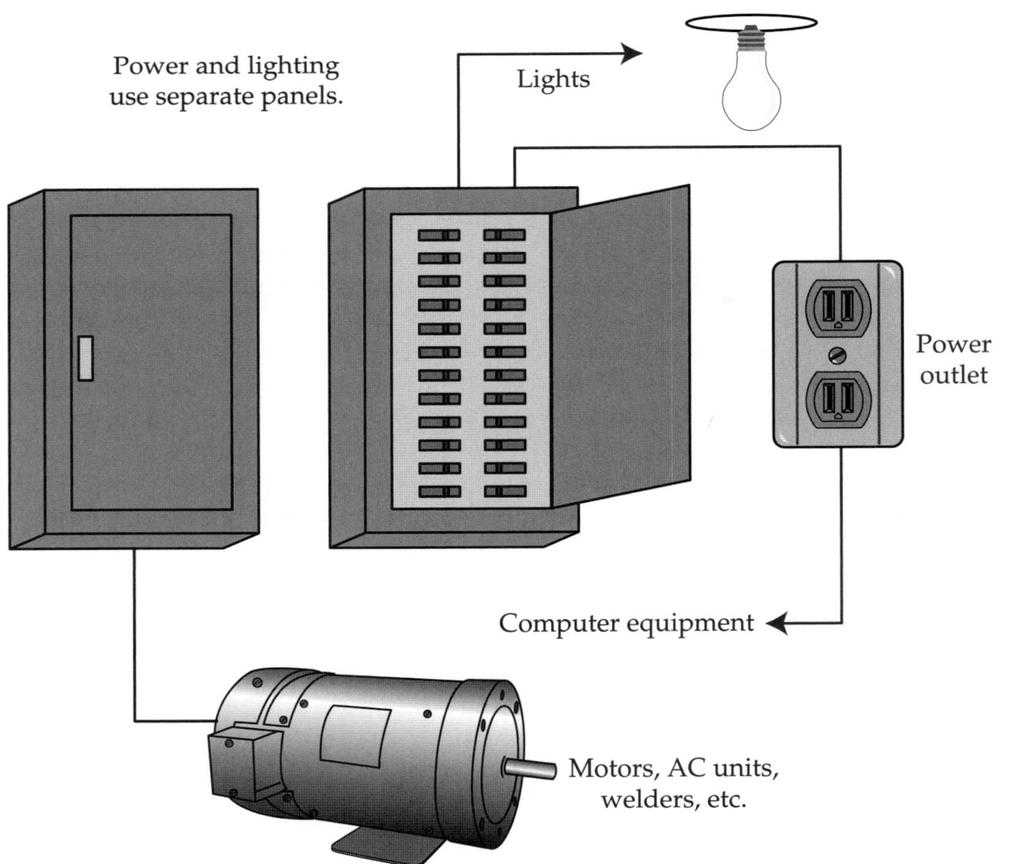

location in the form of a large industrial building can be misleading to a technician. While the immediate environment may look like a typical office setting, the same electrical circuits in the office environment can be serving heavy printing press equipment directly behind the office wall. A surge protector power strip may not be adequate in this type of location. A more reliable approach to ensure dependable operation of this computer system would be the installation of a quality uninterruptible power source (UPS) system. UPS systems are covered later in this chapter.

Dedicated Circuit

A ***dedicated circuit*** is one that is installed in an electrical power distribution system that is designed to serve *only* computer equipment. A dedicated circuit is wired separately from other electrical circuits. A typical installation uses an isolation transformer to separate the computer electrical power from other power circuits. An isolation transformer converts electrical energy to magnetic energy and then back to electrical energy again. The transformer helps to buffer the circuit against voltage spikes generated outside the building as well as from inside the building.

dedicated circuit
a circuit installed in an electrical power distribution system that is designed to serve only computer equipment.

A separate electrical panel is used strictly for the computers in the building. No additional equipment should ever be plugged into the dedicated circuit outlets. If computers connected to dedicated circuits suddenly develop problems that appear to be power related, the technician should look for some type of equipment that may have been plugged into the dedicated outlets. Any noncomputer type equipment that is found should be removed.

Tech Tip:
An interesting, and all too common, occurrence happens to network equipment and office computer systems that are left constantly in the "on" position. When office workers return to work in the morning, they find their computers locked up or crashed. After rebooting, everything appears fine again. However, a few days later, or even the next day, the computer system is down again. This problem is usually solved when it is discovered that the overnight cleaning service is using the dedicated circuits to power their vacuum cleaners.

Grounding

Improper grounding conditions can cause serious problems to computer equipment. After all other attempts to solve a power problem have been exhausted, the technician should investigate the grounding system. An improperly installed or damaged grounding system can cause problems that appear as voltage problems.

To check out the grounding system, a certified electrician or power company technician should make the inspection. There is specialized equipment used to perform grounding tests. It is expensive and special training is needed to use it. This is one time when the computer tech must call on another specialist.

The PC Power Supply

The power supply is responsible for converting standard 120-volt ac power from the wall outlet to dc voltage levels appropriate for the electronics systems

Molex connector a four-wire, D-shaped connector that delivers +12 volt and +5 volt signals from the power supply.

mini connector a two pin connector that delivers a +5 volt signal from the power supply. A variation of this connector has four wires and delivers both +12 volt and +5 volt signals.

of the computer. Typical dc voltage levels are +12, +5, +3.3, -12, and -5. These voltages are provided to the motherboard, which, in turn, distributes these voltage levels to motherboard components and expansion slots. The expansion slots provide the voltage levels required by adapter card electronic parts.

To assist in making the proper voltage level connections, power plugs have a special shape that matches the voltage level required by the device. The larger power supply plug is called a ***Molex connector*** and the smaller plug is called a ***mini connector.*** Disk drives, hard drives, and CD-ROM drives usually use the +12 volt level from the Molex connectors. **Figure 5-18** shows a picture and sketch of the Molex connector. **Figure 5-19** shows the same for the mini connector. This connector is used for 3½″ floppy drives.

Figure 5-20 and **Figure 5-21** illustrate two styles of motherboard power connection. Figure 5-20 shows the older style you might find in a computer with an XT or an AT form factor. Figure 5-21 shows the newer style of power connector you would find in a machine with an ATX form factor.

Figure 5-18.
Molex connector with pin identification.

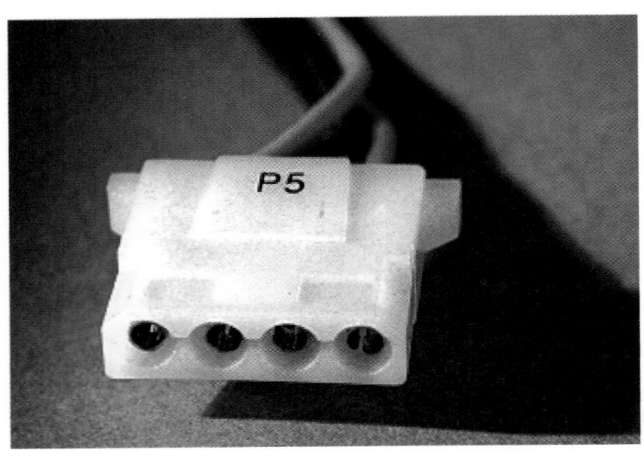

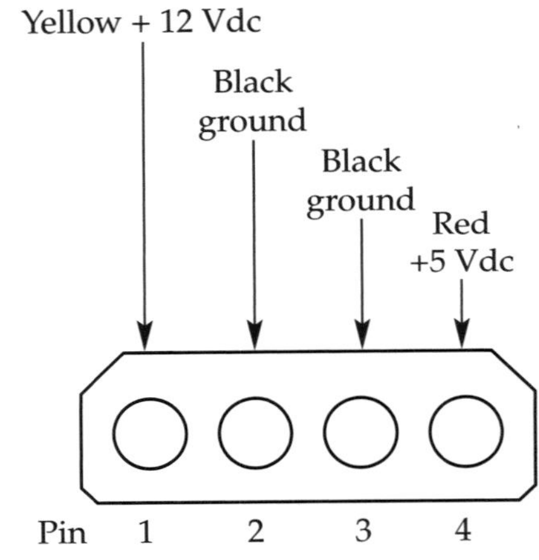

Figure 5-19.
Mini connector. This connector is used to power 3½″ floppy drives. Older floppy drives, like the 5¼″ drive, used the Molex connector. The older style of mini connector had four leads. The newer style of mini has only two.

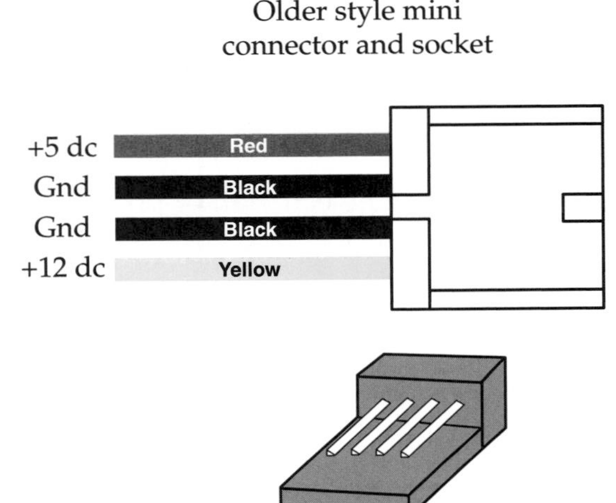

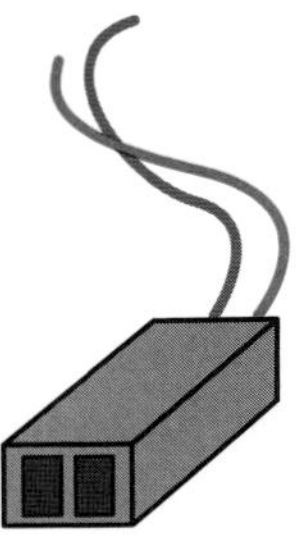

In Figure 5-20, note the connectors are marked P8 and P9. The type of power supply connection for the motherboard is usually marked P8 and P9. The connectors can be plugged into the motherboard in several ways. *Improper connection will result in damage to the motherboard.* It is very easy to connect them to the motherboard in reverse order, thus destroying the motherboard. As a memory aid, remember the saying "black back-to-back." Each power connector has a black wire. The black wires should be side-by-side when connected properly to the motherboard, see **Figure 5-22.**

In **Figure 5-23,** you see a photo of the newer style of motherboard power connector (Figure 5-21). This plug style combines the P8 and P9 connections into one keyed connector. Another feature of this plug is that the plastic is molded to permit the connector to connect to the motherboard in only one way. This prevents an improper connection that will destroy the motherboard.

Power Connection
Point on Motherboard

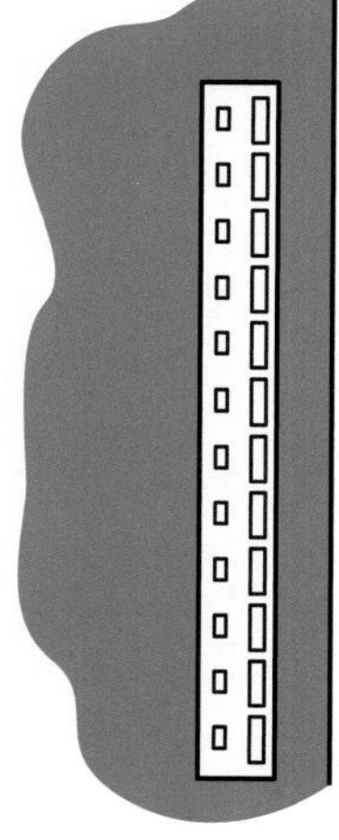

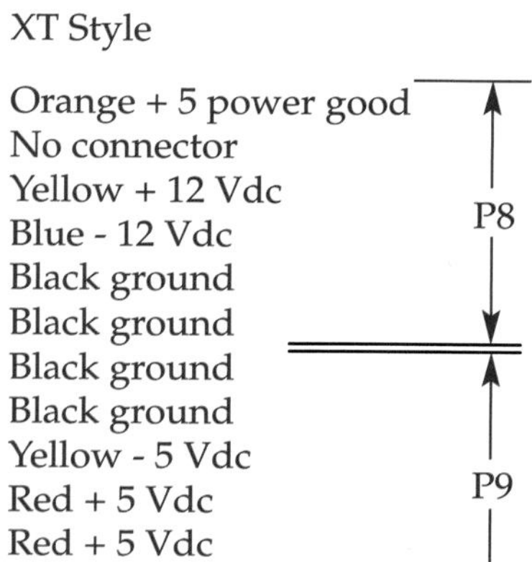

AT Style
Orange + 5 Vdc power good
Red + 5 Vdc
Yellow + 12 Vdc
Blue - 12 Vdc
Black ground
Black ground
Black ground
Black ground
Yellow - 5 Vdc
Red + 5 Vdc
Red + 5 Vdc
Red + 5 Vdc

Figure 5-20. Typical colors and voltages for XT and AT style power supply P8 and P9 connectors.

Typical ATX Form Factor
Power Connections

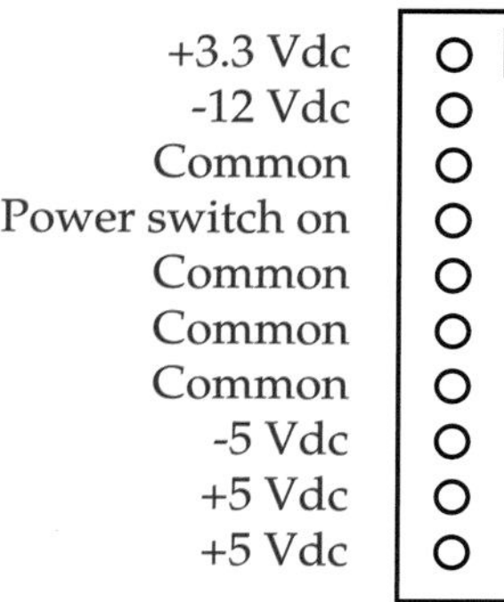

+3.3 Vdc
+3.3 Vdc
Common
+5 Vdc
Common
+5 Vdc
Common
Power good
+5 Vdc standby
+12 Vdc

Figure 5-21. The ATX motherboard power connector takes the place of the P8 and P9 connectors.

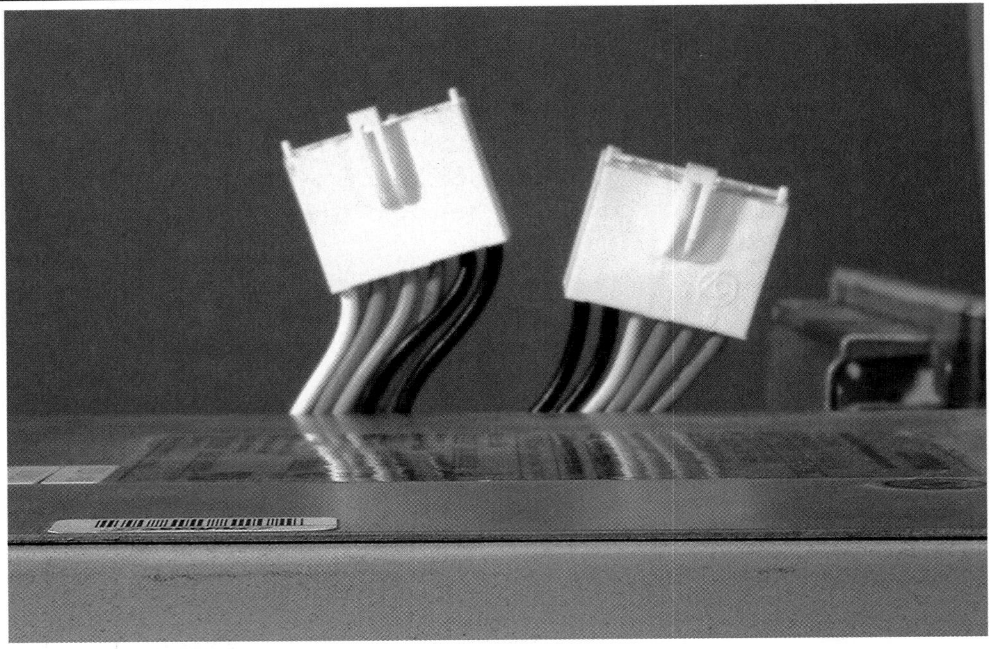

Figure 5-22.
With the P8 and P9 connection, keeping the black wires in the center together is very important.

power good signal
a signal sent from the power supply to the motherboard to verify that it is functioning normally.

Notice the connectors in Figures 5-20 and 5-21 marked "power good." They refer to the power good signal. This signal is transmitted from the power supply to the motherboard and on to the CPU. The ***power good signal*** is used to verify the power supply is working properly during POST.

See **Figure 5-24** for a picture of the inside of a power supply. A power supply is usually sealed to make it difficult to open. In general, there are no serviceable parts inside the power supply. It is considered a field replacement unit. Although it is possible to repair a power supply, it is not cost effective. The cost of most power supplies does not come near the cost of having an electronic technician repair the unit.

Power Supply Form Factor

Power supplies have form factors just as motherboards do. The power supply must fit into the case and also allow room for the motherboard. Some of the standard form factors are named after the motherboard form factors such as AT, Baby AT, LPX, ATX, and NLX. In addition, they can be broken down further to tower or desktop models. Last but not least, you should be aware of a variety of nonstandard power supplies that are proprietary. The color coding on the wiring is not truly standard. You must be careful. As a matter of fact, any implied standardization should not be taken for granted. Always check with the manufacturer's specifications for definitive information about color and voltages.

AT and XT Form Factors

The AT and XT form factors are very similar in design. Close examination is required to see the differences. They are the traditional form factors of older power supply units, but they are still used to some degree.

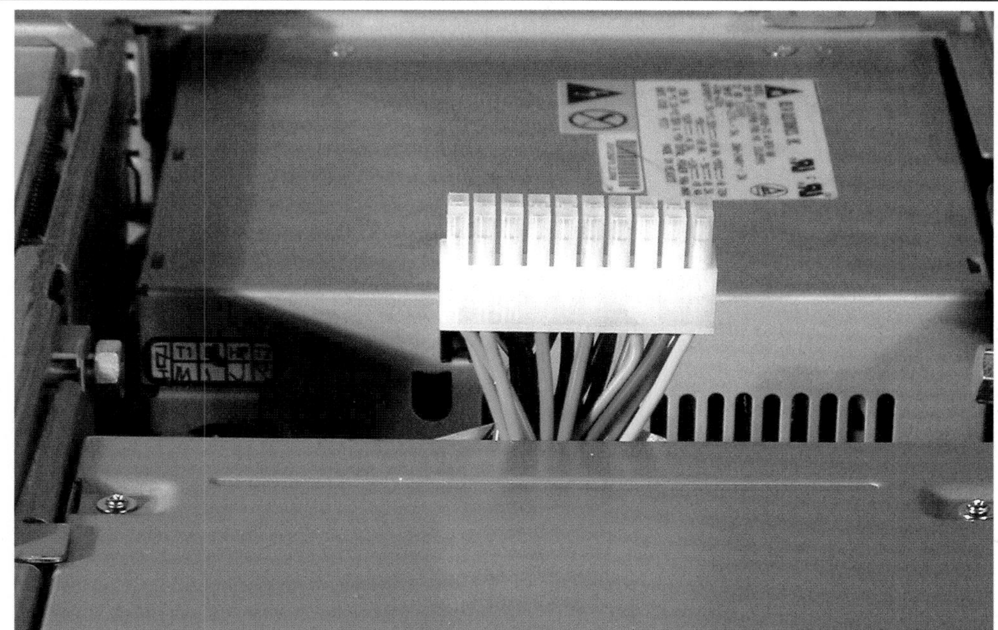

Figure 5-23.
ATX motherboard power connector.

Figure 5-24.
Inside a power supply. Power supplies are field replacement units.

ATX Form Factor

The ATX form factor is an improvement over the AT and XT form factors. It has a *keyed* power connector. Look back to Figure 5-21. This means it is impossible (more or less) to plug the connector into the board incorrectly. Do keep in mind that nothing along these lines is truly impossible. If sufficient force is applied, it can be plugged in backward. The connector should attach easily. If it does not, do not force it.

The ATX form factor also has 3.3-volt power connectors as well as power switch on and standby power connection. ***Standby power connection,*** also called ***soft power,*** provides power to the keyboard when the computer system is in sleep mode. Power is reduced to the entire system, but some power must remain on to reactivate or wake up the system. This is the purpose of the standby power connection. The power on and the standby power connections are also used jointly by Windows 9x software to turn the computer off using software commands rather than a physical switch.

standby power connection provides power to reactivate or wake up a system in standby mode.

soft power another term for the features provided by a standby power connection.

The addition of 3.3 volts at the power connection has eliminated the need for a voltage regulator located at the CPU. The regulator was used to convert the 5 volts from the power supply to the lower voltage required by the new CPU units. ATX has become one of the most popular power supply form factors on the market.

APM Standards

Advanced Power Management (APM) a power saving design that is managed by the operating system.

Advanced Power Management (APM) is a specification developed by Microsoft and Intel. It is a power saving design that is managed by the operating system. There are five power conditions available through APM. See the chart in **Figure 5-25.**

Not all devices are controllable by the APM technology. The device must comply with the APM design before the APM technology can control it.

Troubleshooting the Power Supply

The bulleted list that follows contains signs that a power supply might be bad. Although some of the indicators can be caused by other system components, it is most likely that the power supply has caused the occurrence. Power supply failure is quite frequent when compared to the failure of other computer components.

These common signs of a defective power supply include the following:

- **Inoperable cooling fans:** Cooling fans that are not running are a fairly consistent sign that the power supply has failed. (Cooling fans receive their power directly from the power supply.)
- **Smoke:** Smoke coming from the power supply is an indicator of electronic component or circuit board damage. Electronic components usually burn up from an overload condition. This almost always results in excessive heat, which generates the smoke.
- **Circuit breaker tripping:** If a circuit breaker is tripped, it is most likely caused by the power supply unit in the computer. With the exception of the monitor, no other component will generate a condition to trip the breaker. To verify that the problem is with the power supply, unplug the monitor to isolate the computer power supply.
- **Automatic rebooting:** If the computer reboots itself while on standby or during normal operation, it is a good indication of a bad power supply. The power level dropping and rising is a common occurrence as the power supply breaks down. This fluctuating voltage level causes the computer system to reboot for no apparent reason.

Full On	The system is at full power.
APM Enabled	The APM power system is on and unused devices are powered down.
APM Standby	The system appears asleep. Most devices are shut down but can be powered back up almost instantly.
APM Suspend	The system is not operating and is in a state of suspended animation. Operation parameters have been saved to disk. The system can be brought back to the APM enabled state but with some delay.
Off	The power supply is off. The system is completely shut down.

Figure 5-25. Chart of the five conditions possible with APM technology.

- **Electric shock:** Any electric shock received from the computer case is a sign of a bad power supply or one that is breaking down. *Always use extreme caution when troubleshooting a suspected power supply unit. Remember that 120-volt ac power can be deadly.*
- **Excessive heat:** This troubleshooting diagnosis is made through experience. Even a normally functioning power supply will produce a certain amount of heat. Heat is a normal by-product of electrical equipment. However, excessive heat is a sure sign that complete failure of an electronic component is imminent. The excessive heat in combination with the other signs can leave little doubt that the power supply is failing. If the power supply is too hot to touch, it has excessive heat. Electronic components usually start to break down at 160°F (71°C).

Electronic technicians can repair power supplies, but it is usually not cost effective. The time taken to diagnose the power supply, locate the component, and replace the defective component is simply cost prohibitive. It's much quicker and more economical to replace rather than repair. Power supplies are very low cost components. The cost of labor and availability of replacement parts are the major factors that determine when a unit is repaired or replaced.

Replacing a Power Supply

Replacing a power supply is an easy task. You must make sure the replacement is an acceptable form factor to match the case and motherboard. You must also make sure there is an adequate watt capacity provided by the replacement unit. *The watts capacity should either match or exceed the unit being replaced.*

Steps for power supply replacement:

1. Be absolutely sure the power is off. (Do not use an anti-static wrist strap for this operation.)
2. Sketch of all the connections between the old power supply unit and the other computer components. (This will save you a great deal of time later.)

3. Remove the power connections carefully. Try not to disturb other cable connections on the motherboard or other devices. Also, remove the power cord attached to the power supply.
4. Remove retaining/mounting screws from the case that secure the power supply in place.
5. Place the new power supply into the case and secure the retaining/mounting screws.
6. Reconnect the power connections to the motherboard and devices using your sketch as a map.
7. Place any extra connections from the power supply in a neat bundle. Keep the loose connectors away from the motherboard. A loose connector could easily slip over a motherboard bare jumper causing destruction during power or can catch in the fan blades causing the CPU to overheat.
8. Take one last look around at the connections. Verify that they are all secure, and then power on the computer before replacing the case cover. The cover should be left off until you are satisfied the PC is working properly. Any error messages at this time could be generated by a loose or improper connection during installation.
9. If everything is fine, replace the case cover and power on the PC once more. When replacing the case cover, be careful not to pinch any of the cables between the case frame and cover.

Surge Protection Devices

An electrical surge, brownout, or blackout can happen at any time. A surge is when a higher voltage than desired is present in the electrical system. A brownout is when low voltage is present. In a blackout condition, there is no voltage present. A momentary blackout can happen at any time and go completely unnoticed by the human eye. All that is required is the absence of one electrical cycle of power, or less, to cause a computer crash or lockup. **Figure 5-26** shows a series of cycles with one flatlined. Below it is a series of digital signals with a large group of flat digital pulses in relation to the one cycle.

Surge protection devices are designed to protect computer and other electronic devices against harmful surges of electrical energy. Two of the most common methods of providing protection are the use of power strips and UPS systems. UPS systems also protect against brownouts and blackouts.

UPS System

uninterruptible power supply (UPS) a power supply that ensures a constant supply of quality electrical power to the computer system.

An ***uninterruptible power supply (UPS)*** is designed to ensure a constant supply of quality electrical power to the computer system. Quality power means a power supply that eliminates surges and low voltage as well as complete power outage conditions. **Figure 5-27** illustrates a typical UPS system showing outlets, surge protection, batteries, and charger. **Figure 5-28** shows two typical UPS systems.

A UPS system monitors the power input to the computer while maintaining a fully charged battery. The AC/DC inverter is used to convert some of the 120 Vac

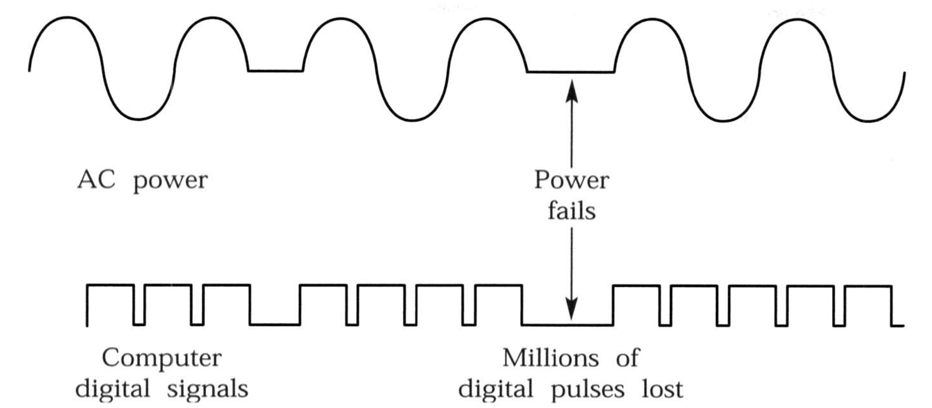

Figure 5-26.
Series of cycles with a few cycles flat lined. Below it is a series of digital signals with a large group of flat digital pulses. A few lost cycles can eliminate many digital pulses.

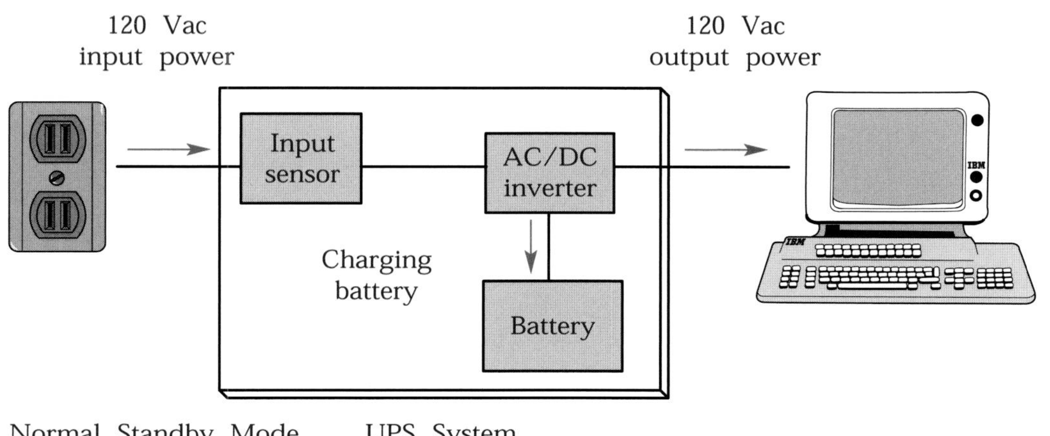

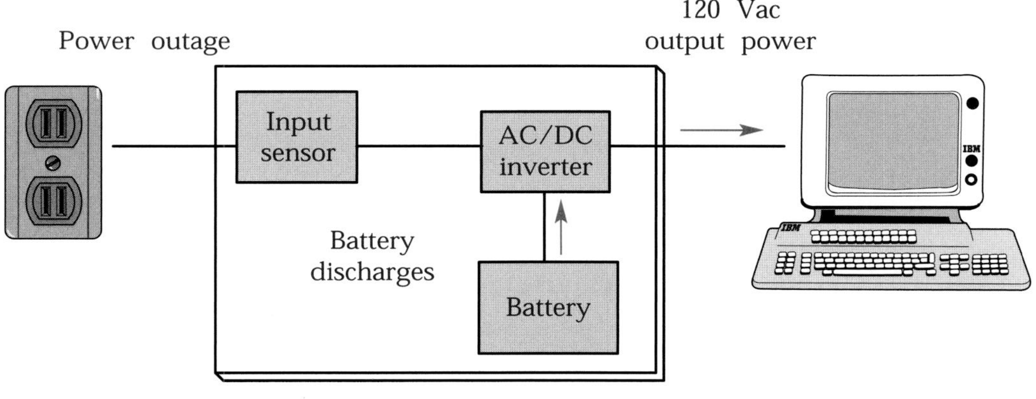

Figure 5-27.
A typical UPS monitors the 120 Vac input. When power is normal, the battery is kept fully charged and ac power is supplied to the computer. When the 120 Vac input fails, the battery discharges through the inverter to create 120 Vac for the computer.

from the outlet to 12 Vdc used to keep the batteries fully charged. When commercial power fails, the inverter changes the 12 Vdc from the battery back into 120 Vac. The 120 Vac is then used to maintain power to the computer until the PC can be properly shut down, preventing the loss of data. Without the UPS system, the PC would crash when the power failed, and all data in RAM would be lost.

Figure 5-28. Uninterruptible power supply systems protect PCs and servers from power loss and power surges. All critical PC systems should be protected by a UPS. (APC)

Low voltage situations and brownouts are common occurrences in electrical distribution systems. Some low voltage occurrences last only a few milliseconds and go completely unnoticed by the users. Even low voltage levels of a few milliseconds can cause a computer crash. Remember that the digital traffic in a computer is traveling at megahertz values. Many commands can be issued in a few milliseconds or thousands of bits of data can be sent. All of it could be lost during the momentary voltage loss. Many computer system lockups are caused by momentary low voltage conditions. This condition can be prevented by using a UPS. A power strip does not provide protection against blackout or brownout conditions.

Power Strips

Not all power strips provide protection against power surges. Some are designed as a strip of convenient outlets to plug equipment into. Power strips that are designed for power surge protection have a ***metal oxide varistor (MOV)*** connected across the internal electrical line.

metal oxide varistor (MOV)
a gate in a surge suppressor that becomes conductive at a given voltage, causing current to bypass the equipment plugged into the suppressor.

The MOV does not normally conduct electricity until a certain voltage level is reached. Then the MOV acts much like a direct short. It provides an alternate path for current. This diverts the current from the path through the electronic equipment that is plugged into the strip.

Power strips offer some degree of protection against power surges. While there is no true protection against extreme power surges, such as those generated by a direct hit from a bolt of lightning, the surge protector does protect against lower forms of power surge. A power surge can occur naturally many times a day in high-voltage power distribution systems. Most of them go unnoticed, but there are some that are quite severe. Surges are produced in the normal course of events such as in the opening and closing of electrical switch gear. Electrical distribution systems are normally rerouted while performing routine or emergency maintenance.

Other sources of voltage surges are caused by running brush-type motors such as those found in vacuum cleaners, drills, saws, and most any type of power tool or appliance. These types of surges show up as line spikes. See **Figure 5-29.**

These surges can produce very large spikes in the electrical system many times greater than the normal voltage. These spikes can damage sensitive electronic equipment. Many electronic components have maximum operating voltages. When a voltage surge exceeds this value, the component is damaged.

Batteries

Computers keep a variety of information stored in their CMOS. In this way, when your computer is turned on, it knows the settings describing the hard drive and floppy drive as well as items like the time and date. This information cannot be stored in ROM since it is constantly changing and different from machine to machine. Yet, computers need to maintain this information even when powered down. Thus, a battery is used to power the CMOS chip when the main power supply to the computer is shut down. Look at **Figure 5-30.**

Batteries are constructed in a simple manner. When two dissimilar metals are placed in contact with a chemical solution, called an electrolyte, a voltage is produced. See **Figure 5-31** for an illustration of the principles behind a battery. It shows two metal plates and an electrolyte with a lightbulb as the load.

The most common types of batteries used for motherboards are alkaline, nickel metal hydride, nickel cadmium (also called NiCad), and lithium. All are rechargeable batteries. The charge on a lithium battery lasts longer than the other three types of battery. This is why lithium is also the preferred choice for laptop computers.

A sure sign of failure of the CMOS battery is the PC's failure to correctly keep the date and time. Battery failure can also cause the system to fail to recognize the hard drive and other devices that store information about themselves in the CMOS settings. A typical PC battery should last five to seven years, but they have been known to fail sooner. You can usually reset the CMOS settings and use the computer as normal until the battery is replaced.

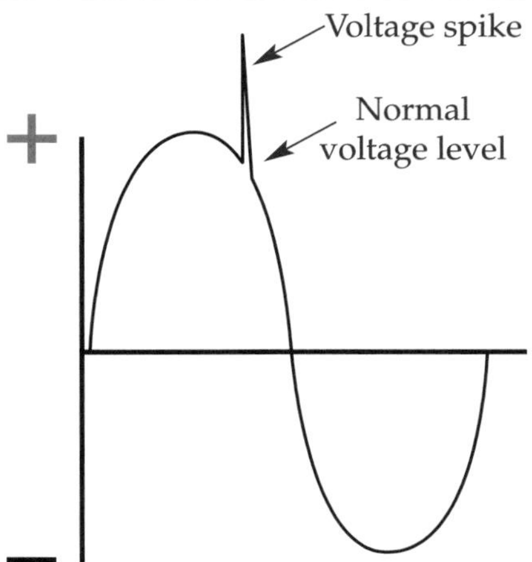

Figure 5-29. Voltage spikes can be caused by many things. The increased voltage in the spike damages electronic components by exceeding the voltage limitation of the component.

Figure 5-30. Typical motherboard battery.

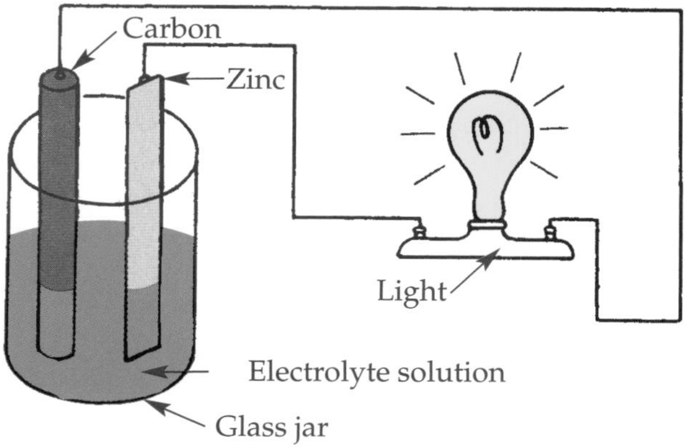

Figure 5-31. Illustration of the battery principles. Two metal plates in an electrolyte solution producing energy to power a light.

The batteries used for a UPS system are usually lead-acid or a jell-type. These batteries can provide power for a substantial period of time. The biggest advantage of jell-type is the lack of regular maintenance required as compared to lead-acid. Newer lead-acid batteries should also be maintenance free. Both types should be periodically inspected for corrosion on the battery terminals.

Battery Disposal

Batteries must be disposed of in the manner outlined by the Environmental Protection Agency (EPA). Most manufacturers will readily accept the old battery in return when purchasing a new one. They have the proper means of disposal at hand that the typical technician does not. You simply do not throw an old battery into the trash, especially large UPS batteries.

More information on battery recycling can be found on the EPA's Web site. The site is located at www.epa.gov.

Summary

- Electrical voltage provides the pressure needed to push electrons through a circuit.
- Amperes or current is used to express the amount or volume of electrical energy flowing through the circuit.
- Electrical current is expressed in amperes.
- Resistance is the opposition to current and is measured in ohms.
- Electrical power is expressed in watts.
- Power is calculated by multiplying voltage times amperes. If the circuit is a dc circuit, this value is expressed in watts (W). If it is an ac circuit, this value is expressed in volt-amperes (VA). Watts is not the same as VA.
- The highest possible resistance reading is called infinity.
- A good fuse or cable has a zero resistance reading.
- Clean electrical power does not have any undesirable electrical characteristics such as spikes or low voltage slumps.
- An auto-range meter selects the proper range automatically.
- A dedicated circuit is used only for computer equipment.
- Computer systems must be properly grounded.
- PC power supplies have form factors to match cases and motherboards.
- Remember "black back-to-back" when connecting power supply connectors to the motherboard.
- Advanced Power Management systems are used to conserve electrical energy.
- A UPS system provides protection against power surges and temporary power outages.
- A surge protector power strip provides protection against power surges.
- An MOV is used to stop voltage surges in electrical power strips and UPS systems.

Review Questions

Answer the following questions on a separate sheet of paper. Please do not write in this book.

1. Define *electrical energy*.
2. Water pressure, expressed in PSI, is similar to what value in electronics?
3. What value in electrical energy is similar to gallons per minute in water?
4. Opposition to electron flow is expressed in _____.
5. Wattage and VA are exactly the same. True or False?

6. The wattage rating on a power supply unit is an indication of how much _____.
   a electrical energy can be safely supplied to the PC's devices
   b electrical energy the power supply will consume
   c. current the power supply unit will draw from the PC's devices
   d. voltage the power supply unit needs to operate the PC
7. What resistance value will a good fuse indicate on a digital multimeter?
8. A blown fuse should indicate how much resistance on an ohmmeter?
9. A good cable should read how much resistance from one end to the other end?
10. What is a dedicated circuit?
11. What are the typical dc voltage levels from a PC power supply unit?
12. How does an ATX form factor power supply differ from an AT or XT power supply?
13. What is the name of the connector that is used to supply power to a hard drive unit?
14. List five APM power conditions.
15. What is a metal oxide varistor used for?
16. What is the difference between an electrical surge and a brownout?
17. A UPS unit delivers a constant level of power to a PC during _____. Select all that apply.
   a. electrical surges
   b. low voltage
   c. power outage conditions
   d. brownouts
18. All power strips provide surge protection. True or False?

Sample A+ Exam Questions

Answer the following questions on a separate sheet of paper. Please do not write in this book.

1. Select the best definition of a PC power supply.
   a. A power supply converts 120 Vac power into 3.3, 5, and 12 Vdc levels that are used by the motherboard and various components.
   b. A power supply converts 120 Vdc power into 3.3, 5, and 12 Vdc levels that are used by the motherboard and various components.
   c. A power supply converts 120 Vac power into 5, 12, and 18 Vdc level that is used by the motherboard and various components.
   d. A power supply converts 120 Vdc power into 5, 12, and 18 Vdc level that is used by the motherboard and various components.

2. Which unit below is used to express electrical pressure?
   a. Ampere
   b. Volt
   c. Watt
   d. Ohm
3. Which electrical characteristics does a digital multimeter measure? Select all that apply.
   a. Voltage
   b. Resistance
   c. Amperes
   d. Wire size
4. Which item listed below ensures a steady and clean supply of electrical energy during power outages?
   a. VOM
   b. DMM
   c. UPS
   d. APC
5. Electrical power is usually expressed by which letter?
   a. V
   b. A
   c. W
   d. R
6. What is the maximum electrical load that may be connected to a typical 120 Vac power strip supplying computer equipment?
   a. 1000 W
   b. 1600 W
   c. 2000 W
   d. 2400 W
7. Which of the following is the closest to the resistance reading of a blown fuse?
   a. 0 Ω
   b. 120 volts
   c. 10 MΩ
   d. Infinity
8. Which is a typical procedure when a power supply is suspected to be bad?
   a. Open the power supply unit and replace the fuse.
   b. Check the output voltage levels of the wall outlet.
   c. Run **msinfo32** from **Run** in the **Start** menu to diagnose the power output.
   d. Put on an anti-static wrist strap and then open the power supply box to replace the fuse.

9. What system was developed by Microsoft to save electrical energy when using a PC?
   a. APM
   b. EES
   c. MOV
   d. ATX
10. Which DC voltage levels are associated with a typical ATX power supply?
   a. 3.3, 5, 12
   b. 5, 12, 18
   c. 3.3, 5, 12, 18
   d. 12, 18, 24

Suggested Laboratory Activities

Do not attempt any suggested laboratory activities without your instructor's permission. Certain activities can render the PC operating system inoperable.

1. Remove a power supply from a typical PC and then reinstall it.
2. Practice taking ohm readings of various conductors.
3. Gather several small batteries of different voltages. Practice taking dc voltage readings.
4. Take voltage readings of the 120 Vac outlets in your classroom. See what the actual voltage levels are. Take readings throughout the day to see if the voltage levels change.
5. Take voltage readings from the output of a typical PC power supply. Take notes of the voltage type (whether ac or dc) and the voltage levels.
6. Take resistance readings of a fuse known to be good and then a fuse known to be blown. Compare the results.
7. Go to a multimeter manufacturer's Web site, such as www.fluke.com, and download a user's manual for one of their digital multimeters.

Interesting Web Sites for More Information

www.apcc.com

www.bestpower.com

www.duracell.com

Chapter 5
Laboratory Activity

Exploring and Replacing the Power Supply

After completing this laboratory activity, you will be able to:

- ❑ Replace a PC power supply unit.
- ❑ Determine if a power supply is defective.
- ❑ Check the voltage input and output of a power supply unit.

Introduction

One of the most common PC problems encountered is a defective power supply unit. The power supply unit is considered a field replacement unit. A field replacement unit is any module in a PC system that is commonly changed in the field and does not need to be brought back to the repair shop to be replaced or upgraded. The power supply is used to convert 120-volt ac input into 12-, 5-, and 3.3-volt dc outputs. It supplies the correct dc voltage to the PC's modules and devices, such as the motherboard, hard disk drive, and CD-ROM drive. Some of the dc voltages are positive while others are negative. Some of the connections will have no voltage indicated at all. These usually indicate a ground used by system components. Power supplies come in a variety of styles and arrangements. Their physical appearance depends on the motherboard and case style.

Power supplies are classified by their wattage ratings. The wattage rating is an indication of how much electrical energy can be safely supplied to the PC's devices. In general, a higher wattage rating means that more devices can be connected to the power supply. In a typical repair scenario, you would replace a power supply with one that has the same wattage rating. However, if additional devices have been added to the machine, then the power supply may need to be upgraded to a higher wattage rating.

In this lab activity, you will remove the existing power supply and then reinstall it in the same PC. After reinstalling the same power supply, you will record the voltage output of the connectors. Note that not all power supplies provide the same voltage levels.

Equipment and Materials

- Typical PC with a 486 or later processor.
- Digital multimeter to take voltage readings.

Procedure

1. ______ Power up the assigned PC and make sure it is working properly. If all is well, properly shut down the unit.

2. ______ Remove the cover from the PC's case.
3. ______ Before removing any of the wiring or attempting to physically remove the power supply unit, *unplug the power cord* that runs from the power supply to the 120-volt outlet.
4. ______ Once the power cord has been removed, make a drawing of the power cables, noting their orientation to the various components. For example, draw the position of the black wires running from the power supply to the motherboard. The connector's orientation can be recorded by the color of the wiring as well as the connector identification marks. The following illustration shows how two power cables connect to the motherboard. The power cable connection to the motherboard may consist of one or two separate power cables, depending on the age of the technology.

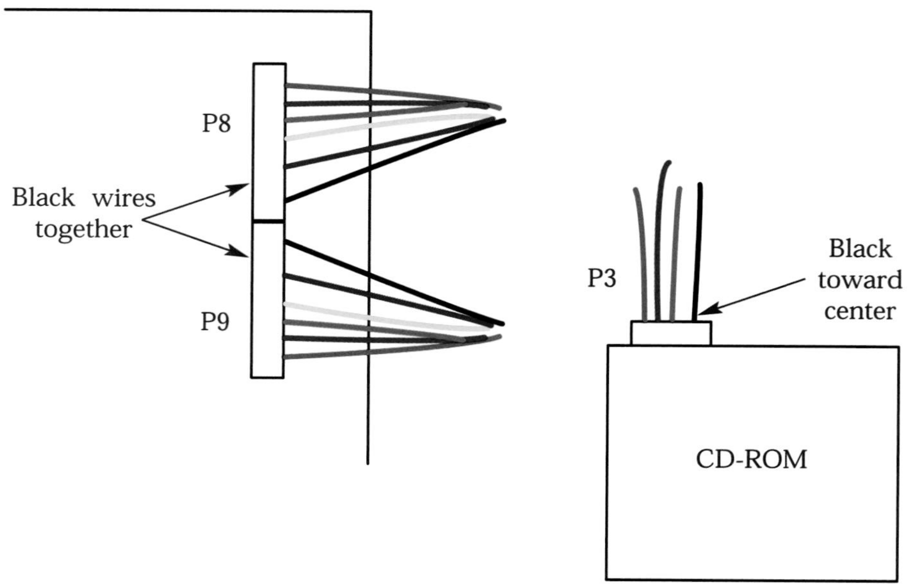

In the drawing, the connector identification marks have been labeled P8, P9, and P3. The orientations of the black wire to the physical devices have also been recorded. It is not necessary to indicate each color wire in the harness. The wiring in the drawing shown here will not necessarily match the wiring in the PC you are working on.

5. ______ Carefully remove each of the power cables from the various devices. As you remove the cables, be careful not to loosen any other connections or adapter cards installed in the PC.
6. ______ After all of the wiring from the power supply has been disconnected, locate the screws that connect the power supply to the case. Carefully remove the screws, being careful not to confuse the power supply mounting screws with the screws used to mount the fan to the power supply. You should not need to remove the power supply fan. Also, do not remove any screws used to fasten the cover to the power supply.

7. ______ After the power supply has been completely removed, call your instructor to inspect your work.

8. ______ Reverse the process to reinstall the power supply. Reconnect all the devices according to your drawing. Do not plug the power cord into the power supply or the outlet until your instructor has inspected your work.

9. ______ After the instructor has approved your reinstallation of the power supply, connect the power cord and power on the PC.

10. ______ Check all devices to make sure they have power. If they do not, call your instructor.

11. ______ Now, take voltage readings at each of the different connectors running from the power supply. You need to turn the power off, sketch the connectors and wiring, disconnect the power cables to the devices, and then reapply power to the power supply. Finally, measure the voltages at each terminal in the various connectors. Use the following illustration as a guide when creating your own sketches. *Be aware that the example given is not intended to match your unit but simply to serve as a model.*

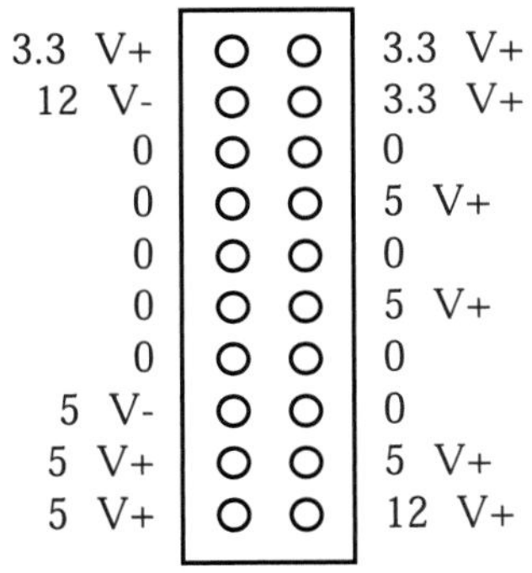

3.3 V+	O	O	3.3 V+
12 V-	O	O	3.3 V+
0	O	O	0
0	O	O	5 V+
0	O	O	0
0	O	O	5 V+
0	O	O	0
5 V-	O	O	0
5 V+	O	O	5 V+
5 V+	O	O	12 V+

Warning:
Disconnecting a power connector from any device while the device is energized could result in permanent damage to the device. This is especially true for the motherboard.

12. ______ After recording all voltages at each power connection, return the PC to its original condition.

Review Questions

Answer the following questions on a separate sheet of paper. Please do not write in this book.

1. What other components of the PC affect the power supply's appearance?
2. Do all power supplies supply the same voltages?
3. What is the power supply function in the PC?
4. What is the wattage rating of the power supply in your test unit?
5. What is the rated input voltage and frequency? (Look on the power supply.)

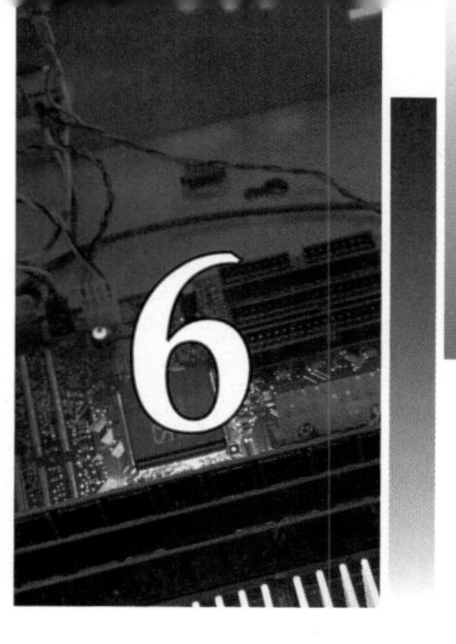

6 Memory

After studying this chapter, you will be able to:

- Identify major issues concerning memory upgrades and replacement.
- Describe how to properly replace and/or upgrade RAM.
- Identify and classify the various types of memory available.
- Identify memory map areas and functions.
- Identify typical memory problems.
- Upgrade system memory.

A+ Exam—Key Points

Know the memory map areas thoroughly as well as DOS file and BIOS locations in memory.

Know the DOS commands related to memory management such as DOS=HIGH, NOEMS, and MEM.

Study and know the maximum amount of RAM accessible by various processors.

Key Words and Terms

The following words and terms will become important pieces of your computer vocabulary. Be sure you can define them.

buffer
conventional memory
dual in-line memory module (DIMM)
dual in-line package (DIP)
dynamic RAM (DRAM)
electrically erasable programmable read only memory (EEPROM)
erasable programmable read only memory (EPROM)
error code correction (ECC)
even parity checking
expanded memory standard (EMS)
extended memory system (XMS)
fake parity
flash memory
flash ROM
heap
high memory area (HMA)
hot swap
memory management software
nanosecond (ns)
odd parity checking
parity
programmable read only memory (PROM)
random access memory (RAM)
read only memory (ROM)
registered memory
reserved memory
safe mode
single in-line memory module (SIMM)
single in-line package (SIP)
static RAM
upper memory

The memory in a computer is one of the most difficult parts of the computer to explain and understand. It is imperative that you carefully examine the illustrations provided in this chapter while studying the concept of memory. You may also need your instructor's help to completely grasp this difficult concept. While memory is, without question, one of the easiest upgrades that can be made to a PC, understanding system memory and its evolution is very complex and confusing.

The original disk operating system (DOS) could only access 1MB of memory for program use. This restriction existed for many years to ensure compatibility with legacy software systems. Consequently, this restriction is still part of memory terminology and structure. With the introduction of Windows 95 and Windows NT, memory could be handled as one large unit, referred to as the *heap*. However, the memory restrictions were in effect in Windows if the PC was using legacy programs (programs designed to run under DOS).

This chapter covers memory types, memory terminology, memory diagnostics, and memory management used by the various Microsoft operating systems. It will also help you understand the complexity of PC memory and develop troubleshooting strategies. A large part of the A+ Certification exams is dedicated to questions regarding memory systems and terminology. The terminology associated with memory can be very confusing, but with a little concentration and effort, you will master the subject of PC memory.

Questions to Ask before Upgrading Memory

Before you begin your study of memory types, let's look at the issues you must consider when upgrading memory. There are a number of items of which you must be aware. Novices simply plug memory modules into motherboards and expect the amount of memory and performance to increase. This will not always be the result. Improperly identified memory modules and improper installation can decrease PC performance and possibly permanently damage the motherboard.

The questions that need to be answered before upgrading memory involve the following:

Physical Shape: What type of memory will be upgraded or replaced? Are you adding SIMMs or DIMMs? Is the machine a laptop requiring a small outline memory package?

Quantity: What is the total amount of RAM desired? Are you adding to existing RAM or replacing it?

Parity or Non-parity: Does the existing memory have parity checking? Does the existing system support parity checking?

Voltage: At what voltage do the memory chips operate (5 or 3.3 volts)?

Type: What type of memory chip will be installed—DRAM, SRAM, etc?

Speed: Will the existing chip speed be matched or exceeded?

These questions should all be answered before attempting a memory upgrade on a PC. Deciding on these issues will save time and money. The rest of this chapter assists with answering these questions. It also covers important concepts that will aid in your understanding of technical manuals and memory issues.

Physical Memory Packages

PC memory chips are packaged in several different physical styles. Some of these are SIP, DIP, SIMM, and DIMM. Physical size of the memory package is very important when the technician is assessing an upgrade or a replacement.

SIP

A ***single in-line package (SIP),*** as the name implies, is a single row of connections that run along the length of a chip, **Figure 6-1.** SIPs are sometimes referred to as SIPPs, single in-line pin packages, because the row of connections along the modules are pins. This type of module is not often used today. It had a high physical profile and the pins were easily bent.

single in-line package (SIP)
a memory chip containing a single row of connections, which run along the length of the chip.

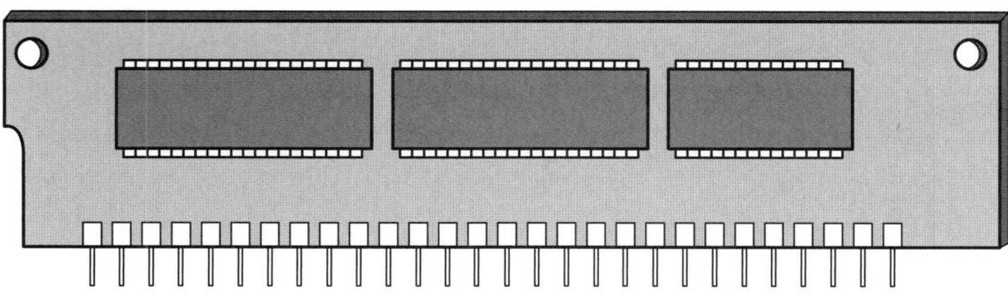

Figure 6-1.
Early PC memory modules were SIPs.

DIP

dual in-line package (DIP)
a memory chip that has two rows of connections, one row per side of the chip.

A ***dual in-line package (DIP)*** is a chip that has two rows of connections, one row per side of the chip, **Figure 6-2.** This style is commonly used for cache memory or for memory that must be mounted permanently on a circuit board. You can see memory of this type on older model motherboards. It is mounted in rows near the CPU unit.

SIMM

single in-line memory module (SIMM)
a memory module containing a row of DIP memory chips mounted on a circuit board.

A ***single in-line memory module (SIMM)*** is a row of DIP memory chips mounted on a circuit board. The circuit board has flat contacts that run along both sides of the bottom edge. This type of connection is called an *edge connector*. The circuit board is then inserted into a SIMM memory slot on the motherboard. The SIMM is designed so that, when plugged into the memory socket, each side of the edge connector is the same circuit. This eliminates easily damaged pins. SIMMs come in 30-pin and 72-pin packages.

Tech Tip:
Flat edge contacts are also referred to as pins.

DIMM

dual in-line memory module (DIMM)
a memory module in which the edge connectors are located directly across the circuit board from each other and do not connect electrically.

A ***dual in-line memory module (DIMM)*** is constructed much like a SIMM. The major difference is that the edge connectors located directly across the circuit board from each other do not connect electrically. They are not the same electrical connection as they are on the SIMM board. The DIMM design allows for more electrical connections per inch than the SIMM design, **Figure 6-3.** DIMMs come in 168-pin packages.

SO-DIMM and SO-RIMM

Small outline DIMM (SO-DIMM) and *small outline RIMM (SO-RIMM)* are a small outline package of regular DIMM and RIMM modules made especially for laptop applications where space is compact. The small outline package is designed to fit easily into the small confines of the interior of the laptop.

Micro-DIMM

Micro-DIMM is a more compact version of the standard SO-DIMM package. Kingmax Semiconductor coined the term "Micro-DIMM" to distinguish it from

Figure 6-2.
Another early form of PC memory was the DIP.

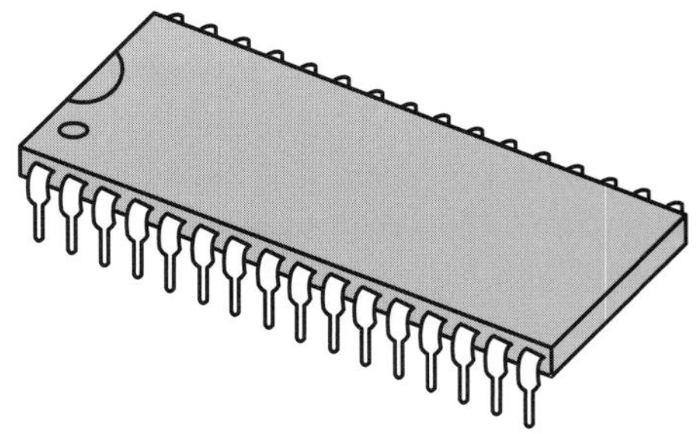

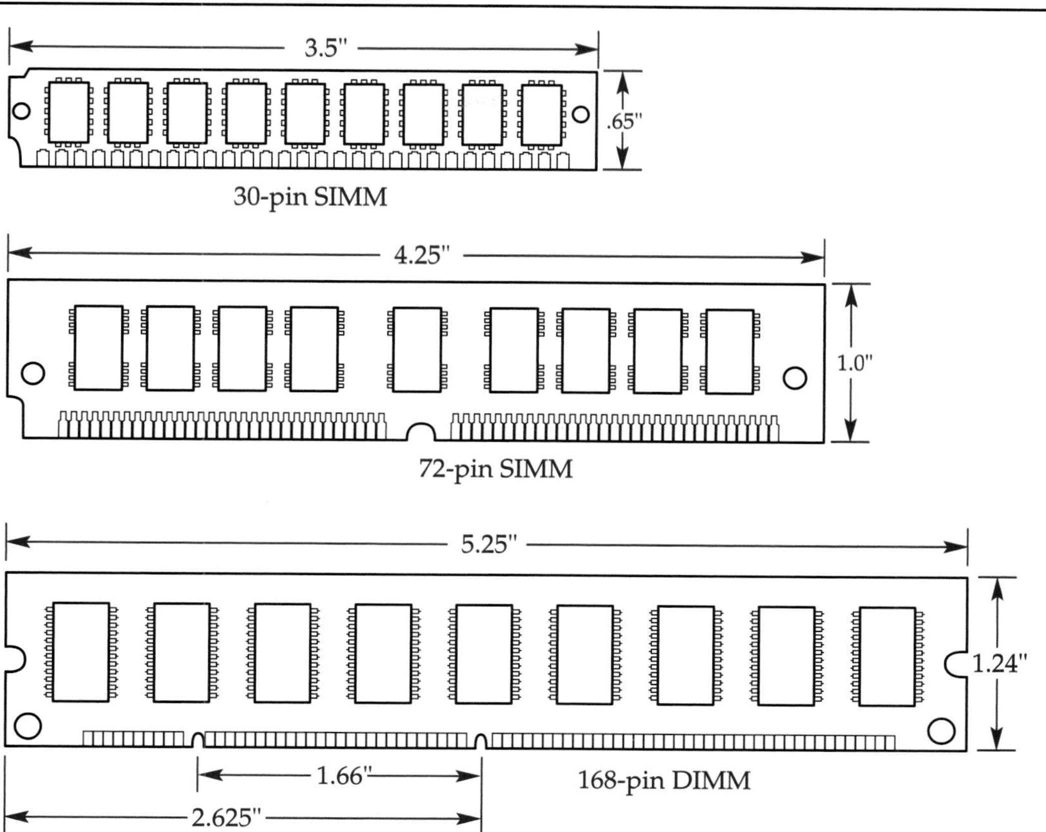

Figure 6-3. The various packages of memory can be easily identified by size. Shown are two SIMMs and the more modern DIMM.

the already existing SO-DIMM package and to emphasize its smaller size. Other memory manufacturers such as Kingston use SO-DIMM as the name of the smaller module. Either way, the module is quickly identified because of the overall smaller dimensions and pin count. The Micro-DIMM has a 172-pin count while the standard SO-DIMM module has a 200-pin count, **Figure 6-4.** The Micro-DIMM memory module is used in many notebook and laptop computers, not in desktops.

ROM and RAM Memory

Computer systems contain both ***read only memory (ROM)*** and ***random access memory (RAM)*** memory. ROM is designed to store the program information in a permanent fashion, while RAM is designed to be loaded with data or programs, which can then be erased and reloaded again and again. All programming and data in RAM is lost when power is removed from the chip. ROM retains any data and programs after power is removed.

read only memory (ROM) memory that stores information permanently.

random access memory (RAM) memory type that can store information, be erased, and have new information written to it.

To help you understand the difference between RAM and ROM, think of a typical "white board" found in classrooms or in corporate boardrooms. The white board requires the use of a nonpermanent marker. If information is written on a white board using a permanent marker, the information will remain on the board forever, similar to the information written in a ROM memory chip. If an erasable marker is used on the white board, the information can be wiped clean from the board, allowing new and different information to be written on the white board. This is similar to RAM.

Figure 6-4.
Micro-DIMM is a compact version of the standard SO-DIMM. Some manufacturers also call the Micro-DIMM a SO-DIMM. (Kingston Technology)

The terms *volatile* and *nonvolatile* are often used to describe computer memory. RAM is considered volatile memory. Like RAM, a volatile memory chip loses its data when power is removed from the computer. ROM chips are nonvolatile. Nonvolatile memory chips retain their information when the power is removed from the computer.

Types of ROM

There has been a good deal of innovation involving ROM memory. Not all ROM chips have programs that are permanently embedded. Many variations of ROM chips can actually be reprogrammed with different data or programs. They are still classified as ROM chips because, in normal applications, they retain their information even after power is removed from the computer.

PROM

The original ROM chips were manufactured with a program etched into the chip. The technically correct term for this type of ROM chip is *mask ROM*. The manufacturer uses a mask to create the circuitry. This circuitry represents the program when the chip is manufactured. Recall the discussion from Chapter 1—Introduction to a Typical PC about the chip manufacturing process. The programs in these chips cannot be altered.

Programmable read only memory (PROM) is similar to mask ROM. It is used extensively in computer program development. Blank ROM chips are purchased and then programmed using a device called a *PROM burner*. A PROM burner is connected to a PC. A program or data is written on the PC and then transferred to the burner where it permanently electrically burns the program into the blank PROM chip. The PROM chip then retains the program indefinitely, but it cannot be reprogrammed.

PROM programmable read only memory.

EPROM

Erasable programmable read only memory (EPROM) was an advancement of the PROM. These chips can be programmed, erased, and then reprogrammed. The EPROM has a small clear window that exposes the miniature circuitry inside the chip. The chip is erased by shining an ultraviolet light through the window. This returns the EPROM back to its original blank state.

EPROM erasable programmable read only memory.

EEPROM

Electrically erasable programmable read only memory (EEPROM) eliminated the need for using an ultraviolet light to erase the memory chip. The EEPROM uses a higher electrical charge to erase the chip than the original charge used to program it. EEPROM was designed to be erased one bit at a time. In this way, part of a program could be erased rather then the entire program at one time.

EEPROM electrically erasable programmable read only memory.

Flash ROM

Flash ROM behaves in a similar manner to RAM. It is possible to replace the memory contents of flash RAM. It is similar to EEPROM, but it uses a much higher voltage to erase the chip and also erases the entire block of memory at one time.

It is important to note that EEPROM and Flash ROM can only be reprogrammed a limited number of times. At some point, the chip will become damaged by the application of the higher than normal voltage used in the erase operation.

flash ROM ROM that can be erased in blocks using a high voltage.

Types of RAM

Random access memory is a matrix of individual storage areas where information can be stored as bits. The name random access means that the CPU can access any bit anywhere in the memory. The CPU does not have to go through the memory in sequential fashion. The early computer systems did not have the advantage of RAM chips or disk drive systems. They used ROM chips and stored data on magnetic tape. The data on the tape was stored sequentially, bit by bit, along the entire length of tape. To access any information on the tape, the tape would have to play back bit-by-bit until the desired information could be retrieved.

Dynamic RAM vs. static RAM

There are two basic forms of RAM. One type, dynamic RAM, uses capacitors to store the information. The second type, static RAM, uses devices called flip-flops.

dynamic RAM (DRAM) a type of integrated circuit that utilizes capacitors to assist in storing data in the transistors.

static RAM (SRAM) an integrated circuit using digital flip-flop components.

Dynamic RAM (referred to as DRAM, pronounced *dee-ram*) is a type of integrated circuit that uses capacitors to assist in storing data in the transistors. Capacitors are capable of storing electrical charges. The presence or absence of the electrical charge in the capacitor represents the binary data being stored. Because of their microscopic size, the capacitors in the integrated circuit lose their charge over a short period of time. To retain the charge, the capacitors must be constantly refreshed (recharged) with electrical energy. Dynamic RAM is used in the CPU because it is very small and is low cost when compared to static RAM.

Static RAM (referred to as SRAM and pronounced *es-ram*) is an integrated circuit technology based on digital flip-flop components. The flip-flop does not use a capacitor to hold the data condition as the dynamic RAM does. It transmits data faster than dynamic RAM because it does not have to be constantly refreshed. To take advantage of the faster data transfer speed, most PC cache systems use static RAM as opposed to dynamic RAM. However, SRAM is approximately four times larger than DRAM, and it is considerably more expensive. Consequently, a computer's RAM will be some variant of DRAM.

DRAM

The basic *dynamic RAM (DRAM)* is the typical memory chip installed in older PCs, **Figure 6-5.** When someone says a computer has 64MB of RAM, they are generally saying that the computer has DRAM. DRAM memory chips must be refreshed periodically to retain the information stored on them.

EDO DRAM

Extended Data Output DRAM (EDO DRAM) is faster than conventional DRAM. Conventional DRAM accesses only one block of memory at a time and then passes the data completely on to the next component before it transfers in new data. EDO DRAM is designed to access and start transferring in new data before the previous data stored on the chip is finished being transferred out. This technique greatly improves the transfer rate of memory.

BEDO DRAM

Burst Extended Data Output DRAM (BEDO DRAM) is an improved version of EDO DRAM. BEDO DRAM can transfer data in groups or bursts of four memory addresses at one time. EDO DRAM cannot keep up with a motherboard bus that runs faster than 66 MHz. Consequently, there are few current applications for this type of memory.

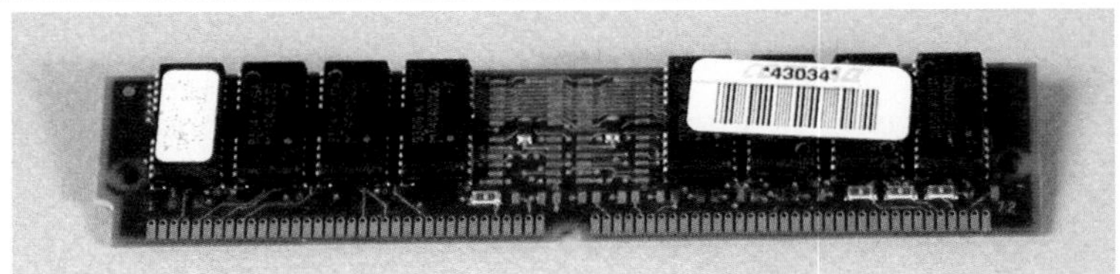

Figure 6-5. Basic DRAM found in older PCs.

SDRAM

Synchronous dynamic RAM (SDRAM) is much faster than conventional DRAM, **Figure 6-6.** SDRAM can transfer data at speeds exceeding 100 MHz. The SDRAM synchronizes the transfer of data with the CPU chip. Synchronizing data transfer timing increases data transfer rates. This is because the chip does not have to wait for the next tick of the CPU clock system to begin transferring data. SDRAM can be found on video cards because of its high-speed transfer rate.

DDR-SDRAM

Double Data Rate-Synchronous DRAM (DDR-SDRAM) is designed to replace SDRAM. As the name *double data rate* implies, this particular design can transmit data at twice the normal data rate.

Normally, data is transferred on each complete digital cycle. That is, one piece of data is transferred for each complete rise and fall of the digital signal. DDR is designed to transmit data on both the rising edge and the falling edge of a typical digital signal. This is how it is able to achieve twice the normal data transfer rate. For instance, a memory module designed to transfer data at 100 MHz can be replaced with a DDR-SDRAM, which can transfer the data at 200 MHz.

The DDR memory standard classification is based on the maximum data transfer rate. The data transfer rate is a product of the motherboard front side bus speed and the memory module data rate. For example, a motherboard bus designed for 100 MBps using a DDR SDRAM designed for doubling the bus data rate (100 MBps × 2 = 200 MBps) would produce a total data transfer rate of 1600 MBps (8 bits × 200 = 1600). The PC1600 standard description identifies the memory module type as one that is used on a front side bus rated at 100 MBps and used as a DDR, producing twice the data rate and moving 8 bits or 1 byte to achieve an overall speed of 1600 MBps, **Figure 6-7.** This speed is identified in the specification label PC1600. See the chart in **Figure 6-8** for other data transfer rate comparisons.

Dual-Channel DDR Memory

Dual-Channel DDR memory takes advantage of dual-channel technology developed by Intel in 2003. The RAM bus system, also known as the front side bus, consisted of a single bus system. The Intel Corporation redesigned the

Figure 6-6. SDRAM found in many desktop PCs.

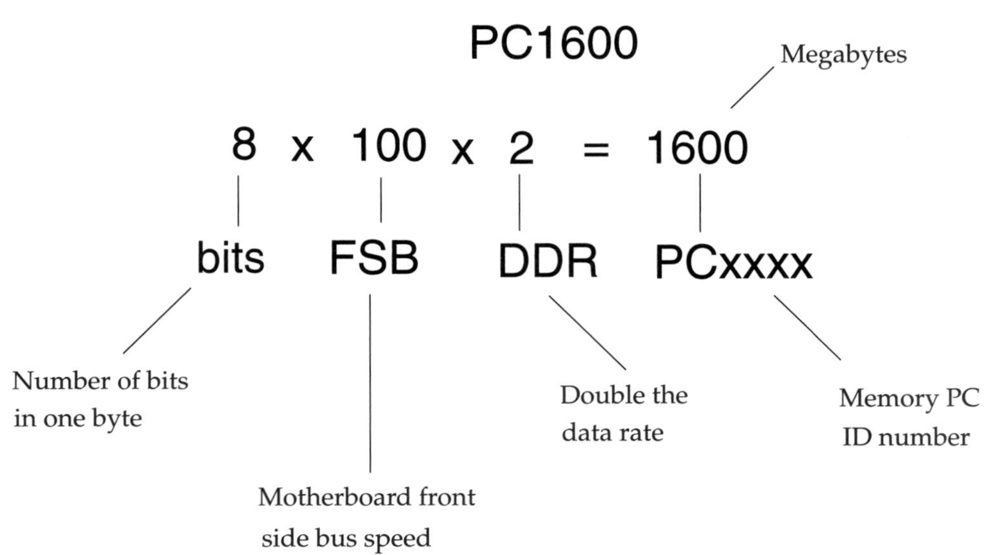

Figure 6-7. The memory PC ID number is derived by multiplying the number of bits by the motherboard's front side bus speed by the double data rate.

Figure 6-8. DDR data transfer rate comparisons. Note the correlation between the DDR specification identification of the memory and the data rate. For example, PC3200 is equal to a single channel rate of 3200 MBps (3.2 GBps).

DDR Specification	PC1600	PC2100	PC2700	PC3200
Bus Speed MHz	100 MHz	133 MHZ	166 MHz	200 MHZ
Data Rate MHz	200 MHz	266 MHz	333 MHz	400 MHz
Single Channel MBps PC	1600 MBps	2100 MBps	2700 MBps	3200 MBps
Dual-Channel MBps DDR	3200 MBps	4200 MBps	5400 MBps	6400 MBps

motherboard to provide two memory busses between the RAM and the north bridge chipset, **Figure 6-9.** The north bridge chipset contains the memory controller, which controls the flow of data between the RAM and CPU. Dual-channel technology doubles the data flow between the chipset and the RAM but does not actually double the data rate to the CPU. There is still at the time of this writing only a single bus between the CPU and chipset. While data rates are significantly higher, they have not reached double the rate when tested in the field.

VRAM

Video RAM (VRAM), also called *Video DRAM (VDRAM),* is a type of RAM used to enhance data transfer rates between the video card and the display unit. It is designed with two paths, one to the CPU and one to the display unit. This design allows for a much higher transfer rate.

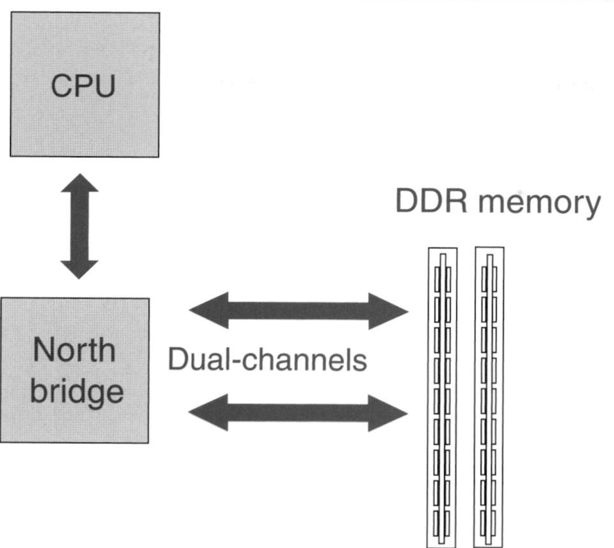

Figure 6-9.
The Intel dual-channel DDR memory motherboard architecture significantly increases the data throughput from the RAM to the north bridge.

WRAM

Windows RAM (WRAM) is specially designed memory used in video adapter cards to enhance Windows multimedia applications. It is much faster than traditional video RAM found in PCs.

SGRAM

Synchronous Graphics RAM (SGRAM) is used to enhance the video qualities of video cards. SGRAM is designed to work with advanced video card systems that contain their own controller. The design moves video RAM as large blocks of data rather than a stream. Moving the video data in large blocks makes for a more efficient system. SGRAM is found in many high performance 3D video card systems.

RDRAM

Rambus DRAM (RDRAM) was developed by Rambus, Inc. RDRAM is a proprietary memory system, **Figure 6-10.** The RDRAM uses a DDR (double data rate) technique to double the speed of the data transfer. Data transfer rates as high as 800 MHz can be accomplished using RDRAM and a motherboard and CPU that supports a 400 MHz front side bus. It is one of the fastest memory chips available. Intel originally incorporated Rambus RDRAM into their line of motherboards but has since discontinued it.

RIMM is the trade name for Direct Rambus memory module. It is longer than a 168-pin DIMM, and it reaches speeds of 800 MHz. It also uses a package capable of dissipating the heat generated by the high-speed data transfer rate. The package is an aluminum sheath, called a *heat spreader,* which covers the chips and acts as a heat sink.

RIMM must be installed in pairs to function. However, one RIMM module may contain more than enough memory for a user. In that case, to achieve the effect of two RIMM modules when using only one RIMM module, a continuity RIMM (C-RIMM) must be installed in the second slot, **Figure 6-11.** The C-RIMM does not contain any memory chips; it simply acts as an electrical connection allowing data to pass through as if there were an additional RIMM installed.

Figure 6-10. RDRAM has data transfer rates of up to 800 MHz.

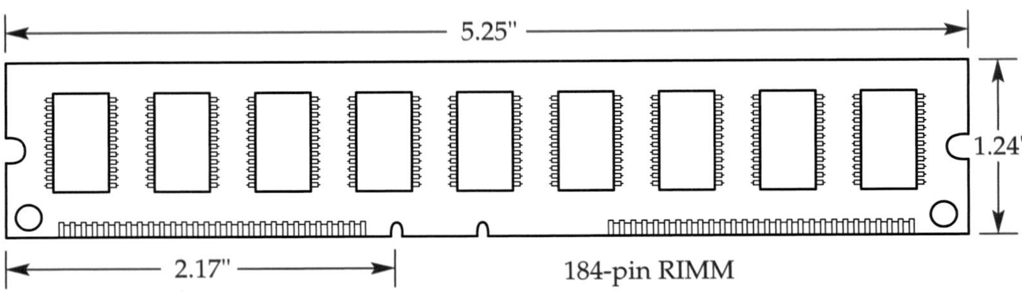

Typical RIMM Module

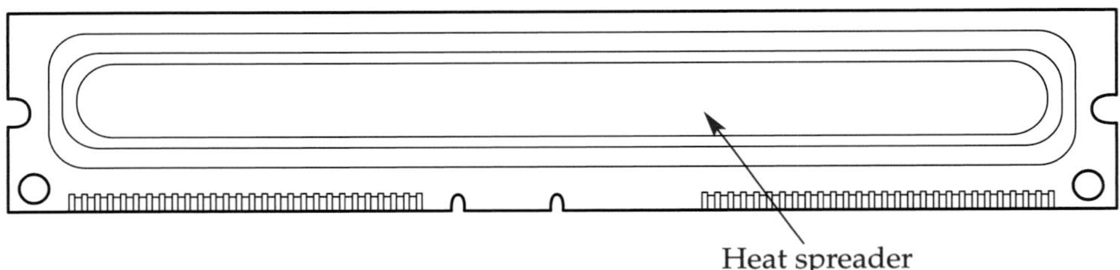

Typical C-RIMM Module

Figure 6-11. Sketch of RIMM and C-RIMM. In the diagram, the RIMM is shown with the heat spreader removed, exposing the individual memory chips.

When C-RIMM is used in conjunction with a RIMM, the exact slot sequence should be checked against the manufacturer's specifications.

SSD

A new technology called solid state disk (SSD) is a Plug and Play storage device designed to replace the traditional hard drive system. It is constructed with no moving parts. This creates greater data transfer rates and lower failure rates. Typically, the SSD is constructed of DRAM chips, a CPU, a BIOS chip, and a battery. It simulates a miniature PC that allows the SSD to communicate independently with the computer's CPU and with other independent devices such as RAM. At this time, it is used only in network servers, but as prices decrease, it will likely be used in standard PCs.

FPM RAM

Fast page mode RAM (FPM RAM), or page mode memory, is a DRAM that allows for faster transfer rates. It was developed mainly for video systems in which large chunks of sequential data are needed for graphic displays. The

RAM uses a technique that divides memory into 512-byte pages, or smaller, and then accesses the pages sequentially. With this technique, only half the normally required address is used.

Memory can be thought of as a matrix of memory cells. Column and row addresses are used to identify the memory cells, **Figure 6-12.** When FPM RAM is applied, the start of the addresses is equated to a certain column and row. After the initial column and row is supplied, only the column is needed for the next series of consecutive addresses. This technique eliminates the need of row identification, thus allowing for faster transfer time.

Tech Tip:
Memory chip technology is rapidly changing. There has been at least one new memory type developed every year for the last five years.

Cache

Cache can be found throughout the computer system. *Cache* is a small amount of high-speed memory designed to speed up the transfer of data between components and peripherals. The term *small* is relative, of course. The cache is small when compared to total system RAM.

An example of a common use of cache is transferring data from system RAM to a hard drive. Transferring and writing data to a hard drive can be very time-consuming compared to the speed of transferring and writing data to RAM. By incorporating a cache on the hard drive circuit board, data transfer can be accelerated, thus releasing the system to perform other tasks. The memory chips used for cache store data at least ten times faster than storing data directly to the hard disk system.

Another important reason for using cache is the data remaining in cache can be accessed faster than accessing the hard disk drive. Anywhere data transfer is

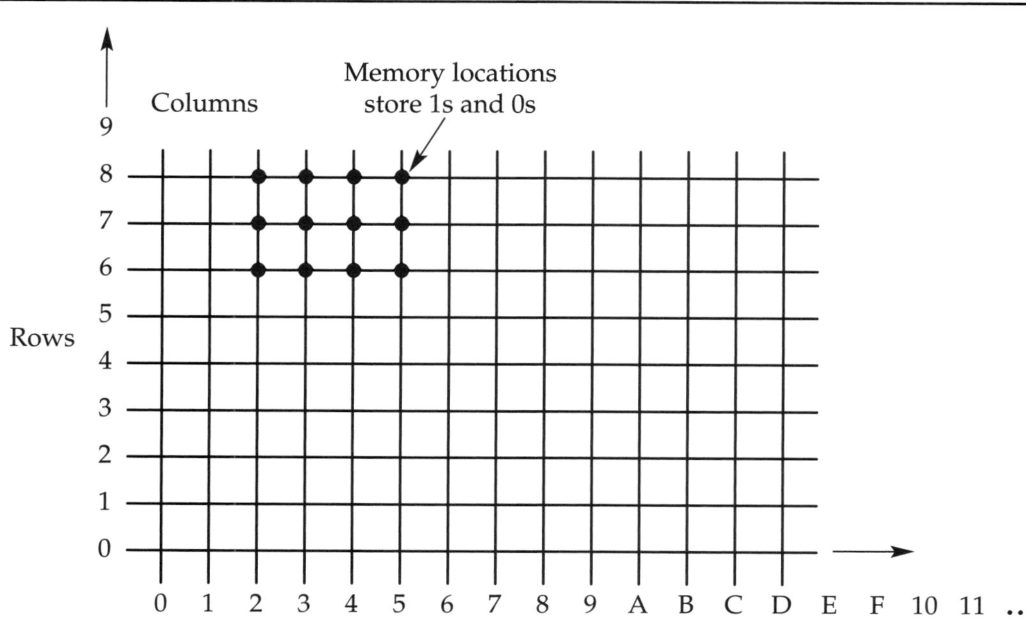

Figure 6-12. Each memory location in the matrix is described by a column and a row hexadecimal number such as 08A2h 3B5Fh.

taking place, you can be sure there is a cache system designed in the circuit board. Discussion of L1, L2 and L3 cache can be found in Chapter 4—CPU.

Installing RAM Modules

Adding memory is one of the easiest upgrades you can make to a computer. You simply insert the module and the computer's BIOS recognizes the new memory when you start your computer. However, the memory and the slots on the motherboard can be damaged if you are not careful, so there are a few important facts to keep in mind when installing memory.

Memory modules are extremely sensitive to static discharge. Always wear a standard static or grounding wrist strap when handling memory chips. You must also properly identify the orientation of the SIMM or DIMM before inserting it into the memory slot. Both the SIMM and DIMM packages are physically designed to prevent backward insertion into the slot. If too much force is applied when inserting the memory modules into the slots, permanent damage may result to both the memory module and the slot.

The SIMM is inserted at a 30° angle, **Figure 6-13.** It is then rotated up to a final position perpendicular to the motherboard. The notch in one end of the SIMM is used for proper insertion into the slot. If the notch does not line up with the locking clip, the SIMM is being inserted backward. Take special note of the notch or notches on the edge connector. The notch or notches are used to identify the proper voltage and the type of memory compatible with the PC system.

DIMM memory is inserted straight into the DIMM slot. You do *not* use the 30° angle used with SIMMs. DIMM modules also use special ejector tabs to assist in the removal and installation of memory, **Figure 6-14.** Again, note the notches along the bottom edge of the DIMM on the tab ejector.

In most instances, SIMM memory modules must be installed in pairs. A few motherboards were produced that allowed single SIMMs to be installed. The reason most SIMM memory modules have to be installed in pairs is because of the way information is transmitted to and from most SIMM modules. Memory access speed is increased when data is stored in a pattern that alternates between the two SIMM modules rather than just one. DIMM modules do not have to be installed in pairs. The DIMM module circuitry is designed to simulate two separate memory modules. Only one DIMM needs be installed to increase memory.

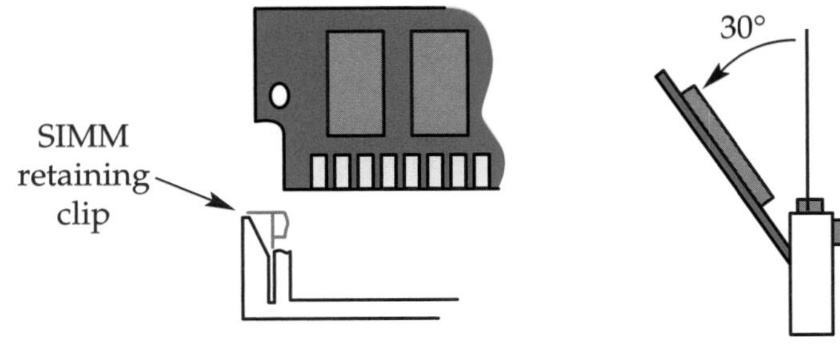

Figure 6-13. With the retaining clips open, a SIMM is inserted at approximately a 30° angle. It is then tilted to the perpendicular. The retaining clips are then closed to lock it in place. The procedure is reversed for removal.

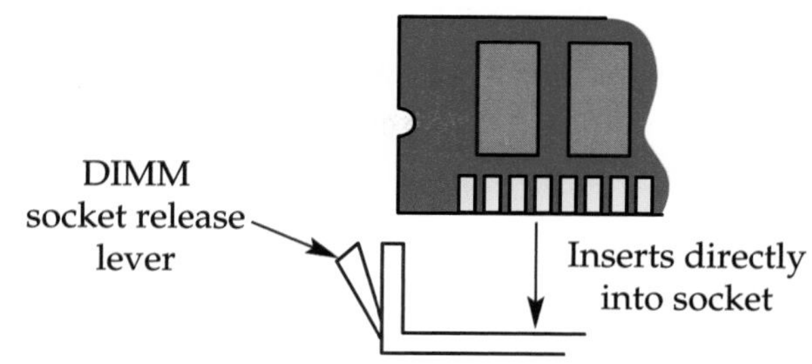

Figure 6-14.
A DIMM is inserted directly into the socket. There is no need to tilt the DIMM. Simply move the DIMM socket release lever outward.

Matching RAM Characteristics

When adding or replacing RAM modules, it is important that certain characteristics of the modules are matched. The two most important characteristics of RAM chips are the speed and the integrity of the chips. These two characteristics need to be studied.

Memory Chip Speed

The speed of the CPU is measured in megahertz (MHz) or gigahertz (GHz). Memory chip speed is measured in nanoseconds. A ***nanosecond (ns)*** is equal to one billionth of a second.

nanosecond (ns) one billionth of a second.

When adding more memory to a PC, it is best to match the speed of the existing memory chips. If faster memory chips are added to an existing slower memory chip bank, the newer faster chips will run at the same speed as the existing chips. The chips will run, so if you have them, they can be used successfully. However, as they will run at a slower speed, they are not cost effective.

Another consideration is the maximum speed that the motherboard system bus can support as well as the chipsets. You must check the PC, chipset, and BIOS documentation before attempting to upgrade RAM. This is especially true if the PC you are attempting to upgrade is several years old.

While faster RAM will slow down to run on a computer with a slower bus speed, RAM modules with a speed slower than that of the motherboard bus will *not* run. For example, a 133 MHz SDRAM module can run on a motherboard with a 100 MHz bus, but will operate at 100 MHz. However, a 100 MHz SDRAM module will not work on a motherboard with a 133 MHz bus, **Figure 6-15.**

Memory Data Integrity

Data can become corrupted while waiting in memory. Some causes of data corruption are electrical voltage leaking from the memory module, electrical interference, power surges, and electrostatic discharges. Even cosmic rays can corrupt data. Think for a moment about a 16MB SIMM memory module. That module is composed of 128 million memory cells, so there is always a possibility of corrupted data being transmitted. Corrupt data that is processed through the RAM can result in mathematical computation errors as well as program run errors that can cause a computer system to lock up. There are two common methods for checking the integrity of data transferred in and out of memory: parity and error correction code.

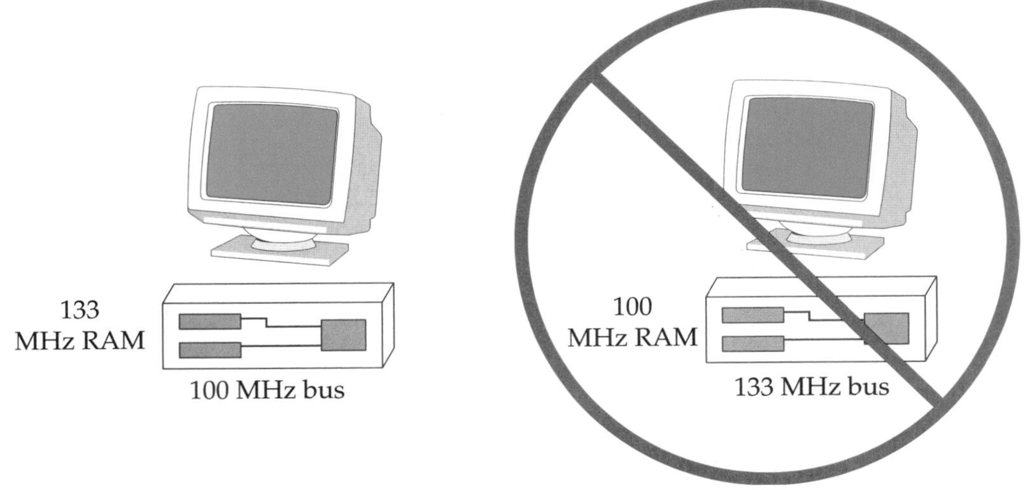

Figure 6-15.
RAM must be as fast or faster than the system bus it is installed in.

Parity

parity
the counting of either odd or even bits being transmitted.

As you have learned, all data transmitted through a PC system is comprised of 1s and 0s together in groups of eight. These groups of eight are known as bytes. ***Parity*** is simply the counting of either odd or even bits of the bytes being transmitted.

To understand the role of parity, we must first look at how memory is constructed. A memory chip consists of millions of tiny cells that store data. Each cell can contain either a zero or one. The 1s and 0s represent the state of electrical charge in the cell. Typically, a five-volt electrical charge represents a one and no electrical charge represents a zero. The cells are grouped together in sets of eight cells (one byte).

When memory chips and data transfer techniques were first developed, they were not as reliable as they are today. Out of the millions of cells designed in the memory module, a few of the individual cells might be flawed. These flawed cells tend to lose their electrical charge. Cells that lose their charge are said to *leak*. If a single cell changes its charge state from five volts to zero while it is stored, then the data it represents also changes. For example, the stored binary number 00001010 represents the decimal number 10. If one cell loses its charge, the binary format of the data could look like 00000010. It now represents the decimal number 2. The data stored as a byte has changed its value from the decimal 10 to the decimal 2. Data stored in a changing byte is not limited to data that represents numbers. The stored byte could represent letters, sound, part of an illustration, or even a program command.

Data can also change while being transferred from one module to another. Remember that data is processed through a PC. It could be loaded from a disk to the memory (RAM) and then moved to the CPU to be manipulated and then routed simultaneously to the screen and to RAM. While the data is being transferred around the PC system, any of the bits that form a complete byte could be changed by outside electrical interference or by a slightly defective part such as a circuit board trace that is starting to fail.

To check that data received by RAM and transferred to other parts is still valid, parity was developed. Instead of just the usual eight bits being stored to represent one byte, an additional bit was added to make a total of nine bits. The ninth bit is referred to as the *parity bit.* The parity bit reflects the number of ones and zeros contained in the data byte.

For example, assume the number of 1s being transmitted to or from the memory is counted. Every time the number of bits counted is *odd,* a parity bit of one is sent to indicate the number of bits is odd. This is an example of ***odd parity checking.*** The system could also be designed to do ***even parity checking*** by transmitting an extra bit each time there was an even number of bits in the byte of data being transmitted. See **Figure 6-16.** Parity checking is not simply limited to memory; it is also used for transmitting data across telephone and network lines.

odd parity checking
a data integrity checking method in which every time the number of bits counted is odd, an extra bit of data is transmitted as a 1 to indicate odd.

The only problem with a parity check using this method is it assumes that only one bit will change. If two bits change, the parity will not change and the error will go undetected.

Today, memory chips and circuit board designs are very dependable. Relatively few errors are generated by individual memory cells or motherboard parts. Many PCs use memory modules that do not check parity, or they use what is described as fake parity. With ***fake parity,*** the parity bit is set to a constant value, say, for instance, a one. This is done by electronic circuit design. Since the parity bit is always set to one regardless of the true number of ones contained in the byte, parity will always match when data is transferred. In other words, a true parity check is never performed. The fake parity bit always confirms the data as good. Some PC systems *require* parity checking memory modules. On systems that require parity checks to be made, fake parity memory modules can be used.

even parity checking
a data integrity checking method in which every time the number of bits counted is even, an extra bit of data is transmitted as a 1 to indicate even.

fake parity
when the parity bit is always set to one regardless of the true number of ones contained in the byte.

The term fake parity can also refer to the manufacture of memory chips that are advertised as containing parity but in reality are fake. Memory designed with actual parity checking costs more than memory that is not designed with actual parity checking. Using fake parity in place of true parity checking memory brings additional profit.

SIMM modules usually contain eight chips used for stored memory and a ninth chip to check parity. The only way to be certain if a memory module uses fake parity checking or not is to check the part number. All information needed about the chip is usually listed on the company Web site.

Example of Parity			
Data byte bit location	0 1 2 3 4 5 6 7	Parity bit	Result
Data bit value	1 0 0 0 1 0 1 0	1	ODD
Data bit value	1 0 1 0 1 1 1 1	0	EVEN

Figure 6-16. Drawing of streams of bytes representing odd and even totals followed by a parity bit. In this example, the parity bit is generated as a one each time the total number of bits that equal one is odd. A zero is generated if it is even.

Error code correction

error code correction (ECC)
an alternative form of data-integrity checking.

Another form of checking the integrity of data is error code correction. ***Error code correction (ECC)*** not only checks for errors but also corrects most errors. Parity checking simply generates an error code, which is displayed on the screen and then stops the program. Error code correction requires an additional chip designed especially for this type of error checking and correcting. ECC cannot correct all errors, only the usual corrupt single bit. If multiple bits are corrupt, the ECC chip cannot correct the data.

ECC is not often found in desktop PCs. It is usually only found in high-end machines such as servers.

Buffered Chips

buffer
an area to temporarily store data before transferring it to a device.

The term ***buffer***, in relationship to a PC, can be likened to a temporary waiting or holding area. Data can be temporarily stored for a few microseconds before continuing its journey. Remember that there are several different bus systems on the computer motherboard, and all of them are running at different speeds. In addition, many of the devices attached to the computer have speeds much slower than memory chips. For this reason, fast memory requires buffering when exchanging data with other components in the PC.

The buffer area can be provided in the motherboard chipset or as an additional chip on the memory module. DIMM memory modules have definitive notch patterns that match the memory module slots on the motherboard. This design prevents improper installation of a buffered DIMM into a motherboard that already contains memory buffer chips. See **Figure 6-17** to view a drawing of notch locations on a DIMM and how they vary.

Registered Memory

registered memory
a memory module that incorporates driver and synchronizing electronics as part of the unit.

Registered memory is a memory module that incorporates a registry chip to drive and synchronize itself without depending on the motherboard. Typical motherboards incorporate a chipset with functions to drive and synchronize the memory unit with the motherboard bus system. Registered memory is sometimes referred to as buffered memory because it works in a similar fashion as buffered memory. Some computer systems incorporate a memory register or buffer on the motherboard. The important thing to remember is that registered and nonregistered memory modules cannot be mixed. Registered memory is not typically found on standard PCs. It is found more commonly on high-end PCs and network servers.

Flash Memory Devices

flash memory
memory type that stores data but does not require a power source to retain the data.

Flash memory is a solid-state, reusable data storage device that can retain data even when the electrical power is disconnected. It is a relatively new technology that is used in many different digital applications. It is derived from EEPROM technology and takes advantage of the EEPROM's ability to be programmed and reprogrammed. However, unlike the original EEPROM, flash memory only stores data, not computer programs. Like the EEPROM, flash memory does not require a power source to retain data. Since it does not require a power source, the size and weight is reduced significantly.

Figure 6-17.
Buffering and voltage can be identified by the position of the notch at the bottom of the DIMM. This is how manufacturers ensure the correct type of DIMM is installed on the motherboard when replacing or upgrading memory modules. The variances in the notch locations on DIMMs are slight but sufficient. Forcing an incorrect DIMM into the slot will result in damage to the DIMM or to the slot. Memory modules should be inserted into the slot with minimum effort.

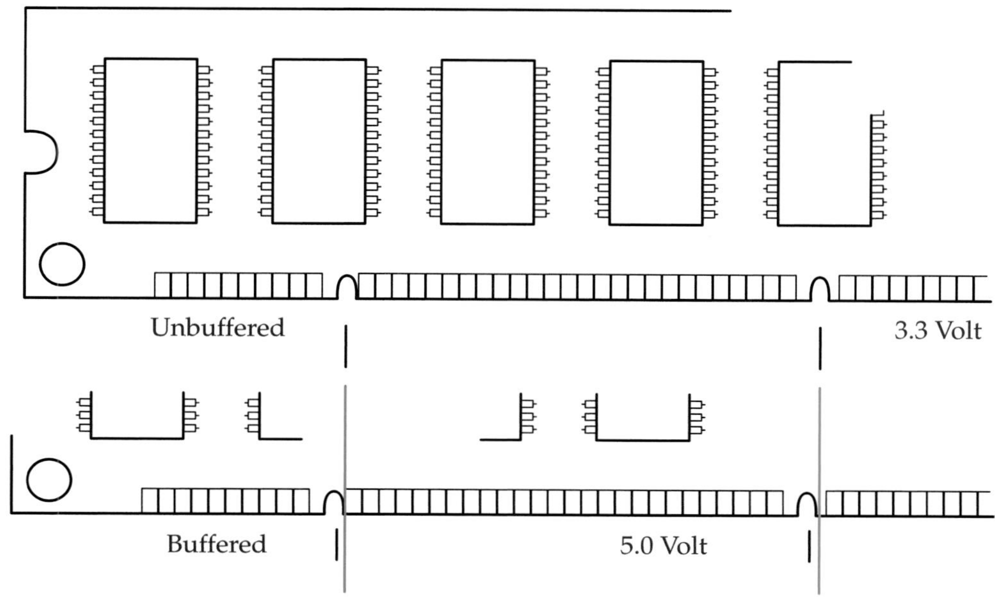

Flash memory devices are often referred to as "Hot Swappable" devices. The term ***hot swap*** means that the device can be plugged into or unplugged from a computer system while the computer is running.

hot swap
a technology that allows a computer device to be plugged into or unplugged from a computer while the computer is running.

Some typical devices that use flash memory technology are miniature data drives, personal digital assistants (PDAs), global positioning systems (GPS), digital cameras, cellular phones, pagers, electronic instruments, MP3 players, and personal computer systems. A few of the many devices commonly found are presented in the following sections.

USB Flash Drives

A typical flash drive is constructed from EEPROM chips. Data is "flashed" to the EEPROM chip similar to the way BIOS chips are flashed. There are many different names used for the EEPROM memory devices such as pen drives, jump drives, micro drives, thumb drives, micro vaults, stick drives, and more. In this textbook, the term USB flash drive will be used. *USB flash drives* are reusable storage systems that connect to the computer system via a USB port, **Figure 6-18.** The electrical power for energizing the USB flash drive is also delivered by the USB port. There is no need for an external power supply. After data is transferred to the USB flash drive, the drive can be removed from the system and will retain the data for a long period of time. The data on the USB flash drive can be transferred to another computer or to a similar device. The USB flash drive can have additional data added to it or it can be completely erased similar to most other storage media.

Figure 6-18.
USB flash drive.

At the time of this writing, USB flash drives range from a modest 16MB to 2GB. A 2GB USB flash drive has the same storage capacity as approximately 1400 floppy drives or 3 standard 650 CD-RW discs. This is an incredible amount of data for such a compact device. USB flash drives will compete with traditional hard disk drives soon and most likely will replace the use of common floppy disks and possibly compact discs. The main advantage of the USB flash drive is it has no moving parts to wear out or misalign. The entire system is designed from integrated chip technology.

When connected to a computer system through the USB port, the device is recognized as a removable hard drive. Look at **Figure 6-19.** The USB flash drive is listed beneath **Devices with Removable Storage** and is identified as **drive F:**.

A USB flash drive is automatically detected and configured when inserted into the computer system's USB port. As a precaution, the USB flash drive should be deactivated before removing it from the USB port. This is especially

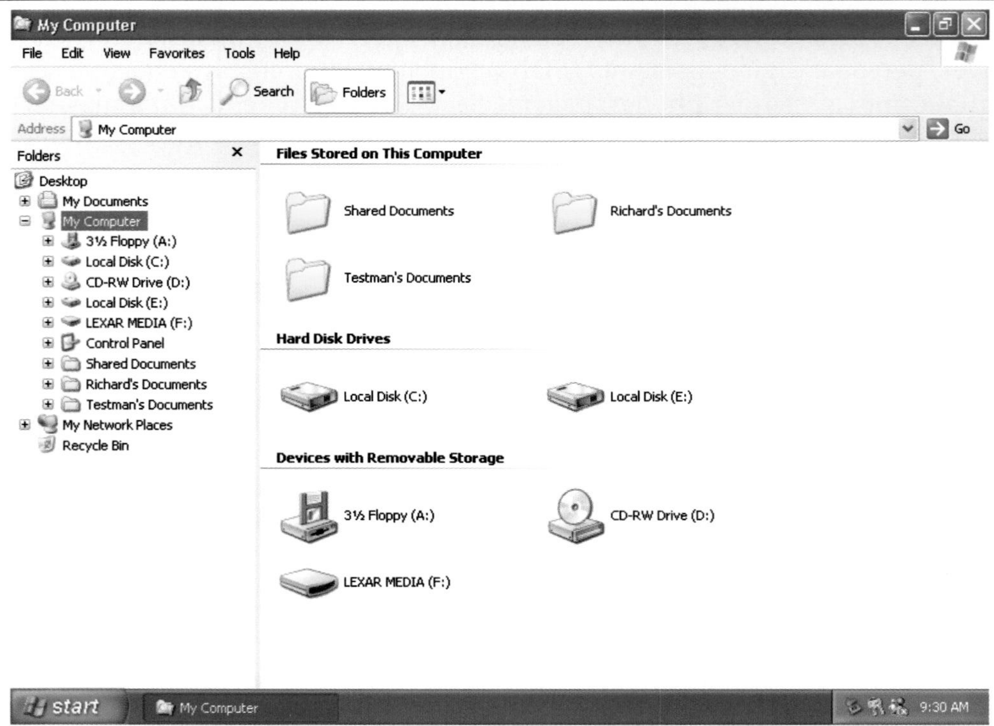

Figure 6-19.
Removable storage devices such as the USB flash drive are automatically detected on boot and are listed in **My Computer** beneath **Devices with Removable Storage**.

true while data is being transferred to or from the USB flash drive. **Figure 6-20** shows a Windows XP Safely Remove Hardware window.

The Safely Remove Hardware Window identifies the USB flash drive as a **USB Mass Storage Device**. The user simply clicks the **Stop** button and then proceeds to unplug the USB flash drive from the USB port. Many users simply unplug the USB flash drive, unaware of the possible damage that could occur to the drive.

Flash Memory Cards

Flash memory cards hold text data, image data, and sound data. Flash memory technology has been incorporated into many digital systems, such as cameras, music players, notebook computers, cell phones, electronic test equipment, MP3 players, cam recorders, and personal digital assistants. Some flash memory cards are especially designed for security systems. They contain user passwords required to log on to the computer system, and they support data encryption.

Flash memory cards go by many different names such as SmartMedia, CompactFlash, MultiMediaCard, Memory Stick, and Secure Digital. The names vary because of the individual competing companies who developed and marketed the flash memory cards. Although they are all designed on the same principles of flash memory technology, they differ in their overall physical design, electrical characteristics, and software system requirements for reading and writing to the media. Because they have different attributes, you have to either match the card type to a particular reader or use one of the readers that support multiple card formats.

One such card reader is the Belkin 8-in-1 Media Reader/Writer, **Figure 6-21,** which reads and writes to eight different types of flash memory cards. The reader connects to any standard PC through the USB port.

Figure 6-20.
The USB flash drive, as with any other removable computer device, should first be stopped with the Safely Remove Hardware program.

Figure 6-21. The Belkin 8-in-1 Media Reader/Writer reads a variety of flash memory card types. (Courtesy of Belkin Corporation)

Memory Map Structure and Development

Memory map structure is a description of the way memory is allocated in the PC. Because of the issue of backward compatibility in the PC industry, the development of the memory structure has become complex and confusing. The desire for the latest computer system to be compatible with ancient 8-bit system technology has created the evolution of a difficult memory structure. There have been many different software attempts to overcome these structural limitations.

The terminology of memory structure dates back to the original PC and the oldest DOS operating system. The early PC could only access 1MB of memory (1,024,000 bytes). The restrictions of 1MB of memory are DOS and Windows 3.x restrictions. They do not apply to Windows 95 or later operating systems. Windows 95 and later follow the DOS memory pattern *only* when dealing with legacy cards or 16-bit software programs. Windows NT, Windows 2000, and Windows XP are not affected at all by DOS memory structure. NT, 2000, and XP operating systems handle individual memory areas as one big block, referred to as the ***heap.*** The memory is then portioned out as needed. Let's look at how the memory system structure was designed and labeled.

heap
how Windows refers to the entire memory.

conventional memory
the first 640KB of a PC's RAM.

upper memory
term for a PC's memory range between 640KB and 1MB.

reserved memory
another term for upper memory.

Conventional Memory

The memory structure is illustrated in **Figure 6-22.** This illustration shows the layout of conventional, upper, high, and extended memory.

The original PC was limited to 1MB (1024KB) of random access memory. This first memory was originally divided in half (512KB each). After the original PC was on the market for a short time, the memory system was redesigned into parts that were no longer equal. The bottom part was given 640KB and was called ***conventional memory.*** The top part was given 384KB and was called ***upper memory*** or ***reserved memory.*** This division of the first 1MB of memory into two unequal parts, conventional (640KB) and reserved (384KB), became the industry standard.

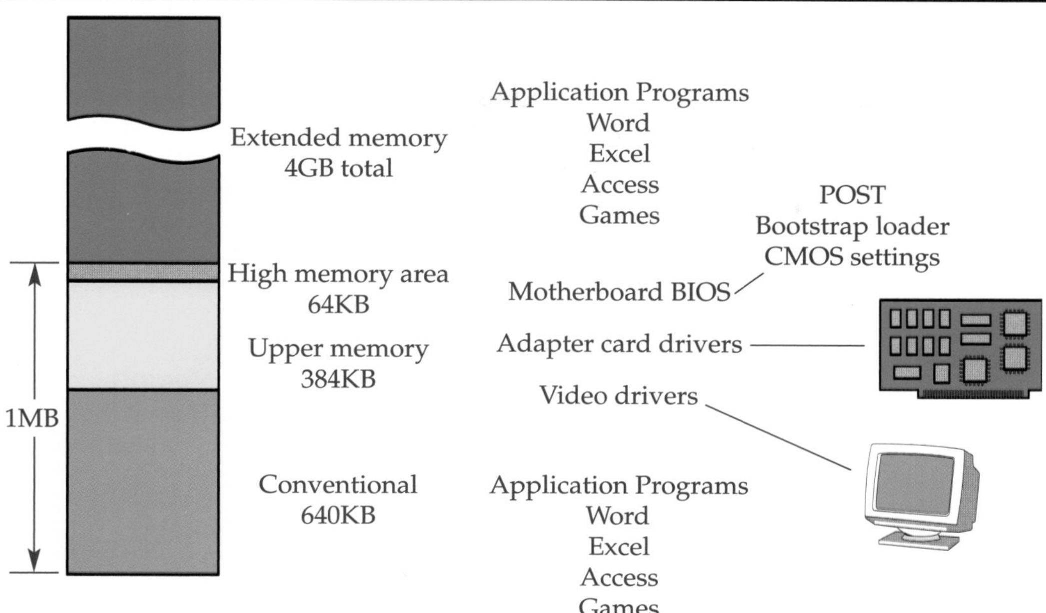

Figure 6-22.
To the right of the memory map are examples of what you might find loaded into each of these portions of memory.

Conventional memory is where application programs are loaded. The reserve memory was reserved for use by the video system, expansion cards, and the BIOS. The reserve memory is dedicated (or reserved) for hardware drivers and cannot be used by application programs. For many years, conventional memory (640KB) was referred to as the *memory barrier*. Early computer programmers were required to write programs that could fit into the 640KB space of conventional memory.

The term conventional memory is still in use. However, the 32-bit operating systems of newer models easily work around the 640KB barrier. Programs, as well as drivers, can be loaded into memory well beyond the first 1MB.

Read through **Figure 6-23.** This illustration diagrams the relation of the various areas in RAM and how they developed.

Upper Memory Area (Reserved Memory)

The upper memory area (UMA), or reserved memory, is the 384KB of memory remaining after the first 640KB of conventional memory. The term reserved means that only the PC system software drivers used to run and interface with the system hardware components can be loaded into this area. The reserved memory cannot be used for application software such as word processor programs, gaming, or other software.

The upper memory is divided into sections that are determined by their function. The first part of the UMA (128KB) is used for the video system. The information about the computer monitor is stored in this area. The next part of the UMA (128KB) is used for adapter boards mounted in slots on the motherboard. Examples of these adapter boards are boards for the modem or network cards. VGA adapter cards sometimes utilize the first 32KB of this area of memory. The last part of the UMA (128KB) is used for the motherboard BIOS, CMOS settings, POST program, and bootstrap program.

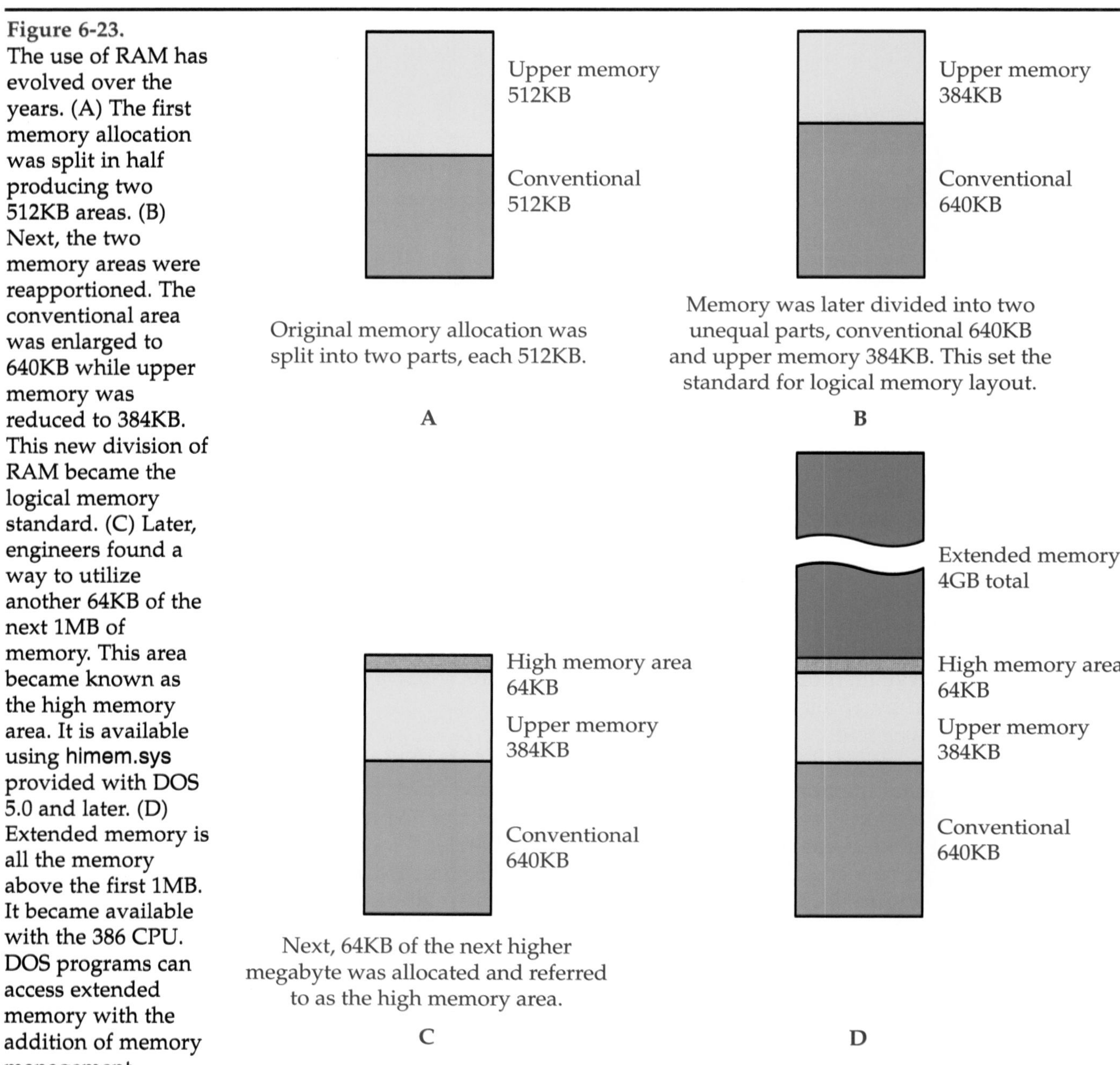
Upper memory
512KB
Conventional
512KB
Original memory allocation was split into two parts, each 512KB.
A
Upper memory
384KB
Conventional
640KB
Memory was later divided into two unequal parts, conventional 640KB and upper memory 384KB. This set the standard for logical memory layout.
B
High memory area
64KB
Upper memory
384KB
Conventional
640KB
Next, 64KB of the next higher megabyte was allocated and referred to as the high memory area.
C
Extended memory
4GB total
High memory area
64KB
Upper memory
384KB
Conventional
640KB
D

Figure 6-23.
The use of RAM has evolved over the years. (A) The first memory allocation was split in half producing two 512KB areas. (B) Next, the two memory areas were reapportioned. The conventional area was enlarged to 640KB while upper memory was reduced to 384KB. This new division of RAM became the logical memory standard. (C) Later, engineers found a way to utilize another 64KB of the next 1MB of memory. This area became known as the high memory area. It is available using himem.sys provided with DOS 5.0 and later. (D) Extended memory is all the memory above the first 1MB. It became available with the 386 CPU. DOS programs can access extended memory with the addition of memory management

Many types of device drivers are also loaded into the UMA. A section of UMA can also be occupied by a memory manager program, which permits certain programs to use memory beyond the 1MB barrier. Again, modern operating systems have no problem accessing RAM beyond the first 1MB. This was a restriction of earlier operating systems.

High Memory Area

high memory area (HMA)
is the first 64KB of the extended memory area.

It is easy to confuse a high memory area with upper memory. The ***high memory area (HMA)*** is the first 64KB of the extended memory area. (Actually it is 16 bytes short of a full 64KB.)

This area was first discovered as a design flaw in the memory access data lines, but it soon became the standard method to gain more conventional memory space. Conventional memory not only holds application programs but also basic DOS files, such as the kernel, needed to operate the PC. The DOS kernel file is approximately 45KB in size. Transferring a DOS kernel to the high memory area releases 45KB of conventional memory space for use by application programs. To use the HMA, the line **DOS=HIGH** is added to the **config.sys** file.

In DOS 5.0 and later versions, the **DOS=HIGH** command loads the DOS program kernel into the high memory area. The high memory area can also be used to store a software driver instead of the DOS kernel, but note that only one program can be stored in the high memory area.

Expanded Memory

Expanded memory was an early method to move past the 1MB memory barrier. ***Expanded memory standard (EMS)*** was designed to increase the amount of memory available for applications. An expanded memory adapter board loaded with memory chips was inserted into a motherboard expansion slot. Unlike RAM, the expanded memory adapter board is not accessed directly by the CPU, but rather by a software-driver program, which is loaded into reserved memory. The software-driver program transfers data to and from the memory adapter board to the 64KB EMS window established in upper memory. See **Figure 6-24** for a memory map illustrating the 64KB EMS window and expanded memory available on the expanded memory adapter board.

expanded memory standard (EMS)
an early method to move past the 1MB memory barrier.

The memory adapter board could contain a maximum data content of 32MB. Data was transferred through the EMS window in 16KB segments, or pages, to and from the memory on the adapter board.

EMS is obsolete, and the memory boards are no longer manufactured. The transfer rate of data with EMS is extremely slow because it is limited to the

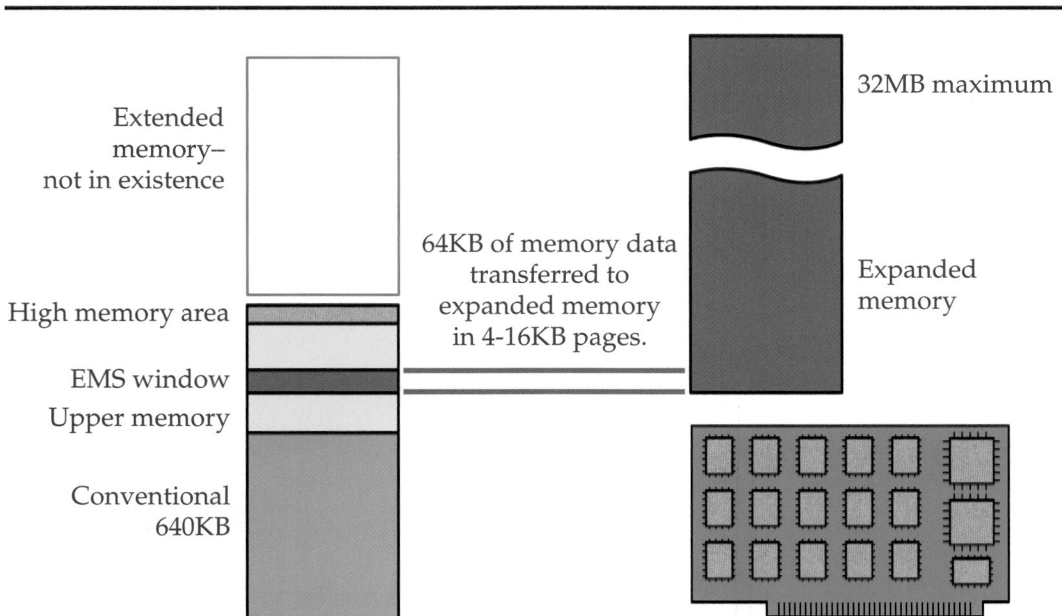

Figure 6-24. Expanded memory is provided by a memory adapter board inserted into a motherboard expansion slot. A small EMS window is set up in the upper memory area and transfers data to and from the expanded memory in increments of 4KB to 16KB pages of data totaling 64KB.

speed of the motherboard bus slot. EMS was designed for the ISA bus slot, which is very slow when compared to the data transfer rates of SIMM or DIMM. SIMM and DIMM connect via the system bus, directly to the CPU. The concept of EMS was readily accepted when memory space was needed and the 1MB barrier was a problem.

A+ Note:
While *expanded memory (EMS)* is obsolete, the possibility that a reference to it could be on the A+ Certification exams exists. The pressure of taking an exam could cause you to mistake it for *extended memory (XMS).*

Extended Memory

extended memory system (XMS) all of the PC's memory beyond the first 1MB when the CPU is running in real mode.

The ***extended memory system (XMS)*** includes all of the PC's memory beyond the first 1MB when the CPU is running in real mode. As PC systems evolved over time, the CPU was designed to access more memory. The 286 and 386 models could address a total of 16MB. The 486, Pentium, and Pentium Pro CPUs can access 4GB. The Pentium II and later models can access up to 64GB. Note that it is currently impossible to use the full 64GB of RAM using a standard PC.

Memory Management Software

memory management software software designed to efficiently utilize valuable memory resources.

Since the 640KB barrier and 1MB maximum RAM restricted early computer systems, memory management software was created. ***Memory management software*** is designed to efficiently use valuable memory resources. To use all available memory to its fullest extent, memory management software systems (such as himem.sys, emm386.exe, and MemMaker) were developed.

Himem.sys

The himem.sys program is used to manage the high memory area (HMA) and to make use of the extended memory area. The extended memory area must be managed to prevent two different programs from simultaneously attempting to use the same area of memory. This is a common problem for Windows while programs are performing multitasking operations. If the extended memory area is not properly managed, the computer system can lock up or crash. If a program that is not designed to work with Windows is used, a program crash can occur if the program directly accesses the extended memory region.

Emm386.exe

The software DOS program emm386.exe was developed for 386 CPUs or later models. It was designed to load programs and device drivers into the upper memory area and to simulate extended memory (memory beyond the first 1MB) called expanded memory (the adapter board loaded with memory chips).

There are two main switches used with emm386.exe. These switches are **ram** and **noems**. The **ram** switch is used with the emm386.exe to give DOS access to the upper memory area and expanded memory. The **noems** switch is used to give DOS access to the upper memory area but not to the expanded memory.

Sample config.sys file lines for loading himem.sys and emm386.exe:

DEVICE=HIMEM.SYS
DEVICE=EMM386.EXE

Tech Tip:
Note that himem.sys must be installed before emm386.exe.

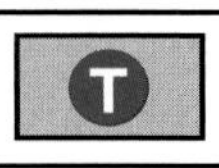

MemMaker

MemMaker is a DOS 6.0 utility that can be used to increase the amount of conventional memory available for DOS applications. MemMaker is a menu driven utility program. It runs in two main modes of operation. These two modes are *express* and *custom*. The express mode involves the least user intervention. The custom mode requires the user to be familiar with memory terminology and drivers. The utility automatically updates and modifies the config.sys and autoexec.bat files to reflect changes that are requested. The following example can also be inserted manually into the config.sys file:

DEVICE=C:\DOS\HIMEM.SYS
DEVICE=C:\DOS\EMM386.EXE NOEMS
DOS=HIGH, UMB

The references made to himem.sys and emm386.exe are easily noticed. The last line loads DOS into the upper memory area. In the following example, notice how Windows loads himem.sys, emm386.exe with the **noems** switch followed by DOS being loaded into the upper memory area.

DEVICE=C:\WINDOWS\HIMEM.SYS
DEVICE=C:\WINDOWS\EMM386.EXE NOEMS
DOS=HIGH, UMB, AUTO
FILESHIGH=80
BUFFERSHIGH=40,4

Real Mode, Protected Mode, and Safe Mode

Real mode is designed on the DOS system of memory access. When operating in real mode, only the first 1MB can be accessed. *Protected mode* includes all of real mode plus extended memory area. Multitasking can only occur in protected mode and not in real mode.

The Windows 95 operating system can be started in ***safe mode*** by pressing the [F5] or [F8] key during the boot process when the "Starting Windows" splash screen first appears. Starting with Windows 98, safe mode can be started by pressing and holding the [CTRL] key during the POST. Starting Windows in safe mode is a common troubleshooting method. By using safe mode to boot the computer, the technician can eliminate 32-bit drivers and some other programs that may be causing the system to fail to boot. This type of information is used to zero in on the cause of system failure. You can access safe mode in Windows 98, Me, 2000, and XP by pressing [F8] when prompted on the display screen during system boot or by pressing [F8] after the POST and before the Windows Splash screen appears.

safe mode
mode that boots the computer without some drivers and programs to allow for troubleshooting.

Gold Vs. Tin Edge Connectors

There are two types of edge connector finishes used on memory modules, gold and tin. The memory module (SIMM or DIMM) edge connector should match the connector finish inside the expansion slot. When two different types of metal are in contact with each other, a condition occurs that causes increased oxidation. When first installed, the memory will not show any signs of a problem. It should work perfectly. But as time goes by, oxidation develops. The PC starts to generate error codes, such as parity errors, more frequently. The amount of use and the conditions of the environment determines how long the oxidation process will take. Once it reaches a point that the electrical connection between the memory edge connector and the slot connector has totally degenerated, errors will constantly occur.

Some oxidation can be removed by simply removing and reinserting the memory module. This action alone may correct the error. However, the condition can also be so bad as to render the motherboard slot useless. Always match the type of metals used.

Memory and Heat

Heat will destroy a chip or cause temporary chaos in a computer. A common symptom of excessive heat causing memory problems is when a PC works fine for a short period of time (20 minutes) and then locks up. At the time the PC locks up, a sufficient level of heat has been generated to cause a circuit problem inside one of the memory chips. This causes the PC to fail. Fans should be checked, filters cleaned, and dirt and dust removed to prevent heat build up.

Summary

- There are many different packages for RAM including: SIPs, DIPs, SIMMs, and DIMMs.
- ROM retains data after the power is removed.
- RAM loses data after power is removed.
- DRAM must be constantly refreshed.
- SRAM does not need to be refreshed.
- Registered memory modules can only be used on systems designed for registered memory.
- Flash memory is derived from EEPROM technology and takes advantage of the EEPROM's ability to be programmed and reprogrammed and to retain data without depending on a power source.
- Hot swap technology allows a computer device to be plugged into or removed from a digital system without requiring the system power to be turned off.
- Windows can utilize RAM as one large block of memory if there are no legacy programs or hardware in the system.
- The four logical areas of RAM are conventional, upper, high memory, and extended memory.
- Conventional memory is the first 640KB of RAM.
- Upper memory is the next 384KB after conventional memory.
- High memory area is 64KB after upper memory or the first 64KB (minus 16 bytes) of the second megabyte of RAM.

- Extended memory is all the memory above the first 1MB of RAM and is used by Windows in protected mode.
- **Emm386.exe** is used to free up unused portions of reserved memory and to access expanded memory.
- Real mode means addressing only the first 1MB of memory.
- Protected mode is an operating mode that supports multitasking and allows access to the extended memory area.

Review Questions

Answer the following questions on a separate sheet of paper. Please do not write in this book.

1. Compare an ink pen and a pencil with an eraser to RAM and ROM memory.
2. RAM chip speed is measured in _____.
3. What is the difference between SO-DIMM and MicroDIMM?
4. What is the maximum data rate for a PC3200 memory module used in a motherboard with a FSB of 200 Mbps?
5. Briefly describe dual-channel DDR memory technology.
6. How much memory can DOS access?
7. What is the difference between expanded and extended memory?
8. What is the maximum amount of RAM that the original PC's processor could access?
9. What are the four logical areas of RAM?
10. Draw the logical memory layout of RAM for DOS and label each part and indicate the size in KB.
11. What is another name used for upper memory?
12. Application programs run from _____ memory.
13. Video drivers are loaded into the _____ memory area of RAM.
14. Theoretically, how much RAM can a Pentium II access?
15. What is the difference between upper memory and the high memory area?
16. What does the **noems** switch do when added to the **emm386** command?
17. System BIOS is transferred into the _____ memory area of RAM.
18. System video BIOS is usually stored in the _____ area of RAM.

Sample A+ Exam Questions

Answer the following questions on a separate sheet of paper. Please do not write in this book.

1. During the system boot, the following error message is displayed onscreen: "Parity check failure!" What particular system component would the message be referring to?
   a. RAM
   b. ROM
   c. HDD
   d. USB
2. In the Windows 98 operating system, how would you display the amount of RAM installed on a PC?
   a. Right-click **My Computer** and then select **Properties** from the shortcut menu.
   b. Right-click **My Computer** and then select **System Status** from the shortcut menu.
   c. Open **Control Panel** and then double-click the **RAM** icon.
   d. Open **Control Panel** and select the **System Memory** icon.
3. Which software program is used to manage memory areas above the first 1MB?
   a. 386mem.exe
   b. himem.sys
   c. noems.386
   d. expmem.sys
4. Which processor mode will only allow access to the first 1MB of memory?
   a. Real mode
   b. Protected mode
   c. Limited mode
   d. Extended mode
5. Which type of memory must constantly be refreshed to retain the stored data?
   a. SRAM
   b. PROM
   c. DRAM
   d. CRIMM
6. A memory location at 2MB would be considered part of which memory area?
   a. Upper memory
   b. Conventional memory
   c. Expanded memory
   d. Extended memory

7. How can you access safe mode when using Windows XP operating system?
   a. Hold down [F1] during the POST.
   b. Press [F8] immediately after the POST.
   c. Press [Ctrl] [Alt] [Delete] at the same time.
   d. You cannot access Safe mode when using a Windows XP operating system.
8. A memory chip's speed is measured in which standard unit?
   a. Megahertz
   b. Gigahertz
   c. Nanoseconds
   d. Cycles per second
9. Which method listed below is used to not only detect memory transfer errors but also to correct them?
   a. ECC
   b. EBO
   c. EDO
   d. CEC
10. Which items listed below should be practiced to ensure correct installation of additional memory? Select all that apply.
   a. Use an ESD wrist strap.
   b. Put the PC into real mode to prevent accessing the upper memory area until after the installation is complete.
   c. Turn off all electrical power to the system.
   d. Disconnect all peripheral components until after complete memory installation has been verified by system setup.

Suggested Laboratory Activities

Do not attempt any suggested laboratory activities without your instructor's permission. Certain activities can render the PC operating system inoperable.

1. Run msinfo32.exe and reveal the properties of the memory.
2. Remove the RAM chips from a lab PC and observe the boot operation. Observe all proper ESD precautions. Does the system boot? If it does, what part of the system startup sequence does not rely on RAM? Also, observe any error messages that are displayed.
3. Add additional memory to a lab PC.
4. Identify any markings on the lab PC (such as the manufacturer, serial number, and model number) and then try to obtain a definitive identification from the Internet Web sites.
5. Go to www.kingston.com and download their memory manual. It contains pages of information about system memory.

Interesting Web Sites for More Information

www.fujitsu.com
www.hitachi.com
www.intel.com
www.kingston.com
www.micron.com
www.mitsubishielectric.com
www.mosys.com
www.nec.com
www.oki.com
www.samsung.com
www.toshiba.com

Chapter 6
Laboratory Activity
Determining the Amount of RAM in a PC

After completing this laboratory activity, you will be able to:

- ❑ Identify the amount of memory installed in a PC.

Introduction

There are several different ways to identify the amount of memory installed on a typical PC. The amount of memory is revealed to the user when the PC runs the power-on self-test (POST). The RAM is tested and the amount of memory is displayed on the screen during the POST. The amount of memory can also be determined by looking in the **System Properties** dialog box, which can be opened by clicking the **System** icon in **Control Panel**. You can receive a detailed accounting of the total amount of memory and where it is allocated by going to the DOS prompt and typing the **mem** command. The System Monitor utility, a very sophisticated diagnostic and monitoring tool, can monitor memory activity and give a good indication if the memory needs to be upgraded.

Equipment and Materials

- Typical PC with 8MB or more of SIMM or DIMM memory and Windows 95, or later, operating system installed.

Procedure

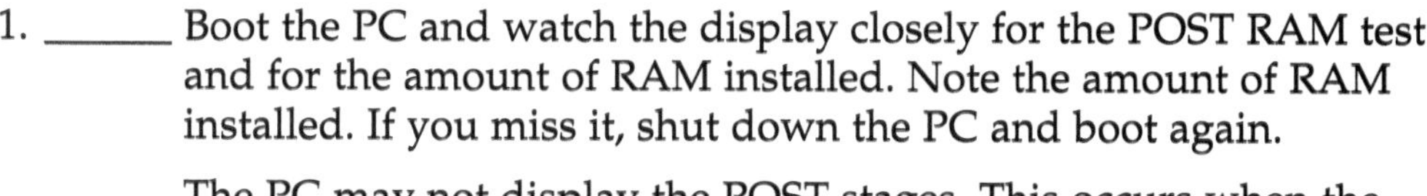

1. ______ Boot the PC and watch the display closely for the POST RAM test and for the amount of RAM installed. Note the amount of RAM installed. If you miss it, shut down the PC and boot again.

   The PC may not display the POST stages. This occurs when the option to show the POST process is disabled in the BIOS setup. This setting can be changed by running the BIOS setup program and enabling the POST display. The display is usually disabled for security reasons. By blanking out the display during the POST, the key combination to access BIOS is hidden from view, as is the memory information. Hiding this information limits unauthorized access to the BIOS setup program.

2. ______ Once the desktop is displayed, open the **System Properties** dialog box. This dialog box is opened through **Start | Settings | Control Panel | System**. Look under the **Performance** and **General** tabs. Write down the memory information in the space provided. The amount of information will be limited, compared to the amount of information provided by the DOS **mem** command.

3. ______ A quick way to access the **System Properties** dialog box is to right-click **My Computer**, and select **Properties** from the shortcut menu. Do so now.

4. ______ Close the **System Properties** dialog box.

5. ______ To access the **Microsoft System Information** dialog box, select the **Run...** option from the **Start** menu and enter **msinfo32**. The **Microsoft System Information** dialog box should appear. This is a very detailed box concerning all system information, hardware and software alike. The default screen should display memory information in the System Information window.

6. ______ Another way to access the **Microsoft System Information** dialog box is to access it through **Start | Programs | Accessories | System Tools | System Information**. Try it now to see if you obtain the same results. The System Monitor utility may or may not be installed on your PC. It is not installed during a normal operating system installation. To run it, select **Start | Programs | Accessories | System Tools | System Monitor**. A screen similar to the one shown should appear.

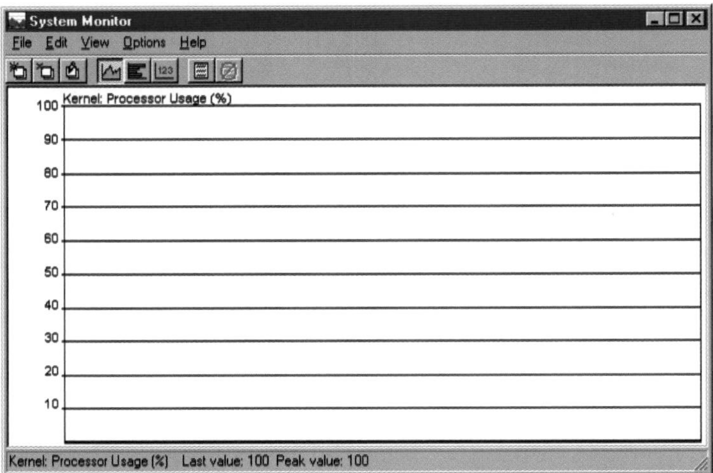

7. ______ If System Monitor is not installed, then install it using **Add/Remove Programs** in **Control Panel**. Select the **Windows Setup** tab in the **Add/Remove Programs Properties** dialog box. Scroll through the **Components:** list, select **System Tools**, and click the **Details** button. Scroll through the **Components:** list, check the box next to **System Monitor**, and click **OK**. Finally, click the **Apply** button, and follow the directions on the screen. Be sure to have the Windows 98 installation CD available, although you may not need it. If System Monitor is not already installed on your machine, install it now.

8. ______ After you successfully install the System Monitor utility, select **Start | Programs | Accessories | System Tools | System Monitor**. This will run the System Monitor.

9. ______ Now, select **Allocated memory** and **Other memory** for monitoring. You select them by opening the **Edit** menu and selecting **Add Item**. A list of categories appears in the **Add Item** dialog box. Choose **Memory Manager** and then select **Allocated memory** from the window on the right. Hold down the [Ctrl] key and select **Other Memory**. Both options should now be highlighted. Click **OK**.

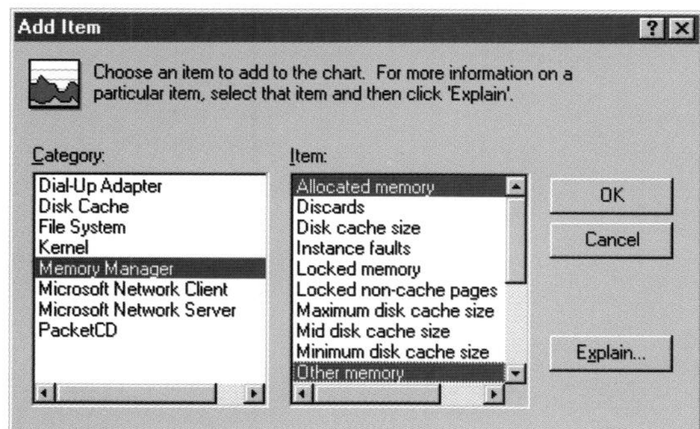

10. ______ The default display will be a line chart form. The data can also be displayed in bar chart and numeric chart forms. The chart styles are changed by selecting a new style from the **View** menu of the **System Monitor** window. Try the options for **Bar Charts** and **Numeric Charts**.

11. ______ To find out more about the options available, highlight a system device you wish to monitor in the **Add Item** dialog box. Next, click the **Explain** button. A dialog box appears with a brief description of the selected item. Try it now. Remember, you must select **Edit | Add Item** from the **System Monitor** window, select a category from the **Components:** list, and then select an item from the **Item:** list before the **Explain** button becomes available.

12. ______ Now, answer the review questions. You may leave the PC on and access **Help** while you answer the following questions. After you complete all of the questions, return everything to its original condition. If your PC did not have System Manager installed when you started, use the **Add/Remove Programs** feature in **Control Panel** to remove it before shutting down the system.

Review Questions

Answer the following questions on a separate sheet of paper. Please do not write in this book.

1. List two ways to access the **Microsoft System Information** dialog box.
2. What memory-related items can be monitored using System Monitor?
3. At the DOS prompt, run **mem/?** and list the option switches that can be used with the **mem** command.
4. What is the effect of using the **/d** and **/p** switches together in the **mem** command?

Input Devices

After studying this chapter, you will be able to:

- Explain how a keyboard scan code is generated.
- Know how to modify input device properties of a keyboard or mouse using DOS.
- Know how to modify input device properties of a keyboard or mouse using Windows Control Panel.
- Explain how devices such as the keyboard, mouse, joystick, scanner, and digital camera operate.
- Explain how to access input device information using Device Manager.

A+ Exam—Key Points

The IRQ assignments are always a source of questions for the A+ Certification exams. It is important to know how and where modifications for these devices are made.

Key Words and Terms

The following words and terms will become important pieces of your computer vocabulary. Be sure you can define them.

bar code reader
Bluetooth standard
carpal tunnel syndrome
digital camera
digitizer pad
input device
light pen
mouse
optical character recognition (OCR)
scan code
scanner
synchronous
touch screen display
track ball
universal peripheral interface (UPI)

input device
a piece of equipment that provides the computer with data.

Input devices included a wide variety of items that are used to communicate with the PC system. The standard keyboard is a common serial input device. It changes keystrokes into computer data. See **Figure 7-1.**

The keyboard is one of the most common and useful input devices, but there is a broad spectrum of input devices for computers. Some devices, such as the mouse, find widespread use in a variety of different computer applications. Other input devices, like bar code scanners, have more specific uses.

Figure 7-1.
A typical keyboard and how it works.

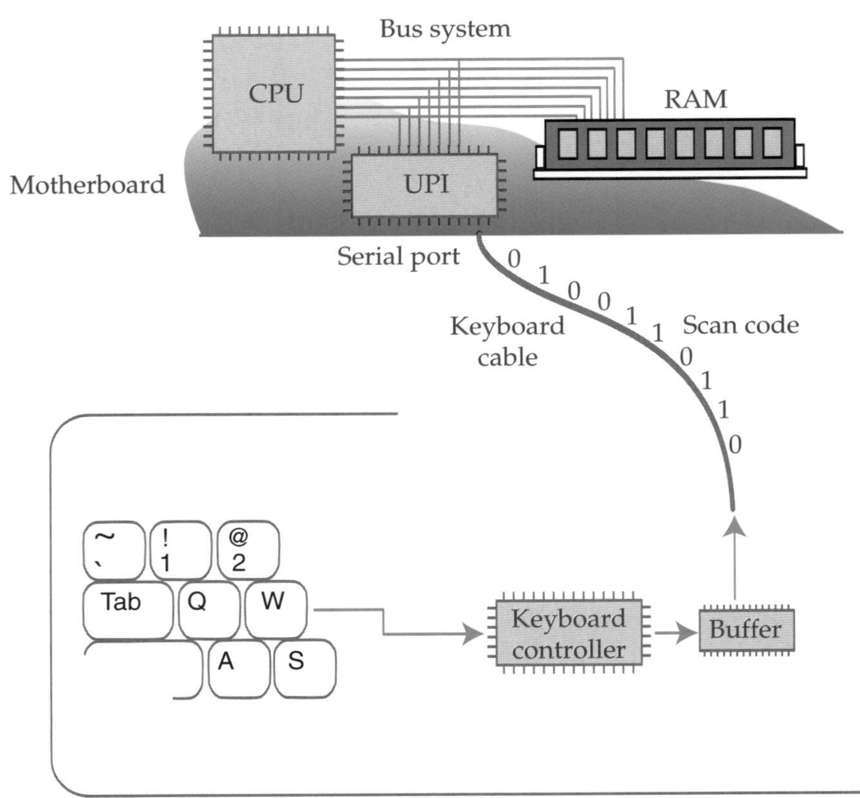

While specific plugs and jacks are common to certain input devices, you may encounter a keyboard, mouse, or other input device that installs in some unique way. Some devices have standard jacks coming off the motherboard. The keyboard and mouse usually attach this way. Other devices require a card be inserted into a motherboard expansion slot. In addition, almost all new input devices are offered in the universal serial bus (USB) format.

Keyboard

The typical keyboard has a small microprocessor chip such as the Intel 8048, 8049, or Motorola 6805 processor installed as a keyboard controller. The keyboard controller is not as powerful as the processor inside a PC. Rather, it is a limited processor used for small device applications such as telephones, automobiles, and appliances. The keyboard also contains a buffer, which is a temporary memory storage device similar to RAM.

When a key or a combination of keys is pressed, an electrical circuit is completed to the keyboard controller. The keyboard controller turns the electrical signal into a ***scan code.*** Look back to the drawing in Figure 7-1. Each key or combination has its own unique scan code. The scan code is sent to the keyboard buffer. The buffer temporarily stores the scan codes.

scan code
a data signal created from electrical signals sent by an input device.

From the buffer, the scan code is sent to the ***universal peripheral interface (UPI)*** mounted on the motherboard. The UPI is a microcontroller device. You can think of a microcontroller as a mini computer that is programmed to do a specific set of tasks. The UPI is manufactured with a small 8-bit CPU and a small amount of ROM and RAM. It will typically accept up to 90 programming instructions. A UPI can be designed to support any peripheral device associated with a computer.

universal peripheral interface (UPI)
a chip on the motherboard that directs communications between the CPU and the input device.

The keyboard UPI chip then sends an interrupt signal (IRQ1) to the CPU, letting it know that the keyboard is attempting to transmit data. The CPU receives the data and determines if it is simply text, a command for the application software, or a command for the CPU such as "save." If it is simply text, the code is temporarily stored in RAM. The code can also be a command for the software application that is loaded in RAM. If so, it will also be transmitted to RAM where the application software is stored.

Key Construction

Several types of switches are used under the keys in keyboards. See **Figure 7-2.** The most common types include the following:

- Mechanical.
- Membrane.
- Rubber dome.
- Capacitor.

The mechanical switch, Figure 7-2A, is constructed from a set of typical electrical contacts that are normally open (separated). When the key is pressed, the contacts snap closed.

A membrane switch, Figure 7-2B, is constructed differently than the typical contact switch. A piece of foam with foil on one side is attached to the switch actuator. A circuit board is used as the base of the switch. The circuit board has a pair of contact points on the surface of the board. When the key is pressed, a

Figure 7-2.
These are the mechanics of the four most common types of keyboard switches.

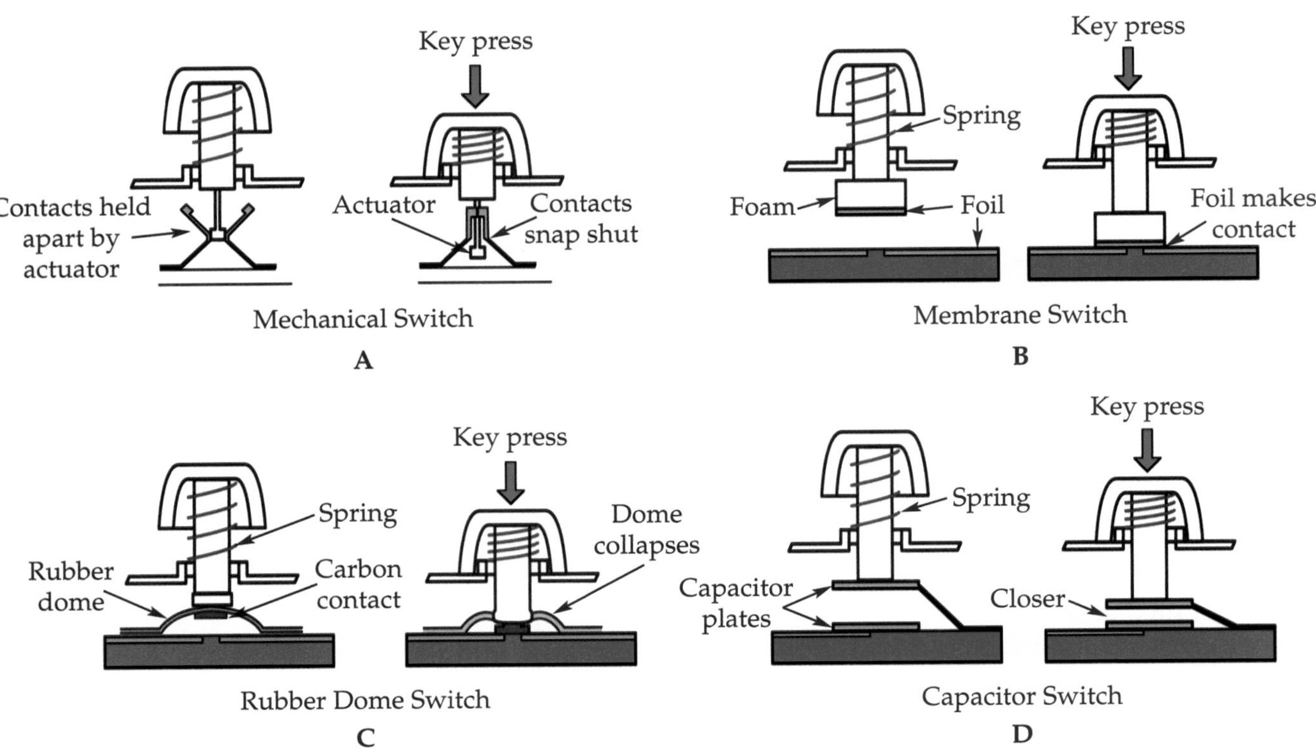

conductive piece of foil located on the foam completes the circuit across the circuit board contact points.

Another type of keyboard switch is the rubber dome, Figure 7-2C. The rubber dome is constructed as the name implies, with a small rubber dome under the actuator. When the key is pressed, the rubber dome folds down. This causes a small carbon contact to complete the circuit on the circuit board. The rubber dome switch is less likely to allow dirt particles to accumulate between the carbon contact and the circuit board contact area. This keeps the switch working reliably.

The last type of switch is the capacitor switch, Figure 7-2D. The capacitor switch derives its name from the fact that it operates on the principle of an electronic capacitor. A capacitor is simply two plates of metallic material in close proximity to each other. The distance between the two capacitor plates directly affects the strength and electrical characteristics of the capacitor. When the key is pressed on the capacitor switch, the plates move closer together, but they never touch. The capacitor switch is the most reliable type of keyboard switch available. Dirt particles or corrosion will not affect the switch. The other three types of switches are susceptible to corrosion, which causes an open circuit and a failure to complete the electrical circuit.

When comparing types of switches, the first obvious difference is the tactile feel of the switch. While the difference in the "feel" of the various switches may not be important to a PC technician, it may be the most important characteristic to a professional typist. Most PC users have a keyboard preference even if they do not realize the reason for the difference. Because of this, you may be required to install an older keyboard when replacing an old PC with a newer one.

Keyboard Scan Codes

The keyboard is a matrix of electrical connections. Each junction in the matrix is a key location. Each position on the matrix has an assigned number. When a key is pressed, the electrical signal (digital binary) is sent to the keyboard controller as a scan code. The scan code is interpreted by the system BIOS and the application software and is turned into an ASCII character. The scan code represents the position of the key being pressed. Another scan code is generated when the same key is released.

The scan code is not the ASCII code nor is it the printed letter, number, or symbol on the physical key. The scan code is used to identify the exact symbol to be displayed on the screen or to be printed on the printer. Keyboards can have multiple sets of scan codes. Programmers use the scan codes to convert the action of a certain key being pressed into an action by the computer. Usually, the action is converting the code to an ASCII character, but not always. The scan codes are what allow multiple languages to be assigned to a particular computer. The scan code from the key is converted into the letter symbol of the language for which the system has been set up.

Look at **Figure 7-3** for a listing of scan codes for several keys. Note that the key press and release codes are expressed in hexadecimal values.

Keyboard Connectors

There are two traditional types of keyboard connectors, 5-pin DIN (XT/AT style) or 6-pin mini-DIN (PS/2). See **Figure 7-4.** The 6-pin mini-DIN is currently the most common style. However, USB connected keyboards are becoming more common.

The difference in the two connectors is their physical shape, not their electrical qualities. Even though the 6-pin mini-DIN has an extra pin connector, the extra pin is a no connects (NC). The NC means that there is no electrical connection made by that particular pin. Each style transmits the same information to the motherboard. There are adapters made that change the physical connection of either plug to make them compatible with the motherboard.

Data is sent through only one of the five connectors. The keyboard is a serial device. The data sent to the motherboard is sequential. After the data reaches

Key	Key Press Code	Key Release Code
A	1E	9E
B	30	B0
Esc	01	81
F2	3C	BC
Home	E047	E0C7
Delete	E053	E0D3
Page Down	E051	E0D1
Space bar	39	B9
4 $	05	85

Figure 7-3. Hexadecimal scan codes for the pressing and releasing of selected keys.

Figure 7-4.
Keyboard plugs and diagrams showing their corresponding plug ends. The 6-pin mini-DIN is newer and more common than the 5-pin DIN.

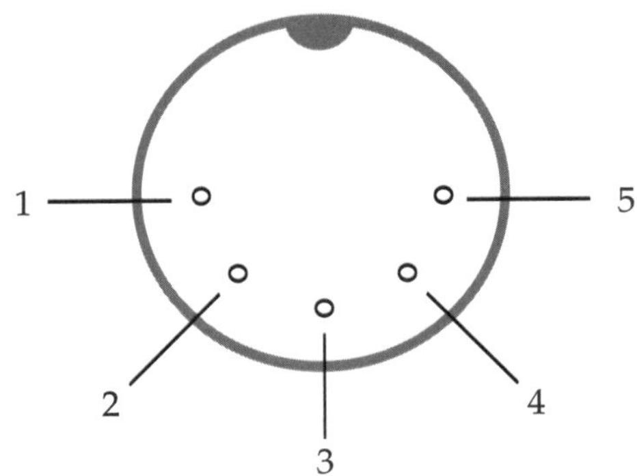

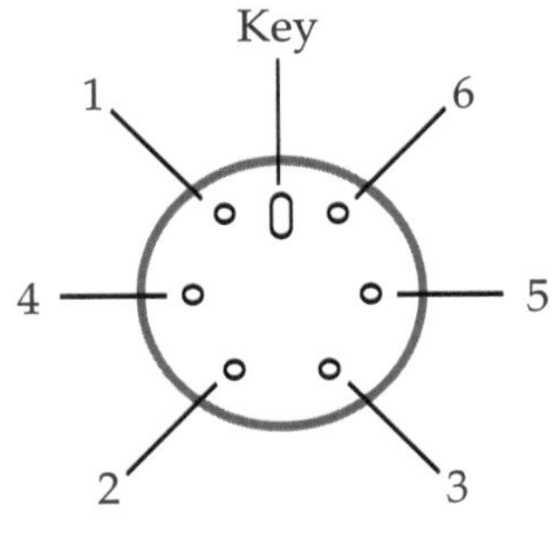

5-pin DIN (XT/AT) Connector

1. Clock
2. Data
3. NC
4. Ground
5. +3.0, +3.3, +5.0 Vdc

6-pin DIN (PS/2)

1. Clock
2. Data
3. NC
4. Ground
5. +3.0, +3.3, +5.0 Vdc
6. NC

the motherboard, it is converted into parallel form, usually two bytes. There is also a clock signal transmitted through the keyboard connector wiring. The keyboard data transfer is ***synchronous.*** This means that the data is transferred based on that clock signal.

synchronous
data transferred on the same timing as the computer.

Ergonomic Keyboards

carpal tunnel syndrome
an inflammation of the tendons in the hands and especially the wrist.

Ergonomic keyboards are keyboards shaped for comfort and to help prevent injury. Many people suffer from carpal tunnel syndrome. ***Carpal tunnel syndrome*** is an inflammation of the tendons in the hands and especially the wrist. Carpal tunnel syndrome is caused by repeating the same movement over and over again without proper rest or support. An example of this type of repetitive movement, and a common cause of carpal tunnel syndrome, is inputting data at a keyboard day after day.

It is believed that by shaping a keyboard so the hands and fingers contact the keyboard in a more natural alignment, carpal tunnel syndrome can be prevented. A variety of different designs for keyboards have been developed. See **Figure 7-5.**

Troubleshooting Keyboards

In general, it is not cost effective to repair damaged keyboards. It is usually cheaper to simply replace the keyboard. However, preventive maintenance can be used to extend the life of a keyboard.

Preventive Maintenance

Most of the problems with keyboards are associated with dirt in and around the keys. As you have seen, the keyboard keys can easily be disabled by dirt or corrosion. A keyboard should be cleaned on a regular basis. A small vacuum cleaner or a can of dry compressed air can be used to clean the keyboard.

When using vacuum cleaners, remember that they generate a lot of electrical noise and static. Electrical noise consists of high voltage spikes. If the vacuum is plugged into the same outlet as the computer being cleaned, be sure the computer is off. Do not equate a computer being off as a computer in a suspended state. When in doubt, unplug the computer. Also, remember that computers other than the one being cleaned might be connected to the same circuit. A battery-operated vacuum is the safest, but be sure it contains sufficient power. Be careful of static electricity. Static electricity is a common and hazardous by-product produced by the plastic parts on a vacuum cleaner. Be sure to follow all anti-static procedures to prevent damage to equipment.

Most computer users understand the hazards of keeping liquids (coffee or soda) near the computer equipment. If a liquid is spilled on the keyboard, the keyboard should be flushed with distilled water as soon as possible. Residue from soda or any other liquid containing sugar will leave a sticky film when dry. This film will quickly collect dirt and dust and the keys will begin to stick. Certain drinks contain materials that are very corrosive to electrical parts. Distilled water does not contain any minerals that will cause corrosion. Flush the keyboard liberally with distilled water.

Keys on the keyboard can be easily removed using a chip puller. A paper clip can also be bent to hook under the individual keys. Care should be used when attempting to remove the space bar. The typical space bar can be very difficult to reconnect to the keyboard after removal.

Figure 7-5. Ergonomic keyboards are designed to relieve stress on the hands and wrists caused by typing with hands in an uncomfortable position.

Warning:
Caution should be exercised when entirely disassembling a keyboard. Many styles of keyboards are assembled at the factory in ways that make them nearly impossible to reassemble.

Adjusting Keyboard Properties

Certain keyboard properties can be adjusted for preference. Windows has a simple graphic interface for adjusting keyboard properties. Look at **Figure 7-6.** This is the Keyboard Properties dialog box found in the Windows 95 operating system and later versions, as well as NT 4.0 and later. The dialog box can be reached through **Start | Settings | Control Panel** and then double-clicking the **Keyboard** icon.

Several adjustments can be made using this window, such as to the repeat rate, repeat delay, cursor blink rate, and language. Under the **Speed** tab, you will find the **Repeat delay** and **Repeat rate** adjustments, which control the actions of a pressed key. These adjustments control the length of a pause after pressing a key and the time required to hold a key in place before it repeats a character. A typical application of this timing method is when a user holds the space bar down to continuously move the cursor across the screen. The number of times per second a character can be typed is usually expressed as characters per second (CPS). The **Cursor blink rate** is simply how fast the cursor blinks on and off. It does not affect your typing in any way.

The **Language** tab, **Figure 7-7,** allows a different language to be displayed on the screen. The computer is an international electronic device marketed worldwide, not just in the United States. This window allows you to add and change the language entered by the keyboard. There are keyboards for all major languages in the world.

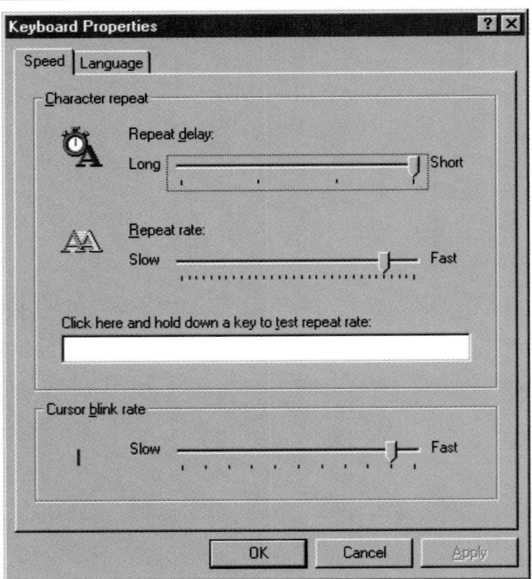

Figure 7-6. Windows Keyboard Properties dialog box. This box is accessible through **Control Panel**.

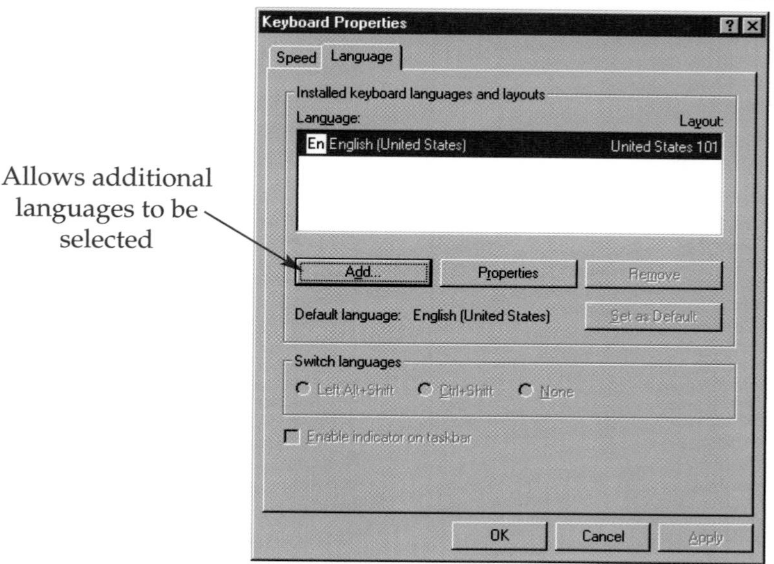

A

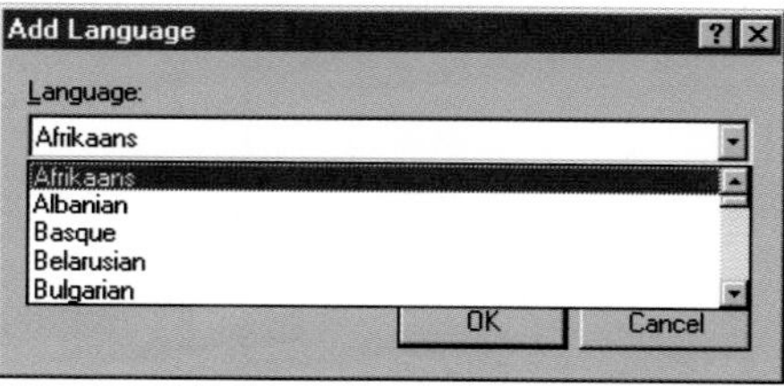

B

Figure 7-7. The **Language** tab in the **Keyboard Properties** dialog box allows you to add a selection of languages to your computer. Clicking **Add...** (Part A) will bring up a selection of languages (Part B).

Mouse

The ***mouse*** is a computer pointing device used to manipulate an on-screen pointer. The mouse can be used to move, select, or change items on your computer screen. There are a variety of mouse styles, **Figure 7-8.** They can come with two or three buttons, and many come with a center wheel or lever that is designed for ease in scrolling through documents or Web pages.

mouse
a computer pointing device used to manipulate an on-screen pointer.

The typical mouse is a very interesting combination of electrical and mechanical applications. See **Figure 7-9.** Take a good look at the major parts of the assembly, the light receiver, light transmitter, shutter disk, and the y-axis and x-axis contact points with the ball. As the ball inside the mouse rolls across the surface of a mouse pad, the movement causes either shutter disk (or both) to rotate. An infrared beam is emitted from an LED (light-emitting diode) across from the shutter. As the shutter disk revolves, it causes the light beam to be chopped. The number of chops is directly proportional to the distance the ball rolls. The combined effect of the x- and y-axis is transmitted to the motherboard as a digital signal. The digital signal plots the new location of the mouse cursor on the screen. The buttons on a mouse close very small microswitches. There is one switch under each button.

The typical ***track ball,*** **Figure 7-10,** is simply a mouse that is configured upside down. The same principles of the mouse apply to the track ball.

track ball
a pointing device similar to a mouse that is operated upside down.

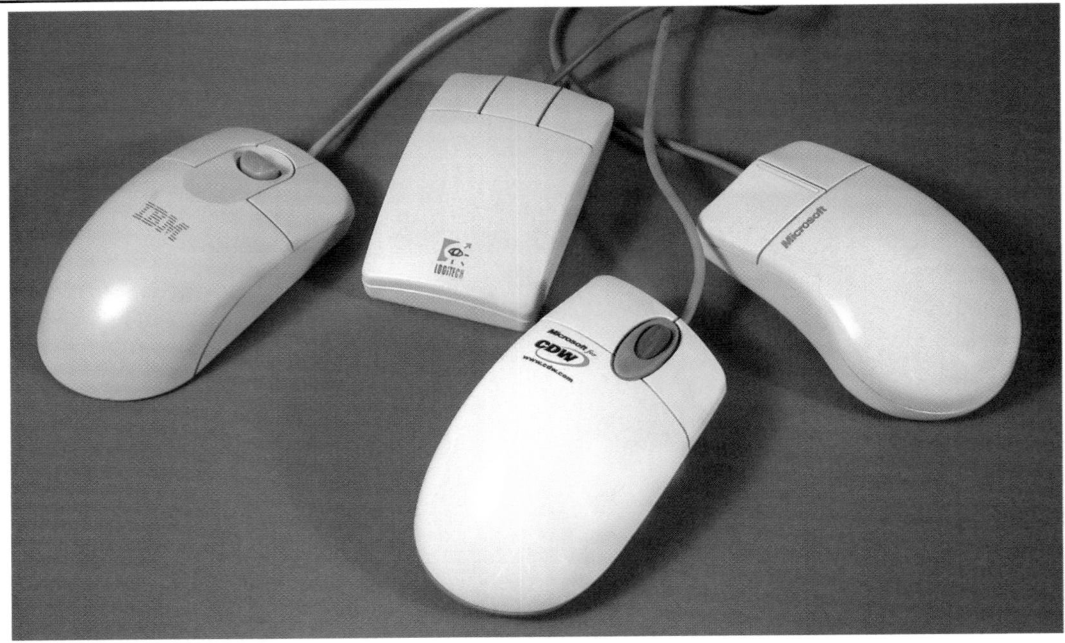

Figure 7-8.
Selection of mouse styles.

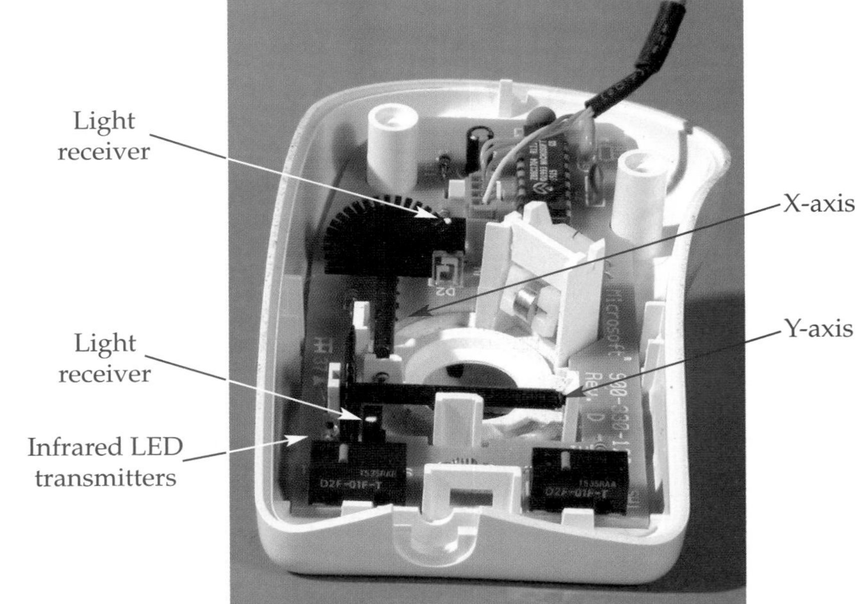

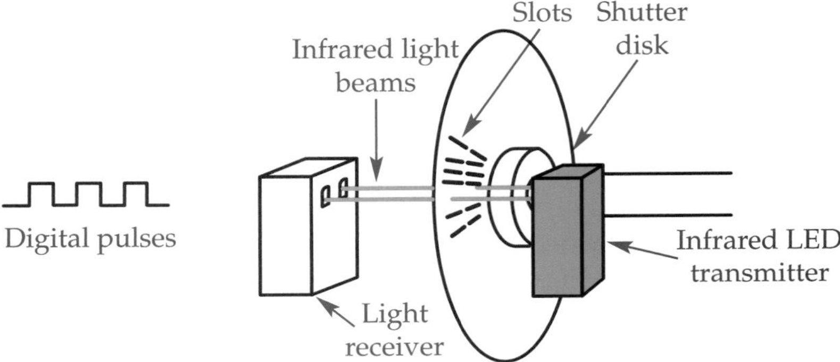

Figure 7-9.
Shown are the insides of a typical mouse. The mouse ball moves two wheels that determine the x- and y-axis movement of a mouse pointer on screen.

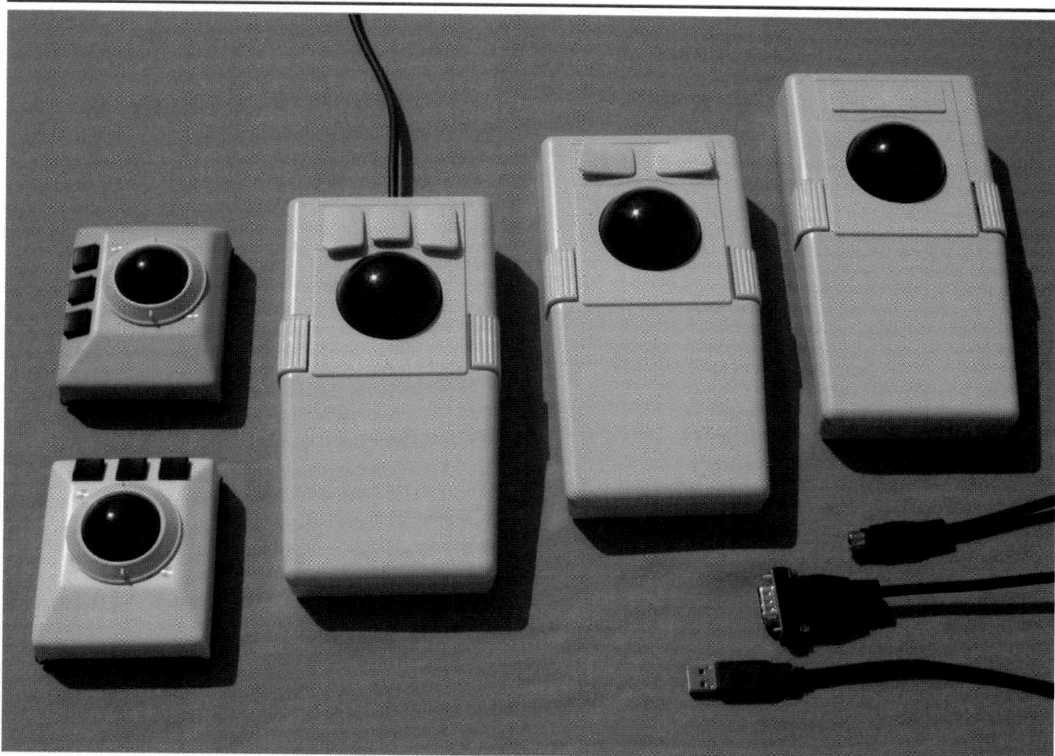

Figure 7-10.
A track ball, like a mouse, can be used to control the position of the cursor and to pick points. (Evergreen Systems International)

Mouse Interface

The mouse is available in four interface styles:

- Motherboard.
- Serial.
- Bus.
- USB.

A mouse connector built into the motherboard is the most common means of connection. The IRQ setting for a motherboard interface mouse connection is most likely IRQ12. The connection for the mouse is usually next to the connection for the keyboard. Generally, both devices use the same type of connection, the 6-pin mini-DIN. However, they are not interchangeable. The two connections are easy to swap by mistake. There should be some indication on the back of the computer showing whether the connection is for the mouse or for the keyboard. If not, refer to your motherboard manual.

The serial interface connects to one of the serial ports such as COM1 or COM2 using a 9- or a 25-pin connector. This is often referred to as RS-232. If the mouse uses COM1, then its IRQ is 4. If it uses COM2, the IRQ is 3. These settings can be viewed through **Device Manager**.

A bus mouse connects to the motherboard through an expansion or adapter card inserted into the bus system. The most common card uses an ISA type bus slot. ISA has the slowest bus speed, though a mouse is actually a very slow device when comparing the transfer rate of data. An ISA bus mouse most likely uses an IRQ setting of 5.

A bus mouse may have a connector that looks like the connector for a motherboard interface mouse. One that looks like a mini-DIN is common. However, a bus mouse is usually not compatible with the other types of mouse devices. Plugging a bus mouse into a motherboard mouse connector could result in damage to the motherboard.

The newest type of connection for a mouse is the Universal Serial Bus (USB). The USB is not compatible physically with the other connector styles, so it is impossible to plug into the wrong socket. While the mouse may not require the speed that USB can provide, the USB is a standard socket that all new PCs have. This makes the USB connection a safe choice for mouse manufacturers.

Optical Mouse

One problem with the traditional mouse is a buildup of dirt in the inner workings of the device. The mouse ball picks up the dirt and transfers it to other parts. The latest input technology for a mouse eliminates the need for the ball, preventing dirt buildup problems. All of the moving parts from a traditional mouse are replaced with a CMOS digital camera.

The optical mouse uses a tiny optical camera that senses motion by taking a rapid series of pictures (1500 pictures per second). A microprocessor inside the mouse compares the pictures of the surface to each other and translates the direction and speed of movement into screen positions. The mouse can be used on any type of surface. No mouse pad is required.

Troubleshooting the Mouse

As with keyboards, it is not cost-effective to spend any large amount of time fixing a malfunctioning mouse. However, proper maintenance and adjustments can make them last longer and work more efficiently.

Mouse Maintenance

Maintenance for a mouse or track ball is very easy. Most failures are caused by a buildup of lint or dirt on the roller that contacts the ball. This buildup is usually caused by a dirty mouse pad or from using the mouse without a pad on dirty furniture surfaces or on pads of paper. Paper tablets contain a great deal of paper lint particles. Using a mouse directly on a paper tablet will cause the mouse to fail after a relatively short period of time.

Another large cause of problems is hand lotion. People who use hand lotion on a regular basis will inadvertently contaminate the mouse ball with a film from the lotion. This film rapidly picks up dust and lint.

The best way to maintain a mouse is to keep the mouse or track ball and socket very clean. The ball under the mouse is easily removed, **Figure 7-11.** A small plate usually twists off and the ball drops out. The rollers inside the mouse can be sprayed with compressed air. The mouse ball itself can be rinsed with water.

Adjusting Mouse Properties

As with keyboards, certain properties of the mouse can be adjusted for preference. Mouse properties can be adjusted in both Windows and DOS.

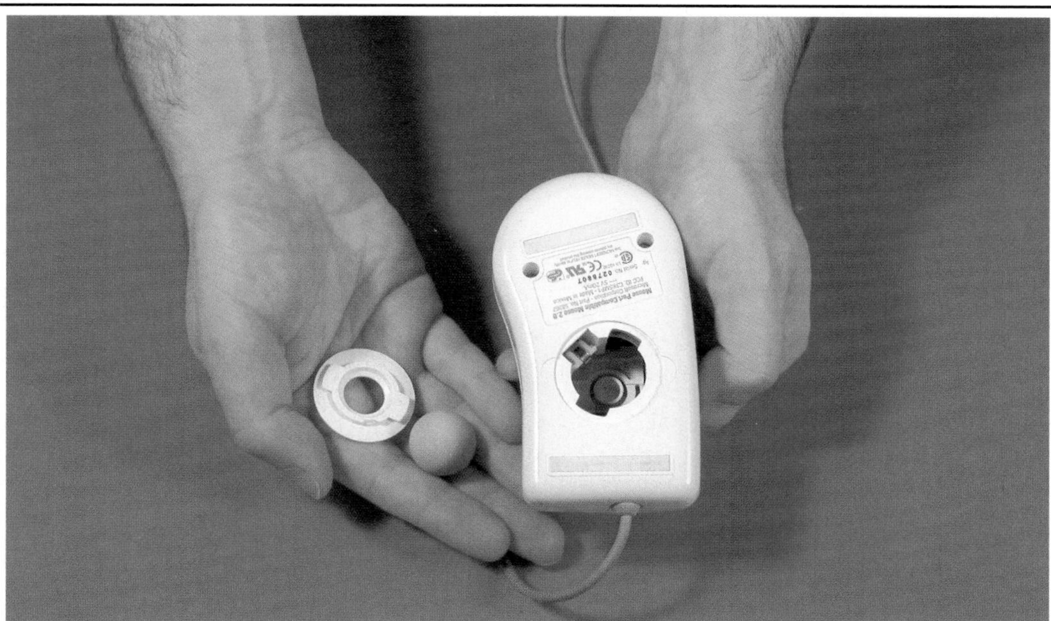

Figure 7-11. Opening a mouse for cleaning is a simple task.

Windows adjustments

There is a Mouse Properties window for making adjustments to the mouse. See **Figure 7-12.** The properties window can be accessed through **Start | Settings | Control Panel** and then double-clicking the **Mouse** icon.

Once the properties window for the mouse is open, adjustments to functionality, such as speed of pointer travel across the screen and the speed used to double-click can be adjusted. The type of mouse being used can be selected. One special change allows you to reverse the features (such as dragging) associated with the right and left buttons. Adjustments for purely aesthetic reasons can be performed here as well. The length of the trailing mouse tail can be adjusted. The style, color, and size of the pointer can also be changed, **Figure 7-13.**

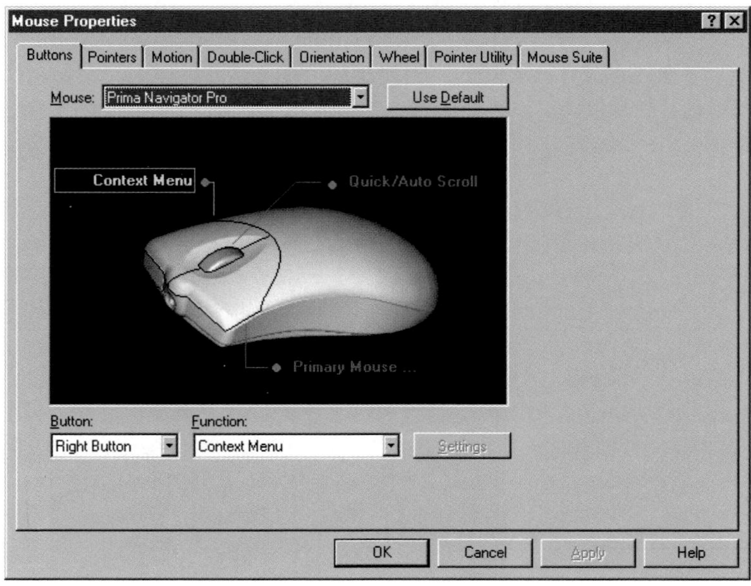

Figure 7-12. **Mouse Properties** dialog box. The appearance of this box will vary depending on the mouse installed.

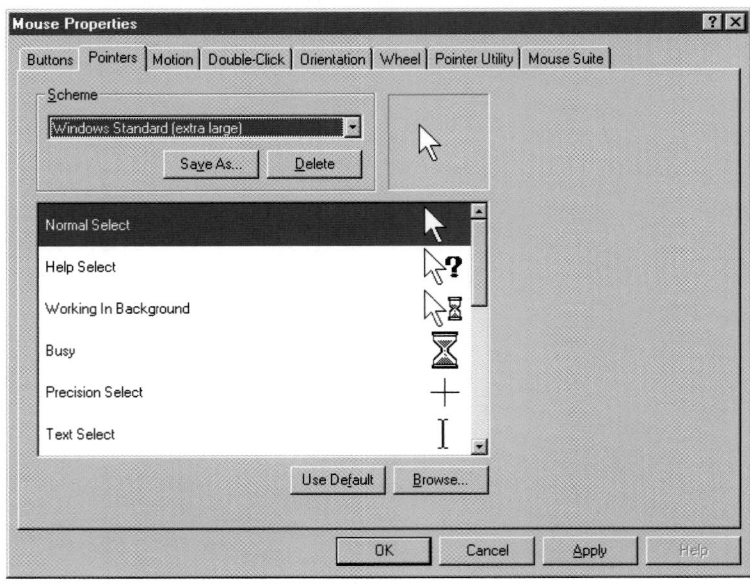

Figure 7-13. The **Mouse Properties** dialog box allows you to adjust the mouse for purely aesthetic reasons in addition to functional reasons.

DOS adjustments

In DOS, the mouse has to be called for and a manufacturer's driver has to be placed on the machine. The mouse must be activated by inserting the command **mouse.sys** into the config.sys or autoexec.bat file. This command calls the mouse driver. Windows 95 and later versions, as well as NT 4.0 and later, do not need this mouse command to run.

Game Controllers

The earliest game controller, other than the keyboard or mouse, was the joystick. The first joysticks were of a simple box construction with a lever extending from the top (the stick), **Figure 7-14.** Often, it had one or two push buttons. When the lever was moved, its position was converted into x- and y-screen coordinates. The buttons operated microswitches concealed inside the box. The buttons were typically fire control buttons for games that used weapons. Today, the simple joystick has evolved into a more complicated game controller. It has the same functions as the original joystick design and more, **Figure 7-15.**

The additional features on most controllers are top hat control and force feedback. The top hat control located at the top of the stick is used as an additional control. It can plot x- and y-coordinates, or it can be used as an additional switch.

The force feedback feature is a method that creates "feel" at the game stick control. A set of servomechanisms is incorporated into the game controller. These operate on feedback from the computer. When a wall is struck in a driving game or a weapon is fired in a shooting game, the game software package generates an electrical signal that is sent to the game stick. The signal activates a servomechanism, which generates movement or vibration in the game controller that simulates the action in the game.

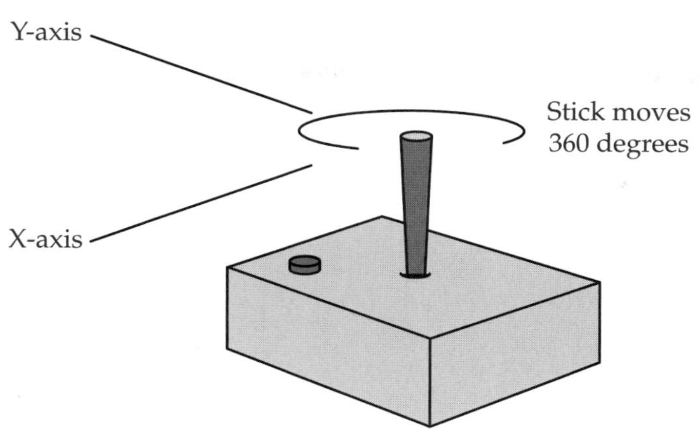

Figure 7-14. Very early (and basic) joystick.

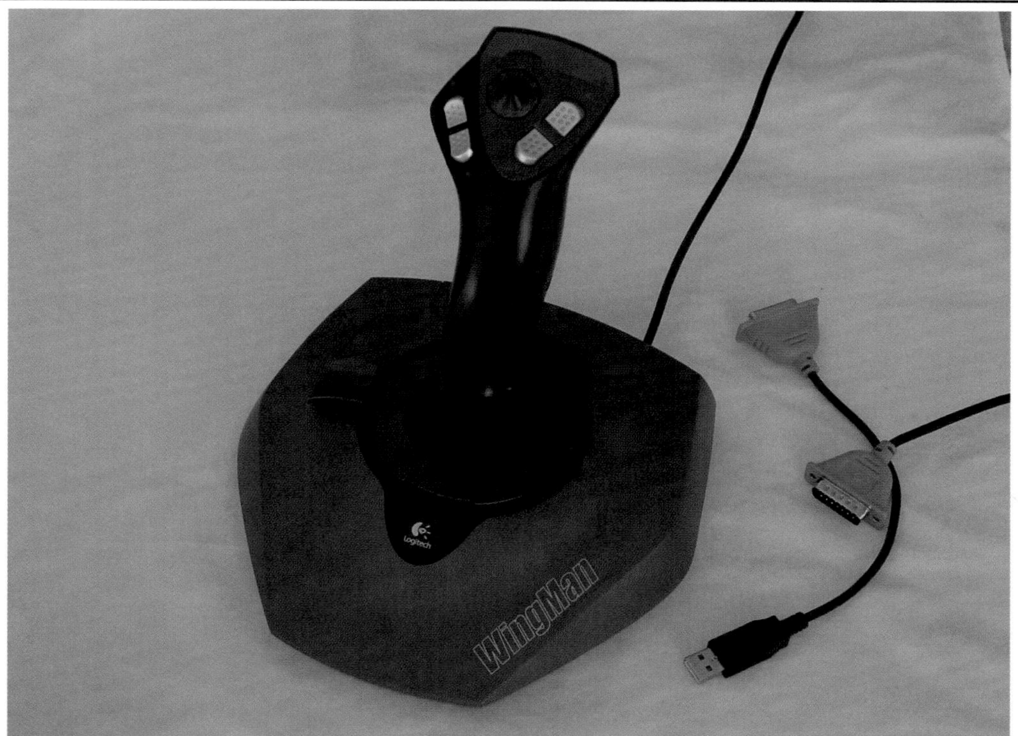

Figure 7-15. Modern joysticks still resemble their predecessors, but they offer many more options. They have more buttons and controls, and some offer force feedback from the games they play.

Game Controller Construction

A game controller is similar in construction to the mouse except that there are many variations on the electrical and mechanical mechanism that generates the electronic positioning signal. The original designs were based on two variable resistors called potentiometers. A potentiometer is a resistor device that is capable of varying its resistance to current. The styles of potentiometer used for gaming devices usually ranges from 0 to 100 kilohms of resistance. One potentiometer is used for the x-axis and the other for the y-axis. The range of resistance

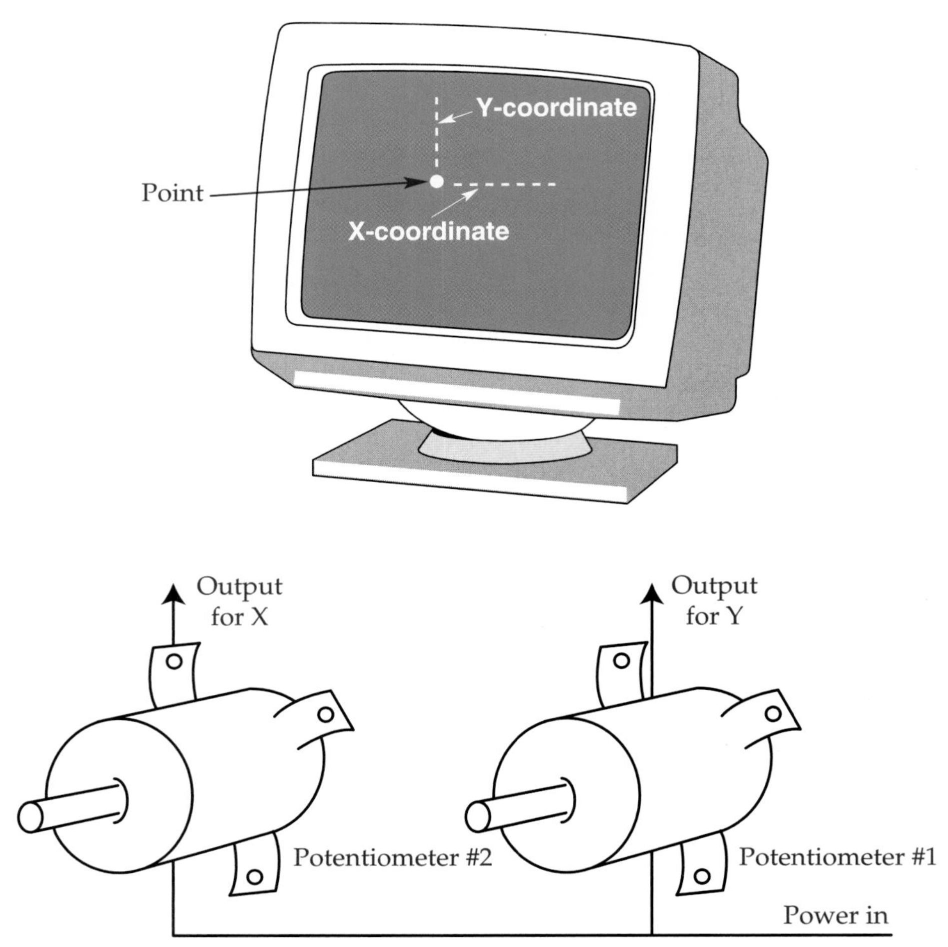

Figure 7-16. Two potentiometers and the screen coordinate they produce.

values is directly proportional to the x- and y-coordinates on the display screen. See **Figure 7-16** for an illustration of a screen and its coordinates.

Game Controller Port

The game port is usually a 15-pin, two row D-shell connector, **Figure 7-17.** The game controller connects to the motherboard through fifteen conductors. The chart in **Figure 7-18** identifies the function of each of the fifteen conductors involved in a typical application. Note that this chart represents a typical application, not a typical game controller. The actual use of pins can vary or be modified for a particular brand of game controller. Also note that this chart reflects conditions for using two game controllers (one called A, and the other B), since many games are set up for two players.

Some game adapters are quite elaborate in appearance. Some are designed to imitate steering wheels with gas and break pedals and aircraft steering yokes with pedals. These types of controls are all based on the same electrical and mechanical principles discussed here.

As with the mouse and keyboard, many new game adapters are coming out with USB connections. These take advantage of the speed and abundance of USB ports.

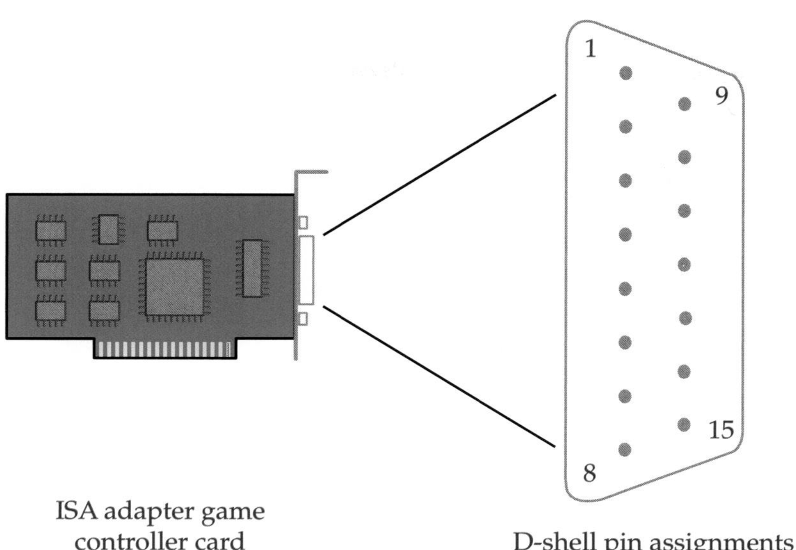

Figure 7-17. Game controller card with a 15-pin D-shell connector.

Pin #	Function Description
1	Provide +5 volts to game controller A.
2	Provide input from switch located on game controller A.
3	Provide input about position along x-coordinate of game controller A.
4	Used as ground.
5	Used as ground.
6	Provide input about position along y-coordinate of game controller A.
7	Provide input from second switch on game controller A.
8	Provide +5 volts to game controller A.
9	Provide +5 volts to game controller B.
10	Provide input from switch located on game controller B.
11	Provide input about position along x-coordinate of game controller B.
12	Used as ground.
13	Provide input about position along y-coordinate of game controller B.
14	Provide input from second switch located on game controller B.
15	Provide +5 volt input to game controller B.

Figure 7-18. Chart of pin use in a typical application of a game controller. Pin use can be modified by the game controller.

Digitizer Pad

A ***digitizer pad*** came into use long before graphical user interfaces, **Figure 7-19.** The pad served the same purpose as the GUI does today. This results in very few current applications for digitizer pads.

digitizer pad
a pointing device consisting of a tablet and a puck or pen-like stylus.

The digitizer pad is connected to the computer motherboard, usually through a serial port. The pad is constructed with a matrix under the symbols

Figure 7-19. Digitizer pad and pucks. (CalComp, Kurta)

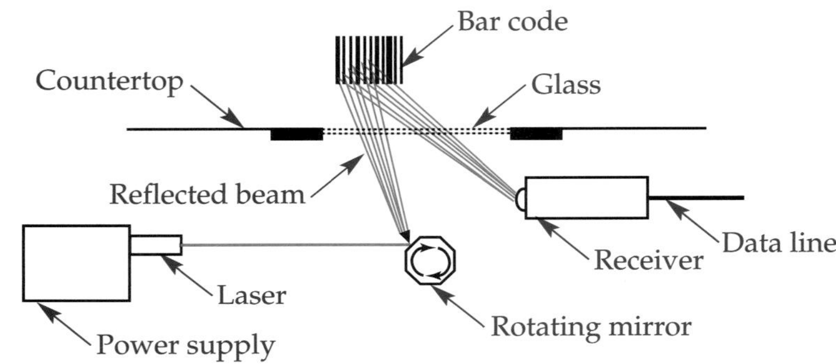

Figure 7-20. Shown are the workings of a bar code reader that can be found at the checkout counter of many stores. Using these fixed readers, objects have their bar codes dragged across the glass for reading.

displayed on the pad. A mouse-like device called a puck is moved across the pad and centered above the desired command. Commands such as circle, line, and square are typical for computer-aided drafting systems. When the pointer button is pressed, the coordinates under the pointer device transmit the coordinates from the digitizer pad to the computer. The software system responds to the appropriate request.

Bar Code Readers

bar code reader a device that converts bar code images into data.

scanner a device that digitizes printed images and text.

A ***bar code reader*** simply converts bar code images into data. The operation of a bar code scanner is simple, **Figure 7-20.** It is designed with a light source transmitter and a light source receiver. The light source transmitter projects a light beam across the bar code. The bar code is made up of dark lines of varying width and spacing. The widths of the dark lines combine with the white spaces to form a code that represents ASCII letters and numbers. Look at **Figure 7-21,** which shows a typical bar code.

The light from the source is reflected by the white spaces and absorbed by the dark lines. The receiver converts the reflected light into electrical pulses

Figure 7-21.
A typical bar code. Note the variation in the thickness of the black lines of the code.

representing the data contained in the bar code. The electrical pulses are then passed along as ASCII data to the PC through either a wireless or a wired connection. The PC has software driver programs that use the ASCII data for application programs that manage inventory or drive a cash register program.

Scanners and Digital Cameras

A ***scanner*** is a tool that takes in an optical image and digitizes it, **Figure 7-22.** Scanners can be used to read text into a computer or to create a digital version of a photo. To read text into a format that can be used with word-processing software, a scanner uses optical character recognition software. This ***optical character recognition (OCR)*** software determines which letters, numbers, and symbols match with images taken by the scanner. The output is a fairly accurate text version of a printed document. A ***digital camera*** takes pictures like a regular camera, but it captures and stores images as digital data instead of on photographic film. See **Figure 7-23.**

The secret to scanner and digital camera operations is the charged-coupled device. Think of a charged-coupled device (CCD) as a series of light-activated

optical character recognition (OCR) a type of software that is able to distinguish between the various letters, numbers, and symbols in a scanned image.

digital camera a type of camera that captures and stores images as digital data instead of on photographic film.

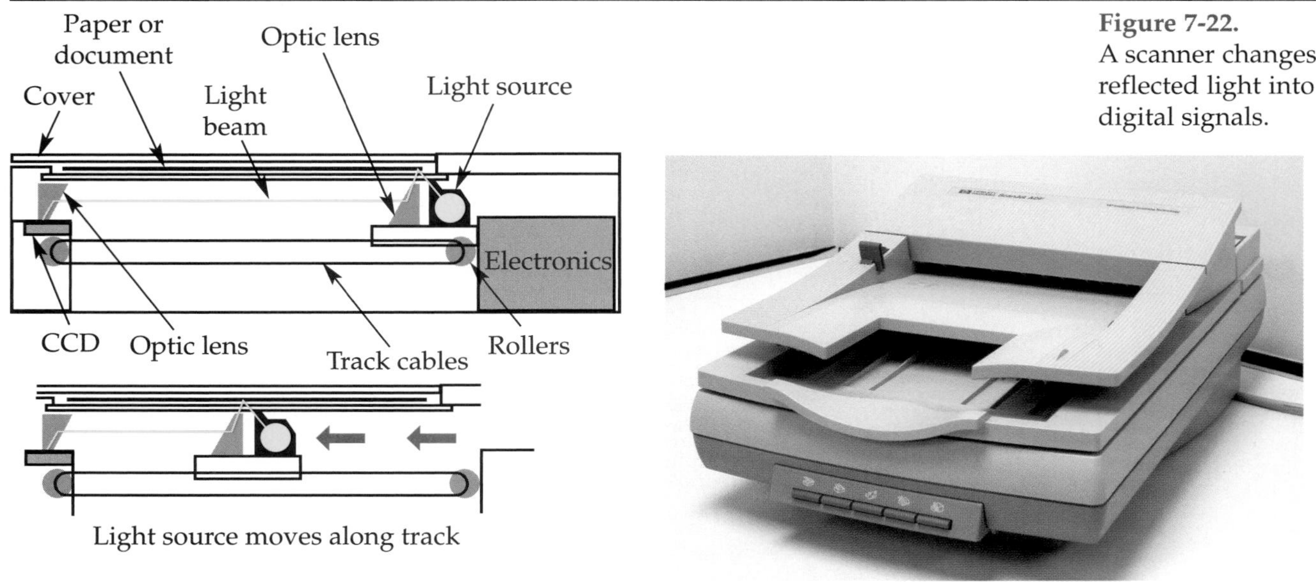

Figure 7-22.
A scanner changes reflected light into digital signals.

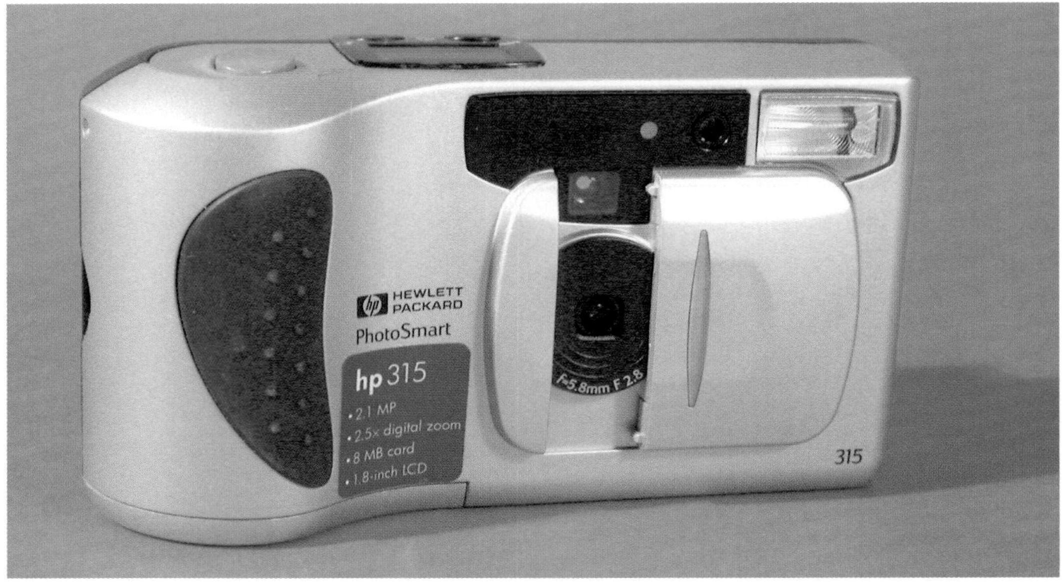

Figure 7-23. Digital cameras are similar to scanners in that they both use charge-coupled devices to produce their images.

transistors contained in a single chip. These transistors convert light into electrical energy. When light strikes the CCD, a voltage is produced in direct proportion to the intensity of the light.

The voltage produced is analog, which means the voltage level is a continuously variable signal. To be utilized by a computer system, the voltage must be converted to a digital signal, a sequence of discrete voltages. A special chip called an *analog-to-digital converter (ADC)* receives the analog electrical charge from the CCD and converts it to a series of digital signals that represent the light intensity of the image. The digital pulses are stored in memory to be accessed by graphical software programs. See **Figure 7-24.**

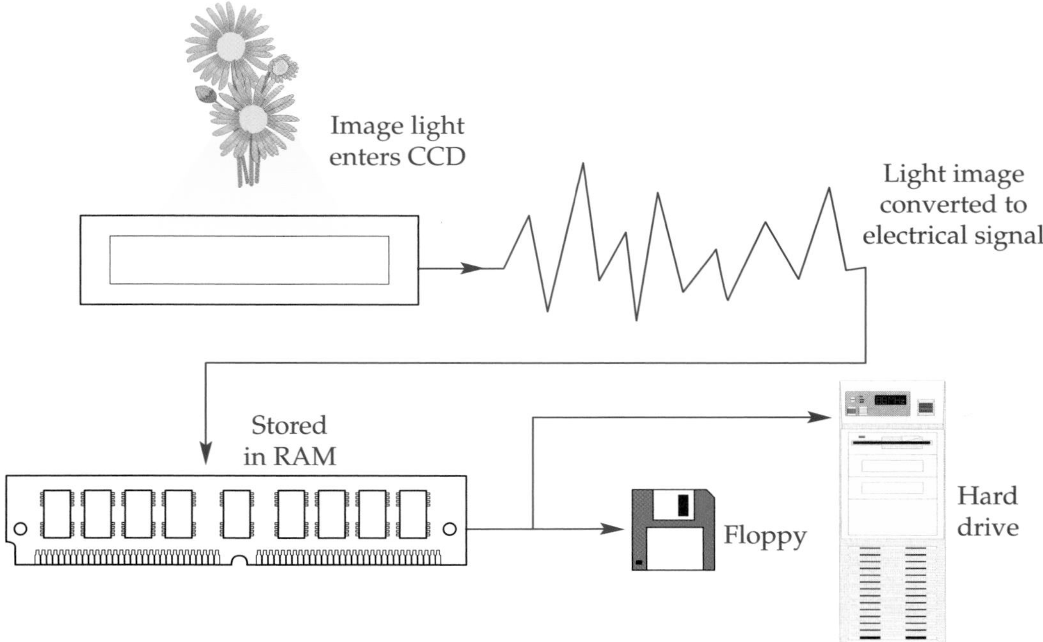

Figure 7-24. Illustration of a graphic stored as impulses.

The flat bed scanner uses a cable to move the light beam along the image placed on the bed of the scanner. The scanner captures the image one line at a time. After a line of the image is captured, the CCD is moved down the image a fraction to capture the next line. This process continues until the entire image has been captured.

The CCD device in a camera consists of an array of tiny windows. The entire image is captured at once rather than line by line as in the scanner application. Color filter lenses are used for color images. Each color is captured separately by incorporating a set of color filters into the lens units.

Windows Imaging Program

In Windows 98 and Me, under **Accessories**, is an imaging program. The program is accessible by going through **Start | Programs | Accessories | Imaging**.

The Kodak Company provides this imaging program for Microsoft to distribute with the operating system. It can be used in conjunction with a scanner, camera, or any graphic objects already loaded in one of the storage systems. **Figure 7-25** shows a screen shot of this free program. You can view many different image files with the program.

Light Pen

Light pens interact with a light beam that strikes the monitor screen. The raster or movement of the light across the screen is explained in detail in Chapter 8—Video Displays and Audio Systems. For now, imagine the computer screen image as being generated by a light beam sweeping across the screen thousands of times a second. The beam moves from left to right. After each pass

light pens
input devices that interact with the light beam that creates the image on the monitor.

Figure 7-25.
This imaging program from Kodak is free with the Windows operating system.

of the beam from left to right, it moves down the screen just a fraction. This process continues until the beam has covered the entire screen. The process is repeated approximately sixty times a second. The light intensity of the beam changes as it crosses the screen to produce an image. The travel of the beam is a product of precise timing of horizontal and vertical electronic controls.

The light pen is plugged into an adapter card that is inserted into one of the expansion slots in the motherboard. The end of the light pen is light sensitive. The light pen can detect the beam from the monitor as it sweeps across the computer display screen. The screen area has a graphical user interface displayed. It can be a menu or a list of products. When the light pen touches the screen area where an image is displayed, the light beam strikes the display screen and actuates the input area of the pen. It is this exact timing of the beam that allows the light pen adapter card to convert the location of the pen into screen coordinates. The software program converts the screen coordinates into user information such as "one hamburger with cheese," or "open bay door number 2." The command can be anything associated with the image on the screen.

Touch Screens

touch screen display computer display that is modified to accept input by touch.

Touch screen displays are computer displays modified to accommodate input information by touch. The input area on the touch screen is activated by a touch, as the name implies, or by using a stylus.

A touch screen system requires a touch screen panel assembly, controller, port connector, and software driver. The controller can be a separate unit attached by cable to the touch screen or incorporated into the edge of the touch screen frame. The typical connection to the computer system is made through a USB port, **Figure 7-26.** Special PCI cards may be used in place of a USB port. The PCI card can serve as a port connection to the computer and incorporate the necessary electronics to act as the system controller.

A software driver program must be installed in the computer system during the installation of the touch screen. The software driver provides the necessary support for interpreting the digital signal sent by the controller. Installing the necessary driver is similar to installing a driver for any other computer input device.

Touch screens are often incorporated into a computer system when a mouse or keyboard would not be a practical input device or as a convenience for users. Touch screen applications have been applied to interactive computer communications such as those in hotel lobby information panels, manufacturing assembly line controls, hospital surgical rooms, and the food service industry.

Touch screen technology falls into five major sensor categories: resistance, capacitance, near field effect, infrared, and acoustical wave. All touch screen technologies operate in a very similar manner. The main difference is the touch screen surface construction and the type of electronic transmitters and receivers or sensors used.

Resistance

Touch screens that utilize the electronic principle of resistance are one of the most common and cheapest to design. The touch screen consists of two layers of conductors separated by very tiny spacers. The first layer is a series of vertical translucent electrical conductors, and the second layer is a series of horizontal

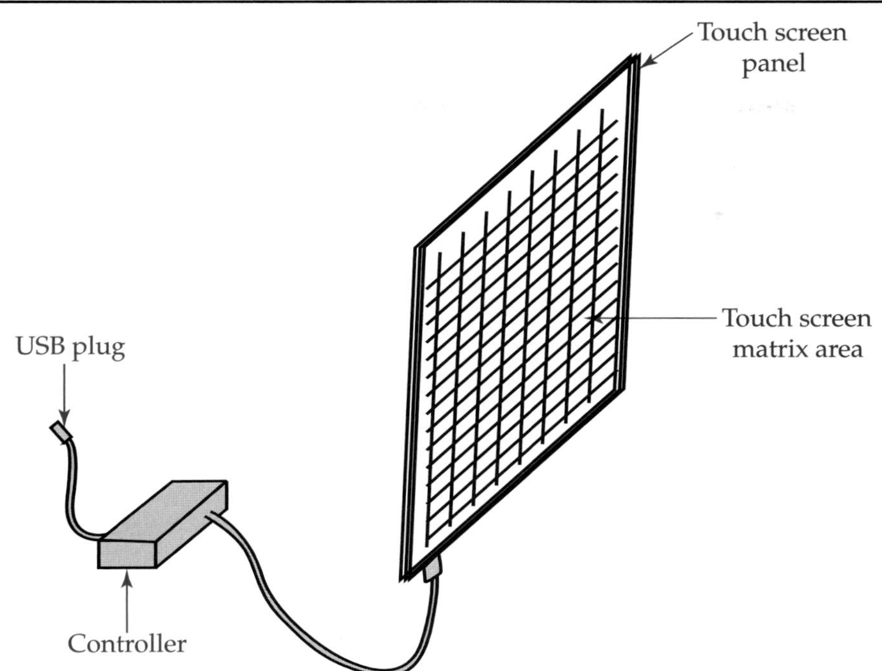

Figure 7-26.
This touch screen connects to the USB port of a PC. The controller is a separate unit attached to the cable.

translucent electrical conductors. The two layers combine to form a matrix pattern. The two layers are assembled into a flexible transparent cover, which fits neatly over the monitor display.

The monitor typically displays command buttons or similar graphics, which represent menu commands such as open, save, view files, and exit. When the screen is touched, a connection is made at that point in the matrix, **Figure 7-27.** Each area on the resistance touch screen produces a unique electrical resistance value. The electrical resistance value is interpreted by the screen controller and then passed to the computer operating system as a screen location. The digital signal is sent into the computer system through a USB port or through a PCI card designed for this purpose. Resistance touch screens work well in dusty or humid environments.

Capacitance

Capacitance touch screens operate on the principle of capacitance. See **Figure 7-28.** The touch screen is coated with a transparent metal oxide. A slight electrical charge is applied to the metal oxide, which creates an equally distributed electrical field across the inside of the touch screen. When the screen is touched, the electrically charged field is disturbed. A drop in the electrical potential at that point in the screen is transmitted to the touch screen controller. Capacitance touch screens do not work well in a humid environment.

Near Field

Near field touch screens also operate on the principle of capacitance. However, the near field touch screen is constructed from two laminates of glass, each with a pattern of a transparent metal oxide coating. The main difference

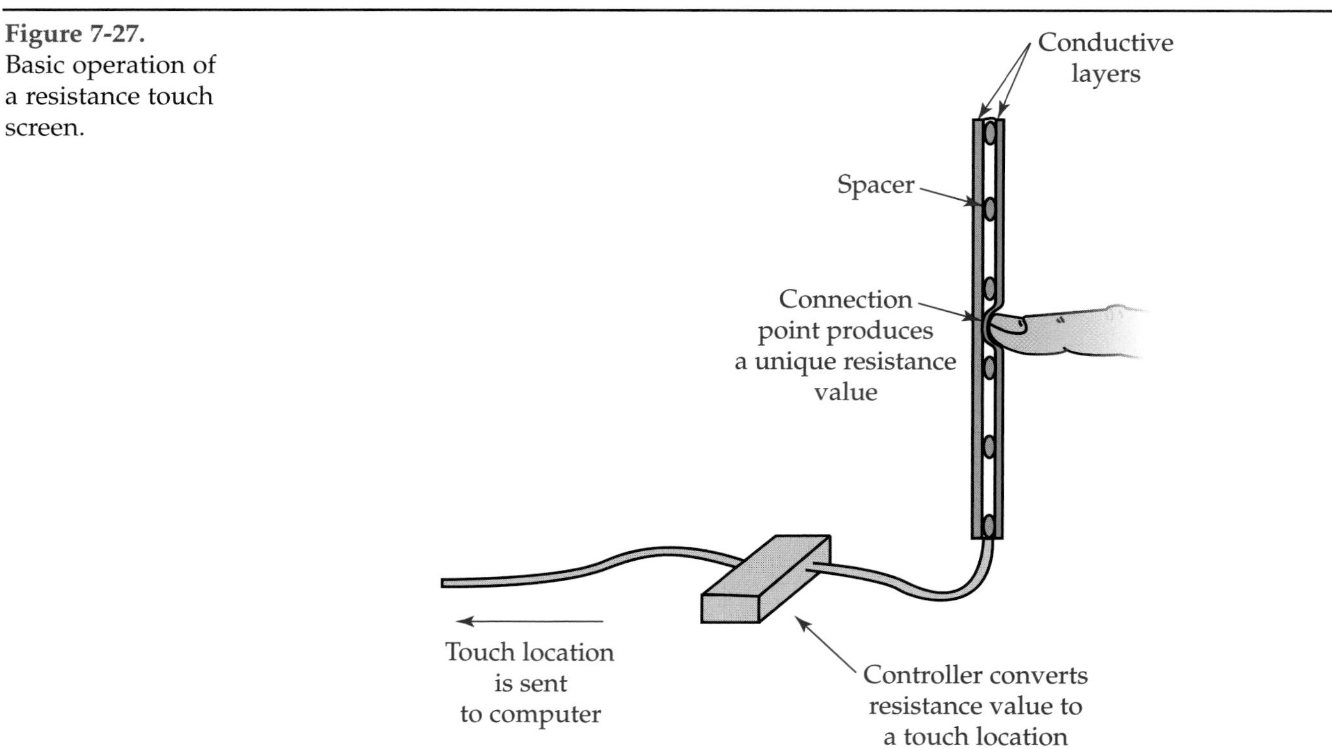

Figure 7-27.
Basic operation of a resistance touch screen.

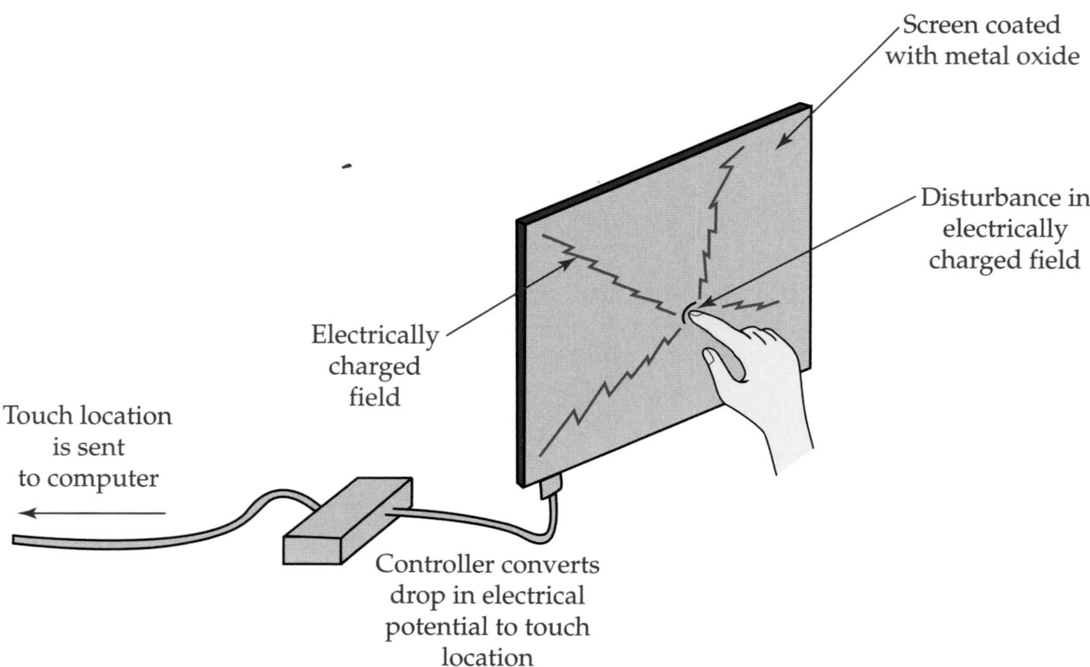

Figure 7-28.
Basic operation of a capacitance touch screen.

between the two technologies is that you need not touch the screen, but rather place your finger near the screen area. A finger or any other pointing device near the screen area is sufficient to disturb the electrical field between the two screen plates. Near field touch screen works well in an industrial or medical application where the user may have gloved hands.

Infrared

The infrared touch screen forms a matrix created by a row of infrared transmitters and receivers along the edges of the screen, **Figure 7-29.** The infrared transmitters are specially designed LEDs that transmit infrared light to the receivers. The receivers are light activated transistors, which act like a switch that is turned on and off by the presence or absence of the infrared light beam. When a touch interrupts the infrared beam, the receivers in that matrix area send a signal to the controller. The controller determines the touch location and sends this location to the computer.

Acoustical Wave

The acoustical wave touch screen is similar in design to the infrared screen. The acoustical touch screen, however, uses a matrix of sound waves. The edges of the panel are lined with acoustical sound wave transmitters and receivers. When an object such as a finger interrupts the sound wave, the location of the interruption is transmitted to the screen controller. The infrared and acoustical do not work well in a dusty environment.

Figure 7-29.
Basic operation of an infrared touch screen.

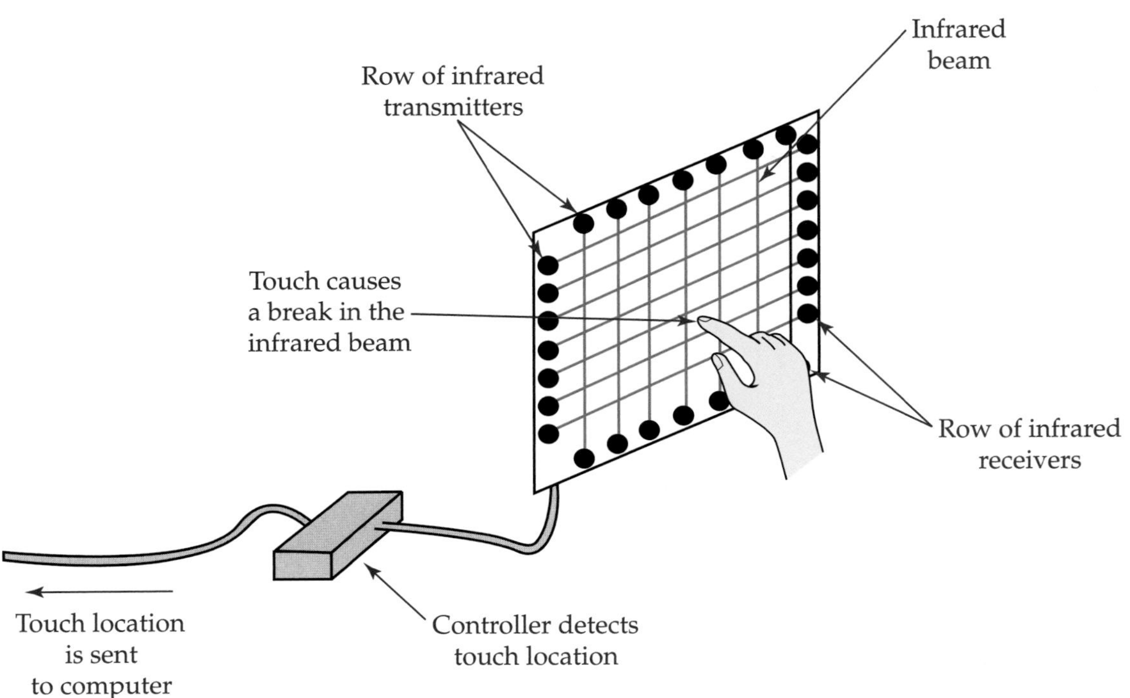

Wireless Input Devices

Wireless input devices operate using infrared light or radio transmission. Infrared technology is the same technology your typical television remote control uses. Infrared devices flash a series of infrared pulses from the transmitter (keyboard, mouse, joystick) to a receiver usually built into the PC case. Radio devices operate by transmitting digital codes similar to Morse code from the transmitter (keyboard, mouse, etc.) to the receiver, a separate device connected to an input port on the PC. The pulses represent the buttons being pushed or the position of the mouse wheel. Some wireless keyboards are a combination keyboard and mouse.

Infrared devices have a limitation that digital radio devices do not. The infrared products must be used in line-of-sight position. This means that the infrared transmitter and receiver must be positioned so the light emitted from the transmitter can reach the receiver unobstructed. No desktop clutter can be in the way. A digital radio device is not limited by typical desktop clutter. It can transmit digital impulses through and around the paper, books, and discs found on a typical desktop.

Bluetooth standard standard that ensures interoperability between different manufactures of wireless devices by requiring that all radio transmission be in the 2.4 GHz radio band and transmit 1 Mbps at a maximum of 10 meters.

Wireless input devices such as keyboards and mouse devices conform to the Bluetooth standard. The ***Bluetooth standard*** was developed to ensure interoperability between different manufactures of wireless devices. The Bluetooth standard requires that all radio transmission be in the 2.4 GHz radio band and transmit up to a maximum of 10 meters. The maximum data transfer rate is 1 Mbs. This may sound slow, but it is more than ample for keyboards, mouse devices, and similar input devices.

Virtual Keyboard

Canesta has developed a virtual keyboard designed to work with PCs, personal digital assistants (PDAs), smart phones, and any application where an input device might be required. The Canesta system consists of three main components: the sensor module, the infrared light source, and the pattern projector, **Figure 7-30.**

The infrared light source and pattern projector work together to create an image of a keyboard. The keyboard image can be projected onto any surface. The light of the keyboard image is reflected off the surface to a set of light sensors. The user simply types on the image just as though it was a real keyboard. The user's finger motions interrupt the light pattern representing the keyboard. The light sensors detect interruptions in the reflected light. The light sensor module converts the interruptions into digital signals that represent the keys touched by the user. See **Figure 7-31.**

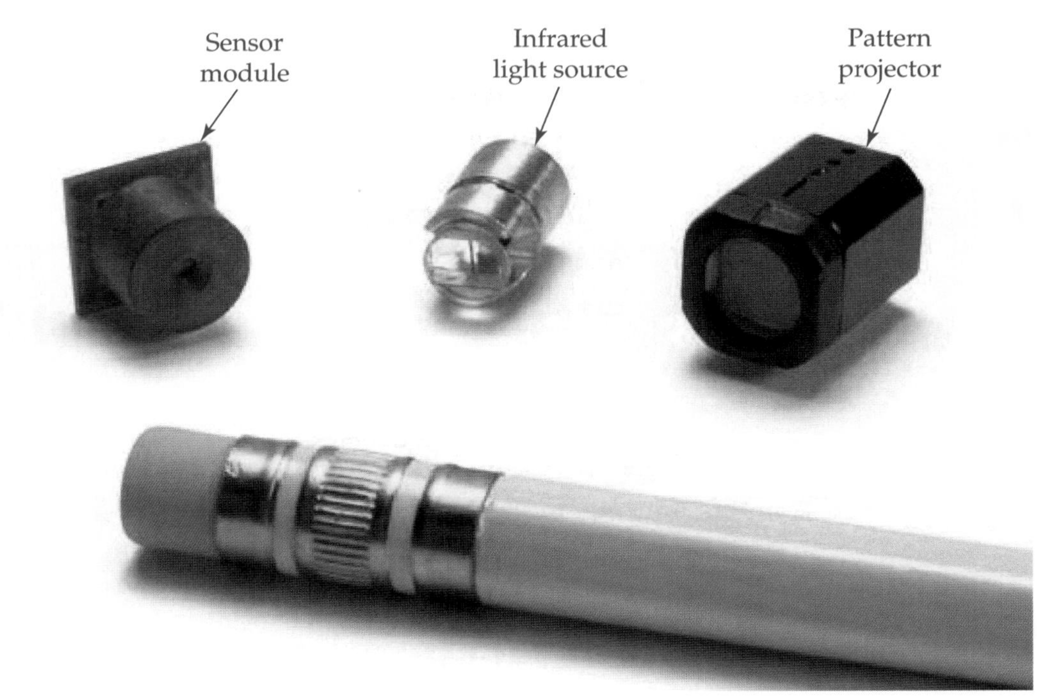

Figure 7-30. The virtual keyboard by Canesta is constructed from three main devices: the sensor module, the infrared light source, and the pattern projector. (Canesta, Inc.)

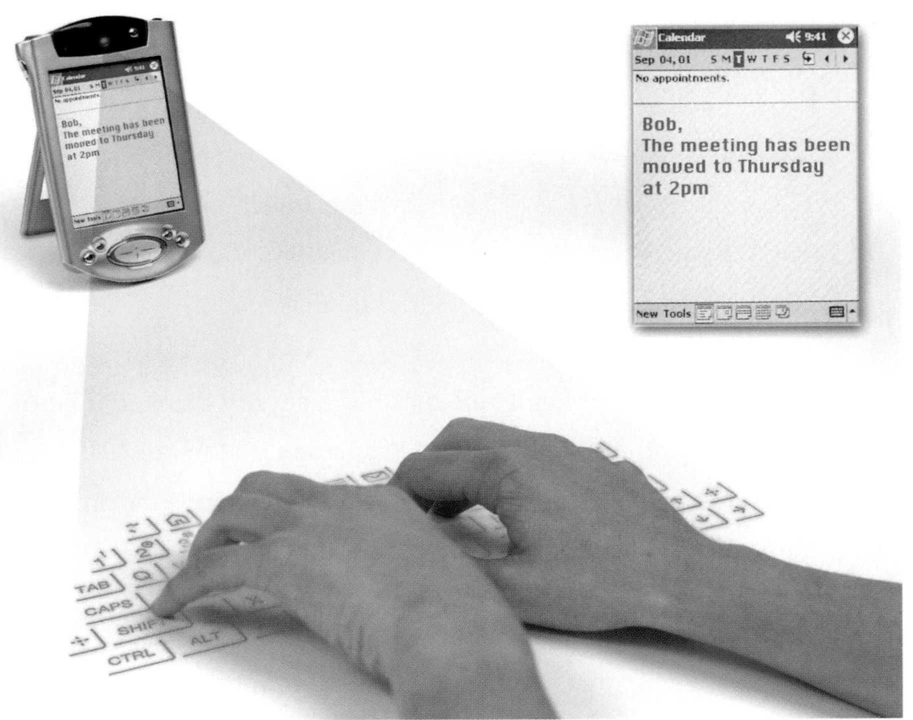

Figure 7-31. The user's finger movements interrupt the light pattern representing the keyboard. The light sensor module detects the interruptions and converts them into digital signals that represent the keys touched by the user. (Canesta, Inc.)

Summary

- There are four standard types of keyboard input switch designs: mechanical, membrane, rubber dome, and capacitor.
- Keyboard scan codes are interpreted by the BIOS and sent to the CPU as an ASCII character.
- Keyboard properties such as characters per second and repeat delay can be adjusted via Control Panel.
- The common styles of keyboard and mouse connectors are the 5-pin DIN, the 6-pin mini-DIN, and the USB.
- Ergonomic keyboards are shaped for comfort and help prevent carpal tunnel syndrome.
- If a mouse uses a COM port for a connection, it is assigned the same IRQ as the COM port (e.g. COM1 gets IRQ4 and COM2 gets IRQ3).
- If a mouse is connected directly to the motherboard, it is usually assigned IRQ12.
- The mouse properties such as size and style of the pointer and the speed of the click are changed in **Control Panel** under the **Mouse** icon.
- The game port usually is a 15-pin, two row D-shell connector or a USB.
- The major touch screen technologies are resistance, capacitance, near field effect, infrared, and acoustical wave.
- Wireless input devices operate using infrared light or radio transmission.
- Wireless input devices such as keyboards and mouse devices conform to the Bluetooth standard.

Review Questions

Answer the following questions on a separate sheet of paper. Please do not write in this book.

1. Scan codes are always equal to ASCII codes. True or False?
2. What are the four types of keyboard switches?
3. What are the two main keyboard connector styles called?
4. Is the keyboard a parallel or a serial device?
5. What is carpal tunnel syndrome?
6. How do you clean a keyboard that has a sugary drink spilled on it?
7. What is the path to the **Keyboard Properties** dialog box?
8. How is a new language assigned to a keyboard in Windows 98?
9. List two advantages of an optical mouse.
10. What is the commonly used IRQ setting for a mouse with a direct motherboard interface?
11. Describe a game port connector. Give the number of pins and shape.
12. What is a CCD?

13. How does a wireless mouse send information to a computer?
14. What standard is associated with wireless keyboard and mouse devices?
15. What is the maximum data transfer rate for a keyboard designed according to the Bluetooth standard?
16. What is the maximum distance typically associated with Bluetooth standard wireless devices?
17. What bandwidth is assigned to Bluetooth technology?
18. Identify five touch screen technologies that are incorporated into the touch screen matrix.
19. What type of touch screen would you use in a dusty environment?
20. What type of touch screen would you choose for a medial surgical room where the staff commonly wears rubber or latex gloves?
21. What three main parts comprise the Canesta virtual light keyboard?

Sample A+ Exam Questions

A+

Answer the following questions on a separate sheet of paper. Please do not write in this book.

1. Which two connection ports are most commonly associated with keyboards? Select two.
   a. 15-pin D shell
   b. PS/2
   c. USB
   d. LPT1
2. What is a keyboard buffer?
   a. A mechanical device designed to keep the individual keys from striking the keyboard backing too severely
   b. A special IC designed to suppress electrical surges directed from the keyboard
   c. An IC designed as a small memory unit to temporarily store keyboard-generated signals
   d. A mechanical device designed to remove debris and shine keyboard keys
3. A mouse is behaving erratically. When moved in certain directions, it seems to work fine. However, when moving in different directions, it skips or stalls. What would most likely remedy the condition?
   a. Reinstall the mouse driver software.
   b. Check the connection for a bent pin.
   c. Clean the mouse ball and rollers.
   d. Open the **Mouse** dialog box in **Control Panel** and adjust the movement speed of the mouse pointer.

4. Which best defines a keyboard scan code?
   a. A keyboard scan code is a signal generated when a key is struck on the keyboard. It determines what symbol is displayed on the monitor.
   b. A keyboard scan code is a signal generated by the keyboard scan generator. It checks to see what key is being pressed and then generates the corresponding ASCII symbol.
   c. A keyboard scan code is a binary code that records the duration that a key is held down.
   d. A keyboard scan code is generated by the CPU and then sent to the keyboard to identify which key is being pressed.
5. The physical design of a keyboard is referred to as what?
   a. Ergonomics
   b. Ecology
   c. Carpelmatics
   d. Physiology
6. Which item below is best for cleaning a keyboard?
   a. Windex
   b. A solution of 50 percent alcohol and 50 percent water
   c. Distilled water
   d. Any vacuum cleaner
7. Which technology does an optical mouse use?
   a. It is a wireless radio communication model.
   b. It uses a rotating wheel that breaks up a light signal into digital pulses.
   c. It uses CCD CMOS technology similar to digital camera technology.
   d. It uses an optical rubber ball that lights the surface of the material it passes over.
8. What are the limitations of a wireless mouse according to the Bluetooth standard?
   a. 10 MBPS at a distance of 1 meter
   b. 1 MBps at a distance of 5 meters
   c. 1 Mbps at a distance of 10 meters
   d. 10 Mbps at a distance of 50 meters

Suggested Laboratory Activities

Do not attempt any suggested laboratory activities without your instructor's permission. Certain activities can render the PC operating system inoperable.

1. Access the **Keyboard** icon in **Control Panel** and change the keyboard properties, such as the **Repeat rate** and **Repeat delay** settings, to see the effects on the keyboard.
2. Try installing a second language for the keyboard. Access the **Keyboard** icon in **Control Panel**, select the **Language** tab, click the **Add** button, and then select a new language from the **Add Language** dialog box. You will most likely need the operating system installation CD.
3. Unplug the keyboard and restart the system. Observe any error codes that may appear. Also, listen for any beep sounds indicating a problem. Repeat the experiment by unplugging the mouse.
4. Double-click the **Mouse** icon in **Control Panel** to open the **Mouse Properties** dialog box. Change the appearance of the tail, the click speed, and the type of icon used for the pointer.

Interesting Web Sites for More Information

www.americanmicrosystems.com

www.logitech.com

www.microsoft.com

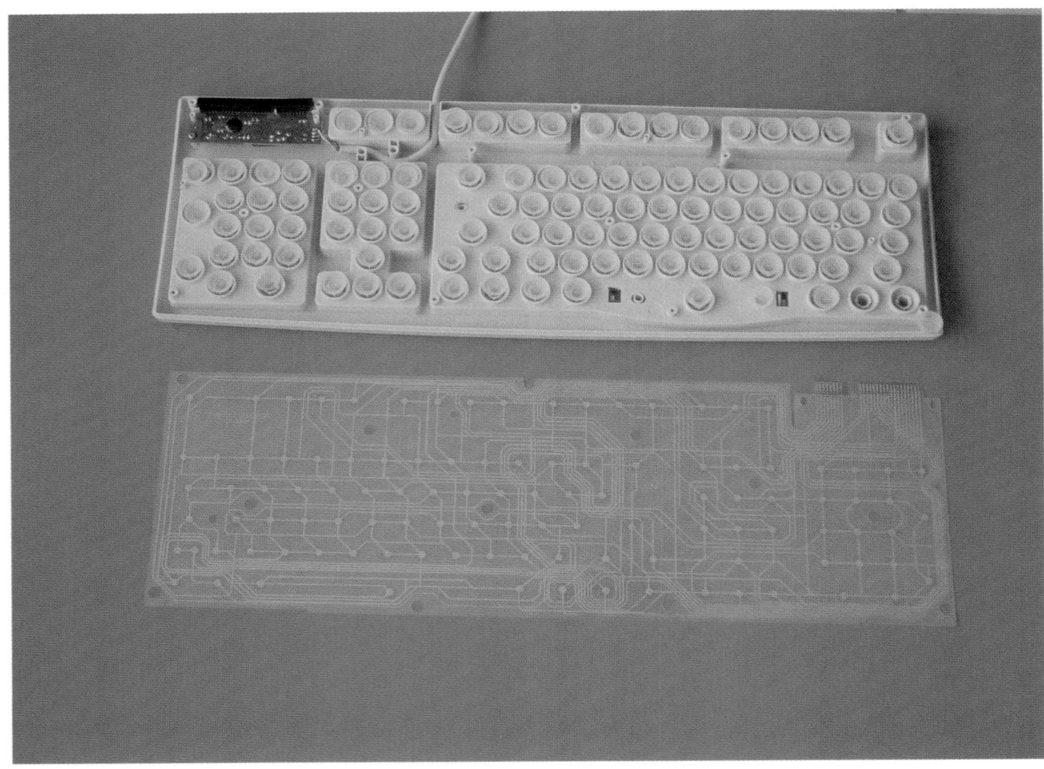

Internal view of a rubber-dome switch keyboard. This type of keyboard has two layers of circuit boards. The circuit boards are made of clear, flexible plastic.

Chapter 7
Laboratory Activity
Keyboard Properties

After completing this laboratory activity, you will be able to:

- ❑ Adjust the typing characteristics of a typical keyboard.
- ❑ Change the default language of the keyboard.

Introduction

As a PC technician, you may be called to make certain adjustments to the keyboard. Many people, especially professional secretaries, are sensitive to keyboard characteristics such as the repeat rate of a key press. In this exercise, you will make adjustments to the keyboard typing rate characteristics. You will also select a set of language characters, other than English, to be output by the keyboard. In addition, you will learn to adjust the English properties to change the layout of your keyboard, such as making it function as a Dvorak style keyboard.

A Dvorak style keyboard has a different physical arrangement, designed for use by the fastest typists. The original keyboard layout was designed to limit the speed of the typist. This prevented the typist from typing too fast, which could jam the typewriter's mechanism. A keyboard layout designed to maximize speed was developed and named after the inventor, Dr. August Dvorak. It is not a very common keyboard style, but it does exist.

Equipment and Materials

- Typical PC with Windows 98 operating system and a typical keyboard.
- Windows 98 Installation CD.

Procedure

1. ______ Boot the PC and wait for the desktop to be displayed.
2. ______ Activate the **Keyboard Properties** dialog box by opening **Control Panel**, right-clicking the **Keyboard** icon, and then selecting **Open** from the menu. (**Start | Settings | Control Panel | Keyboard**.)
3. ______ The **Keyboard Properties** dialog box will appear similar to the one shown in the following screen capture.

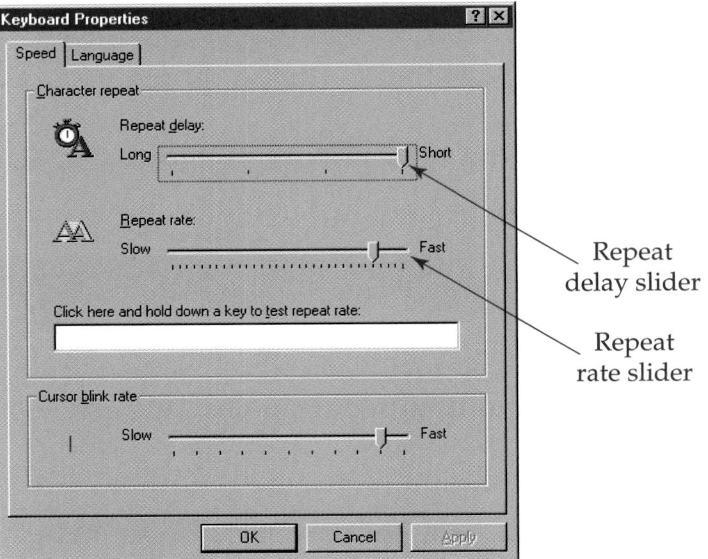

4. ______ Look at the two adjustment sliders, one labeled **Repeat delay** and the other labeled **Repeat rate**. Experiment with the two adjustments until you can answer the following questions:

   When a key is held down, a character will be repeated rapidly across the screen. The rate at which the character repeats is controlled by the repeat delay or the repeat rate?

   When a key is held down, the time delay before the second character appears on the screen is controlled by the repeat delay or the repeat rate?

5. ______ Select the **Language** tab at the top of the **Keyboard Properties** dialog box. The dialog box should appear similar to the one shown in the following screen capture.

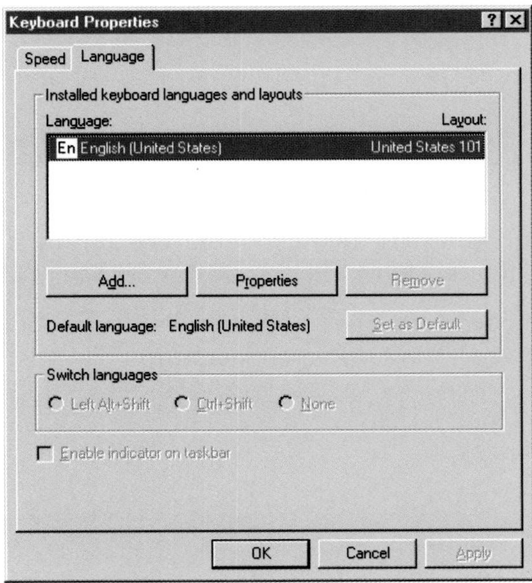

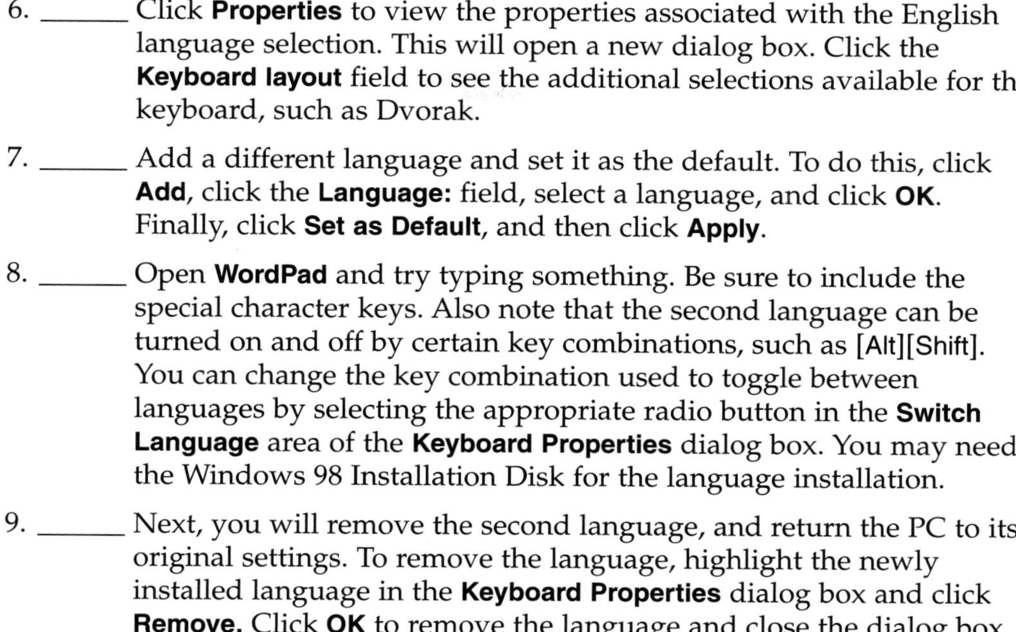

6. ______ Click **Properties** to view the properties associated with the English language selection. This will open a new dialog box. Click the **Keyboard layout** field to see the additional selections available for the keyboard, such as Dvorak.

7. ______ Add a different language and set it as the default. To do this, click **Add**, click the **Language:** field, select a language, and click **OK**. Finally, click **Set as Default**, and then click **Apply**.

8. ______ Open **WordPad** and try typing something. Be sure to include the special character keys. Also note that the second language can be turned on and off by certain key combinations, such as [Alt][Shift]. You can change the key combination used to toggle between languages by selecting the appropriate radio button in the **Switch Language** area of the **Keyboard Properties** dialog box. You may need the Windows 98 Installation Disk for the language installation.

9. ______ Next, you will remove the second language, and return the PC to its original settings. To remove the language, highlight the newly installed language in the **Keyboard Properties** dialog box and click **Remove.** Click **OK** to remove the language and close the dialog box.

Review Questions

Answer the following questions on a separate sheet of paper. Please do not write in this book.

1. How does the **Repeat delay** setting differ from the **Repeat rate** setting?
2. Explain how to add a set of characters for a second language to the keyboard.

The back of a Power Mac is shown here. Can you identify the various connections?

Video Display and Audio Systems

After studying this chapter, you will be able to:

- Describe the basic operation of the CRT.
- Describe the basic operation of an LCD panel.
- Explain screen resolution.
- Define screen pitch.
- Explain the major steps for installation of a video adapter board.
- Explain how to install additional memory to a video adapter board.
- Explain the major steps to install a sound card.
- Define different display systems such as CGA, EGA, XGA, VGA, SVGA, and UVGA.
- Explain how data compression works.
- Explain how MIDI produces sound.
- Compare WAV file and MIDI file types.
- Explain how sampling rate and number of bits determine the quality of analog-to-digital conversion.

A+ Exam—Key Points

Be very familiar with screen resolutions associated with different displays, especially VGA and XGA. A scenario question concerning the assignments of system resources may be asked about a sound or video card.

Key Words and Terms

The following words and terms will become important pieces of your computer vocabulary. Be sure you can define them.

active-matrix display
aspect ratio
bitmap (.bmp)
buffering
cathode ray tube (CRT)
codec
color palette
color/graphics adapter (CGA)
contrast ratio
deflection yoke
digital-to-analog converter (DAC)
dot pitch
electron guns
enhanced graphics adapter (EGA)
extended graphics array (XGA)
field
gas-plasma display
liquid crystal display (LCD)
monochrome
Motion Picture Experts Group (MPEG)
multicolor/graphics array (MCGA)
multimedia
musical instrument digital interface (MIDI)
native resolution
passive-matrix display
persistence
pixel
pixel pitch
polarized light
raster
refresh rate
resolution
response time
run-length encoding (RLE)
sampling
shadow mask
super VGA (SVGA)
thin film transistor liquid crystal display (TFT-LCD)
vector graphics
video graphics array (VGA)
viewing angle

The display system of a computer consists of two main components, the display and the adapter. The video adapter is often called a video card, or graphics card. There are some references made to legacy video systems in this unit. Many of these legacy systems are no longer being manufactured. This brief information, however, will help you understand the development of the computer video system as well as help you identify obsolete systems when you encounter them. There are still a number of these old technologies in existence. Being unable to identify them can be extremely frustrating and embarrassing to any technician.

Warning:
A computer video display can be very dangerous. The inside of a computer monitor has voltages present in excess of 20,000 volts. In addition, the monitor can store high voltages for a long period of time after the power has been disconnected.
A monitor should only be opened by a trained and qualified electronics technician. The scope of this textbook is not to train you as a monitor repairperson but rather give you the necessary skills to install, calibrate, and diagnose common monitor problems. *Do not* open a computer monitor case for any reason.

Display Aspects

There are a number of features common to all monitors. These features, such as dot pitch and size, greatly affect the quality of the picture produced as well as the price you will pay for the unit.

Monitor Size

Sizes of monitors are similar to television sets. The length of a diagonal drawn from one corner to the opposite corner determines the size of a monitor. See **Figure 8-1.**

Standard monitor sizes are 14″, 15″, 17″, 19″, and 21″. The actual viewing area is approximately 10% less than the diagonal measurement, though it varies from monitor to monitor.

A+ Note:
Most PC systems use a three-row 15-pin D-type connector for the monitor. The game port is usually a two-row 15-pin D-type connector. The A+ Certification exams may ask a question about identifying one of these two ports on the PC.

Dot Pitch

The ***dot pitch*** is the distance measured in millimeters between two color dots on the screen. The dot pitch is a measurement that reflects the quality of the image displayed on the screen. Generally, if the monitor has a smaller dot pitch, it produces a higher quality (sharper) image. An acceptable standard dot pitch is from 0.28 mm to 0.25 mm. The dot pitch cannot be adjusted. It is manufactured into the screen.

dot pitch
the distance between two color dots on the screen, measured in millimeters.

Color Display Values

The color display quality is determined by the number of bits used to represent the individual colors of red, green, and blue. The number of bits used to represent each color can determine the possible number of color shades. A byte contains 8 bits. This means that there are a total of 256 possible combinations of 1s and 0s in a byte. This means that an 8-bit color pattern can reproduce 256 intensities of a *specific* color. By mixing the intensities of red, blue, and green, other colors can be produced.

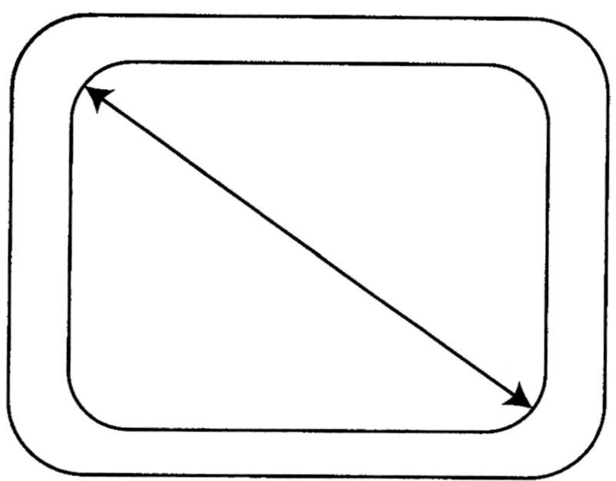

Figure 8-1.
Computer display screen sizes are measured on the diagonal.

Figure 8-2 is a listing of common standard color display values, expressed in bits. As the number of bits increases, so does the number of possible colors produced.

The color mix guide in **Figure 8-3** shows the application of 256,000 color intensities and the total spectrum of color produced by the monitor. This illustration is a screen capture taken from the Edit Colors command from Microsoft's Paint program. Paint can be found in the **Accessories** section of Windows. Using the **Edit Colors** dialog box, you can create your own pallet of colors beyond the standard colors. By moving your mouse across the sample of colors in the display, the amount of red, blue, and green that make up the custom color are varied. In the bottom-right corner are three numeric text boxes. Each box contains the value of the color used to make the color indicated under the cursor. The values correspond to the 8-bit range (0 to 255). This is an example of a 24-bit color system.

Display Resolution

resolution the amount of detail a monitor is capable of displaying.

The term ***resolution*** refers to the amount of detail a monitor is capable of displaying. The term *resolution* is also used to describe the detail produced by printers, digital cameras, and any similar type of graphic equipment. High resolution equals finer, better detail than low resolution. Look at **Figure 8-4** for a comparison of resolution patterns.

Figure 8-2. Common standard color display values.

Color Display Value	Number of Colors
8-bit	256
16-bit (True color)	65,536
24-bit (True color)	16,000,000
32-bit (True color)	4,000,000,000

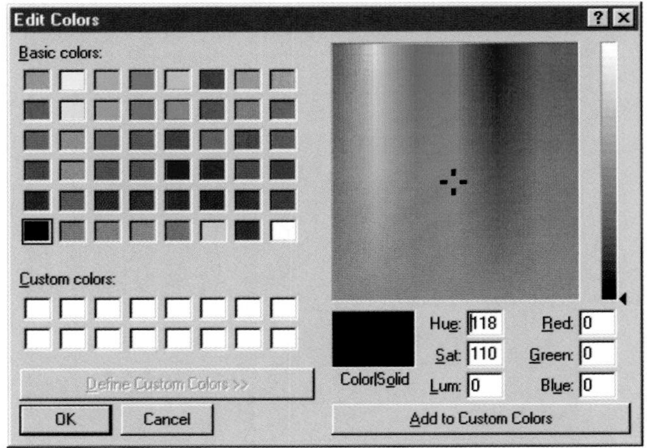

Figure 8-3. With this color mix guide, you can display 256,000 color intensities and the total spectrum of color produced by the monitor.

Figure 8-4.
A comparison of resolution patterns. The image of the PC setup is shown on the left at high resolution (300 dpi). On the right, the same image is shown at a low resolution (72 dpi).

Resolution is measured in pixels (*pict*ure *el*ement). A ***pixel*** is the smallest unit of color in a screen display. Think of it as a small dot. A typical VGA system has a resolution of 640 × 480. This means a VGA has a screen layout of 640 pixels by 480 pixels or a total of 307,200 pixels. The most common resolutions are listed in **Figure 8-5.**

pixel
the smallest unit of color in a screen display.

When PCs first came to the marketplace, most displays were monochrome display adapters (MDA). ***Monochrome*** technology uses only one color. Usually the color was amber or green. The adapters were designed to display text only, not graphics. Graphics required a good deal of memory, and at that time large amounts of memory were too expensive for most users. Early computers were used for business and research, not for entertainment. The screen resolution was 720 × 350, which presented a very sharp, clear image for text only.

monochrome
a monitor type that displays only a single color, usually amber or green.

In 1981, IBM introduced the ***color/graphics adapter (CGA).*** It offered two resolutions: 320 × 200 in four colors (from a choice of sixteen colors) and a higher resolution of 640 × 200 in two colors. Another company offered the Hercules adapter card. It met the requirements of graphics programs (such as AutoCAD) that the IBM adapter could not fulfill. The Hercules adapter card resolution was 720 × 348.

color/graphics adapter (CGA)
a video standard that featured two resolutions: 320 × 200 in four colors and a higher resolution of 640 × 200 in two colors.

Resolution	Acronym	Designation
640 × 480	VGA	Video graphics array
800 × 600	SVGA	Super VGA
1024 × 768	XGA	Extended graphics array
1280 × 1024	UVGA	Ultra VGA

Figure 8-5.
Chart of common resolutions.

enhanced graphics adapter (EGA)
a video standard that improved on the resolutions and color capabilities of the CGA standard.

video graphics array (VGA)
the minimum standard for video adapters, which displays at a resolution of 640 × 480 with 16 colors or 320 × 200 with 256 colors.

color palette
a collection of possible different colors that can be displayed on a monitor.

In 1987, IBM introduced the ***enhanced graphics adapter (EGA)***. The EGA system could display 16 colors in 640 × 200 or 320 × 200 resolution on a standard IBM color monitor. In monochrome, it could display a 640 × 350 resolution. When the EGA was attached to an enhanced color monitor, it could display 16 colors (from a choice of 64) in a resolution of 640 × 350.

The ***video graphics array (VGA)*** is the baseline for video adapters today. The VGA standard was also first introduced in 1987 with the IBM PS/2. VGA is the true minimum standard for video monitors at a resolution of 640 × 480 and 16 colors. Up to 256 colors can be displayed, but the resolution is reduced to 320 × 200.

The VGA palette contains 262,144 (256K) different colors. A ***color palette*** is a collection of possible different colors usually in degrees or shades, which can be displayed on a monitor. The palette contains a large variety of possible colors, but the total number of colors in the palette cannot be displayed at the same time on a monitor. For example, a video system such as VGA that can display up to 256 colors in the 320 × 200 mode can only utilize 256 colors from the total 262,144 colors possible in the palette.

Think of the color palette as the total number of tubes of color an artist has available to purchase from a supplier. While there may be 262,144 colors in the store, the artist can only afford to buy 256 tubes. Thus, the actual number of colors used for the painting is limited to the 256 colors. In the same way, while there are 262,144 colors that can be displayed in VGA, the video adapter can only support 256 of the total number at one time.

Tech Tip:
When a computer system detects a malfunction, it will start in safe mode, which only supports the minimum video standard of VGA. The VGA mode driver is located in the first 1MB of memory while more sophisticated drivers require memory above the first 1MB.

Also in 1987, the PS/2 display adapter 8514 was also introduced. It had better resolution than VGA and offered more colors. It supported a resolution of 1024 × 768 pixels with 256 colors. There were some disadvantages to the system, however. First, the system plugged into IBM micro-channel architecture. Second, in order to take full advantage of its capabilities, an 8514 color display monitor had to be used. This PS/2 display adapter was replaced by the IBM XGA standard.

multicolor/graphics array (MCGA)
a video standard that supported CGA and also provided up to 64 shades of gray.

super VGA (SVGA)
a video standard that supports 16 million colors and various resolutions up to 1600 × 1200 pixels.

It is interesting to note that EGA, VGA, and the PS/2 adapter 8514 came out at about the same time. However, only VGA survived the consumer marketplace.

Another standard of the time was ***multicolor/graphics array (MCGA)***. The MCGA adapter could support CGA, and also provided up to 64 shades of gray when more color variations than the standard CGA were required to be displayed.

Super VGA (SVGA) supports 16 million possible colors and various resolutions such as 800 × 600, 1024 × 768, 1280 × 1024, 1600 × 1200 pixels. The exact number of colors that can be displayed at the same time on an SVGA monitor is determined by the amount of memory. The higher the number of colors produced, the more memory required.

A+ Note:
All the previously mentioned types of display adapters with the exception of VGA have been discontinued. The reason that they are mentioned in this text is to keep you on alert for difficult questions on the A+ Certification exams. For example, if given EGA and XGA as answers for a multiple-choice question about video properties, confusion could result in an incorrect response.

In 1990, IBM introduced the ***extended graphics array (XGA).*** It is capable of a resolution of 640 × 480 while supporting 65,536 colors or 1024 × 768 with 256 colors. It also supports all of IBM's older graphic standards.

extended graphics array (XGA)
a video standard that supports a resolution of 640 × 480 with 65,536 colors, or 1024 × 768 with 256 colors.

Tech Tip:
You will see the label Ultra VGA used in advertising. Ultra VGA is not a true standard but rather a marking terminology that is used by manufacturers to describe their video adapters and monitors in an enhanced description.

Types of Monitors

There are a number of different types of display systems for computers. The two most common types are the *cathode ray tube (CRT)* and the *liquid crystal display (LCD).* See **Figure 8-6** and **Figure 8-7.** As the television industry merges computer and television technology into a single display unit, it will no longer be possible to distinguish a computer monitor from a television. Because of this,

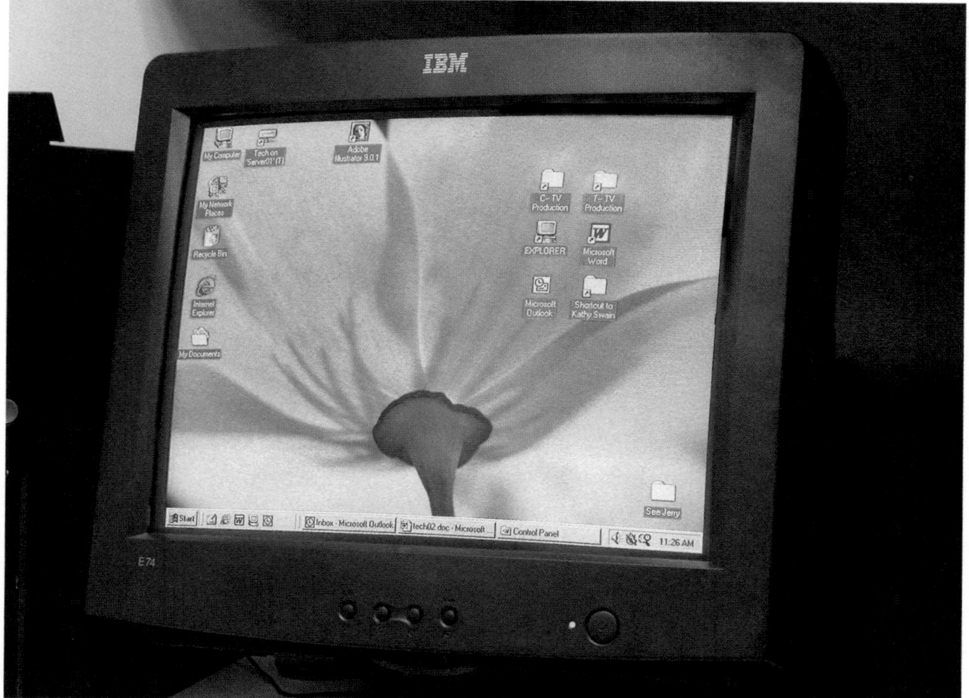

Figure 8-6.
CRT display used with a desktop computer.

Figure 8-7.
The light weight of the LCD makes it perfect for a laptop display.

the gas plasma display will also be discussed in this section. This section covers the basic operation and principles of all three display technologies and the terminology with which they are commonly associated.

Cathode Ray Tube Displays

cathode ray tube (CRT)
a picture tube in which a beam of electrons sweeps across a glass tube, exciting phosphorus dots in the screen.

A ***cathode ray tube (CRT)*** is a glass tube in which electrons are used to produce a picture. To understand how a CRT monitor works, you must first understand some basic electricity concepts. A brief discussion of electron theory will help you understand how the flow of electrons can create an image on a screen.

When electrons flow through a wire, similar to a filament in a lightbulb, heat and light are produced. The filament is placed inside a glass-enclosed vacuum. A vacuum contains no oxygen. Oxygen is needed for supporting fire, thus the vacuum prevents the destruction of the filament by burning. The vacuum prevents the wire from burning while producing the heat and light.

This is the most you usually need to know about a lightbulb. But, in addition to the heat and light, a cloud of electrons forms around the filament. The greater the electron flow through the filament, the larger the cloud of electrons. The movement and direction of the cloud of electrons can be controlled by a magnetic field. By shaping a magnetic field into a ring, the electron cloud can be shaped into a beam of electrons. The beam direction can also be deflected by magnetic fields. The formation of an electron beam and the action of deflecting the direction of the beam are the underlying principles behind producing an image on a computer monitor as well as on a television screen. See **Figure 8-8.**

Figure 8-8. Televisions and CRT computer monitors use the same electronic principles to produce images. (Sylvania-GTE)

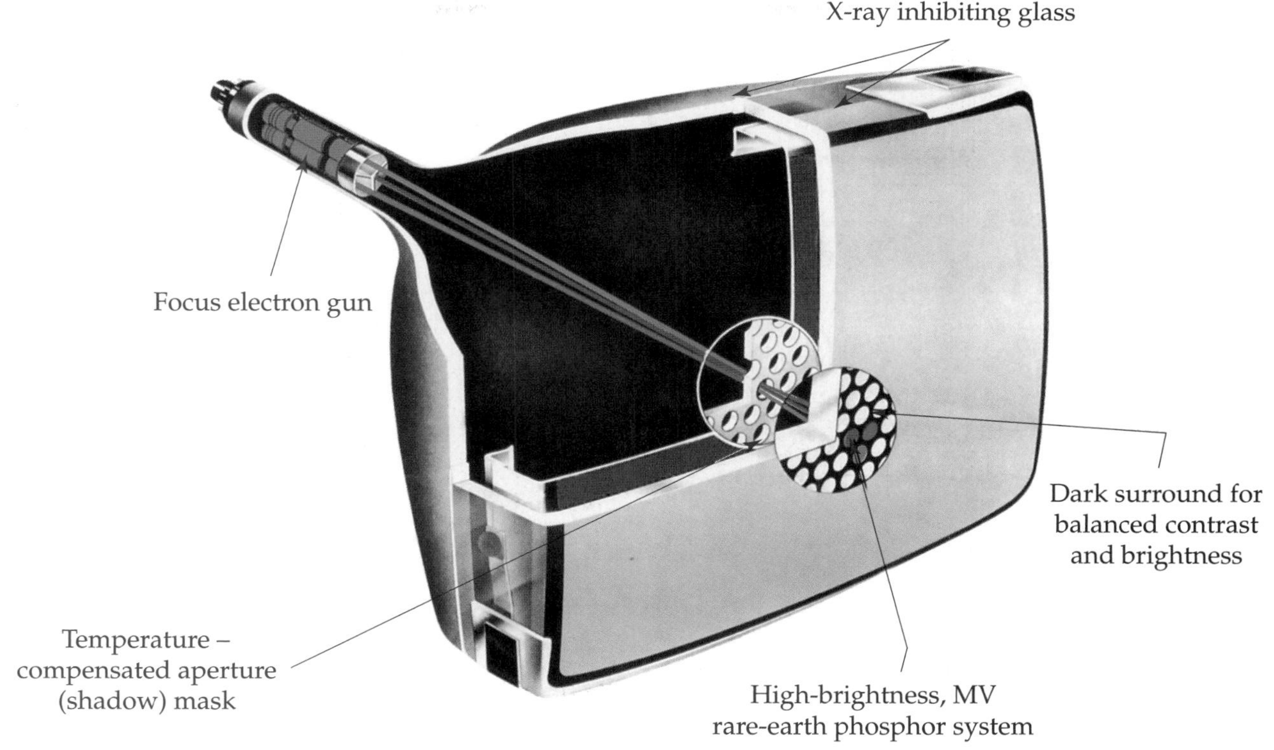

Warning:
A second important safety concern is implosion. A CRT is under a vacuum condition. When broken, the pieces of glass will at first be sucked into the glass envelope and will then burst out into the surrounding area. Severe damage to personnel can occur from a monitor tube bursting.

Three ***electron guns*** are located at the back of the CRT. The guns produce the electron beam, which sweeps across the inside of the monitor screen. The CRT ***deflection yoke*** area contains electromagnets. The intensity of the magnets can be changed to deflect the electron beam horizontally and vertically. The deflection yoke controls the location where each of the three electronic beams strikes the screen area.

The beam then passes through a metal mesh called a ***shadow mask.*** The shadow mask is designed as a pattern of triangular or rectangular holes. The shadow mask pattern of holes limits the area of the screen the electron beam can strike. The design of the shadow mask holes produces a much sharper image than would be produced without the shadow mask. The shadow mask determines the dot pitch of the monitor. The beam passes through the shadow mask and strikes the inside of the display screen. The screen area is coated with phosphorus material. The phosphor material is spread across the screen of the monitor in a pattern of red, blue, and green. When the electron beam strikes the color areas, they glow red, blue, and green accordingly. The intensity of the electron beam is directly related to the intensity of color produced in the area struck by the beam. The phosphor areas continue to glow after the electron beam ceases to strike the area. The continuation of the glow after the beam leaves the

electron guns
the components that produce the electron beam, which sweeps across the inside of the screen.

deflection yoke
the electromagnets used to deflect the electron beam in a CRT.

shadow mask
a metal mesh with triangular or rectangular holes that a CRT's electron beam passes through, creating a crisper image.

persistence
the continuation of the glow after the electron beam ceases to strike the phosphor areas.

area is called ***persistence.*** The persistence of the color glow must last long enough that it does not disappear before the electron beam strikes the phosphor again. By mixing the intensities of the three colors, a complete spectrum of colors can be produced. Look at **Figure 8-9.**

As you can see in the illustration, the color white is produced when each of the three colors is at equal intensity. The color black is produced when there is complete absence of intensity. Varying the degree of intensity of the three-color combinations produces other color hues.

Refresh rate

refresh rate
the rate at which the electron beam sweeps across the screen.

The rate at which the beam sweeps across the screen is called the ***refresh rate.*** The refresh rate of most computer monitors can be adjusted in **Control Panel** using the **Display Properties** dialog box. Often screen flicker can be corrected by increasing the refresh rate. A high refresh rate is good for someone who must spend long hours in front of a computer display because it reduces eyestrain. The downside of a high refresh rate is that it takes away from CPU time that could otherwise be used for processing information. Most current systems will choose their own optimal settings, **Figure 8-10.**

Raster display

raster
the sweep of the electron beam.

field
a complete sweep of the entire video display area.

The electronic beam sweeps across the screen horizontally from left to right. The sweep of the beam is called a ***raster.*** The sweep from left to right is repeated, each time lower on the screen, until the bottom of the screen is reached. This method of producing a picture on a monitor is called raster display. A complete sweep of the entire screen area is called a ***field.*** The entire field is completed sixty times each second.

Not all monitors make one continuous sweep vertically down the screen. Some complete the process in two steps. First, all of the odd number lines are

Figure 8-9.
Red, green, and blue are the basic colors used in a CRT.

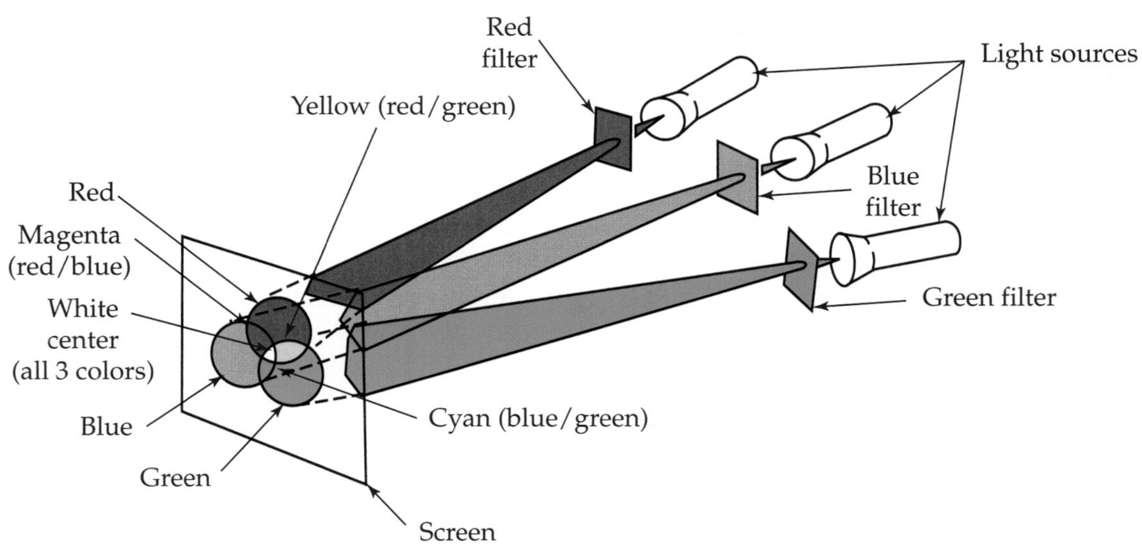

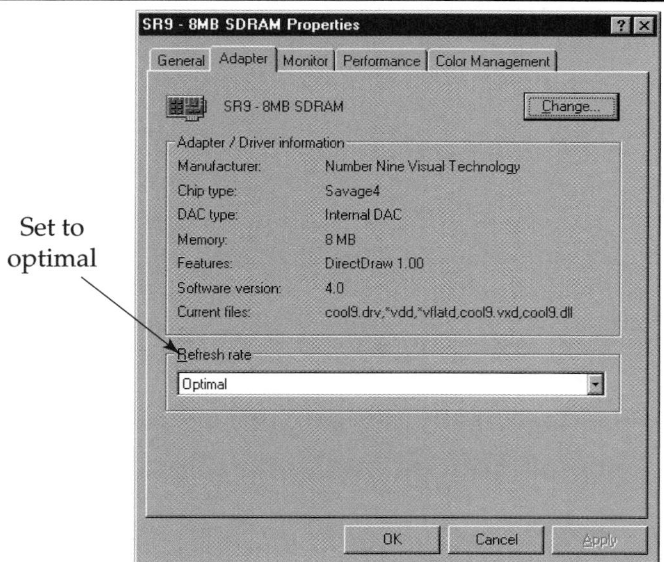

Figure 8-10. Most monitors are by default set to the "Optimal" refresh rate setting. You can find your adjustments for this setting in the **Display Properties** dialog box in **Control Panel.** Click the **Settings** tab. Choose **Advanced** and then choose the **Adapter** tab.

swept, and then all of the even lines are swept. This method of producing a complete frame is called *interlacing*. Some display units, especially LCD panels, use a technique known as progressive scan. *Progressive scan* displays the image on the monitor line by line in sequence from top to bottom.

The time it takes to complete the entire screen sweep is referred to as the monitor's *refresh rate*. The refresh rate of the monitor can be controlled with software in **Control Panel**. The refresh rate can be adjusted higher or lower.

Warning:
The typical PC technician should never disassemble a monitor. If for some reason it is required, *never* wear an anti-static wrist strap when working on a monitor. You must avoid grounding yourself. Remember that a CRT can contain voltage in excess of 20,000 volts even when unplugged! The CRT tube can retain a high voltage charge for some time, similar to a capacitor.

Liquid Crystal Displays

The most common flat-panel display is the ***liquid crystal display (LCD).*** The liquid crystal display operates on two principles. The first is *polarized light*. The second is the effect of an electrical voltage applied to a crystal structure.

liquid crystal display (LCD) a type of monitor that uses polarized light passing through liquid crystal to create images on screen.

polarized light light consisting of waves that have the same orientation.

A typical light beam is composed of numerous waves of light. The waves of light travel in parallel but at different wave angles. When a thin slot is cut in a material such as metal, only light waves with an angle matching the slot can travel through the slot. The light that travels through the slot is polarized light. ***Polarized light*** is light energy composed of light beams with a matching wave angle.

The second principle is based on the effect of electrical voltage applied to a crystal structure. When an electrical voltage is applied to a crystal, the crystal changes shape slightly or twists. The degree of twist is directly related to the amount of voltage applied to the crystal. Light normally passes through the crystal in a straight line. When a light is shined through a crystal and voltage is then applied to the same crystal, the angle of the light wave changes as it passes through the crystal. These two principles, polarized light and voltage effect on crystals, is the basis of how all LCD displays work.

How liquid crystal displays work

To fully understand how the typical liquid crystal display works, follow along while referring to **Figure 8-11.** The LCD panel is constructed of several thin layers of material. A thin fluorescent backlight is used as the source of light energy for the display. When the backlight strikes through the first layer, only light waves with an angle matching the slot can pass through the filter. The light waves that pass through the slot are polarized light because they all have a matching wave angle.

The polarized light passes through the array of crystals. Each crystal has a transistor connected to it. The transistor acts similar to a dimmer light switch, which can be turned on in varying degrees. The amount of voltage applied to each crystal by the individual transistors determines the amount of twist in each crystal. Any crystal that has voltage applied to it causes the angle of the light beam to change as it passes through the crystal. The amount of change in the light wave angle is determined by the amount of voltage applied to each crystal.

The second filter is used to screen out light waves that are no longer polarized. The amount of change in each light wave determines how much of the polarized light can pass through the second filter. For example, a light beam passing through a crystal with a maximum voltage applied will have its angle changed to the extent that none of the light energy will pass through the second filter. This creates a dark pixel image on the display. A light beam passing through a crystal with no voltage applied will not have its angle changed and will therefore pass through the second filter. This creates a full brightness pixel image. The amount of light and dark pixels directly relates to the applied voltage at each crystal.

passive-matrix display
an LCD display in which a grid of semitransparent conductors is run to each of the crystals that make up the individual pixels.

Passive-matrix display

There are two types of electrical circuitry used to energize the crystal area, passive and active, **Figure 8-12.** In a ***passive-matrix display***, a grid of

Figure 8-11.
The liquid crystal is used to twist the light wave.

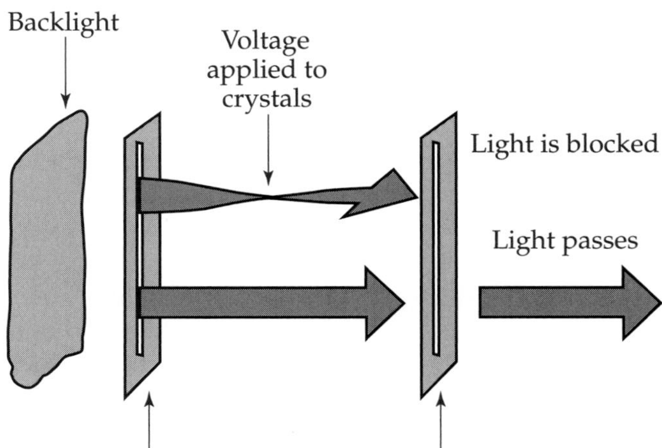

semi-transparent conductors run to each crystal, which is used as part of the individual pixel area. The grid is divided into two major circuits: columns and rows. Transistors running along the top and the side of the display unit head the columns and rows. A ground applied to a row and a charge applied to a column activates a pixel area. The voltage is applied briefly and must rely on screen persistence and a fast refresh rate. Because current must travel along the row and column until it arrives at the designated pixel, response time is slow.

Active-matrix display

In an ***active-matrix display***, each pixel in the grid has its own transistor. The active-matrix provides a better image than the passive-matrix. The active-matrix image is brighter because each cell can have a constant supply of voltage.

active-matrix display an LCD display in which each individual cell in the grid has its own individual transistor.

The most common active-matrix display is the ***thin film transistor liquid crystal display (TFT-LCD).*** Often, this type of display is referred to simply as a TFT display. The TFT display consists of a matrix of thin film transistors spread across the entire screen. Each transistor controls a single pixel on the display. There are over one million transistors in a display, three transistors at each pixel area, one transistor for each color pixel, **Figure 8-13.** The liquid crystals in the TFT display are energized in a pattern representing the data to be displayed.

thin film transistor liquid crystal display (TFT-LCD) a display that consists of a matrix of thin film transistors, in which each transistor controls a single pixel.

The conventional television has used the CRT to display images because the original LCD design had limitations that could not compete with larger display units. As the size of the display unit grew to over 18″, problems developed with the brightness of the display and in converting the analog television signal to a digital signal and to a wide-angle viewing area without image distortions. These problems were solved with the introduction of thin film transistor LCD technology.

Figure 8-12.
In an active-matrix display, each individual cell in the grid has its own individual transistor. The active-matrix provides a better image than does the passive.

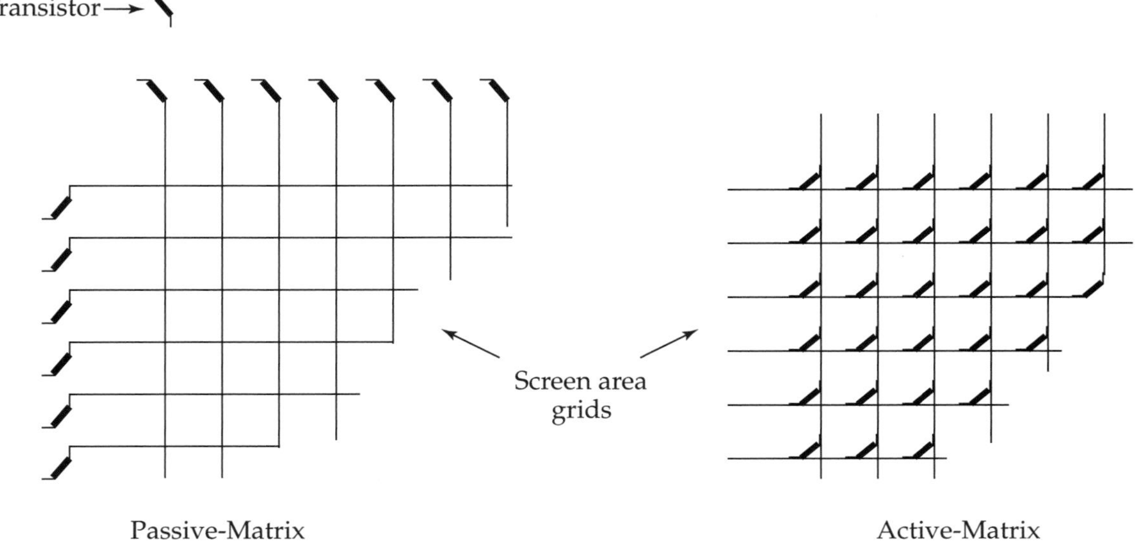

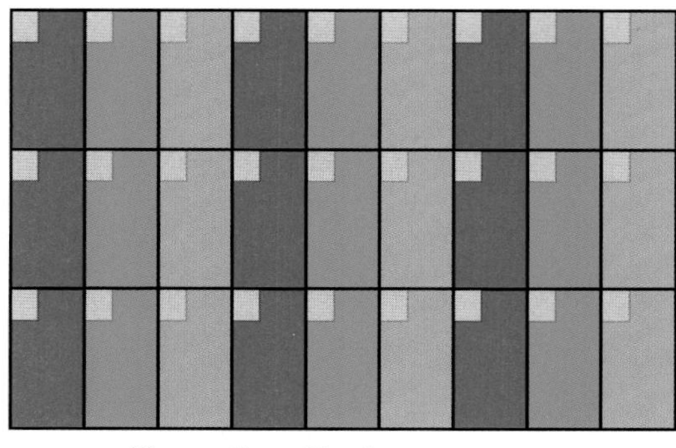

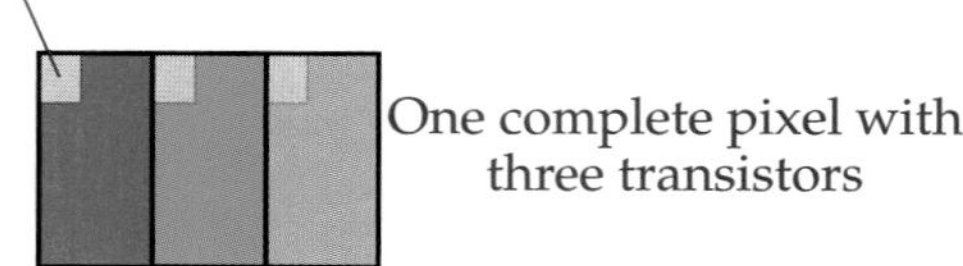

Figure 8-13. Each pixel area on the TFT display consists of three transistor-controlled color fields. The three, color fields—red, green, and blue—are combined to form various shades and hues of color.

Advantages of LCD over CRT displays:

- LCDs can be constructed much smaller and are lighter in weight than CRT displays.
- LCDs are more economical to run because they require less power.
- LCDs generate less heat.
- LCDs create more detailed images.
- LCDs produce less electromagnetic interference (EMI).

Disadvantages of LCD as compared to CRT displays:

- Lack of an industry-wide standard.
- Higher cost for a comparable size.
- Complexity of scaling images without distortion.

Contrast ratio

contrast ratio a numeric expression in the form of a ratio that describes the amount of contrast between the darkest and lightest pixel in the image.

Contrast ratio is a numeric expression in the form of a ratio that describes the amount of contrast between the darkest and lightest pixel in the image. The higher the ratio, the better the colors will be represented on the display unit. This is a very important display characteristic that correlates closely to the overall quality of the display. For example, a display with a high contrast ratio will be able to do a better job of displaying finer details of an image. Contrast ratios typically range from 200:1 to 600:1. A contrast ratio of over 500:1 is considered a high quality display.

Brightness

Brightness in an LCD is produced by the fluorescent backlight. The maximum amount of brightness produced in the display is determined by this light source. Brightness levels typically range form 200 cd/m^2 (candela per square meter) to 250 cd/m^2. A candela is a light measurement based on candle illumination. Many people confuse light measurement with watts or wattage.

Wattage is a measurement of electrical energy, not light energy. While electrical energy often directly relates to the amount of light produced, there is not a direct correlation between electrical energy and light when comparing different light technologies such as the case of incandescent and fluorescent light. For example, a fluorescent light and an incandescent light use two different electrical technologies for generating light. The amount of power consumed measured in watts does not accurately represent the amount of light provided when comparing different technologies. The same is true for computer displays. To accurately compare brightness levels between a CRT display and an LCD, you must use candela per square meter. For a general comparison, a typical CRT screen displays approximately 120 cd/m^2. An LCD screen would need to display at least 120 cd/m^2 to produce the same amount of brightness as a typical CRT display.

Brightness is also a main factor for determining if the monitor will adequately display an image in a bright environment such as an outdoor area.

Viewing angle

The ***viewing angle*** is a measurement of the angle at which a person can adequately see an image on a display without it looking excessively distorted. As a person's angle to the screen increases, the image displayed becomes increasingly washed out until the image disappears. See **Figure 8-14.**

The viewing angle of early models of LCD panels was quite limited and could not compete with CRT screens. Today, the viewing angle is of less concern because almost all LCD panels have a very acceptable viewing angle. The actual viewing angle of a display varies from manufacturer to manufacturer, but the minimum viewing angle is typically 150°. Top of the line displays have a viewing angle of 170° or more. To match the viewing angle of a CRT, the viewing angle of the LCD panel must be at least 170°.

viewing angle
a measurement of the angle at which a person can adequately see an image on a display without it looking excessively distorted.

Pixel pitch

Pixel pitch is similar to CRT dot pitch. Pixel pitch is the distance between two same color pixels on the display area. In other words, pixel pitch is the distance between two red pixels or two green pixels. Each color pixel is

pixel pitch
the distance between two same color pixels on the display area.

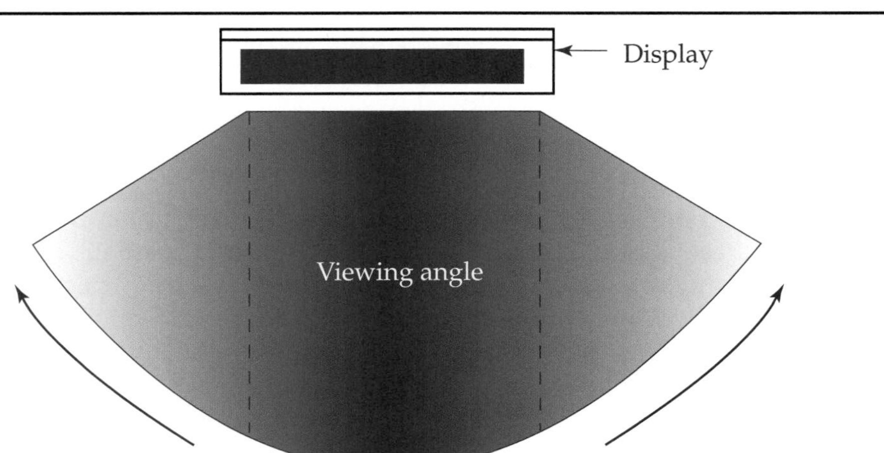

Figure 8-14. The viewing angle defines the locations where the screen can be viewed comfortably without distortion. As the angle of view increases, the image appears increasingly washed out until the image disappears.

composed of three pels, one pel for each of the three colors that compose a pixel. Pixel pitch is expressed in millimeters (mm) per inch.

Native resolution

native resolution the resolution that matches the pixel design of the display.

An LCD is capable of displaying a number of different resolutions. The ***native resolution*** is the resolution that matches the pixel design of the display. For example, if a display has a native resolution of 1280 × 1024 then it will display images best at 1280 × 1024. If a resolution other than the native resolution is chosen, an image will appear slightly blurred in some areas. Earlier in this chapter, bitmap distortion was explained for bitmap images that change scale. The LCD is manufactured with a set number of pixels. Because a set number of actual pixels are used to generate an image, the display will operate as a bitmap device, its image blurring when the scale is changed. When a screen resolution other than native is selected, the display controller must either add or remove pixels from the image before it is displayed on the screen. The process of adding or removing pixels causes the image to appear slightly blurred. This is especially true when displaying a much higher or much lower resolution image.

Response time

response time the amount of time it takes a TFT pixel to display after a signal is sent to the transistor controlling that pixel.

The ***response time*** is the amount of time it takes a TFT pixel to display after a signal is sent to the transistor controlling that pixel. Response time is measured in milliseconds (ms). A typical response time ranges from 15 ms to 40 ms. The lower the response time, the better the quality of the display unit. A quick response time is required for quality animation. A high response time can result in a slight flicker or in breaks in the animation presented on the screen. It is interesting to note that at this time, the CRT is better at displaying animation or full motion video then the LCD. The CRT has an almost instantaneous response time, which produces a better full motion video display.

Monitor size

The monitor size of an LCD is measured in a similar fashion to a CRT screen, in a diagonal line across the front panel of the display. The big difference between the LCD monitor and the CRT monitor is no display size is lost to the area around the perimeter of the screen. As you recall from earlier in the chapter, a CRT monitor has an actual image display smaller than the screen's measured size. An LCD screen size is the same as the image to be displayed. There is no display size loss. A 16″ LCD monitor can and will display a 16″ image, while a 16″ CRT monitor will display less than the measured size.

Aspect ratio

aspect ratio ratio of a display area's height and width.

Aspect ratio refers to the ratio of the display area's height and width. A typical CRT screen is based on the television standard ratio of 4:3. The width is represented by the number 4 and the height is represented by the number 3. A newer wide-aspect ratio became a standard with the introduction of high definition television. The wide-aspect ratio found on most new LCD panels is 16:10. See **Figure 8-15** for a comparison of the two aspect ratios.

The wide-aspect ratio width allows more information to be displayed on the monitor and matches the new high definition television standard for display

Figure 8-15.
The aspect ratio is an expression of the relationship of height to width of the screen area. The aspect ratio for high definition television screens is wider than traditional screens.

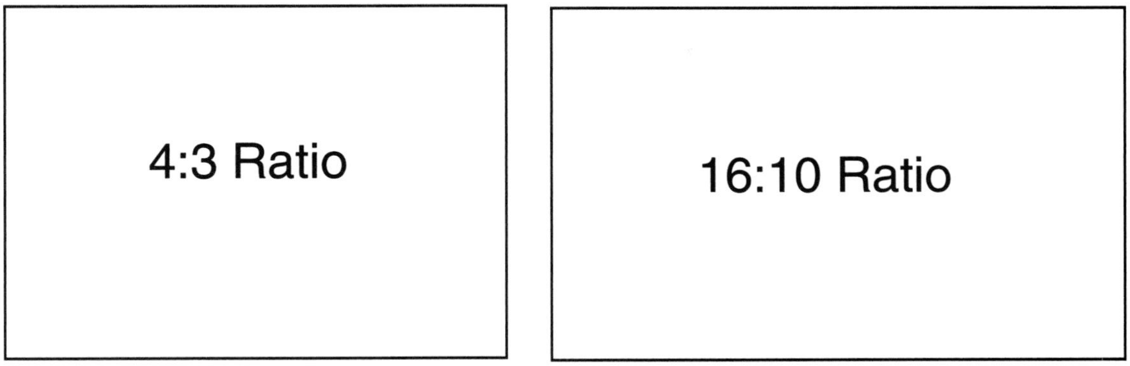

systems. The development of the wide-aspect ratio has created a need for newer video resolution standard identification, which allows a user to select a resolution that more closely matches the design of the monitor. The newer resolution standards designed for wide-aspect ratio use the prefix "W" to describe the modified standard resolution. For example, an XGA resolution based on the traditional 4:3 ratio would be identified as WXGA when based on the 16:10 ratio.

Gas-Plasma Displays

gas-plasma displays a display that operates on the principle of electro-luminescence.

Gas-plasma displays are flat panel displays that operate on the principle of electro-luminescence. *Electro-luminescence* is the display of light created when a high frequency passes through a gas to a layer of phosphor, resulting in the release of photons. The electrical energy from releasing photons is better known as producing light.

A gas-plasma display consists of millions of tiny cells sandwiched between two glass plates. See **Figure 8-16.** Each cell contains an inert gas and is coated with a phosphorous material of red, blue, or green. Transparent electrodes run horizontally behind the front panel on top of the cells. Address electrodes run vertically along the rear glass panel beneath the cells. When the address electrodes and its corresponding transparent electrode are energized, the gas, in an exited, plasma state, releases an ultraviolet light. The ultraviolet light strikes the phosphorus coating inside the cell causing the cell to release a light corresponding to its color. By varying the pulses of current, the entire light spectrum can be duplicated such as orange, yellow, and brown.

The top electrode is called the row electrode and the bottom electrode is called the column electrode. A column and row electrode forms a junction point. Each junction point conforms to a memory address. The microprocessor sends information to the memory address and to the monitor. The junction points become energized in a pattern reflective of the computer memory pattern.

The biggest difference between an LCD and a gas-plasma display is the plasma display does not require a backlight. Each cell in a gas-plasma display generates its own light. For this reason, a gas-plasma display can be manufactured much thinner than an LCD.

Figure 8-16.
Gas-plasma technology.

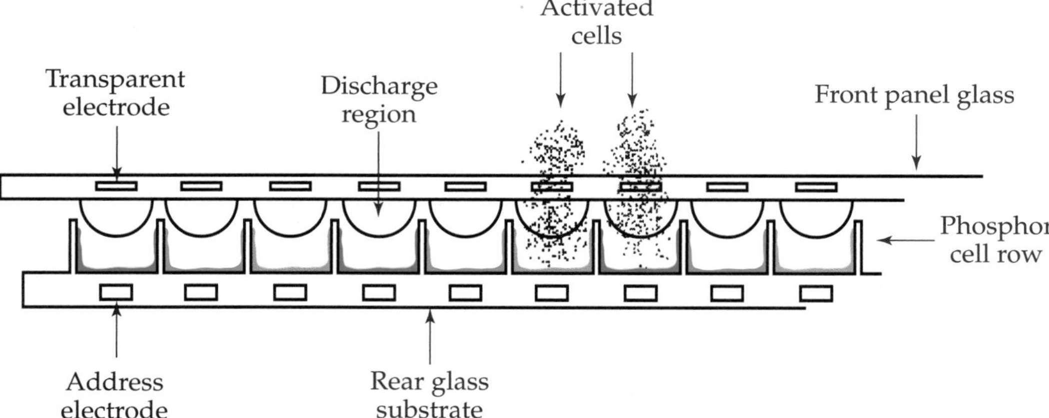

Video Adapter Cards

Monitors can attach to a computer in one of two ways. The monitor can plug into a video adapter card, which is inserted into a PCI or an AGP slot on the motherboard. They can also attach directly to the motherboard, which incorporates the same electronic components found on a video adapter card.

The heart of the video adapter card is a specialized chip known as a digital-to-analog converter. The ***digital-to-analog converter (DAC)*** converts the digital signal from the computer to an analog signal that is displayed on the computer's monitor. The DAC can consist of one single chip or three chips, one chip for each color. The card also contains RAM, ROM, a video processor, and BIOS. The entire video adapter card is similar to a complete computer that has been specialized for video display.

digital-to-analog converter (DAC) a chip that converts the digital signal from the computer to an analog signal that is displayed on the computer's monitor.

A VGA monitor uses a 15-pin connector to connect to the video display adapter card or to the video port on the motherboard. **Figure 8-17** shows a diagram of a standard VGA 15-pin connector. The chart next to the diagram lists the function of each pin on the connector.

Video adapter cards are installed in PCI or AGP slots on the motherboard. As you can see in the chart in **Figure 8-18,** the AGP design produces the highest throughput of the two technologies. The *accelerated graphics port (AGP)* is a slot used strictly for AGP adapter cards. It is designed with graphics as a priority, using a computer's memory to work more effectively with graphics. It also operates at a faster bus speed than PCI slots.

Typically, there is only one AGP slot on a motherboard. The AGP slot looks similar in design to the PCI slot, only in reverse. It is slightly shorter than a PCI slot and it is usually a different color. To readily identify the AGP slot, look for the slot closest to the CPU and offset from the alignment of the PCI slots.

Video performance also depends on the amount of available memory that can be used to create and process images. When the graphics controller is incorporated into the motherboard, the controller uses the RAM that is installed on

Figure 8-17.
Standard VGA 15-pin connector diagram. In this arrangement, pin 5 is used for testing the monitor. Some manufacturers use Pins 4, 11, 12, or 15 to identify or detect the type of monitor connected to the motherboard. Pin 9 is usually missing by design; other pins may be missing as well if not used by that particular manufacturer.

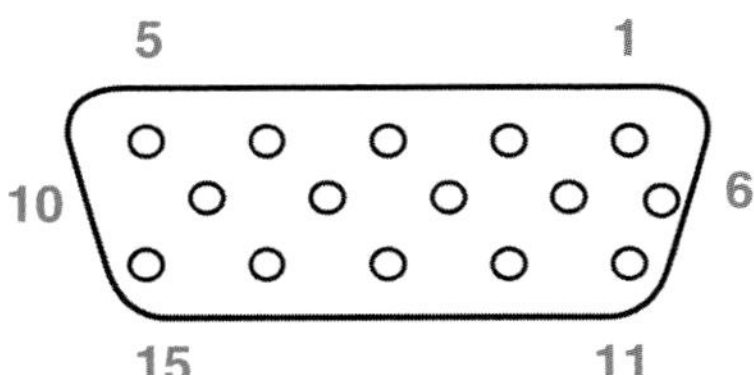

Pin Number	Function
1	Red video
2	Green video
3	Blue video
4	Monitor ID 2
5	TTL ground test pin
6	Red analog ground
7	Green analog ground
8	Blue analog ground
9	Plugged hole
10	Sync ground
11	Monitor ID 0
12	Monitor ID 1
13	Horizontal sync
14	Vertical sync
15	Monitor ID 3

Bus Type	Throughput MBps	Speed in MHz	Width in Bits
PCI	127.2	33	32
PCI 2.1	508.6	66	64
AGP	254.3	66	32
AGP × 2	508.6	66 × 2	32
AGP × 4	1,017.3	66 × 4	32
AGP × 8	2,034.4	66 × 8	32

Figure 8-18.
Comparison of video adapter card bus types.

the motherboard for video images. This means that the motherboard RAM must be used for all software functions that require RAM as well for video performance. When a video adapter card is used, the performance is greatly increased. The total effect on video performance is determined by how much RAM is incorporated into the video adapter card. As a general rule, the more video RAM incorporated into the video adapter card, the better the overall video performance. Other factors that influence video performance are the version of operating system, the motherboard chipset, and the video adapter card BIOS.

Installing a Video Adapter Card

Installing a video adapter card is easy. The steps that follow are generic in nature, but there should not be much variation in installation between different cards.

Warning:
Before beginning any installation of hardware, always back up critical computer files. It is very easy to accidentally destroy data on a computer. Sometimes drivers do not work the way they should resulting in a total lockup of the computer system. In the course of recovering the system, most anything can happen. The worst-case scenario is losing hard drive data. Always back up the hard drive or critical data before working on a PC.

Steps for installing an adapter card:

1. Back up all computer files.
2. Power off the computer and unplug the power cord from the wall outlet.
3. Read the installation procedures and specification sheet that came with the adapter card. Verify that your new card is compatible with the type of display unit being used.
4. Take normal static precautions.
5. Before attempting to insert the video adapter card into the expansion slot, check for debris in the slot.
6. Insert the card by applying even force to the top of the card. Do not rock the card into the slot.
7. Connect the monitor to the new card and turn on the PC. The card should auto detect if it is Plug and Play and you are using a modern Windows operating system.
8. If Windows cannot find its own driver when the system attempts to detect the card, it will ask you to supply a new driver. The driver should have been packaged with the expansion board either as a floppy disk or a CD-ROM. It is also a good idea to check the card manufacturer's Web site for any patches or upgrades needed for the driver. Prepackaged drivers will often be dated. The most up-to-date drivers can be downloaded from their Web sites.
9. As the drivers are loading, follow the screen prompts to complete the installation.
10. A message box will display on the screen when the installation is complete. If a problem occurs, a message will appear saying that the installation is not complete. Reread the installation procedures. Also, check for bent pins on the video adapter. A pin can easily bend when assembling the system. Another area to check is your computer's BIOS. In particular with older machines, you may need to upgrade the BIOS on the motherboard to use your new card.

If problems still persist, check both the card manufacturer's and the motherboard manufacturer's Web site. Some motherboards have a video adapter integrated into the circuit board. If this is the case, you may have to disable the integrated system before the new adapter board will work. It is *always* a good idea to consult the Web site of the motherboard manufacturer for the latest updates before you begin.

11. If all has gone well, you should be able to close up the case and reboot the system.

Adding Memory to an Existing Video Adapter Card

Adding memory is also a simple operation to perform. Adding more memory to your video card can increase video performance, but remember the important topics covered in Chapter 6—Memory. The most important item to remember is that you must determine what type of memory you need to install. Check the video adapter card's specification sheet or visit the manufacturer's Web site for the information. Remember, it is important to match existing memory if you are upgrading. You can write down the part numbers of the existing memory and check what type of memory it is. Most manufacturers have a cross-reference chart to identify other compatible chips.

Steps for adding memory to a video card:

1. Back up all computer files.
2. Power off the computer and unplug the power cord from the wall outlet.
3. Take normal static precautions.
4. Unplug the monitor from the video adapter card and remove the case. Use a screwdriver to remove the screw securing the video adapter card to the frame.
5. Remove the video card from the motherboard expansion slot. It will be easier to add memory chips with the board removed from the computer motherboard. The card may be a very snug fit. Be careful to not rock the board if possible. Do not pry the board out of the slot with a screwdriver or with any other device. If the connectors inside the slot are damaged, you will not be able to continue the operation. The card slot will be damaged beyond normal repair.
6. Orient the new memory (SIMM or DIMM) correctly. Take your time and be sure. Check documentation or look at the existing memory modules.
7. Reinsert the video card in the same slot. Do not rock the card into place. Simply use a steady, even force along the top edge of the card.
8. Connect the monitor connector to the video adapter card.
9. Power on the PC and look for any possible error codes.

This is a simple operation and should go well if you take your time. If there is a problem, check for bent pins on the 15-pin connector from the monitor. Also double-check your installation procedures. If problems persist, reverse the procedure and remove the new memory modules to see if the problem clears up. You may have installed defective memory chips. Use the system diagnostics program to verify that the amount of video memory has increased. If not, the memory may be defective.

Changing Display Properties

In the Windows operating system, many adjustments can be made to the display. These adjustments are made in the **Display Properties** dialog box, **Figure 8-19.** The **Display Properties** dialog box can be accessed through **Start | Settings | Control Panel** and double-clicking the **Display** icon.

There are a number of options in the properties of the video display. This dialog box allows you to change "look and feel items" like the desktop theme, screen saver, or computer wallpaper. It also allows you to adjust hardware issues such as the monitor's refresh rate or the type of display used (e.g. CRT or flat panel).

Television and Computers

Computer and television technology has rapidly merged since the development of HDTV and the availability of flat panel display technology such as TFT and gas-plasma. It is not unusual for a display unit to be designed to serve as both a television display and a computer display, **Figure 8-20.** The merger of the two technologies has produced many conflicting standards within the television and computer industry. This conflict in standards has resulted in a variety of connector designs used to connect various displays to computers and television receivers. **Figure 8-21** shows some of the connection designs associated with computer and television systems.

All of the connection designs carry the acronym DVI, which stands for digital video interface. The DVI-I is a combination-type connector designed for both digital and analog connections. The DVI-D is designed for a digital only

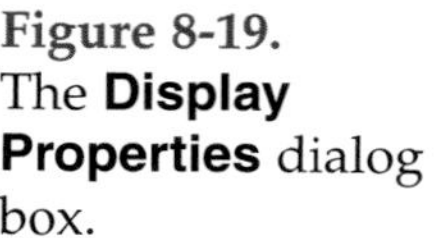

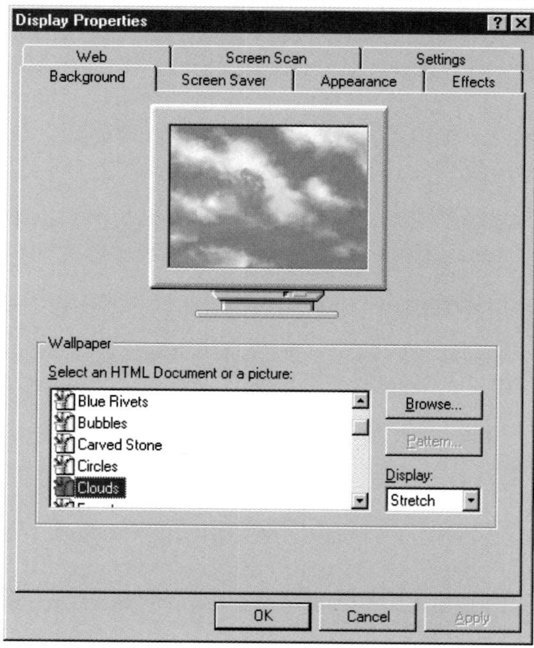

Figure 8-19. The **Display Properties** dialog box.

Figure 8-20.
This flat-panel, gas-plasma TV is capable of both television and computer applications. (ViewSonic Corp.)

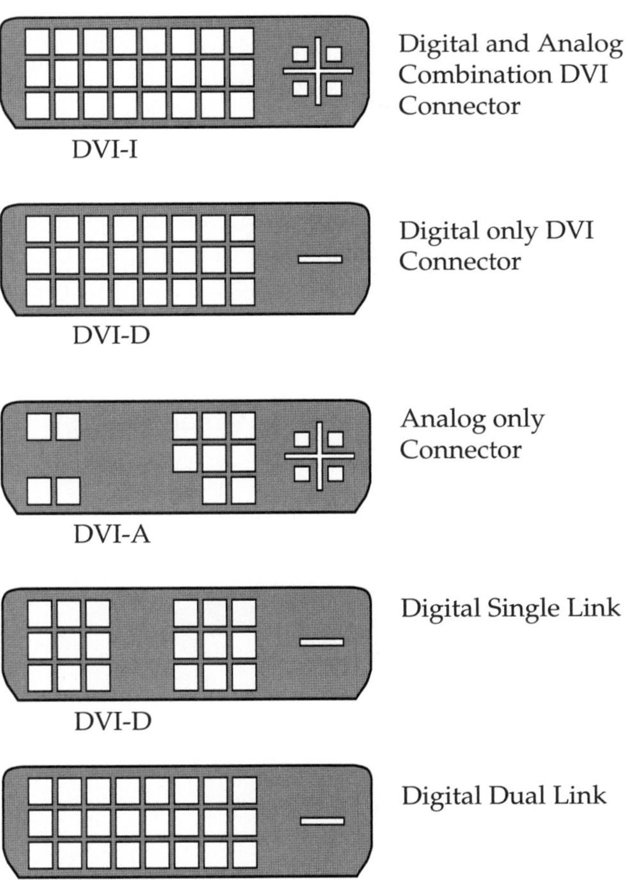

Figure 8-21.
Various connection designs.

connection. It can be used to connect devices that support compatible digital resolutions. The DVI-A is used with digital-to-analog conversion. It is not commonly used today because of rapid advances in digital video and the fading out of analog systems.

The references to DVI-D single link and DVI-D dual link relate to the amount of bandwidth that can be transmitted by each connection design. The single link can carry a bandwidth equal to 165 MHz, which is the matching bandwidth for HDTV. It is capable of producing a maximum resolution of 1920 × 1080 at 60 Hz. The dual link can carry twice the bandwidth of the single link and can produce a resolution as high as 2048 × 1536.

Some video adapter cards provide several connection types to choose from. **Figure 8-22** shows a video adapter card with a variety of video display ports: a DVI port, a TV port, and a DB-15 VGA monitor port.

Some video adapter cards are manufactured to support two monitors at the same time. Web page designers often require more than one display unit while designing Web pages. By having more than one display connected to the computer station, they can view the Web page they designed at different resolutions.

Bitmapped Graphics

bitmap (.bmp) a graphics standard for uncompressed encoding of images.

There are many different methods used to code the data of an image. One of the standards is the ***bitmap (.bmp),*** also referred to as a ***raster image.*** A display screen or printed image is made from thousands or millions of pixels. As discussed earlier, a pixel is the smallest screen element. The number of bits used to encode the pixel determines the color and shades of that color.

For example, an 8-bit code is capable of 256 different binary number patterns. Each of the binary number patterns can represent a different color or shade of gray. On a color monitor, each pixel is actually a combination of three different colors: red, blue, and green. Each color has an 8-bit binary code that can represent 256 shades of the color. The three individual 8-bit colors combine to form a 24-bit code that represents the actual color of the pixel image, see **Figure 8-23.** The 24-bit color code is referred to as *true color* and can produce over 24 million colors when mixed together.

Figure 8-23 is a screen capture of the Edit Colors tool in Microsoft's Paint program. Take note of the color reference window. All the different possible

Figure 8-22. This video card is equipped with a variety of video display ports.

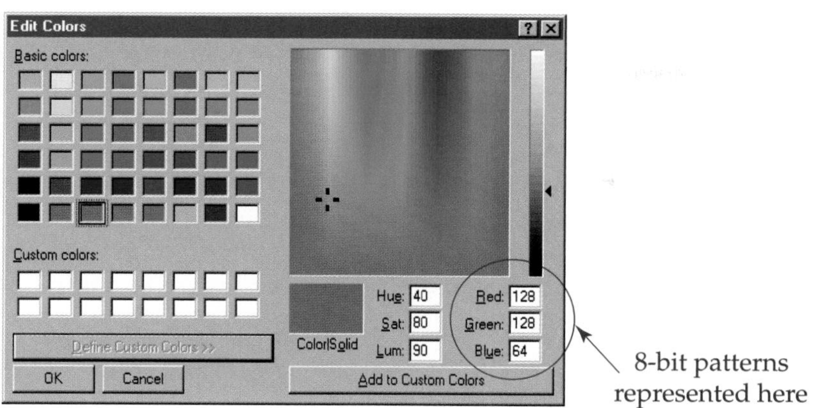

Figure 8-23. In Microsoft's Paint program, you can see three 8-bit patterns forming a 24-bit pattern to represent the final color. The three patterns are represented by three 8-bit numbers, which describe the amount of red, green, and blue used.

colors in the window are created from mixing various shades of red, blue, and green. At the bottom right are the three colors listed with a box beside each. Displayed in the boxes is a numeric value that can be varied from 0–255. Notice that these are the same total number of values that an 8-bit binary code can represent. By varying the numeric value displayed in the boxes, the three colors (red, blue, and green) can be mixed to form new colors in addition to the basic 28 colors that are given in the Paint program for drawing bitmap pictures. This technique of mixing colors is standard for most drawing programs.

Vector Graphics

vector graphics a graphic standard based on a series of mathematical formulas that can be converted into geometric shapes representing the image to be displayed.

Vector graphics is based on a series of mathematical formulas that can be converted into geometric shapes representing the image to be displayed. Vector graphics are typically produced by drawing programs, not by photographic images. One main advantage of vector images is they can be resized or scaled without losing the quality of the image. When a bitmap image is enlarged or reduced in size, the number of pixels must be increased or decreased accordingly. This means adding or removing pixels, which distorts the original image. The software program performing the bitmap conversion must decide what color to add as the image is increased. It chooses the pixel color closest to the original pixel. When the image is reduced, the software erases an existing pixel.

Since vector graphic images use mathematical formulas to represent the lines in the figures, the picture retains its original picture quality no matter which size it is changed to. The lines that compose the image are simply multiplied or divided by the applied scale factor. For example, all the line segments and circle diameters are multiplied by 2 for a drawing that is to be increased in scale by 200%.

A vector drawing could scale an infinite number of times and never lose its quality. In comparison, a bitmap image that was resized only a few times would become completely distorted.

Tech Tip:
Software programs that produce bitmap images are often referred to as *paint programs*. Software programs that produce vector images are often referred to as *draw programs*.

Vector image technology is used in critical drawing applications such as computer aided drafting (CAD) programs and in many different animation software programs. Bitmap is mostly associated with photographic images. It is important to note that you can convert a vector image to a bitmap image, but you cannot convert a bitmap image to a vector image.

Graphic Compression

Graphics applications require a lot of memory space for storage. Even a small graphic can require several million bytes of memory depending on the resolution and the number of colors used to create the graphic. To decrease the amount of memory space needed, drawing data can be compressed. There are many different compression methods. However, they all use similar techniques to accomplish the compression.

A close inspection of a typical graphic reveals the color pixels repeated many times sequentially in an area of the picture. **Figure 8-24** shows a series of apple images. Each successive photo in this series looks progressively closer at the apple to expose the pixel pattern of colors. In the first image, you see what appears as very subtle variations of shades of green and red. As the picture is enlarged, you can see that many of the pixels are the same color. These repeating pixels of the same color are the secret to file compression. Instead of describing every pixel, a compressed file can describe a series of similar pixels with a short piece of code.

For a file compression technique to be effective, it must convert the same information stored in the image but use less memory space. This image was saved as a Windows true color image, meaning that the image pixels are each composed of three 8-bit bytes. Consequently, each picture element shown uses 24 bits to represent the pixel. Look at the magnified images of the apple. Notice several continuous rows of pixels. If a row has 20 pixels, it would require 60 bytes of information.

One compression method worth looking at is run-length encoding. ***Run-length encoding (RLE)*** replaces a series of repeated pixels with a single pixel and the length of the series (run). The longer the runs and the greater number of runs there are, the greater the compression that will be achieved.

run-length encoding (RLE)
a graphics compression format that reduces image file sizes by recording strings of identical pixels.

Figure 8-25 shows a comparison of labeled binary codes. The first set of binary codes represents the color white for 20 pixels. The second set of binary codes shows a condensed version of the same information.

In the compressed file, the first byte gives the location of the first pixel. The next three bytes represent the color white, which is equal to decimal 255 (or binary code 11111111). The color white is composed of equal parts of red, blue, and green. Thus, the color is coded as three bytes, all consisting of eight 1s. The last byte of information contains the number of times necessary to repeat the pattern of white pixels. In the example, the last byte represents the decimal number 20. As you can see, the size of the compressed file, containing only 6 bytes, is very small in comparison to the original file that required 60 bytes of data.

Figure 8-24.
What appears to be finely detailed can be broken down into a series of pixels, some of which repeat.

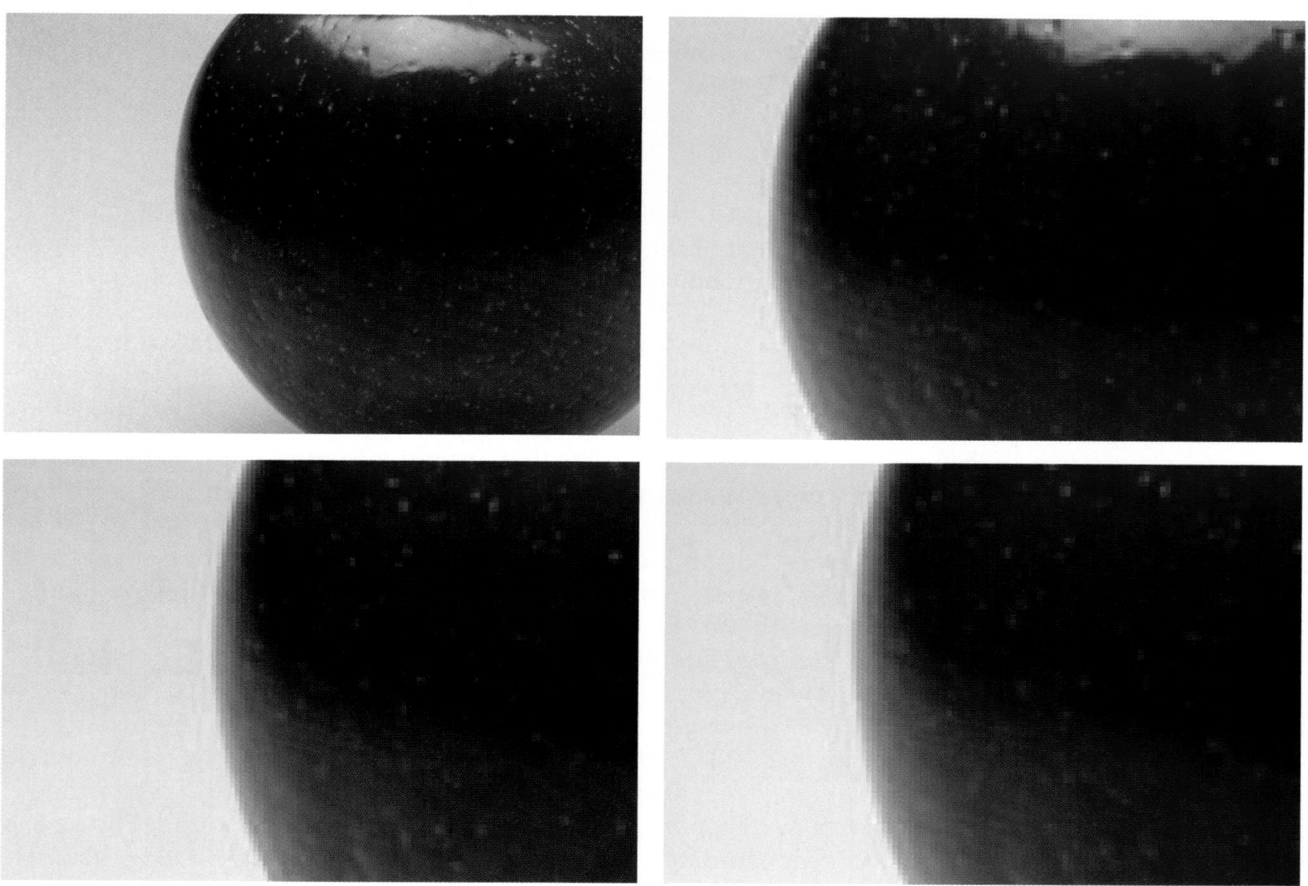

The color white is equal to equal color parts of red, green, and blue.

Red	Blue	Green			
11111111	11111111	11111111	11111111	11111111	11111111
11111111	11111111	11111111	11111111	11111111	11111111
11111111	11111111	11111111	11111111	11111111	11111111
11111111	11111111	11111111	11111111	11111111	11111111
11111111	11111111	11111111	11111111	11111111	11111111
11111111	11111111	11111111	11111111	11111111	11111111
11111111	11111111	11111111	11111111	11111111	11111111
11111111	11111111	11111111	11111111	11111111	11111111
11111111	11111111	11111111	11111111	11111111	11111111
11111111	11111111	11111111	11111111	11111111	11111111

Original file information needed for the row of white pixel images.

10010011 11100111	11111111 11111111 11111111	00010100
Location of first pixel	The three colors	Repeat (length of run)

Compressed file information for same section.

Figure 8-25.
Compression techniques can tremendously reduce the amount of code used to store an image or text. Here repeated data is reduced from 60 bytes to 6 bytes.

Looking back to Figure 8-24, you can see many different colors that form a repeating pattern in the image. Each of these areas can be encoded the same way. This is the basic concept of compression. There are many different programs available to compress files. While they all do not work exactly as demonstrated, they do work in a similar fashion. File compression techniques are used not only for graphics but also for other forms of data such as sound files. Some compression techniques can achieve a compression ratio as high as 12:1.

Audio

Audio is the second half of the multimedia experience. All PCs come with a small internal speaker, but that is not enough for most users. Fancy sound cards, subwoofers, and microphones have become standard equipment on many systems. The first step in learning audio systems is to understand sound itself and how it is created. The next step is to see how audio devices interface with the PC.

What Is Sound?

Sound is comprised of vibrations that are put into motion through a medium such as air or water. We are most familiar with air as the medium. The air itself actually carries a vibrating wave action. If you place a piece of tissue paper in front of a speaker, you can see it move from the sound vibration. If you are anywhere near some cars that have megawatt speakers turned up very loudly, you are familiar with the "feel" of sound.

If all air is removed and only a vacuum exists, there would be no sound. A vacuum is completely empty, there is no medium to carry the vibrations produced that we call sound. This concept can be demonstrated by placing an alarm clock inside a sealed, glass container. In this experiment, air is removed from the container. When the alarm goes off, it cannot be heard. There is no medium present to transport the pattern of vibrations called sound, **Figure 8-26.**

The human ear can detect sounds from approximately 20 Hz to 20 kHz. This is known as the frequency response range of the human ear. Vibrations above or below this range go undetected by human ears.

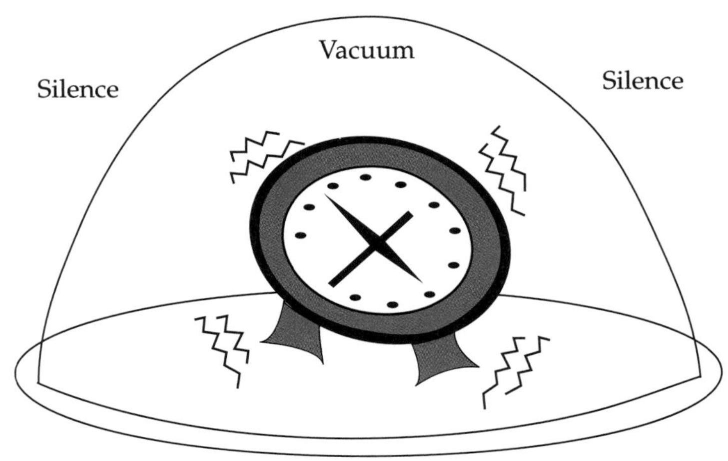

Figure 8-26.
The alarm can be set off in a vacuum, but no sound will be transmitted.

Sampling

Measuring an analog signal at regular intervals is called ***sampling.*** Sampling is required before converting an analog signal into a digital signal. The quality of any type of analog-to-digital conversion is based primarily on the sampling rate and number of bits used to represent the height or voltage level of the signal. Sampling rates are incorporated into many different technologies. Weather radar units, security systems based upon voice and image identification, and automatic piloting of aircraft are only a few examples.

sampling
measuring an analog signal at regular intervals.

A high frequency of sampling (frequent samples taken) results in a better quality of sound. **Figure 8-27** shows two different sampling rates taken from the same wave. See how the resultant waves differ with high and low sampling rates by comparing the reconstructed analog wave shapes.

A high sampling rate gives a better representation of an analog signal shape. In the illustration, an analog wave shape is sampled at two different rates. When the two wave shapes are reconstructed by connecting the points of sampling, you can see that the higher sampling rate gives a shape closer to the original analog wave shape. The quality of the sampling is directly affected by the sampling rate and by the number of bits used to indicate the height of the signal at the sampling points. The size of the file storing the signal data needed to reconstruct the sound wave also increases proportionately with the sampling rate.

Several factors affect the choice of sampling rates. Sampling rates vary depending on what is being recorded. Music would require a high sampling rate in comparison to a simple voice recording. The quality of sound may not be an issue when leaving a voice mail message. However, most listeners are fairly discriminating regarding the quality of their music.

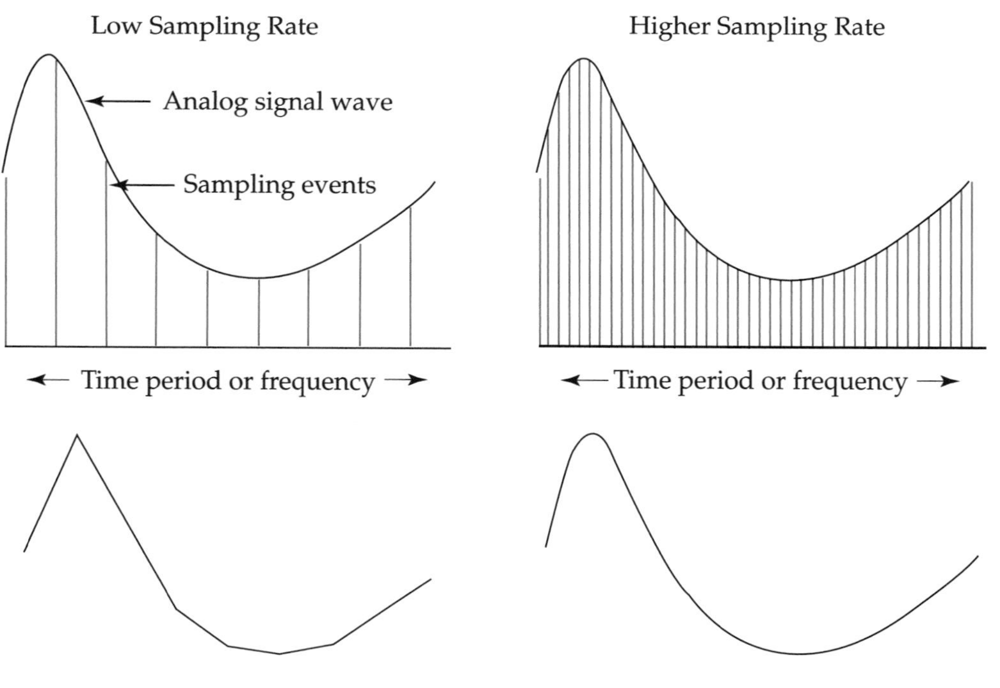

Figure 8-27.
A higher sampling creates a more accurate reproduction of the original waveform.

Shown in **Figure 8-28** are the properties of a sound to be used when a new e-mail arrives. In these details of the Sounds Properties dialog box, you can see properties of the audio format such as its frequency (22,050 Hz). Note that it is 16-bit and in stereo. The path to this window is **Start | Settings | Control Panel | Sounds**. Click the event you are interested in to highlight it and then click **Details.** This brings up the dialog box to the right of the Sounds Properties window. You can use the Sounds Properties dialog box to change any of the sounds assigned by Windows.

Eight-Bit and Sixteen-Bit Sound

The original sound card was an 8-bit card. Today most quality sound cards are 16-bit. You can record a better image of the original sound using 16-bit rather than 8-bit. A system based on 8-bit sound is limited to using 256 levels, or binary codes, to store a binary image of the sound wave sample. A 16-bit sound card can use 65,536 binary codes to store the sound wave pattern during each sampling. The 16-bit system can save a more detailed representation of the analog sound wave pattern than an 8-bit system.

Think in terms of graphic picture resolution. A better graphic image can be produced using 16 bits, rather than 8 bits, per pixel. Look back to Figure 8-27 where sampling rate and reconstructed analog wave shapes are illustrated. In the illustration of sampling rates, the height of the sample is measured in bits. A more detailed graph can be reconstructed by using more bits for the initial readings taken.

musical instrument digital interface (MIDI) a file standard developed for music synthesizers.

MIDI Files

Musical instrument digital interface (MIDI) is a file standard developed for music synthesizers. Synthesized music is electronically simulated music sounds

Figure 8-28.
Dialog box showing new mail notification sound properties.

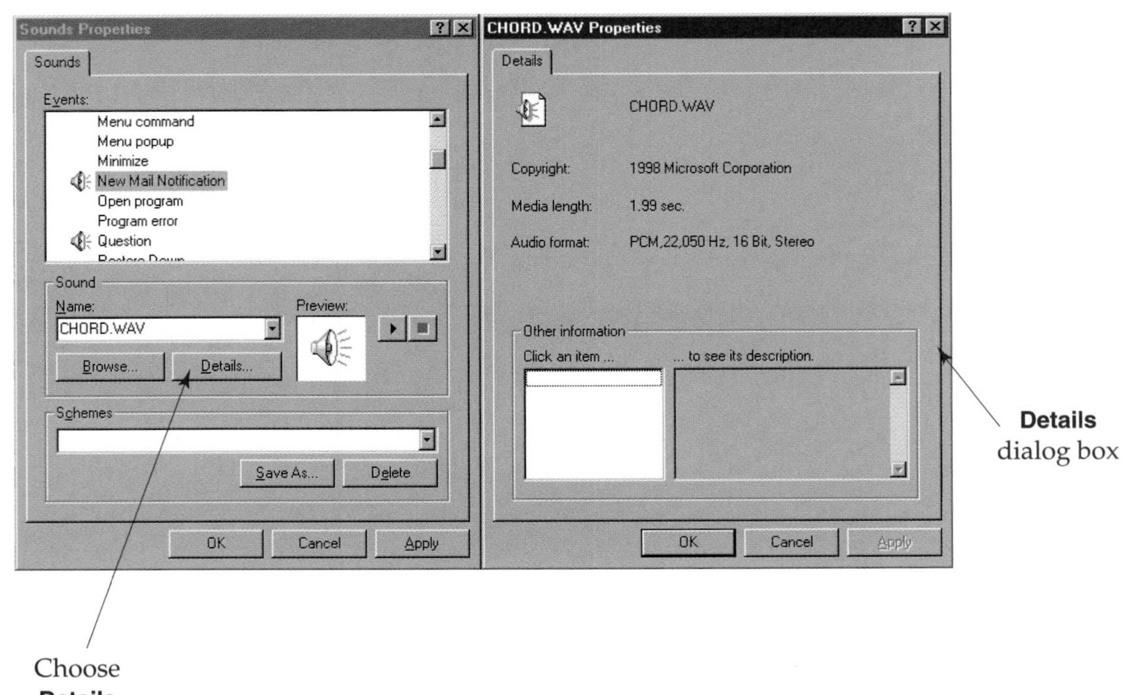

rather than recorded sounds. A chip, or set of chips, can produce the sounds of many instruments, **Figure 8-29.** To play music, input through the chips is made from a database containing information such as the type of instrument to play, the actual note to play, the length of sound, and any special effects such as an echo chamber effect. The music is actually a sequence of coded instructions sent to the chips that make the sounds. An advantage of MIDI is that it is a universal file format. A disadvantage is that many MIDI audio systems sound like artificial music to the ear. After all, they are artificial sounds produced by chips rather than real instrument recordings.

MIDI can be created electronically by connecting a PC to a sound synthesizer or keyboard, **Figure 8-30.** The keyboard has selector switches from which the user can select dozens of different instruments. A song can be recorded in

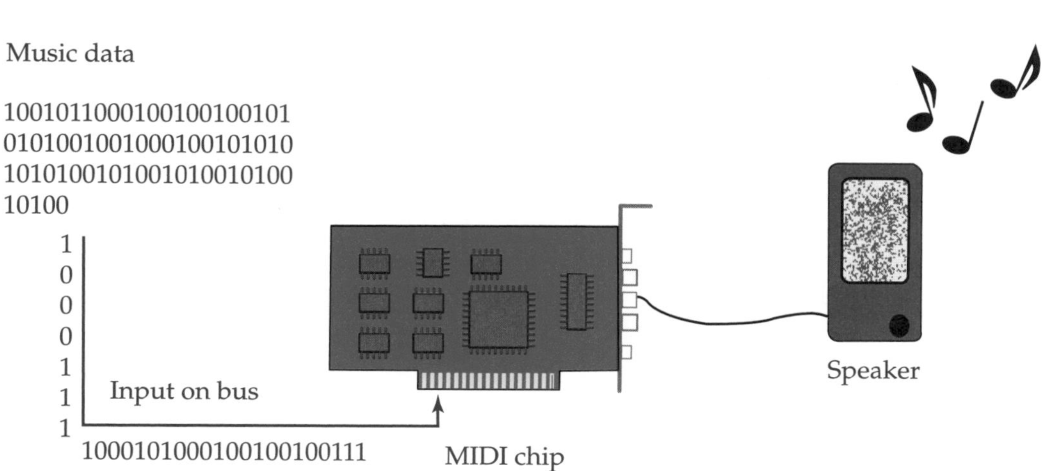

Figure 8-29.
A MIDI chip is capable of reproducing sound from a selection of instruments that are stored in its memory.

Figure 8-30.
A typical keyboard (left) with its MIDI interface (right).

MIDI data format to be saved and played back on the PC. Once the sound track is saved, it can be manipulated to add special effects. A single musician can create music similar to a complete orchestra of instruments.

Audio Devices

There are numerous audio devices for the PC. They include both input devices, such as the microphone, and output devices, such as the speaker. Most of these devices are tied into the PC through the sound card.

Microphones

A *microphone* is a simple electronic device used to convert sound waves into electrical energy. The microphone converts the air vibration that strikes it into voltage levels that are in direct proportion to the strength and frequency of the vibrations. The electrical energy is analog in nature. **Figure 8-31** shows sound waves striking a microphone and their conversion to digital data.

When the signal reaches the sound card, the analog electrical signal is converted to a digital signal, which allows it to be stored in RAM, on a hard drive, or on a CD. When the sound is stored as a digital code, it is often referred to as a "wave" file because it usually has a wav file extension. A one-minute .wav file can vary in size from 500KB to over 20MB depending on variables. Some of these variables are the speed of the sampling frequency, whether monaural or stereo sound is being recorded, whether 8-bit or 16-bit sampling is used, and what compression technique is being used (if any).

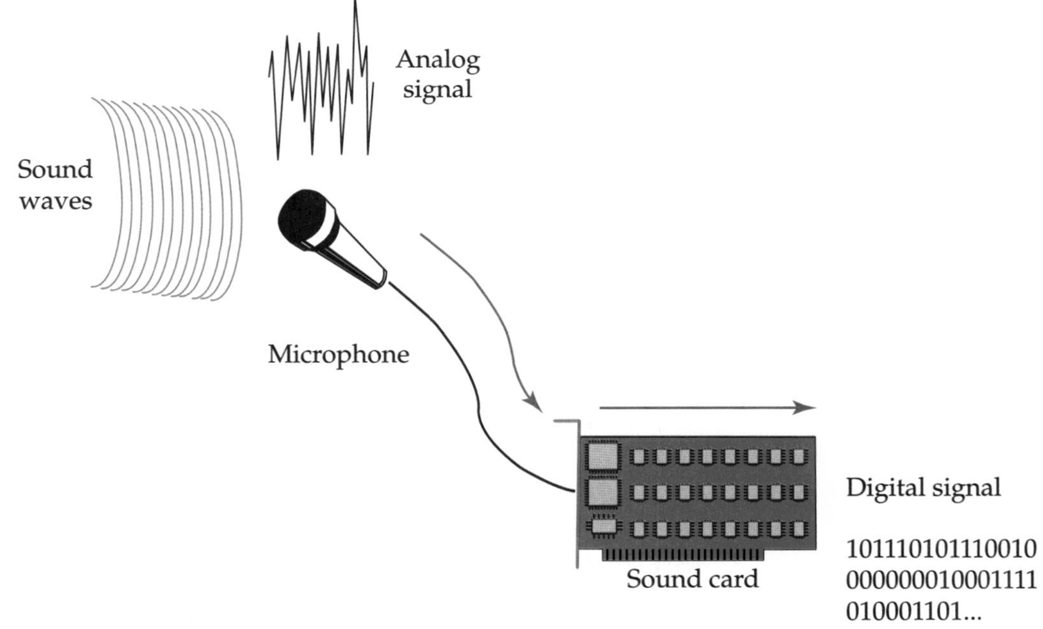

Figure 8-31. An analog sound signal is turned into an analog electrical signal by a microphone and then into a digital electrical signal by a sound card.

Speakers

A *speaker* converts electrical energy back to sound energy. Look at **Figure 8-32** to see a digital sound passing through a sound card and out through a speaker.

To listen to stored digital code, the code is sent back through the sound card and is then converted back to an analog electrical signal. As the electrical energy

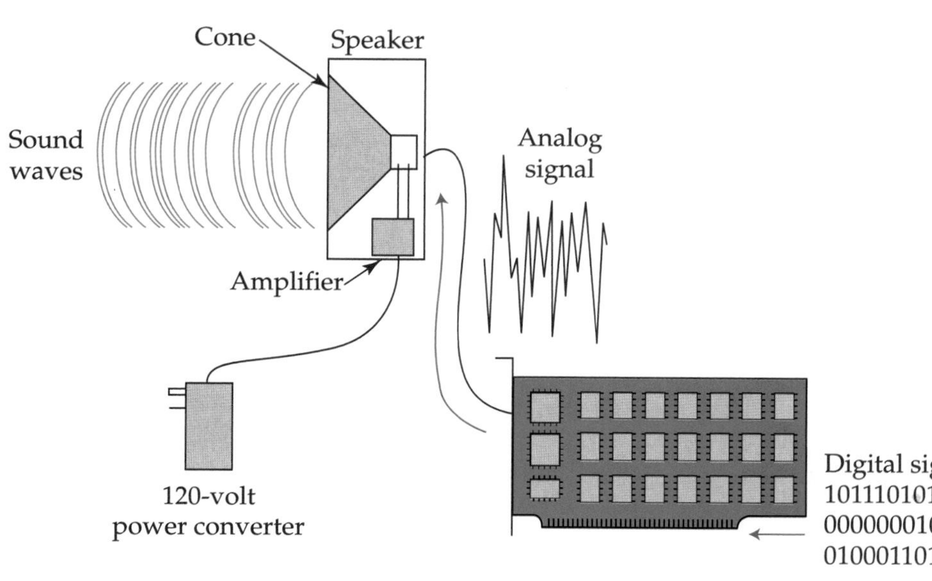

Figure 8-32.
The sound card changes a digital signal back into an analog electrical signal. This electrical signal is used to produce sound by the speaker.

varies in strength, the speaker cone is vibrated at a rate proportional to the analog electrical signal.

Take note of the 120-volt converter unit. The 120-volt converter unit is used to power the amplifier inside the speaker. The speaker amplifier takes the small analog signal it receives from the sound card and powerfully reproduces it. A typical sound card cannot provide ample power to drive a speaker. Most sound cards only produce approximately 2 watts of energy. This is sufficient to drive only a headphone set, not a desktop speaker. When a speaker has its own built-in amplifier, it is called an active speaker. A speaker without amplification is called a passive speaker.

Sound Cards

Most sound cards purchased today are PCI adapter cards. This means they are Plug and Play technology. All system resources (IRQ, DMA, I/O port addresses, memory addresses) are automatically detected and assigned. Older 8-bit ISA adapter type cards will most likely require system resources to be manually assigned through software or physically assigned by setting jumpers or dip switches.

System conflicts are quite common for older ISA type cards. Always check the system resource assignments when problems arise, especially after newer hardware has been installed to an existing system. Software diagnostic programs included in most operating systems can diagnose conflicts. Windows 98 and higher versions have diagnostic software to assist you with conflicts with system resources. These tools can be accessed through **Start | Programs | Accessories | System Tools | System Information**. **Figure 8-33** shows the Microsoft System Information dialog box. It can assist you when solving system resource conflicts. You can use this window to analyze conflicts arising from system resource assignments.

Sound Card Installation

Installing a sound card before Plug and Play could be very frustrating. The source of frustration came from system resource assignments. There was almost a guarantee of a system resource conflict appearing with legacy sound cards.

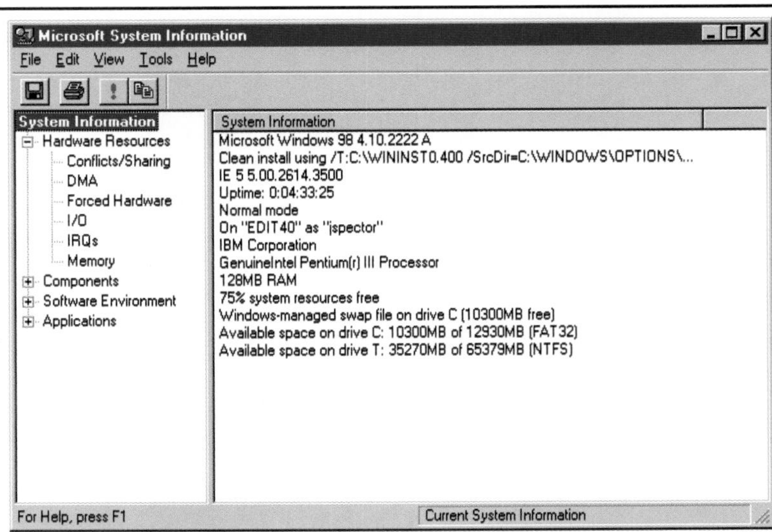

Figure 8-33. The Microsoft System Information dialog box can be used to help troubleshoot conflicts. It shows the IRQs, DMAs, and I/O port addresses a computer's components are using.

Multimedia type cards use all areas of system resources. Before installing any legacy sound card, review the following areas: IRQs, DMA, memory addresses, and I/O port address covered earlier in the textbook.

Although Plug and Play should eliminate most conflicts, there can still be problems, especially when upgrades are performed. As new technologies evolve, there will be the need to upgrade current technologies. In other words, Plug and Play operates well now, but a new technology will appear in the future that will also require Plug and Play to be upgraded or redesigned. The following steps are used for the installation of a typical sound card:

1. Power off the computer and unplug the power cord from the wall outlet.
2. Read the card procedure and specification sheet.
3. Take normal static precautions.
4. Check for debris in the expansion slot.
5. Insert the card into the slot by applying even force to the top of the card. Do not rock the card into the slot.
6. Check if there are any cables that might interfere with the sound card. Voltages can be induced by wires in close proximity to the sound card. This can cause distortion of the sound quality. Keep cables away from sound cards.
7. Connect the speakers to the computer and connect the speaker's power supply to the speakers. Turn the speakers on before powering on the computer.
8. Power on the computer.

The card should be auto detected if it is Plug and Play. You may have to supply the driver for the new adapter card when the system detects the card. The Windows system may not have the correct driver for the card. The driver should have been packaged with the sound card either as a floppy or CD-ROM. Also check the manufacturer's Web site for the latest patch or upgrade for the driver. Follow the screen prompts to complete the installation. If all has gone well, you should be able to turn off the power, install the cover, and then reboot the system. If the installation failed, reread the installation procedure. Check for simple things first. For example, is the power supply module for the speakers plugged in? Or, is there a bent pin at one of the connection points? Check if the volume is turned up. You may also need to upgrade the BIOS on the motherboard. Check the Web site of the motherboard manufacturer and the sound card manufacturer for the latest updates.

Multimedia

Interaction with audio and video is referred to as ***multimedia.*** Attempts to create and play multimedia files more quickly and clearly has been one of the major driving factors in the computer industry. The computing power needed to render three-dimensional images and the storage needed to store or even play movies have caused the processing speeds of CPUs and the RAM considered "minimum requirements" on PCs to increase over the last few years. The greatest recent changes in PC operating systems are changes to how they handle multimedia.

multimedia
incorporating sound or video.

MPEG Formats

Motion Picture Experts Group (MPEG)
a standard format for recording motion picture video and sound.

The ***Motion Picture Experts Group (MPEG),*** (pronounced empeg), is an organization made up of professionals from all areas of the motion picture industry. The goal of the organization was to develop a standard format for recording motion picture video and sound. Together they developed data compression standards and file formats for storing both audio and video data. The two main formats are MPEG-1 and MPEG-2. MPEG-1 is similar to videotape quality. MPEG-2 is a higher quality compression used for PC CD video, digital versatile disc (DVD) (also called digital video disc), and High-Definition Television (HDTV).

The MP3 standard (short for *MP*EG layer 3) is used for music. It is a derivative of the MPEG-2 standard. (To avoid confusion, MP3 is also a well-known Web site, but the site takes its name from the format.) MPEG-4 came out in 1999, and there are several more MPEG standards under development. Check the Web page provided by the Motion Picture Experts Group for the latest updates.

Codecs

codec
any hardware, software, or combination hardware and software that can compress and decompress data.

A term frequently used in compression is codec. The term codec is a contraction of the two words *co*mpression and *dec*ompression. A ***codec*** is any hardware, software, or combination hardware and software that can compress and decompress data. The term is used most often in the video industry and telecommunications. MPEG is only one form of codec. There are others such as Indeo, Cinepak, QuickTime, and DVsoft. When setting up properties for audio and video equipment using Windows, the many compression techniques will be referred to as choosing a method of codec.

Buffering

buffering
a technique used to play a downloaded file without skips or quiet spots during playback.

Buffering is a technique used to play a downloaded file without skips or quiet spots during playback. When downloading music from a site, it must travel hundreds or even thousands of miles from the source to your PC. Unless you have a high-bandwidth connection such as a T1 or cable, you will have difficulty maintaining a steady stream of data from the other site. In Chapter 13—Modems and Transceivers, more detailed information about various connection mediums, such as T1 lines, will be presented.

Data is sent across phone lines to your PC in packets that average 1500 bytes each. As noted earlier, data for sound is quite large. A music sample may be constructed from thousands of the 1500-byte packets. The data does not arrive as a consistent series of packets. Many data packets will even arrive out of their original order. The reason the data packets can arrive out of order is that the data route to and from the site is constantly being updated. The Internet is composed of millions of miles of lines. Many of the lines become congested with data traffic. At times, data packets are rerouted to achieve a faster transmission rate. If a quicker route is discovered by the transmission system while data is transferred, the balance of the data will be transmitted through the new route, **Figure 8-34.** If another route is discovered or the present one becomes very busy, an alternate route is chosen. As the routes continue to change, some of the packets arrive out of the original order.

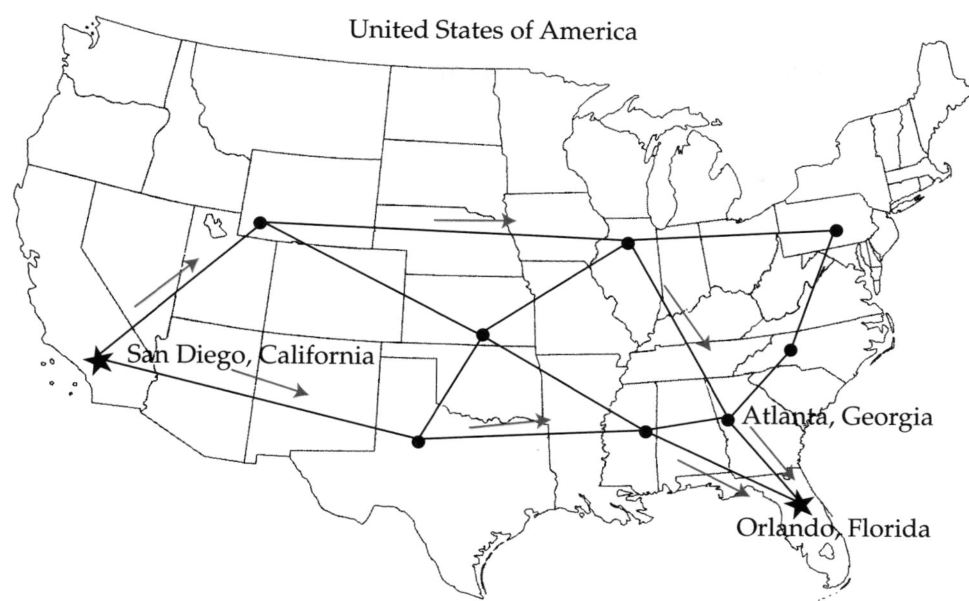

Figure 8-34. Different routes for data flow. The shortest route is not always the quickest.

In addition, the steady stream of packets can be momentarily stopped due to congestion on the lines. In the last few years, the dramatic increase in video and audio data packets has created a lot of traffic on the data lines resulting in an apparent slow down of the entire system. A good example of these seemingly slow systems can be seen on many college campuses where scores of students are downloading music and video files from the Internet at one time.

The packets must be reassembled at their destination. Buffering collects all the downloaded data and reassembles it in its original order. It then provides a steady stream of data. In the case of downloading a song, the act of buffering means the song data is downloaded into RAM. It is then assembled and transferred to the player. The player plays the song from a steady stream of data located in RAM rather than from the site. With buffering, there are no interruptions in the continuous stream of music.

Audio and Video Players

To access sound and video tracks recorded on the PC or taken from the Internet, you need a player which is often called a *plug-in*. A player is used to decode compressed multimedia files converting them to audio and video. Players can convert more than one type of compression, but when a new or enhanced compression format is developed, you will need to download an updated version of the player. See **Figure 8-35.**

A large variety of media players are available through the Internet at no charge. Some of the players are only designed to allow you to play through the Internet browser. They will not actually record.

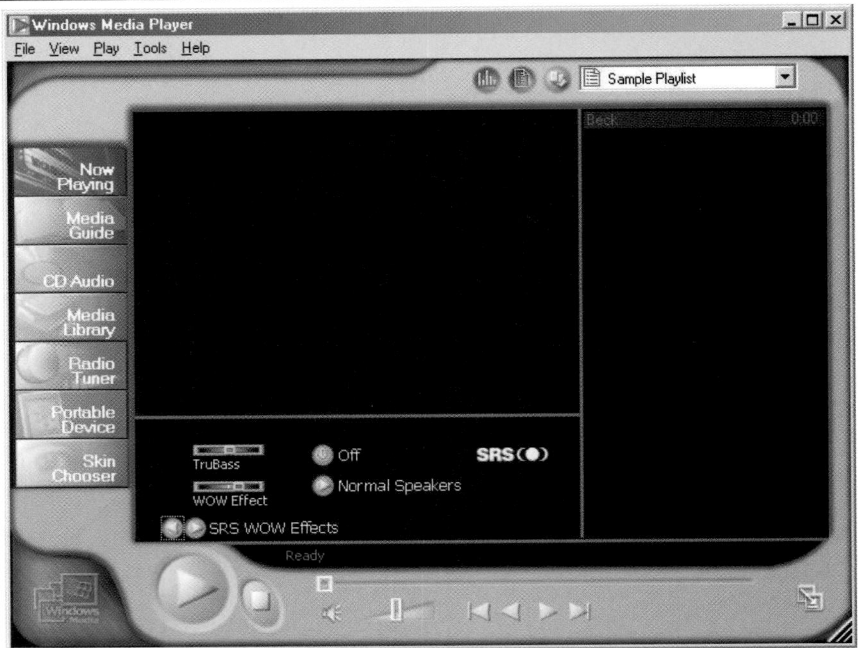

Figure 8-35. Microsoft includes Windows Media Player with its operating system.

Tech Tip:
The quality of the multimedia presentation is directly related to the quality and capacities of the computer system you use. However, upgrading a single component on an existing system may not show any real improvement. Too often, novices assume that upgrading the CPU or adding more RAM will greatly improve the performance. A system needs to be studied as a whole before a decision is made about enhancing multimedia performance. For example, upgrading the CPU and adding more memory will do little to improve the quality of the multimedia performance if the system uses an 8-bit sound card inserted into an ISA slot. A major improvement may have resulted by simply replacing the sound card with a 16-bit PCI sound card.

Summary

- There is a danger from high voltage levels inside a CRT-type computer monitor. Never open a computer monitor.
- There is a danger from implosion when handling computer CRT-type monitors.
- Pitch is the distance between pixels on a video screen.
- All colors produced on a display monitor are derived from red, blue, and green.
- Screen resolution expresses the amount of detail that can be displayed on a screen or in an image. Resolution is usually measured in pixels.
- An image is formed on a CRT-type monitor by a stream of electrons striking the phosphorous coating inside the CRT.
- A shadow mask ensures a sharp image on a CRT-type display.
- Liquid crystal material twists when energized.
- The two main types of LCD panels are active and passive.

- Contrast ratio is a measurement of contrast between the darkest and lightest pixel that can be displayed.
- Aspect ratio expresses the relationship of height to width of a display.
- Native resolution is the resolution that is based on the number of actual pixels designed in the monitor.
- Analog-to-digital conversion takes a periodic sample of the voltage levels in an analog signal and stores them in digital format.
- Digital-to-analog conversion converts the stored digital information patterns back into analog wave shapes.
- Gas-plasma displays do not require a backlight.
- AGP was developed strictly for use by video cards.
- Most sound card problems are generated by system resource conflicts.
- A bitmap image distorts when changed to a different scale; a vector image does not.
- A vector image is stored as a series of mathematical formulas that represent the image.
- Compressing a file is a technique that summarizes redundant information contained in a file.
- Codec is any technology that compresses and decompresses a file.
- Buffering is a technique that downloads a stream of data packets and reassembles them in correct order before using the data in an application.

Review Questions

Answer the following questions on a separate sheet of paper. Please do not write in this book.

1. What two dangers should you be concerned with when working around CRTs?
2. How is monitor size determined?
3. The distance between two color pixels is called _____ _____.
4. Dot pitch is measured in _____.
5. The smaller the dot pitch the (better, worse) the screen resolution.
6. What is a pixel?
7. Which type of standard display has the highest resolution?
   a. VGA
   b. XGA
   c. SVGA
   d. UVGA
8. Which type of standard display has the lowest resolution?
   a. VGA
   b. XGA
   c. SVGA
   d. UVGA

9. What three colors are produced by the electron guns inside a color CRT?
10. What is raster?
11. Describe the difference between progressive scan and interlacing.
12. What is the difference between passive and active matrix?
13. What two factors determine the quality of converting an analog signal into a digital signal?
14. Define the term "contrast ratio" when describing LCD displays?
15. What is the unit of measure for a LCD display?
16. What is "native resolution"?
17. What affect does a high response time have on animation?
18. Why does a gas-plasma display not require a backlight?
19. What type of image retains its quality after resizing?
20. Explain how a picture image is compressed.
21. What is codec?
22. What does the acronym DVI represent?

Sample A+ Exam Questions

Answer the following questions on a separate sheet of paper. Please do not write in this book.

1. When a PC boots in safe mode, which video mode is used by the system?
   a. VGA
   b. SVGA
   c. XGA
   d. CGA
2. Which of the following is the best definition of dot pitch?
   a. The distance between two color dots measured in pixels
   b. The distance between two color dots measured in inch fractions
   c. The distance between two color dots measured in millimeters
   d. The distance between the diagonal of the screen corners measured in millimeters
3. Which screen resolution provides the greatest image detail?
   a. VGA
   b. XGA
   c. SVGA
   d. UVGA

A+

4. Which is a standard VGA resolution?
   a. 640 × 480
   b. 860 × 1280
   c. 320 × 480
   d. 1280 × 960
5. A typical VGA monitor connects directly into which type of adapter card connector?
   a. 9-pin D shell
   b. 15-pin D shell
   c. 25-pin D shell
   d. Any of the above may be used.
6. A customer complains of eyestrain when using a CRT-type monitor. Which action would most likely remedy the problem?
   a. Increase the monitor's refresh rate.
   b. Lower the screen intensity and resolution.
   c. Increase the screen contrast and resolution.
   d. Lower the monitor's refresh rate.
7. Which example would provide the best quality for a sound recording?
   a. An 8-bit, high frequency sampling rate
   b. A 16-bit, high frequency sampling rate
   c. An 8-bit, low frequency sampling rate
   d. A 16-bit, low frequency sampling rate
8. The term *codec* best relates to which of the following answers?
   a. Sound quality measurement
   b. Picture quality measurement
   c. A compression and decompression technique
   d. A sound transmission media type
9. A music file is being downloaded and played at the same time. The music constantly starts, stops, and skips repeatedly. What is most likely the reason?
   a. Insufficient amount of RAM. The amount of memory should be increased.
   b. The modem speed needs to be increased to 112 baud.
   c. This is a normal effect caused by low download speeds.
   d. The DMA channels are blocked by too much bus traffic.
10. The smallest picture element on a monitor display is called what?
    a. Raster element
    b. Pixel
    c. Byte mark
    d. Color element

Suggested Laboratory Activities

Do not attempt any suggested laboratory activities without your instructor's permission. Certain activities can render the PC operating system inoperable.

1. Make sound recordings and experiment with changing the sampling rates.
2. Use Control Panel to install and modify the properties of a digital camera input system.
3. Open **Control Panel** and double-click the **Sounds** icon. In the **Sounds Properties** dialog box, create a new set of sounds for closing, opening, and maximizing windows.
4. Adjust the refresh rate of the monitor and observe the effects. This is usually accomplished by clicking the **Advanced** button in the **Settings** tab of the **Display Properties** dialog box. Next, the **Adapter** tab should be selected from the video adapter **Properties** dialog box. A list of available refresh rates can be found near the bottom of the dialog box, but be aware that not all video cards and monitors allow adjustments to the refresh rate. After you have experimented with changing the refresh rate, return the refresh rate back to its default setting.

Warning:
Some video cards and monitors cannot support higher than normal refresh rates.

5. Locate and identify the driver for the monitor. This information should be provided in the video adapter's **Properties** dialog box. Detailed instruction for accessing this dialog box is given in the previous activity.
6. Download new audio clips from the Web. Use one of the audio clips to greet PC users after they boot the system. Remember that new system sounds are assigned by accessing **Start | Settings | Control Panel | Sounds**.
7. Experiment with various wallpapers in the **Background** tab of the **Display Properties** dialog box. Change the screen saver by selecting the **Screen Saver** tab of the **Display Properties** dialog box.
8. Create a unique desktop wallpaper using the Windows Paint program.
9. Download a Paint Shop Pro or SnagIt trial program and create a unique animated screen saver.
10. Use a digital camera to create a unique desktop wallpaper for your assigned PC. Make it a computer "techie" theme.
11. Install a new multimedia system, including a newer sound card, video card, and CD-ROM drive, in an older PC. Before starting, make sure the PC is upgradeable. Check the PC and multimedia manufacturers' Web sites for hardware concerns, such as BIOS support.

Interesting Web Sites for More Information

www.alesis.com
www.bell.com
www.ddwg.org
www.echoaudio.com
www.korg.com
www.lucent.com
www.microsoft.com
www.midiman.com
www.mp3.com
www.roland.com
www.sony.com
www.soundblaster.com
www.vesa.org
www.yamaha.com

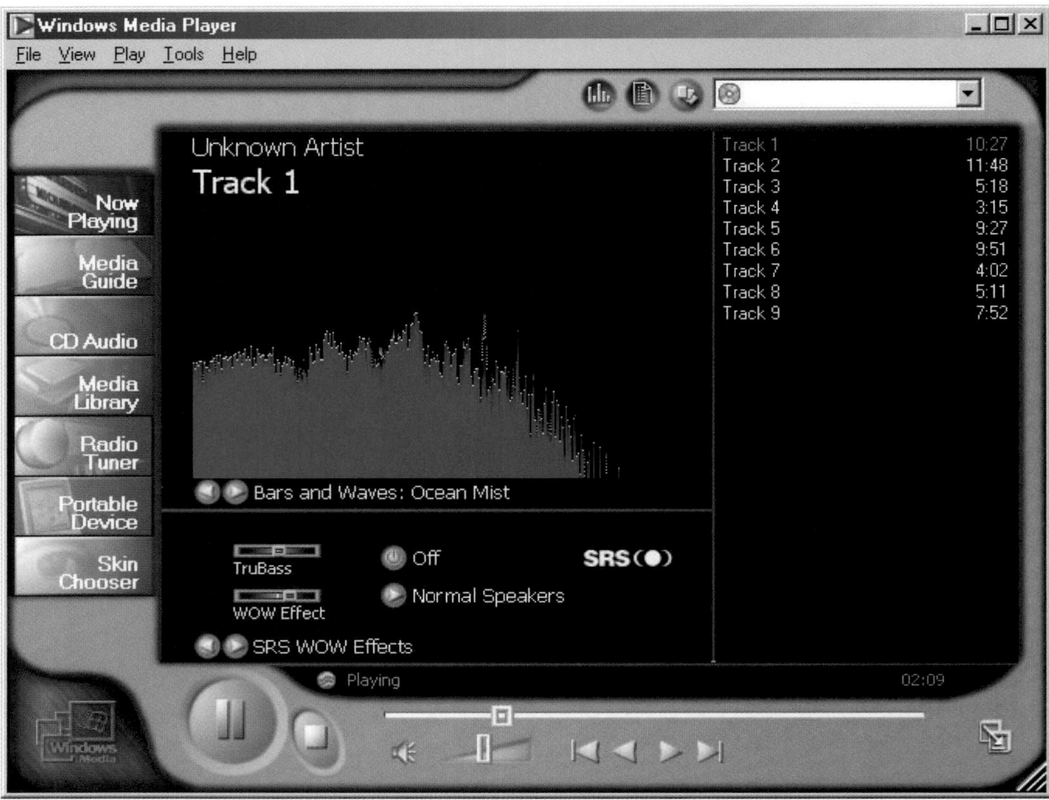

Various media players, like Microsoft's Windows Media Player, allow you to use your PC as you would a CD player. The software gives you the same controls over your music and discs as a traditional CD player.

Chapter 8
Laboratory Activity
Display Properties

After completing this laboratory activity, you will be able to:

- ❑ Modify the appearance of the desktop area and screen saver.
- ❑ Adjust the screen size.
- ❑ Set password protection in the **Display Properties** dialog box.
- ❑ Change the monitor settings that affect display performance.

Introduction

This laboratory activity will familiarize you with the many setting options available for a standard display. You will change many of the display settings, and then restore the original settings. Throughout the laboratory activity, you will be prompted to write down the settings before you change or experiment with them. This will assist you when attempting to restore the system to its original configuration.

The **Display Properties** dialog box can be used to change the appearance of the desktop, screen saver, windows, and dialog boxes. The more advanced settings in the **Display Properties** dialog box affect the technical performance of the monitor, such as refresh rate and energy management. The variety and effect of display-setting options depends on the display manufacturer's hardware and drivers. For example, not all monitors allow you to change the refresh rate. For some monitors, refresh rate is determined entirely by the hardware and the driver software.

Some of the settings will be viewed but not used. Do not make any permanent changes to the desktop area. If you follow the information in the lab activity, you will not permanently change any of the settings. The settings you change will only be temporary.

Equipment and Materials

- Typical PC with a SVGA monitor and Windows 98 installed. (A VGA monitor may be substituted.)

Procedure

1. ______ Boot the PC and wait for the desktop display.
2. ______ Click the **Display** icon located at **Start | Settings | Control Panel | Display**.
3. ______ The **Display Properties** dialog box should appear similar to the one that follows.

4. ______ List the tabs found in the **Display Properties** dialog box. For example, the first tab is **Web**.

5. ______ First, click the **Settings** tab. Next, click the **Advanced** button. This opens a dialog box that incorporates your video card name in its title bar. List the names of the tabs available in this dialog box.

6. ______ Compare the sets of tabs available in this dialog box and the **Display Properties** dialog box. Can you tell which set is used for cosmetic purposes and which set is used for the display's technical settings?

7. ______ Now go back to the **Display Properties** dialog box by clicking the **Cancel** button in the new dialog box.

8. ______ Select the tab marked **Background**. This is where the screen's background can be changed. Another name for the background is wallpaper. A window in the center of the dialog box lists all of the files in the selected directory that can be used as wallpaper. The currently selected wallpaper is highlighted in the list. In the space provided, write down the name of the current wallpaper so that you can restore it when you are finished.

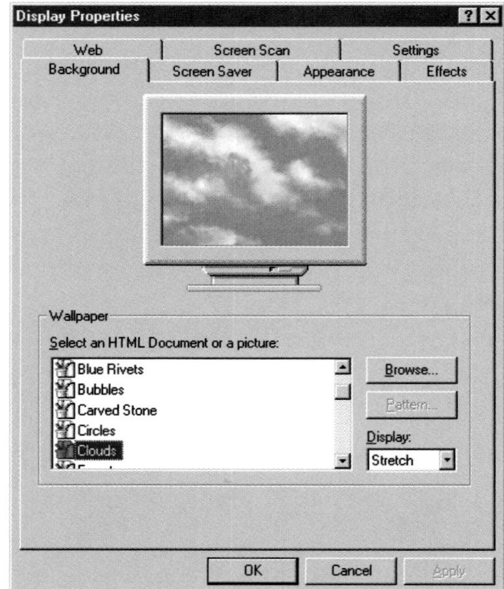

9. ______ Scroll through the list and select Pinstripe. After Pinstripe is selected, click in the **Display:** field and select **Tile** from the menu. Click **Apply** and watch the effect on the monitor.

10. ______ Select several other types of wallpaper and watch their effect on the display.

11. ______ Restore the original wallpaper selection.

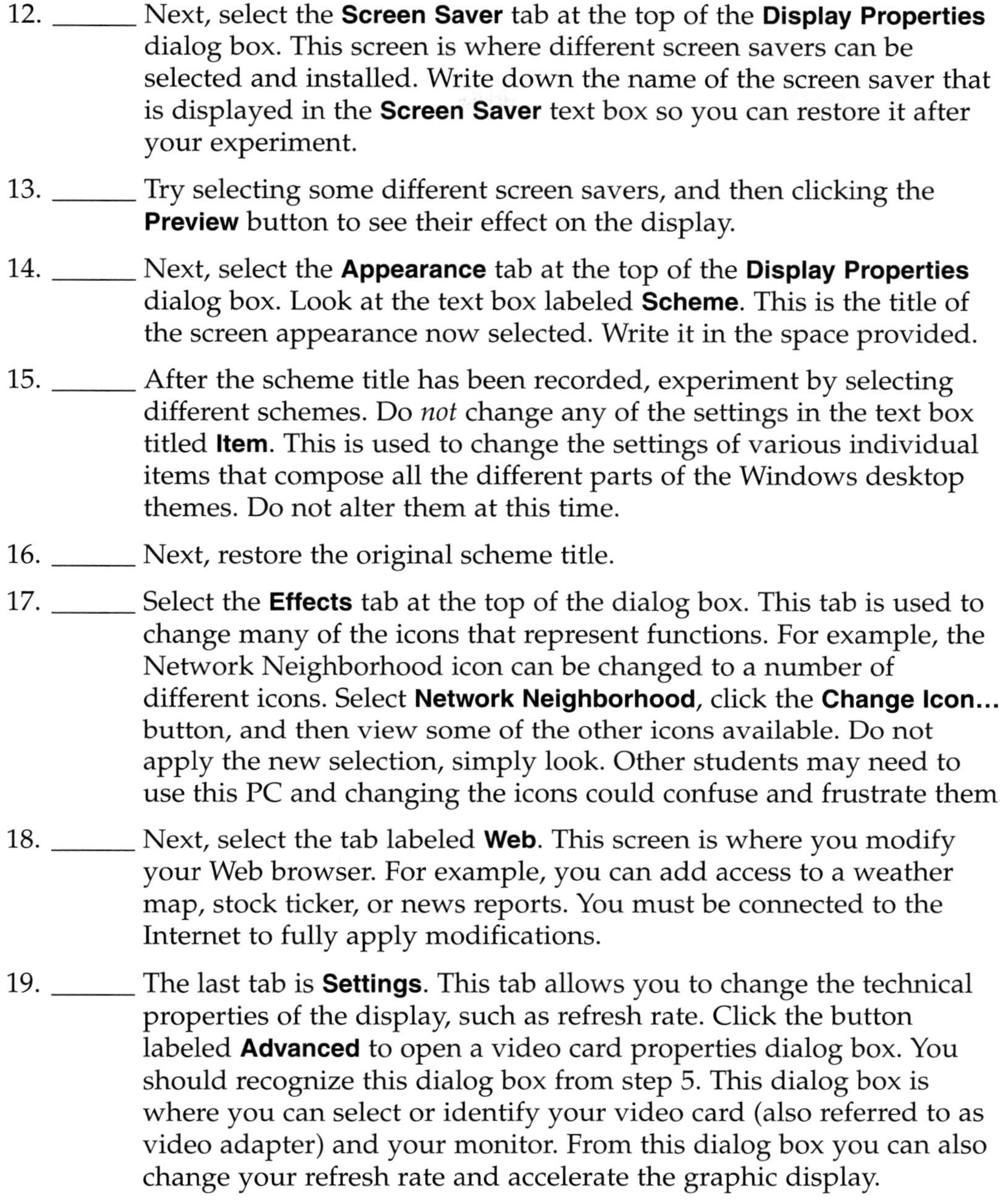

12. ______ Next, select the **Screen Saver** tab at the top of the **Display Properties** dialog box. This screen is where different screen savers can be selected and installed. Write down the name of the screen saver that is displayed in the **Screen Saver** text box so you can restore it after your experiment.

13. ______ Try selecting some different screen savers, and then clicking the **Preview** button to see their effect on the display.

14. ______ Next, select the **Appearance** tab at the top of the **Display Properties** dialog box. Look at the text box labeled **Scheme**. This is the title of the screen appearance now selected. Write it in the space provided.

15. ______ After the scheme title has been recorded, experiment by selecting different schemes. Do *not* change any of the settings in the text box titled **Item**. This is used to change the settings of various individual items that compose all the different parts of the Windows desktop themes. Do not alter them at this time.

16. ______ Next, restore the original scheme title.

17. ______ Select the **Effects** tab at the top of the dialog box. This tab is used to change many of the icons that represent functions. For example, the Network Neighborhood icon can be changed to a number of different icons. Select **Network Neighborhood**, click the **Change Icon...** button, and then view some of the other icons available. Do not apply the new selection, simply look. Other students may need to use this PC and changing the icons could confuse and frustrate them.

18. ______ Next, select the tab labeled **Web**. This screen is where you modify your Web browser. For example, you can add access to a weather map, stock ticker, or news reports. You must be connected to the Internet to fully apply modifications.

19. ______ The last tab is **Settings**. This tab allows you to change the technical properties of the display, such as refresh rate. Click the button labeled **Advanced** to open a video card properties dialog box. You should recognize this dialog box from step 5. This dialog box is where you can select or identify your video card (also referred to as video adapter) and your monitor. From this dialog box you can also change your refresh rate and accelerate the graphic display.

Note:
The refresh rate can be changed to a higher setting to help relieve eyestrain. The optimal setting is usually fine, but at times it may need to be faster to relieve eyestrain. The eye can perceive the raster moving across the screen even though the brain allows us to see only the image presented. Nevertheless, the action of the raster can cause eyestrain and headaches after a long period. A screen that has an apparent flicker usually needs a higher refresh rate.

20. ______ Take the rest of the time allocated for this lab activity to experiment with the settings available in the **Display Properties** dialog box. Before changing any settings, write down the current setting. After you have experimented with a new setting, immediately restore the original setting before changing the next. Change only one setting at a time. Changing several settings at the same time can lead to confusion when trying to return the display to its original state. For your first experiment, change the **Screen area** setting, which is listed under the **Settings** tab. See how this affects the screen display area.

21. ______ You may leave the PC on and the **Display Properties** dialog box open while answering the review questions. After you have answered all the questions, return all display properties to their original settings and properly shut down the PC.

Review Questions

Answer the following questions on a separate sheet of paper. Please do not write in this book.

1. How do you add access to the weather on your desktop?
2. Where can you access the options to change to a higher contrast for the Windows display?
3. How can the icon for My Computer be changed?
4. Where can you adjust the resolution of the screen display?
5. What happens to the size of the screen icons when you select a higher resolution on the Screen area slider control? Remember that the **Screen area** slider is located under the **Settings** tab of the **Display Properties** dialog box.

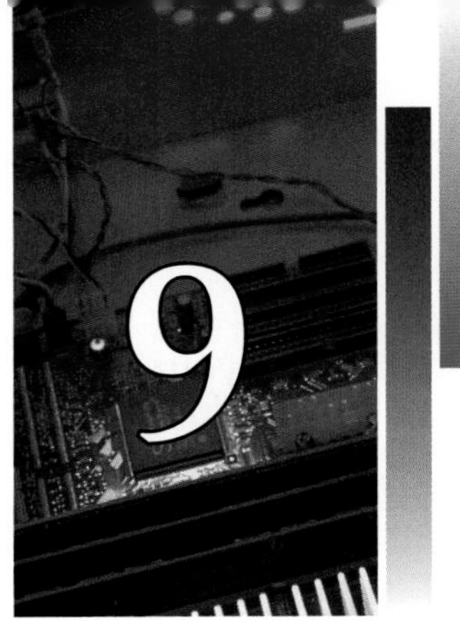

9 Magnetic Storage Devices

After studying this chapter, you will be able to:

- Explain how magnetic principles are used for data storage.
- Understand disk geometry.
- Explain how disk fragmentation occurs.
- Explain the purpose of using ScanDisk.
- Identify major parts of common disk storage units.
- Select the appropriate file storage system.
- Explain how to install a second hard drive.

A+ Exam—Key Points

This entire unit is very important for test preparation. Hard drive installation and replacement is one of the most common jobs for a PC technician and will be weighted heavily on the examination.

Be familiar with how to prepare a hard disk drive using the **fdisk** and **format** commands as well as with the **fdisk** menu options for creating partitions. Know the various file systems, their limitations, and which operating systems they are associated with. Be able to explain the use and features of hard drive utilities such as ScanDisk and Disk Defragmenter.

In addition, thoroughly familiarize yourself with the hard drive terminology listed in the Key Words and Terms section.

Key Words and Terms

The following words and terms will become important pieces of your computer vocabulary. Be sure you can define them.

active partition
actuator arm
AT Attachment (ATA)
basic disk
benchmark tests
cluster
cylinder
defragment
dual boot system
dynamic disk
encrypted file system (EFS)
Enhanced Integrated Drive Electronics (EIDE)
FAT16
FAT32
floppy disk
floppy drive
formatting
fragmented
High Performance File System (HPFS)
high-level format
Integrated Drive Electronics (IDE)
interleave factor
logical drive
logical unit number (LUN)
low-level format
LS-120 drive
master
Master Boot Record (MBR)
multiple zone recording (MZR)
New Technology File System (NTFS)
NTFS5.0
partition
read/write head
ScanDisk
SCSI ID number
sector
slave
Small Computer System Interface (SCSI)
track
virtual file allocation table (VFAT)
volume mount points
Zip disk

This chapter will prove to be one of the most important units covered in the entire textbook. It will give you incredible insight as to how an operating system organizes, stores, and retrieves data. This information can prove invaluable when troubleshooting system failures. Magnetism has been used to record data for many years. Magnetic storage devices have been the mainstays of the PC industry. This unit thoroughly covers magnetic storage systems such as hard drives, floppy disks, and tape systems. First, electromagnetic principles are explained to provide the proper foundation for understanding how magnetic storage devices work.

Electromagnetic Principles

To understand complex devices like hard drives and other disk drives, you first need some background in electromagnetic principles. These principles allow hard drives and floppy disks to store volumes of data. However, these principles also place restrictions on their use and construction.

Converting Data to Magnetic Patterns

Electrical energy can produce magnetism, and magnetism can produce electrical energy. This principle is the basis of magnetic storage device operation. A fine layer of iron oxide covers the data storage area of a typical storage device such as tape or a disk platter. Iron oxide is easily magnetized when it is exposed to an energized conductor. A *conductor* is any material that allows for the easy flow of electricity. Any energized conductor is surrounded by a rotating magnetic field. The direction of the rotation determines the north and south characteristics of the magnetic field. The direction of rotation around the conductor is determined by the direction of current in the conductor. Look closely at **Figure 9-1.**

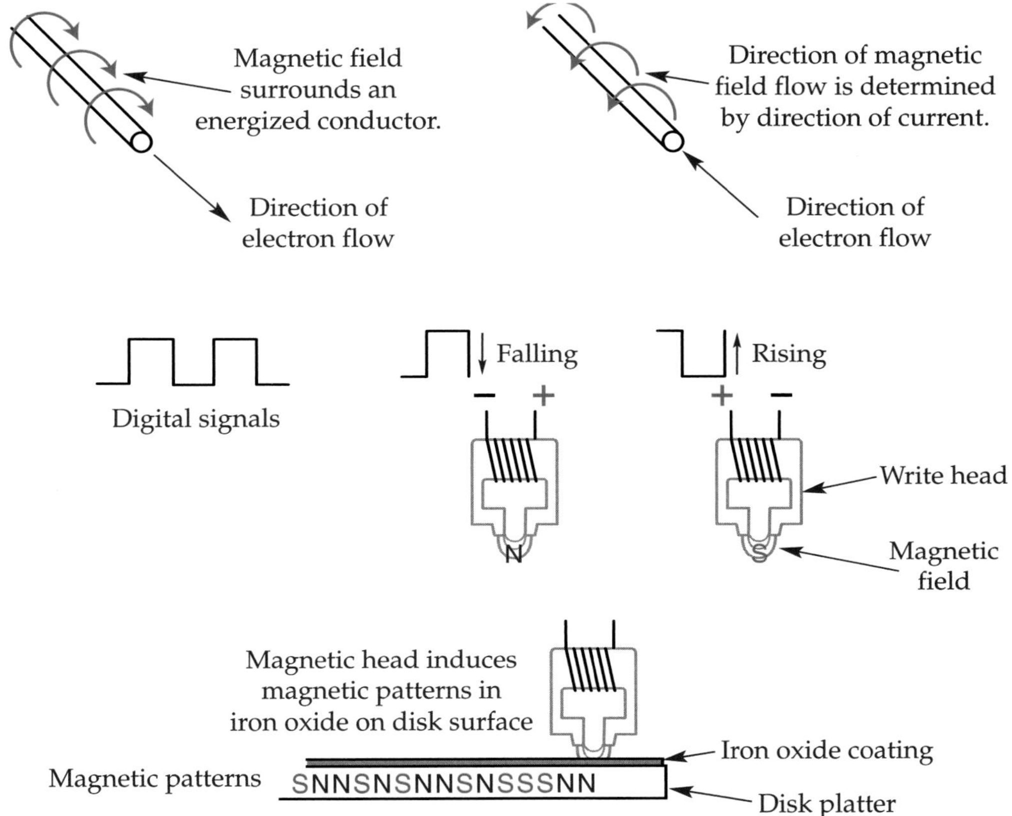

Figure 9-1.
At the top, current flowing through a conductor produces a magnetic field. This field is concentrated in a magnetic write head (middle). The write head is then used to create patterns on a disk or tape surface (bottom).

In Figure 9-1, you can see the relationship of current direction and the magnetic field surrounding a conductor. The conductor is wound around the top of the magnetic ***read/write head*** to increase the amount of magnetic energy created by the electrical current. At the bottom of the magnetic head, there is a gap. This gap is used to transfer the magnetic energy to the oxidized surface of a floppy disk, hard disk, or magnetic tape. All magnetic recording devices use this same principle.

read/write head
the mechanism that records information to and reads information from a magnetic medium.

A digital signal is composed of rising and falling voltage levels. These rising and falling voltage levels produce a changing current direction. As the current (digital signal) changes direction through the conductor wound around the read/write head, the magnetic field at the gap changes. As the digital signal flows through the read/write head, a magnetic pattern is impressed on the iron oxide. The magnetic pattern represents the digital pattern sent to the read/write head. This is how data is stored on a magnetic disk or tape.

Converting Magnetic Patterns into Computer Data

To read the data back from a disk or tape, an electrical signal is generated from the magnetic patterns. Electrical energy can be produced by the motion of a magnetic field near a conductor. Look at **Figure 9-2.** The direction of the current produced in the conductor is directly related to the north and south property of the magnetic field.

As you now know, a magnetic disk has a magnetic pattern along its surface. As the magnetic pattern on the surface of the disk passes rapidly under the read/write head, electrical energy is produced in pulses. The electrical pulses that are generated match the pattern on the magnetic code stored on the disk. The pulses of electrical energy are very small, so an amplifier circuit is needed. The amplifier magnifies the electrical energy produced from the magnetic patterns stored on the media to a level high enough to be utilized by the computer circuitry and components. The amplifier is integrated into the electronic circuitry on the media drive's circuit board.

Hard Disk Structure

actuator arm the device that moves the read/write head over the disk.

A typical hard drive consists of several platters in a stack. The platters can be made from glass, an aluminum alloy, or even ceramic. The top and bottom of the platter are coated with a thin film of metal oxide. The metal oxide records the magnetic patterns introduced to the disk platter by the read/write head. The read/write head is located at the end of an ***actuator arm,*** which moves the head over the disk.

Tech Tip:
At one time, the head itself was constructed of very small wire coils. Read/write head technology has now evolved to such microscopic size that the same technology used to manufacture chips, is also used to create the read/write head. The read/write head can produce extremely compact magnetic patterns exceeding 10,000 bits per inch.

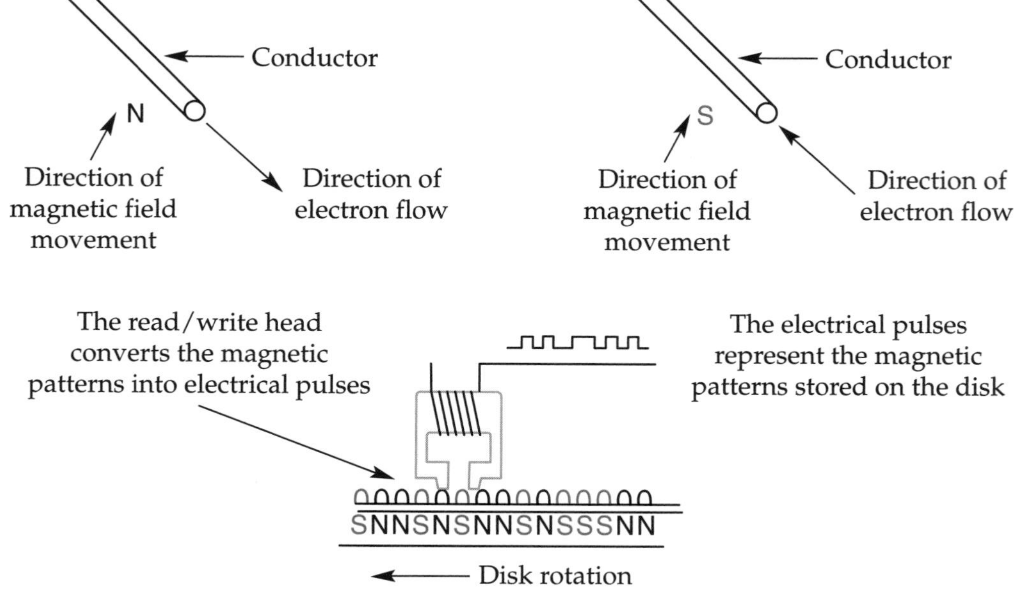

Figure 9-2. The magnetic patterns stored on a disk platter are converted back to electrical pulses representing the data stored on a disk. As the platters spin rapidly under the read/write head, the magnetism creates electrical energy in the read/write head.

The hard disk drive is simple in design but very impressive when you consider the tolerances within which it operates. See **Figure 9-3.** The read/write head does not actually touch the platter. Instead, it rides over the platter on a cushion of air. The distance from the surface of the disk platter is only a few microns. Since the head travels so closely to the platter, the platter must be absolutely flat and free of defects. Any defect on the surface of the platter would destroy the read/write head upon contact.

Hard drives have filters to catch any microscopic particles that might be produced during normal read/write operations. Remember that the actuator mechanism is mechanical and will produce some particles through friction between the moving parts.

Disk Geometry

Before a floppy or hard disk can be used to store data, it must be formatted. ***Formatting*** a disk prepares it to receive data in a systematic, organized manner. The surface of the disk is divided into sections that are used as storage areas for the data. The layout of the sections on the disk surface must be recognized by the computer operating systems. The sections used to record data on a disk drive are described in terms such as sectors, clusters, tracks, and cylinders, **Figure 9-4.**

formatting preparing a disk to receive data in a systematic, organized manner.

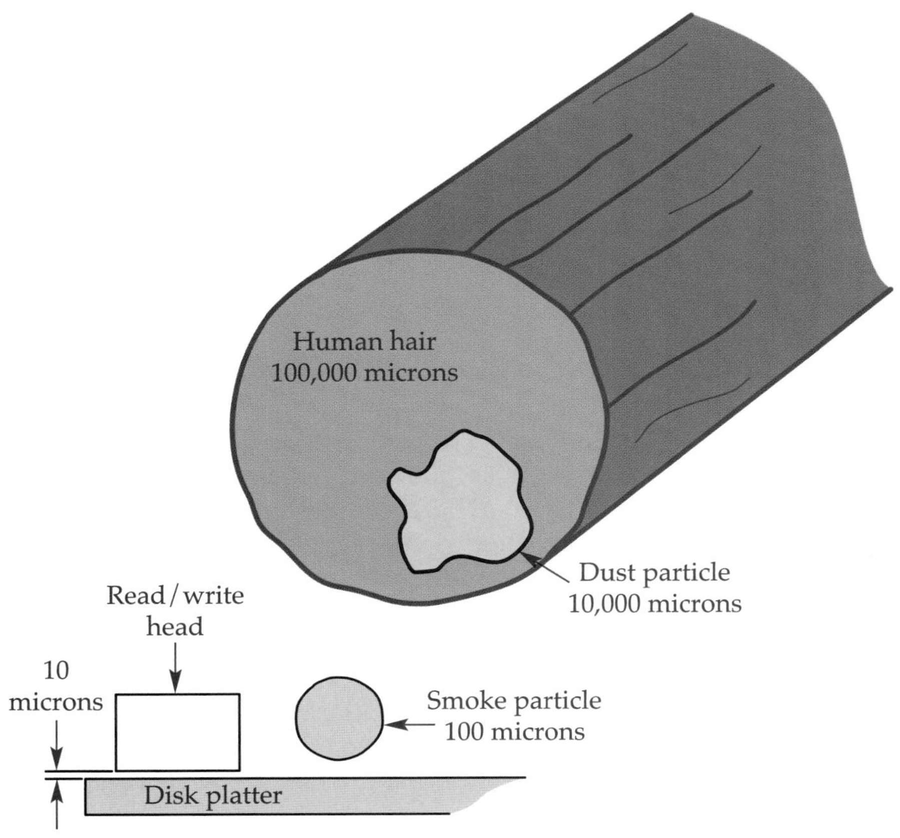

Figure 9-3. The read/write head floats just above the spinning disk of a hard drive.

Figure 9-4. Typical disk geometry. Disks can be subdivided into sectors, tracks, and cylinders.

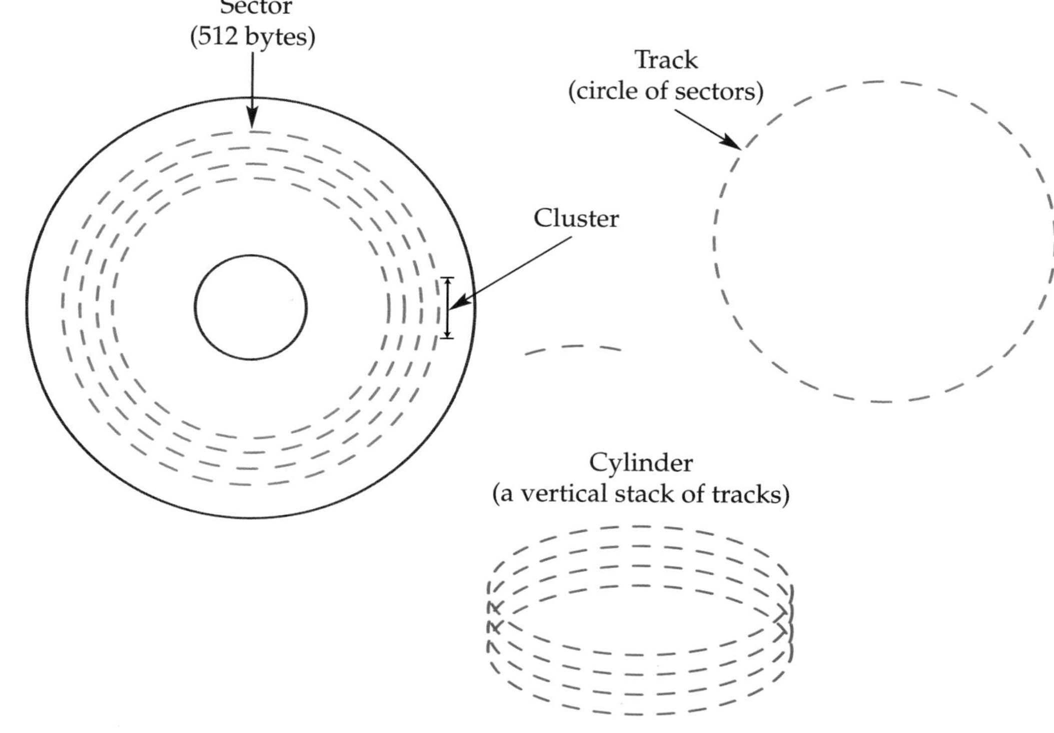

tracks
the concentric circles of data storage areas on a disk.

clusters
composed of one or more sectors and are the smallest unit that a file will be stored in. Also referred to as *allocation units.*

sector
subdivisions of tracks, usually about 512 bytes in size.

A set of concentric circles represents the ***tracks*** where data is stored. The tracks are subdivided into physical sections called ***sectors.*** The term ***cluster*** (also referred to as *allocation units*) is used as a description of file storage space and usually consists of one or more sectors. The smallest sector or cluster size is 512 bytes.

Tech Tip:
A sector is a "*physical*" description of a portion of a track. A cluster is a "*logical*" file storage unit, which may span several sectors.

cylinder
a vertical collection of one set of tracks.

While a floppy disk is a single layer, a hard disk drive consists of a stack of platters. Each platter has its own tracks, clusters, and sectors. A ***cylinder*** is a vertical collection of one set of tracks. There is one cylinder for every stack of tracks. The read/write heads move across the platters in unison. All tracks are written to simultaneously. Thus, data files are stored in cylinders for fast access.

When writing to a disk, each head writes data to the disk sequentially. Head 1 writes data on the first available sector on the top surface of platter one. When another sector is needed, head 2 writes data on the bottom of the top platter. Head 3 writes data on the top of the second platter and so on. This scheme of data recording is continued using the read/write heads in sequence until all the data has been recorded. Thus, the data of a single file can be spread over several disk platters.

A typical cluster size range is from 4KB to 32KB each. It is important to note that the size of the cluster is directly related to the size of the hard disk drive when using certain file systems such as FAT12, FAT16, FAT32, and NTFS. These file systems are discussed in detail later in this chapter.

Tech Tip:

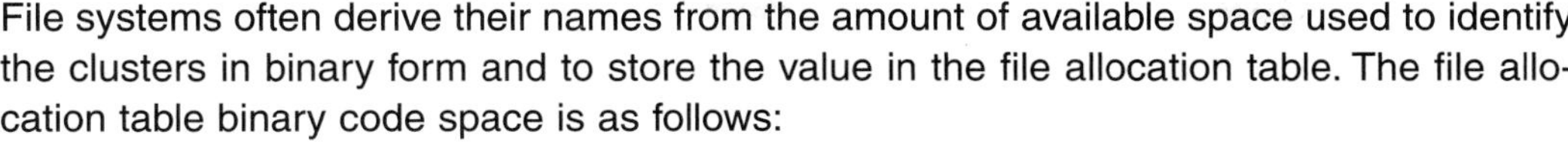

File systems often derive their names from the amount of available space used to identify the clusters in binary form and to store the value in the file allocation table. The file allocation table binary code space is as follows:

FAT12 = 2^{12} entries

FAT16 = 2^{16} entries

FAT32 = 2^{28} entries

FAT32 only uses 2^{28} of the available 2^{32} possible entries. It saves the rest as spares for future development.

Data or a typical program stored on disk will span many clusters. There needs to be an organized way to keep track of all the clusters of data on a disk. Clusters open for storage space and those filled with data must be identified. The computer needs to know where clusters of a particular data group begin and end. The computer must also know which clusters on a disk are already being used for storage and which clusters are available for storage. Special areas on a disk are used to organize and keep track of all of this information. The Master Boot Record contains partition information and a small amount of executable code that starts the computer operating system.

In a FAT16 or FAT32 formatted system, the file allocation table (FAT) contains information about where each file starts on the disk. In a system formatted as NTFS, a master file table (MFT) contains similar information for the NTFS system. See **Figure 9-5.**

Two DOS commands are used to prepare a disk for storage: **fdisk** and **format**. These commands are covered in detail later in the text. The disk geometry is created by the command format. When the format command is issued, the disk is prepared to store data by organizing the surface of the magnetic media into tracks containing sectors and clusters. To keep track of how the clusters are organized on a disk, a boot record is installed when the disk is formatted.

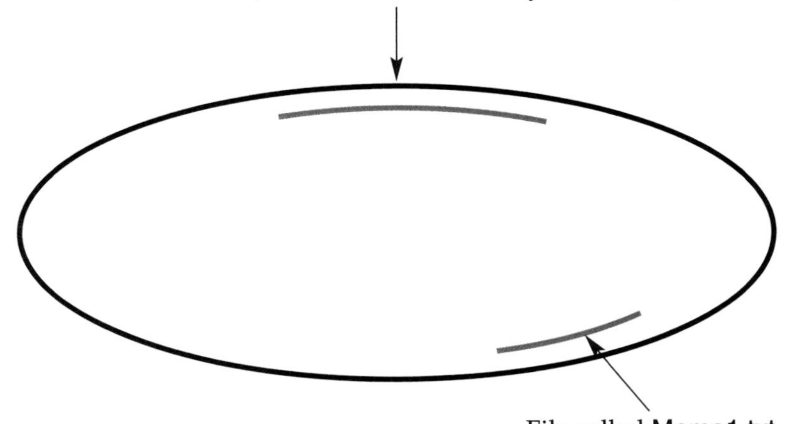

Figure 9-5. Three pieces of information are necessary to locate a file on a disk: the drive letter (to locate the drive the data is stored on), the name of the file or directory, and the cluster locations of the file.

Multiple Zone Recording

Early disk drive geometry provided an equal number of sectors on the inner- and outermost tracks. To improve storage capacity of the platters, a new method of sectoring the tracks was developed. Because there is wasted space in the outer tracks on the platter, multiple zone recording was developed. ***Multiple zone recording (MZR),*** also called zone bit recording, provides twice as many sectors in the outermost tracks as compared to the innermost tracks. See **Figure 9-6.**

multiple zone recording (MZR) a method of sectoring tracks so there are twice as many sectors in the outermost tracks as there are in the innermost tracks.

Master Boot Record

The most important area on a hard disk is the Master Boot Record. The ***Master Boot Record (MBR)*** contains information about the disk partition areas such as the number of bytes per sector, number of sectors per cluster, number of clusters per track, number of tracks, total number of clusters, number of read/write heads, and the type of storage media (floppy disk or hard drive). It also contains the boot software program used to access or transfer control of the computer system to the operating system.

master boot record (MBR) an area of the hard disk that contains information about the physical characteristics of the drive, the disk partitions, and the boot procedure. Also referred to as the boot sector.

The MBR is created when a disk is partitioned, and it is located at sector one, cylinder zero, head zero. **Figure 9-7** shows the critical files pattern on a hard disk. This pattern is standard for FAT16 file systems. Other compatible systems have also followed this design to maintain downward compatibility.

A bad sector or cluster anywhere on a disk simply causes a loss of that particular file. Often, parts of a file can be recovered using a third party utility program, such as Norton Utilities. When the MBR is corrupted or infected by a virus, access to the entire disk is lost. The MBR *may* be recoverable if precautions have been taken. One method of recovery is to have a copy of the MBR saved on floppy disk so that it can be reinstalled to replace the corrupted sector that contains the MBR.

Figure 9-6. Multiple zone recording allows for more sectors on the outer tracks of a disk. The disk on the left reflects the older style for setting up sectors on a hard drive. Inner and outer tracks contain the same number of sectors. The disk on the right shows multiple zone recording. There are more sectors on outer tracks than inner tracks with multiple zone recording.

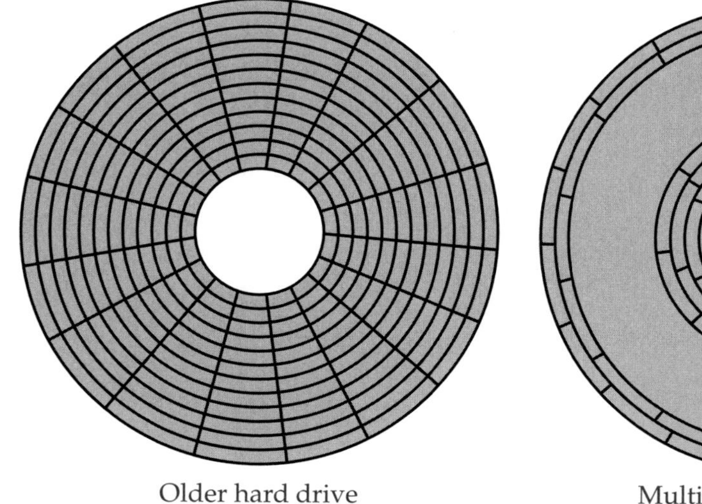

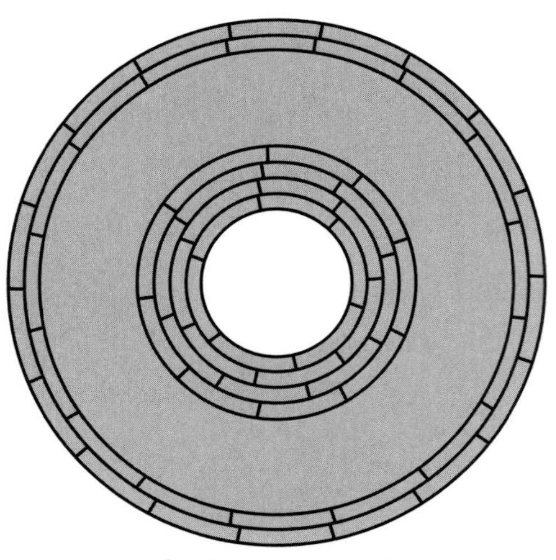

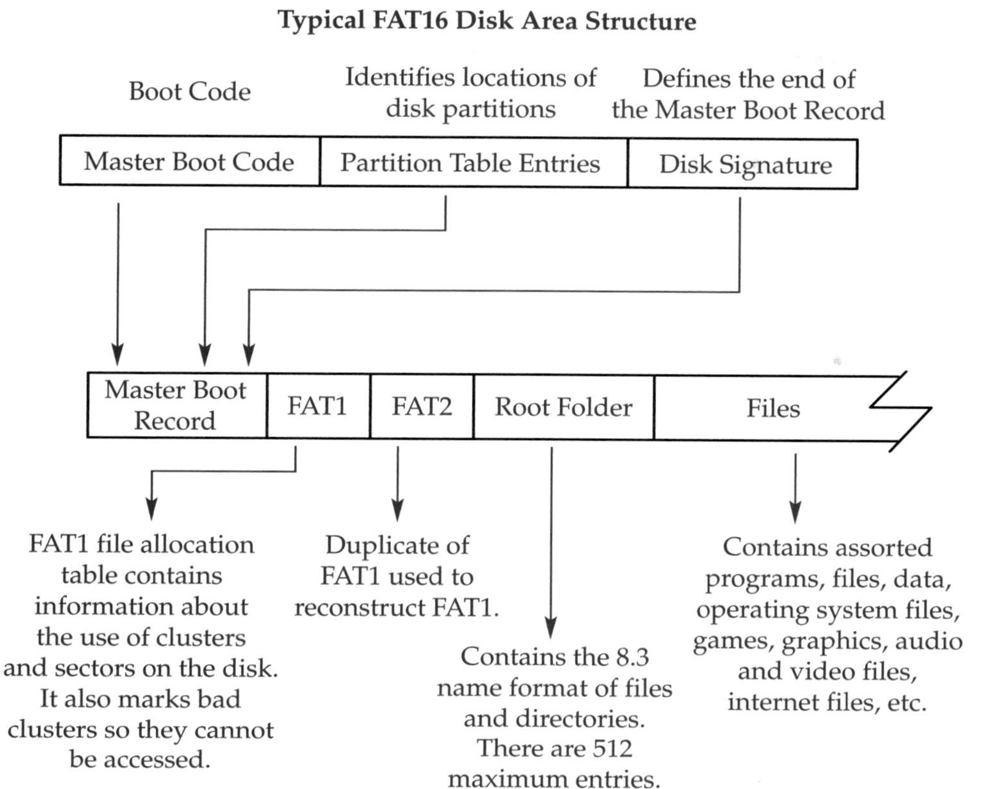
Typical FAT16 Disk Area Structure
Boot Code
Identifies locations of disk partitions
Defines the end of the Master Boot Record
Master Boot Code
Partition Table Entries
Disk Signature
Master Boot Record
FAT1
FAT2
Root Folder
Files
FAT1 file allocation table contains information about the use of clusters and sectors on the disk. It also marks bad clusters so they cannot be accessed.
Duplicate of FAT1 used to reconstruct FAT1.
Contains the 8.3 name format of files and directories. There are 512 maximum entries.
Contains assorted programs, files, data, operating system files, games, graphics, audio and video files, internet files, etc.

Figure 9-7. Layout of a typical FAT16 system.

A hard drive can be divided into two or more logical drives called ***partitions.*** Having one hard drive with multiple partitions simulates having multiple hard drives. Each partition has its own boot record, but one partition must contain the master boot record. The master boot record is located on the partition that is used to boot the computer operating system. See **Figure 9-8.**

partitions
areas on a hard drive that simulate separate drives. Also referred to as logical drives.

Tech Tip:
There can be a lot of confusion concerning proper terminology of the Master Boot Record. Often, the MBR is referred to as the boot record, boot sector, master boot sector, and boot program. This text uses terminology as defined by Microsoft in the *Microsoft Resource Kit.*

Root Directory

The *root directory* identifies the files and directories by name. It also identifies files that are associated with various directories and their location on the disk. It stores information such as the file extension, file attribute, time, date, and location of the first cluster.

FAT16 has a limit to the number of files (512) that can be contained in the root directory. This does not imply that a hard disk storage unit can only contain 512 files. It means that there can be only 512 unique names of files and directories in the *root directory* of a FAT16 file system. There can be more files on the hard disk by the use of directories and subdirectories. A directory in the root directory appears as a single file, but it can have an unlimited number of files contained under it as files and subdirectories.

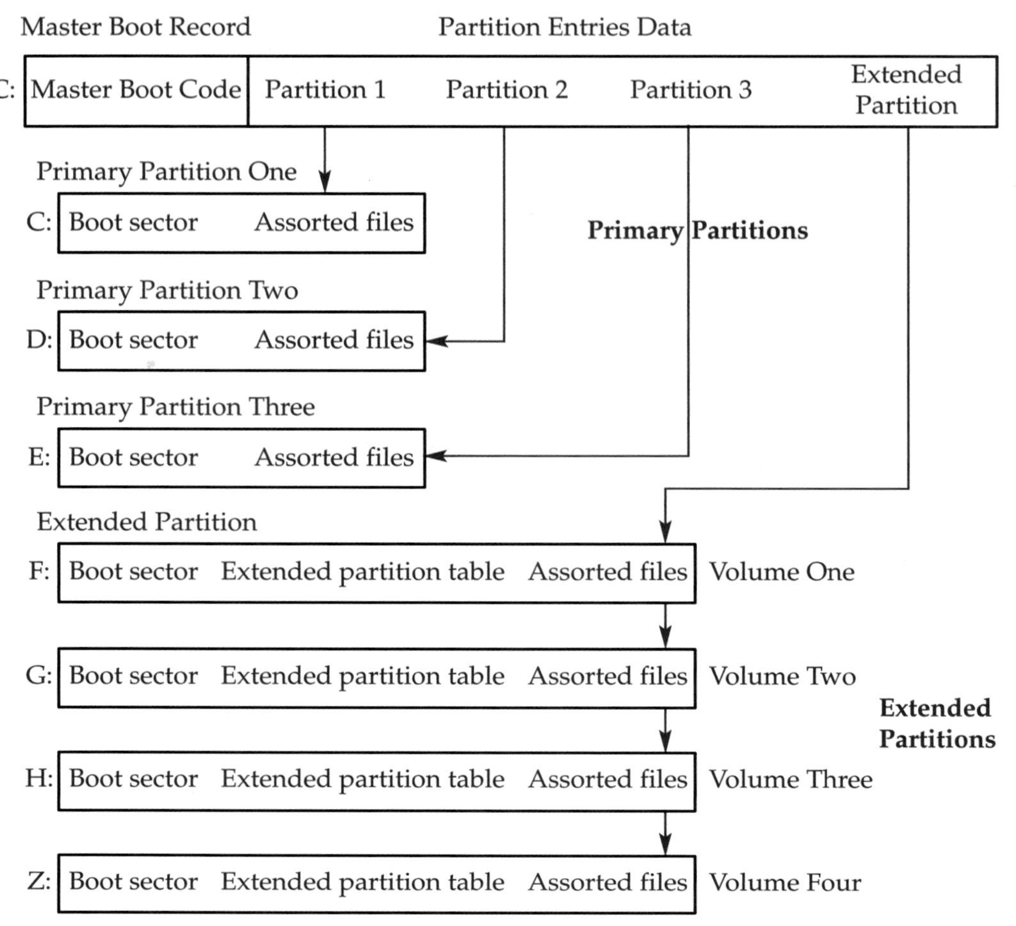

Figure 9-8. A disk drive can be divided into many sections called partitions. Each partition is identified with a drive letter such as C, D, E, up to the letter Z.

Disk Partitions and Fdisk

Hard drives are partitioned for several reasons. The user may wish to have more than one operating system on a computer. When two logical drives are created from one hard drive, one partition drive could be used for Windows XP and the other for Linux. A multiple operating system installation is usually referred to as a ***dual boot system.*** When the computer boots, the user is prompted to choose which operating system is to be used. If no selection is made, the default system is booted after a given length of time.

dual boot system a system in which multiple operating systems are stored. The user chooses the operating system when the computer boots.

Hard drives can also be divided into several partitions to separate different types of files such as business files and games. This important aspect of partitioning makes it easy for the user to make backups of critical files. If the original is destroyed or lost, a backup still exists on another partition.

It is normal to partition a disk that is larger than 2GB when using DOS. One of the limitations of DOS is that it can only directly access a maximum of 2GB of space. For example, a drive with 8GB of storage space may be partitioned into four 2GB areas. All areas can be used for storage of programs and data. Each of the partitioned areas of the drive will have a unique drive letter (C, D, E, and F).

logical drives separate storage areas on a single drive that simulate separate drives. Also referred to as partitions.

When a disk is partitioned, it is divided into separate storage areas. The separate storage areas are often referred to as ***logical drives.*** Logical drives are not physically separate drives even though they appear to the user as a separate drive. See **Figure 9-9.** In this screen capture, a 10GB hard drive has been partitioned into several areas. Notice how many hard drives are displayed. You can see five hard drives indicated by the letters C, D, E, F, and G. These are five logical hard drives created from one large physical hard drive.

Another reason for partitions is security. In Figure 9-9, drive C is set up on a network as a share. The hand under the drive is the symbol for a shared drive. The term *shared* means that the drive can be used or shared by other computers on the network. The other drives on this computer are not shared and cannot be accessed by other users on the network.

The **fdisk** command is used to partition a hard drive. When multiple partitions are created on a hard drive, only one of the partitions is designated as the active partition. The ***active partition*** is where the operating system will boot. It is the designated boot disk for the system. The master boot record can be reconstructed using the command **fdisk/mbr**. It is a commonly used method of restoring the hard disk once the disk failure has been analyzed and determined to have bad or corrupt MBR.

active partition the designated boot disk for the system.

Warning:
The use of the **fdisk** command destroys any existing data on the hard drive. In addition, you do not necessarily have to issue the command **fdisk** to obtain the same disastrous results. It is common for the computer to ask if you want to partition or repartition a hard drive while installing an operating system.

The minimum amount of space a file can occupy is a cluster. The size of clusters on a hard drive is directly related to the size of the hard drive. Larger hard drives have larger clusters. The hard drive can have clusters as large as 64KB. With 64KB clusters, even if a file size were only a few hundred bytes total, the entire 64KB cluster would be required for storing the small file. Examine **Figure 9-10.**

By partitioning a hard drive, smaller cluster sizes can be used. Since the cluster size is directly related to partition size, you can have more efficient use of disk space by using more than one partition. For example, a 20 GB hard drive formatted with FAT32 as one partition will contain 16 KB clusters. The same

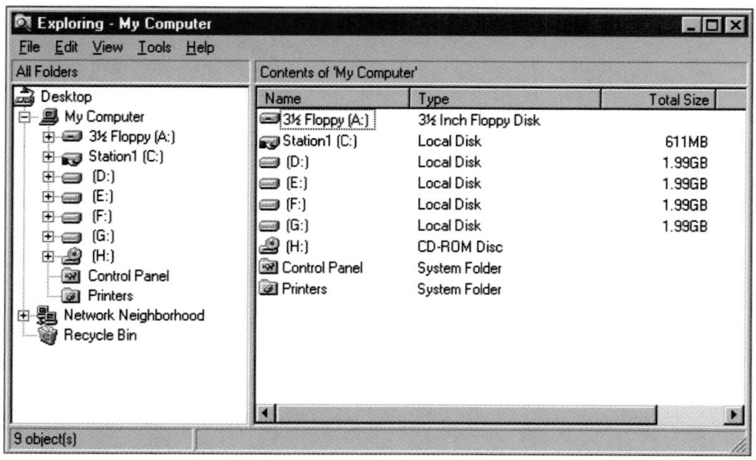

Figure 9-9. Windows Explorer showing a 10GB hard drive partitioned into drives C through G.

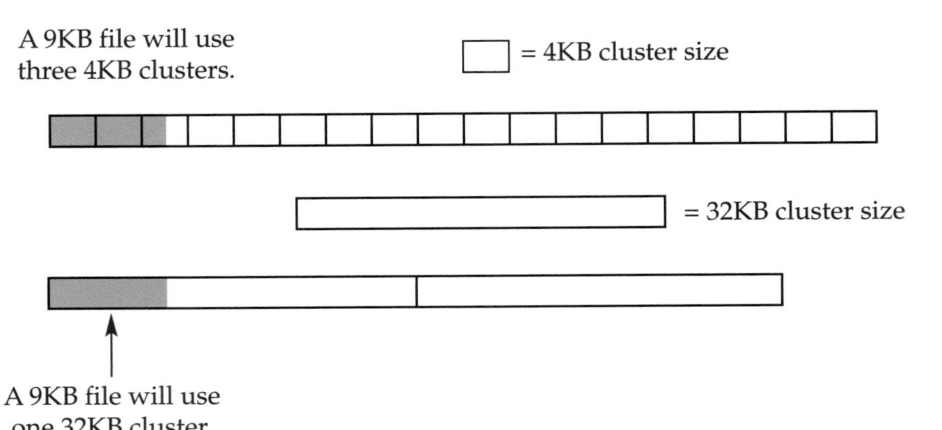
A 9KB file will use
three 4KB clusters.
= 4KB cluster size
= 32KB cluster size
A 9KB file will use
one 32KB cluster.

Figure 9-10. Comparison of cluster utilization of disk storage area for a 9KB file. The 4KB cluster format wastes only 2KB of storage space when storing the file. The 32KB cluster format wastes 23KB of space.

20 GB hard drive formatted with FAT32 but divided into two equal partitions will contain 8 KB clusters. Partitioning improves the efficiency of disk storage space.

The size of the cluster is also dependent on the FAT system used. The chart in **Figure 9-11** details cluster size in relation to hard drive size and the FAT system used. Note the NTFS cluster sizes compared to FAT16 and FAT32. The NTFS system uses much smaller cluster sizes than FAT16 and FAT32. This results in better utilization of hard disk space.

File Allocation Tables

The file allocation area is referred to as the file allocation table (FAT). The FAT contains information about how the clusters on the disk are being used and which ones are associated with each other. For example, a file may span four clusters of storage on the disk. The FAT retains a record of which clusters are used to store a particular file, such as clusters 127, 128, 129, and 130. It is important to note that there are two file allocation tables on a disk. One is the primary FAT and the other is a duplicate of the first. The second FAT is used to reconstruct the first in case of corruption.

FAT16
a file system in which file storage information is recorded with 16 bits of data.

FAT32
a file system in which file storage information is recorded with 32 bits of data.

virtual file allocation table (VFAT)
a method of programming the FAT16 file system to allow long file capabilities similar to FAT32.

FAT16 and FAT32

There are several forms of FAT. The original DOS and the original release of Windows 95 used ***FAT16.*** The 16 represents the number of bits used to identify stored data. The maximum storage area for a FAT16 system is limited to 2GB.

As demand for greater storage capability evolved, the ***FAT32*** system was designed. Starting with Windows 95 OSR 2, this new FAT was available. Windows 95 OSR 2 and later Windows 9x operating systems can use either FAT16 or FAT 32. FAT32 uses 32 bits to identify stored data, and its upper limit for storage is theoretically 2 terabytes (TB). However, Windows 2000 limits the size to 32GB. A number of different operating systems and their file systems are listed in the table of **Figure 9-12.**

VFAT

Virtual file allocation table (VFAT) is not a truly independent file allocation table system but rather a method of programming related to the existing FAT16 root directory. This programming allows the FAT16 to appear to have long file

Volume or Partition Size	FAT16 Cluster Size	FAT32 Cluster Size	NTFS Cluster Size
7MB–16MB	2 KB	NA	512 bytes
17MB–32MB	512 bytes	NA	512 bytes
33MB–64MB	1KB	512 bytes	512 bytes
65MB–128MB	2KB	1KB	512 bytes
129MB–256MB	4KB	2KB	512 bytes
257MB–512MB	8KB	4KB	512 bytes
513MB–1024MB	16KB	4KB	1KB
1025MB–2GB	32KB	4KB	2KB
2GB–4GB	64KB	4KB	4KB
4GB–8GB	NA	4KB	4KB
8GB–16GB	NA	8KB	4KB
16GB–32GB	NA	16KB	4KB
32GB–2TB	NA	NA	4KB

Based on Windows 2000 Resource Book.

Figure 9-11. Comparison of cluster size for FAT16, FAT32, and NTFS. NTFS allows the smallest cluster for larger partitions.

Operating System	File System(s) Supported
DOS	FAT16
Windows 95/98/Me	FAT16, VFAT, FAT32
Windows NT4.0	FAT16, NTFS
Windows 2000/XP	FAT16, FAT32, NTFS4.0, NTFS5.0
OS/2	FAT16, HPFS
LINUX	FAT16, FAT32, NTFS

Figure 9-12. File systems. Note that each of the file systems maintains downward compatibility with the original DOS FAT16 system.

capabilities similar to FAT32. The long file names span over several normal 8.3 file name spaces on the FAT16 file allocation table, thus allowing the system to reflect long file names. This system is used for operating systems prior to Windows 95 OSR 2.

The VFAT system of storing file names in its root directory significantly reduces the total number of root directory files it can handle. NTFS and the Windows 2000 dynamic disk system has long file name capabilities without limiting the number of files that can be listed in the root directory.

NTFS

The ***New Technology File System (NTFS)*** was designed specifically to operate with the Windows NT operating system. Microsoft Corporation realized the limitations of FAT that included a 2GB size limit for a volume on a hard drive and large cluster sizes. These factors resulted in wasted disk space. The NTFS was designed to ensure that much larger hard drives could be

New Technology File System (NTFS) a file system found in Windows NT and Windows 2000. NTFS features improve security and storage capacity and are compatible with FAT16.

accommodated. The maximum hard drive volume that can be used with NTFS is 16EB (exabytes). NTFS also limits the size of clusters, which results in less wasted space on the hard drive.

NTFS supports long file names for user convenience and security access features that are not available in FAT systems. NTFS is compatible with FAT16 but not with FAT32. Windows 2000 further developed the NTFS with additional features and called its file system *dynamic disk.* NTFS is not as common as FAT16, but has steadily gained popularity. NTFS is more commonly found on a file server or an NT workstation than on a typical PC. However, with the introduction of Windows XP, Microsoft is moving the home user to an NTFS-based file system.

Since the introduction of the dynamic disk file system, the name has been changed to NTFS5.0. The original NTFS is now called NTFS4.0. This can lead to a lot of confusion. Technical literature written during and before the year 2000 uses the terms NTFS and dynamic disk, while literature produced post 2000 uses NTFS4.0 and NTFS5.0. Microsoft still uses the term dynamic disk in their own literature when describing the new file system, but publications that originate outside of Microsoft use NTFS5.0. In addition, Microsoft refers to FAT16, FAT32, and the original NTFS as *basic disk systems.*

Encrypted file system

The ***encrypted file system (EFS)*** is the native encryption system used with NTFS. NTFS uses a file encryption key (FEK) to encrypt and decrypt the file contents. A single file, folder, or a complete data drive may be encrypted. A common way to use EFS is to create a folder in a directory and then set the properties of the folder to encrypt. After the folder is set for encryption, any file that is dropped into the folder will be encrypted. The encryption and decryption process is transparent to the authorized user of the file. EFS is an ideal security measure that can prevent confidential data from being accessed by unauthorized users.

encrypted file system (EFS) an NTFS native encryption system that uses a file encryption key (FEK) to encrypt and decrypt the file contents.

The compression and encryption features in Windows XP can be accessed by right-clicking the item to be encrypted (file, folder, or data drive), selecting **Properties,** and then **Advanced**. **Figure 9-13** shows the Advanced Attributes dialog box.

EFS is not available in Windows XP Home Edition because the Home Edition does not support NTFS. Also, you cannot encrypt a file that is compressed.

NTFS Compression

NTFS supports its own file compression system. The NTFS file compression allows you to compress a single file, a folder, or an entire volume. Like file encryption, file compression is transparent to the user. A compressed file opens and closes in a fashion typical to an uncompressed file. The only time file compression is obvious to the user is during the initial compression of a large folder or volume. An entire volume could take hours to compress. After it is compressed, the time it takes to open and close is comparable to an uncompressed volume.

Compression does not always achieve the desired effect. For example, if a user is trying to create more disk space by compressing graphic files, they may notice very little difference in file size after compression. Most graphic file systems such as JPEG and GIF already use a file compression technique. Additional compression has little or no effect on the file size. Also be aware that files that are compressed may be difficult or impossible to recover after a complete system failure.

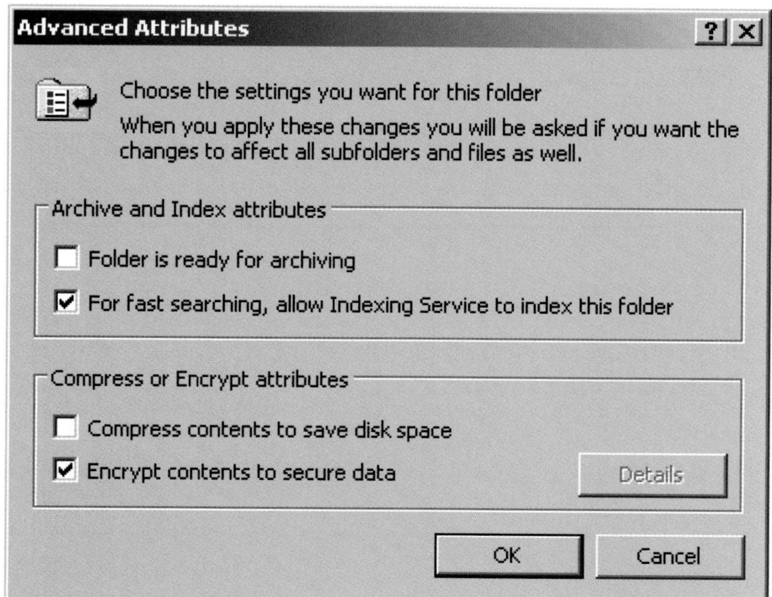

Figure 9-13. The Advanced Attributes dialog box can be used to encrypt or compress a file in an NTFS directory system.

HPFS

High Performance File System (HPFS) was developed jointly by Microsoft and IBM for the IBM series of computers. HPFS was first introduced as part of the OS/2 operating system, which is also unique to IBM. This file system was written to overcome the limitations of DOS and is similar to NTFS. It provides security and multiple naming conventions. Although HPFS is not compatible with NTFS4.0, HPFS is compatible with the DOS version of Windows 3.0. HPFS was designed to meet the needs of a larger computer system, such as those encountered on a network, but it can be used on a desktop.

High Performance File System (HPFS) file system developed for IBM PCs to overcome the limitations of DOS.

A+ Note:
There are many more file systems in existence than the ones listed here. The others are very limited or proprietary in nature. The CompTIA examination is based on the Microsoft family of file systems at this time. For the current exam, you may need to know that HPFS is an IBM file system and is not compatible with NTFS4.0.

Dynamic Disk (NTFS5.0)

Windows 2000 Professional handles two types of disk configurations: basic disk and dynamic disk. ***Basic disk*** refers to the traditional FAT16, FAT32, and NTFS file storage system. ***Dynamic disk*** is based on NTFS technology, but with significant improvements. It has improved disk security as well as lifted

basic disk the traditional FAT16, FAT32, and NTFS file storage systems.

dynamic disk an improved version of the NTFS file system.

restrictions normally associated with NTFS. As discussed, dynamic disk is often referred to as ***NTFS5.0.***

Tech Tip:
Note that NTFS5.0 also supports the FAT32 file system. Earlier versions of NTFS would not support FAT32 until service pack 4.

While Microsoft recommends you use dynamic disk, you can set your system to use basic disk. You might wish to use a basic disk file system because of compatibility features. Some software may not run on the NTFS5.0 system.

Tech Tip:
Microsoft Active Directory can only be installed on a drive that is formatted as dynamic disk (NTFS5.0).

You can install a basic disk file system on your machine and upgrade at any time without losing data, but you probably will not be able to reverse the operation without losing data. Microsoft recommends against reversing the process, though there are some third party utilities that claim they can do the job. Use them at your own risk.

There are a number of important changes for NTFS5.0. *Disk quotas* can be set using NTFS5.0. That means when a hard disk drive is shared by several users, each user can be allocated a portion of the disk for storage and cannot use more space than they have been allocated. This prevents one user from using up all the disk space for photos and such.

In addition, the traditional method of allocating additional space on a large disk system by using partitions and additional logical drives is no longer needed. Dynamic disk treats the entire disk as one large volume of data. It appears seamless to the user. The usual long list of additional drive letters such as R, P, S, and Z is no longer required to appear on the screen to the user. Instead, a system of volume mount points can be established. This gives the user an illusion of one long continuous file structure.

volume mount points
allow a volume or additional hard drive be attached to a directory structure. Volume mount points can be used to unify dissimilar file systems into one logical file system.

Volume mount points allow a volume or additional hard disk drive to be attached to a directory structure. Traditionally, adding a new hard disk drive required a new partition and new directory assigned such as E: or F:. With the volume mount point feature, a new volume or disk can be attached to an existing directory. See **Figure 9-14.**

When the new disk is installed, it can be spliced into an *existing* file structure rather than appear as a separate drive with an individual drive letter. Basic file systems are limited in the number of drives that can be installed and in the maximum number of partitions that can be created. The maximum number of partitions is equal to the letters of the entire alphabet minus the letters used for assignment to floppy drives, CD-ROM drives, and other disk drives. Since the volume mount point technology does not require a separate drive letter, there is no practical limitation to the number of drives assigned to a system. This is especially important on network systems.

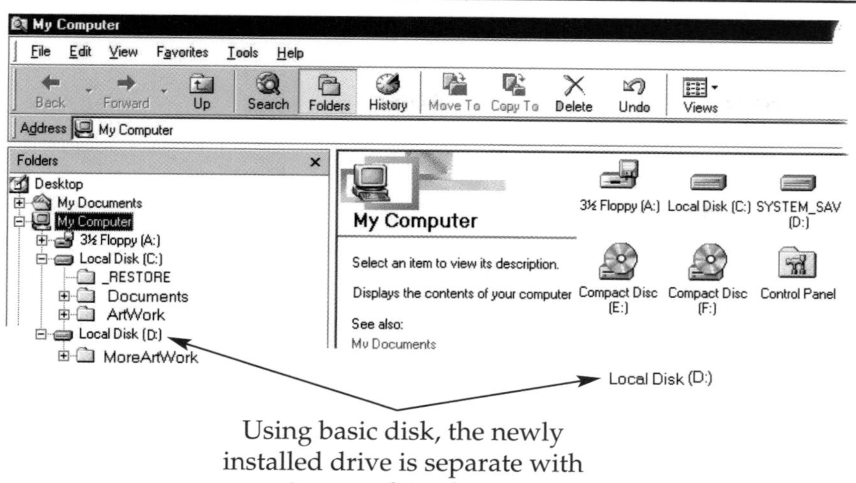

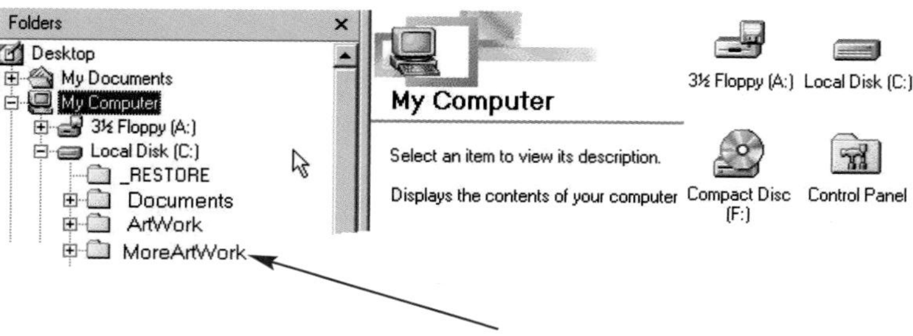

Using dynamic disk volume mount point technology, the new drive can be added as a folder rather than a separate drive.

Figure 9-14. The volume mount points, new in NTFS5.0, allow additional volumes or disk drives to appear as a folder in the existing directory rather than as a separate drive letter.

Format

The **format** command is used to prepare the disk for data storage. The command creates a new root directory and a file allocation table. The **format** command also checks for bad areas on the disk surface. When a bad area is found, it is identified in the file allocation table so that it will not be used to store data.

There are two classifications of formatting for hard drives: low-level format and high-level format. Generally, a hard drive comes with low-level formatting already performed at the manufacturer. The ***low-level format*** performs operations that determine the type of encoding to be done on the disk platter and the sequence in which the read/write heads will access stored data. The sequence is referred to as the interleave factor.

Interleave factor describes the way the sectors are laid out on a disk surface. Many times you will see an illustration showing sectors laid out side-by-side. In reality, they are staggered across the tracks, **Figure 9-15.** If the actual sectors were in sequential order side-by-side, disk access would be slow. At the end of each cluster or sector is information about the location of the next sector or cluster. If the sectors were side-by-side, the read/write head would pass the next sector before the location information could be processed. This means the

low-level format
a process that determines the type of encoding to be done on the disk platter and the sequence in which the read/write heads will access stored data.

interleave factor
describes how the sectors are laid out on a disk surface to optimize a hard drive's data access rate.

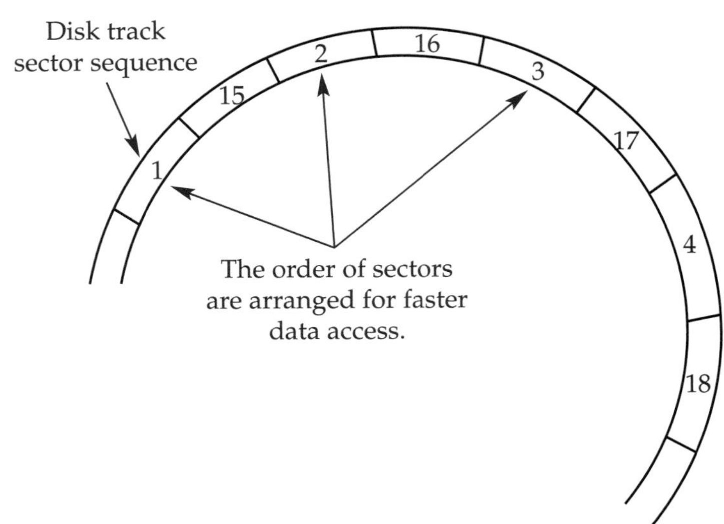

Figure 9-15.
The interleave factor describes the pattern in which sectors are laid out on a disk. Sequential sectors are not side-by-side.

disk would need to make a complete revolution before the data could be read from the next sector. By staggering the sectors across the disk track area, a hard drive's data access rate is optimized. When the read/write head passes over the end of the sector, all information about the location of the next storage sector can be processed before the read/write head reaches it. This means the disk read/write head does not need to wait for a complete disk revolution to read the stored data in the next data storage sector.

The interleave factor is unique to each disk design. It takes into account disk rpm, the speed of data transfer across the bus, and the speed of transfer through the chips and the read/write head. Because these factors differ greatly from manufacturer to manufacturer, the interleave factor also varies greatly. The interleave factor is only important for performing a low-level format. The low-level format arranges the locations of the sectors on the disks. High-level formats performed by the **format** command simply identify the sector locations and construct the file allocation tables.

high-level format
a process that prepares the disk for storage of files.

High-level format prepares the disk for file storage. It determines the file allocation table, checks the physical condition of all sectors, marks bad sectors so that they cannot be used to store data, and identifies the operating system being used. A low-level format actually destroys all data on a disk. While a high-level format is said to destroy all data, in actuality, the sectors/clusters still contain the original data. A high-level format erases only the contents of the file allocation table so that no file name is associated with the data clusters.

Data can be recovered after a high-level format takes place. The collection of clusters that contain the file data can be identified and given a file name using third party tools. Also, certain third party disk editor utilities can display the ASCII contents of a file after the disk has been formatted or the file deleted.

Windows offers two high-level format methods, full format and quick format. Quick format is used on a disk that has already been formatted once. Rather than prepare the entire disk surface for storage, only the FAT table and the root directory are changed. This is much quicker than the full formatting process, which prepares the entire disk. The full formatting process typically would be used for an unformatted disk. This process was useful when floppy disks were sold unformatted. Since disks are now formatted during manufacture, this process is not needed as often.

File Fragmentation

File fragmentation is a common occurrence on disks. Files are assigned to disks by clusters. A file is ***fragmented*** when the clusters used for storage of the data are not consecutive. File fragmentation occurs through normal disk activities such as saving new files, erasing older files, opening files, and adding additional data to files.

fragmented stored in non-consecutive clusters on the disk.

Figure 9-16 illustrates a possible sequence of events leading to fragmented files on the hard drive. The first three files saved (A, B, and C), show no file fragmentation. Each file is stored in a consecutive series of clusters. When file B is erased, it creates an opening in the sequence of clusters, which can now be used for the storage of new data. When file D is saved, it uses the two clusters left open by the deletion of file B as well as three additional clusters. File D is a fragmented file because the clusters used to store the data are not sequential. Next, file C is opened and used by the computer. As file C is used, it grows in size. When file C is saved back to the disk, it uses the four original clusters and two additional clusters at the end of the file system. File C is now fragmented also.

The more often files are opened, modified, closed, or erased from a disk, the more fragmented the system becomes. The more fragmented a file becomes, the longer it takes to load and use the file. It is more difficult for a data recovery

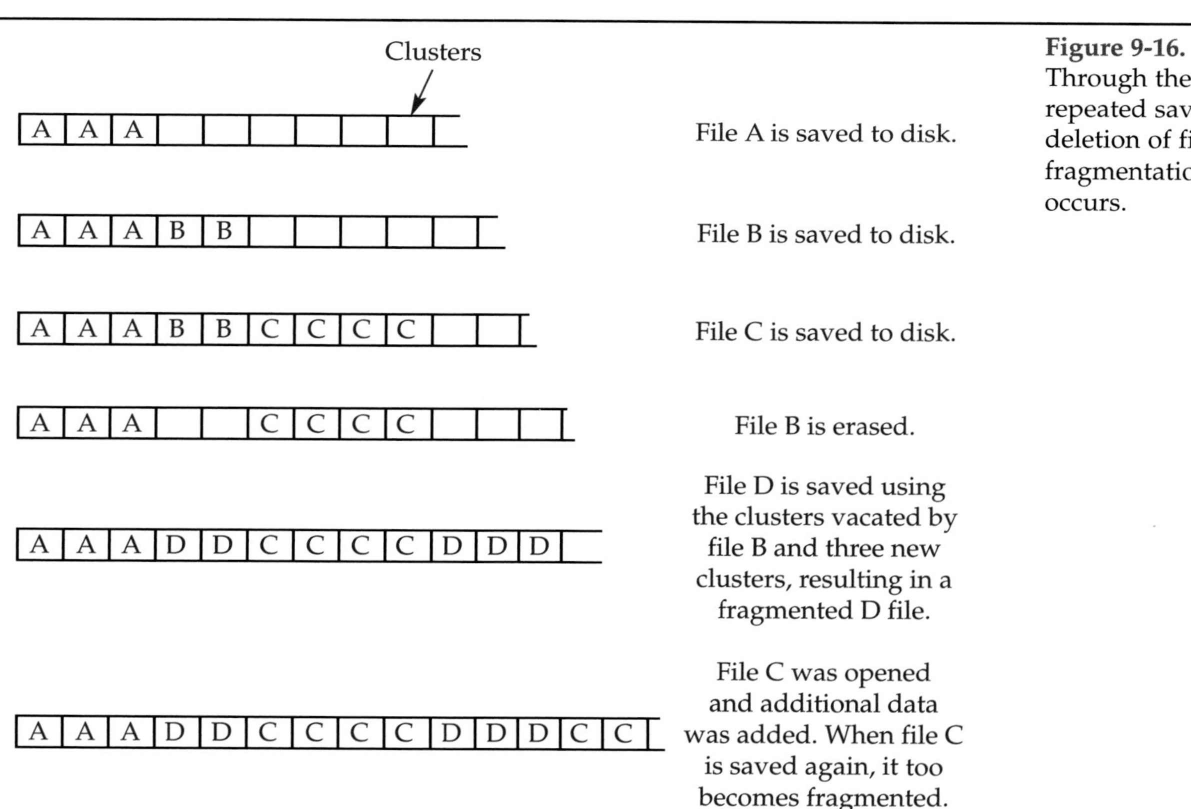
Clusters
A A A
File A is saved to disk.
A A A B B
File B is saved to disk.
A A A B B C C C C
File C is saved to disk.
A A A C C C C
File B is erased.
A A A D D C C C C D D D
File D is saved using the clusters vacated by file B and three new clusters, resulting in a fragmented D file.
A A A D D C C C C D D D C C
File C was opened and additional data was added. When file C is saved again, it too becomes fragmented.

Figure 9-16. Through the repeated saving and deletion of files, fragmentation occurs.

defragment
rearranging clusters on the disk so each file is stored in consecutive clusters.

utility to identify the cluster sequences of fragmented files. As part of routine file maintenance, a hard disk should be defragmented (defragged) on a regular basis. When you ***defragment*** your hard drive, the computer moves the clusters around so that all files have their clusters organized sequentially. The defragmentation utility program is located at **Start | Programs | Accessories | System Tools | Disk Defragmenter**. **Figure 9-17** illustrates a disk defragmenter.

In the screen capture, you see what the defragment program looks like while it is in operation. Each small square represents a cluster on the disk. The progress of the program is displayed in graphic form on the screen. A color code is used to indicate items such as damaged areas on the disk, data that is currently being read, and free disk space. Windows 2000 automatically prevents fragmentation of files by only storing files in sequential clusters. This operation is accomplished by skipping over small clusters of available storage space that are not large enough to contain the file being saved.

Tech Tip:
Defragmenting can take a long time to complete, especially on large hard drive systems. Performing routine disk defragmentation can save time. The more operations performed between defragmentation, the longer the time required.

ScanDisk
a program, included in Windows operating systems, used to inspect the surface of disk storage and identify bad and lost clusters on the disk.

ScanDisk

The ***ScanDisk*** program is used to inspect the surface of a disk and identify bad and lost clusters on the disk, **Figure 9-18.** Many times the program will repair lost clusters.

After ScanDisk has inspected disk surface integrity, a report can be viewed, similar to the one in Figure 9-18. The report summarizes the findings by identifying bad sectors, reporting the number of files, and reporting the available disk

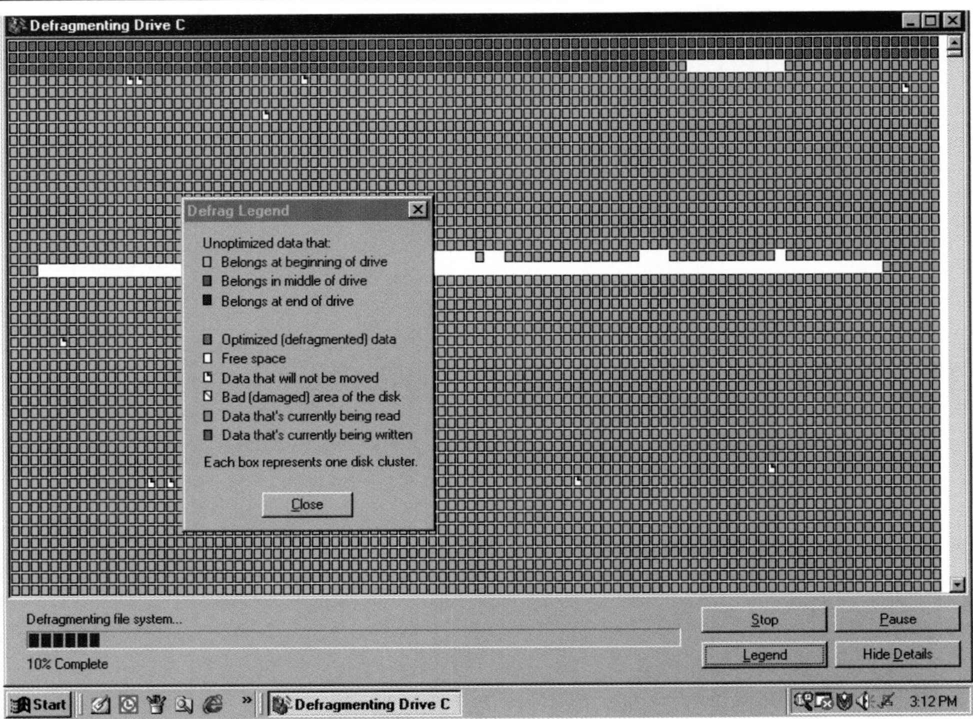

Figure 9-17. Disk defragmentation in process. This tool reorganizes your files to optimize hard disk access times.

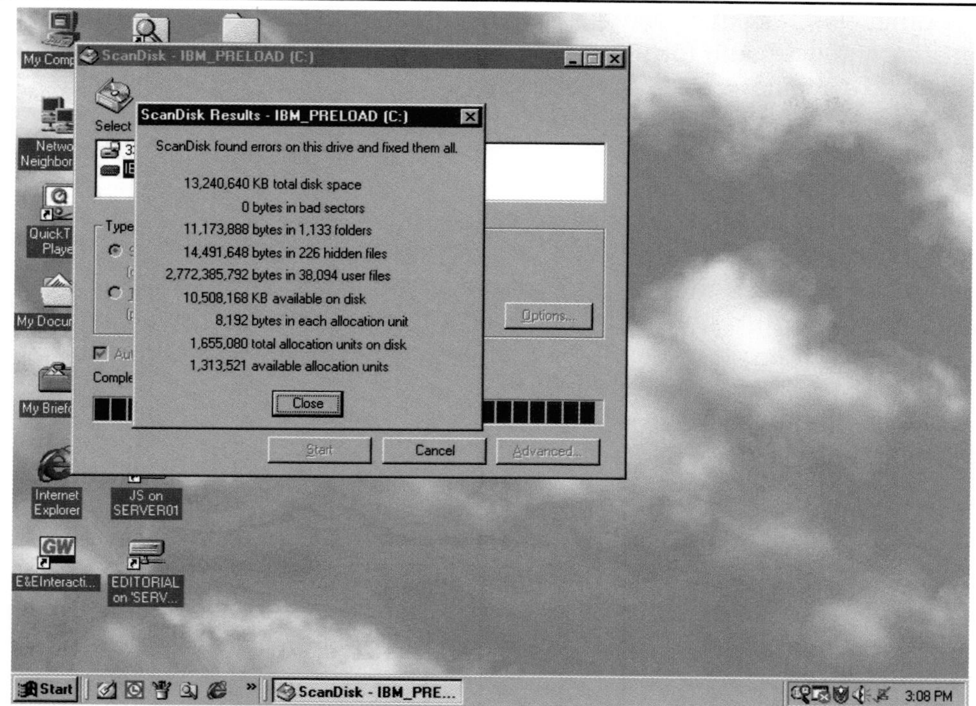

Figure 9-18. ScanDisk program in operation.

space. The ScanDisk program can be accessed through **Start | Programs | Accessories | System Tools | ScanDisk**. ScanDisk is useful when troubleshooting a possible data storage problem.

Tech Tip:
ScanDisk is a DOS utility program. There are two versions of ScanDisk available. The oldest version from Windows 95 OSR1 supports only 8.3 file names. Versions from Windows 95 OSR2 and later support long file names. If you use the older version on a file system that contains long file names, the long names will be converted to a 8.3 file name. Always label the versions of repair disks that you create.

Performance Measures

benchmark tests performance tests used to compare different hardware and software.

Benchmark tests are performance tests that are conducted to compare different hardware and software. Industry journals and third party organizations often do comparisons to rate the quality of hardware and software. Many times these same performance tests are conducted by the manufacturer and then used in advertisement campaigns. Always look to see who conducted the performance test. Based on this information, the results of the test should be viewed with caution.

Hard drive performance is judged on such items as *access time, latency,* or *seek time.* Access time, latency, and seek time mean the same thing when it comes to performance. These terms refer to the amount of time taken to position the read/write head over the proper sector. This is usually measured in microseconds (ms).

Another standard of measure is data transfer rate. This rate refers to the speed of transfer of data to and from the disk. The actual time it takes must include the fact that cache memory is used to give the appearance of higher transfer rates. Disk data transfer rates are usually measured in megabytes per second.

The fastest and easiest way to compare disk drive systems is to load the two drives that are to be compared with a Windows operating system. Place one or two typical software applications in the system's Startup folder so that they launch when Windows opens. The two systems should then be booted. Compare the length of time it takes to boot and load the software systems. Any technician can perform this simple test. When comparing two devices, all other hardware must be equal. The only variation can be the actual piece of hardware or software being compared in the test.

AT attachment (ATA) a standard for disk drive interface that integrates the controller into the disk drive. Often referred to as IDE or EIDE.

Integrated Drive Electronics (IDE) an early standard for a disk drive interface that integrated the controller into the disk drive. The term is still commonly used when referring to the AT Attachment.

Enhanced Integrated Drive Electronics (EIDE) an enhanced version of the IDE disk drive controller standard. The term is commonly used when referring to the AT Attachment.

ATA (IDE and EIDE) Hard Disk Interface

IBM introduced the first hard drive in 1957. It was constructed of fifty 24-inch platters with a total storage capacity of 5MB. IBM would not sell the hard disk, but, at that time, it could be leased for approximately $35,000 per year. The entire disk drive system was physically enormous by today's standards. It was as big as a refrigerator box. Today's hard disk has a thousand times more storage space at a fraction of the size and cost.

Early PC hard drive controller circuitry was mounted on an adapter card and installed into an ISA slot. A cable ran from the adapter card to the hard disk drive. A second hard disk drive standard was introduced by IBM and was used with the MCA slot. It was used to interface with the MCA bus system. It is now obsolete.

As the hard disk drive became more popular, the card was integrated into the hard drive device so that the adapter card and physical hard disk drive became one unit. This was the beginning of a third standard called the ***AT Attachment (ATA),*** developed for the 80286 model. The original ATA was a 16-bit data transfer system using a 40-pin cable connector that attached to the motherboard and to the circuit board mounted on the hard disk drive.

The ATA design is in use today and is referred to as IDE or EIDE. The term ***Integrated Drive Electronics (IDE)*** came from the adapter card being integrated into the hard drive device. ***Enhanced Integrated Drive Electronics (EIDE)*** was a term introduced by Western Digital Corporation, a major hard drive manufacturer. EIDE hard drives originally used a new ATA standard known as ATA-2, Fast ATA, or Fast ATA-2.

Tech Tip:
IDE may be referred to as either Integrated Drive Electronics or as Intelligent Drive Electronics. In this textbook, we will use Integrated Drive Electronics as the norm.

Programmed Input Output (PIO) was introduced in 1995. The PIO standard was used in relation to early ATA and ATA-2 systems to classify data transfer rates, **Figure 9-19.** The PIO ATA system used the CPU to process the data transfer before DMA became standard. PIO is only mentioned because it is still listed in the CompTIA A+ exam objectives.

ATA Version	PIO	MBps
ATA	0	3.3
ATA	1	5.2
ATA	2	8.3
ATA-2	3	11.1
ATA-2	4	16.6

Figure 9-19.
ATA PIO data rates.

All the different terminology around the ATA/IDE drive connection can prove very confusing. Some manufacturers didn't wait for new standards to be implemented and came out with similar sounding names. Other manufacturers have changed the requirements for their standard. The requirements for EIDE have changed many times. Refer to **Figure 9-20** for ATA standards.

Some ATA designs use an adapter board inserted into the PCI slot to take advantage of higher data transfer speeds. When using the expansion slot to upgrade to a higher ATA standard, check if the motherboard chipset will support the higher ATA standard. Otherwise, the desired higher transfer speed of the newer ATA design may not be reached.

After all these advancements, many people still refer to the ATA design as IDE or EIDE, so when you are in the field talking to other technicians, remember that they are talking about the connection to the mass storage devices other than SCSI.

ATA Hard Disk Installation

Figure 9-21 illustrates two drives, one slave and one master, connected to a motherboard using an IDE interface connection point. Typical motherboards provide two sets of connections identified as IDE0 and IDE1. They provide two channels of communication to hard drives and to other devices such as CD-ROM, CD-RW, or tape drive systems. Each channel can provide an interface with the computer bus system for two hard drives, creating a total of four separate physical drives. Each channel consists of one drive designated as a master and the other designated as a slave. Moving jumper settings on the hard drive sets the designation of master and slave. See **Figure 9-22.**

When two or more drives are installed on the same PC system, one drive must be designated the ***slave*** and the other the ***master.*** The jumper settings are required because the two drives share the same communication cable. Failure to configure one device as master and the other as slave can result in hard drive failure. Think about the partitions in the hard disk drive system. When the PC is booted, it must be able to differentiate between the two or more drives. How can the BIOS system search out the active boot partition if it cannot tell the difference between the two hard disk drives installed on the same PC? By making one the master and the other the slave, one drive becomes the extension of the other. The BIOS system can now differentiate between the two drives and try each one out as it searches for the master boot partition.

slave
a secondary drive on an IDE channel.

master
the primary drive on an IDE channel.

Figure 9-20.
ATA standards.

Drive Specification	Features
ATA-1	The original ATA design released in 1988 used a 40-pin ribbon cable connector and featured a master, slave, and cable select option. It also used a programming technique to automatically identify itself to the BIOS system during setup.
ATA-2	Released in 1996, it allowed other storage devices to be connected to the bus system not just hard disk drives. It allowed disks up to 8.4GB to be accessed easily. It was also called Fast ATA because it featured faster DMA data transfer speeds than ATA-1.
ATA-3	A revised ATA-2 that allowed password protection for hard disk drive security and a few other minor changes.
ATA-4	A 1998 revision that allowed data transfer rates as high as 33 MBps. It is also referred to as UDMA/33 and Ultra ATA/33. ATA-4 also introduced an optional 80-conductor ribbon cable for the standard 40-pin connector. This modification reduced electrical effects that limited data transfer rates. The ATA-4 specification also integrated the ATAPI standard, which allows for the attachment of CD-ROM, tape drives, and other forms of mass storage devices that required an ATAPI interface.
ATA-5	Introduced in 1999 with a standard 80-conductor ribbon cable. The 80-conductor ribbon cable allowed for transfer rates as high as 66 MBps as long as the motherboard is designed to take advantage of the ATA-5 design. If not, the transfer rate is only 33 MBps. The ATA-5 is also referred to as UDMA/66.
ATA-6	ATA-6, released in 2000, offers transfer rates as high as 100 MBps. An 80-conductor-ribbon cable is again used with this design. If the motherboard is not designed for the ATA-6 specification, then the highest transfer speed will probably be 33 MBps.

Serial ATA

Serial ATA (SATA) was developed to overcome the limitations of the ATA drive. The SATA 1.0 maximum transfer rate is 150 MBps. The transfer rate is expected to reach as high as 600 MBps as other versions of SATA are developed and released. SATA has a higher performance than ATA because it moves data to the motherboard in a series of packets in a similar fashion to USB and Firewire. The ATA transfer rate is slower because it is limited to the clock frequency of the motherboard and to the effect of induction caused by the design of the flat ribbon cable. The SATA design can achieve a higher data rate because it generates its own frequency for the data transfer, and its cable is designed to reduce the effects of electrical induction. As you recall from earlier chapters, induction can limit the frequency of data traveling through a conductor, reducing data transfer speeds.

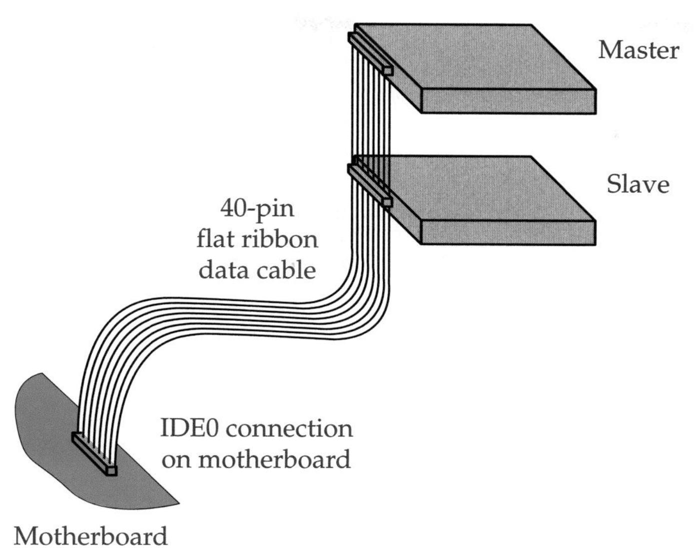

Figure 9-21. Illustration of two IDE hard drives connected to a motherboard. Two hard drives are connected as shown. One hard drive is the *master* and the other is the *slave.*

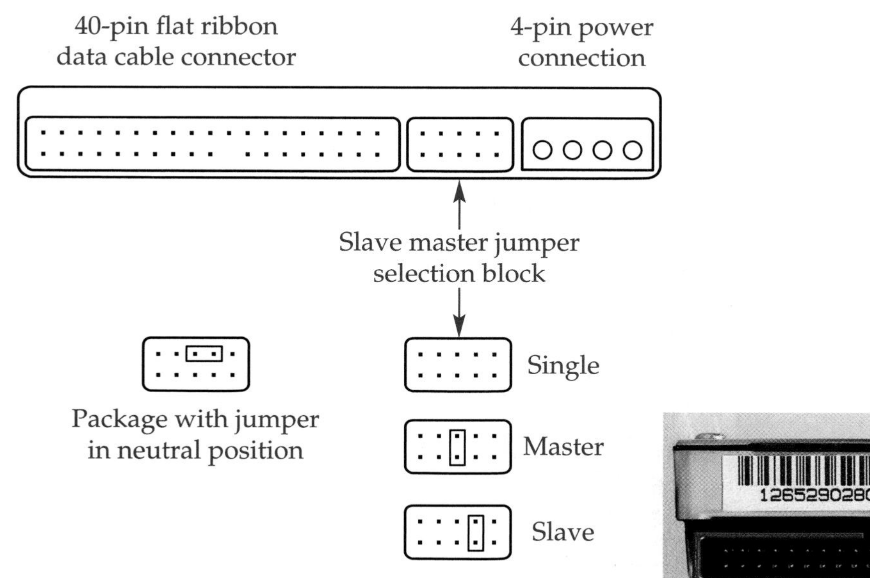

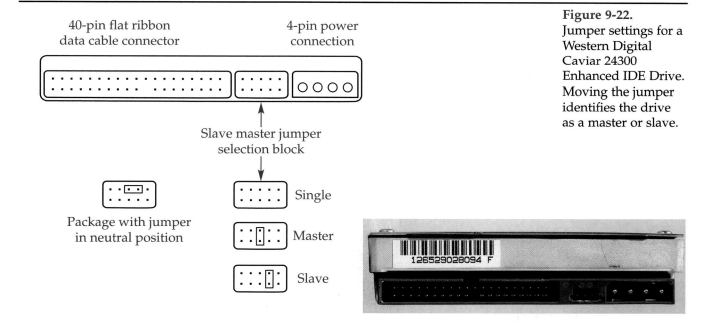

Figure 9-22. Jumper settings for a Western Digital Caviar 24300 Enhanced IDE Drive. Moving the jumper identifies the drive as a master or slave.

The SATA drive uses a thin, flat or round cable with 7 conductors and a 7-pin cable connector. This is quite a reduction in cable width compared to the width of the 40-pin and 80-pin ATA cables. Because of the width reduction, the SATA cable is much easier to route inside the computer chassis.

Look at **Figure 9-23.** Three of the seven conductors in the illustration are identified with the letter G, which represents ground. The pair of conductors used to transmit data are marked DT– and DT+. The pair of conductors used to receive data are marked DR– and DR+. The pairs of cables and the grounds are twisted together to reduce the negative effect of electrical induction on the data transfer rate.

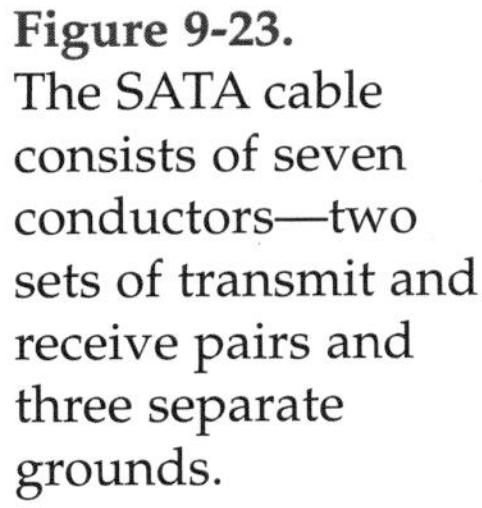

Figure 9-23.
The SATA cable consists of seven conductors—two sets of transmit and receive pairs and three separate grounds.

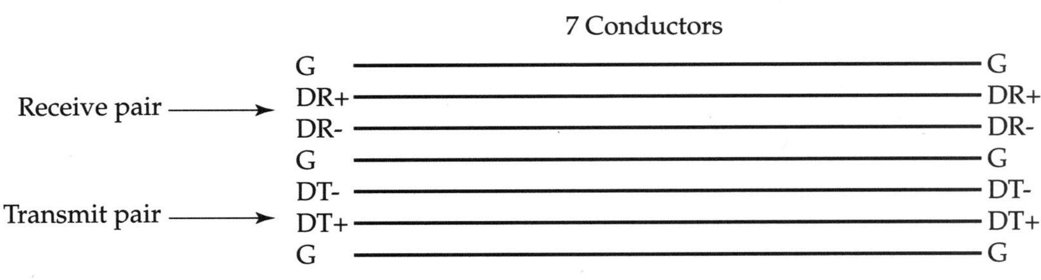

The SATA cable connectors are keyed to prevent a user from connecting the cable to the motherboard or to the hard drive incorrectly. The SATA cable is connected to the motherboard at locations identified as SATA 0 and SATA 1, **Figure 9-24.**

The SATA drive is designed with only two sets of connectors, power and data, **Figure 9-25.** There are no master/slave jumper pin connections to worry about. Each device is automatically set as master. There is no slave in the SATA design.

An existing computer system may be upgraded to SATA by using a SATA host adapter card. The host adapter card is installed in an available PCI slot. The SATA drive is then connected to the host adapter card using a SATA cable.

Figure 9-24.
SATA connections on a motherboard.

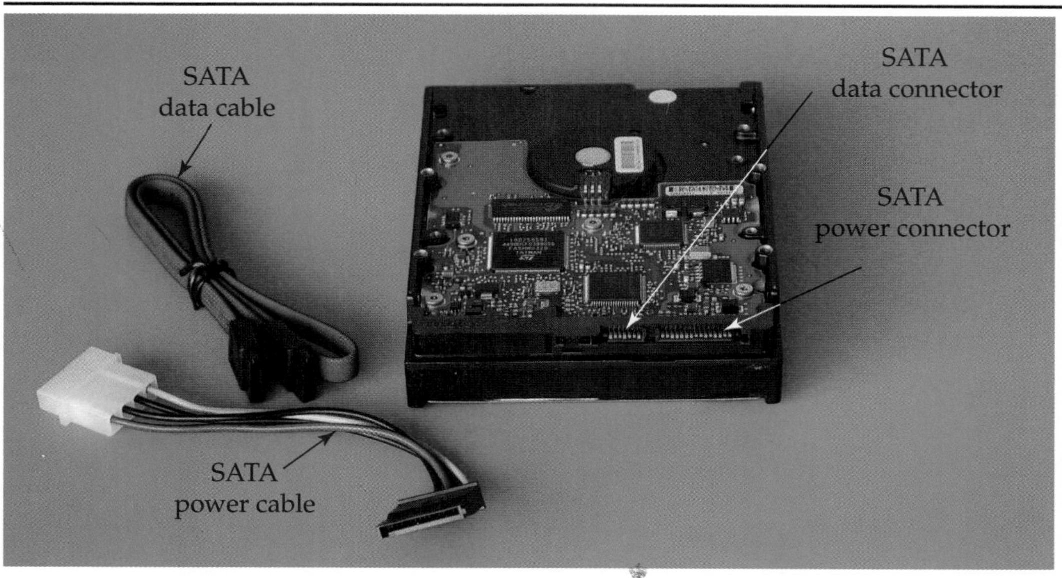

Figure 9-25. SATA drive and cables. A SATA drive has only two connectors: a data connector and a power connector.

When using a host adapter card, you must check that the BIOS and motherboard will support the SATA technology. Even if SATA is supported, the motherboard BIOS may report the SATA drive as a SCSI drive. The SATA system should perform normally even if it is identified as a SCSI drive. Also note that only one SATA drive can be connected on a SATA cable. This means that there can only be a total of two SATA drives connected to motherboard or to the host adapter card.

Tech Tip:
During the early implementation of SATA, regular ATA drives were fitted with a bridge adapter and a SATA conversion chip at the manufacturers and then marketed as SATA drives.

SCSI Interface System

Small Computer System Interface (SCSI), pronounced *skuzzy,* uses an adapter board and connects up to seven devices on one flat ribbon cable. This is the standard system used by Macintosh/Apple and many UNIX mainframe systems to connect peripherals. Because it was fairly expensive, SCSI technology was slow coming to the PC market. It was first used in the IBM market for file servers that required a lot of disk storage. File servers are like super PCs that control network systems. They are covered in more detail in later chapters.

small computer system interface (SCSI)
the standard interface used by Macintosh/Apple and many UNIX mainframe systems to connect peripherals.

The SCSI standard was developed, in part, to remedy compatibility problems between PCs and aftermarket hardware. Original market concerns created proprietary systems in early PCs. PC upgrading and expansion was a challenging task because of the compatibility issues. SCSI was designed to eliminate some of these issues by creating a standard that was available to all manufacturers.

The SCSI system was also designed to free the CPU from the burden of processing all data transactions. SCSI interfaces with a PC through an intelligent controller card inserted into the expansion bus. A SCSI bus cable connects the SCSI card to a series of devices. These devices, as directed by the controller card, can communicate freely along the bus cable, eliminating the need for the CPU's involvement.

Figure 9-26 shows a typical SCSI-1 installation. The SCSI-1 standard allows for eight devices at maximum to be connected to a SCSI-1 cable. One of these is the host adapter card. The ID numbers assigned range from 0 to 7 (eight numbers total). SCSI-2 allows for 15 devices to be assigned.

A+

A+ Note:
The quantity of SCSI devices allowed can make for a tricky question on the A+ Certification exams. When asked how many devices can be connected to a SCSI-1 cable, the correct answer is eight. However, eight may not be one of the multiple-choice answers. In that case, the answer is seven. Look to see how the question is worded. Eight devices can be connected to the cable. Seven devices can be connected to a host adapter card. In various reference materials, you will see it written that seven devices can be connected to a SCSI-1 cable. This is written because the host adapter card is understood to be a necessary part of the installation. Read and answer the question carefully.

There are many styles of SCSI that have developed over the years. The main three classifications are SCSI-1, SCSI-2, and SCSI-3, **Figure 9-27.** There are variations of these three SCSI styles that can easily be confusing. Some of the names are Wide SCSI, Fast SCSI, Fast Wide SCSI, Ultra SCSI, Ultr-2 SCSI, Ultra2 SCSI, and Wide Ultra2 SCSI. When selecting SCSI hardware to install or replace, you

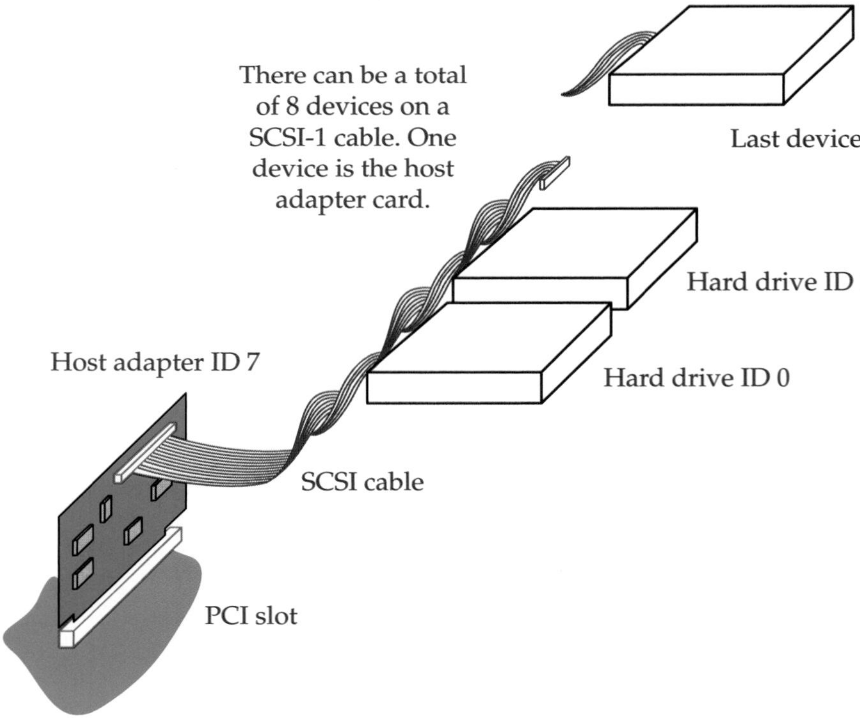

Figure 9-26.
Typical SCSI setup. There can be a total of eight devices including the adapter card.

Controller	Maximum Number of Devices	Typical Devices	General Information
SCSI-1	8–the host adapter plus seven devices	Hard drive, CD-ROM, scanner	Low transfer rate 5 MBps
SCSI-2	8 to 16–the host adapter plus 7 or 15	Hard drive, CD-ROM, CD-RW, DVD, tape drive, scanner	Fast SCSI is 10 MBps Fast Wide is 20 MBps
SCSI-3	16–the host adapter plus 15	Hard drive, CD-ROM, CD-RW, DVD, tape drive, scanner	Various speeds from 20 MBps to 160 MBps

Figure 9-27
SCSI standards.

must exercise caution. Though SCSI was originally created to help solve compatibility problems, many of the SCSI systems are still not compatible with each other. The problem lies in the many proprietary variations.

You must be careful to match the device to the proper SCSI technology. *SCSI-1* uses an 8-bit system and supports data transfer rates as high as 5 MBps. It was the first SCSI technology. It uses a 25-pin flat ribbon cable. *SCSI-2* is similar to SCSI-1, but it uses a wider, 50-pin connector and supports up to seven devices on one cable. *Wide SCSI* uses a wider cable with 68-pins, hence the name "Wide SCSI." Wide SCSI can transfer 16-bits of data at one time. *Fast SCSI* uses an 8-bit bus similar to SCSI-1, but has a much higher transfer rate of 10 MBps. There are also Fast-20, Fast-40, and Fast-80 SCSI systems. The last two digits of the name reflect the speed of data transfer in megabytes per second. The speed of each can be doubled by the use of a Fast/Wide device. Hence, a Fast/Wide-20 will produce a data transfer speed of 40 MBps.

Tech Tip:
Be careful when checking the speed of a device. When abbreviated, megabits per second is Mbps while megabytes per second is MBps. The small change in the case of the "b" means a very large change in the speed of the device.

Serial Attached SCSI (SAS) is the latest development for SCSI technology. Serial attached SCSI is similar in design to SATA. The SCSI device transfers data in serial fashion rather than in parallel. The SAS design allows 128 devices to be attached directly and can be expanded to as many as 4,032 storage devices. The SAS can be expanded to 4,032 devices total through the use of edge expander devices.

SAS has achieved data transfer rates as high as 3 Gbps. Note that a SAS is expressed in gigabits per second (Gbps) not gigabytes per second (GBps). Gbps is used as a measurement for *serial* type data transfers. Since SAS transfers data in a serial fashion, Gbps is technically correct. For comparison to other SCSI standards, 3 Gbps is equal to 375 GBps. This is more than twice as fast as the 160 MBps transfer rate associated with the SCSI-3 standard.

Advanced SCSI programming interface (ASPI) is a programming language developed by Adaptec, Inc. It was developed for issuing commands between SCSI devices. It is the standard for programmers developing SCSI utility programs.

Advantages of SCSI

One advantage of SCSI is that SCSI devices can be connected inside or outside the computer case, leaving some flexibility for the user. IDE and EIDE are designed to install hardware inside the case. SCSI also has very high data transfer rates. Older SCSI hard drives were much faster than IDE hard drives. (New EIDE drives have closed that gap.) Most SCSI devices are also fully compatible with the Windows Plug and Play specification making installation simple. Some older SCSI systems may not be Plug and Play compatible.

A big advantage of SCSI in a multitasking environment is its ability to disconnect the communication between devices when the device is not needed, thus conserving resources. For example, when a tape is rewinding, it does not need to maintain its connection to another device. SCSI can disconnect the communication to and from the tape for a period of time and then go back and check if it is ready for additional communication.

In the SCSI technology system, equipment can be easily exchanged. At the most, the driver may need to be upgraded. To a SCSI host adapter, all hard drives look the same, as do other SCSI devices such as printers and optical drives. Of course the total capacity of the drives may differ. There is no need for slave and master arrangements as there is with IDE/EIDE. Each device is given its own unique ID number.

SCSI ID

SCSI ID number a unique number assigned to a device on a SCSI chain and used to identify that device.

SCSI devices must have a unique ***SCSI ID number.*** The ID range for the typical SCSI-1 is from 0 to 7 (eight ID numbers). When two devices attempt to control the SCSI bus at the same time, the device with the highest number takes control.

While any device connected on the SCSI cable can have any ID number assigned, there are some common assignments. The host adapter is usually assigned the number 7, and hard drives are usually assigned 0 and 1. The host adapter is usually given the highest priority number. These are normal SCSI assignments, but they are not mandatory nor a recognized standard. It is simply a general practice.

The original SCSI limit of eight devices was first expanded by the use of SCSI bus extenders. The bus extenders were integrated circuit cards that connected as SCSI devices. They allowed an additional seven devices to be connected within a SCSI system. See **Figure 9-28.** As the SCSI-1 system was expanded, an additional system of identification was needed. The additional devices connected to the SCSI extender are identified using ***logical unit numbers (LUN)*** from 0 to 7.

logical unit numbers (LUN) an identifier used with SCSI extenders to distinguish between (up to) eight devices on the same SCSI ID number.

Expanders can also be found in some SCSI-2 systems. They may be referred to as expanders, repeaters, and regenerators. The use of LUN ID is not limited to only SCSI storage drives. LUN ID is often used to identify nonstorage devices connected on a common SCSI cable, such as SCSI compatible CD-ROM, DVD, and tape drives.

SCSI ID Jumpers

Older SCSI systems used jumpers to identify devices. Look at **Figure 9-29.** The picture illustrates how a set of pins and jumpers might look on a SCSI device. The pins are actual electrical connections and the jumpers are used to make an electrical connection across the pairs of pins. The jumpers are set in the

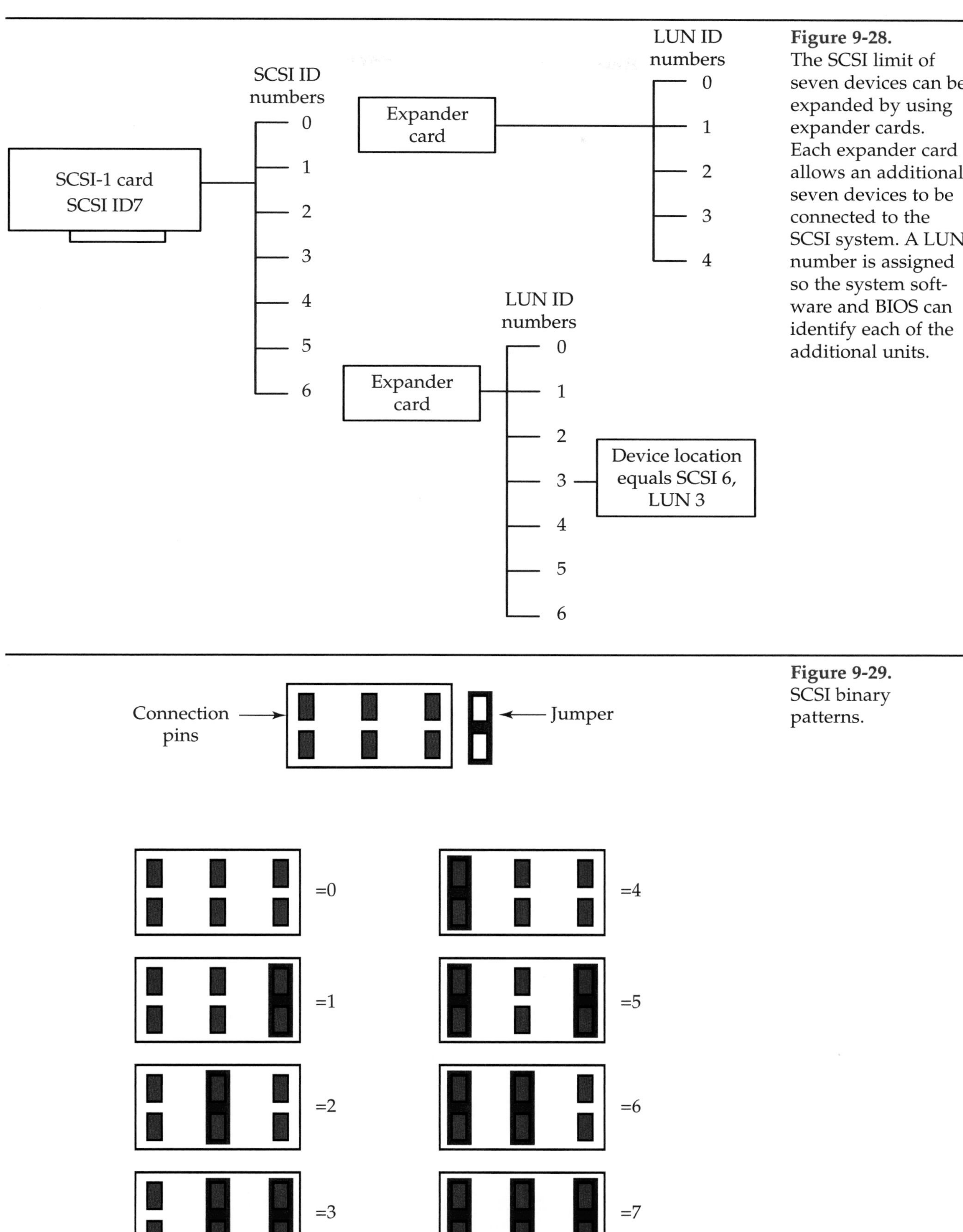

Figure 9-28.
The SCSI limit of seven devices can be expanded by using expander cards. Each expander card allows an additional seven devices to be connected to the SCSI system. A LUN number is assigned so the system software and BIOS can identify each of the additional units.

Figure 9-29.
SCSI binary patterns.

binary pattern that represents the SCSI ID number. If you have trouble interpreting the jumper patterns, you may wish to review the first chapter in the textbook, which illustrates and discusses binary numbers.

LVD and HVD

SCSI systems communicate using two different voltage levels identified as *High Voltage Differential (HDV)* and *Low Voltage Differential (LVD)*. HVD uses 5 volts for a high and 0 volts for a low. LVD uses 3.3 volts for a high and 0 volts for a low. The high and low voltage levels are represented by a binary one or zero respectively. The advantage of HVD is that data can be transmitted on longer cables than on LVD. HVD can transmit data on cables up to 25 meters long while LVD is limited to cables 5 meters long.

The SCSI trade organization has excellent reference material, such as detailed charts of SCSI connectors, at their Web site www.scsita.org. Also, Adaptec and other hard drive manufacturers listed at the end of this chapter contain SCSI information.

SCSI Commands and Terminology

In the SCSI system, there are two classifications of hardware that relate to communication between SCSI devices. They are targets and initiators. The SCSI host adapter card is usually the *initiator*, while the devices connected to the SCSI bus (printers, hard drives, tape drives, and other SCSI devices) are usually the *targets*.

SCSI has its own set of commands, which are used to control the flow of data and the communications between devices, targets, and initiators. There are also nine special control signals used in a SCSI system. They are as follows:

1. **C/D (Control/Data):** This control signal allows the target to signal if it will return a command or data to the initiator. The initiator will wait for the data or command.
2. **I/O (Input/Output):** This indicates whether the target will be sending or receiving on the data bus.
3. **MSG (Message):** The target uses this control signal to send error messages or status conditions back to the initiator.
4. **REQ (Request):** This control signal allows the target to obtain data from the bus.
5. **ACK (Acknowledge):** This is a reply signal sent back after the REQ signal. It acknowledges the REQ signal and takes control of the bus.
6. **BSY (Busy):** This control signal lets other devices know that a device is busy.
7. **SEL (Select):** This control signal is used to select a target device.
8. **ATN (Attention):** This control signal informs the target that a message is coming.
9. **RST (Reset):** This control signal resets all devices on the bus system.

These signals are sent on wires inside the complete cable assembly. By placing a high or low voltage level on the wire, a signal is sent between initiator and target devices. Additional wire in the cable assembly supplies data and power. These commands are invisible to the user.

SCSI Cable

SCSI cables are designed in many variations, **Figure 9-30.** The cable itself is either single-ended or differential. A single-ended cable simply carries the signal from the initiator to the target. Each wire carries the signal to the target and to a common ground. There is a terminating resistor located at each end of the cable to absorb stray signals.

In the other design, called differential, a pair of wires is used for each signal transmitted. By using a pair, the signal travels simultaneously from the initiator to the target and from the target to the initiator. This transmission cancels the effects of electrical noise generation. The system still uses terminating resistors at each end to absorb the signals. The main advantage of the differential design is that it can be used for greater distances, up to 25 meters. In high-speed data transmissions, single-ended cable may be required to be as short as 1.5 meters.

SCSI Termination

Each end of the SCSI cable must be terminated immediately after the last device on the end of the cable. Without the terminators, data would be garbled. The high-speed transmission of data through the cable would produce an effect similar to radio broadcast waves. These waves would echo and return to the ends of the cable causing the data to be garbled.

Cable termination is classified as either active or passive. *Passive termination* uses resistors to terminate the cable on each end. Passive termination is powered through the cable itself and is good for short runs of up to one meter. Passive termination works well for cables limited to the inside of the PC case. *Active termination* requires the use of an external power supply. It uses a voltage regulator and resistors to control the amount of voltage transmitted inside the cable and to absorb the signals at the end of the cable. The active terminator allows greater lengths of SCSI cable to be used. It is typically used for cable runs outside the computer case to connect devices such as flat bed scanners.

Figure 9-30.
Typical SCSI device and cabling. The back of this SCSI CD-RW drive has two SCSI cable connectors. The photo on the right shows the ends of a cable connector. Compare the cable connector on the left (SCSI) to the cable connector on the right (parallel).

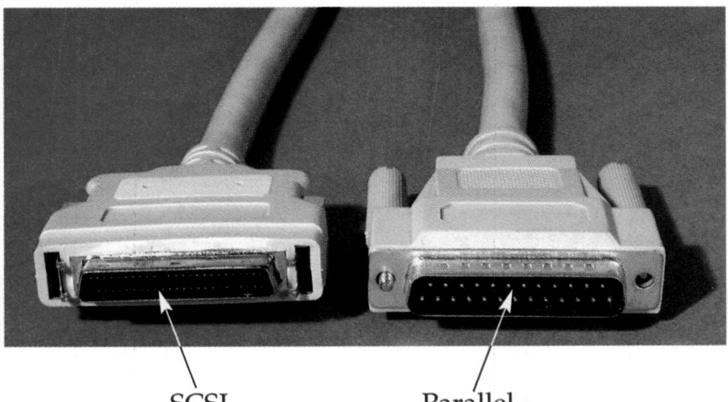

SCSI Bus Operation

The first part of communication on the SCSI bus is the control of the bus. The control of the bus can only be attempted while there is no active BSY or SEL signal on the bus. Both BSY and SEL must be idle. Only one device can communicate on the bus at a time, so the device must gain exclusive control of the bus. The device that has control is the initiator. When a device is attempting to take control of the bus, it is called the *arbitration phase.* Once a device (the initiator) has taken control of the bus, it identifies the target device. Identification of the target device is called the *selection phase.*

The individual devices negotiate the control of the SCSI bus. When two devices attempt to take control of the bus at the same time, the device with the highest assigned ID number wins control. This is the reason that the host adapter is usually assigned the highest number. In a SCSI-2 system, the host adapter is usually assigned the number 7.

The initiator sends a BSY signal a SEL signal. After the initiator has transmitted data or a command, it then releases the BSY signal. The target then receives the data and issues a BSY signal until a reply with data or a command such as ACK is transmitted. The following steps are an example of how a typical communication might take place between two devices:

1. The system checks that the bus is idle with no BSY or SEL signal.
2. Arbitration takes place until the device chosen as the initiator takes control.
3. Selection of the target takes place.
4. The target device acknowledges the communication link.
5. The target notifies the initiator that it is ready to receive data.
6. The data is transferred to the target device.
7. Status of the data transfer is maintained. For example, are there any errors?
8. A message indicating all the data has been transferred is sent.
9. The bus is released to all devices.

Tech Tip:
When putting a SCSI system together with multiple devices, one device at a time should be installed after the host adapter card is installed. Using this method, it is easy to isolate a problem with an individual device if it arises during assembly. Also, note that all devices on your SCSI chain must support (or not support) parity. Some SCSI devices use parity and others do not.

SLDRAM

SyncLink DRAM (SLDRAM) is a new technology called solid state disk (SSD). It is a Plug and Play storage device designed to replace the traditional hard drive system. It is constructed with no moving parts, which creates greater data transfer rates and lower failure rates. Typically, the SSD is constructed of DRAM chips, a CPU, a BIOS chip, and a battery. It actually simulates a miniature PC that allows the SSD to communicate independently with the computer's CPU and with other independent devices such as RAM. At this time, it is used only in network servers, but as prices decrease, it will likely be used in standard PCs.

Tape Drive

Magnetic tape storage was the earliest removable storage media used with computer systems. Tapes can hold a tremendous amount of data and have long been used for backing up large amounts of data. Tape drives were also the preferred method of sending data from one location to another before the full development of the Internet, **Figure 9-31.**

A storage tape is created by covering a plastic tape with a thin flexible coating of metal oxide, similar to the coating on floppy disks and hard disk platters. A read/write head transfers data to and from the tape. The data is stored on the tape as a long series of magnetic pulses. The principles used to store and retrieve data on a hard drive also apply to the magnetic tape system, **Figure 9-32.**

Figure 9-31.
Typical tape drive.

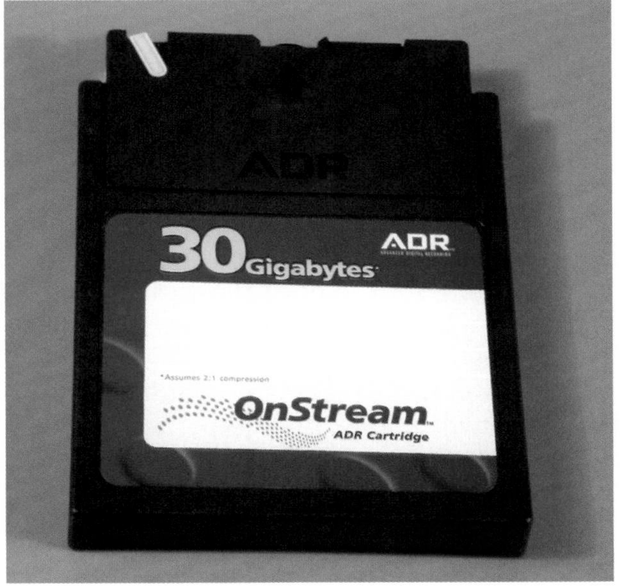

Figure 9-32.
Large storage tapes are often used to back up systems. This tape can hold 30GB of data.

The tape uses a format similar to disks. A file allocation table is used to keep track of sectors on the tape. A tape must also be formatted before it can be used. Formatting a tape is similar to formatting a disk except that it takes a great deal of time because of the tape's large capacity. Tapes are generally preformatted when they are purchased, saving hours of valuable time. Some of the top-of-the-line tape systems can format a tape as they are being used.

The one main disadvantage of using tape is that the data must be read sequentially. That is to say you must start at the beginning of the tape and search through the data sequentially until you find what you need. Hard drives, floppies, and CD-ROMs allow you to access data anywhere on the disk without having to pass through all of the data saved previously. Still, for inexpensive, dependable backups of large data systems, the tape has been the preferred media. However, with the development of CD-RW and DVD disc systems, tape drives have diminished in popularity. CD-RW and DVD give the advantages of both large storage capabilities and random access. Tape systems will continue in industry as conversion from tape to disc continues, but they will soon be obsolete.

Tech Tip:
The importance of system backups cannot be overemphasized. Once total loss of data or programs has been experienced, the need to back up becomes obvious. Most cases of a total loss of data revolve around the failure of a hard drive that contained all original data. While operating system software can be reinstalled, original data can be lost forever. Data recovery techniques are discussed later. However, data recovery techniques are not always successful, and they are certainly more time-consuming than replacing files with copies from a backup disc or tape.

Tape Formats

Early tape drive systems were not standardized. If data was saved on any particular manufacturer's tape drive system, it most likely could not be read by a different tape drive system. Manufacturers used different recording schemes and, at times, even the physical sizes of the tapes were not compatible. Due to the demand for standardization, the Quarter-Inch Cartridge (QIC) was developed by a group of manufacturers. Tapes are identified by a combination of letters and numbers such as QIC-40 or QIC-80. The numbers are strictly identification numbers. They do not correlate to the length of tape or the amount of data.

In 1983, the first tapes were based on the 4 × 6 × 5/8 original size of recording tapes. Later the 3¼ × 2½ × 3/5-inch cartridge was developed. The larger cartridge would not install in a typical PC bay, hence the need for the smaller physical size standard. The larger cartridge was referred to as a data cartridge (DC), and the smaller tape cartridge was called a minicartridge (MC). Minicartridges can contain over 13GB of data on a single tape. By using compression techniques, some tape standards such as digital linear tape can reach capacities of over 70GB.

Minicartridges are not all compatible. The compatibility issue is caused by mechanical differences between tape drives, especially in the read/write mechanism. Never assume that a mini tape recorded on one system can be read by a different tape drive. If the tape is to be used exclusively by one tape drive, there should be no problem.

There are other common tape systems. While QIC is the most common tape media, there are quite a few others that have been developed. Digital audio tape (DAT) uses a system to record data similar to the music industry. Exabyte Corporation has an 8 mm tape similar to the video industry. Digital Linear Tape (DLT) is a technology with very high storage capacities and long lasting tapes. It is an expensive system, but it has rapidly gained favor for backing up network systems. The 3M Company created the Travan cartridge tape as a patented proprietary system. Its different styles are identified as T-1 through T-4 type tapes.

Choosing a Tape Drive

When choosing a tape backup system, there are some things that should be considered. These factors include the following:

- The amount of data that needs to be backed up.
- The capacity for future growth of the system.
- The compatibility with other tape systems in the same or affiliate companies.
- The overall cost of the system as compared to other data backup systems.
- The speed of data recording and retrieval.

A balance between all factors should be made. Not all scenarios will require the same equipment for a backup system.

Floppy Disks and Drives

Floppy disks are soft magnetic disks used for storing small to moderate amounts of information, **Figure 9-33.** It is similar in design to the hard drive except that the media disk is readily accessible. The ***floppy drive*** reads and writes to floppy disks, and it has been a standard device on PCs for quite some time. There have been many predictions about the end of the floppy drive, but they are still hanging in there, **Figure 9-34.**

floppy disk
soft magnetic disks use for storing small amounts of information.

floppy drive
a device that reads and writes to floppy disks.

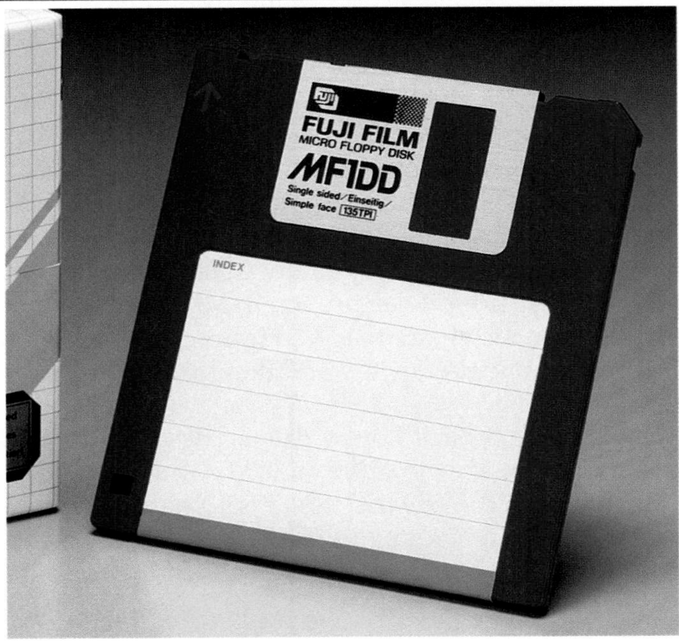

Figure 9-33.
Early floppy disks were very flexible, earning them the name "floppy." Today's disks have hard shells that have little flexibility.

Figure 9-34.
Typical floppy disk drive.

Think of a floppy drive as an unsealed hard drive package. In the hard drive system, the data is stored on platters. In the floppy drive system, the data is stored on removable diskettes.

The original disk media was a thin, Mylar (plastic) disk covered with metal oxide. It was stored inside a paper jacket when not in use. This media was easily exposed to the environment, and data was often lost due to improper handling. Users were taught not to touch the disk media with bare hands and to avoid laying the disk down without the protective jacket. These early disks were easily damaged. The 3½″ diskette was designed with a durable plastic case surrounding the entire disk media. The protective jacket and the data media were supplied as a single unit rather than as two separate pieces. This provided much more security for the disk. The data on the media was well protected when not inserted in the floppy drive. The added rigidity of the plastic case of the 3½″ diskette gave even more protection. The original floppy disks could easily be bent or warped resulting in failure of the disk inside the disk drive. Data on the newer plastic diskettes is protected from dust and lint particles. The older style floppy was exposed to contaminants even when properly stored.

The floppy drive, as we know it, has evolved from a large 8″ disk, to a 5¼″ disk, and to the standard 3½″ disk with which we are all familiar, **Figure 9-35.** The early 8″ and 5¼″ diskettes were packaged in a hard paper or thin layer of cardboard or plastic. Today's diskettes are packaged in a thicker, durable plastic. However, the diskette inside the package is still "floppy," giving the medium its name. With the improvement of manufacturing capabilities, the physical size of diskettes steadily decreased while the amount of storage available on a diskette greatly increased. The 3½″ floppy has proven to be one of the most dependable and popular devices ever installed on a PC. **Figure 9-36** shows a table listing the three common storage capacities for the 3½″ floppy. The 1.44MB format is the widely accepted format.

Figure 9-37 diagrams a typical floppy drive. The operation of a floppy drive is simple. The disk spins inside the drive at 300 revolutions per second. A read/write head, similar to the one discussed with hard drives, moves across the disk's surface through an opening in the disk cover called the head window. The read/write head moves into position over one of the concentric tracks to read or write as necessary.

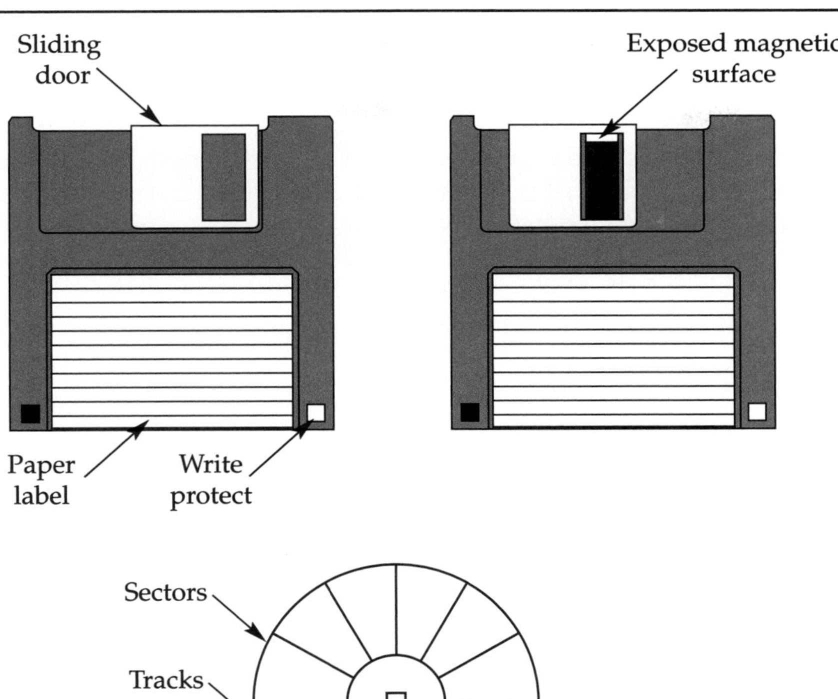

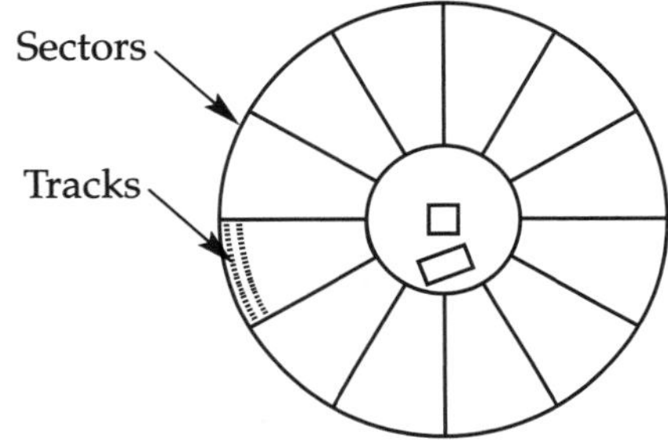

Figure 9-35. The features of a typical floppy disk.

Physical Size	Type	Capacity
3.5	Double density	720KB
3.5	High density	1.44MB
3.5	Extra-high density	2.88MB

Figure 9-36. Floppy disk capacities.

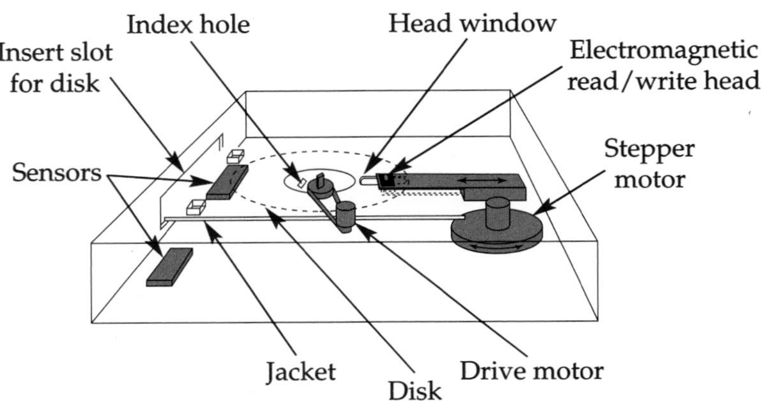

Figure 9-37. Parts of a floppy disk drive.

Figure 9-38 shows power and cable connections for a floppy drive. The data cables for floppy drives have a twist near one of the connectors. The connector near the twist is attached to the drive unit.

The file system on a floppy disk is similar to that on a hard disk with the exception of partitions. A floppy disk cannot be partitioned. As with hard drives and tapes, floppy disks must be formatted before they can be used to store data. Most disks today are preformatted when purchased.

The Windows operating system gives the user two options for formatting a diskette, quick or full, **Figure 9-39.** The quick format simply erases the FAT. The full format erases information across the entire disk and checks for bad sectors.

Floppy Disk Drive Repairs

Repairing a floppy drive is practically obsolete. The replacement of a 3½″ drive is so inexpensive that labor costs for a typical disk repair far exceed replacement.

Figure 9-38. Cable and power connections for a floppy drive. The data cabling is the same for all floppy drives. However, many drives come with a two-jack mini power connector.

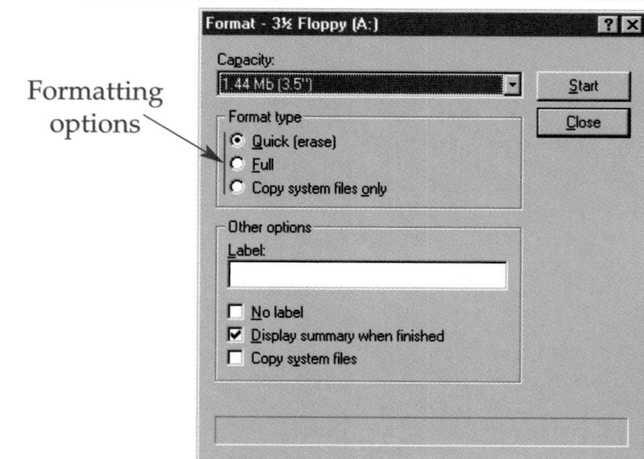

Figure 9-39. When formatting a floppy disk, there are two formatting options, quick and full. Quick can only be used on a floppy that has been previously used or formatted. Most floppy disks are now formatted by the manufacturer.

Cleaning

Floppy drive repair is usually limited to cleaning the read/write head. A commercial head cleaner kit can be used and is recommended over cleaning the head manually with alcohol and a foam swab. Cleaning the head manually involves removing the floppy drive from its mount. A commercial kit involves inserting a special cleaning floppy disk.

Disk Drive Alignment

Disk alignment is important. A misaligned disk drive will probably go unnoticed… until you attempt to use a floppy disk created on another computer. A misaligned disk drive will not read a disk from a properly aligned disk drive, or the material it does read will seem to be plagued with data errors. A misaligned disk drive will also find errors when attempting to read a floppy disk from an original software package.

Disk alignment is a questionable repair. The easiest and quickest solution is to replace the drive. Attempting to realign the read/write head is typically a waste of valuable time. Correcting a misaligned head involves purchasing software to assist in the realignment, as well as mechanically adjusting the head alignment.

Tech Tip:
Before replacing a misaligned disk drive, remember to copy all floppy material to the hard drive or to some other backup media. Once the drive has been replaced, all of the old floppy disks will become unreadable. Just as a misaligned floppy drive cannot read data from an aligned floppy drive, an aligned floppy drive will not be able to read the disks created on the old misaligned floppy drive.

If there is a large amount of data stored on floppies created by the old drive, there is one other solution. You can install an additional 3½″ drive in an available bay space on the PC. With this option, the original misaligned floppy drive is still around allowing you to access any disk recorded with the old drive. As each old disk is discovered, the data can be transfered from the bad drive to the new 3½″ drive.

LS-120 Drive

The ***LS-120 drive,*** also called a ***floptical,*** is a very high capacity disk drive that is able to store 120MB of data, **Figure 9-40.** This is quite an increase when compared to the 1.44MB capacity of an ordinary floppy disk. The *optical* part of fl*optical* infers that an optical system is part of this drive. However, the optical system is not used to record data. Data is recorded in a manner similar to any typical floppy drive or hard drive. The difference between the floptical and regular floppy drive is in the size and number of tracks per disk. The LS-120 uses many more tracks in thinner lines. It can also simultaneously write to 20 tracks, creating a much higher data transfer rate than the typical disk drive.

LS-120 (floptical) drive
a very high capacity disk drive that is able to store 120MB of data on a single disk.

This technology requires a much more precise alignment than the typical alignment found on a 3½″ drive. An optical system guides the read/write head

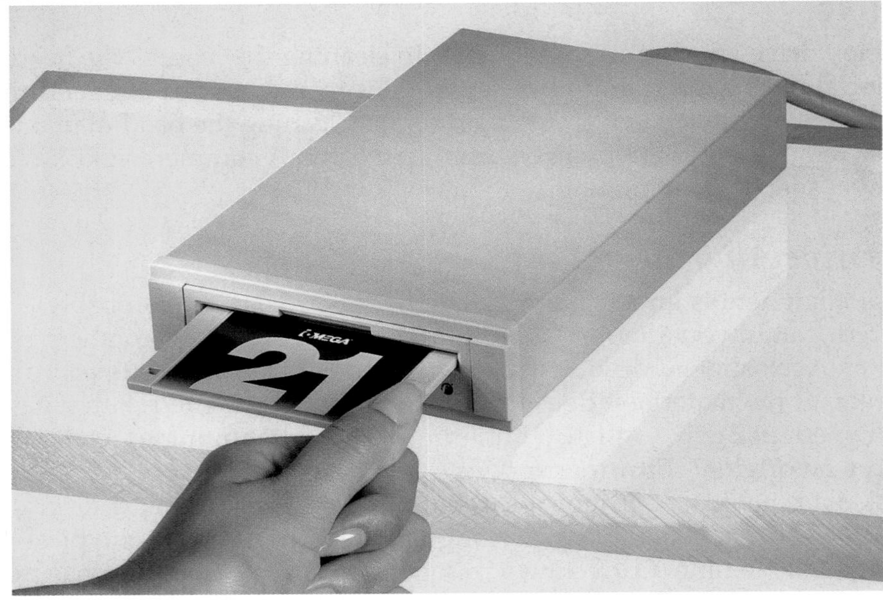

Figure 9-40. Floptical drives, like the one shown here, can read and write to regular floppy disks as well as to their own high storage disks.

into proper alignment each time the disk is run. An alignment track is permanently etched into the recording disk. A laser beam is reflected from the alignment etch and this keeps the read/write heads in perfect alignment each time data is transferred to or from the disk. The laser alignment is used in place of the typical mechanical alignment of a read/write head. By using the laser for tracking the alignment, the disk can store over 80 times the data of a typical floppy disk of the same size. An additional advantage of the LS-120 is that it can also read/write to regular floppy disks.

Zip Drives

Zip disk
a form of removable computer data storage that can contain over 100MB of data.

A ***Zip disk,*** **Figure 9-41,** is another form of removable computer data storage. The Zip disk is similar to a floppy disk in physical size. Like the floppy disk, a Zip disk contains a flexible metal oxide covered disk surrounded by a hard plastic shell. The typical Zip disk, however, can contain over 100MB of data.

The Zip drive, **Figure 9-42,** differs from conventional floppy disks in the head design. The head used for reading and writing in a Zip drive is approximately one-tenth the size of that used for a floppy drive. This allows the Zip drive to write data using 2118 tracks as compared to 135 tracks on a floppy.

Zip drives also use the multiple zone recording (MZR) technique used on modern hard drives. This technique, as discussed earlier in this chapter, allows for more sectors on the outer portions of the disk leaving little wasted space. A typical floppy disk has the same number of sectors on the outside track as on the innermost track.

The Zip drive can be installed internally or externally. Internal installations use either SCSI or (E)IDE technology. Externally, a Zip drive typically uses the

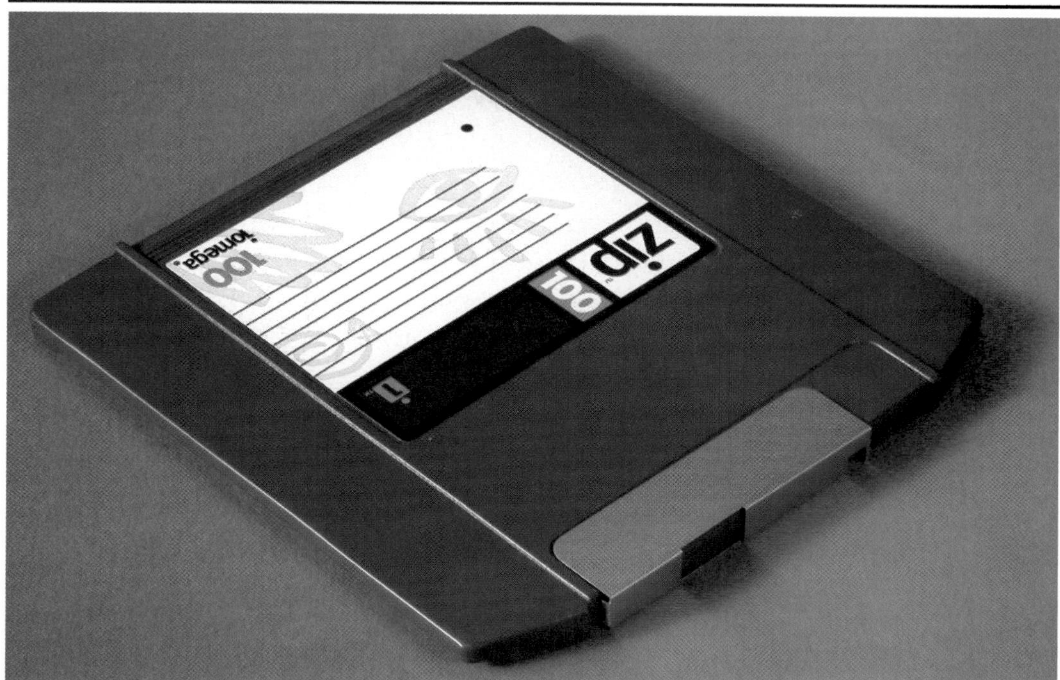

Figure 9-41.
A Zip disk is slightly larger than a floppy disk.

Figure 9-42.
Standard external Zip drive.

parallel port. Before CD-ROM drives were common, a portable Zip drive connected to the parallel port was a popular way to back up or transfer files.

Summary

- The hard drive is divided into sectors, cylinders, and tracks.
- A sector spans 512 bytes of storage space.
- The smallest unit of storage on a disk is a cluster.
- A cluster is composed of one or more sectors.
- Another name for cluster is allocation unit.
- Tracks are concentric circles of data storage areas on a disk.
- A cylinder is a vertical collection of tracks spanning two or more platters.
- Hard drives can be divided into multiple partitions to simulate additional drives.
- **Fdisk** and **format** are commands used to partition and format disks.
- The file allocation table contains information about how the clusters on a disk are being used and which clusters are associated with others.
- FAT16, FAT32, and NTFS are common file storage technologies.
- Encrypted file system (EFS) is the native encryption system used with the NTFS file system.
- Files become fragmented under normal disk operations.
- FAT16 is compatible with most operating systems.
- The ScanDisk program checks the disk surface integrity.
- The manufacturer of the hard disk drive performs low-level formats. Technicians or users generally perform high-level formatting.
- SCSI is a bus system that typically connects up to seven devices on a high-speed connection to a PC. There are many different styles of SCSI.
- SCSI devices connect to the PC through an adapter board, and each device will have its own ID number.
- SCSI must be terminated at each end of the cable. There are two types of SCSI terminator used: active and passive.
- Floppy drives are common, useful tools for recording small files.
- Tape drives can be used to back up large amounts of data.
- An LS-120 drive, also called a floptical, can store 120MB of data, and it can read/write to a standard 3½″ 1.44MB floppy disk.
- Zip drives are like large floppies that can be used to store over 100MB of data.

Review Questions

Answer the following questions on a separate sheet of paper. Please do not write in this book.

1. The magnetic polarity produced by a conductor is directly related to the direction of _____ through the wire.

2. The magnetic patterns left on a disk represent _____ numbers.
3. What is another term used for allocation units?
4. What DOS command is used to partition a hard disk?
5. What is multiple zone recording?
6. When is the MBR created?
7. Each primary partition or volume must contain a _____ _____ _____.
8. What is the maximum size hard drive that can be formatted using a FAT16 file system without more than one partition?
9. What information is contained in the file allocation table?
10. What are the three major interface technologies used for hard disk systems?
11. On which file system can EFS be used?
12. What is the maximum number of physical hard drives that can be installed on a typical PC with two IDE channels?
13. How many drives are designated as master on a PC with two channels and four physical hard drives?
14. How many logical drives can a typical PC designate?
15. What is the maximum data transfer rate of SATA 1.0?
16. How many SATA drives can be connected to a SATA cable?
17. How many hard drives can be installed on a type SCSI-1 interface?
18. How many devices can be attached to a SCSI-1 cable?
19. How many devices can be attached to a SCSI-2 cable?
20. What is the data transfer rate of SAS?
21. What is the expected high voltage level of SCSI HDV and LDV?
22. How is so much more data stored on a Zip drive diskette as compared to a conventional 3½″ high-density floppy?

Sample A+ Exam Questions

Answer the following questions on a separate sheet of paper. Please do not write in this book.

1. You install a new second hard drive to increase the total storage capacity of a PC. Both hard drives are installed on the same data cable. When you boot the system, the computer displays the BIOS information and the RAM test on the screen. After the RAM test is completed and passed, the PC hangs up. What is most likely the problem?
   a. The BIOS needs to be upgraded to match the new hard drive.
   b. A virus has been introduced into the system from the new hard drive.
   c. The jumper settings identifying master and slave are incorrect.
   d. The two drives' positions are reversed on the data cable.

2. Where in a FAT16 file system is the MBR located?
   a. In the first disk sector
   b. In the last disk sector
   c. The exact location varies according to the number of cylinders.
   d. An MBR is only on a hard disk system formatted for NT4.0.
3. Which command is used to partition a hard drive?
   a. **format**
   b. **format /s**
   c. **fdisk**
   d. **fdisk /part**
4. Windows 98 operating system can be installed on which of the following file formats? Choose all that apply.
   a. FAT16
   b. FAT32
   c. VFAT
   d. NTFS4.0
5. When preparing a new disk, the **format** command performs which of the following functions?
   a. Creates a root directory
   b. Sets the first partition to active
   c. Checks for bad sectors on the disk surface
   d. Creates a master boot record
6. A certain file consists of 12 sectors. The sectors are not contiguous but rather they are divided into two separate areas of the disk. Which technical term listed below is used to describe this condition of file storage?
   a. Cross-linked sectors
   b. File fragmentation
   c. Multiple zone recording
   d. Multiple sector storage
7. Which of the following technologies is not used for disk storage?
   a. ATA
   b. IDE
   c. SCSI
   d. DDS
8. What is the size, in bytes, of the smallest typical disk sector?
   a. 256
   b. 512
   c. 1024
   d. 2048

9. What is the maximum number of hard drives that can be installed on a SCSI-2 configuration?
   a. 5
   b. 9
   c. 15
   d. 24
10. On a Windows 98 operating system, the ScanDisk utility is located where?
    a. In **Control Panel**, under **DOS Utilities**
    b. **Start | Programs | Accessories | System Tools | ScanDisk**
    c. **Start | Programs | Utilities | ScanDisk**
    d. In **Control Panel** under **Disk Utilities**

Suggested Laboratory Activities

Do not attempt any suggested laboratory activities without your instructor's permission. Certain activities can render the PC operating system inoperable.

1. Using a lab PC identified by your instructor, experiment with the **fdisk** command. Try to set up multiple partitions on one physical drive. Also, try to create FAT32 and FAT16 file systems. Boot the system before formatting any of the partitions to observe the error generated. Format the same hard drive and reboot the system to observe the error generated. Now format the partition using the **/s** switch, which installs system files to the partition. Boot the system once more to see if any errors are generated.
2. Install a second disk drive sharing the same data cable as the original drive.
3. Use the **fdisk/status** command issued from the DOS prompt to reveal information about the hard drive's partition tables.
4. Access Seagate or Western Digital's Web site. Download any hard drive utilities that are available. There are usually hard drive utilities that will identify the type of hard drive installed, perform diagnostics, or allow access to hard drives too large for DOS and older BIOS systems.
5. Check a floppy disk and a hard drive with ScanDisk. Choose to perform a thorough scan.
6. Access the BIOS setup utility and find information about the hard drive configuration. See if it is auto detected or assigned a number. See if there is information about the number of heads, cylinders, and sectors. See if you can find controls to change the boot order (which boots first, floppy, hard drive, or CD-ROM drive). Do not make any changes to the BIOS setup without your instructor's approval.

Interesting Web Sites for More Information

www.maxtor.com
www.adaptec.com
www.quantum.com
www.scsita.org
www.seagate.com
www.westerndigital.com
www.ibm.com

Chapter 9
Laboratory Activity
Typical ATA (EIDE) Hard Drive Installation

After completing this laboratory activity, you will be able to:

- ❑ Replace a hard drive on a typical PC.

  or

- ❑ Add a second hard drive to a PC.

Introduction

The replacement of a hard disk drive is a common PC repair. Fortunately, the mechanics of the replacement are very simple. Back up any important data before beginning this activity. When replacing a hard drive or adding an additional hard drive to a PC, *always* back up important files. The original hard drive can be inadvertently damaged during the installation process. For example, confusion or distraction could result in executing commands such as **fdisk** or **format** to the wrong drive.

This laboratory activity, with slight alterations, can be used to add an additional hard drive to a computer. If your instructor has you add an additional hard drive, skip the removal portion of the activity (steps 2 through 7).

Equipment and Materials

- Typical PC with Windows 95 operating system or later.
- Additional hard drive.

Procedure

1. ______ Back up your data!
2. ______ Be sure the power is off to the PC. Remove the cover of the PC unit. Follow all anti-static procedures.
3. ______ Inspect the position of the hard drive and cables. Make a drawing of all cable positions if necessary.
4. ______ Remove the cables (power and data) from the existing hard drive. Do not forcibly pull on the cables. Make sure you remove the cables by pulling on the connector and not the cable itself. Some cable assemblies are poorly made, and the cable can be pulled apart from the connector.
5. ______ Hard drives mount in various ways. Inspect the mounting carefully before removing any of the screws. Unscrew the hard drive mounting screws. Place the screws in a safe location so they will not be lost. A paper cup or small container will prove very handy.

6. ______ Slide the drive out of the mounting. *The drive should remove easily.* If there is a lot of resistance when trying to remove the drive, check for an additional screw.

7. ______ If there is more than one hard drive on the computer you are working with, check the jumper positions on the hard drive you have removed for slave or master identification.

8. ______ Check the jumper settings on the hard drive you are about to add. Make sure the master/slave jumper on the new drive is set to match the drive removed. If there will be only one hard drive in the machine, the jumper should be set to master or single (no setting).

   If you are installing an additional hard drive, the jumper setting will be determined by where you install the drive and what is already installed in your machine. If you are adding the drive to an empty cable, the drive can be set as master or single. If you are adding the device to a cable that already has an EIDE device attached, the settings of the preinstalled and new device must be checked. One device must be set as a master and one device must be set as a slave. (Note that the hard drive you will be booting from must be set as a master.)

9. ______ Insert the new drive. Mount it into position using the mounting screws.

10. ______ Attach the power and data cables. When attaching the flat ribbon data cable, be sure to align pin 1 on the hard drive to the colored stripe on the cable assembly. Pin 1 on the hard should be identified by a number stamped on the drive. It is usually the pin closest to the power connection. The stripe on the cable is most often red, though it can be blue. Some cables will have a 1 printed on the proper conductor. See the illustration.

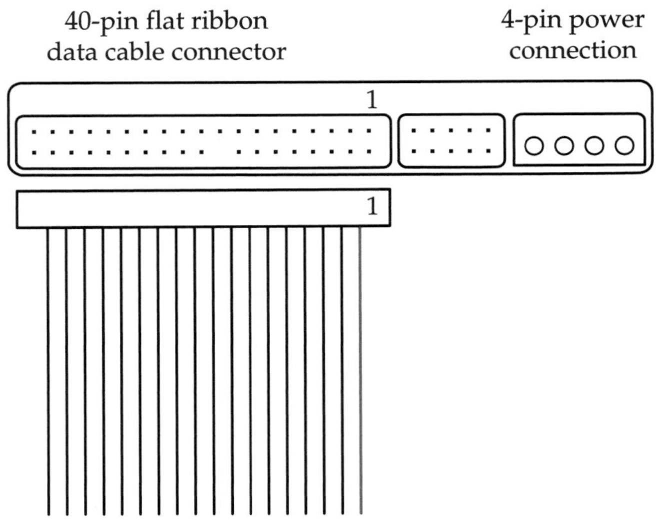

11. ______ Before closing the PC cover, power on the PC and boot the system.

12. ______ The new drive should be automatically detected by the Windows operating system. If the drive is not detected, you may have to adjust the CMOS settings. Some drive manufacturers supply a disk with software for their hard drives should a problem arise.

13. ______ When everything is normal, power down the system and attach the PC case.

14. ______ After the new hard drive has been installed, you need to perform an fdisk to setup partitions on the new drive, even if it will only have one partition. After you perform the fdisk, proceed to format each partition.

If the computer will not boot up, check that all cables are connected properly. Cables can come loose when installing a new component inside the PC. Also, check if the BIOS supports the drive you are installing. You may need to upgrade the BIOS. Check the Web site of the drive manufacturer for the latest information. Many manufacturers provide free downloads of diagnostic software for their drives.

Tech Tip:

In the field, before you replace a suspected bad hard drive, you will want to verify that the hard drive is actually bad. Try installing the suspect drive in another PC to verify it is indeed bad. There are many items, such as the data cable, the EIDE on the motherboard, or a boot sector virus, that would make the hard drive appear to be defective.

Review Questions

Answer the following questions on a separate sheet of paper. Please do not write in this book.

1. What is the first thing you should do before you install a new hard drive? Why?
2. What are the possible jumper settings if your PC has only one hard drive? What are your jumper options with two hard drives?
3. How is proper data cable alignment assured to prevent connecting the cable backward to the hard drive or motherboard?

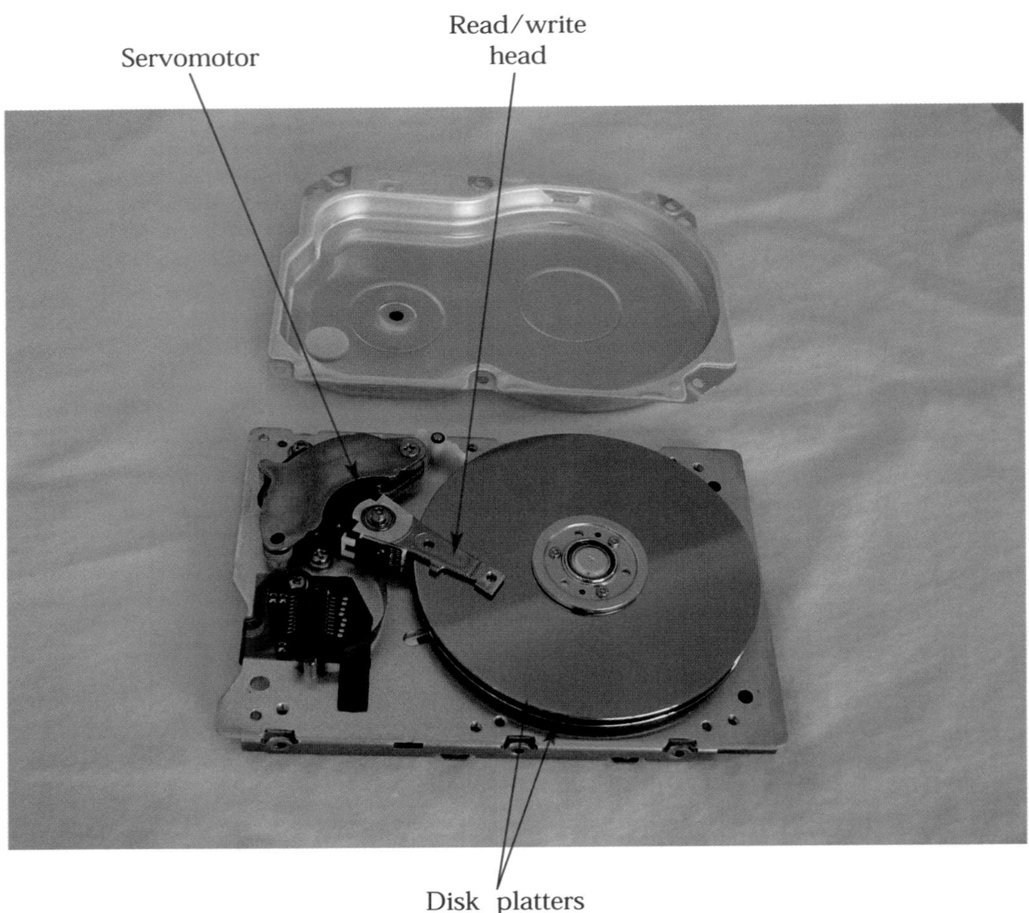

Disassembly of an older (or nonfunctioning) hard drive will allow you to see how the mechanical and electronic parts of a hard drive work together. Do not attempt to open any hard drive that you intend to use again for data storage. Once a hard drive case has been opened, the drive cannot be used.

CD Technology

After studying this chapter, you will be able to:

- Explain how data is stored and retrieved using optical storage devices.
- Describe how CD and DVD discs are constructed.
- Explain different CD formats such as CD-ROM, CD-R, CD-RW, and DVD-RW.
- Describe major parts of a CD and DVD storage device.
- Define Sierra format.
- Explain the steps for installing an optical drive.
- Discuss the compatibility of different CD and DVD formats.
- Explain the CD file systems, ISO 9660, and UDF.

A+ Exam—Key Points

- Know the differences between CD types and DVD types of discs.
- Be familiar with the different storage capacities of disc types.
- Be familiar with disc compatibility.
- Know the various ways that disc drives can be added to an existing computer system, such as SCSI, EIDE, USB, and FireWire.
- Be familiar with the disc standard (colored) books. Know which colors describe which specifications.

Key Words and Terms

The following words and terms will become important pieces of your computer vocabulary. Be sure you can define them.

access time
Advanced SCSI Programming Interface (ASPI)
AT Attachment Packet Interface (ATAPI)
CD-ROM File System (CDFS)
colored books
Compact Disc Read Only Memory (CD-ROM)
Compact Disc Rewritable (CD-RW)
Compact Disc-Recordable (CD-R)
constant angular velocity (CAV)
constant linear velocity (CLV)
data transfer rate
Digital Versatile Disc (DVD)
High Sierra format
ISO 9660
land
magneto-optical (MO) drive
packet writing
photocell
pit
Universal Disk Format (UDF)

Optical data storage began with the CD-ROM. It revolutionized the methodology for storing and retrieving data. Great amounts of data could be stored in much smaller physical areas. The CD-ROM paved the way for economical computer storage of music, graphics, and video. This unit discusses and explains CD and DVD technology associated with the PC.

CD-ROM

Compact Disc Read Only Memory (CD-ROM)
an optical disc able to store very large amounts of data.

In 1978 Philips and Sony Corporations developed the ***Compact Disc Read Only Memory (CD-ROM),*** an optical disc able to store large amounts of data. CD technology was originally developed to replace plastic records and tapes used in the music industry and not directly for computer storage, **Figure 10-1.**

Tech Tip:
Note that spelling *disc* with a *c* is a common practice to indicate optical disc or CD. Spelling *disk* with a *k* is used when discussing floppy and hard disks.

The first CD-ROM devices were large 12″ platters. By 1982, the 4.72″ platter became the standard.

To see the layers built into a CD-ROM, look at **Figure 10-2.** A typical CD-ROM is composed of a polycarbonate (plastic) wafer approximately 1.2 mm thick. The base of the wafer is coated with an aluminum alloy. This is where the actual data is encoded. A final layer of plastic polycarbonate is used to seal the aluminum alloy layer. A label is then placed on the top of the CD. The data is read from the bottom of the CD, not the label side. Data is recorded on the aluminum disc as a series of pits and lands.

pits
the holes etched into a compact disc in order to record data.

lands
the flat areas between the pits in a compact disc.

The ***pits*** are holes etched into the disc and ***lands*** are the flat areas. The lands reflect the light of the laser beam. The pits disperse the light rather than reflect it back. Digital data is recorded to the CD track as a series of pit and land sequences. The pits and lands convey the binary values of 1 and 0. Changes from lands to pits and pits to lands create 1s. Lack of change for defined periods of time creates 0s.

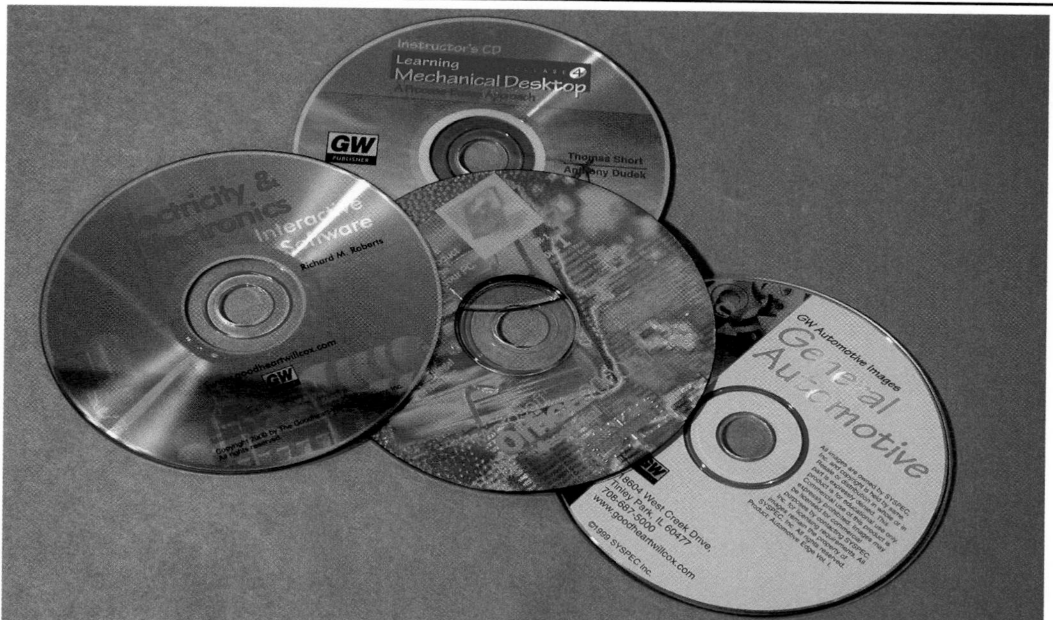

Figure 10-1. Typical CDs. CDs can hold 650MB to 700MB of information.

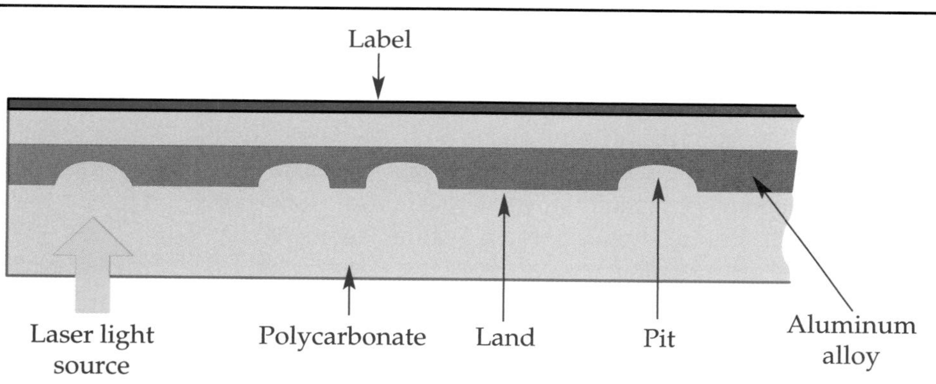

Figure 10-2. Cutaway view of a typical CD.

Most CD-ROMs are mass-produced using a laser to etch the surface of a disc known as the *master*. The master is then used to stamp out copies of the original data pattern onto many more plastic discs. The mass-produced discs are copies of the original. The plastic disc is then coated with a thin film of aluminum reflective material. The aluminum material follows the pits and lands etched into the plastic. An additional layer of plastic seals the aluminum material, and the outside is given a smooth finish to allow the laser light to pass freely through the surface.

A CD-ROM drive uses a laser diode to read the disc, **Figure 10-3.** The laser diode produces a laser light when energized. The laser produces a low-energy infrared beam. A servomotor in the drive follows commands issued by software to position the beam on the track on the disc. The pits defuse the light, while the lands reflect the light. The reflected light strikes a photocell, which is sometimes referred to as a photo detector. A ***photocell*** is an electronic component that changes light energy into electrical energy.

photocell
an electronic component that changes light energy into electrical energy.

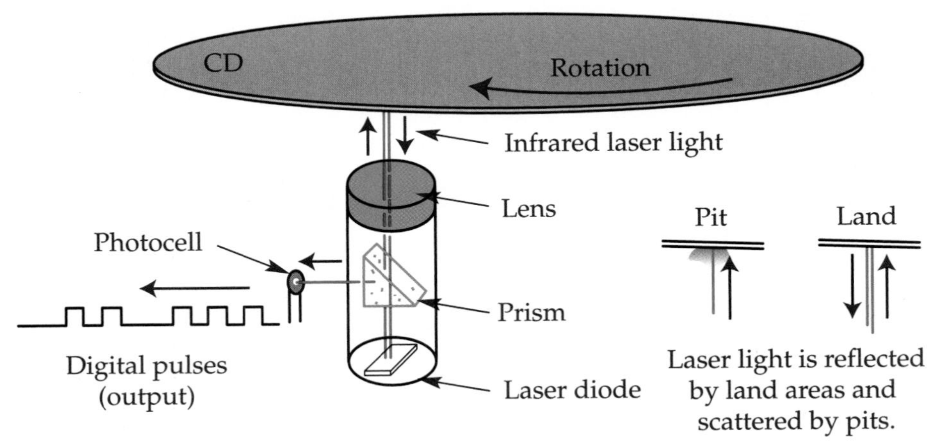

Figure 10-3. A laser diode sends a beam of light through a prism and onto the CD. If the light hits a land, the light is reflected. Pits disperse the light. The reflected light travels back through the prism, which sends some of the light to a photocell. The photocell turns the light into digital electrical pulses.

The light reflected off the CD produces a pattern that replicates the data stored on the disc. The light is reflected to the photocell where it generates electrical pulses. These electrical pulses are reproduced as a digital signal (on or off), and they represent the binary codes used to encode the data on the CD. Once the information stored on the CD is converted to digital signals, it can be utilized by the computer system. A typical CD-ROM contains between 650MB and 700MB of information.

Warning:
Caution should be taken when working with any laser source. Permanent damage can result to the retina of the eye. There are specially designed safety glasses for working on lasers. As a computer technician, you should never work directly on the parts inside a CD device. The CD device is considered a field replacement unit.

The CD data is organized somewhat differently than on a hard drive platter. The CD uses a spiral technique to record data rather than dividing the platter into sectors, **Figure 10-4.** By using a spiral technique, it is possible to increase storage capacity. There is no wasted space as is found on the conventional hard disk platter.

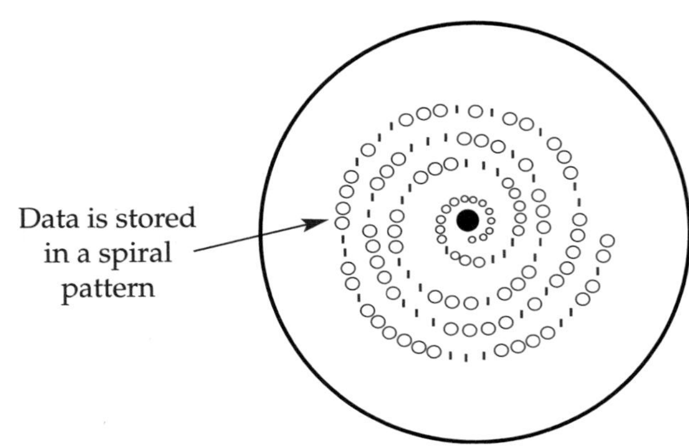

Figure 10-4. CDs store data differently than hard drives. CDs do not use sectors.

Two major advantages of optical storage over magnetic storage are capacity and stability of data storage. Using the same physical amount of storage area, much more data can be stored using optical systems than magnetic systems. Optical systems are also more stable than magnetic systems. Magnetic systems such as floppy disks and hard drives maintain data for approximately five to eight years before they must be refreshed (written again). Optical storage does not have this limitation. There is debate over how long a CD-ROM can last before it degrades to a point where it cannot be read. Some estimate 10 to 25 years. Other estimates put the lifespan of the discs at over 100 years.

CD-R

With ***Compact Disc-Recordable (CD-R)*** technology, you have a CD upon which you can write data. This type of disc was first called CD-WORM (Write Once Read Many). With CD-R data *can be* erased and the disc *can be* written to again. However, it cannot be written to a previously recorded sector. A previously recorded area *cannot* be recorded on again. When an area on the CD is said to be *erased,* the data is actually still present. It simply can no longer be accessed. Consequently, every time a file is updated on a CD-R, the existing file is made inaccessible and a new section of the CD-R is used to store the newest version of the file. **Figure 10-5** shows a typical CD-R disc.

Compact Disc-Recordable (CD-R) an optical storage media that uses photosensitive reflective dye to simulate the pits and lands of a standard CD.

A CD-R is designed with a photosensitive transparent organic dye layer placed against an aluminum alloy layer inside the CD. The photosensitive layer reflects light in its natural state. Thus, in its natural state, it appears as one long land to the CD reader. When exposed to the recording laser light, the photosensitive layer changes from a reflective state to an opaque state. Instead of reflecting light, it absorbs the light from the laser similar to the pits used in the standard CD.

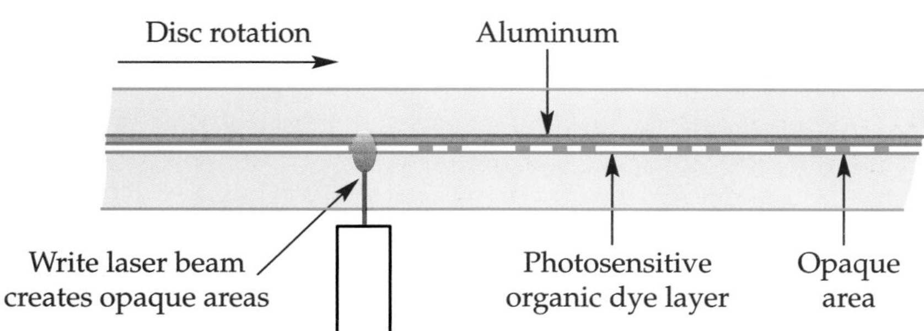

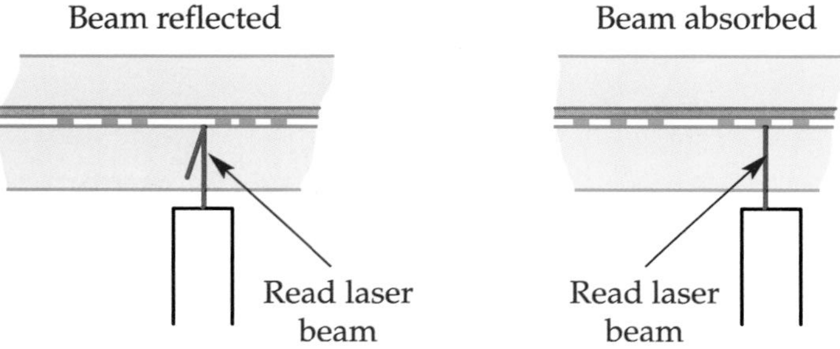

Figure 10-5. One laser writes to the CD-R while a second laser is used for reading.

Note that with these discs you can actually see where you have recorded your data. With the stamped CDs, the entire disc has universal shine. With CD-R discs, the area that has been recorded reflects light differently than the unrecorded area, **Figure 10-6.**

CD-R is being rapidly replaced by CD-RW (discussed next). You will still encounter the CD-R in existing PCs for some time, but virtually all new PCs come with combination CD-RW and DVD recordable systems.

CD-RW

Compact Disc-ReWritable (CD-RW) an improvement over the CD-R technology, featuring special discs that can be erased and rerecorded.

The ***Compact Disc-ReWritable (CD-RW)*** is an improvement over the CD-R. The CD-RW read and write technology allows the same sections of a CD to be written to many times instead of only once. A special polycrystalline structure is sandwiched inside the plastic platter, **Figure 10-7.** The polycrystalline is a composite silver-indium-antimony-tellurium layer.

This technology uses a laser beam that has two states of intensity: low heat and high heat. When the polycrystalline structure is exposed to the high heat 932°F–1292°F (500°C–700°C), it loses its reflective quality. When the low power beam of the laser 392°F (200°C) is applied, it changes the surface back to a reflective quality. By applying the high and low beam heat effects on the polycrystalline structure, the reflective quality of the disc can be arranged (and rearranged) into a state similar to the land and pit technique. This means that previously recorded areas of the disc can be rewritten to, allowing for a

Figure 10-6. Notice the change in the appearance of the CD-R disc. Data has been recorded on the inner circle.

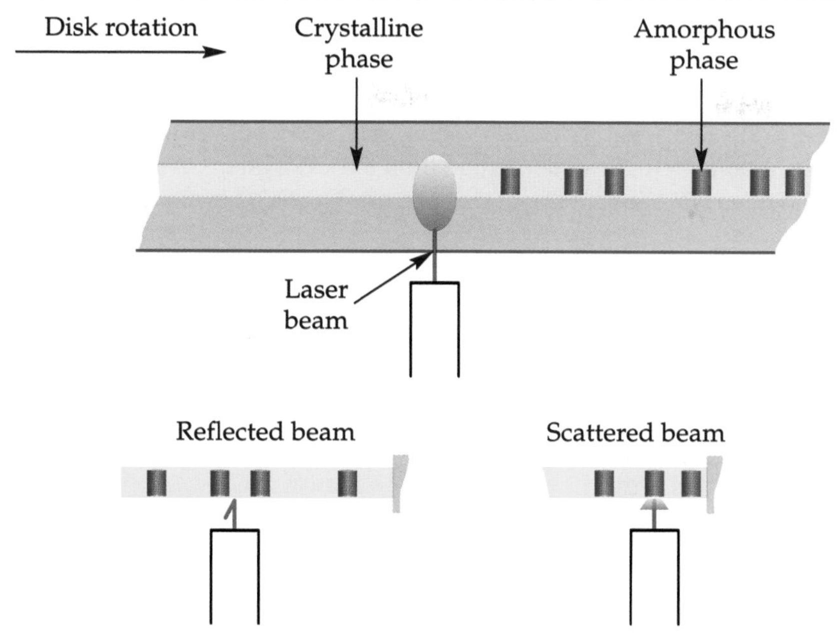

Figure 10-7. With the CD-RW process, firing a laser at its high intensity causes the disc to lose its reflective quality. The firing of a low intensity beam returns the reflective quality to the material.

data-recording media similar to a hard drive or floppy disk. The CD-RW has become a cost-effective media for low-volume data backups.

Compatibility issues have, at times, plagued the CD industry. Older CD players will often not be able to play new CDs, in particular CD-RWs. This lack of recognition is related to the intensity of the light used to represent the lands and pits on newer discs. The original CD standards required that the CD reflect at least 70% of the light striking the land. With the pits, no more than 28% of the light could be reflected. On the modern CD-RW, the land areas reflect no more than 15% to 25% of the light striking the surface of the land. This is well below the early standard of 70%.

Today's modern CD and CD-RW systems can read older technologies and make adjustments for the various light reflective intensities. However, the older technologies cannot make these adjustments. Consequently, a CD-RW made on a PC today, may not be readable by a CD system that is not CD-RW capable. Typically, only a CD-RW can exchange data with another CD-RW.

CD Specifications

Two of the most common CD specifications are data transfer rate and access time. The ***data transfer rate*** is a measurement of how much data can be transferred from the CD to the PC random access memory in a set period of time. This standard is usually given in KBps or MBps. If a manufacturer claims a transfer rate of 1MBps, they are claiming that the CD can transfer a steady stream of data at 1 megabyte per second. Data transfer rate is more important if you transfer a lot of data from a CD on a continual basis. Playing games off of a CD is one use where you would like a high data transfer rate.

data transfer rate a measurement of how much data can be transferred from a CD to RAM in a set period of time.

Tech Tip:
Be careful when reading manufacturers' claims. Sometimes, they use the numbers based upon compression techniques rather than true data transfer time. Another method of producing a higher-than-normal transfer figure is by incorporating software that uses your hard drive as a buffer to cache information from the CD system. With this type of software, any CD-ROM drive will appear to be faster and any CD-ROM system can be used this way.

access time
the amount of time that passes between the issue of the read command and when the first data bit is read from the CD.

The access time for a CD is measured in much the same way as it is for a hard disk. The ***access time*** is the amount of time that passes between the issue of the read command and the point in time when the actual first data bit is read after it has been located on disc. Because the amount of time delay will vary according to where the data is physically located on the CD, the rating is usually an average. If you run applications where you periodically access a CD, access time becomes a more important time factor.

When upgrading a CD-ROM drive, be sure of what you are trying to achieve. Consider why you are upgrading. A better access time and transfer rate will not deliver a significant difference in performance to the average user. However, if the drive is being used as part of a tower in a network system, it can make an important difference in the performance. **Figure 10-8** shows a comparison of CD-ROM drive access and data transfer rates.

constant linear velocity (CLV)
a method of reading data from a CD where the speed of the CD drive adjusts so that points on the inside and outside of the disc are read at a constant linear velocity.

Note that CD-ROM drives are commonly advertised as 8X, 24X, or 40X. This naming convention is relative to the speed at which the disc is spinning, with 1X set by the speed at which the early CD-ROM drives turned.

There are two methods of reading data from a CD, constant linear velocity and constant angular velocity (CAV). ***Constant linear velocity (CLV)*** was used on earlier CD drives. It varied the speed at which the CD was spinning to keep points on the inside and outside of the disc spinning at a constant linear velocity. To better understand this concept, we must look at the relationship of

Figure 10-8.
Table showing the access times and the data transfer rates of a selection of speeds of CD-ROM drives.

Speed	Access Time	Data Transfer Rate
1X or Single-speed	600 ms	150 KBps
2X	320 ms	300 KBps
3X	250 ms	450 KBps
4X	135–180 ms	600 KBps
6X	135–180 ms	900 KBps
8X	135–180 ms	1.2 MBps
10X	100–150 ms	1.6 MBps
12X	100–150 ms	1.8 MBps
16X	100–150 ms	2.4 MBps
24X	100–150 ms	3.6 MBps
32X	100–150 ms	4.8 MBps
40X	50–100 ms	6.0 MBps

The X represents the base speed of the original music CD. For example, a 24X CD spins 24 times faster than a 1X CD.

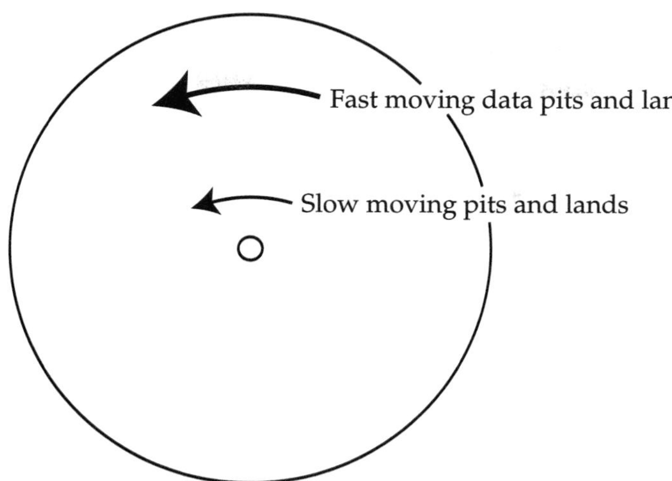

Figure 10-9. Although the *rpm* of a CD remains constant, the *speed* of the CD varies from point to point. A point farther out on the disc has a longer distance to travel per revolution. Consequently, the point moves at a faster speed.

data location on the disc and the speed of disc rotation. **Figure 10-9** shows the relationship between the speed of rotation on the surface of a disc and the distance from the center of the disc.

All points on the surface of a disc that is spinning at a constant speed rotate at the same rpm. However, the farther any point is from the center, the faster that point will move. The point farther from the center has a longer distance to travel to complete its revolution, yet it has the same amount of time in which to complete it. Thus, data patterns at the outer edge of a CD move more quickly than data patterns in the center of the disc. CLV technology maintains the same speed of data transfer by varying the speed of the disc. When reading data from the outer areas of the disc surface, the rpm is reduced. When reading data from the inside areas, rpm is increased. By varying the speed of the spinning disc, a steady stream of data flow is maintained.

Modern drives use constant angular velocity technology. ***Constant angular velocity (CAV)*** maintains the same rpm regardless of the data location. These drives permit the data flow rate to change. With CAV technology, there is no more lost time while the CD-ROM drive adjusts its speed. Thousands of revolutions could be wasted with the CLV method while the drive sped up or slowed down to the proper speed.

constant angular velocity (CAV) a method of reading data from a CD where the drive maintains the same RPM regardless of the data location.

CD-ROM Formatting

Without some standard method for coding CDs, a CD generated on one CD device would be unreadable to a CD device made by a different manufacturer. Producers of CD technology foresaw these problems and met to set some standards for the industry. The first set of standards became what is known as the High Sierra format. This format was later modified into ISO 9660. This format is the worldwide standard for CD-ROMs. An additional format, UDF, was developed for ***packet writing*** of information. This format was developed primarily for the CD-RW and DVD systems.

packet writing records data in small blocks similar to the way hard drives store data.

High Sierra Format

High Sierra format
a standard for compact discs that was created so that CDs could be read on any CD device.

The ***High Sierra format*** is a standard for compact discs that was created so that CDs could be read on any CD device. The format got its name from the meeting place at the High Sierra Hotel near Lake Tahoe. CD-ROM industry representatives were interested in combining their efforts to achieve a common format they could all share. All members would benefit if they could use their CDs on any type of CD device.

The following explains the standard in simple terms. The first track on the CD identifies the CD itself as the media. It also synchronizes the CD with the drive mechanism. The disc also identifies the directories of data on the volume. The CD contains a Volume Table Of Contents (VTOC). This tells the CD drive how the data is laid out on the disc, similar to the FAT on a hard drive.

The spiral path of data on the CD does have sectors and clusters, but there is no need of tracks since the disc consists of one long spiral. The CD also contains a directory. The directory is used for organizing the data stored on the CD, but in contrast to the DOS system that relies on the directory structure to access information, a CD system can directly access files and information without going through the directory.

ISO 9660

ISO 9660
the file system standard that CD-ROMs use, an update on the High Sierra format.

CD-ROM File System (CDFS)
another name used for ISO 9660.

In 1988, the High Sierra format was transformed into ***ISO 9660.*** The two standards are identical in content. However, the exact formatting is different. The ISO 9660 format is the CD-ROM format used today. An interesting note to the ISO acronym is that it is also a Greek word "iso," which translates to mean "equal." The ISO 9660 is also called ***CD-ROM File System (CDFS).***

The ISO 9660 is a file system structure very similar to FAT16 but with many improvements. There is no limit to the size of the root directory, and it can contain up to eight levels of files and directories. Look at the example that follows:

F:\LEV1\LEV2\LEV3\LEV4\LEV5\LEV6\LEV7\LASTFILE

The root directory is F: and then there are seven levels of subdirectories ending with the file LASTFILE.

ISO 9660 supports long file names. However, if you intend to use it with an operating system like DOS, you must use the eight by three naming convention. The ISO standard for CD-ROMs allows only upper case letters, digits, and the underscore when naming a file or directory. Remember DOS allows the use of many special symbols in the name. The CD-ROM files are stored by sectors, usually 2048 bytes long, but they can be made larger or smaller. The sectors are numbered consecutively starting with sector zero.

UDF

Universal Disk Format (UDF)
the file system standard accepted for CD-RW, magneto-optical disc, and DVD technology.

The Optical Storage Technology Association (OSTA) was formed by manufacturers to create a file system structure that could be used for CD-RW, magneto-optical disc, and DVD technology. The file structure called ***Universal Disk Format (UDF)*** defines the new file system structure. It is the successor to the ISO 9660 file structure.

One of the greatest improvements of the UDF file system structure is that it allows for a bootable disc. One of the reasons CD-RW discs cannot be read by CD-ROM technology is the way the UDF file structure is organized.

Disc System Standards

Disc system standards are outlined in a series of specifications referred to as the ***colored books.*** Each set of specifications is classified by book color. The *red book* describes the physical properties of compact disc audio and graphics. The *yellow book* was written to describe the requirements of using CD technology for computer data storage systems. The *green book* describes the specifications of interactive CD technology (CD-i). The *orange book* standard describes recordable CD media. The *white book* is used for video standards. The *blue book* is an expanded version of music standards referred to as *CD Plus* or *Enhanced Music CD* discs.

colored books
the set of books that outline disc system specifications.

The CD standards contain information about the physical description of tracks and overall physical dimensions as well as data formats, data encoding, disc compression, light reflection intensities, and error correction techniques. The standards are designed to allow for compatibility between different manufacturers in the industry.

Magneto-Optical Drives

Magneto-optical (MO) drives combine magnetic and optical principles to store and retrieve data on a CD-like disk. The MO disk is constructed of a magnetically sensitive metal crystal that is sandwiched between two plastic disks.

magneto-optical (MO) drives
disk drives that combine magnetic and optical principles to store and retrieve data.

When writing to the MO disk, a laser heats the plastic surrounding the metallic crystal. This allows the crystal to change its orientation on the disk when exposed to the magnetic field of the write head. When the plastic cools, the metallic crystal is aligned along the disk track representing the binary information, **Figure 10-10.**

To read the data from the disk, the CD is spun while the laser is focused on the track. This time the laser uses much less power and simply provides light to be reflected back to the photodiode. The reflected light is slightly polarized by the magnetic domain. The direction of the polarization represents the bit pattern stored on the disks. For example, a north pole orientation may represent a binary one, while a south pole orientation may represent a binary zero.

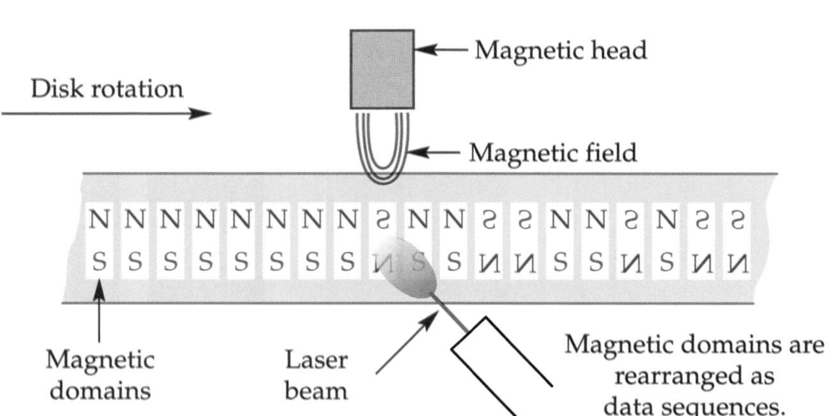

Figure 10-10.
The crystals on a magneto-optical disk are fixed until the plastic around them is heated with a laser. During this heating process, the crystals are susceptible to having their orientation changed to store data.

DVD

Digital Versatile Disc (DVD)
the highest storage capacity of all laser-based CD storage types. Also called *digital video disc.*

Digital Versatile Disc (DVD) offers the highest storage capacity of all laser-based CD types thus far. The very same technology is also referred to as *digital video disc.* DVD is a standard that was pushed by the motion picture industry so that they could release films on CD rather than traditional tape systems. DVD obtains its higher storage capacity by using a shorter wavelength of light, **Figure 10-11,** to record and play back data. DVD uses a shorter wavelength red light as opposed to the infrared used by CDs. DVDs with an even shorter wavelength, blue laser are starting to appear. DVDs also use a smaller track technology, smaller pit and land length, and advanced data compression techniques such as MPEG-2.

The DVD Forum developed DVD-RW standards, which are not compatible with DVD-RAM developed by manufacturers that did not wait for a standard to be developed. DVD-Read Only Memory (DVD-ROM) was developed mainly to focus on multimedia in order to store video and sound on the same disc space. DVD-ROM is a playback only media and cannot be used to record. DVD-RAM is made to be written to and played back many times and also features random access of data. The directory does not have to be accessed first to locate a particular file, photo, or special sequence of data.

DVD Disc Structures

The DVD disc comes in several structure styles to increase data storage capacity. See **Figure 10-12** for a drawing of DVD disc structures.

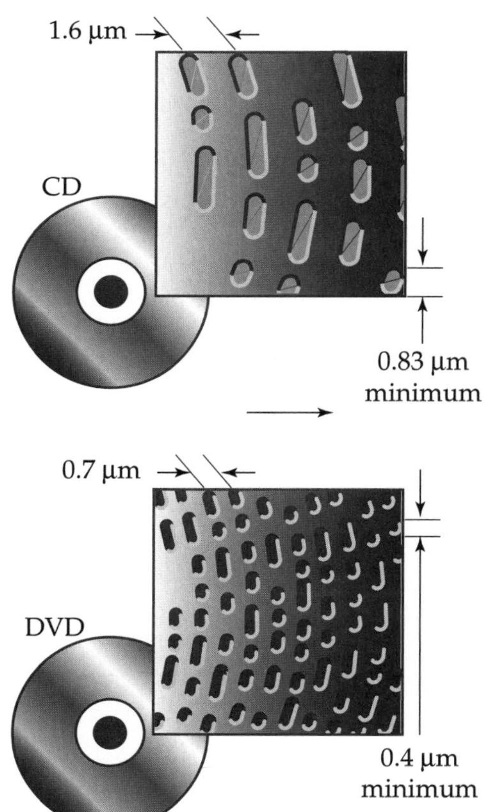

Figure 10-11.
DVD players use a laser with a shorter wavelength than the infrared of traditional CD players. This allows data to be more tightly packed.

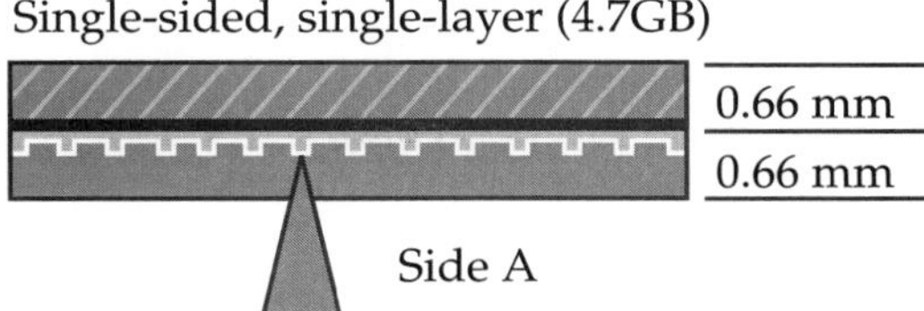

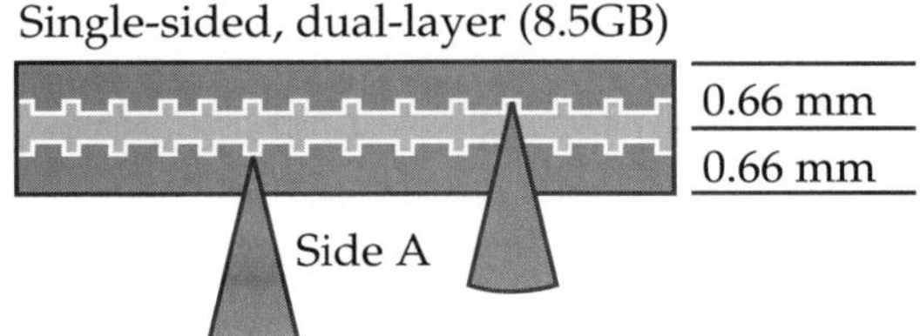

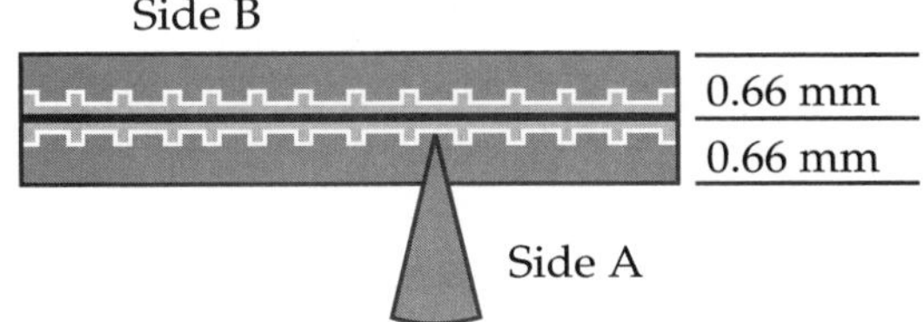

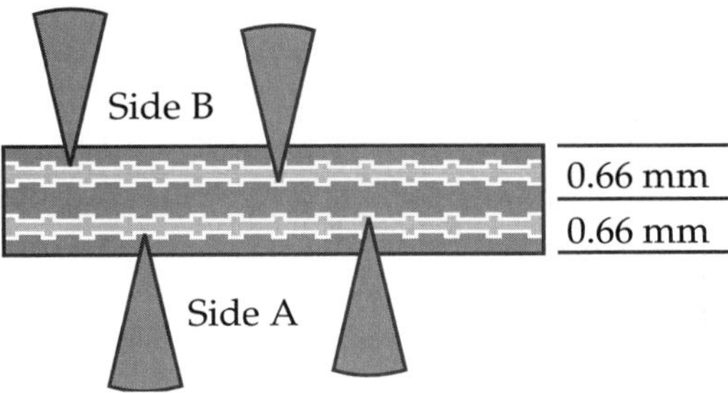

Figure 10-12. Different DVD structures allow for a variety of storage capacities. DVDs can store up to 17GB of data.

The 4.7GB single-sided, single-layer DVD disc structure consists of a single layer of reflective film that contains the pit and land areas that represent stored data. It is similar in construction to the typical CD-ROM. However, the 4.7GB DVD storage capacity far surpasses the CD-ROM's 650MB capacity, **Figure 10-13.**

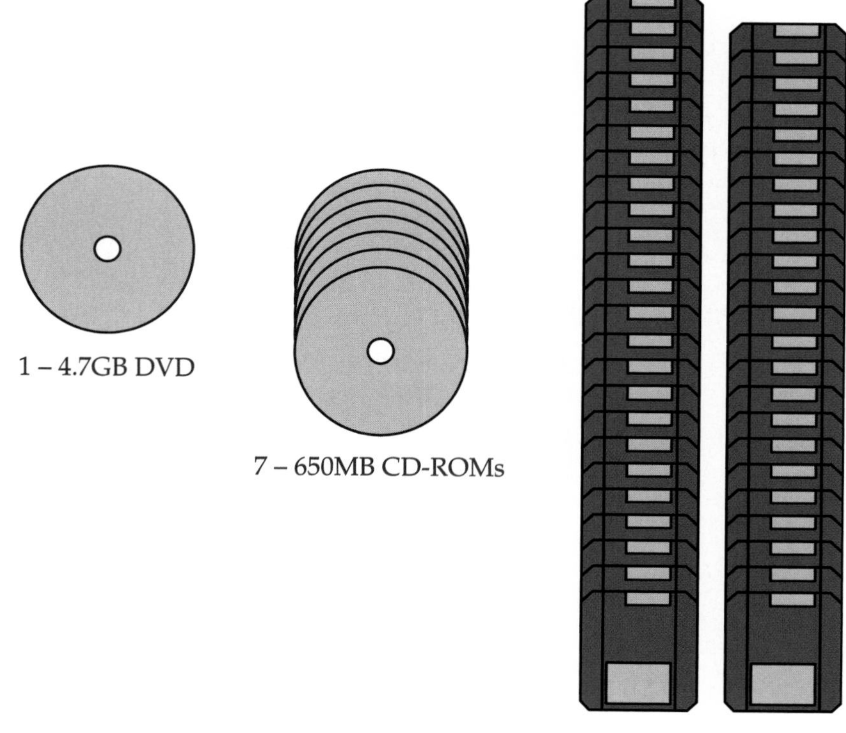

Figure 10-13.
The storage capacity of a DVD is a significant increase above the CD, and a tremendous increase above the old storage king, the Zip disk.

The 8.5GB dual-layer, single-sided structure contains two reflective film layers, a gold layer and a silver layer. For this technology to operate, the laser beam is run at two different intensities. The first layer is gold. When the laser is run at high intensity, this layer is partially transparent to the laser beam. This allows the data on the second layer, the deepest silver reflective film, to be read. When intensity is lowered, it cannot penetrate through the gold reflective layer. The gold layer data is read when the beam is in low intensity mode.

The 9.4GB single-layer, double-sided disc structure is accessed from both sides. Think of the 9.4 single-layer, double-sided disc as two 4.7GB back-to-back. The double-sided disc works with a DVD drive that has two lasers, one to read the top and another to read the bottom of the disc. If the DVD drive has only one laser head, the disc must be turned over to read the other side.

The 17GB is dual-layer and double-sided. It is similar to two 8.5GB dual-layer, single-sided discs joined back-to-back. The same technology of a gold/transparent layer is applied to this disc structure. Again, as with the 9.4GB double-sided disc, there must be two laser heads or the disc must be turned over to access data on both sides of the disc.

In a race to have the first dual-layer, double-sided discs available to the public, some compatibility problems developed. The manufacturers did not wait for a standard to be fully developed and implemented. Usually, if the disc is referred to as 17GB DVD-Random Access Memory (DVD-RAM), it is not compatible with 17GB DVD-RW.

Advantages of DVD

In addition to the obvious advantage of tremendous storage capacity, there are several other advantages to DVDs and DVD drives. One of the best advantages of purchasing a DVD drive is its downward compatibility with CD technology. A DVD drive will read most older CD technologies in addition to the new DVDs. DVD players have no trouble reading CD-ROMs, however, some players may have difficulty with CD-Rs and CD-RWs. The newer DVD players should be able to handle all the older CD technologies. Unfortunately, older CD technology drives will not read DVD discs because the laser intensities are different.

Another advantage of DVD is that video cards can incorporate MPEG standards of decompression directly onto the adapter card. This eliminates the use of the processor to decompress the files. This means faster overall performance.

DVD Compatibility Issues

Manufacturers raced to release DVD technology to dominate the market, and the consumer was therefore left with enormous compatibility issues. Consequently, there are several DVD standards that are not compatible with each other. This is a common cause of customer complaints about making a DVD on one DVD recorder and not being able to access it on another. Presently, there are two formal organizations dictating standards, the DVD-RW Alliance and the DVD Forum. Interestingly there are some manufacturers like Sony and Ricoh that are members of both organizations. The following section covers DVD format standards for both groups.

DVD-R

DVD-R is a write once DVD recordable format introduced by the DVD Forum. The DVD-R format is compatible with most DVD players. DVD-R comes in two types, general use and authoring. The authoring type is a higher quality than the general type. The DVD-R type must match the recorder being used for the initial writing, but it can be read back on either type.

DVD-RW

DVD-RW is a ReWritable format introduced by the DVD Forum. DVD-RW can be reused over 1000 times. Most DVD players will read DVD-RW, but not all. It is not as compatible as the DVD-R format.

DVD+R

DVD+R was introduced by the DVD+RW Alliance and functions similar to DVD-R. There are some minor differences that are sufficient to prevent compatibility with the DVD-R format. It is also interesting to note that DVD+R is not compatible with all DVD+RW players. Most DVD players support both DVD+R and DVD+RW formats.

DVD+RW

DVD+RW is again similar to DVD-RW except for minor differences in the format structure. One of the main differences is that DVD-RW was designed to allow drag-and-drop file exchange, which earlier formats did not support. The drag-and-drop capability is often referred to as the Mount Rainier drag-and-drop support. The Mount Rainier version is also referred to as +MRW.

Early DVD players will have the most problem reading the variety of formats available. Today it is common to purchase a DVD player that cannot only read, but can also write in any of the mentioned formats.

DVD-RAM

DVD-RAM is used primarily as a video format but originally was designed as a data storage format. One problem with DVD-RAM is it will not work in a standard DVD-ROM player.

CD and DVD Interface

Advanced SCSI Programming Interface (ASPI) an interface that allows CD devices to communicate with SCSI system components.

There are several ways to interface CD or DVD technology with existing PC technology. They include SCSI/ASPI, IDE/ATAPI, and parallel port. Exterior connections can also be made easily using USB or FireWire ports.

The ***Advanced SCSI Programming Interface (ASPI)*** was developed by Adaptec to allow CD devices to communicate with the SCSI system components. ASPI became the de facto standard for SCSI CD devices. Remember that SCSI was used in PCs before the CD became standard equipment. Beginning with SCSI-2, the CD device could be installed as part of the internal or external system.

Tech Tip:
De facto standards are standards that have not been defined by an organization. They are standards that have become so widely used they are accepted as the standard by industry.

AT Attachment Packet Interface (ATAPI) the interface used for standard IBM PC AT and compatible systems for accessing CD devices.

The IDE port was designed as a hard drive interface. As CD technology became popular, the IDE system was modified to accept a CD upgrade, hence the development of ***AT Attachment Packet Interface (ATAPI).*** ATAPI is the interface used for standard IBM PC AT and compatible systems for accessing CD devices. ATAPI drives are also referred to as Enhanced IDE drives.

Tech Tip:
When upgrading a PC with a CD attached to the IDE port on the motherboard, it is advisable *not* to connect the CD to the same IDE that connects the hard drive. Depending on the software that is running and the purpose of the CD, the IDE channel can have problems sharing the channel. For example, when recording music on a CD-RW, it is desirable to avoid interruptions in the data transfer process. Having the CD-RW share the same IDE channel with a hard drive can create problems arising from use of the hard drive. SCSI is a preferred way of connecting a CD device because of the much higher data transfer rates of which it is capable. Also, the CD device can completely take control of the SCSI bus, allowing for fewer problems caused by interruption of the data transfer process.

The easiest way to add a new CD or DVD drive to a PC is through the use of the parallel port, FireWire port, or USB port. The PC does not have to be opened, and the drive can be used for more than one PC. Before purchasing a new drive for a business, look at the corporate environment. It may not be necessary to install a CD-RW on every PC in the corporation. A portable CD-RW can be used to upgrade software systems and for installing large programs. A CD tower can be shared over a networked system.

Physical Connections

The connection points on a CD or DVD drive are similar to a hard disk drive with the addition of an audio and digital output connection. See **Figure 10-14.** This figure shows the back and front view of a typical CD device. The power and data connection cables are similar to the ones found on the hard disk drive unit.

The difference between the hard drive and the CD or DVD drive is the audio and the digital output connections. The CD or DVD audio connection connects to the sound card. This connection provides sound from the disc drive to the sound card. The digital output connection can be connected to an audio-tape or other recording device for direct data transfer to the device. Installation of CD and DVD technologies can be made using EIDE as well as SCSI. SCSI is the preferred method for high data transfer rates, but EIDE is most common and works well for most consumers.

Note that master/slave selection jumpers must also be installed if the CD or DVD drive is to share a channel with another EIDE device such as a hard drive. It is recommended that hard drive channels not be shared with a CD or DVD device if possible. Sharing the same channel with the CD or DVD device can cause some unusual problems.

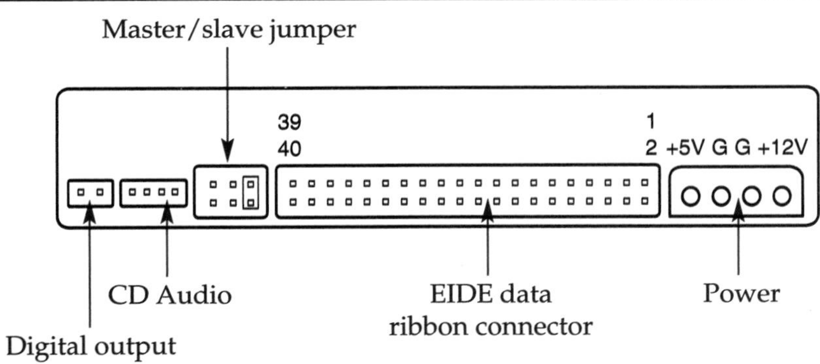

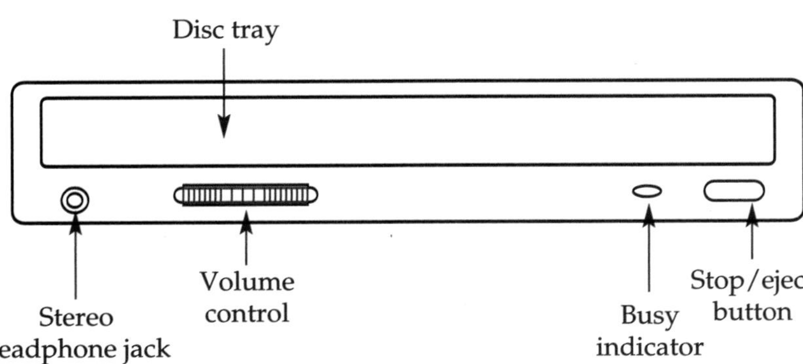

Figure 10-14. Connections for a typical CD or DVD drive.

Summary

- CD and DVD technology use laser light reflected from the CD disc to generate electrical pulses that represent the data stored on the disc.
- Patterns known as land and pit areas represent data stored on a CD-ROM.
- A typical CD-R uses a chemical that changes from a transparent to an opaque color when exposed to laser light.
- A typical CD-RW uses a special crystalline structure that changes its reflective quality after exposure to heat generated by laser light.
- Most CD-ROM drives cannot read CD-RW discs.
- Magneto-optical drives use a combination of laser and magnetic properties to store data. The magnetic properties are used to polarize reflected light from the magneto-optical storage disc.
- DVD offers the same flexibility that a CD has only at much higher storage density.
- Higher storage for DVD was accomplished by using a shorter wavelength of laser light, smaller pit and land areas, and closer track spacing.
- While DVD can read CDs, CD drives cannot read DVD discs.

Review Questions

Answer the following questions on a separate sheet of paper. Please do not write in this book.

1. When was the CD-ROM introduced?
2. How do pit and land areas affect the laser light?
3. What does a photocell do?
4. What is the typical storage capacity of a CD-ROM?
5. What precaution should be taken when working around lasers?
6. How does the track on a CD differ from the track arrangement on a hard drive?
7. Why must a CD-R use a new section of the CD to store a file after the file is modified?
8. What other CD acronym could be used in place of CD-WORM?
9. How does a typical CD-RW have the ability to reuse the same areas for storage of data?
10. What is the difference between a CD-ROM and a CD-R?
11. What is the difference between a CD-R and a CD-RW?
12. Why is a drive designed as a CD-ROM player *not* able to read a CD-RW disk?
13. What does data transfer rate mean when used in specifications?
14. What does access time mean when used in specifications?
15. What does the "X" represent on a CD drive when printed as 24X?

16. What is High Sierra format?
17. What four factors give DVD a higher storage capacity than CD-ROM?
18. What is the typical storage capacity of the smallest capacity DVD disc?
19. What are the four ways in which DVD discs are constructed? List them starting with single-sided, single-layer.
20. After installing a CD-RW to an EIDE, it fails to work. What might be some of the reasons for failure?

Sample A+ Exam Questions

Answer the following questions on a separate sheet of paper. Please do not write in this book.

1. Which is the most appropriate and advisable scenario for the installation of a CD drive?
   a. Install the new CD drive on the same IDE interface and data cable as the existing hard drive. This allows the remaining IDE interface to be used for future expansion.
   b. Install the new CD drive and format it using FAT16 to ensure compatibility with the existing hard drive.
   c. Do not install the new CD drive on the same IDE interface as the existing hard drive to avoid possible conflicts.
   d. Install the new CD drive on either IDE interface, but you must format the new CD drive using the same file system as the hard drive.
2. Which is true about MO disk technology?
   a. The read/write head uses intense magnetic fields to change the arrangement of the magnetic particles embedded in the disk drive.
   b. The read/write process uses laser technology to heat the plastic surrounding the magnetic storage particles being written to.
   c. The laser head is used to melt the reflective material embedded in the plastic disk leaving a bit pattern matching the data.
   d. The read/write head cuts small notches, which represent binary data, into the surface of the plastic disk. The individual notches reflect laser light back, which is then interpreted as data by the BIOS system.
3. Which are the standards for CD file storage? Select two.
   a. UDF
   b. CDUF
   c. CDRW
   d. CDFS
4. The amount of storage on a typical CD-ROM is equal to __________.
   a. 2.88MB
   b. 650MB
   c. 1.6GB
   d. 1.44GB

5. Which interface can be used for a CD drive installation? Choose all that apply.
   a. EIDE
   b. ATA
   c. USB
   d. IEEE1394
6. Which of the following technologies offers the greatest storage capacity?
   a. MO
   b. CD-RW
   c. DVD
   d. CD-ROM
7. Which book describes the standards for audio and graphics compact discs?
   a. The red book
   b. The yellow book
   c. The brown book
   d. The cyan book
8. How does CD-RW technology work?
   a. A typical CD-RW uses a special crystalline structure that changes its reflective quality after exposure to heat generated by laser light.
   b. A typical CD-RW uses metallic particles suspended in plastic, which are heated by a laser and moved magnetically into patterns representing the data.
   c. The CD-RW technology is based on polarized light formation caused by a polarizing magnetic light read/write head crossing the plastic surface.
   d. A typical CD-RW is exactly the same as a CD-ROM only using a much more powerful laser.
9. A couple brings in their computer and complains that when they make a music CD using their new CD-RW drive, the CD plays music perfectly from the new CD-RW drive, but won't play on the CD-ROM drive on their old computer. What is most likely the problem?
   a. The CD is copy protected and it is impossible to make a copy of the original.
   b. The new CD-RW has a much more powerful laser than the older CD-ROM and has burned the middle layer beyond recognition by the older CD player.
   c. The BIOS of the older system needs to be upgraded to match the newer CD-RW.
   d. The laser intensities are different on the two drives. The disc made on the CD-RW will not be readable from the older CD-ROM drive.

10. What is the purpose of the VTOC on a CD-ROM?
    a. Its function is similar to a FAT. It describes how the data is laid out on the disc.
    b. It controls the volume level on the disc so that it will not blow the speaker system during playback.
    c. It controls the speed of the compact disc to make it compatible with other systems such as DVD.
    d. It is a special identification data tag to protect against copyright infringements.

Suggested Laboratory Activities

Do not attempt any suggested laboratory activities without your instructor's permission. Certain activities can render the PC operating system inoperable.

1. Format and then copy a file to a CD-RW disk. You can go to the CD-RW manufacturer's Web site and access information about the steps necessary to record data.
2. Install a CD-RW into a PC. After installation, test the CD-RW by accessing data from an existing CD.
3. Install a CD-ROM, CD-RW, or a DVD in combination with a sound card.
4. Check the Microsoft hardware compatibility list at Microsoft's Web site (www.microsoft.com/hwtest/hcl) to see if all CD drive and DVD drive systems are compatible with Windows 98, Windows 2000, Windows Me, and Windows XP operating systems.
5. Open up **Device Manager** and see what the system resource assignments are for an existing CD drive.
6. Download a driver for a CD drive from a manufacturer's Web site.

Interesting Web Sites to Visit

www.hp.com

www.iomega.com

www.philips.com

www.sony.com

www.verbatim.com

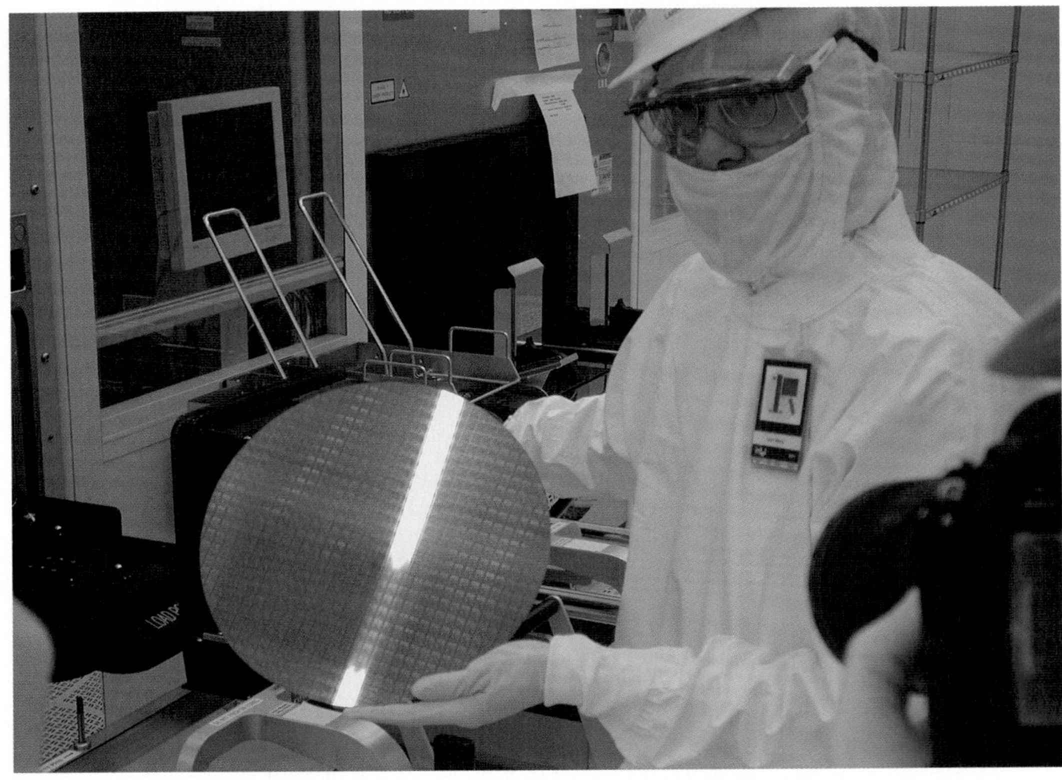

An Intel technician holds a wafer of microprocessor chips. Each small square on the wafer is a microprocessor. (Source: Intel Corporation)

Chapter 10
Laboratory Activity
CD Drive Installation

After completing this laboratory activity, you will be able to:

- ❑ Install any type of IDE CD drive.
- ❑ Identify common problems associated with CD drive installation.
- ❑ Identify the major parts required for CD drive installation.

Introduction

In this laboratory activity, you will either be installing a new drive in a PC that didn't previously have one, or you will be replacing or upgrading an existing CD drive. The exact type of procedure will be assigned by your instructor. The installation process is similar for both types of installation.

Installing a CD drive system is a simple task. The installation can be more complicated when a sound card is used in combination with the CD drive. When a sound card is incorporated with the CD drive for enhanced audio, some problems may develop. Usually the sound card and CD will share the same IRQ assignment.

Another common problem is Plug and Play's failure to properly identify the new drive. If the CD drive is not identified automatically, or is incorrectly identified by the Plug and Play feature, the CD drive will not operate properly. In this case, you may need to disable the Plug and Play feature. The Plug and Play feature can usually be disabled in the BIOS setup program.

Loading the proper driver can be another problem when installing a CD drive. New drives are placed on the market daily. The operating system you are using may not contain the very latest drivers needed for the installation. The driver is usually included when the CD drive is purchased. It is a good idea to check the manufacturer's Web site for the latest driver for the unit as well as information about known problems. Checking the Web site can save many frustrating hours during an installation.

Proper connection of the CD drive can be another troublesome area during the installation. When installing a CD drive, avoid sharing the IDE connection with the hard drive. Sharing the same IDE connection can create compatibility problems between the CD drive and the hard drive. One problem is resolving the master/slave issue between the two devices. The other is the data transfer speed. An older hard drive will most likely have a much slower data transfer rate than the newer CD drive. This condition will cause the CD drive to transfer data at the lower rate, matching the hard disk drive and thus hurting the performance of the CD drive.

The following illustration of a typical CD drive shows the connection points on the end of the drive. Note the master/slave jumper selection area. The master/slave jumper setup is similar to that found on hard drives. When more than one device is connected to an IDE or EIDE connection, one device must be designated the master and the other, the slave.

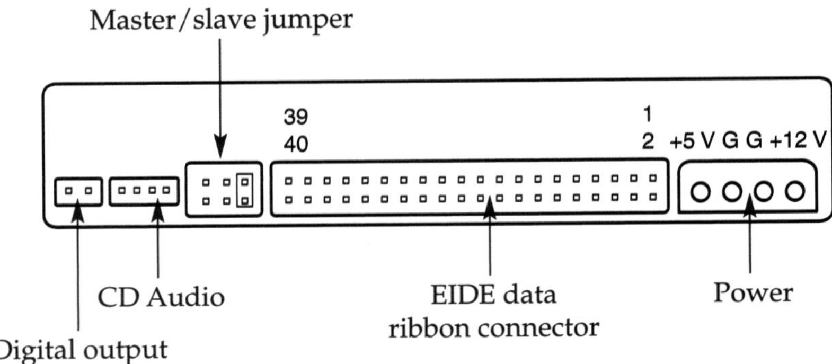

The mechanics of installing a CD drive are quite simple. The only real concern is the possibility of loosening a connection to one of the other drives while installing the CD drive cables.

Equipment and Materials

- Typical PC (486 or later CPU recommended).
- CD drive, such as a CD-RW.

Procedure

1. ______ Boot the PC to be sure it is working before you begin the installation procedure.
2. ______ Once you have verified that the assigned PC is in working order, properly shut it down and turn off the power.
3. ______ Remove the PC cover and select the bay in which the new CD drive will be installed. If you are replacing an existing drive, sketch the drive and its cable connections. Take care to mark the proper orientation of the cables, as you will most likely have to reinstall the original drive at the end of the lab. Once you have sketched the drive setup, disconnect the cables and remove the mounting screws from the mounting rails. Slide the CD drive out of its bay. This procedure will vary based on the make and model of the drive and the case.
4. ______ If you are performing a new installation, install the mounting rails to the bay now. For a unit replacement, check the existing mounting rails for compatibility with the new CD drive. You may need to remove the existing mounting rails and replace them with a set of rails compatible with the new CD drive. Before securing the CD drive into the case, check the master/slave jumper settings. Be sure to choose the correct setting for the installation. Check the CD drive documentation or look on the side of the CD drive for a chart of jumper settings.

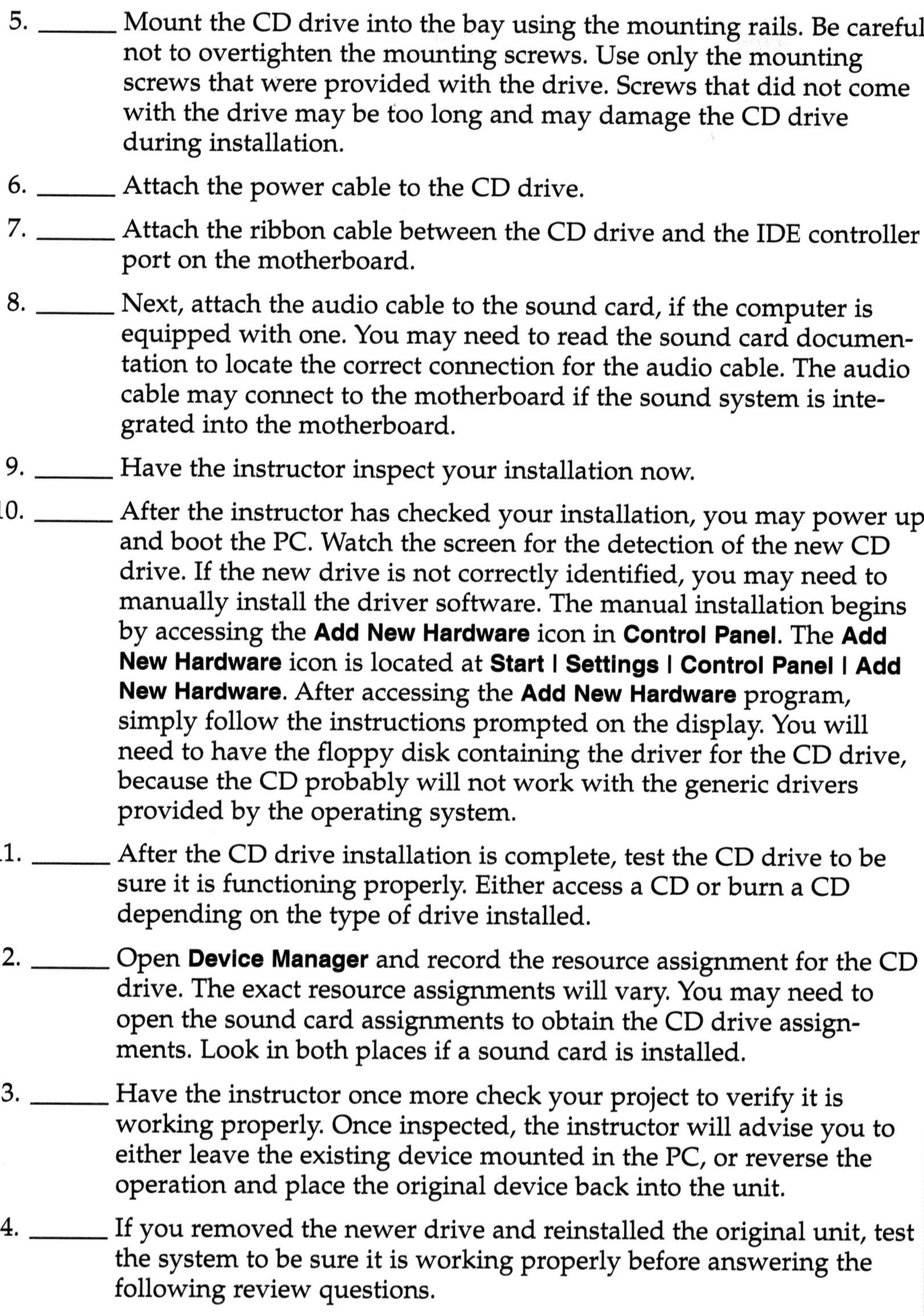

5. ______ Mount the CD drive into the bay using the mounting rails. Be careful not to overtighten the mounting screws. Use only the mounting screws that were provided with the drive. Screws that did not come with the drive may be too long and may damage the CD drive during installation.
6. ______ Attach the power cable to the CD drive.
7. ______ Attach the ribbon cable between the CD drive and the IDE controller port on the motherboard.
8. ______ Next, attach the audio cable to the sound card, if the computer is equipped with one. You may need to read the sound card documentation to locate the correct connection for the audio cable. The audio cable may connect to the motherboard if the sound system is integrated into the motherboard.
9. ______ Have the instructor inspect your installation now.
10. ______ After the instructor has checked your installation, you may power up and boot the PC. Watch the screen for the detection of the new CD drive. If the new drive is not correctly identified, you may need to manually install the driver software. The manual installation begins by accessing the **Add New Hardware** icon in **Control Panel**. The **Add New Hardware** icon is located at **Start | Settings | Control Panel | Add New Hardware**. After accessing the **Add New Hardware** program, simply follow the instructions prompted on the display. You will need to have the floppy disk containing the driver for the CD drive, because the CD probably will not work with the generic drivers provided by the operating system.
11. ______ After the CD drive installation is complete, test the CD drive to be sure it is functioning properly. Either access a CD or burn a CD depending on the type of drive installed.
12. ______ Open **Device Manager** and record the resource assignment for the CD drive. The exact resource assignments will vary. You may need to open the sound card assignments to obtain the CD drive assignments. Look in both places if a sound card is installed.
13. ______ Have the instructor once more check your project to verify it is working properly. Once inspected, the instructor will advise you to either leave the existing device mounted in the PC, or reverse the operation and place the original device back into the unit.
14. ______ If you removed the newer drive and reinstalled the original unit, test the system to be sure it is working properly before answering the following review questions.

Review Questions

Answer the following questions on a separate sheet of paper. Please do not write in this book.

1. What problems might arise during a CD drive installation?
2. How do you correct a wrong IRQ assignment by the Plug and Play feature?
3. How is Plug and Play usually disabled?
4. Why should you avoid connecting the CD drive on the same IDE controller on the motherboard?
5. What does the stripe running along the ribbon cable indicate?
6. Where could you locate the latest driver for the CD drive you are installing?
7. Why should you use only the screws designed for the mounting of the drive unit?

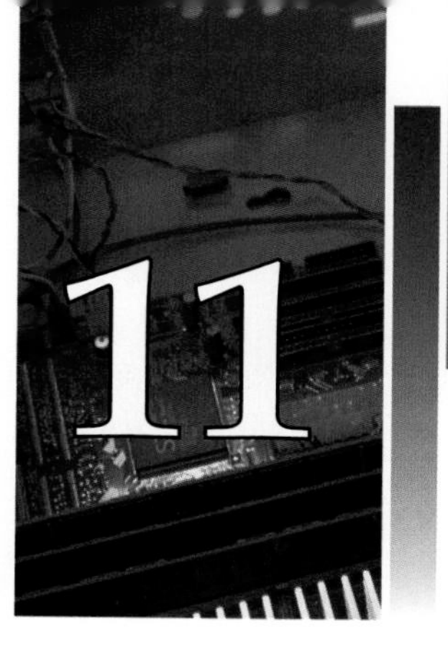

Printers

After studying this chapter, you will be able to:

- Explain the operating principles of a laser printer.
- Explain the operating principles of an inkjet printer.
- Explain the operating principles of a dot matrix printer.
- Explain how to install a printer.
- Install print driver software.
- Complete printer setup and installation.
- Identify and diagnose common laser printer faults.
- Explain how fonts are generated and installed.

A+ Exam—Key Points

The A+ Certification exams usually feature a few questions about the function of the major parts of the laser printer, such as the primary corona wire. Study the major parts and the steps of the laser printer process.

You should also understand how printer drivers are installed and how to solve common printer problems.

Key Words and Terms

The following words and terms will become important pieces of your computer vocabulary. Be sure you can define them.

bubble jet printer
CMYK
color thermal printer
dot matrix printer
dye-sublimation printer
electrophotographic process (EP)
font
inkjet printer
local printer
paper jam
paper train
pitch
point
printer
queue
solid ink printer
spooling

printer
an electromechanical device that converts computer data into text or graphic images printed to paper or other presentation media.

A ***printer*** can be defined as an electromechanical device that converts computer data into text or graphic images printed to paper or other presentation media. PC technicians are responsible for the installation, setup, modifications to, and troubleshooting of printer systems. A PC technician is not usually responsible for making physical repairs to the electromechanical parts of the printing engine, but a good knowledge base of the electromechanical operation of printers can prove valuable when troubleshooting a printer system. The electromechanical repair of printers is a specialization area. In this unit, you will learn the basic operation of the most common styles of printer.

Laser Printer Operation

electrophotographic process (EP)
a photographic process that uses a combination of static electricity, light, dry chemical compound, pressure, and heat.

Traditional printing is based on wet ink applied to paper using several different processes. Laser printing uses a process called the electrophotographic process. ***Electrophotographic process (EP)*** is a combination of static electricity, light, dry chemical compound, pressure, and heat. To better understand this process and the role that the major parts of the laser printer perform in the printing process, view the step-by-step series of illustrations shown in **Figure 11-1,** parts A through G. A black-and-white laser printer is shown here.

Step One. Charging the Drum (Part A):

The primary corona wire is charged to approximately 6000 volts. The high voltage creates an electrical condition known as *corona*. The corona is a static charge surrounding a high voltage conductor. The primary corona wire is in close proximity to the drum. The primary corona wire applies a large negative charge of approximately 600 to 1000 volts to the surface of the drum.

Warning:
The laser printing process utilizes extremely high levels of voltage. Never attempt to repair or disassemble a laser printer. Repairing a laser printer requires special training and safety precautions. PC technicians do not normally replace printer parts other than toner cartridges.

Step 2. Writing the Image (Part B):

The image is written to the drum using laser light. The laser light changes intensity according to the light and dark patterns encoded by the data

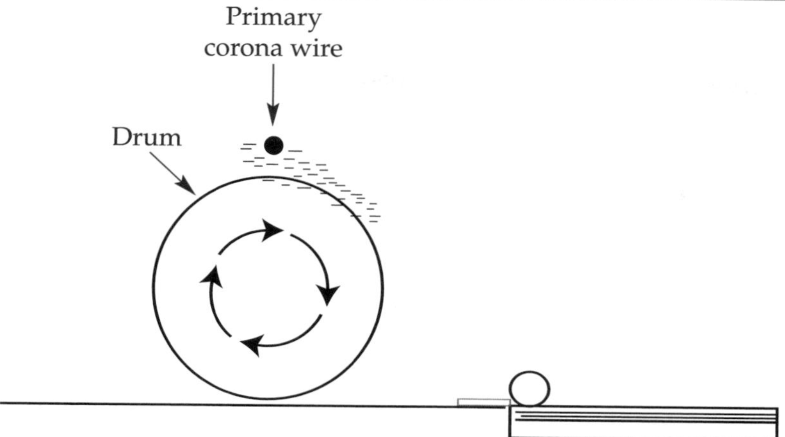
Primary
corona wire
Drum
Step 1. The primary corona wire charges the surface of the drum with a negative negative charge of approximately 600-1000 volts.
A

Figure 11-1A
Charging the drum.

describing the image. A rotating pentagon-shaped mirror reflects the laser beam horizontally across the surface of the drum.

After each horizontal trace is complete, the drum rotates by a small increment and the next trace begins. A typical laser printer makes 300 to 1200 increments of rotation per inch. The drum is coated with a light sensitive photoconductive material. The special coating on the drum conducts electricity when struck by intense light. As the laser beam is reflected across the drum, the areas struck by the beam become conductive and lose most of their negative static charge. For example, when a typical image or business letter is to be printed, the white areas of the image are struck by the laser beam while the dark areas, such as letters and lines, are not struck by the laser light. The parts of the drum that are not exposed to the light retain the 600- to 1000-volt negative charge.

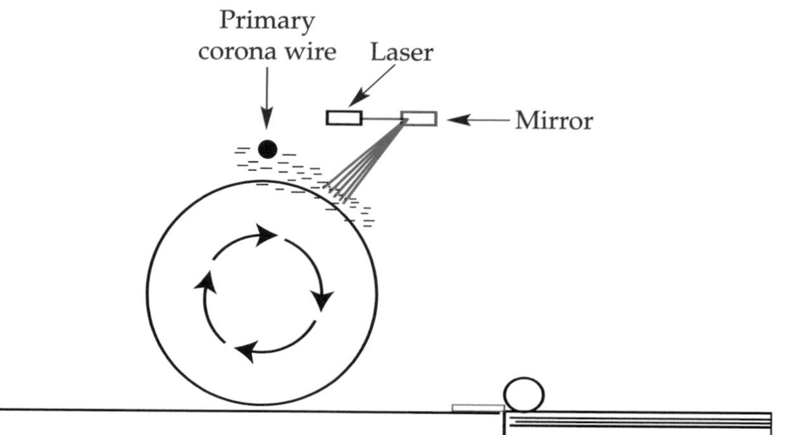
Primary
corona wire
Laser
Mirror
Step 2. A laser beam pulses to a spinning mirror which reflects light across the negatively charged drum. The laser light draws the outline of the image to be produced.
B

Figure 11-1B.
Writing the image to the drum with a laser.

Step 3. Developing the Image (Part C):

As the drum turns, the image created by low and high static charges on the drum pass by the toner cartridge. The toner is attracted to the static charge on the drum. Think of toner as a form of very fine plastic dust particles.

A roller is incorporated in the toner cartridge to assist with dispersing the toner from the cartridge. The image to be printed is now formed on the drum.

Figure 11-1C. Toner is drawn to the drum.

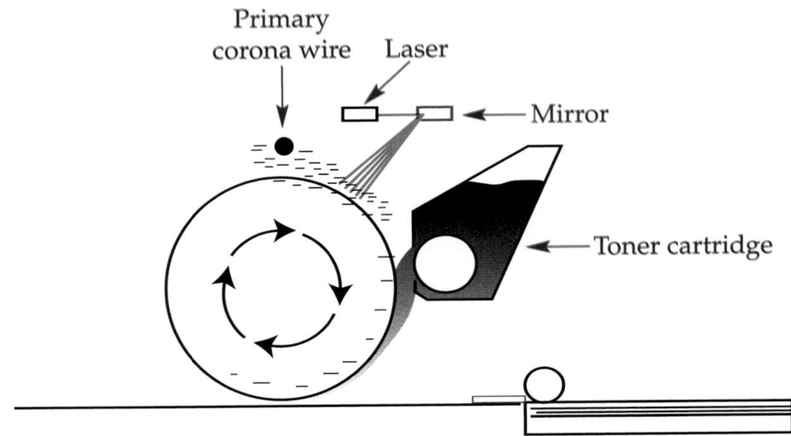

Step 3. The toner is attracted to the static charge on the drum. The static charge is in the shape of the image to be printed.

C

Step 4. Transferring the Image (Part D):

As the drum continues to rotate, the paper is fed under the drum. A set of rollers called pickup rollers lift one sheet of paper at a time from the paper tray. The paper is fed into position under the drum. A device known as a *separator* makes sure only one sheet of paper is sent into the drum area. The separator is located at the edge of the paper tray near the pickup rollers.

Just before the paper passes under the drum, it is given a positive charge by the transfer corona wire. The transfer corona wire works much like the primary corona, only using the opposite charge. The paper now has a positive charge of static applied to its surface. As the positively-charged paper passes under the negatively-charged toner on the drum, the toner is attracted to the paper. (As you should remember from a basic physics class, opposite charges attract.)

Step 5. Fusing the Image (Part E):

There is no longer a need for the static positive charge on the paper. A static brush makes contact with the paper and drains off any charge remaining on the paper. If the charge were not removed from the paper, it would cause the paper to stick to the negatively charged drum and would also make the paper difficult to handle after leaving the printer.

Covered with a dry toner image, the paper passes through the fuser. The fuser consists of a pair of rollers, one of which is heated to a very high temperature. As the toner-covered paper passes through the fuser rollers, the heat and pressure melt the toner, fixing it to the paper's surface.

Usually, a quartz lamp is used to produce the high temperature of the fusing unit. The lamp generates a temperature of over 356°F (180°C). As a safety precaution, there is usually a temperature sensor installed near the fusing unit. This sensor will shut off power to the fusing unit if the temperature gets too high.

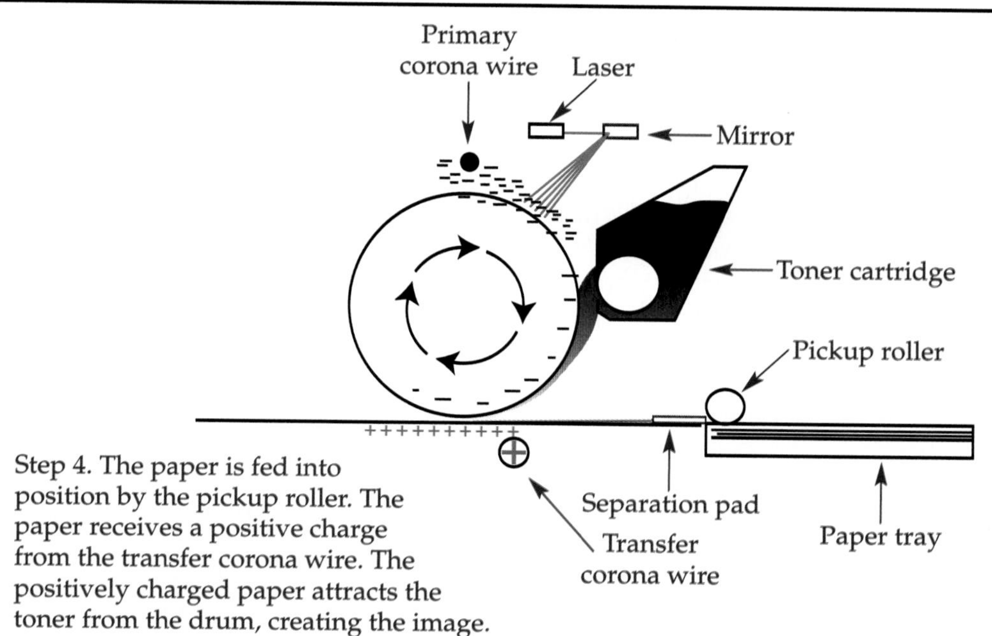

Step 4. The paper is fed into position by the pickup roller. The paper receives a positive charge from the transfer corona wire. The positively charged paper attracts the toner from the drum, creating the image.

D

Figure 11-1D. The paper is charged and drawn under the drum.

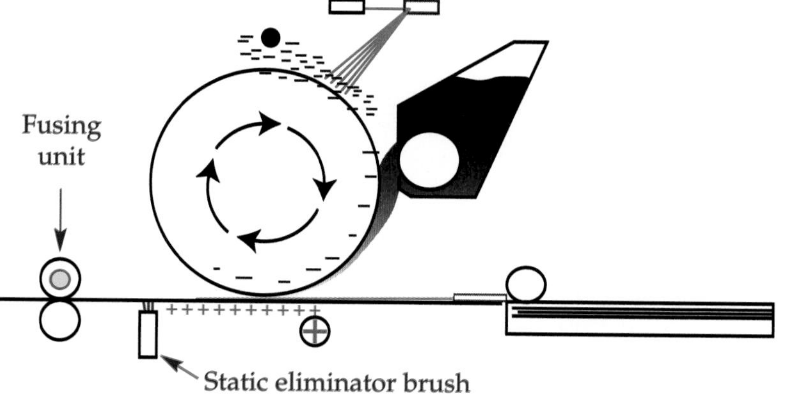

Step 5. The fusing unit rollers heat the toner and paper until the toner melts and bonds to the paper. The static eliminator brush removes the static charge from the paper.

E

Figure 11-1E. Toner is fused to the paper.

Warning:
The area around the fusing unit in the printer can cause severe burns when touched. Never attempt to work inside a laser printer unless it has been off for at least 15 minutes.

Step 6. Cleaning the Drum (Part F):

The drum must be prepared before the next image can be printed. A cleaning unit removes any toner that might still be on the drum. The unit consists of a simple rubber scraper or blade that removes any residual toner left on the drum. The particles of toner are collected inside the cleaning unit container. The blade or scraper is specially designed not to scratch the drum surface. Any scratches on the drum would remove the photosensitive finish. This would result in poor quality printed images.

A high intensity light is also beamed onto the drum to remove any remaining charge from the drum's surface. The drum is now ready to be charged again by the primary corona wire, and the printing process can be repeated. Part G of Figure 11-1 shows all the parts together.

Note that in the example of the laser printing process, the drum illustrated was negatively charged. The same process can occur using opposite polarities. Different manufacturers use different charging levels and polarities to create the same printing process that was shown in our example.

These principles of operation employed in the black-and-white laser printer can also be applied to a color laser printer. A color laser printer uses four separate print engines, one for each of the major colors. The major colors used in a color laser printer are blue, red, yellow, and black. Often the blue color is represented by the color cyan and the red is represented by the color magenta.

Figure 11-1F. The drum is cleaned of excess electrical charge and toner.

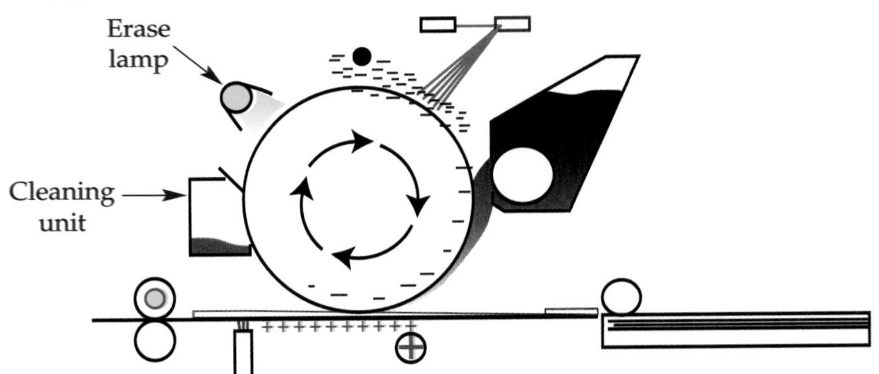

Step 6. The cleaning unit removes any residual toner that might remain on the drum. The erase lamp shines a bright light on the drum to remove any remaning charge. The drum is now ready to begin the process over again.

F

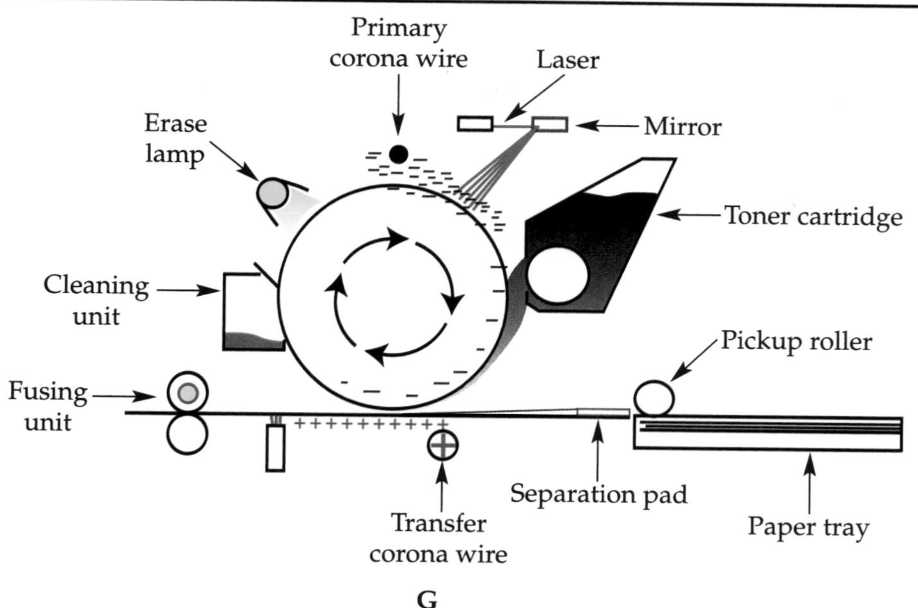

Figure 11-1G. Shown here are the vital parts of the laser printer in relation to each other. This illustration shows a negatively charged drum. Some printers place a positive charge on the drum and a negative charge on the paper. The process is the same with the polarities reversed.

Color Inkjet Printer Operation

inkjet printer printer that uses specially designed cartridges that spray a fine mist of ink as they move horizontally in front of a sheet of paper.

bubble jet printer an inkjet printer.

An ***inkjet printer*** uses specially designed cartridges that spray a fine mist of ink as it moves horizontally in front of a sheet of paper. Some inkjet printers are commonly referred to as ***bubble jet printers.***

The inkjet printer head is the part that fires the ink onto the paper. The construction of an inkjet printer head is fairly simple, **Figure 11-2.** Ink must be forced out of the printer head. The two most common types of inkjet printers use either a *thermoresistor* or *piezocell crystal* to produce a force that fires a drop of ink through a nozzle directly onto the paper.

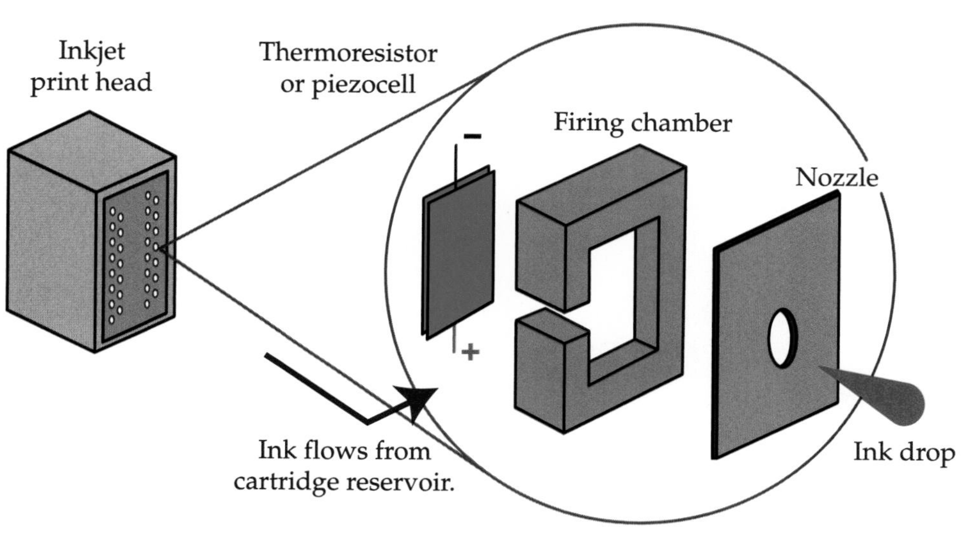

Figure 11-2. Exploded diagram of typical color inkjet printer head.

Figure 11-2 is an exploded view of a single nozzle and its major parts: the nozzle, the firing chamber, and (in this model) a thermoresistor. The ink flows into the firing chamber from the ink cartridge reservoir. An electrical pulse from the computer enters the thermoresistor and the ink in the firing chamber is instantly heated to over 1112°F (600°C). The extreme heat expands the ink in the chamber, causing it to fire through the nozzle and onto the paper. As the chamber cools, a vacuum is created that draws more ink into the firing chamber from the ink cartridge reservoir. An inkjet printer can fire its chamber many times a second.

The single ink droplet is quite small. A typical low-cost inkjet printer can produce 720 × 720 dots per square inch (dpi). High quality inkjet printers can produce a dpi of 1200 × 1200 and higher.

A piezocell could be used instead of the thermoresistor. A piezocell is a crystal that deflects or bends when energized by an electrical pulse. When a piezocell is used in place of the thermoresistor, the piezocell flexes every time an electrical pulse is sent. When the piezocell crystal flexes, the ink drop is fired through the nozzle. When the electrical pulse stops, the crystal returns to its original shape. This creates a vacuum in the firing chamber (like with the thermoresistor), which draws more ink into the chamber.

A color inkjet printer uses four hues of ink: cyan, magenta, yellow, and black. This is a standard combination of colors often referred to simply as ***CMYK***. Note that the letter K is used to signify black rather than B, which is used for blue in the RGB (red, green, blue) system. See **Figure 11-3.** These colors are standard in the printing industry. They can be mixed to make other hues such as green, orange, brown, and gray.

CMYK
standard combination of colors (cyan, magenta, yellow, and black) used by color inkjet printers.

Inkjet Printer Cleaning Guidelines

Inkjet printers operate on the principle of controlling a fine mist of ink to print images on the paper. Because of this printing technique, the mist of ink often collects on the inside and outside of the printer case. To remove ink deposits from the outside of the printer case, you should use a soft cloth and water. If the case will not clean properly with water, you may use a mild detergent diluted in water. The water should be distilled water. Cleaning a printer with water that has severe mineral deposits can make the printer case look worse than before it was cleaned. Never clean a printer case with alcohol or any form of strong commercial cleaners. Harsh chemicals will ruin many plastics.

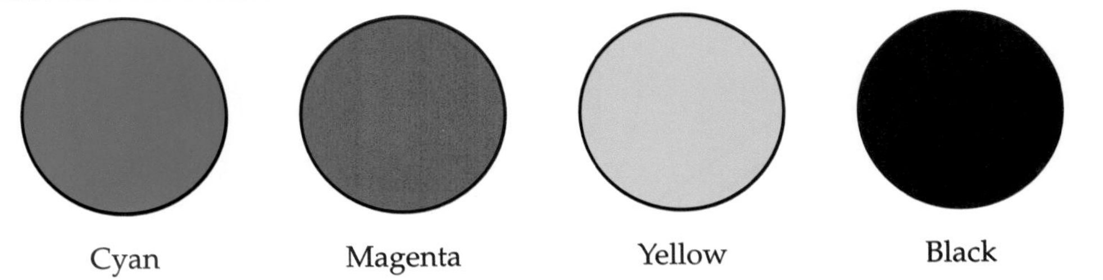

Figure 11-3.
CMYK stands for cyan, magenta, yellow, black. These are the colors used for ink printing. They can be mixed to produce a broad spectrum of colors.

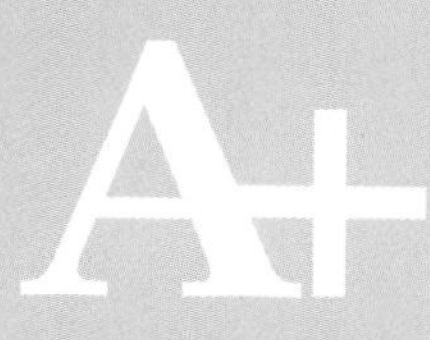

A+ Note:
The A+ Certification exam will most likely only list water or very mild detergent as the correct answer.

Most printer designs have been engineered to allow for some accumulation of ink inside the printer. In general, you should never attempt to clean the inside of the printer with alcohol or any commercial solvents. Alcohol, solvents, and water can damage the electrical components inside the printer. The only areas inside the printer that may require cleaning are the printer cartridges. The printer should only be turned off after the printing process has completed. When the printer has finished printing, the ink cartridge is returned to "home" position. The home position is engineered to cover the ink ports to prevent them from drying out. Inkjet ports often dry out because of long periods of nonuse.

A small, fine brush or an anti-static vacuum should be used to remove paper dust and lint. Do *not* use compressed air to remove dust. The compressed air may actually force the dust deeper inside the printing mechanism and result in more harm than good.

Never attempt to lubricate parts inside the inkjet printer. Lubricants can cause an increased buildup of dust and lint inside the printer. Lubricants can also damage electronic components.

The above are general guidelines to follow and may vary somewhat when working with specific printers. The best policy is to download a copy of maintenance and cleaning instructions for the exact printer model from the manufacturer's Web site.

Dot Matrix Printers

The ***dot matrix printer*** derives its name from the pattern, or matrix, of very small dots it prints to create text and images. Dot matrix printers were some of the earliest printers. They are now much less common and tend to be used only for special purposes.

dot matrix printer printer that uses a pattern of very small dots to create text and images.

The dot matrix print head consists of a line of small metal rods called print pins, **Figure 11-4.** In appearance, they look much like a series of small nails. An electrical coil, called a solenoid, controls each print pin. When energized, the solenoid creates a magnetic field. The print pin is constructed with a magnet at one end. When the solenoid is energized, the magnetic end of the pin is attracted to the coil and the print pin rapidly moves forward, striking an ink ribbon. Each energized solenoid causes that individual print rod to strike the ribbon, leaving a dot of ink on the paper.

To form a letter, such as the letter A in the illustration, a series of electrical pulses is sent to the print head. The pulses are coded in a sequence that forms the letter A on the paper as the entire print head moves horizontally across the paper. The two most common print head styles are 9-pin and 24-pin.

Dot matrix printers are quite slow and noisy. To achieve finer detail, the print head may have to make multiple passes on the same line. They are used today primarily for spreadsheets and other text applications in businesses. When graphics with fine detail are desired, other printers such as inkjet or laser are typically used.

Figure 11-4.
The dot matrix print head close up. Dot matrix printers generate a pattern of dots to create images.

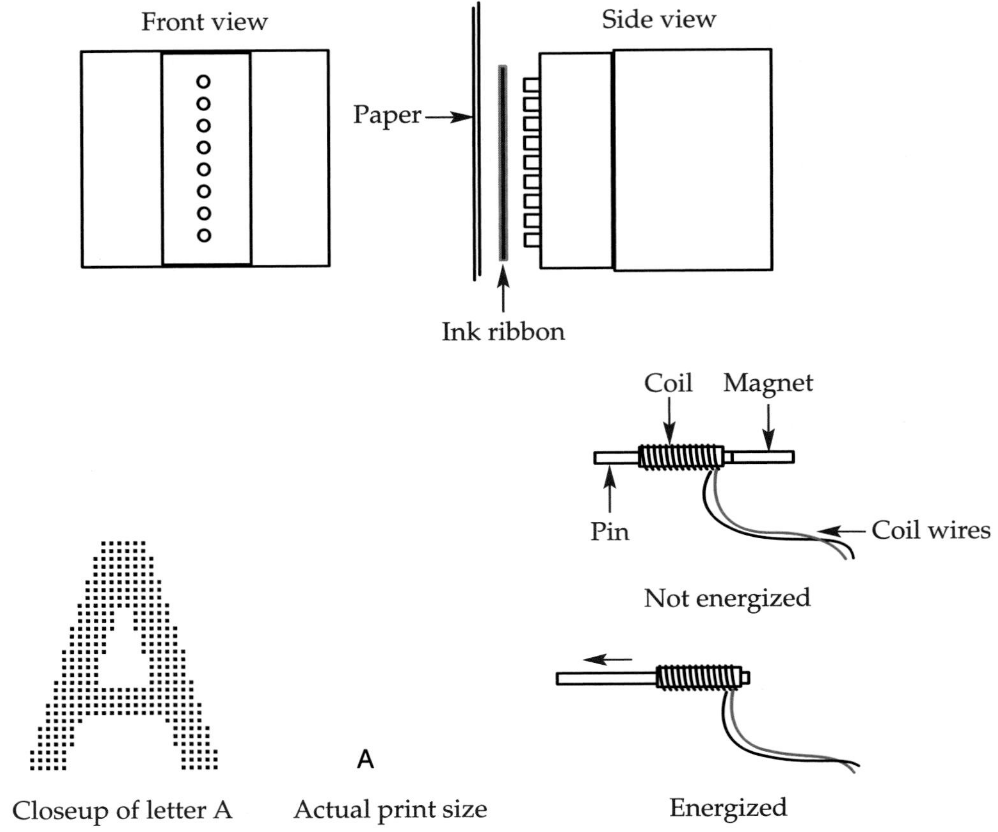

Color Thermal Printer Operation

color thermal printer printer that applies color by heating a special ribbon that is coated with wax-like material.

Color thermal printer operation is based on the principle of applying color by heating a special ribbon that is coated with wax-like material. Heat is used to melt the wax. The wax is then sealed to the surface of the paper by Teflon coated rollers. See **Figure 11-5.**

The heating unit consists of an array of small heaters that melt the wax in small dots. The small dots of heated wax represent the data sent from the PC to the printer. The paper must be run through the process four separate times. Each time the paper is run through, a new color is added to the paper. The colors are cyan, magenta, yellow, and black (CMYK). The process is similar to the dye-sublimation process described in the next section. The difference is that in dye sublimation the color actually penetrates the paper, while in thermal print operation the color is printed to the surface of the paper.

Figure 11-5.
Sketch of a color thermal printer.

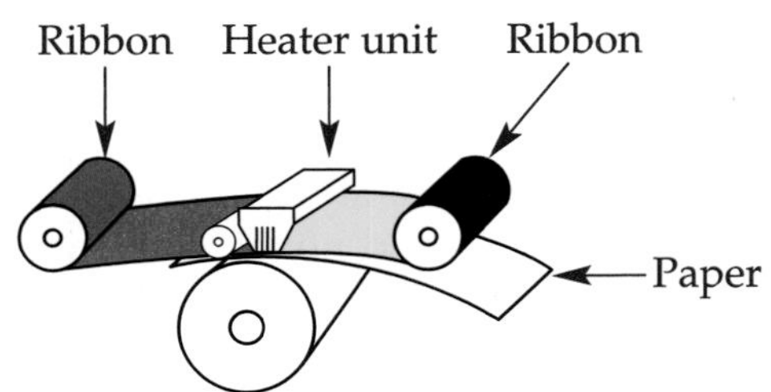

Color thermal printers are used for high quality presentation drawings and illustrations. Many corporations use them for special applications such as CEO reports to the board when color photos and charts are required. They are not commonly found in home use. They have high quality print but at a relatively high cost per sheet since they use special paper and expensive color wax supplies. Color thermal printers are not used for mass copies, just high quality.

Dye-Sublimation Printer Operation

dye-sublimation printer
printer that produces near photo quality printed images by vaporizing inks, which then solidify onto paper.

Dye-sublimation printers produce near photo quality printed images by vaporizing inks, which then solidify onto paper. *Sublimation* is a scientific term that means changing a solid material into a gas.

The major parts used in the dye-sublimation process are the drum, transfer roll, and heater, **Figure 11-6.** A special paper is mounted directly on the drum. The transfer roll is a long sheet of plastic material coated with CMYK colors. As the drum rotates, the plastic transfer sheet (roll) passes under the drum and across the heater.

The heater consists of thousands of tiny heating elements arranged in a close array. These elements heat up in patterns representing the data patterns sent from the computer system. The heating elements can heat to 256 different temperature levels, which cause the dye to be transferred at 256 different levels of intensity.

The drum rotates four times. During each revolution of the drum, a different color passes from the transfer roll into the paper. The color is absorbed into the fibers as opposed to coating the top of the paper. The four colors sublimate to the paper and combine to create over 16 million colors.

Dye-sublimation printers and materials are very expensive. However, the dye-sublimation process gives much higher resolution and better color representation than the laser or inkjet processes.

Solid Ink Color Printer Operation

solid ink printer
printer that uses solid ink cartridges similar to wax.

A ***solid ink printer*** uses solid ink cartridges similar to wax. The print head consists of four long rows of many individual nozzles. Each of the four rows produces one of the CMYK colors. The four colors are heated and flow into individual reservoirs. As the paper passes by the print heads, the nozzles are fired, releasing a fine mist of color to the paper.

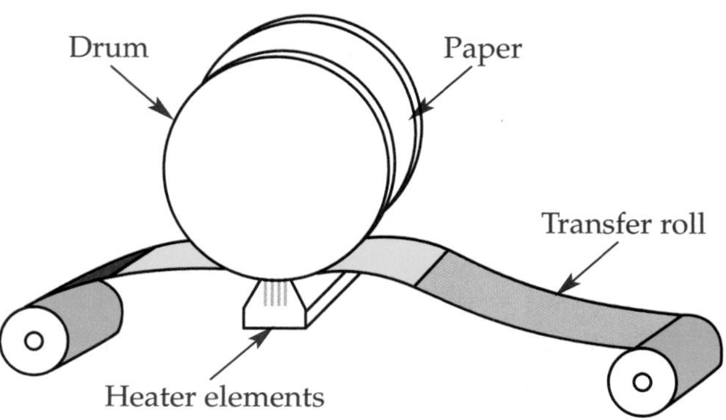

Figure 11-6. The important parts of a dye-sublimation printer.

An advantage of the solid ink color printer is that it uses ordinary paper for its process. However, printer and ink supplies are expensive when compared to laser and inkjet supplies.

All-In-One Products

In recent years, manufacturers have introduced all-in-one products, especially for home and small office use. The all-in-one units are a combination of four common office devices that rely on printing techniques to accomplish their tasks. They are a combination of printer, fax, copier, and scanner. The all-in-one devices are a cost-effective way to purchase office equipment. The downside is that when the all-in-one device fails, typically you cannot use any of the devices.

Common Printer Connections

Printers can be connected to a computer using various media such as USB, IEEE 1394, RJ-45, SCSI, serial, infrared, and wireless. The most common connections encountered today in homes and small offices are USB, IEEE 1394, wireless, and RJ-45.

Local Printer Installation

local printer printer that connects directly to a specific PC.

The term ***local printer*** refers to a printer that connects directly to a PC. The printer is *local* to that particular PC. Not all printers are local printers. A printer can be connected to a PC through a network and shared by many different PCs. This type of connection is covered later.

When a printer is connected to a PC, a port address must be assigned before the PC can communicate with the printer. Common computer ports are given a name such as LTP1 or COM1 rather than a port number such as 037Fh. The usual choices for a printer are LPT1, LPT2, COM1, COM2, COM3, or COM4. Originally, the letters LPT represented *line printer terminal,* but today, it's simply *printer.* The letters COM were an abbreviation for communication.

During the DOS era, printers were a real challenge to set up. They had to be set up manually. The printers were usually equipped with several DIP switches that had to be set (flipped) into certain positions to match the type of ASCII code it was to use. Switches also controlled other printer characteristics or commands. For example, placing a carriage return after every line of text or double spacing between lines of text could be set by mechanical adjustments or by software commands. It could take many hours to set up a printer correctly.

Today, most systems are Plug and Play compliant, which usually means an easy, automatic setup. However, not all setups are simple. Sometimes, parts of the setup program must be accomplished manually. A technician must become familiar with the setup options and properties available for printer systems. Be aware that the users you serve are easily frustrated by inoperable equipment or by new computer equipment that does not perform to expectations. Knowledge can generate confidence in the user and lessen some frustrations during setup or repair.

Printer installation begins with opening the printer folder. One way to open the folder is by accessing it through **Start | Settings | Printers**. See **Figure 11-7.**

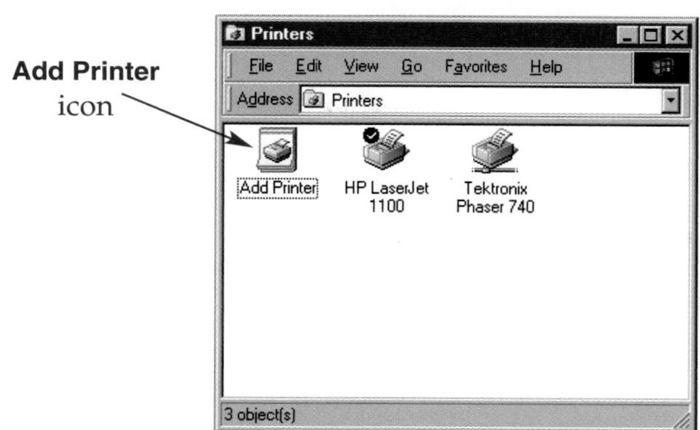

Figure 11-7.
Screen capture of the Windows **Printers** folder.

After accessing the **Printers** folder, any printers for which the PC has been set up will appear in the window. In the illustration, two printers are identified: an HP LaserJet 1100 and a Tektronix Phaser 740. The printers listed will vary depending on what has been installed. Notice the **Add Printer** icon to the left in the folder. This icon is in all **Printers** folders. The **Add Printer** icon is activated to add a new printer to the PC. When activated, the **Add Printer Wizard** screen appears, **Figure 11-8.**

This wizard steps you through the installation procedure when adding a new printer. You will be required to manually intervene, even when using the wizard. In one of the wizard steps, you must select the printer for which the drivers are to be installed, **Figure 11-9.**

In the illustration, you see the window used to identify the printer for which the drivers must be installed. A printer driver contains the code necessary to allow the computer to communicate to the printer. Without the correct driver, the printer may operate incorrectly or may not operate at all. When you attempt to print without the correct driver, some common actions are a constant ejection or feed of paper, printing copy with no margins, and printing gibberish or unrecognizable symbols. The correct driver for the printer is essential to ensure proper printing of the desired text or image.

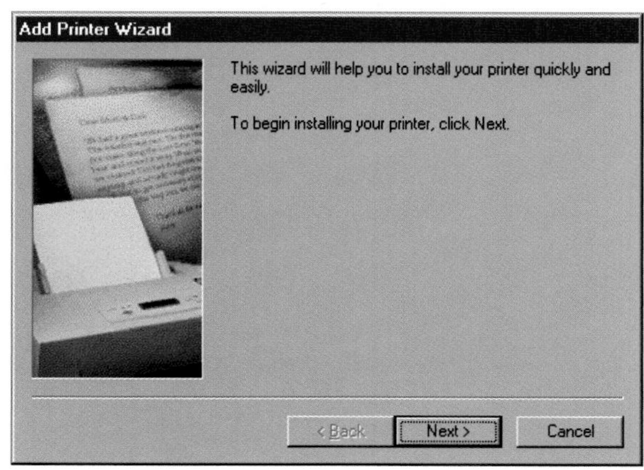

Figure 11-8.
The **Add Printer Wizard** takes you through the installation of a new printer.

Look again at Figure 11-9. On the left side is a list of printer manufacturers. After a printer manufacturer is selected, the models of the printers associated with the manufacturer appear on the right. Windows has over 800 models from which to choose. Some technicians load all available printer drivers on the hard disk as part of a regular installation procedure. This way, all the printer drivers at the time of the OS release are available on the hard drive. This is not always the case. If the driver needed was not loaded during installation, when you click on the **Next** button after choosing your printer, the wizard will ask you to insert your Windows OS CD-ROM and to click the OK button. The wizard will then find the correct driver on the CD.

Sometimes, the printer you are installing will not be listed. New models of printers are constantly being developed and the desired driver may not be present. When the model to be installed is not listed, choose the **Have Disk** option shown in Figure 11-9. With this option, you supply the driver from floppy disk or CD. A floppy disk or CD with drivers should come in the packaging with the printer. (Though, don't forget to check for the latest drivers at the manufacturer's Web site.) Choosing the **Have Disk** option brings up the screen shown in **Figure 11-10.** If the drivers included with the printer are on a CD, be sure to change the **A:** to **D:** (or to the correct CD drive letter for your PC).

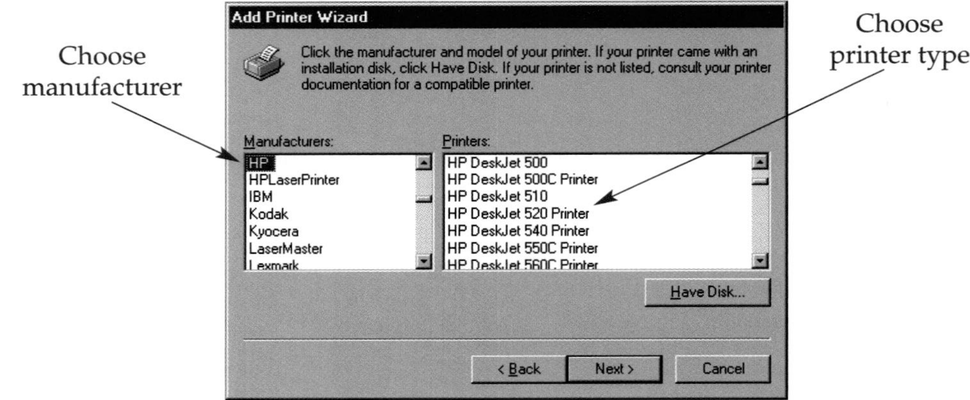

Figure 11-9. The wizard offers a selection of manufacturers to choose from. First choose your manufacturer. Next, pick out the model you are installing.

Figure 11-10. To use a driver supplied by a manufacturer, choose **Have Disk** and then enter the path to the driver (floppy or CD). If you have downloaded a driver from a manufacturer's Web site, you need to point to the folder on your hard drive in which you saved the file.

PC Printer Resources

Your printer may use any of your COM ports or your LPT ports. Remember that the four COM serial ports share two IRQs. Typically, COM1 and COM3 share IRQ4, while COM2 and COM4 share IRQ3. If you have two devices connected to the same COM IRQ, you can only use one of the devices. The two ports assigned the same IRQ cannot be used simultaneously. See **Figure 11-11.**

Generally, the LPT port is chosen by default. Occasionally, you may need to select another port or different system resources. When selecting different system resources, such as the IRQ assignment, you may need to disable the Plug and Play feature of the computer. The Plug and Play feature can be usually disabled in the BIOS setup program. Once Plug and Play has been disabled, you simply open **Device Manager** and assign the system resources of your choice. Next, you can reactivate the Plug and Play feature and the computer will assign the remaining system resources without changing the ones you have now previously assigned manually.

The number of serial and LPT ports on new computers has been reduced with the emergence of USB and FireWire. As this trend continues, serial and LPT ports may be completely replaced by USB and FireWire.

Sharing Printers

There are several common methods of sharing printers between many PCs. One common way is through the use of a network system. Any printer connected directly to a PC on the network or to the network cabling can be shared by any or all PCs connected to the network system. Networking printers will be covered in more detail in Chapter 16—Introduction to Networking.

Another common way to share printers among multiple PCs is through mechanical selector switches. A selector switch can connect several PCs to one common printer. This method is very common for dot matrix printers, but is not recommended for printers that contain elaborate electronics such as a laser printer. Mechanical selector switches can damage laser printer electronics, especially if they are switched while printing is in process.

Printer Spooling

In early computer systems, no other operation could be accomplished until the computer finished printing. Today, when a file is sent to the printer, other activities can be performed on the PC without waiting for the printer to

	IRQ Assigned	Port Address	Comment
COM1	4	3F8h-3FFh	Serial port
COM2	3	2F8h-2FFh	Serial port
COM3	4	3E8h-3EFh	Serial port
COM4	3	2E8h-2EFh	Serial port
LPT1	7	378h-37Fh	Parallel port
LPT2	Any available	278h-27Fh	Parallel port

The lowercase letter h signifies a hexadecimal number.

Figure 11-11.
COM and LPT ports and their resources.

spooling
a technique that stores data to be printed into memory so that printing operations can be completed in the background while other tasks are performed by the PC user.

queue
list of print jobs waiting to be completed and their status.

complete its job. This is accomplished through a technique called ***spooling.*** Many I/O devices and operations use spooling to temporarily store data, freeing up CPU resources and allowing other activities to be performed on the PC. When a printer uses spooling, it stores the data to be printed in a buffer. The printing operation can be completed in the background while the user performs other tasks on the PC.

Many printer jobs can be sent to the printer at the same time. The computer, rather than sending multiple printer jobs directly to the printer, sends them to the spooling buffer. The buffer can be RAM or hard disk area. With the data in the buffer, the documents can be accessed by the printer one at a time as the printer completes its printing jobs. Print jobs waiting to be completed are stored in the print ***queue*** (pronounced like the letter Q). Figure 11-12 shows a print queue with multiple documents in line. You can check a printer's queue at any time. It is accessed through the **Printers** folder by double-clicking the icon for the printer you wish to inspect.

The print jobs are displayed in a Windows print queue window. The status of each print job is shown. If the printer is shared by more than one PC, the owner of the job will be displayed. In Figure 11-12, the same print job is repeated several times. This is a very common occurrence. When a page fails to print, a novice user will attempt to print the document several times before calling for technical support. One of the first things a technician should do when responding to a print call is to purge all the duplicate print files from the queue. Sometimes a printer is locked up because of a document sent by a shared user. By purging a particular user's document, the printing problem may be cleared and the remaining documents will print as they should.

Printer Memory

Printers usually have memory in the form of SIMMs or DIMMs. The amount of memory with which a printer is equipped determines the resolution and size of the subject to be printed. If a printer does not have sufficient memory to print a file, it will generate an error code. Error codes are common when printing large, memory-intensive, graphic images. The exact error code will depend on the printer manufacturer and model. When a printer prints only a portion of an image, it is a sure sign of insufficient memory.

Installing more printer memory is a relatively simple task. Once the printer documentation is consulted about the appropriate memory type to use, the memory installs just as it would to the RAM banks on a motherboard. Review the *Installing RAM Modules* section from Chapter 6—Memory. The amount of memory in the printer can usually be verified by a self-test performed at the menu on the printer.

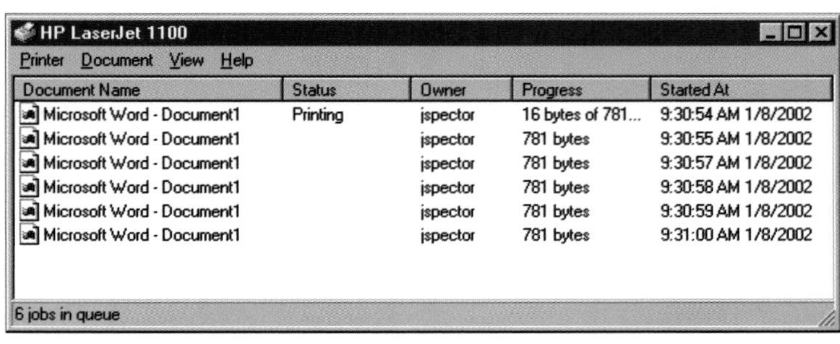

Figure 11-12. The printing queue shows you the status of your current printing job as well as what else is lined up to follow.

Error Codes

Error codes produced on some printer LCD displays provide a frequent source of confusion. Some errors generated are straight forward such as "Paper Jam" or "Refill Paper Tray." Other errors are cryptic and require decoding. They simply refer to a number such as "40 ERROR" or "22 ERROR." Some of these errors can be translated by using the owner's manual. Other times, you may need to access the manufacturer's Web site.

Some of the codes are not published for the general public. The manufacturers feel these repairs involve work beyond the typical user's expertise.

Paper Jams

Paper jams are when a printer pulls one or more sheets through its mechanism and the paper becomes wedged inside. They are a very common problem associated with most printers. With proper care, most printer jams can be avoided. There are many causes of paper jams.

Paper quality is an important issue when it comes to paper jams. Low-quality paper produces a lot of paper lint. Paper lint accumulates in all printers. Accumulation around sensitive printer parts can cause jams.

paper jam
when a printer pulls one or more sheets through its mechanism and the paper becomes wedged inside.

Another issue is moisture. When paper arrives from an outside storage area that is not climate controlled, condensation (moisture) can be created due to the change in temperature. This can make the paper damp. Damp paper is almost sure to jam in a printer. Paper should be stored at the same room temperature and humidity level as the printer for approximately twenty-four hours.

Another common cause of paper jams is worn parts along the paper train. The ***paper train*** is the route that the paper follows through the printer. The train consists of several rubber rollers and a paper separator pad. The paper separator pad is designed to allow only one sheet of paper at a time to enter the paper train from the paper tray. As the paper separator pad wears, jams become increasingly more common. In this case, the only remedy is to replace the separator pad. Worn pickup rollers can also cause jams. Sometimes, cleaning the rollers or removing paper lint can solve the problem. Other times, the pickup rollers have to be replaced.

paper train
the route the paper follows through the printer.

The direction of paper can influence the number of jams created in the printer. Most paper is manufactured with a natural curve. Typically, the outside wrapper of the paper will indicate the side of the stack of paper that should be used first in any printer or copy machine. The wrapper is often marked with an arrow. Not all paper packages are marked with an indicating arrow, however. If you are experiencing a definite curl to the finished printed page, check for markings on the paper wrapper for the correct positioning of the paper into the paper tray.

Tech Tip:

One way to avoid paper jams is to discard the first sheet of paper where the fold of the wrapper comes together. Many times this sheet of paper contains glue residue from the sealing process. The glue can collect inside the printer on the rollers and separator as well as on the fusing unit or drum. *Always* discard the first sheet from a new package of paper.

Toner Spills

When working with laser printers, a toner spill is almost inevitable. It is good practice to use a facemask and plastic gloves to clean up toner spills. Breathing in toner dust is not recommended.

Use a soft, dry, lint-free cloth or a brush to wipe up the toner or use a specially designed vacuum. Do not try to clean up toner with a household vacuum. The toner can damage a household vacuum cleaner. The toner is very fine dust and can pass through the vacuum's filters. The toner dust can collect on the vacuum motor, where a great deal of heat is generated. This heat can cause the toner to melt, thus causing a host of problems for the motor. There are specially designed vacuum cleaners that are used to clean printers and copy machines that use toner.

The use of compressed air to blow out toner deposits should also be avoided. This causes the toner to spread even further and can force the toner deep inside the printer.

Toner residue on the skin or clothes should be cleaned up with cold water. Hot water can cause the toner to set.

Diagnosing Laser Printer Problems

Laser printers are the most common printer you will encounter. Understanding the complete printing process of the typical laser printer based on the electrophotographic process will give you a quick insight to the problem. Most printers are equipped with a self-test program as part of a diagnostic routine. Running the printer self-test can eliminate many printer faults.

The following is a list of twelve most common problems you may encounter with a laser printer. Examine them along with their causes and solutions.

1. Printing Gibberish:

If the printer is printing gibberish or unintelligible symbols, **Figure 11-13,** but prints fine during the self-test, you probably have the wrong printer driver loaded or a corrupted driver.

Figure 11-13.
If your printed page looks like this, there is likely a problem with your printer driver.

```
$$%34693%@%&&#^&bsr   ]]]]]]]]]]]]]]]]]]]]]]]]]]]
#^tbsss$%^^%#$#%$%^%%^%&LK$J^$%JYS}
}}}$@L#K!!K@#LL$K#$T)$U))_$          #KS)$%)LFX
)$I)$#  )#$L      )$##@)#^&B%PO("R
@!@RGXR^*&*)%Y%^%&&R(T)(+ {&^@$^%^%E
R^*^R<LTG*&T<A#$^E&I&R*KFEA$^%E&HEW$
#^%DB$%&%4985)(*&(()*)(Q@LJ9984jlk
094/94"3434W%$))$E)$I)@LR_%%+@<V<
%)$##########)I$#$%& *()_&E<?""})_(%#R$%*(&
:$*&L(MN?){"_W^((D%^*(*E$^JJ&*O)(PAE$^^%
*P_VHJ*%&K<M?": "?><O)*%$#&(**>&T%$#^*&
&())?><R$%E$%O*&#^%*&)(*&^%Q%*D*$B^&(
*@R****D^U^E&I^%*R*KS%$*&T(IAY$Q@$%*(*
JYR#^%E(*&(OYT$A^%(*&(HRE^%&(I^R*%*UI&
^O$%*D%&%&Y^%*IKM^%^&^)%%%%%%%
%%%%%%%%%%
```

An incorrect printer driver can be loaded when a user attempts to use a disk from another PC with a different printer installed. Some word processing packages save the printer setup as well as the document to disk. When the document is loaded on a different PC with a different printer, it can cause the printer to print gibberish or just continually print a series of blank pages. Check the **Printers** window located at **Start | Settings | Printers**. If you see printers other than the one you are using, this is most likely the problem.

You may also have a corrupt printer driver and may need to reinstall the printer driver. A computer "hiccup" can corrupt a driver. Reinstalling the printer driver will correct this problem. Reinstalling the driver is done just like the initial installation, using the **Add Printer Wizard**. The computer will install the new driver over the old, corrupt driver.

2. Pages Have Light Streaks:

If pages are printing light images or have light streaks vertically down the page, **Figure 11-14,** the printer is low on toner. Remove the toner cartridge, shake it gently from side to side, and then reinstall it. If the quality of the printed pages improves, replace the toner cartridge.

3. Pages Print Solid Black:

When pages print solid black or if there is a great deal of gray in the areas that should be white, the most likely problem is the toner cartridge is seated improperly, allowing toner to dump on the paper, **Figure 11-15.** It is also possible that the toner cartridge is defective. Fixing an improperly seated toner cartridge is as simple as removing the cartridge and replacing correctly.

Although less likely, there is also the possibility that the laser may not be working or the mirror may be defective. The primary corona wire could also be at fault. When the primary corona wire is at fault, there is no initial charge

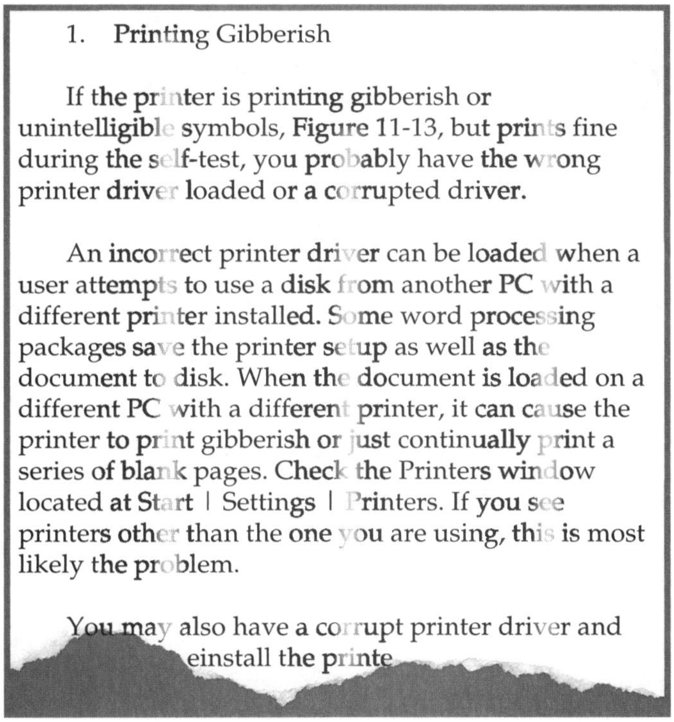

---

1. Printing Gibberish

If the printer is printing gibberish or unintelligible symbols, Figure 11-13, but prints fine during the self-test, you probably have the wrong printer driver loaded or a corrupted driver.

An incorrect printer driver can be loaded when a user attempts to use a disk from another PC with a different printer installed. Some word processing packages save the printer setup as well as the document to disk. When the document is loaded on a different PC with a different printer, it can cause the printer to print gibberish or just continually print a series of blank pages. Check the Printers window located at Start | Settings | Printers. If you see printers other than the one you are using, this is most likely the problem.

You may also have a corrupt printer driver and einstall the printe

Figure 11-14. When toner cartridges run low, the printed page will show insufficient toner coverage.

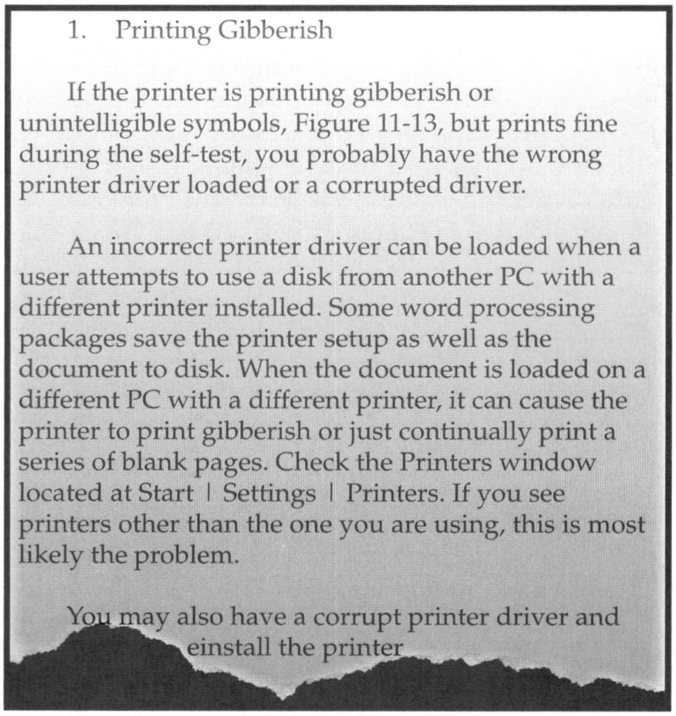

Figure 11-15. If extra toner appears on a page, you should first check if the toner cartridge is seated correctly.

1. Printing Gibberish

If the printer is printing gibberish or unintelligible symbols, Figure 11-13, but prints fine during the self-test, you probably have the wrong printer driver loaded or a corrupted driver.

An incorrect printer driver can be loaded when a user attempts to use a disk from another PC with a different printer installed. Some word processing packages save the printer setup as well as the document to disk. When the document is loaded on a different PC with a different printer, it can cause the printer to print gibberish or just continually print a series of blank pages. Check the Printers window located at Start | Settings | Printers. If you see printers other than the one you are using, this is most likely the problem.

You may also have a corrupt printer driver and einstall the printer

placed on the drum. Remember that the polarities used depend on the manufacturer. The polarities used determine if the page prints totally black or totally white. You must first determine whether the laser on the printer writes the images or writes the background. If any of these parts have gone bad, a qualified technician needs to be contacted.

4. Pages Print Blank:

Always check the easy things first. A common error that causes blank pages occurs when the toner cartridge is changed. Often users fail to remove the sealing tape that keeps the toner slot closed during shipping and transfer. If you are getting blank pages, always remove the toner cartridge first to ensure that the sealing tape has been removed.

The wrong driver or a corrupt driver can also cause blank pages. If only alternate pages or just the first page is blank, it is probably a printer setup problem. The driver is the place to look. Try reinstalling.

If all the pages of the print job are blank, the transfer corona may be at fault. Without a charge on the paper, it cannot attract toner from the drum. A qualified technician must be called for this problem.

5. Printer Quality Has Suddenly Become Poor:

With poor quality prints, first check that the toner cartridge is not low on toner or completely empty. Also, check if the printer is set up for economy or draft mode. The economy or draft mode is used to conserve on toner. This option usually can be accessed in the printer dialog setup window of the operating system and through the printer menu options controlled by the buttons on the printer. Usually, any settings on the printer will override settings created with the operating system interface.

6. Toner Smears on Paper:

As stated earlier, always check the simplest thing first. With toner smears, the easiest thing to check is if the printer was loaded with the wrong type of paper. Some printers require special paper. If there are multiple types of printers at a location, there is a chance the wrong type of paper may have been placed into the paper tray.

However, when toner smears across the paper when touched, **Figure 11-16,** it is a good indication that the fusing unit is out. With the fusing unit out, the toner is never melted to the paper.

7. The Printer Acts Completely Dead:

If a printer acts dead, check if the printer is offline. If there is no response, check the printer cables, as they may have become loose. Of course, never forget to check the power cable and to make sure there is power at the outlet.

A dead printer can also be a driver problem.

8. Printed Characters Are Fuzzy:

With fuzzy printing, check the type of paper loaded into the printer. If the wrong type of paper is used, the toner may scatter outside the character outline.

9. Constant Dark or White Spots:

If you find dark or white spots that appear in the same place on multiple printed sheets, it is likely that the drum is scratched. With a scratch on the drum, it may not be able to hold toner or it may hold toner on the spot at all times. Replacement drums can be purchased and installed fairly easily for most laser printers.

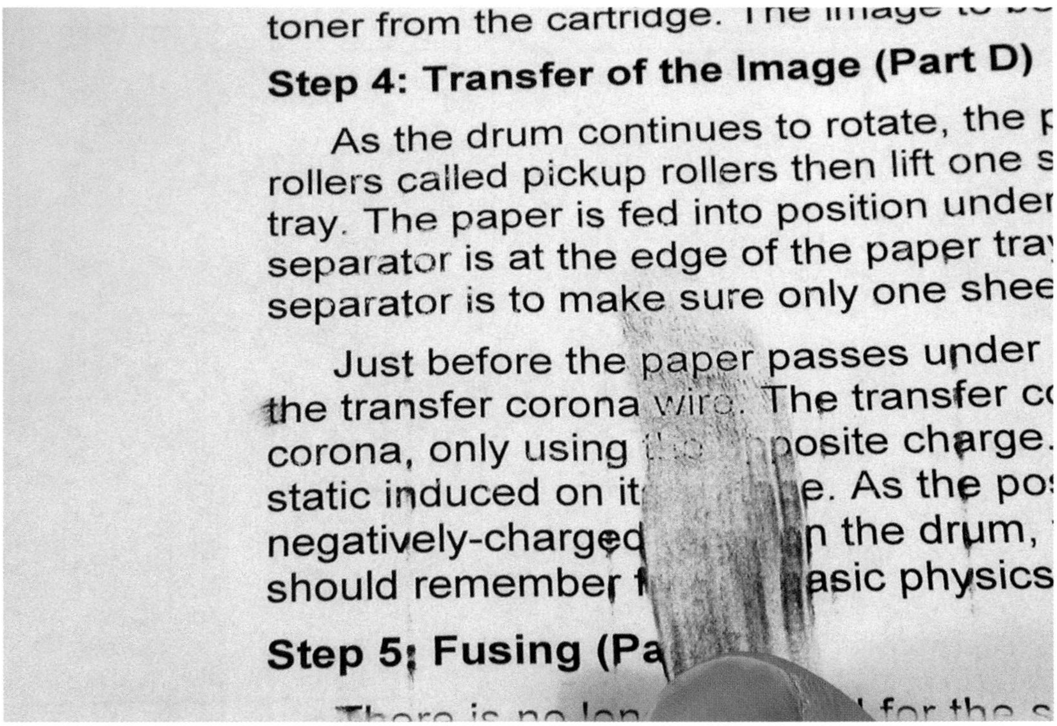

Figure 11-16.
If toner is not sealed properly to paper, it smears easily.

10. Ghost Images on the Paper:

A ghost image is a second image that appears on the paper in the background of the image you are trying to print, **Figure 11-17.** A ghost image is usually a sign that the erase lamp is burnt out. When the erase lamp is out, the image of the last print run will remain on the drum.

11. Blank Areas Appear in Parts of the Printing Job:

If blank areas are appearing on the printing job, there is a good chance the wrong paper length has been selected at setup. Check if there is a mismatch in paper length.

12. Printer Trips the Circuit Breaker:

If the circuit breaker trips when the printer is running, it is a good sign that electronic or other parts of the printer are failing. However, you must remember that a printer uses heat to fuse the toner to the paper. A printer may draw as much as 15 amps of current while processing a page. If the printer is on the same circuit as another piece of heavy-load equipment, the two running at the same time can trip a breaker. A coffeepot, copy machine, toaster oven, and microwave are good examples of equipment that may be found on the same circuit breaker as the printer. The combination of these types of equipment sharing the same breaker as the printer can cause frequent breaker trips. Check carefully. A circuit can span more than one room. The overloaded equipment may not be near the printer location.

Diagnosing USB Printer Problems

The USB connection has become the standard cable type connection for printers replacing the parallel cable and earlier serial connections. While USB is easy to install and typically configures automatically, there are several problems commonly associated with this type of connection.

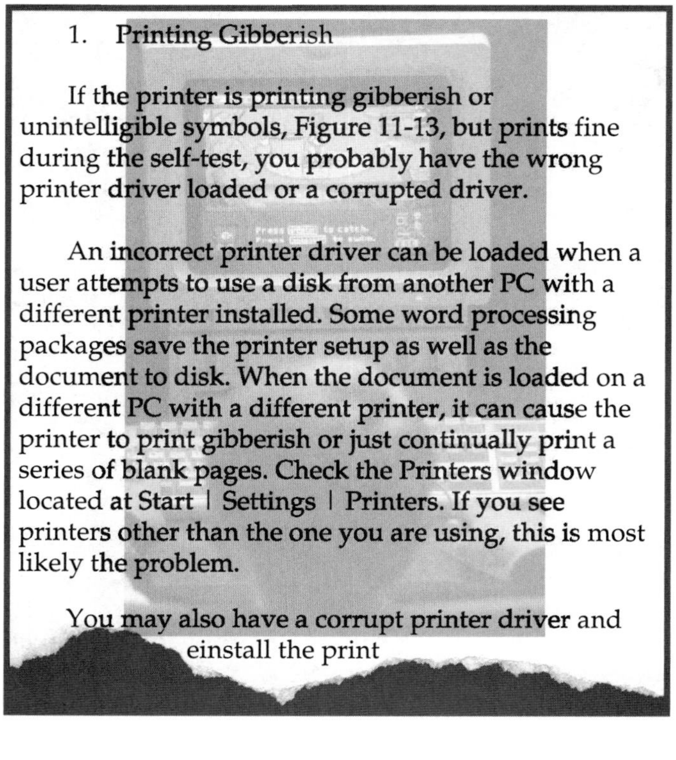

Figure 11-17. Ghost images appear when the image from a previous print is not erased from the drum.

1. Printing Gibberish

If the printer is printing gibberish or unintelligible symbols, Figure 11-13, but prints fine during the self-test, you probably have the wrong printer driver loaded or a corrupted driver.

An incorrect printer driver can be loaded when a user attempts to use a disk from another PC with a different printer installed. Some word processing packages save the printer setup as well as the document to disk. When the document is loaded on a different PC with a different printer, it can cause the printer to print gibberish or just continually print a series of blank pages. Check the Printers window located at Start | Settings | Printers. If you see printers other than the one you are using, this is most likely the problem.

You may also have a corrupt printer driver and einstall the print

Insufficient or No Electrical Power

It is most important to mention that you should always check for the simplest and easiest solution first when dealing with printer problems. Check if the printer is turned on and is online. An LED generally indicates power to a printer. If the LED is lit, the USB port selected for the printer connection may not be providing sufficient electrical power to operate the printer. While the majority of electrical power is supplied to the printer through its own electrical plug, the USB cable also provides a small amount of energy required to run the printer. This problem is easily remedied by installing a powered USB hub capable of supplying the higher electrical power needed by the printer.

Printer Is Offline

A printer can have power but be offline or on standby. A printer cannot print while in the offline mode. An offline printer may sound like too simple of a problem or too obvious, but the problem often occurs. When giving support over a telephone, the power source and whether the printer is offline should be checked first. Don't be surprised if the person on the other end of the telephone does not exactly know what you mean by "offline."

Conflicting Devices

USB devices are not supposed to conflict, but this is in theory only. Occasionally, conflicts do arise and are generally caused by either the BIOS setup program or the USB device driver. One of the devices may be programmed to take over the bandwidth of the port, causing the other devices to go into a hibernation state or simply lockup.

Microsoft furnishes basic device code to developers to use and modify for their USB devices. Microsoft will also test the software and the hardware compatibility for a small charge. If the device passes Microsoft testing, the device is added to the Microsoft Hardware Compatibility List (HCL) for the operating system version for which it was tested. However, some manufacturers develop their own driver software and only refer to the Microsoft guidelines. For whatever reason, they do not submit their code for testing or it is tested after the release of the hardware device. If a problem is found, the manufacturer will simply provide a "patch" at their Web site.

To troubleshoot a USB device, remove all other USB devices from the port that the printer is connected to. This will help eliminate the possibility of a conflict between the devices connected to the same port.

Check Device Manager for a problem with the USB port indicated by an exclamation mark or question mark. These symbols indicate that the printer is not properly recognized or configured and are most likely related to the printer driver or BIOS setup. The software drivers or BIOS, or both, may need to be upgraded. Check the printer manufacturer's Web site for more information.

Windows Assistance

Windows provides a troubleshooting dialog box under their Help feature that can be accessed and utilized to help with printer problems. **Figure 11-18** shows the printer troubleshooter in the Windows Help dialog box. This troubleshooting box can be accessed through **Start | Help | Contents | Troubleshooting | Windows Troubleshooters | Print**.

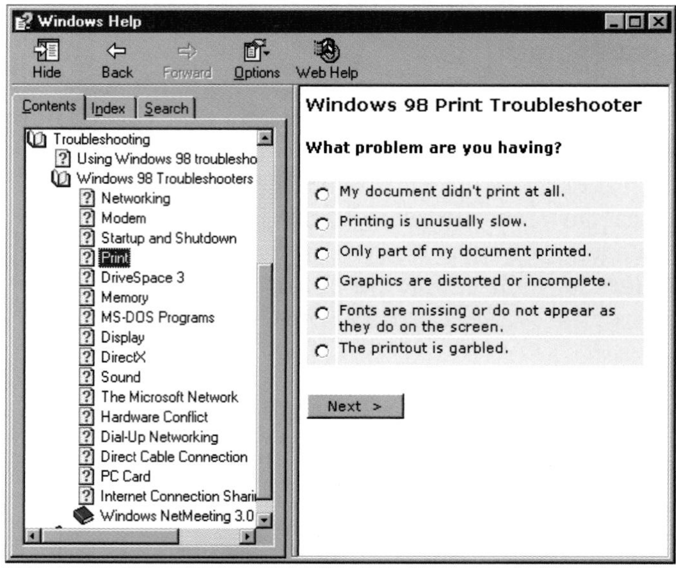

Figure 11-18. Windows print troubleshooting dialog box.

Windows Help will ask you a series of questions about the printing problem and provide you with possible solutions. There are many topics about printers in the Windows Help dialog box. The Help dialog box is a reference tool with information about adding a printer, setting up a printer on a network, changing printer settings, and many more topics.

Fonts

font
a design for a set of symbols, usually text and number characters. A font describes characteristics associated with a symbol such as the typeface, size, pitch, and spacing between symbols.

points
unit of measure for the height of a font. Each point is equal to 1/72 of an inch.

pitch
unit of measure for the width of a font.

A ***font*** is a design for a set of symbols, usually text and number characters. A font describes characteristics associated with a symbol such as the typeface, size, pitch, and spacing between symbols. Look at **Figure 11-19.**

The two main classifications of fonts are *bitmap* and *vector.* Bitmap fonts use a pattern of dots to represent each letter. The bitmap images of the text are stored in memory. As you type, the bitmap images are placed on the screen by a process similar to a cut-and-paste process. Each and every different font requires a different bitmap pattern. A bitmap font must also use a separate bitmap for each size of the letter.

A vector font is also referred to as an outline font. A vector font draws the outline of the letter rather than storing a separate bitmap pattern for each font. The angles, turns, and distances are calculated for each character. A vector font is easily scaled to larger or smaller sizes because the letter is based on an algorithm.

Bitmap fonts look better than vector fonts when displayed on low-resolution devices such as monitors. On high-resolution devices, such as some printers, vector fonts look better than bitmap fonts.

The physical size of a font is described in points and pitch. The height of a letter is measured in ***points.*** The width is measured in ***pitch.*** Each point is equal to 1/72 of an inch.

Sample Fonts

This is a sample of Times New Roman 8 point font.

This is a sample of Times New Roman 12 point font.

This is a sample of Times New Roman 18 point font.

This is a sample of Courier 8 point font.

This is a sample of Courier 12 point font.

This is a sample of Courier 14 point font.

This is a sample of Brush Script 16 point font.

This is a sample of Brush Script 20 point font.

This is a sample of Tahoma 10 point font.

This is a sample of Tahoma 14 point font.

This is a sample of Myriad 10 point font.

This is a sample of Myriad 16 point font.

This is a sample of Myriad 16 point italic font.

This is a sample of Myriad 16 point bold font.

Figure 11-19. Samples of common typefaces and point-sizes.

Vector fonts are used with Page Description Language (PDL). Common PDLs are Adobe PostScript and Microsoft TrueType. A page description language treats everything on a page as a graphic image. The PDL translates the picture on the monitor into a set of printer codes that will exactly duplicate the image seen on the screen. This is often referred to as "what you see is what you get" (WYSIWYG).

Figure 11-20 shows all the ways the Word program can manipulate a font. The manipulation feature is typical in most word processing packages. Available fonts can be viewed by accessing the folder located at **Start | Settings | Control Panel | Fonts**. See **Figure 11-21.** You can print a sample of the selected font by right-clicking the folder and selecting **Print** from the shortcut menu.

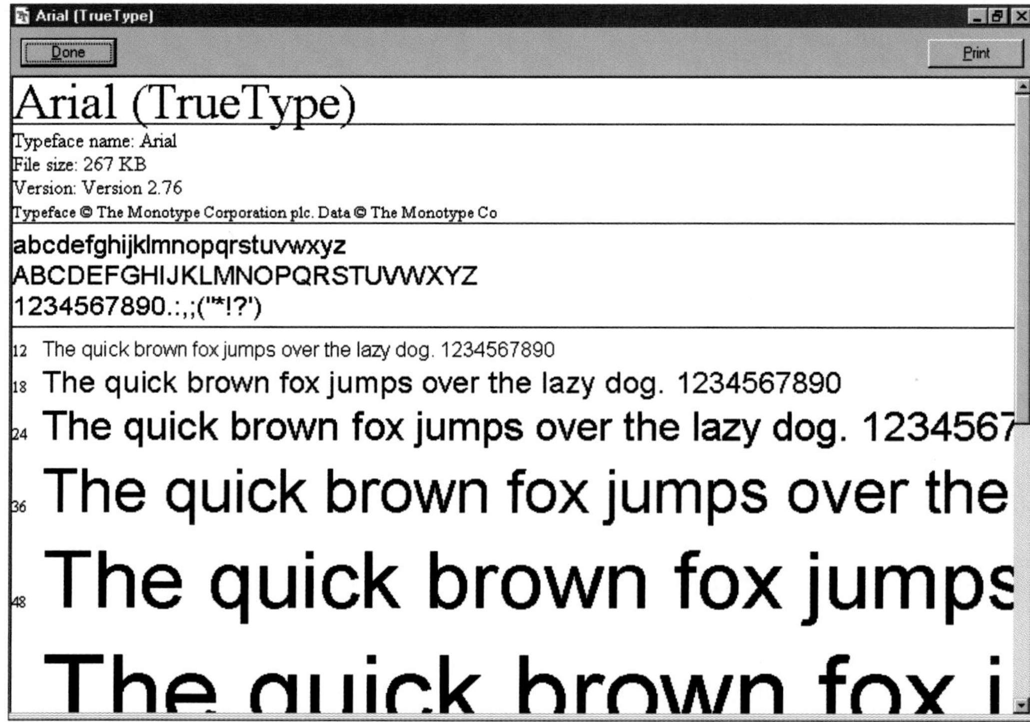

Figure 11-20. A sample of Arial Italic printed from the **Font** folder in **Control Panel**.

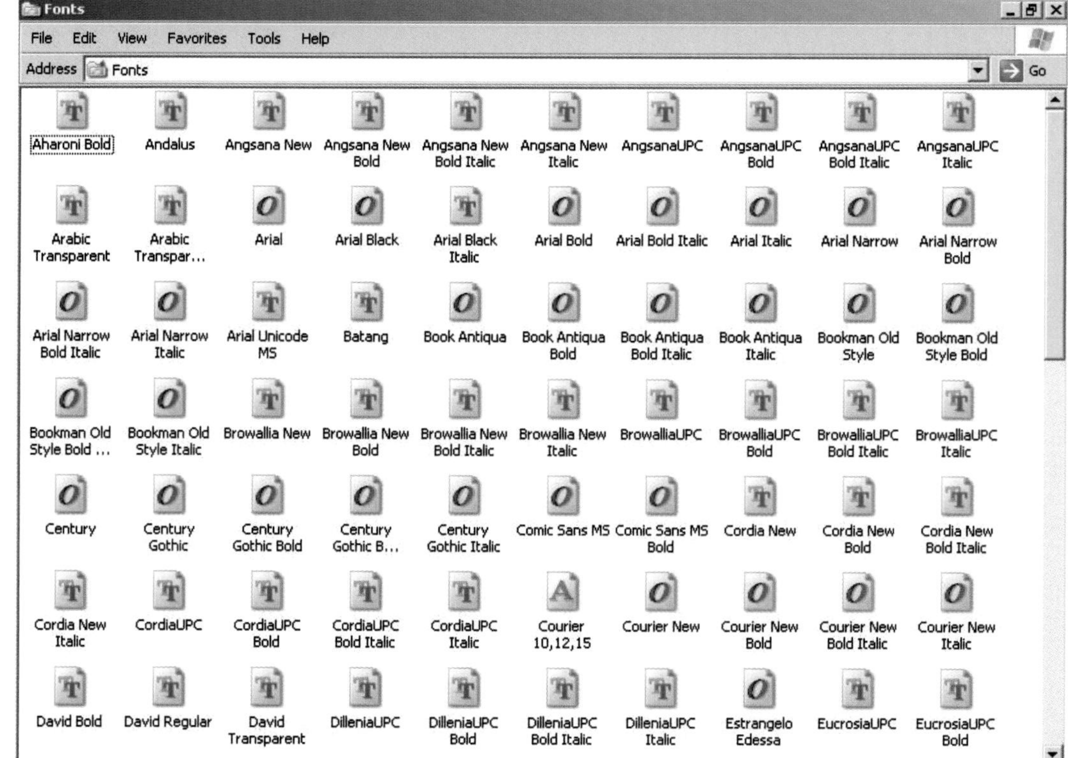

Figure 11-21. Windows fonts folder showing just a few of the available fonts.

Summary

- A printer is an electromechanical device used to print an image or text to paper or other presentation media.
- The six laser printing stages are charging the drum, writing the image, developing the image, transferring the image, fusing the image, and cleaning the drum.
- Inkjet printers use either a photoresistor or a piezocell crystal to produce the force needed to spray a fine mist of ink onto paper.
- COM1 and COM3 share IRQ 4.
- COM2 and COM4 share IRQ 3.
- Many printer problems are simple and can be easily solved by users or technicians.
- A font is a description of the characteristics of a symbol such as letters and numbers and describes the attributes of the symbol.

Review Questions

Answer the following questions on a separate sheet of paper. Please do not write in this book.

1. After a laser printer prints a page of text, the toner smears when touched. What might be the problem?
2. A paper jam constantly occurs when using a printer. This is a recent problem. What might be the cause?
3. An error code appears on the printer panel that you are not familiar with. What should you do?
4. Place the following steps in the correct order.

   Toner is attracted to the drum.

   The static brush removes the charge from the paper.

   The laser writes the image on the drum.

   The transfer corona charges the paper.

   The fusing section melts the toner.

   The drum is erased of all charge.

   The primary corona wire places a charge on the drum.
5. Describe what print spooling does.
6. What is the print queue?
7. What is the difference between a bitmap font and a vector font?
8. How can the font folder be accessed? Start with **Start** | _____ | _____ | _____.
9. The height of a font is measured in _____.
10. The width of a font is measured in _____.

Sample A+ Exam Questions

Answer the following questions on a separate sheet of paper. Please do not write in this book.

1. What type of printer utilizes piezoelectric technology?
   a. Laser
   b. Dot matrix
   c. Dye-sublimation
   d. Inkjet
2. What type of printer utilizes pins driven by a solenoid striking a ribbon to make dots conforming to letters, symbols, and pictures?
   a. Laser
   b. Dot matrix
   c. Dye-sublimation
   d. Inkjet
3. Which type of printer utilizes thermoresistors to force the ink from a reservoir?
   a. Laser
   b. Dot matrix
   c. Dye-sublimation
   d. Inkjet
4. In the electrostatic process, the term *fusing* can best be described as which of the following answers?
   a. The protective device installed in electrostatic laser printers to prevent electrical overload of the circuits.
   b. The transfer of toner to the paper to construct the printed image.
   c. The bonding of the toner to the paper.
   d. A special module that prevents the voltage from exceeding the 600 volts positive charge.
5. Which of the following includes all the correct processes in correct order for electrostatic printing?
   a. Charging the drum, writing the image, developing the image, transferring the image, fusing the image, cleaning the drum.
   b. Charging the drum, transferring the image, writing the image, developing the image, fusing the image, cleaning the drum.
   c. Cleaning the drum, charging the drum, transferring the image, developing the image, charging again, writing the image, fusing the image.
   d. Writing the image, charging the drum, developing the image, transferring the image, fusing the image, cleaning the drum.

6. The acronym LPT represents which of the following?
   a. Local printer transferring-port
   b. Line printer terminal
   c. Local printer terminal
   d. Line port terminal
7. What does the printer term *spooling* mean?
   a. It describes the mechanical device that holds the ribbon in place on a dot matrix printer.
   b. It is a method of connecting a local printer to an area network printer group.
   c. It is the method used to store print jobs waiting to be processed in an orderly fashion.
   d. It is a method of determining the amount of rotation or "print spooling" required for blank spacing between lines of text in a document.
8. LPT1 is usually assigned to which IRQ?
   a. 5
   b. 6
   c. 7
   d. 8
9. A paper comes out of a laser printer, and its printed surface is completely black. What is most likely the cause?
   a. The toner cartridge is seated improperly.
   b. The charge is too low on the drum.
   c. The laser is defective.
   d. The fuser is overheating the paper.
10. A laser printer prints a page, and the document smears when touched. What is the most likely cause of the image smear?
    a. The primary corona is defective.
    b. The transfer corona is defective.
    c. The toner is damp.
    d. The fuser is defective.

Suggested Laboratory Activities

Do not attempt any suggested laboratory activities without your instructor's permission. Certain activities can render the PC operating system inoperable.

1. Install a printer on a PC. Use a printer that is not identified in the list of printer drivers used by the Windows operating system for a real challenge. You must use a printer that requires downloading a printer driver file from a Web site.
2. Practice downloading a printer driver file.
3. Set up a printer to print to paper in landscape orientation.
4. Send the same print job to a printer three or four times. Open the **Printers** folder located under the **Start** menu and look for a listing of files being printed. Stop the file printing process and purge the duplicate files.
5. Try printing to a printer while it is turned off and observe the error code.
6. Go to a major printer manufacturer's Web site and access information about how to care for the printer. What is the routine maintenance that should be performed?
7. Using a laser printer that cannot be salvaged, carefully disassemble the printer and identify all the major parts. You may try to use the manufacturer's Web site to assist you. Do not be surprised if you cannot find information about the disassembly process. Usually the manufacturer does not want persons who are not fully qualified to disassemble their printers.
8. Add memory to an existing laser printer. Go to the manufacturer's Web site for step-by-step instructions. Do not attempt to disassemble a working laser printer without instructions on how to access the memory chips. Attempting to access the memory chips without knowing how can result in damaging the printer's plastic assembly.
9. Draw out the step-by-step electrostatic printing process. When presented, this is one of the most commonly missed questions on the A+ Certification exam by PC technicians.
10. Go to the HP Web site and download a list of common error codes associated with an HP4L printer.

Interesting Web Sites for More Information

www.epson.com

www.hp.com

www.ricoh.com

Chapter 11
Laboratory Activity
Setting Up a Printer

After completing this laboratory activity, you will be able to:

- ❑ Install and set up a typical printer.
- ❑ Explain the various printer options available.

Introduction

The installation of a new printer is a common procedure. During the early years of personal computers, printer installation could be quite difficult. Now, in the era of Plug and Play and wizard programs, printer installation is much easier. In this exercise, you will install a printer driver. For the purpose of lab instruction, an HP laser printer is used, although the exact model will not be specified. You should substitute the manufacturer and model of your own printer in its place.

A printer driver is necessary for communications between the software that uses a printer and the printer hardware. The driver translates the communications between processor and printer. The processor communicates in hexadecimal or binary codes. The printer driver translates those and reissues them as commands that the printer can understand. In turn, the printer starts a new page, changes font size or style, copies an image from RAM, or prints a line.

If the correct driver is not selected, many things go wrong. An endless stream of paper may be ejected from the printer, completely blank or filled with unintelligible symbols. The printer may simply sit there and appear dead.

To install a printer, access the printer installation program located at **Start | Settings | Printers**. The printer installation program can also be accessed by double-clicking the **Printers** icon located at **Start | Settings | Control Panel**. Once the Printers window is open, double-click the **Add Printer** icon and follow the instructions in the **Add Printer Wizard** dialog box to install the printer.

Equipment and Materials

- Typical PC with Windows 98 operating system.
- Windows 98 Installation CD.
- HP laser printer or any equivalent printer.

Note:
The lab is compatible with most printers. Simply substitute the brand and model you are using in place of references made to the HP laser printer.

Procedure

1. ______ Boot the PC and wait for the Windows desktop to appear.
2. ______ Access the **Printers** dialog box located at **Start | Settings | Printers**.
3. ______ Double-click the **Add Printer** icon. The **Add Printer Wizard** dialog box should appear, similar to the one shown.

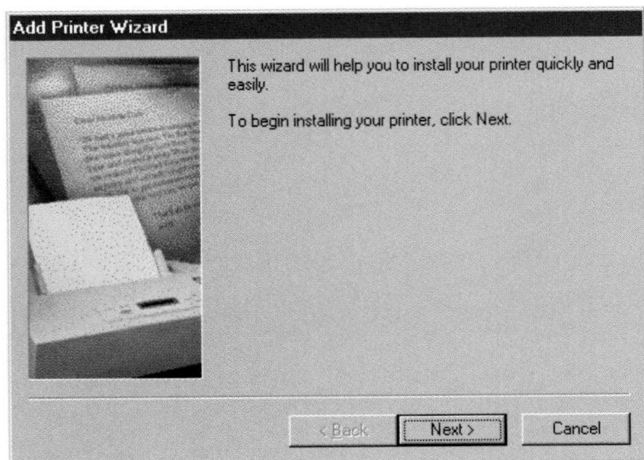

4. ______ Next, click the **Next** button and follow the onscreen prompts.
5. ______ The **Add Printer Wizard** dialog box should now appear similar to the following illustration. You must make a choice of printer connection by selecting either the **Local printer** or **Network printer** radio button.

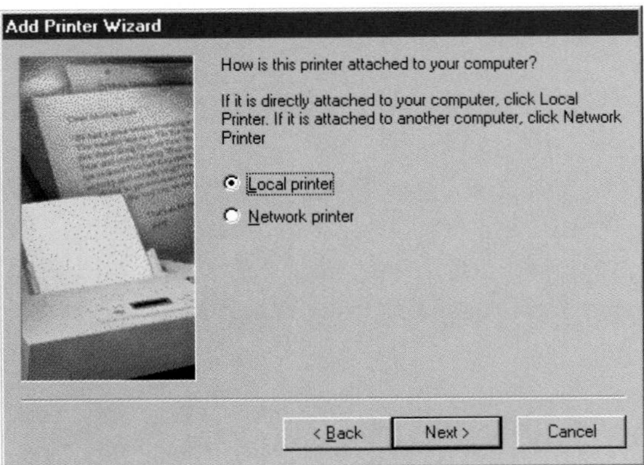

A local printer is one that is directly connected to the PC, while a network printer is one that is accessed via a network. In this lab activity, you should select the **Local printer** radio button.

6. ______ When installing a local printer, the **Add Printer Wizard** dialog box will ask you to identify the manufacturer and model of the printer you are installing. The list of manufacturers is on the left side of the dialog box, and the list of models from the selected manufacturer is on the right side of the dialog box. Use the scroll bar to locate the printer manufacturer and then select the manufacturer by clicking its name. The screen should appear similar to the following illustration.

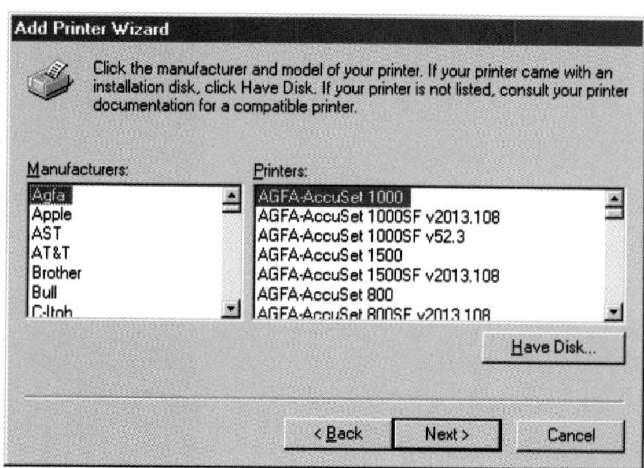

7. ______ Locate the model in the right panel by using the scroll bar on the right side listings. Select the model by clicking it. After the manufacturer and model have been selected, click the button labeled **Next**. Once this is done, Windows will automatically load the correct software driver for the printer. At times, the exact model will not be listed, and you will need to have a disk containing the correct printer driver for your printer.

8. ______ Next, the dialog box asks you to identify a port for the printer to connect to. See the following screen capture.

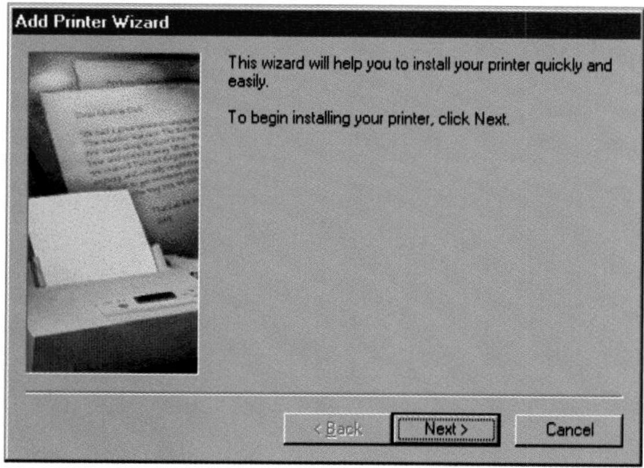

The usual choices are **COM1:**, **COM2:**, **FILE:**, and **LPT1:**. COM1 and LPT1 are commonly associated as printer ports. When the serial ports of COM1 or COM2 are selected, you may need additional information such as type of parity, number of data bits, and number of stop bits. This information can usually be found in the printer manual. For this exercise, select **LPT1: Printer Port**. The most modern printers used today can use USB ports as well. It is also common to purchase printers that have an RJ-45 port that is used for networking a printer. When a printer is networked, it is accessible to other computers on a network. This is found in both industry and in the home office. Printer connections for networks will be discussed in later chapters.

9. ______ The next screen in the **Add Printer Wizard** dialog box contains a **Printer Name:** text box. A new name can be typed in this field if you wish to rename the printer. This option will assist you and others in identifying the printer. The ability to rename the printer is especially useful when you have several printers that can be accessed, such as in a network environment.

10. ______ Below the **Printer Name:** text box is a prompt that asks if you wish to use the new printer as the Windows default printer. Select the **Yes** radio button.

11. ______ Next, the dialog box asks if you wish to print a test page after installation. Select the **Yes (recommended)** radio button. If everything prints correctly, you are finished. If the printer does not print correctly, you can enter the Windows Troubleshooters program by simply replying **No** when prompted.

12. ______ If everything is correct with the printer, you may close all Windows programs and shut down the PC. If things are not correct or if you have questions, please call your instructor.

Review Questions

Answer the following questions on a separate sheet of paper. Please do not write in this book.

1. Which two physical ports are typically used to connect to an older model printer?
2. What does the printer driver do?
3. What is the difference between a COM port and an LPT port?
4. If a printer prints unintelligible characters or symbols when first installed, what is most likely the problem?

12 Portable PCs

After studying this chapter, you will be able to:

- ❑ Distinguish between laptops, notebooks, palmtops, and personal digital assistants.
- ❑ Identify the parts that are different in full-size PCs and portable PCs.
- ❑ Explain the difference between the types of batteries used in portable PCs.
- ❑ Identify the three standard PCMCIA cards.
- ❑ Define what the Bluetooth standard does.
- ❑ Describe how Briefcase is used.
- ❑ Describe Direct Cable Connection communications.

A+ Exam—Key Points

You can count on at least one question about PCMCIA cards and batteries. You also may be asked a question about a null modem cable, its use, or construction.

Key Words and Terms

The following words and terms will become important pieces of your computer vocabulary. Be sure you can define them.

access point
ad-hoc network
alkaline battery
application service provider (ASP)
Bluetooth
docking station
encryption
fuel cell
laptop
lithium-ion (Li-ion) battery
nickel-cadmium (NiCd) battery
nickel-metal hydride (NiMH) battery
notebook
palmtop
PCMCIA card
personal digital assistant (PDA)
port replicator
smart card
Windows CE

The portable PC is a computer that is designed to go wherever the user needs it. There are a variety of portable PCs on the market. They go by names such as laptops, notebooks, palmtops, pocket PCs, and personal digital organizers. All modern portable PCs are battery-powered devices that use some type of flat-panel screen technology to keep weight and power consumption to a minimum.

Portable PCs generally have equal computing power to full-size PCs, though they are more expensive than the equivalent full-size model. However, as their numbers have increased, their price per unit has come down. When electronic devices are manufactured in limited numbers and with the latest technology, the prices are always higher. The classic electronic calculator is an excellent example. The first calculators, which provided only basic mathematical functions, cost $325 or more. Now, a small-sized calculator, which can perform nearly any desired mathematical function, preprogram math formulas, and plot graphs on an LCD screen, can be purchased for much less. This same trend is in progress with laptops, palmtops, and personal digital assistants.

laptop
lightweight, portable computer with the monitor, motherboard, processor, disk drives, keyboard, and mouse molded into one unit.

notebook
lightweight, portable computer with the monitor, motherboard, processor, disk drives, keyboard, and mouse molded into one unit.

palmtop
portable computer that can rest in the palm of the hand.

Laptops, Notebooks, and Palmtops

There are several types of true portable computers including laptops, notebooks, and palmtops, **Figure 12-1.** All are lightweight, portable machines with the monitor, motherboard, processor, disk drives, keyboard, and mouse molded into one unit. ***Laptops*** are the largest of the group. Each classification is determined by the physical size of the computer. Laptops are considered slightly larger than ***notebook*** computers, which are slightly smaller and thinner. However, this is a little ambiguous. When exactly does a laptop become a notebook computer? For the purpose of this textbook, the term *laptop* and *notebook* will be used interchangeably.

With a palmtop computer, there is no argument. The ***palmtop,*** as the name implies, rests in the palm of the hand. Despite its size, the palmtop is a true

Figure 12-1. Typical portable PCs.

portable computer that provides the services that its full-size PC counterpart provides.

Even newer devices such as cellular phones are becoming more and more accessible for use as wireless computers. These devices can be even smaller than a palmtop.

Parts of Portable PCs

A portable PC functions very similarly to a full-size PC. However, alterations have been made to the design of the portable PC to allow it to be carried easily, used anywhere, and connected quickly to other PCs and networks. To allow this functionality, laptop computers are equipped with some parts that full-size PCs don't have (large storage batteries) and have had other common PC components altered significantly (such as the mouse). In addition, to keep laptops adaptable like their full-size counterparts, PCMCIA cards were developed. PCMCIA cards allow new devices to be added to laptops easily.

Batteries

Batteries are a vital part of portable computing, **Figure 12-2.** There are four major types of batteries found in use for portable computers:

- Alkaline
- Nickel-cadmium (NiCd)
- Nickel-metal hydride (NiMH)
- Lithium-ion (Li-ion)

The type of battery is extremely important when selecting a portable PC. The type of battery determines the number of hours a PC can be used independently, and it also greatly affects the weight of the PC. All four types of batteries are rechargeable.

Figure 12-2.
There are a variety of battery choices for the portable PC. On the left is a lithium-ion battery. This type is found in most modern portable PCs. On the right is a nickel-metal hydride battery. This type is found in some older laptops.

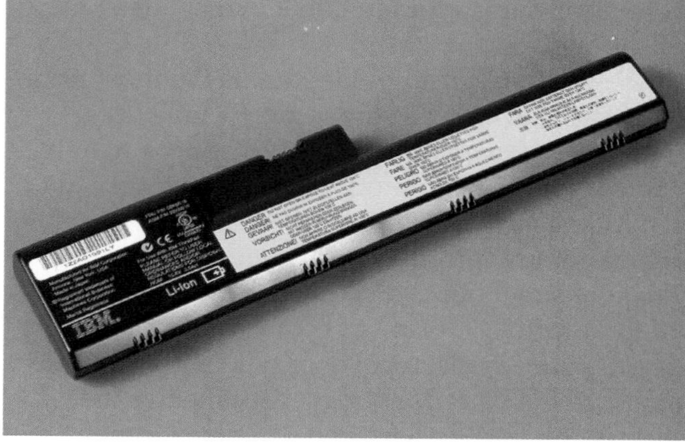

alkaline batteries
common batteries found in small devices such as TV remote controls and some palmtops.

nickel-cadmium (NiCd) battery
rechargeable battery used in early portable computers. Had problems with memory effect.

nickel-metal hydride materials (NiMH) batteries
second generation of rechargeable battery used for portable computers. Has no problem with memory effect and holds a charge longer than the NiCd battery.

lithium-ion (Li-ion) batteries
rechargeable battery found in most new portable computers. Has no problem with memory effect and holds a charge longer than NiCd and NiMH batteries.

fuel cell
a type of battery that uses hydrogen or methanol to produce electrical energy.

Alkaline batteries are common batteries found in small devices such as TV remote controls and some of the older palmtops. They are not used much today with computers.

The ***nickel-cadmium (NiCd) battery,*** called ***NiCad*** for short, was a standard portable computer battery for many years. It is one of the least expensive batteries. However, NiCad has some drawbacks. NiCad batteries could take up to 12 hours to fully recharge. Also, older NiCad batteries were subject to a phenomenon known as *memory effect.* When NiCad battery-powered equipment was recharged before the battery was completely drained, the battery would operate for a shorter time before it appeared to be completely discharged. Batteries that were not fully drained could not be fully recharged. They showed a *memory* of previous use. For example, a battery should last four hours, but the equipment is only run for one hour and then recharged. With future uses, the battery will appear completely drained after one hour. This is not such a problem with more modern batteries. Cadmium is a very toxic material, which presents a problem with disposal of spent batteries.

All batteries have limits to the number of recharges. With NiCad, the average number of recharges is approximately 1000. This number of recharges can last an average user up to 2 1/2 years.

Nickel-metal hydride (NiMH) batteries were an improvement over the NiCad batteries. They can store up to 50% more charge time than NiCad batteries. They do not have the memory effect problem, so they can be recharged anytime during their discharge cycle. The NiMH batteries have a shorter number of total recharges then NiCad. They can usually only be recharged about 500 times.

Lithium-ion (Li-ion) batteries have the highest electrical potential of all the batteries discussed here. As with NiMH batteries, they also do not suffer from a memory effect. Lithium-ion is both lightweight and compact, making it the most popular battery type used for laptop computers. Lithium-ion batteries also contain no poisonous metals and are relatively safe for the environment. The only disadvantage to lithium-ion batteries is that they are more expensive than their counterparts.

A fifth type of battery, ***fuel cell,*** is expected to take the place of batteries for low wattage applications such as cell phones, PDAs, and laptops. NASA began utilizing fuel cell technology for space exploration in the 1960s. The fuel cell proved to be practical for space applications, but very expensive.

There are many different fuel cell technologies. Most are either too large for portable applications, or the fuel requires large storage tanks, which also would not be practical for portable applications.

Toshiba Corporation recently released a practical model that is the most promising for portable electronic devices. The fuel cell developed by Toshiba uses methanol as fuel, which allows the storage tank to be reduced to approximately 1/10 the size of that required for hydrogen, the common fuel used for fuel cells. The methanol model is called the *direct methanol fuel cell (DMFC).* In October of 2003, Toshiba introduced DMFC as a practical product in the computer industry. The output power of the DMCF is quite small but can be used to supply electrical power to a small electronic device for 4 to 10 hours based on the fuel tank size. A DMFC can be utilized to either directly supply electrical energy to a portable electronic device or simply used to recharge the batteries already installed in the device. DMFC for electronic devices is still in the early stages of development. Toshiba expects to be mass marking the DMFC by 2006.

Laptop battery disposal

Most rechargeable batteries are regulated because of the hazardous waste materials they contain. The exact method of disposal varies according to local government authority such as cities, counties, state, and the federal government. Almost all states have adopted their own set of guidelines that exceed the federal regulations. Following is a list of common battery types and why they can be dangerous:

- **NiCad batteries:** NiCad batteries contain the toxic metal cadmium.
- **Mercury batteries:** Mercury batteries contain the toxic metal mercury.
- **Lithium-ion batteries:** Lithium-ion batteries contain lithium, which is highly reactive with water. (Not all lithium-ion batteries are considered a waste hazard.)
- **Lead-acid and lead-gel batteries:** These batteries contain the toxic metal lead.

In most areas, there is a recycling facility that takes old batteries and either recycles them or sends them to another facility for recycling.

If a battery is rechargeable, it is usually recyclable. Do not attempt to disassemble a battery for recycling. It takes a highly skilled and trained individual and special safety equipment to disassemble a battery for recycling.

Warning:
Never attempt to incinerate a battery.
Never attempt to solder wire leads to a battery.
Never short circuit (connect the positive and negative terminal with a wire or any conductive material) a battery. Batteries can explode or catch fire.
Never puncture, crush, or physically damage a battery. (Some battery vapors are hazardous.)

As a PC technician, you and your company will encounter more than the average number of recyclable batteries. You must adhere to all laws and regulations when disposing of batteries. The regulations vary according to the amount of batteries accumulated over a set period.

Docking Station

A ***docking station*** is like an electronic cradle for the laptop. The laptop slides into the docking station and snaps into place. Once in place, the laptop can operate from power provided by the docking station rather than from a battery or a battery charger. Some docking stations contain slots for expansion devices and bays for additional storage devices. Many times the docking station automatically connects the laptop to the company network or the Internet.

docking station an electronic cradle that provides power for a laptop, allowing users to turn the laptop into a full-size PC.

Docking stations essentially allow users to turn their laptops into full-size PCs when portability isn't necessary. By connecting to the docking station, you can easily connect a full-size keyboard, mouse, or other less portable equipment to your machine.

Normally, a portable computer needs to have the desired configuration identified while docking or undocking. For example, a laptop is equipped with an LCD screen but a docking station may use a CRT screen as a display. When the laptop is connected to the docking station, the video must be configured for the CRT display. When the laptop is removed from the docking station, it must be reconfigured for the LCD screen. Windows XP, however, automatically configures the laptop video. Windows XP introduced a new feature called *hot docking*. The hot docking feature allows users to dock or undock their laptop computer without the need to change hardware configurations. Windows XP automatically detects when a portable computer is placed into or removed from a docking station.

Port Replicator

port replicator an external computer device that provides additional ports to be used by a computer system.

A ***port replicator*** is an external computer device that provides additional ports to be used by a computer system. The most common computer systems to use a port replicator are notebook computers, cell phones, and PDAs. Portable devices typically have a very limited number of ports available due to their compact design. For the same reason, it is often difficult or impossible to add additional ports by using expansion cards. Adding a PCI card to a laptop, cell phone, or PDA is not a practical solution. A port replicator solves the problem of adding additional ports.

A port replicator allows for the addition of devices such as a printer, camera, joystick, external CD or DVD drive, monitor, extra hard drive, external modem, scanner, keyboard, mouse, or any other digital device utilized by a full-size PC. In many ways, the port replicator serves the same function as a docking station. The use of a port replicator is not limited to just small digital devices. You can also use a port replicator to add additional ports that are not usually found on a typical computer, such as SCSI ports. It is also important to note that a USB hub designed to add additional USB ports can also be classified as a port replicator.

Portable Motherboards

Portable PC motherboards do not follow a standard form factor, **Figure 12-3.** The form factors are proprietary. To help keep the PCs small, most portable PCs incorporate the processor directly into the motherboard. The processor is often purposely set to run at a lower speed than it is capable of if installed in a full-size PC. The reason for the slower speed is to reduce heat in the portable PC. Because of the compact design, portable PCs leave little room for cooling. They incorporate large, flat heat sinks inside the case, but there is not sufficient room for a full-sized cooling fan.

Mouse

To avoid having to find a flat surface to work a mouse, portable PCs incorporate a mouse or a mouse substitute into the case of the computer. The mouse can be incorporated into the portable PC as a simple roller ball alongside two flat switches. Some computers use an eraser-looking joystick that is located in the middle of the keyboard, **Figure 12-4A.** A small touch pad is standard on other models, **Figure 12-4B.**

If room to work is available, many people prefer to add a standard, full-size mouse to the laptop. This is easily accomplished by connecting a mouse to an available port on the laptop.

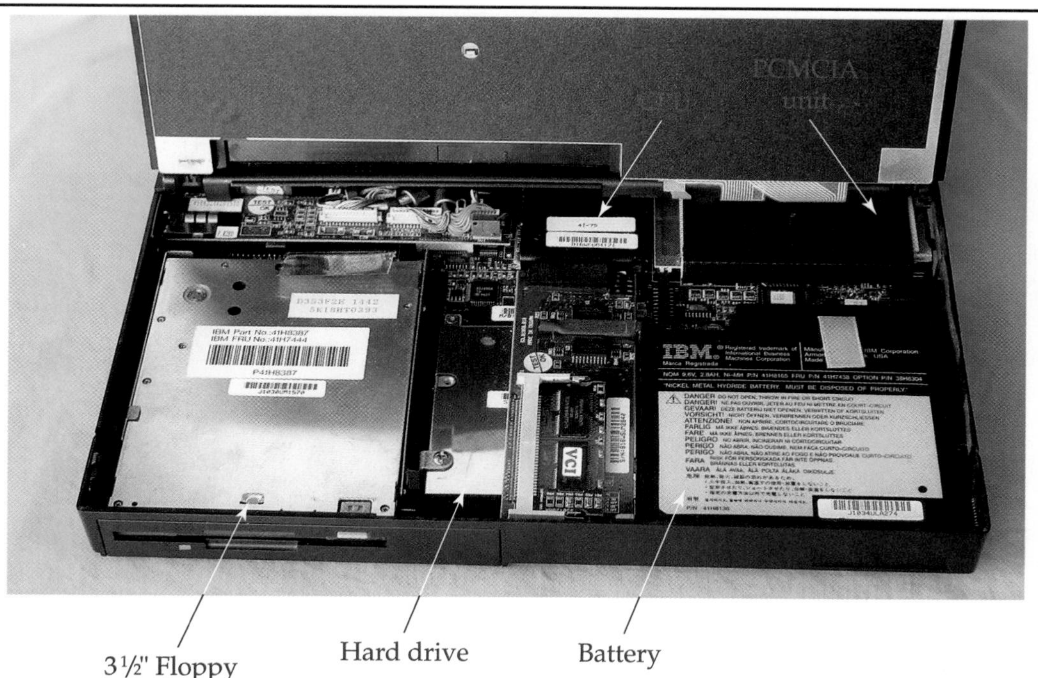

Figure 12-3. Laptop PCs, such as this unit, have the same internal components as full-size PCs. However, the layout of a laptop machine is very different to keep size and weight down.

Infrared Devices

Data is often transferred between computer devices using infrared beams of light. One of the most common uses of this transfer is to move data from full-size PCs to laptops and vice versa. Almost all laptops are equipped with an infrared port for this purpose. The infrared beam of light is broadcast from an infrared transmitter located on one PC to another PC. Infrared ports can also transmit to other equipment, such as a printer.

The infrared port is sometimes referred to as an *IrDA transceiver port.* The IrDA stands for Infrared Data Association, a group responsible for a set of standards for infrared transmission of data. The term *transceiver* is used because the term implies a device that cannot only transmit a signal but can also receive a signal. Think of the term transceiver as a combination of the words *transmit* and *receive.*

Printers and many other devices that are not designed with infrared ports can be modified to accept the infrared signals. An infrared port can be added to existing equipment typically through the serial COM port, a USB port, or by adding an expansion card to an expansion slot. If the Plug and Play feature does not recognize the device during startup, the device can then be set up manually through **Control Panel | Add New Hardware.**

The infrared light beam is pulsed in patterns representing the data being transferred. Transfer rates as high as 115 kbps are typical through a standard serial port. Speeds as high as 4 Mbps can be achieved going directly to and from infrared transceivers.

Figure 12-4.
A—Some portable computers have a small joystick-like device mounted on the keyboard. This device, along with two buttons below the keyboard, takes the place of a mouse. B—Other keyboards come with a touch pad instead.

PCMCIA Cards

PCMCIA card
card designed by the Personal Computer Memory Card International Association (PCMCIA) to add memory or expand a portable PC. The PCMCIA card is often referred to as simply a "PCM" or "PC" card.

The Personal Computer Memory Card International Association (PCMCIA) designed a set of standards for adding memory and expanding a portable PC through the use of devices resembling thick credit cards. These cards are called ***PCMCIA cards.*** PCMCIA cards are installed in PCMCIA slots on the side of the PC. These slots are used in place of expansion slots as the way to install additional devices. As with USB connections, many PCMCIA cards are hot swappable (can be swapped without powering off the machine).

All PCMCIA cards have the same rectangular (85.6 mm by 54 mm) shape, but they vary in thickness, **Figure 12-5.** Their thickness classifies the cards. There are three classifications of cards. The classifications are as follows:

- **Type I:** 3.3 mm thick. These cards are used primarily to add memory to the PC.
- **Type II:** 5.0 mm thick. These cards are usually used to add modems and network cards to the PC. The cards are equipped with either RJ-11 or RJ-45 connectors. The RJ connectors look like telephone jacks.
- **Type III:** 10.5 mm thick. These cards are designed to support hard drives or to support external CD, DVD, or tape drives.

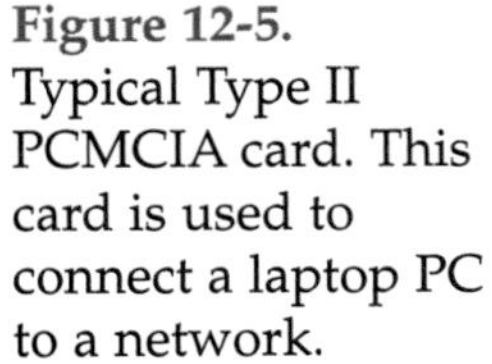

Figure 12-5.
Typical Type II PCMCIA card. This card is used to connect a laptop PC to a network.

There is a selection of slots to go with the cards. A Type I slot can hold one Type I card. Type II slots can hold one Type II card or two Type I cards. Type III slots can hold one Type III card or one Type I card and one Type II card. All of the smaller cards will fit into larger slots on their own.

Type IV cards are in the works, but they have not been ratified by the PCMCIA consortium at this time. Type IV cards are expected to be 16 mm thick. They will be used for large-capacity hard drives.

Power Management

Many portable devices use power management techniques to reduce heat and conserve battery power. Heat producing and power consuming devices such as the hard drive, display, and CPU are put into a *sleep mode* when inactive. This mode saves valuable battery life.

Some CPU systems can run at a reduced clock speed while in normal use. A high-speed CPU is not necessary to run many software applications such as word processing. High speed is desirable when doing mathematical calculations, using video-intense graphic programs, or playing games.

Portable Operating System

When installing the Windows operating system on a computer, you usually have four choices for the installation process: typical, portable, compact, and custom. Each type contains certain feature packages. The *typical installation* is a set of programs installed for a typical desktop or tower model PC. The *custom installation* option allows you to select each feature or program from a list as it is being installed. *Compact installation* is used for machines that do not have a lot of storage room. Only the minimum features are installed in this process.

The *portable installation* is an installation package intended for use on portable PC systems. Certain features are either entirely or partly left out. Features such as multiple language support, screen savers, document templates, games, imaging software, Paint, Real Audio Player, Macromedia Shockwave Player, System Monitor, and many more files can be omitted. However, the portable installation includes a number of programs that would often be left out in a typical installation. The programs include Virtual Private Networking, HyperTerminal, and Direct Cable Connection. These features are associated with connecting the portable PC to a home or office when traveling. Any feature left out at the time of installation can be added later with an installation CD.

It is not required to use the portable installation option when setting up a portable PC. Any of the four types of installations can be chosen. However, many of the desirable features a portable PC would use to connect to another computer are not installed with the typical installation, as they would be with the portable installation option.

Windows CE

For personal digital assistants and palmtops, Microsoft has an operating system called ***Windows CE.*** The CE is thought to stand for *compact edition.* Space is limited on palmtop and very limited for personal digital assistants. The Windows CE operating system has been modified to meet the needs of the smaller units. The Windows CE program is similar in appearance to any of the

Windows CE version of Windows designed for less powerful devices, such as PDAs or smart appliances.

Windows operating systems. It has a control panel and uses the registry system to control devices and users. Files and directories are arranged in the same way. Windows CE also supports a number of third party software programs.

Windows CE is not just for computers. It is also installed in some stereos, telephones, and other electronic items where programmable features such as memory storage are desired. When programmed through an operating system such as Windows CE, these units are often referred to as *smart appliances.* These systems are being regularly incorporated into common toys.

Windows CE will not run correctly on a standard PC because it is designed to work on RISC-type processors. Remember from Chapter 4—CPU, a RISC (reduced instruction set computing)-based CPU is designed to run on a smaller instruction set. Windows CE is not designed to support graphics-intensive programs.

Microsoft has developed a stereo system for cars that uses the Windows CE operating system called AutoPC. It is a voice-controlled car stereo that can check and read e-mail, dial a cellular phone, and give directions to the driver's destination.

Personal digital assistant (PDA) portable computer comparable in size to a palmtop. Has a limited amount of memory and is used mostly to retain to-do lists, store personal data, connect to the Internet, and send and receive e-mail.

application service provider (ASP) provides software applications to a personal digital assistant (PDA) or palmtop by downloading the application from a provider as needed.

Personal Digital Assistants

Personal digital assistants (PDA) are not as powerful as laptop or palmtop computers are. They are limited in memory space because of their overall physical size, but they do perform many valuable services. They can be used to retain to-do lists and store personal data such as phone numbers, addresses, and company information. They connect to the Internet to display text-only versions of Web pages. They can check and transmit e-mail.

With the innovation of application service providers, they will function more like the palmtop. An ***application service provider (ASP)*** can provide software applications such as word processing packages, spreadsheets, databases, or even games. However, the operational concept is to download the application from a provider as needed rather than to permanently load it on the machine. By using an ASP, valuable storage space is saved on the PDA or palmtop. Also, by using an ASP, the latest version of the software is always available.

One important difference between a PDA and a palmtop is that a PDA does not have a keyboard. A palmtop does. Without a keyboard, the PDA relies on a stylus for inputting data. A *stylus* is a small pen-like object used to write on a touch screen. Software like Microsoft Transcriber converts cursive or printed handwriting entered by the stylus into data recognized by the operating system. Some PDA systems use a small onscreen keyboard for entering data.

A second big difference between the PDA and a palmtop is that a PDA does not have a hard drive. All data is stored in RAM and held there by battery backup. The RAM can be proportioned by software into two sections. One section is used as traditional RAM that will be erased when power is removed. The other section is used for storage similar to a hard drive. This difference may disappear as experimental hard drives are being developed that have no moving parts—the entire hard drive storage consists of memory technology similar to RAM. Because of the lack of a hard drive, memory modules are often used to retain data and serve to function as a PDA hard drive.

The last major difference between a palmtop and a PDA is the screen. Palmtops usually have a high-resolution color screen while PDAs usually have monochrome screens with fairly low resolution.

A PDA can come with many accessories, such as a docking station that has a built-in charger. A keyboard can also be purchased as an input device. An automobile charger is always a nice accessory, too. A charge on a PDA can last for two weeks or more, but it is always convenient to have a charger when needed.

PDAs can upload to full-size PCs using an infrared portal, a telephone modem, a USB port, or a network connection. The PDA can also be synchronized with a CD-ROM on a desktop model enabling it to download programs and files.

Bluetooth Standard

Bluetooth is the name of a standard developed for short-range radio links between portable computers, mobile phones, and other portable devices. The standard was created by many of the world's leaders in mobile computing equipment. It is a royalty-free standard enabling major manufacturers to develop compatible equipment. PCs, PDAs, and mobile phones using the Bluetooth standard are able to communicate with one another. A small transmitter and receiver are incorporated into the devices. They transmit data and commands on a 2.45 GHz radio band. Bluetooth standards support data transfer speeds as high as 1 Mbps. Actual speed, however, is 700 kbps to 800 kbps. The use of the standard allows for many innovative applications. Some examples include the following:

Bluetooth royalty-free standard developed for short-range radio links between portable computers, mobile phones, and other portable devices so that major manufacturers could develop compatible equipment.

- **Office:** You arrive at your office or worksite and your PDA automatically downloads files from home or downloads entries that you may have made while on the road. As you inspect an industrial location, you download information about each piece of equipment as you pass by. Items such as total running hours, number of items manufactured, next and scheduled downtime are recorded to be later downloaded at the office.
- **Home:** When you arrive at home, you can automatically open the garage door, unlock the door, turn on outside lights, turn off the security system, and turn on the heater, stereo, or TV. If an item operates on electricity, it can be turned on, off, or have its settings modified so long as the item is Bluetooth compliant.
- **Travel:** You arrive at an airport and automatically check in using your PDA rather than standing in a long line. Arriving at your destination, you automatically notify the car rental and have your car sent to you. If you are a tourist on vacation, you can automatically download maps or directions to your PDA. You can automatically check in or check out of a hotel. You can also monitor your billing at the hotel or resort. You can check on a restaurant, download its menu, and check on the waiting time for the next available table.

Wireless Data Transfer

A wireless connection is commonly used to connect a notebook PC to a full-size PC or to join a small network. A wireless connection can be made using radio waves or by using infrared light. A much more detailed description of wireless networking is covered later in this textbook. This section covers terminology related to wireless data transfer.

Ad-Hoc Network

When a wireless network is formed between two or more wireless devices such as a workstation and a notebook, it is called an ***ad-hoc network.*** You can think of an ad-hoc network connection as a direct cable connection that uses radio waves as the connection media rather than cable. Look at **Figure 12-6.**

ad-hoc network
a wireless network formed between two or more wireless devices such as a full-size PC and a notebook PC.

access point
a device that is used to support communications between wireless devices and a hard-wired network system.

Wireless Infrastructure

Another classification of wireless connection is called infrastructure. An *infrastructure* differs from an ad-hoc system in that it contains a network access point. An ***access point*** is a device that is used to support communications between wireless devices and a hard-wired network system, **Figure 12-7.** An access point is often referred to as a network bridge. A *bridge* is a special networking device that is used to connect two dissimilar networks. In this example, the access point is bridging the connection between the hard-wired network and the wireless network.

Wireless Devices

Wireless devices for PCs are designed in three general styles—as PCMCIA cards, PCI adapter cards, and USB devices. A PCMCIA wireless card is the preferred device for the portable computer, **Figure 12-8.** Some portable computers are purchased with a wireless device already installed as standard equipment.

On a PC, a wireless PCI adapter card, **Figure 12-9,** or a USB wireless device are the most common choices. Be careful when purchasing a PCI wireless device. Many are designed in two separate pieces (and as two separate

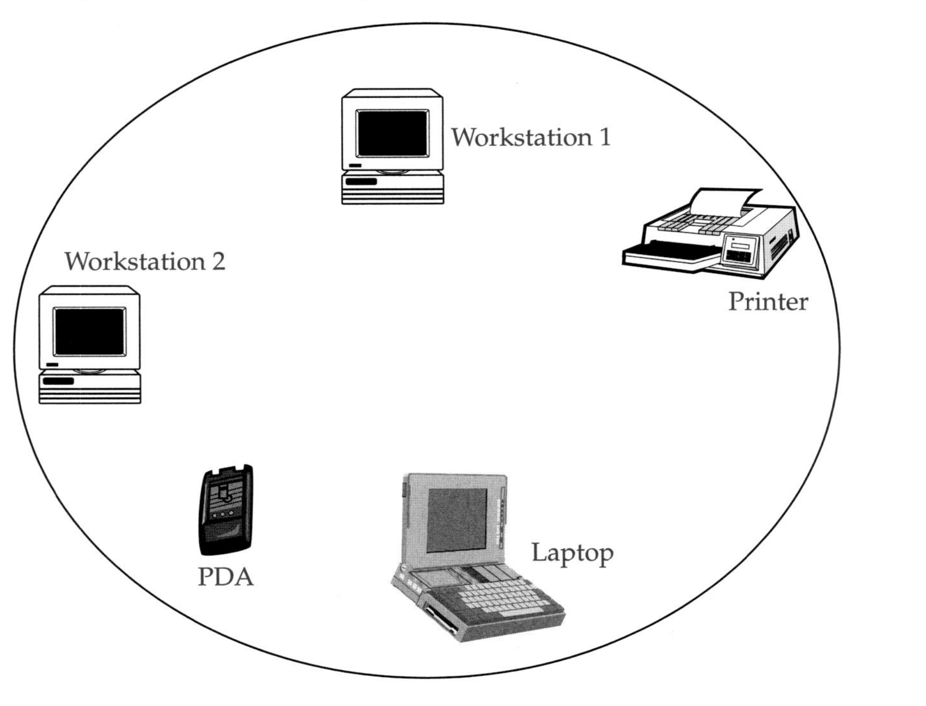

Figure 12-6. Some devices connected together by radio waves in an ad-hoc network. An ad-hoc network can consist of 2 to 64 wireless devices.

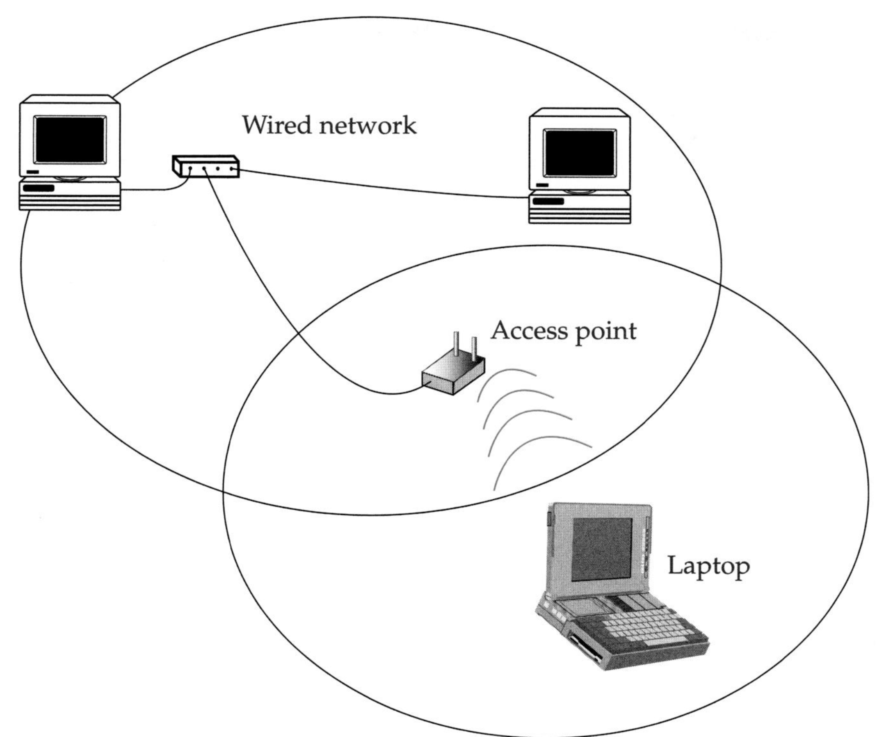

Figure 12-7.
A wireless access point acts as a bridge between the wireless device and the wired network system.

Figure 12-8.
A PCMCIA wireless network card.

purchases)—a PCI cardholder and a PCMCIA card. The PCMCIA card is installed in the cardholder.

Radio Waves

Radio waves are used to deliver or exchange information all over the world. To prevent radio waves from interfering with each other, radio frequencies are regulated by the FCC. The FCC assigns specific radio frequencies to various types of equipment. For example, toy remote control cars are typically 27 MHz and 40 MHz. When you tune your car radio, you are actually selecting a radio frequency. When you select a radio station such as 104.5 FM, you are tuning the

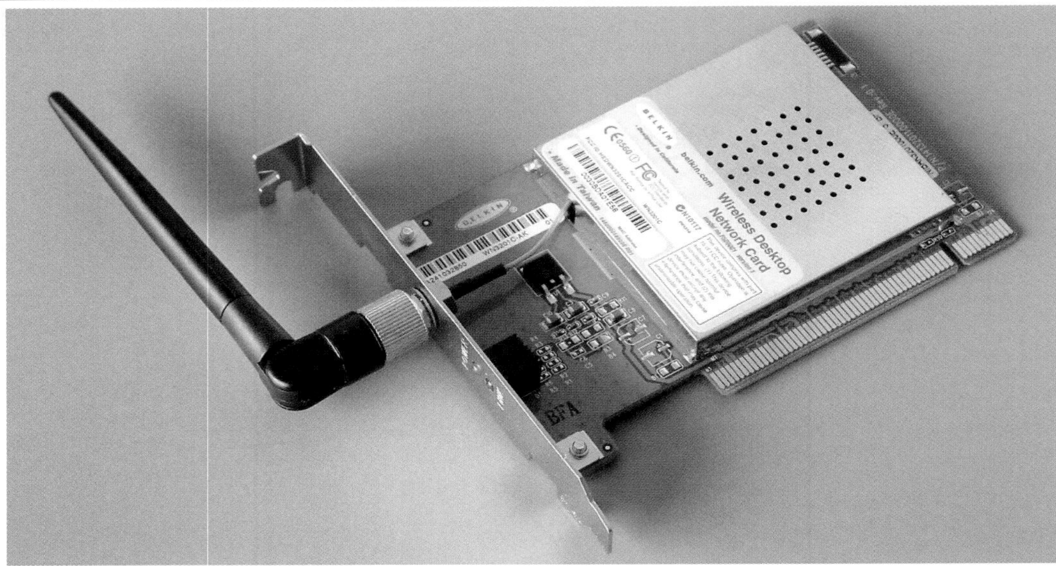

Figure 12-9. A PCI wireless network card. The antenna attached to the PCI card can be easily removed and replaced using an antenna on a length of cable. Replacing the attached PCI card antenna with a cable-type antenna will typically improve wireless signal reception.

radio receiver to a transmitted carrier wave of 104.5 MHz. The carrier wave is a set frequency, which is used to carry the information from the transmitter to the receiver.

Radio Signal Interference

Radio signal interference is a radio wave transmission that corrupts a desired radio wave signal. Some common sources of wireless computer communication devices are, wireless telephones, medical equipment, microwave ovens, and cell phones. While all electronic equipment generates some interference, these specific devices share the same radio wave frequencies that wireless network cards use, approximately 2.48 GHz. Other electrical devices and appliances containing electrical motors can also cause problems.

A wireless connection rated at 11 Mbps, may actually be only 5 Mbps or as low as 1 Mbps or less. Another major factor that affects wireless communication is the distance between the source and destination. As the distance between the source and destination increases, the throughput decreases. This is because the greater the distance of the transmitted radio signal, the weaker the signal becomes. As the signal becomes weaker, it is more susceptible to radio interference.

On average, the maximum advertised distance for IEEE 802.11b wireless devices is approximately 250 meters indoors and 450 meters outdoors. There is no definitive maximum distance because of the variables that affect radio waves. Realistic distances for wireless transmissions will be much shorter distances than advertised because wireless systems rarely operate in ideal environments.

Another factor that affects radio signals is physical objects in the radio wave area. Objects placed directly between the source and destination weaken the radio signal. The most common object that affects radio signals are building partitions, file cabinets, furniture, fireplaces, appliances, and similar objects. The density and material these objects are made from affect the signal. For example, a wall constructed of concrete block will weaken a signal more than a wall constructed of sheet rock. A metallic partition commonly used to create an office cubicle will block a radio signal. A wireless connection to exchange data directly between a notebook computer and a PC should not be affected by building structures. If you are using a notebook on a patio to access an Internet connection through a PC inside the home, the distance and building materials will affect the signal to a great extent. Windows XP and wireless device manufacturers have utilities that allow you to monitor the wireless network. **Figure 12-10** shows the strength of the wireless signal displayed as a bar graph. The speed of the data is also displayed as 11.0 Mbps.

Wireless Standards

The IEEE organization has developed and released several standards that deal specifically with wireless communication. The standards serve as a guideline for how the equipment should function. Remember that standards are developed so that equipment developed by different manufacturers can communicate with each other. The wireless standards, 802.11, 802.11a, 802.11b, and 802.11g, recommend characteristics and specifications for wireless networking. Some of the items specified are frequencies, maximum bandwidth, and communication procedures.

The original 802.11 standard was first developed to standardize wireless devices that would transmit data at 1 Mbps and 2 Mbps. The frequency, or radio band, assigned to 802.11 by the FCC is 2.48 GHz. It was a very short time before it had to be modified to provide for higher data rates and was soon followed by 802.11a and 802.11b. Although both standards were released at the same time, 802.11b became the de facto standard for small office and home wireless devices.

The 802.11a standard specifies a frequency of 5.8 GHz and a maximum bandwidth of 54 Mbps. While 802.11a has a much higher bandwidth than 802.11b, it has less range, approximately half that of 802.11b. It is not backward compatible with 802.11.

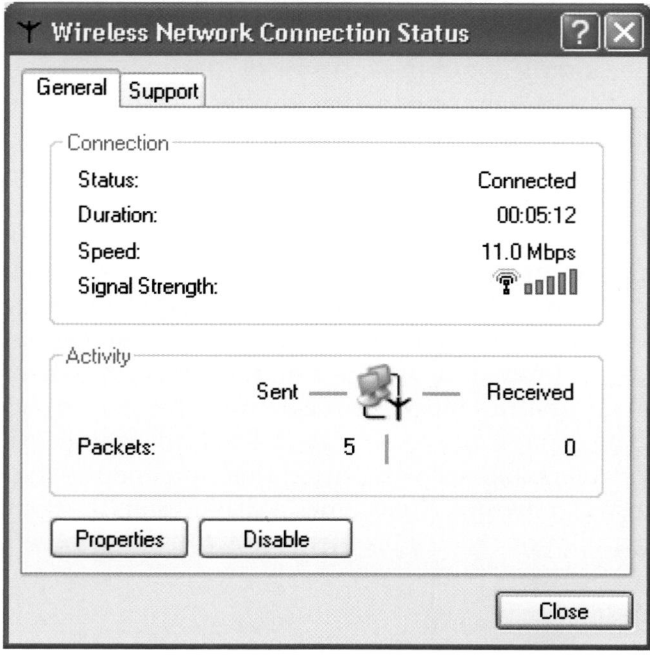

Figure 12-10. The Wireless Network Connection Status screen displays the strength of the signal and the speed of the transmission.

The 802.11b standard allows for data transmission rates at 1 Mbps, 2 Mbps, 5.5 Mbps, and 11 Mbps. The 11 Mbps throughput, however, is only achieved at optimal conditions. Optimal conditions are short distances with no radio interference and only two devices. As distance increases between two wireless devices, the bandwidth drops drastically. Building materials and furnishings can also interfere with radio wave transmissions. Other devices such as portable phones, microwave ovens, wireless industrial communication control devices, and wireless medical devices assigned to the same frequency, can generate radio interference. 802.11b is backward compatible with 802.11 and is assigned the same 2.48 GHz frequency.

The 802.11g standard was the next to be developed. It operates at the 2.4GHz frequency with a maximum transmission rate of 54 Mbps. It is compatible with 802.11 and 802.11b.

Tech Tip:
Wireless technology has not fully developed to one set of de facto terminology to describe the wireless systems. Do not be surprised to see that terms vary among manufacturers. For example, Basic Service Set (BSS) may be listed as Independent Basic Service Set (IBSS). Also, be aware that the specified frequency of a standard will vary. For example, 802.11b may be presented as 2.5 GHz, 2.4 GHz, and 2.45 GHz. The frequency for 802.11a may be presented as 5 GHz, 5.1 GHz, and 5.8 GHz. In actuality, the frequency is not one set frequency, but a range of frequencies. Below are the actual assigned frequency ranges:

- IEEE 802.11 = 2.4 GHz–2.4835 GHz
- IEEE 802.11a = 5.15 GHz–5.850 GHz
- IEEE 802.11b = 2.4 GHz–2.4835 GHz
- IEEE 802.11g = 2.4 GHz–2.4835 GHz

Installing Ad-Hoc Network Connection

Setting up an ad-hoc network connection between a full-size PC and a portable PC can be simple. Both the full-size PC and the portable PC must be equipped with a wireless communication device. Installing a wireless card in a computer is simple. Most Microsoft operating systems automatically detect the presence of a wireless device and launch the Found New Hardware Wizard, as shown in **Figure 12-11.**

At this point, you can allow the wizard to automatically install the necessary drivers and configure the device, or you can perform the installation manually. When performing a manual installation, Windows 2000 or Windows XP may issue a warning that the drivers are not signed. Microsoft thoroughly tests a driver or software program and assigns a digital signature when approved. Assigning a digital signature means that Microsoft has found the driver or software program to be capable of working with their operating system with no problems. Many drivers and software programs came on the market after the operating system was released. Most times a driver that has not been "digitally signed" will generally not cause a problem, and you can proceed to install the wireless device.

Figure 12-11. The Found New Hardware Wizard gives you the choice to automatically install the necessary drivers or to manually install the necessary drivers. If installing the drivers manually, you will be prompted for the location of the driver files.

When using Windows XP, you typically have two ways to control the wireless device. You can use the wireless management software incorporated into Windows XP to manage the connection, or you can use the wireless manager that comes with the wireless device.

The Belkin dialog box in **Figure 12-12** shows some of the typical options available by the Belkin NetShare utility. You can set up file or print sharing, view network information, and change the workstation name or the workgroup to which the device belongs. Workgroups, file sharing, and other aspects of networking are covered in detail in Chapter 17—Network Administration.

After the device has been installed, it appears in **Control Panel | Network Connections**. Most wireless devices install with default settings, which makes it very easy to set up communications between the portable PC and the full-size PC. However, there is a security concern when default settings are used. Wireless systems are easily compromised when default settings are used. Anyone with a similar wireless equipped notebook can access the ad-hoc network. When default settings are used, all stations have the same assigned communications channel and the same security set identifier (SSID) such as WLAN. The *SSID* is a string of characters, which typically represent the name of the collection or group of wireless communication devices. Each small network group needs an assigned name to identify other devices that belong to that same group. By using two different SSIDs, you could have two different wireless networks communicating in the same area and they would not be aware of each other.

Look at the Windows XP Wireless Network Properties dialog box in **Figure 12-13.** The SSID "Home" has been entered into the **Network name (SSID):** box. In **Figure 12-14,** the SSID "Home" is listed in the **Preferred networks:** box and is ready for automatic connection.

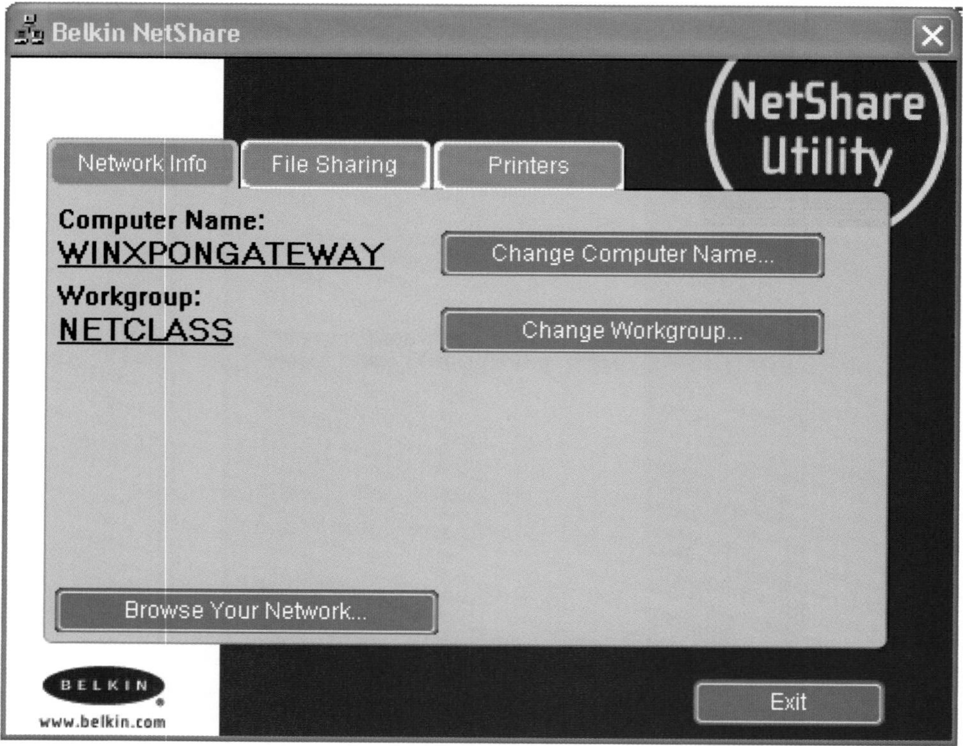

Figure 12-12. Typical options available in the Belkin NetShare utility.

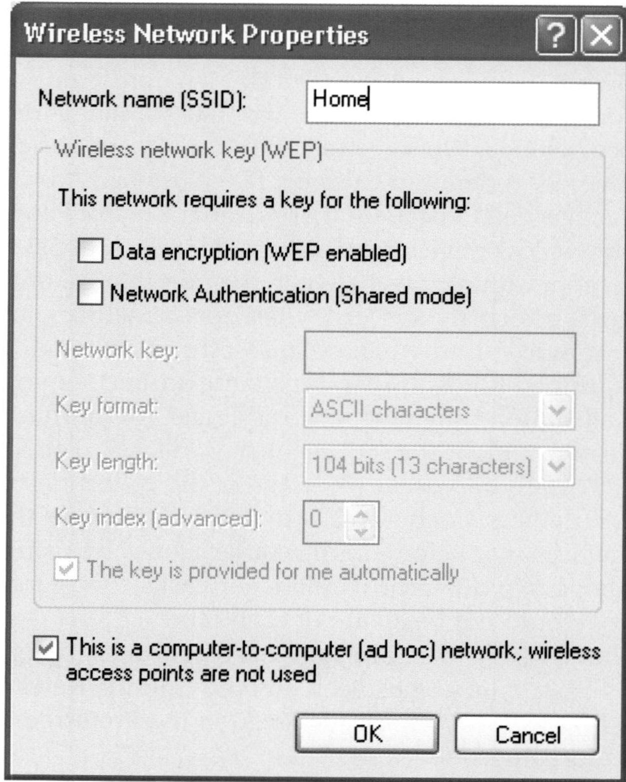

Figure 12-13. Entering the name "Home" in the Network name (SSID) field identifies this computer as part of the wireless network called "Home."

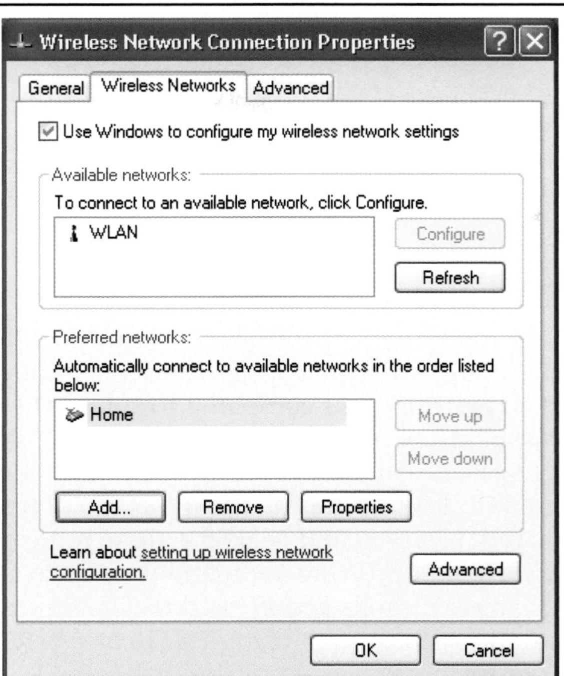

Figure 12-14.
This computer is set to automatically connect to the wireless network "Home."

When a wireless infrastructure is configured, each access point requires a *Basic Service Set (BSS) ID* for identification. The BSS ID is a string of characters used to identify the area served by the access point. A typical BSS ID is a name that identifies the wireless access point area. For example, WlanRoom123 identifies a wireless access point located in room 123. An *Extended Service Set (ESS) ID* is required for a wireless network consisting of more than one access point. As with the BSS ID, a descriptive name such as WlanBld10 is typically used as the ESS ID. An ESS ID is used to support roaming. A person using a portable PC, such as a laptop, can move throughout the wireless LAN areas as long as they stay within the range of an access point. Fully understanding the configuration of a wireless infrastructure requires additional networking skills, such as a fundamental understanding of IP and MAC addresses. These topics will be covered in detail in later chapters.

Security

Security is a high priority at all times, especially when dealing with portable PCs. The portable PC may contain important company information such as customer lists, contract information, proposed business ventures, and other sensitive communications. Information for connecting to the company network may also be contained on the hard drive. Security is even more important for portable PCs issued to people in police departments, the FBI, or the CIA. As you can see, laptop security is a vital issue.

encryption
method of encoding data that must be converted back to meaningful words by using an encryption key. The encryption key is a mathematical formula for substituting values in strings of data.

Encryption

Encryption is used as part of the security system. ***Encryption*** is a way to code data that cannot be converted back to meaningful words without an encryption key. The encryption key is not a physical device but rather a mathematical formula for substituting values in strings of data. For example, a text-based code could be developed based on the number five. The data in a file would be stored with every letter changed to one that is four places further in the alphabet. See **Figure 12-15.**

The message is rewritten in code and then stored. To read the message, you would need the code. This is a simple example. A true encryption code is more complex.

NTFS versus FAT

The NT kernel that comes with Windows NT, Windows 2000, and Windows XP provides many security features needed for this security. It is very difficult to hack into an NT station as compared to some other home operating systems. Security was an important design issue for the NT system.

A typical security system using FAT16 or FAT32 allows for only two types of file access when shared: full access and read only. These options are set when a file or directory is shared. NTFS4.0 and NTFS5.0 allow more choices when file and directory security are set up. There are many options to choose from when a file share is created. These options are referred to as permissions.

For example, a Windows 9x system using FAT16 or FAT32 can only set file access options to either full access, read only, or no access. With full access capabilities, another user can do anything to the file that the file originator can do. The user can delete the file completely, copy the file, or create a new file. When the NTFS system is used, access to the shared file can be controlled through more precise options. These options include read only, modify, read and execute, write, and list files. The people who have the right to modify or delete the file can be tightly controlled.

Tech Tip:
A FAT system can be set up with similar file restrictions used for NTFS when running the NT operating system. However, the file restrictions are lost when the files are transferred to another directory or operating system.

Figure 12-15.
Very simple encryption code.

Sample message:

THIS IS THE TIME FOR ALL GOOD MEN...

Change the position of all letters by four positions in the alphabet.

A B C D E F G H I J K L M N O P Q R S T U V W X Y Z
E F G H I J K L M N O P Q R S T U V W X Y Z A B C D

Coded message:

XLMW MW XLI XMQI JSV EPP KSSH QIR...

The strongest security feature for NTFS is its encryption capabilities. NTFS allows for file encryption. FAT does not. This means that a low-level disk editing utility can be used to access the contents of a hard drive formatted with FAT. NTFS system files are protected.

Figure 12-16 shows a text file that was created and saved to the hard drive of a FAT system and viewed through the Norton Disk Editor. The Norton Disk Editor program is used to inspect the disk storage system and reveal the contents of the clusters byte by byte. In the figure, you can see the contents of a file located at cluster 291,629. The Norton Disk Editor reveals the contents as ASCII code on the right side of the screen and as hexadecimal codes on the left side.

Notice the hexadecimal number 73 in the center field of hexadecimal numbers. The number 73 is equal to the ASCII character code for the letter *s*. If you count the hexadecimal position locations, you can see that the hexadecimal code 73 occurs at the fourth, seventh, and eleventh position in the line of hexadecimal characters. These three locations correspond to the location of the ASCII text for the letter *s* on the right.

With NTFS, you could not view the file system this way. NTFS has encryption capabilities built into the system. The files created by the user can be saved as encrypted files that would have no meaning to the person opening them in Norton Disk Editor.

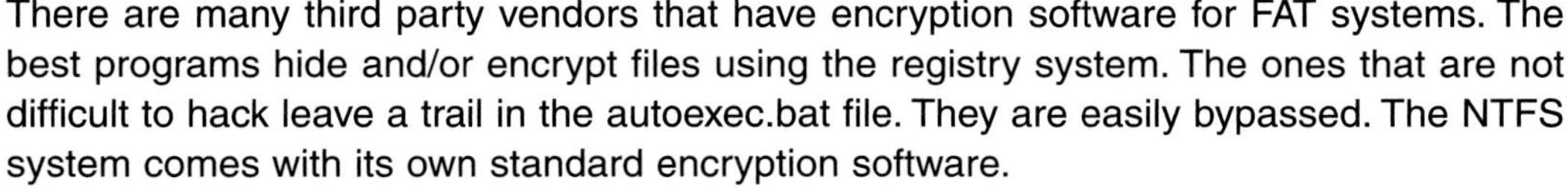

Tech Tip:
There are many third party vendors that have encryption software for FAT systems. The best programs hide and/or encrypt files using the registry system. The ones that are not difficult to hack leave a trail in the autoexec.bat file. They are easily bypassed. The NTFS system comes with its own standard encryption software.

Figure 12-16.
An unencrypted text file viewed through a disk editor. The ASCII code can be read and translated.

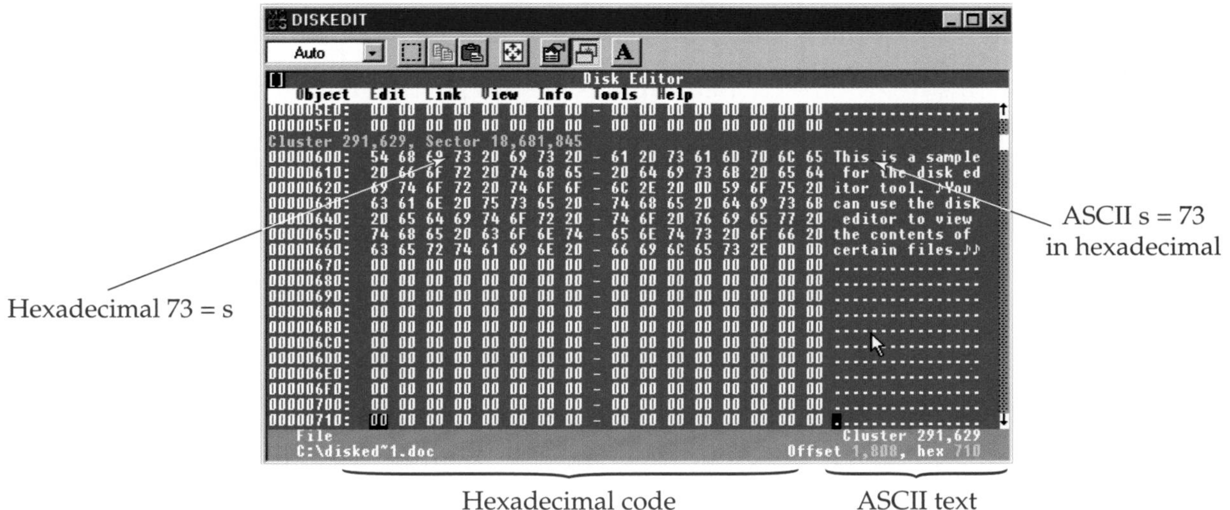

Another feature of NTFS that makes it more suitable than FAT for portable PCs is NTFS uses smaller cluster sizes when formatting the drive. Portable systems generally have less storage space available than full-size PCs because of their physically smaller hard drives. The smaller NTFS cluster sizes results in less wasted space on a hard drive system, making it the preferred storage file system for portable PCs.

Smart Cards

smart card credit card-like device with a chip imbedded in the plastic. The chip allows the card to be used for a variety of purposes.

Use of a smart card is another clever way to protect your laptop. A ***smart card*** is identical in size and feel to a credit card. Smart cards store information on a chip located within the body of the card. These chips can hold a variety of information. They can be used commercially for retail or vending operation. They can be used with pay phones or for gaming. With portable computers, they work very well for security. A smart card setup can be used to allow you to access the laptop (or full-size) PC. Without the card, the computer cannot be accessed. The smart card works in conjunction with a smart card reader, which is placed in the PC. The typical smart card connects through a standard RS-232 connection or a Type II PCMCIA card slot. The smart card is supported by all the latest Microsoft operating systems and by many other operating systems.

Wireless Security

Wireless networks have an inherent security problem because the communications media they use is radio waves. All wireless devices, however, are capable of using *wired equivalent privacy (WEP)* which is an encryption technique used for wireless transmissions. WEP uses 64- and 128-bit encryption keys to encode and decode messages. Wireless devices are assigned a unique coding key that encrypts and decrypts messages. Anyone without the unique encryption key can still receive or send messages, but they will not be able to decode them.

Another common practice is to encrypt the files located on the wireless devices. The Windows NTFS encrypted file system (EFS) is typically used to encrypt files located on the devices such as laptop computers.

Exchanging Data with Full-Size PCs

Laptops need to exchange data with full-size PCs for a variety of reasons. One common reason is to allow you to bring work home from the office or from home to the office. Often, laptops are used to maintain a profile of a PC system that is installed on new computers. For example, in a corporate environment most PCs have a standard set of software loaded that is dependent on the department in which the PC is located. One way of doing a standard installation is to load a laptop with the software that is used by a particular department. When new PCs are delivered, the PCs can be loaded with department software from the laptop rather than from individual software disks. The technician can easily transport the laptop to any area of the corporation.

You can exchange data with a full-size PC by using a bidirectional parallel cable, a serial null modem cable, or an infrared port. Windows comes with a program called Direct Cable Connection that can be used to connect two PCs. Direct Cable Connection is an optional program that is not installed during a typical Windows installation. It must be added. To add it, you simply access **Control Panel** and then select the **Add/Remove Programs** icon. Look in the

Windows Setup tab under **Communications**. It is listed there. It must be selected and installed. You need the Windows installation CD to install the program. After installation, the program can be found under **Start | Programs | Accessories | Communications | Direct Cable Connection**. There are other transfer methods, such as network connections, but these will be presented later in the text while discussing networking fundamentals.

To communicate between the laptop and full-size PCs, a null modem or special parallel cable must be used. The null modem is a special serial cable. Normally a standard cable supports communication in only one direction, from the PC to the peripheral device. When connecting two PCs, there is communication in both directions between the devices. A normal serial cable cannot support communications in both directions. A null modem cable supports communications in both directions.

A null modem cable differs from the normal cable construction in that the transmit and receive terminal located at one end are reversed. Look closely at **Figure 12-17.** You will notice that the null modem cable reverses the connections so that it will support two-way communications.

Briefcase

Briefcase is a Microsoft program that is designed to exchange programs between laptops and full-size PCs while keeping the most recent version on both devices. For example, you want to take several files in which to work on while away from the office. You can simply copy the file to a floppy disk or use

DB-25 connection

Pin	Pin
2	3
3	2
7	7

DB-9 connection

Pin	Pin
3	2
2	3
5	5

3-wire serial null modem cable pinout connections

Pin	Pin
2	15
15	2
3	13
13	3
4	12
12	4
5	10
10	5
6	11
11	6
25	25

11-wire parallel null modem cabel pinout connections

Figure 12-17. A null modem cable is designed by switching the transmit and receive connections on one end of the cable. This allows data from the transmit connection on one computer to be sent to the receive connection on the other.

Briefcase. Many people have difficulty when copying files to/from floppies and PCs. They become confused as to which is the latest edition of a file. Briefcase determines which file has the latest changes, and it issues warnings about updating a file before action is taken.

Briefcase can be copied across a network or loaded to a floppy. To use the Briefcase system, simply copy the files you wish to work on to the **Briefcase** icon on the desktop. You can simply drag each file onto the **Briefcase** icon. Then drag the briefcase icon onto a 3 1/2″ floppy. Take the PC home, complete your work, and then reverse the operation.

Briefcase icon

Upgrade and Repair

Notebooks and laptops can be upgraded easily. Memory or hard drive upgrades are not difficult. Although, some of the internal parts for laptops are smaller and more delicate than their full-size PC versions, so handle all parts with care. The CPU upgrade is usually not an option because of the design. Since most are soldered directly to the motherboard, it is a very difficult task even for an experienced electronics technician. PDAs and palmtops also have limited upgrades. You can add additional memory or any accessory through a port. Hardware repairs must usually be made at an authorized factory. Software is another matter. By now you are aware that most computer repairs are required because of software or operator error. Third party downloads and add-ons can cause a system lockup or crash. Most repair techniques related to software or operator error that are used for a full-size PC work equally as well on portables.

Summary

- Several types of portable computers include laptops, notebooks, and palmtops.
- A palmtop computer is small enough to rest in the palm of the hand.
- The most common battery types associated with portable equipment are alkaline, nickel-cadmium (NiCad), nickel-metal hydride (NiMH), and lithium-ion (Li-ion).
- Portable PCs usually use lithium-ion type batteries because they are relatively lightweight and have a greater charge holding capability than other types of batteries.
- Portable computers can expand their capabilities through the use of PCMCIA cards rather than the use of expansion slots used in a typical full-size PC.
- There are three types of PCMCIA card: Type I for memory, Type II for communication devices such as modems and network connectors, and Type III for hard drives or CD drives.
- Portable computers rely on energy management software to lengthen the life of the batteries.
- A port replicator is used to provide additional ports for computer devices.
- The portable option in the Windows installation installs additional features that are used with portable computers.

- NTFS is the preferred file system for portable computers because of its encryption capabilities and its ability to use smaller clusters than those used by FAT16 and FAT32.
- IEEE 802.11a transmits at 5.8 GHz and has a maximum bandwidth of 54 Mbps.
- IEEE 802.11b transmits at 2.48 GHz and has a maximum bandwidth of 11 Mbps
- IEEE 802.11b devices transmit farther than IEEE 802.11a devices.
- IEEE 802.11g transmits at 2.48 GHz and has a maximum bandwidth of 54 Mbps.
- Other radio devices in the same assigned frequency as well as other electrical devices and appliances can interfere with wireless communications.
- As the distance between two wireless devices increases, the transmission rate decreases.
- Wired equivalent privacy (WEP) is used to encode wireless transmissions.
- Data can be exchanged between two computers using a null modem cable, a parallel cable, or infrared technology.

Review Questions

Answer the following questions on a separate sheet of paper. Please do not write in this book.

1. What is the difference between a PDA and a palmtop?
2. Name four types of batteries commonly associated with portable PC products.
3. Which battery is the preferred choice for portable PCs?
4. Which type of battery has memory effect?
5. What is the most lightweight and compact battery?
6. What type of PCMCIA is used for hard drives?
7. What type of device is associated with a Type I PCMCIA card?
8. Which type of PCMCIA card is the thickest?
9. What is the function of a docking station?
10. What device can be used to provide additional ports for a portable or compact digital device?
11. List five devices that can be connected through a port replicator.
12. What are the three styles of wireless devices used for personal computer systems?
13. What is the frequency and the maximum bandwidth associated with IEEE 802.11b devices?
14. What is the frequency and bandwidth associated with IEEE 802.11a devices?

15. Which wireless standard can communicate over the greatest distance?
16. How does distance affect wireless device communications?
17. What items can interfere with radio wave communications?
18. Why is security so critical for a portable PC?
19. What does the acronym WEP represent?
20. What role does WEP play in wireless communications?
21. How does a palmtop communicate to a full-size PC?
22. Why is it difficult to upgrade the CPU in a portable PC?

Sample A+ Exam Questions

Answer the following questions on a separate sheet of paper. Please do not write in this book.

1. A Type I PCMCIA card port is typically used for which application?
   a. It is typically used to install a PCMCIA hard drive.
   b. It is typically used to install a PCMCIA CD-ROM.
   c. It is typically used to install additional RAM.
   d. It is typically used to install a floppy drive connection.
2. When installing an operating system for a laptop computer, which choice is usually selected because it installs the programs associated with portable PC systems such as a laptop computer?
   a. Windows CE
   b. Windows 98 portable
   c. Windows 98 compact
   d. Windows 98 typical
3. When exchanging information directly from a laptop PC to a full-size PC, which cable would you most likely use?
   a. Rollover cable
   b. Straight through network cable
   c. 15-pin D shell serial connection cable
   d. Null modem cable
4. Which is the best example of battery memory effect?
   a. A battery supplies the same level of voltage when connected to various types of laptop computers because it remembers the voltage level required the last time it was used.
   b. A battery loses its charge after the amount of time lapse of its last usage, even if the battery is designed to last longer.
   c. A battery is designed to remember the total length of warranty and will cease supplying voltage after the expiration date.
   d. A battery remembers the orientation of the connection polarity after being removed from the case for reinstallation at a later date.

5. Which type of battery would you most likely find in a new laptop computer?
   a. Lithium-ion
   b. Alkaline
   c. NiCad
   d. Nickel-metal hydride
6. When using a Windows 98 operating system, which program, located under **Accessories**, would you most likely use to transfer data to and from a laptop PC to a full-size PC?
   a. Direct Cable Connection
   b. Direct Dialup Networking
   c. Modem Connection
   d. Mail and Fax
7. Which statement is true for proper disposal of a laptop battery?
   a. They must be disposed of by incineration to protect the environment.
   b. You must follow local, state, and federal guidelines.
   c. Any container that is lined in plastic can be used.
   d. Lithium-ion batteries do not need to be disposed of because they can be recharged indefinitely.
8. Which situation best describes an ad-hoc network?
   a. An Ethernet network with two wireless access points: one for WAN and the other for LAN service
   b. A notebook PC connected to a full-size PC transferring files by radio signal
   c. A group of computers using radio waves to communicate through a centralized access point on a 1000BaseT network
   d. A network consisting of several access points each using a different frequency
9. What is the maximum data transfer described by the IEEE 802.11b standard?
   a. 2 Mbps
   b. 5 GHz
   c. 11 Mbps
   d. 54 GHz
10. What form of security is typically implemented on an IEEE 802.11b network system to prevent compromising sensitive data?
    a. PPTP
    b. WEP
    c. PGP
    d. SLIP

Suggested Laboratory Activities

Do not attempt any suggested laboratory activities without your instructor's permission. Certain activities can render the PC operating system inoperable.

1. Set up a laptop PC to access your home or school PC. You will need a laptop with a modem port or you can install a PCMCIA modem card into the laptop.
2. Transfer a file from a laptop to a full-size PC using a Direct Cable Connection.
3. Try installing and using the Briefcase program available through Microsoft Windows.
4. Locate and use the infrared port feature to transfer files from a laptop to a full-size PC.
5. Explore the power management settings on a typical portable PC. Be sure to record the settings before changing any.
6. Set up a portable PC for use by multiple users. Each user should have their own password and they should be able to retain their personnel desktop settings. For example, change the desktop display so each user has a different desktop.

Interesting Web Sites for More Information

www.comdex.com

www.hp.com

www.ibm.com

www.bluetooth.com

www.motorola.com

www.compaq.com

www.3com.com

www.palm.com

www.sun.com

Chapter 12
Laboratory Activity
Direct Cable Connection

After completing this laboratory activity, you will be able to:

- ❑ Describe the various ways to transfer data from a laptop to a full-size PC.
- ❑ Define the host and guest as it applies to direct cable connections.
- ❑ Explain how to install the Direct Cable Connection utility.
- ❑ Setup a share on a resource located on one PC to be accessed by another PC.

Introduction

This laboratory activity introduces you to the various ways to directly connect a laptop to a full-size PC and then access or transfer files. You can transfer data between two PCs by using a special parallel cable, a special serial cable, or an infrared port. Files can also be transferred by connecting the laptop PC and the full-size PC to a network. This networking option is covered in later chapters.

What makes the direct connection cable special is the way the cable is wired from end to end. With a normal cable, all the individual wires connect straight through. Each pin is connected to an exact matching pin number on the opposite end. The cable used to make a direct connection between two PCs is referred to as an *interlink cable* or a *null modem cable.*

The direct connection cable comes in two main styles, serial and parallel. The parallel cable connection is much faster than the serial cable connection. Examine the drawing that follows to view the pin connections of a typical serial cable and a typical parallel cable used for direct connection between two PCs. When a straight-through cable is used, for example, between a PC and a printer, the transmit signal is sent to the receive pin on the printer. There is no need to switch the pin assignments around. However, when connecting a PC directly to another PC, a special cable is required so that the send and receive pins are correctly connected. If a straight-through cable was used, the transmit pin on one PC would be connected to the transmit pin on the other PC. No communications would take place.

pin 5	pin 5
pin 3	pin 2
pin 7	pin 8
pin 1 + 6	pin 4
pin 2	pin 3
pin 8	pin 4

9-pin serial cable

pin 2	pin 15
pin 3	pin 13
pin 4	pin 12
pin 5	pin 10
pin 6	pin 11
pin 15	pin 2
pin 13	pin 3
pin 12	pin 4
pin 10	pin 5
pin 11	pin 6
pin 25	pin 25

25-pin parallel cable

Before you can establish a connection between two PCs for this laboratory, you will most likely need to install the software for doing a direct cable connection. When a typical Windows operating system installation has been performed, not all of the various programs are installed. There are a number of programs that you might find useful listed under the **Windows Setup** tab of the **Add/Remove Programs** dialog box. Direct Cable Connection is one of the programs usually not configured in a typical Windows desktop installation, though it is for a portable installation. To install the Direct Cable Connection program, you will need to use a Windows installation CD. After you obtain the Windows installation CD, open **Control Panel** and click **Add/Remove Programs**. The **Windows Setup** tab needs to be selected. You should see the following:

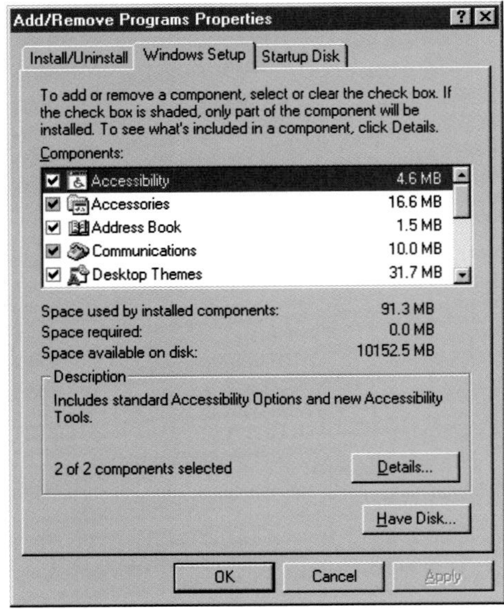

Double-click the line that says **Communications**. You should see the following:

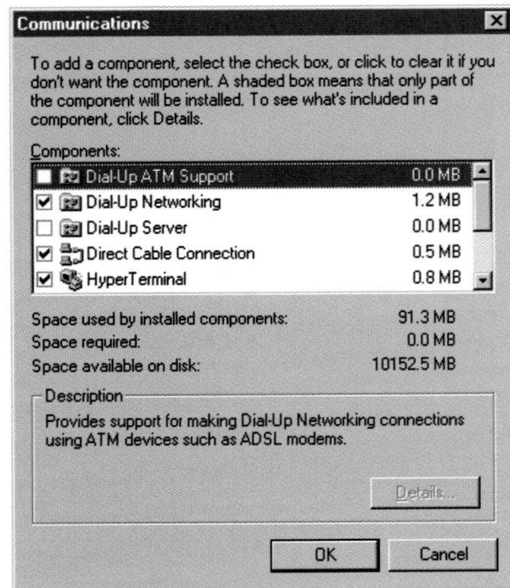

After the **Communications** dialog box appears on the screen, place a check mark in the **Direct Cable Connection** box. Follow the screen prompts and the Direct Cable Connection program will be successfully installed. Once the program has been installed, you can access it through **Start | Programs | Accessories | Communications | Direct Cable Connection**.

When the program activates, you will see a series of windows as the cable connection wizard program walks you through the setup. In the first window, you must choose Host or Guest. A short definition of each appears beside the choice.

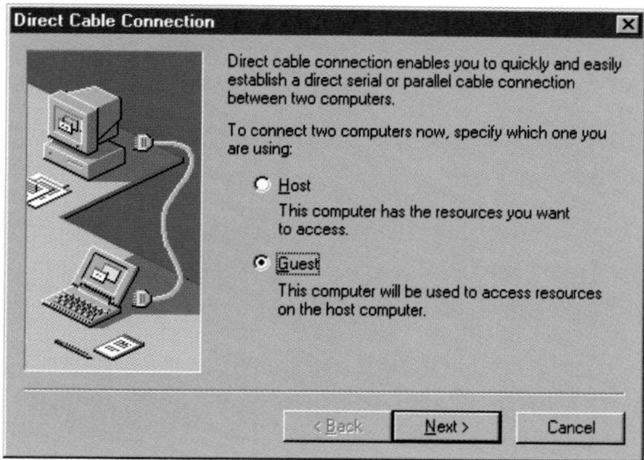

The next window asks what type of port you plan to use: serial or parallel.

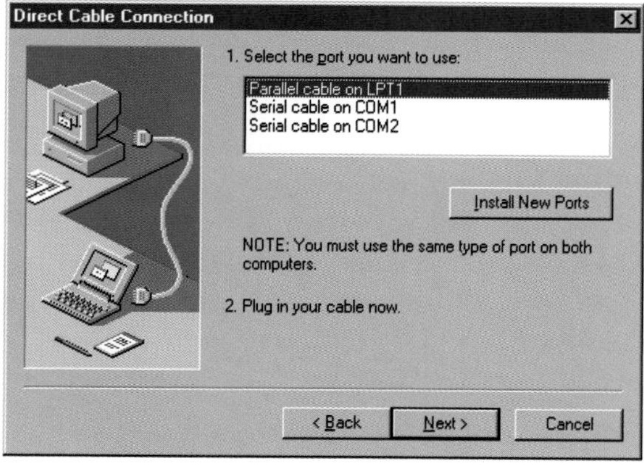

The final window verifies the completion of the Direct Cable Connection wizard setup. You are now ready to verify your connection between the host and guest.

You use the same program to transfer files between the guest and host when an infrared port is available. When using an infrared port, no cables are necessary. The infrared port can also be used to transfer files to a printer that is equipped with an infrared receiver. An infrared receiver can be adapted to a printer through the parallel printer port located on the printer.

Equipment and Materials

- Typical PC with Windows 98 or later operating system.
- Portable PC with same operating system (second full-size PC can be substituted).
- Windows installation CD.
- A parallel PC to PC cable or a null-modem serial cable.

Procedure

1. ______ Gather the materials required for the laboratory exercise. Your instructor will identify the type of cable to use.
2. ______ Boot both the laptop PC and the full-size PC. Be sure the operating systems are working.
3. ______ If it has not already been installed, install the Direct Cable Connection program on the full-size PC. Review the instructions in the introduction to locate the file.
4. ______ Activate the Direct Cable Connection program selecting the program through **Start | Programs | Accessories | Communications | Direct Cable Connection**.
5. ______ When the program starts, follow the directions as they appear on the screen.
6. ______ After the cable connection wizard is complete, try viewing the contents of the text file from the host to the guest. If there is a problem, look at the following notes. If there are no problems, move on to Step 7.

   If the Direct Cable Connection program does not work, check if **File and Print Sharing** has been activated on the host computer. It is located under the **Network** icon in **Control Panel**. Activate the Network icon and a dialog box will appear with a button on it labeled **File and Print Sharing**. The dialog box should look similar to the following:

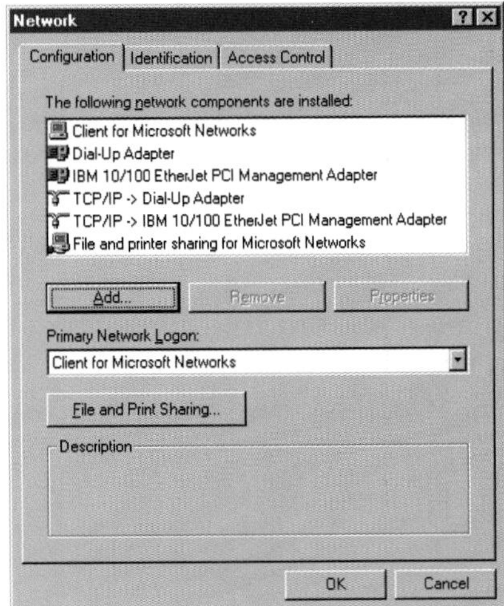

Click the **File and Print Sharing** button and follow the onscreen dialog boxes to activate file and print sharing capabilities. Attempt to access the files once more.

You also may want to check if the access is controlled by a password. If so, this could be the reason you cannot make a successful connection. Try changing the role of host and guest to see if this clears the problem. Also, check if you are using a PC-to-PC parallel cable and not a regular printer cable.

If none of this helps, check the system IRQ settings for a conflict.

7. ______ After you have successfully connected the two PCs, experiment with setting up different shares and using passwords to protect the files being shared. Use the word "password" as the password. Do not use any other password unless instructed to do so by the instructor.
8. ______ After successfully experimenting with Direct Cable Connection, return the system to its original condition and return all materials to the instructor.
9. ______ Answer the following review questions.

Review Questions

Answer the following questions on a separate sheet of paper. Please do not write in this book.

1. Which transfers data faster, a serial cable or a parallel cable?
2. How do you access the direct cable program starting with the **Start** button?
3. The PC that permits files to be accessed is called the _____ (host, guest).
4. When a PC is used to access files on a portable PC, the portable PC is called the _____ (host, guest).
5. Why do you think using a password is an option to accessing the files rather than a "must do" requirement?

The PC tablet is the newest portable computer that competes with laptops and notebook computers. The PC tablet comes with many different accessories to enhance its features and allow it to perform as a desktop system. (ViewSonic Corporation)

Modems and Transceivers

After studying this chapter, you will be able to:

- Identify basic features of telephone wiring systems.
- Explain the operation of a modem.
- Install and use Windows Communications options.
- Explain how modems negotiate a connection.
- Set up a standard modem.
- Use the Dial-Up Properties dialog box.
- Explain ISDN, DSL, cable, and T-carrier lines.
- Identify several basic AT commands.
- Diagnose common modem problems.

A+ Exam—Key Points

Telephone applications and setup will be on the A+ Certification exams. More questions will be included on the tests as more computer telephone services develop. Be familiar with standard modem negotiation terminology and acronyms such as CD, RTS, and CTS. Also, be able to compare and contrast ISDN, DSL, cable, and telephone modem characteristics.

Key Words and Terms

The following words and terms will become important pieces of your computer vocabulary. Be sure you can define them.

bandwidth
baud rate
cable modem
Data Over Cable Service Interface Specification (DOCSIS)
digital subscriber line (DSL)
integrated services digital network (ISDN)
Internet Service Provider (ISP)
modem
protocol
T-carrier line
telephone jack
universal asynchronous receiver-transmitter (UART)

One of the basic functions of the modern PC is communication with other computers, usually through Internet access. In this section, you will learn about the modem, basic residential telephone system wiring, modem installation, and communications software setup. Some of the material covered here will be seen again in the chapters discussing the basics networking.

Modems allow you the freedom to surf the Internet, connect with others through e-mail, send pictures around the world, take part in conference calls, and participate in many other activities relating to communications. While the modern modem is a Plug and Play device, there is still much to learn about modems and modem-related issues. We will begin this chapter with a brief description of the public telephone system and residential telephone wiring.

Public Telephone System

To understand the complete communications model, we must first take a look at the standard telephone system. The public telephone system has been serving the general public for over 100 years. As telephone system technology evolved, it has retained its own downward compatibility to existing equipment. The original telephone system was designed to transmit voice as an analog signal across the country and world. This system only had to be able to accommodate the frequency spectrum of sound associated with voice communications. The voice frequency spectrum for the telephone industry operated between 200 Hz and 4000 Hz. This frequency spectrum is more than adequate for carrying voice. However, it is not adequate for high-speed modem connections. High-speed connections demand higher *bandwidth.* This is the main reason why people switch to cable television carriers for Internet access. The cables used for cable television can carry much higher frequencies than the simple twisted-pair telephone cable. This large bandwidth allows for much more information to be transported in shorter spans of time.

bandwidth
the range of frequencies that an electronic cable or component is designed to carry.

The ***bandwidth*** of a cable or device is the range or limit of frequency that an electronic cable or component is designed to carry. For example, a cable with a bandwidth of 4 kbps is designed to carry a maximum frequency of 4 kbps. Note that *bandwidth* is also used to describe a portion of the frequency spectrum. For example, television channels use a bandwidth of 6 MHz for each channel. This means that each channel has a frequency range of 6 MHz.

Telephone technology has made tremendous advances over the years, but the downward compatibility issue has made it difficult to implement all the latest technologies. The main bottleneck of the entire telephone system is the last few hundred feet of connection that serve each building, especially in private homes. Most of the public telephone network system (PTNS) is constructed of high-speed fiber-optic cables, microwave transmitters and receivers, digital equipment, and computerized telephone control units. While all of these major parts of the telephone network system are composed of cables and media that have high data transfer rates, the last few hundred feet of twisted pair from the main system to the individual connection point severely limit the speed of data transmission.

Tech Tip:
The public telephone system is often referred to as POTS, which is an acronym for *plain old telephone system.*

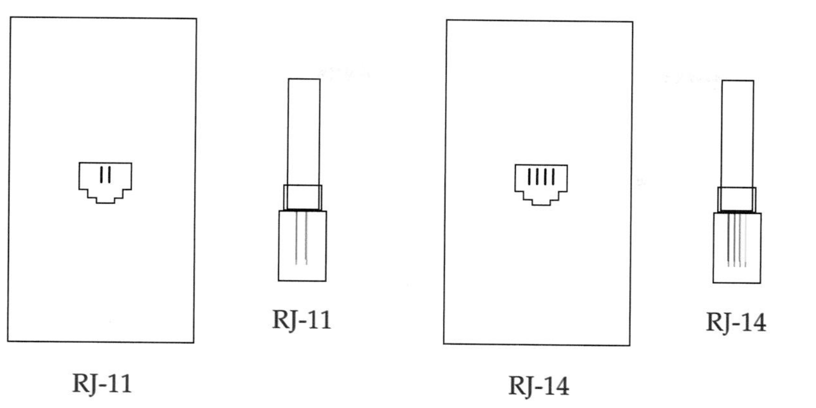

Figure 13-1. Most modern homes are wired with RJ-14 four-wire cable. Two wires are used for one telephone connection. The other two wires can be used for an additional phone line or for electrical power for phone lighting.

Residential Telephone Wiring System

The typical residential telephone wiring system is simple in design while a system for a commercial enterprise will be somewhat more complicated. The simple residential system consists of two to four wires running throughout the residence and connecting to telephone jacks. See **Figure 13-1.**

Tech Tip:
RJ-11 and RJ-14 connectors look very similar. Their physical shape is the same. The difference in classification is determined by the number of electrical contacts inside the connector. Four contacts for four wires is an RJ-14, and two contacts for two wires is an RJ-11.

The telephone wiring in a residential dwelling is typically #22 copper conductor run in a daisy chain fashion throughout the residence. Older homes may have a two-wire system, but four-wire systems are most common. Two wires are the minimum number used for one telephone to communicate with another telephone. The pair of connections are referred to in telephone technician terminology as the "tip and the ring." The additional two wires from the four-wire system can be used for an additional phone or to connect to electrical power for electrical lighting or other electrical device on the phone.

Phone lighting does not use 120 volts. A transformer is used to step the voltage level down to 12 volts, which is used to light the phone dial. The voltage level at the phone jack is considered low voltage. It reaches an approximate 48 volts when the phone is ringing. This voltage can be felt by touch, but is not considered deadly. To see how a typical phone line might be run through a home, look at **Figure 13-2.** As you can see, the cable runs through the residence from room to room. This is the usual style, but each individual jack could have its own run of cable from a junction box. The daisy chain style is preferred because it uses less cable, which means it is less expensive.

Warning:
Never work on a telephone line when there is a storm in the area. Lightning strikes can travel many miles across a telephone system and exit anywhere along the system. You could be injured during a lightning storm.

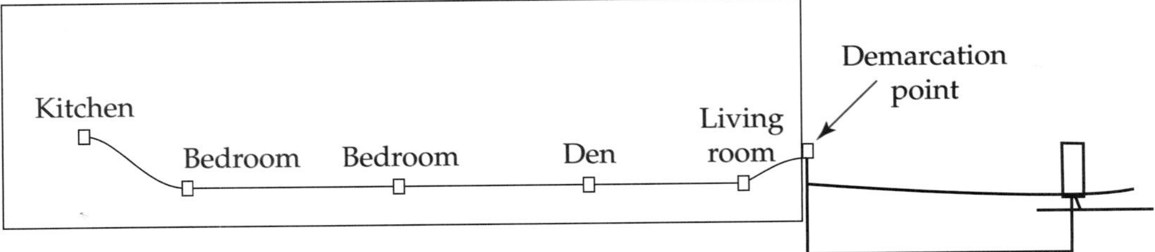

Figure 13-2.
The telephone jacks in a home are run using one common line.

telephone jack
where the telephone line connects into the cabling. This is a standard connection used to attach devices such as modems and telephones to the wiring system.

A ***telephone jack*** is where the telephone line connects into the cabling. This is a standard connection used to attach devices such as modems and telephones to the wiring system. The telephone jack is usually an RJ-11 or an RJ-14. The RJ-11 is a two-wire system, while the RJ-14 is a four-wire system. Since the deregulation of the public telephone system some years ago, the wiring inside the residence is typically the responsibility of the owner and not the local telephone company. A *point of demarcation* is where the telephone company system ends and the residence ownership begins.

Modems

modem
an electronic device that is used to convert serial data from a computer to an audio signal for transmission over telephone lines and vice versa.

A ***modem*** is an electronic device that is used to convert serial data from a computer to an audio signal for transmission over telephone lines and vice versa. The term modem is a contraction of two words: *mo*dulator and *dem*odulator. It is derived from the field of electronics. A modem can be integrated into the motherboard, it can be installed in the form of an adapter card, or it can even be connected outside the computer case as a peripheral device. A modem must be used to transmit data across traditional telephone lines. The modem simply converts a digital signal into an analog signal, and then transmits a signal across telephone lines. Another modem on the receiving end converts the analog signal back to a digital signal. See **Figure 13-3.**

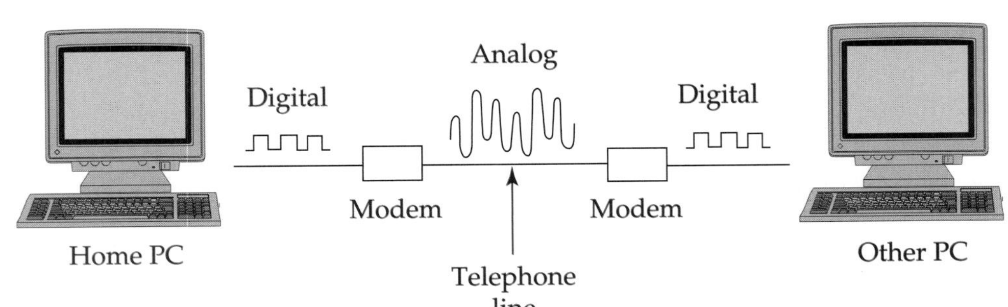

Figure 13-3.
These two computers are connected by a modem. The signal coming from the first computer is digital until it passes through its modem. The modem coverts the digital signal to an analog signal and passes it through the phone lines. The second computer's modem receives the analog signal and converts it back to a digital signal that the computer can read.

Two computers can communicate using modems. The modem converts the digital signal from the computer system to an analog signal that can be carried over telephone lines. When the analog signal reaches the destination PC, the modem converts the analog signal back to a digital signal. Some common uses for modems are to gather information across the Internet, to connect to an office PC from home, to connect to a home or office PC from a laptop while on the road, and to establish a connection to a mainframe computer system. Sending and receiving facsimiles (faxes), pictures, and music or having a simple telephone conversation while working at the computer are all examples of applications of a modem.

Windows Communications Options Menu

A modem allows you to utilize the many features provided through the Windows communications menu. This menu is located at **Start | Programs | Accessories | Communications**. When opened, there are several choices such as HyperTerminal, Phone Dialer, Dial-Up Networking, and Direct Cable Connection. A variety of services are provided under this menu. Your computer can be used to place and receive telephone calls, make conference calls (include sharing a computer white board), or send faxes. It can also be used to directly connect two computers via cable or infrared ports, connect to the Internet or bulletin boards, or to your home computer from your office. Nearly anything that can be done with a phone can also be done with a computer terminal.

Some of these communications options may not be installed on your machine. To try them out, you will need to add them to your PC. First, we will cover installing the options. Then, we will look at a few of the programs.

Installing Communications Options

Many of the options placed in the Communications folder are not installed automatically during a typical Windows operating system installation. For example, a typical Windows 98 installation installs Dial-Up Networking, NetMeeting, and Phone Dialer but does not install Dial-Up Server, Direct Cable Connection, HyperTerminal, Microsoft Chat, or Virtual Private Networking. These additional programs can be added later or by performing a custom installation while installing the operating system.

To add additional communications programs, access **Control Panel** and double-click **Add/Remove Programs**, **Figure 13-4.** A dialog box similar to the one in **Figure 13-5** will appear. Select the **Windows Setup** tab at the top middle of the dialog box. This is where you will select the type of software you wish to install or remove. **Figure 13-6** shows the selection for **Communications** software.

After the Communications software options have been selected, a dialog box similar to **Figure 13-7** appears. The various optional components are listed. Simply click the check box directly to the left of the program you desire to install. A check that is already in the check box means the component has previously been installed. You can remove any component that is installed by clicking inside the check box. This will remove the check mark and will set the component for removal.

Dial-Up Networking

Dial-Up Networking allows you to make a connection to a remote network. It is a connection to a network through existing telephone lines. For example,

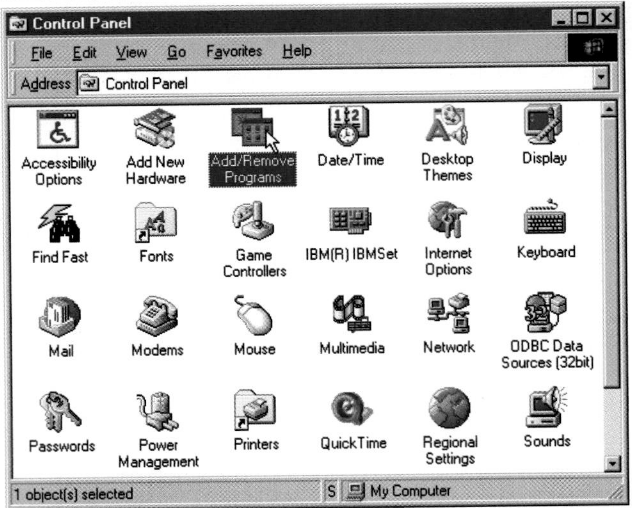

Figure 13-4.
Add/Remove Programs icon.

while away on business, a person can use their laptop to dial into the company network and access files. This type of connection is referred to as remote access service (RAS). Remotely accessing a network is covered in more detail in later chapters dealing with network fundamentals.

Dial-Up Networking is also how an Internet connection is typically established from a PC using a modem. (Remember that the Internet is just a very large network.) Double-clicking the **Make New Connection** icon runs the

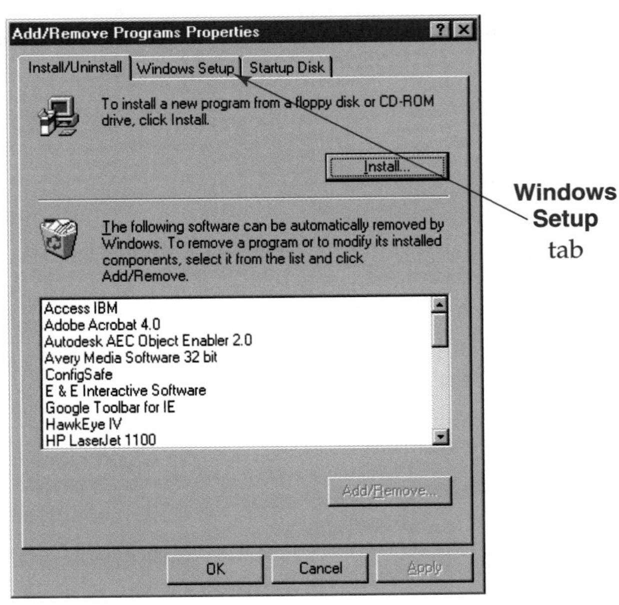

Figure 13-5.
Double-clicking the **Add/Remove Programs** icon brings up this properties dialog box. Choose the **Windows Setup** tab.

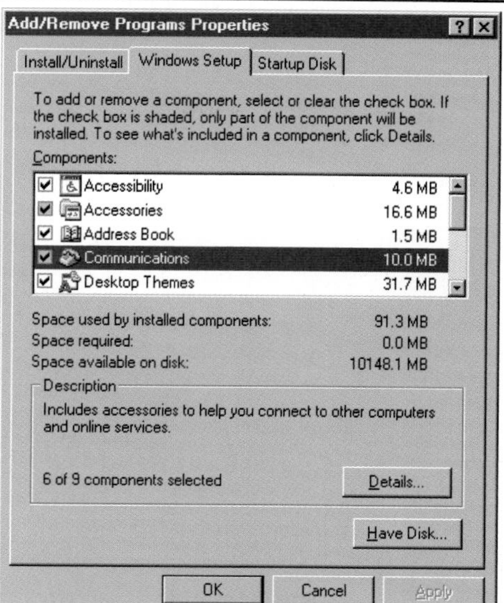

Figure 13-6. There are 9 possible different components listed in this Windows 98 operating system. The first five are shown.

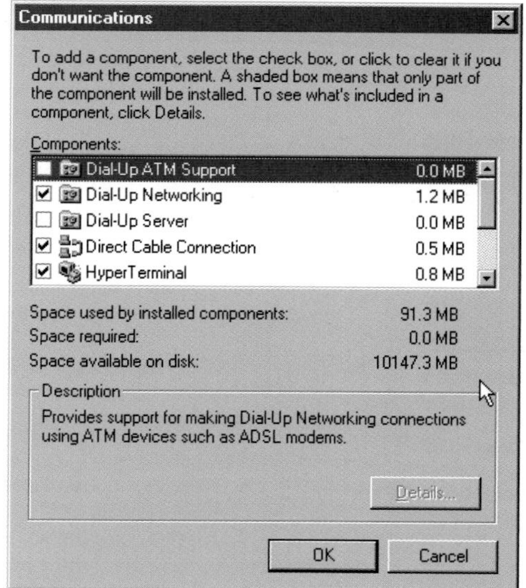

Figure 13-7. Components with check marks have already been installed on this PC. To select an unchecked component, click the box directly to the left of the component listing. Remove the check mark to uninstall a component.

Welcome to Dial-Up Networking wizard. This wizard steps you through the setup of creating a network connection, **Figure 13-8.**

An internal modem connects to the Internet through a COM port, while an exterior modem connects to a serial port. To connect to the Internet, you must use an Internet Service Provider (ISP). Most ISPs will not only provide a connection to the Internet, but they will also provide e-mail service, Web page hosting, chat rooms, local radio station connection, and more.

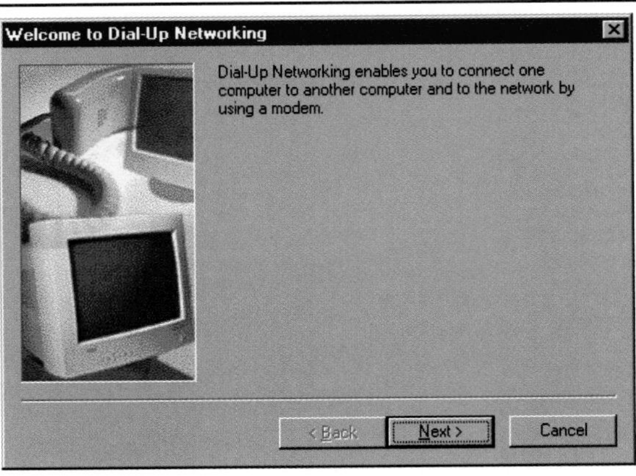

Figure 13-8. The Welcome to Dial-Up Networking wizard makes setting up a new network connection a straightforward process.

Direct Cable Connection

Direct Cable Connection allows you to connect any two PCs using an infrared port, parallel cable, or a null modem serial cable. Once connected, files can be transferred between the two computers. When using the Direct Cable Connection feature, one PC is designated the host and the other is designated the guest, **Figure 13-9.** The host provides the files needed by the guest. This is a common way to communicate between a laptop computer and a desktop PC.

HyperTerminal

HyperTerminal allows you to make a connection between two computers using a modem. Usually, this software is used to connect a PC to a mainframe computer. Once the connection is established, you can send or receive files, connect to a bulletin board, or connect to an online service.

Phone Dialer

Phone Dialer does exactly as its name implies. It allows your computer to be used as a telephone, **Figure 13-10.** You can connect to any computer in the world that allows the service. This method of communication is very inexpensive for long distance calling, especially overseas. You can use a phone credit

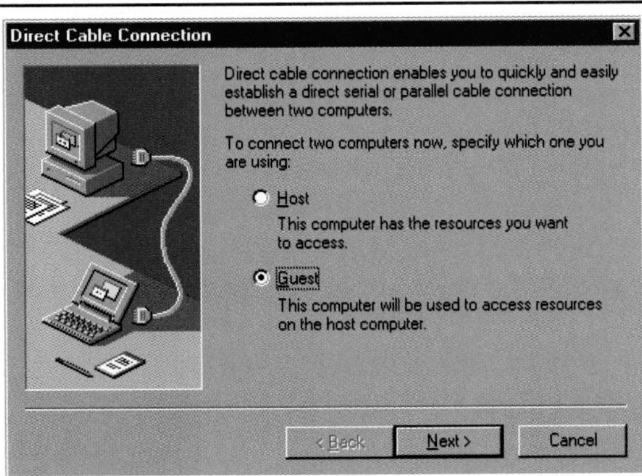

Figure 13-9. The Direct Cable Connection wizard. In the first screen, you can choose to make your PC the host or the guest.

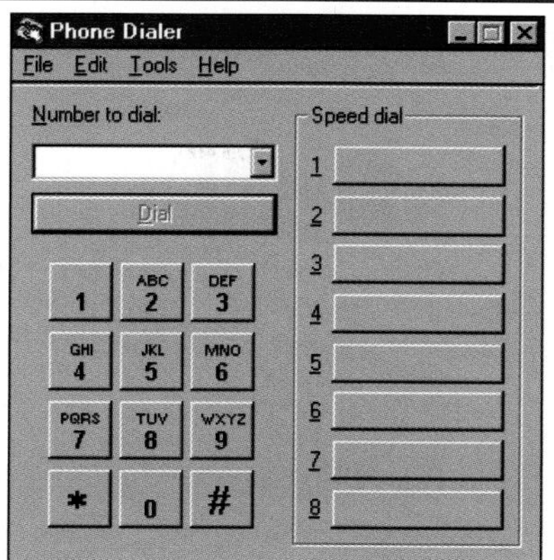

Figure 13-10. Phone Dialer allows you to use your computer as a telephone.

card when placing calls and even set the system for speed dialing. Your calls can be connected and then turned over to a typical telephone device, or, if the PC is equipped with telephony hardware, you can speak directly through the PC. You can even set up a *net meeting* with several people sharing the line all at once.

Modem Construction

The modem is simple in construction and only requires a few electronic components. See **Figure 13-11.** The main chip is the ***universal asynchronous receiver-transmitter (UART).*** The main purpose of the UART is to change parallel data to serial data and vice versa. Data moves as bytes on the computer bus system. The telephone uses a single wire to communicate in one direction. Thus, the byte, which is a parallel arrangement of data, must be converted into a series or single string of data bits.

universal asynchronous receiver-transmitter (UART) main chip in a modem that changes parallel data to serial data and vice versa.

The modem must also change the data into a form that can be transmitted across telephone lines. Digital data from the computer system cannot travel across typical phone lines because of its high frequency and wave shape. To operate over traditional phone lines, the digital signal must be modulated. This means that the digital signal is changed into an analog signal and its frequency is slowed down. The rate of data flow inside the computer is far too high to pass through traditional phone lines.

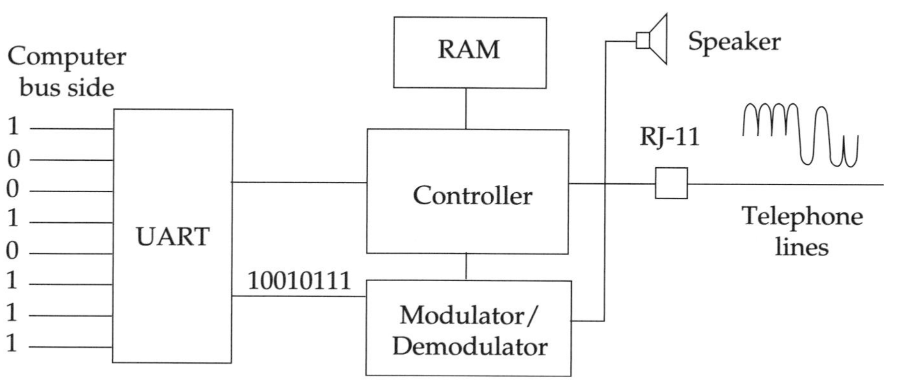

Figure 13-11. There are only a few major components in a modern modem. The UART is the most important.

baud rate
analog frequency rate of modem transmission.

The rate of the analog frequency that a modem transmits at is known as the ***baud rate.*** When the original modem was designed, the baud rate and data transfer rate were very close. Today, the baud rate and data rate are two distinct speeds. Baud rate reflects the actual analog signal rate. However, now there are a number of modulation techniques that can get a higher data transfer rate from the same baud rate. Some of these techniques include *frequency shift keying, quadrature amplitude modulation,* and *phase shift keying.* These systems of encoding are very difficult to fully understand without an adequate electronics background. For now, just know that these techniques allow data to be a multiple of a single baud rate. For example, a baud rate of 900 can be changed to a data rate of 1800 or 3600 bits per second (bps). Even bits per second is not the actual data speed. The actual data speed is increased by data compression techniques as well. Compression techniques were introduced in Chapter 8—Video Display and Audio Systems.

In addition to the components that produce signal modulation, modems need a memory chip component. The data flow from the computer bus is too fast to transmit directly through the modem. Data must be stored in the modem and transmitted more slowly. This is the job of a simple RAM chip incorporated into the modem. The RAM chip holds large chunks of data and sends it at a slower rate, a rate the modem can handle. When a modem receives data, the same action takes place in reverse. The data received is stored in RAM until the computer bus system is ready to receive it.

Modems also come with an audio device, such as a small speaker. This speaker allows you to hear the audible tones being dialed by the modem when activated. This will assist you when troubleshooting. The speaker allows the user to hear the tones used in the transmission of data, usually at start up. When you connect to the Internet through your modem, you can hear the modem dial out to your Internet provider. If you don't hear any tones when the modem is dialing out, the modem may be set up incorrectly or the modem may have failed. However, some people turn off the sound to the modem, so lack of sound does not always indicate a problem.

The job of coordinating the entire operation of the modem is left to the control chip. The control chip controls the flow of data and the interaction of all the parts of the modem. It is similar to a minicomputer and is often referred to as a microcontroller.

Modem Connection Process

There are several steps that must be performed to make and maintain a connection to another computer. The act of connecting to another computer using a modem is often referred to as *modem negotiation.* Often these steps can be observed on an exterior modem through the use of lights (LEDs). The process of making the connection is a series of signals and commands, which include the following:

- Data Terminal Ready (DTR)
- Data Set Ready (DSR)
- Carrier Detect (CD)
- Request to Send (RTS)
- Clear to Send (CTS)
- Transmit Data (TD)

A software program commands a modem with a data terminal ready (DTR) signal, which tells the modem that the user wishes to make a connection to another location. If the modem is ready, it sends a data set ready (DSR) signal back to the software. Both signals must be present before any data can be transmitted. Next, the PC sends a transmit data (TD) signal to the modem. This commands the modem to dial a particular phone number. The modem replies with a receive data (RD) signal and proceeds to open a connection on the phone line, which is referred to as "off the hook". A series of electrical pulses flows from the modem through the telephone line. This is the same as dialing a number. When the other modem receives the hailing signal, it responds back to the originating modem. The modem now uses a carrier detect (CD) signal to let the originating PC know that a carrier signal has been received from the modem. An example of this conversation is shown in **Figure 13-12.**

Figure 13-12.
Modems send signals back and forth to set up a conversation.

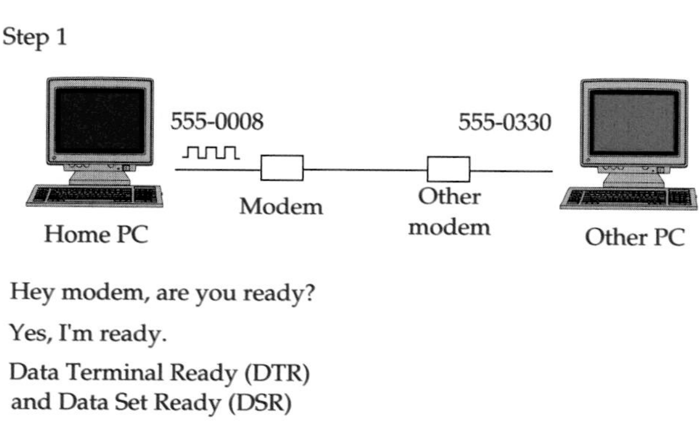

Step 2

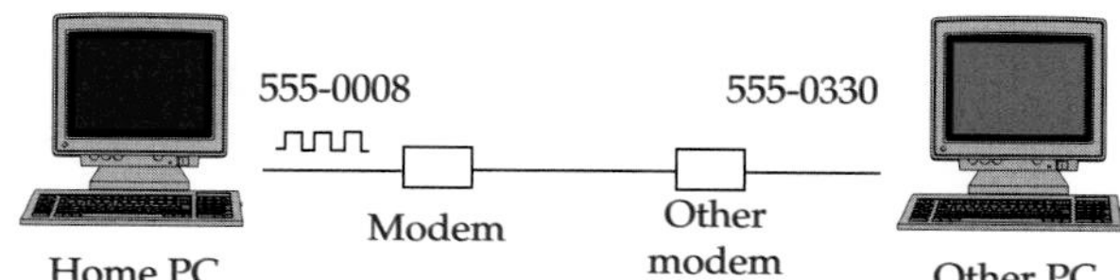

Hey modem, call this number for me: 5550330

OK, will do.

Transmit data (TD) : call the 5550330 number.
Carrier Detect (CD): is there a phone line available?
When line is available, the 5550330 number is dialed.

Step 3

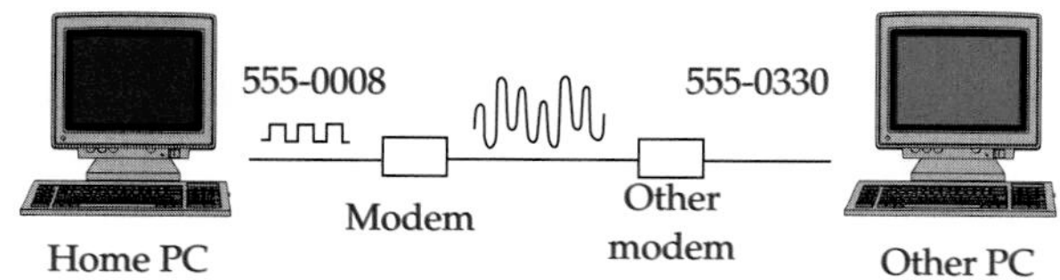

Hey 5550330. I'm calling you.

I'm here 5550008.

How fast do you run?

I run at 28,000 bps. Can you keep up?

No problem. Do you use parity?

Yes.

Odd or even?

How about odd?

That's fine. Are you going to display images on both screens or shall I?

You called, so why don't you do it.

Ok.

The rules of communication have been negotiated.

Step 4

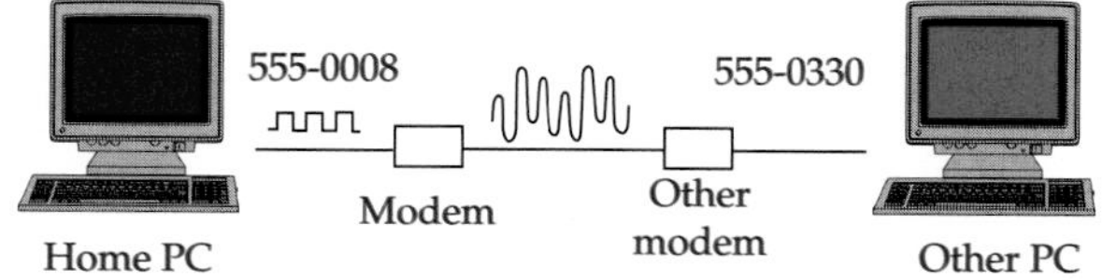

Hey 5550330, I'm going to send you a request to send (RTS) each time I send you some data, and you reply with a clear to send (CTS) if you are ready. I know that the CPU can be quite busy and your RAM could be full.

Thanks 5550008, I'll do the same for you.

The process of data exchange continues until one of the parties hangs up.

There are many different modem styles and software systems, so the two modems now communicate back and forth trying to establish a common ground for exchanging data. The communication includes such matters as the transmission speed, the number of stop and start bits, and the type of parity that will be used. The handling of half/full-duplex must also be resolved. Data speed or baud rate must be the same for both modems. The absolute base speed is 300 baud, but normally it will be above 1200 baud. Start/stop bits must be established.

Data sent across telephone lines by a modem is sent in packets. A single bit is used to mark the beginning of a packet and either one or two bits are used to mark the end of the packet. Look at **Figure 13-13.**

The type of parity must also be agreed on. There are three options: no parity, odd parity, and even parity. Parity is a way to check the accuracy of the data packet being sent. When the number of bits inside the data packet is added up, it will equal an odd or an even number. The systems agree to send an additional bit that represents either an odd number or an even number. A zero can represent odd or even parity and the same is true for a one. The receiving system adds up the bits in the data and compares that number to the parity bit to check for errors.

The last item to resolve is the half/full-duplex condition. The two communicating systems must agree which system will be responsible for half-duplex transmission and which will be responsible for full-duplex transmission. The terminal responsible for full-duplex is responsible to display data on the screen for both PCs. The other PC need not be responsible. If this condition is not agreed on, neither system will display the data on the screen, or both systems will display data on the screen. This means the data will be displayed twice on each screen.

After all the responsibilities have been negotiated between systems, messages can begin to be transmitted. The modem sends a request to send (RTS) signal asking if the other modem is ready to receive data. It replies with a clear to send (CTS) signal. The two computers can send data back and forth in continuous operation and actually both can transmit data over the line at the same time.

Many of these commands and activities can be monitored when using a modem connected outside the PC unit. The exterior type of modem has a series of lights that indicate different stages of activities. **Figure 13-14** is a list of typical light abbreviations and their definitions.

Figure 13-13. Typical modem data packet. Surrounding the data is a start bit, stop bit, and parity bit.

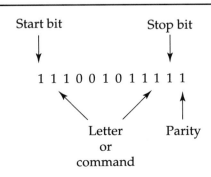

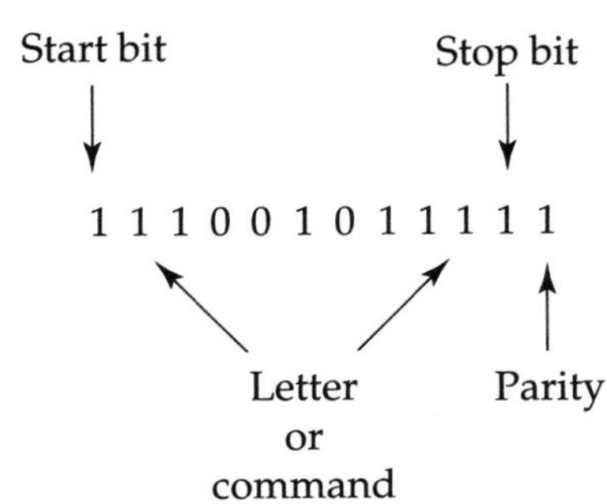

AA (Auto Answer)	Ready to accept incoming calls automatically.
CD (Carrier Detect)	The modem has detected a carrier signal.
HS (High Speed)	The modem is operating at its highest speed.
MR (Modem Ready)	Modem is ready to operate; the power is on.
OH (Off Hook)	Same as taking the receiver off the telephone hook.
SD (Send Data)	Data is being received from the other modem.
TR (Terminal Ready)	Modem indicates it has received a (DTR) from the software package.

Figure 13-14. External modem light abbreviations and definitions.

The entire operation of the modem is a combination of coordination of the operating system software, the modem controller chip, and the UART chip. The entire process seems complicated, but in effect it appears transparent to the typical user. The user simply clicks an icon and connects.

Setting up a Residential Internet Connection

A residential Internet connection can be easily set up. The term *residential* is used because setting up an Internet connection for a network system is different. The requirements for a large network are covered later in this textbook. Most of the residential setup is done using a setup wizard program, but even the setup wizard will need some input of information from you.

The very first step in arranging an Internet connection is to choose an Internet Service Provider. An ***Internet Service Provider (ISP)*** provides connection to the Internet, and it usually provides many other services as well. Services such as e-mail, tools, and space to set up your own Web site, search engines, and local information are provided by most ISPs.

Internet Service Provider (ISP) provides connection to the Internet and other services.

Most ISPs provide CD-ROMs to assist you in automatically connecting with their services. Running these discs starts a wizard that helps you set up your connection to the Internet. In addition, most PCs purchased today have setup software for several ISPs already loaded. These ISPs can be added quickly by clicking the associated icon on the screen. Usually, all this will work automatically. At times, you may be required to do some configuring manually. This is especially true in a business environment or in a PC with a security system such as a firewall.

For a typical home PC, you will need to enter the telephone number of the ISP, your user ID such as JonesB, and a password issued by the Internet service provider. Other items that you may need to enter are the name of the e-mail server being accessed at the ISP location and type of e-mail protocol being used, such as POP3. These last two items are usually provided by the ISP. You might also need to select the type of protocol used to transmit data to the ISP over the telephone line such as PPP or SLIP. Typically, PPP is used.

When you are setting up your Internet connection, you may be required to input a choice of protocol. A ***protocol*** is a set of rules much like the rules that are used by two modems. The standard protocol used for the Internet is TCP/IP, which stands for Transmission Control Protocol/Internet Protocol.

protocol a set of rules for formatting the data stream transmission between two computers or devices and for describing how to transmit data, usually across a network.

A number, called an IP address, is usually associated with TCP/IP. You will have to get this number from your service provider if it is not automatically set up by the software installation. An IP address is a series of numbers that identifies the computer you are using. The numbers are separated by periods (dots) into four groups (for example 192.168.27.132). Each group is called an octet. An octet is a number that is comprised of eight bits. As you know, you can form 256 numbers (0–255) using eight bits. The Internet actually communicates using these series of numbers to identify a site as opposed to using the site name (such as www.goodheartwillcox.com) that you are used to seeing. Software converts the numeric ID (IP address) into the name of the site you are trying to reach.

Since you are connecting to the Internet and expect other Web sites and people to respond to you, your PC also will have an IP address. If you use a dial-up ISP, the IP address you use may not be permanent. Rather, the address is newly issued each time you access the Internet through your service provider. This allows the ISP to have a smaller number of IP addresses and distribute them to users as they need them. The access phone number dialed as you access the Internet is just the phone number of the Internet Service Provider used by your PC. It is not your IP address. If you have a cable modem, you will likely have your own dedicated IP address.

Host Name and Domain Name

The host name and domain name is issued to you by the ISP. The domain name system (DNS) is a software system located on the ISP server that supplies your PC with an identity for Internet communication purposes. The ISP server will issue your PC an identity address for the Internet each time you access the service. You may be asked to supply proxy server information. This information will be covered in the upcoming chapters on networking. Proxy servers are not generally used on residential or individual PC setups.

Modem Properties Dialog Box

Setting up a modem is easy with Plug and Play technology and software wizards. These tools make most of the hardware and software decisions for you. However, there will be times when it will be necessary to access the settings yourself to verify or alter the settings. This is especially true when the person having modem difficulties has already accessed Control Panel and changed some of the settings while attempting a repair.

The **Modem Properties** dialog box can be accessed through **Start | Settings | Control Panel** and then double-clicking the **Modems** icon. This allows you to view or change information such as highest baud rate, parity selection, end bit style, number of data bits, and file compression. See **Figure 13-15.** The **Modem Properties** dialog box can be used to examine modem properties and also to open other dialog boxes such as **Dialing Properties**.

Dialing Properties

Dialing properties are controlled by telephone application programming interface (TAPI). See **Figure 13-16.** The **Dialing Properties** dialog box is where information about the telephone service to be used is entered. Items such as area code, the phone number assigned to the modem, country, and type of modem being used (identified by brand) are included here. Dialing Properties can be

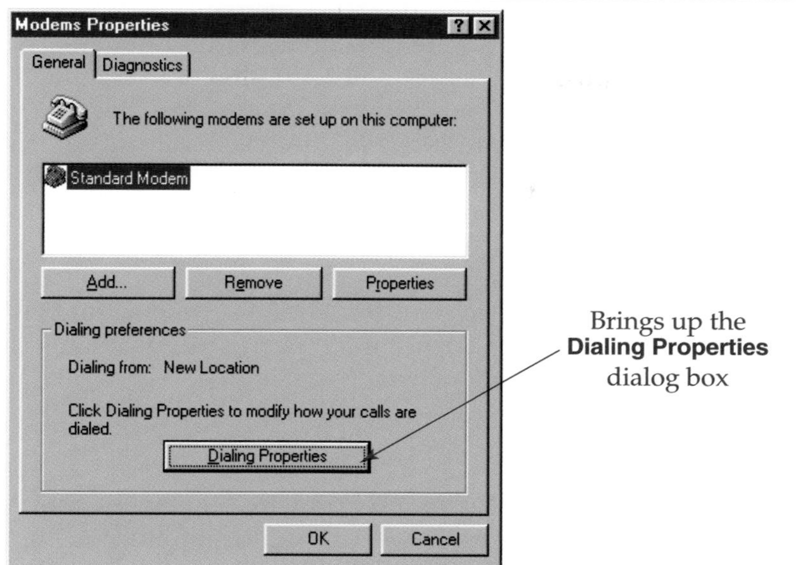

Figure 13-15.
The Modem Properties dialog box allows you to examine and change settings for your modem.

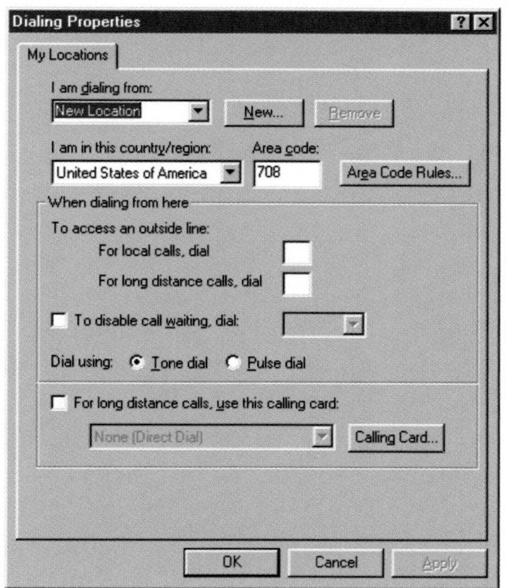

Figure 13-16.
The Dialing Properties dialog box. This tool allows you to enter the number you are dialing from, set up your local area code rules, and disable call waiting.

accessed through a button labeled **Dialing Properties** found in the **Modem Properties** dialog box or by double-clicking the **Telephony** icon in **Control Panel**.

Integrated Services Digital Network

Integrated services digital network (ISDN) is a standard that allows a completely digital connection from one PC to another. Like the regular dial-up service, ISDN uses phone lines to transfer data. Although, to use ISDN services, you must be within approximately 3 1/2 miles of the actual digital equipment of the telephone company. To use ISDN lines for communication, you must use a terminal adapter (TA) rather than a modem. A terminal adapter is like a modem, only it does not need to convert signals back and forth between analog

integrated services digital network (ISDN)
a standard that allows a completely digital connection from one PC to another.

and digital. The signal stays digital. Terminal adapters come in the form of adapter boards or exterior devices that connect directly to the serial port.

ISDN can be used to carry voice and digital information simultaneously. Traditional phone lines only allow voice or data. They can't handle both at the same time. On a standard ISDN line there are three channels, one D channel and two B channels. The D channel is designed to carry control signals and operates in a range of 16 kbps to 64 kbps. The two B channels are used for voice and data and can carry data at speeds up to 64 kbps. The two B channels can be combined to carry data up to 128 kbps.

ISDN provides services for businesses as well as for private use. The price is much higher for digital service than for traditional phone lines. This makes its use prohibitive for many private users.

Digital Subscriber Lines

digital subscriber lines (DSL) provide high-speed Internet access over telephone lines. A DSL can provide a constant connection to the Internet and can send both voice and data over the same line.

Digital subscriber lines (DSL) provide high-speed Internet access over telephone lines and has become one of the most popular methods for connecting to the Internet. There are many different variations of DSL available, such as ADSL, HDSL, VHDSL, and SDHL. In this unit, we will use the acronym DSL to represent the technology in general and will not address any particular type of DSL. A DSL can provide a constant connection to the Internet and can be used to send and receive both voice and data over the same line. Regular telephone lines are designed to carry low frequency voice communications in a range of 0 kHz to 4 kHz. DSL telephone lines are designed to carry much higher frequencies at 25 kHz to 1 MHz. The higher frequencies can be used as a high speed Internet access. DSL is not available in all areas, and it is more expensive than regular telephone line service.

The maximum distance DSL can span is limited by the high frequencies it uses. The typical maximum distance for DSL is 1,000′ to 1,800′ measured from the DSL modem to the telephone central office. The exact limit depends on the type of DSL used and any special equipment, such as loading coils, or media such as fiber optic, that might exist on the telephone line.

A loading coil is used to amplify analog voice signals. It will not amplify a DSL signal. In fact, the loading coil reduces or blocks the higher frequency DSL signal. The media might also change between the subscriber location and the central office. For example, the copper conductor cabling may change to fiber-optic cabling at some point, which will prevent the application of DSL. DSL technology is applied only to copper wiring, not fiber optic.

Another factor that determines the maximum distance DSL can span is the length of the cable. A short cable can pass a much higher frequency than a long cable. High frequency signal strength is affected in direct proportion to the length of the cable. This means that the longer the cable, or greater the distance, the lower the applied DSL frequency must be, resulting in lower data transfer rates.

DSL systems vary in upstream and downstream bandwidth according to the type of DSL used. See **Figure 13-17.** The term downstream is used to describe the data flow direction from the carrier or provider's site to the customer. The term *upstream* is used for the data flow direction from the customer to the carrier. For more information on the various DSL technologies, visit www.xdsl.com.

DSL Type	Upstream	Downstream	Maximum Distance
ADSL	1.544 Mbps	1.5 Mbps – 8 Mbps	12,000′ – 18,000′
HDSL	1.544 Mbps	1.544 Mbps	15,000′
SDSL	1.544 Mbps	1.544 Mbps	10,000′
VDSL	1.5 Mbps – 2.3 Mbps	13 Mbps – 52 Mbps	1,000′ – 4,500′

Figure 13-17.
DSL types and their upload and download speeds. Typical maximum distances are also listed.

Look at **Figure 13-18** to see how a DSL installation might look. The DSL modem is connected between the DSL telephone line and the PC. Notice that the DSL modem connects to the RJ-45 jack on the network adapter card and not to the RJ-11 jack on the telephone modem. Not all DSL modems use a network adapter card for a connection from the DSL modem. A USB port on the PC can serve as the connection point as well. The DSL modem must have electrical power to operate. In the drawing, you can see that the DSL modem has been plugged into a 120 VAC power adapter.

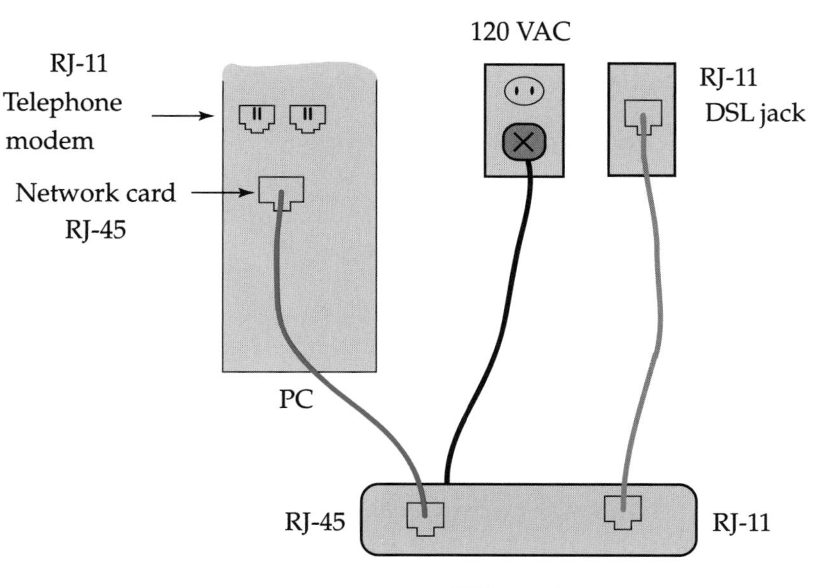

Figure 13-18.
The DSL modem is connected between the DSL telephone line and the network card on the PC.

Cable Modems

cable modem provides high-speed Internet access using lines designed for cable television.

A ***cable modem*** provides high-speed Internet access using lines designed for cable television. Cable modems connect you to the Internet without having to dial in. It can provide you with a continuous connection. Your connection won't time out for lack of use like it may with a dial-up ISP. ISPs set a time-out value, so that they can take back the IP address and make it available to other users. With a cable modem, you have your own IP address. Cable access also provides you with a much higher download speed than phone line networks. However, a drawback of cable modems is that you share the access with other neighborhood cable users. Thus, as more people access and use data intense services on the network system, such as video and audio downloading, your data speeds will slow down. Another downside of this system is there is typically only one choice of cable service provider per neighborhood. So, if you are unhappy with your service provider, the only way to get a new one is to move.

There are two major types of cable media used for access, fiber-optic cable and coaxial cable. See **Figure 13-19.** Coaxial cable consists of a solid copper conductor surrounded by a thick insulating material. An outer conductor is made of braided copper or a foil jacket surrounding the insulating material. An insulating jacket, used to provide physical protection to the cable assembly, covers the entire assembly. Special coaxial cable connectors are crimped on to the ends. Coaxial cable is easily spliced or extended. Coaxial cable has a maximum data transfer speed of 350 MHz. The coaxial cable is used to download from the Internet while conventional telephone lines must make connection to the Internet. The coaxial cable is not currently a two-way data transmission system.

Fiber-optic cable consists of a glass or plastic core. Each core material, glass or plastic, is quite small in cross-sectional area and is very flexible. Fiber-optic cable transmits light rather than an electrical signal through the core. Fiber-optic cable has many advantages over coaxial cable or any type of copper core cable.

Figure 13-19.
A—Coaxial cable. Note the center conductor surrounded by layers of insulation. B—Fiber-optic cable. Fiber-optic cable has several outer layers. The layers protect the cable and reflect the light down the cable.

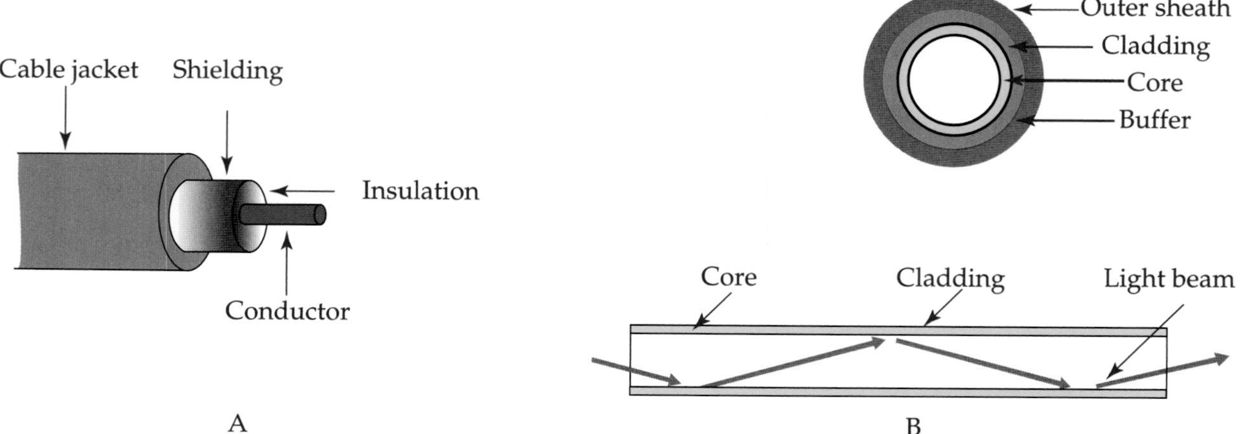

It is lightweight, resistive to corrosion and water, and immune to electrical interference. It also provides excellent security because it is almost impossible to tap into. One very big advantage of fiber-optic cable is that it is immune to strikes by lightning. When lightning strikes traditional metal core cable, a high current can run through the cable and damage sensitive electronic equipment including computers and monitors. Fiber-optic cable can also be run for longer lengths with less signal loss than conventional copper core cables.

The downside of fiber-optic cable is essentially price. Fiber-optic cable is expensive to install. Also, special equipment is required for splicing the cable.

Fiber-optic cable through the television company is usually divided into many different channels. Each channel uses a 6-MHz channel to transmit each separate television channel or network, such as ABC, CBS, or NBC. The same principle is used for Internet connections. Two channels, each 6 MHz, are provided to transmit data to and from the Internet. Currently, there is not a single standard for cable modem specifications. You must check with the local ISP cable company to see what type or brand of cable modem you will need. One standard that has been established for cable modems is called ***Data Over Cable Service Interface Specification (DOCSIS).*** This standard allows any DOCSIS cable modem to communicate with any other DOCSIS cable modem. Also, you will need to install a cable splitter. The cable splitter divides the signal between your modem and your television. Remember, the same cable provides both television and Internet access.

Data Over Cable Service Interface Specification (DOCSIS) standard for cable modems that allows any DOCSIS cable modem to communicate with any other DOCSIS cable modem.

T-carrier Lines

T-carrier lines were first introduced in 1993 by AT&T. They are designed to carry voice and data. The lines have the ability to carry data at a much higher rate than traditional phone lines. An important part of the T-carrier line system is the use of a *multiplexer* and a *demultiplexer.* A multiplexer is a special electronic device that controls the flow of data and voice over a T-carrier line. Think of it as a funnel that combines lower frequency lines together to take advantage of the higher frequency transmission rates of the T-carrier. Look at **Figure 13-20** to view a multiplexer and T-carrier.

T-carrier lines lines designed to carry voice and data at a much higher rate than traditional phone lines.

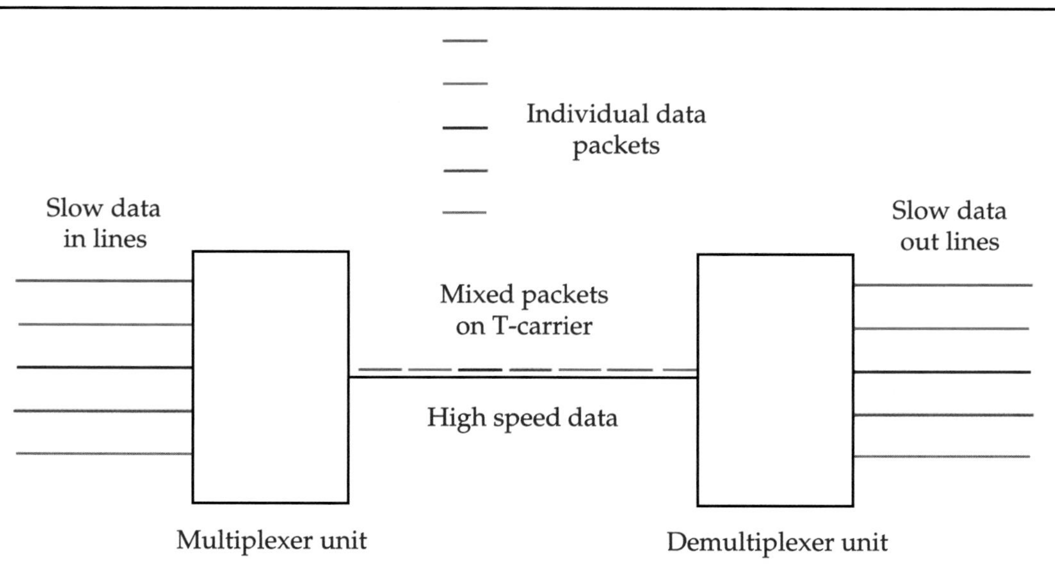

Figure 13-20. A multiplexer organizes slower speed data and voice signals into a series of higher speed data packets. The packets are converted back to a lower speed at a demultiplexer unit.

As you can see in the illustration, there are several low-speed lines tied into the multiplexer. As data is transmitted through the multiplexer, it is reorganized into smaller packages called data packets. The multiplexer sends the data packets through the T-carrier in an organized manner. The data packet then travels at the maximum speed of the T-carrier. At the opposite end of the T-carrier there is a demultiplexer that reverses the process. It rearranges packets back into their original structures and releases them to lower data rate lines. Businesses, government, and educational institutions are the primary customers who lease T-carrier lines. The levels of T-carrier lines are identified in the list in **Figure 13-21.**

An additional label, called a fractional T-1, is a T-1 line that is only partially issued to a customer. Think of a fractional T-1 line as a line being shared among different parties who, individually, do not require full T-1 line capacity.

Modem Signaling Standards

Data sent between two modems must use some type of communication standards after the initial process of setting up communication rules. The standards are used for data compression techniques and error correction after an error has been detected. When there were only a few telephone companies operating, this was not an issue. The Bell Telephone Company developed a set of standards known as the Bell standards. Bell 103 was the first widely accepted standard used for modems operating at 300 baud. Later, Bell 212A was the accepted standard for 1200 bps. After deregulation of the telephone companies in America, however, a number of standards were used.

A dominant standard was the International Telecommunications Union standard (ITU). This was not actually a single standard but rather a collection of standards. The standards resolved issues such as volume, minimum and maximum tone sound, and synchronous or asynchronous transmissions. As the speed of modems increased, new standards had to be developed based on the new techniques and technical parameters. Communication is now a worldwide event and involves standards from Europe also. As computer network systems evolved, another set of standards was developed called the Microcom Networking Protocol (MNP). This was developed in the mid-1980s. This set of standards deals mainly with the rules of communication between two computers.

In addition to the standards, a system is needed for telephone data communication between two points. A modem standard is developed so that two modems can communicate effectively. After a communications standard is established, the modem must have a way to determine data and command codes. A system is needed to show how the electrical pulses and fluctuations will be used to represent data. A modem simply transports packets as a series of

Figure 13-21. T-carrier identifications.

T-carrier
T-1 = 1.544 Mbps or 24 voice channels
T-2 = 6.312 Mbps or 96 voice channels
T-3 = 44.736 Mbps or 672 voice channels
T-4 = 274.176 Mbps or 4032 voice channels

electrical fluctuations. A protocol is needed to represent the data and how it is to be encoded. You can think of a protocol as the organized manner and the rules used to represent the data being transmitted. Some common communication protocols are Kermit, ASCII, Zmodem, Ymodem, and Sealink. There will be much more information about protocols later in this textbook when covering network fundamentals.

Basic AT Commands

There are sets of modem commands that are usually automatically issued by software in the GUI environment. You simply click the feature you want, and it automatically issues the command to the modem for you. However, at times, you may want to use a command directly from the keyboard, especially when using HyperTerminal or troubleshooting a modem.

Tech Tip:

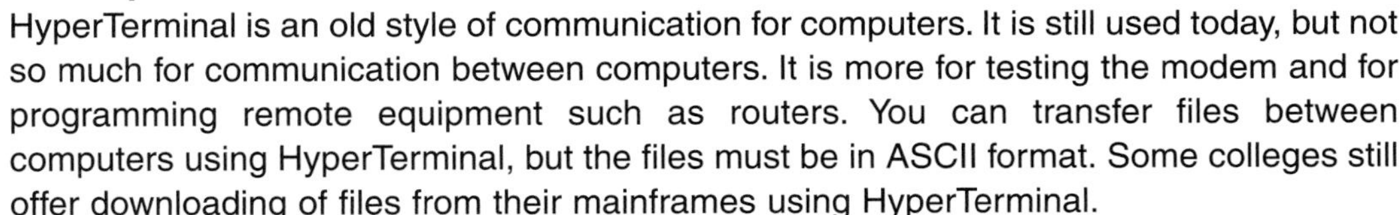

HyperTerminal is an old style of communication for computers. It is still used today, but not so much for communication between computers. It is more for testing the modem and for programming remote equipment such as routers. You can transfer files between computers using HyperTerminal, but the files must be in ASCII format. Some colleges still offer downloading of files from their mainframes using HyperTerminal.

There are many AT commands, but only the basic commands will be covered here. You can download information on more commands from the Internet. You can use the basic AT commands for troubleshooting purposes. For example, you could start HyperTerminal, and then enter **AT** at the command line to verify that the modem and PC are communicating with each other. After the [Enter] key is pressed, the HyperTerminal screen should display "OK" on the screen. You can also type **AT&F** to reset the modem to its original factory settings. Examine some other basic commands in **Figure 13-22.**

Command	Response	Description
AT&F	OK	Restore factory default settings.
ATZ	OK	Soft modem reset.
ATE1	OK	Enable the echo command. This allows commands to be viewed.
ATE0	OK	Turns the echo command off.
A/	OK	Repeat the last command issued.
+++	OK	This command gets the attention of the modem.
ATDT####	Connect ####	This command dials the phone number indicated by the #### symbols.
ATDT#, ##	None	The comma tells the modem to pause after dialing #.

Figure 13-22.
AT commands.

There are other AT commands that can set the number of rings before a phone is answered, set the phone for a manual answer rather than automatic, save the phone profile or setup, cause the modem to briefly turn on, and more. The commands illustrated here are just to familiarize you with AT commands. They can be used when troubleshooting a standard modem.

IrDA

Windows XP introduced a new feature that allows users to place a phone call from a workstation or laptop PC through their cell phone. All that is required is both the PC system and the cell phone be equipped with an infrared transceiver. A transceiver is a device that transmits and receives data. The cell phone must be equipped with an infrared port and the IrCOMM protocol. Using their cell phone like a modem, the user is free to connect to the Internet from almost anywhere.

Modem Troubleshooting

Use the following suggestions when troubleshooting a modem:

- Always check the modem connections first. Do not waste valuable time until you check the most obvious and the most common problem. People tend not to check cabling unless told to do so. A modem connection can be easily disturbed by vacuum cleaners, the plugging in of other equipment, or moving furniture. Always check the cable first.
- Start HyperTerminal and type AT at the command prompt to see if the modem responds. The response should be "OK." The OK response tells you that communication between the PC system and modem is working. Do not start disassembly of the PC.
- Try dialing a local or test telephone number. Use the computer's Phone Dialer to call the phone number of a phone on a neighboring desk. The phone should ring.
- Check the computer's IRQ and COM port settings. Look for conflicts.
- Check the call waiting function on the modem or dialer setup.
- Check if there is a time-out feature being used for the modem. Some modems cut off after a set time period of no activity.
- Check the telephone cable and telephone line. Faulty wiring along the telephone cable can be the cause. Try plugging in a standard telephone.
- Check with the phone company if any lines are out. Look for communications vehicles in the area of the company or residence with a modem problem. If you are called to a business for a modem problem and you see a communication vehicle sitting beside a ditch on your way there, it may save you a lot of frustration troubleshooting the modem if you stop and ask a few questions.
- If the modem is connecting but you are receiving or transmitting gibberish, then you probably have a software issue. Check the manufacturer's Web site for last minute upgrades and patches.
- Always assume that someone has already attempted to correct the problem before you were called. You may have to correct several problems before you detect the original one.

Summary

- An RJ-11 is a standard telephone cable connector.
- The term *modem* is a combination of the words modulate and demodulate, which describe the electronic action of the modem.
- The central electronic component of a modem is the universal asynchronous receiver transmitter (UART), which changes data from parallel to serial output.
- A modem is designed to communicate by converting the digital data from the PC to an analog signal transmitted across telephone lines or other media.
- Baud rate reflects the speed of the analog frequency and not the true data transfer rate.
- Parity is used to ensure the data received is the correct bit pattern.
- Some standard communications media are telephone wiring, coaxial cable, and fiber-optic cable.
- A multiplexer is used to convert multiple individual data inputs into one series of serial data output.
- A demultiplexer is used to separate serial data input to separate parallel output data that matches the original data configurations.
- AT commands are used for modem communications.

Review Questions

Answer the following questions on a separate sheet of paper. Please do not write in this book.

1. What is the most important task of a phone modem?
2. Name several specific tasks that can be done by using a modem.
3. What is the main factor that limits the speed of data transfer over the residential telephone system?
4. What is the designed frequency spectrum for voice communication over traditional telephone lines?
5. What is RJ-11?
6. What was the original modem maximum speed?
7. Describe the difference between baud rate and data rate.
8. Describe the difference between a protocol and a standard.
9. What are four communications programs listed under Windows Communications?
10. Arrange the following commands in the expected order of implementation.
    CTS
    RTS
    DTR
    DSR
    CD

11. Why does a modem negotiate a connection with another modem?
12. What is an octet?
13. Write an example of an IP address.
14. Give five advantages that fiber-optic cable provides over coaxial cable and typical telephone wiring.
15. What does the AT command ATDT5551010 do?

Sample A+ Exam Questions

Answer the following questions on a separate sheet of paper. Please do not write in this book.

1. Which statement best describes the operation of a modem?
   a. A device that converts digital signals from the PC bus system to analog signals that are transmitted across telephone lines.
   b. A device that transmits digital signals across telephone lines.
   c. A device that converts analog signals from a USB port to digital signals that are transmitted data across telephone systems.
   d. A device that sends digital signals across various network systems until a digital signal reaches a predetermined PC connection.
2. Which of the following has the slowest data transfer rate?
   a. ISDN
   b. DSL
   c. Cable modem
   d. Dialup modem
3. Which is the correct example of using an AT command to dial the phone number 555-6186?
   a. AD 555-6186
   b. ATDT5556186
   c. ATD5556186
   d. AutoDial555-6186
4. What does the LED marked "CD" on a modem most likely indicate?
   a. The call has been disconnected: CD = Call Disconnect.
   b. The phone code has been deployed: CD = Call Deployed.
   c. The carrier has been detected: CD = Carrier Detect.
   d. The carrier has been called or dialed: CD = Carrier Dialed.
5. Which of the following is an example of an IP address?
   a. 00 03 A4 34 C5 1F
   b. 123.67.103.114
   c. JohnJK12@hotmail.com
   d. JohnDoel23.456.ACME

A+

6. Which connection type is typically found in a residential home telephone jack outlet?
   a. RJ-45
   b. RJ-11
   c. BNC
   d. AT-45
7. Which program below is typically used to place a telephone call?
   a. HyperTerminal
   b. Dial-Up Networking
   c. Direct Cable Connection
   d. Phone Dialer
8. Which is the correct method of accessing the Direct Cable Connection program in Windows Me?
   a. Right-click **My Computer** and then select **Telephone Connections** from the shortcut menu.
   b. Open **Control Panel** and select the **Modem** icon.
   c. Open **Control Panel** and select the **Cable Connection** icon.
   d. From the **Start** menu, open **Program | Accessories | Communication** and then select **Direct Cable Connection**.
9. What is the maximum bandwidth using an ISDN line?
   a. 56 kbps
   b. 1.54 Gbps
   c. 128 kbps
   d. 256 kbps
10. A T1 line is capable of reaching what data transfer speed?
    a. 56 kbps
    b. 1.54 kbps
    c. 1.54 Mbps
    d. 2.56 Mbps

Suggested Laboratory Activities

Do not attempt any suggested laboratory activities without your instructor's permission. Certain activities can render the PC operating system inoperable.

1. Try ringing a telephone using the Phone Dialer program. This is a good way to quickly test a modem.
2. Experiment with the settings of the Modem Properties dialog box and the Dialing Properties dialog box. Write down all the existing settings before making any changes. Change settings for the baud rate and parity. Try selecting a different protocol. After making changes, attempt to use the modem or Phone Dialer to see what effect the change had on the system.

3. Open **Control Panel** and select **Add/Remove Programs**. Select the **Windows Setup** tab and see what optional programs have not yet been installed for communications on the PC.
4. Install and set up NetMeeting to communicate with another PC.
5. Install and set up HyperTerminal to connect to a remote PC and exchange a file.
6. Inquire about what types of service are available in your area. The services to inquire about are DSL, ISDN, cable modem, and satellite. Use the Internet to inquire about availability in your area.

Interesting Web Sites for More Information

www.56k.com

www.cablelabs.com

www.catv.org

www.usrobotics.com

www.verizon.com

www.xdslresource.com

Chapter 13
Laboratory Activity
Modem Installation

After completing this laboratory activity, you will be able to:

- ❑ Install and configure a typical modem.
- ❑ Configure a dialup network connection.
- ❑ Configure a dialing location.
- ❑ Explain how to test a modem using the telephone dialer program.

Introduction

In this laboratory activity, you will not only install a modem but also access the Internet. The term *modem* is a contraction of the two electronics terms, modulation and demodulation. Modulation is the process of modifying an electrical signal or electronic waveform. A modem allows a PC to access the Internet as well as connect to an office network or another PC.

A PC outputs information as a digital signal. A modem converts that high-speed digital signal into an analog waveform that can be carried over a typical telephone line. A typical telephone line is not designed to transport a high-speed digital signal. Therefore, the signal generated by a computer must be converted into an analog signal before it can be transmitted over the phone lines. When the signal reaches the destination, such as another PC, the modem on the receiving end converts the analog signal back to a digital signal so the signal can be processed by the receiving PC system.

The main electronic component of a modem is a chip called a universal asynchronous receiver-transmitter or UART. The UART converts the parallel digital signal into a serial digital signal. The digital signal is then converted into an analog signal, an electrical signal of varying voltages. See the following illustration.

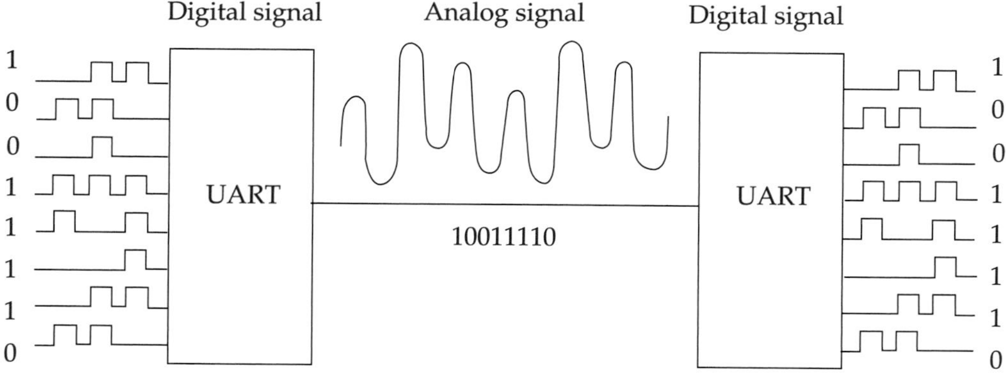

The digital signal of one PC is converted to an analog signal, transmitted on telephone lines, and then converted back into a digital signal at the other PC.

The modem can be integrated into the motherboard (onboard modem), installed as a separate unit outside the PC (external modem), or installed inside the PC as an adapter card (internal modem). In this laboratory activity, you will install an internal modem (adapter card) into the appropriate expansion slot. Once installed into the slot, the card is easily set up by Plug and Play technology.

After installing the modem card, you will need to configure the settings to make a connection over a telephone line. Connecting via phone lines to a network that has a file server is often referred to as dial-up networking (DUN) or remote access service (RAS). You also can connect to the Internet using an Internet service provider (ISP). The difference in the terminology is slight. Dial-up networking (DUN) refers to actually dialing a phone number using a modem to make a connection to a remote network system, usually to your work location. You also use dial-up networking to attach to your ISP. After connecting to your ISP, you can access your network at work by navigating the Internet. Remote access service is a service run on a network file server or PC. When the RAS is installed, it allows users to dial in directly to a computer or file server and make a connection. Dial-Up Server is an optional service that can be installed using the Add/Remove Programs icon in Control Panel. Open the **Add/Remove Programs** and select the **Windows Setup** tab located at the top of the dialog box. The **Dial-Up Server** option is located under **Communications**. When installed, you can access your PC from a remote location over the telephone system.

Another optional component is **Phone Dialer**. It is also located beside the **Dial-Up Server** option. **Phone Dialer** can be used to dial telephone numbers from your PC. This is a very handy utility for checking the condition of a modem. Simply dial an existing telephone number for a cell phone or pager to see if your modem is working.

Equipment and Materials

- Typical PC with Windows 98 or later operating system installed.
- 56K modem card.
- Access to an active telephone line.
- A telephone number to be used by your PC modem and a telephone number to be used as a destination (the number of an Internet service provider).

Note:
Check if a number is required to reach an outside line (usually 9). Check if there is call waiting on the line.

Procedure

1. ______ Boot the PC and wait for the Windows desktop. This verifies the system is working properly.
2. ______ Properly shut down the system.

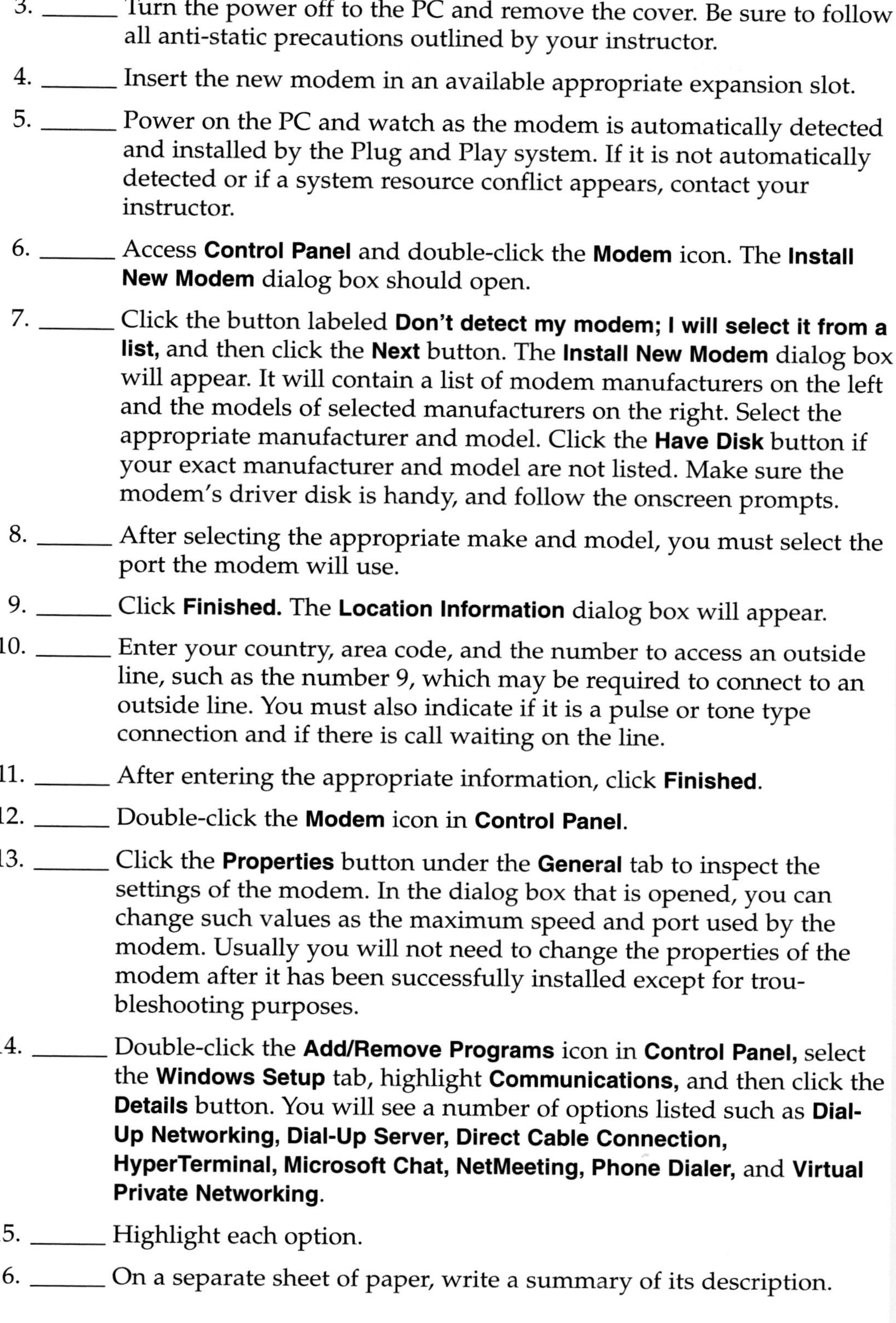

3. ______ Turn the power off to the PC and remove the cover. Be sure to follow all anti-static precautions outlined by your instructor.
4. ______ Insert the new modem in an available appropriate expansion slot.
5. ______ Power on the PC and watch as the modem is automatically detected and installed by the Plug and Play system. If it is not automatically detected or if a system resource conflict appears, contact your instructor.
6. ______ Access **Control Panel** and double-click the **Modem** icon. The **Install New Modem** dialog box should open.
7. ______ Click the button labeled **Don't detect my modem; I will select it from a list,** and then click the **Next** button. The **Install New Modem** dialog box will appear. It will contain a list of modem manufacturers on the left and the models of selected manufacturers on the right. Select the appropriate manufacturer and model. Click the **Have Disk** button if your exact manufacturer and model are not listed. Make sure the modem's driver disk is handy, and follow the onscreen prompts.
8. ______ After selecting the appropriate make and model, you must select the port the modem will use.
9. ______ Click **Finished.** The **Location Information** dialog box will appear.
10. ______ Enter your country, area code, and the number to access an outside line, such as the number 9, which may be required to connect to an outside line. You must also indicate if it is a pulse or tone type connection and if there is call waiting on the line.
11. ______ After entering the appropriate information, click **Finished**.
12. ______ Double-click the **Modem** icon in **Control Panel.**
13. ______ Click the **Properties** button under the **General** tab to inspect the settings of the modem. In the dialog box that is opened, you can change such values as the maximum speed and port used by the modem. Usually you will not need to change the properties of the modem after it has been successfully installed except for troubleshooting purposes.
14. ______ Double-click the **Add/Remove Programs** icon in **Control Panel,** select the **Windows Setup** tab, highlight **Communications,** and then click the **Details** button. You will see a number of options listed such as **Dial-Up Networking, Dial-Up Server, Direct Cable Connection, HyperTerminal, Microsoft Chat, NetMeeting, Phone Dialer,** and **Virtual Private Networking**.
15. ______ Highlight each option.
16. ______ On a separate sheet of paper, write a summary of its description.

Review Questions

Answer the following questions on a separate sheet of paper. Please do not write in this book. Use Windows Help to answer the following questions.

1. What protocol is used for a virtual private network?
2. What is multilink?
3. Can you use your personal computer as a dial-up server?
4. What is a virtual private network (VPN)?
5. What is dial-up networking?
6. What does the acronym UART represent?
7. Does a modem convert analog signals to digital or digital signals to analog?

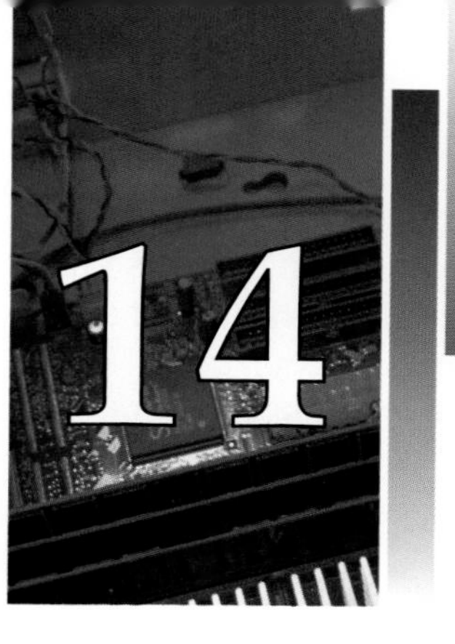

Viruses

After studying this chapter, you will be able to:

- ❑ Identify common virus characteristics.
- ❑ Explain virus detection.
- ❑ Explain how viruses are spread.
- ❑ Explain the prevention of virus infection.
- ❑ Define virus signature.
- ❑ Classify viruses by their action or description.

A+ Exam—Key Points

Data backup may be covered on the examination as well as the installation of antivirus software.

Key Words and Terms

The following words and terms will become important pieces of your computer vocabulary. Be sure you can define them.

back door virus
computer virus
hoax
logic bomb
macro virus
MBR virus
password virus
polymorphic virus
stealth virus
Trojan horse
virus signature
worm

This unit covers the fundamentals of virus infection, protection, and its elimination in the computer environment. Viruses cause a tremendous amount of destruction and aggravation. Sooner or later you will encounter a virus or worm. You must have a knowledge base to deal with these threats. This may be one of the most important chapters you read.

What Is a Computer Virus?

computer virus a maliciously created software program that is written for the express purpose of causing damage to a computer system.

A ***computer virus*** is a maliciously created software program that is written for the express purpose of causing damage to a computer system. It is typically written to duplicate itself and in the process cause problems and often permanent damage to a computer or computer system. A virus usually has three phases: infection, replication, and execution.

The infection arrives from a source such as a floppy disk, CD, e-mail, or network connection to a computer, such as the Internet. Replication is when the virus duplicates itself to other programs, files, drives, or other computers on a network system. If a virus continually replicates itself, it can easily use up all available disk space. Execution can take many forms. Some are harmless and just annoying. Others can be very destructive. They can erase files and lock up hardware.

virus signature combination of characteristics that define a particular virus, including such things as its length, file name(s) used, mode of infection or replication, and more.

Viruses are said to have *signatures.* A ***virus signature*** describes a particular virus. It is a combination of characteristics that include such things as its length, file name(s) used, mode of infection or replication, the areas of the system that are attacked, the type of software programs that are attacked, and the name or length of the file attachment. These signatures are what antivirus software use to catch viruses on your PC.

Virus Classifications

The term computer virus has taken on a very broad definition with the public. Most malicious programs that infect PCs are referred to as viruses. However, the software companies that develop antivirus software programs have developed a variety of classifications. These classifications vary somewhat from company to company. In addition to virus, there are other malicious programs called worms. Each program has its own features. Common classifications of computer infections are Trojan horse, logic bomb, macro, worm, password, back door, and hoax. While some classes will seem similar, there are sufficient variations in their style to allow a classification system to be used. Note that there are many viruses and worms that are composed of the features of multiple classifications.

Worm

worm destructive program that contaminates files on the infected machine and spreads itself to other machines without prompting from the user.

While many viruses attach themselves to other programs to slip into your machine, worms operate on their own. Technically speaking, a ***worm*** is not a true virus but rather its own destructive program. A virus replicates itself on one machine and infects files on that particular machine. A worm contaminates files on the infected machine, but it also spreads itself to other machines without prompting from the user. This method of spreading itself is what makes it different from a virus. Worms are also referred to as *bacterium* virus by some authorities.

It is also important to note that worms are self-replicating. Once infection takes place, the worm can replicate or transmit itself to other machines without user intervention. A classic example of its reproduction is through an e-mail application. When a worm is sent out as a file attachment, it replicates itself by using the list of contacts in the user's e-mail database. The recipients of the e-mail then inadvertently infect the people on their lists. The infection rate is exponential. See **Figure 14-1.** The infamous Melissa and I Love You viruses are both worms.

Trojan Horse

The Trojan horse classification is named after the Trojan horse from Homer's Iliad. In the legend, the Trojans leave a huge wooden horse to the city of Troy, presumed as a gift that symbolized the end of the Trojan War. The horse was taken inside the walls of the city. However, the horse was hollow inside and filled with Greek soldiers. In the secret of night, the Greek soldiers climbed out of the horse, attacked the guards, and opened the gates to the city. This allowed the Greek soldiers to enter and defeat the city of Troy. The city was captured and burned to the ground. The virus acts very much like the Trojan horse in the legend.

The ***Trojan horse*** class of virus appears as a gift. It may be a free download of a program such as a game or utility program, an e-mail attachment, or some other item that is attractive to a user. When opened, the virus becomes activated. Some cause immediate damage. Others wait until a later date. The Trojan horse can have a harmless outward appearance. It often advertises itself as a utility to assist with some sort of computer operation. Since the Trojan is disguised, users may not even realize that they have infected their machine. After a time, unusual operations or glitches appear in the computer. The hard

Trojan horse class of virus that appears as a gift, such as a free download of a game or utility program, an e-mail attachment, or some other item.

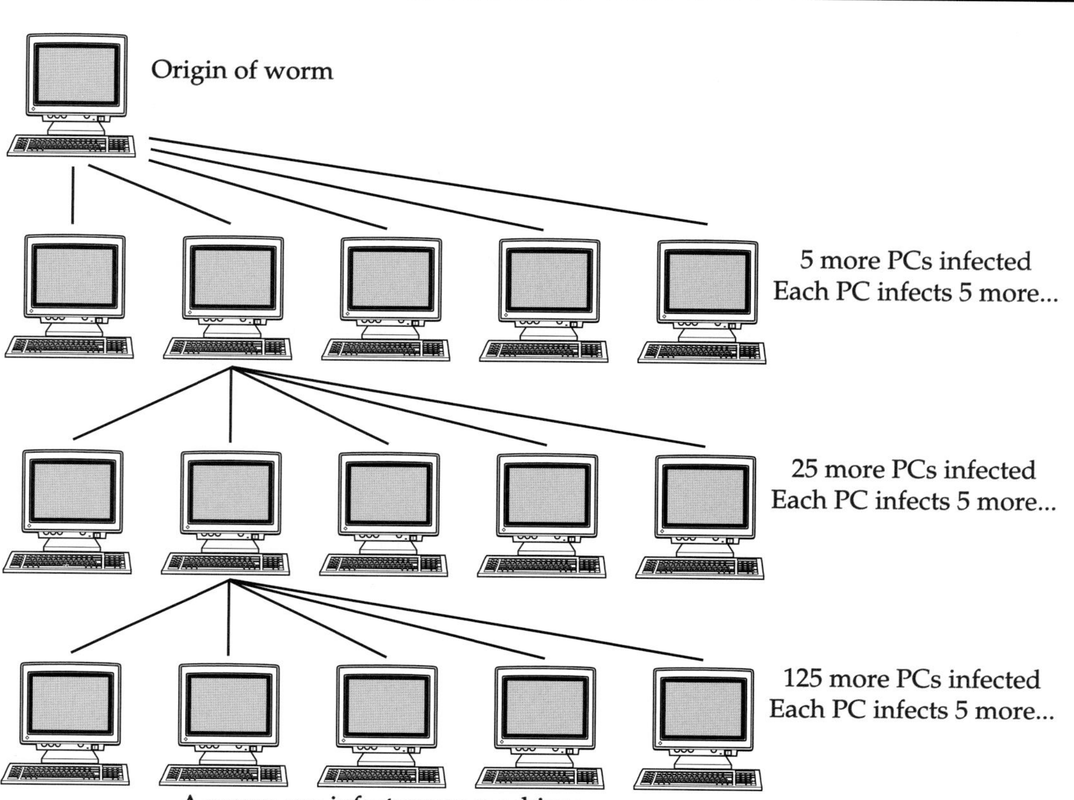
Origin of worm
5 more PCs infected
Each PC infects 5 more...
25 more PCs infected
Each PC infects 5 more...
125 more PCs infected
Each PC infects 5 more...
A worm can infect many machines across the globe very rapidly.

Figure 14-1. E-mail is the most common method of transmitting a worm. Using this method, the worm multiplies at an exponential rate.

drive may be erased or written over leaving no space for any other files to be saved. There are too many possible symptoms of Trojan horses to list them all, but you can expect many unusual operations on the computer and may not recognize the problem until damage has been done.

Macro Virus

macro virus a common virus created using a macro programming language. It is attached to documents that use the language.

A ***macro virus*** is named after the macro software-programming tool. It is a virus created using a macro programming language, and it is attached to documents that use the language. A standard macro program is designed to assist a computer user by converting repetitive tasks into one simple key code or name. Macros can record a set of user keystrokes and then save the set of keystrokes under a file name. When needed, the set of keystrokes can be easily loaded anytime. For example, a set of keystrokes used to create a template that will be used over and over again can easily be created using the macro feature in Microsoft's Word program. A typical letter heading including a company's name, address, phone number, and contact person is an example. When loaded, the macro automatically recreates the keystrokes, producing the desired information.

This same method is used to create some virus programs. They are often distributed as e-mail attachments. Once a machine is infected, the virus attaches itself to any new file created with the infected software application. Macro viruses are very common. In fact, macro viruses are estimated to account for 75% of all viruses.

MBR Virus

MBR virus an extremely destructive virus that attacks the master boot record (MBR) of a hard disk, resulting in hard disk failure.

An ***MBR virus,*** a virus that attacks the master boot record (MBR) of a hard disk, is considered extremely destructive. When activated, the virus plants hexadecimal codes in the master boot record, rendering it useless. This results in hard disk failure. Damage is usually limited to only the master boot record, which can be rebuilt if backups have been made. Many antivirus programs perform MBR backups as part of their installation and require a floppy to save necessary records for rebuilding the system.

T

Tech Tip:
One point of particular interest is the FDISK/MBR command used to repair the MBR. Certain known virus programs, such as the Monkey virus, actually move the location of the MBR. Applying the FDISK/MBR command will not remedy the problem, and it will most likely do more damage when the command reconstructs the MBR with a damaged file and saves the damaged file as the backup copy.

Logic Bomb

logic bomb a destructive program that is slipped into an application and waits dormant until some event takes place, allowing the virus to spread to other machines before releasing its payload.

A ***logic bomb*** is a destructive program that is slipped into an application and waits dormant until some event takes place. The event could be the arrival of some date or time, the entering of a certain number, word, or file name, or even the number of times the application is loaded. The idea behind the design of a logic bomb is to wait for a period of time, allowing the virus to spread to other machines before releasing its payload of destruction.

Back Door Virus

A ***back door virus*** is designed to go undetected and leave a *back door* into your system. A back door is a hole in the security system of a computer or network.

back door virus a virus designed to go undetected and leave a back door into your system. A back door is a hole in the security system of a computer or network.

The back door virus is not designed to be directly destructive like the typical virus or worm. Rather, it is used to breach security systems. Once the back door is created, the PC file system can be accessed in spite of password and other standard security setups. Back doors are usually associated with network systems but can also be used on a single PC.

Password Virus

A ***password virus*** is not designed to destroy a system or replicate itself. Rather, like the back door virus, it is designed to breach security. These viruses steal passwords. The passwords are stolen and then redirected to another location possibly on some other system on the Internet to be accessed later. Often, the system that is housing the stolen passwords is not even aware that it is being used to hold stolen material.

password virus a virus that steals passwords.

A password virus is closely associated with a back door virus, and both may be used in combination. The password virus and back door virus are designed for illegally accessing networks, though either can be used to access a single PC when it is connected to the Internet.

Stealth Virus

A ***stealth virus*** hides from normal detection by incorporating itself into part of a known, and usually required, program for the PC. The signature of a stealth virus is difficult to acquire unless the original PC system has an antivirus program installed when new. When the antivirus program is installed on a clean PC, the program monitors changes in all files, especially those susceptible to a stealth virus. For example, if the important files change in length, it is a sign that it has been infected with a stealth virus.

stealth virus a virus that hides from normal detection by incorporating itself into part of a known, and usually required, program for the PC.

Polymorphic Virus

To resist detection, a ***polymorphic virus*** changes as it evolves. It can randomly change its program length, and it can also change the location or type of file it chooses to infect. By constantly changing its virus profile, it can go undetected by antivirus programs that compare the signature or profile of the known virus. The most modern and dangerous viruses use both the polymorphic and stealth characteristics to protect themselves.

polymorphic virus a virus that changes as it evolves so that it may go undetected by antivirus programs.

Hoaxes

Hoaxes are not actually viruses. Instead, ***hoaxes,*** as the name implies, are false messages spread about a real or unreal virus. These messages could be classified as pranks. While hoaxes do not directly damage the PC or destroy files, they are not harmless.

hoaxes false messages spread about a real or unreal virus.

Hoaxes can cost money through the loss of production time. If a hoax warns of a virus such as a logic bomb that will activate at 12:00 on June 5, people who believe the hoax will stop working and use antivirus software to clean their computer before resuming work. It may take some time before they find out that the message was just a hoax and that no real virus exists. If this message spreads through a large corporation, thousands of computers could be shut down. Another trick used by hoaxes, is to pick the name of a legitimate file used by a computer's operating system and claim that it is a virus. You are then warned to delete the file. Many people lost their ability to read long file names when one of these hoaxes passed through.

A hoax is considered harmful because it too can cause losses. While the damage is not usually directed to the PC or data system files, money is lost in the form of labor costs. The best way to prevent against being fooled by a hoax is to visit one of the Web sites of an antivirus software manufacturer. These sites have pages dedicated to discussing common hoaxes.

Creation of Viruses

By understanding something of how a virus is created, you may better be able to detect a virus. Viruses are created in a number of different ways using many different programming tools. For example, one common way viruses are created is through macros. As discussed in the section on macro viruses, a macro is a short program written to save keystrokes. Macros are written in macro language programs, such as visual basic, for applications or similar programming tools. They were developed to help users. However, the same techniques used to save you time can also be applied for destructive purposes. Programming software such as Visual Basic, C++, and ActiveX are some commonly used tools to develop viruses and worms. Even the simple macro editor that comes with Microsoft Word can be used. There are Web sites that will even sell password, back door, and worm programs. They are advertised "for educational use only."

Most virus and worm paths can be tracked. They can often be traced backward to the original source, especially when delivered by e-mail. Look at **Figure 14-2** through **Figure 14-4.**

In the Figure 14-2, you can see the obvious source of the e-mail in the e-mail listing. This screen box is available under the properties of e-mail. Figure 14-3 and Figure 14-4 reveal more information about the e-mail and routing. The actual TCP/IP address and the e-mail ID number are revealed. Once the TCP/IP address is known, a trace can begin. While the exact user may not be exposed as simply as is illustrated here, the ISP can revoke access to any user who violates privacy or harasses another PC site. Remember that accessing another person's PC without their express permission and distributing a virus is a crime.

Well-Known Viruses

There are many more viruses than the viruses that follow, but these are some of the significant viruses. Each listed virus is well-known and documented. Understanding viruses from the past will help you understand how to identify and defend against new viruses as they continue to arrive.

Michelangelo

On March 6, 1992, millions of computers were predicted to have their hard drives erased. The cause was the Michelangelo virus. The Michelangelo virus was named such because the trigger for this logic bomb was the birth date of the famous artist. Michelangelo was the first virus widely publicized in the media.

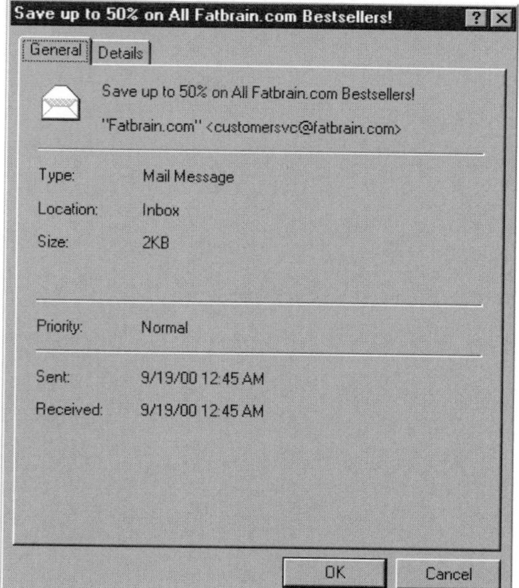

Figure 14-2. By choosing Properties from the File drop-down menu on an open e-mail, you can see basic information on the message sent to you.

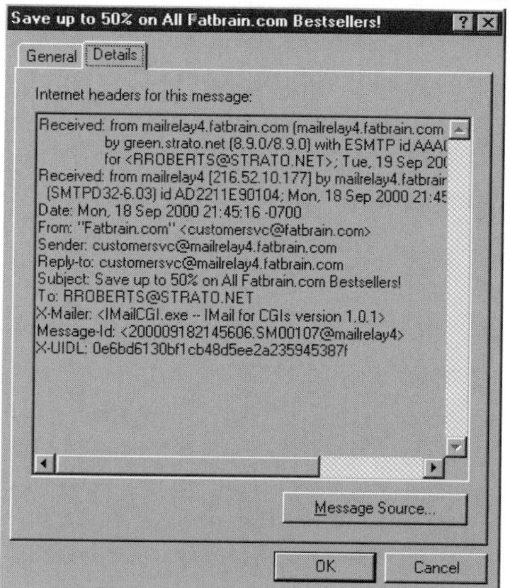

Figure 14-3. Additional information from the e-mail's Properties.

```
Message Source
Received: from mailrelay4.fatbrain.com (mailrelay4.fatbrain.com [216.52.10.177])
        by green.strato.net (8.9.0/8.9.0) with ESMTP id AAA04216
        for <RROBERTS@STRATO.NET>; Tue, 19 Sep 2000 00:45:48 -0400 (EDT)
Received: from mailrelay4 [216.52.10.177] by mailrelay4.fatbrain.com
  (SMTPD32-6.03) id AD2211E90104; Mon, 18 Sep 2000 21:45:16 -0700
Date: Mon, 18 Sep 2000 21:45:16 -0700
From: "Fatbrain.com" <customersvc@fatbrain.com>
Sender: customersvc@mailrelay4.fatbrain.com
Reply-to: customersvc@mailrelay4.fatbrain.com
Subject: Save up to 50% on All Fatbrain.com Bestsellers!
To: RROBERTS@STRATO.NET
X-Mailer: <IMailCGI.exe -- IMail for CGIs version 1.0.1>
Message-Id: <200009182145606.SM00107@mailrelay4>
X-UIDL: 0e6bd6130bf1cb48d5ee2a235945387f

 'Tis the season of summer sports and thrilling
 competition, but it's not all fun and games here at
 Fatbrain.com. From now until September 29th, you'll
```

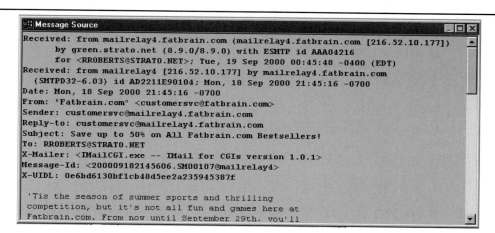

Figure 14-4. Further detail can be found by opening the **Message Source** window.

While certainly not harmless, Michelangelo was not as disastrous as predicted. The prediction of millions of PCs crashing was not achieved, but an estimated 10 to 20 thousand machines did get hit that year. While the virus is still around, it is fairly rare. The destructive nature of this virus keeps it from spreading. By wiping out the hard drive of its host machine, the virus destroys itself as well.

Melissa

The Melissa virus first appeared in March of 1999. Melissa was a macro e-mail virus that, when activated, sent an infected message to the first fifty people on a user's Microsoft Outlook e-mail list. The message sent out from the infected computer would say, "Important message for (insert the person's name from e-mail list)." The body of the message would say, "Here is that document you asked for." The attached document is the infected document. Melissa was also able to infect additional documents on your PC. This means that almost any document could be sent, regardless of whether it was insignificant, high security, or simply embarrassing.

Melissa attracted attention because of how quickly it spread and the large number of PCs it affected. The volume of e-mail generated by machines in some corporate networks forced the networks to shut down temporarily. The Melissa virus is estimated to have caused $80 million in damage.

I Love You

The subject of the e-mail said "I Love You," **Figure 14-5,** and the e-mail body contained the note "Kindly check the attachment." The attached file name was Love-Letter-For-You.txt.vbs. When the attachment was opened, it not only infected the host PC, it also e-mailed itself to all the addressees in the PC's Microsoft Outlook e-mail address book.

While this worm was similar to Melissa in its method of distribution, it was considerably more destructive. The worm would attack any graphics file with a .jpeg or .jpg extension and any file with a .vbs, .vbe, .js, .jse, .css, .wsh, .hta, or .sct extension. The worm would overwrite those files with copies of its source code and then append the .vbs extension to the files. It also caused Windows Explorer to produce a blank page for the home screen. Over twenty variations of this worm were created and released. The I Love You virus spread even faster and did more damage than Melissa.

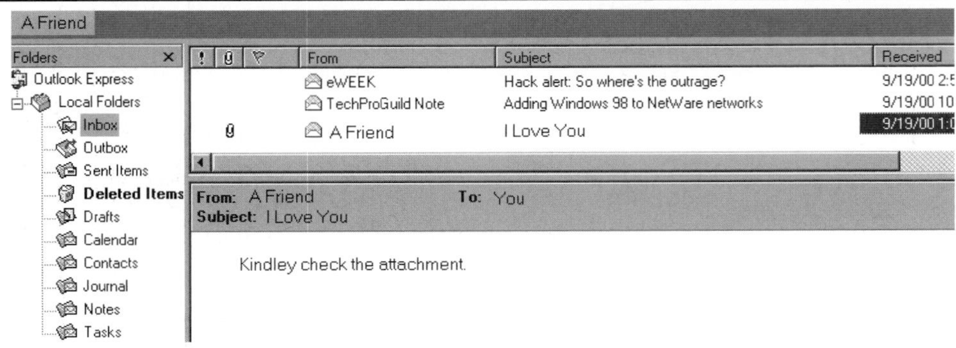

Figure 14-5. The I Love You virus spread quickly across the globe. Unlike Melissa, this virus was destructive to the computers it struck.

Pretty Park

The Pretty Park virus had a combination of malicious features. This program was a worm, Trojan horse, back door, and password-stealing virus. It first appeared in June 1999 and then cropped up again in March 2000. This is a particularly nasty virus. It attaches itself to e-mail and is distributed as Pretty Park.exe. It included an icon as an attachment using a character from South Park, the cartoon show.

When activated, this virus does several things. It hides itself on the user's system by changing its file attribute to hidden. It also creates a file called files32.vxd, duplicates itself, and then places itself into files32.vxd. It then alters the registry so that files32.vxd is called every time the PC attempts to run an executable (.exe) file. If the user erases files32.vxd, none of the .exe files on the PC will operate. The files32.vxd reference in the system registry must be removed first. The virus can be removed easily by changing the registry and removing files32.vxd, but it must be done in that order.

One of the characteristics of the Pretty Park virus is that it attempts to attach the infected computer to one of several chat rooms. By invading a chat room, the author can monitor the chat room and determine which computers are infected. The virus author can invade any infected computer by using the back door that the virus creates. Any files on the system can then be accessed.

Chernobyl

The Chernobyl virus was written as a logic bomb designed to go off on April 26, the anniversary date of the Chernobyl nuclear accident in Russia. Variations of the original virus were created and set to deliver its payload on the 26th of any month. One part of the payload overwrites the hard drive. A second part overwrites the flash BIOS program, effectively killing the PC. A PC attacked by the virus may need a new BIOS chip, or if the BIOS is soldered to the motherboard, it may need a new motherboard.

Interestingly, the Chernobyl virus uses a method of infection called a *fragmented cavity attack.* It looks for unused space in the file it is infecting. Then, the virus breaks itself into smaller pieces and inserts itself into the empty space. Thus, files infected by this virus can be the same size as the original. The Chernobyl virus affects only computers running the Windows 9x line of operating systems. Windows NT and Windows 2000 are not affected.

Kakworm

Kakworm took advantage of a design flaw in Windows Internet Explorer browser and Outlook Express mail programs. This bug limited itself to these two programs and could not affect other browser or mail programs. It was a selective virus. What made this worm unique and dangerous was that you didn't need to open an attachment to become infected. You only needed to view an infected e-mail to infect your PC.

When Kakworm is activated, it plants itself in the Windows startup folder. On the first of any month after 5:00 pm the worm displays the following message "Kagou-Anti-Kro$oft says not today." After the message is displayed, the PC shuts itself down, **Figure 14-6.**

Figure 14-6. This error message indicates that your PC has been infected with Kakworm.

Laroux

Laroux is a macro virus written to attach Microsoft Excel spreadsheets. The code hides in two macros named auto_open and check_files. When activated, it looks for a file called personal and, if found, Laroux is planted inside it. If the personal file is not found, one will be created. The virus does no damage to the PC or its files. It only replicates itself.

Picture Note

Picture Note is a back door and Trojan horse combination virus. It does no direct harm to files or to the system, but it does have the potential for damage. It comes in the form of an e-mail attachment named picture.exe. When activated, it searches for any America Online user information such as the user name and password of the local PC. This information is then sent to a specific e-mail address for retrieval.

Sobig

One of the latest virus programs to cause havoc for Internet e-mail users is the Sobig virus. As of Aug. 2003, it was considered one of the most costly viruses in years. Sobig displays the characteristics of a time bomb, worm, Trojan horse, and a back door virus. When it infects a PC, it lays dormant until the following Friday. It then sends e-mail to everyone on the host computer's e-mail list and to certain Web sites. It continues to send e-mail until the virus is removed. By starting on a Friday, the virus can spread over the weekend, creating the best opportunity to infect a large majority of computers before the start of the business week on Monday morning. When business employees check their e-mail early Monday morning, the Sobig virus is activated through the infected attachments by unsuspecting users. The result is a severe slow down on the Internet because of the heavy traffic generated by businesses opening all of the infected e-mails generated over the weekend. Business e-mail servers are flooded with bogus, infected e-mails. Certain Web sites are also inundated with excess traffic and cannot meet the requests of real users.

The e-mail attachment typically has a .pif extension and a file name such as "Thank_you," "Details," "Application," "wicked_screen," "Movie0045", and others. The subject titles used typically correspond to the file such as, "Your details," "My Details," "Your Approved," "Your Application," "That movie," and others. The virus is not spread until the attached file is opened. The address from the infected system is used in the e-mail "From" textbox.

The lesson to be learned here is that when an unusually large number of e-mails are on the incoming e-mail server, you probably need to suspect the worst.

Virus Prevention

Keeping a PC free of viruses can be a task. Most viruses can be prevented, but with new viruses appearing all the time, it is difficult to prevent them all. Worms make use of existing program security flaws. For worms, there is no other protection than to avoid all contact on networks and the Internet. For most people this is not an option.

Tech Tip:
A virus or worm designed to crack an e-mail list will be specific to a particular e-mail software package. Since each e-mail system has a unique program design, each e-mail software package must have a virus designed especially for that package. This means other e-mail software packages cannot be cracked by the same worm.

Most virus infections can be prevented following some simple practices. Additional practices will help keep the damage to a minimum if you are infected. The following suggestions will help keep your PCs and networks safe:

- Don't accept file attachments on e-mails from unknown sources. It is true that you can still get a virus from a known source. This happens when the friendly source does not know that they are spreading a virus. However, your chances are lessened by accepting attachments from only known sources. Regular acceptance of file attachments from completely unknown sources will almost surely cause a problem sooner or later.
- Turn off Windows scripting if you do not need it (you probably don't). Script files are a way of making a short startup program for remote connection to a network. They also allow the invader to access your information. You can turn off scripting by accessing **Start | Settings | Control Program | Add/Remove Programs | Windows Setup | Accessories | Windows Scripting Host**. If the box marked **Windows Scripting Host** has a checkmark next to it, uncheck the program, click **OK**, and then click **Apply**. If there is no check in the box, your PC may already have had script files disabled, **Figure 14-7.**

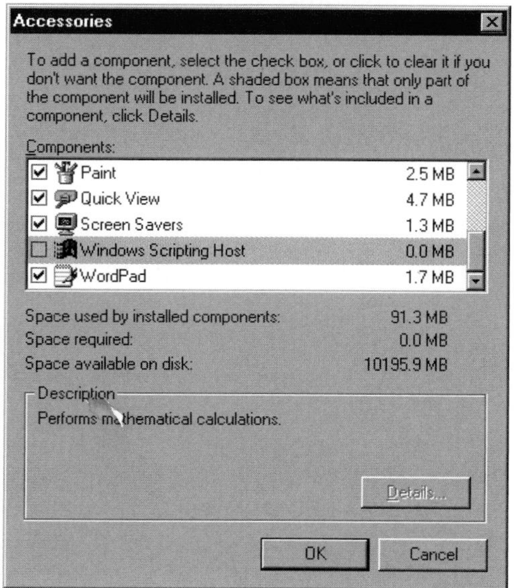

Figure 14-7. Removing **Windows Scripting Host** will protect your computer against any viruses that use Windows Scripting to run.

- Never load a file from a floppy disk or other media that you have not checked first with up-to-date antivirus software. The number of infections that have occurred by simply exchanging disks (especially games) is enormous.
- Before giving anyone a file on disk, make sure it is write-protected. This will prevent a virus from being written to the disk, yet still allow the recipient to download the files they need. For example, someone needs a copy of a proposal you have written. They wish to proofread it and possibly make changes. By write-protecting the disk, you will protect the disk from becoming infected if they attempt to make changes to the file. It's safer for them to print the proposal and give you changes on the hard copy.
- Encrypt your important files. Encrypted files are usually useless to another user without the encryption key. Even if you have files stolen, minimal damage is done.
- Back up your important files.
- Always check for the latest software packages to update security and virus software.

If you have any doubts about taking the time to protect yourself or taking the time to back up your files, ask yourself the following questions regarding your options if a virus destroys your files.

1. Do you have the discs to reload everything, from your operating system to your leisure programs?
2. How much time would it take to reconstruct everything on your computer?
3. How many of the items on your PC are one of a kind?
4. Are there important documents on your hard drive? Do you have term papers, legal papers, financial data, income tax forms, and other unique items stored on your PC?
5. Do you have any hard copies of this information?
6. What happens to you if you are responsible for a corporation?
7. How much would the corporation lose if the PC was wiped out? Could it lose a list of thousands of customers? Could it lose a 200-page catalog sitting on the hard drive or file server?

After thinking about the individual or corporate losses, it is easy to see the benefits of protecting your PC and backing up all of your important files.

Virus Removal

While preventing the arrival of a virus or worm is ideal, there is a good chance that at some point you will encounter an infected PC. Remember that a virus or worm is simply a program designed to annoy, amuse, or destroy. You eliminate a virus that has never been run as you would any unwanted program. You delete it. Place it in the **Recycle Bin** and empty it.

However, once the virus has been activated (run on your machine) it can be a much more complicated task. The removal of some viruses and worms is as easy as locating and erasing the file containing the virus. In most cases, removal often involves removing many various files, installing a software patch, and adjusting registry settings. Most antivirus manufacturers provide a small downloadable program that does many of these tasks automatically. When a widespread virus is first discovered and publicized, your first move should be to go to the Web site of your antivirus provider and check their alert bulletins for a description and remedy.

The first step in virus removal is to identify the virus. Just because a PC is acting strangely does not mean it has contracted a virus. Any number of things can produce the same effects of known viruses. Check your antivirus software manufacturer Web site for information about the particular virus characteristics. The characteristics of a virus, or its signature, can be found there. This will give you a complete description of the virus and what it does. This includes its symptoms and size, where it is generally located, how it spreads, and what areas of the PC system are affected. Most viruses and worms have hidden, system, or read only file attributes set to help protect it.

The next step is the actual removal. Usually, antivirus manufacturers provide a removal tool, which is an executable program you download and run. The executable program does all the complicated steps for you. Behind the scenes it removes all the infected files, and, if need be, corrects any altered registry settings. If there is no removal tool prepared, you can usually find step-by-step instructions on the Web. You will have to manually delete all infected files. If registry changes are needed, you must open the registry program and make the alterations as specified. You must be extremely careful when altering the registry. If you make a typo in your registry alteration, great trouble may ensue.

A virus may make additional copies of itself so that it can re-infect your computer if the original is erased. For example, it can attach itself automatically to any drive when files are saved to that drive. This means that while the bug has not been detected and you save a file to a floppy disk, CD-RW, or even to a network hard drive, the virus also saves a copy of itself to the same media. When the media such as the floppy is used to load a file to a hard drive or to RAM, the virus tags along, loading itself as well. This is one way many viruses spread. As part of eliminating a virus, all floppy disks, CDs, and Zip disks must be scanned. This is the only way to ensure the complete removal of the virus.

Legal Aspects

Legal punishment for the creation and distribution of a virus is severe. In addition, individuals can be held liable for the cost of financial losses suffered by any corporation harmed by the virus. The FBI National Computer Crime Squad (NCCS) has classified computer crimes into certain categories. These categories include the following:

- Intrusions of the public phone system.
- Major computer network intrusions.
- Network integrity violations.
- Privacy violations.
- Industrial espionage.
- Pirated software.
- Other crimes committed by using a computer.

In addition to the federal crime statutes, most states have their own crime statutes that are comparable to the federal statutes. Computer crimes are not taken lightly. An example of harsh consequences can be seen in the cases of a number of young students who have used new computer systems to break these laws. The final outcome is usually simple. While the students serve no time for their mistakes, their entire computer systems have been confiscated, and they may be banned from using a PC for five years or more.

You may be wondering why there are laws dealing with intrusion into the public telephone system. The public telephone system provides a medium for a tremendous amount of Internet use. Many hackers have attempted to gain, or have successfully gained, access to telephone company records. This has allowed them to use other people's identifications when accessing the Internet for illegal purposes. Illegal access to the public telephone system carries severe penalties.

The last classification, "other crimes committed using a computer," is a catchall. If a computer crime is not specifically listed, then the act of any criminal nature committed using a computer will fall under this statute. This law is important because people who are determined to do damage or illegally use computer systems invent new crimes on a continual basis.

Mistaken Identifications (or Oops)

Many times a problem occurs on a PC and the PC software automatically assumes it to be a virus. Some technicians automatically assume that many difficult-to-solve problems are caused by a virus. However, users do make errors when using their computers and often the results can appear similar to problems caused by a virus. A classic problem is when a user accidentally hits a key combination that has devastating effects. For example, a key combination struck in error can cause an entire manuscript to disappear. When the key combination [Ctrl] [A] is struck in Microsoft Word, the entire text document is highlighted. The very next keystroke will replace all text in the document with the next letter typed. A major disaster has now occurred, and the computer user may have no idea that they actually caused the problem. It would be easy to assume that a virus has attacked their computer system.

A follow-up phenomenon is the repeat of the keystroke error. Once a mistake is made, human nature allows that person to repeat the same mistake again. Since the technician will probably never view the error in progress and will only get a verbal description of the situation, it may be difficult to diagnose the problem. A frantic description of time lost on a document does not make for easy computer diagnosis. The assumption is that it must be a virus. A few simple steps can help if the user has not tried to repair the error first. Typing [Ctrl] [Z], the shortcut combination for undo, can save the day if the user has not typed too many additional keystrokes before you arrive.

Users often assume a virus has attacked their computer as things go wrong. However, there are many different reasons that a computer can exhibit unusual actions. Possibilities include power glitches, magnets too close to the PC or monitor, network glitches, and more. A strong magnetic field can completely erase computer disks. When this happens, it will probably be reported as a virus.

Summary

- A computer virus is a software program that is written for the purpose of causing damage to a computer system.

- Virus infection is a real danger that can destroy data, slow down a PC system, fill up unused space on a hard drive, or do relatively nothing.
- A worm contaminates files on the infected machine and also spreads itself to other machines without prompting from the user.
- Viruses are spread easily by e-mail, and passing copies of disks, both floppy and CD.
- Most virus infections can be prevented by not accepting file attachments on e-mails from unknown sources, turning off Windows scripting, and never loading a file from a floppy disk or other media that has not been checked.
- Legal punishment for the creation and distribution of a virus is severe.
- Not all puzzling computer problems are caused by viruses. Human error is one of the leading causes of computer catastrophes.

Review Questions

Answer the following questions on a separate sheet of paper. Please do not write in this book.

1. What are the three major stages of a computer virus?
2. How can replication harm a PC system?
3. What is a Trojan horse virus?
4. What steps can you take to prevent virus attacks?
5. Define *macro*.
6. How is a worm different than a virus?
7. What are the six major categories of computer crime as identified by the FBI?

Sample A+ Exam Questions

Answer the following questions on a separate sheet of paper. Please do not write in this book.

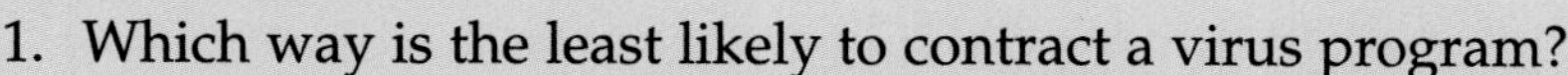

1. Which way is the least likely to contract a virus program?
   a. Loading a game program on a PC from a floppy disk given to you by a trusted friend.
   b. Downloading a file from a reputable Internet site.
   c. Connecting to another computer on a corporate network.
   d. Loading a new operating system from a CD-ROM taken directly from a sealed shrink-wrapped box.
2. Which of the following is the best definition of a macro?
   a. A short program used to diagnose system resources.
   b. A short program used to detect viruses designed to infect text editors.
   c. A software program designed to take repetitive tasks and combine them into one simple set of keystrokes.
   d. A program named for the Macromaniac virus first released in 1993.

3. Worms are typically spread by which of the following methods?
   a. E-mail attachments.
   b. Exchanged floppy disks.
   c. The system BIOS whenever two computers connect together on the Internet.
   d. Exclusively by text editor programs.
4. How does a virus typically cause problems for a PC?
   a. It loads itself into the video ROM, which results in poor video performance.
   b. It resides on the hard disk drive and uses up valuable disk space by replicating itself.
   c. It is loaded as an e-mail attachment. Once it is activated, it spreads to other computers via the e-mail list of users on the PC.
   d. Viruses spread by installing new operating system software supplied through venders.
5. Which is the best definition of a polymorphic virus?
   a. A polymorphic virus is a combination worm and Trojan horse virus.
   b. A polymorphic virus constantly changes its virus profile to resist detection by antivirus programs.
   c. A polymorphic virus can infect multiple parts of the same PC system.
   d. A polymorphic virus lives forever by constantly re-infecting the same PC, thus preventing it from ever being removed.
6. The characteristics which describe the uniqueness of a virus are referred to as a _____.
   a. signature
   b. reputation
   c. payload
   d. morphic synopsis

Suggested Laboratory Activities

Do not attempt any suggested laboratory activities without your instructor's permission. Certain activities can render the PC operating system inoperable.

1. Visit some antivirus manufacturer Web sites. Download and install trial versions of their antivirus program.
2. Open Microsoft's Word program. Explore how macros are made. Make a macro that will automatically type your name and address on a form when a combination of two keys is pressed.
3. Visit www.eicar.org and download their virus test program.
4. Download the latest security patch for Microsoft e-mail. While at the Microsoft Web site, look for other patches to update security for your PC.

Interesting Web Sites for More Information

www.antivirus.com
www.datafellows.com
www.datarescue.com
www.fedcirc.gov
www.mcafee.com
www.norman.com
www.ontrack.com
www.stiller.com
www.symantec.com
www.virusbtn.com

The SANS organization is dedicated to combating viruses and providing security information. Their online Internet Storm Center displays current information about the very latest virus attacks and correlates the information to a map of the world. Check out ics.sans.org for more information about malicious software.

Chapter 14
Laboratory Activity
Virus Test Software

After completing this laboratory activity, you will be able to:

- ❑ Test a typical antivirus program to ensure it is installed correctly.
- ❑ Build the EICAR virus test program.

Introduction

In this laboratory activity, you will access the EICAR Web site at www.eicar.org and download a copy of the EICAR utility. The utility is designed to test an installed version of any antivirus software.

EICAR (European Institute for Computer Antivirus Research) has developed a virus test program that checks if an antivirus program has been installed correctly and is working. The EICAR test file is a simple text file that contains the following symbols:

X5O!P%@AP[4\PZX54(P^)7CC)7}$EICAR-STANDARD-ANTIVIRUS-TEST-FILE!$H+H*

You can copy the line of text above using Notepad or WordPad and save it as a plain ASCII text file named EICAR with the file extension of .com, .dll, or .exe. When typing the line of text, be sure to enter the third letter symbol as the capital letter *O* and not as a zero. All the letters should be entered as uppercase letters.

The antivirus program installed on your computer should prevent you from saving the EICAR antivirus file. When the EICAR file is activated, you should see a window similar to the McAfee dialog box that follows. The look of the dialog box will vary according to the brand of antivirus software you are using.

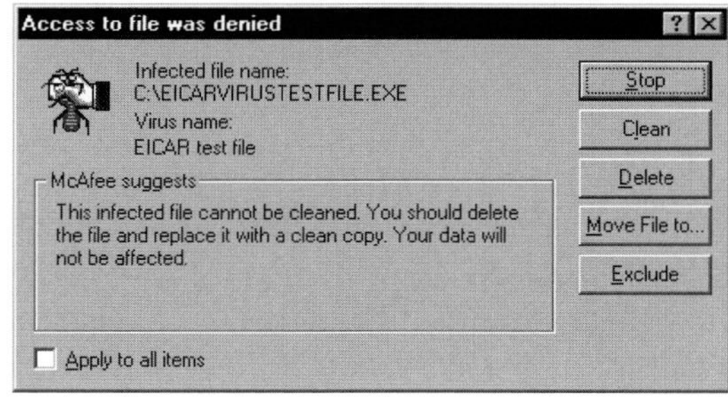

Seeing a window similar to this window means that the software is working. However, it does not ensure that all options for the antivirus utility are correctly configured. It just lets you know that the general antivirus program is installed and working. For example, it does not mean the antivirus program you are using is up-to-date and contains the latest virus definitions or that the program is scanning e-mail automatically.

The following screen captures are another sample of dialog boxes triggered by the EICAR.COM program.

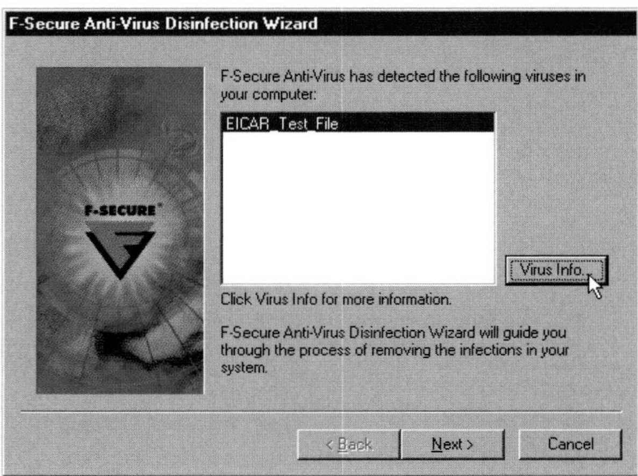

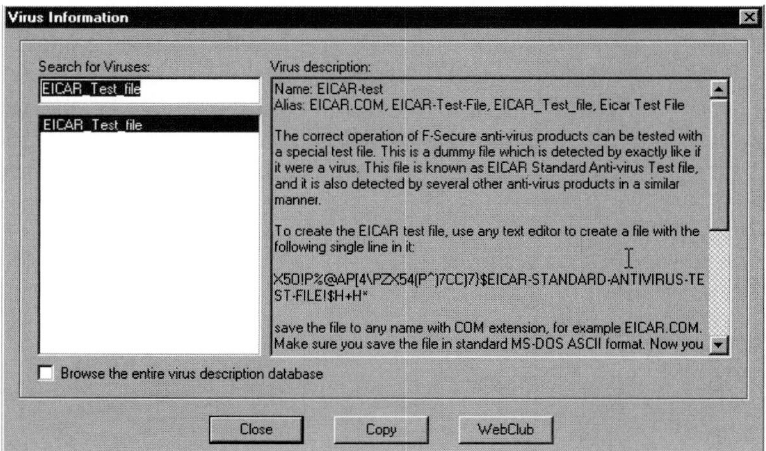

These two images are windows created by the F-Secure Anti-Virus software utility. If your computer is not equipped with an antivirus utility package, you can download an evaluation package from www.fsecure.com. After downloading the evaluation package, install the antivirus utility following the screen prompts. You can either create the EICAR file or download the test file from most antivirus Web sites. The file is free to download and use to test antivirus programs.

Equipment and Materials

- Typical PC with Windows 98 or later operating system, Internet access, and an antivirus program installed. (If you do not have an antivirus program installed, you can download a 30-day antivirus trial version from many different sites including www.symetec.com, www.mcaffee.com, and www.fsecure.com.
- Floppy disk for saving the EICAR file.

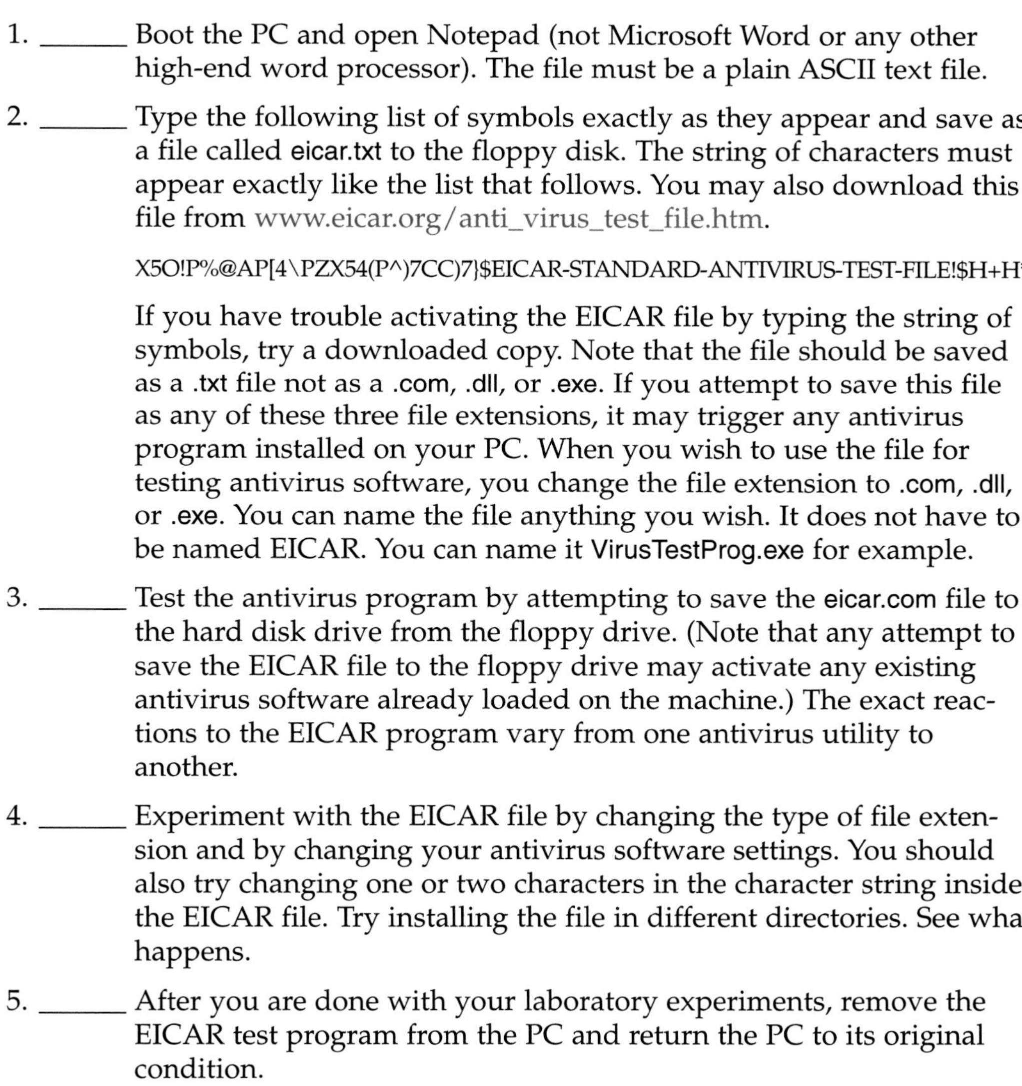

Procedure

1. ______ Boot the PC and open Notepad (not Microsoft Word or any other high-end word processor). The file must be a plain ASCII text file.
2. ______ Type the following list of symbols exactly as they appear and save as a file called eicar.txt to the floppy disk. The string of characters must appear exactly like the list that follows. You may also download this file from www.eicar.org/anti_virus_test_file.htm.

   ```
   X5O!P%@AP[4\PZX54(P^)7CC)7}$EICAR-STANDARD-ANTIVIRUS-TEST-FILE!$H+H*
   ```

   If you have trouble activating the EICAR file by typing the string of symbols, try a downloaded copy. Note that the file should be saved as a .txt file not as a .com, .dll, or .exe. If you attempt to save this file as any of these three file extensions, it may trigger any antivirus program installed on your PC. When you wish to use the file for testing antivirus software, you change the file extension to .com, .dll, or .exe. You can name the file anything you wish. It does not have to be named EICAR. You can name it VirusTestProg.exe for example.
3. ______ Test the antivirus program by attempting to save the eicar.com file to the hard disk drive from the floppy drive. (Note that any attempt to save the EICAR file to the floppy drive may activate any existing antivirus software already loaded on the machine.) The exact reactions to the EICAR program vary from one antivirus utility to another.
4. ______ Experiment with the EICAR file by changing the type of file extension and by changing your antivirus software settings. You should also try changing one or two characters in the character string inside the EICAR file. Try installing the file in different directories. See what happens.
5. ______ After you are done with your laboratory experiments, remove the EICAR test program from the PC and return the PC to its original condition.

Review Questions

Answer the following questions on a separate sheet of paper. Please do not write in this book.

1. What types of file extensions are used with the EICAR virus test program?
2. What does the acronym EICAR represent?

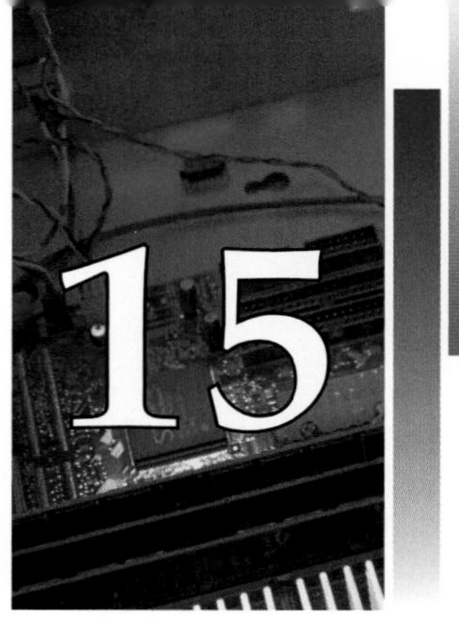

PC Troubleshooting

After studying this chapter, you will be able to:

- ❑ State commonly practiced troubleshooting steps.
- ❑ Recognize common startup problems and understand their causes.
- ❑ Use the tools found in the Microsoft System Information dialog box.
- ❑ Restart a PC in a variety of troubleshooting modes.
- ❑ Step through a PC's boot sequence.
- ❑ Explain how to access, repair, and back up the system registry files.
- ❑ Access and use troubleshooting log files.
- ❑ Explain basic data recovery methods.

A+ Exam—Key Points

The A+ Certification exams place a great deal of weight on knowing the basics of troubleshooting. You need to become familiar with the tools, their limitations, and the purpose of each tool. The best way to become familiar with troubleshooting tools is by using them. Study the menu options, such as safe mode, and how to access them.

It is very important to study the setup readme.txt files that come with each version of Windows setup program CDs. They contain a lot of information that is used on the A+ Certification exams and that is usually not found in textbook material.

Key Words and Terms

The following words and terms will become important pieces of your computer vocabulary. Be sure you can define them.

Automated System Recovery (ASR)
Automatic Skip Driver Agent
blue screen error
clean room
differential backup
DirectX Diagnostic Tool
Disk Cleanup Utility
Dr. Watson
incremental backup
kernel mode
Microsoft System Information
real-mode driver
Registry Checker
Remote Assistance
restore point
startup problem
System Configuration Utility
System File Checker
System Restore
Recovery Console
user mode
Version Conflict Manager
virtual device driver (VxD)
Windows Report Tool

Troubleshooting a PC requires a combination of the technician's knowledge, intuition, and experience. There are many diagnostic tools that are included as standard programs for Microsoft software systems. There are also many diagnostic tools available from third-party vendors that can assist in the troubleshooting process. Third-party vendor programs range from freeware and shareware to systems costing several thousands of dollars, which include diagnostic boards that plug into the PC's expansion slots.

Most problems can be diagnosed without expensive system diagnostics. The value of expensive diagnostic tools is they can be used to save time and money when trying to identify problems that may be caused by two or more components. For example, it can be difficult to determine if a problem is caused by a troublesome CPU or a bad motherboard. When this situation arises, a simple solution is to substitute a known or good CPU for the suspect CPU. However, this substitution alone can be a very expensive proposition.

Common Sense Practices

Remember, when troubleshooting and repairing PCs that "time is money." When diagnosing PC failures and problems, always take the quickest and easiest path first. When troubleshooting, there are some common sense practices you should follow:

- Determine the major area at fault.
- Determine what action occurred just prior to failure or problem.
- Write down settings before you change them.
- Go slowly.
- Think, think, think!

Determining the Major Fault Area

The first step is to try to determine what major area is the most likely source of the fault. There are three major fault areas to be considered:

1. Hardware failure.
2. Software failure.
3. User-generated problems.

The most common error or problem is the user-generated problem. Some users like to tinker with Control Panel, and others will try to solve their problems alone. Users with a little technical knowledge can be the most dangerous. They often attempt to fix a problem alone before calling the technician. When this happens, you may very well be faced with more than one problem. First, the original problem likely still exists, and then there are additional problems created by the user. Repairing computers in a school setting can be the most frustrating. Some students love to experiment on the settings on a school's computer before trying the activity on their personal computer at home.

What Happened Last?

It is critical to determine from the computer user what the last action on the computer was prior to the problem occurring or before computer failure. Often, the last action taken by the user can lead the technician directly to the problem. Find out if the user recently installed some new software. Perhaps, there has been a recent hardware upgrade to the problem PC. Has the user recently downloaded a file from the Internet? Ask as many questions of the user as possible. This can save valuable time.

Proceed Carefully

Do not rush when diagnosing problems. Operating in a hurry will lead to sloppy work. This can create new problems or cause you to overlook something important. In contrast, do proceed in a methodical yet constant pace. Customers will not appreciate a technician who is standing around drinking coffee, talking, socializing, or any other activity that appears to be a nonproductive use of energy. Customers are typically paying a premium price for service and are losing the use of their computers while they are inoperable. Don't waste their money, or, next time there is a problem, someone else will be called.

Write Things Down

Do not rely on your memory alone while performing troubleshooting. Before you change a setting, write down the current setting. If you are going to delete a file, write down the file name. You can make the problem much harder to find if you create another problem along the way. If a problem is not cleared after changing a setting or deleting a file, you should return the system file or setting to the way you found it. Do not simply move on and try something else.

Think

Think the problem through. Don't try operations out of desperation. Desperate technicians will often run the same test twice knowing the results from the first test were valid. These are acts of desperation, and they occur when a technician is stumped.

When you run out of tests—*stop and think* about the situation. Writing things down in a list helps. Make two lists. First, make a list of what you know is not the problem. Then, make a list of possible problems that could still exist. Check the Web site of the manufacturer of the PC, the BIOS, and the operating system. There could be corrections posted for exact symptoms you are encountering. Many times, a problem is discovered that affects a particular setup or particular combination of hardware and software programs.

Don't hesitate to contact the manufacturer of the hardware or software in question by e-mail with a description of the problem. Most questions will be answered in 24 to 48 hours at no cost for the service. You can get much faster replies by calling, but that service is seldom free.

Your fellow technicians are another very important source of information. As you progress in the PC repair world, you will make many friends. It is a standard practice to share information with a colleague who may have encountered a similar problem. A peer may have a quick and easy answer to a problem that you have not encountered before. Other times, simply discussing the problem with a peer can be quite helpful itself. Explaining the problem forces you to summarize the situation and describe it in logical terms. Just the act of verbalizing the problem may allow you to solve it. Never be embarrassed to use this form of assistance.

Some Typical Startup Problems

startup problem problem that causes the computer to lock up during the boot process.

Startup problems are a tough class of computer error that you are bound to run into. ***Startup problems*** are problems that cause the computer to lock up during the boot process. These problems occur too early in the PC operation to be solved by system diagnostic tools. This section details some of the most common and catastrophic boot problems that you will encounter while starting the PC. Each of the following problems is described as a symptom. Possible solutions are provided as a guide. The list of symptoms is condensed and centers on the problems encountered before the boot process is completed. Keep in mind that there are hundreds of possible computer symptoms. What follows are a few of the most common system failures during the boot.

Think about the boot process and the steps involved. System boot failures involve the power supply, CPU, hard drive (boot device), BIOS, CMOS, system configuration, autoexec.bat file, loading of drivers, and the loading of the operating system. Now let's look at some of the most common problems and their symptoms during the boot process.

When reading the list that follows, assume that there is one hard drive labeled C *and a CD drive labeled* D*. Note that these are recommended procedures, not absolute procedures. Also, viruses can imitate some of the described symptoms. Always check for the presence of a virus and protect your disk while doing so.*

Remember, always attempt the simplest tests first. Then, move on to the more complex and labor-intensive tests.

Symptom 1:

There is no power light, no fan running, and no sound of boot operation at all. It appears that the PC is completely dead.

Items to check:

Before you open the case, make sure the PC is plugged in. Next, check the power from the wall outlet or power strip or both. Be sure there is power to the unit. If you have power, then the likely problem is the computer's power supply. Open the case and test the power supply outputs. Swapping out power supplies is generally more cost effective than fixing a broken one.

Symptom 2:

The power light (LED) is on and the fan is running but there is no activity. The system appears dead.

Items to check:

Check the power supply for a power good signal. The *power good signal* is sent back to the BIOS system to signal that the power supply is up and ready. The signal back should be approximately 5 volts. Pin 1 is usually the power good pin. Pull the connector back just far enough to check for 5 volts (+/–1 volt). If the power is very low, there may not be sufficient voltage to power up the system. The power output does not have to be completely dead to affect startup.

If the power good signal checks out, check the connection from the power supply to the motherboard. Reseat this connection. Try reseating the CPU. Sometimes the CPU is not making a good electrical contact. CPUs operate on fairly low voltages. A slight oxidation buildup on one of the CPU's pins that is operating at 3.3 volts is sufficient to render the CPU dead. Cleaning the oxidation will bring it back.

If you perform all of the listed operations and the system still fails to activate, you *probably* have a defective motherboard.

Symptom 3:

The system tries to boot, there are two or more beeps and then nothing (no video). The fan is running and there is a power light.

Items to check:

Make sure the monitor is plugged in correctly (both the data plug and the power cord). Check the video card. Try reseating the card. If those actions don't help, try to decode the beep error code. If you have the manual that came with the motherboard, start there. Newer manuals are often CDs as opposed to the traditional paper booklet. If there is no manual, look up the BIOS chip manufacturer on the Internet. First, copy all information from the BIOS chip and then head to the manufacturer's Web site.

Symptom 4:

You see a setup error indicated on the screen.

Items to check:

This is probably a CMOS setup problem. Access the BIOS setup routine by using the key combination indicated on the screen. If no setup routine is given, try key combinations you are familiar with. Some popular combinations can be found in Figure 3-27 from Chapter 3—Motherboards. You can also look up the keystroke combination for accessing the BIOS at the BIOS manufacturer's Web site.

Normally, CMOS settings do not change. However, sometimes when you install a new hard drive, and the drive is automatically detected, the settings change. Also, if the battery used to hold the CMOS data is going bad, you could lose the settings. The date and time not matching the true date and time is a good indication that your battery is going bad.

Be sure to write down the existing CMOS settings before you make any changes to them. This is extremely important if you are going to try something like the **Return to default settings** option. When that option is selected, many settings will change instantly, and you will not be able to tell which settings have changed or what they changed from. Check the manufacturer's Web site for the correct CMOS settings for your particular model of PC.

Sometimes people get curious and go into the BIOS setup to see what it looks like. They also make changes either intentionally or accidentally. What makes it worse is they generally deny going into the setup program.

Symptom 5:

The PC powers on, but there is no drive activity.

Items to check:

Check the system CMOS settings. Make sure the drive is identified. The drive should be identified in the setup program as far as the number of cylinders, heads, and sectors. In addition, while the PC is booting, the hard drive manufacturer followed by the hard drive model number will often flash on the screen when the BIOS finds it. If the drive is not detected during the boot, the screen will flash something similar to "No Hard Disk Drive."

You should also check the connections between the power supply and the hard drive and the motherboard and the hard drive. They should be tight.

If all that checks out, boot the system with a boot disk. From the command prompt, see if you can access the hard drive. If you can access the hard drive, change your default directory to the C:\windows. When in the Windows directory, type **win** to see if you can start Windows.

Symptom 6:

There is normal boot activity, lights and sounds, but no video.

Items to check:

Check if the monitor is plugged into the computer and that the monitor has power. Swap the monitor out for a monitor that is known to be good. If the system still fails to generate a display, you probably have a bad video adapter card. Try reseating the video adapter card. If the system will still not display, change the video adapter card.

Symptom 7:

The system crashes or reboots for no apparent reason.

Items to check:

Check the power supply and cables. Make sure they are all tight. Check for excessive heat on the CPU and memory chips. Make sure all SIMMs/DIMMs are seated properly. Try reseating the CPU.

If all of that hardware checks out, you likely have a defective motherboard or there is a problem with the hard drive. Swapping hard drives with one you know is working should show you where the problem lies. If the hard drive is causing the problem, check for a virus or a corrupt operating system. Always think about the last thing that occurred on the PC before the problem developed. For example, did you recently install a new software program? The following section looks at hard drive failures in more detail.

Hard Drive Failures

Hard drives fail more often than would be thought. Any component that is an electronic and mechanical combination will fail after a period of time. In addition, hard drives can fail because of software issues. A corrupt MBR can cause hard drives to be unresponsive. It is important for you to determine more than just if a hard drive is bad. You must also determine why it is bad.

A bad hard drive or a corrupt MBR will generate a screen message such as one of the following:

- Invalid partition table.
- Error loading operating system.
- Missing operating system.

If any of these three error messages appear, you most likely have a hard drive problem. To check, try booting the system from a floppy disk. If the system boots normally from the floppy, this will verify a hard drive problem.

Mechanical Hard Drive Failure

Mechanical parts wear out. A sure sign of an upcoming mechanical hard drive failure is an unusual sound coming from inside the computer when it is being accessed (a read or write operation is being done). The sound may be a high-pitched whining sound or a clanking sound. The strange sound coming from the hard drive is mechanical in origin and cannot be repaired. Swapping out the bad hard drive is the only solution.

The only guaranteed method of fully recovering from a hard drive failure is by doing regular backups of your data. You can always reinstall a collection of software when replacing a hard drive, but your data will be lost unless a recent backup has been made. Users should be instructed to back up data regularly, but it is even more important when a hard drive makes strange sounds. Data should be backed up immediately, and a technician should be called to prepare for the crash. You should have parts on hand and be prepared to replace the hard drive.

MBR Failure/Recovery

Hard drives can also fail because of corrupted files and data. The most important area of the hard disk is the master boot record (MBR). If the MBR is damaged, the hard drive will not support the booting process. However, you will still be able to boot from a bootable floppy or CD. Once you boot from the floppy or CD, try to look at the hard drive by entering the **dir C:** command at the command line prompt, **Figure 15-1.** If you can view the files on the hard drive, then you are in a position to do a repair. You probably will be able to remedy the situation. As a precaution, back up all data immediately.

You will not be able to back up the files in every situation. But, if you can see files on the hard drive, you should be able to back up important data to some kind of data storage media. Generally on an older system, you will be forced to do a copy to disk. Though, on some newer systems, you may be able to access the drive via an existing network connection. A modern computer with a bootable CD-RW allows for a quicker and easier backup of system files. You can boot the PC using a system restore CD. The CD is placed in the drive and loads all necessary files to boot the PC. In addition, you may load a driver to support the CD-RW. After the drivers are loaded for the CD-RW, you can copy files that need to be backed up.

Avoid using the **fdisk/mbr** command unless it is as a last resort. The **fdisk/mbr** rewrites the boot code portion of the MBR. The last two bytes in the MBR contain partition and volume information. If the last two bytes in the MBR were deleted by a virus, all partition information will be lost when you use the **fdisk/mbr**. Two situations are made worse by this command. One situation is

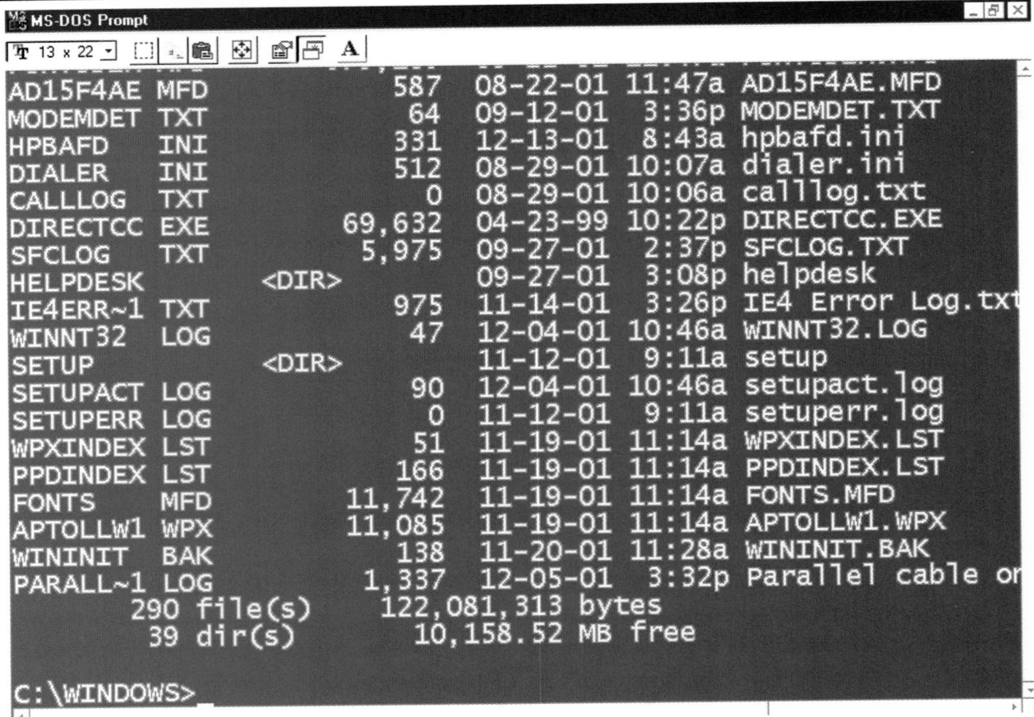

MS-DOS Prompt
13 x 22
AD15F4AE MFD 587 08-22-01 11:47a AD15F4AE.MFD
MODEMDET TXT 64 09-12-01 3:36p MODEMDET.TXT
HPBAFD INI 331 12-13-01 8:43a hpbafd.ini
DIALER INI 512 08-29-01 10:07a dialer.ini
CALLLOG TXT 0 08-29-01 10:06a calllog.txt
DIRECTCC EXE 69,632 04-23-99 10:22p DIRECTCC.EXE
SFCLOG TXT 5,975 09-27-01 2:37p SFCLOG.TXT
HELPDESK <DIR> 09-27-01 3:08p helpdesk
IE4ERR~1 TXT 975 11-14-01 3:26p IE4 Error Log.txt
WINNT32 LOG 47 12-04-01 10:46a WINNT32.LOG
SETUP <DIR> 11-12-01 9:11a setup
SETUPACT LOG 90 12-04-01 10:46a setupact.log
SETUPERR LOG 0 11-12-01 9:11a setuperr.log
WPXINDEX LST 51 11-19-01 11:14a WPXINDEX.LST
PPDINDEX LST 166 11-19-01 11:14a PPDINDEX.LST
FONTS MFD 11,742 11-19-01 11:14a FONTS.MFD
APTOLLW1 WPX 11,085 11-19-01 11:14a APTOLLW1.WPX
WININIT BAK 138 11-20-01 11:28a WININIT.BAK
PARALL~1 LOG 1,337 12-05-01 3:32p Parallel cable or
290 file(s) 122,081,313 bytes
39 dir(s) 10,158.52 MB free
C:\WINDOWS>_

Figure 15-1. Examine your hard drive through the command line prompt. If you can see your files, you should be able to repair the drive and save your data.

when you have a multiple boot system using at least two partitions. The **fdisk/mbr** command can make the second partition inaccessible as well. It overwrites the partition table, the boot sector, and the file allocation table. This essentially erases any record of the other partitions. The second situation affects some older computer BIOS systems that cannot access large disk drives. A third-party tool called an overlay program is used to remedy the large disk access problem. The **fdisk/mbr** command can overwrite the information used by the overlay program to allow large disk support. This can further complicate or compound the program.

Many third-party software systems can repair an MBR, especially if the software is installed before the problem develops. The software recovery systems make a copy of all vital information including creating a copy of the MBR. When an error occurs, the recovery software can use the copy to help recover the damaged system. In addition, third-party software systems can be used to inspect, copy, and modify bytes in each sector of the hard drive. This is a very powerful tool, but using it can be very time-consuming.

Additional Mechanical Problems

There are a number of other mechanical faults that cause problems in PCs. Boards, cards, and cables can go bad, but these occurrences are not all that common. You will find that, along with hard drive failure, most of your other mechanical problems will arise from two areas: improper hardware upgrades and an accumulation of dust in the system.

Problems after Hardware Upgrades

There are many possible system failures after a hardware upgrade. The first thing to check when a system fails to boot is the power and cable connections. Many times while working inside the case, cables are pulled loose. So, the first thing to look for is free-hanging cables. However, cable problems will not always be cables that were not reconnected. Sometimes when a cable is pulled loose, the user will inadvertently replace the cable incorrectly. The cable may be off one pin, or a pin may be damaged. Data cables can also be pinched when systems are reassembled.

Another major problem occurs when mixing different generation technologies together inside the same PC. When a PC has been upgraded several times, problems do arise. An older BIOS chip may not be able to recognize certain new memory module or see the vast new hard drive that has been installed. Check the system resources for conflicts. (Use the **System Properties** dialog box or **Microsoft System Information**.)

Dust Accumulation

The accumulation of dust inside a PC unit is typical. The type of environment in which the PC operates, as well as its age, determines how much dust has accumulated. Large amounts of dust can cause heating problems by blocking air filters and by collecting on processor heat-sink fins and fan components preventing the proper dissipation of heat. The dust acts like an insulator and holds the heat to the CPU rather than allowing the cooling fins to dissipate it. The dust can clog air filters and render a fan inoperable.

Remove dust carefully using a can of compressed air or a special vacuum cleaner designed for PC cleaning. Standard vacuum cleaners can generate a tremendous amount of static electricity, which is very dangerous to computer chips. Use only vacuum cleaners made specifically for electronic equipment.

Warning:
Removing dust from a CRT can be dangerous. Do not attempt to open and remove dust from inside a CRT without special training. There are dangerous voltage levels inside a CRT case that remain even after the CRT has been disconnected from electrical power.

Windows Boot Process Problems

Windows boot problems can be very difficult to diagnose, especially if they are intermittent problems. An extremely useful utility found in the Windows 98 and later versions of the operating system is Microsoft System Information, msinfo32.exe. ***Microsoft System Information,*** displays detailed information about the hardware and software in the system, **Figure 15-2.**

Microsoft System Information
utility that displays detailed information about the hardware and software in the system.

Figure 15-2 shows the window that is displayed after running msinfo32.exe. You can activate it from **Start | Programs | Accessories | System Tools | System Information**, or by typing **msinfo32** at the **Run**. prompt.

Tech Tip:
Note that Windows NT does not respond to **msinfo32**. Windows NT is an older operating system and used a set of three emergency recovery disks when problems occurred.

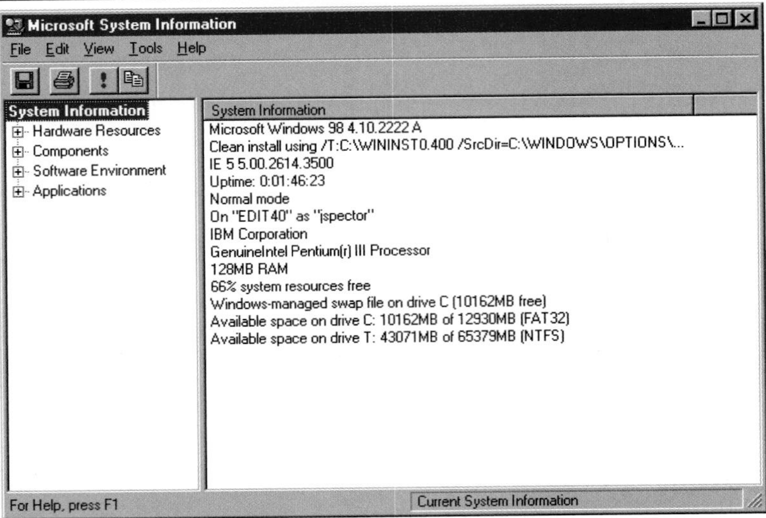

Figure 15-2. Microsoft System Information can be used to find boot problems and other conflicts.

Most Microsoft operating systems carry the same troubleshooting utilities. Hardware devices, system resources, software, and Internet program settings can be displayed from this location. You can readily determine conflicts in system resources, as well as most startup problems. There is also an online help program. This can assist you when you need to know more about your diagnostics utilities. There are several troubleshooting utilities available through this window. The essentials of each will be covered next.

Examine **Figure 15-3.** In the **Tools** drop-down menu, there is a list of diagnostic utilities. All of the following utilities can be found in this location. You need to become familiar with these utilities to save time when troubleshooting a system problem. Let's see how they might be helpful.

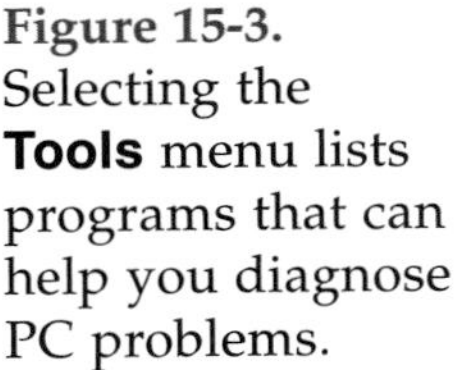
Dr. Watson troubleshooting software that collects information about the computer system during and just before a software application fault.

Dr. Watson

Dr. Watson is a standard Microsoft troubleshooting utility that is used to diagnose software fault problems. Dr. Watson collects information about the

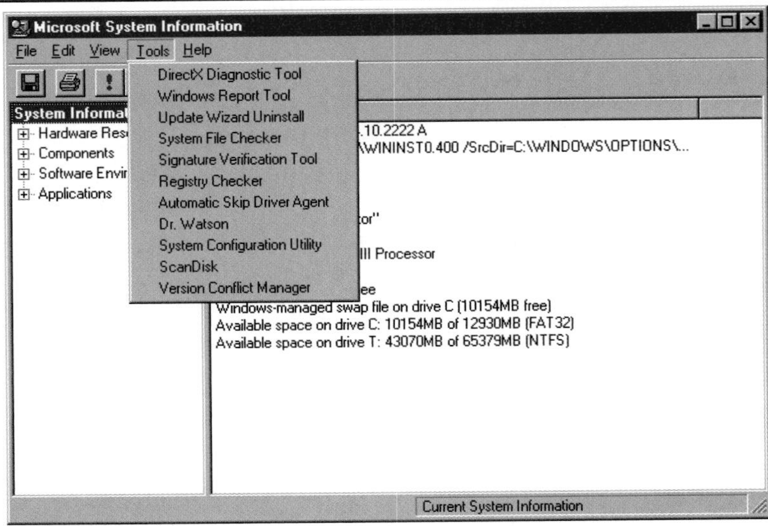

Figure 15-3. Selecting the **Tools** menu lists programs that can help you diagnose PC problems.

computer system during and just before a software application fault. It tracks down the program that caused the fault and reports the part of the memory and the program in which it occurred. This information can be used when contacting product support.

Dr. Watson does not load automatically. To activate Dr. Watson, click **Start | Run**, type **drwatson**, and then click **OK**. The Dr. Watson diagnostic program will appear as an icon in the system tray (bottom right taskbar area). You can then right-click the icon to open it. You can also access Dr. Watson, as mentioned earlier, through **Start | Programs | Accessories | System Tools | System Information**, click on the **Tools** menu, and then choose **Dr. Watson**.

By accessing **View** from the drop-down menu and selecting **Advanced View**, you can view the drivers, startup programs, and many more items, **Figure 15-4.** Dr. Watson can also write to a log to save errors and the descriptions of faults. These descriptions can be used when contacting support. Dr. Watson cannot diagnose a system hang or lockup condition.

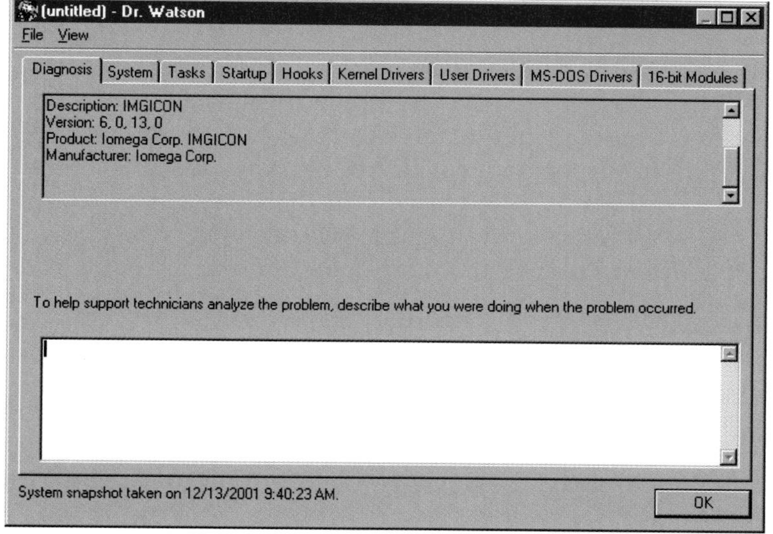

Figure 15-4. The Advanced view in Dr. Watson can be shown by selecting the **View** drop-down menu and selecting **Advanced View**. Running Dr. Watson places an icon in the system tray. You can activate the program from there.

Automatic Skip Driver Agent

This tool is available to assist with a startup problem. The ***Automatic Skip Driver Agent*** is used to detect devices that keep Windows from starting. Items that have been disabled can be viewed and enabled by running this tool. The agent is located with the other diagnostic tools at **Start | Programs | Accessories | System Tools | System Information**. Select the **Tools** menu and then select **Automatic Skip Driver Agent**.

Automatic Skip Driver Agent tool used to detect devices that keep Windows from starting.

System Configuration Utility

The ***System Configuration Utility*** allows you to modify the system configuration. To modify the system configuration, you simply check or uncheck the features listed, **Figure 15-5.**

System Configuration Utility tool that allows you to modify the system configuration.

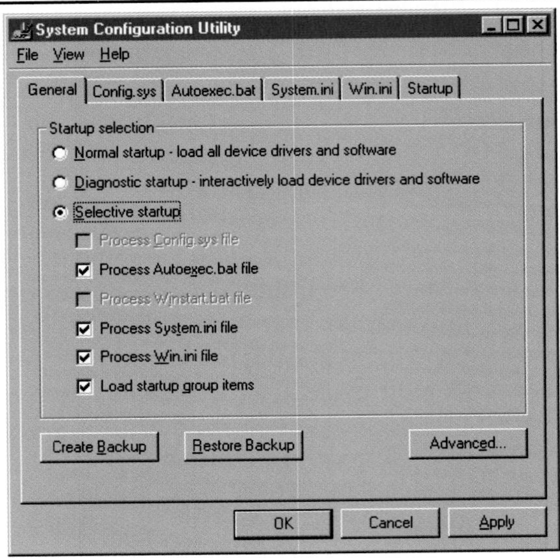

Figure 15-5. The System Configuration Utility gives you fast access to all your startup files.

The System Configuration Utility allows you to modify win.ini, system.ini, the startup files, autoexec.bat, and config.sys. When the suspected problem line is disabled, the file is automatically given a remark such as **REM TSHOOT:** to assist you. By disabling the suspected areas of trouble, you selectively eliminate possible causes of problems. This is much handier than using the System Configuration Editor (sysedit.exe) program because you do not have to go directly into the files to manually remark out any lines.

Registry Checker

Registry Checker utility that will scan, backup, and restore the system registry.

The ***Registry Checker*** utility will scan, back up, and restore the system registry. It is also a system maintenance program from the point of view that it automatically backs up the system's registry on a daily basis. When a serious error is found in the registry, the Registry Checker will restore the registry using the most recent copy from backup files. If a good backup cannot be found, the registry checker will automatically attempt to correct the problem.

The Registry Checker utility maintains five copies, or backups, stored in the backup folder by default. The setting can be adjusted from 0 to a maximum of 99. The backup files are located in the folder at C:windows\sysbckup and are called rb0##.cab where ## represents the number of the copy. For example, rb005.cab is the fifth copy of the registry. The highest number associated with the backup is the most recent file. For example, rb004.cab is more recent than rb003.cab.

Tech Tip:
You should never attempt to repair the registry files directly. An error made in the registry files can render the computer system inoperable. You may have to completely reinstall the system onto a clean hard drive. Simply loading the software over the corrupt registry would do no good. The new installation would inherit the previous corrupt settings.

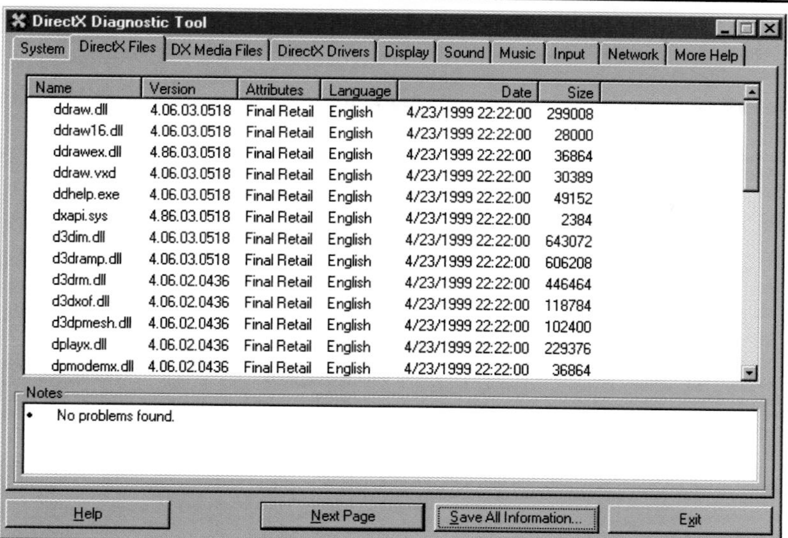

Figure 15-6. The DirectX Diagnostic Tool checks for problems with DirectX files. This check shows no problems.

DirectX Diagnostic Tool

DirectX is a software development tool used for multimedia applications. It allows programmers to directly access many of the built-in features of Windows. A poorly written program using DirectX can cause severe system hangs or crashes. The ***DirectX Diagnostic Tool*** will look at every DirectX program file on the computer, **Figure 15-6.** You can look for non-Microsoft approved program labels here. If it is Microsoft approved, you should not have a problem. That cannot be said for other programmers' tools. DirectX program files are abundant. They are used for game development and all types of multimedia programs.

DirectX Diagnostic Tool tool that looks at every DirectX program file to check for problems.

System File Checker

The ***System File Checker*** (sfc.exe) can be run to check for corrupt, changed, or missing files from Windows-based applications. It can also be used to restore system files. To start the System File Checker program, select it from the **Tools** menu in the Microsoft System Information utility, or type **sfc** at the **Run** prompt. See **Figure 15-7.** In Windows XP, you can access the system file checker by typing **sfc** at the command prompt.

System File Checker tool that can be run to check for corrupt, changed, or missing files from Windows-based applications.

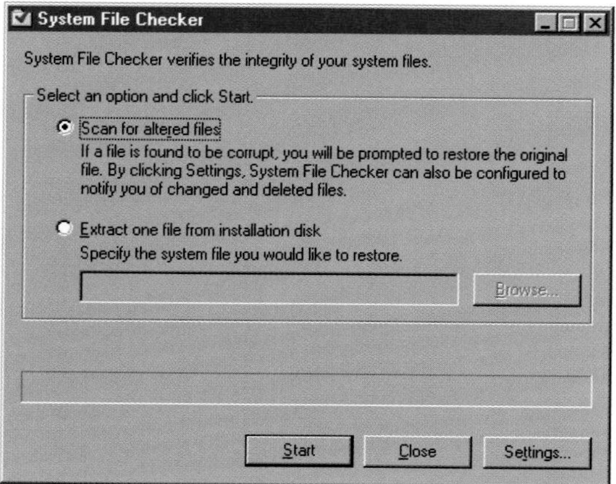

Figure 15-7. System File Checker can by used to check the integrity of your System Files.

Windows Report Tool

Windows Report Tool
utility that allows the PC system settings to be copied and sent to technical support for evaluation.

The ***Windows Report Tool*** is a utility that allows the PC system settings to be copied and sent to technical support for evaluation. Of course, a modem connection is needed and the system must be bootable. **Figure 15-8** shows the Windows Report Tool as it appears in Windows 98 and Me. Text box areas are provided for you to report information about the error.

Figure 15-9 shows the Error Reporting dialog box available in Windows XP. In Windows XP, you can choose to report errors generated by the Windows operating system or by other programs installed on the computer. Some programs may generate an error report each time they are launched or closed. If you find the automatic generation of an error report annoying, there is an option to disable it. The Error Reporting utility can be accessed through the System Properties dialog box in Windows XP, **Figure 15-10.** The complete path to the Error Reporting utility is **Start | Settings | Control Panel | System | Advanced | Error Reporting**.

Version Conflict Manager

Version Conflict Manager
utility that checks for a Microsoft certificate to ensure that only compatible software is installed on the system.

The ***Version Conflict Manager*** utility checks for a Microsoft certificate and for the version number of the software. This ensures that only compatible software is installed on the system. It does provide an option to install an unrecognized software driver program, but it warns you first.

Recovering from System Startup Failure

Recovering from a system startup failure requires the technician to have advanced skills. Many of the utilities described in this section should not be used by the inexperienced user because they can cause additional problems if not used correctly. To become an experienced technician, you should practice

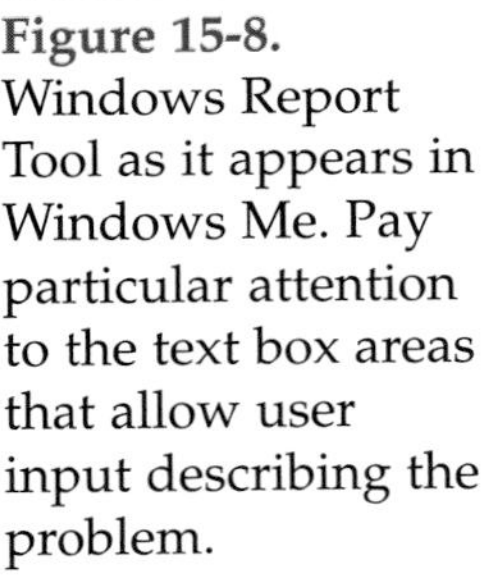

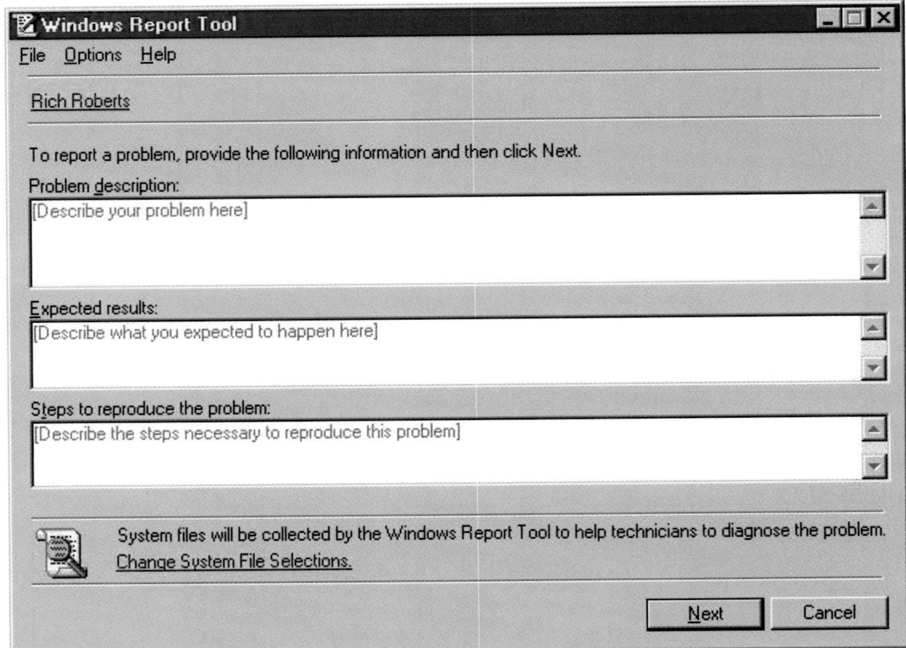

Figure 15-8.
Windows Report Tool as it appears in Windows Me. Pay particular attention to the text box areas that allow user input describing the problem.

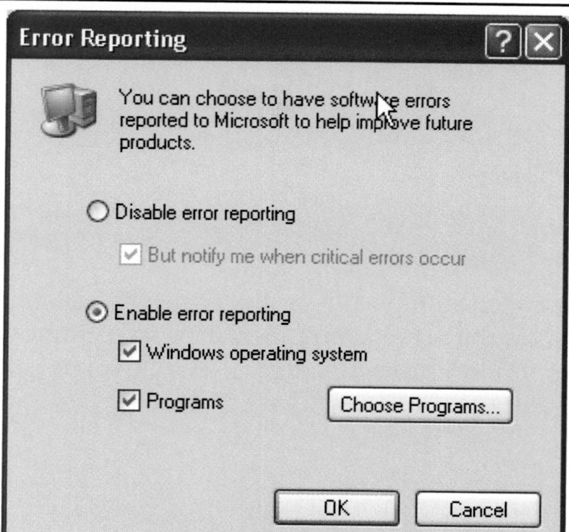

Figure 15-9. An example of the Error Reporting dialog box in Windows XP.

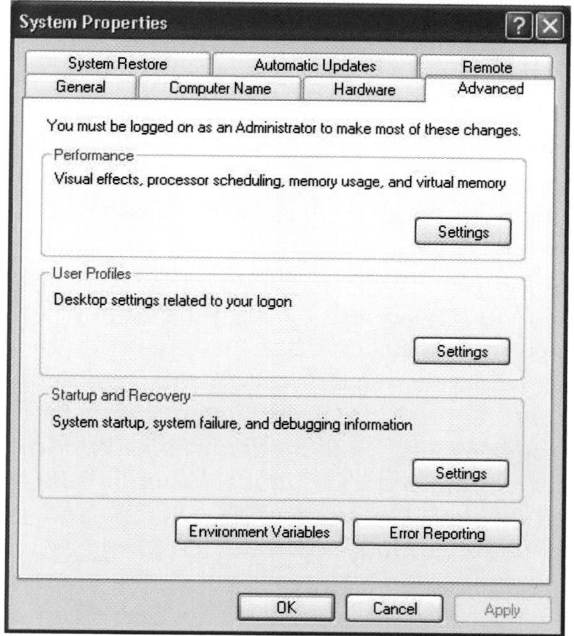

Figure 15-10. Look at the lower-right button marked "Error Reporting" on the System Properties Dialog box. This is used to access the Error Reporting dialog box in Windows XP.

using these utilities in the lab before attempting to use them on a customer's PC. You can also download extensive information about each of the utilities from the Microsoft Support Web site.

Boot Options

There are a number of different modes you can boot your computer into other than the normal mode that your PC boots into by default. The other modes are used for troubleshooting the computer. You can force your computer to boot into these other modes. They are useful if your computer has any of the following symptoms:

- System stalls for an unusually long period of time.
- Printer problems (as a last resort only).
- Video display problems.
- Computer shuts down or locks up for no apparent reason.
- Intermittent error conditions.

Pressing the [F8] function key during the boot process halts the boot process and displays a menu on the screen. These choices vary somewhat depending on the operating system you are using. A typical Windows 98 operating system lists the following options:

- Normal.
- Logged.
- Safe mode.
- Safe mode with network support.
- Step-by-step confirmation.
- Command prompt only.
- Safe mode command prompt only.
- Previous version of MS-DOS.

Normal means that you start the PC as you normally would. The second choice, *Logged,* means that a log of boot activities will be recorded in a file called bootlog.txt stored in the root directory of drive C. The log contains information about which files loaded correctly.

Safe mode will start automatically if Windows detects a system startup failure. In safe mode, Windows uses a basic configuration. Safe mode bypasses startup files such as config.sys, autoexec.bat, the registry, high memory, and parts of the system.ini. You will likely use this very handy option on a frequent basis. In this option, only the essentials are used to start the system giving you a chance to diagnose the computer. Safe mode disables Windows device drivers and starts the display in standard VGA mode. When in safe mode, each corner of the monitor screen displays the words "Safe Mode." You can also force the PC to start in safe mode by holding down the left [Ctrl] key while booting.

Step-by-step confirmation operates as is implied. It allows you the option to carry out or reject boot process files displayed on the screen on a step-by-step basis. This allows you to disable specific drivers called for in each line in the autoexec.bat and config.sys. By disabling each line, one at a time, you can determine which files and drivers are corrupt.

Command prompt only allows the computer to boot to the command line interface, not to the Windows graphical user interface. The command interpreter is loaded. A command prompt appears on the screen, and you are free to issue commands from the prompt such as **scandisk**, **dir**, and **copy**. You can start Windows from the command line simply by typing **Win** and then pressing [Enter].

Safe mode command prompt only starts the computer with only the essential drivers as if in safe mode. It does not load the Windows graphical user interface. The command interpreter is loaded and the command prompt appears allowing commands to be issued.

Depending on the version of Windows you are using, not all options will be available. *Last known good configuration* is available from safe mode of Windows 2000 and XP but not in Windows 98 or Me.

Last known good configuration, when selected, uses the last set of registry data before the system failed. This selection assumes that a change occurred in the configuration of the computer system, which resulted in the system failure.

System Restore

System Restore can be used to restore a system to a previous working state. System Restore first became available in Windows Me and then in Windows XP. ***Restore points***, which are backups of system settings and configurations, make it possible for a computer to revert to an earlier time when the computer system was working properly.

System Restore utility used to restore a system to a previous working state.

restore points backups of system settings and configurations that make it possible for a computer to revert to an earlier time when the computer system was working properly.

Look at **Figure 15-11.** When System Restore first opens, it provides two options: **Create a restore point** and **Open a previous restore point**. Although System Restore automatically creates restore points daily and before a software program is installed, the **Create a restore point** option allows the user to make a backup of the existing system. Creating a restore point manually should always be performed before changing configurations, adding hardware, or installing software. If something is done to the system that results in improper operation, the System Restore feature can be used to return the system to its previous state. This is done by selecting **Open a previous restore point** from the opening screen. System Restore displays a calendar of restore points from which the user can choose, **Figure 15-12.**

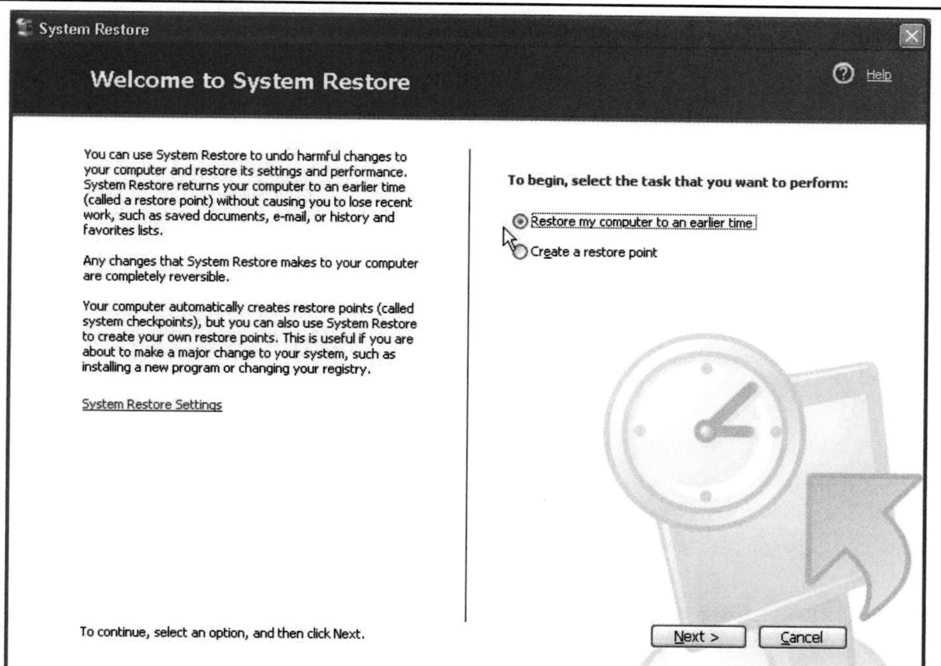

Figure 15-11. System Restore gives the option to restore the computer's system settings and performance to a previous point in time or to create a restore point.

Figure 15-12. Several restore points may be available in a single day. These include scheduled restore points created by the computer and restore points created by the user.

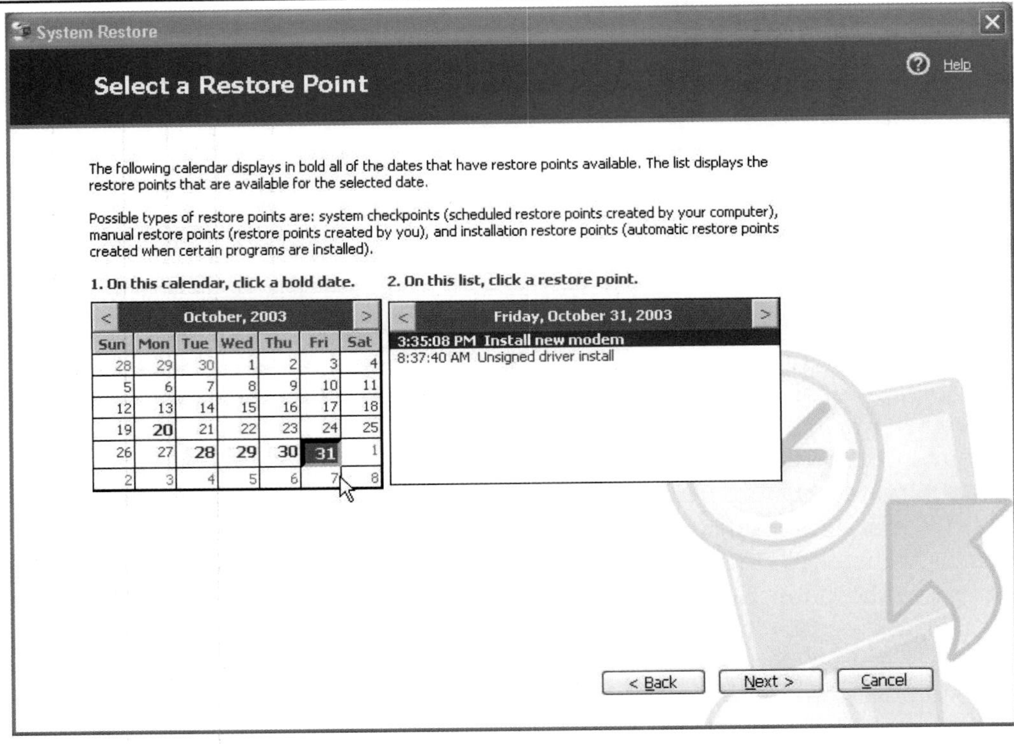

Recovery Console

Recovery Console text-based command-line utility used to enter commands similar to DOS commands to recover from a system startup failure.

The Recovery Console is a last resort recovery utility available in Windows 2000 and XP. ***Recovery Console*** is also referred to as "command console" and "repair console." The Recovery Console is used when the problem is so severe, you cannot access the safe mode startup option. Recovery Console is not a GUI utility. It is a text-based command line utility. Commands are issued at the Recovery Console command line prompt. The commands are very similar to the old style DOS commands issued at the DOS prompt. Many of the commands you are probably already familiar with, but there are some new ones.

Look at the chart in **Figure 15-13.** The chart is a partial listing of the many commands available to use in Recovery Console.

Recovery Console looks very much like the Windows command interpreter, but it is not the same. Recovery Console is not installed by default. Unless the computer system has been previously configured to run Recovery Console from the hard disk drive, you must use the installation CD to start the Recovery Console. To do this, insert the installation CD into a bootable CD-ROM drive. You may need to configure the BIOS settings to allow the CD-ROM drive to be the first device in the boot sequence.

When the PC boots to the installation program, select *R* to repair the system, and *C* to enter Recovery Console. Selecting *R* will command the recovery console to perform an automatic recovery of the system similar to the Last known good configuration option. Choosing *C* displays the Recovery Console command prompt. You can issue commands from the command prompt or copy a missing file from a floppy disk to the operating system directory. The Recovery Console is a last resort utility and should only be used by technicians with advanced troubleshooting experience.

Command	Description
attrib	Clears or sets file attributes.
bootcfg	Used to recover multiboot system failures and to reconfigure the boot.ini file.
cd or chdir	Change directories or folder location.
chkdsk	Checks and may repair bad disk sectors and check the surface of the disk.
copy	Copies a file.
del or delete	Deletes a file.
dir	Displays the contents of a directory.
disable	Disables a service or driver.
diskpart	Manages the partitions on a disk.
enable	Enables a service or file.
exit	Closes the Recovery Console.
expand	Extracts a compressed file known as a cab file.
fixboot	Write a new boot sector on a partition.
fixmbr	Repairs the master boot record.
format	Formats a partition, volume, or logical drive.
help	Displays a list of Recovery Console commands.
listsvc	Lists all available services and drivers.
logon	Lists all Windows 2000 and XP systems and lets you log on to one particular system.
md or mkdir	Create a directory or folder.
rd or rmdir	Removes a directory or folder.
ren or rename	Renames a file.

Figure 15-13. Text-based commands available to use in Recovery Console.

Automated System Recovery

The ***Automated System Recovery (ASR)*** utility is new with Windows XP. ASR is designed to replace the Emergency Repair Disk option used in Windows NT and 2000. The ASR utility automatically restores critical files that were backed up by the Backup utility. The ASR wizard can be accessed through the menu options of the Backup utility and through many third-party troubleshooting utilities. When ASR is used in conjunction with the Backup utility, it is possible to restore critical system files and data files. The Backup utility is available through **Start | Accessories | System Tools | Backup**. The Backup utility can also be accessed by running **NTbackup** from the **Run** dialog box.

Automated System Recovery (ASR) utility that automatically restores critical files that were backed up by the Windows XP Backup utility.

Remote Assistance

Remote Assistance allows a user to invite another user to access their computer and assist them in repairing their computer.

One of the newest features incorporated into Windows XP is Remote Assistance. ***Remote Assistance*** allows a user to invite another user to access their computer and assist them in repair. The user needing help sends an e-mail invitation to another person, such as a technical support person. Technical support can then repair the system while they chat with the user.

Remote Assistance should not be confused with Remote Desktop. Remote Desktop allows a user to connect directly to their computer from another location. For example, a user could connect to their office computer from their home computer. The user would have complete control over their office computer just as if they were sitting at its keyboard. Remote Assistance is a temporary connection, and a person must be present at both locations.

Figure 15-14 shows the remote connection options listed in the **System Properties** dialog box under the **Remote** tab. Both Remote Assistance and Remote Desktop are available in Windows XP Professional, but only Remote Assistance is available in Windows XP Home Edition.

Reinstall the Operating System

If you cannot repair the system using the utilities provided, you will need to reinstall the operating system. This is the very last resort to recovering from a system startup failure. When reinstalling the operating system, first try to perform a system upgrade. This will allow you to retain the data files that reside on the hard drive. Performing a new installation rather than a system upgrade wipes out all existing files on the hard drive, thus losing all data files.

Third-Party Utilities

There are many different third-party utilities available to assist in troubleshooting and maintenance. Two of the most commonly used are ConfigSafe by imageLAN Inc. and Winternals by Winternals Software.

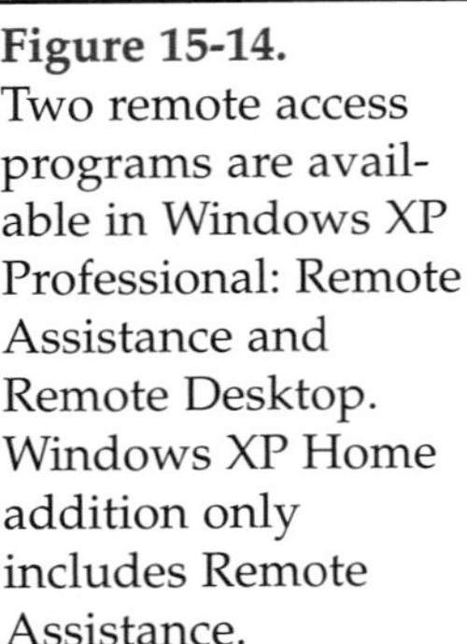

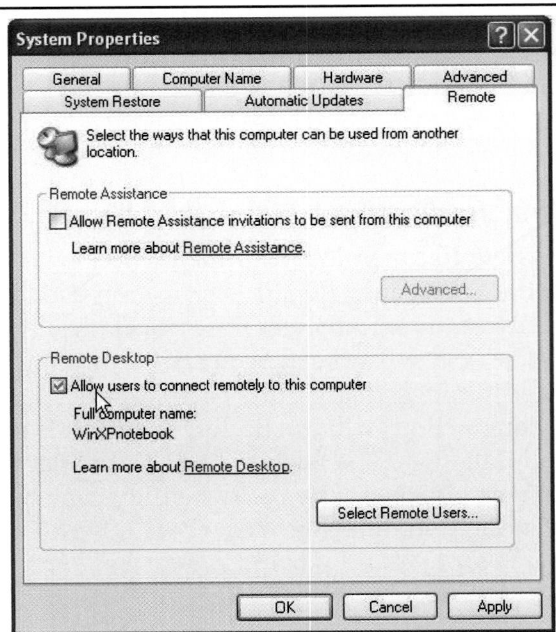

Figure 15-14. Two remote access programs are available in Windows XP Professional: Remote Assistance and Remote Desktop. Windows XP Home addition only includes Remote Assistance.

ConfigSafe

ConfigSafe is a third party software utility that can recover a failed system. It is designed to work with all Microsoft products from Windows 95 to Windows XP. ConfigSafe inspects and provides a list of all critical items installed and configured on the computer system. Changes in the system configuration can be viewed later to assist in troubleshooting. Trial versions of ConfigSafe are available from the imagineLan Web site at www.imaginelan.com/configsafe/.

Winternals and Sysinternals

There is a vast array of troubleshooting and maintenance tools available at both the Winternals and the Sysinternals Web site. The Sysinternals Web site, www.sysinternals.com, distributes freeware utilities while the Winternals Web site, www.winternals.com, distributes commercial versions of the products.

Blue Screen Errors

A Windows ***blue screen error*** is a blue screen that appears with an error code and then freezes the system. Microsoft also refers to blue screen errors as *fatal errors, stop errors,* and *stop error messages* because the system is not recoverable at the time of the error. The system must be restarted before you can attempt to remedy the problem. Some of the most common causes for blue screen errors include the following:

- Defective hardware, such as memory chips and video adapter cards.
- Corrupt files on the hard drive.
- System BIOS settings that are beyond the capabilities of the hardware.
- Third-party software containing bad code.
- Bad code in the Windows operating system.

The error codes displayed on the blue screen can be quite cryptic. You should copy the error code and use it as a reference when searching Microsoft's support Web site.

blue screen error a blue screen that appears with an error code and then freezes the system. Also referred to by Microsoft as fatal errors, stop errors, and stop error messages.

BOOT Sequences

It is imperative that you study the boot sequence of all standard operating systems and compare the differences. One way to accomplish this is to study the programs associated with the boot disk created for each system. The boot disk contains the files necessary to boot the computer as well as some of the various enhancement files. Not all files on a boot disk are necessary for booting the system. Information about a system boot sequence and boot files are usually contained in the readme.txt file of the installation discs (or disks). Always read the readme files of the operating system you are installing for the first time. Also, go to the operating system's Web site for the latest updates and patches.

DOS Boot Sequence

The DOS boot sequence can be divided into three parts:

1. Conducting a POST and adapter POSTs.
2. Locating the volume boot sector and master boot partition.
3. Loading system files.

Conducting POST and adapter POSTs

The power on self-test (POST) is conducted first. The motherboard BIOS contains the software program that conducts the self-test of major system components. The software program is generally referred to as firmware. It is written specifically for the particular BIOS chip and hardware system.

After the POST is completed, any adapter board that contains a ROM BIOS is run. Adapter boards such as video cards contain their own BIOS and memory.

Locating the volume boot sector and master boot partition

The program looks for the volume boot sector located at cylinder 0, head 0, sector 1 on the boot drive. The default order of drive search is first floppy drive A, hard disk drive C, and CD drive D. (Note that not all computers are capable of booting from the CD drive.) The order of this search can be manually changed in the BIOS setup routine and stored in the CMOS. When the volume boot sector is located, the boot program is activated. If no boot sector can be found on the floppy drive, the program searches for the master boot partition on the hard drive.

When the program locates the master boot partition, it tries to locate and load the master boot sector and read the data stored on the master boot partition. The master boot partition contains data describing the setup of the hard drive and file system. It also contains the location of certain programs as well as the type of file system structure being used. If any other partitions are on the hard drive, their locations are stored here. After all this information has been loaded into RAM, the program turns over control to the operating system.

Loading the system files

The io.sys (or ibmbio.com) copies itself into RAM from the hard drive. The io.sys loads the msdos.sys (or ibmdos.com) into memory. The io.sys initializes the basic generic drivers needed to start communication with the computer system. More advanced drivers that enhance the hardware are loaded later.

Next, the contents of the config.sys are loaded into RAM. The config.sys file processes statements and commands that load drivers and provides information about the system configuration. The config.sys file usually contains commands about buffer size and the number of files that can be opened at any one time.

Tech Tip:
Early Windows operating systems, such as Windows 3.x, use win.ini and system.ini to store configuration information. Later Windows systems use the system registry to store system configuration information or a combination of both registry and config.sys when necessary to support legacy hardware and software.

After the config.sys file is loaded and processed, the command interpreter, command.com, loads and executes the autoexec.bat file. The autoexec.bat file contains a list of commands that load software and other options. This is where the command to load a screen menu is presented or from where other software systems can be run. If the autoexec.bat is missing, a simple display prompt will appear on the screen. The PC will then wait for the user to issue a command such as **win** followed by [Enter]. After the command is issued, the Windows GUI and the associated software programs start up. Instead of typing the command at the prompt to start Windows, the command is processed as part of the autoexec.bat file. At this point, the boot process is over and the control of the system has been turned over to the operating system user interface.

Windows 95/98/Me Boot Sequence

Windows 95, 98, and Me are very similar in their boot process, and all can be covered together. With these operating systems, Microsoft started moving away from the use of config.sys, autoexec.bat, and the win.ini and system.ini files. It replaced them with the system registry. The system registry is a database that stores information about the hardware and software systems. The registry is continually referenced by the operating system and software programs. The autoexec.bat, config.sys, command.com, and io.sys have been renamed for Windows 98 by changing the file extensions to .dos. For example, io.sys in Windows 98 is now called io.dos.

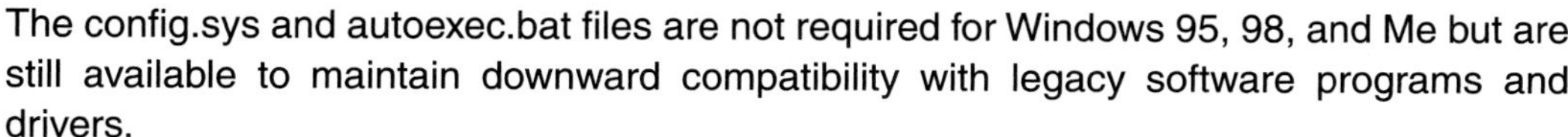

Tech Tip:
The config.sys and autoexec.bat files are not required for Windows 95, 98, and Me but are still available to maintain downward compatibility with legacy software programs and drivers.

It is important to note that when a Windows operating system is upgraded, the old data stored in .ini files is converted to registry settings. Any attempt to change the .ini files will not affect the system configuration. The settings must be changed in the registry file structure. The system registry contains two main files called system.dat and user.dat. The system.dat file contains information that is specific about the machine. The user.dat contains information about the user. A PC may have multiple users, thus there can be multiple user.dat files containing information about each specific user. Such user information would include, but not be limited to, desktop layout preferences and specific documents created by the user.

The boot process in Windows 95, 98, and Me is similar to the DOS boot process until the loading of the bootstrap program. During the BIOS phase, all Plug and Play devices are detected. Other devices and ROM chips with their own BIOS program are also detected here. The Windows startup process will load the config.sys file and then the autoexec.bat file, if they are required for support of legacy programs.

The three core executive files of the Windows 95 and 98 systems are krnl386.exe, gdi.exe, and user.exe. They are loaded in the same order as presented. The krnl386.exe is the kernel file or core program of the operating system. (There is also a krnl286.exe, which was used with earlier models of the operating system.) It manages the processor functions and system resources such as memory DMA channels, IRQs, and port functions. It also loads programs, schedules processor events, and controls the actions of the CPU. The user.exe file is designed to allow the user to manipulate the icons, windows, and elements that make up the user interface. The gdi.exe is the graphic device interface. It is responsible for displaying the screen images used as the interface between the user and the operating system. All three files are located in the directory structure under **Windows | System**.

After these three program files are processed, the logon window appears. The user logs on, and the system processes the user's individual settings.

Windows NT Workstation Boot Sequence

The Windows NT operating system is a complete GUI operating system and is much more powerful than DOS, especially with regard to security and file structure. A DOS-like prompt is available from the NT GUI interface, but NT is not a DOS-based operating system. Instead, NT emulates the DOS system providing users the opportunity to access the commands they are familiar with.

The boot sequence of Windows NT is the same as described in the DOS Boot Sequence section up to the point of loading the volume boot sector from the active partition. From that point on, the boot system process is quite different. The Windows NT system does not use an io.sys or msdos.sys file. It uses a program called NTLDR.

The NTLDR starts the process of detecting hardware and loading the operating system. It also detects the existence of other operating systems. For example, if you load NT with an existing Windows operating system, such as Windows 95, NT provides you with the option of starting the computer with either system. This is referred to as a *dual boot system.* Two different operating systems coexist on the same hard drive, but only one can be run at a single time. All boot option information is stored in a file called boot.ini. Once NT is selected as the operating system, the ntdetect.com file loads and detects the hardware in the PC system.

After the hardware detection is complete, the boot process loads the NT operating system kernel file called ntoskrnl.exe and the hal.dll. The hal.dll is the hardware abstraction layer. NT does not allow software programs to gain direct access to the system hardware the way that traditional Windows programs allow. The hal.dll is a machine language program that serves as the go-between for software and hardware. The hal.dll makes it possible for the computer system to be hardware and device independent. It will support many different CPU platform designs. In other words, the PC does not have to be an IBM clone. It could use a processor such as Digital's Alpha processor. The ntoskrnl.exe file is the heart of the operating system. It initializes the hardware system and drivers. It controls and oversees the entire operating system and the processing of instructions and files.

kernel mode
automatic Windows NT mode of operation that oversees the system resources and processor actions.

user mode
the actual user interface mode for the NT operating system. It is very restrictive and many areas are not accessible by the user or user programs.

The entire boot process is not considered complete until you log on with the [Ctrl] [Alt] [Delete] key combination. Once you log on, the system turns to the user mode of operation. There are two modes of operation, user mode and kernel mode. ***Kernel mode*** oversees the system resources and processor actions. This is an automatic mode requiring no user intervention. ***User mode*** is the actual user interface with the operating system. It is very restrictive in the sense that many areas are not accessible by the user or user programs. This environment is what makes NT such a stable system as compared to other Microsoft Windows products. The stability is due to software and users not being allowed to manipulate hardware resources and features.

Windows 2000 and XP Boot Sequence

Windows 2000 and Windows XP are designed on the NT operating system kernel, not the traditional Windows 95/98 operating system kernel. However, their outward appearance is remarkably similar.

As with the other systems covered so far, these systems start with the POST, load the BIOS program, and look for the boot sector as well as the MBR. Then, Windows 2000 and XP follow the NT system. The NTLDR is loaded, and it in turn loads the program startup files from the boot sector. Part of loading the startup files is the detection of the preferred operating system. Windows 2000 and XP, like NT, allow for the existence of more than one operating system. They will coexist with Windows 95, Windows 98, Windows NT, MS-DOS, and OS/2.

After the preferred operating system has been chosen, NTLDR detects the system hardware. After hardware detection, NTLDR passes control to the Windows 2000/XP kernel. A dialog box will appear on the display, similar to the NT system. The system will request the user to log on. The user *must* be identified by a user name and password. The startup system is complete after the user successfully logs on to the system. The screen settings will match the user's preference.

Linux Boot Sequence

Some common versions of Linux are SuSE, Xandros, Red Hat, Caldera, and Debian. All have graphical user interfaces available and appear similar to the Windows screen display.

Linux is similar to the other systems in that a POST is performed and a BIOS routine is loaded. It is common to boot from a floppy disk when using Linux, but you may also boot from the hard drive. Like any typical startup operating system, after the initial system startup, the Linux operating system takes over. Linux uses a boot manager called *lilo*, which stands for *Li*nux *lo*ader. Lilo looks at the configuration file called lilo.conf to detect operational information. The lilo boot manager allows the user to select other operating systems when more than one exists on the hard drive. Linux operating systems can coexist with Microsoft Windows operating systems. Once the Linux kernel loads, the system runs the init program. The init is the system initialization, similar to DOS or Windows. All the system processes, such as the keyboard, mouse, and network connections, require initialization.

Repairing the System Registry

Never attempt to repair a system registry when there are other methods of repair at your disposal. Direct manipulation of the registry should be the last attempt effort to repair a PC system. Starting with Windows 98, a program called Registry Checker (discussed earlier) was introduced. It automatically checks and backs up the registry everyday. It will also restore the registry if needed. This is the preferred method of dealing with any registry problems.

There is a tool available called Registry Editor (regedit.exe) that is designed for manipulating the registry files. Direct manipulation of registry files should only be attempted by advanced technicians. The wrong entry of a registry file can result in the operating system becoming unstable or unusable. The preferred method for making changes to the registry is to use alternate tools provided by Microsoft to adjust the settings. These preferred tools are the dialog boxes that can be accessed through **Control Panel**. The settings you have been adjusting in these dialog boxes during your laboratories and other practices make changes to the computer's registry. However, when using these dialog boxes, you will receive messages displayed on screen warning of possible system failures or problems resulting from the changes. You are also more limited in the changes you can make. When you directly manipulate the registry, you will *not* receive warning messages and have no limitations to the code that can be entered.

Repairing the registry for Windows 95 requires the manual replacement of user.dat and system.dat files. Start the computer, press [F8], and choose **Command prompt only** from the menu select. Copy the two files, system.da0 and user.da0, to system.dat and user.dat. (Note that the "0" in "da0" is the number zero, not an alpha character.) Before the files can be copied, the hidden, read only, and system attributes must be removed from the file. Removal is accomplished by using the attrib command and adding the **-h**, **-r**, **-s** switches in front of the file names. See the following example:

attrib -h -r -s system.dat

This command removes the hidden, read only, and system attributes from a file called system.dat. You should only have to use this method when dealing with a Windows 95 operating system. For Windows 98 and later versions, this alteration is not necessary.

An alternative to using Registry Checker to back up the registry files is to issue the command **scanreg** from the **Run** dialog box or from the DOS prompt. To restore the registry files, type **scanreg/restore** from the DOS prompt. Windows NT, 2000, and XP do not support these two commands.

Common Troubleshooting Log Files

Log files are created as ASCII text files. They are used to record events that take place or to collect information about hardware and software systems. There can be many different log files on a computer system, not just the ones discussed in this section. These logs are created because many software and hardware manufacturers write their own log file collection programs to assist them (and you) in determining problems that may have occurred during the installation of their hardware or software package. The log files can also be used to relay information to technical support personnel by e-mail or telephone. Sometimes these files can also be accessed remotely by technical support personnel.

Bootlog.txt

The Windows bootlog.txt contains information about the sequence of operations that take place while the system boots. It is an ASCII text file that opens under any text editor program such as Notepad or WordPad. The bootlog.txt file is located in the root directory C:/bootlog.txt. Look at the sample contents extracted from the file in **Figure 15-15.**

As you can see, each driver that is loaded is displayed in the file followed by the status (successful or unsuccessful). The file is very lengthy and averages about 65KB in length. If you are looking for a specific driver or piece of hardware, use the **Find** option from the drop-down menu items in WordPad or in an equal text editor.

The bootlog.txt file is created automatically, one time only, when Windows is started for the first time. If you want to create another more recent version of the bootlog.txt file, access the startup menu by pressing the function key [F8] during the boot process, and choose the **Logged** option.

```
[0005A46E] Loading Vxd = VMM
[0005A46E] LoadSuccess = VMM
[0005A46E] Loading Vxd = vnetsup.vxd
[0005A46E] LoadSuccess = vnetsup.vxd
[0005A46E] Loading Vxd = ndis.vxd
[0005A46D] LoadSuccess = ndis.vxd
[0005A46E] Loading Vxd = JAVASUP.VXD
[0005A46D] LoadSuccess = JAVASUP.VXD
[0005A46D] Loading Vxd = CONFIGMG
[0005A46D] LoadSuccess = CONFIGMG
[0005A46D] Loading Vxd = NTKERN
[0005A46D] LoadSuccess = NTKERN
[0005A46D] Loading Vxd = VWIN32
[0005A46D] LoadSuccess = VWIN32
[0005A46D] Loading Vxd = VFBACKUP
[0005A46D] LoadSuccess = VFBACKUP
[0005A46D] Loading Vxd = VCOMM
[0005A46D] LoadSuccess = VCOMM
[0005A46D] Loading Vxd = COMBUFF
[0005A46D] LoadSuccess = COMBUFF
```

Figure 15-15. Text copied from a typical bootlog.txt file.

Tech Tip:
Studying the bootlog.txt file is an excellent way of learning the steps of the startup sequence that takes place in Windows.

The bootlog.txt file records the loading and initiation of real-mode drivers and virtual device drivers. These are where many startup problems can originate. ***Real-mode drivers*** are the legacy 16-bit drivers such as setver.exe, himem.sys, and emm386.exe. Real-mode drivers were written for the original 16 bit 8086 and 8088 CPU architectures. Windows ***virtual device drivers (VxDs)*** are special device drivers that have access to the operating system kernel. At times, the x between V and D in VxD represents the type of device driver being installed. For example, the extension .vpd would represent a printer driver and .vdd would represent a display driver.

real-mode drivers legacy 16-bit drivers.

virtual device drivers (VxDs) special device drivers that have access to the operating system kernel.

The system attempts to load the device driver and if it is successful, the next line statement says LoadSuccess. See the two lines that follow, which are taken directly from a Windows 98 bootlog.txt file.

[0005A46E] Loading Vxd lmouse.vxd
[0005A46D] LoadSuccess lmouse.vxd

In the example, the loading of the mouse driver and verification of success are displayed in the file. There are more steps to successfully loading a mouse. After the device software driver is successfully loaded, it is tested as a software package only, without the hardware device. This step is called *initialization.*

After the driver software has been successfully initialized, the actual hardware device (the mouse itself) is located and tested. After the hardware device is tested, it is tested again, this time with the software device driver. Once the hardware device has been successfully tested with the software device driver, the entire process of loading the driver and verifying its success for this single device is considered complete and becomes the last entry in the bootlog.txt file for this device.

You can trace the steps described by opening the bootlog.txt file on your PC using a word processor. Use the **Find** option to find every reference to the device you are examining (lmouse in this example).

Setuplog.txt

The setuplog.txt file is an ASCII text file located in the root directory. Setuplog.txt contains information about the system setup and is created during the step-by-step installation of Windows. This file is used by the system to recover from a failed installation or to troubleshoot a failed installation attempt. If the process of installing a new Windows operating system fails, use this log to see the exact step in the installation process that failed.

Detlog.txt

The detlog.txt file records all hardware components that have been detected by the system. The file is located in the root directory. Note that this file is more than just a hidden file. It is a hidden system file. So to see this file, you must have the correct view file options set. You can adjust this setting through the Windows Explorer program. Choose **Folder Options** under the **View** drop-down menu. Then select the **View** tab and pick the **Show all files** radio button. See **Figure 15-16.**

The detlog.txt file is run each time the computer system is started and when **Add New Hardware** is run from **Control Panel**. The detlog.txt file is used to verify

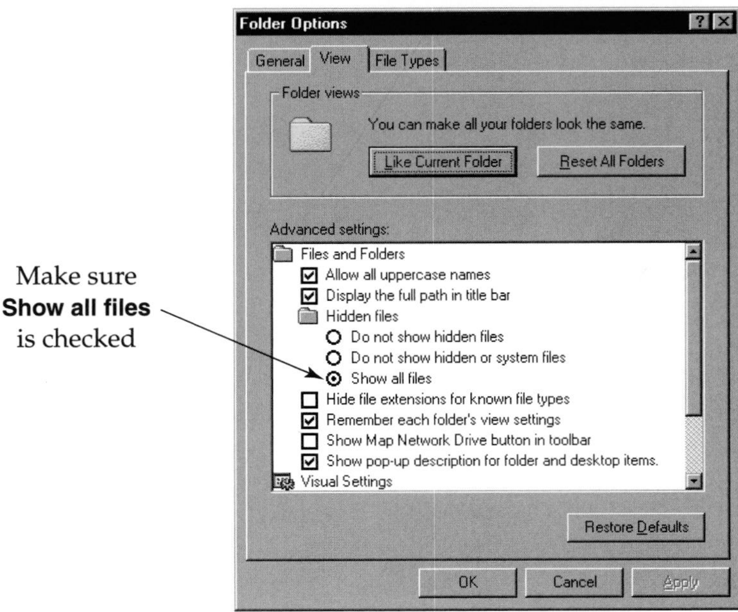

Figure 15-16. If you can't find your detlog.txt file, check if your PC is set to view all files.

that the hardware has been detected by the system, that it is loaded into the correct memory address, and that it is using the appropriate I/O port address, IRQ, and DMA channel.

Detcrash.log

The detcrash.log is created when the system locks up during the hardware detection phase of the system startup process. The last entry in the detcrash.log file would be the appropriate place to start a comparison of the detlog.old file to solve the problem. The detlog.old is created and stored after a successful system hardware detection and startup.

Netlog.txt

The netlog.txt contains information about any network settings and hardware that might exist. This log is used to help determine network connection failures. This log will be addressed in more detail later in the textbook when we discuss networking.

Event Viewer

The Event Viewer, available in Windows 2000 and XP, allows you to view the application, security, and system log files. These log files are named AppEvent.Evt, SecEvent.Evt, and AppEvent.Evt and are only viewable through the Event Viewer program. Each log file can be viewed in chronological order or by categories such as event and user. Since the Event Viewer log files retain a history of events that have occurred on the PC, it can be a very valuable troubleshooting tool. For example, users typically will not want to reveal information about installed software such as games, especially if gaming software is against company policy. A technician can quickly view a list of software changes and obtain objective data that can be used to identify possible causes of system problems.

Data Recovery Techniques

Many times data on a nonfunctioning hard drive is not actually lost, although it cannot be directly accessed. Think about the causes of failure for a hard drive. They include the electronics board mounted on the hard drive, the mechanical parts inside the drive, or simply a boot sector failure. If you can still see the drive directory on drive C when using a boot disk, chances are excellent for recovering the data.

One of the most common ways to recover data is with software. There are a number of third party programs out there designed to read disks that show as bad. **Figure 15-17** shows a disk being accessed by Norton Disk Editor. It can examine the disk and display the sectors in your choice of ASCII, binary, or hexadecimal code. Sections can then be copied to another disk.

Mechanical and electronic repairs should be left to the specialist. Many businesses specialize in this type of data recovery. An electronic circuit board controller mounted on the drive could be destroyed. It can be replaced, but it takes a skilled electronics technician. The circuit conductors are very fragile and easily broken. Also, disk drive platters can be removed and installed on other drives. However, it takes special tools, training, and a clean room (which is not

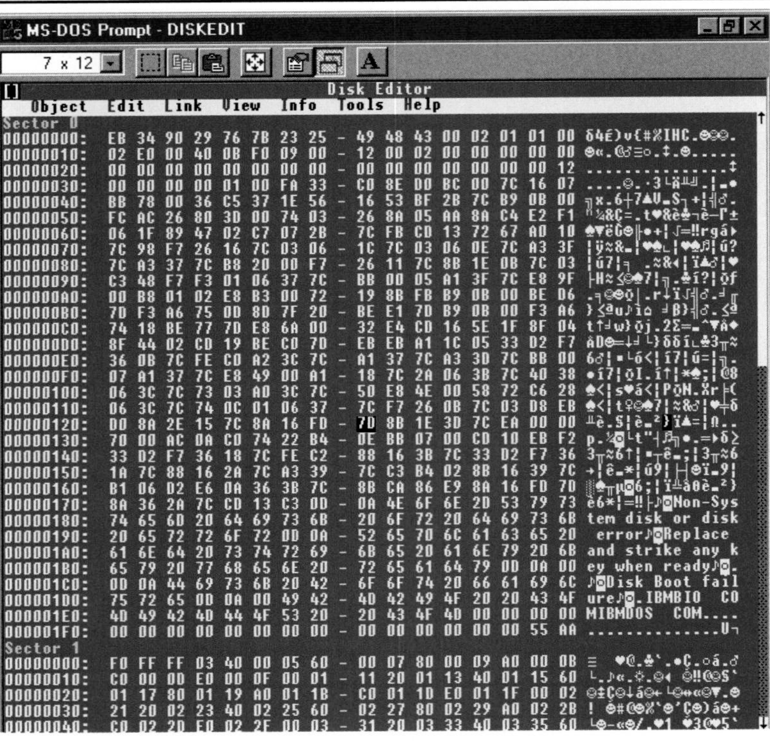

Figure 15-17. Data on a hard drive that stops working can often be accessed using special software. Here a file is being viewed in Norton's Disk Editor.

clean room
a room where dust and foreign particles have been completely eliminated.

just a room that is clean). A ***clean room*** is a room where dust and foreign particles have been completely eliminated.

Preparation for Installing or Upgrading an Operating System

Before installing a new operating system, several appropriate practices should be followed for the ideal setup:

- Check for viruses.
- Defrag the drive.
- Read the readme.txt file.
- Check the operating system's Web site for latest updates, known installation problems, hardware compatibility lists, patches, and updates.

If you are upgrading an existing system, be sure to backup existing system data. You are probably tired of hearing "back up the system data," but it is the *only way* to rebuild a destroyed system. There are two commonly accepted methods of backing up files: *incremental* and *differential.*

The difference between the two is determined by the *archive bit.* The archive bit is designed to indicate if a file has been backed up or not. This issue is important on large data systems where backups are performed daily to ensure against data loss.

incremental backup
operation that backs up select files that have changed since the last backup of files. The archive bit is reset.

An ***incremental backup*** requires a disk or tape for each daily backup. When performing an incremental backup, only the changes in data since the last incremental or last full backup are copied. A copy of the last full data backup plus *each* incremental backup in sequence must be used to reconstruct an entire collection of data, **Figure 15-18.** When performing a ***differential backup,*** *all* the data changes are copied since the last full backup. Only one disk or tape is needed to perform the differential backup because it copies all changes in data since the last full backup was performed. To restore the data, you need only the last full backup and the last differential backup.

differential backup operation that saves files that have changed since the last full backup of all files. The archive bit is not reset.

The reason for selecting an incremental or differential backup is based on the amount of time and disk space required for each type of backup. Since the incremental backup only copies changes from the last incremental backup, there is less data to copy. This results in a shorter time period required to perform the backup. A differential backup copies all data changes since the last full backup. This can require a significant amount of space and time if there is a great number of days between full backups. These differences may seem insignificant at first, but when you are talking about the large volumes of data that some corporations generate, you can be talking about significant periods of time.

Preventive Maintenance

Performing routine maintenance on the PC can help prevent future problems and improve system performance. Some of the most common but often overlooked routine maintenance items are listed in this section. Many of the items can be scheduled to perform automatically.

System Backups

Backups should be performed as part of routine system maintenance. You may not be able to repair a failed computer system, but you can at least restore critical data after installing a clean copy of the operating system. If the system has been configured to perform automatic backups, check if the backups are being performed. The automatic backup configuration may have been turned off or has been corrupted. You can verify that the backup job has run at the

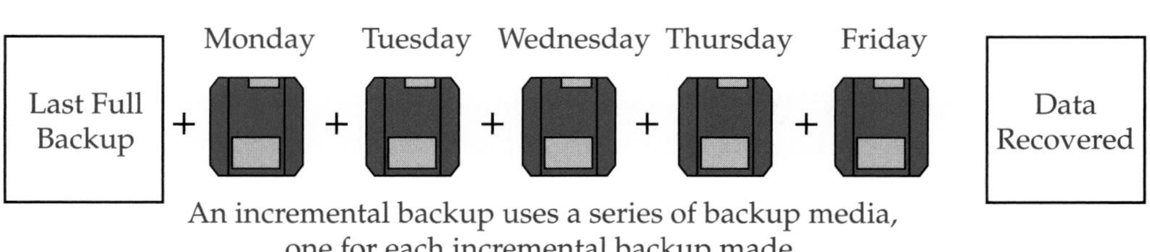

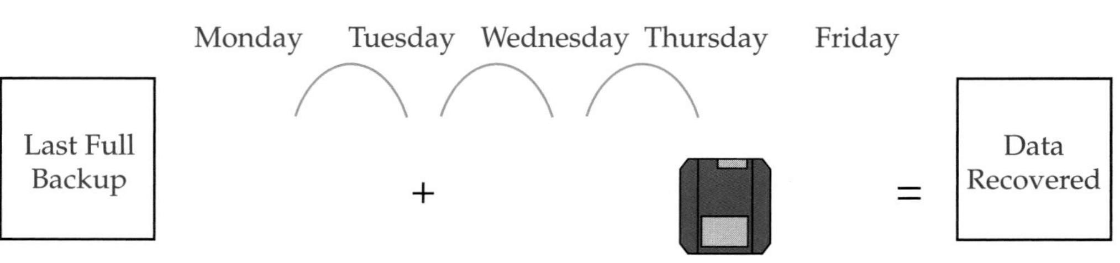

Figure 15-18. The incremental method requires the complete set of disks plus the last full backup to restore the system data. The differential method requires only the last differential backup made plus the last full backup to restore the system.

scheduled time and that the backup was successful by checking the backup log. Most backup programs keep a backup log, which is accessible through the program's main menu. You should occasionally verify that the data could be read and restored from the backup tape. If you have installed a patch, however, you should verify that you could still restore data. Microsoft has many problems with their DLL files. A DLL file used in the restore process could develop a problem after a system patch is installed.

Disk Cleanup Utility

Disk Cleanup Utility
utility that can be used to regain hard drive space such as that consumed by temporary files, files sitting in the Recycle Bin, unused Windows components, unneeded installed programs, and restore points created by System Restore.

The ***Disk Cleanup Utility*** can be used to regain hard drive space such as that consumed by temporary files, files sitting in the Recycle Bin, unused Windows components, unneeded installed programs, and restore points created by the System Restore utility. Some of the temporary files that Disk Cleanup allows you to remove are downloaded program files, temporary Internet files, and offline files. The Disk Cleanup Utility performs the functions of other Windows programs, such as Recycle Bin and Add or Remove Programs. From this one utility the Recycle Bin can be emptied, saving you the extra steps of accessing Recycle Bin and clicking Empty Recycle Bin. Windows components and installed programs can be uninstalled, rather than accessing Add or Remove Programs. The Disk Cleanup Utility can be used to remove all but the most recent restore points created by the System Restore utility. System Restore automatically backs up system information. This information can be used to restore a computer to a previously operational state. Depending on factors such as how much hard drive space is available, how much hard drive space is allocated to System Restore, and the amount of activity on the hard drive, System Restore can save one to three weeks of system information in files called *restore points.*

Disk Defragmenter Utility

As you recall from Chapter 9—Magnetic Storage Devices, files can become fragmented over time by opening, closing, and deleting them and by changing their contents. These activities can result in a file being segmented and stored in various clusters across the hard drive. The Disk Defragmenter utility rearranges all files on your hard drive into a continuous series of clusters, which results in better disk performance. The Disk Defragmenter utility should be run at least once per month depending on the amount of file activity on the system, and especially run after using the Disk Cleanup Utility. Also, be aware that running Disk Defragmenter on a large disk, 80 GB or more, can take a very long time. Schedule to run the Disk Defragmenter when you will not require the use of the computer for an extended period of time.

ScanDisk and Chkdsk

Disk error checking should be performed on a regular basis. Windows 98 and Me use the ScanDisk utility, and Windows NT, 2000, and XP use the chkdsk utility. Both programs inspect the hard disk and correct errors in the file structure, such as bad sectors, lost clusters, cross-linked files, and directory errors.

Install Patches

Check for the latest software patches for your operating system. Patches should be installed on a regular basis, especially as a matter of security. Many operating system security problems are discovered after the release of an operating system. Checking for and installing patches on a regular basis will keep the security level high on the computer system. Some patches can have adverse effects on your computer system. Be sure to backup your system files before installing a patch.

Virus Protection Updates

Virus protection software requires updates on a regular basis. Your virus protection can fail to protect your system if it does contain the latest virus definitions. Check the company Web site of your virus protection software for the latest virus information and updates.

Clean the Physical System

Routinely check and clean the cooling system on the computer. The cooling system includes the power supply fan(s) and the fans located on critical components such as the CPU, chipset, memory modules, and video cards. Also, remove dust accumulations from passive heat sinks located in the same areas. Dust should be removed using a static-free vacuum cleaner.

Also, be sure to remove dust and debris from keyboards, mouse, and the screen areas. Do not use chemicals when cleaning the plastic parts of a computer system or the screen area. First attempt to clean the plastic parts with a dry, soft, lint-free cloth. Next, try a damp cloth, and as a last resort, you may use a mild, soapy water solution. Keep water away from electronic components inside the computer and computer vents. Avoid the use of any harsh chemicals for cleaning the computer and computer components.

Summary

- Try the simple things first when troubleshooting.
- Write down changes made as you progress through the troubleshooting stages.
- The first sector is critical on a hard drive.
- Hard drives have a high failure rate because mechanical systems have a higher failure rate than electronic systems.
- Dr. Watson is used to collect information about the computer system before and during a software failure.
- The Automatic Skip Driver Agent is used to detect devices that keep the Windows operating system from starting.
- The System Configuration Utility allows users to modify the system configuration.
- Msinfo32.exe provides information about the system, as well as online help and access to system troubleshooting tools.
- The Registry Checker scans, backs up, and restores the system registry files.
- By default, there are five backup copies of registry files for Windows 98 and Me.
- The DirectX Diagnostic Tool checks the validity of any existing DirectX software tools and add-ons.
- The System File Checker checks for missing, changed, or corrupt system files.

- You can start the Windows operating system in several different modes, accessed by pressing function key [F8] when the Windows logo appears.
- Safe mode loads the minimum generic drivers and bypasses autoexec.bat and config.sys, if they exist.
- The two methods of backing up files are incremental and differential.
- Performing regularly scheduled maintenance can prevent future problems and improve system performance.

Review Questions

Answer the following questions on a separate sheet of paper. Please do not write in this book.

1. What are the three major fault areas?
2. If there are no power lights and the fan is not running, which is most likely the cause?
   a. Power supply
   b. Motherboard
   c. Hard drive
   d. CMOS settings
3. After booting, an error message appears on the display screen. What is the most likely cause?
   a. Operating system software problem
   b. Bad CMOS battery
   c. Corrupt hard drive
   d. Corrupt io.sys file
4. What program is used to repair a Windows 98 registry?
5. You can start the PC in safe mode after pressing _____.
   a. [Ctrl] [Alt] [Del]
   b. [F8]
   c. [F3]
   d. [Ctrl] [Shift] [Del]
6. How does safe mode differ from a normal boot process?
7. What are some things you should do before installing a new operating system?
8. What troubleshooting utility is available in Windows XP that can be used when you cannot access the GUI interface or safe mode?
9. What is the Windows XP ASR utility?
10. What program is required to allow the user to issue commands from the command prompt in a DOS or Windows environment?
11. What is io.sys called in a Windows 98 environment?

12. How do you start Windows from the command line prompt?
13. What are the three core executive files of the Windows 95/98 operating system?
14. What two major files found in the DOS and early Windows boot process are no longer needed except for running legacy DOS programs starting with Windows 95?
15. What is used in place of the win.ini and system.ini files to store system information?
16. What does the NTLDR program do?
17. What is the gdi.exe used for in the Windows operating system?
18. What is the name of the NT kernel file?
19. What is the final step to the boot process in an NT installation?
20. What other operating system is most like Windows 2000?
21. What boot process steps are similar to all Windows operating systems?
22. What program allows you to directly access the registry files?
23. What is the detlog.old used for?
24. How can you change the drive search order from floppy drive A to drive C as the first drive looked at for booting purposes?
25. What is the difference between an incremental backup and a differential backup system?
26. List seven things to perform during regular system maintenance.

Sample A+ Exam Questions

Answer the following questions on a separate sheet of paper. Please do not write in this book.

1. How do you access the startup menu when using Windows 98?
   a. Press [Ctrl] [Alt] [Del] keys simultaneously and wait for the menu to appear.
   b. Press [F8] while the PC is booting.
   c. Press [F3] while the PC is booting.
   d. Open Control Panel and change the setting in the **Start-Up Menu Select** icon.
2. Which is *not* a typical screen display choice in a Windows 98 startup menu?
   a. Normal
   b. Step-by-step confirmation
   c. Safe mode with fast recovery detect
   d. Logged

3. What answer correctly corresponds to safe mode operation for Windows 98? (Select all that apply.)
   a. Only the essential drivers are loaded into extended memory.
   b. Only the first 1MB of memory is accessed.
   c. Autoexec.bat is not run.
   d. Config.sys is not run.
4. Which of the following files are found in the NT4.0 operating system but not in Windows 98? (Select all that apply.)
   a. NTLDR
   b. MS-DOS
   c. NTDETECT
   d. NTFILESYS
5. What is the name of the NT kernel program used for NT4.0?
   a. ntoskrnl.exe
   b. ntkrnl.exe
   c. kernelnt.exe
   d. ntkrn.exe
6. What keyboard combination is used to access the system logon window in Windows 2000?
   a. [Ctrl] [Shift] [Esc]
   b. [Del] [Alt] [Shift]
   c. [Ctrl] [Alt] [Delete]
   d. [Ctrl] [Alt] [Enter]
7. The two main files associated with Windows 98 registry are _____ and _____.
   a. user.dat, system.dat
   b. OS.dat, machine.dat
   c. user.001, system.001
   d. reg.dat, OS.dat
8. What should be done before upgrading the operating system? (Choose all that apply.)
   a. Back up important documents.
   b. Run a virus check.
   c. Read the readme.txt files on the installation CD.
   d. Check the manufacturer's Web site for latest updates and patches.
9. How often is the system registry in Windows 98 backed up?
   a. It is backed up once a month, but more often if a problem exists.
   b. It is backed up everyday after a successful boot operation.
   c. It is backed up once every hour of use by the user.
   d. The registry is only backed up when the user accesses the Registry Backup program and then launches it from the **Run** dialog box.

10. Where is the record of a system boot sequence kept when using a Windows 98 operating system? Note that drive C is assumed as the default boot drive.

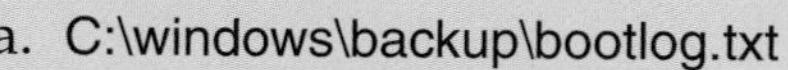

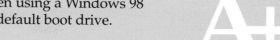

  a. C:\windows\backup\bootlog.txt
  b. C:\win\system\bootlog.txt
  c. C:\bootlog.txt
  d. C:\windows\registry\bootlog.txt

Suggested Laboratory Activities

Do not attempt any suggested laboratory activities without your instructor's permission. Certain activities can render the PC operating system inoperable.

1. Launch the msinfo32.exe program from the **Run** dialog box. Look under the **Tools** menu and list all available tools. Next, access the system help program from the start menu to find out all you can about the various tools before you use them.
2. Start a selection of Windows operating systems in safe mode and write down the safe mode menu options available for each system. Suggested systems are Windows 98, Me, 2000, and XP.
3. Try using the different safe mode menu selections to see their effect. Check for information about the different safe mode options in the system help files available through the startup menu.
4. Using a PC designated for experimentation, try several of the following tests to see how a PC reacts. Be sure you have an installation CD available before you begin. Also be sure you have any drivers you might need for the CD-ROM drive and the video display. *If you are requested to remove any cable, remember to disconnect all power to the PC before removing or reconnecting the cable.*
   a. Remove the data cable from the hard drive and observe the boot process. Replace the cable when done.
   b. Remove the floppy drive data cable and observe the system boot up. Replace the data cable when done.
   c. Reverse the data cable connection to the floppy drive and observe any error messages. Return the cable to its correct orientation.
   d. There are several connection points on most floppy drive data cables. Connect the installed floppy drive to a different connection point on the data cable. (Note that not all PCs have a floppy data cable with more than one connection point.)
   e. Remove certain files from the hard disk drive and then observe the boot process for error codes or symptoms. Try removing: command.com, io.sys, and msdos.sys. Some files can simply be copied from the hard disk drive to a floppy disk and then reinstalled after the experiment. Some must be replaced by doing a system install from the installation CD. Be prepared to do a complete system reinstallation.

5. Access some of the log files found on drive C and see what information is contained in each.
6. Try restoring the registry on a Windows 98, 2000, and an XP system.
7. Go to the Microsoft support page (http://support.microsoft.com/) and look for known troubleshooting issues. Find out what is available there. Examine the many options available at the Web site such as frequently asked questions (FAQs) for different operating systems.
8. Look for Web casts. There are Web casts available from Microsoft for basic troubleshooting techniques of their operating systems.

Interesting Web Sites for More Information

www.sysinternals.com
www.winternals.com
www.configsafe.com

Chapter 15
Laboratory Activity
Accessing the Startup Menu

After completing this laboratory activity, you will be able to:

- ❑ Access the startup menu using [F8] during the system boot.
- ❑ Identify and explain the startup menu options.

Introduction

One of the most important steps in troubleshooting a PC system is accessing the Windows startup menu. This menu is accessed at startup by holding down the [F8] key, or the [Ctrl] key for later operating systems, such as Windows Me. In Windows 98, a menu with six choices appears on the screen. You simply highlight the appropriate option and press [Enter] to select your startup choice.

Typical choices are listed below:

Normal
Logged (\BOOTLOG.TXT)
Safe mode
Safe mode with network support
Step-by-step confirmation
Command prompt only
Safe mode command prompt only
Previous version of MSDOS

Normal is selected to boot the PC as it would be under ordinary conditions or if you have accessed the menu accidentally.

Selecting the **Logged (\BOOTLOG.TXT)** option creates a file, named bootlog.txt, that records the boot process activities. Choose this option if you wish to create a boot log of the activities. The boot log can be later opened in safe mode using notepad. This is a valuable aid for determining the point at which the system locks up during the boot process. The bootlog.txt file is saved in the root directory of drive C.

Selecting the **Safe Mode** option prevents the loading of many drivers and disconnects peripherals. Safe mode disconnects many of the things that commonly cause system startup problems. If a PC is not properly shut down or fails to boot properly, safe mode will be automatically activated.

Selecting the **Safe mode with network support** option allows the drivers that are used with a network system to load.

Selecting the **Step-by-step confirmation** option will step you through the typical startup process. This is a valuable aid for determining the point at which the system locks up during the boot process.

Choosing the **Command prompt only** option loads all the standard components of the operating system except for the Windows graphical interface.

Windows graphical interface can be started from the command prompt by typing the **win** command at the command prompt.

Selecting the **Safe mode command prompt only** option boots the computer using the bare requirements. It does not load Windows.

The **Previous version of DOS** option uses the files that were backed up during the upgrade of Windows. This option is usually used when a problem develops after upgrading to Windows 95.

Depending on the computer's hardware and operating system, some of these options may not appear in the startup menu. For example, you will not see the network options unless the PC is set up to work with a network system.

Equipment and Materials

- PC with Windows 95 or 98 operating system.

Procedure

1. ______ Boot the computer and wait for Windows desktop to be displayed. This step is to ensure that your system is working properly.
2. ______ Look in the root directory to see if the bootlog.txt file exists. Does it? (Note that bootlog.txt is a hidden file.)
3. ______ Shut down the PC, and then restart the computer using the [F8] function key to access the startup menu. If this method fails, hold the [Ctrl] key while booting. If this also fails to access the startup menu, call your instructor.
4. ______ On a separate sheet of paper, list the startup menu options.
5. ______ After listing the options, select the **Safe mode** option.
6. ______ Describe the screen display when the computer is in safe mode.
7. ______ Try opening Windows Explorer by right-clicking **My Computer** and choosing **Explore** from the shortcut menu. Did it work?
8. ______ Try opening the Paint program in **Start | Programs | Accessories**. Can it be accessed?
9. ______ Try opening Device Manager from safe mode. Can it be accessed?
10. ______ After opening Device Manager, open some of the devices such as COM1, COM2, and LPT1. Write down which system resources each is using, such as the IRQ settings and the memory assignments.
11. ______ Use the **Run** option of the **Start** menu to run the program named msinfo32.exe located in the Program Files\Common Files\Microsoft Shared\MSINFO directory. A window labeled Microsoft System Information will appear. The left side of the window displays system information in hierarchical (tree) form, similar to the way

Windows Explorer displays directory structures. Expand the **Hardware Resources** branch by clicking the box to its left. Next, click the **IRQs** branch. Examine the list of IRQs on the right side of the window. Which ones are listed as free?

13. ______ Now select the **I/O** branch. Are any I/O ranges assigned?

14. ______ Now select **Memory** to see the memory assignments. Which memory ranges are assigned?

    Take special note of the information you have just gathered. System resources are not assigned in safe mode.

15. ______ Shut down the system.

16. ______ Reboot the system. This time, select the **Step-by-step confirmation** startup option.

17. ______ What is the first confirmation?

18. ______ What is the second confirmation?

19. ______ Continue through the rest of the step-by-step startup process. It may take a few minutes before the Windows screen appears. Be patient.

20. ______ Now, try experimenting with the other options from the startup menu.

21. ______ When you are finished, please return the PC system to its original condition.

Review Questions

Answer the following questions on a separate sheet of paper. Please do not write in this book.

1. What happens to IRQ settings in safe mode?
2. Can Device Manager be accessed when in safe mode?
3. How might the step-by-step confirmation be used when troubleshooting a boot problem?
4. What does the boot log tell you?
5. Must the PC be rebooted after completing the step-by-step confirmation?
6. What is the difference between the command prompt only and the safe mode command prompt startup options?
7. Can Windows be loaded from the command prompt when the command prompt only option has been chosen?

How is a PC technician able to isolate and correct a problem within a computer with thousands of electrical connections and components? The task is easier than you might think, thanks to the computer's modular design and the systematic diagnostic techniques of the technician.

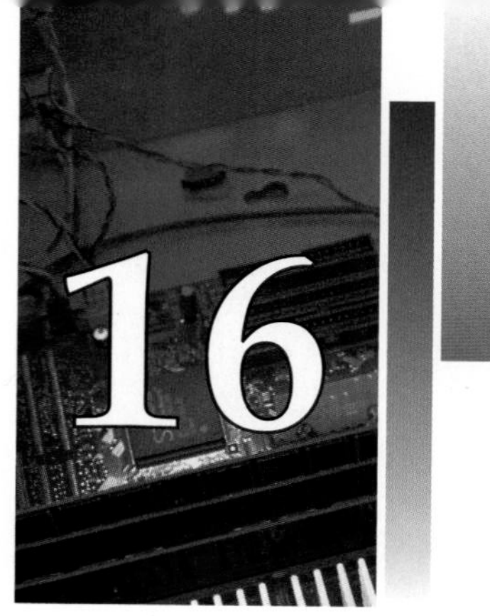

Introduction to Networking

After studying this chapter, you will be able to:

- Identify and describe network topologies.
- Describe the communication theory of a network system.
- Describe the communication principles of Ethernet and Token Ring systems.
- List and describe the layers of the OSI model.
- Describe the installation of a typical network adapter.
- List and describe common network protocols.
- List and describe common network systems.
- Identify common network cabling materials.
- Identify a network's basic hardware devices.

A+ Exam—Key Points

Be sure you can identify the layers of the OSI model and identify the various network topologies. You should be familiar with network protocols. Also, know how to use **Control Panel** to install a network interface card manually.

Key Words and Terms

The following words and terms will become important pieces of your computer vocabulary. Be sure you can define them.

active hub
backoff interval
British Naval Connector (BNC)
bus topology
Carrier Sense Multiple Access with Collision Avoidance (CSMA/CA)
Carrier Sense Multiple Access with Collision Detection (CSMA/CD)
client
client/server model
coaxial cable
cross talk
dedicated server
Ethernet network
fiber-optic cable
hub
hybrid topology
local area network (LAN)
media access code (MAC) address
mesh topology
metropolitan area network (MAN)
Multistation Access Unit (MAU)
network
network interface card (NIC)
node
Open Systems Interconnection (OSI)
packet
passive hub
peer-to-peer network
protocol suite
query
ring topology
segment
sequence number
server
star topology
switching hub
token
token bus network
Token Ring network
topology
twisted pair cable
wide area network (WAN)
wireless topology

The technical support of multiple computers in the home and office requires special skills. As a technician, you must have a basic understanding of the principles and operation of networked computers. The next four chapters will introduce you to the basic knowledge required to successfully network and support a small group of computers and related equipment. All technicians will encounter some form of a network when troubleshooting a computer system. In recent years, CompTIA has increased the percentage of questions related to networking on the A+ Certification exams.

Networks—What Are They?

network
two or more computers connected together for the purpose of sharing data and resources.

A computer ***network*** consists of two or more computers connected together for the purpose of sharing data and resources. Networked computers can share data, hardware, programs, and provide a means of e-mail communications and video conferencing. See **Figure 16-1.**

In the illustration, there are several computer stations connected to a server. A server is usually the most powerful computer in the network system. It contains the network operating system (NOS) on its hard drive. The server also controls network security and communications. There are many benefits to using networks. Networks often increase the productivity, cost effectiveness, and security of the institution using them because they allow different parties to interact and share data quickly. These benefits are worth looking at more closely.

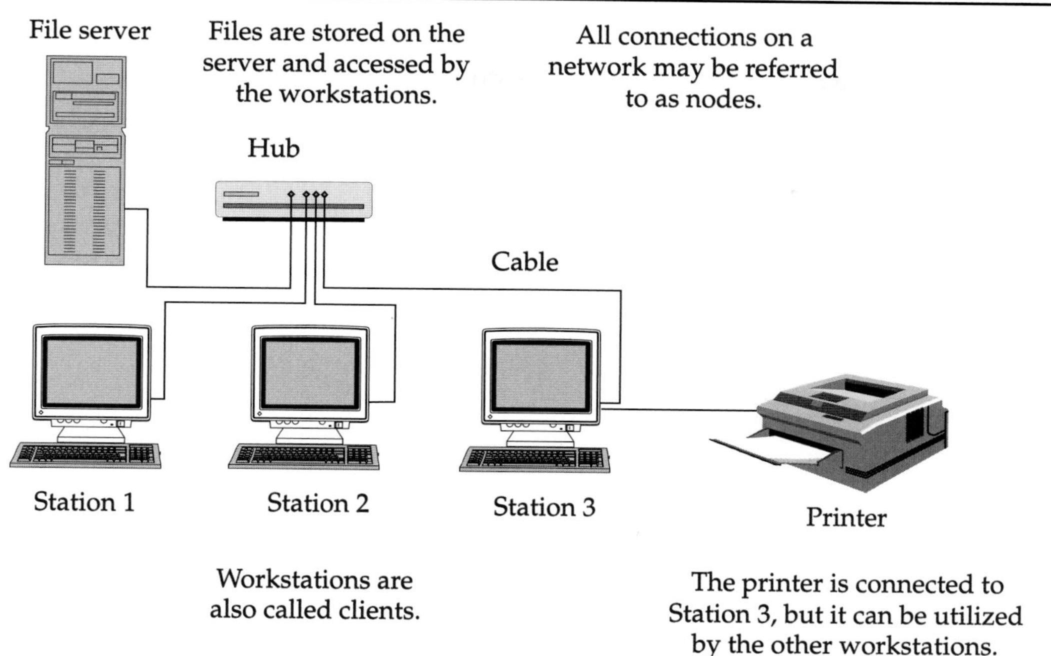
File server
Files are stored on the server and accessed by the workstations.
All connections on a network may be referred to as nodes.
Hub
Cable
Station 1
Station 2
Station 3
Printer
Workstations are also called clients.
The printer is connected to Station 3, but it can be utilized by the other workstations.

Figure 16-1. A simple client/server network.

Shared Resources

Networks provide an economical solution for sharing hardware such as printers. Look again at Figure 16-1. A printer is connected to one of the PC stations. When connected as a network device, the printer can be accessed by any of the stations connected to the network. Through this arrangement, all the computers on the network share a common printer instead of each having its own expensive printer.

Shared Data

The main reason for installing a network system is to simultaneously share data among a large group of computer users. For example, a company that sells computer parts has sales, supply, distribution, and accounting departments. If the company did not have a computer network, daily operation would depend on written or verbal communication between these departments. The various departments would have to work very closely and carefully to organize such complex tasks as ordering inventory for projected seasonal sales trends or reducing sales discounts to slow paying customers.

Before computer networks, this system required a large quantity of paperwork, such as customer order forms, inventory forms, and customer invoices. The completion of these forms consumed personnel time and the exchange of information could take days or even weeks depending on the size of the company. A network system alleviates the lag time required to match customer orders to warehouse inventory and distribution. The sales department has immediate access to the warehouse and distribution system of the company. Customer orders are processed instantly. In addition, there is no need to do a physical inventory of the warehouse because a running tally is kept electronically for each item in the inventory.

As soon as the sales force enters an order, the products can be pulled from the warehouse, sent to distribution, and put in the mail or loaded on a delivery truck. The invoice can be generated at the same time and automatically mailed to the customer. If the inventory levels drop below predetermined limits, the items are automatically reordered or manufactured to replenish the inventory. In addition to the above steps, a customer's information is added to the customer list, which can be used for catalog distribution.

This speed can only be achieved with a computer network. The inventory, billing, and distribution information is stored on the file server and shared by all who require it.

Computer System Management

A network can make the management of a large number of computers much easier. For example, distribution of new software or upgrades can be handled quicker using a network system than individual stations. Think of a large corporate network consisting of hundreds or even thousands of computers. If the word-processing application used by the company's personnel is installed in one central location and accessed by all users, it is relatively easy to upgrade or swap with a new software package. In contrast, loading software onto hundreds of computers can be very time-consuming.

Productivity

A folder of information such as a client list containing telephone numbers, addresses, and e-mail addresses can be easily and instantly shared by users on a network system. A business's inventory can be constantly updated as orders are placed. Shipping can be made automatic.

Cost Effective

A network system is usually expensive, but when compared to the cost of individual workstations needed to accomplish the same scope of work, networks can actually save money. Savings are realized through the sharing of expensive equipment and reduced labor costs.

Security

Security is a major issue in the world today. A network system can limit data access to only authorized personnel. Network system software can determine who can read, copy, or erase the contents of a file. The network can also keep a log of all files accessed, who accessed them, and which workstation they were accessed from. The hours and days of the week that a user is authorized to use the network can be controlled. The network administrator can control the appearance of a workstation display and the programs and information the user can access.

Network Administrative Models

There are two main networking models in use today: client/server and peer-to-peer. We will look at both models and compare them.

Client/Server

The ***client/server model*** is an architecture in which the network is made up of computers that are either clients or servers. ***Servers*** are more powerful computers used to manage network resources and provide services such as security and file sharing. ***Clients*** are individual PCs or workstations that access a Server's resources and shared files. The client/server model provides a method for centralized administration of the network.

A network administrator controls the operation of the file server, which in turn controls the workstations' access to the files located on the server. The network operation software located on the file server also controls how each workstation interacts with other stations, printers, and any devices connected to the network. Devices connected to the network are often referred to as ***nodes.*** Nodes are connected together by a device called a hub. A ***hub*** is used to provide a quick and easy method of connecting network equipment together by cables. The cables simply plug into the hub. A typical client/server network is represented in Figure 16-1.

client/server model
networking model in which the network is made up of computers that are either clients or servers.

server
powerful computers used to manage network resources and provide services such as security and file sharing.

client
individual PC or workstation that accesses a Server's resources and shared files.

node
device connected to a client/server network.

hub
device used to provide a quick and easy method of connecting network equipment together by cables.

dedicated server
server with special functions, such as file servers, print servers, database servers, Web page servers, and administrative servers.

query
locating and extracting data from a database system.

Servers

The server is very similar to the standard PC in design. In fact, early versions of servers were simply PCs designated as servers. Today, many small networks still use a typical PC for the network server. For large network systems, the server is an enhanced, more powerful PC. It may contain two, four, or more CPUs and ten times the amount of RAM normally found on a typical PC. The additional RAM and CPUs allow faster processing of information when connected to many stations. The server is usually equipped with several hard drives. The server may also have a duplicate set of hard drives used to back up the data saved on the first set of hard drives. Backup systems for servers will be covered in greater depth later in the textbook.

A network system may consist of one or more servers, each having a special function. Servers with special functions are referred to as ***dedicated servers.*** Some types of dedicated servers are file servers, print servers, database servers, Web page servers, and administrative servers. A file server is used to store data files that can be accessed by individual workstations. A printer server coordinates printing activities between PCs and network printers. An administrative server may be used to administer network security and activities. A database server contains data files and software programs that query the data. ***Query*** is a term used to describe locating and extracting data from a database system. A common server software system, Microsoft SQL server, is a typical database query software package.

Clients

Clients are computers connected to the client/server network and access network resources controlled by the server. The term client is also used to define the software program that runs on a computer and accesses the resources on the network. For example, an e-mail client is used to send and receive e-mail stored on the network e-mail server. Clients are also cross-platform. For example, you can connect a client running a Microsoft Windows operating system such as Windows XP to a server running Novell NetWare, UNIX, or Linux.

Peer-to-Peer

peer-to-peer network
network administration model in which all the PCs connected together are considered equal.

Another type of network administration model is the ***peer-to-peer network.*** As the name implies, all the PCs connected together on this type of network are considered equal, or peers. A typical peer-to-peer network is represented in **Figure 16-2.** Devices on a peer-to-peer network are also connected together by a hub. On a peer-to-peer network, the workstations are typically standard PCs.

Since a peer-to-peer network has no centralized administration, each PC has equal administrative powers over the network. An individual station must grant permission to the other stations before they can access its files or use its hardware. This model is usually used on very small networks of less than 25 stations. It is very difficult to keep an organized administration of this type of network. For example, if all the workstations had to access a database of the company customers, each user would have to be aware of the file location, as well as any other files or software that they may need. The advantages of a peer-to-peer network is that they are inexpensive to install and simple to administer as long as they remain small. Unlike the client/server model, a peer-to-peer network requires no costly network-specific software. You can build a simple peer-to-peer network using only Windows 95 or later and minimal hardware.

Tech Tip:
Approximately 45% of all networks used in the world today are composed of fewer than 25 computers. This number does not include home networks.

Network Classifications—LAN, MAN, WAN

local area network (LAN)
a small network of computers contained in a relatively small area, such as an office building.

metropolitan area network (MAN)
a group of two or more interconnected LANs operating under a single management.

Networks are classified into three major categories. The categories are used to describe the size and complexity of the system. The three major categories of networks are the local area network (LAN), metropolitan area network (MAN), and wide area network (WAN). These classifications are based on the physical size, management, and use of a telecommunication system, such as the telephone network.

A ***local area network (LAN)*** is a small network of computers contained in a relatively small area, such as an office building. It operates under a single management. An example of a LAN would be the computer network in a small business office.

A ***metropolitan area network (MAN)*** is a group of two or more interconnected LANs operating under a single management. An example of a MAN would be a network system on a university campus. It consists of a group of LANs but is limited to the campus area.

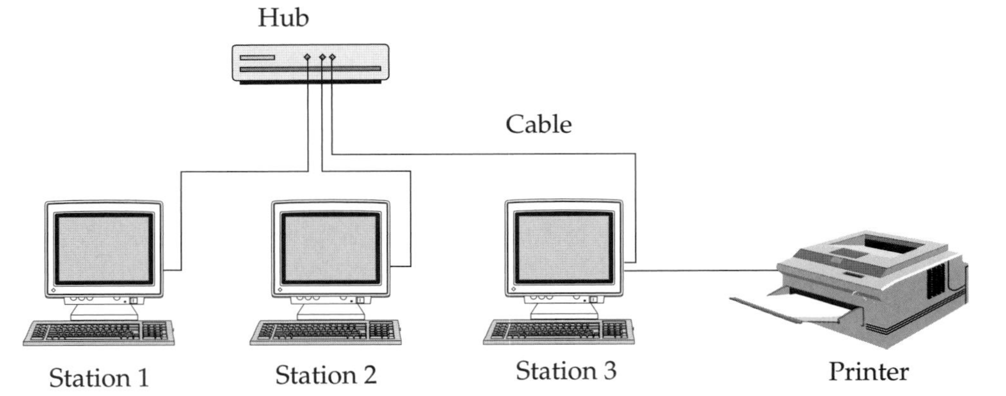

Figure 16-2. A simple peer-to-peer network.

The *wide area network (WAN)* is typically a large number of computers, spread over a large geographic area and under the control of a centrally located administrator. The communication over the large area is made possible by the world's telecommunication network. The Internet is a good example of a WAN. It consists of millions of PCs spread across the entire world. A WAN is usually composed of a group of LANs interconnected through a telecommunication network. See **Figure 16-3.**

wide area network (WAN)
a large number of computers, spread over a large geographic area and under control of a centrally located administrator.

Topologies—Bus, Ring, Star, Hybrid, Mesh, Wireless

The physical arrangement of hardware and cabling in a network system is referred to as the *topology*. The most distinctive identifier of topology is the computer cable arrangement. The three major topologies are the bus, ring, and star. See **Figure 16-4.**

topology
the physical arrangement of hardware and cabling in a network system.

Bus Topology

In a *bus topology,* a single conductor connects to all the computers on the network, Figure 16-4A. A bus topology uses less cable than the other cabled topologies and requires a 50-ohm terminating resistor at each end of the cable. The resistor absorbs the transmitted signals when they reach the end of the bus. Without the terminating resistors, some of the signals being transmitted would be reflected back through the cables, distorting the data being transmitted.

bus topology
a single conductor connects to all the computers on the network.

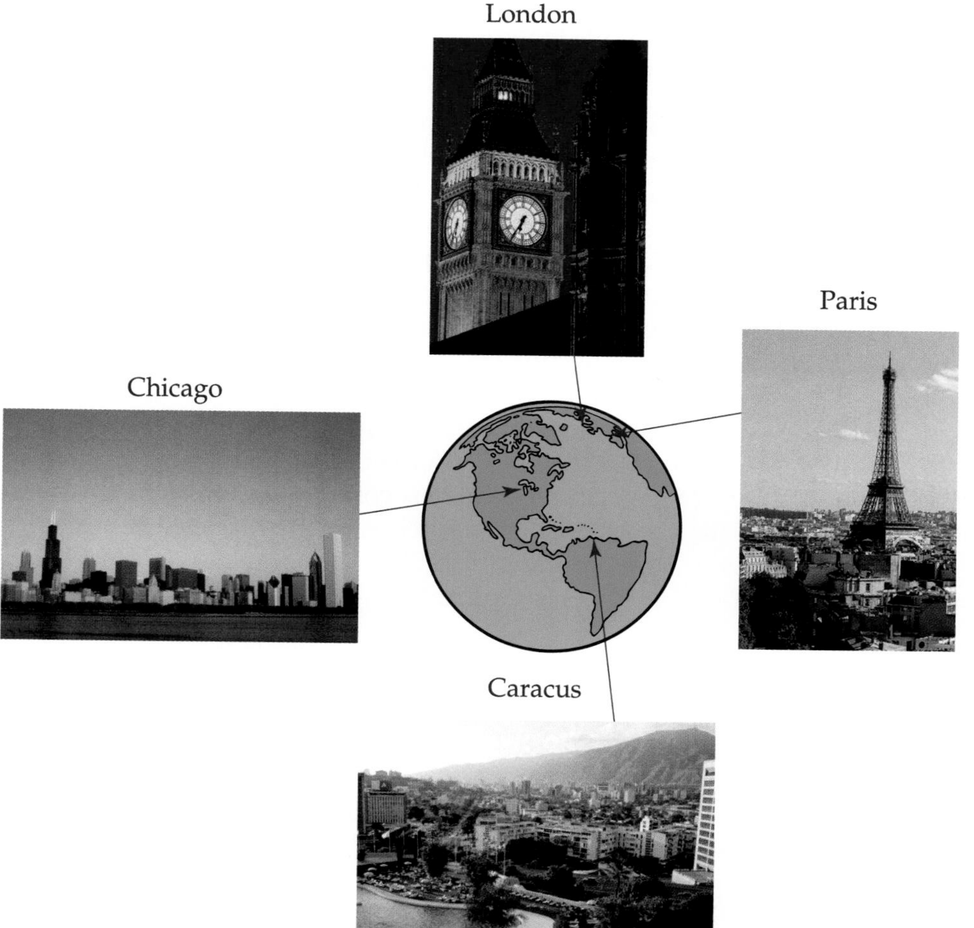

Figure 16-3.
A WAN can be used to connect smaller networks around the globe.

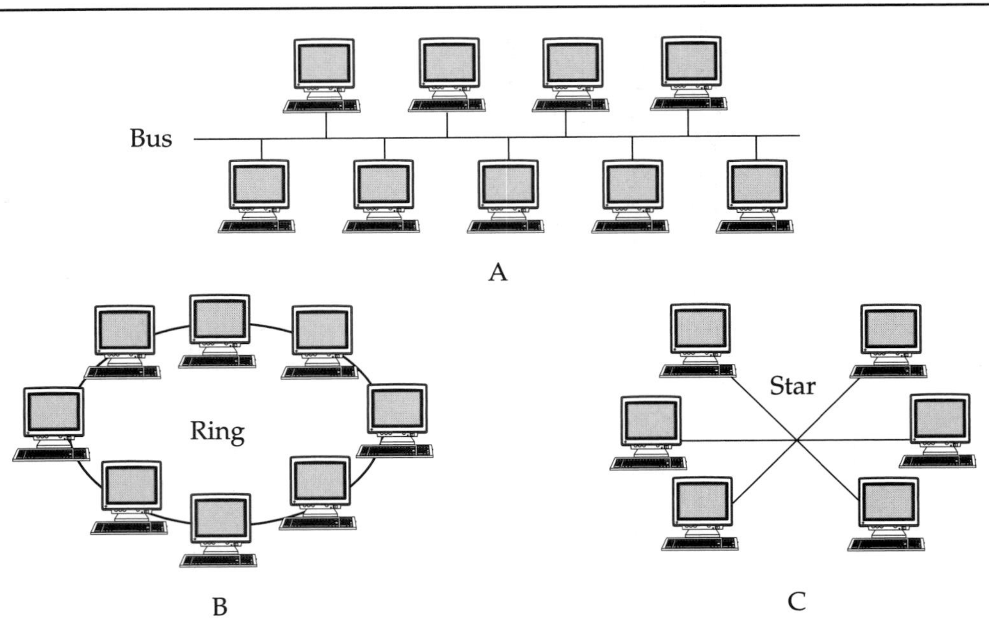

Figure 16-4.
A—An example of bus topology. All workstations are connected to a single conductor known as a backbone. B—An example of ring topology. All workstations are connected in series, forming a closed loop. C—An example of star topology. All workstations are connected to a center point, known as a hub or concentrator.

Tech Tip:
In a bus topology, the single conductor which connects all computers to the network is often referred to as the trunk or backbone.

Ring Topology

ring topology
a single cable that runs continuously from computer to computer.

The ***ring topology*** consists of a single cable that runs continuously from computer to computer, Figure 16-4B. The cable begins and ends at the first computer in the system. The ring must remain unbroken. Depending on the type of equipment and cable being used, a ring topology can resemble a star topology, which is discussed in the following section.

Multistation Access Unit (MAU)
a hub-like device that physically connects computers in a star arrangement while maintaining a ring structure.

When laid out in star form, each computer is wired directly to a central location called a ***Multistation Access Unit (MAU).*** A MAU resembles a hub, but functions differently. A MAU allows quick connection and disconnection of Token Ring cables while maintaining the integrity of the ring topology. The ring's integrity is maintained at the MAU by the use of switches at the access ports. The unused ports act as closed switches, completing the circuit. When a cable is plugged into the access port, the switch is opened. The circuit is completed by the pair of wires running from the PC to the MAU. A MAU is sometimes referred to as MSAU. See **Figure 16-5.**

Star Topology

star topology
a network in which cables run from each computer to a single point, forming a star.

The ***star topology*** is a network in which cables run from each computer to a single point, forming a star, Figure 16-4C. The center of the star is usually a device known as a hub or concentrator. Cables from the network's computers plug into the hub, and it provides a common electrical connection to all the computers in the network.

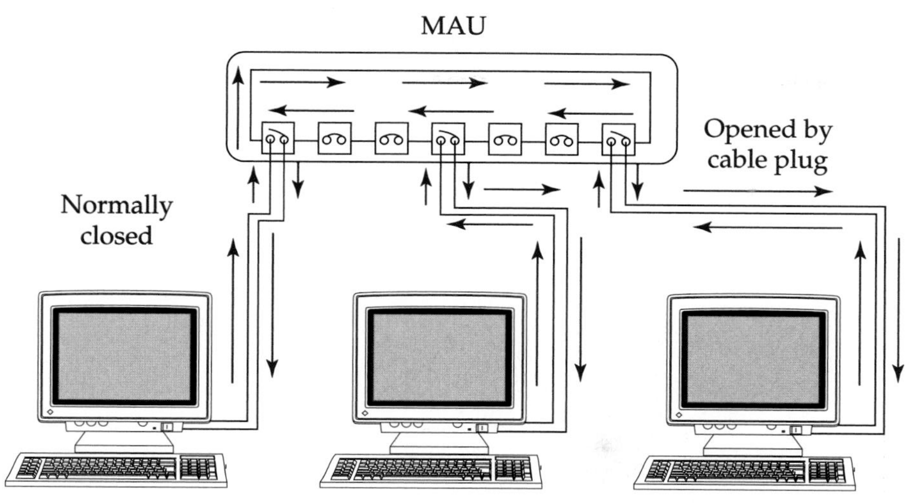

Figure 16-5.
A MAU maintains ring integrity while cables are connected to or disconnected from the network.

Hubs are classified as either active or passive hubs. A ***passive hub*** simply acts as a connection point in the star topography. Transmitted digital signals from one computer are passed to all computers connected to the passive hub and through the hub to other network sections. ***Active hubs*** have a source of power connected to them. When a signal is received by an active hub, it is regenerated. The active hub can be used to extend the range of a signal transmission. The passive hub does not extend the range of the transmission signal.

Some hubs are referred to as switching hubs, or intelligent hubs. ***Switching hubs*** are enhanced active hubs. They can determine whether a signal should remain in the isolated section of the network or be passed through the hub to another section of the network. For this reason, switching hubs are used to divide LANs into different segments.

passive hub
acts as a connection point in the star topography. Transmitted digital signals from one computer are passed to all computers connected to the passive hub and through the hub to other network sections.

active hub
has a source of power connected to it. When a signal is received by an active hub, it is regenerated.

switching hubs
enhanced active hubs. They can determine whether a signal should remain in the isolated section of the network or be passed through the hub to other parts of the network.

A+ Note:
Switching hubs and switches are very similar. In the A+ Certification exams, references to hubs will usually be limited to active and passive hubs, not switching hubs. Switches are referred to as a separate network device, not as a hub. Switches are used to divide networks to make them operate more efficiently. Switches forward network packets based on the packet's destination address.

Examine **Figure 16-6.** Imagine Station 3 is attempting to communicate with Station 1. The switching hub will not allow the data frame to be transmitted through the hub to other parts of the network. The hub directs the frame

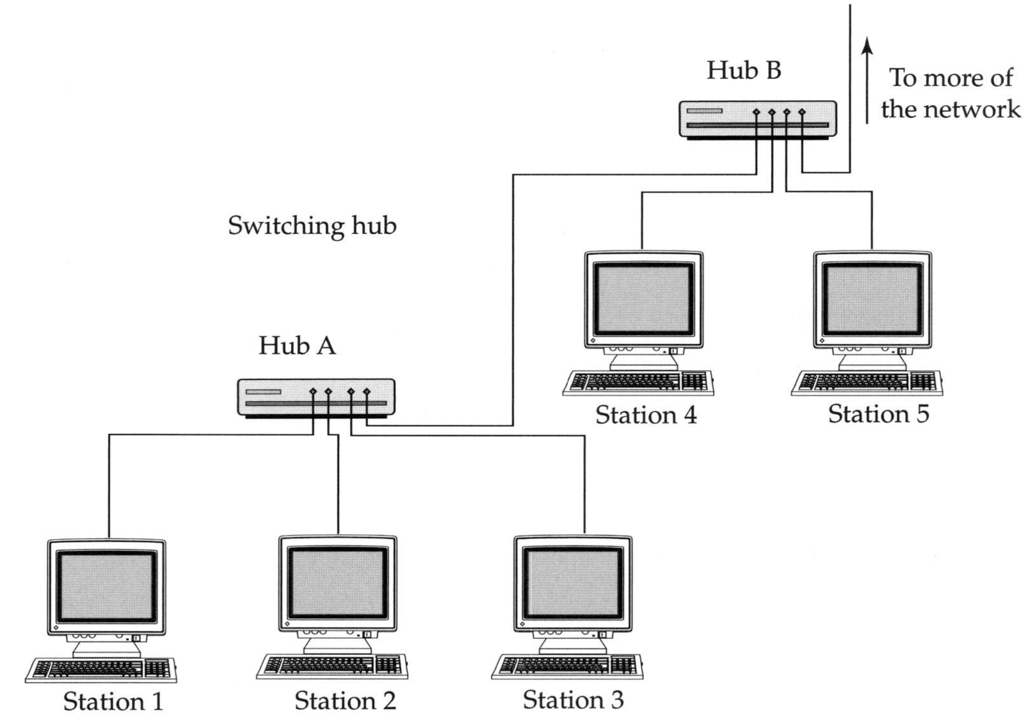

Figure 16-6. Switching, or intelligent, hubs are used to segment the network, reducing unnecessary data traffic.

directly to Station 1. Switching hubs are used to reduce excessive data transmissions on a network. A network with an excessive number of collisions can be broken into segments by adding switching hubs. This can reduce the amount of frames being transmitted over the entire network. This will only reduce the traffic if there are a significant number of transmissions between PCs on the same network segment.

hybrid topology a mixture of star, bus, and ring topologies.

Hybrid Topology

A ***hybrid topology*** is simply a mixture of star, bus, and ring topologies, **Figure 16-7.** Notice the different sections of the network in the example.

mesh topology a network design in which each node connects directly to every other node on the network.

Mesh Topology

Mesh topology is a network design in which each node connects directly to every other node on the network. This is the most reliable network system and the most expensive because of the additional cost of cabling and equipment. A mesh is only practical when the network mission is critical and cost is not a barrier. A network consisting of multiple servers may use a mesh topology to ensure the reliability of the servers. See **Figure 16-8.**

wireless topology uses no cabling system between the computers. It uses either infrared light or radio transmission to communicate between the network devices.

Wireless Topology

As the name implies, a ***wireless topology*** uses no cabling system between the computers, **Figure 16-9.** It uses either infrared light or radio transmission to communicate between the network devices. Unfortunately, infrared transmissions require an unobstructed line of sight between devices to establish connections. This means that nothing can be placed between the computers that would

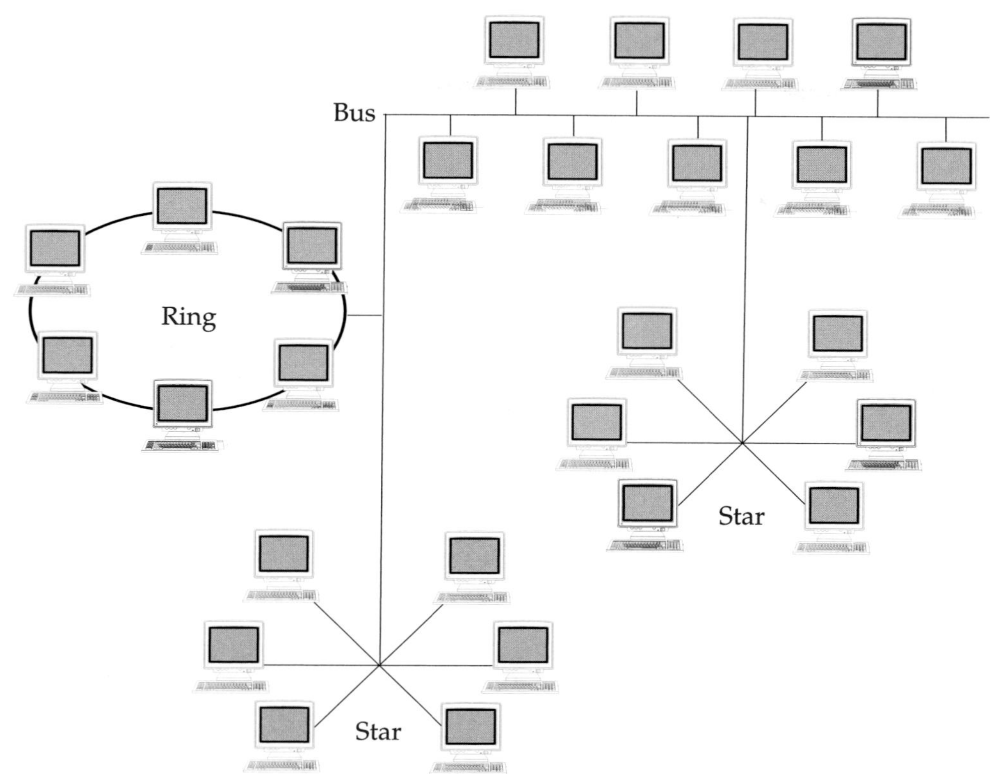

Figure 16-7.
Hybrid topology is a mixture of the other forms of topology. Shown here is a network consisting of all four topology types. Any mixture of topology types, even if it's only two different types, is known as hybrid topology.

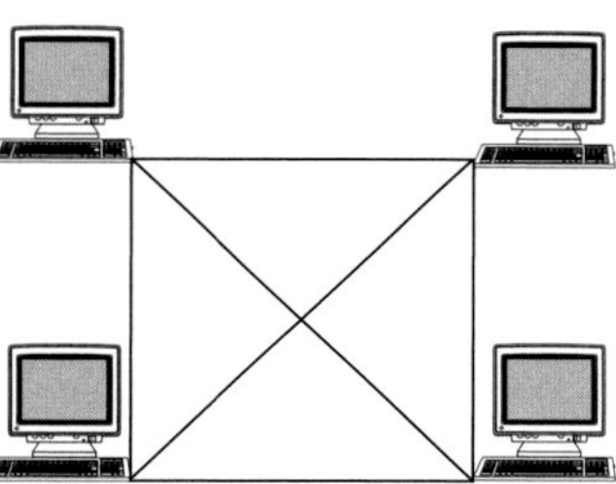

Figure 16-8.
Mesh topology connects each workstation to every other workstation on the network.

block the light beam used for communication. Radio transmission systems don't need a line of sight. However, they can experience difficulties caused by the building structure and other interference generated by a variety of electrical equipment, such as radios, motors, welders, and microwaves.

There are many reasons to use wireless topologies. Wireless topology can be used to connect vehicles to a network. The transmission can originate from a building antenna or even from a satellite, Figure 16-9A. Wireless technology may be used in place of conventional network cabling to bridge a gap between two buildings separated by a wide metropolitan street or a river, Figure 16-9B. Connecting two buildings with cable could be more expensive and time-consuming than installing transmitters and receivers. A wireless system can provide a quick way to reconfigure a computer arrangement, Figure 16-9C. Moving cables to rearrange computer stations may not be as easy.

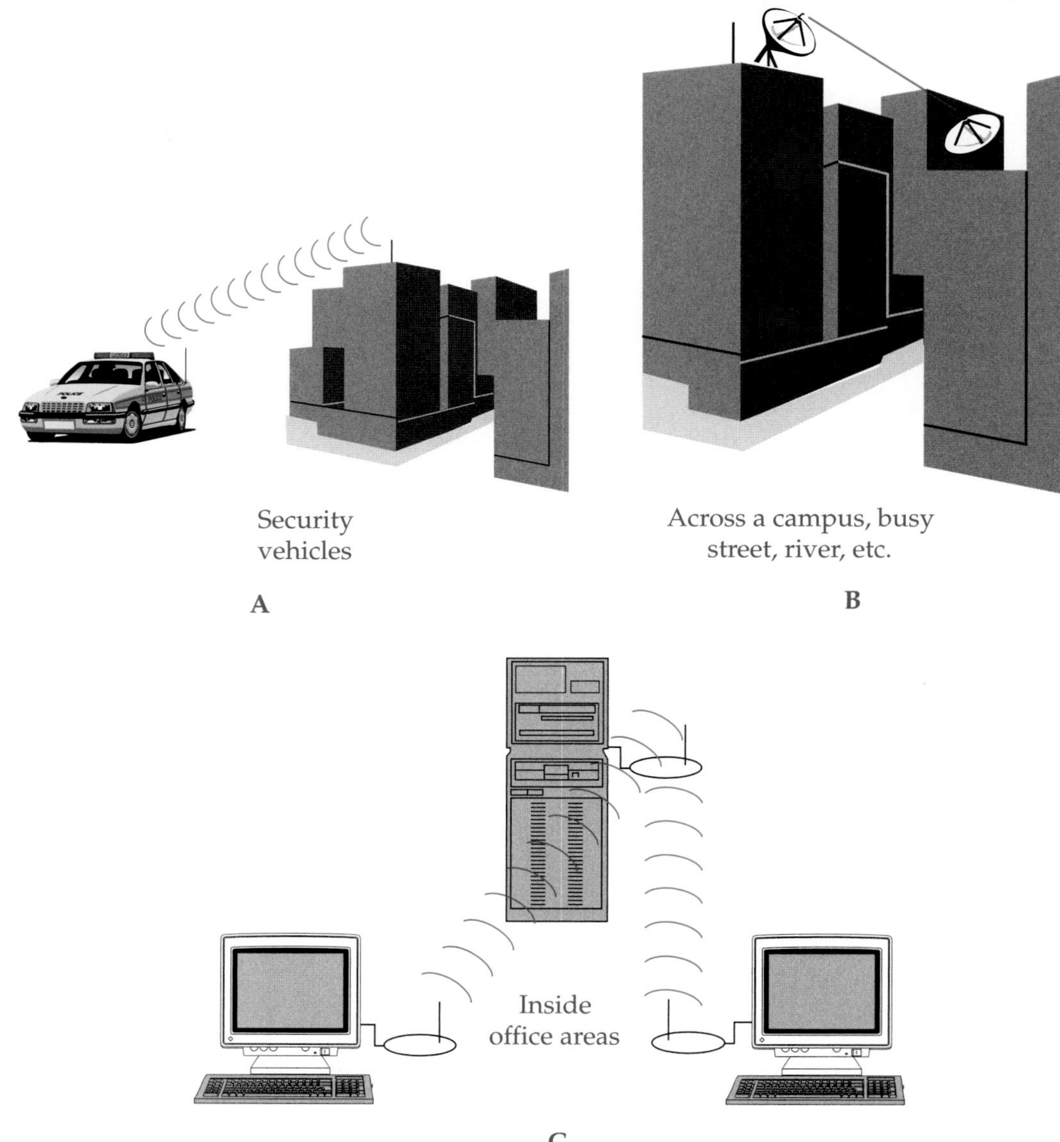

Figure 16-9. A—Wireless topology can be used to connect mobile computers, as found in many police cars, to a stationary network. B—Wireless topology can bridge a gap between buildings where cable connection is impractical. C—A wireless topology can also be used to connect workstations to a server.

Segments

segment a section of cable between two network devices. Also, a portion of a network that shares a common collision or token passing domain.

The term ***segment*** can be applied to a physical portion of a network or to a logical portion of a network. In the physical sense, a segment is a section of cable between two network devices. It can be the backbone or drop cables in a bus topology, the cables between nodes and hubs or hubs and hubs in a star topology, or a single cable in a ring topology, **Figure 16-10A.**

In a logical sense, a segment is a portion of a network that shares a collision or token passing domain. It is often bounded by routers and switches. This definition will become clearer to you when you learn about how networks communicate.

A logical segment varies according to the type of topology to which the term is applied. In a bus topology, a segment is the complete section of backbone and nodes. In a ring topology, it is the complete ring. In a star topology, it is the complete star. See **Figure 16-10B.**

Figure 16-10.
A—Examples of physical segments in various topologies. B—Examples of logical segments in various topologies.

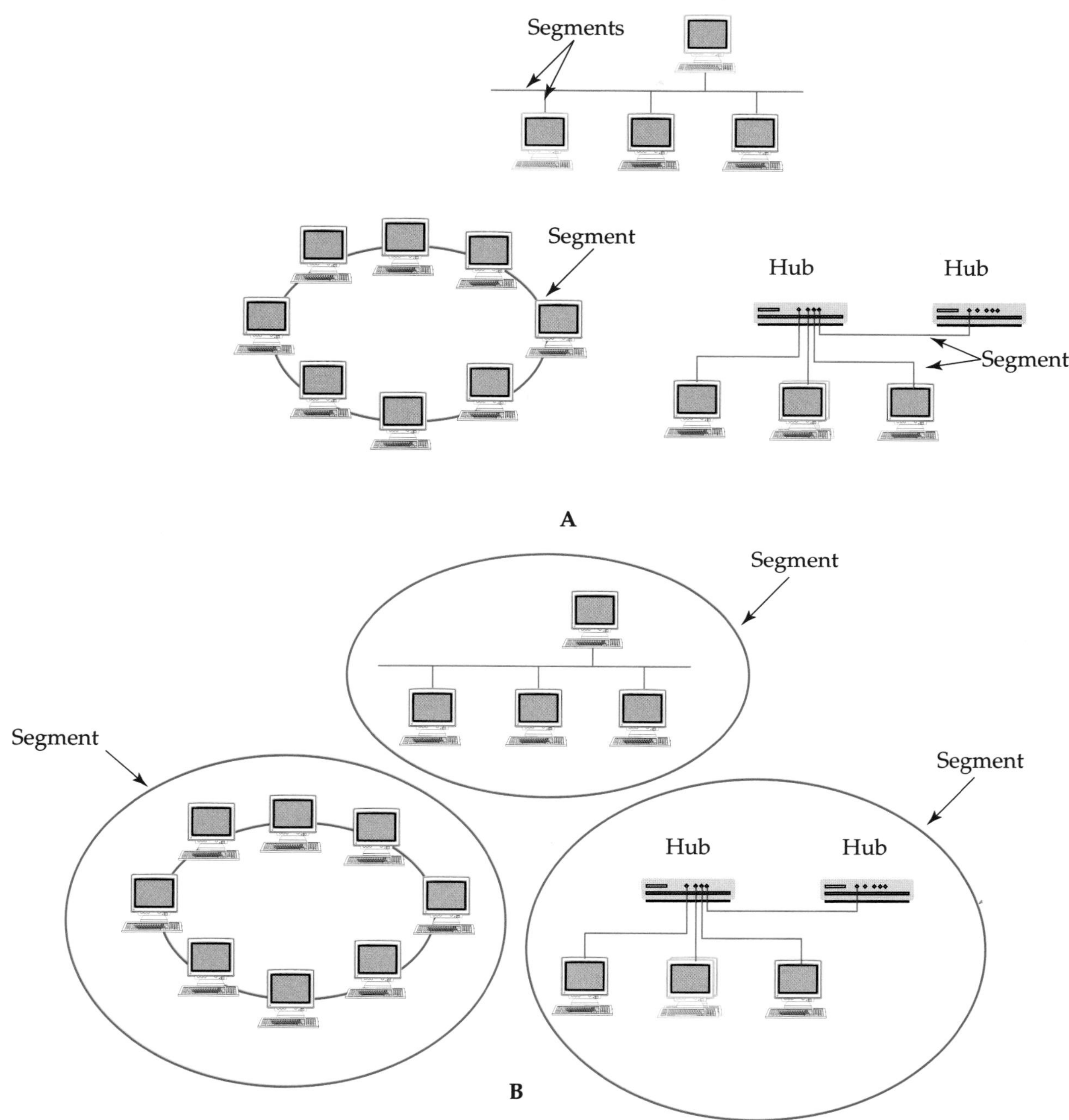

How Networks Communicate

For two or more computers to communicate, they must use the same system of identification and data transfer. There are two main communications schemes used by networks: Ethernet and Token Ring. In each of these types, data is

packet
small unit of data into which larger amounts are divided for passage through a network.

divided into smaller units called ***packets*** or ***frames*** before it is transmitted across the network. Like an envelope going through the mail system, each packet contains the address of the sender and the intended recipient. When all of the packets have arrived at their destination, they are reassembled to form a complete message or file.

How Data Is Packaged

Data is sent across a network in the form of digital pulses, or rapidly changing levels of voltages. For data to be sent across a network from node to node, a common data-packaging scheme must be used. The sequence and length of the information is the key to coding and decoding the data frames.

The digital pulses represent binary and hexadecimal codes, which in turn represent the data that is being transmitted. Different network operating systems use different encoding schemes for transmitting their data. In a typical data frame, the first six bytes represent the *network interface card (NIC)* to which the data is being sent. The NIC is identified by its *media access code (MAC) address.* NICs and MAC addresses are discussed more thoroughly later in this chapter.

The second six bytes represent the NIC that is transmitting the data. Again, the MAC address of the sending NIC is used. Additional blocks of encoded data may contain information such as the length of the particular packet being sent, a sequence number for the packet, and an error checking code. Error checking is incorporated into the packet to ensure the data was not corrupted during transmission. A frame of data has a maximum length, usually approximately 1500 bytes.

sequence number
attached to each packet of data being transmitted, ensuring that the data will be reassembled in the exact order it was transmitted.

A ***sequence number*** is attached to each packet of data. The sequence number ensures the data will be reassembled in the exact order it was transmitted. Some network systems, such as the Internet, are very complex. The various packets of information that make up a message may not be routed through the same path and may not arrive at their destination in the same order they were sent. Packets of information arriving at different times would be garbled when reassembled.

The amount of time it takes data to arrive at its destination is influenced by three major factors:

- Length of route taken.
- Type of media and equipment used to route the data.
- Amount of data traffic on that particular route.

Protocols

For computers to be capable of communicating with each other, they must use the same protocol. A *protocol* is a set of rules for formatting the data stream transmission between two computers or devices and for describing how to transmit data, usually across a network. Data can be transmitted between two computers in small packets or as a steady stream of data. The protocol determines the size of the packets. It also compresses the information to allow for faster transmission rates, verifies that the information transmitted is complete, and reassembles the information packets when they are received. The protocol usually has some error-checking capabilities.

Common protocols are listed here:

- NetBEUI (NetBIOS Enhanced User Interface).
- TCP/IP (Transmission Control Protocol /Internet Protocol).
- FIP (Fast Infrared Protocol).
- IPX/SPX (Internet Packet Exchange /Sequenced Packet Exchange).
- ATM (Asynchronous Transfer Mode).

Protocol Suites

Some protocols are actually a collection, or suite, of protocols. Both TCP/IP and IPX/SPX are examples of a protocol suite. While TCP/IP and IPX/SPX consist of two major protocols (separated by the slash, "/"), they both combine many more protocols to offer a vast array of services to the end user. ***Protocol suites*** are combinations of individual protocols each designed for specific purposes.

protocol suite combination of individual protocols each designed for specific purposes.

Some protocols within a suite guarantee delivery of a data packet while others do not. For example, if a command is issued from one computer on a local network to another on the same local network, delivery is almost guaranteed. No method of checking for delivery is absolutely necessary. If one computer is sending a message to another across the United States, a method needs to be used to verify delivery.

As technology progresses, newer protocols must be added to existing suites. For example, when transmitting a collection of data, such as a large document, there is no requirement that the individual packets that represent the entire document arrive at the destination in proper sequence or with extraordinary speed. The document can be reassembled at the final destination in a reasonable amount of time. However, when transferring data such as sound or video, data must be received in proper sequence in a short period of time. A telephone conversation that is broken into packets and received out of order sounds garbled. Protocols constantly evolve and grow as new technologies emerge.

NetBEUI

NetBIOS is software that provides basic services for the transfer of data between nodes, allowing a computer to communicate with many other computers. NetBEUI is an enhanced version of NetBIOS. IBM and Microsoft jointly developed the *Net*BIOS *E*nhanced *U*ser *I*nterface (NetBEUI) protocol. This simple protocol is used for small network systems of 100 or fewer computers. The ideal small computer network system for NetBEUI consists of 25 computers or fewer. If more than 25 computers are installed on a network using the NetBEUI protocol, the system starts to slow down significantly because of user activity.

TCP/IP

Transmission Control Protocol/ Internet Protocol (TCP/IP) is the standard default Internet protocol used today. It was developed for UNIX to communicate over the Internet. TCP/IP is the combination of two different protocols: transmission control protocol and Internet protocol. TCP is designed to guarantee delivery of all packets. It simply delivers packets and assumes they are received. TCP/IP is the default protocol installed in a Windows operating environment.

FIP

Fast Infrared Protocol (FIP) is used for transmitting data from laptop computers to desktop PCs without the use of cables. This protocol governs the transmission of data by infrared light.

IPX/SPX

Internet Packet Exchange/Sequenced Packet Exchange (IPX/SPX) is the standard protocol suite of Novell NetWare. IPX/SPX controls how packets of data are delivered and routed between nodes and LANS. The IPX protocol does not guarantee the delivery of a complete message, but SPX does.

ATM

Asynchronous Transfer Mode (ATM) is a protocol used for transmitting data, voice, and video simultaneously over the same line. It rearranges the packets in such a way that the quality of the voice or video will not be degraded when transmitted. Data is broken into packets containing 53 bytes each, which are switched between any two nodes in the system at rates ranging from 1.5 Mbps to 622 Mbps.

Ethernet

Ethernet network network that communicates by broadcasting information to all the computers on the network.

An ***Ethernet network*** communicates by broadcasting information to all the computers on the network. This is similar to a room full of people talking and one person yelling, "Bob, do you hear me?" Everyone in the room hears Bob's name being called, but only Bob will reply if he is in the room.

In an Ethernet system, each computer on the network is given a unique name; no two computers can have the same name. A computer name can be most anything you desire, such as Station 1, Accounting 3, or even WildBill. Each computer in the system also has a unique hexadecimal address programmed into the network card inside the computer. The hexadecimal address is six bytes long. For example, C0 0B 08 1A 2D 2F is a hexadecimal address. See **Figure 16-11.** No other computer on the network has the same number. Using the hexadecimal number system to communicate would be difficult for humans. Therefore, a database automatically corresponds the unique number of the network card to the unique name given to the computer.

A typical session on an Ethernet network goes something like this. Bob wants to send a message to Sue using the network. Bob uses Station 1 to send data to Sue at computer Station 4. When Bob sends the message to Sue, he is actually sending the message to all computers on the network. However, only Sue's computer accepts the message. See **Figure 16-12.** Let's take a closer look to see how this happens.

Bob's computer transmits the first six bytes of data, the address of the target computer. Next, six more bytes are sent, the address of Bob's computer. Then the message data is sent, followed by the frame check sequence. When Sue's computer receives the transmission, it recognizes its own address in the first six bytes of data and accepts the packet. When the data packet is accepted, the next six bytes, which identify the sending PC (Station 1), are decoded and stored for a return message. Next, the actual message is decoded, and then the transmission is checked for errors. If there are no errors detected, a return message is transmitted to Bob's PC to verify receipt of the message. If Bob's PC does not receive the return message, it will continue to retransmit the data packets until the return message is received.

Figure 16-11.
Close-up of a network interface card MAC address.

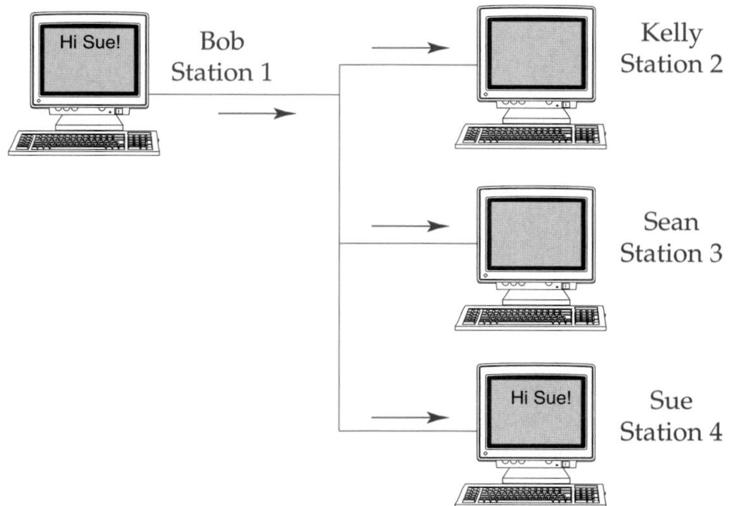

Figure 16-12.
Bob transmits to all the PCs on the network, but only Sue's address can accept the message.

Tech Tip:
The act of sending a message or command to all nodes on the network is referred to as *broadcasting.* Sending a message or command to more than one, but not all nodes, is called *multicasting.*

CSMA/CD

One inherent problem with Ethernet communications is the collision of data being transmitted across the network. When two data packets collide on the network, they both become corrupted and cannot be delivered. Ethernet networks use a protocol called ***Carrier Sense Multiple Access with Collision Detection (CSMA/CD)*** to control and ensure the delivery of data.

Carrier Sense Multiple Access with Collision Detection (CSMA/CD) protocol used by Ethernet networks to control and ensure the delivery of data.

The following passage describes how CSMA/CD works. A workstation listens for data traffic on the network before transmitting data. When the network is silent, the station transmits data to another station. However, another station may choose the same lull in activity to transmit data also. If the data packets from the two stations collide on the network, each station waits a random period of time, known as the ***backoff interval,*** before trying to retransmit the data. The random period is a very small fraction of a second. A typical network can transmit thousands of data packets in one second. Collisions do not usually noticeably affect the performance of a properly installed network. However, a poorly designed network may operate very slowly due to excessive collisions.

backoff interval period of time two network stations wait before trying to retransmit data after data packets from the two stations collide.

CSMA/CA

Wireless communication uses another type of network access called ***Carrier Sense Multiple Access with Collision Avoidance (CSMA/CA).*** This access method is different than CSMA/CD in that it does not detect collisions; it avoids them. There are times when wireless networks cannot detect collisions, so the Ethernet method cannot be used as a media access method.

Carrier Sense Multiple Access with Collision Avoidance (CSMA/CA) protocol used by wireless networks to control and ensure the delivery of data.

Look at **Figure 16-13.** In the drawing, an access point and two computers with wireless adapter cards are connected to a cabled network. The limited range of the wireless network cards does not allow the two computers to communicate directly with each other. They can only communicate with the access point. To prevent both computers from communicating with the access point at the same time, which would cause collisions, each computer must ask permission first. A wireless network card sends a very small packet requesting

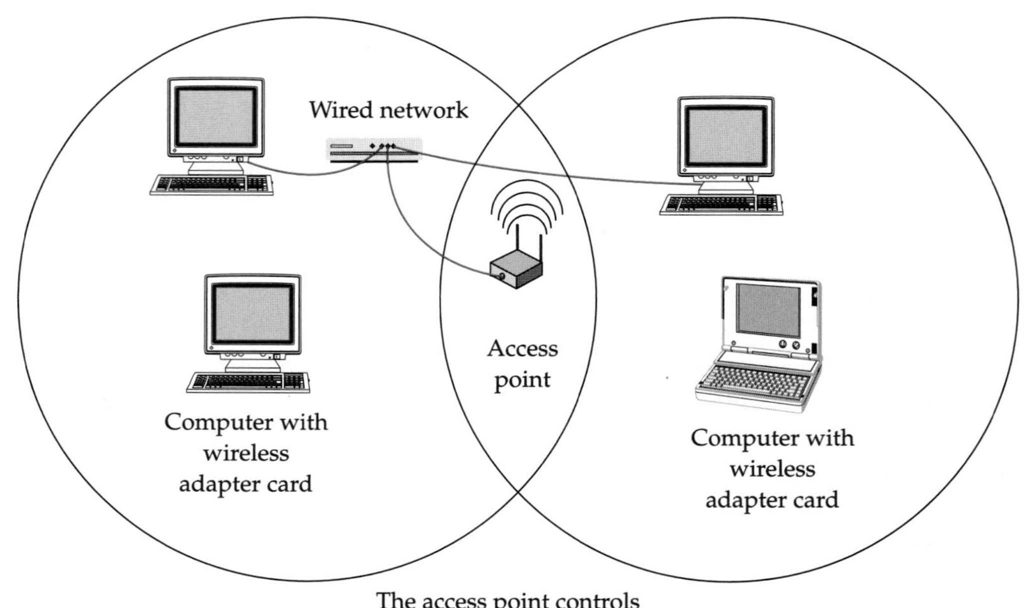

Figure 16-13. Wireless systems use collision avoidance to control communication.

permission to transmit before it sends larger packets to the access point. If the access point is not busy communicating with the other computer on the wireless network, it responds by giving permission for communication. The access point controls all communication. When a wireless network uses a wireless access point to control communications, the wireless network is referred to as an *infrastructure design.* The wireless access point creates a communications bridge between the cable network and the wireless network.

Token Ring

A ***Token Ring network*** is a highly organized system in which each computer must wait its turn to transmit data. A ***token*** is a short binary code generated by the network software and passed from one computer to the next along a ring topology and in some bus topologies. Before a computer station can transmit information over the network, it must seize the token to take control of the network. Unlike the Ethernet design, the Token Ring network was designed to prevent collisions. The data transmission on a Token Ring is organized around the computer that possesses the token.

Token Ring network
a highly organized system in which each computer must wait its turn to transmit data.

token
a short binary code, generated by the network software, that is passed from one computer to the next along a ring topology and in some bus topologies.

A computer or node must possess the token before it can transmit a message or data across the network. Once a computer has control of the token, it attaches a data frame to the token. The token is then passed sequentially to each computer on the network. Each computer checks the destination address in the token. If the destination address does not match the NIC's address, the NIC does not accept the token and it is passed along to the next computer station. If the network card's address matches the token's destination address, the token is accepted and its information is transferred to the NIC's RAM to be processed by the computer. The computer that accepted the token then passes the token on to the next computer and the process is repeated. When the token returns to the originating computer, it is deleted and a new token is created.

By using this scheme, only one machine can control the flow of data at any given time. Although this method may seem time-consuming, you must remember that the process only takes a few milliseconds. One station can control the token for up to 10 milliseconds. After that time, the computer must relinquish its control over the token and wait its turn to resume the data transfer. This prevents one station from dominating the network.

When comparing a Token Ring and an Ethernet network of equal throughput, the Token Ring will process packets faster under heavy traffic conditions than an Ethernet network. This is because Token Ring does not permit packet collisions. As traffic increases in an Ethernet system, so does the number of collisions. When there are an increased number of collisions, the transfer rate slows.

Token Bus

A ***Token Bus network*** operates similarly to a Token Ring. However, a different method is used to pass the token from node to node. In a typical Token Ring, the token is passed to the next physical location on the ring. Since the token bus network uses a bus rather than a ring, a variation of token passing must be used. A list of nodes is created in a database. Each node is identified by a MAC address and computer name. A sequential list of addresses is generated, which becomes the sequence for the token to follow when passing from computer to computer.

Token Bus network
network that uses a token passing system with a bus-type topology.

Network Media

Network media is the means by which an electronic signal is transmitted. An electronic signal can be transmitted via cable-based media or wireless media. Generally, there are three types of cable-based media from which to choose: coaxial, twisted pair, and fiber optic. There are also two types of wireless media: infrared and radio transmission.

Coaxial Cable

coaxial cable
a core conductor surrounded by an insulator.

Coaxial cable, or "coax," consists of a core conductor surrounded by an insulator. The insulator is covered with a shield of either a solid foil or a braided wire layer. The shield protects the cable core from stray electromagnetic interference, which would corrupt the data being transmitted. See **Figure 16-14.** Coaxial cable is difficult to work with and relatively expensive when compared to some of the other wiring media.

BNC (British Naval Connector)
connector used with coaxial cable.

The connectors used with coaxial cable are called ***BNCs (British Naval Connectors).*** **Figure 16-15** shows a typical BNC T-connector, a BNC straight connector, and a terminating resistor. **Figure 16-16** shows an exploded diagram of a BNC coaxial cable connector.

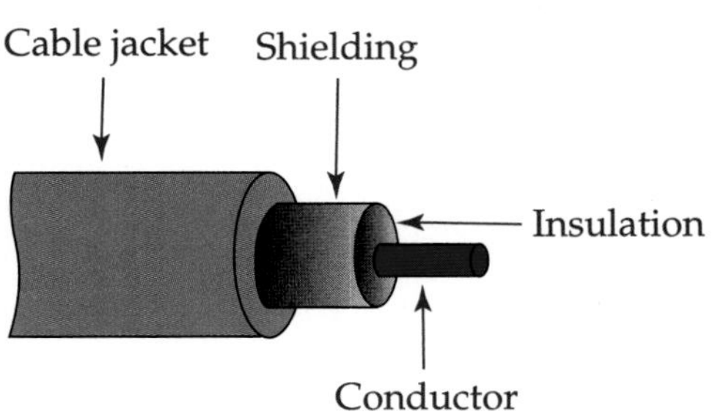

Figure 16-14. The structure of typical coaxial cable is shown here.

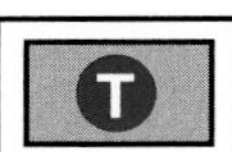

Tech Tip:
The true origin of the BNC acronym is a mystery. The terms British Naval Connectors, Bayonet Nut Connectors, Bayonet-Neill Concelman, Baby N Connector, and BayoNet Connectors all refer to BNCS.

The IBM Data Connector (IDC) and Universal Data Connector (UDC) connectors were developed by IBM to be used on their Token Ring networks. These connectors are rarely encountered today. Token Ring now commonly uses twisted pair and shielded twisted pair.

There are several classifications of network coaxial cable. Coaxial cable use for television is not acceptable for use as a network cable. Its characteristics work well for television transmission but will cause problems if used for computer networks.

The earliest coaxial cable used as network media was thick coaxial cable (10base5), also known as RG-8 or RG-11, or thicknet. Later, thin coaxial cable (10base2), also known as RG-58, or thinnet, was introduced to overcome some of the difficulty associated with the physical attributes of thick coaxial cable. As the name implies, thinnet is much smaller in diameter than thicknet. Thick

Figure 16-15.
A BNC straight connector (left), a BNC T-connector (middle), and a terminating resistor (right).

coaxial cable is difficult to install when compared to thin coaxial cable. Thinnet is more flexible but does not provide the transmission distance that thicknet can provide. Thicknet supports transmissions up to 500 meters per segment while thinnet is limited to 185 meters.

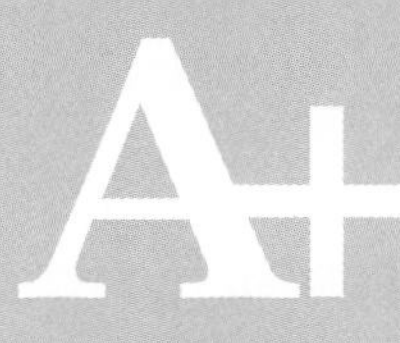

A+ Note:
Be sure to associate RG-58 with thinnet and RG-8 and RG-11 with thicknet.

Computer applications require that the coaxial cable have a 50-ohm rating. RG-8, RG-11, and RG-58 each have the required 50-ohm rating. The coaxial cable used for cable TV has a 75-ohm rating.

A+ Note:
Do not confuse the RG-11 coaxial cable with the RJ-11 connector. They are distinctly different. If an exam question asks about the connector used for a phone jack, don't be confused if RG-11 appears as a possible answer.

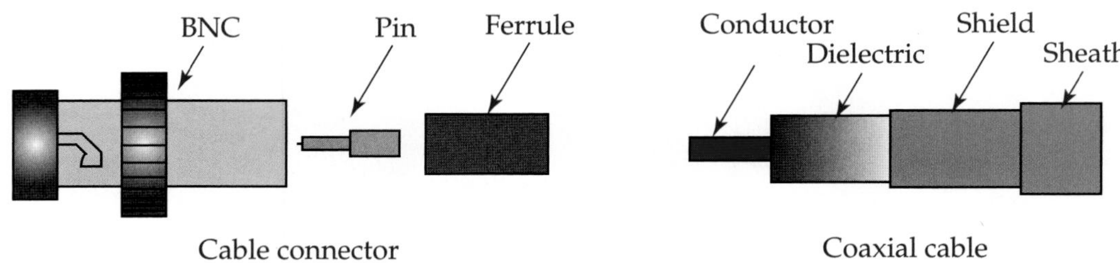

Figure 16-16. Exploded view of a standard coaxial cable connector.

Tech Tip:
The RG prefix is an acronym for Radio Guide. The coaxial cable series was developed primarily as a radio frequency guide (path) for radio signals. Later it was used for video applications, and then much later it was used as a computer signal path.

Twisted Pair Cable

twisted pair cable the most common choice for network wiring. It consists of four pairs of conductors twisted around each other.

Twisted pair cable has been available for many years and was first used to carry voice transmissions by telephone companies. Today, twisted pair is the most common choice for network wiring. It consists of four pairs of conductors twisted around each other.

The common Ethernet network uses only two of the pairs in the cable. Duplex Ethernet uses all four pairs. In a typical standard Ethernet installation, the extra two pairs can be thought of as spares. When only two pairs are used for the network, the remaining two pairs are often used for telephone communication.

cross talk the imposition of a signal on one pair of conductors by another pair of conductors that runs parallel to it.

The twists in the pairs are necessary to eliminate cross talk between the conductors. ***Cross talk*** is the imposition of a signal on one pair of conductors by another pair of conductors that runs parallel to it. Twisting each pair inside the cable greatly reduces the effect of cross talk. This occurs because, when twisted, the two pairs are no longer parallel to each other.

Wire sizes range from #18 AWG to #26 AWG, with #24 AWG used most often. AWG stands for American Wire Gage, a standard method for sizing wire. There are two major classifications of twisted pair cable, UTP (unshielded twisted pair) and STP (shielded twisted pair). The categories or classifications of cable that follow are based on the physical design of the cable. The chart in **Figure 16-17** summarizes the maximum frequency and maximum speed of the most used twisted pair cable types.

Category 1

Category 1 cable consists of two twisted pairs. While this design was sufficient for electrical signals representing voice transmission, it is entirely inadequate for computer networks.

Category 2

Category 2 cable consists of four twisted pairs. This design again is not acceptable for today's networking systems. It was used in some early applications that were limited to 4 Mbps. Today's networks run at a minimum of 10 Mbps.

Category	Maximum Frequency	Maximum Speed
Cat 3	16 MHz	16 Mbps
Cat 4	20 MHz	20 Mbps
Cat 5	100 MHz	100 Mbps
Cat 5e	100 MHz	100 Mbps
Cat 6	250 MHz	1000 Mbps / 1 Gbps
Cat 7	650 MHz	1 Ghz+

Figure 16-17. Common twisted pair cable types and their maximum frequency and speed (bandwidth) ratings.

Category 3

Category 3 cable consists of four twisted pairs, three twists per foot. This can be found on existing networks usually rated at 10 Mbps and 16 Mbps. This is found in many existing telephone installations today.

Category 4

Category 4 cable consists of four twisted pairs. This cable handles 20 Mbps and is only a slight improvement over category 3 cable. It reduced the amount of cross talk generated as well as cable signal loss.

Category 5

Category 5 cable consists of four twisted pairs and offers a transmission speed of 100 Mbps. It is found commonly in 10baseT and 100baseT installations.

Category 5e

The *e* in Cat 5e represents *enhanced.* Cat 5e is an enhanced version of the Cat 5 standard that provides a little less cable loss. It is designed for fast Ethernet and gigaspeed Ethernet transmissions. The Cat 5e standard is actually an addendum to the existing standard to expand the qualities of existing Cat 5 cable.

Tech Tip:

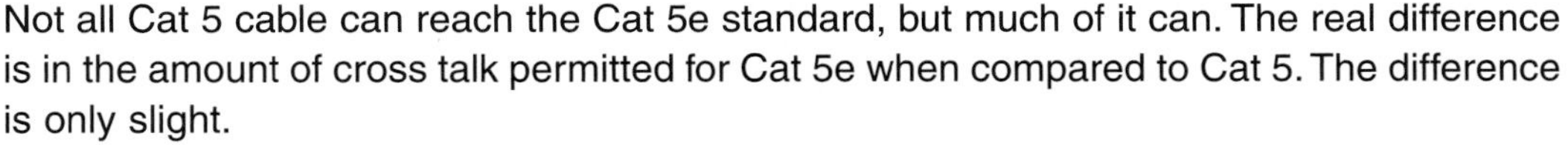

Not all Cat 5 cable can reach the Cat 5e standard, but much of it can. The real difference is in the amount of cross talk permitted for Cat 5e when compared to Cat 5. The difference is only slight.

Category 6

Category 6 cable supports frequencies as high as 250 MHz and data throughput of 1 Gbps. The high data throughput is achieved by using all four twisted pairs of wiring.

Category 7

Category 7 cable provides data transmission speeds to 650 MHz. It uses a different construction technique to achieve the higher transmission speeds. Category 7 is constructed of four pairs of twisted conductors with a protective coating of foil or an electrical conductive braided coating surrounding each pair. In addition to the individual pair protective covering, there is an overall protective foil or conductive braiding surrounding the complete assembly. See **Figure 16-18.**

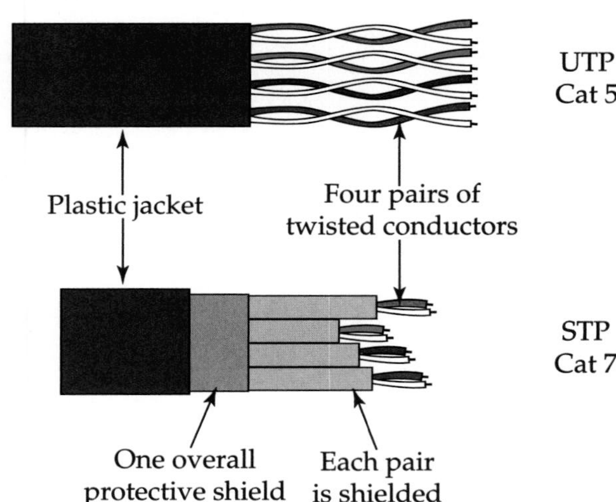

Figure 16-18. Cat 5 is constructed of four pairs of twisted conductors. Cat 6 is similar in construction to Cat 5. Unlike Cat 5 and Cat 6, Cat 7 has individual shielding over each conductive pair, and an overall shield between the plastic outer jacket and the individual-pair shielding.

Fiber-Optic Cable

fiber-optic cable cable that contains a glass or plastic center used to carry light.

Fiber-optic cable, often referred to as fiber, contains a glass or plastic center used to carry light. The electronic signals transmitted from the computer are converted to a signal consisting of a fluctuating beam of light. The fiber-optic cable carries the light signal to its destination where it is converted back to an electrical signal. The use of fiber optics has many advantages over conventional copper wire systems. The advantages include increased security, greater resistance to corrosion, immunity to lightning strikes, longer transmission distances per segment, and decreased weight. Its biggest disadvantages are greater expense and the increased difficulty of field installations. It is ideal for network backbones.

Fiber-optic cable uses two primary types of connections: ST and SC. The main difference between the two is the shape of the physical connector. ST is round, and SC is a square or rectangular shape.

Network Cable Classifications

The Institute of Electrical and Electronic Engineers (IEEE) has classified network cables according to their abilities and physical description. Network cables are classified with a short description such as 10BaseT. The "10" represents the speed of transmission, in this case 10 megabits per second. Note that the speed is rated in bits not bytes. The "Base" refers to baseband, which means data travels across the network one message at a time rather than in multiple simultaneous messages. When a number is used as the last character(s) in the description of coaxial cable, it represents the approximate maximum distance the cable can be used in hundreds of meters. When the last character is a letter, it provides specific information about the cable used. For example, when the last letter is a *T*, the name denotes twisted pair with a maximum distance of 100 meters. An *F* represents fiber-optic cable. The chart in **Figure 16-19** lists the specifications of some common cables. Note that the 10Base2 maximum distance is 185 meters, not 200. However, the 2 serves as a good memory aid.

Classification	Maximum segment distance in meters	Minimum segment distance in meters	Speed in Mbps	Description
10Base2	185	0.5	10	Thin coaxial cable
10Base5	500	2.5	10	Thick coaxial cable
10BaseT	100	0.6	10	UTP
10BaseT4	100	0.6	100	UTP
100BaseTX	100	0.6	100	Two pair of UTP
100BaseFX	2500	1	100	Fiber optic
100BaseVG	100	0.6	100	Four pair of UTP

Figure 16-19. Specifications chart for common cable classifications. Note that 100 meters = 328 feet.

Network Interface Cards

Network interface cards (NICs), also called ***network adapter cards,*** connect the network media, usually twisted pair, to the individual network devices such as workstations, file servers, and printers. The network interface card must be selected to match the motherboard slot type and the network cable styles such as coaxial cable or unshielded twisted pair. See **Figure 16-20.** The card shown in the illustration is equipped with three styles of cable adapter: BNC, RJ-45, and AUI.

The BNC is used to connect to coaxial cable. The DB-15, or AUI, is used to connect to thick coax, and the RJ-45 is used to connect twisted pair. A BIOS chip can be inserted into the ROM socket, allowing the computer to become a diskless station. Diskless stations are covered later in this unit.

network interface card (NIC) connects the network communication media, usually twisted pair, to the individual network devices such as workstations, file servers, and printers.

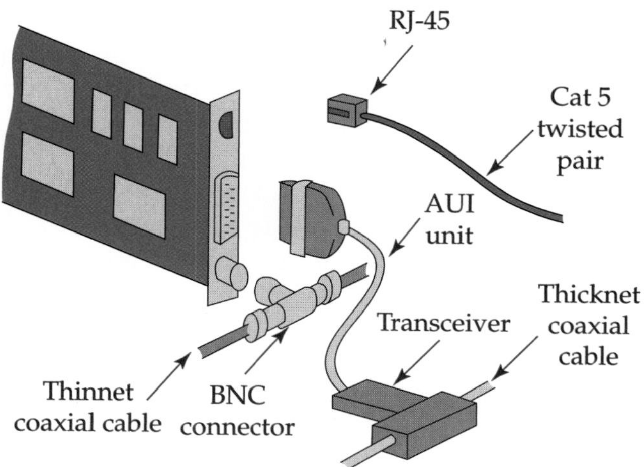

Figure 16-20. The network interface card shown here is equipped with three connector types. The BNC connector is used to connect to coaxial cable. The DB-15, or AUI, connector is used to connect to thick coaxial cable. The RJ-45 connector is used to connect to twisted pair cable.

MAC

media access code (MAC) address a hexadecimal number programmed into the network interface card's chip. The first six digits identify the card's manufacturer. The second six-digit sequence is assigned by the manufacturer and is different on every card produced.

As discussed earlier, each NIC has a unique ***media access code (MAC) address.*** A MAC address is a hexadecimal number programmed into the card's chip. Refer to Figure 16-11. The address is composed of twelve digits divided into two equal sections. The first six digits identify the card's manufacturer. The second six-digit sequence is a number assigned by the manufacturer and is different on every card produced. No two NIC cards can have the same MAC address on the same network. The network uses the MAC address to identify the different nodes on the network. If two cards match, the network cannot communicate properly with either card. The MAC address functions like telephone numbers in a telephone system. If two people had the same telephone number, each one would receive calls that were unintended for them.

The MAC address is often referred to as the *physical address* because it is physically burned into the card. Names used to identify computer stations or network nodes are referred to as the *logical address.* A typical PC has both a physical address assigned through the network adapter card and a logical address assigned by the technician when the NIC is installed. For example, a PC may have a physical address of 0020AF012AB3 and a logical address such as Station12.

The MAC address is also referred to as the Data Link Control (DLC) identifier. In the IEEE 802 standard, the Data Link Layer of the OSI model is subdivided into the LLC (Logical Link Control) layer and the MAC (Media Access Control) layer. The MAC layer communicates directly with the network while the LLC layer uses a protocol such as ARP (Address Resolution Protocol). ARP is part of the TCP/IP protocol suite. The ARP resolves the MAC address to a machine name, such as Station 1. Using the machine name Station 1 is more convenient than trying to remember the hexadecimal code number for the node.

Installation of a Typical Network Interface Card

The NIC must be selected according to the type of slot into which it will be inserted, the type of network connector required, and the speed of the network. Care must be used when handling a NIC, just as with any static-sensitive device.

Firmly push the NIC into the appropriate slot. After it is installed, boot the computer. If you are using Windows 95 or later, the operating system will probably automatically detect the new hardware item, assign the system resources, and install the proper driver. If the operating system does not detect the card automatically, you will have to install it manually.

When manually installing the card, you must also identify the NIC card from a list provided in the **Select a Device** dialog box. You may need to have the driver disk that was packaged with the card. If a disk with the driver files did not come with the card, you will need to download the appropriate driver from the Internet. To avoid a conflict, you must assign the proper IRQ and memory address. By now, you should be very familiar with the proper procedures for assigning IRQ and memory addresses. If not, go back and review Chapter 3—Motherboards. Installing a network adapter card is covered in great detail in your lab activity manual.

Diskless Workstations

A diskless workstation is just as the name implies, a station that works without a floppy or hard disk. Some do have small hard drives, but they are used solely as a cache rather than for data storage. The diskless workstation relies on the file server's hard drive for application software and data storage. As you know from previous study, the hard drive contains the bootstrap program needed to boot the computer station. A diskless workstation is booted from the interaction of the NIC and the file server. The NIC is equipped with a BIOS ROM chip, which contains the boot code needed to boot the station and connect to the network file server.

There are some very strong advantages to diskless workstations. Diskless workstations provide extremely good security. Without a disk system for employees to use, there is no way for data files such as customer lists or account numbers to be electronically duplicated at the workstation. In addition, diskless systems eliminate the possibility of introduction of viruses from floppy disks.

Another consideration is the overall cost of installation. By eliminating the cost of hard drives, floppy drives, and CD drives, there can be substantial savings especially when installing several hundred or thousands of PCs in an enterprise system. Another real advantage is administration of the PCs. Because all workstations are dependent on the file server for their application software, thousands of diskless workstations can be upgraded at the same time. This results in a tremendous savings in man-hour costs of installing software on individual computers. The only real disadvantage is, when the network is down, all workstations are affected.

Hubs

A hub is a device that connects network equipment of a network together quickly and easily. See **Figure 16-21.** The hub in this figure has eight RJ-45 ports for quick connection of twisted pair cable. It may also be equipped with a BNC and AUI connector for coaxial cable.

Hubs may be cascaded to provide more connections or to segment a network (as with switching hubs). See **Figure 16-22.** Compare the daisy chain arrangement to the cascading arrangement. When a network is expanded, the daisy chain arrangement can be used to add additional computer stations to the network. The problem is that most systems are limited to only four hubs connected in this manner. After four hubs, the signal is degraded and data may have to be retransmitted many times before it can be received at its destination. The regeneration of data causes a delay in the delivery of the packets. If the delay is too long, the packet is discarded.

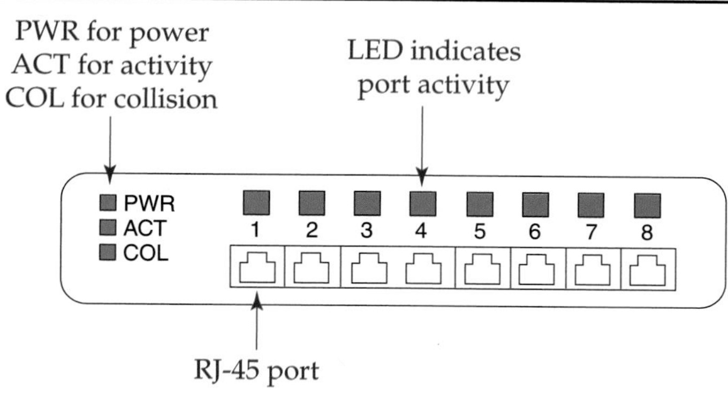

Figure 16-21.
A typical hub. The RJ-45 ports allow twisted pair to be connected. Various LEDs make the hub's current status visible at a glance.

Figure 16-22.
By arranging the network in a cascading hub configuration, data must pass through a maximum of two hubs to reach its destination. With the daisy chain configuration, data may have to pass through as many as four hubs to reach its destination.

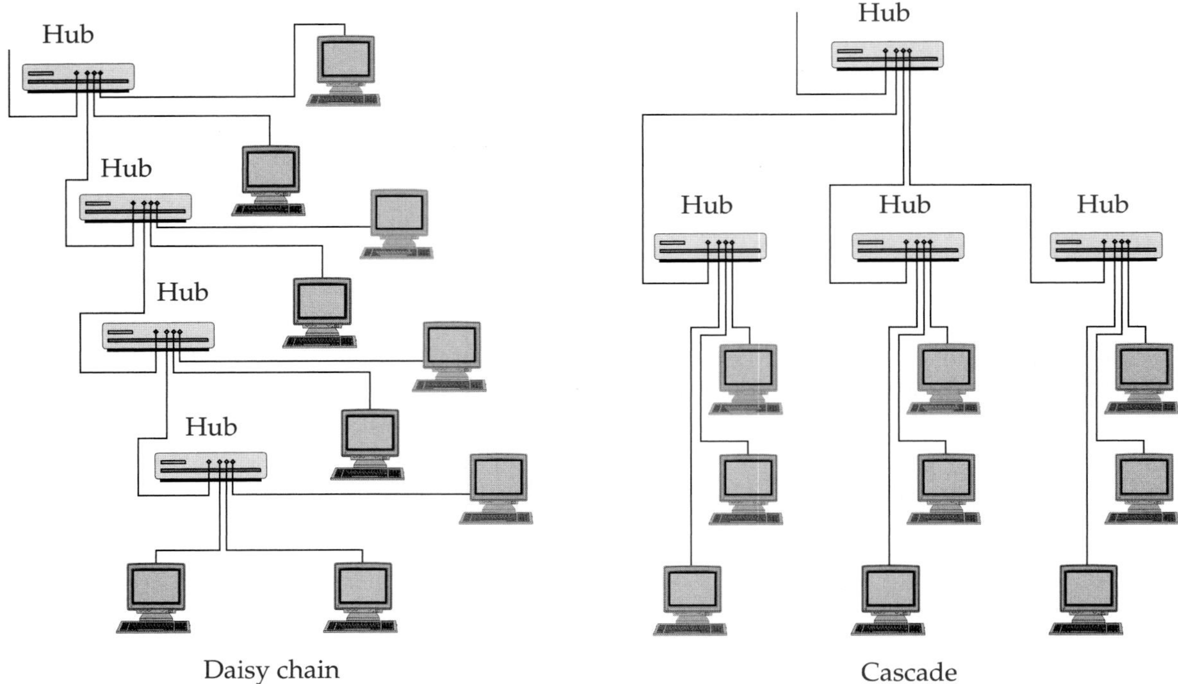

The preferred arrangement is the cascading style. By connecting the hubs in a cascading arrangement as in the illustration, the number of hubs the signal travels through is limited to two. The cascade arrangement allows a greater number of PCs to be connected without traveling through four hubs.

When hubs are cascaded, a crossover cable may be needed. This particular hub is equipped with a selector switch that eliminates the need for a crossover cable. By changing the selector switch to the uplink position, port eight is reconfigured as the uplink port for a cascading hub configuration.

Network Operating Systems (NOS)

The most common network operating systems today are Novell NetWare, Microsoft Windows NT, Microsoft 2000 Server, Windows 2003 Server, Linux, and Unix. The network operating system (NOS) provides communications between the computers, printers, and other intelligent hardware on the network. A network need not consist of a single brand of hardware or software. For example, a network may consist of a Linux server, a Novell server, and client operating systems, such as Windows 98, Windows XP, and Apple all sharing and accessing resources on the network. The NOS is also composed of software programs that provide security, user identity, remote access, and sharing for printers and other devices. Without the NOS, a network would just be a useless collection of parts.

OSI Model

The ***Open Systems Interconnection (OSI)*** reference model was a joint effort of international members to standardize network communication systems. The OSI model describes how hardware and software should work together to form a network communication system. The OSI model consists of seven layers:

- Layer 7—Application.
- Layer 6—Presentation.
- Layer 5—Session.
- Layer 4—Transport.
- Layer 3—Network.
- Layer 2—Data.
- Layer 1—Physical.

Open Systems Interconnection (OSI)
seven-layer reference model that describes how hardware and software should work together to form a network communication system.

Physical Layer

The physical layer is the most basic layer of the model. It consists of the cable and adapter cards. The structure of this layer determines how electrical signals are carried between the devices on a network.

Data Layer

The data layer describes the network's level of operation at which the raw data is packaged for transfer from one network card to another network card. It packages binary numbers (1s and 0s) together into frames or packets for transmission between nodes.

Network Layer

The network layer is responsible for routing packets of data from one card to another across a large network. Routing provides a means of preventing or limiting congestion on large networks. It also can prioritize the transmission of data. As data is being transmitted from one computer to another, several different routes may be used. If the equipment senses too much traffic along one cable section, the data can be transmitted along a different route to avoid the congestion.

Transport Layer

The transport layer's main responsibility is to ensure the data received from a transmission is reliable. It sequences the packets of data and reassembles them in their correct order. The individual data packets that compose a single file or message may arrive by very different routes when transmitted over many miles. Also, the packets of data may not arrive in the same sequence in which they were transmitted, requiring reassembly into the correct order. This correct reassembly is especially important in the transmission of graphic images.

Session Layer

The session layer is the layer at which a connection is established between two different computers. This layer also provides system security based on machine and user name recognition. The session layer and transport layers are sometimes combined. The session layer also resolves compatibility problems between dissimilar systems, such as a PC and a Macintosh or a mainframe.

Presentation Layer

The presentation layer ensures character code recognition. It is responsible for converting the character codes from the originating computer to another form that can be recognized by the receiving computer. An example would be converting ASCII codes to EBCDIC codes. Extended Binary Coded Decimal Interchange Code (EBCDIC) is a character code widely used on mainframe computers while most PCs use the American Standard Code for Information Interchange (ASCII) character code.

Application Layer

The application layer sits on top of the OSI model. The application layer manages network processes such as file transfer, mail service, and file-server database access. Thus far in your study of PCs, when you hear the term *application* you think of application software such as word processing, spreadsheets, and graphic programs. These are not the same applications being illustrated in the OSI model. In the OSI model, the application layer is referring to strictly network applications, such as Web browser and e-mail software. The application is designed as a communication interface for the user. Think of the application layer as a network browser.

The OSI model clearly illustrates the complexity of transmitting data from one machine to another and should be used as a model for a well-designed protocol. Not all software companies follow the strict guidelines of the OSI model. Many systems were already in place long before the model was developed and adopted. Some protocol systems combine two or more layers into a single unit. It is important to remember that the OSI model is simply a guide for future protocol development.

A+ Note:
A+ Certification exams will require some knowledge of the OSI model.

The IEEE 802 Standards

The Institute of Electrical and Electronic Engineers (IEEE—pronounced *I triple E*) is a professional organization that continually develops standards for the networking and communication industry. The organization consists of scientists, students, commercial vendors, and other interested professionals within the industry. The IEEE's network standards are identified with an 802 prefix. Specific standards are listed here:

- 802.1—Bridging and Management.
- 802.2—Logical Link Control and Media Access Control.
- 802.3—CSMA/CD Access Method (Ethernet).
- 802.4—Token Bus.
- 802.5—DQDB Access Method (Token Ring).
- 802.6—Metropolitan Area Networks.
- 802.7—Broadband Local Area Networks.
- 802.8—Fiber Optic.

- 802.9—Isochronous LANs.
- 802.10—Security.
- 802.11—Wireless Local Area Network (WLAN).
- 802.12—Demand Priority Access.
- 802.15—Wireless Personal Area Network (WPAN).
- 802.16—Wireless Metropolitan Area Network (WMAN).

The specifications outlined in the 802 standards are not to be thought of as laws. They are a set of recommended practices that are designed to ensure the quality of a network system. However, if a contract to install a network system refers to the IEEE 802 standards, they should be thought of as law. If a new network is required to meet the IEEE 802 standards and problems arise because the standards were not followed, the installation contractor or designer of the network system can be held liable. The 802 standards will be referred to constantly throughout your studies of network systems. The most up-to-date information on the IEEE 802 standards can be obtained at www.standards.ieee.org/getieee802/portfolio.html.

Summary

- Networks provide a way to share data and hardware.
- The two most common network administration models are peer-to-peer and client/server.
- The client/server model is centrally administered; the peer-to-peer model is not.
- The three classifications of networks are LAN, MAN, and WAN.
- The three common cable topologies are star, ring, and bus.
- Data transmitted on a network is broken down into packets or frames.
- A data frame contains the address of the PC sending the data, the address of the intended recipient, an error-checking program, and a sequence number.
- A protocol is a set of programs that determines the rules for communication between two nodes.
- In general, two computers need to use the same protocol to communicate with each other.
- On an Ethernet network there are many data collisions, which require the data to be retransmitted, resulting in increased traffic on the network.
- Data transmission in an Ethernet network is chaotic.
- Ethernet uses CSMA/CD to ensure the delivery of data.
- The primary choice for Ethernet topology is the star.
- The primary choice of cable for Ethernet is Cat 5 and Cat 5e using RJ-45 connectors.
- Ethernet is inexpensive and easy to install.
- Wireless communications use CSMA/CA to ensure the delivery of data.
- On a Token Ring network, only one node may control the token at any one moment.
- The Token Ring network uses a ring topology.

- Data transmission in a Token Ring network is organized and predictable.
- A Token Ring network is usually expensive and difficult to install.
- The OSI model serves as a guide for troubleshooting and design of network systems.

Review Questions

Answer the following questions on a separate sheet of paper. Please do not write in this book.

1. What are the advantages of using a computer network system?
2. How does a large network server differ from a typical PC?
3. Name three types of dedicated servers.
4. What are the three major classifications of networks used to describe the size and complexity of a network system?
5. The Internet would be best described as a _____.
   a. LAN
   b. MAN
   c. WAN
   d. PAN
6. Six computers connected together in your classroom would most likely be classified as a _____-to-_____ network.
7. Your instructor has a computer that is connected to a powerful computer in another building. This would most likely be a _____/_____ network.
8. Which type of network administrative model has a centralized administration?
9. Rank LAN, MAN, and WAN by their typical sizes, from smallest to largest.
10. What are the three major classifications of network topologies?
11. A bus topology segment is often called a _____.
12. Define a segment for a typical ring and a typical star topology.
13. What does a typical frame of data contain?
14. What three things affect the time it takes for data to arrive at its destination?
15. Describe, compare, and contrast Ethernet and Token Ring systems of network communication?
16. What are the major advantages of fiber-optic cable systems?
17. What are the major disadvantages of fiber-optic cable systems?
18. Name three types of network connectors found on NICs.

19. Convert the following acronyms to complete words and capitalize the letter of the word used to construct the acronym. Example: CPU = Central Processing Unit.
    a. MAU =
    b. LAN =
    c. MAN =
    d. WAN =
    e. ATM =
    f. IPX/SPX =
    g. TCP/IP =
    h. IEEE =
    i. CSMA/CD =
    j. FIP =
    k. NIC =
20. Which layer of the OSI model is mainly concerned with network cables and connectors?
    a. Application
    b. Session
    c. Transport
    d. Physical

Sample A+ Exam Questions

Answer the following questions on a separate sheet of paper. Please do not write in this book.

1. Which statement below best defines a peer-to-peer network?
    a. A group of computers in which each has control of their own resources.
    b. A group of computers controlled by one central computer.
    c. A group of computers in which one is designated the control unit and the rest are defined as peers.
    d. A group of computers in which each computer has the ability to remove any other computer from the group.
2. A network limited to one particular floor of an office building would most likely be classified as a _____.
    a. LAN
    b. MAN
    c. WAN
    d. CAN
3. From the list of answers, choose the one that is *not* a network topology.
    a. Star
    b. Bus
    c. Ray
    d. Mesh

4. Which protocol listed below is commonly associated with Internet communication?
   a. TCP/CPS
   b. IPX/NEX
   c. TCP/IP
   d. TCP/POP3
5. CSMA/CD is closely associated with which type of network listed below?
   a. Token Ring
   b. Ethernet
   c. ARCnet
   d. Subnet
6. The unintentional transfer of data between individual wires inside a network cable, such as Cat 5, is called _____.
   a. impedance
   b. attenuation
   c. cross talk
   d. broadcast storm
7. Which of the following best represents a network card MAC address?
   a. 123.202.16.24
   b. 1673452
   c. 00 A1 23 12 C2 F1
   d. CF12D
8. A Web browser program would be located at which layer of the OSI model?
   a. Presentation
   b. Application
   c. Session
   d. Network
9. Which protocol listed below is associated with transferring data using infrared light?
   a. TCP/IP
   b. PX/SPX
   c. FIP
   d. ATM
10. Cat 5e provides less signal _____ than Cat 5 cable.
    a. strength
    b. loss
    c. quality
    d. cost

Suggested Laboratory Activities

Do not attempt any suggested laboratory activities without your instructor's permission. Certain activities can render the PC operating system inoperable.

1. Construct a small peer-to-peer network using two or more PCs and an active or passive hub.
2. Make a Cat 5 cable for connecting a PC to a hub.
3. Make a crossover cable for connecting two computers.
4. Remove and then install a network card.
5. Inspect and change the various properties found in the **Properties** dialog box under the **Network** icon in **Control Panel**. Be sure to write down all the settings before making any changes. Watch the effect on the PC in the network. You can find more information about each setting at the technical support page at Microsoft's Web site.
6. Set up a network share for a hard drive of a set of files on a PC.
7. Set up a network share for a CD-drive and then access it from another PC.
8. Set up a network share for a printer. Share the printer for two or more PCs.

Note:

There is detailed information located at the Microsoft Web site that can be used to help you accomplish these experiments.

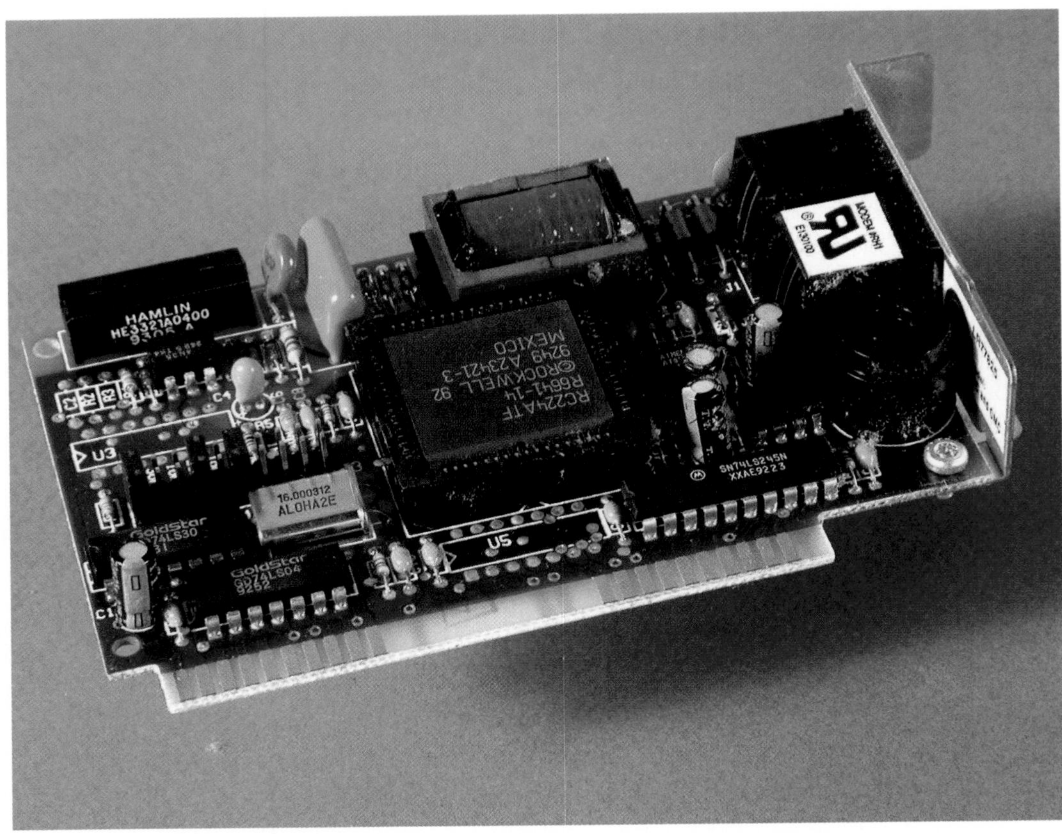

With a standard telephone modem, like the one pictured here, even people in remote rural locations can connect to the Internet, the world's largest WAN.

Chapter 16
Laboratory Activity
Network Adapter Card Installation

After completing this laboratory activity, you will be able to:

- ❏ Install a typical network adapter card.
- ❏ Configure a network adapter card using information supplied by the network administrator.
- ❏ List the requirements needed to communicate on a peer-to-peer network.

Introduction

In this laboratory activity you will install a typical network adapter card, often referred to as a NIC card. The acronym NIC stands for *network interface card.* After the NIC and the proper drivers have been installed, you will select and install the proper protocols for communication across a peer-to-peer network.

The installation of a NIC became much simpler with the introduction of Plug and Play technology. However, there are still times when you will need to configure the NIC properties manually. At other times, you will need to modify or verify NIC properties. In this lab activity, you will verify NIC properties, even if you are using a Plug and Play card.

The following illustration shows the **Network** dialog box. You can access the **Network** dialog box by right-clicking **Network Neighborhood** and then selecting **Properties** from the shortcut menu. It can also be accessed by opening **Control Panel** and clicking the **Network** icon **(Start | Settings | Control Panel | Network)**.

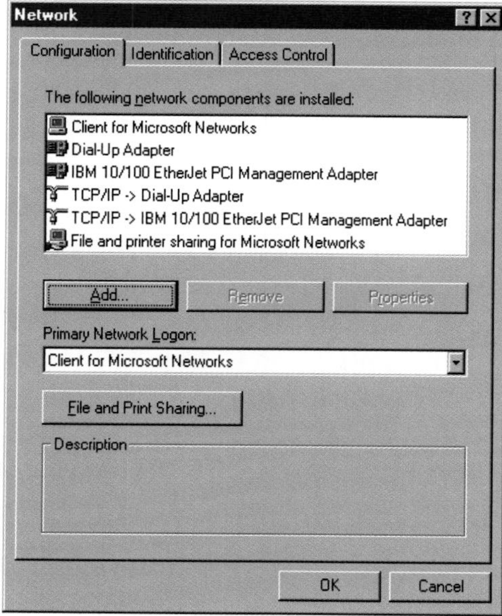

The **Network** dialog box is used to configure the PC on a network. Below is a partial list of some of the things that can be accomplished through the **Network** dialog box:

- Select the type of network protocol to be used.
- Install the drivers for the network card.
- Set up print and file sharing.
- Identify the PC and the workgroup by name.
- Verify and modify Internet properties.

You will use the **Network** dialog box extensively in the next few lab activities. Be sure you know how to access it easily.

Each network adapter has a unique MAC address used to identify the network card to the network system. The MAC address consists of six pairs of hexadecimal numbers, such as 00 1C DF B7 2C DB. The first three pairs of hexadecimal numbers identify the manufacturer, and the last three pairs of numbers uniquely identify the NIC. If two network adapter cards have the same MAC address, the network will be unable to communicate with at least one of the two stations.

The MAC address in the network environment is similar to the unique phone numbers used in the telephone industry. To correctly contact the person you wish to speak to, each telephone must have a unique phone number. The purpose of the MAC address in the network system will become more apparent as you progress through your studies.

After you install the network card, you may not be able to see other computers in the peer-to-peer network. To interact with other computers on the network, you will need to set up a share and be part of the same workgroup. Your instructor will assign you a workgroup name.

Equipment and Materials

- Typical PC with Windows 98 or later operating system.
- Network adapter card with a RJ-45 connection.
- Cat 5 UTP cable with standard RJ-45 connectors.
- Access to a hub to connect your PC to the other PCs.

Procedure

1. ______ Gather all required materials.
2. ______ Before you begin installing the network adapter card, boot the PC to make sure it is functioning properly. If the PC is working properly, shut it down and go on to step 3. If the PC is not working properly, notify the instructor.
3. ______ Make sure the electrical power is turned off to the PC before you remove the case cover. Follow all anti-static procedures as prescribed by your instructor.
4. ______ Before you install the network adapter card, look for the MAC address on the card. Write down the MAC address.

5. ______ Select the appropriate expansion slot (usually a PCI type) in which to install the NIC.

6. ______ Remove the screw that retains the slot cover in place. Save the screw for securing the NIC in place.

7. ______ Insert the NIC into the slot by applying even pressure. Do not rock the card side to side while inserting it into the slot. Rocking the card can damage the conductors that run along the edge of the card. Be sure the card is seated all the way in the slot. See the following illustration.

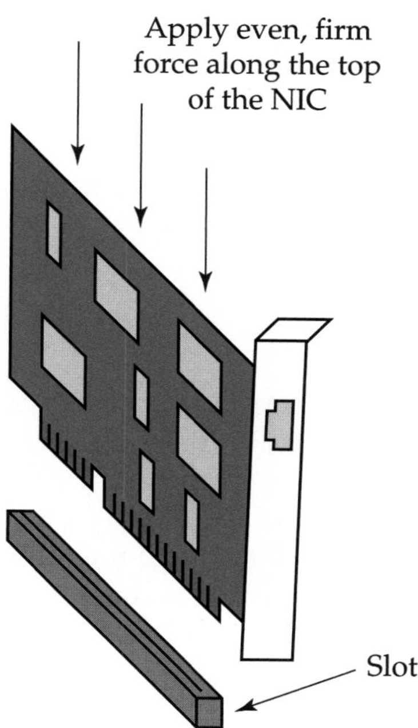
Apply even, firm force along the top of the NIC
Slot

8. ______ Secure the NIC in the slot using the screw removed from the slot cover. Do not skip this step. A loose NIC is one of the most common causes of network problems.

9. ______ Connect the Cat 5 UTP cable between the NIC and the network hub.

10. ______ Boot the PC and see if the card is automatically detected and set up. Normally, the card will be automatically configured through the Plug and Play **Add New Hardware Wizard**. If the card is automatically detected, simply follow the prompts displayed on the screen. If the card is not automatically detected, you may have to install the driver files from the floppy disk that accompany the card. If this happens, ask your instructor for detailed instructions for loading the drivers manually.

11. ______ After the card is successfully installed, double-click the **Network Neighborhood** icon on the desktop to view other PCs that are connected to the network. Other PCs may or may not be seen. To view other PCs, you must be part of the same network, and those computers must be configured to share files. Following is a screen capture of a Network Neighborhood window, which shows the PCs that are connected to the network.

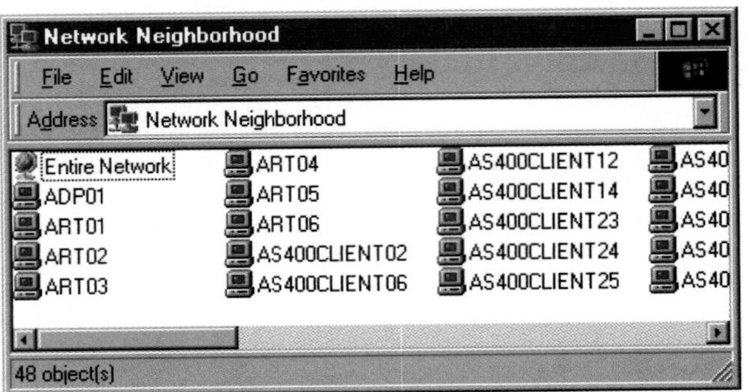

12. ______ Open the **Network** dialog box by right-clicking the **Network Neighborhood** icon and selecting **Properties** from the shortcut menu. This should open the **Network** dialog box. Note the installed network components listed in the large window near the top of the dialog box. This list contains the network adapter card, the protocols being used, and file and print sharing (if it has been enabled). To add a protocol, highlight Client for Microsoft Networks and then click **Add**. This opens a new dialog box that enables you to install additional components, such as other protocols and services.

13. ______ Select the **Identification** tab in the **Network** dialog box. This screen allows you to verify or modify the computer and workgroup names. A short description for the computer, such as "Johns computer in payroll" or "Building A, Room 212, PC#4," may be entered into the **Computer Description:** text box. The description is a great help when dealing with hundreds or thousands of computers. The following illustration shows the layout of the **Identification** tab.

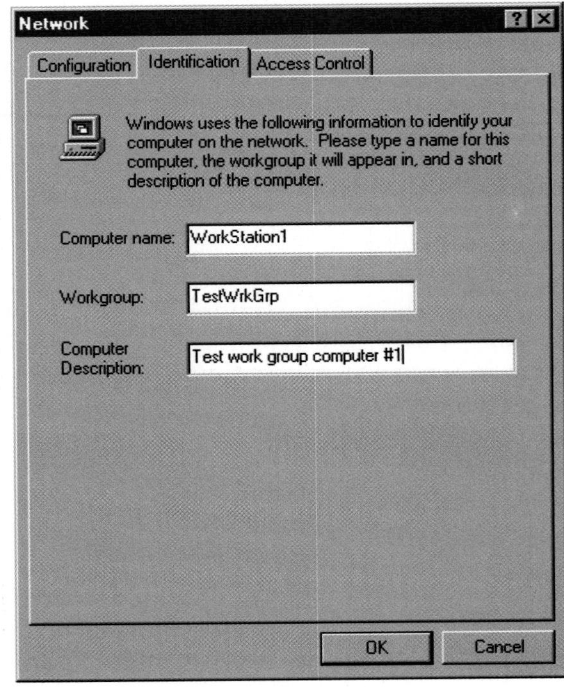

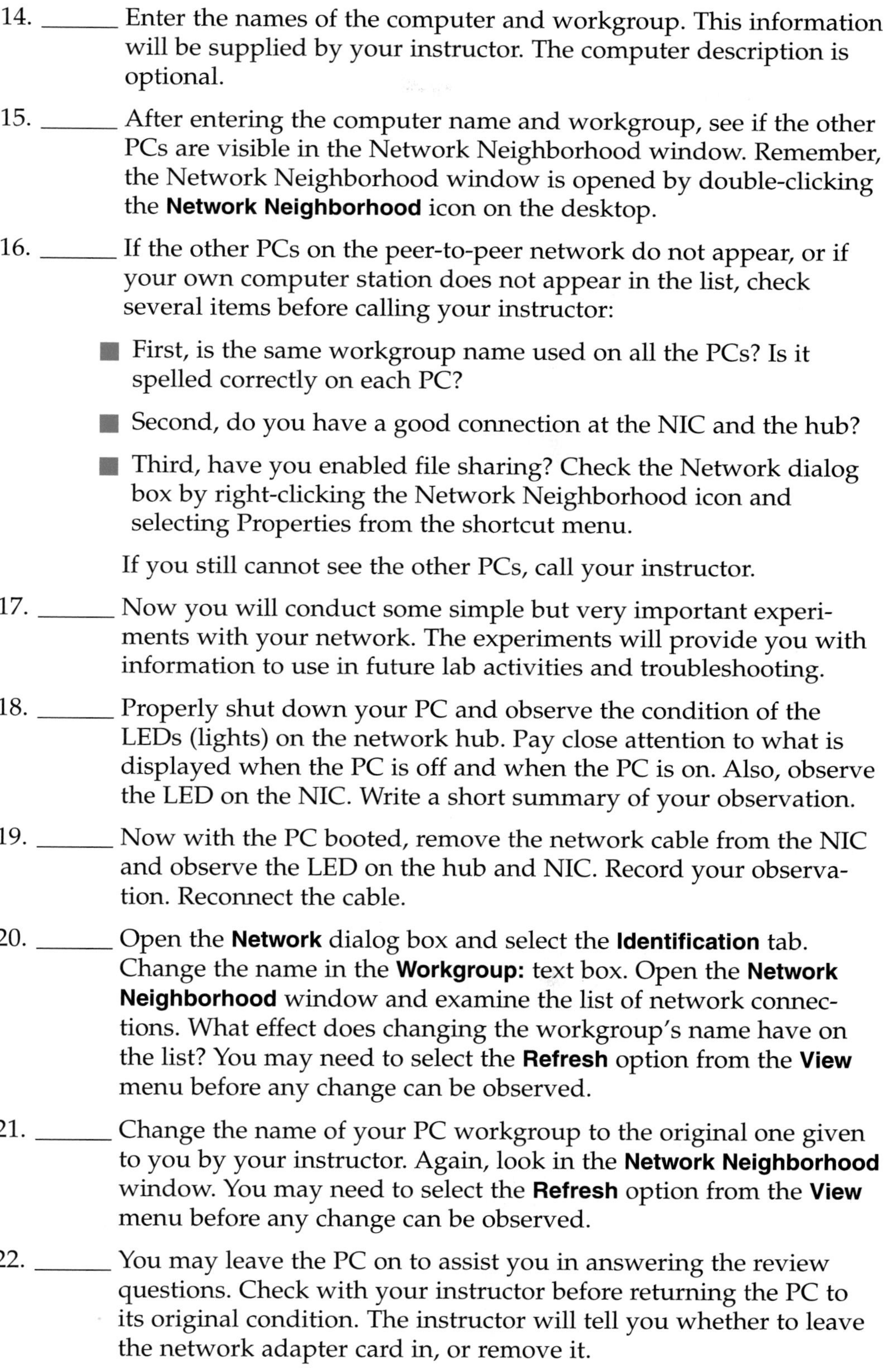

14. ______ Enter the names of the computer and workgroup. This information will be supplied by your instructor. The computer description is optional.

15. ______ After entering the computer name and workgroup, see if the other PCs are visible in the Network Neighborhood window. Remember, the Network Neighborhood window is opened by double-clicking the **Network Neighborhood** icon on the desktop.

16. ______ If the other PCs on the peer-to-peer network do not appear, or if your own computer station does not appear in the list, check several items before calling your instructor:

    - First, is the same workgroup name used on all the PCs? Is it spelled correctly on each PC?
    - Second, do you have a good connection at the NIC and the hub?
    - Third, have you enabled file sharing? Check the Network dialog box by right-clicking the Network Neighborhood icon and selecting Properties from the shortcut menu.

    If you still cannot see the other PCs, call your instructor.

17. ______ Now you will conduct some simple but very important experiments with your network. The experiments will provide you with information to use in future lab activities and troubleshooting.

18. ______ Properly shut down your PC and observe the condition of the LEDs (lights) on the network hub. Pay close attention to what is displayed when the PC is off and when the PC is on. Also, observe the LED on the NIC. Write a short summary of your observation.

19. ______ Now with the PC booted, remove the network cable from the NIC and observe the LED on the hub and NIC. Record your observation. Reconnect the cable.

20. ______ Open the **Network** dialog box and select the **Identification** tab. Change the name in the **Workgroup:** text box. Open the **Network Neighborhood** window and examine the list of network connections. What effect does changing the workgroup's name have on the list? You may need to select the **Refresh** option from the **View** menu before any change can be observed.

21. ______ Change the name of your PC workgroup to the original one given to you by your instructor. Again, look in the **Network Neighborhood** window. You may need to select the **Refresh** option from the **View** menu before any change can be observed.

22. ______ You may leave the PC on to assist you in answering the review questions. Check with your instructor before returning the PC to its original condition. The instructor will tell you whether to leave the network adapter card in, or remove it.

Review Questions

Answer the following questions on a separate sheet of paper. Please do not write in this book.

1. What happens when a new name is entered in the **Workgroup:** text box on one of the computers?
2. What happens to the LED on the hub when the PC is turned off?
3. How is the MAC address identified?
4. What is the **Computer Description:** text box (found in the **Network** dialog box) used for?

Network Administration

After studying this chapter, you will be able to:

- ❑ Describe the characteristics of a strong password.
- ❑ Explain the difference between user-level and share-level security.
- ❑ Explain the role of the network administrator.
- ❑ Describe the characteristics of centralized and decentralized network administration.
- ❑ Describe some of the features that may be implemented to increase network security.

A+ Exam—Key Points

The A+ Certification exams do not go into great depth with networks, but they will test your basic knowledge. You should be prepared to answer questions like the following:

- What is a protocol?
- Who controls system logons?
- Who controls system security?
- How do you log on to a workstation?
- How do you set up a peer-to-peer share?

Also be prepared to explain the difference between user-level and share-level security and to identify the properties of a secure password.

Key Words and Terms

The following words and terms will become important pieces of your computer vocabulary. Be sure you can define them.

account
backup domain controller (BDC)
domain
fault tolerance
group
network administration
permission
primary domain controller (PDC)
RAID
rights
share-level security
shares
system resources
user-level security
user

network administration the use of network software packages to manage network system operations.

Network administration is the use of network software packages to manage network system operations. The central focus of network administration is network security and coordination of shared resources on the network. In this unit, the basics of network administration are covered. It is important to have a basic understanding of network operations when troubleshooting PCs that are connected to a network. You must be able to determine if the problem is PC-related or network-related. This section is not intended to prepare you for the Network+ Certification exam, but it will help you begin the process of achieving that additional certification if you desire.

Network administration in the corporate world is a vast subject requiring years of study and experience. To be competent in a single networking software package can take years. Home and small business networks are becoming more popular everyday. It is imperative that you have a basic understanding of small peer-to-peer networks. The four major network systems will be introduced, and then the majority of the unit will concentrate on the Microsoft Server 2003 network operating system.

Peer-to-Peer Network Administration

Small peer-to-peer networks are rapidly becoming popular, especially in home and small-business offices. Small networks can be set up easily and administered to allow users to share files, printers, hardware, and Internet connections. You can set up a peer-to-peer network using Windows 98, Me, 2000, and XP. These operating systems typically limit the number of simultaneous connections to ten users. Larger networking systems require a client/server operating system.

Administrative functions in a peer-to-peer network are not highly organized and are best described as decentralized. In a decentralized administrative system, no one person controls the network. All users have equal rights on the network, and each user usually controls access to their own files and hardware.

To create a simple peer-to-peer network, all that is required is an operating system that supports peer-to-peer networking and a network adapter card for each PC participating in the network. Microsoft operating systems after Windows 98 are easy to configure as a peer-to-peer network. They use a wizard to ask a series of simple questions. Once the questions are answered, the network's communications are automatically set up. Networks using Windows 98 and prior operating systems require a bit more input during the setup phase.

Shares

Shares are objects that are shared across the network, such as files, hard drives, CD drives, printers, and scanners. Shares are usually set up with some form of security system. In Windows, there are two main security levels for accessing shares on a Windows peer-to-peer network: share-level security and user-level security.

Share-level security is the default security system used on Windows-based networks. Share-level security requires a password to access a share. The other security system, ***user-level security,*** identifies who may have access to a shared resource but does not require a password for accessing the share. A peer-to-peer network usually uses share-level security, while a client/server network usually uses user-level security.

In the client/server network, the client is issued a password and a security level. The clients must supply a user name and password when they log on to the network. Once they successfully log on, they will automatically have the right to access certain files, hardware, and directories.

In a peer-to-peer, it is not necessary to log on as in a client/server network system. Shares on a peer-to-peer network are recommended to be password protected but are not required to be password protected. When shares on a peer-to-peer are password protected, a window appears which is similar in design to a typical logon window. Each share must be accessed using a specific password even though the users belong to a particular group.

shares
objects that are shared across the network, such as files, hard drives, CD drives, printers, and scanners.

share-level security
default security system used on Windows-based networks, which requires a password for access.

user-level security
security system used on Windows-based networks that identifies who may have access to a shared resource but does not require a password for accessing the share.

Tech Tip:
The owner of the share in a peer-to-peer system may choose not to require a password for accessing the share. Not requiring a password is a discouraged security practice.

There are three share-level security options for peer-to-peer access in Windows 95, 98, and Me: Read-Only, Full, and Depends on Password. In Windows XP, NT, and 2000 the share-level security options are Full Control, Change, and Read. See **Figure 17-1** for a complete description of the access level security of each type. As you can see from the figures, user access levels for shares offer varying degrees of security.

Tech Tip:
It is very important that you do set passwords for any shares that you might set up, especially if the same computer station will be connecting to the Internet.

Setting up a Resource Share

Setting up a share for a resource is easy, but you must first allow access to your files and printer. By default, Windows 95, 98, and Me operating systems do not allow other peer-to-peer network users access to your files, printers, and other hardware. Therefore, a share must be created before other users on the network can access your files and hardware. You can use the Network dialog box to change your file- and print-sharing settings. See **Figure 17-2.**

Figure 17-1.
A—Access levels available for shares in Windows 95, 98, and Me and the difference between those levels.

Windows 95, 98, and Me

User Access Level	Description
Read-Only	A user can read and copy the file but not delete or modify a file.
Full	A user can read, copy, modify, delete, move, erase and take ownership of a file or directory.
Depends on Password	A combination of Read-Only and Full access. Each access level has its own password.

A

Figure 17-1. continued.
B—Access levels available for shares in Windows XP, NT, and 2000.

Windows XP, NT, and 2000

User Access Level	Description
Full Control	A user can read, copy, modify, delete, move, erase, and take ownership of a file or directory.
Change	A user can read, create, write, or delete a file.
Read	A user can read and copy a file but not delete or modify a file.

B

Note: Windows XP introduces a new type of file sharing system called "Simple File Sharing." Windows XP Professional can use both Simple File Sharing and the classic file sharing system. When "Simple File Sharing" is enabled, file permissions are hidden from viewing. The Simple File Sharing feature must be disabled to view and modify file share access permissions. Windows XP Home Edition uses "Simple File Sharing" exclusively. It cannot be disabled.

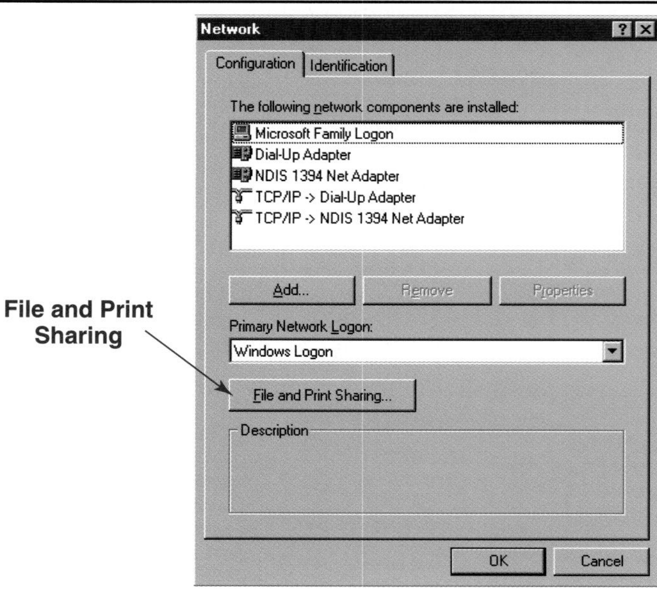

Figure 17-2.
Click on the **File and Print Sharing** button in the **Network** dialog box to set up a share.

To change your file and print-sharing settings in Windows 95, 98, and Me open the **Network** dialog box located at **Start | Settings | Control Panel | Network**. Next, click **File and Print Sharing** and put a check mark next to the appropriate selections. The first selection is **I want to be able to give others access to my files**. Placing a check in this box allows you to set up a share for your drives. See **Figure 17-3.** The second option is **I want to be able to allow others to print to my printer(s)**. Placing a check mark in this box allows you to set up a share for your printer.

Tech Tip:
File and print sharing capabilities are automatically enabled in Windows NT and 2000.

To complete the share for disk drives, open **My Computer** and right-click on the icon of the item you wish to share. Select **Sharing** from the shortcut menu. Activate the **Shared As:** radio button and enter the name of the share in the **Share Name:** field. Click the **Add** button beneath the **Name:** text box, and select the users you wish to share with from the left hand side of the **Add Users** dialog box. Next, select one of the three center buttons to grant the selected user access to your drives. Each button corresponds to one of the access levels described in the previous section. Click the **OK** button in the **Add User** dialog box, and then click the **OK** button in the device's properties dialog box to complete the share. If the share has been successful, the share icon replaces the original icon in the **My Computer** window. See **Figure 17-4.**

To create a shared folder or drive in a peer-to-peer network using Windows XP, locate the file or drive using Windows Explorer. Right-click the file or drive you wish to share and then select **Sharing and Security** from the shortcut menu, **Figure 17-5.** To create a shared folder or drive in a peer-to-peer network using Windows NT or 2000, locate the file or drive using Windows Explorer. Right-click the file or drive you wish to share and then select **Sharing** from the shortcut menu.

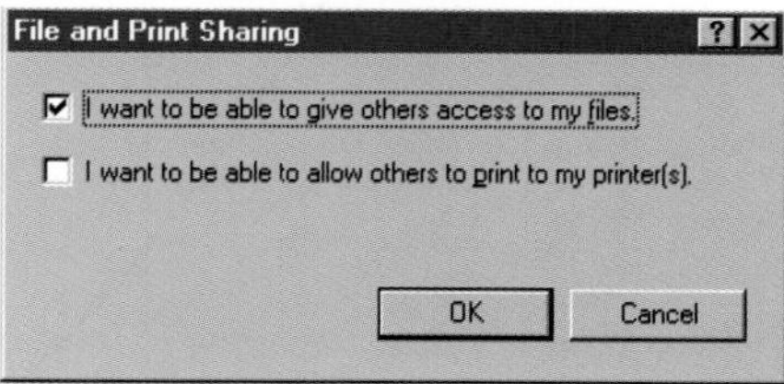

Figure 17-3. Click the appropriate box to share your files or printer.

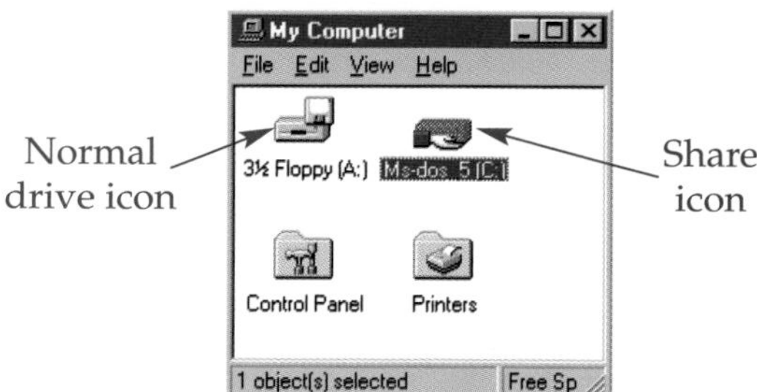

Figure 17-4. After a share has been set up, the drive's normal icon is replaced with the share icon.

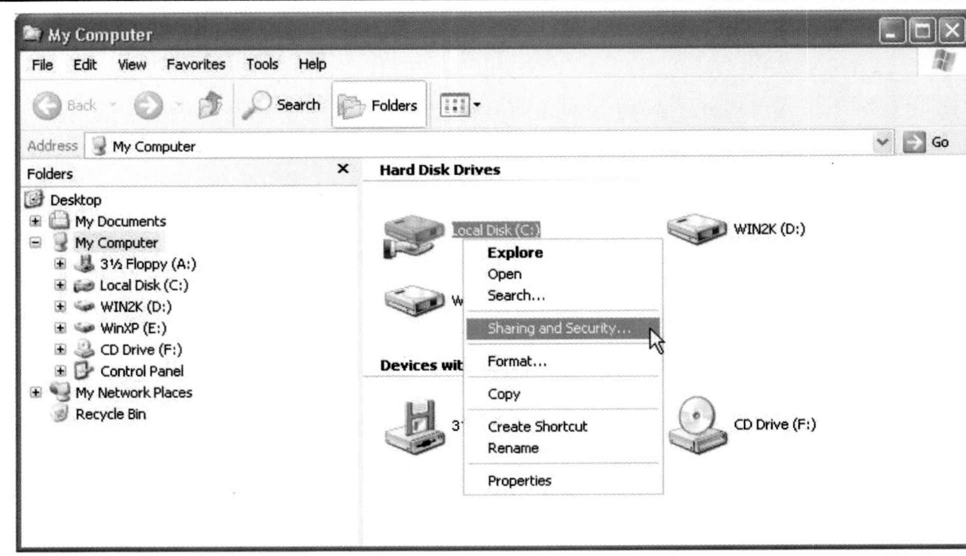

Figure 17-5. File and print sharing are enabled by default in Windows XP, NT and 2000. To set up sharing, simply right-click the file or drive you wish to share and select **Sharing and Security** from the shortcut menu.

A Windows dialog box similar to the one in **Figure 17-6** will appear. You can configure share properties such as a share name, number of users (maximum of ten), permissions, and caching. You can also use this dialog box to remove a share. **Figure 17-7** shows the permissions for the drive C given to the group Everyone.

Creating a printer share in Windows 95, 98, and Me is similar to creating a disk drive or file share in those operating systems. First, the **I want to be able to allow others to print to my printer(s)** option must be selected in the **File and Print Sharing** dialog box. To complete the share, access the **Printers** folder by choosing

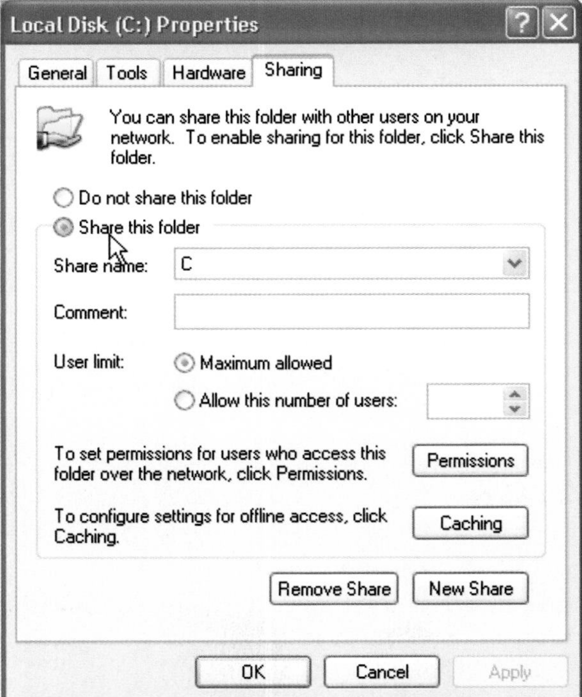

Figure 17-6. Windows XP **Sharing** dialog box.

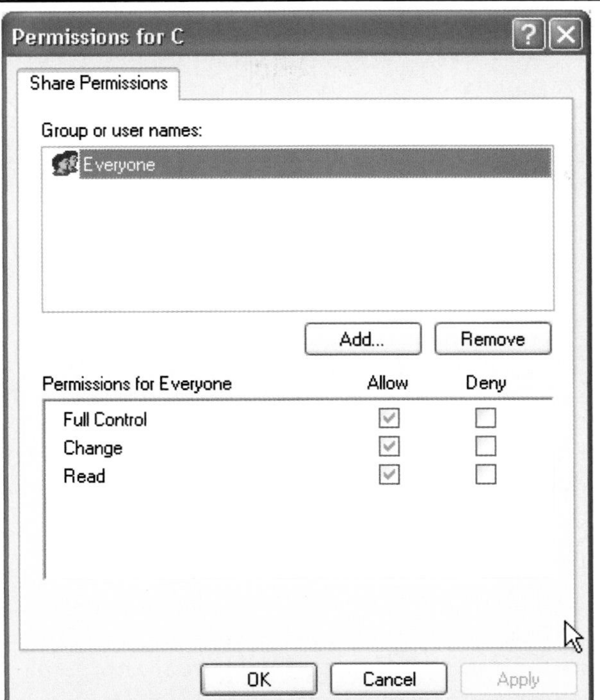

Figure 17-7. **Share Permissions** dialog box. The group Everyone has been given Full Control, Change, and Read rights to drive **C**.

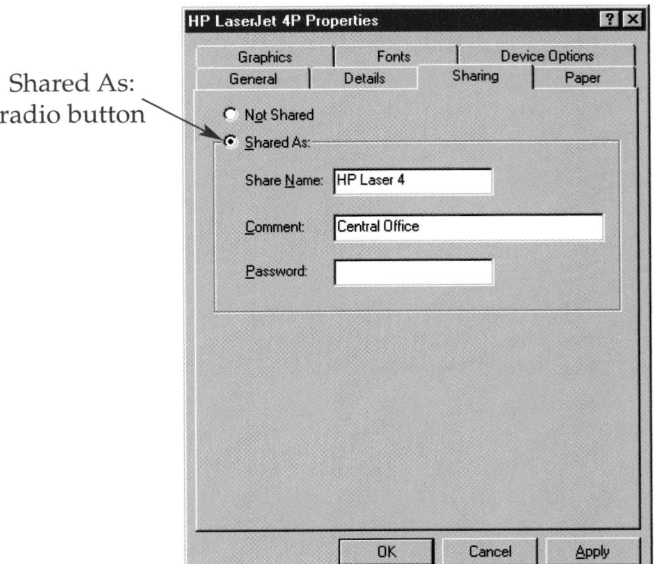

Figure 17-8. A printer share is set up through the printer's **Properties** dialog box.

Start | Settings | Printers. Right-click the name of the printer you wish to share. A shortcut menu will appear and one of the choices will be **Sharing**. Selecting this option will open a dialog box similar to the one in **Figure 17-8.**

Next, activate the **Shared As:** radio button and give the printer share a name. For a small network system, the name can be quite simple, but in a complex network environment, the name should exactly identify the printer share. An example of a printer share name on a complex network might look like HPLaser6Accounting. This name identifies the type of printer and the department in which the printer is located. The building and room can be identified as well. Click the **OK** button in your printer's **Properties** dialog box to complete the share. If the share is successful, the share icon replaces the normal printer icon.

To create a printer share in Windows XP, NT, and 2000, access the **Printers** folder by choosing **Start | Settings | Printers** (**Printers and Faxes** in XP). Right-click the name of the printer you wish to share. A shortcut menu will appear and one of the choices will be **Sharing**. Selecting this option in Windows XP will open a dialog box similar to the one in **Figure 17-9.**

Next, select **Share this printer**. Windows will automatically insert the first seven characters of the printer's name in the **Share name:** text box. You may change this to a more descriptive name. There is also an option to add additional drivers for users running different versions of Windows. This will enable the correct version of the printer driver to be automatically downloaded to a user's system when they add the shared printer. If you do not choose to add the additional drivers, users will be required to provide the drivers themselves, either from the installation CD or from the Windows cab files.

Local User Account

For added security in a peer-to-peer, or workgroup-based, network, a user account should be set up for each user on each computer that the user plans to log on and use. This type of account is called a *local user account.* The main characteristics of a local user account include the following:

- Associated with a peer-to-peer, or a workgroup-based, network.
- Needed to access resources at the local computer.
- Authenticated through the computer at which the account is created.
- Maintained in the computer at which the account is created.

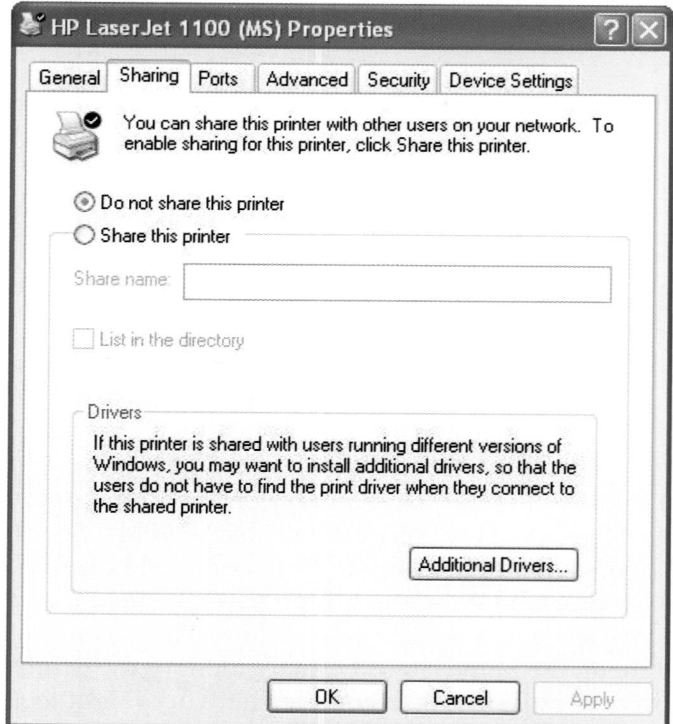

Figure 17-9. Printer **Sharing** dialog box in Windows XP.

Typical Centralized Network Administration

This part of the unit introduces the four major network operating systems: UNIX, Novell NetWare, Microsoft Server 2003, and Linux. There are many more, but these are the most predominate systems in use.

UNIX

UNIX is the oldest of the four network operating systems. It was written in the C programming language and was mainly intended for use on minicomputers. One of the things that made it so popular was that it was not machine specific. In the early days of computers, operating systems were written specifically for certain machines. You could only use an operating system on a specific brand and model of machine. Today, you can run most software across the boundaries of different manufacturers with relatively few restrictions.

UNIX was adopted by IBM and became the standard operating system for their RISC-based systems. UNIX is still used today on many mainframe computers and enterprise servers. The original UNIX operating system required a mainframe computer to meet the operating system hardware requirements. Early PC models did not have sufficient hardware to support the UNIX operating system. Today, many variations of UNIX exist, such as the numerous Linux versions that are designed to run on a PC. Today's PCs have more computing power than the early mainframe computers.

Novell NetWare

Novell NetWare was developed by Novell. It was a very popular network operating system in the 1980s and into the 1990s. The operating system came in several flavors, ranging from Ethernet to Token Ring.

The early versions of NetWare, equipped with a command line interface, were very complex to use. To perform functions, commands had to be typed in at the command line rather than issued by clicking an icon. Today's version incorporates a GUI interface, and you can simply point and click to access its features. Novell's determination and progress in making it possible to share information across diverse platforms has helped NetWare to regain its popularity. Novell set the standard for today's network security systems and has become a tremendously powerful and secure network operating system.

Tech Tip:
The term platform is often used as a synonym for operating system.

Microsoft NT

There are two main versions of Windows NT: one for network servers and the other for individual computers or workstations. The stand-alone workstation version looks very similar to Windows 95, 98, and Me but has many of the characteristics of the server version of Windows NT. The Windows NT workstation version is a much more stable operating system than Windows 95 and 98. The Windows 2000 and XP design is based on Windows NT technology.

The NTFS file system was designed for Windows NT. Windows NT can also use the FAT16 file system. It cannot use the FAT32 file system because FAT32 was designed after the release of Windows NT. The NTFS file system provides greater security than FAT16 or FAT32. The NTFS file system structure provides greater security, flexibility, and detail than FAT file systems. NT also offers file encryption as a security feature.

The mass appeal of Windows NT is due to two things. First, it is relatively user friendly when compared to other systems. It is operated entirely through a graphical user interface, making it very accessible. Second, Microsoft employs brilliant marketing strategies. Microsoft placed trial versions of Windows NT into the hands of many IT specialists and held countless seminars and technical briefings before the software was released to the public.

Microsoft Windows 2000

Windows 2000 was the first major change in the NT operating system. Windows 2000 introduced Active Directory, which removed many restrictions imposed by the NT domain structure and NT file system. Active Directory allowed files and information to be easily shared across large enterprise networks. Active Directory technology is based on the lightweight directory access protocol (LDAP). With the implementation of Active Directory, a user or group member can simply log on once and have complete access to resources across the entire system. In the previous version of NT, users had to be authenticated for each individual domain, and trusts relationships needed to be set up between network domains.

Windows 2000 introduced the terms forest and trees to describe the directory structure. A *tree* is a collection of domains that share a common namespace. A namespace is a name used to identify servers on the Internet, such as www.OurCompany.com. The NT system did not support namespaces. A *forest* is a collection of trees. For example, a forest is a collection of Windows 2000 servers each having a unique namespace.

The Active Directory structure required a newer version of NTFS to be implemented. The newer version of NTFS was named dynamic file system by Microsoft. Other parties referred to the new file system as NTFS 5.0 and the original NTFS file system as NTFS 4.0. Additional changes introduced in Windows 2000 were automatic Plug and Play device detection, enhanced multimedia features, many different setup wizards to assist with common tasks, and many more features. For a complete list of additional features, visit the home page for Windows 2000 at Microsoft's Web site.

Microsoft Net Server 2003

Microsoft introduced Net Server 2003 as the next server operating system after Windows 2000 Server. Net Server 2003 continued with Active Directory as the main directory structure. Some new features included in Windows Net Server 2003 are Automatic System Recovery, Remote Assistance, Web Interface for remote administration, improved Internet Information Service (IIS 6.0), wireless networking support, IP version 6, and more. Many of the features new for Net Server 2003 were introduced in Windows XP. One main area of development is the utilization of the Internet as a medium for accessing and administering the Server. To learn more about the features in Net Server 2003, visit the Net Server 2003 home page at Microsoft's Web site.

Tech Tip:
Microsoft Net Server 2003 is most often referred to as Microsoft Server 2003.

Linux

Linux is one of the latest networking operating systems to be fully developed. Because the source code is available to the public, there are many different Linux operating systems available. Linux has become very popular because its source code is readily available, and it is relatively inexpensive compared to other network operating systems.

Most software companies guard their source code and only release sufficient information about the code to allow third party developers to write software to enhance their product. By having the complete listing of source code for the Linux operating system, programmers can write any feature they desire into the networking software. Anyone with reasonable programming skills can use the open source code to build a network operating system of their own specifications. Even though major software companies now build networking software packages based on Linux, the pricing remains very reasonable.

However, complete access to source code does have a price. In this case, it is security. If you have complete access to the source code, so does every interested hacker in the world. To abide by the Linux software copyright regulations, if you use the Linux source code to develop your software system, you must allow access to any and all modifications to the code when you market it. As far as security goes, everyone has a road map to your system's operations when the source code is freely distributed.

Many network models incorporate a Linux server together with a server of another network operating system. For example, the front-end server, the part that allows users to access the site, uses a standard high security package such as those provided by Novell NetWare or Windows NT and 2003. This provides the security that the site must have. To cut operating cost, the Linux system is used as a mail server or Web server.

System Administrator

When talking about a network, or system, administrator, we will be talking about the centralized model of network administration, the client/server model, rather than the peer-to-peer model. The network administrator is one person (or more) who has the highest security rating on the network. The network administrator is responsible for delegating authority all the way down to the user level. The other users on the network can exercise only the authority granted to them by the network administrator.

Delegated Administrators

The network administrator controls all aspects of the network. However, in a large organization with thousands of users spread all over the country, it would be difficult, if not impossible, for one person to perform all the duties associated with running a network. For this reason, the network administrator usually grants limited administrative powers to a middle management level of administrators. The middle management people take care of routine duties, such as adding or deleting users from the network, setting up printers to be shared, setting up specific files or programs to be shared, and doing routine data backup.

Logging on the network involves identifying the user by name and password. The user name identifies the individual and the password verifies his or her identity. The network administrator issues the user name, and the user's initial password. The administrator can give permission to the user to change their individual logon password following the first successful logon. This is the typical password administrative scenario used.

Choosing User Names

The typical format for a user name is the user's last name followed by the underline symbol and ending in the first letter of user's first name. For example, the author's user name would likely be Roberts_R. There are many different naming styles, but once a naming style is chosen, it should remain consistent as new user accounts are added to the network. Inconsistent naming styles can easily lead to confusion.

Choosing Passwords

Passwords are used to verify that the named user is, in fact, the authorized user. Passwords should be unique and be composed of a mixture of letters (both upper- and lowercase), numbers (0–9), and special symbols ($%&(){}[]+=<>). The special symbols that can be used as part of the password depend on the network operating system. There may be a maximum and minimum length for the password as well. Passwords should not be names or words found in a dictionary. Good passwords are combinations of words and other symbols that do not make sense to a typical person when used together. See **Figure 17-10.**

Letters can be replaced by symbols, such as the dollar symbol for "S," or the "^" for "A," or "[" for "C." The use of symbols improves the security of a password. Many hackers attempt to crack passwords by using a database of dictionary words. Each entry in the database is systematically substituted for the password until the correct word is found or the database is exhausted. The use of symbols and numbers negate the use of a dictionary database as a password breaker.

Figure 17-10. A good password combines numbers, letters, and special symbols in a way that has no meaning to a typical person. Common names, words, and phrases make poor passwords.

Good	Poor
Night$tar1	Star
Brend^01	Brenda
Dog$uper5	BigDog
Pa$$word_1	Password
Acce$$005	Access
Mountain_Blue3	Bluemountain
Rock{123}Surf	RockSurf
[h^rle$_01	Charles

Tech Tip:
Never write your password down and store it at your workstation. This is very obvious to others, especially when you have to look it up to log on to the computer system. Do not let people watch you enter your password. With practice, people can memorize a sequence of keystrokes made by a user when logging on to a network.

Tech Tip:
Microsoft Net Server 2003 requires that the administrative password meet complexity requirements. A blank password cannot be used. The password must contain a mixture of characters—at least 6—and not contain part or all of the user's name.

Network Administration Models

Each major software vender uses its own terminology to describe its network organization. They are all similar for the most part, and terminologies can be easily transferred from one system to another without losing their intended meanings. The terminology used in this unit will be primarily based on the Microsoft network systems. Concentrating on one system in generic fashion will be less confusing than explaining different systems in one unit.

Centralized networks are organized administratively into sections. These sections are called domains, groups, and users. The ***domain*** is an organized collection of all groups and users on the network. ***Groups*** are collections of users organized together by similarities in their job tasks. ***Users*** are the individual people who may use the network system resources.

domain
an organized collection of all groups and users on the network.

group
collection of users organized together by similarities in their job tasks.

user
a person who may use the network system resources.

Tech Tip:
The term domain has two meanings: one for the early Windows server models and another when used to discuss Internet locations. A domain in Windows NT and Windows 2000 means a collection of computers. When discussing the Internet, the term domain refers to a classification of a site such as .com or .org or to represent the Internet site.

Domains

The entire network organization is usually referred to as a domain. For example, ABC Inc. may be a domain. The entire organization is one whole unique network system. Inside the domain are groups of users with related tasks, such as the personnel in the accounting and sales departments. Each of these groups is composed of individual users, such as John Doe in accounting and Jane Doe in sales.

Groups

The next level in the network organization is the group. Groups are workers who share common responsibilities and can be thought of as a set. For example, the payroll, marketing, research, design, and administrative departments of a corporation could easily form five distinct groups of network users. The workers within the group usually require similar ***system resources*** (files, software, printers, etc.) to perform their jobs.

system resources
files, software, printers, and such.

Users

The individual user is at the bottom of the network organization. A user is an individual who uses the network system. Each user is assigned an account, which includes all available information about him or her. The account, which contains such information as the user's password, user name, restrictions, and the group(s) he or she belongs to, is kept in a database on the file server. Each user must have an account before he or she can use the network system. Once the user has an account, he or she can be granted full use of the network and can be given access to any area of the network by the system administrator. The individual user usually belongs to one or more groups, but may belong to no group at all.

Assigning Resources at the Group Level

If the company has several hundred or thousands of employees, the amount of time required to set up individual shares for each employee would be unreasonable. Although access to system resources can be granted to individual users, network administrators can save a great deal of time by assigning resources to groups rather than to individual users. In this case, each group can be allowed access to the normal software programs, files, and hardware required by that group. When it is necessary to add new users to the network, it is quicker and simpler to assign a new individual to an existing group than it is to authorize each individual to use specific network resources.

As you just learned, networks are organized by domains, users, and groups. These groups are often formed from the different divisions or departments in the corporate structure. Although all of these departments are part of the same company and may have many common needs, they each will likely have special needs based on their different job requirements. For example, all departments will need some sort of word-processing package but only a few would need access to the accounting software or payroll database. Each group's needs and security requirements must be determined individually.

Accounts

account contains all the security information describing an individual user.

primary domain controller (PDC) a file server that keeps the master record of all accounts.

backup domain controller (BDC) a file server that keeps a backup record of all accounts in case of failure of the primary domain controller.

Even when resources are assigned at the group level, each employee must still have an account. An ***account*** can be thought of as part of the network administrative security database. The user account contains all the security information describing an individual user. The account usually consists of the user logon name, description, password, and other normal network necessities such as what group they belong to and what user rights they have been assigned. A user must have an account set up before they can access a client/server network system.

In this centralized, administrative structure, all the files pertaining to the users, groups, and computers connected to the system are contained in the file server. A network may be composed of many file servers sharing the burden of the network system. In the early Windows NT system, one file server was known as the primary domain controller, and the others were called the backup domain controllers. The ***primary domain controller (PDC)*** kept the master record of all user accounts, and the ***backup domain controllers (BDC)*** kept backup copies of the user accounts. The redundancy helped to protect against losing information about the users if the primary domain controller should fail or crash. In today's systems, all servers can be configured with equal responsibilities. They no longer require the notation of primary and backup.

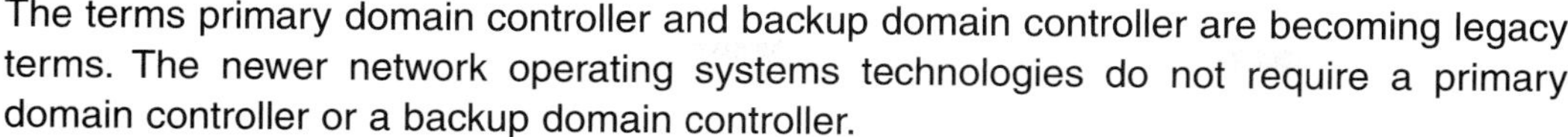

Tech Tip:
The terms primary domain controller and backup domain controller are becoming legacy terms. The newer network operating systems technologies do not require a primary domain controller or a backup domain controller.

When a user account is part of a network administrative security database, the user of that account can do the following:

- Be authenticated through the domain server.
- Access resources anywhere in the network domain.
- Log on through any computer in the domain.
- Access resources anywhere in the domain.

A Quick Tour of Windows Net Server 2003

We will now take a quick tour of a typical Windows Net Server 2003. The following paragraphs illustrate differences between a simple peer-to-peer network and a much more sophisticated network system. This will be a quick tour, not an in-depth study of Windows Net Server 2003. It is intended to introduce you to some of the capabilities of a network operating system. A complete study of Windows Net Server 2003 would require a complete textbook of its own. Remember, a network that uses Windows Net Server 2003 is a client/server type of network. Let's begin by looking at some of the Windows Net Server 2003 Start menu selections. See **Figure 17-11.**

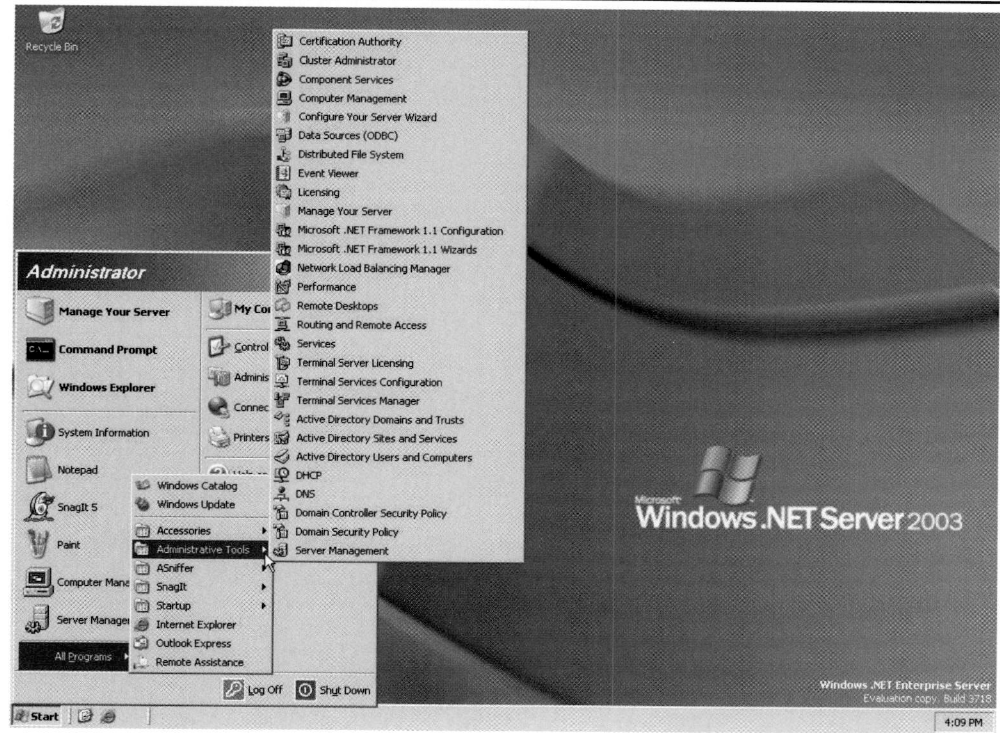

Figure 17-11.
The Windows Net Server 2003 Start menu is similar to previous server versions and workstations.

The Windows Net Server 2003 Start menu contains many different selections not found on a typical PC running Windows 98 or earlier. However, the Windows Net Server 2003 version does look very similar to other Windows 2000 and Windows XP workstation versions and has many of the same features.

User Management

The Active Directory Users and Computers management utility is located at **Start | Administrative Programs | Active Directory Users and Computers**. It is used to enter or examine information about users, groups, domains, and other objects in the Active Directory structure. See **Figure 17-12.** The right-hand window contains a listing of the names and descriptions of the network's users and groups.

From the Active Directory Users and Computers window, you can add or delete users and groups. Microsoft is famous for providing software wizards to assist users with their tasks, and Microsoft Server 2003 is no exception. Microsoft provides several wizards, such as the New Object User shown in **Figure 17-13,** to assist the network administrator. This wizard helps add users to the network in a systematic way, ensuring that no important security features are inadvertently left out.

In addition to adding new user accounts, you can set up, modify, or view security levels for existing users. While the password system on a PC is quite simple, the password system for a network contains a number of added features. These features can be adjusted through the Default Domain Controller Security Settings **Password Policy** directory tree, **Figure 17-14.**

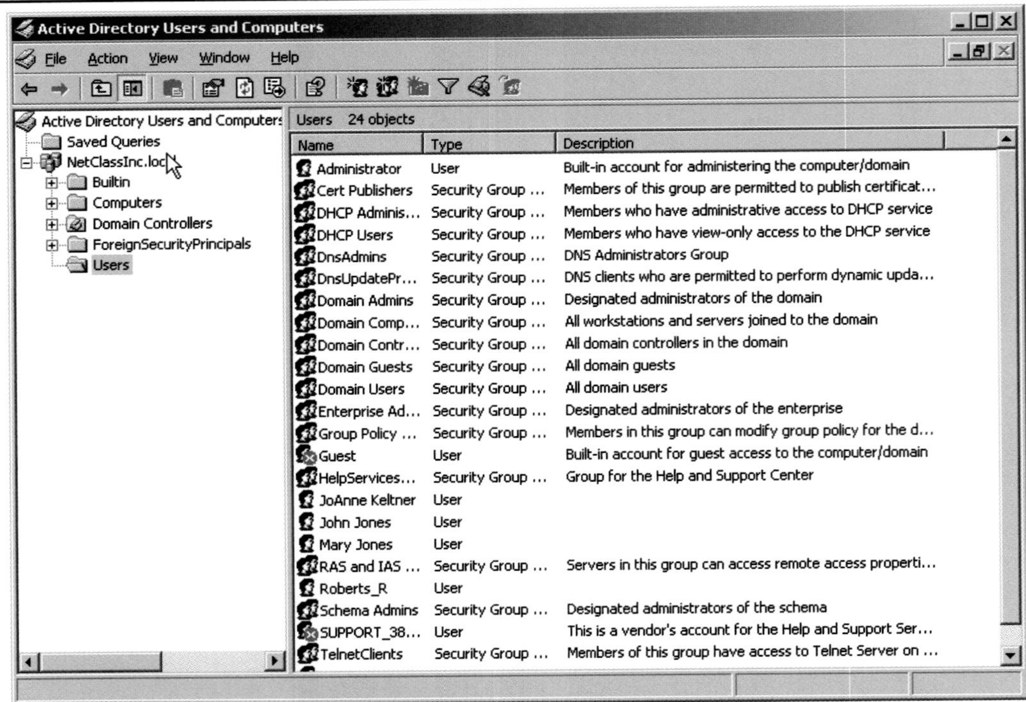

Figure 17-12. Information about groups and users can be examined or changed in the **Active Directory Users and Computers** utility.

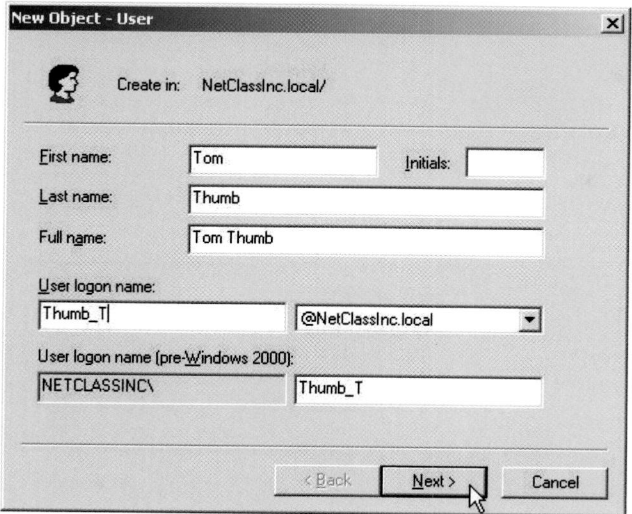

A

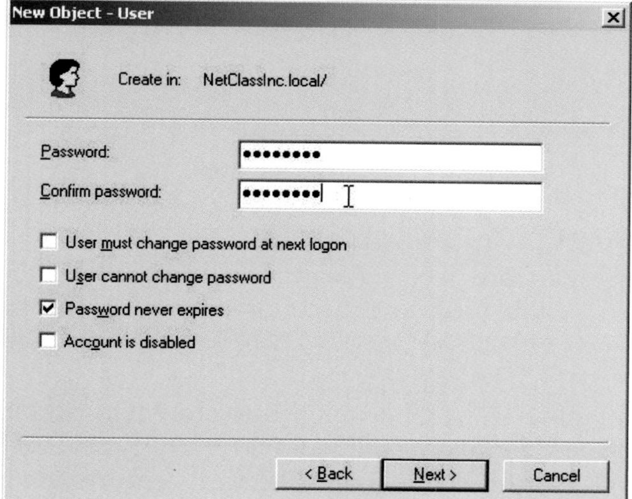

B

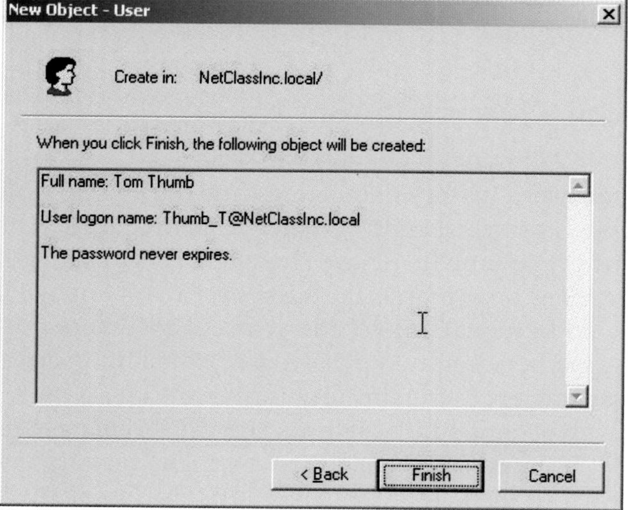

C

Figure 17-13. When adding users to the network system in Windows Net Server 2003, the user is created using the New Object wizard. A—The first dialog box to appear during the creation of a new user in the network system. B—User password settings are entered in the second dialog box. C—The last dialog box allows you to verify the new user's settings.

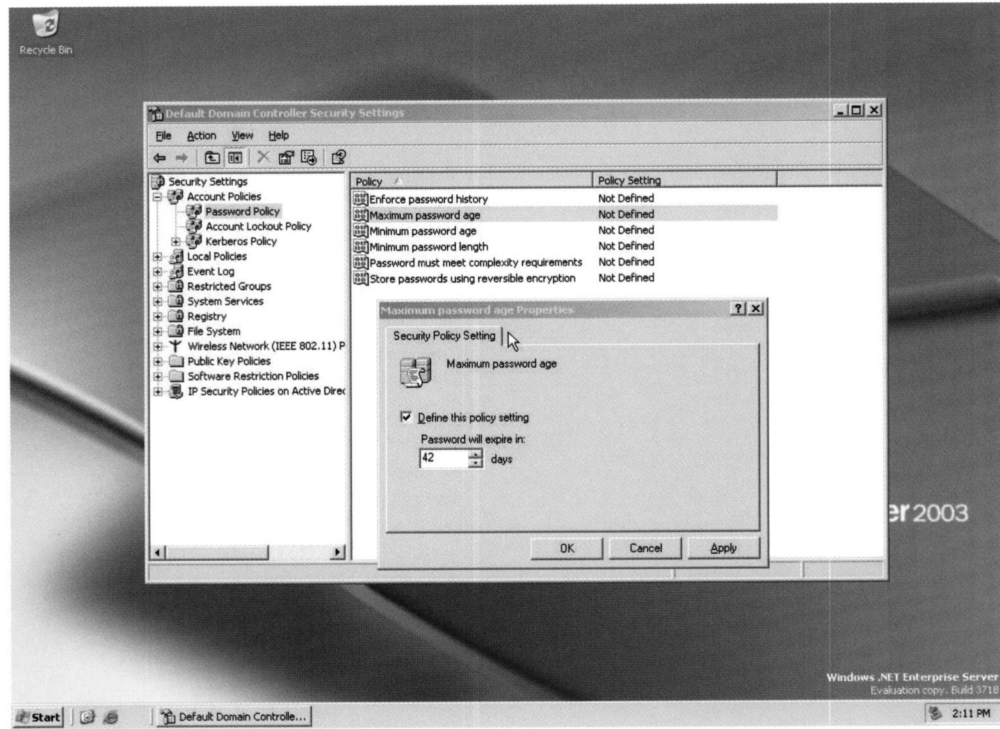

Figure 17-14. In Windows Net Server 2003, password policies are set in the **Default Domain Controller Security Settings** utility. The network administrator can influence the degree of security by setting tough password restrictions.

Security Features

There are many standard security features incorporated into Windows Net Server 2003. These include password, account lockout, audit, and time policies.

Password policy

Look again at Figure 17-14. Choosing **Password Policy** from the left window of the **Default Domain Controller Security Settings** utility reveals 6 password policy features on the right. The following security features are listed:

- Enforce password history.
- Maximum password age.
- Minimum password age.
- Minimum password length.
- Password must meet complexity requirements.
- Store passwords using reversible encryption.

The **Enforce password history** determines how old passwords are remembered by the system. Password controls can be set to require a user to use a different password every time he or she changes passwords. A value can be entered that determines how many times the user must change passwords before being allowed to repeat an old password. If this were not set, the user could simply flip-flop between two passwords, weakening system security.

Maximum password age is maximum number of days a password can be used before it must be changed. Passwords should be changed frequently but not so frequently it becomes a bother to the user. The recommended password age is 30 to 90 days, but the actual range is from 0 to 999 days.

The **Minimum password age** is the number of days old a password needs to be before it can be changed. **Minimum password age** is a required feature when using the password history policy. Values range from 0 to 998 and must be set at a value less than maximum. If there were no minimum password age and a value was set in **Enforce password history** that determined a user must change their password 7 times before being allowed to reuse an old password, a user may change their password to meet the maximum password requirement and then immediately change their password to the original. For example, if a user's original password was "MyPassword_1," the user could create a series of passwords based on the last digit, such as "MyPassword_2," "MyPassword_3," and so on. When the password series reached the value set in **Enforce password history**, the user once more could use the original password, "MyPassword_1." Setting the minimum password age feature to as little as 1 day will prevent a user from cycling through all their old passwords at one sitting.

Minimum password length sets the minimum length a password can be. Enforcing passwords of 6 characters or more can increase security. The length of a password is directly related to the how secure the password is. The longer the password, the longer it takes to "crack." It can also, however, be more difficult to remember. The length of the password must provide a reasonable amount of security and not be too difficult or complex to use.

Microsoft and most security experts recommend a password of at least 6 characters. A longer password of at least 12 characters is not unreasonable. As the length of the password increases and if we also meet complexity requirements of the next section, a lengthy password could be difficult to use. Just remember that the password must be at least 6 characters in length to be considered a minimally secure password.

The **Password must meet complexity requirements** prevents a user from choosing a password that is easily compromised by cracking tools such as dictionaries. Complex passwords require a minimum length and the use of an assortment of letters, numbers, and special symbols in the password. A complex password is extremely difficult to compromise.

Store passwords using reversible encryption hides the user password by encrypting the characters so they cannot be seen by unauthorized probes of the security database.

Account lockout policy

The Account Lockout Policy accessed through **Default Controller Security Settings | Account Policies** allows the system administrator to select a lockout duration for a set number of failed logon attempts. For example, if a person attempts three times to log on to a network system and fails, the system locks the user out for a period of time. The time can range from 0 to 99,999 minutes. The idea is to cause a reasonable delay between login failures to prevent a "dictionary attack" by an unauthorized person. Even a delay of a few minutes will ward off most attacks.

Audit policy

The Audit Policy allows a user's activities to be monitored and recorded in a log file that can be viewed by the system administrator. Audit Policy is accessed through **Default Controller Security Settings | Local Policies**. As you can see in

Figure 17-15, choosing **Audit Policy** in the left-hand window reveals 9 audit policy features on the right. The features allow the network administrator to specify certain events that are recorded in a log for later review.

Take special note of **Audit account logon events** located at the top of the right-hand window. The most common cause of a failed logon attempt is the use of a wrong password. Because the settings in the Audit Policy dialog box specify that failed logon attempts should be recorded, the attempted logon would appear in the system's security log. See **Figure 17-16.** Each security event specified in the Audit Policy dialog box is recorded in the security log and can be viewed and saved. To see a more detailed description of the event, the administrator can simply double-click the individual event. This opens the Event Detail dialog box, which contains a more detailed description of the selected event. See **Figure 17-17.**

In the illustration, the event captured is the attempted logon of a user named Roberts_R. The logon was refused because of improper identification. Either the user was not an authorized user of NETCLASSINC or the user's

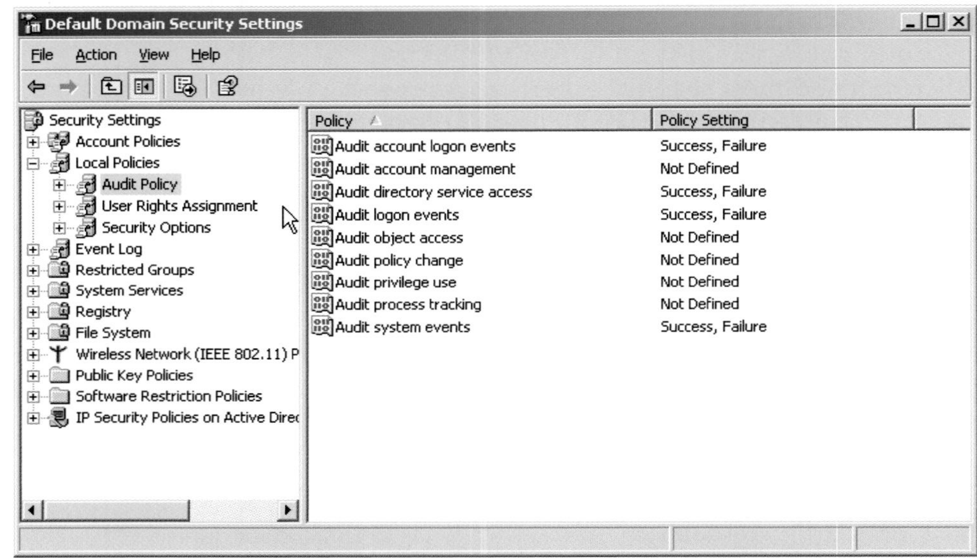

Figure 17-15. Audit policies can be set to record the success or failure of different events. This can be a valuable tool in detecting unauthorized attempts to enter the system.

Event Viewer - Security Log on \\NTSERVER1

Log View Options Help

Date	Time	Source	Category	Event
9/25/00	6:58:41 AM	Security	Logon/Logoff	538
9/25/00	6:54:55 AM	Security	Logon/Logoff	528
9/25/00	6:54:23 AM	Security	Logon/Logoff	528
9/25/00	6:54:22 AM	Security	Logon/Logoff	538
9/25/00	6:54:20 AM	Security	Logon/Logoff	528
9/25/00	6:52:33 AM	Security	Logon/Logoff	529
9/25/00	6:52:30 AM	Security	Logon/Logoff	529
9/25/00	6:52:22 AM	Security	Logon/Logoff	529
9/25/00	6:52:19 AM	Security	Logon/Logoff	529
9/25/00	6:52:02 AM	Security	Logon/Logoff	529
9/25/00	6:51:49 AM	Security	Logon/Logoff	529
9/25/00	6:51:41 AM	Security	Logon/Logoff	529
9/25/00	6:51:28 AM	Security	Logon/Logoff	529
9/25/00	6:51:17 AM	Security	Logon/Logoff	529
9/25/00	6:51:14 AM	Security	Logon/Logoff	529
9/25/00	6:40:40 AM	Security	Logon/Logoff	538

Figure 17-16. All events specified in the **Audit Policy** dialog box are recorded in the security log.

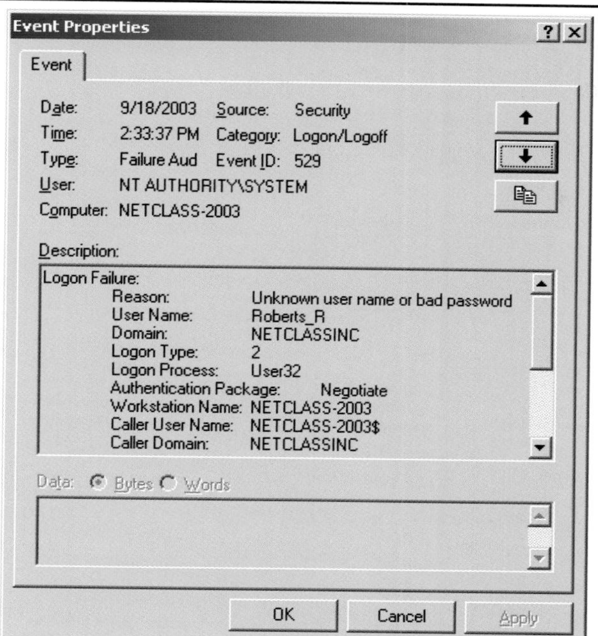

Figure 17-17.
The Event Properties dialog box offers greater detail about the warnings issued in the **Event Viewer**.

password could not be validated. In either case, access to the server was denied. It was also recorded that the unsuccessful access attempt was made from NETCLASS-2003, at 2:33 PM on 9/18/2003. These details could be invaluable if an investigation is necessary.

Time policy

The time (days, hours) that a user may access the network can be easily controlled through an individual's Properties window, **Figure 17-18.** In **Figure 7-19** logon hours are configured so that the user can only access the network system from 6:00 AM to 8:00 PM Monday through Friday. At any other day or time, the user will be denied access to the network. This security feature prevents someone from accessing the network with a stolen user name and password during a business's off hours. One option of this feature forces users off the system when their time expires. Another option allows them to continue (or finish) working in their current program or document but does not allow them to open any new files or services.

Monitoring the System

In addition to monitoring the users on the network, the system can monitor itself, record events in the system log, and alert the system administrator to potential problems. In addition, various other features are available in Windows Net Server 2003 that allow the network administrator to observe and track system performance. The features are discussed in the following sections.

Event Viewer and the system log

The same Event Viewer window that is used to monitor user activity on the network can also be used to monitor the system's performance. This is

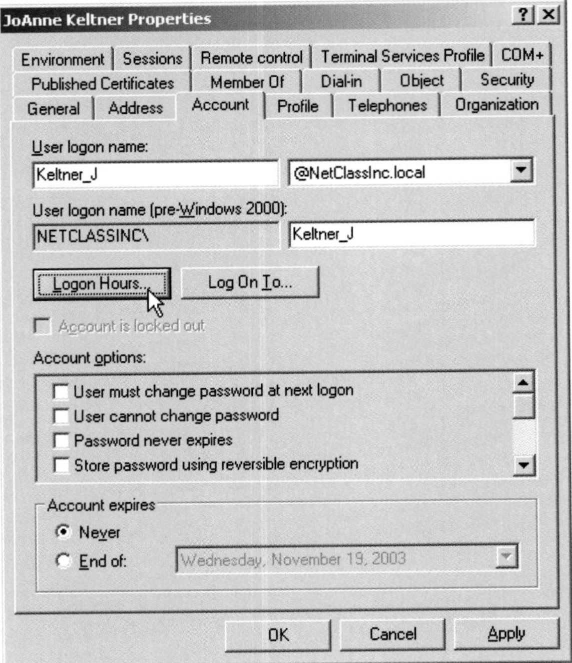

Figure 17-18. **Logon Hours** is accessed through the user's **Properties** settings. The exact days of the week as well as the hours of the day a user may access the system can be restricted by the server.

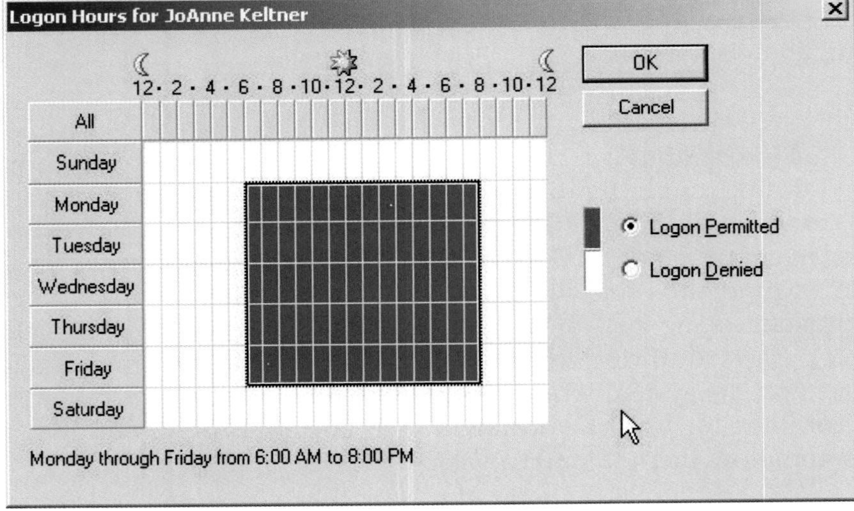

Figure 17-19. Logon Hours dialog box. A user's access to the network can be limited to certain days of the week or hours.

accomplished by loading the system log rather than the security log. In **Figure 17-20,** the Event Viewer window has issued a warning to the administrator. A warning is indicated by the yellow circle and exclamation point. By double-clicking the warning, the administrator can open the Event Properties dialog box. This dialog box explains the warning in greater detail. See **Figure 17-21.** Note in the **Description:** window, there is a notification that a computer was automatically configured with the IP address 169.254.0.22. As you can see, very detailed information can be captured by the system events monitor, which can help analyze system problems.

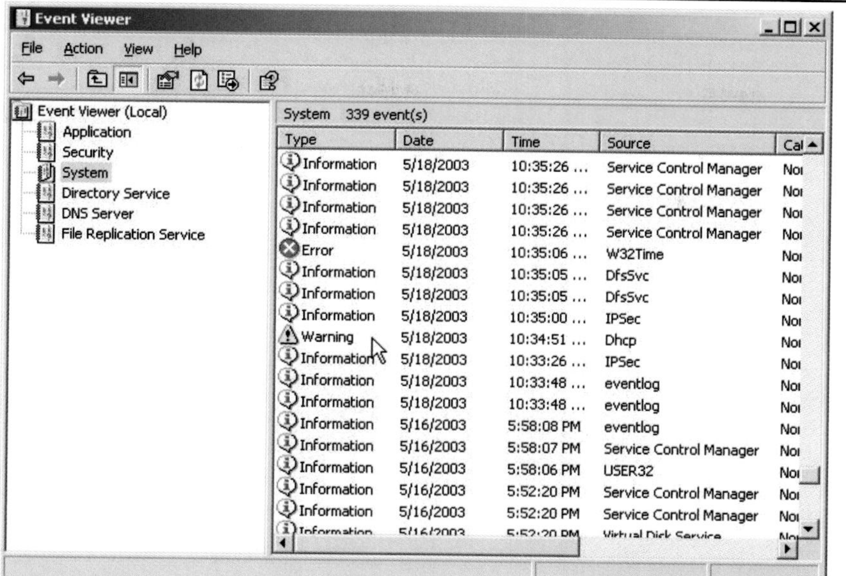

Figure 17-20. The Event Viewer can be used to monitor system performance. Warnings are indicated by an exclamation point inside a yellow triangle.

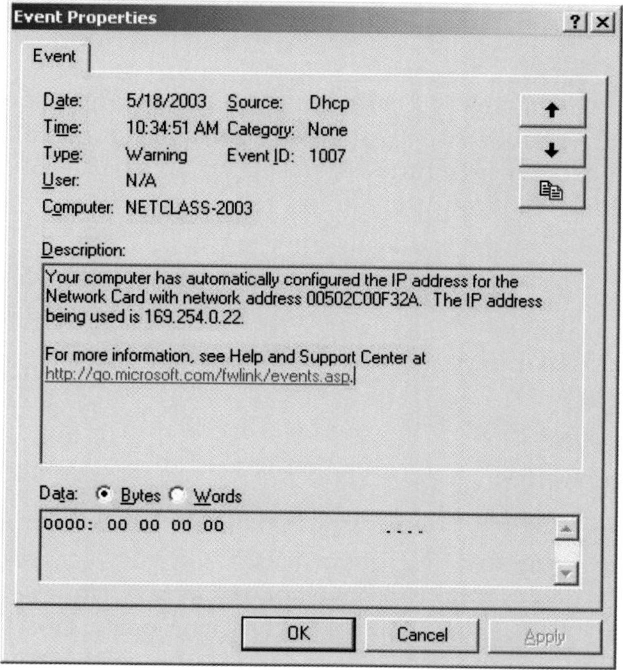

Figure 17-21. Details of a system event warning. Take a close look at the system event indicated in the screen capture. What information does it provide?

Performance Monitor

The administrator can also use the Performance Monitor utility to monitor the performance of some of the computer system components. In **Figure 17-22,** the Performance Monitor is displaying the CPU activity, memory pages, and hard disk on the same graph. The usage is expressed as a percentage from 0 to 100. The administrator can use this tool to diagnose various network problems such as network congestion or failing hardware.

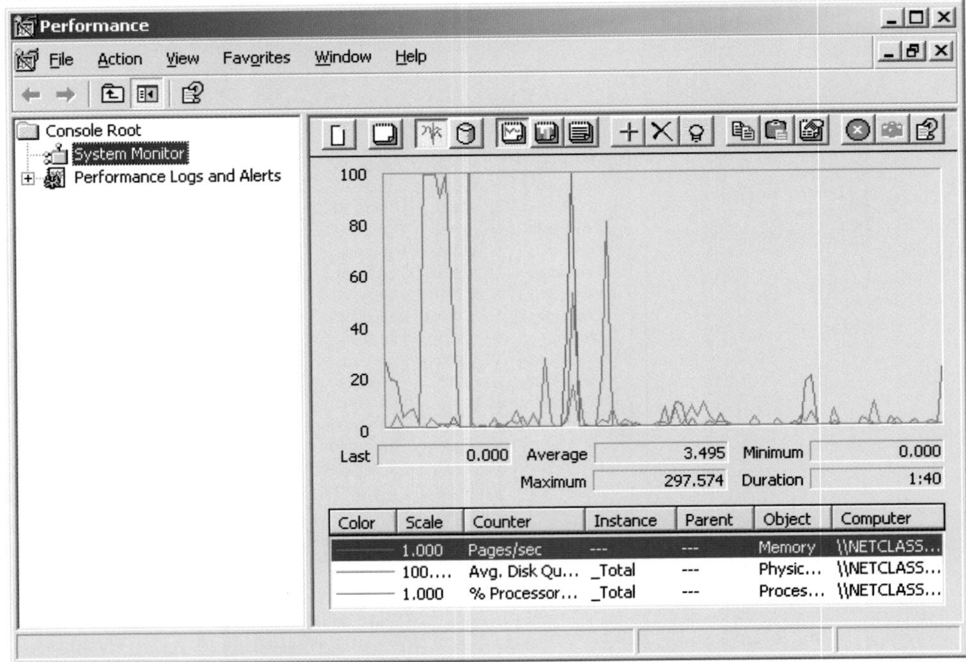

Figure 17-22. The Performance Monitor can display graphs of the system's use of certain resources.

Default Groups

Server operating systems typically have a set of default users and groups. These are the most common user and groups required in most server systems. Default users and groups save time when setting up a server.

Some of the most common users are as follows:

- Administrator
- User
- Guest

Some of the most common groups are as follows:

- Print Operators
- Backup Operators
- DHCP Administrators
- Domain Administrators

The exact title of the user or group account will vary according to the operating system used. Each group can have specific permissions set, which dictate what the members of the group can do, access, or modify. Users are simply added to each group and the user is restricted to the permissions of the group. Additional users and groups can be added to meet the needs of the environment. For example, in a school setting, a group named Teachers and another named Students can be set up on the server. A user named Teacher and a user named Student can be added to the user list. All students can log on using the user name Student. The student would be restricted according to the permissions set in the group called Students. The same scenario can be applied to the teachers. Each teacher can log on using the user name Teacher. The teacher would be restricted according the permissions set in the group named Teachers.

Rights, Properties, Profiles

A network security system maintains a database of security information on all network users. The exact terminology used to describe the individual features varies somewhat according to the network operating system software being used. The database stores information such as the group(s) the user belongs to and their access rights to files and drives. The administrator can alter, copy, delete, or simply read the contents of a profile. There are many aspects to the individual user profile.

Restrictions

In the **Advanced Security Settings for Users** dialog box, **Figure 17-23,** you can see part of the default restrictions assigned to users. Restrictions can be added or removed by checking or unchecking the box next to the item in the list. Remove Run Command from Start Menu, Hide Network Neighborhood, and Hide Drives in My Computer are just a few of the restrictions used to limit an individual user on a Windows Net Server 2003 network. As you can see, the network administrator can place strong limits on a user to ensure a secure network environment. The administrator can limit a user's access so that they may only run the programs and access the files authorized by the network administrator.

Rights and Permissions

The Users Properties dialog box can give users certain abilities, or ***rights***, that are normally reserved for the system administrator, such as the ability to shut down the system or manage auditing and the security log. See **Figure 17-24.** As you can see, users can be given rights as powerful as those of the administrator, or they can have all the typical user rights taken away. There is a wide range of control over users and groups.

rights
system control abilities that are normally reserved for the system administrator.

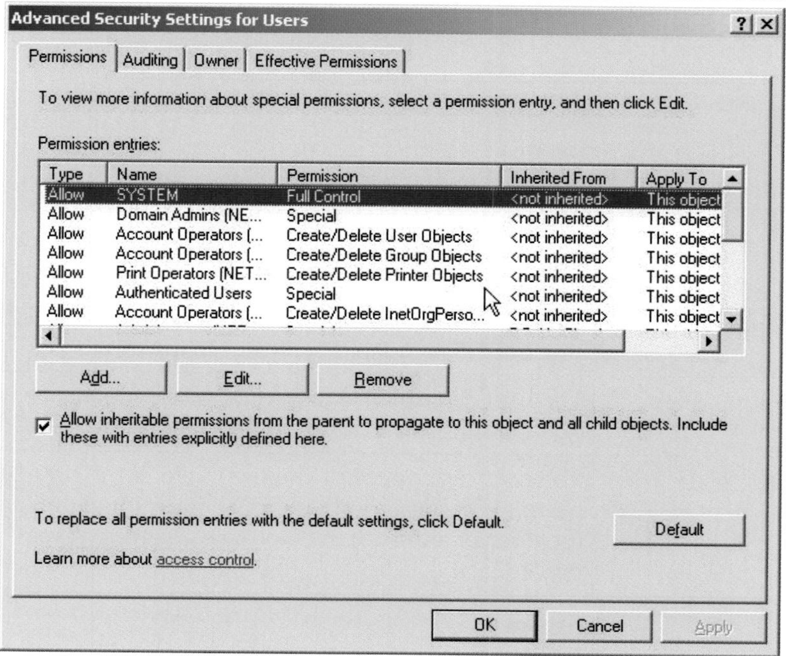

Figure 17-23. The Advanced Security Settings for Users dialog box controls user permission settings. The permission settings control what the user may do based on group membership.

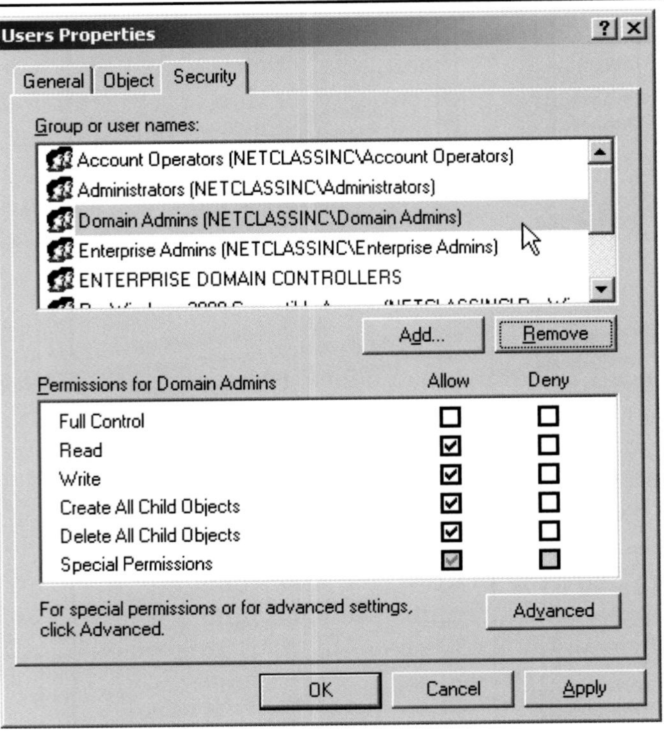

Figure 17-24. User rights are set in the **User Properties** dialog box. Some of the permissions that can be assigned are Full Control, Read, and Write.

permissions the right to perform certain functions.

The process of logging on to the network as part of an assigned group either gives the user the right to access the share or not. The type of access can be limited for a share, such as read-only, full access, execute, write, delete, or no access. These access restrictions are called permissions. ***Permissions*** are the right to perform certain functions. See **Figure 17-25** for a listing of some typical additional permissions that can be assigned to users and/or groups in the Windows Net Server 2003 environment.

Figure 17-25. Typical permissions that can be assigned to users or groups.

Assigned permission	Description
Read	User can execute, read, copy, or print a file but cannot delete, change files, or add to the directory.
Execute	User may run files in shared directory.
Write	User may read, write, create, and change a file in a directory but cannot execute or delete the file.
Delete	The user may delete files from a directory.
Full Access	The user can do anything: read, write, delete, change, and execute files.
No Access	The user cannot access the file. Note: if the user has two permissions assigned, one as an individual and one as a member of a group, the No Access setting takes precedence!

RAID Systems

Fault tolerance is a system's ability to recover after some sort of disaster. The hard drive could fail, the operating system could crash, a user could accidentally erase some files, and many more things could happen. Networks have the ability to recover from these types of disasters. There are many fault tolerance methods available. The two most common methods of fault tolerance are the use of RAID and the use of tape backup. In this section, we will explore common RAID configurations used with Microsoft servers.

fault tolerance
a system's ability to recover after some sort of disaster.

RAID is the acronym for Redundant Array of Inexpensive or Independent Disks. The translation of the acronym varies between the use of the word inexpensive and independent. The exact translation is not important, but the concept behind RAID technology is. A ***RAID*** is a system of several hard drive units arranged in such a way as to ensure recovery after a system disaster or to ensure data integrity during normal operation. There are three forms of RAID associated with Microsoft servers: Levels 0, 1, and 5. See **Figure 17-26.**

RAID
a system of several hard drive units arranged in such a way as to ensure recovery after a system disaster or to ensure data integrity during normal operation.

Level 0

Level 0 is called striped without parity. A striped set is two or more areas across two or more disks to which data is written or from which data is read. The main purpose of a striped set is to speed up the data read and write process. The data is recorded more quickly when it is being written simultaneously to multiple disks. When data is recorded in a striped set, the data is equally divided, and equal portions of the data are written to each hard disk drive.

A striped set spreads the data across two drives or volumes. Data is written alternately to each drive or volume in 64KB blocks of data. When two separate hard drive controllers are used, one for each drive, the read and write times are faster than those of a single drive. The disadvantage to this RAID arrangement is that there is no data protection. When one of the drives fail, all data on that drive is lost. To prevent the loss of data, the arrangement for data storage must use parity. Parity, as you recall, is a technique used to ensure data is correct. See Figure 17-26A.

Level 1

The RAID level 1, or disk mirroring, configuration requires two hard drives. One drive keeps an exact copy of all data on the opposite drive. This way if one drive fails, all its data can be retrieved from its duplicate. See Figure 17-26B.

Level 5

The RAID level 5 configuration can use from three to thirty-two drives of equal partition size to form what is called a stripe set with parity. Parity is used to reconstruct data lost on either of the two drives that are used to store data. For example, data is duplicated on two volumes and the third is used to store the parity of the two. Parity is staggered across all drives when a minimum of three are used. See Figure 17-26C.

Remember from previous units, parity is the sum total of two bytes of data added together. The two bytes will be either odd or even. By reversing the operation, the missing data can be reconstructed using the value stored in the parity section. It is important to remember that none of the techniques discussed are infallible. Anything can happen to destroy data. Regular backups are the only way to ensure some degree of fault tolerance.

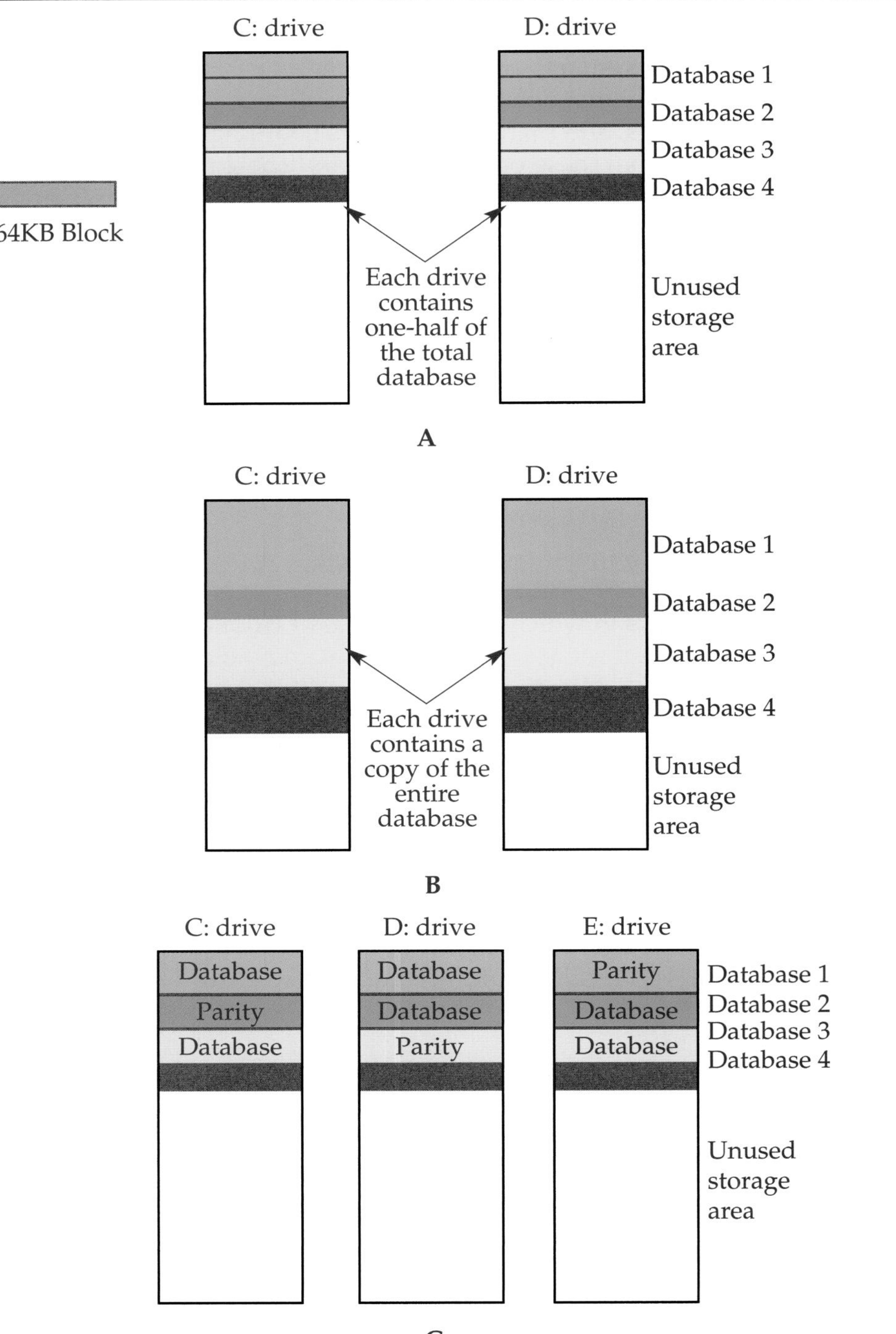

Figure 17-26. The three forms of RAID used on a Microsoft server. A—RAID level 0 offers no data protection. It is used to speed up the read/write process. Data is spread across more than one volume in 64KB blocks. B—RAID level 1 uses at least two volumes to store an exact duplicate of data. If one drive fails, the other still contains an exact copy of the data. C—RAID 5 is a striped set with parity. Parity is used to reconstruct data lost on any of the volumes.

Summary

- Security is one of the main features of a network system.
- Share-level security is the default security system used on Windows-based networks, and requires a password to access a share.
- User-level security identifies who may have access to a shared resource but does not require a password for accessing the share.
- A peer-to-peer network usually uses share-level security.
- A client/server network usually uses user-level security.
- Administrative functions in a peer-to-peer network are not highly organized and are best described as decentralized.
- A centralized administration network system has a single and central network authority that controls all aspects of the network system.
- Centralized networks are organized administratively three sections: domains, groups, and users.
- A domain is the entire network organization of all groups and users on the network.
- Users can be assigned rights and properties on a network system.
- Groups are workers who share common responsibilities and can be thought of as a set.
- RAID is a way to ensure data integrity and fault tolerance through the use of multiple drive volumes.

Review Questions

Answer the following questions on a separate sheet of paper. Please do not write in this book.

1. Who controls a peer-to-peer network?
2. Who controls the access to shares on a peer-to-peer network?
3. What is the default setting of shares when Windows 95, 98, or Me is first set up?
4. Which type of share security is usually found on a peer-to-peer network?
5. Which type of share security is usually found on a client/server network?
6. What are the responsibilities of a network administrator?
7. What are shares?
8. What are the two levels of security on a typical Windows peer-to-peer network?
9. What is the difference in the two levels of security?
10. What is a user account?
11. What is a domain?
12. What is a group?
13. What is a permission?
14. What are the three forms of RAID associated with Microsoft servers?

Sample A+ Exam Questions

Answer the following questions on a separate sheet of paper. Please do not write in this book.

1. Which example below is the best password to use to prevent possible compromise or intrusion?
   a. secret
   b. Big$tar_5
   c. President Roosevelt
   d. Password
2. Which is not a typical Windows XP share permission?
   a. Read
   b. Full control
   c. Partial
   d. Change
3. What does a user need in order to access a network system? Choose all that apply.
   a. User name
   b. Password
   c. Group membership
   d. A security clearance
4. Who determines a user's rights on a client/server network?
   a. Each computer user determines the user rights for their PC station.
   b. Users set their own individual rights based on their total system knowledge.
   c. The network administrator sets individual rights on the network system.
   d. All users automatically have full rights to use the entire network when they are issued an account on the network.
5. In a Windows Net Server 2003 network, user accounts are set up in _____.
   a. Active Directory Users and Computers
   b. Performance Monitor
   c. Event Viewer
   d. User Share Setup
6. In a Windows Net Server 2003 network system, the user password is changed _____.
   a. in the **Active Directory Users and Computers** dialog box
   b. in the **Account Policy** dialog box
   c. at the user's station under the **Change Password** icon in **Control Panel**
   d. A user password can never be changed once it is issued

A+

7. Which program can be used to monitor user activity on a computer system.
   a. Event Viewer
   b. Net Monitor
   c. Performance Monitor
   d. Net Movement
8. Which program would you select to check the total amount of activity through the CPU?
   a. Net Monitor
   b. Performance Monitor
   c. CPU Monitor
   d. CPU Pole Watch
9. When using Windows Net Server 2003, a collection of users who have similar tasks and are consequently assigned the same user rights are generally referred to as a _____.
   a. group
   b. covey
   c. pod
   d. corporate entity
10. In a centralized network, an entire business location is usually referred to as a _____.
    a. corporate entity
    b. select pod
    c. domain
    d. group

Suggested Laboratory Activities

Do not attempt any suggested laboratory activities without your instructor's permission. Certain activities can render the PC operating system inoperable.

1. Set up a client/server network. Choose one PC to be the server. All other PCs must log on through the server to gain access to the network. There is a variety of client/server software available in beta versions as well as free Linux versions. Most Linux systems that use X Windows will be remarkably similar to the Windows operating system.
2. Use an existing network to do the following:
   a. Add a new user to the network.
   b. Restrict the time of day a particular user can access the network.
   c. Set a time limit, by days, during which a user may use the network.
   d. Display a list of users and groups on the network system.
   e. Change an existing user's password.
   f. Set up a minimum password length.

Interesting Web Sites for More Information

www.acterna.com
www.arcnet.com
www.hp.com
www.ibm.com
www.tutorialfind.com

Chapter 17
Laboratory Activity
Creating a Network Share

After completing this laboratory activity, you will be able to:

- ❑ Create a share on a peer-to-peer network.
- ❑ Identify the types of security associated with a peer-to-peer network share.

Introduction

Sharing files and hardware is the main purpose of a network. In this laboratory activity, you will set up a network share. You will share a program on your computer with another person in your lab. You will set up a share for a variety of items such as a hard drive, a CD-ROM drive, a directory, and a file. You will also set up the file with rights such as read only, full rights, and access dependent on a password.

There are two types of security commonly used in networks: share-level and user-level. Share-level security is commonly associated with a peer-to-peer type network and user-level security is associated with a centrally administered network, such as one that utilizes a file server.

Equipment and Materials

- (2) PCs with Windows 95, Windows 98, or Windows Me operating system installed and set up as a peer-to-peer network. *This is a two-station lab activity.*

Procedure

1. ______ Report to your assigned station and power on the PC.
2. ______ After the computer boots, right-click **Network Neighborhood** and select **Properties** from the shortcut menu. When the **Network** dialog box appears, click the **File and Print Sharing** button. The **File and Print Sharing** dialog box will appear. Put a check mark in the **I want to give others access to my files** check box. Click **OK** to accept the changes and close the **File and Print Sharing** dialog box. In the **Network** dialog box, click **OK** to accept the changes and to close the dialog box.
3. ______ Next, select the **Access Control** tab at the top of the **Network** dialog box. Activate the **Share-level access control** radio button. Click **OK** to close the dialog box. You will have to restart the computer for the changes to take effect.

4. ______ When the computer has rebooted, double-click **My Computer**. Right-click the icon for the local hard drive, and select **Properties** from the shortcut menu. Select the **General** tab. In the **Label:** text box, enter the name Station1. The dialog should appear similar to the one in the following illustration.

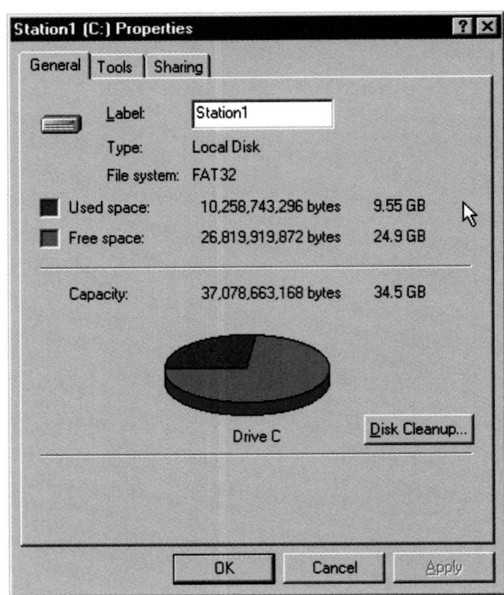

5. ______ Now, select the **Sharing** tab from the top of the dialog box. The dialog box should appear similar to the one shown here.

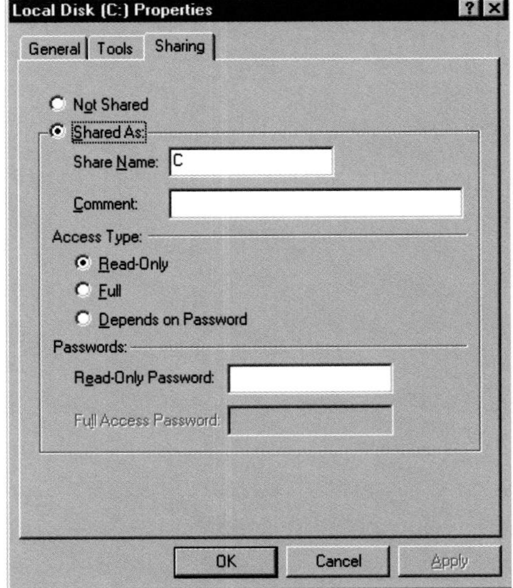

6. _______ With the **Sharing** tab of the hard drive's **Properties** dialog box open, select the **Share As:** radio button. Next, select an access type by selecting the appropriate radio button in the **Access Type:** area of the dialog box. The access options listed are **Read-Only**, **Full**, and **Depends on Password**. Ask your instructor for the proper settings. Next, enable the share by clicking the **OK** button.

7. _______ After your share for the drive has been set up, go to Windows Explorer and look at the directory structure. If the share has been set up correctly, your drive C should be represented by an icon similar to the one shown. The icon has a hand under the hard drive to indicate it is set up as a shared device. If this icon is different or not present, call your instructor.

8. _______ After your hard drive has been set up as a share, experiment with the different access types.

9. _______ Experiment setting up a share for a document. Try changing a document to read-only access and then attempt to access and change the contents of the file. You may need to access the **Help** option from the startup menu for additional information.

10. _______ Leave the PC on while you answer the review questions. After answering the questions, return the PC to its original condition before shutting it down.

Review Questions

Answer the following questions on a separate sheet of paper. Please do not write in this book.

1. What are the three access types associated with a shared device or file?
2. What are the two password types?
3. How can you identify a file or hardware device that is shared?
4. What are the two main types of shares?

Computers installed in classrooms and school labs have created a need for network administrators in the school system.

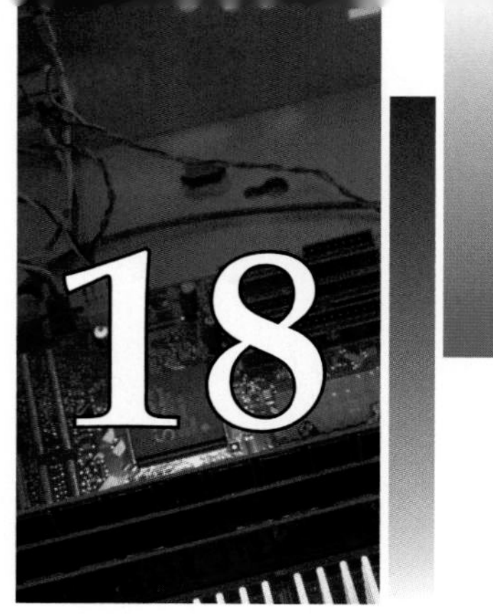

18 WAN

After studying this chapter, you will be able to:

- Explain the difference between a LAN and a WAN.
- Explain how IP addresses are used.
- Explain DNS, WINS, and DHCP services.
- Explain the use of common diagnostic utilities associated with networks.
- Describe the physical structure and evolution of the Internet.
- Identify equipment associated with a WAN.
- Describe the function of several common network troubleshooting software commands.
- Explain how to set up an e-mail account.
- Describe the common features associated with e-mail.

A+ Exam—Key Points

The A+ Certification exams require knowledge of the basic operation of network systems. As a technician, you must know where your responsibility for the repair of a PC ends and where the responsibility of the network administrator begins.

Be sure you are able to distinguish between DNS, WINS, and DHCP services. You may also be asked to identify an example of an IP address and a subnet mask.

Key Words and Terms

The following words and terms will become important pieces of your computer vocabulary. Be sure you can define them.

Archie
ATM
bridge
brouter
Class A network
Class B network
Class C network
Domain Name Service (DNS)
dynamic addressing
Dynamic Host Configuration Protocol (DHCP)
File Transfer Protocol (FTP)
firewall
gateway
Gopher
host
Hypertext Markup Language (HTML)
Hypertext Transfer Protocol (HTTP)
Internet
InterNIC
IP address
IP switch
Multipurpose Internet Mail Extensions (MIME)
octet
Packet Internet Groper (PING)
proxy server
registrar
repeater
router
subnet mask
switch
Telnet
time to live (TTL)
tracert
Uniform Resource Locator (URL)
Windows Internet Naming Service (WINS)

Wide area networks (WANs) are network systems that cover a wide geographical area. Wide area networks require additional networking equipment and different protocols than local-area networks (LANs). WANs use routers, bridges, hubs, brouters, and more. The types of equipment, protocols, and techniques required by a WAN are examined in this chapter. This will provide you with an overall view of how data is delivered over the Internet, the world's largest WAN. Some of the subjects in this section are vast enough to fill textbooks of their own. The purpose of this chapter is to provide you with a basic understanding of how a WAN operates and to explain some of the technical terminology associated with wide area networks, including the Internet.

Today, you must think globally when you think about wide area networks. Many corporations include thousands of computers in their networked system. These systems often stretch across countries or even continents. The networks used by organizations like the United States Postal Service, the combined armed forces, an international bank, and a state school system, are all examples of wide area networks. Many of these networks are connected to the Internet.

You may wonder how the Internet or any WAN handles the volume of data packets generated by all those users. It may seem like all the traffic would slow the Internet down to a snail's pace. There are packets of information being sent everywhere.

In this chapter, you will learn how e-mail gets to its destination and how your browser can locate a particular Web page in the Internet's endless tangle of cables, routers, and computers. The basic concepts of wide area network operation are introduced along with the technologies that make WANs possible. Remember, many of the topics discussed in this unit could fill textbooks of their own. This is only an introduction.

host
a computer or other piece of equipment connected to a TCP/IP network that requires an address; used interchangeably with the term *node*.

TCP/IP Addressing

The TCP/IP protocol is the secret to communication over the Internet and other WANs. The TCP/IP protocol was designed for the Internet and is the dominant protocol for data exchange on a typical LAN, MAN, or WAN. TCP/IP addressing is a method of identification used to identify every node or host on a network. The terms ***host*** and ***node*** are used interchangeably to identify individual PCs, printers, and network equipment that may require an address. *TCP/IP addressing* and *IP addressing* are also interchangeable terms.

IP address
identifying address used for a PC or other equipment on a TCP/IP network.

InterNIC
a branch of the United States government under the direction of the Department of Commerce. It is responsible for regulating the Internet, overseeing the issue of domain names, and assigning IP addresses to them.

InterNIC

In a previous chapter, we discussed how data packets are delivered to the correct computer through various routes. The key to the process is the protocol. The Internet uses TCP/IP protocol to route data packets all over the world. Every network has a unique ***IP address*** assigned to it. IP addresses are regulated and assigned through the organization known as ***InterNIC.***

InterNIC operates under the direction of the Department of Commerce. It is responsible for regulating the Internet, overseeing the issue of domain names, and assigning IP addresses to them. A user does not directly contact InterNIC for an IP address or domain name. Applications are placed through private sector companies, called ***registrars,*** which are regulated by InterNIC (www.internic.org). InterNIC allocates IP addresses much like the way the government issues telephone area codes to long distance carriers and telephone companies. IP addresses must be similarly regulated or there would be chaos in the computer world.

registrar
private sector company, regulated by InterNIC, to whom users apply for an IP address or domain name.

Tech Tip:
The Internet Corporation for Assigned Names and Numbers (ICANN), under the supervision of the Department of Commerce, has recently assumed the name and responsibilities of InterNIC.

IP Addresses

An IP address consists of four octets. An ***octet*** is an 8-bit series of numbers. In a binary expression, each octet is composed of eight digits (0s or 1s). Four octets compose the 32-bit IP address. Periods separate each octet from the neighboring octets. See the example that follows.

octet
an 8-bit series of numbers.

Typical IP address expressed in decimal: 123.104.53.18
Same IP address expressed in binary: 01111011.01101000.00110101.00010010

As you can see in the example, decimal expression of an IP address is much shorter than the binary expression of the same address. The range of each octet's decimal equivalent is from 0 to 255. This is the greatest possible number range using eight binary positions. The relationship of IP addresses to network systems is the same as telephone numbers are to telephone systems. Each telephone is identified with a unique telephone number, and each host on a network is identified by a unique IP number. In the following sections, you will learn how IP addresses are determined.

Class A network large networks that can support up to 16 million hosts on each of 127 networks.

Class B network medium-sized networks that can support up to 65,000 hosts on each of 16,000 networks.

Class C network small networks that can support up to 254 hosts on each of 2 million networks.

Network Class

For the purpose of assigning IP addresses, networks are divided into three classifications. Large networks are assigned a Class A classification. A ***Class A network*** can support up to 16 million hosts on each of 127 networks. Medium-sized networks are assigned Class B status. A ***Class B network*** supports up to 65,000 hosts on each of 16,000 networks. Small networks are assigned a Class C classification. A ***Class C network*** supports 254 hosts on each of 2 million networks. Networks are assigned an IP address based on their network classification. Look at **Figure 18-1.**

In the table, you can see that the class of the network determines the numeric value of the first octet in its IP address. The range for a Class A network is from 1–127; the range for a Class B network is from 128–191; and the range for a Class C network is from 192–223. IP addresses for Class A networks use only the first octet as the network address. The remaining three octets define hosts on the network. The first two octets of a Class B network's IP address

Figure 18-1. The attributes of networks are listed here by class. The *Format* row lists which octets in the network's IP address are used to define the network and which are used to define the host. The *Range of 1st octet* row lists the range of numbers that will appear in the first octet of each class's IP addresses. The *Total hosts per network* row lists the number of hosts that each network can have. The *Total number of networks* row lists the total number of networks that can be supported by a class. The *Typical address* row lists typical addresses for the three classes.

Table of TCP/IP Classes			
	Class A	Class B	Class C
Format	Net.host.host.host	Net.Net.host.host	Net.Net.Net.host
Subnet	255.000.000.000	255.255.000.000	255.255.255.000
Range of 1st octet	1–127	128–191	192–223
Total hosts per network	16,777,214	65,534	254
Total number of networks	127	16,384	2,097,152
Typical address	122.57.103.147	135.200.137.102	198.45.103.67

identify the network. The remaining two octets identify hosts on the network. A Class C network uses the first three octets to identify the network and the last octet to identify the individual hosts. A typical Class C network might have a TCP/IP address of 201.100.100.12. The network is identified by the 201.100.100 and the host is identified as 12.

Subnet Mask

An organizational network may be divided into several smaller networks. These networks within networks are known as subnets. A ***subnet mask*** is used to determine what subnet a particular IP address refers to.

subnet mask
a mask that is used to determine what subnet a particular IP address refers to.

When the subnet mask is encountered, it is usually viewed in decimal form in a series of four three-digit numbers. At first glance, a subnet mask may appear identical to an IP address. However, a subnet mask is distinguishable from an IP address because it begins with one or more octets of 255. An IP address cannot begin with 255. The subnet mask can be used to identify the class of network, but is really intended to allow the network address to be broken down into smaller subnetworks.

The octets of a subnet mask correspond to octets in the IP address. The actual numbers found in a subnet mask depend on the class of the network and the number of subnetworks it is divided into. The subnet mask is combined with the IP address using the bitwise "AND" operation, the details of which are beyond the scope of this text. The resulting address is the *subnet address.* For now, just remember that the subnet mask is used to identify any subnetworks at a network address.

Running WINIPCFG

Both the IP address and the subnet mask can be revealed by running the winipcfg.exe program from the **Run** option of the **Start** menu. Winipcfg is short for Windows IP configuration, and the program is available on all Windows 95, 98, and Me machines. The same information may be obtained for Windows NT, 2000, and XP systems by running ipconfig.exe at the DOS prompt.

Running winipcfg.exe opens a dialog box similar to the one in **Figure 18-2.** It reveals the MAC address (adapter address) of the network interface card, the assigned IP address, the subnet mask being used by the Internet service provider, and the provider's default gateway address. When connecting to the Internet through an ISP, the default gateway is the device located at the Internet service provider that connects the home PC to the Internet. It serves as a "gateway" to the Internet.

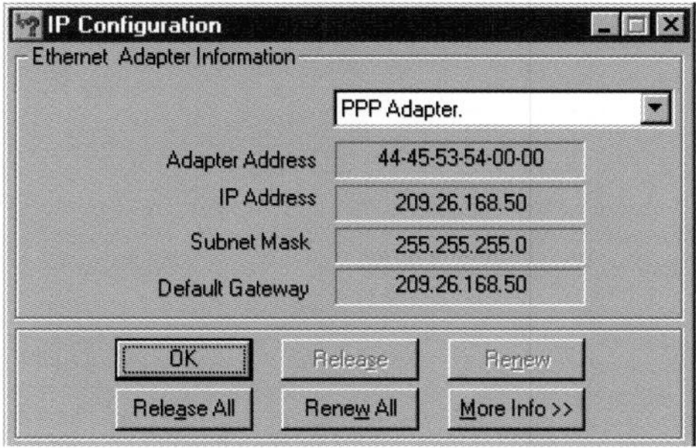

Figure 18-2.
The first screen of the **IP Configuration** dialog box.

By clicking the **More Info>>>** button of the **IP Configuration** dialog box, a second dialog box is revealed with more information about the connection. See **Figure 18-3.** The additional information provided in this dialog box, such as DHCP server and DNS server, will become more relevant as the unit continues.

The IP configuration is a group of settings made on the host that allow it to communicate all over the world. These settings are usually determined automatically by the Internet service provider's software. Occasionally you may have to adjust the settings manually, or verify the information while working with a service provider to troubleshoot a connection.

Dynamic Host Configuration Protocol (DHCP) a protocol written to replace the manual setup of IP addresses on a network by assigning IP addresses dynamically (automatically) to the host PCs.

dynamic addressing the act of automatically assigning IP addresses.

Windows Internet Naming Service (WINS) resolves the computer name to the equivalent IP address on the network.

DHCP

Originally, computers on a network had to have their IP addresses assigned manually as part of the routine to get a PC ready to communicate on a network and over the Internet. When IP addresses are assigned manually, the process is referred to as static IP addressing. This is a time-consuming operation if hundreds or even thousands of hosts are on a network. A log of machine names, locations, MAC addresses, and the assigned IP addresses must be recorded. IP addresses on each host must be unique. Using the same IP address on more than one host causes communication conflicts, resulting in erratic behavior.

Dynamic Host Configuration Protocol (DHCP) was written to replace the manual setup of IP addresses on a network. When a server runs DHCP, the IP addresses are assigned automatically to the hosts. The act of automatically assigning IP addresses is known as ***dynamic addressing.*** The DHCP server is given a pool, or list, of IP addresses. Each host is assigned an address from the pool as it logs on to the network. The IP address is issued to each host temporarily. The address is released after a period and may be reissued to another host later.

WINS

On a typical Windows network, each computer has its own name, such as "Station1" or "BillC". The ***Windows Internet Naming Service (WINS)*** resolves

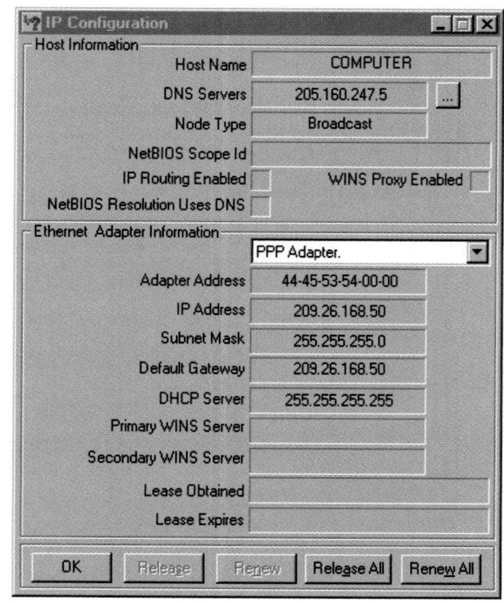

Figure 18-3. The second screen of the **IP Configuration** dialog box. This screen presents more detailed information, including addresses for the DHCP server and the DNS server.

the computer name to the equivalent IP address on the network. DHCP servers assign IP addresses to hosts from a pool of IP addresses. The same host may have a new IP address each time it logs on the local network. To correlate a computer name to its current IP address, WINS works closely with the DHCP server.

DNS

The ***Domain Name Service (DNS)*** is similar to WINS, but instead of translating computer names to IP addresses in the network, DNS translates domain names to IP addresses used on the Internet. The DNS service is used all across the Internet, assisting computers in identifying and talking to each other.

Domain Name Service (DNS) translates domain names to IP addresses used on the Internet.

Domain names are easier to remember than actual IP addresses. When a domain name is typed in, the DNS service searches its database for the matching IP address, and connects the user to that address. Web addresses are entered manually and then passed and copied throughout the Internet by routers. Once a domain is located, the server retains a copy in a database.

Special WAN Equipment

A typical WAN must connect many different and diverse pieces of equipment and handle a tremendous amount of packet traffic. To accomplish this, some special equipment must be used to handle the routing of data to and from hosts all over the network system. Certain pieces of equipment are utilized in a network environment when all the hosts are using the same protocol to communicate. Other types of equipment are used when a mixture of protocols are being used. For example, an IP address consists of four octets that each range from 0–255. IPX uses an eight digit hexadecimal number, using addresses such as A11CA112. AppleTalk (used for Apple computer networks) uses a combination of alphanumeric characters, such as ArtDesign123. Look at **Figure 18-4.**

In the illustration, you see a mixture of different networking protocols. These are only naming convention differences; the data packets created by each system also differ. For the many different protocols to communicate with each other, special hardware and software must be used. This section covers the major types of equipment and briefly explains the function of each in a network environment.

Repeater

A ***repeater*** is a piece of equipment that simply regenerates a weak digital signal. As you know from earlier chapters, there is a maximum length of cable run permissible for transmitting data. To send data across many miles, a repeater is required. A repeater receives a signal, reshapes it to its original form, and sends it on along the cable. Look at **Figure 18-5.**

repeater a piece of equipment that regenerates a weak digital signal.

As a digital signal travels farther from its source, it degrades, eventually becoming unintelligible. At great distances, a network adapter cannot distinguish between the 0s and 1s transmitted through the cable. A repeater receives the degraded digital signal and reshapes it to its original form.

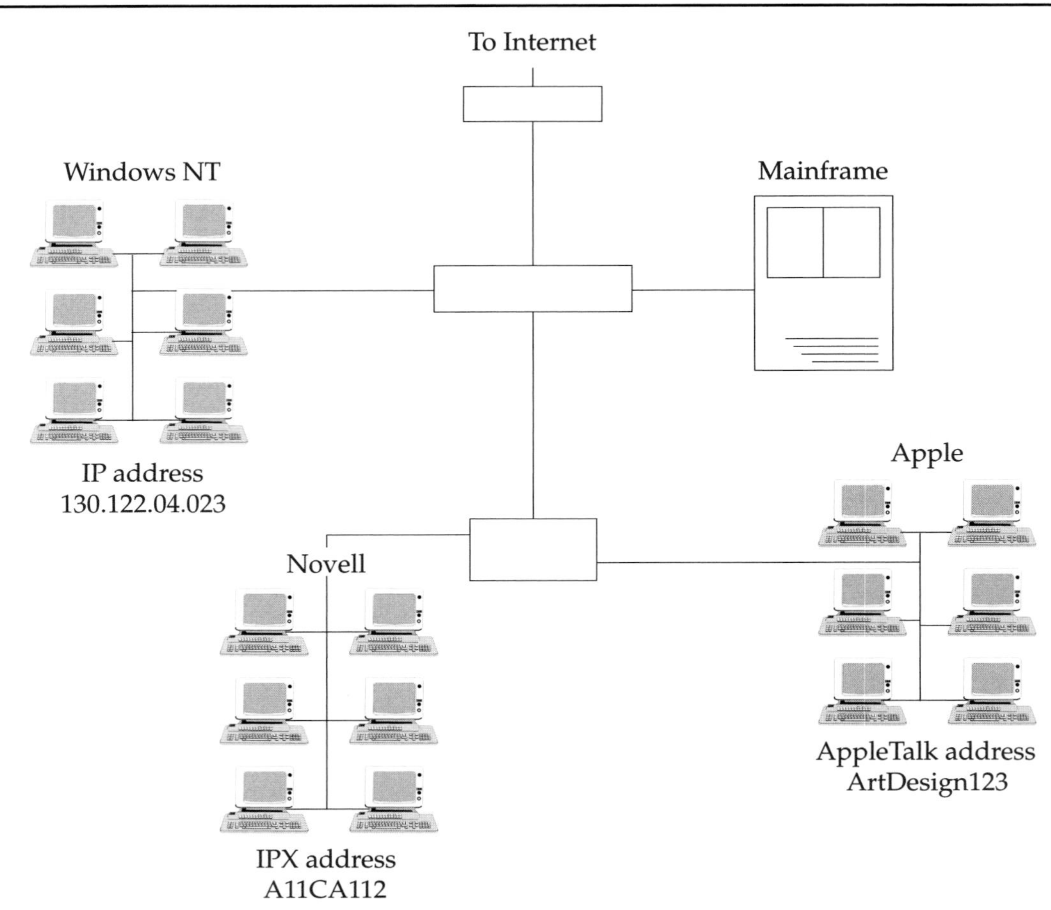

Figure 18-4. This figure demonstrates some of the complexities that occur in a WAN. The individual LANs shown use different operating systems, different forms of address, and different methods for packaging data for transmission. Yet, thanks to a variety of equipment, these networks are able to interact smoothly.

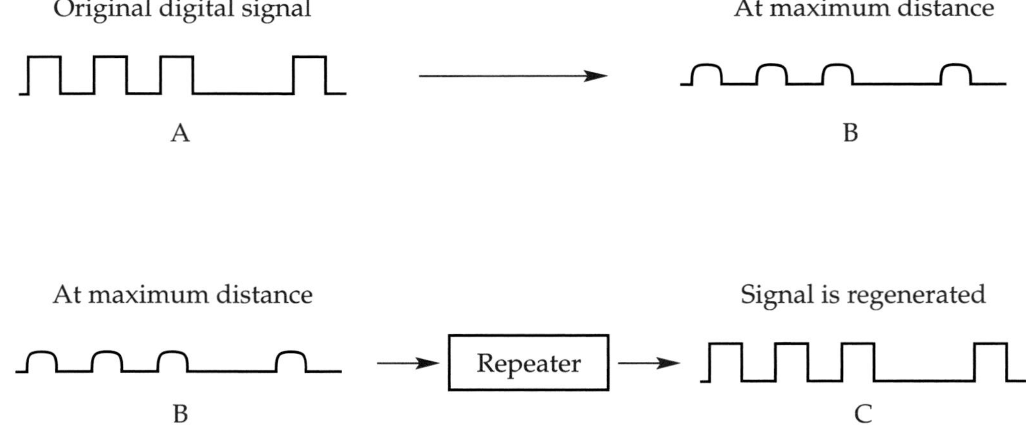

Figure 18-5. A—Digital signal is transmitted. The only values in the signal are 1s and 0s. B—As the signal approaches it's maximum transmission distance, the shoulders of the signal are slumped, creating graduated values (analog) in the transmission. Also note that the crests of the signal are no longer at maximum height. C—The repeater restores the signal to its original strength and shape.

A+ Note:
A repeater is often referred to as an amplifier. Technically speaking, an amplifier increases the original signal strength rather than reshaping the signal back to its original form. On the A+ Certification exams, the only correct answer may equate a repeater with an amplifier. In this case, choose the answer that implies that a repeater works like an amplifier.

Bridge

A ***bridge*** is a special piece of equipment used to join two dissimilar network segments together. For example, you may use a bridge to connect an Ethernet to a Token Ring network. The bridge simply allows the passing of packets from one system to the other regardless of the protocol being used. The bridge maintains a list of MAC addresses that are connected to it so it can filter out data packets. For example, if two network segments are connected by a bridge, the bridge can be programmed to pass only data packets that match the MAC address of hosts on the other side of the bridge. By doing this, data traffic is minimized. See **Figure 18-6.**

bridge
a special piece of network equipment that is used to join two dissimilar networks segments together such as a wireless and an Ethernet 100BaseT network.

Router

A ***router*** is used to connect networks together and to control the flow of exchanged data packets. The term *routing* means moving a packet of data from a source to a destination. A router performs much more complex tasks than a bridge. A router not only connects hosts together on a WAN, it also determines the best route to use. The router actually calculates the cost of a number of different ways to connect the hosts together and uses the least expensive method. The cost is based on the use of leased lines and equipment, the time to transmit, and the distance. Look at **Figure 18-7.**

router
used to control the flow of data to different networks based on IP addresses.

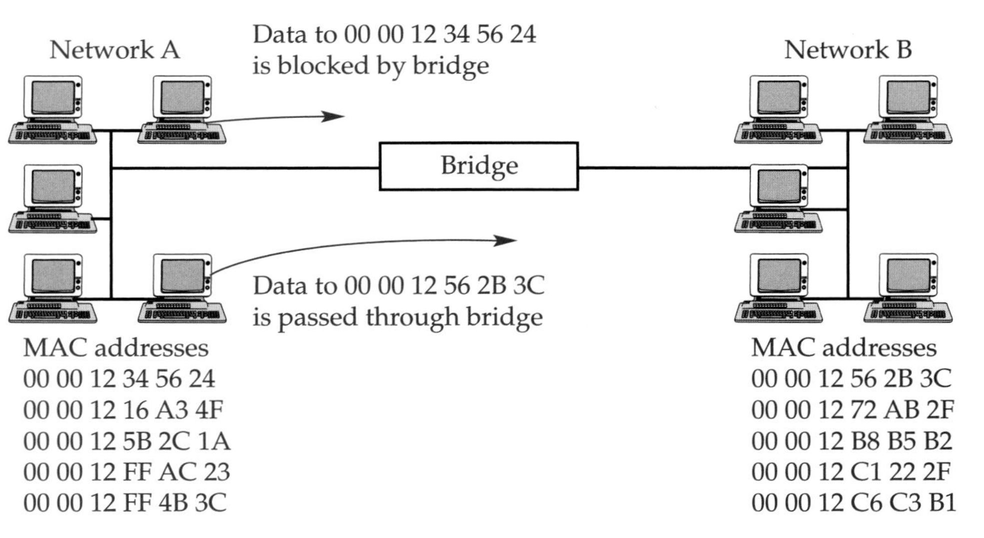

Figure 18-6.
A bridge limits the number of units affected by data broadcasts. The bridge passes or blocks data, based on the MAC address in the destination address in the packet header. If a large network were constructed without bridge techniques, the constant broadcast of data packets would slow the entire network.

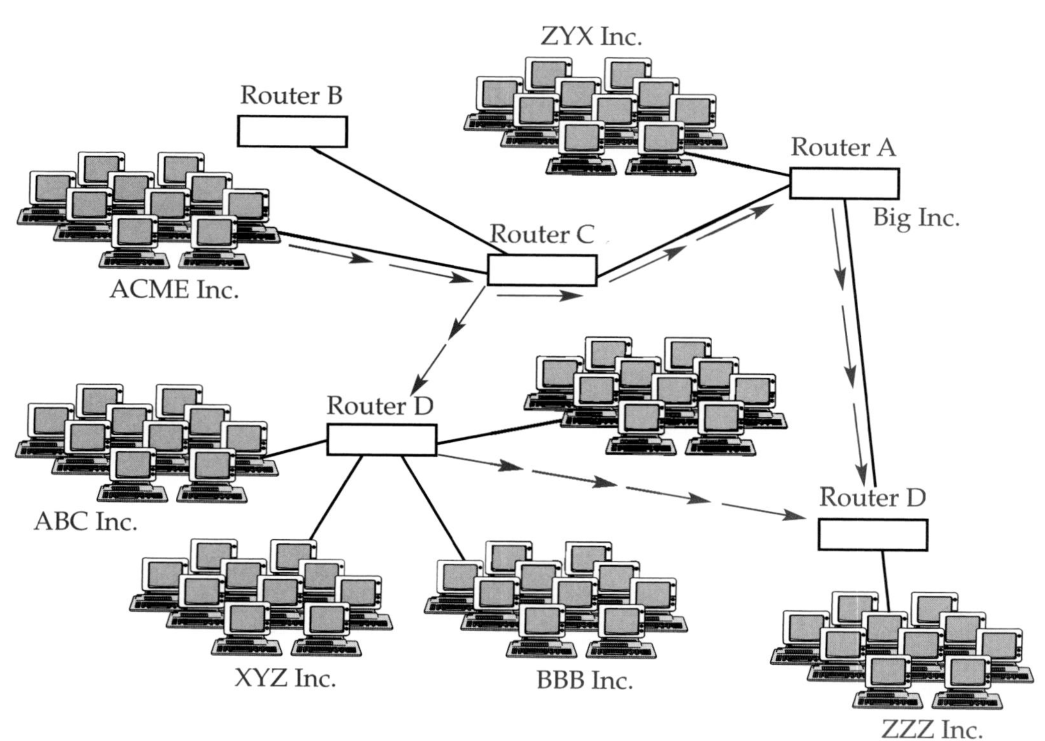

Figure 18-7. Routers route data traffic across the entire world. They also select the cheapest route to use. As you can see, there are several routes that can be chosen to send a data packet from ACME, Inc. to ZZZ, Inc. The job of the router is to select the cheapest.

In the illustration, you can see that the function of the router is to determine the least expensive route from one computer host to another. A router adds information to the data frame surrounding the data packet. The information expands the identification of the packet's origin, its destination, and its route.

Routers are available in two styles: static and dynamic. A static router is programmed with a database of IP addresses, subnet masks, and network IDs. They do not broadcast information on a constant basis. A dynamic router communicates with other routers on the network. Dynamic routers constantly exchange data about each other's location and database tables. See **Figure 18-8** for a quick comparison of bridging and routing.

Brouter

brouter a combination router and bridge.

A ***brouter*** is a combination router and bridge. A brouter applies the best characteristics of both systems.

Figure 18-8. This table offers a short comparison between routers and bridges.

Bridge	Router
Forwards broadcast traffic.	Blocks broadcast traffic.
Uses MAC addresses.	Uses network addresses.
Does not add to packet.	Adds to packet information.
Forwards packets to unknown addresses.	Blocks packets to unknown addresses.

Switch

A ***switch*** filters and forwards packets of data between network segments. Switches are usually intelligent hubs, which means they can determine on which side of the switch a packet's destination is located.

switch filters and forwards packets of data between network segments based on MAC addresses.

There are two types of switching communication used for computer networks, packet switching and circuit switching. Packet switching divides data into packets, which can take a variety of routes to get to their destination. Circuit switching makes a permanent connection for the duration of the transmission, and data is transmitted in a steady stream. For example, when you make a dial up connection with a modem, a circuit switch is closed to keep the modem in constant connection on the telephone line. On the network itself, the packet switching method is used rather than a permanent connection for the duration of the call.

IP Switch

The ***IP switch,*** introduced by Ipsilon Networks, Inc., is designed to pass ATM protocol packets. It is faster than traditional routers, but until ATM is fully implemented, TCP/IP will still be used. As you recall, ***ATM*** is a high-speed network-system design that allows a mixture of voice, video, and data to be transmitted on the same line. To maintain the data flow rate in an ATM system, IP switches rather than conventional routers must be used in the network.

IP switch designed to pass ATM protocol packets.

ATM a high-speed network system design that allows a mixture of voice, video, and data to be transmitted on the same line.

Gateways

Another networking device is the gateway. A ***gateway*** is used to translate information between two networks that use different protocols to communicate. You can think of a gateway as a communications translator because it translates commands and data from one protocol to another, or from one format to another. For example, a gateway can translate information between a Novell network using the IPX/SPX protocol and a Microsoft network using the TCP/IP protocol.

A gateway may be a special piece of equipment or a software package loaded onto a server or a router. It is important to understand that a network server can provide more than one service. A computer can serve as a gateway, a proxy server, a firewall, and a file server. The exact name used for the server is relative to the network service being discussed.

gateway translates information between two LANs using different protocols.

Proxy Server

When dealing with network Internet service, you may hear the term ***proxy server.*** Proxy servers are designed to hide all the PCs in the LAN from direct connection from PCs outside of the LAN. This provides a better security service than if each PC had direct access to outside the LAN. The server acts as a go-between for the distant sites and the user behind the server. The proxy server relays the requested information for the client, leaving the client anonymous outside the network. Users on the outside of the network see only the proxy server and not the client. Also, only one modem is required for a telephone connection, but more can be added to the same server.

The proxy server makes accessing the Web more efficient for the network clients by caching frequently requested Web pages. By caching the frequently accessed Web information, the process of accessing distant pages is sped up.

proxy server designed to hide all the PCs in the LAN from direct connection from PCs outside of the LAN. It relays the requested information for the client, leaving the client anonymous outside the network.

Firewalls

firewall
a barrier that prevents direct contact between computers outside the organization with computers inside the organization.

The term ***firewall*** refers to a barrier that prevents direct contact between computers outside the organization and computers inside the organization. A firewall can be strictly software or a combination software and hardware. All data communications to and from the organization are routed through the proxy server, and the firewall software decides whether to forward the data.

Network Diagnostic Utilities

Standard utility programs are very handy when troubleshooting networked PCs. Ping and tracert are the most common.

PING

Packet Internet Groper (PING)
a utility program that is often used as a troubleshooting tool to verify network connections to Web sites.

The ***Packet Internet Groper (PING)*** is a utility that is often used as a troubleshooting tool to verify network connections to Web sites. The ping utility sends a packet to a distant site and then waits for a reply. Ping is executed as a command from the DOS command prompt. At the prompt, you simply type **ping** followed by the IP address or its URL name, such as www.yahoo.com. **Figure 18-9** shows the results of issuing a **ping** command to the Yahoo Web site. If you are on a network with a firewall, this test may not work. The **ping** command may be blocked by the firewall. Check with the systems administrator.

When the Yahoo site was pinged, the name "Yahoo" was automatically resolved to an IP address. You can see the IP address listed as 216.32.74.50. After the IP address was determined, four packets with 32 bytes of data were sent to that address. The site echoed back with four replies. The average round trip to the site and back was 305 milliseconds.

time to live (TTL)
the length of time the data in the packet is valid.

The ***time to live (TTL)*** is the length of time the data in the packet is valid. Packets are transmitted with the TTL setting recorded in the packet's header. This tells the network to disregard the packet after the set TTL time. There are a number of switches that can be used with the **ping** command to modify it. The additional switches for the **ping** command can be viewed by using **ping** with the help switch or by just typing and entering **ping**.

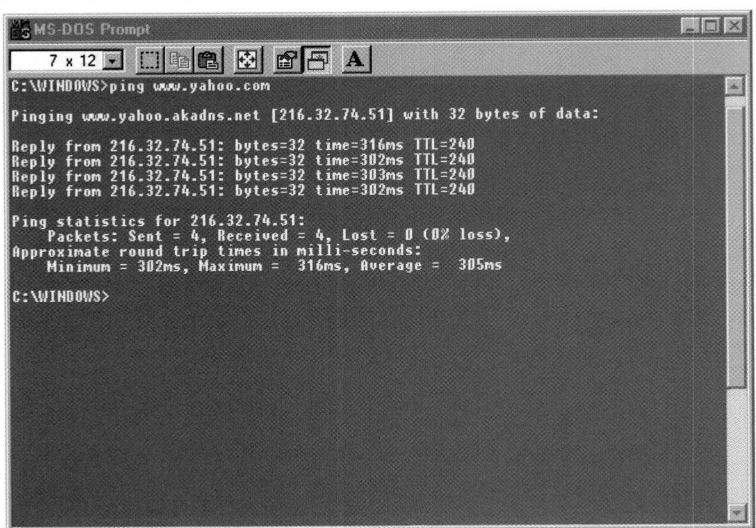

Figure 18-9.
A ping being performed on www.yahoo.com.

A handy way of checking the network card to see if it is responding to TCP/IP transmissions is to ping the card itself. Simply type the **ping** command at the DOS prompt with 127.0.0.1 as the IP address. As an alternative, you may enter **ping localhost** at the DOS prompt. Either method will execute a ping to the local host. The name "localhost" refers to the computer you are using.

Tracert

The utility program ***tracert*** is short for trace route. Tracert is more advanced than the ping utility. Like ping, it sends a packet out and waits for a reply. In addition to the information that ping provides, tracert also displays information about the route that was taken to the destination. See **Figure 18-10.** As with the **ping** command, depending on how the firewall is configured, this test may not work on a network.

tracert
utility program that sends a packet out and waits for a reply. It also displays information about the route that was taken to the destination.

The **tracert** command is issued from the DOS command line. In Figure 18-10, the **tracert** command revealed the actual route taken by the data packet. Among the information provided is the name of the router at strato.net and the names of the different telephone carriers, such as Sprint. The utility also displays the time it takes each packet to reach its destination. This feature is extremely useful in locating bottlenecks along the route.

Many third party software developers offer utilities that further enhance the tracert function. NeoTrace is a commercial product developed and distributed by NeoWorx, Inc. It is a powerful diagnostic and investigation tool. The program traces the route to any destination over the Internet and returns information about the hosts on the route taken. The information includes registered details of each host along the route, such as address, telephone number, e-mail address, and IP address. See **Figure 18-11.** The information can be displayed as a detailed listing similar to a spreadsheet and a graphical display in which the route is displayed on a map.

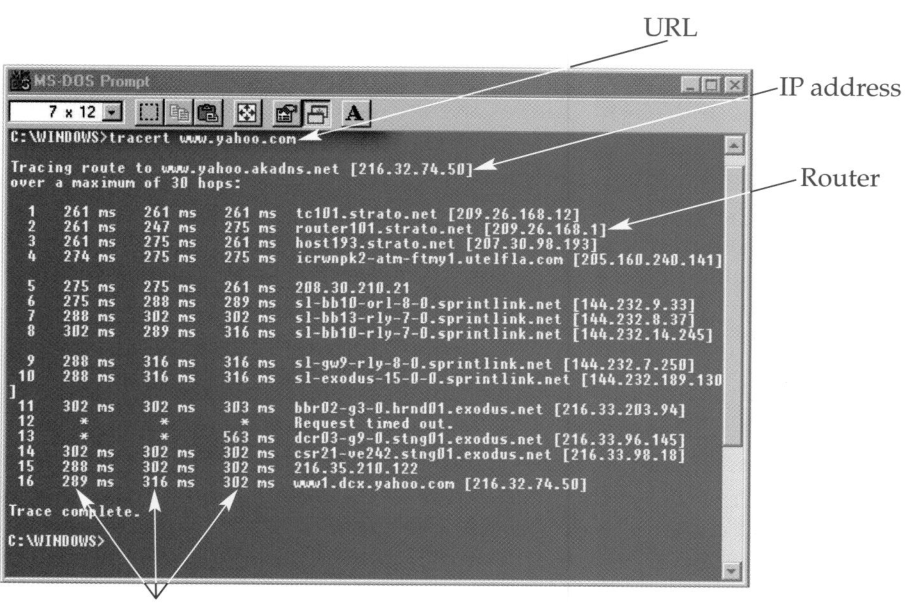

Figure 18-10.
The tracert utility being used to trace the network path to www.yahoo.com.

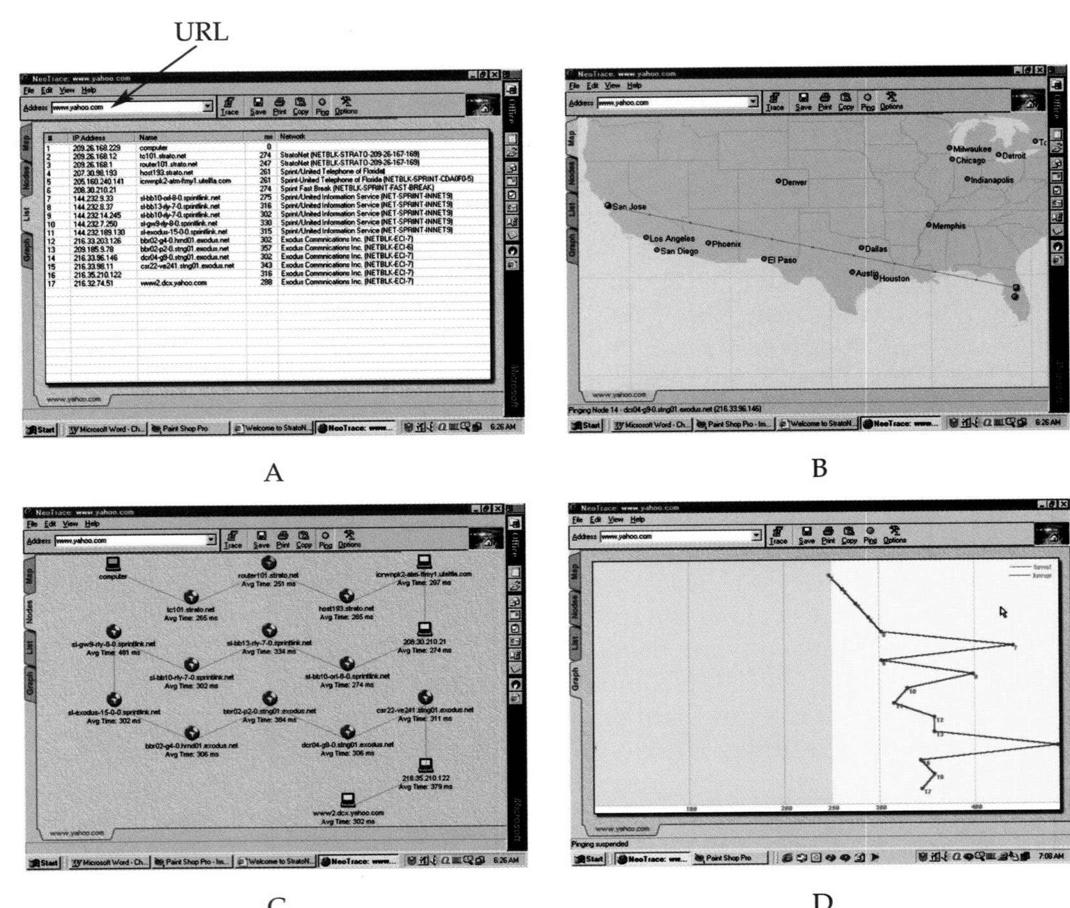

Figure 18-11. A—The network path to www.yahoo.com being displayed in NeoTrace using the **List** tab. B—The network path to www.yahoo.com being displayed using NeoTrace's **Map** tab. C—The network path to www.yahoo.com being displayed using Neotrace's **Nodes** tab. D—The network path being displayed using NeoTrace's **Graph** tab.

Netlog

The netlog.txt contains information about network settings and hardware. It contains information about protocols, clients, binding the protocol to the network card, and more. This makes it very useful for determining network connection failures. It can provide information needed by technical support personnel or system administration.

Because netlog.txt is a hidden file, you must remove the hidden file attribute before you can access or view the file. **Figure 18-12** shows a partial listing of a typical netlog.txt file.

Net Diagnostics Utility

One of the latest utilities developed by Microsoft and first introduced in Windows XP is Net Diagnostics. Net Diagnostics is easily accessed by running msinfo32.exe from the **Run** dialog box at the **Start** menu. Once the System Information dialog box opens, select **Tools** from the main menu and then **Net Diagnostics**. Another way to access Net Diagnostics is through **Help and Support**.

Once the Net Diagnostics tool is run, it displays information about the network system. See **Figure 18-13.** In the screen capture, you can see items that fail tests are displayed in red as "FAILED," and items that pass tests are

```
      C:\WININST0.400\netdi.dll      Version : 4.90.0.3000
      Created : Thu Jun 08 17:00:00 2000
      RETAIL Build

 NETDI: ClassInstall (0x12 on 0x808e:0x318) on TCP/IP at
Enum\Network\MSTCP\0001
 NETDI: SetupFlags=513(SUF_INSETUP)(SUF_FIRSTTIME) BootCount=3
NetSetupFlags=1 (RETAIL)
 NETDI: Examining class Net
 NETDI: Found Enum\V1394\NIC1394\2295E25140CA12 in registry
 NETDI:       Couldn't find an installed driver for NDIS 1394 Net
Adapter
 NETDI:       Set DICIR_SKIP_INSTALL for
Enum\V1394\NIC1394\2295E25140CA12
 NETDI:       NdiCreate[NDIS 1394 Net Adapter] = OK
 NETDI: Found
Enum\PCI\VEN_100B&DEV_0020&SUBSYS_F3111385&REV_00\BUS_00&DEV_0F&F
UNC_00 in registry
 NETDI:       NdiCreate[NETGEAR FA311 Fast Ethernet PCI Adapter] =
OK
 NETDI: Found Enum\Root\Net\0000 in registry
 NETDI:       NdiCreate[Dial-Up Adapter] = OK
```

Figure 18-12. Partial listing of the netlog.txt file.

displayed in green as "PASSED". Critical items are automatically tested, and information can be revealed, such as the MAC address, IP address, DNS host name, and WINS server. The Net Diagnostics utility combines the ping, tracert, and other utilities into one tool.

The Internet Structure

No discussion about WAN systems would be complete without a discussion of the largest WAN in the world, the ***Internet.*** This section will give you a brief historical background of the Internet and its development, and it will make you aware of how complex the Internet really is.

Internet a very large, global, decentralized network.

Development of the Internet

The Internet has actually been in existence since the 1960's and grew from a simple project of the Advanced Research Project Agency (ARPA). The project was designed to test the feasibility of communication between computers over telephone lines. The first experiments were very simple but also very impressive. The original experiments contained only four hosts; today there are millions.

Later ARPA was absorbed by the United States military, renamed DARPA, and operated by the U.S. Department of Defense. As the network grew, the National Science Foundation became involved by awarding grants to many different universities and private companies to develop a communications model for what is now called the Internet.

In 1985, some of the centers connected by the DARPA network's 56 kbps backbone included Cornell University, the National Center for Supercomputing Application at the University of Illinois, the Pittsburgh Supercomputing Center

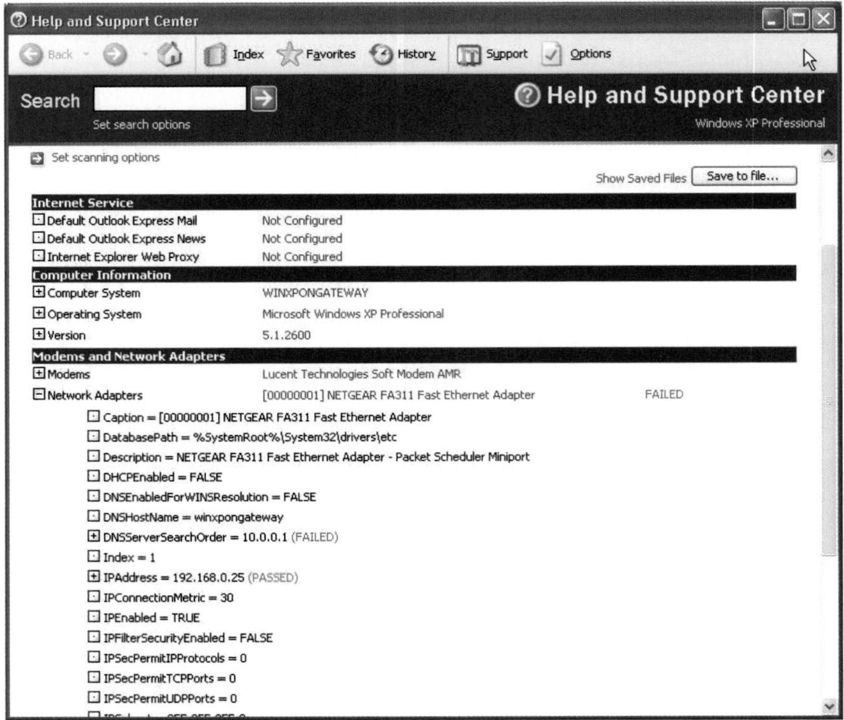

Figure 18-13. Screen capture of the Net Diagnostics utility.

in Pittsburgh, the University of California in San Diego, and Princeton University in New Jersey. This backbone is viewed by many people as the true beginning of what was to become known as the Internet. Over the next several years, many more universities, private companies, and research centers connected to the line. Within three years, the increased traffic forced the original 56 kbps backbone to be replaced with a T-1 line that could carry 1.544 Mbps. The new line connected six diverse regional networks in the United States, including: the National Center of Atmospheric Research in Colorado, the original computer centers previously listed, and the Merit site at the University of Michigan.

Merit would play a significant role in further development of the Internet. In 1990, Merit, IBM, and MCI started a nonprofit organization called Advanced Network and Services, Inc. (ANS). Its major goal was to manage the National Science Foundation backbone and continue to upgrade it. IBM and MCI both contributed four million dollars to the venture. The backbone was expanded to 16 major sites connected by a T-3 line, which could carry 43 Mbps. A T-3 line consists of 672 lines, each with a capability to carry 64 kbps.

By 1993, the National Science Foundation bowed out of the Internet management business. They designed a series of Network Access Points (NAPs) for private companies to connect to the backbone. Private companies could develop their own networks and then tie directly into the backbone, but only at a NAP. Originally, four locations were designated to serve as access to the backbone. The four locations were: San Francisco, operated by Pacific Bell; Chicago, operated by Ameritech; New York, operated by Sprint (the actual NAP is located in Pennsauken, New Jersey, not New York); and Washington DC, operated by Metropolitan Fiber Systems. As demand grew, more locations were added.

Merit was chosen to maintain a database of information about the Internet and act as the arbitrator for disputes. The Internet then came into full power, based on the original ARPA backbone project.

Private communications companies constructed their own backbones as well. Some companies constructed MANs in large metropolitan areas. The MANs were designed to allow businesses to have access to high-speed backbone systems spanning the USA. Growth has continued at an astounding rate. The Internet consists of fiber-optic and copper cables, wireless, infrared, satellites, and millions of miles of old telephone lines. The Internet grows so fast and is so diverse there is no map of all the lines and connections in existence. Individual companies do have information regarding connection and traffic lines, but they only have what is limited to their direct control. There are over 4500 companies making changes to the Internet daily, making it impossible to create an up-to-date and all-inclusive map of the Internet.

The diversity arises from the Internet's practice of sending data along the shortest route between two points. Most Internet providers have agreements allowing each to access the other's backbones and parts of their individually constructed networks. If these agreements were not arranged, the access to the Internet would be very limited.

For example, one customer may use ABC as their Internet provider and another customer may use XYZ as their Internet provider. The two companies are located across the street from each other. However, if it were not for mutually beneficial agreements set up between the two companies, the data sent by one customer to the other customer might very well be routed hundreds or even thousands of miles to a national backbone before making a return trip back on the other provider's lines.

There are thousands of agreements in place between providers to lease line access from one another. In this manner, the route taken by data is considerably shortened. This is one of the main reasons there are so many routers used on the Internet. The routers are constantly updated either manually or automatically to find the least expensive route between two points on the Internet. In short, the Internet is a network of networks that are all interconnected forming a huge spider web of communication circuits.

You might want to conduct an experiment to see how the lines in your own geographic area are accessed. Use the tracert utility to trace the route to some point close by, such as a local business' Web site. You may be surprised to see exactly how far the data must travel. The NeoTrace utility will map out the exact route for you.

Domain Names and URLS

InterNIC was the government agency first responsible for issuing uniform resource locator addresses and domain names. ***Uniform Resource Locators (URLs)*** are the global address for Web sites all over the Internet. The first part of the URL identifies the protocol being used and the second part identifies the domain name.

Uniform Resource Locator (URL) the global address for sites all over the Internet. The first part of the URL identifies the protocol being used and the second part identifies the domain name.

Many people confuse domain names with URLs because they appear so similar. The domain name is an alphanumeric name that identifies one or more IP addresses. The domain name is combined with the protocol type to form the URL. For example, for the URL ftp://www.download.com/freestuff.exe, download.com is the domain. The file freestuff.exe is located at that domain, and can be accessed using the FTP protocol. For the URL http://www.ace.com/index.html, the domain is ace.com. The file, index.html, is a Web page that is accessed using the HTTP protocol.

The Domain Name System (DNS), as mentioned earlier, is a system used to identify domain names of sites on the Internet and resolve them to their IP addresses. When you enter a URL in your Web browser, a query is sent to a local resolver, a database of domain names and matching IP addresses. The query requests a matching IP address for the domain name that you entered. The resolver transmits the requested IP address to your computer, and you are then seamlessly connected to the requested site. If the resolver's database does not contain the requested IP address, it forwards the query to the next resolver in the network. This continues until the IP address is located and you are connected to the requested site, or all of the resolvers are searched without success, resulting in an error message.

Originally and until 1995, InterNIC issued domain names and matching IP addresses. Then the InterNIC commercialized the system, turning it over to the private sector. Today InterNIC retains the control of the system. However, it has delegated the responsibility of dealing with the public to private sector companies. You can access a list of authorized domain name registration companies from the InterNIC site. Domain name suffixes are assigned according to the domain's function. **Figure 18-14** lists some common suffixes found in domain names.

E-mail Communications

E-mail has become one of the most popular uses of the Internet. You can send messages anywhere in the world via the Internet. Originally, e-mail was little more than a system to exchange ASCII text files. It is now a complete communication system that allows not only text-based messages but also attached files. Any type of file can be attached, including reports, spreadsheets, database information, photos, illustrations, animations, and sound. There are numerous e-mail software packages available today. The e-mail software packages wrap themselves around the available Internet e-mail protocols and greatly enhance the user interface.

Figure 18-14. This table lists common domain suffixes and the types of organizations that use them. The bottom portion of the table contains some of the latest domain suffixes and the types of organizations that use them.

Domain	Type of organization
.com	Commercial business
.edu	Educational
.gov	Government
.mil	Military
.net	Host or gateway
.org	Organizations usually, but not necessarily, nonprofit
.store	Merchants
.web	Web activities
.arts	Art and culture
.rec	Recreational and entertainment
.info	Information services
.nom	Individuals

To set up an e-mail account, you must have certain information. First, you need to know your user name and password. You also need to know the name and type of mail server being used for incoming and outgoing messages. Common e-mail protocols include Post Office Protocol (POP3), Internet Message Access Protocol (IMAP), Hypertext Markup Language (HTML), and Simple Mail Transport Protocol (SMTP). A protocol is required to communicate with a mail server that is hosting the e-mail software and the Internet connection.

Your Internet Service Provider (ISP) will provide your user name, password, and e-mail server name. Providers usually have this information on an automatic installation CD. If they do not, you can contact them to get the information. Once the account is established, there are many features you need to understand. Look at **Figure 18-15.**

The e-mail server usually stores all e-mail communications until the user retrieves them. In a strict network environment, e-mails can be delivered directly to the individual PCs. Once you log on to your ISP, you can open your e-mail account, which is stored on the server, and access your personal e-mail.

To send e-mail, you must type in the address of the recipient, such as jsmith@acme.net. Each e-mail user has a unique address. Two or more users can have the same alpha name on the same network, but they are usually given a numeric extension to maintain the uniqueness of the address, such as jsmith23@acme.net. A message is then typed into the letter space and the **Send** button is clicked, sending the e-mail to its destination. The drop-down menus provide the user with many options, including delete and save. There are some options that are unique to e-mail, such as reply, reply to all, resend, and attach file.

MIME and S/MIME

When a non-text file is attached to an e-mail message, it must be converted to a form that can be handled by text-oriented e-mail protocols. The ***Multipurpose Internet Mail Extensions (MIME)*** standard is a specification for formatting non-text-based files for transmission over the Internet. MIME is used for graphics, audio, and video.

Multipurpose Internet Mail Extensions (MIME) a specification for formatting non-text-based files for transmission over the Internet.

A newer version of MIME is S/MIME. The *S* stands for secure. S/MIME allows the sent message to be encrypted and signed with a digital signature, or certificate. Methods used to ensure S/MIME security are discussed in the following section.

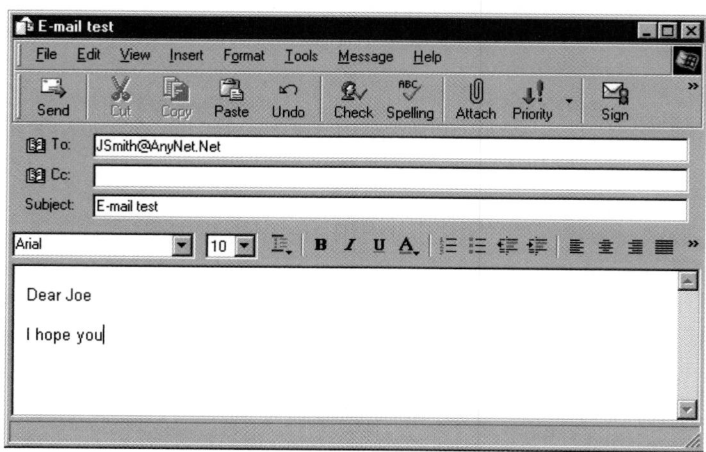

Figure 18-15. There are many features to a typical Internet account.

Digital Signatures and Encryption/Decryption Keys

You obtain a digital ID from a third party software vendor. You make an application using e-mail, and then the certifying authority verifies your identity. Your digital ID will provide you with two digital keys. One key is a private key, which you keep entirely to yourself. The private key can be used to sign your e-mail and also encrypt messages. The receiving party will be warned if a signed message has been tampered with. It also verifies your identity to the recipient. The other key is a public key, which you distribute to people you wish to communicate with. The public key allows others to decode messages encoded with your private key. It also allows them to encode messages that can only be decoded by your private key.

There are three components required to electronically sign and encrypt a message: a public key, a private key, and the appropriate encoding software. When you digitally sign an e-mail, software compresses the message contents to a few lines of text known as a *message digest.* The message digest is then encoded using the sender's private key. The resulting data is the sender's *digital signature.* The digital signature is then added to the end of the message.

The receiver can decode both the signature and the message using the sender's public key. When the signature is decoded, it results in the same message digest used to create it. When the message is decoded, it results in the same data used to create the message digest, and therefore the signature. If the receiver compresses the message, and the resulting message digest does not match the message digest extracted from the key, the recipient knows that the message has been altered.

Internet Protocols

Hundreds of protocols have been developed over the years. Protocols began as simple programs that carried out commands and transported plain ASCII text files but have evolved into sophisticated programs. In the strictest sense, protocols are software programs that establish a set of rules to allow two entities to communicate. As protocols evolve, they take on the appearance of application software and are classified as such. As technology evolves, there will always be new protocols, usually built on top of the older protocols to keep the downward compatibility of the system. The following are a few of the most common protocols used in Internet communications.

HTTP

Hypertext Transfer Protocol (HTTP) protocol that transports Web pages across the Internet.

Hypertext Markup Language (HTML) programming language used to create Web pages.

Hypertext Transfer Protocol (HTTP) is used to transport Web pages across the Internet. ***Hypertext Markup Language (HTML)*** is a programming language used to create Web pages and is often confused with HTTP. HTTP is the mechanism for delivery of HTML pages as well as Web pages developed using other languages. HTTP is not a secure protocol. In fact, the contents of the Web pages it transports can be easily viewed using a protocol analyzer. HTTP was never intended to be used for transmitting secure information such as business transactions involving personal identification and money. Secure Sockets Layer (SSL) was developed by Netscape Navigator to make HTTP-based Internet business transactions secure. When SSL is incorporated with HTTP, the HTTP protocol in the window at the top of the Web browser becomes HTTPS. The *S* indicates that it is a secure transaction. SSL can be used with any protocol in the TCP/IP suite, not just with HTTP.

FTP

File Transfer Protocol (FTP) is a protocol used for transmitting files across the Internet. A special FTP is called anonymous FTP. Many sites accept anonymous FTP, which simply means you can access the files for downloading without using a secret password and identity.

File Transfer Protocol (FTP) a protocol used for transmitting files across the Internet.

Telnet

Telnet is a protocol that allows you to log on to a remote computer and download or upload files. It is often referred to as a terminal emulation protocol because it causes a PC to act as though it is a terminal connected to a mainframe computer. Telnet is part of an entire suite of protocols inside the TCP/IP protocol. It is often used to connect two dissimilar systems, such as a PC running Microsoft Windows and a UNIX mainframe. Telnet is commonly used to program remote routers on wide area networks. It can also be used to control other computer operations remotely.

Telnet a protocol that allows you to logon a remote computer and download or upload files.

Gopher

Gopher was an early Internet protocol designed to search and retrieve documents from distant computers. Gopher was created at the University of Minnesota, the home of the Golden Gophers, hence the name of the protocol. Gopher was originally designed for access only to the computer on the university campus. It was such a success it grew and was soon used all over the country. All that was needed was a telephone modem. Gopher not only provided access, but also organized information into directories such as images, programs, and documents.

Gopher an early Internet protocol designed to search and retrieve documents from distant computers.

Archie

Archie is similar to Gopher and is maintained by McGill University in Montreal. Archie is a program that allows you to search for information on the Internet by filename.

Archie an Internet protocol, maintained by McGill University in Montreal, that allows you to search for information on the Internet by filename.

Network Troubleshooting

Remember the basics of networking. To create or connect a network you need cable, a properly configured adapter card, and software support for the network. Most networking problems are simple problems, such as loose connections. When there are network system problems, check the connections first. The next step is to ping the adapter card (127.0.0.1) to verify that it is communicating the TCP/IP protocol. Finally, try to connect to a known URL using the ping utility. You will not get any results from using ping to a distant host if the modem is not connecting to the Internet service provider.

Adapter settings can be accidentally changed, especially while exploring the network setup dialog boxes. If you are accessing the network by modem, you will have to check the modem setup. You may want to review the unit on modems. Problems can also be created by loading certain Internet-related software programs. Some software packages automatically load from the CD and can change system settings, such as the default protocol and the system configuration. These settings need to be checked closely and are often the root of the problem.

For example, you receive a magazine that includes several software programs, utilities, and games. You place the CD into the CD drive, and it automatically loads. During the installation process, the software attempts to change settings relating to the network. The system may fail, leaving you without access to the network, or the system may begin experiencing recurring problems. In this case, the network settings will have to be verified and reset as necessary.

Another common problem associated with a network is difficulty logging on. Often the user is incorrectly entering his or her name and password or is attempting to use an expired password. As a technician, you will have your own access name and password and will be capable of easily determining if the network is accessible.

Most problems you will be expected to handle as a PC technician are simple in nature. More complex issues may require the assistance of the network administrator. With experience, you will soon be able to determine when you need to consult the system administrator or the Internet Service Provider.

Summary

- Navigation across WAN systems is enabled by network devices, such as bridges, routers, brouters, gateways, and switches.
- Routers connect hosts across network systems using the most economical route. The router communicates by network addresses rather than by MAC address.
- Bridges are used to connect devices by their MAC address.
- Brouters combine the best features of a router and a bridge.
- A gateway translates information between two LANs that use different protocols.
- A proxy server acts as a go-between for the distant Web site and the user behind the server.
- TCP/IP is the most common protocol used for the Internet.
- The netlog.txt file contains information about the network protocols, clients, and adapters.
- Ping and tracert are common diagnostic tools used to check if the network circuit is intact.
- Tracert provides more information than ping.
- The Net Diagnostics utility gathers information about the network setup of the workstation.
- HTTPS displayed in a Web browser URL window indicates that HTTP is using SSL for securing the transaction.

Review Questions

Answer the following questions on a separate sheet of paper. Please do not write in this book.

1. What protocol is predominately used for exchanging data on the Internet?
2. What is InterNIC?

3. What is an octet?
4. What is an octet's numeric range expressed in decimal fashion?
5. How does TCP/IP protocol identify individual networks on the Internet?
6. Identify the class to which a network with an address of 128.204.19.103 belongs.
7. What is a subnet mask?
8. What does winipcfg reveal about a PC connected to a network?
9. What does a DHCP server do?
10. What does DNS do?
11. What is the difference between DNS and WINS?
12. What device extends the maximum length of a network cable run?
13. What is the purpose of a proxy server?
14. What is a firewall?
15. What is the purpose of a ping?
16. What utility reveals the most information about a network system during troubleshooting?
17. What three components are required to send an S/MIME encoded e-mail?
18. What is a digital signature?

Sample A+ Exam Questions

Answer the following questions on a separate sheet of paper. Please do not write in this book.

1. Which is an example of a typical IP address?
   a. 168.23.145.25
   b. 10 2D C4 56 DE FF
   c. JohnH@netcom.org
   d. 255.255.255.000
2. What command issued at the DOS prompt allows you to inspect the IP address on a Windows NT system?
   a. **winipconfig**
   b. **winipcfg**
   c. **ipconfig**
   d. **configip**
3. Which of the following services automatically issues an IP address to a PC when it boots?
   a. WINS
   b. DHCP
   c. IPSETUP
   d. DNS

4. Which of the following services is responsible for resolving domain names to IP addresses?
   a. WINS
   b. DHCP
   c. IPSETUP
   d. DNS
5. Which of the following pieces of equipment is used primarily to extend the length of a network cable run?
   a. Repeater
   b. Hub
   c. Gateway
   d. Router
6. What command can be used as a quick test to see if a network card is functioning?
   a. **Ping 127.0.0.1**
   b. **Tracert 128.10.10.285**
   c. **CardTest**
   d. **NICset**
7. Which of the following is an example of a URL?
   a. JoeB@AcmeNet.Gov
   b. www.GoodheartWillcox.com
   c. 127.34.002.145
   d. BlakeManufacturing@setpoint.com
8. Which command would you use to check cable connectivity between a PC station named Station12 and a file server named Ntserver? (Note that the command is being issued from Station12.)
   a. Ping Station12 Via Ntserver
   b. Ping Ntserver
   c. Ping Ntserver/Station12
   d. Ping Station12/Ntserver
9. An IP address consists of _____.
   a. four octets
   b. 24 binary numbers separated by three colons
   c. a group of 24 hexadecimal numbers
   d. four three-digit decimal numbers ranging from 000–999
10. Which is an example of a class C subnet mask?
    a. 255.255.000.255
    b. 255.255.000.000
    c. 000.255.255.255
    d. 255.255.255.000

Suggested Laboratory Activities

Do not attempt any suggested laboratory activities without your instructor's permission. Certain activities can render the PC operating system inoperable.

1. Install a modem and set up Internet access with an ISP.
2. Inspect the TCP/IP assignment for a PC actively connected to the Internet. Use winipcfg for Windows 95 or 98. Type ipconfig at the DOS prompt for Windows NT-based systems.
3. Set up a PC to be remotely accessed by another PC through a modem line.
4. Use the Windows Help program to see how to set up an Internet connection.
5. Use the Windows Help program to see how to share an Internet connection between two or more computers.
6. Use Windows Help to set up a Virtual Private Network.
7. Set up two PCs and share a game connection. (Instructor's permission is definitely required.)
8. Set up NetMeeting to communicate with another person using a different PC, either through the network in the lab or at home across the Internet.
9. Set up a game connection between two PCs and enable voice chat. This allows two people to talk while sharing a game. Note: Not all games support voice chat. (Again, you must have the instructor's permission.)

Interesting Web Sites for More Information

www.cisco.com
www.domainregistry.com
www.learntcpip.com/OSIModel/OSIModel.html
www.linux.com
www.microsoft.com
www.novell.com
www.pacbell.com
www.unix.com
www.youdzone.com/signature.html

Many metropolitan area networks (MANs) can exist within the same city, interconnecting businesses and college campuses that are under a common management.

Chapter 18
Laboratory Activity
Verify Internet Properties

After completing this laboratory activity, you will be able to:

- ❑ Inspect and modify Internet properties.
- ❑ Assign Internet TCP/IP addresses under the supervision of a network administrator.

Introduction

In this laboratory activity, you will use either the winipcfg or ipconfig utility (depending on the operating system you are using). Winipcfg is used with Windows 95, 98, and Me. The ipconfig utility is used with Windows NT, 2000, and XP. These utilities are used to verify and modify TCP/IP assignments. When issuing the command, you can use a switch to reveal more information, or you can simply click the button on the default window labeled **More info>>** to reveal additional information.

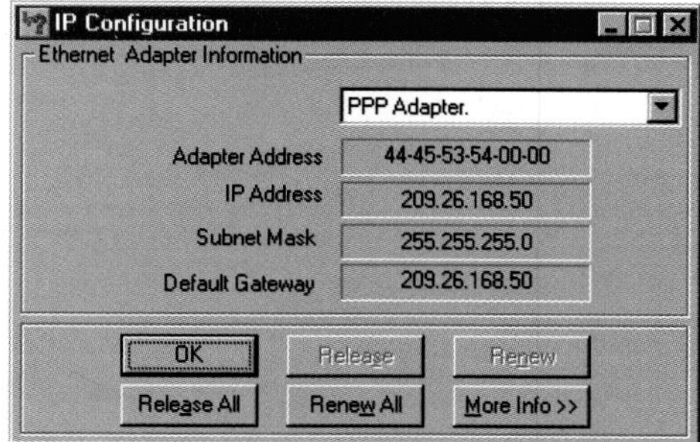

Look at the screen capture that follows to see the typical results of typing at the DOS prompt of a Windows Me operating system **winipcfg** and clicking the **More Info** button or typing **winipcfg/all**. The IP configuration dialog box shown reveals that this is an Ethernet adapter (network card) and is tied to a PPP type protocol. Also displayed is the adapter address (MAC address) of the network card, the IP address assigned to the network card, the subnet mask, and default gateway.

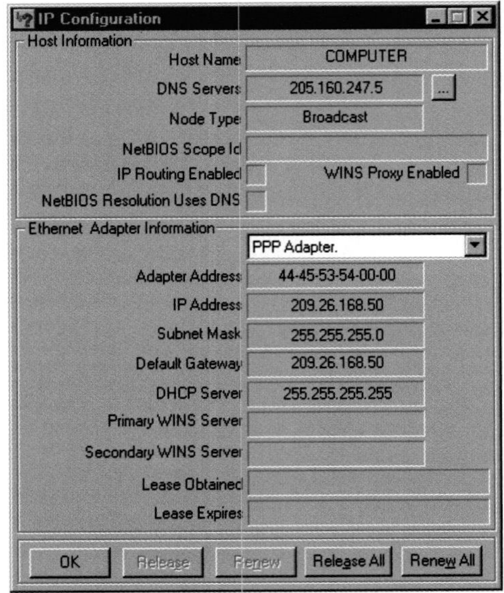

The TCP/IP assignments are the IP addresses used to identify the workstation and other important entities such as the dynamic host configuration protocol server (DHCP), default gateway, and the Windows Internet Naming Service (WINS). The DHCP is used to automatically assign an IP address to the network stations. The WINS servers are used to resolve network NetBIOS names (computer assigned names) to IP addresses. Both systems are critical if needed on the particular network and are assigned by the network administrator. The PC technician is responsible to verify or assign the proper IP addresses while performing a network card installation or during routine troubleshooting involving a network connection. You can find out more about these features in your textbook or by conducting an Internet search using the keywords such as IP, ipconfig, DHCP, WINS, and gateway.

Equipment and Materials

- Typical PC station with Windows 98 or later operating system that is connected to the Internet either through a network or has a direct connection through a modem.

Procedure

1. ______ Boot the PC and ensure that the PC is operating properly.
2. ______ Access the network card and IP assignment information by typing **winipcfg** or **ipconfig** at the DOS prompt. A window similar to the one shown previously should appear. Try using the **/all** optional switch with the command.

3. ______ Write the following information on a separate sheet of paper:

   Host Name

   DNS Server

   Node Type

   Adapter Address

   IP Address

   Subnet Mask

   Default Gateway

   DHCP Server

4. ______ After writing down the information requested in Step 3, go on to answer the review questions that follow. After completing the review questions, shut down the PC.

Review Questions

Answer the following questions on a separate sheet of paper. Please do not write in this book.

1. What command is issued from the DOS prompt on a Windows 98 machine to access the network card IP address information?
2. What command is issued from the DOS prompt of a Windows NT machine to access the network card IP information?
3. What does the DHCP server do?
4. What does WINS do?
5. What is "Host Name?"

WANs help to share needed information across distant locations.

Small-Office/Home-Office (SOHO) Networking

After completing this chapter, you will be able to:

- Determine the best media for use in a SOHO network based on cost and building structure.
- Determine an appropriate Internet access configuration based on the number of PCs and the type of network media used in a SOHO network.
- Design a SOHO network based on the media, the number of PCs, and the type of Internet access that will be used.
- Determine an appropriate level of administration for a SOHO network.
- Identify methods to secure a SOHO network.
- Use the Network Setup Wizard to set up Internet Connection Sharing (ICS) on a host PC.
- Use the Network Setup Wizard to allow a client access to the Internet through a host PC.
- Identify common problems that can occur in a new SOHO network installation.

A+ Exam—Key Points

The A+ Certification exams have increased the percentage of questions asked pertaining to networking. This is due to the growing number of small office and home networks. You need to be familiar with all aspects of home- and small-office networking. It is vital that you have some hands-on experience setting up a small network system with shared Internet access using a variety of media and equipment. The configuration for setting up Internet Connection Sharing (ICS) will most likely be covered in the exams. Be prepared to answer questions concerning shared folders and shared printers.

Key Words and Terms

The following words and terms will become important pieces of your computer vocabulary. Be sure you can define them.

gateway router
Home Phoneline Networking Alliance (HomePNA) technology
HomePNA adapter
Internet Connection Firewall (ICF)
Network Setup Wizard
packet sniffer
powerline communications (PLC)
small-office/home-office (SOHO) network
Universal Naming Convention (UNC)
virtual private network (VPN)

Installing a network in a home or small office is one of the most common tasks for a computer technician. This chapter prepares you for that task by applying many of the concepts presented earlier in the textbook to the installation, configuration, and support of the small-office/home-office (SOHO) network. You will learn how to use the Network Setup Wizard to configure a SOHO network and how to troubleshoot the common problems that can occur in a SOHO network. You will also learn about the many factors that determine SOHO network design.

Designing the SOHO Network

small-office/home-office (SOHO) network
a simple peer-to-peer LAN that is used to share resources and data in a home- or small-office environment.

The ***small-office/home-office (SOHO) network*** is a simple peer-to-peer LAN that is used to share resources and data in a home- or small-office environment. Although any computer hardware connected to the SOHO network can be shared, printers and Internet access devices are the most commonly shared.

As a computer technician, you may be called on to design and configure a SOHO network. There are several factors to consider in its design. These factors include the following:

- Type of media that will be used to connect the PCs together.
- Manner in which the networked PCs will access the Internet.
- Level of administration that will be used to secure resources and data.
- Method of security that will be used to protect the network from intruders.

This section examines each of these factors as it introduces the configurations and technologies commonly used in a SOHO network.

SOHO Media

The four common choices of networking media for SOHO networks are copper cable (Cat 5e and Cat 6), wireless, existing home telephone lines, and existing power lines. The choice is based on cost, building construction, and user or installer preference. For example, copper cable is inexpensive, but the building structure may prove difficult for installing the cables. This is especially true in buildings with open spaces, high ceilings, and concrete floors. Wireless technology is easy to install but has some security issues. Existing telephone lines are economical and convenient but may not be suitable for an office environment. Using existing power lines is inexpensive but undesirable to many people who do not like the idea of connecting the network to 120 volts of ac power.

There are many variables to consider when determining the type of network media to use. The following sections explore each of these variables. We will also look at implementing a mixed network environment and using a prewired home system.

Copper cable

Copper cable has been the choice for many years. However, the main objection to using copper cable is that it is often difficult to run the cable though the walls. To overcome this difficulty, copper cable can be used in one room and another form of network media can be used in a different room. For example, you can use copper cable in one room and wireless technology in the other. This type of network configuration is known as a hybrid, or a mixed network environment, and is discussed later in this chapter.

Wireless

Wireless is a popular choice of SOHO media. It is quick to install, and the location of the networked PCs can be easily changed. It is the ideal solution for a building that is difficult to cable. However, be aware that when using a wireless NIC to access the network, the default settings allow the network to be compromised by an intruder. The default setup configuration uses a default network group name and no data encryption. It is not difficult, though, to change the default network group name and to configure all packets to be encrypted. Doing so increases network security, **Figure 19-1.**

Figure 19-1.
The Wireless Network Properties dialog box provides information about such features as the name used for the wireless network, the type of security, and if the network is Ad Hoc or utilizes an access point.

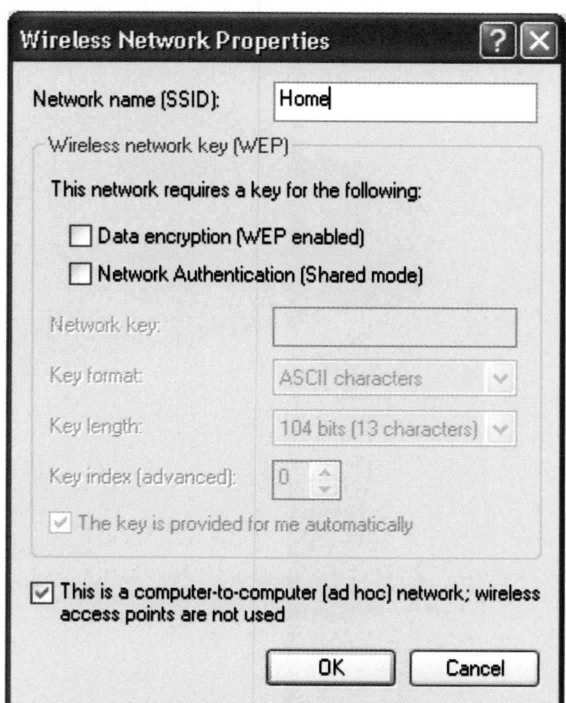

Home Phoneline Networking Alliance (HomePNA) technology
a technology that allows existing home telephone lines to be used for the network media.

HomePNA adapter
a networking device that allows every telephone jack that is connected together physically in a building to be part of the network.

Existing phone lines

Home Phoneline Networking Alliance (HomePNA) technology allows existing home telephone lines to be used for the network media. Any telephone jack can be used as a connection point for the network system. Network cables and a hub are not required for making the connections. All that is needed is a ***HomePNA adapter.*** When a HomePNA adapter is installed, every telephone jack is part of the network. Some HomePNA adapters, like the one in **Figure 19-2,** include two RJ-11 ports. One RJ-11 port is used to connect to the telephone jack and the other is used to connect to either a telephone or to cascade to another HomePNA device, **Figure 19-3.** Cascading HomePNA adapters is useful when there is not an adequate amount of telephone jacks for each PC.

Using existing telephone lines as network media does not interfere with telephone calls. Typical voice and sound data transmitted on a residential telephone system are of relatively low frequencies, usually between 0 Hz and 4 kHz. The HomePNA adapter uses a frequency higher than 4 kHz to transmit data across the existing telephone line. The two frequencies do not interfere with each other.

While HomePNA technology is a practical solution for homes and for some businesses, it is not recommend for commercial buildings. Most corporate offices use a private branch exchange (PBX) as the centralized point of the telephone system. Because the telephone lines for a typical PBX system run directly from each telephone jack to the PBX, a complete network circuit cannot be established. The telephone lines in a home, however, typically run in a daisy chain fashion from one telephone jack to the next, making a complete loop throughout the house.

powerline communications (PLC)
a technology that allows existing power lines to be used as network media.

Existing power lines

Powerline communications (PLC) technology allows existing power lines to be used as network media. A PLC adapter connects a PC to the 120-volt ac outlet, **Figure 19-4.** When a PLC network is implemented, two separate systems can operate over the same media at the same time: a 120-volt ac power source

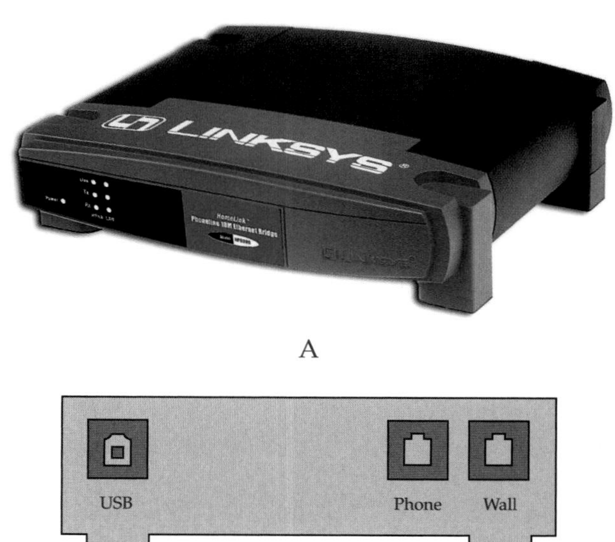

B

Figure 19-2.
A—This HomePNA adapter connects to a PC with a USB cable. (Courtesy of Linksys) B—Back of HomePNA adapter. This adapter includes two RJ-11 jacks: a phone port to connect to a telephone or to another HomePNA adapter and a wall port to connect to the telephone line.

Figure 19-3.
A—PCs connected directly to separate telephone jacks through HomePNA adapters. Telephone jacks must share the same telephone line. B—PCs connected to the same telephone jack through cascading HomePNA adapters.

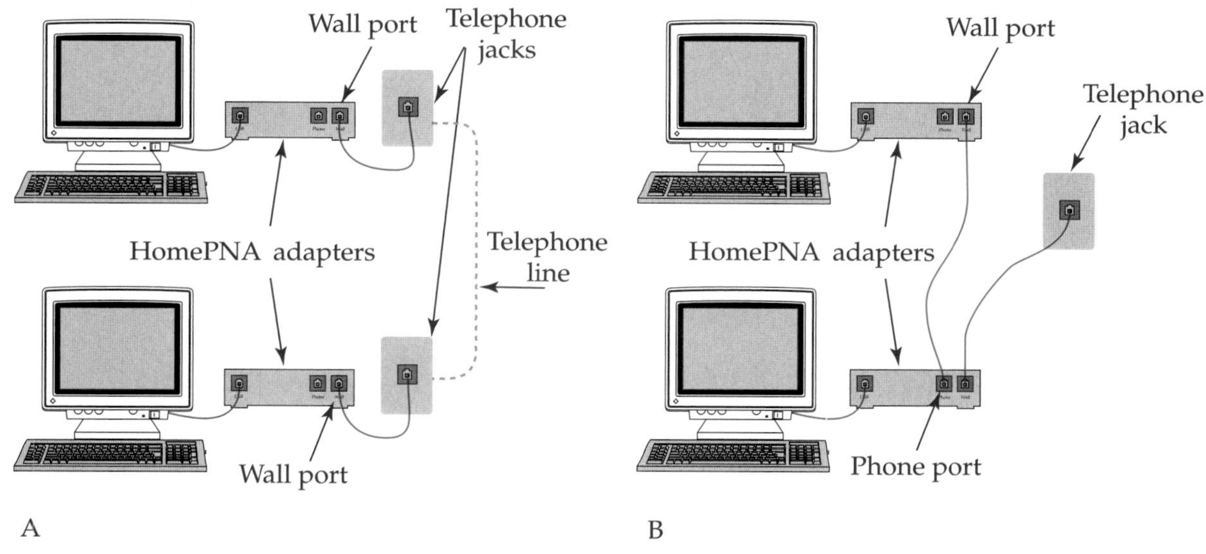

Figure 19-4.
This PLC adapter plugs directly into an ac outlet. Some PLC adapters have a separate power cable. (Courtesy of Linksys)

and an Ethernet network. PLC works in the same fashion as HomePNA technology by transmitting data at a higher frequency than the existing system. Data transmission on the PLC network operates at frequencies much higher than the 60 Hz of the 120-volt ac outlet.

Existing power lines have been used as a network media for some time in Europe, but have been slowly accepted in the United States. The main reason is that people have a natural fear of electricity. The idea of plugging their network equipment directly into a 120-volt ac outlet leaves them somewhat concerned. However, plugging in a PLC device into a 120-volt ac outlet is no more dangerous than plugging in any other electrical device. All electrical and electronic equipment used in the United States is tested for safety by the Underwriters Laboratories (UL). Any equipment designed to plug directly into the power outlet of a home is safe. After all, even the PC plugs directly into the 120-volt ac outlet, and it is safe to use.

PLC has some advantages over HomePNA technology. Typically a room is limited to one telephone jack or possibly two, but power outlets are spaced more conveniently throughout a building. With PLC, there is a connection point for the network just about anywhere in the building.

Mixed network environment

It is not uncommon to have a mixed network environment. For example, a home- or small-office network may use Cat 5e cable in one room and wireless technology in other rooms. When converting from one network media to another, a network bridge is required. A bridge connects dissimilar network media while making no decisions about packet contents, destination, or filtering. Bridges use MAC addresses to communicate. This allows all packets to pass through the bridge, no matter which protocol is used. (Bridges were covered in Chapter 18—WAN.)

Connecting a wireless network to another type of network always requires a wireless bridge. The wireless bridge is referred to as an *access point,* **Figure 19-5.** When a router is used to combine different media and to provide an Internet connection, it is often referred to as a ***gateway router***. The exact terminology used can vary between different vendors.

gateway router a router that combines different media and provides an Internet connection.

Home prewired systems

New homes are often prewired for all types of low-voltage communications systems, such as telephone, audio, television, and computer network systems. Communication equipment suppliers manufacture cabinets to make telephone, television, sound, and computer network system installation simple and convenient. The cabinet shown in **Figure 19-6** provides a common connection point for each home communications system. The cabinet is designed to quickly configure network cables together as needed.

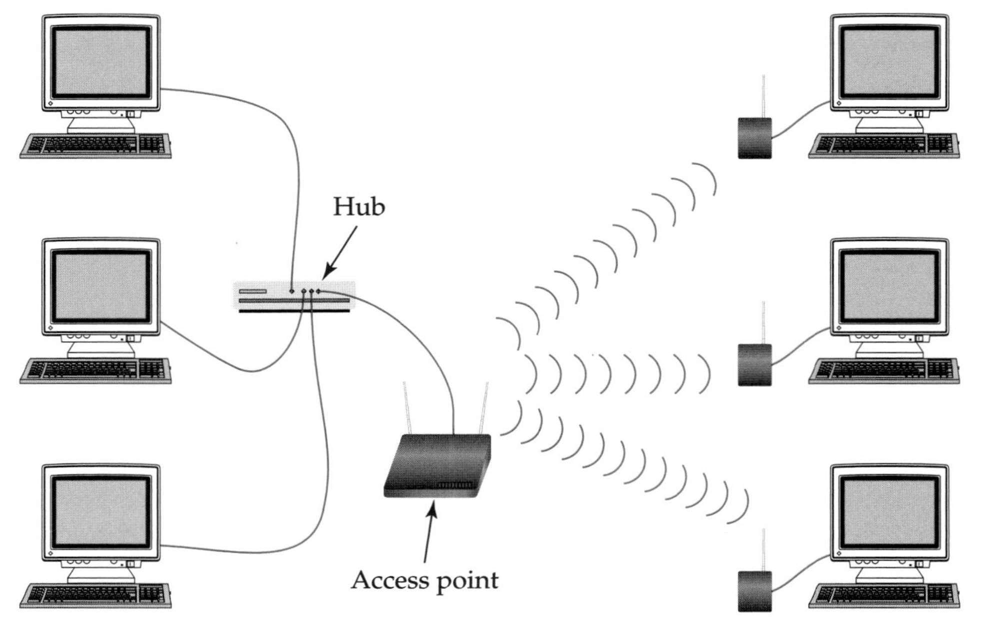

Figure 19-5. An access point functions as a bridge connecting a cabled network to a wireless network.

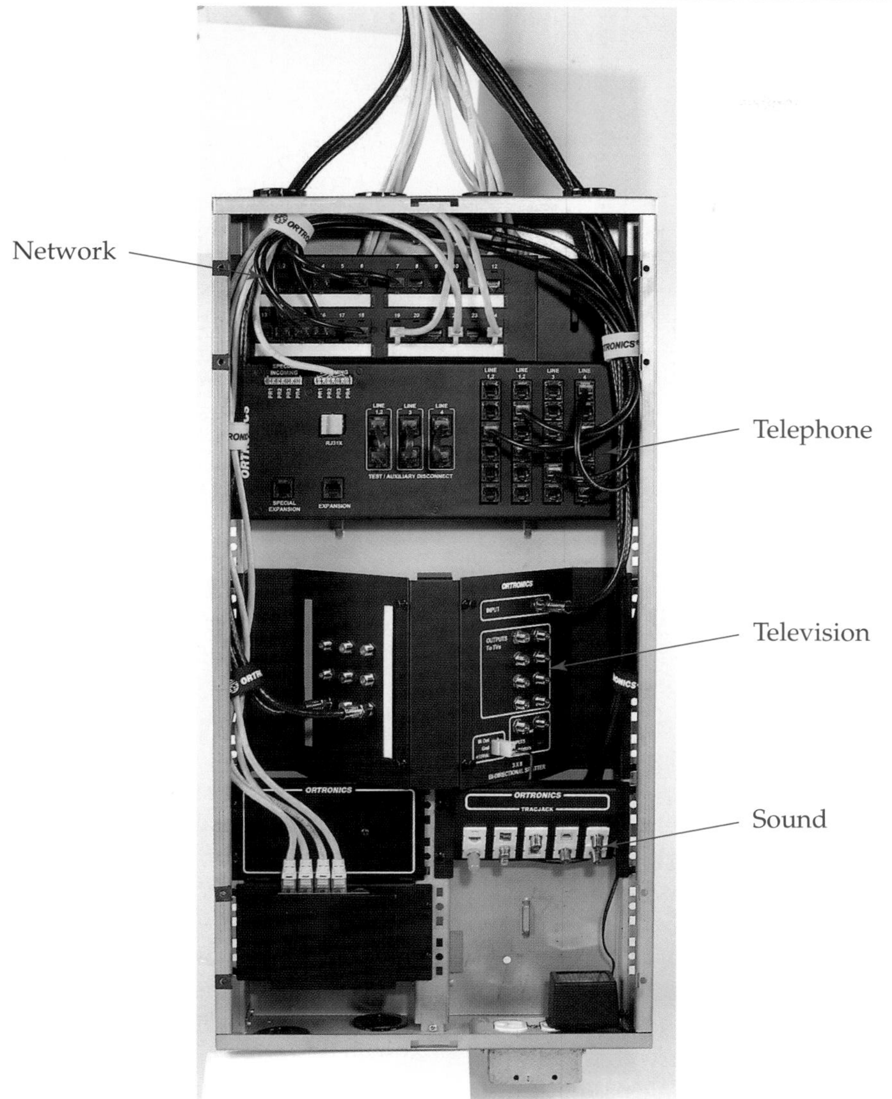

Figure 19-6. A communications cabinet provides a common connection point for home communications systems such as telephone, television, sound, and a computer network. (Courtesy of Ortronics)

Data transfer rates

A comparison of data transfer rates will also help in selecting the best media for the network. The chart in **Figure 19-7** compares commonly used media in a SOHO network. As indicated in the chart, copper cable has the only predictable data rate. Wireless, existing power lines, and existing telephone line data throughputs vary greatly. Often, vendors emphasize the maximum achievable throughput for these media, but this is not the normal throughput. Actual throughput varies because of environmental conditions. For example, a wireless network may advertise a throughput of 11 Mbps but can only achieve that if the wireless network devices are at a close proximity, without radio interference or partitions between the transmitter and receiver. The farther apart the transmitter and receiver, the more the throughput rate drops. If wireless must transmit through walls, the transmission rate also drops, especially if the walls are constructed of a dense material such as concrete.

Figure 19-7.
Data rate comparison for various SOHO network media.

Media	Maximum Data Rate	Remarks
Copper cable	10 Mbps or 100 Mbps	Predictable data rates.
Wireless	11 Mpbs	Can be drastically reduced as low as 1 Mbps by interference.
Existing power lines	No standard	Advertised as high as 10 Mbps, more commonly 4 Mbps.
Existing telephone lines	No standard	Advertised as high as 10 Mbps, more commonly 4 Mbps.

PLC technology has a limited throughput because power line conductors are not designed for data transmission. Also, power line conductors may be connected to sources of interference such as electric motors. Since interference on the power line corrupts packets, the packets have to be retransmitted, thus reducing the actual system throughput.

Using the existing telephone lines is unpredictable because the older generation lines were not designed to carry high frequencies. The length of the telephone cable also reduces throughput. Cable signal losses known as attenuation increase directly with cable length. As cable length increases, the digital signal strength deteriorates which results in corrupt data packets. Each packet that is corrupt must be retransmitted. The loss of data packets and the need to retransmit each lost packet causes the loss of effective bandwidth. The length of the cable will finally reach a point where all data packets are corrupt.

Another cable length factor is cross talk. Older style telephone cable was not designed with twisted pairs. Thus, older cable is much more likely to produce cross talk even on a very short length of cable. The twists in the cable pairs is designed to counter the production of cross talk.

As you can see, the only predictable transmission rates are with traditional network cable. However, the need for a network media that overcomes building structure limitations may outweigh the disadvantages of the lower and unpredictable rates. It is, therefore, the choice of the network user or installer as to the best media to use for the SOHO network.

Internet Access and SOHO Design

There are several typical Internet access configurations that can be used in SOHO networks. The exact configuration depends on the building's environment and the type of Internet access device selected. The common choices of Internet access devices in a SOHO network are the telephone modem, DSL modem, and cable modem. This section covers various network configurations that use a telephone, DSL, or cable modem to access the Internet.

Telephone Modem Internet access

When using a telephone modem as the Internet access device, the configuration varies depending on the number of PCs that are networked. A two-PC network may be connected directly from PC to PC without the use of a hub. **Figure 19-8** shows a two-PC network that uses a telephone modem to connect to the Internet. In this configuration, the two PCs are connected directly from NIC to NIC with a crossover cable. This is the simplest way of connecting PCs together in a SOHO network. Other ways of connecting two PCs can be with a null modem cable, a USB cable, a parallel cable, or infrared hardware.

Tech Tip:
A NIC is generally incorporated in most motherboards today, which means you may not need to purchase them for your network.

Notice that the PC with the internal telephone modem in **Figure 19-9** is designated as the host. It is the *host* because it provides the Internet connection for both PCs. For the host to provide Internet access, Internet Connection Sharing (ICS) must be established. ICS is Microsoft's simple application of the network address translation (NAT) standard. The NAT standard was developed by the Internet Engineering Task Force (IETF) and is described in detail in RFC 1631. NAT was specifically designed as a standard for sharing a single Internet connection and providing a type of firewall protection. NAT can support more clients than ICS and is more versatile than ICS.

The host in a typical ICS configuration is always assigned the IP address 192.168.000.001, and the clients are assigned IP addresses in sequence starting at 192.168.000.002. A PC that accesses the Internet through the host is called a *client*. Setting up an ICS is covered under SOHO Administration.

Tech Tip:
In general, the term *host* describes any computer that provides a service. The term *client* describes a computer that utilizes the service provided by the host. In the example of an ICS system, the host provides Internet access to the client computers that wish to connect to the Internet.

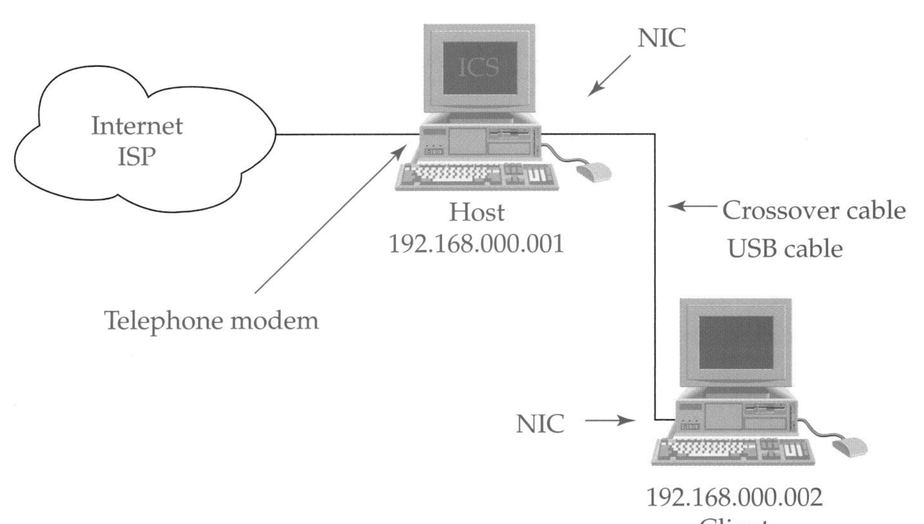

Figure 19-8.
A two-PC network with Internet access via a modem. PCs are connected together with a crossover cable.

Figure 19-9.
A three-PC network with Internet access via a modem. A hub is needed in this configuration to connect the PCs together.

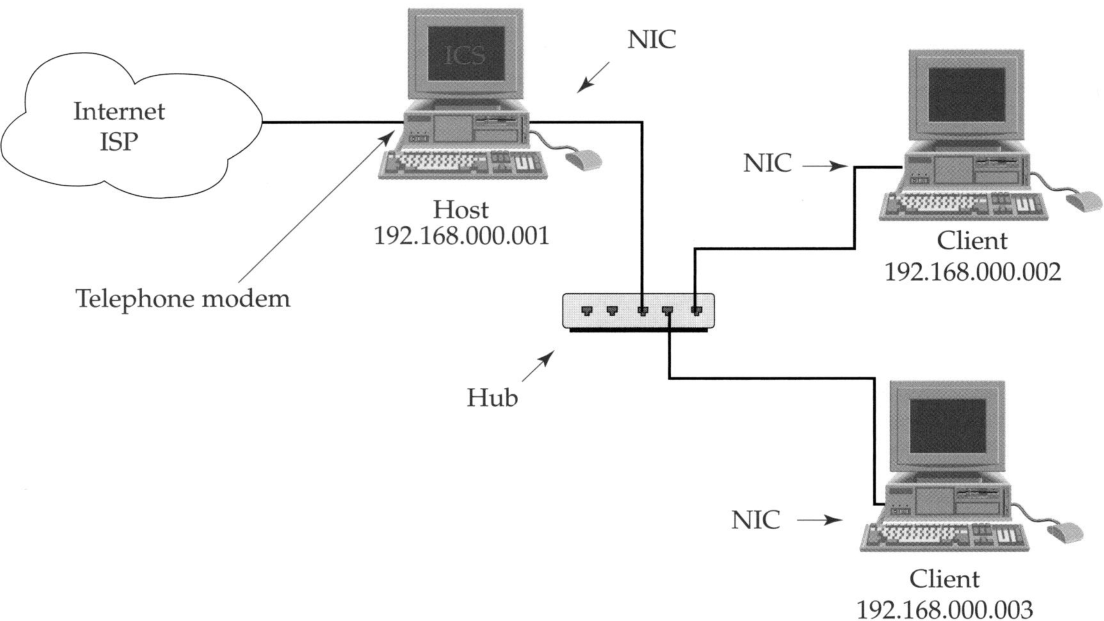

Note that the three PCs in Figure 19-9 are connected together using a hub. This is a typical copper cable arrangement. Again, note that the PC connected to the Internet is the host, while the other two are considered clients. When a client sends a request to access the Internet, the host automatically connects to the ISP. The host must be turned on for the clients to access the Internet.

DSL or cable modem Internet access

A typical DSL modem has several types of connectors with which you need to be familiar. Look at **Figure 19-10.** An RJ-11 jack provides a connection to the DSL service provider. A DSL modem may also have a swapper connection. A *swapper connection* "swaps" the telephone line pairs so that the DSL modem can connect to the DSL signal. This feature is useful in case the DSL service was installed on the nonstandard pair. Cable pairs are often switched by mistake when new cable installers are running cable in a new dwelling during construction. The installer's mistake will go undetected until that particular pair is actually needed. Locating the switched pair using a multimeter or other test equipment could be very time consuming. It is much more convenient to simply use the swapper connection. Some DSL modems have this feature built in rather than offering a second connection point.

The DSL modem is also equipped with a LAN connector. This is an RJ-45 jack that connects directly to the PC or to another network device, such as a router. The DSL modem also requires an electrical power supply. It typically connects to a standard 120-volt ac outlet and then converts the voltage level to approximately 12-volt dc through an inline adapter.

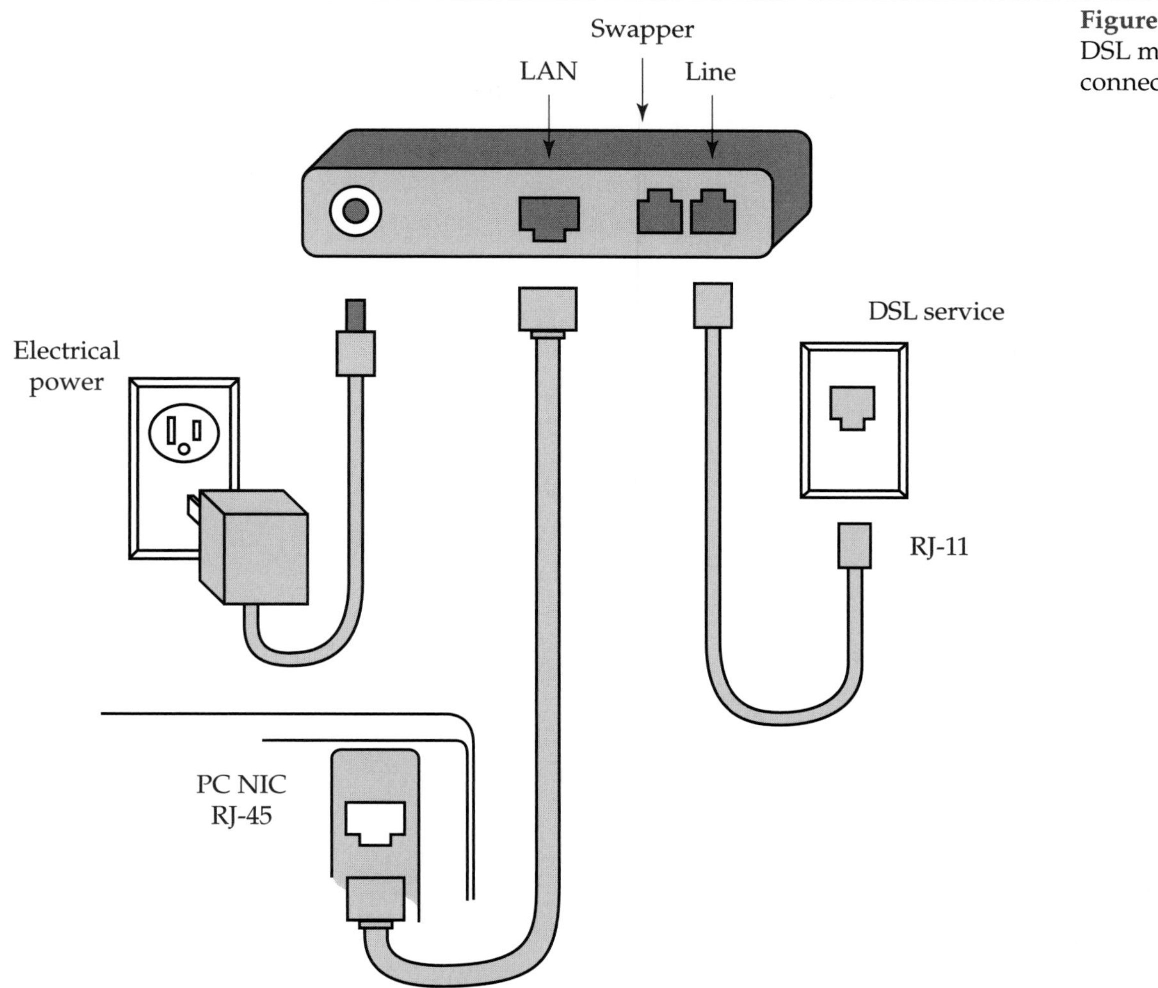

Figure 19-10. DSL modem connections.

A cable modem is installed in a similar fashion as the DSL modem. The main difference is that the cable modem connects to the cable television provider through the use of a coaxial cable F connector rather than an RJ-11 jack. A two-way cable splitter may be required to split the cable connection between the cable modem and the televisions in the dwelling. Software setup is basically the same for DSL and cable modems.

In **Figure 19-11,** a DSL modem is incorporated into a SOHO network. Here the host PC is required to have two NICs installed. One is used to make the connection to the DSL modem, and the other is used to connect to the hub. The network card can be a USB Plug and Play type rather than a PCI type.

To eliminate the need for an extra NIC in the host PC, a router can be incorporated into the network, **Figure 19-12.** A router can configure the SOHO IP addresses independently. A host PC, like the one used in the ICS configuration, is not needed. When using a router to share and control network access, all computers become clients and the router becomes the host. The router controls all access to the Internet and is typically more flexible than a Windows ICS host. Most routers not only supply software wizards to automatically configure the SOHO network, but also incorporate security features such as a firewall.

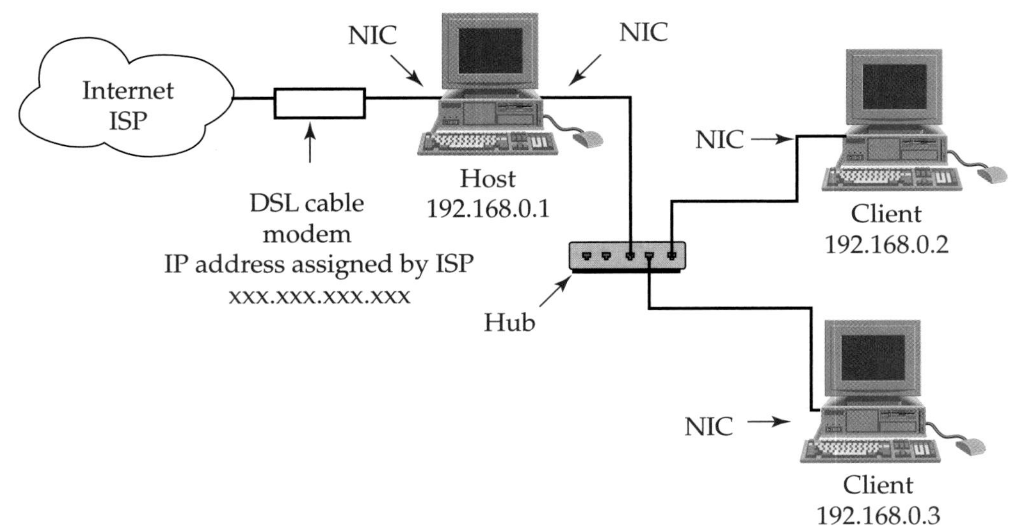

Figure 19-11. A three-PC network with Internet access via a DSL modem. The host PC contains two network cards—one to connect to the hub and the other to connect to the DSL or cable modem.

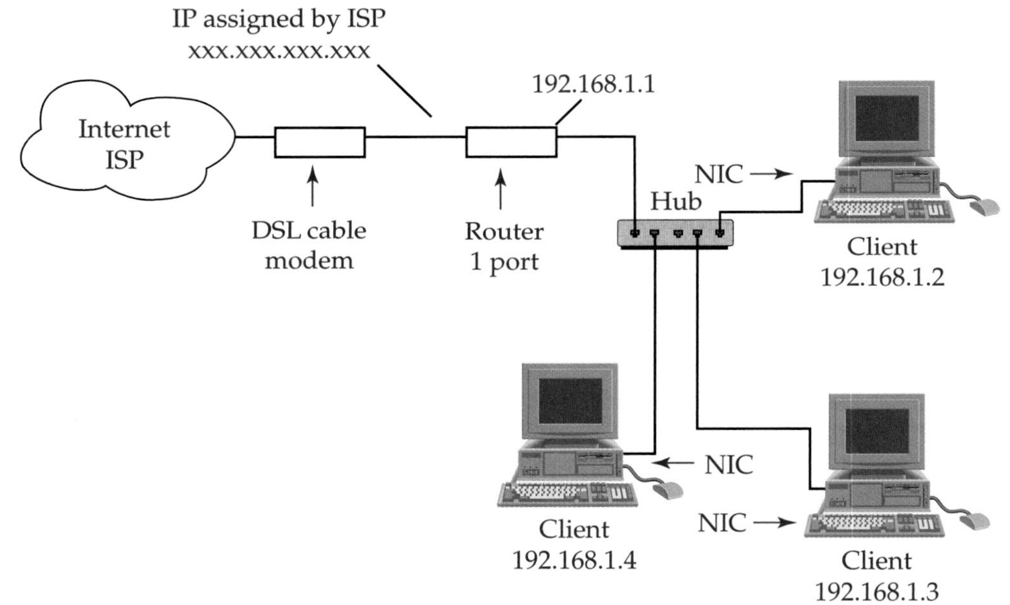

Figure 19-12. The router in this configuration has only one port, so a hub must be used.

A router can be configured to control all port addresses whereas a Windows XP host is limited to the most common port addresses. A router can also be configured to allow a computer in the network to connect directly to the Internet on the public side of the router and avoid port-filtering techniques. This would be useful for situations such as online Internet gaming between one of the SOHO stations and another across the Internet.

Tech Tip:
The router is a complete small computer system. It contains a CPU, memory, and software.

A router can be purchased with one or more LAN connections. When a router with several LAN connectors is used, the hub can be eliminated from the network, **Figure 19-13.** Routers can serve the same function as a hub. The router can incorporate other features, such as firewall protection and VPN support. (Firewalls and VPNs are covered under SOHO Security.) When the router serves both purposes, it reduces the overall complexity of the system. Always check the router specifications to be sure of all the features that are available.

A SOHO network can consist of several different technologies. Remember that when installing a mixture of technologies, a bridge or gateway router is required to connect the different technologies together. The SOHO network in **Figure 19-14** incorporates a DSL modem, router, copper cable, wireless, and HomePNA. This is a perfect example of how various network media can be combined to overcome building structure limitations. This type of SOHO network setup, however, can be challenging when the network devices come from different manufacturers. There can also be some difficulties when mixing media from various manufacturers. It is best to select equipment from the same manufacturer.

An example of a very robust router is the Motorola wireless broadband router model number WR850G. It is a combination cable and wireless router. It incorporates four 10/100BaseT RJ-45 connections and an antenna. This unit is especially designed for offices that require mixed media types.

SOHO Administration

SOHO network administration can be as simple or as complex as you wish to make it. Since the SOHO is a peer-to-peer network, you need not have any real administrative hierarchy. Everyone using the network can have equal access to all files and programs on the network. However, this can be disastrous. With

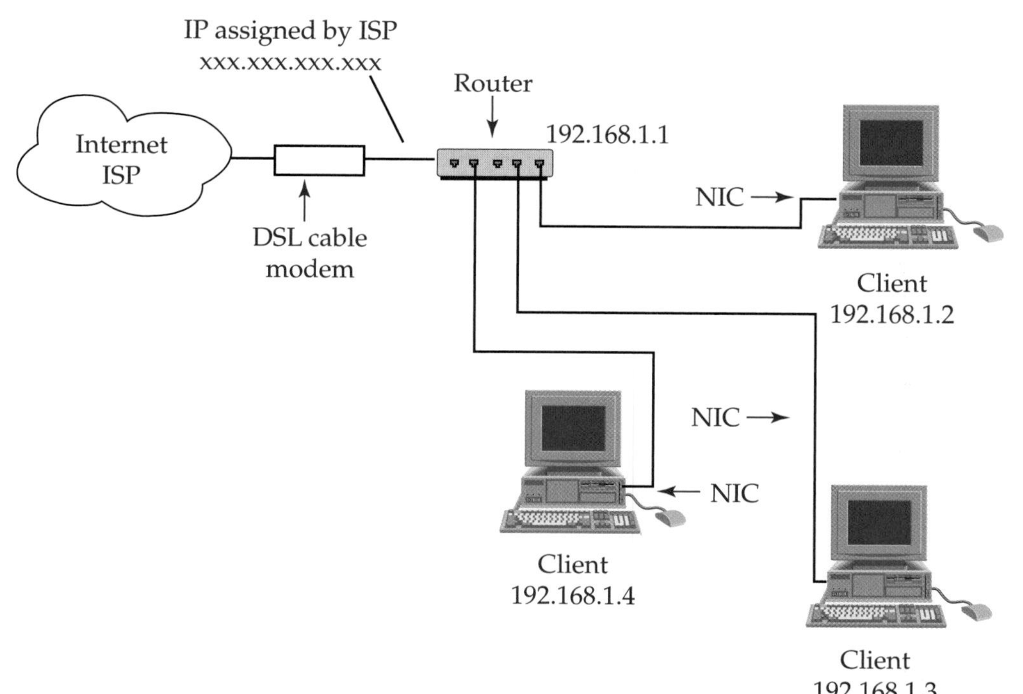

Figure 19-13. In this example, the router has multiple LAN connections so it functions as a hub.

Figure 19-14.
This SOHO network incorporates cable, wireless, and existing telephone lines as its network media.

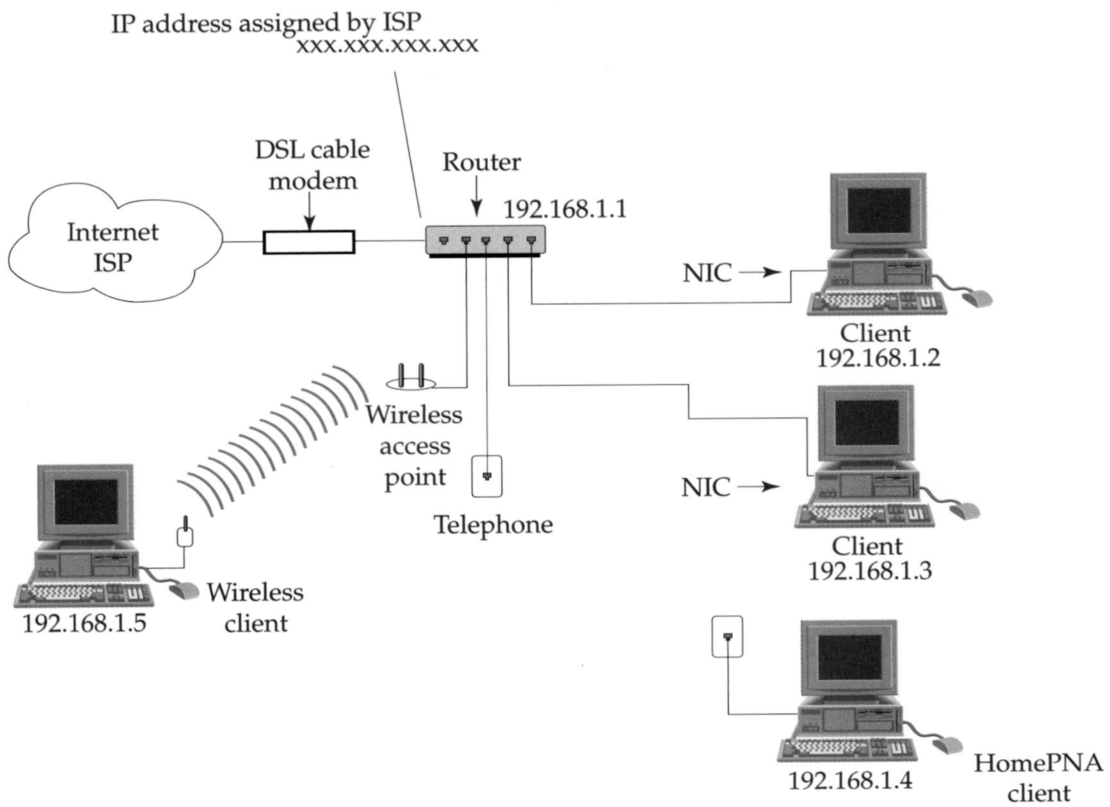

everyone having equal access, anyone can change the properties of any PC in the network. A better scenario would be to have a single administrator with limited authority delegated to other users. The administrator can determine how much control other users have over hardware and software by setting up local and share-level security. (See Chapter 17—Network Administration for a complete discussion of local and share-level security.)

Local security is implemented by creating a local user account on each PC. The local user account allows the user to log on to a single computer where the user account has been created. Remember that a peer-to-peer network uses the workgroup model of security. This model of security maintains a security list at each PC and requires that a local user account be set up at every PC the user will access locally.

Local security protects system settings on a PC. Any changes the user makes to the desktop or to a program is stored in the user's personal settings on that PC. These changes do not affect other local users.

Share-level security protects resources accessed from across the network by requiring a password to access the share or by limiting its access. For example, a network user may only have read-only access to files on another PC, or they may not be able to access the files at all unless they know the password.

Even in a home network, local and share-level security should be implemented to avoid disastrous situations. To reinforce how important security is, let's look at a typical home network in which no security has been implemented.

In the network shown in **Figure 19-15,** two parents use one of the PCs and two children, ages 10 and 16, use the other. Each PC has been set up with a single user account. A color printer is attached to the parent's PC and is shared to allow the children to print to it from their computer. Drive C on the parent's computer is also shared and allows full access to all files. Both of the parents use their PC for work-related activities and for writing checks.

The children use their PC for school assignments and use the color printer to print their school assignments and the graphics they find on the Internet. They also use their PC for their favorite pastime, computer games. The children are constantly downloading sample gaming software and exchanging software games with their friends. The children often need to use the PC at the same time. When this happens, one of them uses the parent's PC.

As you are probably sensing, there are bound to be severe problems because of this lax setup. With everyone using the same local user account, anyone using a PC can make changes on it. For instance, the children could delete important files on their parent's PC, such as banking information. They could even delete important files from across the network if share-level security has not been set up on the parent's local hard drive. Also, one of the children can download a game on their parent's PC and then change the PC's default settings to optimize the game. Or, by simply installing the computer game, a DLL file or some other file can possibly be overwritten. This would lock up, or crash, the PC.

A better scenario would be to secure the network as in **Figure 19-16.** In this configuration, a user account for each family member has been set up on the parent's PC. This ensures that personal settings or files will not be changed or deleted. Also, drive C is no longer shared. The children cannot access it from their own PC and delete important files. The printer is shared with limited access that allows the children to print through it but not change the printer's settings. As you can see, a certain level of security can lessen the opportunity for a problem to occur.

Figure 19-15.
A home network with no security.

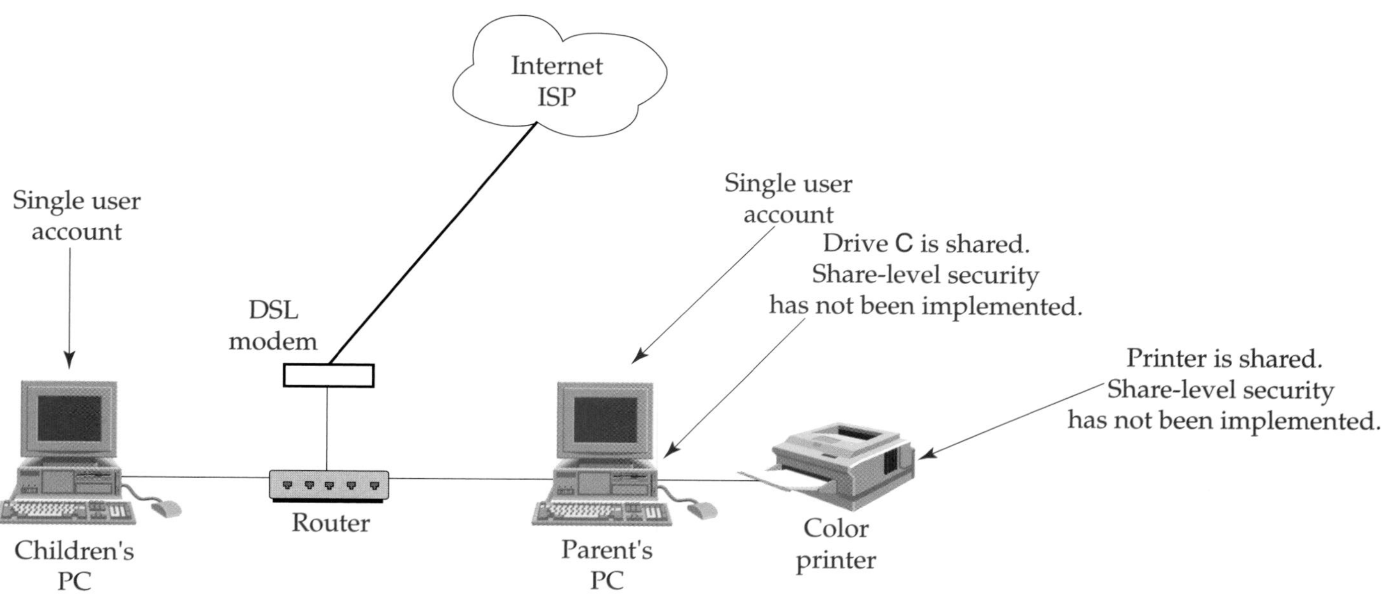

Figure 19-16.
A home network with security.

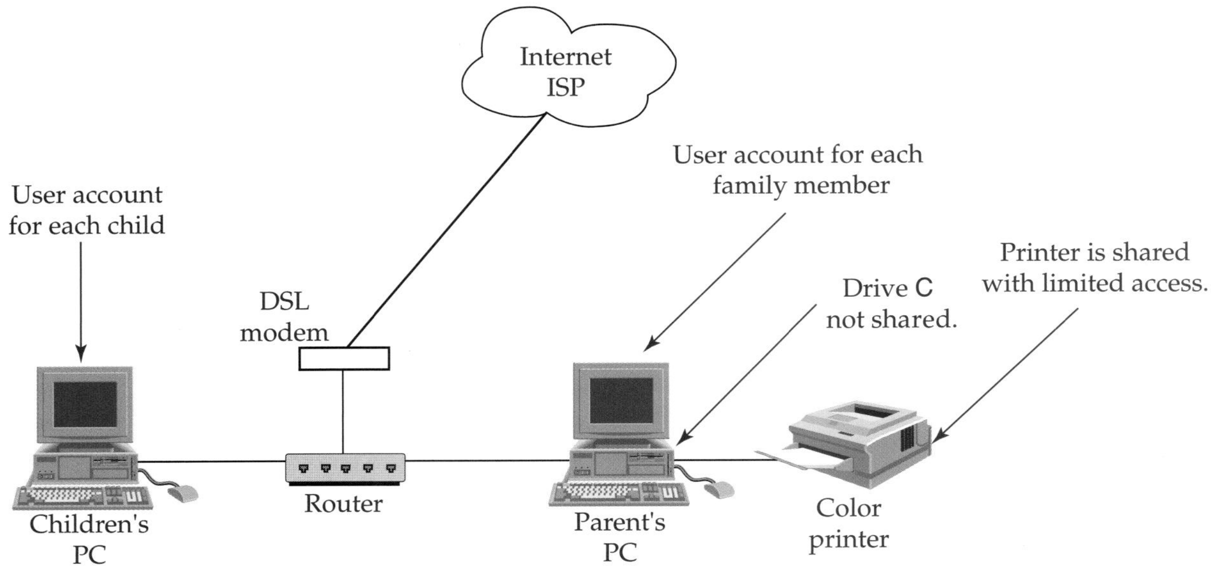

Tech Tip:
Other security practices to keep in mind are to use passwords that are complex, containing uppercase and lowercase letters, numbers, and special symbols. *Never* use a password that matches any word found in a dictionary or a person's name. *Never* leave the password blank. *Always* encrypt important data so even if it is accessed it will be of little use to the intruder.

SOHO Security

PCs in a SOHO network are vulnerable to attacks from outside the LAN if the LAN is connected to the Internet. The Internet is a "public" media. Users from anywhere in the world could access a networked PC through the Internet connection or intercept a PC's message content. There are several ways to set up security to protect the SOHO network from intruders and to protect data as it is travels across the Internet. Two common security implementations that should be configured for the SOHO network are a firewall and a virtual private network (VPN).

Firewall

In Chapter 18—WAN, you learned that a firewall protects a LAN by blocking access to specific ports or by filtering out IP addresses, packet contents, services, and protocols. For example, a firewall can filter out echo requests. This stops a site that is being probed with the ping command from displaying its IP address via echo.

There are times when you may need to block a specific port or open a port. For example, a firewall is set up to block all ports that are not absolutely essential. A person wishes to participate in a game online. The game "Rainbow Six" requires the use of TCP ports 2346, 2347, and 2348 for Internet gaming. These ports can be opened by entering their numbers in the firewall service properties dialog box. Opening these ports allows data to pass through the firewall, allowing two computers to communicate freely during a gaming session. You can view the Microsoft Knowledge Base Article 307554 online to see other port addresses associated with common games and services.

Windows XP comes with a standard firewall, called the ***Internet Connection Firewall (ICF),*** which can be configured to keep unauthorized users from accessing the network. There are also many third party utilities that can be used to increase SOHO security. Using the Network Setup Wizard to install ICF is covered later in this chapter.

Internet Connection Firewall (ICF) software included in Windows XP that can be configured to keep unauthorized users from accessing the network.

Remember that a firewall should only be installed on the host PC. Installing a firewall on more than one PC in the SOHO network adversely affects shares, thus preventing the network's main purpose. Also, do not implement a firewall and a VPN at the same time. The two security systems will conflict.

Virtual private network (VPN)

A ***virtual private network (VPN)*** ensures that data sent across the Internet is not intercepted, read, or modified. It does this by creating a private tunnel between the destination and source PC and encrypting packet contents. As the term *tunnel* implies, all the messages are exchanged privately as though they traveled through the public space of the Internet encapsulated in a security tunnel that no one else can see into or access, **Figure 19-17.**

virtual private network (VPN) a security configuration that ensures data sent across the Internet is not read or modified. It does this by creating a private tunnel between the destination and source PC and encrypting packet contents.

A VPN should be created to ensure security when communicating across the Internet through an ISP. A VPN can also be created if you are permanently connected to the Internet via a cable modem or DSL modem.

Normally, because data is encoded in plain ASCII text, the content of a typical packet is completely viewable through a packet sniffer. A ***packet sniffer*** is a utility that captures packets on a network and displays their entire contents. When a VPN connection is made, all the contents of the packet are encrypted

packet sniffer a utility that captures packets on a network and displays their entire contents.

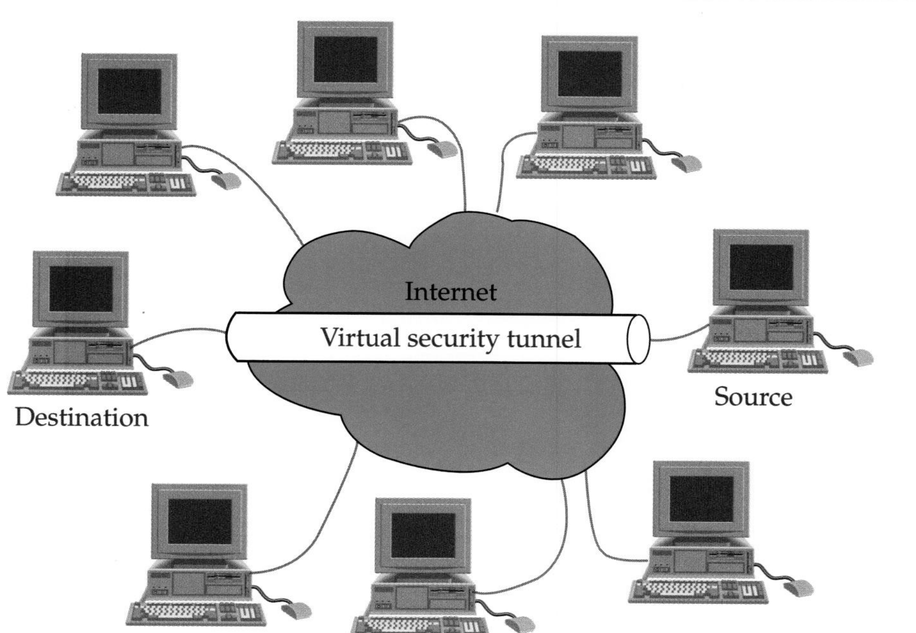

Figure 19-17. A virtual private network (VPN) creates a private tunnel between the destination and source PC. The data flowing between the two PCs cannot be interpreted by other computers on the Internet.

except for the destination address. The destination address remains readable so that it can travel across a series of Internet routers to reach its final destination. The VPN is transparent to users at the destination and the source.

The two main security connection protocols associated with a VPN connection are Point-to-Point Tunneling Protocol (PPTP) and Layer-Two-Tunneling Protocol (L2TP). These protocols also incorporate other protocols, such as IPsec, IKE, and CHAP, to further enhance their security features.

Be aware that many ISPs do not allow VPN connections through their system. The ISP filters out protocols associated with VPNs. To determine if you can use a VPN, check with the ISP. Some ISPs advertise the use of VPN connections to recruit users. Also, since the establishment of a VPN tunnel depends on the destination and source having a unique IP address, using an ISP that assigns IP addresses from a pool of numbers can also create a problem. The VPN will only work with a SOHO network that has a permanently assigned IP address.

There can be problems implementing a VPN connection in a network that uses a firewall or ICS. Microsoft recommends that you do not use the VPN feature at the same time you are using a firewall or ICS. To connect from a SOHO network to a work site using a laptop that is implementing a VPN, it may be best to configure the laptop for an Internet connection separate from the SOHO network. In **Figure 19-18,** a laptop makes a direct connection to the Internet through the DSL modem via a hub. This avoids conflicts between the VPN on the laptop and the firewall in the router. There are third party vendors, though, who market security software and hardware that allow both the firewall and the VPN to run on the same SOHO network.

Configuring the SOHO Network

Ideally, all PCs in the SOHO network would use the latest operating system. This would provide for the easiest installation. Unfortunately, this is not always the case. Many SOHO networks are constructed with various operating systems and equipment. Incorporating legacy computer systems with modern ones can be challenging but can be done if carefully thought out.

Remember to use the PC with the latest or most up-to-date operating system as the host or as the computer that will share other resources, such as a printer. Typically, the latest operating system will have the technology available to support older operating systems. They will also have a wizard that assists in configuring the network. For example, Microsoft Windows XP has the Network

Figure 19-18. Connecting a laptop directly to the Internet access rather than to the network avoids conflicts between the laptop's VPN and the network's firewall.

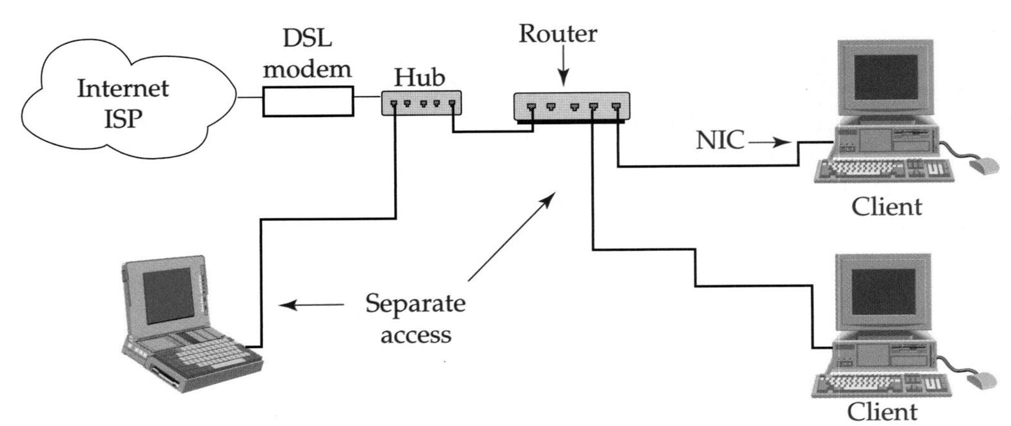

Setup Wizard.

The ***Network Setup Wizard*** makes it easy to set up a SOHO network. It includes a series of dialog boxes that ask for information about the network. The wizard can be accessed by choosing **Start | Settings | Control Panel | Network Connections | Setup a home or small office network**. **Figure 19-19** shows the first dialog box of the Network Setup Wizard. The Network Setup Wizard helps you to share an Internet connection, enable the Internet Connection Firewall (ICF), and enable file and printer sharing.

The Network Setup Wizard is easy to use if you are familiar with networking hardware and terminology. However, if you have never set up a network before, it is easy to provide the wrong information. As an aid, the Network Setup Wizard includes a checklist, **Figure 19-20,** which assists in

Network Setup Wizard
a Windows XP wizard that makes setting up a network easy by including a series of dialog boxes that ask for information about the network.

Figure 19-19. Network Setup Wizard welcome screen.

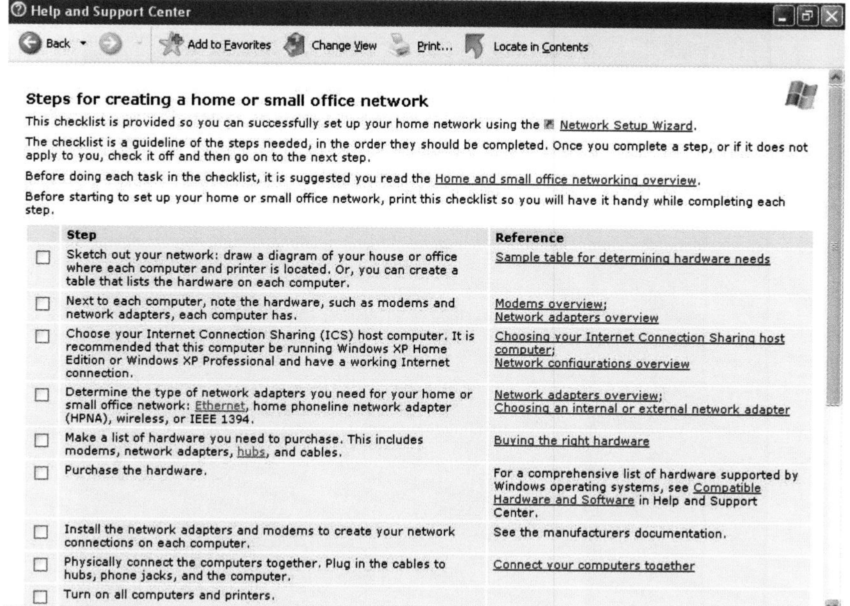

Figure 19-20. This checklist, provided by Windows XP, is a valuable aid for setting up a SOHO network.

setting up a SOHO network. The checklist can be printed and carried with you until you become comfortable with setting up networks.

Share an Internet Connection

One of the main tasks of configuring a SOHO network with Internet access is setting up ICS. ICS can be configured manually or automatically. When configured automatically, choose from the Network Setup Wizard menu "**This computer connects directly to the Internet. The other computers on my network connect to the Internet through this computer**." See **Figure 19-21.** When activated, a series of prompts appear on the screen. Answer the series of questions presented in the dialog boxes.

Using the Network Setup Wizard is by far the easiest method for setting up an Internet connection share. Even a novice can usually configure ICS by responding to the series of dialog boxes. A technician will also use the wizard to set up ICS, but they must know how to configure the same connection manually to be able to perform and understand the results of troubleshooting ICS installation.

After the computer sharing the Internet connection has been set up and configured, you can make a disk that will automatically set up the clients for you. You can make the client disks by simply inserting the Windows XP installation CD. When the first screen appears, select **Additional tasks** from the menu and follow the prompts. A client disk will be made on a floppy, which can be inserted into each client PC. It will automatically configure the client with the appropriate IP address and protocols necessary. If, however, the clients are running Windows XP, you may, as an alternative, run the Network Setup Wizard on those computers and choose **This computer connects to the Internet through another computer on my network or through a residential gateway**. The wizard will automatically configure the client with the appropriate IP address and protocols.

Set up Internet Connection Firewall

The Internet Connection Firewall (ICF) is automatically enabled on the computer that connects directly to the Internet or has ICS installed. When ICF is enabled, it not only protects the computer on which it is configured, but also the

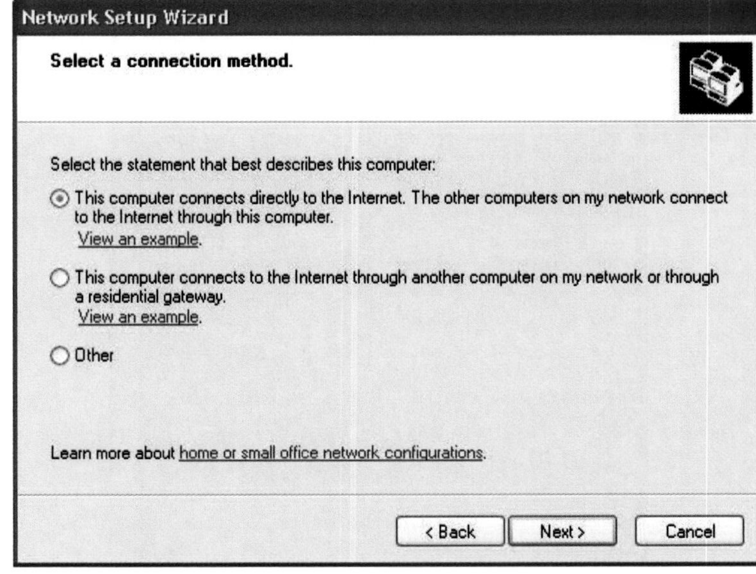

Figure 19-21. The Network Setup Wizard prompts you for a connection method.

other computers on the network. The ICF monitors all communications from the Internet by inspecting the source and destination of each packet sent to the network. The combination of port number and IP address determines if the packet may pass to the network or be discarded. The firewall can also filter packets based on services. Services are identified by port numbers.

Once ICF is enabled, it can be configured manually by accessing the **Network Connection** folder, right-clicking the firewall-enabled connection, and selecting **Properties**. From the **Properties** dialog box, select the **Advanced** tab and then click the **Settings** button. A dialog box like that in **Figure 19-22** will appear, displaying a list of services that can be filtered by the firewall. To select a service, click in the box next to the service. A check mark will appear in the box. If the service exists on another computer in the network, you must enter that computer's name or IP address in the **Service Settings** dialog box, **Figure 19-23.**

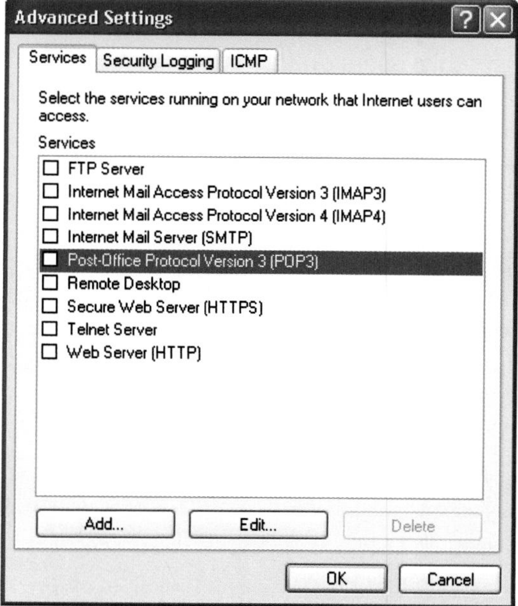

Figure 19-22. Various common network services can be filtered for added security.

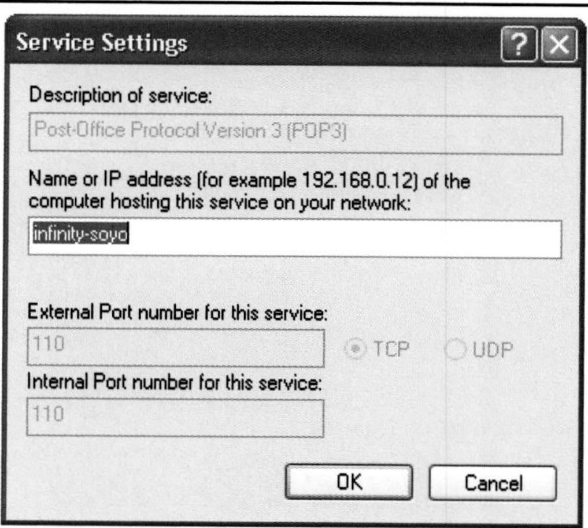

Figure 19-23. Service Settings dialog box set to filter the POP3 service on a computer named "infinity-soyo."

To access the **Service Settings** dialog box, highlight the service to be configured and click the **Edit** button.

In Figure 19-23, the computer hosting the POP3 service is identified by its name, "infinity-soyo." Notice how the POP3 e-mail service corresponds with port 110 indicated in the text box. Port 110 is the default port number for the POP3 service.

A service that is not listed in the **Advanced Settings** may be added by clicking the **Add** button. In this case, the description of the service, the name or IP number of the computer hosting the service, and the external and internal port number for the service must be added.

Share Files and Folders

Folders and files can be easily shared on a small peer-to-peer network. **Figure 19-24** shows a dialog box that appears on a Windows XP system after right-clicking **My Documents** and selecting **Sharing and Security**.

The dialog box gives you two main choices: **Local sharing and security** and **Network sharing and security**. The **Local sharing and security** selection allows a folder to be shared with other users on this computer. Remember that Windows XP allows for local user accounts. In this way, a user's personal files can be protected. If another user logs on to the computer with their own user account name, they will not be able to access the other user's files or folders unless the other user chooses to share them. For a user to share their files and folders locally with other users on the system, a user can simply drag their folder into the shared Documents folder.

Network sharing and security provides access to users connected to the network. To share a folder on the network, click the box next to **Share this folder on the network**. To allow users to make changes to the files, click the box next to **Allow network users to change my files**.

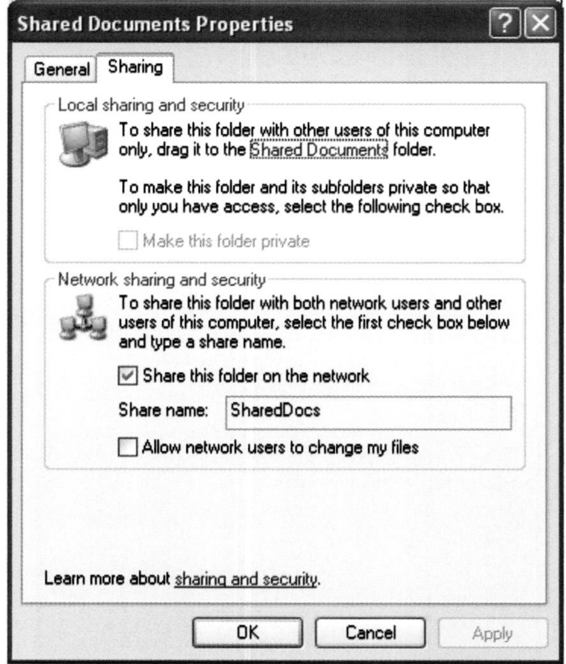

Figure 19-24. The Windows XP My Documents Properties dialog box allows you to easily configure a network share.

Share a Printer

Sharing a printer on a local network is similar to sharing a folder. If the printer is already installed, access the Printers and Faxes folder through **Start | Settings | Printers and Faxes** and right-click the printer. Select **Sharing**.

In the **Sharing** dialog box, select **Share** this printer. The first 8 characters of the printer's name will automatically display in the **Share** name box. You may change this to a more descriptive name. You may also add additional drivers for users running different versions of Windows. This will enable the correct version of the printer driver to be automatically downloaded to a user's system when they add the shared printer. If you do not choose to add the additional drivers, users will be required to provide the drivers themselves, either from the installation CD or from the Windows cab files.

You can also set up user privileges on network to determine who may reconfigure the network printer. To assign printer privileges, you must be logged on as the network administrator.

To connect a computer to a networked printer, access the Printers and Faxes folder through **Start | Settings | Printers and Faxes**. You can then use the Add Printer Wizard to add a printer to the local computer or connect to a printer in the network, **Figure 19-25.**

The next screen in the wizard, **Figure 19-26,** displays two choices: **Local printer attached to this computer** and **A network printer, or a printer attached to another computer**. The first choice is for connecting a printer directly to the PC. When a printer connects directly to the PC it is referred to as the "local" printer. The second choice is for connecting the PC to a printer located on another PC using a network-type connection. Select the second choice, **A network printer, or a printer attached to another computer**. A dialog box will appear similar to the one in **Figure 19-27.**

Figure 19-25. Add Printer Wizard welcome screen.

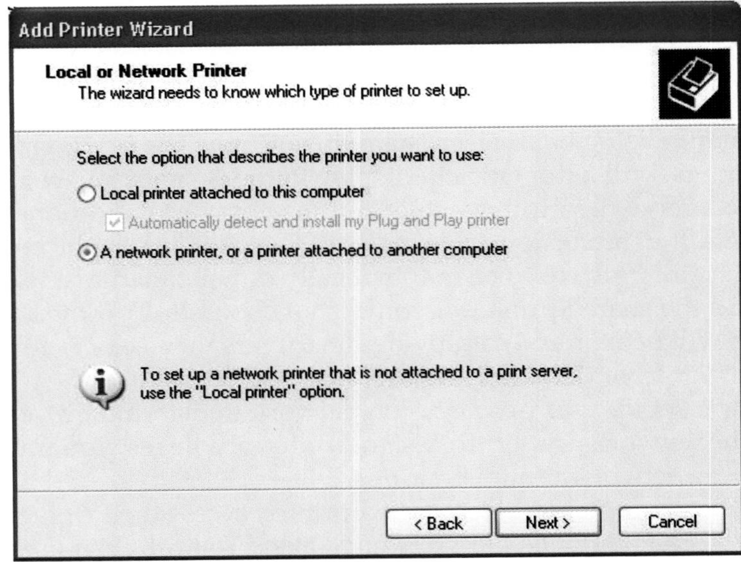

Figure 19-26. To set up access to a network printer, choose **A network printer, or a printer attached to another computer**.

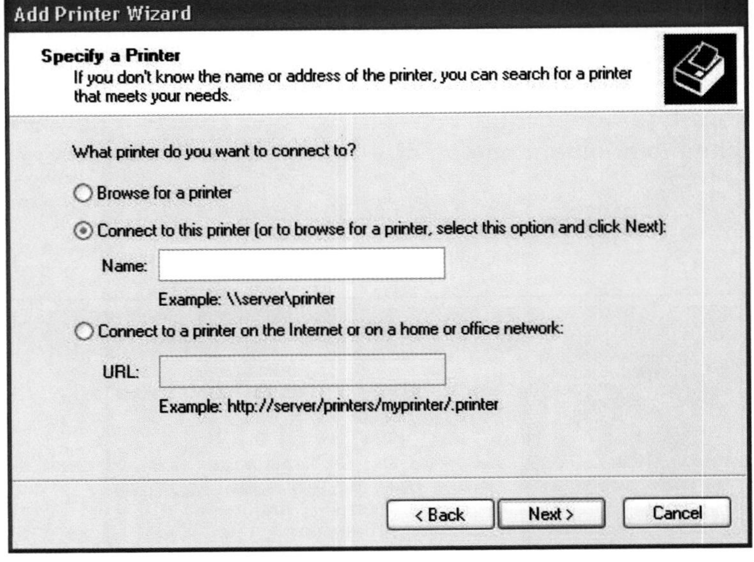

Figure 19-27. To specify a network printer, you may browse the network for it, enter its UNC path, or enter its URL path.

Universal Naming Convention (UNC) a path format that identifies a server and its share and uses backslashes to separate the server name from the share name.

You now have three choices: **Browse for a printer**, **Connect to this printer**, and **Connect to a printer on the Internet or on a home or office network**. Pay particular attention to the way the printer path is displayed in the examples in Figure 19-27. The first example, under **Connect to this printer**, uses the ***Universal Naming Convention (UNC)***. A UNC identifies the server and the share and uses backslashes to separate the server name from the share name. The second example, under **Connect to a printer on the Internet or on a home or office network**, uses a URL to indicate the path. A URL uses forward slashes and must be used to indicate the path for a share on the Internet or on a network using Active Directory as the directory service.

Troubleshooting the SOHO Network

Once you have installed and configured your SOHO network, you may find that you cannot access certain resources or that access is slow. This section covers the most common problems that can occur with a new SOHO network installation. These problems involve firewall installation, VPN and firewall conflicts, improper ICS host configuration, and hardware and software incompatibilities.

Internet Access Is Sluggish

The shared Internet connection can be extremely slow or sluggish if someone on the network is downloading pictures or sound files. Files containing graphics or sound clips are excessively large when compared to text files. Since the bandwidth of the local network is shared by everyone connected to the network, large file transfers can reduce the network response time for everyone connected. This problem can be eliminated by blocking the ports associated with the large file transfers. For example, the music download site Napster uses TCP port 6699. If excessive use of Napster is reducing network performance, simply filter out port 6699.

Cannot Access Resources on the Network

Installing ICF on a computer that is not the ICS host can cause communications problems by blocking transmissions. Users will not be able to share a file with other PCs on the network or access the shared Internet connection on the ICS host. To solve this problem, only configure ICF on the ICS host.

A firewall and VPN on the same SOHO network can also cause access problems. Microsoft does not recommend a firewall and VPN on the same SOHO network. Use one at a time, not both at the same time. An ISP typically assigns only one IP address to a user location. If a computer is configured as a VPN then all other computers in the network will be blocked from accessing the Internet. If the Internet connection is already made to the ICS, then the VPN computer will not be able to access the Internet and complete its connection to the VPN destination.

Some routers will perform multiple duties and support several functions or services simultaneously. For example, a router can provide shared Internet access and support a VPN connection at the same time. This is another example of the superiority of a router used in a small network system. Otherwise, you will need to separate the computer using the VPN from the rest of the network.

Setting up a PC with a different protocol than the other PCs on the network will prevent that PC from accessing resources on the network. This can often happen when the network is set up with a mixture of old and new computers. The older computers may be configured by default with the NetBEUI protocol while the newer computers are configured with TCP/IP by default. There may also be a conflict in the names of computers in a network of mixed operating systems. NetBIOS only allows 15 characters in the name. Windows 2000 and XP can use longer names. The first thing to check on a new network is the correct spelling of the workgroup, computer, and share name.

Cannot Access the Internet through the ICS Host

Do not use any form of server software on any of the local workgroup workstations. For example, a small network system is growing in size and eventually needs to switch to a client/server model. A combination file server and Web server is installed in the existing network. The installation of the server and Web server by an inexperienced technician can cause severe network communication problems. A server is typically configured as a DHCP server or DNS server, which will interfere with ICS host on the network. Remember, the ICS wizard automatically configures IP addresses. If the server is configured for DHCP or DNS, it will also attempt to issue IP addresses, which will cause intermittent access problems or even complete failure of the ICS feature.

Incompatible Hardware/Software

Incompatibility can be a real problem. Check the hardware compatibility list before setting up a SOHO network. If a device that is not on the hardware compatibility list is installed and it is actually incompatible, any unexpected occurrence might happen. The device may try to constantly broadcast, or simply communicate in only one direction. It might respond to text-based commands such as ping and tracert but not communicate at any higher level. If a network is composed of mixed computers (computers with various types of hardware and operating systems), some of the computers may support communication with the odd device and some will not. Anything might happen when using devices that have not been thoroughly tested.

Tech Tip:
Not all devices not listed on the HCL will cause problems. Many function perfectly.

Summary

- A small-office/home-office (SOHO) network is a simple peer-to-peer LAN.
- Typical media used in a SOHO network are copper cable, wireless, existing phone lines, and existing power lines.
- Home Phoneline Networking Alliance (HomePNA) technology uses a frequency higher than the telephone to transmit data over existing telephone lines.
- HomePNA technology is not recommend for use in buildings that use a private branch exchange (PBX) as the centralized point of the telephone system.
- Powerline communications (PLC) technology uses a much higher frequency than 60 Hz to transmit data over existing power lines.
- A mixed network environment requires a bridge to connect dissimilar network media.
- Home communications systems include telephone, sound, television, and computer network systems.
- Copper cabling has the only predictable transmission rate out of all SOHO network media.
- A wireless bridge is referred to as an access point.

- A gateway router is a router that combines different media and provides an Internet connection.
- Common choices of Internet access devices in a SOHO network are the telephone modem and the DSL or cable modem.
- A PC that provides access to the Internet is called a host. A PC that accesses the Internet through the host is called a client.
- The host in a typical ICS configuration is always assigned the IP address 192.168.000.1, and the clients are assigned IP addresses in sequence starting at 192.168.000.002.
- When a DSL or cable modem only provides one RJ-45 connection, an additional NIC can be installed on the host PC or a router can be added to the network to support the other computer workstations.
- A router can function as a firewall and a gateway and can provide Internet Connection Sharing.
- Some routers incorporate other features, such as firewall protection and VPN support.
- When a router contains extra LAN connections, a hub is generally not needed on the network.
- In a peer-to-peer network, a local user account needs to be set up on each PC that the user plans to access locally.
- A firewall should be used to secure an ICS from unauthorized users.
- A virtual private network (VPN) ensures that data sent across the Internet is not intercepted, read, or modified.
- There are many wizards available to help install and automatically configure a SOHO network. Microsoft Windows XP includes the Network Setup Wizard.

Review Questions

Answer the following questions on a separate sheet of paper. Please do not write in this book.

1. Explain some of the limitations associated with each of the SOHO network media.
2. Why may the use of telephone lines as a means of networking an office not work?
3. List the ways two PCs can be connected together in a two-PC network.
4. What is the name of a network device that connects two different types of network media?
5. What Internet access devices are commonly used for a SOHO installation?
6. Draw three possible designs of a SOHO network that has three PCs and will use a DSL modem for Internet access. Include the appropriate network devices for each design.
7. List the benefits of implementing local security and share-level security in a SOHO network.

8. Describe two instances of when a VPN should be created.
9. Windows XP includes the _____ _____ _____ to assist in the configuration of a SOHO network.
10. What are some of the problems you may encounter in a new SOHO network installation?

Sample A+ Exam Questions

Answer the following questions on a separate sheet of paper. Please do not write in this book.

1. Which technology would provide the best protection against unauthorized access from the Internet?
   a. A standard V92 modem
   b. A firewall
   c. A good Internet access password for modem access
   d. Antivirus program
2. Which technology typically will not provide a persistent Internet connection?
   a. DSL
   b. ISDN
   c. Direct cable
   d. Telephone modem
3. What is the typical IP address assigned to an ICS host?
   a. 123.145.000.001
   b. 192.168.000.1
   c. 127.000.000.1
   d. 255.255.255.255
4. A small SOHO network has been set up in a local insurance company, which consists of four Windows XP Professional workstations. Jim has successfully created a local user account on Workstation_1 for his own use. All workstations belong to the same workgroup. Jim is unsuccessful at logging on to the other workstations. What is *most* likely the problem?
   a. Jim does not have a local user account set up on Workstations_2 through Workstation_4.
   b. The network cabling has been disconnected from Workstations_2 through Workstation_4.
   c. Share-level security must be configured on Workstations_2 through Workstation_4.
   d. A user on a peer-to-peer network may not log on to more than one PC at a time.

A+

5. Jim is working late at the office. The office consists of eight computers configured as a peer-to-peer network. The office manager's computer is an ICS host and has a telephone modem installed to access the ISP. The system was installed two months ago and has worked well. Everyone has shut down their computer and has gone home except Jim. Jim attempts to access his e-mail before leaving but finds he cannot access the Internet. What is *most* likely the problem?
   a. The IP address supplied to the ICS host by the ISP has changed.
   b. The connection cannot be established because the ICS host has been shut down.
   c. The Internet Connection Firewall is configured to prevent Jim from accessing the Internet port 110.
   d. The ISP does not provide telephone support after 6 p.m.
6. Which technology allows existing power lines to be used as network media?
   a. VPN
   b. PLC
   c. ICS
   d. HomePNA
7. A _____ ensures that data sent across the Internet is not intercepted, read, or tampered with.
   a. PLC
   b. firewall
   c. ICS
   d. VPN
8. A router that is used to combine different media and to provide an Internet connection is often referred to as a _____ router.
   a. bridge
   b. access
   c. Internet
   d. gateway
9. A SOHO network is a simple _____ LAN.
   a. client/server
   b. client/host
   c. peer-to-peer
   d. wireless
10. The HomePNA adapter uses a higher frequency than _____ to transmit data across the existing telephone line
   a. 4kHz
   b. 10kHz
   c. 2kHz
   d. 15kHz

Suggested Laboratory Activities

Do not attempt any suggested laboratory activities without your instructor's permission. Certain activities can render the PC operating system inoperable.

1. Set up a SOHO network with a shared Internet connection.
2. Configure a printer share on the above SOHO network.
3. Configure a firewall for the SOHO network. Experiment with various firewall port settings to see how they affect the computer stations in the network. Also, attempt to access the SOHO network from outside the immediate network. (Requires at least two modems and two private telephone lines.)
4. Configure a VPN across a peer-to-peer network. Use a packet sniffer to see if it can view the contents of the data packets flowing through the VPN.
5. Design a SOHO network for an existing home that consists of three bedrooms, an office, and a game room. Each bedroom will have one PC and the office and game room will each have a printer. There will be one Internet access point located in the office area. The access point is a DSL line. Make a drawing of the layout. Make a list of materials and costs based on current prices.

Interesting Web Sites for More Information

www.2wire.com

www.microsoft.com

www.3com.com

Chapter 19
Laboratory Activity

Using the Windows XP Network Setup Wizard

After completing this laboratory activity, you will be able to:

- ❑ Set up a SOHO network using the Windows XP Network Setup Wizard.
- ❑ Explain three ways to access the Network Setup Wizard.
- ❑ Explain the various options available through the Network Setup Wizard.

Introduction

One of the many nice features of Windows XP is the different wizards available that make life easier for not only the novice but also the experienced technician. It is very easy to forget something important when performing tasks such as setting up a small network. A wizard is comparable to an automated list of important steps needed to complete a task. While all wizards will not solve every installation problem, they can make installation easier.

Remember, wizards aren't foolproof. Plenty of things do go wrong even when using them on a small network. The advantage of using Windows XP Network Setup Wizard is it is easy to use and requires only a minimum knowledge of networking. The disadvantage is you may leave security holes by relying on the default settings. Security is often left nonexistent, especially by novice users. If you are setting up a share using TCP/IP, keep in mind that not only can all computers in the workgroup see each other's computers outside the workgroup can access all the computers in the workgroup. Be sure to put the proper security in place by doing things such as configuring the firewall or incorporating a gateway.

The Network Setup Wizard is designed for small-office/home-office (SOHO) networks. It is not intended to use on large complicated networks because of the IP addresses that are assigned automatically by the wizard. The Network Setup Wizard typically assigns non-registered IP addresses as identified by the Internet authority.

Non-registered IP Address Ranges
10.0.0.0—10.255.255.255
172.16.0.0—172.16.255.255
192.168.0.0—192.168.255.255

When running the Network Setup Wizard, a series of step-by-step dialog boxes appear on the screen. Be sure to read carefully each screen presentation to avoid missing any important information and making an improper selection. Some installers rapidly go through a wizard clicking "Next" without reading the dialog options or explanations. Default selections do not always work for every possible network configuration. That's why choices are presented in the first place.

Networking wizards are available through a number of operating systems. Most of the wizards generate a disk when you run the wizard for the first time on a network. The disk contains configuration data to be used on other computers in the network. Using the wizard eliminates the need to manually assign IP addresses, the DHCP server location, and WINS server location.

The Network Setup Wizard gives you an option to generate a floppy disk to set up other computers in the SOHO network. The disk generated during the wizard installation contains configuration data identifying the PC with the Internet connection, the workgroup name, and a list of IP addresses that have already been issued. This prevents issuing the same IP address to two or more PCs. Duplicate IP addresses will cause problems in the network. Only one of the PCs among those with the same IP address will be able to communicate on the network.

If all the computers in the peer-to-peer network are using Windows XP, you do not need to use the generated disk. You can use the Network Setup Wizard at these computers. When the Network Setup Wizard is run, it accesses the host PC for the configuration data. Remember that a computer that connects directly to the Internet is referred to as the host and will share the connection with the computers referred to as clients. For the host to provide Internet access, Internet Connection Sharing (ICS) must be established on the host PC. *Always* set up the host first and then configure the clients.

Equipment and Materials

- A minimum of two computers: one with Windows XP and Internet access through a dialup connection and the other with Windows 98, ME, or XP installed. (Do not use Windows NT or 2000 for this laboratory activity.)
- 1–3 1/2" floppy disk.

Note:
You will need to have "Administrator" privileges on each of the workstations to complete this lab activity. A dialup Internet connection is not an absolute necessity for this lab activity. It can be completed without any type of Internet connection or by using another form of Internet connection. If your lab has a security software system installed, you may have some problems with the lab activity. In such cases, set up a small peer-to-peer network without a connection to the Internet or the regular network system.

Procedure

1. ______ Report to your assigned workstation with required materials.
2. ______ Boot the PC to be sure it is in working order. If not, get the instructors attention before proceeding further.
3. ______ Access the Network Setup Wizard by opening **Control Panel** and double-clicking **Network Connections**.
4. ______ From the **Network Tasks** menu on the left side of the screen, select **Set up a home or small office network**.
5. ______ Close the Network Setup Wizard and access the wizard by going through the Start menu: **Start | All Programs | Accessories | Communications | Network Setup Wizard**.
6. ______ Close the Network Setup Wizard and access the wizard once more by right-clicking **My Network Places** and selecting **Properties**.

7. ______ From the Network Tasks menu on the left side of the screen, select **Set up a home or small office network**.

8. ______ Repeat the three access methods indicated in steps 3 through 7 as many times as necessary to be able to remember them in the future before going on.

9. ______ Open the Network Setup Wizard by using any one of the three methods. The "Welcome to the Network Setup Wizard" screen will display.

On a separate sheet of paper, list the four things that can be accomplished with the Network Setup Wizard.

10. ______ Click the **Next** button. The **Before you continue** dialog box will display. Near the top of the dialog box, you are prompted to review the checklist for creating a network. *Do not* click **checklist for creating a network** at this time. Instead, on a separate sheet of paper, list the three steps that should be completed.

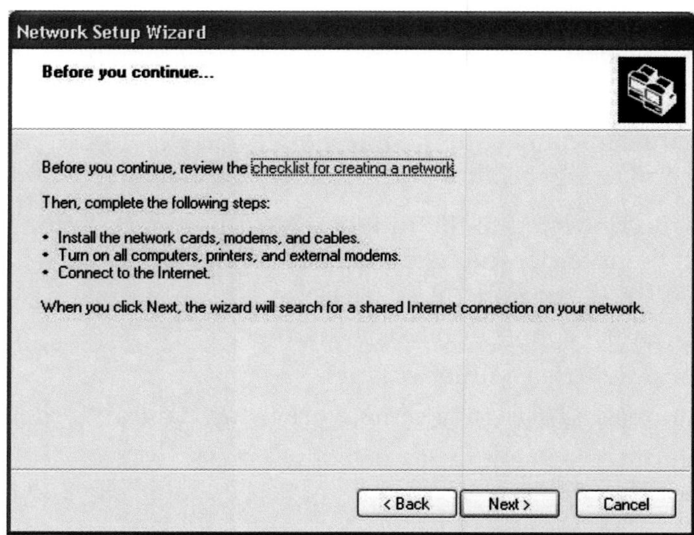

11. ______ Click the **checklist for creating a network**. An extensive listing will appear in a dialog box titled "Help and Support" similar to the one below. The same information provided here can be also accessed through **Start | Help and Support** at any time.

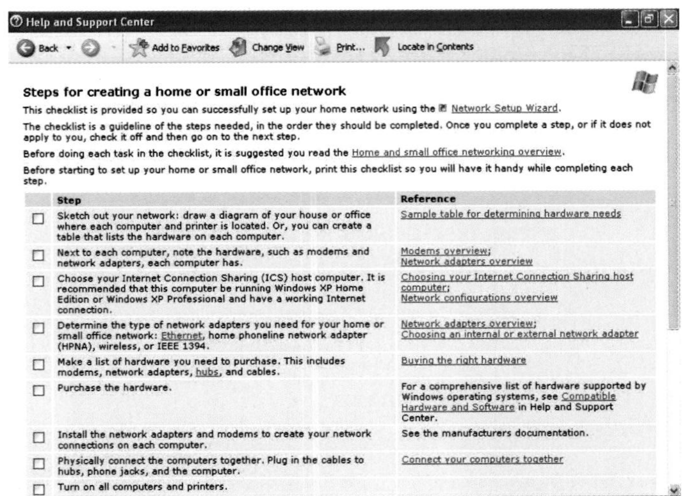

12. ______ Scroll down the listing to see what type of information is available. You may wish to minimize the Help and Support dialog box before moving on so that it can be referenced at any time during the installation process.

13. ______ Click the **Next** button. The **Select a connection method** dialog box will appear. You are prompted to select the statement that best describes the computer on which you are running the Network Setup Wizard. Write these three statements on a separate sheet of paper.

14. ______ Select the appropriate statement and click **Next**.

Note:

The series of screens and selections after the Select a connection method dialog box will vary according to the choice made in this step. Follow the series of screen prompts until the host computer and the clients are all configured. Remember, you can use the 3 1/2″ floppy to create a disk that will assist in setting up the clients.

15. ______ Test the connection to the Internet from each workstation. Be sure you can connect to the Internet. If you experience problems connecting, be sure of the following:

- The host is connected to the Internet. No other workstations will be able to access the Internet unless the host is connected.
- There is no firewall protection activated on any station except the one making a direct connection to the Internet.
- Each computer uses a unique name.
- Each computer is using the same workgroup name.
- Each computer is using the same subnet mask.

16. ______ Set up a shared directory on one of the networked computers. Create a short text file and save it in the shared directory. The text file content can be anything. On a separate sheet of paper, write the complete directory path to the share file.

17. ______ Set up a shared printer on one of the networked computers. On a separate sheet of paper, write the complete path for the printer share. Be careful to use the correct slashes (backward, forward) when writing down the path name.

18. ______ Have your instructor inspect your project.

19. ______ After your instructor has checked your project, return all materials to their proper storage. Your instructor may want you to repeat this lab activity using different Internet connection types as well as a variety of networking materials.

20. ______ Complete the review questions. You may use the "Help and Support" files located on a Windows XP computer.

Review Questions

Answer the following questions on a separate sheet of paper. Please do not write in this book.

1. What are the three ranges of non-registered IP addresses?
2. What does the acronym SOHO represent?
3. List several ways the Network Setup Wizard can be accessed.
4. What does the acronym ICS represent?
5. Which computer is identified as the host in an ICS configuration?
6. What is the name of the file that starts the network setup 3 1/2" floppy?
7. What symbols are not allowed as part of the computer name? (See the Help and Support.)
8. What is the maximum number of characters permitted in a computer name?
9. Can spaces be left in the name–for example "Station 12"?
10. It is best to leave the workgroup name the same as the computer name. True *or* false.

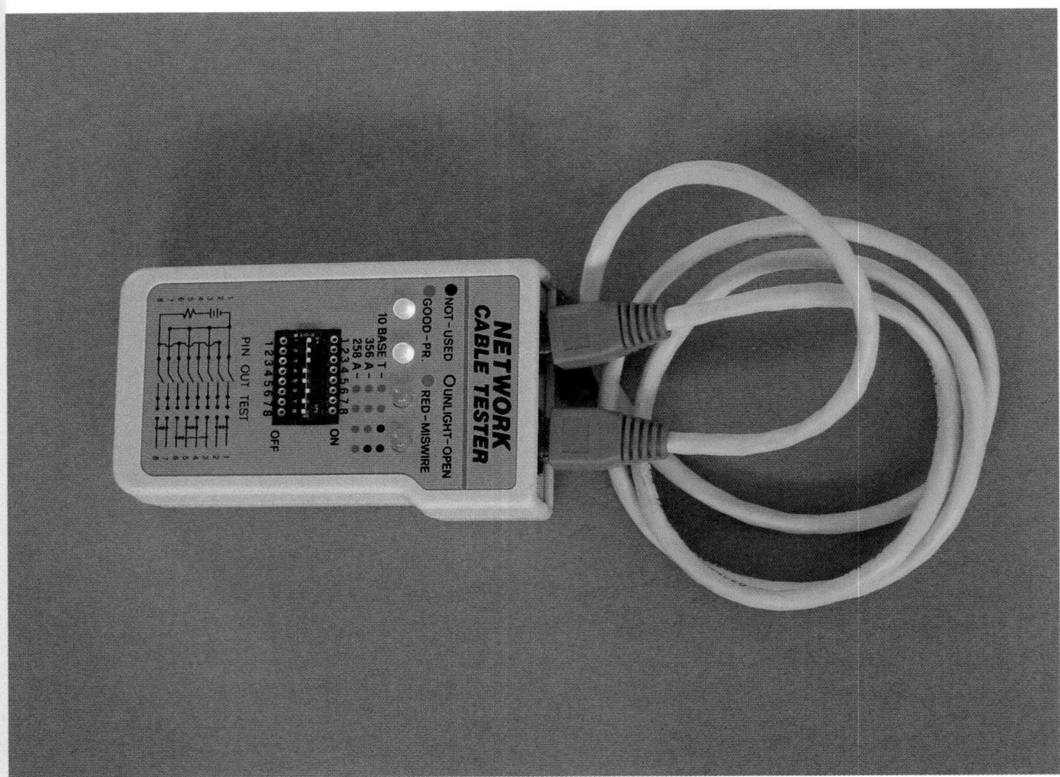

A cable tester is often used to test for continuity in a network cabling system.

A+ Certification Exam Preparation—Core Hardware

After studying this chapter, you will be able to:

- Explain the format of the CompTIA A+ Certification exams.
- Explain eligibility for taking the CompTIA A+ Certification exams.
- Identify strategies for preparing for the CompTIA A+ Certification exams.
- Identify A+ Core Hardware exam objectives and content items.
- Evaluate your readiness for the A+ Certification Core Hardware exam.

A+ Exam—Key Points

Always check the CompTIA Web site for the latest news concerning the A+ Certification exams. The requirements for the exams frequently change. Typically, CompTIA reviews the exams at least once a year, and minor changes are made to the examination objectives. Major changes to the examination objectives occur approximately every three years following the release of the latest operating system. The testing format also changes from time to time. While every attempt is made to provide you with the latest information in this textbook, changes do occur after the release of the textbook. Your best source of exam information is the official CompTIA Web site, www.comptia.org.

You can also check www.RMRoberts.com for additional information about the CompTIA A+ Certification exam and to download additional free practice exams.

Key Words and Terms

The following words and terms will become important pieces of your computer vocabulary. Be sure you can define them.

CompTIA A+ Certification exams
examination objectives
domains
weighted

If you are reading this chapter, you are probably near the completion of your course. You have gained a basic knowledge of computer service and repair and have acquired many skills by performing the lab activities. You have certainly reached a milestone in your education in computer service and repair. Your next step, should you decide to make computer service and repair a career, is to become certified. Certification proves to a potential employer that you have the knowledge and skills needed to perform the typical job duties and tasks of a PC service technician.

The certification you need to acquire is the A+ Certification developed by CompTIA. To receive the A+ Certification you must pass two exams: the A+ Core Hardware exam and the A+ Operating System Technologies exam. This chapter prepares you for the CompTIA A+ Core Hardware exam by teaching you exam preparation skills and study strategies that will help you succeed. A sample exam is also provided to identify areas in which you may need more study. You will find that the material contained in this chapter and in Chapter 21—A+ Certification Exam Preparation—Operating System Technologies, serves as an excellent review for your end of course exam.

A+ Certification Exams

CompTIA A + Certificaton certification awarded by CompTIA to those who pass both the A+ Core Hardware and the A+ Operating System Technologies exams.

examination objectives objectives that are tested for on an exam, and are derived from an industry survey that determines actual job requirements.

The ***CompTIA A+ Certification,*** developed by CompTIA (Computer Technology Industry Association), consists of the A+ Core Hardware exam and the A+ Operating System Technologies exam. You must pass both exams to receive the CompTIA A+ Certification. The CompTIA A+ Certification exams measure the entry-level ability of an IT professional or PC service technician. The entry-level ability is equal to six months of on-the-job experience.

CompTIA provides examination objectives on its Web site, www.comptia.org, for each of the A+ Certification exams. The ***examination objectives*** are derived from industry surveys that determine the actual job requirements of a PC service technician. The objectives state a specific area of knowledge the test taker should know and include examples, or content items, to clarify the objective's meaning. For example, an objective that asks the test taker to identify the names, purpose, and characteristics of system modules will also list the modules that the test taker may have to identify, such as motherboard, memory, and storage devices. The objectives, however, do not provide a complete listing of content items. The list of content items is designed only to provide the testing candidate an idea of what to expect. Content items about a newer technology may not be listed under the examination objectives but maybe included on the actual exam.

A+ Note:
Download the examination objectives and use them as a study guide.

The examination objectives are categorized according to ***domains,*** or topic areas. The domains for the A+ Core Hardware exam and their percentage of coverage on the exam are listed in the chart in **Figure 20-1.**

domains
topic areas into which examination objectives are divided.

Requirements

CompTIA recommends that a test candidate have at least 500 hours of work experience. The 500 hours is a recommendation, not a requirement. In fact, anyone is eligible to take an A+ Certification exam. There are no prerequisites. However, work experience alone does not ensure that a candidate will pass the exam. Formal training provides the best opportunity for passing the A+ Certification exams.

There are some candidates who do pass the exams by using self-study techniques, but this is rare. Your best preparation for passing the exams is a combination of structured classroom-related experiences and hands-on laboratory activities that reinforce classroom training and textbook studies.

When you feel you are ready to take an A+ Certification exam, you must make an appointment to test at a registered testing center. When reporting to the testing center, you must show two proofs of identification. One is typically a photo ID and the other is a document with your signature, such as a credit card. Always check the requirements for identification before reporting to the testing center. After proving your identity, you will be assigned a workstation in the testing area at which you will take your exam. You will not be allowed to bring any reference material into the testing area. You are provided with scrap paper

A+ Core Hardware Domain	Percentage of Questions	Approximate Number of Questions
1.0 Installation, Configuration, and Upgrading	35%	28
2.0 Diagnosing and Troubleshooting	21%	17
3.0 Preventive Maintenance	5%	4
4.0 Motherboard, Processors, and Memory	11%	9
5.0 Printers	9%	7
6.0 Basic Networking	19%	15
Total Percentage	100%	80

Figure 20-1.
A+ Core Hardware domains and the percentage of questions that represent that domain.

on which you may want to do a quick "brain dump" of I/O port numbers, IRQs, and other material you think you may have problems remembering during the exam. *Do not* waste your time by writing down exam questions to share with others who are studying for the exam. You must turn this paper over to the proctor (exam attendant) before you leave the testing center.

Exam Format

The A+ Certification exams do not require any hands-on or practical testing. They are multiple-choice exams. The exams typically consist of 80 questions.

The difficulty level of each question varies from simple identification of a component or part to more demanding scenario problems, which require analytical thinking and some experience. There may be more than one correct answer, but only one answer is the most likely or most practical. Always choose the most practical or most likely. When there are two or more correct answers, read the question carefully to look for clues that point to the most likely correct answer.

weight
a method of applying a measure or score to an individual question.

Exam questions are not scored, or ***weighted,*** equally. This means that exam questions are worth different amounts of points. It is impossible to determine the exact weight of a question because CompTIA does not reveal it. However, the weight of one question compared to another is often rather obvious. A question that asks you to identify a component carries less weight than a question that asks you to apply analytical thinking. For example, a question that asks which component on a motherboard is responsible for processing instructions carries less weight than a question that asks you to identify the order of the Windows XP boot process.

A+ Note:
The A+ Certification exams are graded on a scale from 100 to 900. A minimum score of 467 is needed to pass the A+ Core Hardware exam, and a minimum score of 469 is needed to pass the Operating System Technologies exam. Because each question is weighted, it is difficult to translate these passing scores into a percentage.

The number of questions on an A+ Certification exam can vary because CompTIA sometimes adds a few extra questions that do not count toward the score. The additional exam questions are field-test questions. By answering them, you are helping CompTIA develop new exam questions. Field-testing ensures that the question has been clearly written and the correct answer is clearly indicated in the list of answers. If an experimental exam question is too difficult to understand or does not have a clear, correct answer, it is evident to CompTIA by a higher than average number of incorrect responses to the question. These questions are rewritten and tested again before becoming a valid exam question.

Exam Preparation

To successfully prepare for an A+ Certification exam you must design an exam preparation strategy. A few possible strategies are presented. Using them will increase your chances of passing an A+ Certification exam on your first attempt.

Establish a Study Schedule

Establish a realistic study schedule. Use a calendar and write in the dates and times for study. You will know best how much time to allocate. You can also ask your instructor for input on how many hours of additional study you might need before taking the exam. Having a planned schedule for study allows you to set times for other things such as movies, dates, family plans, and television. If you have a set study schedule, you will most likely think twice about those other activities and will schedule your study time around them.

Get Hands-On Experience

Hands-on experience provides you with many of the required skills that are tested on in the A+ Certification exams. You should spend as much time as possible practicing many of the skills that are tested. For example, you should practice setting up and formatting partitions on a hard drive, rather than just reading and memorizing procedures. For many of the skills tested, there is no substitute for hands-on experience. The series of lab activities designed to accompany this textbook should provide you with many of those skills. It is highly recommended you practice performing the lab activities and review the questions at the end of each lab. Many of the lab review questions are designed to prepare you for an A+ Certification exam. Begin your review at the beginning of the lab manual. Often students forget the basics that were covered early in the course.

Read a Variety of Computer-Related Material

It is helpful to read a variety of computer-related material. Sometimes reading the same topic in a different book or manual can illuminate the information in a new way or can commit better to memory. Some material you should read, besides this textbook, are installation manuals, Readme files, instructional Web pages and Web sites.

Textbook material

Review the textbook material covered in the course. Just as it was suggested for the lab activities, start your review at the beginning of the textbook. Do you still remember the definition of multitasking? Review all tests, end of chapter Review Questions, pop quizzes, and classroom handouts.

Installation manuals

Installation manuals are vast sources of excellent study material. Seagate, Maxwell, Sony, Samsung, 3COM, Microsoft, and many other manufacturers have a lot of valuable information directly related to the exam in their installation manuals. You can learn by reading the installation manual for a hard drive, a network adapter card, or a multimedia card. An installation manual reinforces what you have already learned in the course by showing you how that knowledge is applied. Most of these manuals can be downloaded from the Internet. Simply go to the manufacturer's support page on their Web site, locate the desired manual, and download the PDF file.

Readme files

The Readme files that accompany an operating system installation CD-ROM contain valuable study material. This is especially true for the A+ Operating System Technologies exam, since a large portion of the exam deals with installing and configuring an operating system. Search the CD-ROMs for the document containing the installation information. Also, check the operating system's Web site for information about the installation. Many exam content items have been derived directly from this source of information.

Instructional Web pages and Web sites

There are hundreds of Web pages available today to assist you in learning more about computer technology. Seeing the same material presented in a different format by a different writer can be extremely helpful especially when learning difficult concepts. For example, if you have difficulty learning the differences in RAID types, you could search the Internet for "RAID" or "RAID types." You will find many sources about RAID, including short tutorials.

Create a Study Guide

A great technique to use in preparing for the A+ Certification exams and reviewing for the course is to make your own study guide. Teacher handouts are convenient, but are seldom studied in-depth by the average student. There are also many study guides located on the Internet. Some are free, and some are costly. Some commercial and free study guides contain material that is no longer required for the exam or is not included in the examination objectives. To increase your retention of the subject matter, it is recommended that you make your own study guide. One suggested method of creating a study guide is to list the examination objectives on a sheet of paper, leaving ample space in which to write your own notes between the content items.

A better way to copy the examination objectives is to use a word processor. Add an ample amount of space between the content items listed. When studying, write in by hand the information you have collected about each objective and content item. See **Figure 20-2.** Using this method will not only give you a set of notes matching the exact exam objectives, it will serve as an excellent study tool.

When filling in your study guide, be aware that many content items are listed under more than one objective. When you see a content item that is listed more than once, look for key words in the related objective that identify the desired information for that content item. For example, if a USB port is listed under more than one objective, one occurrence may be under an objective that is concerned with the USB port's identification and characteristics and the other occurrence may be concerned with troubleshooting. Write your notes about the content item according to the specifics of each objective.

Figure 20-2.
Sample study guide.

My Study Guide

1.5 Identify the names, purposes, and performance characteristics, of standardized/common peripheral ports, associated cabling, and their connectors. Recognize ports, cabling, and connectors by sight.

Content may include the following:

Port types :

Serial

Parallel

USB ports

IEEE 1394/FireWire

Infrared

Join or Form a Study Group

A group formed of individuals that are serious about preparing for the A+ Certification exams can be an excellent way to prepare. Here are some general guidelines to follow:

- Stay on task.
- Set a regular schedule of dates, times, and duration. (Every day is best, but not always possible.)
- Write practice exam questions for each other.
- Share resources such as sample exams or Web sites that support your studies.

A study group can make exam preparation a little more fun and provide you with the additional motivation you need to study. The members of the study group help keep one another on task. For example, you may plan to study every night for the next two weeks for three hours each night. However, when it comes to executing the plan, you may easily find a reason not to study. When two or more of you plan to study together, each member feels more obligated to meet at the established time.

The study group can also share some of the burden of exam preparation. Each member of the study group can take a particular area covered on the exam and write a set of questions for the other members. When you meet at your regularly scheduled time, you can exchange the questions. You can also share resources such as sample exams or Web sites that you have found helpful in your personal studies.

One word of caution, though, is to make sure the study group functions as a study group and not as a social group. A group of friends gathered for study can quickly get off track and spend a lot of time discussing football, movies, and other events. It is critical that the study group remains focused on the task at hand—exam preparation.

Take Practice Exams

Practice exams are an excellent way to determine your test readiness and to identify weak areas. You may discover that you do not know the printing process as well as you thought. Practice exams are an important ingredient to your exam preparation strategy. You can use the practice exams to design the content for your review sessions. After taking a practice exam, identify the topics you feel you need more help in. Make a list, and then review materials covering those topics.

There are numerous Web sites offering free on-line or downloadable practice exams. While many are quite reputable, some are rather questionable. There are hundreds of sample exams located throughout the Internet. These exams provide only a sampling of a full test bank. Some have been found to be flawed, misleading, and definitely designed to have the test taker fail. The marketing idea is to show the student how little they know about the subject so that the student may be lured into purchasing the full test bank of questions. You may take the free sample exams because they still have many good questions, but do not consider them a true measure of your ability to pass the exam.

Some Web sites contain free practice exams that are at an appropriate level are listed below:

- www.learnthat.com—This site also contains links to free on-line courses and tutorials.
- www.RMRoberts.com—This site contains practice exams, textbook updates, and other student and teacher resources.

The next two sites are also good sources of free practice exams. Since they have occasionally changed their address, use the following key words in a search engine to locate these sites:

- Aplus Omega—Aplus Omega has A+ and Network+ sample exams.
- Pagesbydave A+ Test Prep—Pagesbydave also has both A+ and Network+ sample exams.

Many students want to score a 100% on their A+ Certification exam. They constantly take practice exams and may continuously achieve a score that is less than 100%. Because of this, they never feel prepared for an A+ Certification exam. While scoring a 100% on a practice exam is a worthy goal, it is unrealistic for many students. To determine if you are prepared to take an A+ Certification exam, consider a passing score of 80% on a practice exam as a good indication. Remember that a student who does pass the exam on the very first attempt is well prepared and confident. A student who fails an A+ Certification exam is obviously not prepared and has not been committed to a set study schedule.

Schedule a Test Date

Scheduling a test date is an excellent component to add to the established study schedule. As soon as you think you know the amount of preparation you will need, set a time and date for the exam. Do not wait until you know the material 100%. Chances are you will most likely never feel you know the material 100%. Procrastinating setting a test date will quickly put you out of date with the material you have studied. Set a date to give yourself a deadline for preparation.

Sample A+ Core Hardware Exam

Taking the practice exam provided in this chapter is one of the best ways to prepare for the real thing. In doing so, you will become familiar with the exam's format, the topics covered, and the varying difficulty of the questions. The provided sample exam identifies the areas tested on the A+ Core Hardware exam and the depth of the questions asked. Exam questions are grouped according to the six A+ Core Hardware domains and are preceded by the domain's objectives.

After taking the exam, your instructor can score it to determine the areas where you need additional review. The answers to the exam are provided in the Instructor's Manual that accompanies this textbook.

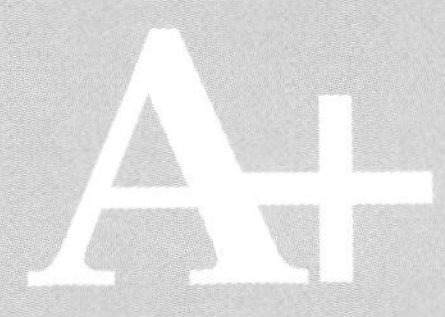

A+ Note:
Because of the vast amount of topics covered on the CompTIA A+ Certification exams, it is rare that anyone passes the exams with a 100% score. *Do not* let this keep you from taking the actual exam. Remember that a passing score of 80% on a practice exam is a good indication you are prepared to take an A+ Certification exam.

Domain 1—Installation, Configuration, and Upgrading

- **1.1 Identify the names, purpose, and characteristics of system modules. Recognize these modules by sight or definition.**

  Examples of concepts and modules are: Motherboard, firmware, power supply, processor /CPU, memory, storage devices, display devices, adapter cards, ports, cases, riser cards.

- **1.2 Identify basic procedures for adding and removing field-replaceable modules for desktop systems. Given a replacement scenario, choose the appropriate sequences.**

  Desktop components: Motherboard; Storage device: FDD, HDD, CD/CDRW, DVD/DVDRW, tape drive, removable storage; Power supply: AC adapter, AT/ATX; Cooling systems: fans, heat sinks, liquid cooling; Processor /CPU; Memory; Display device; Input devices: keyboard, mouse/pointer devices, touch screen; Adapters: network interface card (NIC), sound card, video card, modem, SCSI, IEEE 1394/FireWire, USB, wireless.

- **1.3 Identify basic procedures for adding and removing field-replaceable modules for portable systems. Given a replacement scenario, choose the appropriate sequences.**

  Portable components: Storage devices: FDD, HDD, CD/CDRW, DVD/DVDRW, removable storage; Power sources: AC adapter, DC adapter, battery; Memory; Input devices: keyboard, mouse/pointer devices, touch screen; PCMCIA/mini PCI adapters: network interface card (NIC), modem, SCSI, IEEE 1394/FireWire, USB, storage (memory and hard drive); Docking station/port replicators; LCD panel; Wireless: adapter/controller, antennae.

- **1.4 Identify typical IRQs, DMAs, and I/O addresses, and procedures for altering these settings when installing and configuring devices. Choose the appropriate installation or configuration steps in a given scenario.**

  Content may include the following: Legacy devices (e.g., ISA sound card); Specialized devices (e.g., CAD/CAM); Internal modems; Floppy drive controllers, Hard drive controllers; Multimedia devices; NICs; I/O ports: serial, parallel, USB ports, IEEE 1394/ FireWire, infrared.

- **1.5 Identify the names, purposes, and performance characteristics of standardized/common peripheral ports, associated cabling, and their connectors. Recognize ports, cabling, and connectors by sight.**

Content may include the following: Port types: serial, parallel, USB ports, IEEE 1394/FireWire, infrared; Cable types: serial (straight through vs. null modem), parallel, USB; Connector types: serial (DB-9, DB-25, RJ-11, RJ-45), parallel (DB-25, Centronics [(mini, 36))]; PS/2 (mini-DIN); USB; IEEE 1394.

- **1.6 Identify proper procedures for installing and configuring common IDE devices. Choose the appropriate installation or configuration sequences in given scenarios. Recognize the associated cables.**

  Content may include the following: IDE interface types: EIDE, ATA/ATAPI, serial ATA, PIO; RAID (0, 1 and 5); Master/slave/cable select; Devices per channel; Primary/secondary; Cable orientation/requirements.

- **1.7 Identify proper procedures for installing and configuring common SCSI devices. Choose the appropriate installation or configuration sequences in given scenarios. Recognize the associated cables.**

  Content may include the following: SCSI interface types: narrow, fast, wide, ultra-wide, LVD, HVD; Internal vs. external; SCSI IDs: jumper block/DIP switch settings (binary equivalents), resolving ID conflicts; RAID (0, 1 and 5); Cabling: length, type, termination requirements (active, passive, auto).

- **1.8 Identify proper procedures for installing and configuring common peripheral devices. Choose the appropriate installation or configuration sequences in given scenarios.**

  Content may include the following: Modems and transceivers: dial-up, cable, DSL, ISDN; External storage; Digital cameras; PDAs; Wireless access points; Infrared devices; Printers; UPS (uninterruptible power supply) and suppressors; Monitors.

- **1.9 Identify procedures to optimize PC operations in specific situations. Predict the effects of specific procedures under given scenarios.**

  Topics may include: Cooling systems: liquid, air, heat sink, thermal compound; Disk subsystem enhancements: hard drives, controller cards (e.g., RAID, ATA-100, etc.), cables; NICs; Specialized video cards; Memory; Additional processors.

- **1.10 Determine the issues that must be considered when upgrading a PC. In a given scenario, determine when and how to upgrade system components.**

  Issues may include: Drivers for legacy devices; Bus types and characteristics; Cache in relationship to motherboards; Memory capacity and characteristics; Processor speed and compatibility; Hard drive capacity and characteristics; System/firmware limitations; Power supply output capacity.

  Components may include the following: Motherboards; Memory; Hard drives; CPU; BIOS; Adapter cards; Laptop power sources: lithium ion, NiMH, fuel cell; PCMCIA: Type I, II, III cards.

Domain 1—Practice Exam Questions 1–28

1. Identify the device shown in the following figure.

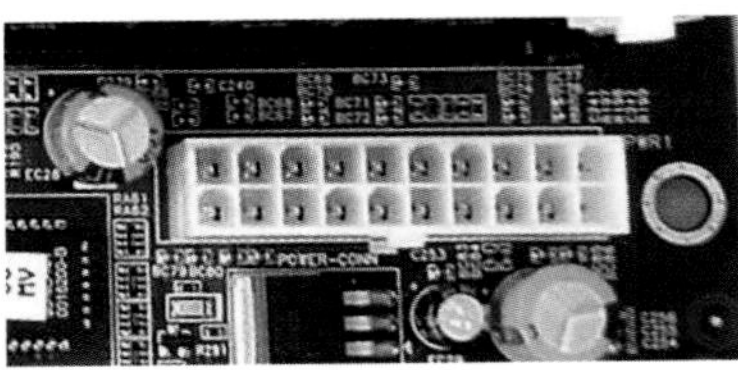

   a. ATX power connector
   b. Multimedia connector
   c. AT power connector
   d. RS232 connector
2. What is the purpose of RAM?
   a. Configures and saves information about system hardware.
   b. Retains data generated by software programs after the power has been removed from the PC.
   c. Provides an area for loading software programs from the hard drive.
   d. Controls the flow of information across the motherboard bus system.
3. A technician has replaced the standard keyboard on a desktop computer with an upgraded version that has programmable keys. The programmable keys provide features such as instant access to user games, contact persons, Web sites, and e-mail. The keyboard was automatically detected and indicates no problems when viewed in Device Manager, however, the programmable keys fail to work. What is the *most likely* problem?
   a. The CMOS settings need to be reconfigured to detect the new keyboard.
   b. Software drivers need to be loaded to allow the programmable keys to function.
   c. The programmable keys are not compatible with the operating system.
   d. The operating system must be reinstalled after the addition of a new hardware device such as the special keyboard.
4. A technician is upgrading the memory of a PC. Currently the PC's motherboard has two 128MB, 184-pin RIMM modules. The technician replaces the two RIMM modules with one 184-pin 512MB RIMM module. What does the technician need to do next?
   a. Replace or upgrade the system BIOS.
   b. Add a C-RIMM in the remaining empty memory slot.
   c. Access the system BIOS setup and check if the additional memory is detected.
   d. Add a software driver so that the motherboard can detect the new memory modules.

5. When assembling a PC, what should be installed between the motherboard and the PC case?
   a. Heat dissipation paste.
   b. Spacers to protect the motherboard components from touching the metal case.
   c. A 12 × 16 insulation shield or anti-static mat.
   d. A protective coating of varnish to prevent moisture buildup.
6. A customer has a notebook computer, which they wish to connect to their home network. The home network consists of two PCs connected to a hub and a laser printer shared by both PCs. They wish to be able to access both PCs, as well as use the printer. What would be the best solution?
   a. Install a wireless PCMCIA type I card and configure it to access the domain.
   b. Install a PCI wireless card and configure it to access the wireless workgroup.
   c. Install a wireless PCMCIA type I card into the notebook and add a wireless access point to the existing home network.
   d. Install a PCI network adapter card into the notebook and then connect the notebook to the network through a network cable.
7. Identify the two common ports used to connect a PC to a DSL modem. (Select two.)
   a. USB
   b. RJ-45
   c. RJ-11
   d. RS-232
8. By using which method listed below are IRQ settings typically reconfigured? Assume you are using a standard PC running Windows 98.
   a. The BIOS CMOS setup program.
   b. Device Manager.
   c. The installation disks used for installing the operating system.
   d. The IRQ settings cannot be reconfigured; they are unique to each PC system.
9. Which IRQ is typically assigned to the primary hard drive controller?
   a. 1
   b. 5
   c. 7
   d. 14

10. A technician has replaced an existing dot matrix printer with a newer laser printer. The dot matrix was connected to the PC by a parallel port connection. The laser printer uses the USB port and is Plug and Play. After the new printer has been plugged in and detected, what should be done next?
    a. The laser printer needs to be selected as the default printer in Printers.
    b. The USB port needs to be enabled.
    c. The system BIOS needs to be updated.
    d. The parallel port must be disabled.
11. Identify the port shown in the following figure.

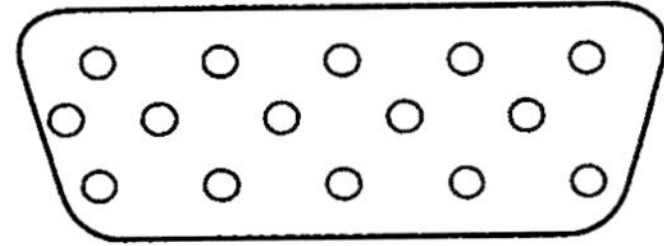

    a. PS/2
    b. USB
    c. IEEE 1394
    d. DB-15
12. Which port or cable type would provide the highest data throughput?
    a. RS-232
    b. Parallel printer port
    c. USB 2.0
    d. Infrared
13. Which type of connector is commonly used to connect a TFT-LCD type monitor to a PC? (Select two.)
    a. DVI-D
    b. HD-15
    c. Serial
    d. RS-232
14. A customer complains that they have just installed a new version of a graphics program on their PC and their PC runs very slowly whenever the program is running. What is the *most likely* problem, and what is the best way to remedy it?
    a. The PC has an insufficient amount of hard disk space. A new or additional hard drive needs to be installed.
    b. The new software program requires more RAM. More RAM needs to be installed.
    c. The software is not compatible with the existing BIOS. The BIOS software needs to be replaced or upgraded.
    d. The new version of the software program introduced a virus into the system, which is running in the background and using up processor time. A virus protection program should be installed, and the virus should be removed.

15. Which is the correct sequence for installing a hard drive?
    a. Install the hard drive into the drive bay; set the selection jumper to slave or master; format the hard drive; and partition the hard drive.
    b. Partition the hard drive; format the hard drive; set the selection jumper to slave or master; install the hard drive in the drive bay.
    c. Set the selection jumper to slave or master; install the hard drive in the drive bay; partition the hard drive; format the hard drive.
    d. Install the hard drive in the drive bay; partition the hard drive; format the hard drive; and set the selection jumper to slave or master.
16. A technician has just replaced a defective floppy disk drive on a PC. When the PC is rebooted, the activity LED on the floppy disk drive stays lit. What is the *most likely* cause of the problem?
    a. The new floppy disk drive is defective.
    b. The cable used to connect the floppy disk drive to the motherboard is defective.
    c. The cable connected to the floppy disk drive is reversed.
    d. A pin on the motherboard FDD connection is bent.
17. Which is the proper orientation for a data cable connected to a hard drive?
    a. The red-striped side of the cable connects to pin 1 on the hard drive and to pin 1 on the motherboard.
    b. The red-striped side of the cable connects to pin 40 on the hard drive and to pin 1 on the motherboard.
    c. The red-striped side of the cable connects to pin 1 on the hard drive and to pin 40 on the motherboard.
    d. The red-striped side of the cable connects to pin 50 on the hard drive and to pin 50 on the motherboard.
18. What voltage levels are commonly associated with an ATX power supply?
    a. 3.3, 5, 12
    b. 6, 12, 18
    c. 3.3, 6.6, 18.8
    d. 2.1, 3.3, 5, 6
19. Which PCMCIA card type is used for notebook wireless network cards?
    a. Type I
    b. Type II
    c. Type III
    d. Notebook computers never use the PCMCIA port for network cards.
20. Which motherboard slot type has the highest expected data throughput?
    a. PCI
    b. PCMCIA
    c. AGP
    d. ISA

21. A Pentium IV processor would *most likely* be installed in which type of motherboard socket or slot?
    a. Slot 1
    b. Socket 5
    c. Slot A
    d. Socket 478
22. Which hard drive parameters listed below are typically stored in the CMOS? (Choose four.)
    a. Master and slave IDE location identification
    b. Drive speed
    c. Number of heads
    d. Drive capacity
    e. Number of cylinders
    f. Boot sector address
23. Which PC resource is assigned to hardware devices and used to notify the CPU that it requires the services of the CPU to process data?
    a. DMA
    b. IRQ
    c. I/O address
    d. Base memory
24. Which devices would normally be found connected to a SCSI cable? (Select three)
    a. CD-ROM
    b. Hard drive
    c. Tape drive
    d. Video monitor
    e. Keyboard
    f. Mouse
25. A customer wants to ensure that the data on their PC is protected from data loss caused by a hard drive failure and protected against power outages. Which solution would best meet the customer requirements?
    a. Install a UPS and a RAID 1 system.
    b. Install a power strip with surge protection and add a tape backup to the PC.
    c. Install a UPS and a DVD writer that can be used to backup data files every day.
    d. Install a UPS and a RAID 0 system.
26. Which item listed below is *not* considered an FRU?
    a. Motherboard
    b. Hard drive
    c. ATX power supply
    d. CRT high voltage supply

27. A conflict arises when installing a Plug and Play device. You must disable the Plug and Play feature so that you can manually assign the IRQ for the new device. Where do you disable the Plug and Play feature for the PC?
    a. You must reinstall the operating system and select non-Plug and Play support during the hardware detection sequence.
    b. You can disable Plug and Play in Control Panel.
    c. You must disable the Plug and Play feature in the BIOS setup.
    d. Plug and Play cannot be disabled; you must use only Plug and Play compliant devices.
28. Which of the following memory types are used for video RAM? (Select two.)
    a. WRAM
    b. DRAM
    c. VRAM
    d. CMOS

Domain 2—Diagnosing and Troubleshooting

- **2.1 Recognize common problems associated with each module and their symptoms, and identify steps to isolate and troubleshoot the problems. Given a problem situation, interpret the symptoms and infer the *most likely* cause.**

  Content may include the following: I/O ports and cables: serial, parallel, USB ports, IEEE 1394/FireWire, infrared, SCSI; Motherboards: CMOS/ BIOS settings, POST audible/visual error codes; Peripherals: Computer case: power supply, slot covers, front cover alignment; Storage devices and cables: FDD, HDD, CD/CDRW, DVD/DVDRW, tape drive, removable storage; Cooling systems: fans, heat sinks, liquid cooling, temperature sensors; Processor /CPU; Memory; Display device; Input devices: keyboard, mouse/pointer devices, touch screen; Adapters: network interface card (NIC), sound card, video card, modem, SCSI, IEEE 1394/FireWire, USB; Portable systems: PCMCIA, batteries, docking stations/port replicators, portable unique storage.

- **2.2 Identify basic troubleshooting procedures and tools and how to elicit problem symptoms from customers. Justify asking particular questions in a given scenario.**

  Content may include the following: Troubleshooting/isolation/problem determination procedures; Determining whether a hardware or software problem; Gathering information from user: customer environment, symptoms/error codes, situation when the problem occurred.

Domain 2—Practice Exam Questions 29–45

29. What is a good sign that a PC's power supply is dead?
    a. The operating system reboots every 2 minutes.
    b. The video monitor goes into sleep mode.
    c. The PC locks up after the POST is completed.
    d. The PC's case cooling fan is not running.

30. A PC operated fine yesterday, but today, after the system is booted, the video display is distorted and fuzzy. Which component and problem is the *most likely* cause?
    a. The POST sequence is corrupted.
    b. The video card RAM is failing.
    c. A virus has infected the boot sector of the hard drive.
    d. The BIOS setup program has changed the video settings.
31. Which program or system is responsible for making the initial check of RAM to verify it is functioning properly?
    a. Windows registry
    b. Dr. Watson
    c. **command.com**
    d. POST
32. You boot a PC and it runs through POST and then a black screen appears and displays the following message: Operating System not found. Which hardware component has *most likely* failed?
    a. ROM
    b. RAM
    c. Hard drive
    d. Video card
33. You are working the help desk when a call comes in stating that the customer cannot get onto the Internet. The customer clicks the Internet Explorer icon and the modem keeps redialing. What is the *most likely* problem?
    a. The user is trying to use the wrong user name or password.
    b. The ISP server has been assigned a new IP address.
    c. The RJ-11 connection is loose.
    d. The modem needs an upgraded driver installed.
34. What type of connector is typically used with Cat 5e?
    a. RJ-11
    b. RJ-45
    c. BNC
    d. RS-232
35. A PC is operating well, but after approximately 10 minutes, the PC locks up. After a period of time, the PC can be restarted, but locks up again after a short period of time. What would be the *most likely* cause of the problem?
    a. A defective cooling fan mounted on the CPU.
    b. A network adapter card with a corrupt driver.
    c. A corrupt printer driver.
    d. A back door virus has been activated causing the PC to lock up each time.

36. While booting a PC, an error code indicating a "parity error" appears on the screen. What is the *most likely* problem?
    a. A defective hard drive.
    b. A conflict with an assigned IRQ.
    c. A smart card device is defective.
    d. The motherboard RAM has a problem.
37. A PC displays the error "Non-system disks" on the screen, and the Window's logon box fails to appear. What is the *most likely* problem?
    a. The BIOS system settings are corrupt.
    b. The DoomsDay virus has just infected the motherboard RAM.
    c. The system registry is corrupt.
    d. There is a floppy disk in the floppy disk drive.
38. Which problem is indicated in the following figure?

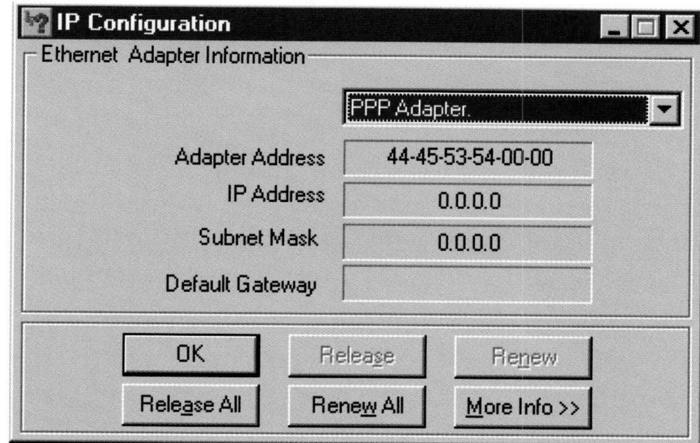

    a. The PC telephone modem is not connected to the ISP.
    b. The network card failed to initiate.
    c. The network card MAC address has been corrupted.
    d. The POST failed during the boot sequence.
39. Why should dust be removed from the inside of a computer case as part of a regular routine maintenance program?
    a. The accumulated dust short-circuits the motherboard, causing catastrophic failure.
    b. The accumulated dust reduces the cooling effect of fans, causing the system to overheat and fail.
    c. The accumulated dust creates bad connections between system components.
    d. Excessive dust cannot harm a PC.
40. What methods are commonly used to effectively cool a CPU? (Select three.)
    a. Freon
    b. Heat sinks
    c. Fans
    d. Liquid cooling systems

41. A customer calls to complain that the new PC they just bought has a bad DVD drive. Every time they make a DVD at home, it fails to play at work. You ask the customer if the DVD plays at home correctly, and they indicate it does. What is the *most likely* problem?
    a. The customer does not know how to format a DVD.
    b. The customer has a different DVD drive standard at work.
    c. The customer is using the wrong DVD media.
    d. The customer needs to upgrade the driver for the DVD at home.
42. A new multimedia card has been installed in a PC and operates well. Later, the PC can no longer connect to the office network. What is the *most likely* problem?
    a. The device driver that came with the multimedia card was infected with a virus.
    b. There is not sufficient RAM installed on the motherboard to support both a multimedia card and a network card.
    c. The network card and multimedia cards have a system resource conflict.
    d. No possible relationship exists between a multimedia card and a network card that would cause the network card to fail.
43. The original display settings for a monitor were 1280 × 1024, 32-bit color quality. After performing an operating system upgrade on a PC, the screen display resolution is set to 800 × 600 at 16-bit color quality. A higher quality is not available through the Display Properties dialog box. What is the *most likely* problem?
    a. The wrong display driver is installed.
    b. There is insufficient RAM on the motherboard to support a higher resolution.
    c. There is insufficient disk space on the hard drive to support a higher resolution.
    d. The Display Properties dialog box is not working properly.
44. After physically installing a second hard drive on the primary controller, a technician boots the PC and finds that the second hard drive failed to be detected by the system. What is the *most likely* problem?
    a. The new hard drive is bad.
    b. The new hard drive was not configured as "slave."
    c. The new hard drive has a corrupt boot sector.
    d. The new hard drive has been infected with a virus.
45. A customer complains that when they attempt to move the cursor across the display it jumps radically and even stops responding. At other times it seems to work OK. They are using a traditional mouse equipped with a rubber mouse ball. What is the *most likely* problem and how should it be corrected?
    a. There is excessive dust and lint on a positioning roller inside the mouse. The lint should be removed, or the mouse should be replaced.

b. There is insufficient memory to support both running programs and the mouse program. The customer needs to add more memory or remove some programs from the hard drive.

c. There is insufficient memory installed in the PC. The memory should be upgraded.

d. The mouse driver is corrupt and should be upgraded immediately.

Domain 3—PC Preventive Maintenance, Safety, and Environmental Issues

- **3.1 Identify the various types of preventive maintenance measures, products, and procedures and when and how to use them.**

  Content may include the following: Liquid cleaning compounds; Types of materials to clean contacts and connections; Nonstatic vacuums: chassis, power supplies, fans; Cleaning monitors; Cleaning removable media devices; Ventilation, dust and moisture control on the PC hardware interior; Hard disk maintenance: defragging, ScanDisk, chkdsk; Verifying UPS (uninterruptible power supply) and suppressors.

- **3.2 Identify various safety measures and procedures and when/how to use them.**

  Content may include the following: ESD (electrostatic discharge) precautions and procedures: what ESD can do; how it may be apparent, or hidden; common ESD protection devices; situations that could present a danger or hazard; Potential hazards and proper safety procedures relating to: high-voltage equipment, power supply, CRTs.

- **3.3 Identify environmental protection measures and procedures and when/how to use them.**

  Content may include the following: Special disposal procedures that comply with environmental guidelines: batteries, CRTs, chemical solvents and cans; MSDS (Material Safety Data Sheet).

Domain 3—Practice Exam Questions 46–49

46. Which would you use as an objective source of information about the safe handling and disposal of a printer chemical such as toner?

    a. The product MSDS

    b. The system administrator

    c. Any standard encyclopedia

    d. Microsoft's technical support Web pages

47. What should be done to prevent damage from static electricity when handling electronics parts?

    a. Wash your hands thoroughly before handling any static-sensitive parts.

    b. Use insulating hand oil before handling delicate or sensitive electronics parts.

    c. Use an anti-static wrist strap for handling static-sensitive parts.

    d. There is no known preventive measure for handling sensitive electronics parts.

48. Which item is best for cleaning a PC monitor screen?
    a. A lint free soft cloth.
    b. A soft cloth and window cleaner.
    c. A soft cloth and alcohol.
    d. A soft cloth and soapy water.
49. A technician discovers that a slot cover is missing from the back of a PC. What should the technician do?
    a. Replace the slot cover to prevent dust buildup and to circulate the cooling air.
    b. Do nothing; the PC obviously was overheating, and the last technician removed the cover to cool the CPU.
    c. Most PCs have at least one cover missing by design.
    d. Slot cover removal is a basic practice that eliminates ESD.

Domain 4—Motherboard, Processors, Memory

- **4.1 Distinguish between the popular CPU chips in terms of their basic characteristics.**

  Content may include the following: popular CPU chips (Pentium class compatible), voltage, speeds (actual vs. advertised), cache level I, II, III, sockets/slots, VRM(s).
- **4.2 Identify the types of RAM (random access memory), form factors, and operational characteristics. Determine banking and speed requirements under given scenarios.**

  Content may include the following: Types, EDO RAM (extended data output RAM), DRAM (dynamic random access memory), SRAM (static RAM), VRAM (video RAM), SDRAM (synchronous dynamic RAM), DDR (double data rate), RAMBUS; Form factors: (including pin count), SIMM (single in-line memory module), DIMM (dual in-line memory module), SoDIMM (small outline DIMM), MicroDIMM, RIMM (rambus inline memory module; Operational characteristics: memory chips (8-bit, 16-bit, and 32-bit), parity chips vs. non-parity chips, ECC vs. non-ECC, single-sided vs. double-sided.
- **4.3 Identify the most popular types of motherboards, their components, and their architecture (bus structures).**

  Content may include the following: Types of motherboards: AT, ATX; Components: communication ports, serial, USB, parallel, IEEE 1394/FireWire, infrared; Memory, SIMM, DIMM, RIMM, SoDIMM, MicroDIMM; Processor sockets: Slot 1, Slot 2, Slot A, Socket A, Socket 7, Socket 8, Socket 423, Socket 478, Socket 370; External cache memory (Level 2); Bus architecture: ISA, PCI (PCI 32-bit, PCI 64-bit), AGP (2X, 4X, 8X ([Pro])); USB (universal serial bus); AMR (audio modem riser) slots; CNR (communication network riser) slots; Basic compatibility guidelines: IDE: ATA, ATAPI, ULTRA-DMA, EIDE; SCSI: Narrow, Wide, Fast, Ultra, HVD, LVD(Low Voltage Differential); Chipsets.

- **4.4 Identify the purpose of CMOS (Complementary Metal-Oxide Semiconductor) memory, what it contains, and how and when to change its parameters. Given a scenario involving CMOS, choose the appropriate course of action.**

  CMOS Settings: Default settings; CPU settings; Printer parallel port: uni., bi-directional, disable/enable, ECP, EPP; COM/serial port: memory address, interrupt request, disable; Floppy drive: enable/disable drive or boot, speed, density; Hard drive: size and drive type; Memory: speed, parity, nonparity; Boot sequence; Date/time; Passwords; Plug and Play BIOS; Disabling on-board devices; Disabling virus protection; Power management; Infrared.

Domain 4—Practice Exam Questions 50–58

50. Which CPU would be expected to produce the highest processing throughput while running a data intensive software program?
    a. A CPU equipped with 500MB of L1 cache.
    b. A CPU equipped with 500MB of L2 cache.
    c. A CPU equipped with 500MB of L3 cache.
    d. A CPU equipped with 250MB of L1 cache.
51. Which type of RAM is most often found in a notebook computer?
    a. SIMM
    b. DIMM
    c. SoDIMM
    d. COAST
52. Under which condition should you disable a workstation's antivirus program?
    a. While running the Disk Defragmenter program.
    b. While setting up a user share.
    c. While installing an additional hard drive.
    d. While changing settings in the system BIOS setup program.
53. Where can you locate information about a hard drive IRQ assignment?
    a. The IRQ assignment is listed on the hard drive label.
    b. The IRQ assignment can be viewed through Device Manager.
    c. The IRQ assignment can be revealed by typing **ipconfig** at the DOS prompt.
    d. The IRQ assignment is always 9 for a hard drive.

54. A user has forgotten the BIOS password used to access the BIOS setup program. What can be done to correct the problem?
    a. A new BIOS chip must be installed on the motherboard.
    b. The CMOS settings must be erased by removing the battery from the motherboard or moving the password jumper position located near the BIOS chip.
    c. The user must back up important data on the hard drive and then reformat the hard drive to remove the password.
    d. Nothing can be done locally, the computer must be sent back to the manufacturer who can replace the BIOS password.
55. A newly installed DVD stops working. What is the normal method used by technicians to verify that the power cable is connected and working?
    a. Open the case and check the power supply leads using a multimeter.
    b. Press the open/close button on the DVD drive and observe the action of the DVD tray.
    c. Open Device Manager and verify the DVD is listed in the tree structure.
    d. Open the command prompt and enter **dir D:** and observe if the directory of the DVD is listed.
56. What keyboard combination is used to access the Windows 2000 logon box?
    a. [Ctrl] [Shift] [Esc]
    b. [Del] [Alt] [Shift]
    c. [Ctrl] [Alt] [Delete]
    d. [Ctrl] [Alt] [Enter]
57. Which utility is used to check the disk drive for errors and correct them in Windows XP?
    a. ScanDisk
    b. Chkdsk
    c. Fdisk
    d. Format
58. What is the purpose of CMOS memory?
    a. To store the CMOS setup program.
    b. To store software programs that permit compatibility between the CPU and devices such as the hard drive and CD-ROM.
    c. To store user data.
    d. To store information about the computer hardware.

Domain 5—Printers

- **5.1 Identify printer technologies, interfaces, and options/upgrades.**

  Technologies may include: Laser, ink dispersion, dot matrix, solid ink, thermal, dye sublimation.

  Interfaces include: Parallel, network, SCSI, USB, infrared, serial, IEEE 1394/FireWire, wireless.

Options/upgrades include: Memory, hard drives, NICs, trays and feeders, finishers (e.g., stapling, etc.), scanners/fax/copier.

- **5.2 Recognize common printer problems and techniques used to resolve them.**

  Content may include the following: Printer drivers, firmware updates, paper feed and output, calibrations, printing test pages, errors (printed or displayed), memory, configuration, network connections, connections, paper jam, print quality, safety precautions, preventive maintenance, consumables, environment.

Domain 5—Practice Exam Questions 59–65

59. What is the most common cause of paper jams?
    a. Low toner volume
    b. Excessive laser heat
    c. Defective fuser
    d. Paper quality
60. Which is the correct printing sequence of a typical laser printer?
    a. Cleaning, charging, writing, developing, transferring, fusing.
    b. Charging, writing, transferring, developing, fusing, transferring.
    c. Writing, charging, transferring, developing, fusing, cleaning.
    d. Cleaning, writing, charging, transferring, fusing, assembling.
61. What is the *most likely* cause of toner smearing on the paper after the printing process is complete?
    a. Defective drum
    b. Wrong type of toner
    c. Defective fusing unit
    d. Paper lint buildup on the laser
62. Which is the correct UNC for a printer called Laser1 connected to a workstation called Station1 used by John Doe?
    a. \\Station1\Laser1\JohnDoe
    b. \\Station1\Laser1
    c. //Laser1/Station1
    d. //JohnDoe/Station1/Laser1
63. A user calls the help desk complaining that they cannot print any documents on the shared network printer. The printer was operating fine yesterday. What would be the first recommendation to the user?
    a. Check the IP address configuration of the printer.
    b. Check if the printer is on-line.
    c. Open Device Manager and see if the printer has a problem.
    d. Save your document to disk and see if you can print the document from a different workstation.

64. A printer has just been installed and the drivers have been loaded from the CD-ROM disk that came with the printer. When a page is printed, it contains an assortment of meaningless ASCII characters all over the document. What is the *most likely* problem?
    a. The printer is setup for the wrong language.
    b. The wrong printer driver is installed.
    c. The wrong type of printer cable is used.
    d. An incorrect font was selected for the document.

65. A graphic is sent to a printer, and each time only half of the graphic prints on the paper. The second half of the page is blank. What is the *most likely* problem?
    a. The printer driver is corrupt.
    b. The print drum is excessively worn.
    c. The printer needs additional memory.
    d. The fuser is starting to go bad.

Domain 6 Basic Networking

- **6.1 Identify the common types of network cables, their characteristics, and connectors.**

  Cable types include: Coaxial: RG6, RG8, RG58, RG59; Plenum/PVC; UTP: CAT3, CAT5/e, CAT6; STP; Fiber: single-mode, multi-mode.

  Connector types include: BNC, RJ-45, AUI, ST/SC, IDC/UDC.

- **6.2 Identify basic networking concepts including how a network works.**

  Concepts include: Installing and configuring network cards; Addressing; Bandwidth; Status indicators; Protocols: TCP/IP, IPX/SPX (NWLINK), AppleTalk, NetBEUI/NetBIOS, full-duplex, half-duplex; Cabling: twisted pair, coaxial, fiber optic, RS-232; Networking models: peer-to-peer, client/server; Infrared; Wireless.

- **6.3 Identify common technologies available for establishing Internet connectivity and their characteristics.**

  Technologies include: LAN, DSL, Cable, ISDN, dial-up, satellite, wireless.

  Characteristics include: Definition, speed, connections.

Domain 6—Practice Exam Questions 66–80

66. A small office network consisting of four workstations share one color laser printer. One morning, no one is capable of sending a print job to the printer. What should be checked first?
    a. Check if the correct driver is loaded.
    b. Check if one of the workstation's network cables is loose.
    c. Check if the printer is on-line.
    d. Check if a virus has infected the network.

67. Identify the connector shown in the following figure.

 a. RJ-45
 b. ST
 c. SC
 d. BNC

68. Which Internet access device can establish the highest throughput?
 a. 56K modem
 b. DSL modem
 c. ISDN
 d. Cable modem

69. Tom has just been hired as a new office employee for a company that publishes a weekly business newsletter. A new Windows XP Professional workstation has been added to a small peer-to-peer network consisting of five Windows 98 workstations, making the total numbers of workstations six. After installing the newest workstation, Tom is unable to access the company newsletter that is setup as a share on another workstation. He can see the other workstations when he uses My Network Places. What is the *most likely* problem?
 a. Adding the sixth workstation exceeded the number of workstations allowed on a peer-to-peer network, thus disabling the ability of the workstation to communicate.
 b. The network adapter card is improperly configured.
 c. Tom does not have rights to the newsletter share.
 d. The network firewall is preventing Tom from accessing the newsletter share.

70. What is the default protocol used for communication across the Internet?
 a. PPP
 b. TCP/IP
 c. IPX/SPX
 d. HTML

71. What identifies the network portion of an IPv4 address?
 a. The third octet always identifies the network address.
 b. The WINS server is responsible for identifying the network address.
 c. The subnet mask identifies the network address.
 d. The entire IPv4 address is the network address.

72. Which device can be used to access the Internet through an ISP for a home-office network designed with ICS?
    a. 56K modem
    b. Cable modem
    c. DSL modem
    d. Any of the devices can be used with ICS.
73. Which device listed below requires a telephone modem to operate?
    a. DSL
    b. ISDN
    c. Satellite
    d. T1
74. Which media listed is also referred to as thinnet?
    a. RG6
    b. RG8
    c. RG56
    d. RG58
75. What is the main difference between single mode and multimode fiber?
    a. Multimode contains more than one core for carrying data.
    b. Single mode carries data further than multimode.
    c. Multimode can be used for more than one type of data, but single mode can only be used for one type of data.
    d. Single mode requires an SC connector, and multimode requires an ST connector.
76. The IPX/SPX protocol is directly associated with which network operating system?
    a. Microsoft Server 2003
    b. Novell Network 4.0 and earlier
    c. Apple peer-to-peer networks
    d. Wireless IEEE 802.11b
77. Which cable typically uses a braided or solid metal shield surrounding a conductor?
    a. RG58
    b. CAT5 UTP
    c. UTP patch cable
    d. 100BaseF
78. What type of connectors would you expect to find on a standard DSL modem used in a SOHO network?
    a. Two RJ-45s
    b. One RJ-45 and one RJ-11
    c. Two RJ-11s
    d. One RJ-11 and one BNC

79. Which is the closest definition of a half-duplex network device?
    a. The device has only half the throughput of any other device on the network.
    b. The device can communicate in two directions, but only in one direction at a time.
    c. The device can communicate in two directions at the same time.
    d. The device can only communicate either in one direction or both directions at the same time.
80. How is the IP address assigned to a PC that is accessing the Internet through a telephone modem and an ISP?
    a. IP addresses are assigned at the manufacturer and are unique to each network adapter.
    b. The IP address is assigned by the telephone modem and is unique to each modem.
    c. The PC's IP address is assigned when the user runs the BIOS setup program and is retained in the CMOS.
    d. An IP address is assigned by the ISP.

Scoring the Exam

Copy the following chart onto a separate sheet of paper and fill in your scores. Please do not write in this book.

A+ Core Hardware Domain	Your Score (Number of correctly answered questions)
1.0 Installation, Configuration, and Upgrading	
2.0 Diagnosing and Troubleshooting	
3.0 Preventive Maintenance	
4.0 Motherboard, Processors, and Memory	
5.0 Printers	
6.0 Basic Networking	
Total Number of Questions	

As a quick indication of how you performed on the practice exam, refer to the chart in **Figure 20-3.** The chart shows the total number of questions in each domain and the number of correctly answered questions you need to have in order to score an 80% in that domain.

A+ Note:
The exam objectives discussed in the chapter were the current objectives at the time of writing. Always check the CompTIA Web site for the latest information on the A+ Certification exams.

Figure 20-3.
Use this quick reference chart to determine if you have achieved an 80% on the practice exam or in any of the tested domains.

A+ Core Hardware Domain	Total Number of Questions on the Exam	Number of Correct Questions Needed to Score an 80%
1.0 Installation, Configuration, and Upgrading	28	22
2.0 Diagnosing and Troubleshooting	17	14
3.0 Preventive Maintenance	4	3
4.0 Motherboard, Processors, and Memory	9	7
5.0 Printers	7	6
6.0 Basic Networking	15	12
Total Number of Questions	80	64

Summary

- The CompTIA A+ Certification exams measure the entry-level ability of an IT professional or PC service technician.
- The CompTIA A+ Certification consists of two exams: the A+ Core Hardware exam and the A+ Operating System Technologies exam.
- The requirements for the A+ Certification exams change frequently. Always check the CompTIA Web site for the latest news concerning the A+ Certification exams.
- The examination objectives are categorized according to domains and are based on industry surveys that correlate exam content to actual job requirements.
- CompTIA recommends that a test candidate have at least 500 hours of work experience. This is not a requirement.
- When reporting to the testing center, you must typically show two proofs of identification. Always check the requirements for identification before reporting to the testing center.
- The A+ Certification exams are multiple-choice tests.
- To ensure success on an A+ Certification exam, establish a realistic study schedule and stick to it.

- Hands-on experience provides you with many of the required skills that are tested on the A+ Certification exams.
- Additional study resources include installation manuals, Readme files, and instructional Web pages and Web sites.
- Creating your own study guide will improve your overall retention of the subject matter.
- A group formed of individuals that are serious about preparing for an A+ Certification exam can be an excellent way to prepare.
- Taking practice exams helps evaluate your weak areas.

Review Questions

Answer the following questions on a separate sheet of paper. Please do not write in this book.

1. The CompTIA A+ Certification exams are a standard _____-_____ exam.
2. Questions on the CompTIA A+ Certification exam carry different _____ and are therefore not scored equally.
3. CompTIA recommends that a test candidate have at least _____ hours of work experience.
4. _____ manuals provided by manufacturers are excellent learning resources.
5. _____-_____ experience is the best way to obtain the required skills that are tested for on an A+ Certification exam.

Suggested Lab Activities

1. Form a study group of students who are serious about preparing for the A+ Certification exams.
2. Make a date to take an exam and construct a schedule of study times and dates.
3. Write practice exams for other members in your study group.
4. Make 3 × 5 flash cards with A+ Certification exam questions. Include the answers on the opposite side. Use the cards to test your knowledge.
5. Create your own study guide using the examination objectives provided by CompTIA.
6. Write your own exam questions using the examination objectives provided by CompTIA. If you have formed a study group, you can try the exam questions out on each other. You will be surprised how many questions written by you will be similar to ones found on the A+ Certification exams.

Traditional study techniques are the key to good performance on a computerized test.

A+ Certification Exam Preparation—Operating System Technologies

After studying this chapter, you will be able to:

- ❑ Identify the study resources that can help you specifically prepare for each domain area covered in the A+ Certification Operating Systems Technologies exam.
- ❑ Identify A+ Operating System Technologies objectives and content items.
- ❑ Evaluate your readiness for successfully passing the A+ Operating System Technologies exam.
- ❑ Identify the areas in which you need further review.
- ❑ Construct a study guide based on the A+ Operating System Technologies Examination Objectives.

A+ Exam—Key Points

Concentrate on the knowledge identified in the A+ Operating System Technologies Examination Objectives. Do not be distracted by outlines available for download on the Internet.

Students tend to study areas they particularly like rather than areas they may be weak in. Do an objective analysis of your strengths and weaknesses.

You need to have hands-on experience with each of the operating systems tested: Windows 98, Me, 2000, and XP. Studying from textbook material and practice tests is not enough.

This chapter briefly reviews the study strategies covered in the previous chapter. It also demonstrates how some of the study resources you learned about can be specifically used to help you prepare for the A+ Operating System Technologies exam. A practice exam is also provided in this chapter, as well as the objectives and content items in each A+ Operating System Technologies domain area. Use this practice exam to gauge the areas in which you may need more study.

The Operating System Technologies Exam Format

The A+ Operating System Technologies exam consists of four major areas: Operating System Fundamentals; Installation, Configuration, and Upgrading; Diagnosing and Troubleshooting; and Networks. The chart in **Figure 21-1** shows the percentages assigned to each of the four domains and the approximate number of questions in each.

There are 80 questions on the exam and no more than 90 questions are presented (the extra questions are for field testing). A minimum score of 469 is required to pass, and you have ninety minutes to complete the exam.

A+ Note:
The exam objectives discussed in the chapter were the current objectives at the time of writing. Always check the CompTIA Web site for the latest information on the A+ Certification exams.

Test Preparation Strategies

The test preparation strategies you learned in the previous chapter can also be applied to your study for the A+ Certification Operating System Technologies exam. Some of the information sources you learned about in the previous chapter can be specifically applied to the study of each domain area

Figure 21-1. A+ Operating System Technologies domains and the percentage of questions that represent that domain.

A+ Operating System Technologies Domain	Percentage of Questions	Approximate Number of Questions
1.0 Operating System Fundamentals	28%	22
2.0 Installation, Configuration, and Upgrading	31%	25
3.0 Diagnosing and Troubleshooting	25%	20
4.0 Network	16%	13
Total	100%	80

covered in the A+ Certification Operating System Technologies exam. Two sources that can help you prepare for the Installation, Configuration, and Upgrading domain are the Microsoft Readme files included on the Windows installation CDs and the Microsoft Support Web pages.

The Readme files provide critical information about system upgrading and installation. It is strongly recommended that you familiarize yourself with these files since 31% of the exam covers installation and upgrading. Also, read the support page for known installation issues and problems. The most recent information will be located at Microsoft's Support Web site.

To help you prepare for questions from the Diagnosing and Troubleshooting domain, check the Microsoft Support Web site for known operating system problems. The site also contains detailed information about various Microsoft troubleshooting utilities. The section on troubleshooting is a vast topic that produces literally thousands of questions. It is highly recommended that you review all lab activities, especially the review questions aimed at troubleshooting.

To help you prepare for the Networking domain, read the installation manuals for DSL modems, cable modems, routers, and telephone modems. Many installation manuals are available for download from various manufacturers. You should also practice installing and setting up these devices. Doing so will help you gain a thorough understanding of basic networking principles.

An often-overlooked source of information, located on PC itself, is Microsoft's Help and Support. Help and Support provides a wealth of information related to all of the A+ Operating System Technologies domains. Some helpful information you will find are a glossary of computer terms, a command line reference, information on Windows support tools, and tips on setting up a SOHO network. To access Help and Support, go to **Start | Help and Support**. Some of the things you can do from the opening page of Help and Support are perform a search, pick a Help topic, and pick a task.

Sample A+ Operating System Technologies Exam

A sample exam has been provided to not only help you identify the areas tested, but to give you an idea of the depth of the questions asked on the A+ Operating System Technologies exam. In taking the practice exam, you will get a sense of the A+ Operating System Technologies exam's format, the topics covered, and the varying degree of difficulty of the questions. Taking the practice exam is one of the best ways to prepare for the real thing.

After completing the practice exam, score the exam with your instructor's assistance and use it as a guide in identifying the areas in which you may require more study. Answers to the exam are provided in the Instructor's Manual that accompanies this textbook.

Domain 1—Operating System Fundamentals

- **1.1 Identify the major desktop components and interfaces, and their functions. Differentiate the characteristics of Windows 9x/Me, Windows NT 4.0 Workstation, Windows 2000 Professional, and Windows XP.**

Content may include the following: Contrasts between Windows 9x/Me, Windows NT 4.0 Workstation, Windows 2000 Professional, and Windows XP; Major operating system components: registry, virtual memory, file system; Major operating system interfaces: Windows Explorer, My Computer, Control Panel, Computer Management Console, Accessories/System Tools, Command line, Network Neighborhood/My Network Places, taskbar/systray, Start Menu, Device Manager.

- **1.2 Identify the names, locations, purposes, and contents of major system files.**
  Content may include the following: Windows 9x specific files: IO.SYS, MSDOS.SYS, AUTOEXEC.BAT, COMMAND.COM, CONFIG.SYS, HIMEM.SYS, EMM386.exe, WIN.COM, SYSTEM.INI, WIN.INI, registry data files (SYSTEM.DAT, USER.DAT); Windows NT-based specific files: BOOT.INI, NTLDR, NTDETECT.COM, NTBOOTDD.SYS, NTUSER.DAT, registry data files.
- **1.3 Demonstrate the ability to use command-line functions and utilities to manage the operating system, including the proper syntax and switches.**
  Command line functions and utilities include: Command/CMD, DIR, ATTRIB, VER, MEM, SCANDISK, DEFRAG, EDIT, XCOPY, COPY, FORMAT, FDISK, SETVER, SCANREG, MD/CD/RD, Delete/Rename, DELTREE, TYPE, ECHO, SET, PING.
- **1.4 Identify basic concepts and procedures for creating, viewing, and managing disks, directories, and files. This includes procedures for changing file attributes and the ramifications of those changes (for example, security issues).**
  Content may include the following: Disks: partitions (active partition, primary partition, extended partition, logical partition); Files systems (FAT16, FAT32, NTFS4, NTFS5.x); Directory structures (root directory, subdirectories, etc): create folders, navigate the directory structure, maximum depth; Files: creating files, file naming conventions (most common extensions, 8.3, maximum length), file attributes (read only, hidden, system, and archive attributes), file compression, file encryption, file permissions, file types (text vs binary file).
- **1.5 Identify the major operating system utilities, their purpose, location, and available switches.**
  Content may include the following: Disk management tools: DEFRAG.EXE, FDISK.EXE, Backup/Restore Utility (MSbackup, NTBackup, etc.), ScanDisk, CHKDSK, Disk Cleanup, format; System management tools: Device Manager, System Manager, Computer Manager, MSCONFIG.EXE, REGEDIT.EXE (view information/backup registry), REGEDT32.EXE, SYSEDIT.EXE, SCANREG, COMMAND/CMD, Event Viewer Task Manager; File management tools: ATTRIB.EXE, EXTRACT.EXE, EDIT.COM, Windows Explorer.

Domain 1—Practice Exam Questions 1-22

1. Which operating systems have the System Recovery utility installed by default? (Choose two.)
   a. Windows Me
   b. Windows 98
   c. Windows 2000
   d. Windows XP
2. Which command will allow you to access the registry in Windows XP?
   a. **regedit**
   b. **regedit32**
   c. **regeditXP**
   d. **sysedit**
3. The ntdetect.com file can be found on which operating systems? (Choose two.)
   a. Windows 98
   b. Windows Me
   c. Windows 2000 Professional
   d. Windows XP Home Edition
4. Which file contains a list of all operating systems installed on the PC?
   a. ntuser.dat
   b. boot.ini
   c. autoexec.bat
   d. command.com
5. What are the expected results of the **xcopy c:/Winmax d:** command issued from the DOS prompt?
   a. All files and directories in the Winmax directory will be copied to drive D and will retain the same names.
   b. The file called Winmax will be copied to drive D, but none of the subdirectories associated with the file will be copied.
   c. The file Winmax will be copied to drive D and checked automatically for an exact match of all data.
   d. All files on drive D will be copied to drive C and placed in a directory called Winmax.
6. Which command listed below is used to partition a hard drive?
   a. **format**
   b. **fdisk**
   c. **partition**
   d. **partrun**

7. Which file system is recommended by Microsoft for Windows 2000 installations?
   a. FAT16
   b. FAT32
   c. NTFS
   d. HPFS
8. Which file system can be used with Windows NT file encryption? (Choose all that apply.)
   a. HPFS
   b. FAT16
   c. FAT32
   d. NTFS
9. Which files are necessary for a Windows XP boot disk? (Select two.)
   a. ntdetect.com
   b. autoexec.bat
   c. boot.ini
   d. command.com
10. What will happen when **attrib -h c:mynote.txt** is issued at the command prompt?
    a. An archive backup of the file mynote will be made.
    b. The hidden attribute will be removed from the file mynote.
    c. The file mynote will be displayed in hexadecimal form.
    d. The file mynote will have the file attribute set to hide.
11. Where is the command.com file found on a Windows 98 operating system installed on drive C?
    a. C:\command.com
    b. C:\Programs\Windows\System\command.com
    c. C:\Windows\command.com
    d. C:\My Documents\command.com
12. Which utility or program displays a summary of information about the software or hardware installed on the PC and provides a menu that allows you to select troubleshooting tools for the Windows XP operating system?
    a. Registry Editor
    b. System Communications Editor
    c. System Configuration Editor
    d. Microsoft System Information Tool
13. Which command, when run, displays the autoexec.bat, config.sys, win.ini, and sys.ini files?
    a. **regedit32**
    b. **sysedit**
    c. **msinfo**
    d. **edit**

14. A technician is setting up a dual boot operating system on a PC. The technician first installs Windows XP and then Windows 98. When the technician is finished, the PC automatically boots directly into Windows 98 with no option for accessing Windows XP. What is the most likely problem? (Choose all that apply.)
    a. The hard drive jumpers need to be set to CS.
    b. The technician installed the operating systems in the wrong order.
    c. The technician needed to remove the boot sector from the hard drive before installing the second operating system.
    d. You cannot dual boot the Windows XP and Windows 98 operating systems. Only Windows XP and Windows 2000 can be dual booted.
15. What should be done before performing a Windows XP upgrade? (Select three.)
    a. Disable the antivirus program.
    b. Backup data files and system settings.
    c. Create a clean partition on the hard drive.
    d. Check the HCL.
16. How do you create a system installation floppy disk set for Windows XP Professional?
    a. Open **Control Panel**, select **Software Install**, and then select **Create Setup Disks**.
    b. Place a floppy disk in the floppy disk drive and then issue the **sys A:** command at the command prompt.
    c. You cannot create a set of Windows XP installation disks. You must download them from the Microsoft Support Web site.
    d. You cannot create a set of installation disks for Windows XP. You must use a set of disks for Windows 2000 to start the setup process.
17. Which is the best definition of the term "clean install" when used in context with Microsoft software products?
    a. An installation process where everything went correctly and there were no problems.
    b. An installation process that is an upgrade of a previous operating system.
    c. An installation process that completely replaces any existing operating system.
    d. An installation process that requires the hard drive be defragmented and scanned for viruses before beginning the operating system installation process.

18. What command will generate the screen in the following figure?

```
Reply from 127.0.0.1: bytes=32 time<10ms TTL=128
Reply from 127.0.0.1: bytes=32 time<10ms TTL=128
Reply from 127.0.0.1: bytes=32 time<10ms TTL=128
Reply from 127.0.0.1: bytes=32 time<10ms TTL=128

Ping statistics for 127.0.0.1:
    Packets: Sent = 4, Received = 4, Lost = 0 (0% loss),
Approximate round trip times in milli-seconds:
    Minimum = 0ms, Maximum =  0ms, Average =  0ms
```

   a. **deltree**
   b. **setver**
   c. **tracert**
   d. **ping**

19. Which file system supports encryption on a Windows XP Professional PC? (Choose all that apply.)
   a. FAT16
   b. FAT32
   c. NTFS
   d. EXT2

20. What utility removes temporary Internet files?
   a. Disk Cleanup
   b. CheckDisk
   c. ScanDisk
   d. Disk Defragmenter

21. Which utility improves disk storage space and storage efficiency by rearranging the files?
   a. CheckDisk
   b. ScanDisk
   c. Disk Defragmenter
   d. Fdisk

22. What utility allows an administrator to create collections of commonly used tools referred to as snap-ins?
   a. Microsoft Management Console
   b. Dr. Watson
   c. Device Manager
   d. Service and Applications

Domain 2—Installation, Configuration, and Upgrading

- **2.1 Identify the procedures for installing Windows 9x/Me, Windows NT 4.0 Workstation, Windows 2000 Professional, and Windows XP, and bringing the operating system to a basic operational level.**
  Content may include the following: Verify hardware compatibility and minimum requirements; Determine OS installation options: installation type

(typical, custom, other), network configuration, file system type, dual boot support; Disk preparation order (conceptual disk preparation): start the installation, partition, format drive; Run appropriate set-up utility: Setup, Winnt; Installation methods: bootable CD, boot floppy, network installation, drive imaging; Device driver configuration: load default drivers, find updated drivers; Restore user data files (if applicable); Identify common symptoms and problems.

- **2.2 Identify steps to perform an operating system upgrade from Windows 9x/Me, Windows NT 4.0 Workstation, Windows 2000 Professional, and Windows XP. Given an upgrade scenario, choose the appropriate next steps.**
  Content may include the following: Upgrade paths available; Determine correct upgrade startup utility (e.g. WINNT32 vs WINNT); Verify hardware compatibility and minimum requirements; Verify application compatibility; Apply OS service packs, patches, and updates; Install additional Windows components.
- **2.3 Identify the basic system boot sequences and boot methods, including the steps to create an emergency boot disk with utilities installed for Windows 9x/Me, Windows NT 4.0 Workstation, Windows 2000 Professional, and Windows XP.**
  Content may include the following: Boot sequence: files required to boot, boot steps (9x, NT-based); Alternative boot methods: using a startup disk, Safe/VGA-only mode, Last Known Good configuration, command prompt mode, booting to a system restore point, Recovery Console, Boot.ini switches, dual boot; Creating emergency disks with OS utilities; Creating emergency repair disk (ERD).
- **2.4 Identify procedures for installing/adding a device, including loading, adding, and configuring device drivers, and required software.**
  Content may include the following: Device driver installation: Plug and Play (PNP) and non-PNP devices, install and configure device drivers, install different device drivers, manually install a device driver, search the Internet for updated device drivers, using unsigned drivers (driver signing); Install additional Windows components; Determine if permissions are adequate for performing the task.
- **2.5 Identify procedures necessary to optimize the operating system and major operating system subsystems.**
  Content may include the following: Virtual memory management, Disk defragmentation, Files and buffers, Caches, Temporary file management.

Domain 2—Practice Exam Questions 23-47

23. What should you do before performing an operating system upgrade? (Choose two.)
    a. Back up important files.
    b. Replace the BIOS chip with the latest version.
    c. Run a virus scan before installing the operating system.
    d. Compress all data files to ensure there will be sufficient room for the new operating system.

24. You are installing the Windows XP operating system on a stand-alone PC. When is the Administrator account created?
    a. After the operating system has been completely installed and boots the very first time.
    b. Automatically during the installation process.
    c. There is no Administrator account on a stand-alone PC.
    d. The Administrator account must be created before the installation process begins.
25. A new PC has been added to an existing peer-to-peer network. You are installing Windows XP Professional on the new system. During the installation process, you are prompted to choose between joining a domain or a workgroup. Which should you select and why?
    a. You should select domain because any collection of PCs is still considered a domain.
    b. You should select workgroup because peer-to-peer networks are typically workgroups.
    c. You should choose both domain and workgroup because all networked PCs are members of a domain and a local set of PCs are a workgroup.
    d. Select neither until the installation process is complete. Then have the system administrator create an account for the new PC. After the new account is set up, configure the workstation as a member of the workgroup.
26. A technician is upgrading a workstation from Windows NT to Windows XP Professional. The workstation is connected to a network domain. What must be done to ensure the user and workstation will still be a member of the domain?
    a. A new account must be set up on the network server.
    b. Windows XP Professional cannot be used on a network domain.
    c. A new network adapter must be installed and then configured.
    d. Nothing needs to be done. All information needed to join the domain is preserved during an upgrade.
27. A customer wishes to install Windows XP Professional on their existing Windows 2000 machine. What are the minimum requirements for installing Windows XP Professional?
    a. Intel Pentium 233MHz, 64MB of RAM, 2GB of hard drive space.
    b. Intel Pentium II, 1GHz, 256MB of RAM, 10GB of hard drive space.
    c. Intel Pentium IV, 1.4GHz, 512MB of RAM, 6GB of hard drive space.
    d. Intel Pentium III, 1.2GHz, 128MB of RAM, 600MB of hard drive space.
28. Which is the correct path to locate the system installation file for performing a Windows 2000 upgrade? Assume the CD-ROM is drive letter D.
    a. D:\i386\winnt32.exe
    b. D:\WinNT\Upgrade.exe
    c. D:\NT\Install.exe
    d. D:Install\Win2000.exe

29. You are installing Windows XP Professional on a new PC. How is NTFS installed?
    a. Using the system startup disks, partition and then format the new partition with NTFS.
    b. The NTFS file system is selected and installed during the Windows XP Professional installation process.
    c. The hard drive is furnished from the disk manufacturer with NTFS already on the drive in a single partition.
    c. Windows XP must be installed on a FAT16 partition and then upgraded to NTFS after the first boot.
30. Which partition must be created first?
    a. Primary partition
    b. Extended partition
    c. Logical partition
    d. Any partition can be created first.
31. Which file system is required for the support of Active Directory?
    a. FAT16
    b. FAT32
    c. NTFS5.0
    d. HPFS
32. A corporation executive has brought his personal notebook computer to work and wants to have the technician set it up to automatically connect to the corporate client/server network while at the office. The notebook has Windows XP Home Edition installed as the operating system. When the technician attempts to join the network domain, he cannot locate the dialog box for entering the domain name. What is the most likely problem?
    a. The notebook is infected with the DomainLoss virus.
    b. The domain name is not needed, simply set the notebook for DHCP.
    c. The Windows XP Home Edition needs to be reinstalled because it is corrupted.
    d. Windows XP Home Edition does not support the automatic domain name feature.
33. When performing a system upgrade, which command line option adds the Recovery Console to the Windows XP startup menu?
    a. **winnt32/AddConsole**
    b. **winnt32/CommandConsole**
    c. **winnt32/cmdcons**
    d. **winnt32/addall**
34. Which command line option allows you to run the Upgrade Advisor without installing Windows XP?
    a. **winnt32/checkupgradeonly**
    b. **winnt32/chkup**
    c. **winnt32/check**
    d. **winnt/check**

35. You are installing Windows 2000 on a new PC with a 40GB hard drive. You wish to divide the hard drive into two equal partitions 20GB each. Which scenario would you follow?
    a. Using a boot disk, use the Fdisk utility to partition the drive into two equal partitions.
    b. During the Windows 2000 installation process, you are presented with an option to use the entire disk or to set up a partition.
    c. Immediately after completing the Windows 2000 installation, you can open the Disk Management dialog box and portion the drive into two equal partitions.
    d. You may use any of the three methods outlined in answers A, B, and C.
36. While performing a Windows 98 installation, you are prompted with a screen asking if you would like to use large disk support. What will answering "no" do to the system?
    a. The installation process will be aborted.
    b. Windows 98 will install on an NTFS partition.
    c. Windows 98 will install on a FAT16 partition.
    d. Windows 98 will install on a FAT32 partition.
37. What should you do before performing a software upgrade on a Windows Me operating system? (Select two.)
    a. Back up important files.
    b. Set a system restore point.
    c. Defragment the hard drive.
    d. Run the ScanDisk utility.
38. What are the two most common methods recommended by Microsoft for installing multiple copies of a Microsoft operating system on more than one PC?
    a. Disk imaging using the Sysprep tool.
    b. Unattended setup using a batch file.
    c. A set of core operating system floppies installed through a direct cable connection.
    d. Microsoft does not permit a single copy of an operating system to be installed on multiple PCs.
39. During an operating system installation, a Plug and Play modem card generates a message telling you that a driver for the device cannot be found. What should you do next?
    a. Select the option to install the device manually using the device driver that came on the modem disk.
    b. Replace the modem card with a different model.
    c. Install the modem manually and select the model number that closely matches the one creating the error.
    d. You cannot manually configure a Plug and Play card. You must replace the card.

40. Where would you determine if the video card is compatible with the Windows 2000 operating system? (Select two.)
    a. Check the HCL at the Microsoft Web site.
    b. Check the video card manufacturer Web site.
    c. Check the back of the operating system's Resource Technical Manual.
    d. Check the FCC Web site at www.fcc.gov.
41. Which command is used to perform a system upgrade?
    a. Winnt
    b. Winnt32
    c. Winupgrd
    d. Wininstall
42. When should you apply a service pack for a clean install of an operating system?
    a. After approximately 2 weeks with no errors.
    b. Immediately after the clean install.
    c. Before beginning the clean install process.
    d. After every hardware upgrade.
43. Where would you locate the very latest driver for a DSL modem?
    a. At the operating system Web site.
    b. At the motherboard manufacturer's Web site.
    c. At the Microsoft Support Web page.
    d. At the DSL modem manufacturer's Web site.
44. When can you change the label of a drive partition?
    a. Only while installing the operating system on that same partition.
    b. The label can be changed only before installing an operating system.
    c. Before or after installing the operating system.
    d. Partition labels can never be changed.
45. Where is virtual memory located?
    a. Virtual memory is the RAM memory located above the 1MB of RAM.
    b. Virtual memory is a portion of the hard drive used as additional RAM space.
    c. Virtual memory is located between conventional memory and extended memory.
    d. Virtual memory is located in L2 cache.
46. How are additional Windows components such as Desktop Themes added to an existing operating system?
    a. Additional components can be added under the **Add/Remove Programs** icon located in **Control Panel**.
    b. Additional system components cannot be added after the installation is complete and the computer successfully boots for the first time.
    c. Additional system components can be added through **Start | Programs | Accessories | Additional Components**.
    d. Additional system components are located on the installation CD in **Windows/System/Components**.

47. Which are requirements when using the Sysprep tool to install Windows XP? (Select two.)
    a. Use only when performing a clean install.
    b. All PCs require similar hardware.
    c. Requires a server for the installation process.
    d. Use only when performing system upgrades.

Domain 3—Diagnosing and Troubleshooting

- **3.1 Recognize and interpret the meaning of common error codes and startup messages from the boot sequence, and identify steps to correct the problems.**
  Content may include the following: Common error messages and codes: Boot failure and errors (invalid boot disk, inaccessible boot device, missing NTLDR, bad or missing Command interpreter), startup messages (error in CONFIG.SYS line XX, HIMEM.SYS not loaded, Missing or corrupt HIMEM.SYS, Device/Service has failed to start), a device referenced in SYSTEM.INI, WIN.INI, Registry is not found, Event Viewer (event log is full), failure to start GUI, Windows protection error, user-modified settings cause improper operation at startup, registry corruption; Using the correct utilities: Dr. Watson, Boot Disk, Event Viewer.

- **3.2 Recognize when to use common diagnostic utilities and tools. Given a diagnostic scenario involving one of these utilities or tools, select the appropriate steps needed to resolve the problem.**
  Utilities and tools may include the following: Startup disks: required files for a boot disk, boot disk with CD-ROM support; Startup modes: safe mode, safe mode with command prompt, safe mode with networking, step-by-step/single step mode, automatic skip driver (ASD.exe); Diagnostic tools, utilities and resources: user/installation manuals, Internet/Web resources, training materials, Task Manager, Dr. Watson, boot disk, Event Viewer, Device Manager, WinMSD, MSD, Recovery CD, CONFIGSAFE; Eliciting problem symptoms from customers; Having customer reproduce error as part of the diagnostic process; Identifying recent changes to the computer environment from the user.

- **3.3 Recognize common operational and usability problems and determine how to resolve them.**
  Content may include the following: Troubleshooting Windows-specific printing problems: print spool is stalled, incorrect/incompatible driver for print, incorrect parameter; Other common problems: general protection faults, blue screen error (BSOD), illegal operation, invalid working directory, system lock up, option (sound card, modem, input device) or will not function, application will not start or load, cannot log on to network (option—NIC not functioning), applications don't install, network connection; Viruses and virus types: what they are, TSR (terminate stay resident) programs and virus, sources (floppy, e-mails, etc.), how to determine presence.

Domain 3—Practice Exam Questions 48-67

48. A Windows XP Professional system had failed to properly boot. Which is the best way to recover system boot files that are corrupted or missing?
    a. Boot the system using the Windows XP installation CD-ROM and begin the ASR process.
    b. Boot the system using a standard boot disk and use the **sys** command to recover the system.
    c. Boot the system and then reinstall the entire operating system.
    d. Boot the system using either Windows XP Professional or Windows XP Home Edition, and then use the ASR disk.
49. When booting in safe mode, which item can be disabled by safe mode menu selection?
    a. VGA device
    b. Hard drive
    c. Keyboard
    d. Network adapter
50. Which Recovery Console command will create a new boot sector in the system partition?
    a. **fdisk /s**
    b. **fdisk /mbr**
    c. **fixboot**
    d. **fixboot /bootsector**
51. Which utility is designed to make a capture of program errors as a program executes and sends the information to a log that can be viewed or sent to technical support?
    a. System Configuration Editor
    b. Command Interpreter
    c. Dr. Watson
    d. ScanDisk
52. Which utility can be used to easily disable startup programs while troubleshooting?
    a. Microsoft Configuration Utility
    b. Dr. Watson
    c. Driver Rollback
    d. Device Manager
53. What condition typically causes a system general protection fault?
    a. Hard drive failure
    b. DVD failure
    c. Corrupt boot.ini file
    d. Memory conflict between two programs

54. A Windows 2000 PC fails to start or fails to complete the boot process. Which is the most appropriate method for accessing the NTFS file system on the hard drive for inspection?
    a. Hold down the [F8] key during the boot process and enter safe mode. Use standard commands to view the drive's areas of concern.
    b. Place the ASR disk in the floppy drive and boot the system, and then run the appropriate commands to access the NTFS file structure.
    c. Place a DOS boot disk in the floppy drive, reboot the system, and then use the **dir** command to view the contents of the NTFS directory.
    d. Place the installation CD in the drive, reboot the system, and then use the recovery console feature.
55. What will happen when [Ctrl] [Alt] [Delete] is pressed while Windows XP is running?
    a. A system crash will occur.
    b. The Windows Security dialog box appears on the screen.
    c. The command prompt window appears on the screen.
    d. The system will automatically reboot.
56. You are providing telephone support for a Windows Me customer. The customer recently installed a game they downloaded from the Internet. Now the video display isn't correct and they want it fixed. They are not concerned with preserving the game. What would be the easiest way to help the customer immediately repair their system?
    a. Guide the customer through the use of System Restore.
    b. Guide the customer through the use of System Configuration Editor.
    c. Simply have the customer reinstall the Windows Me operating system.
    d. Have the customer edit the registry to remove the software program.
57. Which program contains information about programs, security, and system events on a PC?
    a. Performance Monitor
    b. Event Viewer
    c. Disk Management
    d. System Configuration Editor
58. Which file type is most likely to create a system or performance error?
    a. dll
    b. txt
    c. gif
    d. doc
59. A large block of files has been sent to Recycle Bin. Now they need to be restored. What can be done?
    a. Nothing; the files have been lost.
    b. The system registry needs to be edited to regain the files.
    c. Right-click the **Recycle Bin** icon and select **Empty** to empty the contents onto the Desktop so that you can then select the file you wish to restore.
    d. Right-click the **Recycle Bin** icon, select **Open**, and then select **Restore all items**, or select the specific files you wish to restore.

60. You open Device Manager and see a yellow icon next to the USB host controller. What does the yellow icon most likely indicate?
    a. The USB port is in use.
    b. There is a problem with the USB host controller.
    c. The USB port is full and no more devices can be added to the chain.
    d. Someone unauthorized is trying to access the USB port.
61. You have just installed a new USB game controller on a PC. The controller does not appear in Device Manager. What is most likely the problem?
    a. The system BIOS needs to be upgraded.
    b. A system virus has disabled the USB port.
    c. The autoexec.bat file needs to be modified or configured.
    d. The system.ini file needs to be configured for the new device.
62. Which devices can be affected by a DirectX program? (Select all that apply.)
    a. Video display
    b. Sound
    c. Keyboard functions
    d. 3-D acceleration chips
63. What program entered and run from the startup menu will reveal the contents of the boot.ini file?
    a. **msconfig**
    b. **sysedit**
    c. **regedit**
    d. **drwatson**
64. Which key combination would allow you to view a list of programs running on a Windows Me PC?
    a. [Ctrl] [Alt]
    b. [Alt] [Esc] [Shift]
    c. [Ctrl] [F12]
    d. [Ctrl] [Alt] [Delete]
65. You suspect that a PCI network adapter card is causing a workstation to lock up after logging on? How could you disable the network adapter card?
    a. Start the PC with the network cable unplugged from the card.
    b. Start the PC by pressing the [F8] key, and then selecting **Safe Mode**.
    c. Open the sysedit file, and then disable the driver.
    d. Open the autoexec.bat file, and then disable the driver.
66. How can a startup disk be made using Windows Me?
    a. Open **Control Panel**, select **Add/Remove Programs**, and then select the **Startup Disks** tab.
    b. Open the **Start** menu, and then select **Programs | Accessories | Startup Disks**.
    c. Open the installation CD-ROM and copy the files located in **Windows/System/StartupDisks**.
    d. The startup disks can only be made while installing the operating system.

67. What is the purpose of the oakcdrom.sys file located on the Windows 98 startup disks?
    a. It is used to create shadow ROM.
    b. It is used to create virtual memory support on the hard drive system.
    c. The file is used to ensure file compression compatibility.
    d. It is the generic driver for ATAPI CD-ROM support.

Domain 4—Networks

- **4.1 Identify the networking capabilities of Windows. Given configuration parameters, configure the operating system to connect to a network.** Content may include the following: Configure protocols: TCP/IP (gateway, subnet mask, DNS (and domain suffix), WINS, static address assignment, automatic address assignment (APIPA, DHCP)); IPX/SPX (NWLink); Appletalk; NetBEUI/ NetBIOS; Configure client options: Microsoft, Novell; Verify the configuration; Understand the use of the following tools: IPCONFIG.EXE, WINIPCFG.EXE, PING, TRACERT.EXE, NSLOOKUP.EXE; Share resources (understand the capabilities/limitations with each OS version); Setting permissions to shared resources; Network type and network card.
- **4.2 Identify the basic Internet protocols and terminologies. Identify procedures for establishing Internet connectivity. In a given scenario, configure the operating system to connect to and use Internet resources.** Content may include the following: Protocols and terminologies: ISP, TCP/IP, e-mail (POP, SMTP, IMAP), HTML, HTTP, HTTPS, SSL, Telnet, FTP, DNS; Connectivity technologies: dial-up networking, DSL networking, ISDN networking, cable, satellite, wireless, LAN; installing and configuring browsers: enable/disable script support, configure proxy settings, configure security settings; Firewall protection under Windows XP.

Domain 4—Practice Exam Questions 68-80

68. Which protocol is used to send e-mail to a mail server?
    a. SMTP
    b. POP
    c. IMAP
    d. FTP

69. A customer wants to install Internet access at their home. They want to know which access type has the highest bandwidth.
    a. V92 modem
    b. ISDN
    c. DSL
    d. All methods support the same bandwidth.

70. A wireless SOHO network consists of two different PCs each in a different room approximately 60 feet apart. The 802.11b wireless network adapter claims a throughput of 11Mbps. After configuring the network, you see in the properties window of the connection that the throughput is actually less than 5Mbps. What is the most likely problem?
    a. The wireless network adapter has the wrong driver.
    b. There is too much data being transferred across the network.
    c. The system BIOS needs to be upgraded.
    d. This is normal for wireless network adapters set 60 feet apart.

71. Which is the default protocol for communication on the Internet?
    a. IPX/SPX
    b. NWLINK
    c. NetBEUI
    d. TCP/IP

72. Which network system uses CSMA/CD method to access the network media?
    a. Ethernet
    b. Token Ring
    c. Wireless
    d. All networks use CSMA/CD.

73. Which networking media supports the highest data throughput?
    a. Cat3
    b. Cat4
    c. Cat5e
    d. Fiber

74. A small network consists of two workstations each with a 10/100Mbps network adapter, a 10Mbps hub, connected with Cat5e cable. What is the highest expected throughput for this configuration?
    a. 10Mbps
    b. 100Mbps
    c. 200Mbps
    d. 250Mbps

75. Which command reveals the workstation assigned IP address, subnet mask, and default gateway?
    a. **ping**
    b. **tracert**
    c. **ipconfig**
    d. **wins**

76. Which tool or utility would you use to determine the URL that matched an IP address?
    a. Nslookup
    b. FTP
    c. IMAP
    d. SNMP

77. What is the best method to secure a Windows XP PC from intruders on the Internet?
    a. Enable the ICF feature.
    b. Enable the ICS feature.
    c. Enable the HTML feature.
    d. Enable the DNS feature.
78. What type of cable connector would be installed on a typical DSL modem?
    a. One RJ-45 and one RJ-11
    b. Two RJ-45s
    c. One USB and one RJ-45
    d. Two USB
79. Which service is responsible for issuing IP addresses automatically to individual workstations?
    a. DNS
    b. WINS
    c. DHCP
    d. FTP
80. Which example below is a domain name?
    a. jbrown@g-w.com
    b. g-w.com
    c. http:/www.g-w.com/Files/Download/test4/pdf
    d. jbrown/g-w.com

Scoring the Exam

Copy the following chart onto a separate sheet of paper and fill in your scores. Please do not write in this book.

A+ Operating System Technologies Domain	Your Score (Number of Correctly Answered Questions.)
1.0 Operating System Fundamentals	
2.0 Installation, Configuration, and Upgrading	
3.0 Diagnosing and Troubleshooting	
4.0 Networks	
Total Correct	

As a quick indication of how you performed on the practice exam, refer to the chart in **Figure 21-2.** The chart shows the total number of questions in each domain and the number of correctly answered questions you need to have to score an 80% in that domain.

Now that you have scored your exam, you can identify the areas in which you need additional study. You may wish to construct an outline based on the A+ Operating System Technologies Examination Objectives that includes only those areas. After constructing the outline, go through the objectives and make notes on each subject. Use the sources mentioned at the beginning of this chapter as reference materials for completing the study guide.

After studying this textbook, completing the lab activities, the practice tests, and a thorough review of the subject material, you should be ready to pass both parts of the CompTIA A+ exams. Remember, there is a possibility that you will fail an A+ Certification exam when you take it, especially on the first try. There is no disgrace in failure. Simply take the examination again after you better prepare yourself. Also, be aware that many jobs do not require you to be certified when you start employment, but do require certification later. Some employers will reimburse you either fully or partially when you pass the examination. Some college programs also award college credit hours for many of the IT certificates earned such as the A+ Certification.

A+ Operating System Technologies Domain	Total Number of Questions	Number of Questions Needed to Score an 80%
1.0 Operating System Fundamentals	22	18
2.0 Installation, Configuration, and Upgrading	25	20
3.0 Diagnosing and Troubleshooting	20	16
4.0 Networks	13	10
Total	80	64

Figure 21-2.
Use this quick reference chart to determine if you have achieved an 80% on the practice exam or in any of the tested domains.

Summary

- The A+ Operating System Technologies exam consists of four major areas: Operating System Fundamentals; Installation, Configuration, and Upgrading; Diagnosing and Troubleshooting; and Networks.
- Always check the CompTIA Web site for the very latest news concerning the A+ Certification exams.
- Readme files found on operating system installation CDs provide critical information about system upgrading and installation.

- For help in preparing for questions on diagnosing and troubleshooting operating system problems, check the Microsoft Support Web site for common problems.
- Installation manuals for DSL modems, cable modems, routers, and telephone modems can help you prepare for the networking portion of the A+ Operating System Technologies exam.
- Microsoft's Help and Support is an often-overlooked source of information.
- Take the practice exam to evaluate your weak areas and improve overall retention of subject matter.

Review Questions

1. List the four domains covered on the A+ Operating System Technologies exam.
2. List four resources that can specifically help you prepare for the A+ Operating System Technologies exam.
3. An often-overlooked study resource is Microsoft's _____ and _____.
4. If you fail the A+ Operating System Technologies exam, you should _____.
   a. immediately retake the exam
   b. choose another career
   c. review your weak areas and then retake the exam
   d. seek employment with a company that does not require their computer service technicians to be A+ certified

Suggested Laboratory Activities

1. Make a date to take the A+ Operating System Technologies exam and construct a schedule of study times and dates.
2. Create your own study guide using the A+ Operating System Technologies Examination Objectives provided by CompTIA.
3. Download and read various installation manuals from the Web sites of major Internet access device manufacturers.

Employment and Advanced Education

After studying this chapter, you will be able to:

- Conduct a job search.
- Identify appropriate interview skills.
- Discuss a variety of computer careers and the associated educational requirements.
- Define entrepreneur and entrepreneurship.
- Identify career information sources.
- Identify advanced training options.
- List the elements of a successful resume.
- Outline ideas for a successful job search.

This unit discusses ways to gain employment and ways to advance your career in the future. Because the world of technology is constantly advancing, careers in the computer technology field require continuing education. New ideas become reality everyday. To keep up with the rapid changes in technology, you must form an action plan. Your plan must include strategies for keeping up-to-date with the changes in technology and using that newfound knowledge to create career advancement opportunities. See **Figure 22-1.**

Employment issues are discussed in this chapter. Although you may already be employed in a computer repair or related job, this chapter can help you better define your career goals. First, let's look at some of the many job titles found in the computer industry.

A Career Working with Computers

By successfully reaching this point in the textbook, you have probably decided whether or not to pursue a career working with computers. If you have the interest, desire, and ability, you can find a very rewarding career in the computer technology field. By completing this course, you have attained the first level of expertise. You may elect to go on for additional training in a more advanced field of computer technology. PC technician is only one broad area in a field rich in choices.

Figure 22-1. Once you land a job in the information technology field, you must continue to learn about new software and hardware or your skills will quickly become obsolete.

Some of the many other fields from which you can choose are:

- Network installation and support.
- Network administration.
- Digital electronics.
- System analysis.
- Technical sales.
- Help desk support.
- Web support.
- Computer programming.
- Computer engineering.

Because the tools of the trade are constantly changing, a PC technician must continuously learn new software, operating systems, and hardware. You can expand your knowledge to make yourself even more valuable as a PC technician or just to satisfy your own curiosity. There are no limits to your education in the field of computer technology. In fact, if you stop learning, the entire technology will soon pass you by. It would only take a few years before you would feel as obsolete as some of the equipment on which you may work.

Some possible career positions are as follows:

- Entry-level help desk operator.
- PC support professional.
- Technical sales and marketing professional.
- Technical writer.
- Application developer.
- Customer service representative.
- Security specialist.
- Internet Web site developer.
- Internet systems administrator.
- Database specialist.
- Network hardware specialist.
- Network engineer.
- Systems engineer.
- Software engineer.
- Programmer.
- Analyst.
- Chief information officer.
- Telecommunications data specialist.
- Voice-over IP engineer.
- Data communications engineer.
- ATM engineer.
- Web master.
- Web developer.
- Industrial control engineer.

- IT consultant.
- PC support.
- Service/help desk technician.
- PC installation.
- Network support.
- Software programming specialist.
- Network security specialist.
- Training specialist.

You may be considering a career that requires a college-level education. There are many outstanding career opportunities for persons who earn a computer science or related degree, **Figure 22-2.** Some college level training programs offer specialized degrees in many of the areas listed. Some colleges award credit based on technical certifications or work experience.

If you are interested in science and math in high school, you would probably enjoy studying computer science at a four-year college. Mathematics is a large part of computer-related college education. If you do not like mathematics and still want a good career, you may choose to pursue an alternative educational path.

One alternative path you may consider is the training offered in the armed forces. The various branches of the military offer many specialized areas of study in the computer technology field. The opportunities for education are very good in the military services, and valuable work experiences are gained along the way.

Another alternative educational path might be the completion of a special technical program offered at a local school, college, or technical center. These programs typically consist of advanced courses leading to certifications that are recognized worldwide. For example, Novell, Microsoft, Cisco Systems, and

Figure 22-2. Many universities offer an extensive information technologies curriculum.

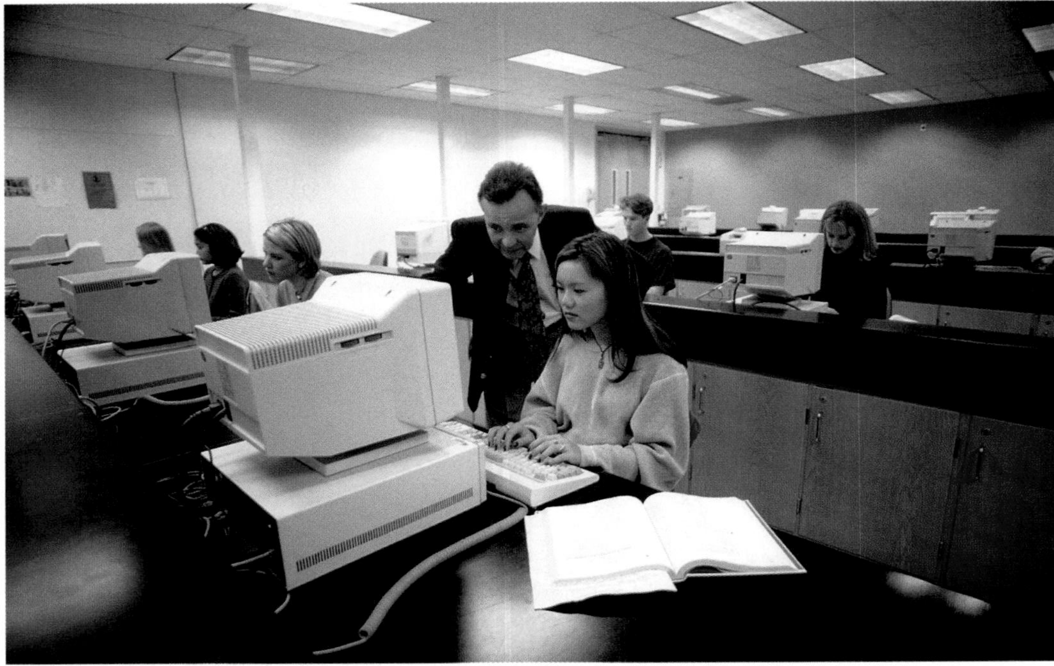

many other companies offer certification examinations in many advance fields of study. One of the most demanding certifications offered by Microsoft is called the Microsoft Certified Systems Engineer (MCSE). To receive certification you must pass a series of examinations designed to test your knowledge and competency. It can easily take one or two years of study to pass all the different examinations required for the certification.

Each person must ask himself or herself several questions before going further into the computer arena. Have you enjoyed this PC textbook and the laboratory activities? The fact that you are studying the PC is a good indicator of an interest in this area. Have you taken other classes in computer technology? Did you like them? Did you do well? Give serious thought to the questions before responding. Your answers may provide you with the insight you need to choose a rewarding career.

Careers in the Information Technology Industry

As we have noted, there are a wide variety of career options in the information technology (IT) industry. Computers, communications, and information systems play a major role in our daily life. Think of all the things that depend on computer systems today. For example, our communication systems—telephone, television, and radio—are all linked to computers. Hollywood studios use advanced computer graphics software to create special effects that were impossible before the advent of the computer, **Figure 22-3.**

The manufacturing industry uses computer controlled robots and automated assembly lines. In the business world, computers tie a company's sales department to its accounting and shipping departments for seamless transactions. The entire banking industry relies on computers to track money exchanges, post records of interest and earnings, and compile mortgage

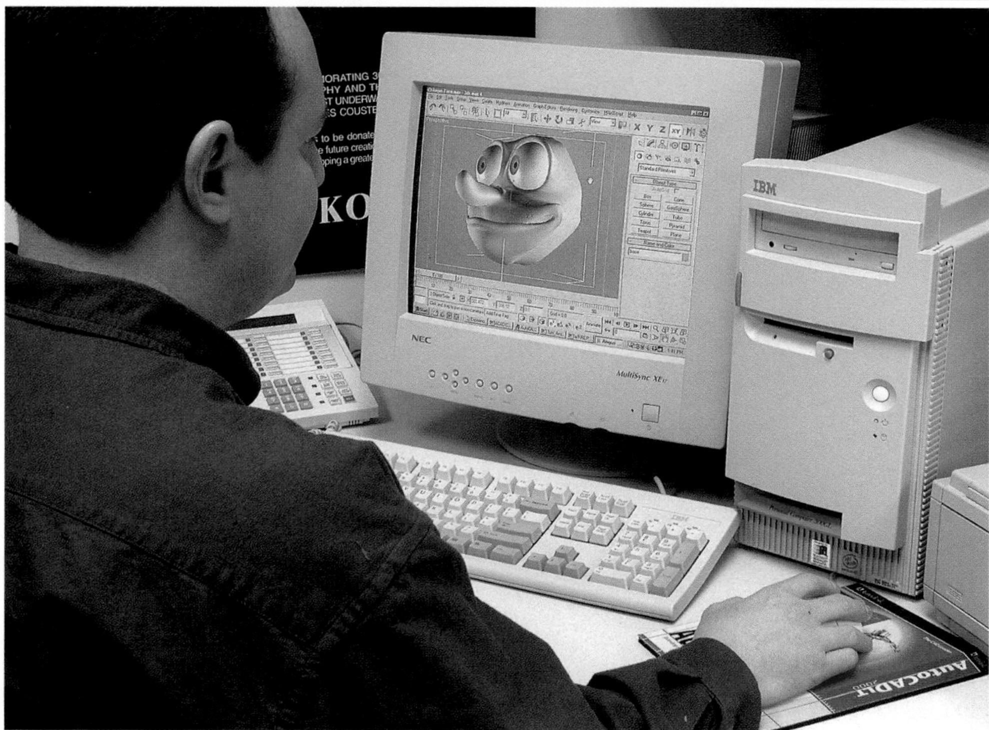

Figure 22-3. Computer-generated animation has become very popular in Hollywood.

statistics. Computer technology has also saturated the field of medicine. Surgeons can now perform computer-assisted surgeries. Patient medical records are all computerized, **Figure 22-4.** MRI scans can be transmitted instantly across a network to a specialist in a distant city for expert evaluation.

With development of each new application for the computer, many highly skilled technicians must be trained to maintain and service it. The need for people with PC technology training will continue to grow rapidly into the next century. Law enforcement, the military, and other governmental units rely a great deal on computers. Architects and engineers use computers to design structures. With computers, they cannot only design the structure but also get a realistic first-person view of the design as they take a virtual stroll through its corridors. As computer technology integrates into every aspect of our world, the need for highly trained and skilled technicians grows.

Entrepreneurs

Entrepreneurs own and operate their own businesses. These small businesses make up 97% of businesses in the United States. They also provide 58% of the jobs in America. Entrepreneurs usually start with an idea for filling a gap in the marketplace, perhaps where a new product or service is needed. Typically, a business plan is produced before a group or individual decides to open a private business. A business plan will always be required if financial support is being sought to open a business. This plan outlines goals for the business, an action plan, and a timetable for meeting those goals. A business plan is vital if the business is to succeed.

Figure 22-4. Medical records are computerized, allowing for immediate access in case of emergency, automated scheduling, and a reduced risk of misplacement.

In addition to a sound business plan, a successful entrepreneur possesses a good knowledge of his or her business, industry, service, or product. This knowledge allows the owner to make smart business decisions. The successful entrepreneur also has sound management skills. These skills allow the owner to successfully manage money, time, and employees. Management of each of these is critical to success, and poor management in any of these areas leads to certain failure.

Entrepreneurial skills, or the ability to think and move creatively and wisely, are also very important for the successful entrepreneur. These skills allow the business owner to control the business and move it in the right direction. Entrepreneurial opportunities are vast in the information technology industry. The tremendous growth in the PC market has triggered a similar growth in the demand for computer services. These highly demanded services include PC maintenance and repair, training, and Internet services.

Consulting is yet another growing business in the information technology industry, **Figure 22-5.** Consultants work for clients on special or individual projects. The specific job they do often depends on what work is needed. Clients pay a consultant for his or her expertise. When the job is completed, the consultant is free to move on to a new job and client.

Career Information Sources

The Occupational Outlook Handbook offers information on careers in many industries. It is published by the United States Department of Labor and the Bureau of Statistics. Most high school, community college, university, and public libraries have copies of this book. It can also be viewed online at www.bls.gov/oco.

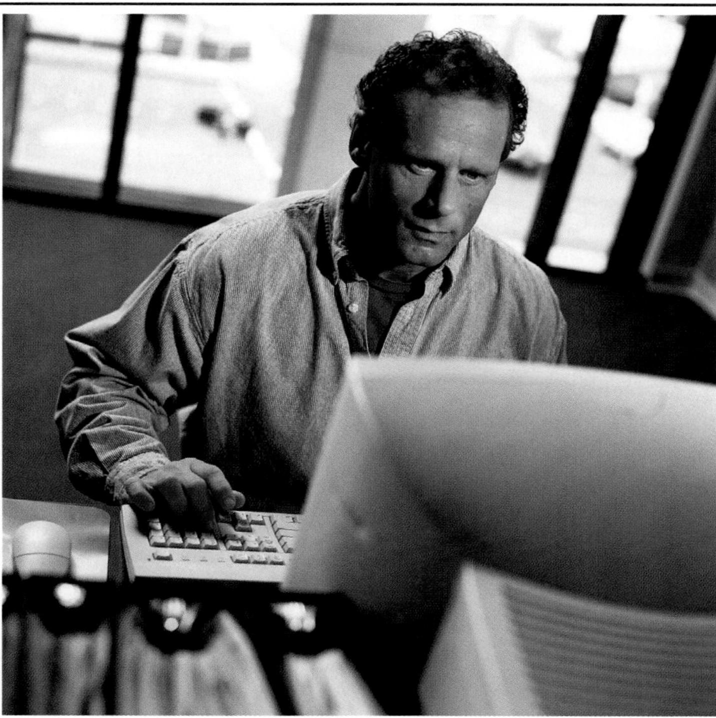

Figure 22-5. Consultants are computer experts who offer their services on a per job basis.

School guidance counselors, local labor markets, and one-stop offices are other outstanding sources of career information. They can help you find information on particular careers, colleges, and other programs that offer training in areas that you are interested in. These people are typically well-informed and ready to help in your search for jobs or training. Many colleges offer job information and placement services as well.

The Internet also contains a great amount of career and training information. Many private company sites list employment opportunities. Usually the listing includes the required skills and educational levels and a brief job description with a list of duties.

Education

The educational requirements for jobs in the information technology industry vary. However, a minimum of a high school education is a solid foundation on which to build. Some high school graduates enter industry directly and receive specialized education in employer sponsored training programs. However, many of these workers do not stop at this point. They continue to study to keep abreast of all the changes and new technologies that develop in the industry.

As discussed, specialized training can also be found in colleges, technical schools, or the military. Advanced degrees are becoming more commonplace as a means of moving ahead. Many state and private universities offer engineering and computer science degrees. Talk with your school counselor to learn locations and entry requirements.

Advanced Certification

Often, people who work in the field of computer technology have minimal certification. They must study at night for the certification exams, while working during the day in a related job. They most likely work under the supervision of another person who already has the certification. This can limit their career advancement.

Certification is a way to advance your knowledge and career in the information technology industry. Certification combined with work experience is a way to prove your abilities to a potential employer. It is also a way to advance within a company and gain job security. As an IT professional, you will be learning the rest of your life. The knowledge base of the computer industry is ever expanding. Part of what you know now may very well be obsolete in a few years. If you did not learn another thing from this point forward, your skills would be very weak in just a few short years.

Obtaining your A+ Certification should be just the beginning for you. You should immediately start advancing toward another area of certification. Network+ or i-Net+ certification is a good place to continue. These two areas will serve as a springboard to other more advanced certificates.

You may choose to not pursue another certification, and this decision is acceptable as long as you keep your skills up-to-date. Subscribe to, and read, professional journals in your area of work. Take as many courses as you can, such as digital electronics, to enhance your PC repair skills.

Home-study groups and courses are becoming commonplace. A student simply signs up from home and takes courses online. Gateway offers many such programs, but there are many other sources as well. Unfortunately, this type of study takes a lot of self-discipline. Most people do not have the drive needed to stick with this type of schooling. Another drawback is the lack of hands-on activities, which are essential to be successful in technical areas of study. Without the hands-on application, simple memorization of facts is useless. If you are already employed in a technology field and do not have time to attend school on a regular basis, home study may be best for you. You will not be looked down on for earning your certification through home study. The place you study and the method you use to learn your skills are not indicated on your certificate.

After you enter the workforce at an entry-level position, you will want to consider further developing your technical skills. If you feel you have a future with the company, you should match the certification route to the company's needs. For example, if the company network system is based on Microsoft 2000, you should pursue the Microsoft line of certificates. If the company uses a system such as Novell, UNIX, or Linux, you should seek certification in one of these areas.

The time required to earn any certification depends on the individual's abilities. Some people are able to complete certification within a year; others lack the necessary aptitude and will never earn their certification. A good rule of thumb is at least two years experience and one year of study before attempting most certifications.

Let's look at some other certifications you may wish to obtain.

CompTIA Certifications

The CompTIA organization offers certification by examination in many areas. Receiving an A+ Certification from CompTIA is just the beginning. They offer advanced certificates that you may elect to pursue, such as CDIA+, i-Net+, Network+, Server+, and Linux+. Visit CompTIA's Web site (www.comptia.org/certification) for more detailed information about the various certifications.

CDIA+

The CDIA+ (Certified Document Imaging Architect) is a good, advanced certification. Today, there is a great demand for persons with expertise in computer imaging. The CDIA+ examination tests your knowledge of imaging systems, including scanners, displays, printers, graphic file types, file conversion, and image enhancement. Typical questions include those about storage systems, transition speeds across networks, and PC performance, as they relate to imaging. There is a tremendous need for technicians who can quickly and efficiently convert text pages and illustrations into formats recognized by computer systems.

i-Net+

The i-Net+ Certification proves competency working with the Internet services. The scope of the certification includes the installation, updating, and modifying of Web sites and other Internet communications. The i-Net+ certification exam includes questions about Internet system administration, application development, security, e-commerce, and site design. The competencies are similar to those for Network+, but with greater emphasis on Internet communication, construction, and design.

Do not confuse this with Web design graphics. Web design graphics is more like commercial art. It involves the presentation of the Web site, including sequencing and the general artwork. The i-Net+ Certification is more concerned with the behind-the-screens of a Web site. This includes equipment, protocols, networking system, and hardware requirements.

Network+

The Network+ Certification is designed to test knowledge of small and large network systems. The ideal candidate should have 18 to 24 months of networking experience. Experience alone, however, will not prepare you for the examination. You need to prepare for the test by taking an instructor-led course, a distance-learning course, or a self-study program. The test is not vendor specific. This means that the test is not based solely on Windows NT, Windows 2000, Novell, or any other brand name of software or hardware. The examination tests knowledge of the universal concepts of network systems.

Although you need to know the basics of network administration to pass the Network+ Certification exam, the knowledge is only intended as a foundation before going on to network administration certification. The Network+ Certification is required prior to many advanced certificates. For example, the Network+ Certification can be used toward Novell's Certified Engineer (CNE) program and Lotus's CLP Domino Messaging Administrator R4 certification, among others.

Tech Tip:
The A+, Network+, and Server+ Certifications count as electives toward the MCSA Certification.

Server+

The Server+ Certification is designed to test a person's knowledge about network server hardware and software. The candidate will be tested on installation, configuration, and diagnosis of network server hardware and network operating systems. The examination requires an in-depth knowledge of protocols, backup system standards, and system security.

Linux+

The Linux+ Certification covers the installation, configuration, and troubleshooting of the Linux operating system for the single PC as well as the network server. The Linux operating system is similar to the operating systems you have studied thus far. However, there are enough significant differences to warrant a separate certification. This is not unusual. In fact, Microsoft has offered separate certifications for their different systems, such as Windows 2000 and Windows 2003, even though they are similar in design and presentation.

Security+

The CompTIA Security+ Certification is one of the newest certifications to be offered. The test is designed to measure the candidate's mastery of general security concepts. Areas covered include communications, infrastructure, cryptography, and organizational security. Candidates are recommended to have at least two years experience in networking, a good knowledge of TCP/IP, some experience in related network security, and possess the Network+ certification. While these are recommended, they are not required before taking the exam.

It has rapidly become recognized internationally as an excellent verification of basic security principles and application. The CompTIA Security+ certificate can be used to award credit toward other certifications offered by companies such as Microsoft, Novell, and Symantec. You should consider the Security+ Certification if you plan to stay in information technology as a career.

Check CompTIA's Web site for the very latest information concerning certification credit.

Microsoft Certification Areas

Microsoft has a rich offering of various certifications such as MOS, MCP, MCDST, MCSE, MCSA, MCSD, and MCDBA. The series of Microsoft certifications are designed to support the Microsoft family of products. These individual certifications usually require two or more separate examinations. In addition to the certification offered for specialized areas, Microsoft offers examinations and certification for their operating systems, such as Windows 2000 and Windows 98. Visit the Microsoft Training Web page (www.microsoft.com/learning/training) for more details on all certification areas.

MOS

The Microsoft Office Specialist (MOS) certification process tests knowledge of Microsoft Office software such as Word, Excel, Access, Power Point, Project, and Outlook. There are presently three levels of certification: Master, Expert, and Specialist.

To earn a Specialist certification, the user must demonstrate the ability to use the software's basic features, such as cut, copy, and paste. To earn an Expert certification, the user must be able to use all of the features included in the Specialist certification, plus more advanced features. For Microsoft Word, these features would include modifying the contents of tables, setting up automatic calculations for tables, and embedding worksheets. To earn a Master certification, you must demonstrate expert-level skill in five Office products. You must also be able to embed in and freely exchange information between the five products.

As a technician and not a secretary, why would you want to learn these products in detail? When you become a technical support person for a large or small company, people automatically think of you as somewhat of an expert in all areas of computers and system information. Automatically, they feel you are qualified to advise them about software, monitors, and even Internet service providers. For example, a person may want to know how to perform a mail merge in Word. After all, you are supposed to be the expert on computers. If you are unable to answer the question, the customer may perceive you as being poorly trained, even if the question falls outside the scope of your job.

A good way to increase your value to a company is to master popular software, such as Word, Access, Excel, and Power Point. You will probably be asked more questions about these products than questions about hardware, operating systems, or drivers.

MCP

The Microsoft Certified Professional (MCP) certificate denotes expertise in one or more of the Microsoft software products. An MCP certificate is commonly earned while in the pursuit of a more advanced certificate such as MCSE. It is a way of gaining instant certification as soon as you pass one of the exams that lead to the MCSE certification. It states that you are expert in one of the many areas required for MCSE, but are not an MCSE as of yet.

MCDST

The Microsoft Certified Desktop Support Technician (MCDST) is one of the very latest of the Microsoft certifications. It is designed to measure the skills necessary to support end users and troubleshoot Microsoft desktop environments. The certification consists of two core examinations. One exam centers on a Microsoft desktop operating system and the other on Microsoft desktop applications. A candidate must pass both exams to become an MCDST. This is a certification you may wish to obtain after finishing this course. It is a likely certification step toward a job as a help desk specialist or as part of a network support team in a corporate environment. Many of the skills learned for PC support are directly related to the skills required for the MCDST.

MCSE

The Microsoft Certified Systems Engineer (MCSE) is a certification based on the ability of the candidate to design, implement, maintain, upgrade, troubleshoot, and administer a network system based on the Microsoft's Windows 2000 and 2003 platform. Some job titles requiring this certification are systems engineer, technical support engineer, systems analysts, network analysts, and technical consultant. It is not unusual for a person seeking this certificate to dedicate one to two years of constant study.

There is not one test but a series of examinations leading to certification. A typical candidate is a person who has been working with large network systems of between 200 and 26,000 users spread over 5 to 150 physical locations. This certification requires expertise in a desktop operating system, network design, and administration. Requirements are constantly changing. Check the Microsoft Web site for up-to-date information.

MCSA

The Microsoft Certified Systems Administrator (MCSA) certificate is designed to prove competency and skills required to implement, administer, and troubleshoot a Windows 2000 or 2003 network system. This certification is designed for a person who wishes to specialize in network support and administration. MCSA certification is not as difficult to obtain as MCSE certification. It requires a less intense series of exams. The MCSA can be obtained while working toward the MCSE. Many of the required series of examinations are the same as those required to receive MCSE certification

If you choose to earn several CompTIA certifications, it can help you earn an MCSA certificate. A+ certification in combination with Network+ or Server+ certification will count toward this particular Microsoft certification. Always check the Microsoft and CompTIA Web sites for the very latest information about reciprocal certification agreements.

MCSD

The Microsoft Certified Solution Developer (MCSD) certificate is awarded to individuals who prove they have the ability to design, implement, and administer business solutions using Microsoft Office or BackOffice products. In other words, they can set up a network system for a business based on the individual business needs, select the appropriate software packages, design the hardware requirements or specifications, and install and maintain the system. This certification area would be most appropriate for persons who work in sales and promotion of specific office products rather than a technician.

MCDBA

The Microsoft Certified Database Administrator (MCDBA) certificate is earned by proving expertise in creating, maintaining, optimizing, installing, and managing the SQL databases server (a Microsoft database server design). Database technology is used extensively by business, government, educational, and research institutions.

Novell Certification Areas

Novell offers several certifications, such as CNA, CNE, and Master CNE. The certifications are tied directly to Novell software products such as NetWare 6. The Novell certifications are similar to the Microsoft certifications. However, they prove knowledge of Novell network products rather than Microsoft products. You can learn more detailed information about the Novell certifications by visiting Novell's website (www.novell.com/education).

CNA

The Novell Certified Network Administrator (CNA) certificate is awarded for skills necessary to set up and manage user stations and manage network system resources such as files, printers, and software. It requires that the person understand how to monitor network performance, provide remote access to the network, and possess various other network skills. Novell recommends that a CNA candidate have a CompTIA Network+ certification.

CNE

The Certified Network Engineer (CNE) certificate proves expertise in a wider range of network applications than the CNA. You must prove expertise in WAN and LAN design, development, implementation, support, and troubleshooting. The CNE may specialize in one particular area of network software such as NetWare 5 or NetWare 6.

Cisco Training and Certificates

Cisco Corporation provides training opportunities at the high schools and colleges all over the United States. The Cisco sites are referred to as networking academies. These academies emphasize network design, implementation, and troubleshooting using Cisco products. Cisco products are widely used for network communications. The academy courses are designed as a combination of lecture, textbook, on-line learning, and hands-on laboratory activities.

Some of the certificates available through Cisco are Cisco Certified Network Associate (CCNA), Cisco Certified Design Associate (CCDA), Cisco Certified Network Professional (CCNP), Cisco Certified Design Professional (CCDP), and

Cisco Certified Internet Expert (CCIE). The certificates are obtained by passing specific Cisco examinations. You can learn more about the certifications offered and locate the Cisco academy nearest you by going to the Cisco Web site (www.cisco.com).

Other Certifications

Many other companies have certification programs as well as the ones outlined in these sections. These companies include 3-Com, Corel, Nortel Networks, Compaq, Red Hat Linux, and Oracle. Check the related Web sites for in-depth information about the exams including exam outlines, study materials, schools and training available, and prerequisites.

Job Search Ideas

Finding a job can be a time-consuming and difficult task. The Occupational Outlook Handbook has excellent tips for conducting a job search. Start by talking to your parents, neighbors, teachers, and guidance counselors. These people may know of job openings that have not been advertised. Read the classified ads in the newspaper, especially the Sunday editions. Look through the Yellow Pages to generate a list of local companies, their addresses, and phone numbers. Companies are grouped according to industry in the Yellow Pages. You may see companies to contact.

City, county, and state employment services may also provide useful job leads. Private employment agencies might also provide leads, but they often charge a fee for a job placement.

The Internet is a valuable source of job information. Almost every computer related site has a section devoted to job opportunities. You can often complete an application online. There are also many Web sites that will allow you to post a resume.

Job Interviews

The three most important factors that determine your ability to land a job are your work history, technical expertise, and the job interview. A work history tells the employer a lot about you as a future employee, even if the job experiences are unrelated to the job you are applying for. You may just be entering the IT profession, but a solid recommendation from a past employer can make the difference. A recommendation from a former employer shows that you have been a valuable and dependable employee. A person with no work history is a gamble in most employers' eyes.

Prior technical experiences can prove to be a real asset, whether they are past jobs or formal training. Other applicants may have no technical employment history or technical training. They may have simple, informal experience helping friends with their home computer and now believe they can handle the job. This is where your training and work history puts you ahead of others.

The job interview is the major factor in determining if an applicant gets the job. The job interview gives the employer a chance to evaluate the applicant through a series of questions. The way a question is answered is at times more important than the answer itself. For example, if an employer asks, "What would you do if you could not fix a PC problem?" The way you answer the question may tell the employer about your character, your confidence, and your ability to work with others. The employer is looking for certain traits in the individual he or she is about to hire. Some common traits are honesty, confidence, dependability, and the ability to work well as a team member. And while your physical attractiveness may not be important to an employer, your neat and clean appearance shows that you take pride in yourself and your work. Even if the job is a "backroom" position, dress well for the interview. Blue jeans and a T-shirt are never appropriate.

Employers may not ask the same questions of all applicants and will not usually be direct about the qualities they are seeking. The employer will ask questions to probe for the character and job related qualities they want. For example, an employer may ask you to describe a time you had a problem with a fellow employee. How was it resolved? The answer to this question can tell an experienced interviewer a lot about the character of the applicant. Once you have secured an interview, it is important to be prepared for it. Read the following tips for a successful interview.

Preparation for the Interview

An interview is perhaps the most critical stage in a job search, and a process that you can control to a great extent. A good interview can cause an employer to overlook a lack of experience or education. On the other hand, a poor interview can cause even the most qualified candidate to be passed over. The following are a few tips to help you prepare for your interview.

- Always learn about the prospective employer and the position. Many times this information is available on their Web site. This preparation lets the employer know you are truly interested in the company and that you possess the personal initiative to research and learn.
- Have a specific job or jobs in mind, generally at an entry level. Most companies do not begin a new employee in a high level job until they have proven their worth to the company.
- Review your qualifications for the job. Make sure your qualifications match those desired by the employer. Do not waste their time or yours by interviewing for a job that is far beyond your level.
- Prepare to answer broad questions about yourself. It is wise to practice interviewing with someone who has knowledge about job interviews. A family member or friend who regularly does hiring for a company can be a great help, even if they do not work in the field you are seeking. Practicing the interview will help you learn to control your natural nervousness and become more relaxed for the real thing.
- A quality resume can make a favorable impression on an employer. Use a good quality paper and a cover sheet. Make sure you have produced an original copy that they may keep.
- Arrive at least 15 minutes prior to the scheduled time of your interview, **Figure 22-6.** Showing up late for your interview does not enhance your prospects for the job. It displays a lack of care for the job, the company, and your interview person or committee. Locate the building in advance and figure how much time it will take to get there. Consider the traffic conditions for that time of day. Do a practice run so that you will know exactly how to get to the interview and the length of time it will take you to arrive.
- If you really want that job, have a backup plan in case you have difficulty with your transportation.

Figure 22-6. Arrive fifteen minutes early for your interview. Make a practice run to the location of your interview a day or two before the actual interview. This will help you predict how long it will take you to arrive at the interview site.

Personal Appearance

The first impression you make on an employer is critical. People are summarily judged on their outward appearance. If you look and act professional, you will make a favorable impression on your interviewer and future coworkers.

- Dress appropriately and be well groomed.
- Blue jeans and a T-shirt are never appropriate. Regardless of the job conditions, men and women should always dress up rather than down for an interview. Do not dress for a party. Dress for a formal business setting.
- Smile and use a firm handshake when you introduce yourself. This shows your confidence, **Figure 22-7**.
- Do not chew gum, eat candy, or smoke at any time when you are on the company premises. This is not a social visit and you may likely encounter your prospective supervisor on the property prior to your interview.

The Interview

Once the interview begins, your responses to questions are being actively evaluated. The interviewer is trying to determine your work ethic, attitude, intelligence, and competency based on your answers and body language. The following are tips to help you avoid creating the wrong impression on the interviewer.

Figure 22-7. A neat appearance, good posture, and a firm handshake demonstrate self-confidence.

- Answer all questions to the best of your ability, and if you do not know the answer, simply say so. Do not try to make an answer up. Express your willingness to learn any new topics with which you may not be familiar. The person conducting the interview is an expert. You will not fool them by trying to invent an answer. Admit your limitations, and you will find they will most likely respect your honesty.
- Use proper English and avoid slang. Speak slowly and concisely. Never use foul language, even in a joking manner.
- Use good manners. Always address the persons who are conducting the interview as "Sir" and "Ma'am." Even if you are personally acquainted with your prospective employer, treat them with polite formality. Do not become complacent or presume you have the job.
- Convey a sense of cooperation and enthusiasm. Your body language will convey a lot about your personality. Keep smiling. Have a look of confidence. Sit up straight and look the interviewer directly in the eyes. Do not slump, or look away as you talk.
- You can ask questions about the position and the organization, but limit your questions to operations or conditions that you do not understand. Much information regarding a job can be obtained prior to the interview, especially if the information was posted. Unless it has not been covered in a job posting, uncovered through your research, or discussed by your prospective employer during the interview, do not ask questions regarding salary.
- Remember that the interview has not ended when you start asking questions. As a matter of fact, your questions can reveal even more to the employer. Asking how many breaks you will get during a day will send an undesirable message to the employer. It is not required that you ask questions, especially if the interview has been thorough, but do not hesitate if you believe that there is pertinent information that you must know.
- Remember that there will be additional time to make any clarifications or salary negotiations after you are offered the job.

Employer Testing

Employer testing is very common today as part of the job interview process. An employer can tell a lot about your technical knowledge and communications skills through a test, especially if handwritten answers are required. Written responses reveal a lot about an interviewee, **Figure 22-8.**

- Be sure you understand all written test directions. If you are unclear about the instructions, verbally confirm them before you begin the test.
- Read each question carefully.
- Write legibly and clearly. Printing helps if your handwriting is poor.
- Budget your time wisely and don't dwell on one question.

Information to Bring to an Interview

The common information required at an interview is social security number, driver's license number, and a copy of your resume. On your resume, make a complete and chronological list of your education and training. List all of your

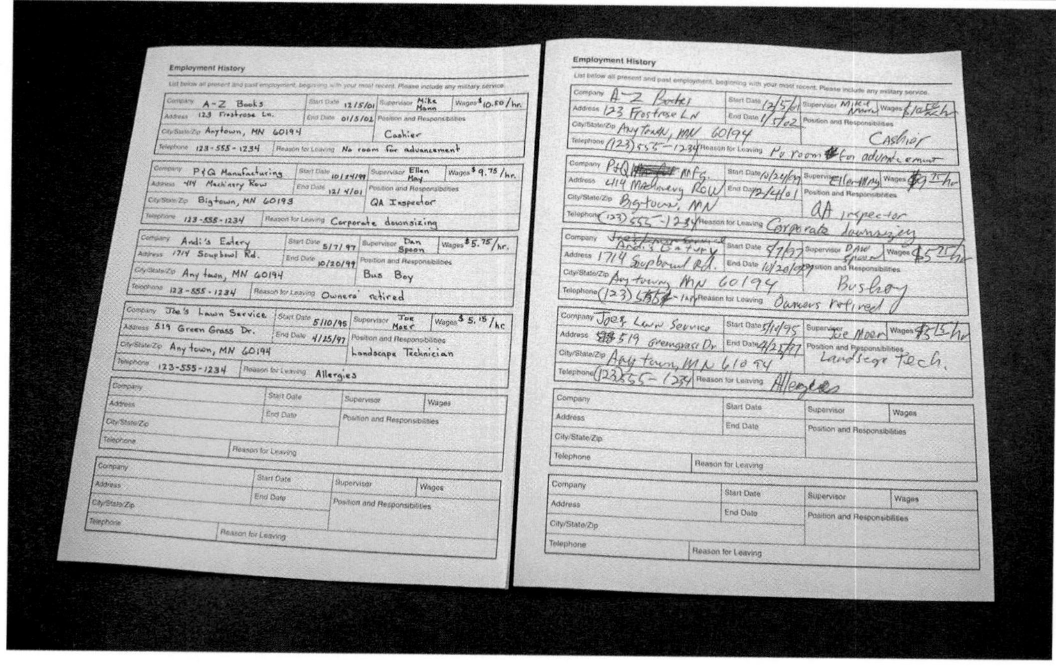

Figure 22-8.
Write neatly (application on left) when filling out employment applications or taking tests. Poor penmanship (application on the right) can make a bad impression on a prospective employer.

past employment in sequence, and do not leave blank dates. If you stopped your employment to go to school, note the dates. This ensures that your potential employer does not think you are trying to leave out an employer who may not give you a good reference. List the reasons for any breaks in your employment history.

You may wish to include copies of training and award certificates, transcripts, and letters of reference with your resume. Typically, these will be verified anyway if listed on your resume. Including copies with your resume may speed up the verification procedure.

Three References

It is customary to provide references for a job. The quality of your references can mean a great deal to the employer. Some good reference people are teachers, past employers, supervisors, and fellow employees. Friends, family, and your clergy are not considered good references. Get permission from people before using them as a reference. For each reference, provide name, address, telephone number, and occupation. Also, note if the person was a past supervisor.

Summary

- An information technology (IT) position requires continuous education.
- A recognized certification is a way of proving your expertise in a computer technology specialty.
- An entrepreneur owns and operates a private business.
- CompTIA offers examinations for A+, CDIA, i-Net+, Network+, Server+, and Linux+ certifications.

- After gaining A+ Certification, Network+ is a good next step in your career advancement.
- Microsoft, Novell, Cisco, and many other companies also offer certifications based on examinations.
- Arrive early or on time for your interview.
- Smile and show a sense of cooperation and enthusiasm during the interviewing process.
- If tested by the prospective employer, be sure you understand instructions for the examination.
- When you are interviewing for a new job, be sure to take your social security card, driver's license, and a quality resume.
- Be able to produce a list of at least three references, including addresses and phone numbers. List only people who have agreed to be references.

Review Questions

Answer the following questions on a separate sheet of paper. Please do not write in this book.

1. Why is continuing education required for an employee in the IT industry?
2. What is an entrepreneur?
3. What items should you take to a job interview?
4. What information must be provided in your list of references?

For Discussion

1. What type of career would you like to have? How much training and education will this career require?
2. What traits do you think are required of successful entrepreneurs?
3. What professional goals do you hope to accomplish in the next five years? The next ten years?

Suggested Laboratory Activities

1. Download the requirements for a Microsoft System Engineer Certificate and a Microsoft System Administrator Certificate. Go to Microsoft's Web site for the latest list of requirements and exams that must be taken.
2. Download the test information for a Windows 2003 exam.
3. Download the test information for MCDST certification.
4. Go to Novell's Web site and download the requirements for Novell CNA and CNE.
5. Do a search to see what colleges will give degree credit for certifications. See how much credit can be obtained and under what conditions.
6. Locate the Cisco Academy nearest you. How much does it cost, and how long does it last?

PC technicians must continuously learn about new software and hardware to meet their employer's changing demands and keep abreast of new technology.

Appendix A

List of Acronyms

A

ac	alternating current
ACK	acknowledge
ACPI	Advanced Configuration and Power Interface
ADSL	asymmetrical digital subscriber line
AGP	accelerated graphics port
AI	artificial intelligence
AIFF	Audio Interchange File Format
ALU	arithmetic logic unit
AM	amplitude modulation
AMD	Active Matrix Display *also* Advanced Micro Devices
ANSI	American National Standards Institute
AOL	America Online
APC	American Power Conversion
API	application program interface
APM	Advanced Power Management
ARCnet	Attached Resource Computer network
ARP	Address Resolution Protocol
ARPANET	Advanced Research Project Agency Network
ASCII	American Standard Code for Information Interchange
ASP	application service provider
ASPI	Advanced SCSI Programming Interface
ASR	Automated System Recovery
ATA	AT Attachment
ATAPI	AT Attachment Packet Interface
ATM	Asynchronous Transfer Mode
AUI	Attachment Unit Interface
A/V	audio/video
AWG	American Wire Gauge

B

BASIC	Beginner's All-purpose Symbolic Instruction Code
BAT	batch file
BBS	bulletin board system
BCC	blind carbon copy
BCD	binary coded decimal
BCU	Bus Controller Unit *also* BIOS Configuration Utility
BDC	backup domain controller
BEDO DRAM	Burst EDO Dynamic Random Access Memory
BFT	Binary File Transfer
BGP	Border Gateway Protocol
BIOS	basic input/output system
BIT	binary digit
BIU	Bus Interface Unit
BMP	bit map
BNC	British Naval Connector, *or* Bayonet Nut Connector, *or* Bayonet-Neill Concelman
BOOTP	Bootstrap Protocol
bps	bits per second
Bps	bytes per second
BRI	Basic-Rate Interface
BSD	Berkeley Software Distribution UNIX

C

CA	Certificate Authority
CAD	computer-aided design, *or* computer-aided drafting
CAD/CAM	computer-aided design/computer-aided manufacturing
CAL	Client Access License *also* Computer-Assisted Learning *also* Computer-Aided Logistics
CAM	computer-aided manufacturing
CAV	constant linear velocity
CBT	computer-based training
CCD	charge-coupled device
CCITT	Comité Consultatif International Téléphonique et Télégraphique
CD	carrier detect *also* compact disc *also* collision detect
CDFS	CD-ROM File System
CD-R	Compact Disc Recordable
CD-ROM	Compact Disc Read Only Memory
CD-RW	Compact Disc Rewriteable
CD-WO	Compact Disc, Write-Once
CD-WORM	Compact Disc, Write-Once Read-Many
CGA	color/graphics adapter
CGM	Computer Graphics Metafile
CHAP	Challenge Handshake Authentication Protocol
CHS	Cylinder, Head, Sector
CID	Certified ID *also* caller identification
CIDR	Classless Inter-Domain Routing
CIFS	Common Internet File System
CISC	complex instruction set computer
CLV	constant linear velocity
CMOS	complementary metal oxide semiconductor
CMTS	Cable Modem Termination System
CMYK	cyan, magenta, yellow, black
CNA	Certified Netware Administrator *also* Cisco Networking Academies
COA	Certificate of Authority
COBOL	common business oriented language
codec	compressor/decompressor
cpi	characters per inch
cps	characters per second *also* cycles per second
CPU	central processing unit
CRC	cyclic redundancy check
CRT	cathode ray tube
CSMA/CA	Carrier Sense Multiple Access with Collision Avoidance
CSMA/CD	Carrier Sense Multiple Access with Collision Detection
CSU/DSU	Channel Service Unit/Data Service Unit
CTS	clear to send

D

DAC	digital-to-analog converter
daemon	Disk and Execution Monitor
DARPA	Defense Advanced Research Projects Agency
DAT	digital audio tape
dB	decibel
dc	direct current
DCC	Direct Cable Connection
DDL	Dynamic Data Link *also* Document Description Language *also* Data Definition Language
DDR	Double Data Rate *also* Dynamic Desktop Router
DDR-SDRAM	Double Data Rate Synchronous Dynamic Random Access Memory
DEC	Digital Equipment Corporation
DEK	Data Encryption Key
DHCP	Dynamic Host Configuration Protocol
DHTML	Dynamic HTML
DIB	Dual Independent Bus
DIMM	dual in-line memory module
DIN	Deutsche Industrie norm (connector)
DIP	dual in-line package
DLC	Data Link Control
DLL	Dynamic Link Library
DMA	direct memory access

DNS	Domain Name System, *or* Domain Name Service
DOCSIS	Data Over Cable Service Interface Specification
DoD ARPA	Department of Defense's Advanced Research Project Agency
DoS	denial of services
DOS	disk operating system
dpi	dots per inch
DRAM	dynamic random access memory
DRDRAM	Direct Rambus Dynamic Random Access Memory
DSIMM	dual single in-line memory module
DSL	digital subscriber line
DSR	data set ready
DSS	digital satellite system
DTE	Data Terminal Equipment
DTR	data terminal ready
DUN	Dial-Up Networking
DVB	Digital Video Broadcasting
DVD	Digital Versatile Disc, *or* Digital Video Disc
DVDR	Digital Video Disc Recordable
DVI	Digital Video Interactive
DVM	Data/Voice Multiplexer

E

EBCDIC	Extended Binary-Coded Decimal Interchange Code
ECC	error correcting code
ECMA	European Computer Manufacturers Association
ECP	Enhanced Capabilities Port
EDO	Extended Data Output
EDO DRAM	Enhanced Data Output Dynamic Random Access Memory
EDSI	Enhanced Small Devices Interface
EEPROM	electrically erasable programmable read only memory
EFS	encrypted file system
EGA	enhanced graphics adapter
EHF	extreme high frequency
EIA	Electronics Industries Association
EIDE	Enhanced IDE
EIGRP	Enhanced Interior Gateway Routing Protocol
EISA	Extended Industry Standard Architecture
EMI	electromagnetic interference
EMM	Expanded Memory Manager
EMP	Electromagnetic Pulse
EMS	expanded memory standard
ENIAC	Electronic Numerical Integrator Analyzer and Calculator
EOF	end of file
EOT	end of transmission, *or* end of text, *or* end of table
EP	electrophotographic process
EPA	Environmental Protection Agency
EPP	Enhanced Parallel Port
EPROM	erasable programmable read only memory
EPS	Encapsulated PostScript
ERD	Emergency Repair Disk
ESC	escape
ESD	electrostatic discharge
ESDI	Enhanced Small Device Interface
ESDRAM	Enhanced Synchronous Dynamic Random Access Memory
ESMTP	Extended Simple Mail Transfer Protocol
ESP	Encapsulated Security Payload *also* Enhanced Serial Port
ETSI	European Telecommunications Standards Institute
EXT	external

F

FAQ	frequently asked questions
FAT	file allocation table

FC	fiber channel
FCC	Federal Communications Commission
FCPGA	Flip Chip Pin Grid Array
FDD	floppy disk drive
FDDI	Fiber Distributed Data Interface
FDHD	floppy drive, high-density
FDI	flat display *also* floppy drive *also* floppy disk *also* full duplex
FDM	Frequency Division Multiplexing
FF	form feed
FIFO	first in first out
FLOPS	floating-point operations per second
FM	frequency modulation
FORTRAN	formula translator
FPM	Fast Page Mode
FPU	floating-point unit
FRU	field replaceable unit
FSB	front side bus
FTP	File Transfer Protocol, *or* File Transport Protocol

G

Gb	gigabit
GB	gigabyte
GDI	Graphical Device Interface
GHz	gigahertz
GIF	graphics interchange format
GUI	graphical user interface

H

HCL	Hardware Compatibility List
HD	hard disk *also* high density
HDD	hard disk drive
HDSL	High Bit-rate Digital Subscriber Line
HDTV	High-Definition Television
HMA	high memory area
HP	Hewlett-Packard
HPFS	High Performance File System
HTML	Hypertext Markup Language
HTTP	Hypertext Transfer Protocol
Hz	Hertz

I

IANA	Internet Assigned Numbers Authority
IBM	International Business Machines
IC	integrated circuit
ICANN	Internet Corporation for Assigned Names and Numbers
ICF	Internet Connection Firewall
ICMP	Internet Control Message Protocol
ICS	Internet Connection Sharing
ID	Identification
IDE	Integrated Development Environment *also* Integrated Drive Electronics, *or* Intelligent Drive Electronics
IDN	Integrated Digital Network
IDSL	ISDN Subscriber Line
IE	Internet Explorer
IEEE	Institute of Electrical and Electronics Engineers
IETF	Internet Engineering Task Force
IIS	Internet Information Server
IMAP	Internet Message Access Protocol
I/O	input/output
IP	Internet Protocol
IPX	Internet Packet Exchange
IR	infrared
IRC	Internet Relay Chat
IrDA	Infrared Data Association
IRQ	interrupt request line
ISA	Industry Standard Architecture
ISDN	integrated services digital network
ISO	International Organization for Standardization
ISP	Internet Service Provider
IT	Information Technology
ITSP	Internet Telephony Service Provider
ITU	International Telecommunications Union

J

JPEG	Joint Photographic Experts Group

K

Kbps	kilobits per second
KBps	kilobytes per second
KHz	kilohertz

L

LAN	local area network
LBA	logical block addressing
LCD	liquid crystal display
LCN	Logical Cluster Number
LDAP	Lightweight Directory Access Protocol
LEC	local exchange carrier
LED	light emitting diode
Li-ion	lithium-ion
LLC	Logical Link Control
LPT	line printer terminal
LQ	letter quality
LSB	least significant bit
LSI	large-scale integration
LUN	logical unit number

M

MAC	media access code *also* media access control
MAN	metropolitan area network
MAPI	Message Application Programming Interface
MAU	Media Attachment Unit *also* Media Access Unit, *or* Multistation Access Unit
MB	megabytes *also* motherboard
Mb	megabit
MBps	megabytes per second
Mbps	megabits per second
MBR	Master Boot Record
MCA	Micro Channel Architecture
MCGA	multicolor/graphics array, *or* multicolor/graphics adapter
MDRAM	Multibank Dynamic Random Access Memory
Me	Millennium Edition (Windows)
MFT	Master File Table
MHz	megahertz
MIDI	musical instrument digital interface
MIME	Multipurpose Internet Mail Extensions
MIPS	million instructions per second
MO	magneto-optical
MODEM	modulator-demodulator
MOV	metal oxide varistor
MPEG	Moving Picture Experts Group
MSB	most significant bit
MS-DOS	Microsoft Disk Operating System
MZR	multiple zone recording

N

NAK	negative acknowledge, *or* not acknowledged
NAP	Network Access Point
NAS	Network Access Server *also* network attached storage
NAT	Network Address Translation
NBT	NetBIOS on TCP/IP
NDS	Netware Directory Services, *or* Novell Directory Services
NetBEUI	NetBIOS Enhanced User Interface
NetBIOS	Network Basic Input Output System
NFS	Network File System
NIC	network interface card
NiCad	nickel-cadmium
NiCd	nickel-cadmium
NiMH	Nickel-Metal Hydride
NOS	network operating system
NSP	Network Service Provider
NT	New Technology (Windows) *also* network terminator

NTFS New Technology File System

NVRAM Non-Volatile Random Access Memory

O

OC Optical Carrier

OCR optical character recognition

OCX OLE Custom Control, *or* OLE Control Extension

OEM original equipment manufacturer

OLE Object Linking and Embedding

OOP object-oriented programming

OOPL object-oriented programming language

OS operating system

OSI Open Systems Interconnection

OSPF Open Shortest Path First

OSR 2 OEM Service Release 2 (Windows 95)

OTDR Optical Time Domain Reflectometer

P

P2P peer-to-peer *also* point-to-point

PAP Password Authentication Protocol

PBX private branch exchange

PC personal computer *also* printed circuit

PCI Peripheral Component Interconnect

PCMCIA Personal Computer Memory Card International Association

PDA personal digital assistant

PDC primary domain controller

PDF Portable Document Format

PDL Page Description Language

PDU Protocol Data Unit, *or* Packet Data Unit

PEL Picture Element

Perl Practical Extraction and Report Language

PGA pin grid array *also* Professional Graphics Adapter

PGP Pretty Good Privacy

PIC Lotus Picture File

PIF Program Information File

PIN personal identification number

PING Packet Internet Groper

PIO Programmed Input/Output, *or* Programmable Input/Output

pixel Picture Element

PLC powerline communications

PLD Programmable Logical Device

PnP Plug and Play

PoP Point of Presence

POP Post Office Protocol

POP3 Post Office Protocol Version 3

POSIX Portable Operating System Interface for UNIX

POST power-on self-test

POTS plain old telephone service

PPGA Plastic Pin Grid Array

ppm page(s) per minute

PPP Point-to-Point Protocol

PPTP Point-to-Point Tunneling Protocol

PRI Primary Rate Interface

PROM programmable read only memory

PS/2 Personal System 2

PSTN Public Switched Telephone Network

PVC permanent virtual circuit

Q

QIC Quarter-Inch Cartridge

QoS quality of service

R

RAID Redundant Array of Independent Disks, *or* Redundant Array of Inexpensive Disks

RAM random access memory

RAS Remote Access Server *also* Remote Access Service

RD receive data

RDRAM	Rambus Dynamic Random Access Memory
RF	radio frequency
RFC	Request for Comments
RGB	red, green, blue
RIMM	Rambus In-line Memory Modules
RIP	raster image processor *also* Routing Information Protocol
RISC	reduced instruction set computer
RJ-11/12/45	Registered Jacks
RLE	run-length encoding
ROM	read only memory
RS (RS-232)	recommended standard
RTF	rich text format
RTS	request to send

S

SAM	Security Accounts Manager
SANS	System Administration, Networking and Security Institute
SAP	Service Advertising Protocol
SCSI	Small Computer System Interface
SDRAM	Synchronous Dynamic Random Access Memory
SDSL	Symmetric Digital Subscriber Line
SEC	Single Edge Contact
SET	Secure Electronic Transaction
SGML	Standard Generalized Markup Language
SGRAM	Synchronous Graphic Random Access Memory
SIMM	single in-line memory module
SIP	single in-line package
SLDRAM	Sync Link Dynamic Random Access Memory
SLIP	Serial Line Internet Protocol
SMB	Server Message Block
SMM	System Management Mode
SMTP	Simple Mail Transfer Protocol
SNA	Systems Network Architecture
SNMP	Simple Network Management Protocol
SOHO	small-office/home-office
SOM	Start of Message *also* System Object Model
SONET	Synchronous Optical Network
SPARC	Scalable Processor Architecture
SPX	Sequenced Packet Exchange
SQL	structured query language
SRAM	static random access memory
SSL	Secure Sockets Layer
STP	shielded twisted pair *also* Secure Transfer Protocol
SVC	switched virtual circuit
SVG	Scalable Vector Graphics
SVGA	super video graphics array

T

TAPI	Telephony Application Programming Interface
TB	terabytes
TCO	Total Cost of Ownership
TCP	Transmission Control Protocol
TCP/IP	Transmission Control Protocol/Internet Protocol
TDM	Time Division Multiplexing
TDR	Time Domain Reflectometer
TFT	thin film transistor
TFT-LCD	thin film transistor liquid crystal display
TFTP	Trivial File Transfer Protocol
TI	Texas Instruments
TIFF	Tagged Image File Format
TLD	top-level domain
TPI	tracks per inch
TSR	terminate and stay resident
TTF	TrueType Font
TTL	time to live *also* transistor-transistor logic

TTY	Teletypewriter
TWAIN	Technology without an Interesting Name, *or* Toolkit without an Interesting Name

U

UART	universal asynchronous receiver-transmitter
UCS	universal character set
UDF	Universal Disk Format
UDMA	Ultra Direct Memory Access
UDP	User Datagram Protocol
UHF	ultra-high frequency
ULSI	ultra large scale integration
UMB	Upper Memory Block
UNC	Universal Naming Convention, *or* Uniform Naming Convention
UPI	universal peripheral interface
UPS	uninterruptible power supply
URI	Universal Resource Identifier
URL	Uniform Resource Locator
USB	Universal Serial Bus
UTP	Unshielded Twisted Pair

V

VAR	value-added reseller
VB	Visual Basic
VC	Virtual Circuit
VCN	Virtual Cluster Number
VDSL	very high data-rate digital subscriber line
VDT	video display terminal
VESA	Video Electronics Standards Association
VFAT	virtual file allocation table
VGA	video graphics array
VHF	very high frequency
VLAN	virtual local area network
VLB	Video Electronics Standards Association (VESA) local bus
VLSI	Very Large-Scale Integration
VMS	Virtual Memory System
VMM	Virtual Memory Manager
VoIP	voice over Internet protocol
VOM	volt-ohmmeter *also* volt-ohm milliameter
VPN	virtual private network
VR	virtual reality
VRAM	video random access memory
VxD	virtual device driver

W

W3C	World Wide Web Consortium
WAN	wide area network
WATS	wide area telephone service
WINS	Windows Internet Naming Service
WLAN	wireless local area network
WMF	Windows Metafile Format
WORM	write once, read many
WRAM	Windows Random Access Memory
WWW	World Wide Web
WYSIWYG	what you see is what you get

X

XGA	extended graphics array
XML	Extensible Markup Language
XMS	extended memory system

Y

Y2K	the year 2000

Z

ZIF	zero insertion force

Appendix B

Binary Math

Binary math accurately represents digital circuitry. In digital electronics, a circuit is either on or off or a voltage condition is high or low. For example, a digital circuit may have two distinct conditions: 5 volts present or 0 volts present.

Binary math uses only 2 numbers, 1 and 0, to represent an infinite range of numbers. The binary number system accomplishes this in basically the same way the decimal number system does, by placing numbers into discrete digit positions. The decimal number system fills these digits with values 0 through 9. The first digit position is commonly referred to as the 1s. The maximum value that can be entered here is 9. The second digit position must therefore be the 10s. If the maximum value of 9 is entered in both the 10s position and the ls position, the resulting number is 99. The third position must therefore be the 100s position, and so on. Notice in **Figure B-1** that each of the positions can be expressed as an exponent of the base 10.

Digit Positions	1s	10s	100s	1,000s	10,000s	100,000s
Exponent	10^0	10^1	10^2	10^3	10^4	10^5
Range	0–9	10–99	100–999	1000–9999	10,000–99,999	100,000–999,999

Figure B-1.

Note:

The Range row indicates the range of number for which the selected digit position would be the leftmost digit, not the range of number that could contain that digit position.

Look at the number 2753.
There are:

2-1000s	2000
7-100s	700
5-10s	50
3-ls	3
Total	2753

Add the values together for a total of 2753.

Binary numbers are expressed in similar fashion. However, instead of each digit position being 10 times greater than the position before it, the value of each position is double that of the position before it. See **Figure B-2.**

Digit Positions	1s	2s	4s	8s	16s	32s	64s	128s
Exponent	2^0	2^1	2^2	2^3	2^4	2^5	2^6	2^7
Range	0–1	2–3	4–7	8–15	16–31	32–63	64–127	128–255

Figure B-2.

Look at the binary number 101011000001 for example.

There are:

1-2048s	2048
0-1024s	0
1-512s	512
0-256s	0
1-128s	128
1-64s	64
0-32s	0
0-16s	0
0-8s	0
0-4s	0
0-2s	0
1-ls	1
Total	2753

As you can see, 101011000001 is the binary equivalent of 2753, **Figure B-3.**

2048s	1024s	512s	256s	128s	64s	32s	16s	8s	4s	2s	1s
1	0	1	0	1	1	0	0	0	0	0	1

Figure B-3.

To convert the binary number to a decimal number, simply insert the value assigned to the location when a binary number 1 is in the location and then add the decimal numbers together. See **Figure B-4.**

32s	16s	8s	4s	2s	1s
1	0	1	1	0	1
32	+	8 +	4	+	1 = 45

Figure B-4.

When converting a decimal number to a binary number, you simply reverse the previous operation. For example, to convert the decimal number 178 to a binary number, you must divide it by a series of "powers of 2." The "powers of 2" are 1, 2, 4, 8, 16, 32, 64, 128, 256, 512, 1024, 2048, and so on.

To convert the decimal number 178 to binary, start by finding the largest "power of 2" that does not exceed 178. The largest "power of 2" value that does not exceed 178 is 128 (2^7). Place a 1 in the binary number position that represents 128. See **Figure B-5.**

Powers of 2	128	64	32	16	8	4	2	1
Binary Digit	1							

Figure B-5.

Subtracting 128 from 178 leaves 50. Fifty is less than 64 (2^6), the next smaller "power of 2." Therefore, you must insert a 0 in the 64s position, as seen in **Figure B-6.**

Powers of 2	128	64	32	16	8	4	2	1
Binary Digit	1	0						

Figure B-6.

Next, 50 is larger than 32 (2^5), so place a 1 in the 32s position. See **Figure B-7.**

Powers of 2	128	64	32	16	8	4	2	1
Binary Digit	1	0	1					

Figure B-7.

Next, subtract 32 from 50 and the difference is 18. The 18 is larger than 16 (2^4), so place a 1 in the 16s position. See **Figure B-8.**

Powers of 2	128	64	32	16	8	4	2	1
Binary Digit	1	0	1	1				

Figure B-8.

Subtracting 16 from 18, leaves 2. The 2 is smaller than the next two "powers of 2," 8 (2^3) and 4 (2^2). That means the next two positions in the binary number are both 0s. See **Figure B-9.**

Powers of 2	128	64	32	16	8	4	2	1
Binary Digit	1	0	1	1	0	0		

Figure B-9.

The next "power of 2" is 2 (2^1), and the number remaining from the last step is also 2. Therefore, a 1 goes into the 2s position. See **Figure B-10.**

Powers of 2	128	64	32	16	8	4	2	1
Binary Digit	1	0	1	1	0	0	1	

Figure B-10.

There are no decimal numbers remaining, so the ls position should be filled with a 0. The binary equivalent of the decimal number 178 is 10110010, **Figure B-11.**

Powers of 2	128	64	32	16	8	4	2	1
Binary Digit	1	0	1	1	0	0	1	0

Figure B-11.

Appendix C

Number Conversion Table			
Decimal	Binary	Octal	Hexadecimal
0	000000	0	0
1	000001	1	1
2	000010	2	2
3	000011	3	3
4	000100	4	4
5	000101	5	5
6	000110	6	6
7	000111	7	7
8	001000	10	8
9	001001	11	9
10	001010	12	A
11	001011	13	B
12	001100	14	C
13	001101	15	D
14	001110	16	E
15	001111	17	F
16	010000	20	10
17	010001	21	11
18	010010	22	12
19	010011	23	13
20	010100	24	14
21	010101	25	15
22	010110	26	16
23	010111	27	17
24	011000	30	18
25	011001	31	19
26	011010	32	1A
27	011011	33	1B
28	011100	34	1C
29	011101	35	1D
30	011110	36	1E

Number Conversion Table (continued)			
Decimal	**Binary**	**Octal**	**Hexadecimal**
31	011111	37	1F
32	100000	40	20
33	100001	41	21
34	100010	42	22
35	100011	43	23
36	100100	44	24
37	100101	45	25
38	100110	46	26
39	100111	47	27
40	101000	50	28
41	101001	51	29
42	101010	52	2A
43	101011	53	2B
44	101100	54	2C
45	101101	55	2D
46	101110	56	2E
47	101111	57	2F
48	110000	60	30
49	110001	61	31
50	110010	62	32
51	110011	63	33
52	110100	64	34
53	110101	65	35
54	110110	66	36
55	110111	67	37
56	111000	70	38
57	111001	71	39
58	111010	72	3A
59	111011	73	3B
60	111100	74	3C
61	111101	75	3D
62	111110	76	3E
63	111111	77	3F

Appendix D

Table of Standard ASCII Characters		
0	NUL	Null
1	SOH	Start of header
2	STX	Start of text
3	ETX	End of text
4	EOT	End of transmission
5	ENQ	Enquiry
6	ACK	Acknowledgment
7	BEL	Bell
8	BS	Backspace
9	HT	Horizontal tab
10	LF	Line feed
11	VT	Vertical tab
12	FF	Form feed
13	CR	Carriage return
14	SO	Shift out
15	SI	Shift in
16	DLE	Data link escape
17	DC1	Device control 1
18	DC2	Device control 2
19	DC3	Device control 3
20	DC4	Device control 4
21	NAK	Negative acknowledgment
22	SYN	Synchronous idle
23	ETB	End of transmit block
24	CAN	Cancel
25	EM	End of medium
26	SUB	Substitute
27	ESC	Escape
28	FS	File separator
29	GS	Group separator
30	RS	Record separator
31	US	Unit separator
32	SP	Space
33	!	
34	"	
35	#	
36	$	
37	%	
38	&	
39	'	
40	(	
41	)	
42	*	
43	+	
44	,	
45	-	
46	.	
47	/	
48	0	
49	1	
50	2	
51	3	
52	4	
53	5	
54	6	
55	7	
56	8	
57	9	
58	:	
59	;	
60	<	
61	=	
62	>	
63	?	
64	@	
65	A	
66	B	
67	C	
68	D	
69	E	
70	F	
71	G	
72	H	
73	I	
74	J	
75	K	
76	L	
77	M	
78	N	
79	O	
80	P	
81	Q	
82	R	
83	S	
84	T	
85	U	
86	V	
87	W	
88	X	
89	Y	
90	Z	
91	[	
92	\	
93	]	
94	^	
95	_	
96	`	
97	a	
98	b	
99	c	
100	d	
101	e	
102	f	
103	g	
104	h	
105	i	
106	j	
107	k	
108	l	
109	m	
110	n	
111	o	
112	p	
113	q	
114	r	
115	s	
116	t	
117	u	
118	v	
119	w	
120	x	
121	y	
122	z	
123	{	
124	|	
125	}	
126	~	
127	DEL	

Glossary

A

A+ Certification: Certification awarded on successful completion of the A+ Core Hardware and A+ Operating Systems Technologies exams.

Accelerated Graphics Port (AGP): A bus designed exclusively for the video card. It supports data transfer of 32 bits at 254.3 MBps, 508.6 MBps, 1.017 GBps, and 2.034 GBps.

access point: A bridge that connects a wireless network to a cabled network.

access time: The amount of time that passes between the issue of the read command and when the first data bit is read from the CD.

account: Contains all the security information describing an individual user.

active hub: Has a source of power connected to it. When a signal is received by an active hub, it is regenerated.

active partition: The designated boot disk for the system.

active-matrix display: An LCD display in which each individual cell in the grid has its own individual transistor.

actuator arm: The device that moves the read/write head over the disk.

address bus: A bus system that connects the CPU with the main memory module. It identifies memory locations where data is to be stored or retrieved.

ad-hoc network: A wireless network formed between two or more wireless devices such as a full-size PC and a notebook PC.

Advanced Power Management (APM): A power saving design that is managed by the operating system.

Advanced SCSI Programming Interface (ASPI): An interface that allows CD devices to communicate with SCSI system components.

alkaline batteries: Common batteries found in small devices such as TV remote controls and some palmtops.

alternating current (ac): Electrical current that reverses direction cyclically.

amperes: A scale used in measuring the volume of electron flow in a circuit.

analog: A system using a continuous, infinite range of values.

anti-static wrist strap: A strap, typically worn around the wrist, that connects the technician to ground and bleeds off any electrostatic charge.

application service provider (ASP): Provides software applications to a personal digital assistant (PDA) or palmtop by downloading the application from a provider as needed.

application software: Software designed for a specific purpose such as creating databases or spreadsheets, word processing, producing graphics, or just for entertainment.

Archie: An Internet protocol, maintained by McGill University in Montreal, that allows you to search for information on the Internet by filename.

arithmetic logic unit (ALU): A CPU component that performs mathematical functions on data stored in the register area.

ASCII (American Standard Code for Information Interchange): The first attempt to standardize computer character codes among the varieties of hardware and software.

aspect ratio: Ratio of a display area's height and width.

assembly language: A low-level language in which a CPU's instruction set is written.

AT attachment (ATA): A standard for disk drive interface that integrates the controller into the disk drive. Often referred to as IDE or EIDE.

AT Attachment Packet Interface (ATAPI): The interface used for standard IBM PC AT and compatible systems for accessing CD devices.

ATM: A high-speed network system design that allows a mixture of voice, video, and data to be transmitted on the same line.

Automated System Recovery (ASR): Utility that automatically restores critical files that were backed up by the Windows XP Backup utility.

Automatic Skip Driver Agent: Tool used to detect devices that keep Windows from starting.

B

back door virus: A virus designed to go undetected and leave a back door into your system. A back door is a hole in the security system of a computer or network.

backfeed: A type of ohmmeter reading in which the resistance is measured through the circuit components even though the circuit is open.

backoff interval: Period of time two network stations wait before trying to retransmit data after data packets from the two stations collide.

backplane: A circuit board with an abundance of slots along the length of the board.

backup domain controller (BDC): A file server that keeps a backup record of all accounts in case of failure of the primary domain controller.

bandwidth: The range of frequencies that an electronic cable or component is designed to carry.

bar code reader: A device that converts bar code images into data.

basic disk: The traditional FAT16, FAT32, and NTFS file storage systems.

basic input/output system (BIOS): Special firmware that permits the compatibility between the CPU and devices such as the hard drive, CD-ROM drive, and monitor.

battery: The component that supplies voltage to the CMOS chip. Without the battery, the information stored in the CMOS chip would be lost every time the computer was shut off.

baud rate: Analog frequency rate of modem transmission.

benchmark tests: Performance tests used to compare different hardware and software.

binary number system: A system in which all numbers are expressed as combinations of 0 and 1. Also known as the base 2 number system.

BIOS: A read only memory module designed to initiate three different activities: The power-on self-test (POST), the CMOS Setup program, and communications between the system hardware and operating system.

bit: Short for binary digit. A bit is a single binary unit of one or zero.

bitmap: A graphics standard for uncompressed encoding of images.

blue screen error: A blue screen that appears with an error code and then freezes the system. Also referred to by Microsoft as fatal errors, stop errors, and stop error messages.

Bluetooth: Royalty-free standard developed for short-range radio links between portable computers, mobile phones, and other portable devices so that major manufacturers could develop compatible equipment.

Bluetooth standard: Standard that ensures interoperability between different manufacturers of wireless devices by requiring that all radio transmission be in the 2.4 GHz radio band and transmit 1 Mbps at a maximum of 10 meters.

BNC (British Naval Connector): Connector used with coaxial cable.

booting: The process of starting the computer and loading the operating system.

bootstrap program: A short program that loads some basic files into memory, and then turns the startup operation over to the operating system.

bridge: A special piece of network equipment that is used to join two dissimilar networks segments together such as a wireless and an Ethernet 100BaseT network.

brouter: A combination router and bridge.

bubble jet printer: An inkjet printer.

buffer: An area to temporarily store data before transferring it to a device.

buffering: A technique used to play a downloaded file without skips or quiet spots during playback.

bugs: Errors in programming.

bus: A collection of conductors that connect multiple components, allowing them to work together for a specific purpose.

bus mastering: A feature of some buses that allows data to be transferred directly between two devices without the intervention of the CPU.

bus topology: A single conductor connects to all the computers on the network.

bus unit: The network of circuitry that connects all the other major components together, accepts data, and sends data through the input and output bus sections.

byte: Equal to eight bits.

C

cabinet (cab) files: Compressed files that contain the operating system software.

cable modem: Provides high-speed Internet access using lines designed for cable television.

cache: A temporary memory area that is used to separate and store incoming data and instructions and to speed up data transfer between components and peripherals.

carpal tunnel syndrome: An inflammation of the tendons in the hands and especially the wrist.

Carrier Sense Multiple Access with Collision Avoidance (CSMA/CA): Protocol used by wireless networks to control and ensure the delivery of data.

Carrier Sense Multiple Access with Collision Detection (CSMA/CD): Protocol used by Ethernet networks to control and ensure the delivery of data.

cathode ray tube (CRT): A picture tube in which a beam of electrons sweeps across a glass tube, exciting phosphorus dots in the screen.

CD-ROM File System (CDFS): Another name used for ISO 9660.

central processing unit (CPU): The brain of the computer. Most of the computer's calculating takes place in the central processing unit. In PCs, the central processing functions are carried out by a single chip, which is called a microprocessor.

chip: A semiconductor containing an integrated circuit.

chipset: A name for the collection of electronic circuitry required to carry out certain common motherboard functions.

Class A network: Large networks that can support up to 16 million hosts on each of 127 networks.

Class B network: Medium-sized networks that can support up to 65,000 hosts on each of 16,000 networks.

Class C network: Small networks that can support up to 254 hosts on each of 2 million networks.

clean room: A room where dust and foreign particles have been completely eliminated.

client/server model: Networking model in which the network is made up of computers that are either clients or servers.

client: Individual PC or workstation that accesses a Server's resources and shared files.

clock doubling: Running the CPU at a multiple of the bus frequency.

clusters: Composed of two or more sectors and are the smallest unit that a file will be stored in. Also referred to as allocation units.

CMOS Setup (or BIOS Setup): A program that allows you to identify the type of hard drive and other storage systems in the PC, set up a password for accessing the PC and the CMOS Setup program, select certain power management features, and select the boot order of bootable devices.

CMYK: Standard combination of colors (cyan, magenta, yellow, and black) used by color inkjet printers.

coaxial cable: A core conductor surrounded by an insulator.

codec: Any hardware, software, or combination hardware and software that can compress and decompress data.

cold boot: Turning on the computer at the power switch.

color palette: A collection of possible different colors that can be displayed on a monitor.

color thermal printer: Printer that applies color by heating a special ribbon that is coated with wax-like material.

color/graphics adapter (CGA): A video standard that featured two resolutions: 320 × 200 in four colors and a higher resolution of 640 × 200 in two colors.

colored books: The set of books that outline disc system specifications.

Compact Disc Read Only Memory (CD-ROM): An optical disc able to store very large amounts of data.

Compact Disc-Recordable (CD-R): An optical storage media that uses photosensitive reflective dye to simulate the pits and lands of a standard CD.

Compact Disc-ReWritable (CD-RW): An improvement over the CD-R technology, featuring special discs that can be erased and rerecorded.

compiler: A special program that translates the higher-level language into machine language based on the CPU's instruction set.

complementary metal oxide semiconductor (CMOS): The chip that stores the BIOS Setup program data.

complex instruction set computer (CISC): A CPU with a more complex instruction set.

CompTIA: A not-for-profit, vendor-neutral organization that certifies the competency level of computer service technicians.

computer: An assemblage of electronic modules that interact with software to create, modify, transmit, store, and display data.

computer virus: A maliciously created software program that is written for the express purpose of causing damage to a computer system.

configured: Setup for use with specific hardware and software.

constant angular velocity (CAV): A method of reading data from a CD where the drive maintains the same RPM regardless of the data location.

constant linear velocity (CLV): A method of reading data from a CD where the speed of the CD drive adjusts so that points on the inside and outside of the disc are read at a constant linear velocity.

continuity: A state of connectedness. In electronics, an unbroken circuit is said to have continuity.

contrast ratio: A numeric expression in the form of a ratio that describes the amount of contrast between the darkest and lightest pixel in the image.

control bus: A bus which delivers command signals from the processor to devices.

control unit: A CPU component that controls the overall operation of the CPU.

conventional memory: The first 640KB of a PC's RAM.

cooling fan: A fan that supplies a constant stream of air across the computer components.

cooperative multitasking: One program dominating the operating system but allowing another program to run while the primary program is idle.

cross talk: The imposition of a signal on one pair of conductors by another pair of conductors that runs parallel to it.

current: The electron flow in a circuit.

cycle: The completed sequence of flow, first in one direction and then in the other.

cylinder: A vertical collection of one set of tracks.

D

data: Information, which can be presented in alpha/numeric form (such as ABC or 123), visual form (pictures), and audible form (like music or voices).

data bus: A bus used to move data between components.

Data Over Cable Service Interface Specification (DOCSIS): Standard for cable modems that allows any DOCSIS cable modem to communicate with any other DOCSIS cable modem.

data transfer rate: A measurement of how much data can be transferred from a CD to RAM in a set period of time.

decode unit: A CPU component that decodes instructions and data and transmits the data to other areas in an understandable format.

dedicated circuit: A circuit installed in an electrical power distribution system that is designed to serve only computer equipment.

dedicated server: Server with special functions, such as file servers, print servers, database servers, Web page servers, and administrative servers.

deflection yoke: The electromagnets used to deflect the electron beam in a CRT.

defragment: Rearranging clusters on the disk so each file is stored in consecutive clusters.

device bay: A drive bay designed to accommodate the easy hot swap of devices such as hard disk drives, tape drives, CD-RW drives, and DVD drives.

differential backup: Operation that saves files that have changed since the last full backup of all files. The archive bit is not reset.

digital: A system that uses discrete values.

digital camera: A type of camera that captures and stores images as digital data instead of on photographic film.

digital subscriber lines (DSL): Provide high-speed Internet access over telephone lines. A DSL can provide a constant connection to the Internet and can send both voice and data over the same line.

Digital Versatile Disc (DVD): The highest storage capacity of all laser-based CD storage types. Also called digital video disc.

digital-to-analog converter (DAC): A chip that converts the digital signal from the computer to an analog signal that is displayed on the computer's monitor.

digitizer pad: A pointing device consisting of a tablet and a puck or pen-like stylus.

direct current (dc): Electrical current that flows in one direction.

direct memory access (DMA): A combination of software and hardware that allows certain system devices direct access to the RAM.

directories: A file used to group other files together in a hierarchical file structure. A directory is analogous to a file folder in a conventional, paper filing system. Directories are referred to as folders in many operating systems.

DirectX Diagnostic Tool: Tool that looks at every DirectX program file to check for problems.

Disk Cleanup Utility: Utility that can be used to regain hard drive space such as that consumed by temporary files, files sitting in the Recycle Bin, unused Windows components, unneeded installed programs, and restore points created by System Restore.

disk operating system (DOS): An operating system typically requiring the user to issue text line commands to perform operations.

docking station: An electronic cradle that provides power for a laptop, allowing users to turn the laptop into a full-size PC.

domain: An organized collection of all groups and users on the network.

Domain Name Service (DNS): Translates domain names to IP addresses used on the Internet.

DOS system boot disk: A floppy disk that contains the files necessary to run a computer with DOS.

dot matrix printer: Printer that uses a pattern of very small dots to create text and images.

dot pitch: The distance between two color dots on the screen, measured in millimeters.

Dr. Watson: Troubleshooting software that collects information about the computer system during and just before a software application fault.

drivers: Software that enables proper communication between the PC and peripheral devices.

dual boot system: A system in which multiple operating systems are stored. The user chooses the operating system when the computer boots.

dual independent bus (DIB): A bus system architecture in which one bus connects to the main memory and the other connects with the L2 cache.

dual in-line memory module (DIMM): A memory module in which the edge connectors are located directly across the circuit board from each other and do not connect electrically.

dual in-line package (DIP): A memory chip that has two rows of connections, one row per side of the chip.

dye-sublimation printer: Printer that produces near photo quality printed images by vaporizing inks, which then solidify onto paper.

dynamic addressing: The act of automatically assigning IP addresses.

dynamic disk: An improved version of the NTFS file system.

dynamic execution: A term coined by Intel to describe the enhanced, the superscalar, and the multiple branch prediction features associated with the Pentium II processor.

Dynamic Host Configuration Protocol (DHCP): A protocol written to replace the manual setup of IP addresses on a network by assigning IP addresses dynamically (automatically) to the host PCs.

dynamic RAM (DRAM): A type of integrated circuit that utilizes capacitors to assist in storing data in the transistors.

E

EEPROM: Electrically erasable programmable read only memory.

EISA: An I/O (expansion) bus with a 32-bit data bus. Designed in response to IBM's MCA bus system. EISA buses are backward compatible with ISA cards. This means that an ISA card would fit and function in an EISA expansion slot.

electron guns: The components that produce the electron beam, which sweeps across the inside of the screen.

electrophotographic process (EP): A photographic process that uses a combination of static electricity, light, dry chemical compound, pressure, and heat.

electrostatic discharge (ESD): A release of energy (electrical current), created when an object with an electrostatic charge makes contact with a conductor.

encrypted file system (EFS): An NTFS native encryption system that uses a file encryption key (FEK) to encrypt and decrypt the file contents.

encryption: Method of encoding data that must be converted back to meaningful words by using an encryption key. The encryption key is a mathematical formula for substituting values in strings of data.

enhanced graphics adapter (EGA): A video standard that improved on the resolutions and color capabilities of the CGA standard.

Enhanced Integrated Drive Electronics (EIDE): An enhanced version of the IDE disk drive controller standard. The term is commonly used when referring to the AT Attachment.

Enhanced Parallel Port (EPP): A parallel port standard that allows a throughput as high as 2 MBps. The EPP is also referred to as the IEEE-1284 standard.

EPROM: Erasable programmable read only memory.

error code correction (ECC): An alternative form of data-integrity checking.

Ethernet network: Network that communicates by broadcasting information to all the computers on the network.

even parity checking: A data integrity checking method in which every time the number of bits counted is even, an extra bit of data is transmitted as a 1 to make the count odd.

expanded memory standard (EMS): An early method to move past the 1MB memory barrier.

expansion card slots: Connectors that allow devices to be quickly and easily plugged into the bus system.

expansion cards: A board that can be easily installed in a computer to enhance or expand its capabilities.

Extended Capabilities Port (ECP): A parallel port standard that provides for bidirectional communication and has extended capabilities to support multiple devices.

extended graphics array (XGA): A video standard that supports a resolution of 640×480 with 65,536 colors, or 1024×768 with 256 colors.

extended memory system (XMS): All of the PC's memory beyond the first 1MB when the CPU is running in real mode.

extension: The second part of a filename. An extension is typically three characters long and indicates the function of the file.

external commands: Individual, executable files that extend DOS's functionality beyond the limits of its internal commands.

F

fake parity: When the parity bit is always set to one regardless of the true number of ones contained in the byte.

FAT16: A file system in which file storage information is recorded with 16 bits of data.

FAT32: A file system in which file storage information is recorded with 32 bits of data.

fault tolerance: A system's ability to recover after some sort of disaster.

fiber-optic cable: Cable that contains a glass or plastic center used to carry light.

field: A complete sweep of the entire video display area.

field replacement unit (FRU): Any major part of a computer system that could be completely replaced on site rather than repaired.

file: A collection of data that forms a single unit.

file allocation table (FAT): A table used by the operating system to record and recall the locations of files on the disk.

File Transfer Protocol (FTP): A protocol used for transmitting files across the Internet.

firewall: A barrier that prevents direct contact between computers outside the organization with computers inside the organization.

FireWire (IEEE 1394): A bus system that provides a high rate of data transfer (speeds of 400 Mbps). A single IEEE 1394 port can serve up to 63 external devices in daisy chain fashion.

flash BIOS: BIOS that is stored on a reprogrammable chip, allowing for easy upgrades.

flash memory: Memory type that stores data but does not require a power source to retain the data.

flash ROM: ROM that can be erased in blocks using a high voltage.

floppy disk: Soft magnetic disks use for storing small amounts of information.

floppy drive: A device that reads and writes to floppy disks.

font: A design for a set of symbols, usually text and number characters. A font describes characteristics associated with a symbol such as the typeface, size, pitch, and spacing between symbols.

form factor: The physical shape or outline of a motherboard and the location of the mounting holes. Also called a footprint.

formatting: Preparing a disk to receive data in a systematic, organized manner.

fragmented: Stored in nonconsecutive clusters on the disk.

front side bus (FSB): Another term for local bus.

fuel cell: A type of battery that uses hydrogen or methanol to produce electrical energy.

fuse: An inexpensive, passive component that is engineered to burn open at a predetermined amperage, protecting the rest of the circuit from overload.

G

gas-plasma displays: A display that operates on the principle of electro-luminescence.

gateway: Translates information between two LANs using different protocols.

gateway router: A router that combines different media and provides an Internet connection.

Gopher: An early Internet protocol designed to search and retrieve documents from distant computers.

graphical user interface (GUI): An operating system interface that allows the user to perform functions by selecting on-screen icons rather than by issuing text line commands.

group: Collection of users organized together by similarities in their job tasks.

H

hard drive: A magnetic storage media consisting of a set of magnetic disks and read/write heads housed inside a hard case.

heap: How Windows refers to the entire memory.

hexadecimal number system: A system in which all numbers are expressed in combinations of 16 alphanumeric characters (0–F). Also known as the base 16 number system.

high memory area (HMA): The first 64KB of the extended memory area.

High Performance File System (HPFS): File system developed for IBM PCs to overcome the limitations of DOS.

High Sierra format: A standard for compact discs that was created so that CDs could be read on any CD device.

high-level format: A process that prepares the disk for storage of files.

hoaxes: False messages spread about a real or unreal virus.

Home Phoneline Networking Alliance (HomePNA) technology: A technology that allows existing home telephone lines to be used for the network media.

HomePNA adapter: A networking device that allows every telephone jack that is connected together physically in a building to be part of the network.

host: A computer or other piece of equipment connected to a TCP/IP network that requires an address; used interchangeably with the term *node*.

hot swap: 1. A technology that allows a computer device to be plugged into or unplugged from a computer while the computer is running. 2. To plug in or unplug a device while the PC is running.

hub: Device used to provide a quick and easy method of connecting network equipment together by cables.

hybrid topology: A mixture of star, bus, and ring topologies.

Hypertext Markup Language (HTML): Programming language used to create Web pages.

Hypertext Transfer Protocol (HTTP): Protocol that transports Web pages across the Internet.

I

I/O bus: A bus that connects the processor to the expansion slots.

I/O port address: A memory address expressed in hexadecimal notation, which is used to identify a computer device such as a video card.

incremental backup: Operation that backs up select files that have changed since the last backup of files. The archive bit is reset.

Industry Standard Architecture (ISA): An I/O (expansion) bus system featuring a 16-bit data bus.

inkjet printer: Printer that uses specially designed cartridges that spray a fine mist of ink as they move horizontally in front of a sheet of paper.

input device: A piece of equipment that provides the computer with data.

instructional set: A set of basic commands that control the processor.

instructions: Commands given to the processor.

integrated circuit: A collection of transistors, resistors, and other electronic components reduced to an unbelievable small size.

Integrated Drive Electronics (IDE): An early standard for a disk drive interface that integrated the controller into the disk drive. The term is still commonly used when referring to the AT Attachment.

integrated services digital network (ISDN): A standard that allows a completely digital connection from one PC to another.

interleave factor: Describes how the sectors are laid out on a disk surface to optimize a hard drive's data access rate.

internal bus: Part of the integrated circuit inside the CPU.

internal commands: A set of programs that are wholly contained within the command processor program (command.com).

Internet: A very large, global, decentralized network.

Internet Connection Firewall (ICF): Software included in Windows XP that can be configured to keep unauthorized users from accessing the network.

Internet Service Provider (ISP): Provides connection to the Internet and other services.

InterNIC: A branch of the United States government under the direction of the Department of Commerce. It is responsible for regulating the Internet, overseeing the issue of domain names, and assigning IP addresses to them.

IP address: Identifying address used for a PC or other equipment on a TCP/IP network.

IP switch: Designed to pass ATM protocol packets.

IRQ: IRQ is an acronym for interrupt request. An IRQ is a signal that interrupts the processes taking place in the CPU and requests that the processor pay attention to a specific device.

ISO 9660: The file system standard that CD-ROMs use, an update on the High Sierra format.

K

kernel: The core of the operating system.

Kernel mode: Automatic Windows NT mode of operation that oversees the system resources and processor actions.

L

L1 cache: A cache contained within the processor that is designed to run at the processor's speed.

L2 cache: A cache mounted outside of the processor. The Pentium III, however, incorporates the L2 cache in the processor chip.

L3 cache: The cache mounted on the motherboard when L1 and L2 caches are incorporated into the CPU chip.

lands: The flat areas between the pits in a compact disc.

laptop: Lightweight, portable computer with the monitor, motherboard, processor, disk drives, keyboard, and mouse molded into one unit.

legacy: Older technology kept intact for use by newer technology systems.

light pens: Input devices that interact with the light beam that creates the image on the monitor.

liquid crystal display (LCD): A type of monitor that uses polarized light passing through liquid crystal to create images on screen.

lithium-ion (Li-ion) batteries: Rechargeable battery found in most new portable computers. Has no problem with memory effect and holds a charge longer than NiCd and NiMH batteries.

local area network (LAN): A small network of computers contained in a relatively small area, such as an office building.

local bus: A bus system that connects directly to the CPU and provides communications to high-speed devices mounted closely to the CPU.

local printer: Printer that connects directly to a specific PC.

logic bomb: A destructive program that is slipped into an application and waits dormant until some event takes place, allowing the virus to spread to other machines before releasing its payload.

logical drives: Separate storage areas on a single drive that simulate separate drives. Also referred to as partitions.

logical unit numbers (LUN): An identifier used with SCSI extenders to distinguish between (up to) eight devices on the same SCSI ID number.

low-level format: A process that determines the type of encoding to be done on the disk platter and the sequence in which the read/write heads will access stored data.

LS-120 (floptical) drive: A very high capacity disk drive that is able to store 120MB of data on a single disk.

M

macro virus: A common virus created using a macro programming language. It is attached to documents that use the language.

magneto-optical (MO) drives: Disk drives that combine magnetic and optical principles to store and retrieve data.

master: The primary drive on an IDE channel.

master boot record (MBR): An area of the hard disk that contains information about the physical characteristics of the drive, the disk partitions, and the boot procedure. Also referred to as the boot sector.

math coprocessor: A component of the CPU that improves the processor's ability to perform advanced mathematical calculations.

MBR virus: An extremely destructive virus that attacks the master boot record (MBR) of a hard disk, resulting in hard disk failure.

media access code (MAC) address: A hexadecimal number programmed into the network interface card's chip. The first six digits identify the card's manufacturer. The second six-digit sequence is assigned by the manufacturer and is different on every card produced.

memory address range: An assigned section of memory used as a temporary storage area for data before it is transferred.

memory bus: A bus that connects the processor to the memory.

memory management software: Software designed to efficiently utilize valuable memory resources.

mesh topology: A network design in which each node connects directly to every other node on the network.

metal oxide varistor (MOV): A gate in a surge suppressor that becomes conductive at a given voltage, causing current to bypass the equipment plugged into the suppressor.

metropolitan area network (MAN): A group of two or more interconnected LANs operating under a single management.

Micro Channel Architecture (MCA): An I/O (expansion) bus system featuring a 32-bit data bus. MCA and ISA cards and slots are not physically compatible.

Microsoft System Information: Utility that displays detailed information about the hardware and software in the system.

mini connector: A two pin connector that delivers a +5 volt signal from the power supply. A variation of this connector has four wires and delivers both +12 volt and +5 volt signals.

MMX processor: A processor with an additional 57 commands that enhance its abilities to support multimedia technology.

modem: An electronic device that is used to convert serial data from a computer to an audio signal for transmission over telephone lines and vice versa.

Molex connector: A four-wire, D-shaped connector that delivers +12 volt and +5 volt signals from the power supply.

Monochrome: A monitor type that displays only a single color, usually amber or green.

motherboard: A circuit board covered by a maze of conductors, which provide electrical current to the computer components and expansion slots. Also used to refer to the main circuit board and all of its electronic components (chipset).

Motion Picture Experts Group (MPEG): A standard format for recording motion picture video and sound.

mouse: A computer pointing device used to manipulate an on-screen pointer.

multicolor/graphics array (MCGA): A video standard that supported CGA and also provided up to 64 shades of gray.

multimedia: Incorporating sound or video.

multiple branch prediction: A technique that predicts what data element will be needed next, rather than waiting for the next command to be issued.

multiple zone recording (MZR): A method of sectoring tracks so there are twice as many sectors in the outermost tracks as there are in the innermost tracks.

Multipurpose Internet Mail Extensions (MIME): A specification for formatting non-text-based files for transmission over the Internet.

Multistation Access Unit (MAU): A hub-like device that physically connects computers in a star arrangement while maintaining a ring structure.

multitasking: Running two or more programs at the same time.

musical instrument digital interface (MIDI): A file standard developed for music synthesizers.

N

nanosecond (ns): One billionth of a second.

Native resolution: The resolution that matches the pixel design of the display.

network: Two or more computers connected together for the purpose of sharing data and resources.

network administration: The use of network software packages to manage network system operations.

Network interface card (NIC): Connects the network communication media, usually twisted pair, to the individual network devices such as workstations, file servers, and printers.

Network Setup Wizard: A Windows XP wizard that makes setting up a network easy by including a series of dialog boxes that ask for information about the network.

New Technology File System (NTFS): A file system found in Windows NT and Windows 2000. NTFS features improve security and storage capacity and are compatible with FAT16.

nickel-cadmium (NiCd) battery: Rechargeable battery used in early portable computers. Had problems with memory effect.

nickel-metal hydride materials (NiMH) batteries: Second generation of rechargeable battery used for portable computers. Has no problem with memory effect and holds a charge longer than the NiCd battery.

node: Device connected to a client/server network.

north bridge: The portion of the chipset that controls higher data speed systems such as graphics and DVD hardware.

notebook: Lightweight, portable computer with the monitor, motherboard, processor, disk drives, keyboard, and mouse molded into one unit.

O

octet: An 8-bit series of numbers.

odd parity checking: A data integrity checking method in which every time the number of bits counted is odd, an extra bit of data is transmitted as a 1 to make the count even.

Open Systems Interconnection (OSI): Seven-layer reference model that describes how hardware and software should work together to form a network communication system.

operating system (OS): Software that provides the user with a file system structure and allows the user to communicate with the computer system's hardware.

optical character recognition (OCR): A type of software that is able to distinguish between the various letters, numbers, and symbols in a scanned image.

overclocking: Forcing a processor to operate faster than its approved speed.

P

packet: Small unit of data into which larger amounts are divided for passage through a network.

Packet Internet Groper (PING): A utility program that is often used as a troubleshooting tool to verify network connections to Web sites.

packet sniffer: A utility that captures packets on a network and displays their entire contents.

packet writing: Records data in small blocks similar to the way hard drives store data.

palmtop: Portable computer that can rest in the palm of the hand.

paper jam: When a printer pulls one or more sheets through its mechanism and the paper becomes wedged inside.

paper train: The route the paper follows through the printer.

parallel: Side-by-side. In parallel transfer, more than one bit of data is transferred at a time.

parity: The counting of either odd or even bits being transmitted.

partitions: Areas on a hard drive that simulate separate drives. Also referred to as logical drives.

passive hub: Acts as a connection point in the star topography. Transmitted digital signals from one computer are passed to all computers connected to the passive hub and through the hub to other network sections.

passive-matrix display: An LCD display in which a grid of semitransparent conductors is run to each of the crystals that make up the individual pixels.

password virus: A virus that steals passwords.

pathname: A string of characters used to identify a file's location in the directory structure.

PCMCIA card: Card designed by the Personal Computer Memory Card International Association (PCMCIA) to add memory or expand a portable PC. The PCMCIA card is often referred to as simply a "PCM" or "PC" card.

peer-to-peer network: Network administration model in which all the PCs connected together are considered equal.

Peripheral Component Interconnect (PCI): A bus system featuring a 32-bit data bus that provides a high-speed bus structure needed for faster CPUs.

peripherals: Optional equipment used to input or output data.

permissions: The right to perform certain functions.

persistence: The continuation of the glow after the electron beam ceases to strike the phosphor areas.

photocell: An electronic component that changes light energy into electrical energy.

pin grid array (PGA): The pattern of pins on a CPU.

pitch: Unit of measure for the width of a font.

pits: The holes etched into a compact disc in order to record data.

pixel: The smallest unit of color in a screen display.

pixel pitch: The distance between two same color pixels on the display area.

Plug and Play (PnP): A BIOS function that enables the automatic detection and configuration of new hardware components. Also the automatic assignment of system resources such as DMA channels, interrupts, memory, and port assignments.

points: Unit of measure for the height of a font. Each point is equal to 1/72 of an inch.

polarized light: Light consisting of waves that have the same orientation.

polymorphic virus: A virus that changes as it evolves so that it may go undetected by antivirus programs.

port replicator: An external computer device that provides additional ports to be used by a computer system.

power: The amount of electrical energy provided or used by equipment.

power bus: A bus system that sends electrical power for small consumption devices such as speakers, lights, and switches.

power good signal: A signal sent from the power supply to the motherboard to verify that it is functioning normally.

powerline communications (PLC): A technology that allows existing power lines to be used as network media.

power-on self-test (POST): A routine check of the computer's hardware that executes every time the computer is turned on.

preemptive multitasking: Multiple programs sharing control of the operating system.

primary domain controller (PDC): A file server that keeps the master record of all accounts.

printer: An electromechanical device that converts computer data into text or graphic images printed to paper or other presentation media.

PROM: Programmable read only memory.

protected mode: An operating mode which supports multitasking and allows access to memory beyond the first 1MB.

protocol: A set of rules for formatting the data stream transmission between two computers or devices and for describing how to transmit data, usually across a network.

protocol suite: Combination of individual protocols each designed for specific purposes.

proxy server: Designed to hide all the PCs in the LAN from direct connection from PCs outside of the LAN. It relays the requested information for the client, leaving the client anonymous outside the network.

Q

query: Locating and extracting data from a database system.

queue: List of print jobs waiting to be completed and their status.

R

RAID: A system of several hard drive units arranged in such a way as to ensure recovery after a system disaster or to ensure data integrity during normal operation.

random access memory (RAM): A volatile memory system into which programs and data are loaded. When the computer's power is shut off, all programs and data stored in RAM are lost.

raster: The sweep of the electron beam.

read only memory (ROM): Memory that stores information permanently.

read/write head: The mechanism that records information to and reads information from a magnetic medium.

real mode: An operating mode in which only the first 1MB of a system's RAM can be accessed. Also an operating mode in which the 286 or later processor emulates an 8088 or 8086 processor.

real-mode drivers: Legacy 16-bit drivers.

Recovery Console: Text-based command-line utility used to enter commands similar to DOS commands to recover from a system startup failure.

reduced instruction set computer (RISC): A type of CPU architecture that is designed with a fewer number of transistors and commands.

refresh rate: The rate at which the electron beam sweeps across the screen.

register unit: A CPU component containing many separate, smaller storage units known as registers.

registered memory: A memory module that incorporates driver and synchronizing electronics as part of the unit.

registers: Small pockets of memory, within the processor, that are used to temporarily store data that is being processed by the CPU.

registrar: Private sector company, regulated by InterNIC, to whom users apply for an IP address or domain name.

registry: A database that stores configuration information.

Registry Checker: Utility that will scan, backup, and restore the system registry.

Remote Assistance: Allows a user to invite another user to access their computer and assist them in repairing their computer.

repeater: A piece of equipment that regenerates a weak digital signal.

reserved memory: Another term for upper memory.

resistance: The opposition to the flow of electrical energy.

resolution: The amount of detail a monitor is capable of displaying.

response time: The amount of time it takes a TFT pixel to display after a signal is sent to the transistor controlling that pixel.

restore points: Backups of system settings and configurations that make it possible for a computer to revert to an earlier time when the computer system was working properly.

rights: System control abilities that are normally reserved for the system administrator.

ring topology: A single cable that runs continuously from computer to computer.

root directory: The directory at the top of the file structure hierarchy. A root directory is analogous to a file cabinet drawer in a conventional, paper filing system. A root directory is also referred to as the root.

router: Used to control the flow of data to different networks based on IP addresses.

run-length encoding (RLE): A graphics compression format that reduces image file sizes by recording strings of identical pixels.

S

safe mode: Mode that boots the computer without some drivers and programs to allow for troubleshooting.

sampling: Measuring an analog signal at regular intervals.

scan code: A data signal created from electrical signals sent by an input device.

ScanDisk: A program, included in Windows operating systems, used to inspect the surface of disk storage and identify bad and lost clusters on the disk.

scanner: A device that digitizes printed images and text.

SCSI ID number: A unique number assigned to a device on a SCSI chain and used to identify that device.

sector: Subdivisions of tracks, usually about 512 bytes in size.

segment: A section of cable between two network devices. Also, a portion of a network that shares a common collision or token passing domain.

sequence number: Attached to each packet of data being transmitted, ensuring that the data will be reassembled in the exact order it was transmitted.

serial: Occurring one at a time. In serial transfer, data is transmitted one bit at a time.

server: Powerful computers used to manage network resources and provide services such as security and file sharing.

shadow mask: A metal mesh with triangular or rectangular holes that a CRT's electron beam passes through, creating a crisper image.

share-level security: Default security system used on Windows-based networks, which requires a password for access.

shares: Objects that are shared across the network, such as files, hard drives, CD drives, printers, and scanners.

single edge contact (SEC): A processor configuration in which the CPU is mounted on a circuit board and the edge of the circuit board inserts into the motherboard socket.

single in-line memory module (SIMM): A memory module containing a row of DIP memory chips mounted on a circuit board.

single in-line package (SIP): A memory chip containing a single row of connections, which run along the length of chip.

slave: A secondary drive on an IDE channel.

small computer system interface (SCSI): The standard interface used by Macintosh/Apple and many UNIX mainframe systems to connect peripherals.

small-office/home-office (SOHO) network: A simple peer-to-peer LAN that is used to share resources and data in a home- or small- office environment.

smart card: Credit card-like device with a chip imbedded in the plastic. The chip allows the card to be used for a variety of purposes.

soft power: Another term for the features provided by a standby power connection.

solid ink printer: Printer that uses solid ink cartridges similar to wax.

source code: The programming code used to make the operating system.

south bridge: The portion of the chipset that controls the slower devices associated with the PCI and ISA buses.

spooling: A technique that stores data to be printed into memory so that printing operations can be completed in the background while other tasks are performed by the PC user.

standby power connection: Provides power to reactivate or wake up a system in standby mode.

star topology: A network in which cables run from each computer to a single point, forming a star.

startup problem: Problem that causes the computer to lock up during the boot process.

static RAM (SRAM): An integrated circuit using digital flip-flop components.

stealth virus: A virus that hides from normal detection by incorporating itself into part of a known, and usually required, program for the PC.

subdirectories: A file that subdivides the contents of a directory. A subdirectory is analogous to a folder within a folder in a conventional, paper filing system. Subdirectories are referred to as subfolders in many operating systems.

subnet mask: A mask that is used to determine what subnet a particular IP address refers to.

super VGA (SVGA): A video standard that supports 16 million colors and various resolutions up to 1600 × 1200 pixels.

superscalar: Processing multiple instructions simultaneously.

switch: Filters and forwards packets of data between network segments based on MAC addresses.

switching hubs: Enhanced active hubs. They can determine whether a signal should remain in the isolated section of the network or be passed through the hub to other parts of the network.

synchronous: Data transferred on the same timing as the computer.

System Configuration Utility: Tool that allows you to modify the system configuration.

System File Checker: Tool that can be run to check for corrupt, changed, or missing files from Windows-based applications.

System Management Mode (SMM): A standby mode developed for laptop computers in order to save electrical energy when using a battery.

system resources: Files, software, printers, and such.

System Restore: Utility used to restore a system to a previous working state.

T

T-carrier lines: Lines designed to carry voice and data at a much higher rate than traditional phone lines.

telephone jack: Where the telephone line connects into the cabling. This is a standard connection used to attach devices such as modems and telephones to the wiring system.

Telnet: A protocol that allows you to logon a remote computer and download or upload files.

text line command: Commands issued by entering text at a command prompt.

thin film transistor liquid crystal display (TFT-LCD): A display that consists of a matrix of thin film transistors, in which each transistor controls a single pixel.

time to live (TTL): The length of time the data in the packet is valid.

token: A short binary code, generated by the network software, that is passed from one computer to the next along a ring topology and in some bus topologies.

token bus network: Network that uses a token passing system with a bus-type topology.

Token Ring network: A highly organized system in which each computer must wait its turn to transmit data.

topology: The physical arrangement of hardware and cabling in a network system.

touch screen display: Computer display that is modified to accept input by touch.

tracert: Utility program that sends a packet out and waits for a reply. It also displays information about the route that was taken to the destination.

track ball: A pointing device similar to a mouse that is operated upside down.

tracks: The concentric circles of data storage areas on a disk.

Trojan horse: Class of virus that appears as a gift, such as a free download of a game or utility program, an e-mail attachment, or some other item.

twisted pair cable: The most common choice for network wiring. It consists of four pairs of conductors twisted around each other.

U

Uniform Resource Locator (URL): The global address for sites all over the Internet. The first part of the URL identifies the protocol being used and the second part identifies the domain name.

uninterruptible power supply (UPS): A power supply that ensures a constant supply of quality electrical power to the computer system.

universal asynchronous receiver-transmitter (UART): Main chip in a modem that changes parallel data to serial data and vice versa.

Universal Disk Format (UDF): The file system standard accepted for CD-RW, magneto-optical disc, and DVD technology.

Universal Naming Convention (UNC): A path format that identifies a server and its share and uses backslashes to separate the server name from the share name.

universal peripheral interface (UPI): A chip on the motherboard that directs communications between the CPU and the input device.

Universal Serial Bus (USB): A bus system designed to replace the function of expansion slots with a data transfer rate as high as 480 Mbps. The USB is accessed by plugging a USB device into the bus at a port opening in the case. Additional devices (up to 127) can be connected to the bus in a daisy chain configuration.

upper memory: Term for a PC's memory range between 640KB and 1MB.

user: A person who may use the network system resources.

user mode: The actual user interface mode for the NT operating system. It is very restrictive and many areas are not accessible by the user or user programs.

user-level security: Security system used on Windows-based networks that identifies who may have access to a shared resource but does not require a password for accessing the share.

V

vector graphics: A graphic standard based on a series of mathematical formulas that can be converted into geometric shapes representing the image to be displayed.

Version Conflict Manager: Utility that checks for a Microsoft certificate to ensure that only compatible software is installed on the system.

Video Electronics Standards Association (VESA) local bus: A bus system that could handle a higher data transfer rate than MCA or EISA. The VL-Bus was developed by a consortium of video adapter and monitor manufacturers.

video graphics array (VGA): The minimum standard for video adapters, which displays at a resolution of 640 × 480 with 16 colors or 320 × 200 with 256 colors.

viewing angle: A measurement of the angle at which a person can adequately see an image on a display without it looking excessively distorted.

virtual device drivers (VxDs): Special device drivers that have access to the operating system kernel.

virtual file allocation table (VFAT): A method of programming the FAT16 file system to allow long file capabilities similar to FAT32.

virtual mode: An operational mode in which the processor can operate several real mode programs at once and access memory higher than the first 1MB.

virtual private network (VPN): A security configuration that ensures data sent across the Internet is not read or modified. It does this by creating a private tunnel between the destination and source PC and encrypting packet contents.

virus signature: Combination of characteristics that define a particular virus, including such things as its length, file name(s) used, mode of infection or replication, and more.

voltage: The amount of electrical pressure present in a circuit or power source.

volt-amperes (VA): An alternative scale for measuring electrical power.

volts: A scale used in measuring electrical pressure (electromotive force).

volume mount points: Allow a volume or additional hard drive be attached to a directory structure. Volume mount points can be used to unify dissimilar file systems into one logical file system.

W

warm boot: Using the reset button or key combination to restart a computer that is already running.

watts (W): A scale used in measuring electrical power.

wide area network (WAN): A large number of computers, spread over a large geographic area and under control of a centrally located administrator.

Windows CE: Version of Windows designed for less powerful devices, such as PDAs or smart appliances.

Windows Internet Naming Service (WINS): Resolves the computer name to the equivalent IP address on the network.

Windows Report Tool: Utility that allows the PC system settings to be copied and sent to technical support for evaluation.

Windows system disk: A disk containing all the files necessary to start the PC and load the operating system.

wireless topology: Uses no cabling system between the computers. It uses either infrared light or radio transmission to communicate between the network devices.

word: The total amount of bytes a computer can process at one time.

worm: Destructive program that contaminates files on the infected machine and spreads itself to other machines without prompting from the user.

Z

zero insertion force (ZIF) socket: A processor socket equipped with a lever to assist in the installation of the processor chip.

ZIP disk: A form of removable computer data storage that can contain over 100MB of data.

Index

K

L

M

N

O

P

Q

R

S

T

W

X

Z